NOTIS

WITHDRAWN

ORDER FORM

Prices are for current editions only.
Call 1-800-FILMBKS or 213/471-8066 for more information.

YES! PLEASE SEND THE FOLLOWING BOOKS:

QTY.	ANNUAL DIRECTORIES	PRICE	CA. TAX	TOTAL
____	FILM DIRECTORS—8th Ed.	$59.95	$4.95	$____
____	PRODS/STUDIOS/ AGENTS & CASTING DIRECTORS—3rd Ed.	49.95	4.12	$____
____	CINEMATOGRAPHERS PRODUCTION DESIGNERS COSTUME DESIGNERS & FILM EDITORS—3rd Ed.	49.95	4.12	$____
____	FILM WRITERS—3rd Ed.	49.95	4.12	$____
____	FILM COMPOSERS—1st Ed.	29.95	2.47	$____
____	TV WRITERS—2nd Ed.	49.95	4.12	$____
____	TV DIRECTORS - 1st Ed.	29.95	2.47	$____
____	FILM ACTORS GUIDE—1st Ed.	49.95	4.12	$____
____	SPECIAL EFFECTS & STUNTS—2nd Ed.	39.95	3.30	$____

SUBTOTAL $____
ADD IN SHIPPING $____
TOTAL ORDER $____

UPS SHIPPING CHARGES CONT. USA/CANADA
First Directory $6.00 $10.00
Add'l. Directory $2.50 $5.00

SHIPPING CHARGES (Overseas)
	AIRMAIL	SURFACE
Film Directors	$45.00	$12.50
Other Directories	$35.00	$12.50

For Faster Service
Call 213/471-8066 (CA) or
1/800-FILMBKS

FAX ORDERS ACCEPTED: 213/471-4969

PAYMENT IS BY:
Check ____ Money Order ____ Visa ____ MC ____ AMEX ____
Card No. _____ Exp. Date _____
Signature _____
(exactly as it appears on your card)

SHIP BOOKS TO:
NAME _____
COMPANY _____ PHONE _____ (very imp't.!)
ADDRESS _____
CITY/STATE/ZIP _____

BUSINESS REPLY CARD
FIRST CLASS PERMIT NO. 4842, BEVERLY HILLS, CA.

POSTAGE WILL BE PAID BY:

LONE EAGLE PUBLISHING CO.
9903 Santa Monica Blvd. #204
Beverly Hills, CA 90212-9942

NO POSTAGE NECESSARY IF MAILED IN THE UNITED STATES

BUSINESS REPLY CARD
FIRST CLASS PERMIT NO. 4842, BEVERLY HILLS, CA.

POSTAGE WILL BE PAID BY:

LONE EAGLE PUBLISHING CO.
9903 Santa Monica Blvd. #204
Beverly Hills, CA 90212-9942

NO POSTAGE NECESSARY IF MAILED IN THE UNITED STATES

BUSINESS REPLY CARD
FIRST CLASS PERMIT NO. 4842, BEVERLY HILLS, CA.

POSTAGE WILL BE PAID BY:

LONE EAGLE PUBLISHING CO.
9903 Santa Monica Blvd. #204
Beverly Hills, CA 90212-9942

NO POSTAGE NECESSARY IF MAILED IN THE UNITED STATES

BUSINESS REPLY CARD
FIRST CLASS PERMIT NO. 4842, BEVERLY HILLS, CA.

POSTAGE WILL BE PAID BY:

LONE EAGLE PUBLISHING CO.
9903 Santa Monica Blvd. #204
Beverly Hills, CA 90212-9942

NO POSTAGE NECESSARY IF MAILED IN THE UNITED STATES

FILM WRITERS
GUIDE

Third Edition

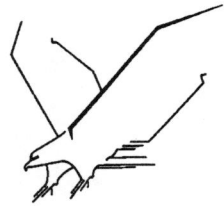

FILM WRITERS
GUIDE

Third Edition

Compiled and Edited by Susan Avallone

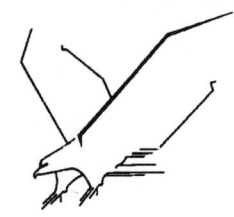

LONE EAGLE

FILM WRITERS GUIDE
Third Edition

Copyright © 1991 by Susan Avallone

All rights reserved. No part of this book may be reproduced or utilized in any form or by any means, electronic or mechanical, including photocopying, recording or by any information storage and retrieval system, without permission in writing from the publisher. Inquiries should be addressed to:

LONE EAGLE PUBLISHING CO.
2337 Roscomare Road—Suite 9
Los Angeles, California 90077-1815
213/471-8066

Printed in the United States of America

Book designed by Liz Ridenour and Heidi Frieder

This book was entirely typeset using an Apple Macintosh SE, Apple Macintosh II, LaserwriterPlus, Microsoft Word and Aldus Pagemaker.

Printed by McNaughton & Gunn, Saline, Michigan 48176

ISBN: 0-943728-48-7

NOTE: We have made every reasonable effort to ensure that the information contained herein is as accurate as possible. However, errors and omissions are sure to occur and are unintentional. We would appreciate your notifying us of any which you may find.

* Lone Eagle Publishing is a division of Lone Eagle Productions, Inc.

LONE EAGLE PUBLISHING STAFF
Publishers .... Joan V. Singleton
                                            Ralph S. Singleton
Editorial Director .... Bethann Wetzel
Advertising Director ...... Lori Copeland
Editorial Assistant .... Steve LuKanic
Art Director .... Heidi Frieder
Computer Consultant .... Glenn Osako

LETTER FROM THE PUBLISHERS

This is the first time we have included interviews in our FILM WRITERS GUIDE. I hope you have time to read and re-read the fascinating interviews that Susan has done with Jeffrey Boam, Naomi Foner, Robbie Fox and Bruce Joel Rubin. If you are a writer, you will find it stimulating to peek into the minds of these prolific and creative writers and compare notes, so to speak. For those of you who produce, direct, run studios, etc., it will be equally stimulating to get a glimpse into the worlds of these minds who create the basic foundation for all the success in our industry. For without the writers, we would have nothing to produce or direct or market.

This book has grown in exponential proportions from its first edition only three years ago. We know how badly you want and need accurate information and are striving to be your best source. As Susan explains, we are the only guide that gives you listings of screenplays which have not yet made it into production—a goldmine for those of you in development looking for the next hot writer and hit project.

As with all the guides we publish, and we now do nine (!), we are dependent on you to keep us up to date on your contact information. As these guides are used not only for research, but also for hiring purposes, it is in your best interests to keep us posted. Please include us on your change of address/change of agent notices. As always, we appreciate your comments and suggestions.

See you at the movies!

Joan V. Singleton   *Ralph S. Singleton*
Joan V. Singleton and Ralph S. Singleton
Publishers

Luke Skywalker had Yoda...

© 1980 LUCASFILM LTD. ALL RIGHTS RESERVED

...Bellamy has you.

Kids know it takes someone very special to make dreams come true. Someone just a bit different, who cares a bit more. The STARLIGHT FOUNDATION is a non-profit organization that makes dreams come true for critically, chronically, and terminally ill children. Kids whose biggest dream probably won't come true.

Through local STARLIGHT chapters, trained volunteers, and corporate donations, STARLIGHT fulfills hundreds of wishes a month for kids from all over the country. And the only requirement is that a wish really come from the child.

Like Bellamy, who has bone cancer. His wish for a toy shopping spree came true.

Please support the STARLIGHT FOUNDATION, and be a force for good in a kid's life.

Call 1-800-274-STAR. Or write to: The STARLIGHT FOUNDATION, 10100 Santa Monica Blvd., Suite 785, Los Angeles, CA 90067.

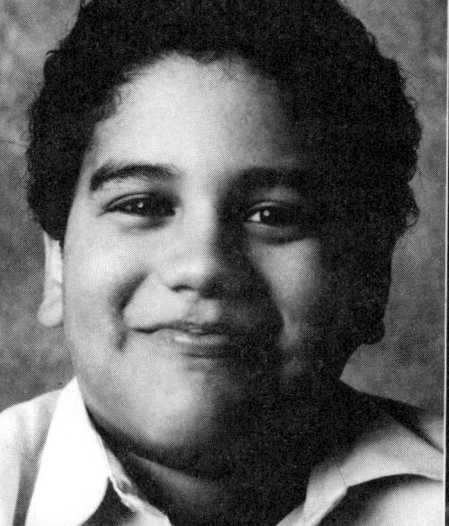

Photograph by Harris Welles

Starlight Foundation

TABLE OF CONTENTS

FILM WRITERS GUIDE

LETTER FROM THE PUBLISHERS v

INTRODUCTION ix

DIALOGUE — Interviews
    Jeffrey Boam 2
    Naomi Foner 6
    Bruce Joel Rubin 10
    Robbie Fox 14

KEY TO ABBREVIATIONS 20

FILM WRITERS
    Alphabetical Listing 21

INDEX — By Film Title 323

OTHER INDICES
    Academy Awards & Nominations 393
    Agents & Managers 399
    Guilds 406
    Advertisers 413

ABOUT THE EDITOR 414

INTRODUCTION

FILM WRITERS GUIDE

We thought we'd never make it, but finally we've reached the **Third Edition of the FILM WRITERS GUIDE** and as promised, it's grown by leaps and bounds, now including an uncountable number of writers and credits. We've added a lot more credits: movies that have come out since last year's edition, earlier films, and new writers whose screenplays are in circulation.

The main purpose of this book is to provide an easy, practical and comprehensive reference to screenwriters and their work. **FILM WRITERS GUIDE** continues to emphasize professionals who are currently active in the industry and their feature film credits over the past ten years. Although we do not include credits for deceased persons in the main section, we have included their credits in the index, noted with a "†" by the person's name. Our next edition will feature an additional section for those writers and their credits.

WHAT'S HERE, WHAT'S NOT
Included are feature film titles produced and unproduced, cable features and miniseries, and stageplays. As the focus of this directory is the feature film world, network television credits are not listed, though there is a sampling of cable television credits, as some of those films are distributed theatrically in the U.S. and abroad. Lone Eagle also publishes **TELEVISION WRITERS GUIDE**, edited by Lynne Naylor, which contains *only television credits*. That book can be used in conjunction with **FILM WRITERS GUIDE** to provide more comprehensive information on a working writer.

Our focus is on English-language writers, though there are many foreign writers included, primarily if they are also directors. Certain foreign writers were singled out (Jean-Claude Carriere, Tonino Guerra) for having sole screenplay credits, but for example, Federico Fellini's co-writers are not listed separately though they are included within his credits.

When a writer has both scripted and directed a project, it is so indicated. Short films are included because for many beginning writers, their short film is their calling card and occasionally become a feature-length script. Likewise a selection of stageplays are listed as they too are often submitted to studios and producers as writing samples. If the play also exists as a screenplay by the playwright, that is indicated.

Story and adaptation credits are now included, though some may have slipped through since we weren't tracking these credits in previous editions. However, for the sake of brevity, the story credit is not indicated if the writer also has screenplay credit. A typical example: Michael Mahern has shared screenplay credit on *MOBSTERS* with Nicholas Kazan, but his sole story credit is not indicated.

We've gone back farther than 1960 this time, probably to 1940 or even 1930 for some writer's listings. Academy award winners (★★) and nominees (★) are noted, and this time we've included a list at the front of the book covering the past 30 years of screenwriting Oscars and nominations.

The Dreaded Contact Info
Contact information is the hardest part of doing this book, and we've provided as many contacts for the writers listed as we could find. Those that are Writers Guild of America members are noted (an asterisk follows a guild member's name). If WGA is listed as the contact, that means that at the time we went to press either the WGA had no contact information or the writer recently left the agency that WGA had listed for them. You can contact writers by writing to them care of the WGA (the address is in the back of this book). We've also noted Directors Guild or Screen Actors Guild members as an alternate route to contact a director or actor who has written for the screen.

The biggest problem this year was that although a number of agencies—from the smallest to the largest—cooperated and confirmed their client lists, probably an equal number would not provide assistance. Therefore, many writers who recently switched agents were left without contact information. Writers who are WGA members should remember to let the Guild know when you switch—it's very hard to find out where you are otherwise. And for writers listed who are not Guild members, please let us know where you can be contacted. This information seems to change overnight and we appreciate any help we can get for future editions.

FILM WRITERS GUIDE

"Unproduced" No More—But They're Still Here
Listing "unproduced" screenplays in the previous editions always caused a ruckus so this time we're just calling them "screenplays." There was much arguing over the meaning of the word "unproduced," so the name of the category has changed, but what's included there has stayed the same: screenplays that are available, in development, or actually in production or post-production. Since the writing credit during production is often different from the final screen credit, many movies that were not released by the time we went to press are listed as screenplays. For movies with several writers during production, some titles are listed under a number of writers, but without referencing each other as they may be working independently. For example, *Machine Gun Kelly* is listed for the original writer Michael Werb, as well as for rewriters Anna Hamliton Phelan and Stephen Metcalfe. When the movie is released, the credit will go to the writer who receives final credit and the other listings will be removed.

The very inclusion of unproduced screenplays is still an issue. One agent asked, "Why do you include all those 'nobodies' along with Robert Towne?" The answer is that people in the business still need to know who wrote what, and the discussions at studios and production companies concern the scripts in development as much as the movies that have already been produced. It's been suggested that we only include those projects currently in development, but that's nearly impossible to confirm (and what studio would give us their development reports?), and then we'd have to worry about turnaround, etc. We still believe the guide should contain as much information as possible—and because of the inclusion of unproduced screenplays our writers book has more information than any other on the market.

Pseudonyms
Pseudonyms are a researcher's nightmare, and we tried to catch them all, but certainly some clever ones slipped through. If a writer's pseudonym was deciphered, we'll direct you from the pseudonym to the writer, as well as list under that writer the name used for that credit. It's a sticky business, and though our hope is to provide the true writer's name for each feature, we have honored some writers' personal requests to keep a credit off their list—but only if they took a pseudonym for that credit.

Thanks, etc.
Any reference book is a continual work-in-progress; information must be added almost daily. The letters and resumes we continue to receive are greatly appreciated, and provide the best resource. Please keep sending comments and suggestions so we can continue to improve our service. Additional data is always welcome and is especially helpful the more information you provide.

A great deal of thanks to the patient Phil Haggood at the Writers Guild-West for answering questions daily, and to Aaron Zimmerman at Writers Guild-East for answering a long list of questions all at once. Numerous thanks to the agents and agencies who offered their support. Many agencies were helpful—but I want to single out for special thanks Holly Harter and Jennifer Phillips at CAA, Byrdie Lifson Pompan at United Talent Agency, Rachel at William Morris Agency, Rob at InterTalent, and Andrew Lester at Triad Artists, for each taking time from their busy jobs to help me get through a great deal of information.

Lots and lots of thanks to the writers who agreed to be my first interviews, and blessed me with wonderful responses to my unpracticed questions: Jeffrey Boam, Naomi Foner, Robbie Fox and Bruce Joel Rubin. An additional thanks to my buddy Mark Levin for introducing me to Bruce.

New thanks to Carlton Cuse for helping me catch a few glitches, and for providing handy tips for a beginning development executive. Also thanks to Susan Kaufman for being my kind of hairpin.

Continuing thanks to Jack Lechner for research assistance (and now that he's in London our information about British writers will surely get better); to fellow editor Steve LuKanic for still being there to lend a hand; to Joan Singleton for support and encouragement; and to Bethann Wetzel for her sanity in the face of chaos. Biggest thanks of all to my incredibly "jefftastic" husband Carr D'Angelo for helping me out when he has lots of his own work to do, and for being the best person to go to the movies with (he doesn't talk and he helps me remember the credits from the previews).

Susan Avallone

DIALOGUE

JEFFREY BOAM

EW WRITERS CAN CLAIM TWO MOVIES IN THE TOP TEN at the same time, but in the summer of 1989, Jeffrey Boam's *LETHAL WEAPON 2* and *INDIANA JONES AND THE LAST CRUSADE* were each a rousing success. These character-driven action movies followed scripts ranging from a highly regarded adaptation of Stephen King's *THE DEAD ZONE* to the science fiction comedy *INNERSPACE*. He has an exclusive deal at Warner Bros. in a producing partnership with Carlton Cuse, where they are looking forward to producing their first feature, which Boam will write and direct. He is currently working on a draft of *LETHAL WEAPON 3*.

SUSAN AVALLONE: How do you approach a rewrite? Is each one different?
JEFFREY BOAM: Each script that I read suggests its own procedure. If I rewrite something, it's because I see in the script a movie that hasn't been realized. I haven't done any rewrites that have been polishes. Every rewrite that I've received credit for has been a page-one rewrite.

Do you know that you are the last writer, that yours will be the definitive draft?
Well I never know that, I'm never sure. There's no guarantee. It has turned out that way but I don't write under that premise because I can't.

With sequels you're writing for well-established characters. Is it your goal to create in these movies a memorable character of your own?
In both *LETHAL 2* and *INDY 3*, I used the same device to inject new life into the series—introducing a new character. In Indy, of course, it was Professor Henry Jones, Indy's father. In Lethal, Joe Pesci's character, Leo Getz, is a variation on a character I created for an earlier script called *THE GOOD GUYS*, which was a very broad comedy based on the ABSCAM scandal. In that script, the character was a professional con man who teams up with a rookie FBI agent. *THE GOOD GUYS* came very close to being made several times, but now it's a dead issue. I'm glad I was able to sneak its best character into another movie.

How did you arrive at writing screenplays?
I did it as a substitute for directing in the theater arts department at UCLA. I just wasn't interested in the process of raising money and asking friends for favors, selling my car, whatever it took to make movies. I guess the people who did that are now directors. I came out of art school, and as an artist you work very much alone. You have no real physical obstacles to overcome beyond the obstacles the medium you're working in presents. That's all you have to master. So going into film school I came with those same sets of conditions and requirements. I didn't want to have to deal with other people. I just wanted to do what I wanted to do. I felt I couldn't do that directing, so writing was the next best thing. Sit down, put the paper in the typewriter and just write whatever I want, without anybody intruding or any other obstacles to overcome.

Screenwriting is still not as solitary pursuit as being a novelist or a painter. Your work is taken away from you and certain things happen to it.
Once you become a professional it is no longer a solitary experience because then you have meetings with executives and producers, actors, a variety of people. But trying to break into the business is still pretty solitary. You go off and write your spec scripts, just keep writing until someone reads a screenplay and likes it.

How did your break happen?
Really in the traditional way. A friend of a friend was an agent. A screenplay of mine got to her, she read it and liked it and she became my agent. Then the scripts began circulating and I had meetings with producers and executives. Jobs were offered, in a real clean kind of way.

Is directing still a goal for you? How do you feel about writers directing?
Anybody who gets a chance to direct and wants to do it should take it. Whether or not writers make better directors than editors or cinematographers, I don't know. That's something you could probably quantify very easily by making a list of people who've succeeded from different fields. But I still want to direct. I'm tired of working for other people; tired of trying to please them.
Some directors will give you moments that they like, and these moments have no context, so what good are they? It's just a moment that the director wants, without considering what it takes to get there. You have to do a lot of work to get to that moment and they don't like it. All they like is their "moment." For them the moment exists in some black hole in space, with nothing surrounding it. But it should be obvious that you can't have a moment without something before and after it.

Many writers want to direct to gain control over something they've written, but even as a director there are producers and studios to deal with.
When I write a screenplay and I know it's going into production I don't feel it's my screenplay anymore. It's also the producer's screenplay. It's the studio executive's screenplay. It's the director's screenplay. It's speaking with so many different voices that it's not mine anymore. So I don't care about creative control over it.

The cost of *LETHAL WEAPON*-type movies has come under fire recently. Is the action genre in trouble because of cost?
I think it's in trouble because it's being used up—by *DIE HARD* and *LETHAL WEAPON* and a few others in that genre. And people may be getting tired of them. But I don't think the budgets of these films are the problem. You need those bigger budgets. It's hard to make a *HOME ALONE* in the action genre. You're not going to make a sleeper in the action genre. People need to see high-priced action stars in these movies. And they want to see stunts and lots of explosions and a lot of things that are expensive. It's hard to make a small, intimate action movie. It's prob-

ably impossible to do that. You can make a cheap one, but it's not going to bring you the big rewards that the studios really need.

People think a "bad" script is one with bad dialogue, but many times it's the action writing that you can't follow. What does it take to write the action so that the reader can imagine what the writer is seeing?

More work. Dialogue comes out very spontaneously. I can write a page of dialogue quite fast. It just starts clicking and it works. But with an action scene, I've got to think about it a long time and constantly revise, revise, revise, so that I'm evoking the right images in the right order, for the right length of time. It's hard to do, because I'm trying to control or manipulate the reader to see the movie that I see. I write it and rewrite it and rearrange it and make things that are in lower case letters in capital, underline things, or just play around with the paragraphing. Whatever it takes to create the rhythm. I think rhythm is very important in an action scene. The way it's cut together is the dynamic that makes it work. You have to suggest that, and you can do so by writing it in a way that forces the reader to read it in cuts.

How important is research in your writing? INDIANA JONES AND THE LAST CRUSADE, for example, has so many historical elements.

The less I know about something the more research I have to do. *FUNNY FARM* was the only script I didn't have to research. Indy was hard to research because the grail is mired in different mythologies and folklore. Much of the script that sounds like information or history is made up.

How does adapting a novel compare to writing your own screenplay or rewriting a screenplay?

Whatever I'm doing, I always feel that the other ones would be easier to do. The truth is, writing a screenplay is so difficult that the degree of difference between adaptations, original screenplays or rewrites is so small as to be inconsequential. They're all so hard to do successfully.

Writing is such a personal pursuit, it's hard to ask someone "how do you write?" because it's a different experience for everyone.

Everybody has certain principles or rules of craft. Everybody's working method is different but it doesn't give you much insight into writing, does it? The hardest thing, I think, is to write a script that needs to be made into a movie. A script may be good, and you can see that the writer's a talented writer, but you know that it will never get made into a movie.

> *"The hardest thing, I think, is to write a script that needs to be made into a movie....Excellence is not enough. Sometimes it's not even necessary...A lousy script with a commercial idea is more valuable than a really well-written script that will ultimately be a movie that no one wants to see."* — Jeffrey Boam

And there's some scripts that aren't well-written that you know will make movies. Excellence is not enough. Sometimes it's not even necessary. I think a commercial idea is almost better than a good script. A lousy script with a commercial idea is more valuable than a really well-written script that will ultimately be a movie that no one wants to see.

Perhaps that's because of the way the studio system is set up—maybe the fine-tuning process works better for bad scripts with good ideas than vice-versa.

I think so. A good idea that's badly written needs the input of other people. I'd rather rewrite that script than an extremely well-written script that's just not commercial. If somebody gave me *CHINATOWN*, for example, and said this is a really well-written script we just don't think there's enough rooting interest in the character, we want the audience to really cheer at the end, I would have no idea how to do that. I just don't think it's possible. But if they gave me some badly written version of *JAWS* I'd say, "Yeah, I'd like to do this, I get it, I know how to make this work." I think that's why many scripts are being sold now for a lot of money. They probably contain some commercial ideas.

But the *Basic Instinct* script by Joe Eszterhas sold for a lot of money, and read like it could be shot as it was, and still there had to be changes made.

Well, the director comes along and he's got his own vision. If Eszterhas got to direct it, he would be shooting the first draft. I think this is one of the secrets to why John Hughes can be so prolific. He is in a position where he can shoot his first draft. Probably many of his scripts could've been improved by more work, but it just wouldn't have made a difference. Movies don't have to be perfect. They work or they don't work. And studios are terrible about not really knowing when it's as good as it needs to be.

What's your process for writing? Should beginners all follow the Syd Field rules, the index cards, etc.?

One thing you never learn is how to create. I've never read those books or taken those courses but probably there's some truth to them. The rules that they've discovered come from analyzing good work and finding things that they all have in common. If you can't do it instinctively then I guess it's good to have a little ruler next to your desk to measure with to see if you're being accurate.

What gets you started writing, the first scene, or knowing the ending?

I have a lot of scenes in mind. I need to have the basic shape of it in my head. I need to know what it's about, what the characters are about. Occasionally I use cards, it's a good organizational tool, but basically I try to just live with it, think about it, and make it have a life in my imagination. Once it starts taking root up there, it can come out. I need to know what the ending is, then it's just moving towards the ending.

What's the attraction a feature writer has to moving into television? The writing is more sacred, the director more for hire?

That's the nice thing. My experience in television so far has been that writers are in control. But I don't have enough experience beyond that to talk about it.

You've achieved a very high level of success as a writer. Do you still have to

be a salesman for your own ideas even though you've proven yourself?

It's no different writing now than it was when I first started. It's no easier. It's not like the road is any less bumpy.

Do you think writers are asking for the wrong things, like casting input, and being allowed to visit the set during production?

We're treated so badly, and now we're going hat in hand. It's pathetic. I really believe that there is an unstated conspiracy among producers and directors and studio executives to make writers feel they're unimportant. Because if they were allowed to know how important they are, they'd want more money, they'd want more power, they'd want more influence.

I feel at some point, back in the twenties maybe, they said, "Look, sound is coming along. The writer's going to become too powerful. He's going to become king. It's going to be his show. We've got to right now not allow that to happen. We'll hire him. We'll fire him. We'll make him feel like dogfood and we'll keep his esteem real low." And I think that's what they still do.

They think now that they're giving writers more money, and that's a big thing.

But not nearly as much as directors and actors are getting. If you compare what I made on *LETHAL WEAPON 2* to what Mel Gibson made, it's like the difference between what I make and what my poolman makes. The only reason writers are getting more money is because the studios are realizing that it's cheaper to spend a lot on a screenplay that they feel is almost ready to shoot than it is to develop something from scratch, where there's a lot of manpower and rewrites and WGA health benefits, etc., to pay for. That's the only reason writers have gotten a lot of money recently for spec scripts. Not because they suddenly feel that writers are underpaid. It's not that at all.

BRI

BRUDER RELEASING, INC.

Program Suppliers to the Pay-Per-View, Cable and Broadcast Markets

* REPRESENTING OVER 100 INDEPENDENT PRODUCERS AND DISTRIBUTORS

* PROGRAM PLACEMENTS ON HBO, SHOWTIME, USA, VIEWERS CHOICE, ETC.

* OVER 500 PLACEMENTS MADE ON U.S. CABLE AND SATELLITE SYSTEMS IN 1990

* OVER 20 YEARS OF EXPERIENCE IN PRODUCTION, PROMOTION AND DISTRIBUTION

CALL US. WE CAN HELP YOU GET YOUR FILM PLACED!

2020 BROADWAY SANTA MONICA, CA. 90404
TEL 213-289-2222   FAX 213-289-0202

NAOMI FONER

OR HER SCREENPLAY OF *RUNNING ON EMPTY*, Naomi Foner received a Golden Globe, a Pen International Best Screenplay Award and an Academy Award nomination for Best Original Screenplay. After starting as a producer in children's television working on such series as *Sesame Street* and *The Electric Company*, she emerged as a unique voice known for well-developed characters. She hopes one of her latest screenplays, an adaptation of the Mary McGarry Morris novel *A Dangerous Woman*, set up at Amblin' Entertainment, will be the next of her many works to reach the screen.

SUSAN AVALLONE: There's a common belief that RUNNING ON EMPTY is based on a true story. How did it in fact come about?
NAOMI FONER: There actually isn't a true story that's any relationship to the movie. There was a newspaper article that [producers] Amy Robinson and Griffin Dunne saw about some modern-day radicals who were arrested with a big stash of guns and things in the house, and their kids were taken into welfare care. The only basis in the story that triggered the concept was what was going to happen to their kids. That seemed like a very original way into dealing with people who had political commitments. But those kids were babies, and I immediately thought, it's not interesting, the kids have to have some kind of decision-making possibilities to give this any drama. And that was the jumping off point. Everything else is fictionalized, based on tons of research and a lot of first-person knowledge about friends and people I interviewed that lived this way. People have insisted that this was such-and-such a family in such-and-such a place who did such-and-such. They don't want to know that it's not. There was actually a trial that came up afterwards in which people used the movie in their defense. The whole point of it was to capture the spirit of that time and place, which it obviously did in terms of people identifying with it.

So in this case the producers brought a story idea to you—
They thought that I could handle this subject area well, so we were looking for some way to do it. People have tried to deal with the sixties for a long time, and the kids were the way in. So the story is basically an original story, but that happens often where somebody says, "I want to make a movie about coal miners." Producers are often looking for subject arenas, or they have a book or something that they want to do. It used to be, much more than it is now in Hollywood, that the writer would go to the producer or the studio. But these days it's turned around a great deal, where the studios like to think of themselves as creative entities, so they come to you with an arena and an array of stories that they've come up with. I think that's unfortunate on some level because the craft of screenwriting is a little diminished by the fact that there isn't more corporate access for your stories.

Is it the difference between the writer trying to sell an original script versus being a writer for hire?
It was always writing for hire, but in this case there's a distinct if subtle difference between being hired to write something that someone thinks they've given to you to do, or you saying, "I think this would make an interesting movie," and having someone say, "Yes you're right, go write it." Authorship hangs on those distinctions. And more and more these days if they've hired you to do their story as they think of it—even if there is no story and you actually have to come up with one—the studios feel freer to dismiss you and then they'll find six, eight writers on a script. Then you're more like a plumber who's come in to fix a broken pipe than you are someone who's designed and built a house. Writers need to feel if they're any good that they have some authorship of their material. I think that's terribly important. And studios, if they really want good material, are going to have to understand that and nurture it. The way that writers have gone about getting it back has been to write spec scripts, which they then sell for a lot of money and the studios don't like it.

Does being a producer on your own material make the development process less uncomfortable?
It means that when they've bought it they can't leave you behind. It's a way to assure at least a superficial ongoing dialogue in the process. That's extremely important because these days we're negotiating with directors and the studio executives to have an ongoing dialogue, which is what one would assume you would have out of common courtesy. Nobody's even asking for any power, they're just asking to be considered a part of the creative team, so that when the director signs on to do your script they meet with you at least once.

Is an area like casting a place where a writer wants more say?
A director, if he's smart, asks you who you thought of playing the part. And if you can make a working relationship where you know what the protocol is—working on a movie's like being in an operating room. You don't talk to the actors on the set. You don't say what you think in casting sessions. A lot of directors like to have writers on the set, but they're afraid because they've had relationships with writers who don't know what the protocol is and do the wrong thing. It goes in both directions. I think it is a responsibility of writers to understand that someone has to be driving the train.

In children's television, how did you make the change from producing to writing?
I did it so long with others as a producer that by the time I did write, it was something I knew how to do, at least in craft. And then you either can do it or you can't. I was very lucky, my first script got produced, then I immediately got an

agent based on that, and another job. I have never written when I wasn't being paid, so I've worked as a professional writer way before I probably ought to have. For the first six, eight scripts I wrote, I just wrote them and they hired me to do something else and they didn't get made. And I thought, well, this is an interesting job, writing scripts that don't get made, and I actually began to believe that that's what you did. The first thing I wrote that was made [VIOLETS ARE BLUE] was a huge surprise to me. Once one of your scripts gets made people tend to look at your scripts differently, more like they will get made. But it's still a process in which they have a 15 to 1 set-up here and whether your script gets made or not has little to do with the quality of your work and much more to do with circumstance. I don't want to be a snob about this but a lot of things that are less quality are more likely to get made because they're more accessible. So writing screenplays can be very bad for your self-esteem.

Would you ever want to write one of those more obviously commercial movies?

I don't know how to do that. My writing is very character-based. I can't start without doing all that background character research, that's my strength. I can't write gags. I can write humor that comes out of the people. I can't write those broad, huge, one-dimensional things, where the people aren't really people but prototypes. Actually I think it's another kind of skill. I don't want to put it down either. I have been asked to come in on things like that and make characters where there are no characters—there are films that don't have my name on them that I have done rewrites on—to give some more meat to it. I don't want to sound self-righteous but I can't do things that I don't feel. My life is finite, my work-time is finite. It has to mean something to me, it has to be something I can take my kids to see. There are very popular movies that are important, and the people writing them should know that they have a huge responsibility. Whoever's writing PRETTY WOMAN is setting a sort of cultural standard, and it's saying something. So if I get a chance to write something for which there's going to be a wide audience, I'd jump to do it because I think that's exactly where we should be working. I don't want to write movies for eight people to see in art houses. RUNNING ON EMPTY was intended to be a very accessible picture about very real people, and I don't think we made a movie that was only accessible to a small audience. But I can't

> "The real hard work is that every character has to be specific and real. You need to know who they are before they walk into your first scene, whole backstories you may never use but they're good to know."
>
> *—Naomi Foner*

write DIE HARD 2 and I wouldn't. There are things I'd say no to on just political grounds. Then there are things I can't do, and I have respect for the people who can do them.

I would hope it would help that many actresses have their own production companies actively looking for good characters for those women to portray.

That helps, but we're living in a world where there is presently one actress who can get a movie financed and it is not Meryl Streep, it's Julia Roberts. And there's a list of ten men. If you ask a studio executive, there has to be a man in it to make the movie go, except for Julia Roberts. So for all the success that Geena Davis and Susan Sarandon have with THELMA AND LOUISE, these are not women who are going to be able to get a movie financed on their own. And for women writers who are writing subject matter and characters for women, there's a certain reality to what apparently the marketplace bears. There was an article in the Los Angeles Times saying that men over 55 are perceived as elegant and distinguished and women as basically old bags. This is crazy. You don't want to hear it, but unfortunately this is what's going on. I have several ideas for grown-up love stories for people who've lived, who have a little wisdom.

With all the ancillary markets it seems there should be a greater number of "small" films because the profit is there to be made.

You get very sanguine about this stuff, or else you drop out of doing it, because pretty soon it's quite clear that in American studio filmmaking this is an uphill battle. There's another way to do it. My husband [director Stephen Gyllenhaal] had a film at Cannes, PARIS TROUT, so we went. I didn't realize that all these little European movies get made for $5 million, and we can do that too. There are all kinds of schemes that could make that happen, like people working for a minimum and taking a *real* percentage of *real* reported profits. There are major actors, writers, directors and producers who would work that way for things they really care about if they knew they could bet on themselves and get it back at the other end. So in the meantime you just keep pushing that rock up the hill. And hope it doesn't roll over and flatten you.

How did getting the Academy Award nomination affect your standing as a writer?

What really talks to them still is money, someone who has just made them $100 million. The Academy Award isn't going to make that much difference, but the nomination helps—it gives you a certain credibility. It means that when you come into the office they listen to you more attentively. They will take a chance a little bit more with you. There is a certain validation. And also it had an affect on me. It gave me a sense of calmness which I didn't have before. I said, "Okay, I can do this." There's a certain level of accomplishment that is acknowledged. The biggest thing you'll find with people who are serious about their work is they'll say it will let me get something else done. It does help a little bit, there's no question about it, but practically it's still always a struggle to do anything that's out of the ordinary. That's because this is show *business*, and it doesn't matter that it's been proven over and over again that anything out of the ordinary is exactly what people are looking for. It's an ongoing struggle, if you keep the energy up, and you do it for the right reasons. It gets done, it just takes longer. It's harder, it's more uncomfortable. But life is complicated. I have days when I get up and say, "What am I doing this for?" And particularly writing—it's so lonely, it's so isolated.

But screenwriting inevitably involves other people.

Yes, but you have two or three months when you're sitting by yourself doing it. My most favorite time is going out to a meeting, or talking to someone after there's a draft in. Or working with the director, being on the set when it's happening. I've been very lucky to have such wonderful directors who included me in the process. That's great. What's hard is sitting and facing the blank page by yourself, because you can go to the office and sit there for 12 hours and, if you haven't done anything, you haven't been to work. Most people I know who are really good writers hate it. There's something very painful about it. You can always see what you can't get to, or what you haven't done or why it isn't exactly the way you'd like to make it. You're facing yourself and your own limitations in some way or another that's disturbing. This isn't funny enough. Or how do I get it funnier? Well I guess I'm not funny. What do I do now? For me anyway, that's always part of the process.

You've been working with Paul Newman on a screenplay he's interested in. How is it different writing with a particular actor in mind?

Paul Newman really came out on the page. What I usually do in the first draft is write the character, and if something needs to be changed afterwards, my work is usually done on the character. Really good actors don't want to play themselves anyway, they want to play the character. The real hard work is that every character has to be specific and real. You need to know who they are before they walk into your first scene, whole backstories you may never use but they're good to know. I think an actor does similar kind of work in preparing to act, and if you've done that already, there are unspoken things in the characters that are enormous help to them. I love to work with really good actors about a character. If I write something and give it to Dustin Hoffman or Paul Newman or Meryl Streep, their comments are going to be as astute about writing as anything you can get. With *RUNNING OF EMPTY*, River Phoenix knew instantly when something was wrong with his character and I always trusted him. Because when you give a character to an actor it's like you've got the frame of the house and they're going to paint it and furnish it, hang the pictures, and live in it. They know, because they're inhabiting it, things that sometimes are creaky or rusty because you didn't look in that corner, and they have to look in that corner to walk. That's the best part of this process.

In reading the script of *RUNNING ON EMPTY*, the character of Lorna [Martha Plimpton] could have been misinterpreted. She's played as sad and vulnerable, but on the page is cold or bratty because her language is that way.

Lorna's my most favorite character. I have a lot of problems with people reading my scripts, because I tend to write surface dialogue that plays against the character. That character was someone in my mind who was very vulnerable, who was tough on the outside to cover that stuff up. And when you read the words they just read tough. Most writers who do this for a while write a draft that is just for the studio in which all that is in the stage direction. I'll sometimes say, "She doesn't know what she's doing here but she pretends she does," so that when the dialogue is read you know that this is Katharine Hepburn putting on a tough-girl act and underneath she's ready to melt. You need to know that, but there's no way to know that on the page unless you put it down. Sidney Lumet took everything like that out for the actors because he wanted them to come to it themselves. He didn't want them to have that kind of direction from the writer. I always say when I teach a class [at UCLA], if somebody's late for lunch and you're sitting and waiting for them and you're pissed off, and they come and sit down and say "Gee I'm awfully sorry," no matter how pissed off you are you're not going to say, "And don't let it happen again." You usually say, "It's okay," but what you're doing with your fork is an indication of what you're really thinking. People rarely say what they're thinking. Well the screenplay can tell you both things at the same time. I'm going to say I'm not angry but I really am pissed off. In a play they have to say, "I'm really pissed off," somehow, it has to be in the dialogue because you can't see it from the stage. And in a novel you get to say all that stuff any way you want. So every one of those forms is different and I like the game of trying to say all the things at the same time. The levels that you can get, that's my most fun when I'm writing screenplays.

> *"When you give a character to an actor, it's like you've got the frame of the house and they're going to paint it and furnish it, hang the pictures, and live in it. They know, because they're inhabiting it, things that sometimes are creaky or rusty because you didn't look in that corner, and they have to look in that corner to walk. That's the best part of this process."*
> *—Naomi Foner*

BRUCE JOEL RUBIN

IT WAS A LONG ROAD TO SUCCESS FOR BRUCE JOEL RUBIN and then it all seemed to happen at once. In the summer of 1990 was a phenomenon called *GHOST*, resulting in incredible box-office and earning him an Oscar for Best Original Screenplay. Then in the Fall came the disturbing and unique *JACOB'S LADDER*, a script that had been included in *American Film*'s list of ten best unproduced screenplays. He hopes the success of *GHOST* will start a new wave of emotional stories on screen: "I want people to vote with their hearts. So many people vote with their intellect. And a film that appeals only to intellect is not satisfying.

SUSAN AVALLONE: Your scripts read like literature. Do you have any desire to be a novelist?
BRUCE JOEL RUBIN: I have great admiration for novelists but I don't think I could write a novel if I wanted to. I don't have that certain depth of perception into the inner workings of specific people's natures in the way that the novelist does. I'm much more involved in the surface and trying to use the surface as a way in, rather than looking inside as a way of seeing what's out. I admire novelists, and in my deepest dreams I would like to be one. But I'm more attracted to the short form of the screenplay. It's a kind of shorthand, and I'm one of these people who's always frustrated with how long it takes to do anything. A screenplay you can write in a given amount of time. If you had to, you could do it in a week.

I never wanted to be a writer and I'm still amazed that people say I write well because I never particularly thought of myself as a writer, I always wanted to be a director. I don't think of myself as a particularly great writer, but I feel in touch with the emotions I'm trying to convey. I think some of those get on the paper and in some places have gotten on the screen and that's a wonderful experience. Mostly I think of myself as a storyteller who's just trying to weave a tale. It's campfire talk, sitting around the campfire and elaborating and getting into the mood and emotion of a scene and trying to elaborate it in such a way that your audience is with you in terms of their own imagination, and that you're joining together in some communal imagination. I find that entering into that communal space is what's really thrilling about storytelling. Because you can lead people on adventures that often they can't lead themselves on. It's not a very common experience in the Western world right now. People do that sitting in the cinema, but in a way it's much more concrete, because they're not journeying through the communal mind they're journeying into someone else's mind. Storytelling is to enter a space that is shared. It's a lost art. When radio died, it really was the end of this kind of storytelling. The novel in a way takes us into that space, where two people meet instead of a group of people. That's what I love about reading a good novel, this privileged opportunity to see another psyche at work. In film you don't have that quite so much because there are so many psyches that impinge upon the final product. You have the mark of the original writer, which should be very strong, but you have so many interpreters of that original image that you don't have a total pure product. You have something that emerges of its own nature. Ultimately, there's no one author of a movie, there's an author of the screenplay but that's only one element in the making of that work and it's hard for a lot of writers to accept that.

An interesting conflict is that writers hate being rewritten but they are often willing to rewrite another writer. How do you reconcile that?
First of all, the process of rewriting is the most lucrative part of writing in Hollywood. So there's a temptation. Writers can often look at another work and judge its weakness much more readily than they can look at their own work and judge its weakness. So the opportunity to go in and fix something is appealing. The proper approach to rewriting—and not all writers have said this because of the 51% rule [you get screen credit for writing 51% of a screenplay]—is to serve the material, to write in the voice of the previous writer as much as you can, and have the film work. To be as invisible a creative partner as you can make yourself. And that's really what I've tried to do, in my last two rewrites I did not try to get credit. I just felt as a favor to these people, I knew how to make these films work. I knew how to take problem areas and fix them. And I knew how to do it in such a way that you'd never know I touched the screenplay. If we could find a lot of writers who thought that way I think we would be in a much better position about being rewritten.

Have you had a bad experience with someone rewriting a screenplay of yours?
I was rewritten once, on *BRAINSTORM*, by a friend [Phil Messina], and actually the work that he did was extraordinary. He did the first rewrite of the film. At that point I was no longer considering myself a writer and I suggested that he do the rewrite. The draft that he created was always the one that I wanted to see reach the screen. And it didn't. He got rewritten by other writers and in the end the film lost all of its integrity, or most of it. But Phil did what I was talking about. He brought the quality of care to the material. Other writers came into it and as fast as they could they got in the way of the material. Their first choice was to change all the names of the characters, which is just an anathema to me. The character's name is everything—when you come up with a character's name, that's the person. A lot of writers know that, so their first order of business is make them "my" characters. I think that's wrong in rewriting.

With *GHOST* and *JACOB'S LADDER* you were able to be the one doing the rewriting. How did that happen?
I insisted on that as much as I could. The way to accomplish that, the way to be your own rewriter, is to be open. As soon as you are closed and you are the only one who knows how this film should go, you're in danger because you have a direc-

11

tor who may not agree with you and the director will have the power. If you can stay open, engage in an honest dialogue with the director, and not be threatening to that director, you'll have the opportunity to rewrite your own work. The directors will have enormous ideas, and often exciting ideas, for the material. If they have ideas you don't agree with at least you can be there to have the kind of honorable battle that is necessary to prevent the destruction of your material. Adrian Lyne and I fought endlessly on *JACOB'S LADDER*, but we would always say to each other "with all due respect" and then we would jump into this harangue. But because it was respectful we could say anything because we both knew that we were passionate, that we had deep and very important feelings about the material and that we wanted that material to be well-realized. And so we never got in each other's way. In the end we fought for the betterment of the script.

If anything got muted from the early *JACOB'S LADDER* drafts it was the apocalyptic Biblical aspects. Do you think that the things you removed will show up in other works of yours?

What I have to say as a writer, a lot of the things I deal with, will re-emerge, and reappear in other work. I do have a particular vision, and that vision is not going to be sublimated by the material, it will always find its way through. I may not ever get to see *JACOB'S LADDER* the way I had dreamt that I would see it. In many ways the movie's close and in some ways it's better, but the big problem for me will always be the ending. That's where the battle that I had with Adrian rested primarily. I wanted a film that was more about resurrection and Adrian wanted one that was more about redemption. I wanted a film that had more of a spiritual climax and involved some deeper messages than the film finally communicates. What I'm grateful about is that even without those messages the film has integrity, that it still works and still has its own message. You cannot go into a film expecting a hundred-percent perfection. If you do you're going to be a very unhappy person in this world. There are a lot of very unhappy writers in Hollywood for just that reason. I don't walk around being unhappy, it's just not worth it. And I always have my screenplays. Though there is joy in seeing your movie get made and in seeing the public respond to it, the real joy of writing is writing. And if you don't feel that, if your whole life is about winning awards or being recognized on the street, don't be a writer. In the aftermath of *GHOST* and *JACOB'S LADDER* my experience is still that the greatest pleasure was the creation of the scripts. You feel very cut off from the actual final achievement, because it's not your own achievement. You stand in

> *"Ultimately, there's no one author of a movie, there's an author of the screenplay but that's only one element in the making of that work and it's hard for a lot of writers to accept that." —Bruce Joel Rubin*

the back of the theater and see so many efforts combined to make the movie happen. You don't feel personal pride but you feel good. You don't feel like the universe is smiling on you then, the universe smiled on you while you were writing. If you don't appreciate that moment, you're in the wrong business.

Did you have any idea, from previews or early comments from people in the business, that *GHOST* was going to be a success?

Before *GHOST* opened, my biggest concern was not that it was a good movie because I knew that it was, but would anybody go see it? Several days before it opened I would tell people I'd written the movie *GHOST* and they'd say "Oh, Bill Cosby" [*GHOST DAD*]. I would say "No, no, no. Patrick Swayze and Whoopi Goldberg and Demi Moore." And they would look at me with their eyes crossed, like give me a break. I would feel so embarrassed. Then we went to see a sneak preview with my parents in Detroit, a week before it opened. I was so nervous that nobody would be in the theater. And in fact just the opposite, we're sitting in the theater and people are coming in, and coming in, there are lines around the theater, they had to turn people away. And I was saying, "This is incredible." My most exciting moment was that realization that people were going to see the preview and then the weekend that it opened we ended up sleeping over at Jerry Zucker's house, we had a brake failure on my car, and had spent the evening running around looking at all the lines at the various theaters. And we woke up at six o'clock in the morning with this phone call from the studio telling us the numbers that the film had done and they were spectacular. And that's when we sensed we had a real movie on our hands. It was against all odds. Nobody had predicted it.

How do you feel about the trend some say *GHOST* started? Lots of ghost stories and love stories seem to be in the pipeline, and your movie will always be the point of comparison when these movies eventually come out.

What can you say? That's Hollywood. The hardest thing in writing is to write a love story in which you really feel that love on the screen. To really convey emotion and not be *about* emotion is very difficult. If we can have films that achieve that, it will be wonderful but if we have a whole rash of films that don't, the genre will slip away very quickly. I hope what's been opened up by *GHOST*, more than just a rash of ghost movies and love stories, is that all the rules are out the window. And until the new rules come in, people can write their hearts out and come up with films that we haven't seen before—that would be wonderful.

Is part of the appeal of *GHOST* the fantasy element, the chance to really escape at the movies?

People call *GHOST* a fantasy, but I think it's true appeal is that it deals with something real. For a lot of people this film is a fantasy, but I think there's a certain part of the population that recognizes that what we're dealing with is a cosmological truth. There's something deep inside many people that vibrates to that affirmation. We're not a film speculating about the idea that a human being preexists his physical life and continues beyond it, we are affirming it. And I think that affirmation is one of the major reasons that film is successful. It has a very strong spiritual world view and that's why the film appeals, even if people don't understand it intellectually. And I think a lot of people who did understand it intellectually rebelled against it. The *People* magazine critic said Jerry Zucker and I should go to Hell for making that film. And I figure we touched something here that this guy didn't want touched, and I felt bad for him. I was personally offended that he would say I would go to Hell for writing a movie. I don't think he knows what he's saying and I think he may have felt he was being cute. But I take that seriously.

Would you ever want to tackle your personal themes in a different kind of movie, like an action picture or comedy?

If I thought I could. I tried to do that with the rewrite I did on *SLEEPING WITH THE ENEMY*. My job was the second act. They had created a character for the Julia Roberts character to fall in love with who was almost as reprehensible as the man she had just left. So the movie didn't work on that level. You didn't like this guy that she was going to for refuge. My job was in three weeks to come in and create a character who you could like and feel her liking and establish him in the second act. Which meant I had to establish him very quickly, you had to like him instantaneously. So I came up with this idea of having her see him outside the window singing a song from *WEST SIDE STORY* and watering the lawn. I felt if this grabbed you, then you're going to like this guy for the rest of the movie. To figure this out was a wonderful challenge. I felt I helped the movie, and I walked away from it feeling very good.

What happens when you write a movie and you're completely unhappy with the finished product and want to distance yourself from it?

What happened to *DEADLY FRIEND* was horrible. I found a way to make it a film that had some redeeming values, particularly by turning it into a love story. On paper, believe it or not, it read very emotionally. A studio executive called me and said she cried when she read it, and we made a movie which conveyed some of that. But director Wes Craven's audience was absolutely outraged we had given them a movie about emotion and not about bloodletting. So the studio made us shoot six scenes, each one bloodier than the preceding one. They changed the name from *FRIEND* to *DEADLY FRIEND*. They put on an ending that the head of the studio came up with, which was a total embarrassment for me and for which I got all the blame. It was a very sad experience.

Particular songs mentioned in screenplays often seem out-of-place, like the writer is putting together the soundtrack of hits. You use music in a way that adds to the scene emotionally. How important is the music to you?

It's not always my forte but there are certain things along the way that I will punch up because I think that's what belongs there at a given moment. "Unchained Melody" for *GHOST* was a brilliant choice and that was producer Lisa Weinstein's idea. She told me and I thought, this is great, and then she brought in the tape for Jerry Zucker to listen to and we all started crying, we just knew that it was so perfect and it really worked in the movie.

I'm a major opera fan and often in writing scripts I will listen to opera because it talks to the emotions, nothing else. It really gets me into a place where I can start to dredge up this stuff that I want to get onto the screen. I love films that address emotions, I cannot stand going to a movie that has not appealed to me as a whole being. So many films appeal either to my kishkas, or to my head, but nothing seems to unite the fact that I exist on all these levels. I have all these aspects of personality that want to be addressed. The great novels—Tolstoy, Dostoevsky—take you in as a whole entity and they put you through it. And it's wonderful.

What films inspire you?

To me, a film like *THE WIZARD OF OZ*, is one of the greatest films ever made. I never tire of it. Every time I see it, it works. It is a vastly entertaining movie that somehow digs into us. A movie like that affects me very deeply, I would love to make movies that have a life beyond me. I would love it if *GHOST* becomes something like that, and time will tell. But to be able to pull that off as a writer, to be able to leave something now that a hundred years from now will still have impact, is thrilling. To be able to touch a universal chord and not just the chord of the moment.

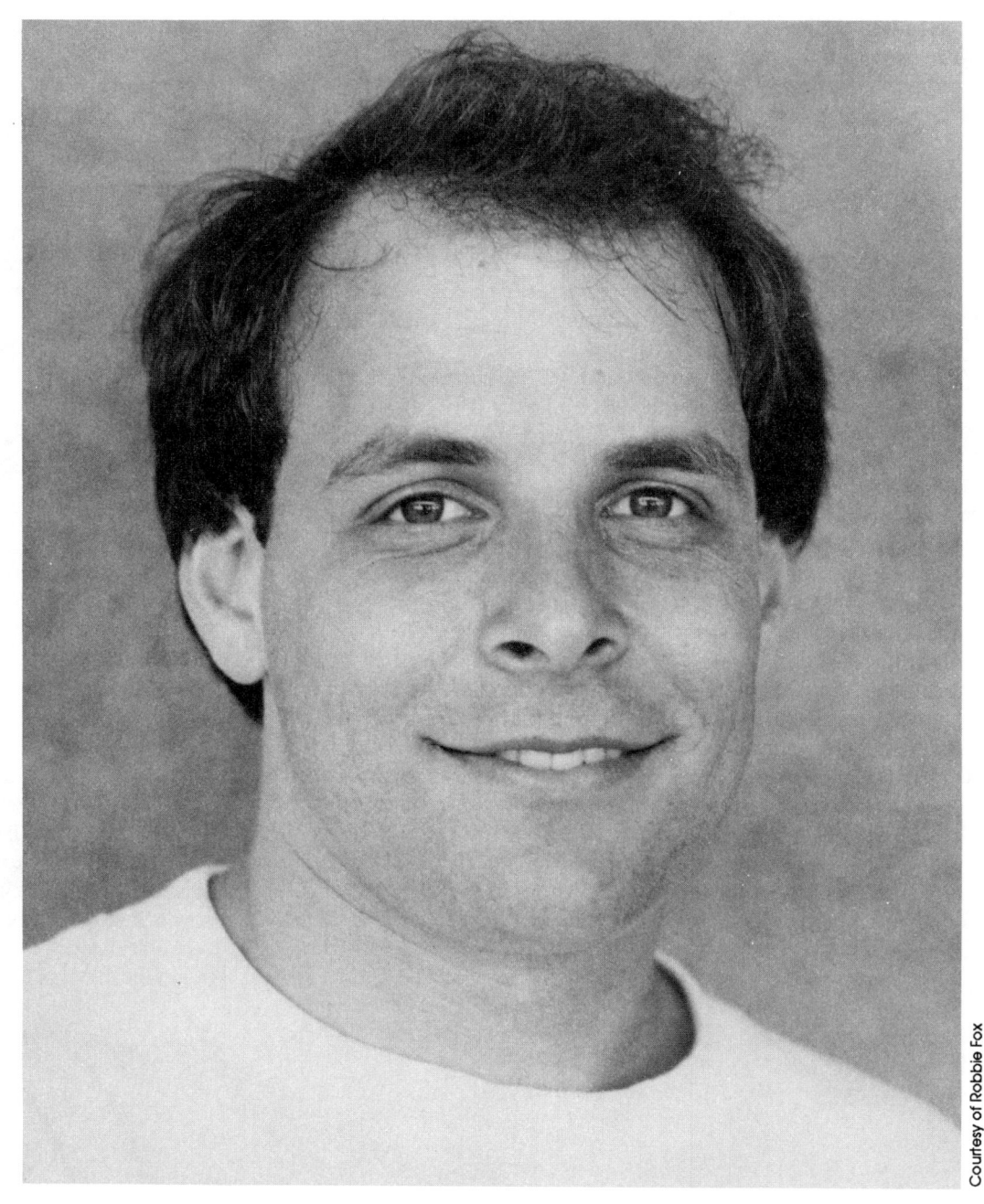

ROBBIE FOX

ROBBIE FOX IS A PERFECT EXAMPLE OF WHY WRITERS with only unproduced screenplays are included in this directory. This 27-year-old came to the attention of Hollywood through a short film he wrote and directed for the Discovery Program called *THE GREAT O'GRADY*. Since then he's been a working writer: every one of his screenplays has been optioned, he gets hired for rewrites, and has a studio deal to develop television projects. And perhaps at last he'll see his name on the screen: one of his scripts, *SHOOTING ELIZABETH*, appears to be nearing production.

SUSAN AVALLONE: When did you know you wanted to be a writer?
ROBBIE FOX: My father, Charlie Fox, is a film composer and songwriter, so he used to take me out of school for dubbing. He'd take me to scoring and I'd hang out on the set, so I kind of grew up in his hip pocket.

Were you a film addict?
I always loved films and I was always a writer. We used to make *Super 8* films when I was younger, from eight years old on. The roof of our house leaned over the swimming pool, so in every movie we made the climax would be a guy getting shot and falling off the roof and into the pool. Whatever the plot was—it could be a love story, it could be about three dogs—it always ended with a gunfight on the roof, one guy gets shot. Then we put a dummy filled with stuffed-up paper in somebody's clothes to fall into the pool. And then we'd put the actor in the pool, put ketchup on him and he would float to the bottom and die. My dad's office looked out onto the pool area, and one day he looked into the backyard and saw my brother floating in the pool, bleeding Heinz ketchup. He opened the door—shoes, shirt, everything—and dove into the pool to save my brother. He ruined the shot, needless to say.

When you got started writing, did you weigh taking a development deal versus the spec script market?
Spec scripts are very deceiving because you only read about the ones that sell for $1 million or $800,000. If you read about a script selling for $200,000 or $300,000 it's almost a disappointment. However the scripts that sell count for probably one percent of the scripts overall that are written on spec. A studio executive always looks better improving a project that he already has money into rather than taking a chance on a new project, so they say they want to hear new ideas but the ideas are all variations of existing ideas. "Well, I have a story that's kind of similar we're developing" or "We don't have Eddie Murphy so there's no sense in us developing a project for that kind of guy." A spec script can be a tricky thing because people can love the script but it just doesn't fit into the twelve pictures that they're going to make. When people buy a spec script they're not paying $100,000 up front, they're committing to $12 to 20 million. Because what's the point of buying a finished script if you don't like it? You could rewrite it a million times but it's going to cost you a lot of money. So you've got to think, do we want to make this movie, not develop it. When you're selling just an idea to a studio, it's a kernel of an idea and anything could happen.

Have you sold mostly scripts or ideas?
All my scripts have sold, not all my ideas have sold. There was that goose love triangle story that the studios didn't seem to get. All my scripts have been on assignment, since the first script I sold, which was *Slightly Panicked*. Then I worked on a feature as the director for a year and a half, but somebody else ended up directing. It was a catering dispute. I felt we should have a salsa bar and they wanted dim sum.

I know you have a good rewrite story.
The true irony of the business. I have many original ideas and I only want to do my original ideas. I've written thirteen drafts of a screenplay over two and a half years, for two different studios, with different stars attached to it at times, different directors, a "go" picture in three different regimes. It's kind of a broad, romantic comedy. After thirteen drafts the studio decided that they wanted a polish to be done by an established, successful writer. They hired a woman who writes really wonderful, small, touching films. And of course it upset me very much, it was my baby. And it was so atypical for her to write this kind of film. And then I got a call recently to come work on a script that was a small, sensitive story and it turned out she was the writer on it. Which makes so little sense that it makes sense. You can't get angry, it's just part of the process. They bring in different people to do different things and that's the way it goes.

When I read one of your scripts it struck me that there's a certain technique that a lot of the "young" writers have in common —
First, you're just a writer trying to sell your script, and you're this "young writer." And then you sell your script and you're a "hot young writer." Then the script goes into turnaround and you go back to "young." Then you lose your hair a little and you're just a "writer." And then people aren't buying your ideas and then you're in the real estate business. That's my theory.

Many descriptive passages in your script, like a lot of other scripts, have little jokes directed at studio readers and development people. Are you trying to insure a favorable response by speaking directly to the reader?
Reading scripts is the dullest thing you could possibly do in your life, it's harder than writing scripts. It's not entertaining, it's not enjoyable, it's technical. It's like showing somebody blueprints and saying, "Doesn't this building look great?" So the point is you want to make it interesting. The way most people read scripts is right down the middle of the page, just the dialogue. The first thing an executive or producer does when he looks at a script is see how many pages it is. If it's 103, 104, you'll see a smile come over his face. If it's

131 pages, it's gonna go last on his pile. Your first scene should be great, funny, exciting. If your first block of words is half a page of description and the dialogue starts in the middle of the page, 99 percent of the people go to the middle of the page and they make up in their mind what it's telling them. You want to be entertaining, your job is to bring it to life.

Do you think by being entertaining in the descriptions you're forcing the person to read every single word?

People don't read very closely. On a project once, the director and I wrote into the script—just to see if the studio really read it closely—one line where the character says, "Wait a minute. I died in the last draft. What am I doing in here?" No one saw it, no one picked up on it. Scripts are very easy to skim. Screenplays are terrible to read.

Since you've written only comedies, would you ever want to turn your attention to a full-fledged drama?

You just want to add weight to the comedy. Comedy is very important. Arnold Schulman wrote some great comedies, romantic stories. *GOODBYE COLUMBUS* had real weight to it. It was funny, it was entertaining, but there was a real view of a relationship that society said couldn't work. You deal with the same themes that are in dramas, but your characters, that's how they deal with life. The other day I was at lunch with a director and producer. And the director got his eggs, and the producer got his pancakes, and I got somebody's steak fries. And I said, "Why does everyone get their meal right and I don't?" And the director said, "I like it that way. I like you in pain. It makes you funnier." Mel Brooks said "Tragedy is when I hurt my finger. But comedy is when a little old lady falls down 25 steps into a manhole." Pain is funny. Adversity is funny. Conflict is funny. I want something and can't get it is funny. And how I try to get it and how I can't get it—that's funny. You can deal with the greatest issues. No movie is more moving than *ANNIE HALL* or *MANHATTAN*. I would love to write *KRAMER VS. KRAMER* but mine would be funnier. And *ONE FLEW OVER THE CUCKOO'S NEST* was hysterical, it just had substance. I don't think there's anything shameful about comedy. I don't think comedy means "non-serious." Comedy just means, look it's funny but it can still grab you. *THE GRADUATE*, I guess, is a comedy, but that movie changed the way people made films.

I'm assuming that you also want to direct or produce or both—

The writer/director in Hollywood is king, the auteurs like Paul Mazursky,

> *"Be unique. There's no such thing as a side character—supporting characters don't move the story ahead or change the plot, but they're little delights for the audience. If you have a cashier, make him a fat, angry cashier. If you have a cab driver, make him a depressed cab driver. Give the audience little treats and joys." —Robbie Fox*

Woody Allen. The writer is nothing in Hollywood. As producer you get into a whole other element. I definitely don't want to produce. Money makes me nervous. I don't want to be telling a lighting designer, "I'd like to go with the 60 watt, it's just not in the budget." I don't want to know about it. It's distracting. Yes, to a director the look of a film is key. But for my films the look would be always important but secondary to the performances and the themes and what you're trying to say in the comedy. Getting the joke on the screen. I don't want to be distracted by a two-hour conversation about shadows.

The writer/director isn't completely independent though, they still have to work within the system, within certain constraints.

The studio gives you the money to go make a film. It entitles them to anything they want to say. Never buck the system. The system's great. The system works. The system makes you rich and famous. The system gets your movies made. And most important the system gives you the opportunity to do something that's so wonderful, which is what I did at eight years old, to make movies in the backyard. And they pay you to go do it.

Do you feel lucky? Or is it still a struggle?

Recently a studio executive turned down a screenplay of mine saying, "Honestly? This is my favorite script I've ever read. I'd wait in line all night to see this movie. I just can't figure out if other people would too." Everything I do is hard. I sometimes feel like Willy Loman, walking around with this bag of jokes, telling people stories that they all laugh and love and think are great and invariably I get a call the next day, saying, "We all liked it, but we have this other project that's kind of..." or "We lost money on a movie that's kind of...." And you hear it more than you don't hear it. Even the ones I've sold are still filled with the day-to-day, "I think we went backwards with this draft." It's hard every step along the way. Every one of my pictures has been a "go" picture at one point.

What would be your words of advice to someone who's getting started as a writer?

Be unique. There's no such thing as a side character—supporting characters don't move the story ahead or change the plot, but they're little delights for the audience. If you have a cashier, make him a fat, angry cashier. If you have a cab driver, make him a depressed cab driver. Give the audience little treats and joys. And in your main characters, be different. Hollywood is very short—as many ideas as they have, there are not that many great, original ideas and the ones that are great and original aren't always written great and original. Be original and stick with it. All the scripts that I wrote at NYU that I got Cs and Ds on, I've since sold. Times change, people change, the buyers change, the market changes, the audience changes. But keep the quality of the work constant and eventually somebody will see it. My dad, as the son of a window washer from the Bronx with no money, used to say about his writing, "I don't know how many people wanted to do what I wanted to do, or how talented they were. I just knew that when the rest of the world went to sleep, I was willing to stay up and work."

**Locations full of texture and life
Legend that feeds creativity
Instant response and one-stop convenience
(312) 744-6415**

**Kathryn Darrell, Director
Charles Geocaris, Coordinator**

174 W. Randolph St., Chicago, IL. 60601

**Chicago Office of
FILM and ENTERTAINMENT**

"TERRIFIC BOOK"
...Hollywood Reporter

"**Something for the bookshelf:** Michael Singer has a handsome new edition (the seventh) just out of his indispensable **Film Directors: A Complete Guide**, something that gets more action moving on and off my shelf than any other single tome...Besides being an invaluable research tool, the books makes for great fun simply when tooling through the pages, running into facts and/or credits that have been forgotten, or never know. Like the fact that Terrence Malick has directed only two films (Badlands and The Days of Heaven) while Norman Mailer, much more a novelist than a film helmsman, has directed four features. Or being reminded that Barry Gordy once directed a film (Mahogany 1975) and noting the number of actors who've directed one but one movie, i.e., Marlon Brando, Klaus Maria Brandauer, Burt Lancaster, Jack Lemmon, Richard Harris, Dom DeLuise, Larry Hagman, Raymond St. Jacques, John Stockwell and others...It's also sobering to see names such as Ida Lupino, Dorothy Arzner, Anne Bancroft, Nancy Walker and others, then realize how few women have ever been invited into the directing ranks. Terrific book."

LONE EAGLE PUBLISHING COMPANY
2337 Roscomare Road, Suite 9
Los Angeles, CA 90077
213/471-8066
1/800-FILMBKS
FAX 213/471-4969

Order your copies today
Eighth Edition - 59.95

Robert Osborne
The Hollywood Reporter
July 3, 1989

WRITERS

LISTINGS

KEY TO ABBREVIATIONS

(CTF) = **CABLE TELEFEATURE**
Motion pictures made for cable television with an on-air running time of 1 to 4 hours.

(CMS) = **CABLE MINISERIES**
Motion pictures made for cable television with an on-air running time of 4 hours or more.

(FD) = **FEATURE DOCUMENTARY**
Documentary films made for theatrical distribution of feature length (1 or more hours.)

(CTD) = **CABLE TELEVISION DOCUMENTARY**
Documentary films made for cable television of feature length (1 or more hours.)

(AF) = **ANIMATED FEATURE**

(P) = **STAGEPLAY**

KEY TO SYMBOLS

* = denotes membership in the Writers Guild of America

★ = after a film title denotes an Academy Award nomination

★★ = after a film title denotes an Academy Award win

† = (in Index listing only) denotes deceased writer

S = (in Index listing only) denotes unproduced screenplay

A

PAUL AARON*
Agent: CAA - Beverly Hills, 213/288-4545

THE OCTAGON   American Cinema, 1980,
   Story w/Leigh Chapman

SHEPARD ABBOTT*
Contact: WGA - Los Angeles, 213/550-1000

C.H.U.D.   New World, 1984, Story

LEWIS ABERNATHY*
Agent: Harris & Goldberg - Los Angeles, 213/553-5200

DEEPSTAR SIX   Tri-Star, 1989, w/Geof Miller

JIM ABRAHAMS*
Agent: United Talent Agency - Beverly Hills,
   213/273-6700
Business: Abrahams Boy, Inc., 11777 San Vicente Blvd. -
   Suite 600, Los Angeles, CA 90049, 213/820-1942

THE KENTUCKY FRIED MOVIE   United Film Distribution,
   1977, w/David Zucker & Jerry Zucker
AIRPLANE!   Paramount, 1980, w/David Zucker &
   Jerry Zucker, co-directed
TOP SECRET!   Paramount, 1984, w/Martyn Burke,
   David Zucker & Jerry Zucker, co-directed
THE NAKED GUN: FROM THE FILES OF POLICE
   SQUAD!   Paramount, 1988, w/Pat Proft, David
   Zucker & Jerry Zucker
HOT SHOTS!   20th Century Fox, 1991,
   w/Pat Proft, directed

JACK ABRAMOFF
RED SCORPION   Shapiro Glickenhaus, 1989,
   Story w/Robert Abramoff & Arne Olsen

ROBERT ABRAMOFF
RED SCORPION   Shapiro Glickenhaus, 1989,
   Story w/Jack Abramoff & Arne Olsen

CELIA ABRAMS
EASY WHEELS   Fries Entertainment, 1989, w/David
   O'Malley & Ivan Raimi

IAN ABRAMS*
Agent: Susan Smith & Associates - Beverly Hills,
   213/852-4777

Screenplays:
CLOAK & DIAPER
THE DUST DEVIL
JOY
MR. WONDERFUL
THE WIZARD OF SANTA MONICA

JEFFREY (J.J.) ABRAMS*
Agent: ICM - Los Angeles, 213/550-4000

TAKING CARE OF BUSINESS   Buena Vista, 1990,
   w/Jill Mazursky
REGARDING HENRY   Paramount, 1991

Screenplays:
THE REST OF DANIEL
UNDER THE GUN   w/Jill Mazursky
GONE FISHIN'   w/Jill Mazursky

JOVAN ACIN
Contact: Yugoslavia Film, Knez Mihailova 19, 1100 Belgrade,
   Yugoslavia, 011/625-860

HEY BABU RIBA   *DANCING ON WATER*   Orion Classics,
   1986, directed

HAL L. ACKERMAN*
Business Manager: Gary Goldstein, 213/659-9511
Office: 6010 Wilshire Blvd., Los Angeles, 213/936-2446

SECOND WIND   Health and Entertainment Corporation of
   America, 1976

Screenplays:
HOLMEYER'S BRIDGE
BENJAMIN'S BABIES
I'LL GET THERE, IT BETTER BE WORTH THE TRIP

ALLEN ACTOR
THE DUNGEONMASTER   Empire Pictures, 1985

CATLIN ADAMS*
Agent: Triad Artists, Inc. - Los Angeles, 213/556-2727

STICKY FINGERS   Spectrafilm, 1988, w/Melanie
   Mayron, directed

Screenplays:
SERENADING LOUIE   w/Lee Grant

RICHARD ADCOCK*
Contact: WGA - Los Angeles, 213/550-1000

HYPER SAPIEN   Tri-Star, 1986, w/Christopher
   Blue & Marnie Paige

ALAN J. ADLER*
Agent: APA - Los Angeles, 213/273-0744

PARASITE   Embassy, 1982, w/Frank Levering &
   Michael Shoob
THE CONCRETE JUNGLE   Pentagon/Aquarius, 1982
METALSTORM: THE DESTRUCTION OF JARED-SYN
   Universal, 1983
THE ALCHEMIST   Empire Pictures, 1986

WARREN ADLER*
Agent: Triad Artists, Inc. - Los Angeles, 213/556-2727

Screenplays:
CRIES OF LAUGHTER

ELEONORE ADLON
Contact: German Film & TV Academy, Pommernallee 1, 1 Berlin 19, 0311/302/6096

BAGDAD CAFE   Island Pictures, 1987, w/Percy Adlon
ROSALIE GOES SHOPPING   Four Seasons Entertainment, 1990, w/Percy Adlon & Christopher Doherty

PERCY ADLON
Contact: German Film & TV Academy, Pommernallee 1, 1 Berlin 19, 0311/302/6096

CELESTE   New Yorker, 1981, directed
SUGARBABY   Kino International, 1985, directed
BAGDAD CAFE   Island Pictures, 1987, w/Eleonore Adlon, directed
ROSALIE GOES SHOPPING   Four Seasons Entertainment, 1990, w/Eleonore Adlon & Christopher Doherty, directed

NORMAN ALADJEM
FIREWALKER   Cannon, 1986, Story w/Robert Gosnell & Jeffrey Rosenbaum

REZA ALAMEHZADEH
THE GUESTS OF HOTEL ASTORIA   Melior Films, 1989, directed

JORDAN ALAN
TERMINAL BLISS   Distant Horizon, 1990, directed

EDWARD ALBEE*
Contact: WGA - Los Angeles, 213/550-1000

A DELICATE BALANCE   American Film Theatre, 1975, from his play

ALAN ALDA*
Agent: United Talent Agency - Beverly Hills, 213/273-6700

THE SEDUCTION OF JOE TYNAN   Universal, 1979
THE FOUR SEASONS   Universal, 1981, directed
SWEET LIBERTY   Universal, 1986, directed
A NEW LIFE   Paramount, 1988, directed
BETSY'S WEDDING   Buena Vista, 1990, directed

ROBERT ALDEN*
Contact: WGA - Los Angeles, 213/550-1000

STREETWALKIN'   Concorde/Cinema Group, 1985, w/Joan Freeman & Diane Gonciarz

PHILLIP ALDERTON
THE EXPENDABLES   Concorde, 1989
THE FACE OF THE ENEMY   Tri-Culture Pictures, 1990

WILL ALDIS*
(Will Porter)
Agent: William Morris Agency - Beverly Hills, 213/274-7451

BACK TO SCHOOL   Orion, 1986, w/Steven W. Kampmann, Harold Ramis & Peter Torokvei
THE COUCH TRIP   Orion, 1988, w/Steven W. Kampmann & Sean Stein
STEALING HOME   Warner Bros., 1988, w/Steven W. Kampmann, co-directed
CLIFFORD   Orion, 1992, w/Steven W. Kampmann

Screenplays:
DID SHE LEAVE ME ANY MONEY?

SCOTT ALEXANDER*
Agent: ICM - Los Angeles, 213/550-4000

PROBLEM CHILD   Universal, 1990, w/Larry Karaszewski
PROBLEM CHILD 2   Universal, 1991, w/Larry Karaszewski

Screenplays:
JUPITER NEEDS PARKING   w/Larry Karaszewski

SCOTT LAWRENCE ALEXANDER
SPACED INVADERS   Buena Vista, 1990, w/Patrick Read Johnson

RICHARD ALFIERI*
Agent: The Irv Schechter Company - Beverly Hills, 213/278-8070

CHILDREN OF RAGE   LSF Productions, 1975
ECHOES   Entertainment Professionals, 1983

DAN ALGRANT
Agent: CAA - Beverly Hills, 213/288-4545

Screenplays:
SANDY   THE NEW YORK PROJECT
THE NOVICE
CALL MY BROTHER BACK
DUET

TED ALLAN*
Contact: WGA - Los Angeles, 213/550-1000

LIES MY FATHER TOLD ME ★   Columbia, 1975
FALLING IN LOVE AGAIN   International Picture Show Company, 1980, w/Steven Paul & Susannah York
LOVE STREAMS   Cannon, 1984, w/John Cassavetes, from his play
BETHUNE: THE MAKING OF A HERO   Filmline International, 1990

Screenplays:
WEDDING BAND (from his play "The Third Day Comes w/John Cassavetes)

CHRIS ALLEN
THE LAST REMAKE OF BEAU GESTE   Universal, 1977, w/Marty Feldman
IN GOD WE TRUST   Universal, 1980, w/Marty Feldman

COREY ALLEN*
Agent: The Irv Schechter Company - Beverly Hills, 213/278-8070

AVALANCHE   New World, 1979, w/Claude Pola, directed

CURTIS ALLEN*
Agent: Preferred Artists - Encino, 818/990-0305

WALKING THE EDGE   Empire Pictures, 1985
HARRY'S MACHINE   Cannon, 1986

BLOODSTONE   Omega Pictures, 1989,
  w/Nico Mastorakis
BLIND VENGEANCE (CTF)   Spanish Trail Productions,
  1990, w/Henri Simoun

IRWIN ALLEN
Business: Irwin Allen Productions, Warner Bros., 4000
  Warner Blvd., Burbank, CA 91521, 818/954-3601

THE ANIMAL WORLD (FD)   Warner Bros.,
  1956, directed
THE STORY OF MANKIND   Warner Bros.,
  1957, directed
THE BIG CIRCUS   Allied Artists, 1959, w/Charles
  Bennett & Irving Wallace
THE LOST WORLD   20th Century-Fox, 1960,
  w/Charles Bennett, directed
VOYAGE TO THE BOTTOM OF THE SEA   20th
  Century-Fox, 1961, w/Charles Bennett, directed
FIVE WEEKS IN A BALLOON   20th Century-Fox,
  1962, w/Charles Bennett & Albert Gail, directed

JAMES ALLEN*
Contact: WGA - Los Angeles, 213/550-1000

HIDDEN AGENDA   Hemdale, 1990

JANIS ALLEN
MEATBALLS   Paramount, 1979, w/Len Blum & Dan
  Goldberg
DOUBLE NEGATIVE   Best Film and Video, 1980,
  w/Thomas Hedley Jr. & Charles Dennis

JAY PRESSON ALLEN*
Agent: ICM - New York, 212/556-5600

THE FIRST WIFE (P)
A LITTLE FAMILY BUSINESS (P)
TRU (P)
THE BIG LOVE (P) w/Brooke Allen
MARNIE   Universal, 1964
THE PRIME OF MISS JEAN BRODIE   20th
  Century-Fox, 1969
CABARET ★   Allied Artists, 1972
TRAVELS WITH MY AUNT   MGM, 1972,
  w/Hugh Wheeler
FUNNY LADY   Columbia, 1975, w/Arnold Schulman
JUST TELL ME WHAT YOU WANT   Warner
  Bros., 1980
PRINCE OF THE CITY ★   Orion/Warner Bros., 1981,
  w/Sidney Lumet
DEATHTRAP   Warner Bros., 1982

Screenplays:
THE AMERICAN FLAG
STONE   w/J. Calley

J.T. ALLEN*
Agent: William Morris Agency - Beverly Hills,
  213/274-7451

Screenplays:
PRINCESS OF PLUTO
LIKE ANGELS
CLUB TABOO

WOODY ALLEN*
(Allen Stewart Konigsberg)
Agent: ICM - New York, 212/556-5600
Business Manager: Jack Rollins/Charles Joffe, 212/582-1940

DON'T DRINK THE WATER (P)
THE FLOATING LIGHT BULB (P)
WHAT'S NEW PUSSYCAT?   United Artists, 1965
TAKE THE MONEY AND RUN   Cinerama Releasing
  Corporation, 1969, w/Mickey Rose, directed
BANANAS   United Artists, 1971, w/Mickey Rose, directed
PLAY IT AGAIN, SAM   Paramount, 1972, from his play
EVERYTHING YOU ALWAYS WANTED TO KNOW ABOUT
  SEX* (*BUT WERE AFRAID TO ASK)   United Artists,
  1972, directed
SLEEPER   United Artists, 1973, w/Marshall
  Brickman, directed
LOVE AND DEATH   United Artists, 1975, directed
ANNIE HALL ★★   United Artists, 1977, w/Marshall
  Brickman, directed
INTERIORS ★   United Artists, 1978, directed
MANHATTAN ★   United Artists, 1979, w/Marshall
  Brickman, directed
STARDUST MEMORIES   United Artists, 1980, directed
A MIDSUMMER NIGHT'S SEX COMEDY   Orion/Warner
  Bros., 1982, directed
ZELIG   Orion/Warner Bros., 1983, directed
BROADWAY DANNY ROSE ★   Orion, 1984, directed
THE PURPLE ROSE OF CAIRO ★   Orion, 1985, directed
HANNAH AND HER SISTERS ★★   Orion, 1986, directed
RADIO DAYS ★   Orion, 1987, directed
SEPTEMBER   Orion, 1987, directed
ANOTHER WOMAN   Orion, 1988, directed
NEW YORK STORIES   Buena Vista, 1989, "Oedipus
  Wrecks," directed
CRIMES AND MISDEMEANORS ★   Orion, 1989, directed
ALICE ★   Orion, 1990, directed
SHADOWS AND FOG   Orion, 1992, directed

NESTOR ALMENDROS
Agent: Smith Gosnell Nicholson & Associates - Pacific
  Palisades, 213/459-0307

IMPROPER CONDUCT (FD)   Cinevista, 1984, directed

MICHAEL ALMEREYDA
Agent: William Morris Agency - Beverly Hills, 213/274-7451

CHERRY 2000   Orion, 1988
TWISTER   Vestron, 1989, directed

Screenplays:
THE FUTURE
TESLA
THE RED HANDS
MANDRAKE THE MAGICIAN

PEDRO ALMODOVAR
Agent: ICM - Los Angeles, 213/550-4000

PEPI, LUCI & BOM   Figaro, 1981, directed
  (rereleased 1989)
LABYRINTH OF PASSION   Cinevista, 1982, directed
DARK HABITS   Cinevista, 1984, directed
WHAT HAVE I DONE TO DESERVE THIS?   Cinevista,
  1985, directed
MATADOR   Cinevista, 1986, directed
LAW OF DESIRE   Cinevista/Promovision International,
  1987, directed

AI

FILM WRITERS GUIDE

WOMEN ON THE VERGE OF A NERVOUS BREAKDOWN   Orion Classics, 1988, directed
TIE ME UP! TIE ME DOWN! *ATAME!*   Miramax, 1990, directed
HIGH HEELS   Miramax, 1991, directed

ARTHUR ALSBERG*
Contact: WGA - Los Angeles, 213/550-1000

NO DEPOSIT, NO RETURN   Buena Vista, 1976, w/Donald R. Nelson
GUS   Buena Vista, 1976, w/Donald R. Nelson
HERBIE GOES TO MONTE CARLO   Buena Vista, 1977, w/Donald R. Nelson
HOT LEAD AND COLD FEET   Buena Vista, 1978, w/Donald R. Nelson & Joe McEveety

EMMETT ALSTON
NEW YEAR'S EVIL   Cannon, 1981, Story w/Leonard Neubauer, directed
NINE DEATHS OF THE NINJA   Crown International, 1985, directed
HUNTER'S BLOOD   Concorde, 1987

GREG ALT*
Contact: WGA - Los Angeles, 213/550-1000

ZORRO, THE GAY BLADE   20th Century-Fox, 1981, Story w/Hal Dresner, Don Moriarty & Bob Randall

RICHARD ALTABEF
THE KISSING PLACE (CTF)   Wilshire Court Productions, 1990, w/Cynthia A. Cherbak & Michael Wing

ERIC ALTER*
Contact: WGA - Los Angeles, 213/550-1000

HARDBODIES   Columbia, 1984, w/Steven Greene & Mark Griffiths
HARDBODIES 2   CineTel Films, 1986, as "Curtis Wilmot," w/Mark Griffiths
THE EXPERTS   Paramount, 1988, w/Steven Greene & Nick Thiel

Screenplays:
MARRYING UP w/Steven Greene

ROBERT ALTMAN*
Agent: ICM - Los Angeles, 213/550-4000
Business: Sandcastle 5 Productions, 502 Park Avenue - Suite 156, New York, NY 10022, 212/826-6641

McCABE & MRS. MILLER   Warner Bros., 1971, w/Brian McKay, directed
IMAGES   Columbia, 1972, directed
THIEVES LIKE US   United Artists, 1974, w/Joan Tewkesbury & Calder Willingham, directed
BUFFALO BILL AND THE INDIANS or SITTING BULL'S HISTORY LESSON   United Artists, 1976, w/Alan Rudolph, directed
3 WOMEN   20th Century-Fox, 1977, directed
A WEDDING   20th Century-Fox, 1978, w/John Considine, Allan Nicholls & Patricia Resnick, directed
QUINTET   20th Century-Fox, 1979, w/Frank Barhydt & Patricia Resnick, directed
A PERFECT COUPLE   20th Century-Fox, 1979, w/Allan Nicholls, directed
HEALTH   20th Century-Fox, 1980, w/Frank Barhydt & Paul Dooley
BEYOND THERAPY   New World, 1987, w/Christopher Durang, directed

Screenplays:
SHORT CUTS w/Frank Barhydt

SHELLY ALTMAN*
Agent: The Gersh Agency - New York, 212/997-1818

SWEET LORRAINE   Angelika Films, 1987, w/Michael Zettler

MARINO AMARUSO
BEACH HOUSE   New Line Cinema, 1982, w/John Gallagher

ROD AMATEAU*
Agent: CAA - Beverly Hills, 213/288-4545

HOOK, LINE AND SINKER   Columbia, 1968
WHERE DOES IT HURT?   American International, 1972, directed
THE WILBY CONSPIRACY   United Artists, 1975, w/Harold Nebenzal
THE GARBAGE PAIL KIDS MOVIE   Atlantic Releasing Corporation, 1987, w/Melinda Palmer, directed
SUNSET   Tri-Star, 1988, Story

Screenplays:
PURSUIT MANUMIT w/Harold Nebenzal

DAVID AMBROSE*
Agent: William Morris Agency - Beverly Hills, 213/274-7451

BATTLE FOR ROME   CCC Filmkunst, 1969
THE 5TH MUSKETEER   Columbia, 1979
THE FINAL COUNTDOWN   United Artists, 1980, w/Gerry Davis, Thomas Hunter & Peter Powell
THE SURVIVOR   Hemdale, 1981
A DANGEROUS SUMMER   Filmco Ltd., 1982
AMITYVILLE 3-D   Orion, 1983, as "William Wales"
D.A.R.Y.L.   Paramount, 1985, w/Jeffrey Ellis & Allan Scott
BLACKOUT (CTF)   1985
TAFFIN   MGM/UA, 1988
THE FRENCH REVOLUTION   Films Ariane/Films A2/Laura Films/Antea, 1989

Screenplays:
YEAR OF THE GUN
TREASURE HUNT
THE LIARS
THE RESCUE OF GENERAL DOZIER (CTF)
SPECTER
TREACHEROUS
INSIDE OUT
KISS OR KILL (CTF)
THE SEDUCTRESS
THE BOOKBINDER
QUEEN CHRISTINA
GOOD MORNING, HE LIED

GIANNI AMELIO
OPEN DOORS   Orion Classics, 1990, w/Vincenzo Cerami & Alessandro Sermoneta, directed

DEBORAH L. AMELON*
Agent: Shapiro/Lichtman - Los Angeles, 213/859-8877

Screenplays:
MY SENIOR YEAR

CHRISTOPHER AMES*
Agent: United Talent Agency - Beverly Hills, 213/273-6700
Business: North Beach Productions, 818/591-2222

CLASS ACTION   20th Century Fox, 1991, w/Carolyn Shelby & Samantha Shad

Screenplays:
LEADER OF THE PACK w/Carolyn Shelby
IT'S NOT THE MONEY w/Carolyn Shelby
BLACK AND BLUE w/Carolyn Shelby
CHAPEL OF LOVE w/Carolyn Shelby
THE MAGIC COTTAGE w/Carolyn Shelby

TAYLOR AMES
Agent: Gray/Goodman Inc. - Beverly Hills, 213/276-7070

HE'S MY GIRL   Scotti Bros., 1987, w/Charles F. Bohl

GIDEON AMIR*
Contact: 213/461-0467

AMERICAN NINJA   Cannon, 1985, Story w/Avi Kleinberger
P.O.W. THE ESCAPE   Cannon, 1986, Story w/AviKleinberger, directed

MARTIN AMIS
Agent: Georges Borchardt Literary Agency - New York, 212/753-5785

SATURN 3   AFD, 1980

ALLISON ANDERS*
Agent: Triad Artists, Inc. - Los Angeles, 213/556-2727

BORDER RADIO   International Film Marketing, 1988, w/Dean Lent & Kurt Voss

Screenplays:
THE LOST HIGHWAY

ANDY ANDERSON
Agent: Triad Artists, Inc. - Los Angeles, 213/556-2727

POSITIVE I.D.   Universal, 1987, directed

GERRY ANDERSON
THUNDERBIRD SIX   United Artists, 1968, w/Sylvia Anderson
JOURNEY TO THE FAR SIDE OF THE SUN   Universal, 1969, w/Sylvia Anderson & Donald James

HESPER ANDERSON*
Agent: InterTalent - Los Angeles, 213/271-0600

TOUCHED BY LOVE   Columbia, 1980
CHILDREN OF A LESSER GOD ★   Paramount, 1986, w/Mark Medoff

Screenplays:
BECOMING THE BUTLERS
GRANDE ISLE
THE COLOR OF EVENING w/Tamara Lynn Roth
MORNING, WINTER AND NIGHT
THE WOMEN WHO RODE AWAY
FATHER AND SON REUNION
FOR NORA
WASSAJA
BILLY BUDD
IT TAKES TWO TO MAKE ONE— THE TOTIE FIELDS STORY

HOWARD L. ANDERSON*
Agent: Ken Sherman & Associates - Beverly Hills, 213/273-8840

Screenplays:
F AS IN PHILADELPHIA
SAGITTARIUS PART I — DUBLINERS
ANNIE II

MIKEL ANDERSON
Agent: Warden & White Associates - Beverly Hills, 213/852-1028

Screenplays:
SNUGGLEFOOT w/Peter Jensen
KISS KISS, KILL KILL w/Peter Jensen
CRASH AND BURN w/Peter Jensen

ROBERT ANDERSON*
Agent: ICM - Los Angeles, 213/550-4000

THE LAST ACT IS A SOLO (P)
TEA AND SYMPATHY   MGM, 1956, from his play
UNTIL THEY SAIL   MGM, 1957
THE NUN'S STORY ★   Warner Bros., 1959
THE SAND PEBBLES   20th Century-Fox, 1966
I NEVER SANG FOR MY FATHER ★   Columbia, 1969, from his play

WILLIAM C. ANDERSON*
Contact: WGA - Los Angeles, 213/550-1000

BAT-21   Tri-Star, 1988, w/Marc Norman

TINA ANDREWS
Agent: William Morris Agency - Beverly Hills, 213/274-7451

Screenplays:
MISTRESS OF MONTICELLO
FRANKIE: THE FRANKIE LYMON STORY

JAMES ANDRONICA
NUNZIO   Universal, 1978

DAVID H. ANDRUS*
Agent: Sanford, Skouras, Gross & Associates - Los Angeles, 213/208-2100

Screenplays:
BOLT UPRIGHT
HARRY
GHOST BOY
PILGRIM

An

FILM WRITERS GUIDE

FILM WRITERS

MARK ANDRUS*
Agent: Richland/Wunsch/Hohman Agency - Los Angeles, 213/278-1955

LATE FOR DINNER   Castle Rock/Columbia, 1991

Screenplays:
THE M WORD
QUARTER TIME
HARDCOVER DREAMS
THE NEIGHBORHOOD

THEO ANGELOPOULOS
Contact: Greek Film Centre, 10 Panepistimiou Street, Athens 134, Greece, 01/618924

THE TRAVELLING PLAYERS   Kino International, 1975, directed
LANDSCAPE IN THE MIST   New Yorker, 1988, directed

EDWARD ANHALT*
Agent: William Morris Agency - Beverly Hills, 213/274-7451

PANIC IN THE STREETS ★   20th Century-Fox, 1950, w/Edna Anhalt & Richard Murphy
THE SNIPER ★   Columbia, 1952, w/Edna Anhalt
A GIRL NAMED TAMIKO   Paramount, 1952
THE MEMBER OF THE WEDDING   Columbia, 1953, w/Edna Anhalt
NOT AS A STRANGER   United Artists, 1955, w/Edna Anhalt
THE PRIDE AND THE PASSION   United Artists, 1957, w/Edna Anhalt
IN LOVE AND WAR   20th Century-Fox, 1958
THE YOUNG LIONS   20th Century-Fox, 1958
THE RESTLESS YEARS   Universal-International, 1959
THE SINS OF RACHEL CADE   Warner Bros., 1960
THE YOUNG SAVAGES   United Artists, 1961, w/J.P. Miller
GIRLS, GIRLS, GIRLS   Wallis-Hazen, 1962, w/Allan Weiss
WIVES AND LOVERS   Paramount, 1963
BECKET ★★   Paramount, 1964
BOEING-BOEING   Paramount, 1965
THE SATAN BUG   United Artists, 1965, w/James Clavell
HOUR OF THE GUN   United Artists, 1967
IN ENEMY COUNTRY   Universal, 1968
THE BOSTON STRANGLER   20th Century-Fox, 1968
THE MADWOMAN OF CHAILLOT   Warner Bros., 1969
JEREMIAH JOHNSON   Warner Bros., 1972, w/John Milius
LUTHER   American Express, 1973
THE MAN IN THE GLASS BOOTH   American Film Theatre, 1975
ESCAPE TO ATHENA   AFD, 1979, w/Richard S. Lochte
GREEN ICE   Universal/AFD, 1981, w/others
THE HOLCROFT COVENANT   Universal, 1985, w/George Axelrod & John Hopkins

KEN ANNAKIN*
Contact: WGA - Los Angeles, 213/550-1000

THOSE MAGNIFICENT MEN IN THEIR FLYING MACHINES ★   20th Century-Fox, 1965, w/Jack Davies, directed
THOSE DARING YOUNG MEN IN THEIR JAUNTY JALOPIES   Paramount, 1969, w/Jack Davies, directed
THE NEW ADVENTURES OF PIPPI LONGSTOCKING   Columbia, 1988, directed

JEAN-JACQUES ANNAUD
Agent: ICM - Los Angeles, 213/550-4000

BLACK AND WHITE IN COLOR   LA VICTOIRE EN CHANTANT   Allied Artists, 1978, w/Georges Conchon, directed

Screenplays:
THE LOVER   w/Gerard Brach & Marguerite Duras (directing)

JOSEPH ANSOLABEHERE*
Agent: ICM - Los Angeles, 213/550-4000

Screenplays:
SURFIN' CIA   w/Stephen Viksten
EXTERMINATORS   w/Stephen Viksten

RICHARD J. ANTHONY
ECHOES   Continental, 1983

STEVE ANTIN
Contact: Monkey Productions - 213/930-2349

Screenplays:
INSIDE MONKEY ZETTERLAND

MICHELANGELO ANTONIONI
CACCIA TRAGICA (THE TRAGIC PURSUIT)   Lux, 1947, w/others
IL GRIDO (THE CRY)   Astor, 1957, w/Elio Bartolini & Ennio de Concini, directed
L'AVVENTURA   Janus, 1961, w/Tonino Guerra & Elio Bartolini, directed
LA NOTTE   Lopert, 1961, w/Ennio Flaiano & Tonino Guerra, directed
L'ECLISSE   Times, 1962, w/others, directed
RED DESERT   Rizzoli, 1965, w/Tonino Guerra, directed
BLOW-UP ★   Premier, 1966, w/Tonino Guerra & Edward Bond, directed
ZABRISKIE POINT   MGM, 1970, w/Fred Gardner, Tonino Guerra, Clare Peploe & Sam Shepard, directed
THE PASSENGER   PROFESSIONE: REPORTER   MGM/United Artists, 1975, w/Mark Peploe & Peter Wollen, directed

Screenplays:
THE CREW   w/Mark Peploe (directing)

GREG ANTONACCI*
Agent: The Irv Schechter Company - Beverly Hills, 213/278-8070

Screenplays:
TIL DEATH DO US PART

LEAH APPET*
Agent: The Gersh Agency - Beverly Hills, 213/274-6611

EVERY TIME WE SAY GOODBYE   Tri-Star, 1986, w/Rachel Fabien & Moshe Mizrahi

Screenplays:
THE WAY WE ARE
VALENTINE
UNFINISHED BUSINESS
THE BLUE VEIL

MAX APPLE*
Contact: WGA - Los Angeles, 213/550-1000

SMOKEY BITES THE DUST   New World, 1981

SHIMON ARAMA
Business: Nova International Films, 1800 Century Park East, Suite 300, Los Angeles, CA 90067, 213/551-0240

TRIUMPH OF THE SPIRIT   Nova International Films, 1989, Story w/Zion Haen

PAUL ARATOW*
Contact: WGA - Los Angeles, 213/550-1000

PURGATORY   New Star Entertainment, 1989, w/Felix Kroll

DENYS ARCAND
Address: 4921 Coronet - Suite 12, Montreal, Quebec, Canada, 514/341-6139

THE DECLINE OF THE AMERICAN EMPIRE   Cineplex Odeon, 1986, directed
JESUS OF MONTREAL   Orion Classics, 1990, directed

MANUEL ARCE*
Contact: WGA - New York, 212/245-6180

EL SUPER   Columbia, 1979, w/Leon Ichaso
CROSSOVER DREAMS   Miramax, 1985, w/Leon Ichaso & Ruben Blades

JEFFREY ARCH
Agent: Warden & White Associates - Beverly Hills, 213/852-1028

FOR SALE (P)

Screenplays:
SLEEPLESS IN SEATTLE
FRENCH TOAST
FREE AGENTS
THE BELL TOWER

EVAN P. ARCHERD
AMERICAN ANTHEM   Columbia, 1986, w/Jeff Benjamin

DARIO ARGENTO
Address: via G. Devoti 16, Rome, Italy, 06/438-5341

THE BIRD WITH THE CRYSTAL PLUMMAGE   UMC, 1970, directed
CAT O'NINE TAILS   National General, 1971, directed
SUSPIRIA   International Classics, 1977, w/Dario Nicolodi, directed
UNSANE   *TENEBRAE*   Bedford Entertainment/Film Gallery, 1982, directed
CREEPERS   *PHENOMENA*   New Line Cinema, 1985, directed
INFERNO   20th Century Fox, 1986, directed

ADAM ARKIN
Agent: Susan Smith & Associates - Beverly Hills, 213/852-4777

IMPROPER CHANNELS   Crown International, 1981, w/Morrie Rubinsky & Ian Sutherland

ALICE ARLEN*
Agent: ICM - New York, 212/556-5600

SILKWOOD ★   20th Century-Fox, 1983, w/Nora Ephron
ALAMO BAY   Tri-Star, 1985
COOKIE   Warner Bros., 1989, w/Nora Ephron

Screenplays:
MODERN BRIDE w/Nora Ephron & Joan Taylor
I THOUGHT I SAW YOU
SKINNER
DEMOCRACY
TROUBLESHOOTER

FRANK ARMITAGE
(See John Carpenter)

GEORGE B. ARMITAGE*
Agent: The Artists Agency - Los Angeles, 213/277-7779

GAS-S-S-S!...OR HOW IT BECAME NECESSARY TO DESTROY THE WORLD IN ORDER TO SAVE IT!   American International, 1970
HIT MAN   MGM, 1972, directed
PRIVATE DUTY NURSES   New World, 1972, directed
NIGHT CALL NURSES   New World, 1974
DARK TOWN STRUTTERS   New World, 1975
VIGILANTE FORCE   United Artists, 1976, directed
THE LAST OF THE FINEST   Orion, 1990, w/Jere Cunningham & Thomas Lee Wright
MIAMI BLUES   Orion, 1990, directed

Screenplays:
DANCING IN THE STREET
HYPE

CURTIS ARMSTRONG*
Contact: WGA - Los Angeles, 213/550-1000

Screenplays:
HOLLYWOOD SCANDAL w/John Doolittle

MICHAEL ARMSTRONG
HORROR HOUSE   THE HAUNTED HOUSE OF HORROR   American International, 1970, w/Peter Marcus, directed
THE BLACK PANTHER   Impics, 1977
HOUSE OF THE LONG SHADOWS   Cannon, 1984

ROBIN ARMSTRONG
Agent: CAA - Beverly Hills, 213/288-4545

ONE CUP OF COFFEE   Miramax, 1991, w/D.M. Eyre Jr., directed

EDDIE ARNO
MURDER STORY   Contracts International/Elsevier-Vendex Film, 1989, w/Markus Innocenti, co-directed

FRANK ARNOLD
HUMANOIDS FROM THE DEEP   New World, 1980, Story w/Martin B. Cohan

DAVID ARNOTT*
Contact: WGA - Los Angeles, 213/550-1000

THE ADVENTURES OF FORD FAIRLANE   20th Century Fox, 1990, w/James Cappe & Daniel Waters

Ar

FILM WRITERS GUIDE

LARRY ARNSTEIN*
Agent: United Talent Agency - Beverly Hills, 213/273-6700

Screenplays:
MULTIPLE CHOICES w/David Hurwitz

WILLIAM ASHER
Agent: The Cooper Agency - Los Angeles, 213/277-8422

BIKINI BEACH   American International, 1964, w/Robert Diller & Leo Townsend, directed

PIERS ASHWORTH*
Agent: William Morris Agency - Beverly Hills, 213/274-7451

Screenplays:
WAGES OF SIN
THE BARTENDER
FAMILY DIES
THE FRUIT PALACE

SAMSON ASLANIAN
TORMENT   New World, 1986, w/John Hopkins

OLIVIER ASSAYAS
Contact: French Film Office, 745 Fifth Avenue, New York, NY 10151, 212/832-8860

SCENE OF THE CRIME   1986, w/Pascal Bonitzer & Andre Techine
RENDEZ-VOUS   Spectrafilm, 1987, w/Andre Techine

DYANNE ASSIMOW*
Agent: Triad Artists, Inc. - Los Angeles, 213/556-2727

Screenplays:
SIGHTSEER
GOLDEN GATE w/Roger Simon
A WILD SANCTUARY w/Roger Simon
PERSONAL LEAVE
MADCAP
PANAMA
TAKING CHARGE
THE BELA LUGOSI STORY
HARD FEELING

PATTI ASTOR
ASSAULT OF THE KILLER BIMBOS   Empire, 1988, Story w/Ted Nicolau & Anita Rosenberg

J.D. ATHENS
(See J. F. Lawton)

PETER ATKINS
Agent: William Morris Agency - Beverly Hills, 213/274-7451

HELLBOUND: HELLRAISER 2   New World, 1989

Screenplays:
HELLRAISER 3

LARRY ATLAS*
Agent: William Morris Agency - New York, 212/586-5100

TOTAL ABANDON (P)

Screenplays:
BLUE HORIZON
TELL ME TRUE

PAUL ATTANSIO*
Agent: CAA - Beverly Hills, 213/288-4545

Screenplays:
CAMPAIGN w/Andy Wolk
MOVING TARGET
THE BOBBY DARIN STORY
THE QUIZ SHOW PROJECT
DONNIE BRASCO (directing)
SLOW BURN
STRANGERS IN THE NIGHT

JOHN P. AUERBACH*
Agent: ICM - Los Angeles, 213/550-4000

STEPFATHER II   Millimeter Films, 1989

MICHAEL J. AUERBACH*
Agent: APA - Los Angeles, 213/273-0744

Screenplays:
PIROUETTE w/Daniel Faraldo
BLINDFOLD w/Daniel Faraldo
KABYLIA
ALWAYS REMEMBERED
LINE OF FIRE
THE DEATH SHIP
HELL-BENT
DETONATOR
PLASMA CELL REPORT
TERMINAL STATION

BILLE AUGUST
Agent: ICM - Los Angeles, 213/550-4000

TWIST AND SHOUT   Miramax Films, 1984, w/BjarneReuter, directed
PELLE THE CONQUEROR   Miramax Films, 1988, directed

Screenplays:
HOUSE OF THE SPIRITS

JOE AUGUSTYN
Business: Paragon Arts International, 6777 Hollywood Blvd., Suite 700, Hollywood, CA 90028, 213/465-5355

NIGHT OF THE DEMONS   International Film Marketing, 1988
NIGHT ANGEL   Fries Entertainment, 1990, w/Walter Josten

SAM AUSTER
SCREEN TEST   CineTel Films, 1986, w/Laura Auster, directed

IRVING AUSTIN
WARLORDS OF THE 21ST CENTURY   New World, 1982, w/John Beech & Harley Cokliss

MICHAEL AUSTIN*
Agent: ICM - Los Angeles, 213/550-4000

THE SHOUT   Films Inc., 1979, w/Jerzy Skolimowski
FIVE DAYS ONE SUMMER   The Ladd Company/Warner Bros., 1982
GREYSTOKE: THE LEGEND OF TARZAN, LORD OF THE APES ★   Warner Bros., 1984, w/P.H. Vazak
KILLING DAD   Scottish Television Film Enterprises, 1989, directed

Screenplays:
WILD BILLY
MADNESS OF A SEDUCED WOMAN
TIMOTHY GEDGE
BARRICADE
SAINT HARRY
COSMIC CHARLIE

HOWARD (HIKMET) AVEDIS*
Contact: Jerome E. Weinstein, Weinstein & Hart, 433 N. Camden Dr., Suite 600, Beverly Hills, CA 90210, 213/274-7157

SCORCHY   American International, 1976, directed
THE FIFTH FLOOR   Film Ventures International, 1980, Story w/Marlene Schmidt, directed
MORTUARY   Artists Releasing Corporation/FilmVentures International, 1983, w/Marlene Schmidt, directed
THEY'RE PLAYING WITH FIRE   New World, 1984, w/Marlene Schmidt, directed
KIDNAPPED   Virgin Vision, 1987, directed

RUTH AVERGON
NIGHT SCHOOL   Paramount/Lorimar, 1981

ROBERT J. AVRECH*
Contact: WGA - Los Angeles, 213/550-1000

BODY DOUBLE   Columbia, 1984, w/Brian De Palma
DARK TOWER   Spectrafilm, 1989, w/Ken Weiderhorn & Ken Blackwell

Screenplays:
CLOSE TO EDEN
THE CONSPIRACY w/William Bairn
LEDA AND SWAN
THE LADY KILLER
THE GAITS OF THE FOREST
BEAST
HOUR OF THE ANGEL
MAIDEN RUN
MABEL
HORSEMEN OF THE SILVER WALL

GABRIEL AXEL
Agent: ICM - Los Angeles, 213/550-4000

BABETTE'S FEAST   Orion Classics, 1987, directed
CHRISTIAN   Chrysalide Films/Victoria Films/Ellepi Film/Dania Film/DMV Distribuzione/Reteitalia, 1989, directed

DAVID AXELROD*
Agent: ICM - Los Angeles, 213/550-4000

CHARLIE CHAN AND THE CURSE OF THE DRAGON QUEEN   American Cinema, 1981, w/Stan Burns

GEORGE AXELROD*
Agent: Camden-ITG - Los Angeles, 213/289-2700

WILL SUCCESS SPOIL ROCK HUNTER (P)
GOODBYE CHARLIE (P)
PHFFFT   Columbia, 1954
THE SEVEN YEAR ITCH   20th Century-Fox, 1955, w/Billy Wilder, from his play
BUS STOP   20th Century-Fox, 1956
BREAKFAST AT TIFFANYS ★   Paramount, 1961
THE MANCHURIAN CANDIDATE   United Artists, 1962
HOW TO MURDER YOUR WIFE   United Artists, 1964
PARIS WHEN IT SIZZLES   Paramount, 1964
LORD LOVE A DUCK   United Artists, 1966, w/Larry H. Johnson, directed
THE SECRET LIFE OF AN AMERICAN WIFE   20th Century-Fox, 1968, directed
THE LADY VANISHES   Rank, 1979
THE HOLCROFT COVENANT   Universal, 1985, w/Edward Anhalt & John Hopkins
THE FOURTH PROTOCOL   Lorimar, 1987, Story

ALAN AYCKBOURN
Agent: Margaret Ramsay Ltd. - London, 011/441/240-0691

ABSENT FRIENDS (P)
WOMAN IN MIND (P)
THE NORMAN CONQUESTS (P)
RELATIVELY SPEAKING (P)
MAN OF THE MOMENT (P)
HENCEFORWARD... (P)
TAKING STEPS (P)
ABSURD PERSON SINGULAR (P)
A CHORUS OF DISAPPROVAL   South Gate Entertainment, 1989, w/Michael Winner, from his play

DAN AYKROYD*
Agent: CAA - Beverly Hills, 213/288-4545

THE BLUES BROTHERS   Universal, 1980, w/John Landis
GHOSTBUSTERS   Columbia, 1984, w/Harold Ramis
SPIES LIKE US   Warner Bros., 1985, w/Lowell Ganz & Babaloo Mandel
DRAGNET   Universal, 1987, w/Tom Mankiewicz & Alan Zweibel
GHOSTBUSTERS II   Columbia, 1989, w/Harold Ramis
NOTHING BUT TROUBLE   Warner Bros., 1991, directed

Screenplays:
LAW OF THE YUKON

PETER AYKROYD
NOTHING BUT TROUBLE   Warner Bros., 1991, Story

JON AYRE
SURF NAZIS MUST DIE   Troma, 1987

ALEX AYRES
Agent: The Roberts Company - Los Angeles, 213/552-7800

Screenplays:
THE DEVIL'S ADVOCATE
FREE AT LAST

GERALD AYRES*
Agent: Broder-Kurland-Webb-Uffner - Los Angeles, 213/656-9262

FOXES   United Artists, 1980
RICH AND FAMOUS   MGM, 1981

Screenplays:
CHANGE OF HEART w/J.P. Miller
STEPPING
SMALL HOTEL
LADY FINGERS

RAFAEL AZCONA
AY, CARMELA!   Prestige Films, 1991

B

BETH B
VORTEX B Movies, 1982, w/Scott B, co-directed
SALVATION! Circle Films, 1987, w/Tom Robinson, directed

SCOTT B
Agent: The Tantleff Office - New York, 212/941-3939

VORTEX B Movies, 1982, w/Beth B, co-directed

THOMAS BABE*
Agent: Select Artists - New York, 212/586-4300

REBEL WOMEN (P)
KID CHAMPION (P)
A PRAYER FOR MY DAUGHTER (P)
FATHERS AND SONS (P)
TAKEN IN MARRIAGE (P)
SALT LAKE CITY SKYLINE (P)
BORN EVERY MINUTE (P)
BILLY IRISH (P)
BURIED INSIDE EXTRA (P)
MURDER IN THE DESERT (P)
GREAT SOLO TOWN (P)
HOME AGAIN, KATHLEEN (P)
WHEN WE WERE VERY YOUNG (P)

Screenplays:
GRAD WEEK
DEATH IN THE DESERT
PHOTO

HECTOR BABENCO
Agent: ICM - Los Angeles, 213/550-4000

LUCIO FLAVIO Unifilm/Embrafilme, 1978, directed
PIXOTE Unifilm/Embrafilme, 1981, directed
AT PLAY IN THE FIELDS OF THE LORD Saul Zaentz Co., 1991, w/Jean-Claude Carriere, directed

DANIEL F. BACANER
Business: Fremont II, 8489 W. 3rd St., Los Angeles, CA 90048, 213/852-0934

SCARED STIFF International Film Marketing, 1987, w/Richard Friedman & Mark Frost

DANILO BACH*
Agent: InterTalent - Los Angeles, 213/858-6200

BEVERLY HILLS COP ★ Paramount, 1984, Story w/Daniel Petrie, Jr.
APRIL FOOL'S DAY Paramount, 1986

Screenplays:
BEVERLY DRIVE
THE TRACE
FOXBAT
ACTUARY
EL SALVADOR
ENDANGERED
HORSE OPERA
TRIALS & TRIBULATION

TOM BADAL*
Agent: Thal Literary Management - Los Angeles, 213/659-4946

OUT ON BAIL Trans World Entertainment, 1989, w/Jason Booth & Michael D. Sonye
VIETNAM, TEXAS Epic Productions, 1990, w/C. Courtney Joyner

R.M. (RANDALL) BADAT*
Agent: Camden-ITG - Los Angeles, 213/289-2700

SURF II Arista, 1983, directed

Screenplays:
SWEETHEART
FOREVER 17
THE DEVILS EYE
THE CUTTING EDGE
CHINESE HANDCUFFS

GEOFFREY BAERE*
Contact: WGA - Los Angeles, 213/550-1000

SCHOOL SPIRIT Concorde/Cinema Group, 1985
CAMPUS MAN Paramount, 1987, w/Matt Dorff & Alex Horvat
CORPORATE AFFAIRS Concorde, 1990, w/Terence H. Winkless

Screenplays:
TEETH'N'SMILES
DATELINE: PARIS

TED BAFALOUKAS*
Contact: WGA - Los Angeles, 213/550-1000

ROCKERS New Yorker, 1979, directed

Screenplays:
SOUTH OF HEAVEN

MILTON BAGBY JR.
REBEL LOVE Troma, 1985, directed

ROSS BAGDASARIAN
Business: Bagdasarian Productions, 4400 Coldwater Canyon, Suite #315, Studio City, CA 91604, 818/769-3210

THE CHIPMUNK ADVENTURE (AF) Samuel Goldwyn Company, 1986, w/Janice Karman

FREDERICK BAILEY
DESERT WARRIOR Concorde/Cinema Group, 1985

Screenplays:
QUICK
KENTUCKY BLUE

PATRICK BAILEY*
Contact: WGA - Los Angeles, 213/550-1000

SPACECAMP 20th Century Fox, 1986, Story w/Larry B. Williams

ROBERT BAILEY*
Contact: 213/443-6155

YOR, THE HUNTER FROM THE FUTURE   Columbia, 1983, w/Anthony M. Dawson

SANDRA K. BAILEY*
Agent: Irvin Arthur Associates - Beverly Hills, 213/278-5934

HAMBONE AND HILLIE   New World, 1984, w/Michael Murphey & Joel Soisson
KGB: THE SECRET WAR *LETHAL*   Cinema Group, 1986
PRETTYKILL   Spectrafilm, 1987
FALSE IDENTITY   RKO Pictures, 1990

GARY L. BAIN
ICE CASTLES   Columbia, 1978, w/Donald Wrye

BERYL BAINBRIDGE
SWEET WILLIAM   World Northal, 1982

JON ROBIN BAITZ
Agent: William Morris Agency - New York, 212/586-5100

POLLOCK (P)
MIZLANSKY/ZILANSKY (P)
THE FILM SOCIETY (P)
DUTCH LANDSCAPE (P)
THREE HOTELS (P)
SUBSTANCE OF FIRE (P)

Screenplays:
JACK & JILL (CTF)
FINALE

DORIS BAIZLEY*
Agent: The Gage Group - Los Angeles, 213/859-8777

CATHOLIC GIRLS (P), also screenplay
MRS. CALIFORNIA (P)
HEARTS ON FIRE (P)

Screenplays:
WIVES
MR. RIGHT

BART BAKER*
Agent: Barrett, Benson, McCartt & Weston - Los Angeles, 213/247-5500

RELAY (P), also screenplay

Screenplays:
TAKE IT BACK
LIVE WIRE

MARK H. BAKER
Agent: Lake & Douroux - Beverly Hills, 213/557-0700

FLIGHT OF THE NAVIGATOR   Buena Vista, 1986, Story

RALPH BAKSHI*
Agent: CAA - Beverly Hills, 213/288-4545
Business: Ralph Bakshi Productions, 8125 Lankershim Blvd., North Hollywood, CA 91605, 818/985-4463

FRITZ THE CAT (AF)   American International, 1972, directed
HEAVY TRAFFIC (AF)   American International, 1973, directed
COONSKIN *STREETFIGHT* (AF)   Bryanston, 1974, directed
WIZARDS (AF)   20th Century-Fox, 1977, directed
HEY GOOD LOOKIN' (AF)   Warner Bros., 1982, directed
FIRE AND ICE (AF)   20th Century-Fox, 1983, directed

Screenplays:
3 DAYS, 4 NIGHTS

RENE BALCER*
Agent: ICM - Los Angeles, 213/550-4000

Screenplays:
ARMED RESPONSE w/Steve Gaydos
DARK PASSION
I FOUGHT THE LAW
BURDEN OF PROOF
WARHEAD
MONIMBO
NUTS & BOLTS
PROJECTIONS

DAVID BALL*
Agent: Shapiro/Lichtman - Los Angeles, 213/859-8877

HARD ROCK ZOMBIES   Cannon, 1985, w/Krischna Shas

ANNE BANCROFT
Business: Brooksfilms Limited, 20th Century Fox, P.O. Box 900, Beverly Hills, CA 90213, 213/203-1375

FATSO   20th Century-Fox, 1980, directed

CHARLES BAND
Business: Full Moon Entertainment, 6930 Sunset Blvd., Los Angeles, CA 90028, 213/957-0091

PUPPET MASTER   Full Moon, 1989, Story w/Kenneth J. Hall

Screenplays:
DOCTOR MORDRID w/C. Courtney Joyner (directing)

WALTER BANNERT
THE INHERITORS   Island Alive, 1985, w/Eric A. Richter, directed

JACK BARAN*
Agent: The Daniel Ostroff Agency - Los Angeles, 213/278-2020

ROOMMATES   Pantages, 1971, directed
BAND OF THE HAND   Tri-Star, 1986, w/Leo Garen
GREAT BALLS OF FIRE   Orion, 1989, w/Jim McBride

Screenplays:
DON'T HOLD BACK w/Leo Garen
LATIN JERRY & HOT HOT TOMATOS
CONFESSIONS OF A DANGEROUS MIND w/Jim McBride

JEAN BARASH
Agent: Circle Talent Associates - Beverly Hills, 213/285-1585

Screenplays:
THE SPRAY w/Ellen Erwin
THE IMMORTALIST w/Ellen Erwin

Ba

BENNY BARBASH
BEYOND THE WALLS Warner Bros., 1985, w/Eran Pries
ONE OF US Israfilm, 1990

JOSEPH BARBERA
Business: Hanna-Barbera Productions, Inc., 3400 Lankershim Blvd. West, Los Angeles, CA 90068, 213/851-5000

HEIDI'S SONG (AF) Paramount, 1982, w/Jameson Brewer & Robert Taylor, directed

NEAL BARBERA*
Contact: Wayne Alexander, Esq. - 213/312-4104

THE PROWLER Sandhurst Corporation, 1982, w/Glenn Leopold
TOO SCARED TO SCREAM Moviestore Entertainment, 1985, w/Glenn Leopold
P.K. AND THE KID Castle Hill Productions, 1987

MALCOLM BARBOUR
P.O.W. THE ESCAPE Cannon, 1986, w/James Bruner, Jeremy Lipp & John Langley

ANN LOUISE BARDACH*
Agent: William Morris Agency - Beverly Hills, 213/274-7451

Screenplays:
BACKTRACK
COMPOSURE
THE CANVAS
RECLAIMED

ILANA BAR-DIN
Agent: The Goldstein Company - Los Angeles, 213/659-9511

THE JAMIE FORT STORY (Short), directed

Screenplays:
FRIDA AND DIEGO
LOST IN TRANSLATION (Shared)

FRANK BARHYDT*
Agent: The Gersh Agency - Beverly Hills, 213/274-6611

QUINTET 20th Century-Fox, 1979, w/Robert Altman & Patricia Resnick
HEALTH 20th Century-Fox, 1980, w/Robert Altman & Paul Dooley

Screenplays:
SHORT CUTS w/Robert Altman

LEORA BARISH*
Agent: William Morris Agency - Beverly Hills, 213/274-7451

DESPERATELY SEEKING SUSAN Orion, 1985

Screenplays:
DESIRE w/Henry Bean & Frederic Raphael
LABYRINTH 9 w/Henry Bean
EL DORADO w/Henry Bean
COUNT FROM ONE TO TEN
DAYLIGHTING

CLIVE BARKER*
Agent: CAA - Beverly Hills, 213/288-4545

UNDERWORLD Limehouse, 1985, w/James Caplin
RAWHEAD REX Empire Pictures, 1987
HELLRAISER New World, 1987, directed
NIGHT BREED 20th Century Fox, 1990, directed

Screenplays:
THE BIG NOWHERE

LYNN BARKER*
Agent: The Chasin Agency - Beverly Hills, 213/278-7505

Screenplays:
RESURRECTIONS w/Bob Skotak
ACES
HEROES

IRA BARMAK*
Contact: Marvin Meyer, Esq. - 213/858-7700

HOTEL COLONIAL Columbia, 1987, w/Enzo Monteleone, Cinzia Torrini & Robert Katz

JOSLYN BARNES
TOUCH OF A STRANGER Raven-Star Pictures, 1990, w/Brad Gilbert

PETER BARNES
Agent: Margaret Ramsay Ltd. - London, 011/441/240-0691

OFFBEAT British Lion, 1960
RING OF TREASON RING OF SPIES British Lion, 1963, w/Frank Launder
NOT WITH MY WIFE YOU DON'T Warner Bros., 1966, w/Larry Gelbart & Norman Panama
THE RULING CLASS Avco Embassy, 1972, from his play

DEBORAH R. BARON*
Agent: Barrett, Benson, McCartt & Weston - Los Angeles, 213/247-5500

Screenplays:
JUST BETWEEN US
STILL FRIENDS
STEAM HEAT
FLIP SIDE

DANNIEL BARON
Agent: United Talent Agency - Beverly Hills, 213/273-6700

HANG E'M REALLY HIGH (Short) 1989, w/Chris Faber, directed

Screenplays:
ASSAULT ON EMPIRE STATE MOUNTAIN (CTF) w/Chris Faber (directing)
FAT CHANCE w/Chris Faber
JACKPOT w/Chris Faber
THE BIG PLUNGE w/Chris Faber

JEFF BARON*
Agent: Warden & White Associates - Beverly Hills, 213/852-1028

Screenplays:
HOUSE SWAP
MAID OF HONOR

DOUGLAS BARR*
Business Manager: Jamner, Pariser & Meschures - Los Angeles, 213/652-0222

Screenplays:
CONUNDRUM

JACKSON BARR
BODY CHEMISTRY   Concorde, 1990

Screenplays:
TRANCERS II
VOICE OF A STRANGER   w/Christopher Wooden

MATTHEW F. BARR*
Agent: Barry Perelman Agency - Los Angeles, 213/274-5999

DEADLY BLESSING   United Artists/Polygram, 1981, w/Glenn M. Benest & Wes Craven

EARL BARRET*
Business Manager: Jamner, Pariser & Meschures - Los Angeles, 213/6520222

SEE NO EVIL, HEAR NO EVIL   Tri-Star, 1989, w/Andrew Kurtzman, Arne Sultan, Eliot Wald & Gene Wilder

BRUNO BARRETO
Agent: ICM - Los Angeles, 213/550-4000

DONA FLOR AND HER TWO HUSBANDS   New Yorker, 1977, directed
GABRIELA   MGM/UA Classics, 1983, w/Leopoldo Sarran, directed

LEZLI-AN BARRETT
Agent: Casaratto Company - London, 01/287-4450

BUSINESS AS USUAL   Cannon, 1987, directed

MICHAEL BARRIE*
Agent: APA - Los Angeles, 213/273-0744

AMAZON WOMEN ON THE MOON   Universal, 1987, w/Jim Mulholland
OSCAR   Buena Vista, 1991, w/Jim Mulholland

Screenplays:
AFTER THE FOX   w/Jim Mulholland
THE CATCH   w/Jim Mulholland

CHUCK BARRIS*
Contact: WGA - Los Angeles, 213/550-1000

THE GONG SHOW MOVIE   Universal, 1980, w/Robert Downey, directed

ARTHUR BARRON
JEREMY   United Artists, 1973, directed

FRED BARRON*
Agent: CAA - Beverly Hills, 213/288-4545

BETWEEN THE LINES   Midwest Film Productions, 1977
SOMETHING SHORT OF PARADISE   American International, 1979
GOING ALL THE WAY   Paramount, 1980

Screenplays:
FUN WHILE IT LASTED   w/Joan Micklin Silver

ZELDA BARRON
Agent: The Artists Agency - Los Angeles, 213/277-7779
Business: Limelight Films, 1724 Whitley Ave., Los Angeles, CA 90028, 213/464-5808

SECRET PLACES   TLC Films/20th Century-Fox, 1984, directed

JULIAN BARRY*
Agent: William Morris Agency - Beverly Hills, 213/274-7451

JEAN SEBERG (P), also teleplay
SECRET AGENT FIREBALL   1966
RHINOCEROS   American Film Theatre, 1974
LENNY ★   United Artists, 1974
THE RIVER   Universal, 1984, w/Robert Dillon

Screenplays:
ME, MYSELF AND I
FLYING TIGERS
THE GUY WHO COULD FIX BIKES
ONE MORE TIME
MERCY MAN
JOSEPHINE BAKER
AN INTERRUPTED LIFE
STOLEN MOMENTS
BARRY MARTIN STORY (CTF)
SLIGHTLY OUT OF FOCUS
CARROLL SHELBY
AN AMERICAN PLACE
DEAD BEAUTY
SHOWTIME
SORRENTO
NO MORE BLUES
SINGLES WEEKEND
A PLACE TO COME TO
SWINGER
TOUGH CUSTOMERS
STRINGS
TENNIS
TAKE THAT
LAST LURID MOMENT

PAUL BARTEL*
Agent: ICM - Los Angeles, 213/550-4165

CANNONBALL   New World, 1976, w/Donald C. Simpson, directed
EATING RAOUL   20th Century Fox International Classics, 1982, w/Richard Blackburn, directed
NOT FOR PUBLICATION   Samuel Goldwyn Company, 1984, w/John Meyer, directed

Screenplays:
BLAND AMBITION   w/Richard Blackburn
FRANKENCAR   w/Richard Blackburn

KEVIN BARTELME
INSIDE OUT   Hemdale, 1986, w/Roy Teicher

HALL BARTLETT*
Business: Hall Bartlett Films, Inc., 9200 Sunset Blvd., Suite 908, Los Angeles, CA 90069, 213/278-8883

UNCHAINED   Warner Bros., 1955, directed
ZERO HOUR!   Paramount, 1957, w/John Champion & Arthur Hailey, directed
DRANGO   United Artists, 1957, co-directed
ALL THE YOUNG MEN   Columbia, 1960, directed
THE CHILDREN OF SANCHEZ   Lone Star, 1978, w/Cesare Zavattini, directed

WILLIAM S. BARTMAN
Agent: Tom Klassen, 73 Market Street, Venice, CA 90291, 213/396-5937

O'HARA'S WIFE   Davis-Panzer Productions, 1982, w/James Nasalla, directed

DANIEL BARTOLINI*
Agent: United Talent Agency - Beverly Hills, 213/273-6700

Screenplays:
MAN'S FATE
IF I SHOULD DIE IN NO MAN'S LAND
THE LAST ILLUSION
HEATLIGHTNING

HAL BARWOOD*
Agent: ICM - Los Angeles, 213/550-4000

THE SUGARLAND EXPRESS   Universal, 1974, w/Matthew Robbins & Steven Spielberg
THE BINGO LONG TRAVELING ALL-STARS & MOTOR KINGS   Universal, 1976, w/Matthew Robbins
MACARTHUR   Universal, 1977, w/Matthew Robbins
CORVETTE SUMMER   MGM/United Artists, 1978, w/Matthew Robbins
DRAGONSLAYER   Paramount, 1981, w/Matthew Robbins
WARNING SIGN   20th Century Fox, 1985, w/Matthew Robbins, directed

Screenplays:
THE GRID w/Matthew Robbins
NEWSREEL w/Matthew Robbins
WITNESSES w/Matthew Robbins
HOME FREE w/Matthew Robbins
NIGHT SHADE w/Matthew Robbins
OTHERWHERE

RON BASE
HEAVENLY BODIES   MGM/UA, 1985, w/Lawrence Dane

RONALD BASS*
Agent: CAA - Beverly Hills, 213/288-4545

CODE NAME: EMERALD   MGM/UA, 1985
BLACK WIDOW   20th Century Fox, 1987
GARDENS OF STONE   Tri-Star, 1987
RAIN MAN ★★   MGM/UA, 1988, w/Barry Morrow
SLEEPING WITH THE ENEMY   20th Century Fox, 1991

Screenplays:
MANHATTAN GHOST STORY
HOSTILE WITNESS
BLAKE
SIGNIFICANT OTHER
TEARS OF THE SUN
LIME'S CRISIS w/David Field
TARGET w/Ulu Grosbard
PASSION OF MIND
REUNION
SECOND SON
THE PRESIDENT ELOPES
WINDWARD PASSAGE
THE DIVE
TRADEOFF

LAWRENCE BASSOFF
Business: Dauntless Director, 228 Main Street - Suite D, Venice, CA 90291, 213/553-5380

WEEKEND PASS   Crown International, 1984, directed
HUNK   Crown International, 1987, directed

WILLIAM E. BAST*
Agent: CAA - Beverly Hills, 213/288-4545

HAMMERHEAD   Columbia, 1968, w/Herbert Baker
THE VALLEY OF GWANGI   Warner Bros., 1969
THE BETSY   Allied Artists, 1978, w/Walter Bernstein

KENT BATEMAN
Agent: ICM - Los Angeles, 213/550-4000

THE LAND OF NO RETURN   International PictureShow, 1981, w/Frank Ray Perilli
THE HEADLESS EYES   J.E.R. Pictures, 1983, directed

JOE BATTEER*
Agent: The Gersh Agency - Beverly Hills, 213/274-6611

CURIOSITY KILLS (CTF)   MCA Television Entertainment, 1990, w/John Rice

BRADLEY BATTERSBY*
Agent: Richland/Wunsch/Hohman Agency - Los Angeles, 213/278-1955

BLUE DESERT   Neo Motion Pictures, 1991, w/Arthur Collis, directed

LLOYD BATTISTA
COMIN' AT YA!   Filmways, 1981, w/Wolf Lowenthal & Gene Quintano
TREASURE OF THE FOUR CROWNS   Cannon, 1983, w/Jim Bryce & Jerry Lazarus

FRED BAUER
UNDER THE RAINBOW   Orion/Warner Bros., 1981, w/Pat McCormick, Harry Hurwitz, Martin Smith & Pat Bradley

DAVID BAUGHN
BEYOND EVIL   IFI-Scope III, 1980, Story
GRADUATION DAY   IFI-Scope III, 1981, Story

THOMAS BAUM*
Agent: The Artists Agency - Los Angeles, 213/277-7779

HUGO THE HIPPO (AF)   1975
CARNY   United Artists, 1980
SIMON   Orion/Warner Bros., 1980, Story w/Marshall Brickman
THE SENDER   Paramount, 1982
THE MANHATTAN PROJECT   20th Century Fox, 1986, w/Marshall Brickman

Screenplays:
UNRAVELLED
LOUIE, LOUIE
CADAVERS
ACTS OF GOD
SHARUN

PETER S. BEAGLE*
Agent: Robinson, Weintraub, Gross & Associates - Los Angeles, 213/653-5802

THE DOVE   Paramount, 1974, w/Adam Kennedy
THE LORD OF THE RINGS (AF)   United Artists, 1978, w/Chris Conkling
THE LAST UNICORN   Jensen Farley Pictures, 1982

Screenplays:
A FINE AND PRIVATE PLACE

DAVID BEAIRD*
Agent: William Morris Agency - Beverly Hills, 213/2747451

OCTAVIA   International Film Marketing, 1984, directed
MY CHAUFFEUR   Crown International, 1985, directed
THE PARTY ANIMAL   International Film Marketing, 1985, directed
SCORCHERS   Goldcrest Films, 1991, from his play, directed

JOHN BEAIRD*
Agent: The Gersh Agency - Beverly Hills, 213/274-6611
Business: John Beaird Productions Inc., 6708 Hillpark Dr,, Los Angeles, CA 90068, 213/851-4142

MY BLOODY VALENTINE   Paramount, 1981
BAKER COUNTY USA   TRAPPED   Jensen Farley Pictures, 1982

Screenplays:
DANCE FEVER
ANNE BONNY THE PIRATE QUEEN
WATCH THE SKY
TANGERINE
PLAYING TO WIN

HENRY S. BEAN*
Agent: William Morris Agency - Beverly Hills, 213/274-7451

RUNNING BRAVE   Buena Vista, 1983, w/Shirl Henryx
INTERNAL AFFAIRS   Paramount, 1990

Screenplays:
DEEP COVER w/Michael Tolkin
DESIRE w/Leora Barish & Frederic Raphael
EL DORADO w/Leora Barish
LABYRINTH 9 w/Leora Barish
CAR THIEVES
WHO YOU KNOW
THE BIG U
THE EDNA BUCHANAN STORY

NICHOLAS BEARDSLY
SAVAGE ISLAND   Empire Pictures, 1985, w/Michelle Tomski, directed

CRISTINE BEATO
Agent: The Wright Concept - Hollywood, 213/461-3844

Screenplays:
THERE'S A RUSSIAN IN MY FRIDGE

ANNE BEATTS*
Agent: Broder-Kurland-Webb-Uffner - Los Angeles, 213/656-9262

GILDA LIVE (FD)   Warner Bros., 1980, w/others

Screenplays:
THE WOMEN
WHERE THE GIRLS WERE
CARIBBEAN WOMAN
COMMUNITY PROPERTY

WARREN BEATTY*
Agent: CAA - Beverly Hills, 213/288-4545

SHAMPOO ★   Columbia, 1975, w/Robert Towne
HEAVEN CAN WAIT ★   Paramount, 1978, w/Elaine May, directed
REDS ★   Paramount, 1981, w/Trevor Griffiths, directed

GORMAN BECHARD
Business: Generic Films, Inc., P.O. Box 2715, Waterbury, CT 06723, 203/756-3017

CEMETARY HIGH   Titan Productions, 1989, w/Carmine Capobianco, directed

BARRY BECKERMAN*
Agent: William Morris Agency - Beverly Hills, 213/274-7451

SHAMUS   Columbia, 1972
ST. IVES   Warner Bros., 1976

Screenplays:
HALLIBURTON
BATTLE OF THE PHILLIPPINE SEA
RHYTHM & BLUES

GEORGE BECKERMAN*
Agent: Robinson, Weintraub, Gross & Associates - Los Angeles, 213/653-5802

Screenplays:
IN DEEP

JAY BECKNER
Agent: William Morris Agency - Beverly Hills, 213/274-7451

Screenplays:
SAFE AT HOME

MICHAEL BECKNER*
Contact: Bloom, Dekom & Hergott - Los Angeles, 213/278-8622
Business: Beckner-Gorman Productions, Hollywood Pictures, 818/567-5180

Screenplays:
SNIPER
TEXAS LEAD AND GOLD w/Jim Gorman
CUTTHROAT ISLAND (Story w/Jim Gorman)
HOSTLIE TAKEOVER w/Jim Gorman

DICK BEEBE*
Agent: CAA - Beverly Hills, 213/288-4545

BAYOU CONFIDENTIAL (P)
THE RAPTURE-TWO STEP (P)

Be

FILM WRITERS GUIDE

HEAVENZAPOPPIN' (P)
VAMPIRES IN KODACHROME (P)
ANDROSCOGGIN FUGUE (P)
THE GUITEAU BURLESQUE (P)
OH, CLORIS (P)
NAKED CHAMBERS (P)
DRACULA (P)
FAREWELL TO FLESH (P)
PRISON STORIES: WOMEN ON THE INSIDE (CTF) Francine LeFrak Productions/HBO Showcase, 1991, "New Chicks" w/Martin Jones & Jule Selbo

Screenplays:
EXIT WOUNDS
HE'S ALL MINE
CITIZEN SICK
BIJOU DREAMS (CTF)
ONLY THE LONELY: ROY ORBISON BIOGRAPHY (CTF)
THE LAST PELT (CTF)

JOHN BEECH
WARLORDS OF THE 21ST CENTURY   New World, 1982, w/Irving Austin & Harley Coklis

GREG BEEMAN
TALES OF THE UNKNOWN   AIP Home Video, 1990, "The Big Garage," directed

JEFF BEGUN
SATURDAY THE 14TH   New World, 1981, Story

MARC BEHM
HELP!   United Artists, 1965, w/Charles Wood
THE PARTY'S OVER   Allied Artists, 1966
THE BLONDE FROM PEKING   Paramount, 1968, w/Nicholas Gessner
THE MAD BOMBER   Cinemation, 1973, Story
HOSPITAL MASSACRE   Cannon, 1982
NANA   Cannon, 1983

EDWARD BEHR
HALF MOON STREET   20th Century Fox, 1986, w/Bob Swaim

IRA STEVEN BEHR*
Agent: Triad Artists, Inc. - Los Angeles, 213/556-2727

Screenplays:
HICKOCK AND CODY
WAR BOYS

JACK BEHR*
Agent: ICM - Los Angles, 213/550-4000

BIRDY   Tri-Star, 1984, w/Sandy Kroopf

Screenplays:
B STREET   w/Sandy Kroopf
PUBLIC SECRETS   w/Sandy Kroopf
MATINEE   w/Sandy Kroopf
RUNAWAY   w/Sandy Kroopf
ALIAS EDDIE SHERBERT   w/Sandy Kroopf
WITNESS TO WAR   w/Sandy Kroopf
BOOK OF EPPE   w/Sandy Kroopf
THE MONKEY WRENCH GANG   w/Sandy Kroopf
PERFECT COUNTERFEIT   w/Sandy Kroopf
SPEECHLESS   w/Sandy Kroopf
SERIOUS LIVING   w/Sandy Kroopf

THIN ICE
ENDANGERED
EASY STREET

JEAN-JACQUES BEINEIX
Contact: French Film Office, 745 Fifth Ave., New York, NY 10151, 212/832-8860

DIVA   United Artists Classics, 1982, w/Jean Van Hamme, directed
THE MOON IN THE GUTTER   Triumph/Columbia, 1983, directed
BETTY BLUE   37.2 DEGREES LE MATIN   Alive Films, 1986, directed

Screenplays:
ICE MAIDENS

ADAM BELANOFF
Agent: Circle Talent Associates - Beverly Hills, 213/285-1585

Screenplays:
BALONEY BOY
CASEY SPEAKS   w/P.J. Pesce

ELISA BELL
Agent: Susan Smith & Associates - Beverly Hills, 213/852-4777

WRITER'S BLOCK (CTF)   USA Network/Wilshire Court Productions, 1991, from her Short film

Screenplays:
SLOW BURN
VIRTUE

JEFFREY BELL*
Agent: Jim Preminger Agency - Los Angeles, 213/475-9491

RADIO INSIDE (Short), directed, also screenplay

Screenplays:
LOST SOUL   w/Stephen Volk
HYMN TIME IN THE LAND OF ABANDON

NEAL BELL*
Agent: Brett Adams, Ltd. - New York, 212/765-5630

COLD SWEAT (P)
READY FOR THE RIVER (P)
TERMINAL CHOICE   Almi Pictures, 1985

ROBERT BELL
FREE RIDE   Galaxy International, 1986, w/Lee Fulkerson & Ronald Zwang

ROSS BELL
CRACKDOWN   Concorde, 1990, w/Daryl Haney

BRUCE BELLAND*
Contact: WGA - Los Angeles, 213/550-1000

WEEKEND WARRIORS   The Movie Store, 1986, w/Roy M. Rogosin

DONALD P. BELLISARIO*
Agent: Broder-Kurland-Webb-Uffner - Los Angeles, 213/656-9262
Business: Bellisarius Productions, Universal Studios, 818/777-3381

LAST RITES   MGM/UA, 1988, directed

STEPHEN F. BELLO*
Agent: Triad Artists, Inc. - Los Angeles, 213/556-2727

CIRCLE OF POWER   *MYSTIQUE/BRAINWASH/THE NAKED WEEKEND*   Televicine, 1983, w/Beth Sullivan

MARCO BELLOCCHIO
Address: Viale Angelico 36/B, Rome, Italy

FIST IN HIS POCKET   Peppercorn-Wormser, 1965, directed
CHINA IS NEAR   Royal Films International, 1967, directed
LEAP INTO THE VOID   Summit Features, 1979, directed
THE EYES, THE MOUTH   Triumph/Columbia, 1983, directed
HENRY IV   Orion Classics, 1985, w/Tonino Guerra, directed
DEVIL IN THE FLESH   Orion Classics, 1987, w/Enrico Palandri, directed

PETER BELLWOOD*
Agent: Lake & Douroux - Beverly Hills, 213/557-0700

PHOBIA   Paramount, 1981, w/Lew Lehman, James Sangster, Gary A. Sherman & Ronald Shusett
ST. HELENS   Davis-Panzer Productions, 1981, w/Larry Ferguson
HIGHLANDER   20th Century Fox, 1986, w/Larry Ferguson & Gregory Widen
HIGHLANDER 2: THE QUICKENING   Davis-Panzer Productions, 1991

Screenplays:
THE LAST LAUGH   w/Larry Ferguson
MALACHI   w/Larry Ferguson

VERA BELMONT
Contact: French Film Office, 745 Fifth Ave., New York, NY 10151, 212/832-8860

ROUGE BAISER   *RED KISS*   Circle Releasing Corporation, 1986, w/Guy Konopnicki, directed

JERRY BELSON*
Agent: CAA - Beverly Hills, 213/288-4545

HOW SWEET IT IS   National General, 1968, w/Garry Marshall
THE GRASSHOPPER   National General, 1969, as "Gary Belsen," w/Garry Marhsall
SMILE   United Artists, 1975
FUN WITH DICK AND JANE   Columbia, 1977, w/David Giler & Mordecai Richler
THE END   United Artists, 1978
SMOKEY AND THE BANDIT - PART II   Universal, 1980, w/Brock Yates
JEKYLL AND HYDE...TOGETHER AGAIN   Paramount, 1982, w/Monica Johnson, Michael Leeson & Harvey Miller, directed

SURRENDER   Warner Bros., 1987, directed
ALWAYS   Universal, 1989

Screenplays:
LOVE, ROGER   w/Garry Marshall
KIDS
CAPTAIN YAWK & THE SILVER STREAK
CARS
THE GREAT CAPE GIRARDEAU LEAP

JAMES A. BELUSHI
Agent: CAA - Beverly Hills, 213/288-4545

NUMBER ONE WITH A BULLET   Cannon, 1987, w/Gail Morgan Hickman, Andrew Kurtzman & Rob Riley

MARIA LUISA BEMBERG
MISS MARY   New World, 1986, w/Jorge Goldenberg, directed
I, THE WORST OF ALL   Gea Cinematografica, 1990, w/Antonio Larreta, directed

JONATHAN BENAIR*
Agent: William Morris Agency - Beverly Hills, 213/274-7451

Screenplays:
TROLLOPS   w/Meredith Brody
BEETHOVEN'S TENTH
JAGGED EDGE 2

PETER BENCHLEY*
Agent: ICM - Los Angeles, 213/550-4000

JAWS   Universal, 1975, w/Carl Gottlieb
THE DEEP   Columbia, 1977, w/Tracy Keenan Wynn
THE ISLAND   Universal, 1980

Screenplays:
AMAZON RUN

LAWRENCE BENDER
INTRUDER   Phantom Productions, 1989, w/Scott Spiegel

BARBARA BENEDEK*
Agent: CAA - Beverly Hills, 213/288-4545

THE BIG CHILL ★   Columbia, 1983, w/Lawrence Kasdan
IMMEDIATE FAMILY   Columbia, 1989
MEN DON'T LEAVE   The Geffen Company/Warner Bros., 1990, w/Paul Brickman

Screenplays:
BEGINNERS   w/Harriet Frank Jr. & Irving Ravetch

TOM BENEDEK*
Agent: United Talent Agency - Beverly Hills, 213/273-6700

COCOON   20th Century Fox, 1985

Screenplays:
MADAME BUTTERFLY
MONSOON
FREE WILLY
SPELLS   w/Abbie Bernstein
HALFWAY HOUSE
SHATTERED SILENCE
ORANGE COUNTY RED
ROLLING NOWHERE
RED ROOSTER

Be

FILM WRITERS GUIDE

FILM WRITERS

ROBERT BENEDETTO*
Agent: United Talent Agency - Beverly Hills, 213/273-6700

ALOHA SUMMER   Spectrafilm, 1988, w/Mike Greco

GLENN M. BENEST*
Agent: Jim Preminger Agency - Los Angeles, 213/475-9491

DEADLY BLESSING   United Artists/Polygram, 1981, w/Matthew Barr & Wes Craven

TOMAS BENITEZ
SALSA   Cannon, 1988, w/Boaz Davidson & Shepard Goldman

JEFF BENJAMIN*
Agent: Robinson, Weintraub, Gross & Associates - Los Angeles, 213/653-5802

AMERICAN ANTHEM   Columbia, 1986, w/Evan Archerd

ALAN BENNETT
Agent: A.D. Peters & Co., Ltd. - London, 011/441/580-9592

A PRIVATE FUNCTION   Island Alive, 1985
PRICK UP YOUR EARS   Samuel Goldwyn Company, 1987
102 BOULEVARD HAUSSMANN   BBC Enterprises, 1991

BILL BENNETT*
(William Regis Bennett)
Contact: Australian Film Commission, 9229 Sunset Blvd., Los Angeles, CA 90069, 213/275-7074

BACKLASH   Samuel Goldwyn Company, 1987, directed

CHARLES BENNETT*
Agent: H.N. Swanson, Inc. - Los Angeles, 213/652-5385

BLACKMAIL   British International Pictures, 1929, w/Alfred Hitchcock & Benn W. Levy, from his play
THE CLAIRVOYANT   Gainsborough, 1934, w/Robert Edmunds & Bryan E. Wallace
THE MAN WHO KNEW TOO MUCH   Gaumont-British, 1934, w/A.R. Rawlinson, D.B. Wyndham Lewis, Edwin Greenwood & Emlyn Williams
THE THIRTY-NINE STEPS   Gaumont-British, 1935, w/Alma Reville
A WOMAN ALONE   *SOBOTAGE*   Gaumont, 1936, w/others
THE SECRET AGENT   Gaumont, 1936
FOREIGN CORRESPONDENT   United Artists, 1940, w/Joan Harrison, James Hilton, Robert Benchley
THEY DARE NOT LOVE   Columbia, 1941, w/Ernest Vajda
UNCONQUERED   Paramount, 1947, w/Frederic M. Frank & Jesse Lasky Jr.
THE SIGN OF THE RAM   Columbia, 1948
BLACK MAGIC   United Artists, 1949
MADNESS OF THE HEART   GFD, 1949, directed
WHERE DANGER LIVES   RKO, 1950
THE GREEN GLOVE   United Artists, 1952
DANGEROUS MISSION   RKO, 1954, w/W.R. Burnett, James Edmiston & Horace McCoy
NIGHT OF THE DEMON   Columbia, 1957, w/Hal E. Chester
THE STORY OF MANKIND   Warner Bris,m 1957, w/Irwin Allen
THE BIG CIRCUS   Allied Artists, 1959, w/Irwin Allen & Irving Wallace
THE LOST WORLD   20th Century-Fox, 1960, w/Irwin Allen
VOYAGE TO THE BOTTOM OF THE SEA   20th Century-Fox, 1961, w/Irwin Allen
FIVE WEEKS IN A BALLOON   20th Century-Fox, 1962, w/Irwin Allen & Albert Gail
WAR-GODS OF THE DEEP   *THE CITY UNDER THE SEA*   American International, 1965, w/Louis M. Heyward

Screenplays:
BLACKMAIL (remake)

HARVE BENNETT*
Business Manager: Barry Greenfeld, 213/282-0477

STAR TREK II: THE WRATH OF KHAN   Paramount, 1982, Story
STAR TREK III: THE SEARCH FOR SPOCK   Paramount, 1984
STAR TREK IV: THE VOYAGE HOME   Paramount, 1986, w/Peter Krikes, Steve Meerson & Nicholas Meyer
STAR TREK V: THE FINAL FRONTIER   Paramount, 1989, Story w/David Loughery & William Shatner

PARKER BENNETT*
Agent: Triad Artists, Inc. - Los Angeles, 213/556-2727

MYSTERY DATE   Orion, 1991, w/Terry Runte

RICHARD BENNETT
(See Bert I. Gordon)

VALERIE BENNETT
Agent: United Talent Agency - Beverly Hills, 213/273-6700

Screenplays:
TIMERS w/Ian Seeberg
HIGHER GROUND w/Ian Seeberg
MORT w/Ian Seeberg

WALLACE BENNETT*
Agent: Harold R. Greene Inc. - Los Angeles, 213/852-4959
Business: 5598 South Rim St., Westlake Village, CA 91362

SILENT SCREAM   American Cinema, 1980, w/Jim Wheat & Ken Wheat
THE PHILADELPHIA EXPERIMENT   New World, 1984, Story w/Don Jakoby
RAGE OF HONOR   Trans World Entertainment, 1987, w/Robert Short

TYLER BENSINGER
Agent: United Talent Agency - Beverly Hills, 213/273-6700

Screenplays:
HOME
SPADE & GRAVE

ROBBY BENSON*
(Robby Segal)
Agent: The Brandt Company - Studio City, 818/506-7747

ONE ON ONE   Warner Bros., 1977, w/Jerry Segal
THE MILER   Warner Bros., 1978, Shared
DIE LAUGHING   Orion/Warner Bros., 1980, w/Jerry Segal & Scott Parker

WHITE HOT *CRACK IN THE MIRROR* Triax Entertainment Group, 1988, as "Robert Modero," directed
MODERN LOVE Skouras Pictures, 1990, directed

ROBERT BENSON
SEXBOMB Phillips & Mora Entertainment, 1989

ROBERT BENTLEY*
Agent: The Mitchell J. Hamilburg Agency - Los Angeles, 213/657-1501

SHANGHAI SURPRISE MGM/UA, 1986, w/John Kohn

ROBERT BENTON*
Agent: ICM - New York, 212/556-5600

BONNIE AND CLYDE ★ Warner Bros., 1967, w/David Newman
THERE WAS A CROOKED MAN... United Artists, 1970, w/David Newman
WHAT'S UP DOC? Warner Bros., 1972, w/Buck Henry & David Newman
BAD COMPANY Paramount, 1972, w/David Newman
THE LATE SHOW ★ Warner Bros., 1977, directed
SUPERMAN Warner Bros., 1978, w/David Newman, Leslie Newman & Mario Puzo
KRAMER VS. KRAMER ★★ Columbia, 1979, directed
STILL OF THE NIGHT MGM/UA, 1982, directed
PLACES IN THE HEART ★★ Tri-Star, 1984, directed
NADINE Tri-Star, 1987, directed

LUC BERAUD
LIKE A TURTLE ON ITS BACK New Line Cinema, 1981, w/Claude Miller, directed
HEART OF DESIRE Triumph/Columbia, 1984, w/Claude Miller, directed
SINCERELY CHARLOTTE New Line Cinema, 1986, w/Caroline Huppert & Joelle Gordon, directed

ERIC BERCOVICI*
Agent: InterTalent - Los Angeles, 213/858-6200

THE DAY OF THE EVIL GUN MGM, 1968, w/Charles Marquis Warren
CHANGE OF HABIT Universal, 1969, w/James Lee & Lewis Meltzer
HELL IN THE PACIFIC Cinerama Releasing Corporation, 1969, w/Alexander Jacobs
THE CULPEPPER CATTLE CO. 20th Century-Fox, 1972, w/Gregory Prentiss

Screenplays:
DUNN'S CONUNDRUM
TRACKS END

LUCA BERCOVICI*
Business Manager: Cindy S. Matyas, 818/509-1811

GHOULIES Empire Pictures, 1986, w/Jefery Levy, directed
ROCKULA Cannon, 1989, w/Jefery Levy & Christopher Verweil, directed

BRUCE BERESFORD
Agent: William Morris Agency - Beverly Hills, 213/274-7451

THE ADVENTURES OF BARRY McKENZIE Double Head Productions, 1972, w/Barry Humphries, directed
BARRY McKENZIE HOLDS HIS OWN Satori, 1974, w/Barry Humphries, directed
MONEY MOVERS South Australian Film Corporation, 1978, directed
BREAKER MORANT ★ New World/Quartet, 1980, w/Jonathan Hardy & David Stevens, directed
THE FRINGE DWELLERS Atlantic Releasing Corporation, 1986, w/Phoison Beresford, directed

PHOISON BERESFORD
THE FRINGE DWELLERS Atlantic Releasing Corporation, 1986, w/Bruce Beresford

A. SCOTT BERG*
Contact: WGA - Los Angeles, 213/550-1000

MAKING LOVE 20th Century-Fox, 1982, Story

DICK BERG*
Business: Stonehenge Productions, 10202 W. Washington Blvd., Culver City, CA, 90232, 213/280-7350

SHOOT Avco Embassy, 1976

JUDITH BERG*
Agent: APA - Los Angeles, 213/273-0744

ALMOST SUMMER Universal, 1978, w/Sandra Berg & Martin Davidson

SANDRA BERG*
Agent: APA - Los Angeles, 213/273-0744

ALMOST SUMMER Universal, 1978, w/Judith Berg & Martin Davidson

ALAN BERGER*
Agent: APA - Los Angeles, 213/273-0744

SAVE THE LAST DANCE FOR ME Swann American Pictures, 1981, w/Kathy Gori

Screenplays:
THE BUFF w/Kathy Gori
THE GOLD COAST w/Kathy Gori
MERCY GIRLS w/Kathy Gori
I'M NOT CHARLIE w/Kathy Gori
THE MAN SHE KNEW w/Kathy Gori
HER SAINTED HUSBAND w/Kathy Gori
GOODBYE FOREVER w/Kathy Gori
RICH LITTLE POOR GIRLS w/Kathy Gori & Joan Rivers
FOR BETTER OR FOR WORSE w/Kathy Gori
ROCKET MAN LIFE ON EARTH w/Kathy Gori
NATIONAL PARK w/Kathy Gori
LADIES DAY w/Kathy Gori
UNDER WRAPS w/Kathy Gori
SHAGGY w/Kathy Gori

PAMELA BERGER
THE IMPORTED BRIDEGROOM Lara Classics, 1990, directed

ANDREW BERGMAN*
Agent: CAA - Beverly Hills, 213/288-4545
Business: Lobell-Bergman Productions, 9336 W. Washington Blvd., Culver City, CA, 90230, 213/202-3362

SOCIAL SECURITY (P)
BLAZING SADDLES Warner Bros., 1973, w/Mel Brooks, Richard Pryor, Norman Steinberg & Alan Uger
THE IN-LAWS Warner Bros., 1979

Be

FILM WRITERS GUIDE

SO FINE   Warner Bros., 1981, directed
OH GOD! YOU DEVIL   Warner Bros., 1984
FLETCH   Universal, 1985
BIG TROUBLE   Columbia, 1986, as "Warren Bogle"
THE FRESHMAN   Tri-Star, 1990, directed
SOAPDISH   Paramount, 1991, w/Robert Harling

Screenplays:
HONEYMOON IN VEGAS (directing)
THE SCOUT
RHAPSODY IN CRIME
AIR PARADISE
NIGHT OF THE TOY SOLDIERS   THE SNATCH
HOLLYWOOD AND LEVINE
SUCCESS STORY
TALL DOG
THE BIG KISS-OFF OF 1944

ANDREW C.J. BERGMAN*
Contact: WGA - Los Angeles, 213/550-1000

Screenplays:
DOUBLES
MIRACLE AT MOOSEHEAD

INGMAR BERGMAN
Agent: Paul Kohner, Inc. - Los Angeles, 213/550-1060

THE DEVIL'S WANTON   Terrafilm, 1949, directed
ILLICIT INTERLUDE   SOMMARLEK   Janus, 1951, w/Herbert Grevenius, directed
SECRETS OF WOMEN   Janus, 1952, directed
MONIKA   Janus, 1953, directed
SAWDUST AND TINSEL   THE NAKED NIGHT   Janus, 1953, directed
A LESSON IN LOVE   Janus, 1954, directed
DREAMS   Janus, 1955, directed
SMILES OF A SUMMER NIGHT   Janus, 1955, directed
WILD STRAWBERRIES   Janus, 1957, directed
THE SEVENTH SEAL   Janus, 1957, directed
THE MAGICIAN   Janus, 1958, directed
THE DEVIL'S EYE   Janus, 1960, directed
THROUGH A GLASS DARKLY ★   Janus, 1962, directed
WINTER LIGHT   Janus, 1962, directed
THE SILENCE   Janus, 1963, directed
ALL THESE WOMEN   NOW ABOUT THESE WOMEN...   Janus, 1964, directed
PERSONA   United Artists, 1966, directed
HOUR OF THE WOLF   United Artists, 1968, directed
SHAME   United Artists, 1968, directed
THE PASSION OF ANNA   United Artists, 1969, directed
THE TOUCH   Cinerama Releasing Corporation, 1971, directed
CRIES AND WHISPERS ★   New World, 1972, directed
SCENES FROM A MARRIAGE   Cinema 5, 1973, directed
FACE TO FACE   Paramount, 1976, directed
THE SERPENT'S EGG   Paramount, 1978, directed
AUTUMN SONATA ★   New World, 1978, directed
FROM THE LIFE OF THE MARIONETTES   Universal/AFD, 1980, directed
FANNY AND ALEXANDER ★   Embassy, 1983, directed
AFTER THE REHEARSAL   Triumph/Columbia, 1983, directed
BEST INTENTIONS   Samuel Goldwyn Company, 1992

LINDA BERGMAN*
Contact: 213/284-7800

THE LOOKALIKE (CTF)   Gallo Entertainment, 1990, w/Martin Tahse
MATTERS OF THE HEART (CTF)   Tahse-Bergman/MCA, 1990, w/Martin Tahse

PETER BERGMAN*
Agent: Abrams Artists & Associates - Los Angeles, 213/859-0625

HE'S MY GIRL   Scotti Bros., 1987, Story w/Taylor Ames & Terence H. Winkless

ROBERT BERGMAN
SKULL: A NIGHT OF TERROR   Geonib Properties, 1989, w/Gerard Ciccoritti, directed
A WHISPER TO A SCREAM   Distant Horizon and Lighthouse Communications, 1989, w/Gerard Ciccoritti, directed

ERIC BERGREN*
Agent: Favored Artists - Los Angeles, 213/653-3191

THE ELEPHANT MAN ★   Paramount, 1980, w/Christopher DeVore & David Lynch
FRANCES   Universal/AFD, 1982, w/Christopher DeVore & Nicholas Kazan

Screenplays:
A WRINKLE IN TIME w/Chris DeVore
CHRIS LUCAS STORY

ELEANOR BERGSTEIN*
Agent: CAA - Beverly Hills, 213/288-4545

IT'S MY TURN   Columbia, 1980
DIRTY DANCING   Vestron, 1987

HOWARD BERK*
Agent: Barry Perelman Agency - Los Angeles, 213/274-5999

TARGET   Warner Bros., 1985, w/Don Peterson

JEANNIE BERLIN
Contact: 212/888-0080

IN THE SPIRIT   Castle Hill Productions, 1990, w/Laurie Jones

MICHAEL BERLIN*
Agent: William Morris Agency - Beverly Hills, 213/274-7451

Screenplays:
TAX MAN w/Eric Estrin
RED BIRD DOWN w/Eric Estrin

JEFF BERMAN*
Agent: William Morris Agency - Beverly Hills, 213/274-7451

Screenplays:
ON THE AIR w/Jerry Rapp
THE TOURISTS w/Jerry Rapp

TED BERMAN*
Contact: 818/956-2612

THE FOX AND THE HOUND (AF)   Buena Vista, 1981,
  Story w/others, directed
THE BLACK CAULDRON (AF)   Buena Vista, 1985,
  Story w/others, directed

JUDD BERNARD*
Agent: CAA - Beverly Hills, 213/288-4545

THE MARSEILLE CONTRACT   Warner Bros., 1974
THE CLASS OF MISS MacMICHAEL   Brut
  Productions, 1978
ENTER THE NINJA   Cannon, 1981, w/Menahem Golan

SAM BERNARD*
Agent: The Gage Group - Los Angeles, 213/859-8777

RAD   Tri-Star, 1986, w/Geoffrey Edwards
3:15   Dakota Entertainment, 1986, w/Michael Jacobs

SANDRA BERNHARD*
Agent: Irvin ArhturAssociates - Beverly Hills, 213/278-5934

WITHOUT YOU I'M NOTHING   MCEG, 1990, from her
  play, w/John Boskovich

JEFFREY S. BERNINI*
Agent: The Gersh Agency - Beverly Hills, 213/274-6611

TAKE THIS JOB AND SHOVE IT   Avco Embassy, 1981,
  Story w/Barry Schneider

ABBIE BERNSTEIN*
Contact: WGA - Los Angeles, 213/550-1000

Screenplays:
SPELLS   w/Tom Benedek
HITCHHIKERS GUIDE TO THE GALAXY
SHATTERED MOON
NOTHING HUMAN
RAIN CRYSTALS

ARMYAN BERNSTEIN*
Agent: CAA - Beverly Hills, 213/288-4545
Business: Beacon Pictures, Warner-Hollywood Studios,
  213/850-2651

THANK GOD IT'S FRIDAY   Columbia, 1978
ONE FROM THE HEART   Columbia, 1982,
  w/Francis Coppola
WINDY CITY   Warner Bros., 1984, directed
CROSS MY HEART   Universal, 1987, w/Gail
  Parent, directed

JANE BERNSTEIN
Agent: Shapiro/Lichtman - Los Angeles, 213/859-8877

SEVEN MINUTES IN HEAVEN   Warner Bros., 1986,
  w/Linda Feferman

NAT BERNSTEIN*
Agent: United Talent Agency - Beverly Hills, 213/273-6700

OPPORTUNITY KNOCKS   Universal, 1990,
  w/Mitchel Katlin

Screenplays:
ON THE AIR   w/Mitchel Katlin
WHEN THE WIFE'S AWAY   w/Mitchel Katlin
LORD OF THE MANOR   w/Mitchel Katlin

WALTER BERNSTEIN*
Agent: ICM - New York, 212/556-6810

THAT KIND OF WOMAN   Paramount, 1959
HELLER IN PINK TIGHTS   1960, Paramount,
  w/Dudley Nichols
PARIS BLUES   United Artists, 1961, w/Irene Kamp &
  Jack Sher
FAIL SAFE   Columbia, 1964
THE TRAIN   United Artists, 1964, w/Franklin Coen &
  Frank Davis
THE MONEY TRAP   MGM, 1966
THE MOLLY MAGUIRES   Paramount, 1970
THE FRONT ★   Columbia, 1976
SEMI-TOUGH   United Artists, 1978
THE BETSY   Allied Artists, 1978, w/William Bast
AN ALMOST PERFECT AFFAIR   Paramount, 1979,
  w/Don Peterson
YANKS   Universal, 1979, w/Colin Welland
LITTLE MISS MARKER   Universal, 1980, directed
THE HOUSE ON CARROLL STREET   Orion, 1988

Screenplays:
F.B.I. STING
HOMAGE TO CATALONIA
LOW DOWN
SPOOKWAFFE
STAR QUALITY

JAY BERNZWEIG
Agent: The Wright Concept - Hollywood, 213/461-3844

Screenplays:
SQUEAKY CLEAN

CLAUDE BERRI
Agent: Artmedia, 10 Avenue Georges V, 75008 Paris,
  France, 04/723-7860
Business: Renn Productions, 10 rue Lincoln, 75008 Paris,
  France, 04/256-2590

ONE WILD MOMENT   Quartet/Films Incorporated,
  1978, directed
JEAN DE FLORETTE   Orion Classics, 1987, w/Gerard
  Brach, directed
MANON OF THE SPRING   Orion Classics, 1987,
  w/Gerard Brach, directed

GINA BERRIAULT*
Agent: The Gersh Agency - Beverly Hills, 213/274-6611

THE STONE BOY   TLC Films/20th Century-Fox, 1984

DAVID BERRY
THE WHALES OF AUGUST   Alive Films, 1987,
  from his play

JULIAN BERRY
AFTER THE FALL OF NEW YORK   Almi Pictures, 1985,
  w/Martin Dolman & Gabriel Rossini

Be
FILM WRITERS GUIDE

MICHAEL BERRY*
Agent: United Talent Agency - Beverly Hills, 213/273-6700

SHORT TIME   20th Century Fox, 1990,
    w/John Blumenthal

Screenplays:
BLUE STREAK w/John Blumenthal
CHUMPS w/John Blumenthal
NIGHT WORK

TOM BERRY
CRAZY MOON   Miramax, 1987, w/Stefan Wodoslawsky

WILLIAM BERRY*
Agent: United Talent Agency - Beverly Hills, 213/273-6700

Screenplays:
BLUE MURDER

BERNARDO BERTOLUCCI
Agent: ICM - Los Angeles, 213/550-4000

BEFORE THE REVOLUTION   New Yorker,
    1964, directed
THE SPIDER'S STRATAGEM   New Yorker, 1970,
    w/Eduardo de Gregorio & Marilu Parolini, directed
THE CONFORMIST ★   Paramount, 1971, directed
LAST TANGO IN PARIS   Universal, 1973,
    w/Franco Arcalli, directed
1900   Paramount, 1976, w/Franco Arcalli & Giuseppe
    Bertolucci, directed
LUNA   20th Century-Fox, 1979, w/Giuseppe
    Bertolucci & Clare Peploe, directed
TRAGEDY OF A RIDICULOUS MAN   The Ladd
    Company/Warner Bros., 1982, directed
THE LAST EMPEROR ★★   Columbia, 1987,
    w/Mark Peploe, directed
THE SHELTERING SKY   Warner Bros., 1990,
    w/Mark Peploe, directed

DAN BESSIE
HARD TRAVELING   New World, 1986, directed

LUC BESSON
Agent: ICM - Los Angeles, 213/550-4000

LE DERNIER COMBAT   Gaumont/Les Films du Loup/
    Constantin Alexandrof Productions, 1983
SUBWAY   Island Alive, 1985, w/Marc Perrier, directed
THE BIG BLUE   Columbia/WEG, 1988, w/Robert
    Garland, directed
LA FEMME NIKITA   Gaumont, 1991, directed

GIL BETTMAN*
Contact: WGA - Los Angeles, 213/550-1000

NEVER TOO YOUNG TO DIE   Paul Releasing, 1986,
    w/Anton Fitz & Steven Paul, directed

JONATHAN BETUEL*
Contact: WGA - Los Angeles, 213/550-1000

THE LAST STARFIGHTER   Universal, 1984
MY SCIENCE PROJECT   Buena Vista, 1985, directed

Screenplays:
INTERCEPTORS (directing)

RADHA BHARADWAJ*
Agent: Sanford, Skouras, Gross & Associates - Los Angeles,
    213/208-2100

CLOSET LAND   Universal, 1991, directed

WILLIAM BICKLEY*
Agent: The Irv Schechter Company - Beverly Hills,
    213/278-8070

HAWMPS   Mulberry Square, 1976,
    w/Michael Warren

ANN BIDERMAN*
Agent: ICM - Los Angeles, 213/550-4000

AMERICAN DREAMER   Warner Bros., 1984, Story

Screenplays:
THE WOMEN
HEADING WEST
MIAMI STORY
THE CHELSEA
LIBERTY CITY
THE THREE "C"S

KATHRYN BIGELOW*
Agent: CAA - Beverly Hills, 213/288-4545

THE LOVELESS   Atlantic Releasing Corporation,
    w/Monty Montgomery, 1981, co-directed
NEAR DARK   Warner Bros., 1987,
    w/Eric Red, directed
BLUE STEEL   MGM/UA 1990, w/Eric Red, directed

Screenplays:
THE BLUNDERER
EVERY BREATH
NIGHT BY NIGHT
UNDERTOW w/Eric Red

DANNY BILSON*
Agent: United Talent Agency - Beverly Hills,
    213/273-6700

FUTURE COP *TRANCERS*   Empire Pictures, 1985,
    w/Paul De Meo
ZONE TROOPERS   Empire Pictures, 1986, w/Paul
    De Meo, directed
ELIMINATORS   Empire Pictures, 1986,
    w/Paul De Meo
THE WRONG GUYS   New World, 1988, w/Paul
    De Meo, directed
ARENA   Empire Pictures, 1988, w/Paul De Meo
PULSEPOUNDERS   Empire Pictures, 1988, w/Paul
    De Meo
THE ROCKETEER   Buena Vista, 1991, w/Paul De Meo

CARL BINDER*
Agent: H. N. Swanson, Inc. - Los Angeles,
    213/652-5385

Screenplays:
A DAY IN THE AFTERLIFE
LIGHT BLACK
HOTEL DO

JOHN BINDER*
Contact: WGA - Los Angeles, 213/550-1000

HONEYSUCKLE ROSE   Warner Bros., 1980, w/Carol
    Sobieski & William Wittliff
ENDANGERED SPECIES   MGM/UA, 1982,
    w/Alan Rudolph
UFORIA   Universal, 1984, directed

Screenplays:
REVOLUTIONARY WAR

MIKE BINDER*
Agent: Triad Artists, Inc. - Los Angeles, 213/556-2727

COUP DE VILLE   Universal, 1990

Screenplays:
THE BRIDGE (directing)
NORTHERN LIGHTS

STEVE BING*
Contact: WGA - Los Angeles, 213/550-1000

MISSING IN ACTION 2: THE BEGINNING   Cannon, 1985,
    w/Arthur Silver & Larry Levinson

BRAD BIRD*
Agent: ICM - Los Angeles, 213/550-4000

BATTERIES NOT INCLUDED   Universal, 1986,
    w/Brent Maddock, Matthew Robbins & S.S. Wilson

SARAH BIRD
Agent: ICM - Los Angeles, 213/550-4000

THE BOYFRIEND SCHOOL   Hemdale, 1990

DAVID BIRKE
Agent: The Goldstein Company - Los Angeles,
    213/659-9511

Screenplays:
BLACK BLOOD
MR. ADVENTURE
THE CROOKED TREE
THE POLICEMAN
NOCTURNUS
CAPTAIN JACK AND THE MUFFIN TWINS
HOMESICK
BORDER TOWN

ANDREW BIRKIN*
Agent: William Morris Agency - Beverly Hills, 213/274-7451

THE PIED PIPER   Paramount, 1972, w/Jacques
    Demy & Mark Peploe
FLAME   Goodtime Entertainment, 1975
THE FINAL CONFLICT   20th Century-Fox, 1981
KING DAVID   Paramount, 1985, w/James Costigan
THE NAME OF THE ROSE   20th Century Fox, 1986,
    w/Gerard Brach, Howard Franklin & Alain Godard
BURNING SECRET   Vestron, 1988, directed

Screenplays:
FIELDS OF HONOR w/Wolfgang Petersen
INSIDE THE THIRD REICH
LITTLE LORD FAUNTLEROY
THE GLORY & THE DREAM
PETER PAN
THE CEMENT GARDEN
RUNAWAY

STUART BIRNBAUM*
Agent: The Gersh Agency - Beverly Hills, 213/274-6611

SMOKEY AND THE BANDIT PART 3   Universal, 1983,
    w/David Dashev
THE ZOO GANG   New World, 1985, Story w/David
    Dashev, Pen Densham & John Watson
SUMMER SCHOOL   Paramount, 1987, Story w/David
    Dashev & Jeff Franklin

Screenplays:
THE SILVER CROSS w/David Dashev
CHAMPAGNE FOR CAESAR   CHANCE OF A LIFETIME
    w/David Dashev
SOME OF MY BEST FRIENDS w/David Dashev
THUNDERBOAT w/Dennis Hackin
LAST CHANCE TO DANCE
THE RESTLESS SWORDS OF SHERWOOD FOREST
PRANKSTER CHRONICLES
KING OF THE SHADOWS

LARRY BISCHOFF*
Contact: WGA - Los Angeles, 213/550-1000

DREAMER   20th Century-Fox, 1979, w/James Proctor

JOHN BISHOP*
Agent: CAA - Beverly Hills, 213/288-4545

THE PACKAGE   Orion, 1989

Screenplays:
THE TRIP BACK DOWN
CHAPPIE
BORDERLINES

SHEM BITTERMAN
THE RAMP (P)
IOWA BOYS (P)
TULSA (P)
BEIJING LEGENDS (P)
1 + 1 = 3 (P)
SELF STORAGE (P) w/Tony Spiridakis
HALLOWEEN 5: THE RETURN OF MICHAEL MYERS
    Galaxy International, 1989, w/Michael Jacobs &
    Dominique Othenin-Girard

Screenplays:
OUT OF THE RAIN (from his play 1 + 1 = 3)

EMERSON BIXBY
DISTURBED   Odyssey-Cinecom International, 1990,
    w/Charles Winkler
BIKINI ISLAND   Curb-Esquire Films, 1991

CAROL BLACK*
Agent: United Talent Agency - Beverly Hills, 213/273-6700
Business: The Black/Marlens Company, 1440 S. Sepulveda
    Blvd., Los Angeles, CA, 90025, 213/444-8100

SOUL MAN   New World, 1986

Screenplays:
THE JUMPING OFF POINT w/Neal Marlens

BI

FILM
WRITERS
GUIDE

FILM WRITERS

43

DON BLACK
GULLIVER'S TRAVELS   Sunn Classic, 1981

JOHN D.F. BLACK*
Contact: WGA - Los Angeles, 213/550-1000

GUNFIGHT IN ABILENE   Universal, 1967
THE RIDE TO HANGMAN'S TREE   Universal, 1967
NOBODY'S PERFECT   Univeral, 1968
SHAFT   MGM, 1971, w/Ernest Tidyman
THE CAREY TREATMENT   MGM, 1972
TROUBLE MAN   20th Century-Fox, 1982

NOEL BLACK*
Agent: The Chasin Agency - Beverly Hills, 213/278-7505

MISCHIEF   20th Century Fox, 1985

SHANE BLACK*
Agent: InterTalent - Los Angeles, 213/858-6200

LETHAL WEAPON   Warner Bros., 1987
THE MONSTER SQUAD   Tri-Star, 1987, w/Fred Dekker
LETHAL WEAPON 2   Warner Bros., 1989, Story
   w/Warren Murphy
THE LAST BOY SCOUT   Warner Bros., 1991

Screenplays:
SHADOW COMPANY

TERRY BLACK*
Agent: CAA - Beverly Hills, 213/288-4545

DEAD HEAT   New World, 1988

Screenplays:
THE FERRET

RICHARD C. BLACKBURN*
Agent: Paul Kohner, Inc. - Los Angeles, 213/550-1060

EATING RAOUL   20th Century-Fox International
   Classics, 1982, w/Paul Bartel

Screenplays:
BLAND AMBITION w/Paul Bartel
FRANKENCAR w/Paul Bartel

WILLIAM BLACKBURN
CHALLENGE THE WIND   Sell Entertainment, 1990,
   w/Ken Howard & Marla Young, directed

KENNETH G. BLACKWELL*
Agent: Preferred Artists - Encino, 818/990-0305

DEADLY FORCE   Embassy, 1983, as "Ken Barnett,"
   w/Robert Vincent O'Neil & Barry Schneider
TRIUMPHS OF A MAN CALLED HORSE   Jensen Farley
   Pictures, 1984, w/Carlos Aured & Jack DeWitt

RICKY BLACKWOOD*
Contact: Attorney Linda Lichter, 213/858-7888

Screenplays:
PLAISIR D'AMOUR
ST. JUDE

RUBEN BLADES
Agent: Harris & Goldberg - Los Angeles, 213/553-5200

CROSSOVER DREAMS   Miramax, 1985, w/Manuel Arce
   & Leon Ichaso

DENNIS BLAIR
EASY MONEY   Orion, 1983, w/Rodney Dangerfield,
   Michael Endler & P.J. O'Rourke

MICHAEL BLAKE*
Agent: The Daniel Ostroff Agency - Los Angeles,
   213/278-2020

STACY'S KNIGHTS   Crown International, 1983
DANCES WITH WOLVES ★★   Orion, 1990

Screenplays:
POODLE SPRINGS
MUSTANG

BEVERLY BLAKENSHIP
SHAME   Skouras Pictures, 1988, w/Michael Brindley

KEN BLANCATO*
Agent: ICM - Los Angeles, 213/550-4000

STEWARDESS SCHOOL   Columbia, 1987, directed

JOEL BLASBERG*
Agent: William Morris Agency - Beverly Hills, 213/274-7451

Screenplays:
PAROLE OFFICER

RICHARD BLASUCCI*
Agent: InterTalent - Los Angeles, 213/858-6200

Screenplays:
SIDEKICK w/Paul Flaherty

JERRY BLATT
DIVINE MADNESS   Warner Bros., 1980, w/Bette Midler &
   Bruce Vilanch

WILLIAM PETER BLATTY*
Contact: WGA - Los Angeles, 213/550-1000

THE MAN FROM THE DINERS CLUB   Columbia, 1963
A SHOT IN THE DARK   United Artists, 1964,
   w/Blake Edwards
JOHN GOLDFARB, PLEASE COME HOME   20th Century-
   Fox, 1965
PROMISE HER ANYTHING   Paramount, 1966
WHAT DID YOU DO IN THE WAR, DADDY?   United Artists,
   1966, w/Blake Edwards
GUNN   Warner Bros., 1967, w/Blake Edwards
THE GREAT BANK ROBBERY   Warner Bros., 1969
DARLING LILI   Paramount, 1970, w/Blake Edwards
THE EXORCIST ★★   Warner Bros., 1973
THE NINTH CONFIGURATION   Warner Bros., 1979,
   rereleased under title TWINKLE, TWINKLE, KILLER
   KANE by United Film Distribution in 1980, directed
THE EXORCIST III   20th Century Fox, 1990, directed

BARRY BLAUSTEIN*
Agent: APA - Los Angeles, 213/273-0744

POLICE ACADEMY 2: THEIR FIRST ASSIGNMENT
   Warner Bros., 1983, w/David Sheffield
COMING TO AMERICA   Paramount, 1988,
   w/David Sheffield

Screenplays:
BOOMERANG   w/David Sheffield
THE GELFAN   w/David Sheffield
OPTIMUM   w/David Sheffield
BUTTERSCOTCH KID   w/David Sheffield
LAST HOLIDAY   w/David Sheffield
BROTHERS KEEPERS   w/David Sheffield
SAVIN A FACE

COREY BLECHMAN*
Agent: CAA - Beverly Hills, 213/288-4545

THE WHITE LIONS   Alan Landsberg Productions, 1979
DOMINICK & EUGENE   Orion, 1988, w/Alvin Sargent
MAX AND HELEN (CTF)   Citadel Entertainment, 1990

ROBERT BLEES*
Business Manager: Joseph Miller, 213/556-2472

PAID IN FULL   Paramount, 1949, w/Charles Schnee
ALL I DESIRE   Universal-International, 1953,
   w/James Gunn
THE GLASS WEB   Universal-International, 1953,
   w/Leonard Lee
PLAYGIRL   Universal-International, 1954
CATTLE QUEEN OF MONTANA   RKO, 1954,
   w/Howard Estabrook
MAGNIFICENT OBSESSION   Universal, 1954
ONE DESIRE   Universal-International, 1955,
   w/Lawrence Roman
SLIGHTLY SCARLET   RKO, 1956
AUTUMN LEAVES   Columbia, 1956, w/Jack Levne &
   Lewis Meltzer
THE BLACK SCORPION   Warner Bros., 1957,
   w/David Duncan
SCREAMING MIMI   Columbia, 1958
FROM THE EARTH TO THE MOON   Waverly, 1958,
   w/James Leicester
FROGS   American International, 1972, w/Robert
   Hutchinson
WHO SLEW AUNTIE ROO?   American International,
   1972, w/Jimmy Sangster
DR. PHIBES RISES AGAIN   American International,
   1972, w/Robert Fuest
SAVAGE HARVEST   20th Century-Fox, 1981,
   w/Robert Collins

WILLIAM BLEICH*
Agent: CAA - Beverly Hills, 213/288-4545

THE HEARSE   Crown International, 1980

BERT BLESSING
(See Frank Gilroy)

TONE BLEVINS*
Contact: 213/659-4216

BOOK OF DAYS   The Stutz Company, 1991,
   w/Meredith Monk

BERTRAND BLIER
Contact: French Film Office, 745 Fifth Avenue, New York,
   NY 10151, 212/832-8860

GOING PLACES   *LES VALSEUSES*   Cinema 5,
   1974, directed
FEMMES FATALES   *CALMOS*   New Line Cinema,
   1976, directed
GET OUT YOUR HANDKERCHIEFS   New Line Cinema,
   1978, directed
BUFFET FROID   Parafrance, 1979, directed
BEAU PERE   New Line Cinema, 1981, directed
MY BEST FRIEND'S GIRL   European International, 1983,
   w/Gerard Brach, directed
SEPARATE ROOMS   *NOTRE HISTOIRE*   Spectrafilm,
   1984, directed
MENAGE   *TENUE DE SOIREE*   Cinecom, 1986, directed
TOO BEAUTIFUL FOR YOU   *TROP BELLE POUR TOI*
   Orion Classics, 1990, directed

WILLIAM BLINN*
Agent: William Morris Agency - Beverly Hills, 213/274-7451

PURPLE RAIN   Warner Bros., 1984, w/Albert Magnoli

ROBERT BLOCH*
Agent: Shapiro/Lichtman - Los Angeles, 213/859-8877

THE CABINET OF CALIGARI   20th Century-Fox, 1962
THE COUCH   Warner Bros., 1962
STRAIT JACKET   Columbia, 1963
THE NIGHT WALKER   Universal International, 1964
THE PSYCHOPATH   Paramount, 1966
THE DEADLY BEES   Paramount, 1967, w/Anthony Marriott
TORTURE GARDEN   Columbia, 1968
THE HOUSE THAT DRIPPED BLOOD   Amicus, 1970
ASYLUM   Amicus, 1972

JOEL BLOCK
NOBODY'S PERFECT   Moviestore Entertainment, 1990,
   w/Annie Korzen

LAWRENCE J. BLOCK*
Contact: WGA - Los Angeles, 213-550-1000

THE FUNHOUSE   Universal, 1981

Screenplays:
URIAH
SPOTTERS
FANTASTIC FOUR

MICHAEL BLODGETT*
Agent: The Agency - Los Angeles, 213/551-3000

RENT-A-COP   Kings Road, 1988, w/Dennis Shryack
HERO AND THE TERROR   Cannon, 1988,
   w/Dennis Shryack
TURNER & HOOCH   Buena Vista, 1989, w/Dennis
   Shryack, Daniel Petrie Jr., Jim Cash & Jack Epps
RUN   Buena Vista, 1991, w/Dennis Shryack

Screenplays:
CAPTAIN'S BLOOD
LUCIFER'S REEF
COBRA II
MAN OF HONOR

BL

FILM WRITERS GUIDE

ERIC L. BLOOM*
Agent: Jim Preminger Agency - Los Angeles, 213/475-9491

EYES OF A STRANGER   Warner Bros., 1981, w/Mark Jackson

GEORGE ARTHUR BLOOM*
Business Manager: 213/277-7782

THE LAST FLIGHT OF NOAH'S ARK   Buena Vista, 1980, w/Steve Carabatsos & Sandy Glass
MY LITTLE PONY (AF)   DEG, 1986

JEFFREY BLOOM*
Contact: WGA - Los Angeles, 213/550-1000

SNOW JOB   Warner Bros., 1972, w/Ken Kolb
DOGPOUND SHUFFLE   Paramount, 1974, directed
11 HARROWHOUSE   20th Century-Fox, 1974
SWASHBUCKLER   Universal, 1976
THE STICK UP   Trident-Barber, 1978, directed
BLOOD BEACH   Jerry Gross Organization, 1981, directed
NIGHTMARES   Universal, 1983, w/Christopher Crowe
FLOWERS IN THE ATTIC   New World, 1987, directed

MAX BLOOM*
Contact: WGA - Los Angeles, 213/550-1000

FISTFIGHTER   Taurus Entertainment, 1989

STEVEN L. BLOOM*
Agent: CAA - Beverly Hills, 213/288-4545

THE SURE THING   Embassy, 1985, w/Jonathan Roberts
LIKE FATHER LIKE SON   Tri-Star, 1987, w/Lorne Cameron

Screenplays:
AFTER ALL
ROGUES

PHILIPPE BLOT
THE ARROGANT   Cannon, 1989, directed

NOAH BLOUGH
CROSS FIRE   Silvertree Pictures, 1989, w/Anthony Maharaj

CHRISTOPHER BLUE
HYPER SAPIEN   Tri-Star, 1986, w/Richard Adcock & Marnie Paige

DEBORAH BLUM*
Business: Blum-Ganz Productions, 8265 Sunset Blvd. - Suite 202, Los Angeles, CA 90069, 213/654-1411

VIBES   Columbia, 1988, Story w/Lowell Ganz & Babaloo Mandel

EDWIN BLUM*
Agent: Harry Gold & Associates - Studio City, 818/769-5003

THE CANTERVILLE GHOST   MGM, 1943
THE BOOGIE MAN WILL GET YOU   Columbia, 1944
DOWN TO EARTH   Columbia, 1947, w/Don Hartman
SOUTH SEA WOMAN   *PEARL OF THE SOUTH PACIFIC*   United Artists, 1953
STALAG 17   Paramount, 1953, w/Billy Wilder
THE BAMBOO PRISON   Columbia, 1955, w/Jack deWitt
GUNG HO   Paramount, 1986, Story w/Lowell Ganz & Babaloo Mandel

LEN BLUM*
Agent: CAA - Beverly Hills, 213/288-4545

MEATBALLS   Paramount, 1979, w/Janis Allen, Dan Goldberg & Harold Ramis
STRIPES   Columbia, 1981, w/Dan Goldberg & Harold Ramis
HEAVY METAL (AF)   Columbia, 1981, w/Dan Goldberg
SPACEHUNTER: ADVENTURES IN THE FORBIDDEN ZONE   Columbia, 1983, w/Dan Goldberg, Edith Rey & David Preston
FEDS   Warner Bros., 1988, w/Dan Goldberg

Screenplays:
RABBIT BOY   w/Dan Goldberg
WIDOWS   w/Dan Goldberg

JOHN BLUMENTHAL*
Agent: United Talent Agency - Beverly Hills, 213/273-6700

SHORT TIME   20th Century Fox, 1990, w/Michael Berry

Screenplays:
BLUE STREAK   w/Michael Berry
CHUMPS   w/Michael Berry

DON BLUTH
Business: Sullivan/Bluth Studios, 2501 W. Burbank Blvd. - Suite 201, Burbank, CA 91505, 818/840-9446

THE SECRET OF NIMH (AF)   MGM/UA, 1982, Story Adaptation w/Will Finn, John Pomeroy & Gary Goldman, directed
ALL DOGS GO TO HEAVEN (AF)   MGM/UA, 1989, Story w/others

JEFFREY BOAM*
Agent: CAA - Beverly Hills, 213/288-4545

STRAIGHT TIME   Warner Bros., 1978, w/Edward Bunker & Alvin Sargent
THE DEAD ZONE   Paramount, 1983
INNERSPACE   Warner Bros., 1987, w/Chip Proser
THE LOST BOYS   Warner Bros., 1987, w/Janice Fischer & James Jeremias
FUNNY FARM   Warner Bros., 1988
INDIANA JONES AND THE LAST CRUSADE   Paramount, 1989
LETHAL WEAPON 2   Warner Bros., 1989

SAM BOBRICK*
Contact: 213/550-0535

MURDER AT THE HOWARD JOHNSON'S (P)   w/Ron Clark
NORMAN, IS THAT YOU?   MGM/United Artists, 1976, w/Ron Clark & George Schlatter, from his play w/Ron Clark
JIMMY THE KID   New World, 1982

STEVEN BOCHCO*
Contact: Attorney Frank Rohner - Los Angeles, 213/477-5001
Business: Bochco Productions, 10201 W. Pico Blvd., Los Angeles, CA 90035, 213/203-2400

SILENT RUNNING   Universal, 1971, w/Michael Cimino & Deric Washburn

YUREK BOGAYEVICZ
Agent: CAA - Beverly Hills, 213/288-4545

ANNA   Vestron, 1987, w/Agnieszka Holland, directed

JOSEF BOGDANOVICH
Agent: ICM - Los Angeles, 213/550-1000

BOXOFFICE   Bee Movies, 1982

PETER BOGDANOVICH
Agent: CAA - Beverly Hills, 213/288-4545

THE WILD ANGELS   American International, 1966
TARGETS   Paramount, 1968, directed
THE LAST PICTURE SHOW ★   Columbia, 1971, w/Larry McMurtry, directed
AT LONG LAST LOVE   20th Century-Fox, 1975, directed
NICKELODEON   Columbia, 1976, w/W.D. Richter, directed
SAINT JACK   New World, 1979, w/Howard Sackler & Paul Theroux, directed
THEY ALL LAUGHED   United Artists Classics, 1982, directed
TEXASVILLE   Columbia, 1990, directed

MICHAEL BOGERT
DEAD END CITY   Action International, 1989, w/Peter Yuval

WARREN BOGLE
(See Andrew Bergman)

NICHOLAS BOGNER*
Agent: Warden & White Associates - Beverly Hills, 213/852-1028

Screenplays:
MATING SEASON
QUEEN BEE
ZERO VISIBILITY

NORMAN BOGNER
Agent: Barrett, Benson, McCartt & Weston - Los Angeles, 213/247-5500

Screenplays:
SNOWMAN
THE MADONNA COMPLEX

WILLY BOGNER
FIRE AND ICE   20th Century-Fox, 1983, directed

ERIC BOGOSIAN*
Agent: ICM - Los Angeles, 213/550-4000

DRINKING IN AMERICA (P)
FUN HOUSE (P)
SUBURBIA (P)

TALK RADIO   Universal, 1988, w/Oliver Stone, from his play (w/Tad Savinar)
SEX, DRUGS, ROCK & ROLL   Avenue Pictures, 1991, from his play

Screenplays:
BLUE SMOKE
STAND UP
MITTY

LESLIE BOHEM*
Contact: WGA - Los Angeles, 213/550-1000

A NIGHTMARE ON ELM STREET 5: THE DREAM CHILD   New Line Cinema, 1989
HOUSE III: THE HORROR SHOW   MGM/UA, 1989, w/Allyn Warner

Screenplays:
UNIVERSAL SOLDIER w/Richard Rothstein
DAYDREAMS w/M. Robinson
ON THE LINE
BRICK DUST
VIDEO KILLED THE RADIO STAR
GUITAR
MIGHTY, MIGHTY
KID
CRYSTAL KNIGHTS
LIVE WIRE

CHARLES F. BOHL*
Contact: WGA - Los Angeles, 213/550-1000

HE'S MY GIRL   Scotti Bros., 1987, w/Taylor Ames

Screenplays:
MY ILLEGAL ALIEN

DON BOHLINGER*
Agent: Stone Manners Agency - Los Angeles, 213/275-9599

THE KILLING TIME   New World, 1987, w/Bruce Franklin Singer & James Nathan

Screenplays:
SMOKESCREEN w/James Nathan

JEROME BOIVIN
BAXTER   Backstreet Films, 1990, w/Jacques Audiard, directed

JOSEPH BOLOGNA*
Business Manager: Zipperstein & Kantor, 818/986-4640

LOVERS AND OTHER STRANGERS ★   Cinerama Releasing Corporation, 1970, w/Renee Taylor & David Z. Goodman
MADE FOR EACH OTHER   20th Century-Fox, 1971, w/Renee Taylor
MIXED COMPANY   United Artists, 1974, w/Renee Taylor
IT HAD TO BE YOU   Limelite Studios, 1989, w/Renee Taylor, from their play, directed

CRAIG BOLOTIN*
Agent: CAA - Beverly Hills, 213/288-4545

NO SMALL AFFAIR   Columbia, 1984, w/Michael Leeson, as "Charles Bolt"

Bo

BLACK RAIN   Paramount, 1989, w/Warren Lewis
SAPPHIRE MAN   (Short), 1991, directed

Screenplays:
THAT NIGHT   (directing)
AMERICAN EXPRESS   w/Richard Kletter
HEARTS
PRIVATE PICTURES
STRAIGHT TALK

CHARLES BOLT
(See Craig Bolotin)

ROBERT BOLT
Agent: Margaret Ramsay Ltd. - London, 011/441/240-0691

LAWRENCE OF ARABIA ★   Columbia, 1962
DOCTOR ZHIVAGO ★★   MGM, 1965
A MAN FOR ALL SEASONS ★★   Columbia, 1966, from his play
RYAN'S DAUGHTER   MGM, 1970
LADY CAROLINE LAMB   United Artists, 1973, directed
THE BOUNTY   Orion, 1984
THE MISSION   Warner Bros., 1986
WITHOUT WARNING: THE JAMES BRADY STORY (CTF)   Enigma Television Productions, 1991

Screenplays:
NOSTROMO   w/Christopher Hampton
BUDDHA
PLUMED SERPENT
PITCAIRN ISLAND

JAMES BOND III
Contact: Screen Actors Guild - Los Angeles, 213/465-4600

DEF BY TEMPTATION   Troma, 1990, directed

JULIAN BOND*
Contact: 01/839-2556

TRIAL BY COMBAT   *CHOICE OF WEAPONS*   Warner Bros., 1976, w/Steven Rossen & Mitchell Smith
THE SHOOTING PARTY   European Classics, 1984
THE WHISTLE BLOWER   Hemdale, 1987
A SEASON OF GIANTS (CTF)   TNT/RAI 1, 1991, w/Vincenzo Labella

Screenplays:
BURMESE DAYS   w/Hugh Stoddart

TIMOTHY BOND
Agent: The Gersh Agency - New York, 212/997-1818

HAPPY BIRTHDAY TO ME   Columbia, 1981, w/John Saxton & Peter Jobin

VITTORIO BONICELLI
AN INFAMOUS LIFE   *UNA VITA SCELLERATA*   Artisti Associati International, 1990, directed

BOB BONNEY
THE NIGHT THE LIGHTS WENT OUT IN GEORGIA   Avco Embassy, 1981

JOHN BOORMAN
Agent: ICM - Los Angeles, 213/550-4000

LEO THE LAST   United Artists, 1970, w/William Stair, directed
ZARDOZ   20th Century-Fox, 1974, directed
EXCALIBUR   Orion/Warner Bros., 1981, w/Rospo Pallenberg, directed
HOPE AND GLORY ★   Columbia, 1987, directed
WHERE THE HEART IS   Buena Vista, 1990, w/Telsche Boorman, directed

Screenplays:
BROKEN DREAMS   w/Neil Jordan

TELSCHE BOORMAN
WHERE THE HEART IS   Buena Vista, 1990, w/John Boorman

JON BOORSTIN*
Agent: Camden-ITG - Los Angeles, 213/289-2700

DREAM LOVER   MGM/UA, 1986

PAUL BOORSTIN*
Agent: Robinson, Weintraub, Gross & Associates - Los Angeles, 213/653-5802

MOVING VIOLATIONS   20th Century Fox, 1985, Story w/Sharon Boorstin
FIRE WITH FIRE   *CAPTIVE HEARTS*   Paramount, 1986, w/Sharon Boorstin, Bill Phillips & Warren Skaaren

Screenplays:
PREGGERS   w/Sharon Boorstin
NAKED REVERSE   w/Sharon Boorstin
SAVAGE   w/Sharon Boorstin
FAERIE TALE   w/Sharon Boorstin
HOT MINUTE   w/Sharon Boorstin

SHARON BOORSTIN*
Agent: Robinson, Weintraub, Gross & Associates - Los Angeles, 213/653-5802

MOVING VIOLATIONS   20th Century Fox, 1985, Story w/Paul Boorstin
FIRE WITH FIRE   *CAPTIVE HEARTS*   Paramount, 1986, w/Paul Boorstin, Bill Phillips & Warren Skaaren

Screenplays:
PREGGERS   w/Paul Boorstin
NAKED REVERSE   w/Paul Boorstin
SAVAGE   w/Paul Boorstin
FAERIE TALE   w/Paul Boorstin
HOT MINUTE   w/Paul Boorstin

JAMES BOOTH*
Agent: CAA - Beverly Hills, 213/288-4545

SUNBURN   Paramount, 1979, w/John Daly & Stephen Oliver
PRAY FOR DEATH   American Distribution Group, 1985
AVENGING FORCE   Cannon, 1986
AMERICAN NINJA 2   Cannon, 1987, w/Gary Conway

JASON BOOTH
OUT ON BAIL   Trans World Entertainment, 1989, w/Tom Badal & Michael D. Sonye

JOSE LUIS BORAU
Business: El Iman S.A., Alberto Alcocer 42, Madrid 16, Spain, 250-5534

ON THE LINE   Miramax, 1987, w/Barbara P. Solomon, directed

LIZZIE BORDEN
(Linda Elizabeth Borden)

BORN IN FLAMES   First Run Features, 1986, directed
WORKING GIRLS   Miramax, 1986, w/Sandra Kay, directed

ALVIN BORETZ*
Contact: WGA - Los Angeles, 213/550-1000

MADE IN AMERICA (P)
BRASS TARGET   MGM/UA, 1978

Screenplays:
BAKER AND BERNSTEIN

DOUGLAS STEFEN BORGHI*
Agent: ICM - Los Angeles, 213/550-4000

Screenplays:
TREASURE

ROBERT BORIS*
Agent: Harris & Goldberg - Los Angeles, 213/553-5200

ELECTRA GLIDE IN BLUE   United Artists, 1973
SOME KIND OF HERO   Paramount, 1982, w/James Kirkwood
DOCTOR DETROIT   Universal, 1983, w/Bruce Jay Friedman & Carl Gottlieb
OXFORD BLUES   MGM/UA, 1984, directed
STEELE JUSTICE   Atlantic Releasing Corporation, 1987, directed

Screenplays:
GYPSY
DIAMOND MAN
THE LAST SAFARI   DANGERFIELD'S SAFARI
CATWALKER
SWEET BERLIN
AIN'T NO HEROES
CONGO
THE DISTRICT
BOMBAY CROSSING
PEEKSKILL
THE DAY THE INDIANS BEAT ST. LOUIS
I AM NO LEGEND
THE BILLIONAIRE
SAN JOSE MILE

ANDY BOROWITZ*
Agent: William Morris Agency - Beverly Hills, 213/274-7451

Screenplays:
YOUNG BUCKS
SCOUTMASTER
AMERICAN WIFE
NEVER SAY DIE
HOW TO MARRY A MILLIONAIRE
CLEVELAND ROCKS

JIM BORRELLI
CAT CHASER   Vestron, 1990, w/Elmore Leonard & Alan Sharp

CLAY BORRIS
QUIET COOL   New Line Cinema, 1986, w/Susan Vercellino, directed

PHILLIP BORSOS
Agent: United Talent Agency - Beverly Hills, 213/273-6700

ONE MAGIC CHRISTMAS   Buena Vista, 1985, Story w/Barry Healey & Thomas Meehan, directed

TERRY BORST
Agent: APA - Los Angeles, 213/273-0744

PRIVATE WAR   Smart Egg Pictures, 1989

CHRIS BORTHWICK
ANNIE'S COMING OUT   Film Australia, 1981, w/John Paterson
A TEST OF LOVE   Universal, 1985, w/John Paterson

MICHAEL BORTMAN*
Agent: CAA - Beverly Hills, 213/288-4545

THE GOOD MOTHER   Buena Vista, 1988
CROOKED HEARTS   MGM-Pathe, 1991, directed

Screenplays:
CHEEK TO CHEEK

AIDA BORTNIK*
Agent: William Morris Agency - Beverly Hills, 213/274-7451

THE OFFICIAL STORY ★   Historias Cinematograficas, 1985, w/Luis Puenzo
OLD GRINGO   Columbia, 1989, w/Luis Puenzo

Screenplays:
HOUSE OF THE SPIRITS
FADEOUT

JOHN BOSKOVICH
WITHOUT YOU I'M NOTHING   MCEG, 1990, w/Sandra Bernhard, directed

ROY BOULTING
Agent: John Redway and Associates Ltd., 5 Denmark St., London WC2H 8LP, England, 71/836-2001

HIGH TREASON   Rank, 1951, w/Frank Harvey, directed
JOSEPHINE AND MEN   Charter, 1955, w/Nigel Balchin & Frank Harvey, directed
HAPPY IS THE BRIDE   British Lion, 1957, w/Jeffrey Dell, directed
BROTHERS IN LAW   British Lion, 1957, w/Jeffrey Dell & Frank Harvey, directed
MAN IN A COCKED HAT   CARLTON-BROWNE OF THE F.O.   Show Corporation, 1960, w/Jeffrey Dell, co-directed
A FRENCH MISTRESS   British Lion, 1960, w/Jeffrey Dell, co-directed
TWISTED NERVE   National General, 1969, w/Leo Marks, directed
UNDERCOVERS HERO   SOFT BEDS AND HARD BATTLES   United Artists, 1975, w/Leo Marks, directed

Bo

FILM WRITERS GUIDE

FILM WRITERS

Bo

JOHN BOWEN
Agent: Margaret Ramsay Ltd. - London, 011/441/240-0691

TREVOR (P)

Screenplays:
BRIEF ENCOUNTER

DOUGLAS BOWIE
THE BOY IN BLUE   20th Century Fox, 1986

ANTHONY J. BOWMAN
Agent: Barrett, Benson, McCartt & Weston - Los Angeles, 213/247-5500

RELATIVES   Archer Films, 1985, directed
CAPPUCCINO   Archer Films, 1989, directed

Screenplays:
ROMANTIC HERO

KENNETH BOWSER
Agent: Lucy Kroll Agency - New York, 212/877-0627

IN A SHALLOW GRAVE   Skouras Pictures, 1988, directed

DON BOYD
EAST OF ELEPHANT ROCK   Boyd's Company, 1976, directed
TWENTY-ONE   Triton Pictures, 1991, w/Zoe Heller, directed

WILLIAM BOYD
Agent: Georges Borchardt Literary Agency - New York, 212/753-5785

STARS AND BARS   Columbia, 1988
TUNE IN TOMORROW...   Cinecom, 1990
MISTER JOHNSON   Avenue Pictures, 1991

RICHARD BOYLE*
Contact: WGA - Los Angeles, 213\550-1000

SALVADOR ★   Hemdale, 1986, w/Oliver Stone

BILL BOZZONE*
Agent: William Morris Agency - New York, 212/586-5100

FULL MOON IN BLUE WATER   Trans World Entertainment, 1988
THE LAST ELEPHANT (CTF)   Ritti Entertainment Inc./ Quintex Entertainment Inc., 1990, w/Richard Guttman

GÉRARD BRACH
Agent: ICM - Los Angeles, 213/550-4000

DO YOU LIKE WOMEN?   Francoriz, 1964, w/Roman Polanski
REPULSION   Royal Films International, 1965, w/Roman Polanski
CUL-DE-SAC   Sigma III, 1966, w/Roman Polanski
SECRET WORLD   1966 w/J. Glagg
THE FEARLESS VAMPIRE KILLERS, OR PARDON ME BUT YOUR TEETH ARE IN MY NECK   DANCE OF THE VAMPIRES   MGM, 1967, w/Roman Polanski
WHAT?   Avco Embassy, 1973, w/Roman Polanski
THE TENANT   Paramount, 1976, w/Roman Polanski
LE POINT DE MIRE   Warner Bros.-Columbia, 1977
BYE BYE MONKEY   Fida, 1978
TESS   Columbia, 1980, w/John Brownjohn & Roman Polanski
I SENT A LETTER TO MY LOVE   CHERE INCONNUE   Atlantic Releasing Corporation, 1981, w/Moshe Mizrahi
L'AFRICAIN   Renn Productions, 1982, w/Philippe de Broca
QUEST FOR FIRE   20th Century-Fox, 1982
MY BEST FRIEND'S GIRL   European International, 1983, w/Bertrand Blier
FAVORITES OF THE MOON   1984, w/Otar Iosseliani
MARIA'S LOVERS   Cannon, 1984, w/Marjorie David, Andrei Konchalovsky & Paul Zindel
THE NAME OF THE ROSE   20th Century Fox, 1986, w/Andrew Birkin, Howard Franklin & Alain Godard
PIRATES   Cannon, 1986, w/Roman Polanski
SHY PEOPLE   Cannon, 1987, w/Marjorie David & Andrei Konchalovsky
JEAN DE FLORETTE   Orion Classics, 1987, w/Claude Berri
MANON OF THE SPRING   Orion Classics, 1987, w/Claude Berri
FRANTIC   Warner Bros., 1988, w/Roman Polanski
THE BEAR   Tri-Star, 1989

Screenplays:
THE LOVER w/Jean-Jacques Annuad & Marguerite Duras
TRISTAN w/G.V. Hughes & R. Scott
SATAN & EVE
CRAZY & DAISY

JACOB BRACKMAN*
Contact: WGA - Los Angeles, 213/550-1000

THE KING OF MARVIN GARDENS   Columbia, 1972
TIMES SQUARE   AFD, 1980

RAY BRADBURY*
Contact: WGA - Los Angeles, 213/550-1000

MOBY DICK   Warner Bros., 1956, w/John Huston
SOMETHING WICKED THIS WAY COMES   Buena Vista, 1983

AL BRADLEY
IRON WARRIOR   Tri-Star, 1987, w/Steven Luotto

DAVID BRADLEY
Agent: CAA - Beverly Hills, 213/288-4545

Screenplays:
OTIS

ELIZABETH BRADLEY*
Agent: United Talent Agency - Beverly Hills, 213/273-6700

COCOON: THE RETURN   20th Century Fox, 1988, Story w/Stephen McPherson

Screenplays:
GOING HOME w/Stephen McPherson
OUTWARD BOUND w/Stephen McPherson
MAD DASH w/Stephen McPherson
TO THE MANOR BORN w/Stephen McPherson
THE GRAY GHOST   MIDNIGHT FLYER w/Stephen McPherson

PAT BRADLEY
UNDER THE RAINBOW   Orion/Warner Bros., 1981,
　　w/Pat McCormick, Harry Hurwitz, Martin Smith &
　　Fred Bauer

MELVYN BRAGG
Business: The South Bank Show, London Weekend
　　Television

THE HIRED MAN (P)
PLAY DIRTY   United Artists, 1969, w/Lotte Colin
ISADORA   THE LIVES OF ISADORA   Universal, 1969,
　　w/Clive Exton
THE MUSIC LOVERS   United Artists, 1970
JESUS CHRIST SUPERSTAR   Universal, 1973,
　　w/Norman Jewison

MALCOLM BRALY
ON THE YARD   Midwest Film Productions, 1978

KENNETH BRANAGH
Contact: British Academy of Film & Television Arts,
　　195 Piccadilly, London W1, England, 71/734-0022

HENRY V   Renaissance Films, 1989,
　　Adaptation, directed

LARRY BRAND*
Agent: Robert Eisenbach Agency - Los Angeles,
　　213/962-5809

BACKFIRE   New Century/Vista, 1987,
　　w/Rebecca Reynolds
THE DRIFTER   Concorde, 1988, directed
MASQUE OF THE RED DEATH   Concorde, 1989,
　　w/Daryl Haney, directed
OVEREXPOSED   Concorde, 1990, w/Rebecca
　　Reynolds, directed

DAVID BRANDES*
Contact: WGA - Los Angeles, 213/550-1000

THE DIRT BIKE KID   Concorde/Cinema Group, 1985,
　　w/Lewis Colick

RICHARD BRANDES
PARTY LINE   SVS Films, 1988
MARTIAL LAW   Image Organization, 1990

Screenplays:
THE CHILEAN PUZZLE

GARY BRANDNER*
Contact: WGA - Los Angeles, 213/550-1000

HOWLING II...YOUR SISTER IS A WEREWOLF
　　Thorn-EMI, 1986, w/Robert Sarno
CAMERON'S CLOSET   SVS Films, 1989

CLARK BRANDON
FAST FOOD   Fries Entertainment, 1989, w/Lanny Horn

CHARLOTTE BRANDSTROM
Agent: ICM - Los Angeles, 213/550-4000

STORMY SUMMER   MGM-Pathe, 1991, w/Nicolas
　　Bernheim, directed

JOHN F. BRASCIA*
Contact: WGA - Los Angeles, 213/550-1000

THE BALTIMORE BULLET   Avco Embassy, 1980,
　　w/Robert Vincent O'Neill

FRED BRAUGHTON
ANOTHER 48 HRS.   Paramount, 1990, Story

ANDREW BRECKMAN*
Agent: ICM - Los Angeles, 213/550-4000

MOVING   Paramount, 1988
ARTHUR 2 ON THE ROCKS   Warner Bros., 1988
TRUE IDENTITY   Buena Vista, 1991,

Screenplays:
MONEY
TODDLERS

PHILIP M. BREEN
Business: Rolling Hills Productions, 204 S. Beverly Dr.,
　　Suite 166, Beverly Hills, CA 90212, 213/275-0872

SWORD OF THE VALIANT   Cannon, 1984, w/Howard C.
　　Pen & Stephen Weeks

GREGORY BREHM*
Contact: Bloom, Dekom & Hergott - Los Angeles,
　　213/278-8622

Screenplays:
JADE
AND THE HOME OF THE BRAVE

STEPHEN BREIMER
NIGHT WARNING   ComWorld, 1983, w/Boom Collins &
　　Alan Jay Glueckman

TERENCE (TERRY) BRENNAN*
Agent: William Morris Agency - Beverly Hills, 213/274-7451

ROOFTOPS   New Century/Vista, 1989

Screenplays:
OUT OF THE DARKNESS
BLATNOY
THE SEARCH FOR TYPHOID MARY
WONDER WHEELS

RICHARD BRENNE*
Agent: Triad Artists, Inc. - Los Angeles, 213/556-2727

Screenplays:
CHANGING LABELS
HEADING HOME

ARTHUR J. BRESSON, JR.
BUDDIES   New Line Cinema, 1985, directed

ROBERT BRESSON
Contact: French Film Office, 745 Fifth Avenue, New York,
　　NY 10151, 212/832-8860

THE LADIES OF THE PARK   Brandon, 1945,
　　w/Jean Cocteau, directed
DIARY OF A COUNTRY PRIEST   Brandon, 1950, directed

AU HASARD, BALTHAZAR   Cinema Ventures,
   1966, directed
LE DIABLE PROBABLEMENT   Gaumont, 1977, directed
L'ARGENT (MONEY)   Cinecom, 1983, directed

MARTIN BREST*
Agent: CAA - Beverly Hills, 213/288-4545
Business: City Lights Films, Universal Pictures,
   818/777-1325

HOT TOMORROWS   American Film Institute,
   1977, directed
GOING IN STYLE   Warner Bros., 1979, directed

JASON BRETT*
Agent: United Talent Agency - Beverly Hills, 213/273-6700

Screenplays:
ROUTE 66 w/Thom Bishop
THE STREET WHERE YOU LIVE w/Thom Bishop
SILENT SERVICE

JAMESON BREWER*
Contact: Jerome S. Siegel Associates, 213/850-1275

GHOST TOWN   United Artists, 1956
THE INCREDIBLE MR. LIMPET   Warner Bros., 1964,
   w/John C. Rose
TERROR IN THE WAX MUSEUM   Bing Crosby
   Productions, 1973
ARNOLD   Avco Embassy, 1973, w/John Fenton Murray
HEIDI'S SONG (AF)   Paramount, 1982, w/Joseph
   Barbera & Robert Taylor

E. KIM BREWSTER
FOOD OF THE GODS II   Concorde-Centaur, 1989,
   w/Richard Bennett

MARSHALL BRICKMAN*
Agent: ICM - Los Angeles, 213/550-4000

SLEEPER   United Artists, 1973, w/Woody Allen
ANNIE HALL ★★   United Artists, 1977, w/Woody Allen
MANHATTAN ★   United Artists, 1978, w/Woody Allen
SIMON   Orion/Warner Bros., 1980, directed
LOVESICK   The Ladd Company/Warner Bros.,
   1983, directed
THE MANHATTAN PROJECT   20th Century Fox, 1986,
   w/Thomas Baum, directed
FOR THE BOYS   20th Century Fox, 1991, w/Neal
   Jimenez & Lindy Laub

Screenplays:
NORTH BY SOUTH

PAUL BRICKMAN*
Agent: CAA - Beverly Hills, 213/288-4545

THE BAD NEWS BEARS IN BREAKING TRAINING
   Paramount, 1977
CITIZEN'S BAND   HANDLE WITH CARE
   Paramount, 1977
RISKY BUSINESS   The Geffen Company/Warner Bros.,
   1983, directed
DEAL OF THE CENTURY   Warner Bros., 1983
MEN DON'T LEAVE   The Geffen Company/Warner Bros.,
   1990, w/Barbara Benedek, directed

LESLIE BRICUSSE*
Contact: WGA - Los Angeles, 213/550-4000

ROAR OF THE GREASEPAINT, SMELL OF THE
   CROWD (P) w/Anthony Newley
OUT OF THE BLUE (P)
AN EVENING WITH BEATRICE LILLIE (P)
LADY AT THE WHEEL (P)
ONE SHINING MOMENT (P)
CHARLEY MOON   British Lion, 1956
BACHELOR OF HEARTS   Rank, 1958,
   w/Frederic Raphael
THE SWINGING MAIDEN   THE IRON MAIDEN   Anglo
   Amalgamated, 1962, w/Vivian Cox
THREE HATS FOR LISA   Seven Hills, 1965,
   w/Talbot Rothwell
STOP THE WORLD - I WANT TO GET OFF   Warner Bros.,
   1966, w/Anthony Newley
DR. DOOLITTLE   20th Century-Fox, 1967
SCROOGE   National General, 1970, from his play
SUNDAY LOVERS   United Artists, 1981, w/Francis Veber
   & Gene Wilder
BULLSEYE!   21st Century Film Corporation, 1991,
   w/Maurice Gran & Laurence Marks

Screenplays:
CHARLIE MOON
EAST COAST, WEST COAST
MUSICAL CHAIRS
THE GREAT MUSIC CHASE

JAMES BRIDGES*
Agent: CAA - Beverly Hills, 213/288-4545

THE APPALOOSA   Universal, 1966, w/Roland Kibbee
COLOSSOS: THE FORBIN PROJECT   Universal, 1969
THE BABY MAKER   National General, 1970, directed
LIMBO   Universal, 1972, w/Joan Micklin Silver
THE PAPER CHASE ★   20th Century-Fox, 1973, directed
9/30/55   SEPTEMBER 30, 1955   Universal, 1977, directed
THE CHINA SYNDROME ★   Columbia, 1979, w/Mike Gray
   & T.S. Cook, directed
URBAN COWBOY   Paramount, 1980, w/Aaron
   Latham, directed
MIKE'S MURDER   The Ladd Company/Warner Bros.,
   1984, directed
PERFECT   Columbia, 1985, w/Aaron Latham, directed
WHITE HUNTER, BLACK HEART   Warner Bros., 1990,
   w/Burt Kennedy & Peter Viertel

Screenplays:
HEARTS
SWEET LIBBY

MATTHEW BRIGHT
FORBIDDEN ZONE   Sutton Marketing, 1980, w/Richard
   Elfman, Nick James & Nick L. Martinson
WILDFIRE   Cinema Group, 1986, w/Zalman King

JOHN BRILEY*
Agent: ICM - Los Angeles, 213/550-4000

INVASION QUARTET   MGM, 1961, w/Jack Trevor Story
POSTMAN'S KNOCK   MGM, 1961, w/Jack Trevor Story
CHILDREN OF THE DAMNED   MGM, 1964
POPE JOAN   Columbia, 1972
THAT LUCKY TOUCH   United Artists, 1975
THE MEDUSA TOUCH   Warner Bros., 1978, w/Jack Gold
EAGLE'S WING   International Picture Show, 1979

GANDHI ★★ Columbia, 1982
ENIGMA Embassy, 1983
MARIE MGM/UA, 1985
TAI PAN DEG, 1986, w/Stanley Mann
CRY FREEDOM Universal, 1987

Screenplays:
GENGHIS KHAN
WARRIORS OF THE RAINBOW
WEST WITH THE NIGHT
HENDERSON, THE RAIN KING
THE LOVES OF KAFKA
THE FOURTH SEASON
A FRAGILE LIFE
WHY DID I EVER LEAVE HORSES? CAPTAIN BARNES, LIEUTENANT FARNUM
OFFERING
TO DIE A STRANGER
THE VEIL
THE GREAT BABY BLUE
HOW SLEEP THE BRAVE
MISTER GOD, THIS IS ANNA
THE BIG APPLE
THE DEADLY INHERITANCE

MICHAEL BRINDLEY
SHAME Skouras Pictures, 1988, w/Beverly Blakenship

BO BRINKMAN
ICEHOUSE Upfront Films, 1989, from his play "Ice House Heat Waves," directed

MORT BRISKIN*
Agent: ICM - Los Angeles, 213/550-4000

WALKING TALL Bing Crosby Productions, 1973
FRAMED Paramount, 1974

JEFF BROADSTREET
SEXBOMB Phillips & Mora Entertainment, 1989, Story w/Robert Benson, directed

DEBORAH BROCK
Business: Concorde Pictures, 11600 San Vicente Blvd., Los Angeles, CA 90049, 213/826-0978

SLUMBER PARTY MASSACRE II Concorde, 1987, directed
ROCK'N'ROLL HIGH SCHOOL FOREVER Concorde, 1991, directed

JOHN BRODERICK
Agent: Associated Talent International - Beverly Hills, 213/271-4662

THE WARRIOR AND THE SORCERESS New Horizons, 1984, directed

OSCAR BRODNEY*
Contact: WGA - Los Angeles, 213/55-1000

SHE WROTE THE BOOK Universal, 1946, w/Warren Wilson
ARE YOU WITH IT? Universal-International, 1948
MEXICAN HAYRIDE Universal, 1948, w/John Grant
SOUTH SEA SINNER Universal-International, 1949, w/Joel Malone
YES SIR, THAT'S MY BABY Universal-International, 1949
CURTAIN CALL AT CACTUS CREEK Universal-International, 1949
FRENCHIE Universal-International, 1950
COMANCHE TERRITORY Universal-International, 1950, w/Louis Meltzer
DOUBLE CROSSBONES Universal-International, 1950
LITTLE EGYPT *CHICAGO MASQUERADE* Universal International, 1951, w/Doris Gilbert
SCARLET ANGEL Universal-International, 1952
WALKING MY BABY BACK HOME Universal-International, 1953
THE SIGN OF THE PAGAN Universal-International, 1954, w/Barre Lyndon
THE BLACK SHIELD OF FALWORTH Universal-International, 1954
THE GLENN MILLER STORY Universal-International, 1954, w/Valentine Davies
THE SPOILERS Universal-International, 1955
THE PURPLE MASK Universal-International, 1955
LADY GODIVA Universal International, 1955, w/Harry Ruskin
CAPTAIN LIGHTFOOT Universal-International, 1955, w/W.R. Burnett
A DAY OF FURY Universal, 1956, w/James Edmiston
TAMMY AND THE BACHELOR Universal-International, 1957
BOBBIKINS 20th Century-Fox, 1959
TAMMY TELL ME TRUE American-International, 1961
TAMMY AND THE DOCTOR American-International, 1963
I'D RATHER BE RICH Universal-International, 1964, w/Norman Krasna & Leo Townsend
THE BRASS BOTTLE Universal-International, 1964
GHOST FEVER Miramax, 1987, w/Ron Rich

HUGH BRODY
Contact: British Academy of Film & Television Arts, 195 Piccadilly, London W1, England, 01/734-0022

1919 Spectrafilm, 1985, directed

HENRY BROMELL*
Contact: WGA - Los Angeles, 213/550-1000

Screenplays:
CLARKSVILLE

REX BROMFIELD
HOME IS WHERE THE HART IS Atlantic Releasing Corporation, 1987, directed

VALRI BROMFIELD*
Agent: ICM - Los Angeles, 213/550-4000

Screenplays:
HOUSEWIVES IN PRISON
LUCKY IN LOVE
THE KID WHO ATE HER PARENTS

DAN BRONSON*
Agent: Triad Artists, Inc. - Los Angeles, 213/556-2727

THE LAST INNOCENT MAN (CTF) HBO Pictures/Maurice Singer Productions, 1987

Screenplays:
BLOOD MONEY

PETER BROOK
Contact: British Academy of Film & Television Arts, 195 Piccadilly, London W1, England, 71/734-0022

LORD OF THE FLIES   Continental, 1963, directed
SWANN IN LOVE   Gaumont, 1983, w/Jean-Claude Carriere & Marie-Helene Estienne

GREG BROOKER*
Agent: InterTalent - Los Angeles, 213/858-6200

Screenplays:
THE FALL AND RISE OF GLEN SPRING '61

ADAM BROOKS
ALMOST YOU   20th Century-Fox, 1982, Story, directed

ALBERT BROOKS*
Business Manager: Gelfand, Rennert & Feldman - Los Angeles, 213/553-1707

REAL LIFE   Paramount, 1979, w/Monica Johnson & Harry Shearer, directed
MODERN ROMANCE   Columbia, 1981, w/Monica Johnson, directed
LOST IN AMERICA   The Geffen Company/Warner Bros., 1985, w/Monica Johnson, directed
DEFENDING YOUR LIFE   The Geffen Company/Warner Bros., 1991, directed

JAMES L. BROOKS*
Agent: ICM - Los Angeles, 213/550-4000
Business: Gracie Films, 20th Century Fox, 213/203-3770

STARTING OVER   Paramount, 1979
TERMS OF ENDEARMENT ★★   Paramount, 1983, directed
BROADCAST NEWS ★   20th Century Fox, 1987, directed

Screenplays:
HOLDING ON   DOUBLE FAULT   w/Allan Burns

JOSEPH BROOKS
Business: Chancery Lane Films, Inc. 41-A East 74th St., New York, NY 10021, 212/759-8720

YOU LIGHT UP MY LIFE   Columbia, 1977, directed
IF EVER I SEE YOU AGAIN   Columbia, 1978, w/Martin Davidson, directed
HEADIN' FOR BROADWAY   20th Century-Fox, 1980, w/Hilary Henkin & Larry Gross, directed

MEL BROOKS*
Agent: CAA - Beverly Hills, 213/288-4545
Business: Brooksfilms Limited, 20th Century Fox, P.O. Box 900, Beverly Hills, CA 90213, 213/203-1375

THE PRODUCERS ★★   Avco Embassy, 1967, directed
THE TWELVE CHAIRS   UMC, 1970, directed
BLAZING SADDLES   Warner Bros., 1973, w/Andrew Bergman, Richard Pryor, Norman Steinberg & Alan Uger, directed
TEN FROM YOUR SHOW OF SHOWS   1973, w/others
YOUNG FRANKENSTEIN ★   20th Century-Fox, 1974, w/Gene Wilder, directed
SILENT MOVIE   20th Century-Fox, 1976, w/Ron Clark, Rudy DeLuca & Barry Levinson, directed
HIGH ANXIETY   20th Century-Fox, 1977, w/Ron Clark, Rudy DeLuca & Barry Levinson, directed
HISTORY OF THE WORLD - PART 1   20th Century-Fox, 1981, directed
SPACEBALLS   MGM/UA, 1987, w/Ronny Graham & Thomas Meehan, directed
LIFE STINKS   MGM-Pathe, 1991, w/Rudy DeLuca & Steve Haberman, directed

RICHARD BROOKS*
Contact: WGA - Los Angeles, 213/550-1000

WHITE SAVAGE   Universal, 1943
COBRA WOMAN   Universal International, 1944, w/Gene Lewis
BRUTE FORCE   Universal International, 1947
TO THE VICTOR   Warner Bros., 1948
KEY LARGO   Warner Bros., 1948, w/John Huston
ANY NUMBER CAN PLAY   MGM, 1949
CRISIS   MGM, 1950, directed
STORM WARNING   Warner Bros., 1950, w/Daniel Fuchs
MYSTERY STREET   MGM, 1950, w/Sidney Boehm
THE LIGHT TOUCH   MGM, 1951, directed
BATTLE CIRCUS   MGM, 1952, directed
DEADLINE USA   20th Century-Fox, 1952, directed
THE LAST TIME I SAW PARIS   MGM, 1954, w/Philip G. Epstein & Julius J. Epstein, directed
THE LAST HUNT   MGM, 1955, directed
THE BLACKBOARD JUNGLE ★   MGM, 1955, directed
SOMETHING OF VALUE   MGM, 1957, directed
THE BROTHERS KARAMAZOV   MGM, 1958, directed
CAT ON A HOT TIN ROOF ★   MGM, 1958, w/James Poe, directed
ELMER GANTRY ★★   United Artists, 1960, directed
SWEET BIRD OF YOUTH   MGM, 1962, directed
LORD JIM   Columbia, 1964, directed
THE PROFESSIONALS ★   Columbia, 1966, directed
IN COLD BLOOD ★   Columbia, 1967, directed
THE HAPPY ENDING   United Artists, 1969, directed
$ DOLLARS   Columbia, 1971, directed
BITE THE BULLET   Columbia, 1975, directed
LOOKING FOR MR. GOODBAR   Paramount, 1977, directed
WRONG IS RIGHT   Columbia, 1982, directed
FEVER PITCH   MGM/UA, 1985, directed

ROBERT BROOKS
TATTOO   20th Century-Fox, 1981, Story

PETER BROSNAN
HIT LIST   New Line Cinema, 1989, w/John Goff

LARRY BROTHERS*
Agent: William Morris Agency - Beverly Hills, 213/274-7451

AN INNOCENT MAN   Buena Vista, 1989
FEVER (CTF)   Saban/Scherick, 1991

BARRY ALEXANDER BROWN
LONELY IN AMERICA   Arista Films, 1990, w/Satyajit Joy Palit, directed

BRYAN BROWN
Agent: CAA - Beverly Hills, 213/288-4545

SWEET TALKER   New Visions, 1991, Story w/Tony Morphett

CURTIS BROWN
THE GAME   Visual Perspectives, 1989, w/Julia Wilson, directed

EDWIN SCOTT BROWN
THE PREY   New World, 1984, w/Summer Brown

JAMIE BROWN*
Contact: 514/288-1638

TOBY MCTEAGUE   Spectrafilm, 1986, w/Djordje Milicevic & Jeff Maguire

JULIE BROWN*
Agent: ICM - Los Angeles, 213/550-4000

EARTH GIRLS ARE EASY   Vestron, 1988, w/Charlie Coffey & Terrence E. McNally

LEIGH BROWN*
Contact: 813/472-9594

A CHRISTMAS STORY   MGM/UA, 1983, w/BobClark & Jean Shepherd

MITCH BROWN
IN DANGEROUS COMPANY   Manson International, 1988

PAUL BROWN*
Agent: ICM - Los Angeles, 213/550-4000

THRASHIN'   Fries Entertainment, 1986, w/Alan Sacks

Screenplays:
BLUE TATTOO

RITA MAE BROWN
Agent: Robinson, Weintraub, Gross & Associates - Los Angeles, 213/653-5802

SLUMBER PARTY MASSACRE   Santa Fe, 1982

Screenplays:
TABLE DANCING

SAM O. BROWN
(See Blake Edwards)

STEVE BROWN*
Agent: Jim Preminger Agency - Los Angeles, 213/475-9491

SECOND THOUGHTS   Universal, 1983

SUMMER BROWN
THE PREY   New World, 1984, w/Edwin Scott Brown

TONY BROWN
Business: Tony Brown Productions, Inc., 1501 Broadway - Suite 2014, New York, NY 10036, 212/575-0876

THE WHITE GIRL   Tony Brown Productions, 1990, directed

JANET BROWNELL*
Contact: WGA - Los Angeles, 213/550-1000

SWEET REVENGE (CTF)   Turner Pictures/The Movie Group, 1990

ROD BROWNING*
Agent: Preferred Artists - Encino, 818/990-0305

OH HEAVENLY DOG   20th Century-Fox, 1980, w/Joe Camp

GLENN A. BRUCE*
Agent: United Talent Agency - Beverly Hills, 213/273-6700

KICKBOXER   Cannon, 1989

PEGGY BRUEN
ALEXA   Platinum Pictures, 1989, w/Sean Delgado

JAMES BRUNER*
Agent: The Chasin Agency - Beverly Hills, 213/278-7505

AN EYE FOR AN EYE   Avco Embassy, 1981, w/William Gray
MISSING IN ACTION   Cannon, 1984
INVASION U.S.A.   Cannon, 1985, w/Chuck Norris
SWORDS OF HEAVEN   Trans World Entertainment, 1985, w/Britt Lomond, William P. O'Hagan & Joseph Randazzo
THE DELTA FORCE   Cannon, 1986, w/Menahem Golan
P.O.W. THE ESCAPE   Cannon, 1986, w/Malcolm Barbour, John Langley & Jeremy Lipp
BRADDOCK: MISSING IN ACTION III   Cannon, 1988, w/Chuck Norris

FRANCO BRUSATI
SUNDAY IN AUGUST (DOMENICA D'AGOSTO)   Colonna, 1950, w/others
THE GIRL WHO COULDN'T SAY NO   INC, 1956, w/Ennio de Concini, directed
ROMEO AND JULIET   Paramount, 1968, w/Masalino D'Amico
THE GARDEN OF THE FINZI-CONTINIS   Cinema 5, 1971, w/others
BREAD AND CHOCOLATE   World Northal, 1978, w/Iaia Fisstri & Nino Manfredi, directed
THE SLEAZY UNCLE (LO ZIO INDEGNO)   Ellepi Film, 1989, w/Leonardo Benvenuti & Piero De Bernardo

CHRIS BRYANT*
Agent: Lake & Douroux- Beverly Hills, 213/557-0700

THE MAN WHO HAD POWER OVER WOMEN   Avco Embassy, 1971, w/Allan G. Scott
DON'T LOOK NOW   Paramount, 1974, w/Allan G. Scott
THE GIRL FROM PETROVKA   Universal, 1974, w/Allan G. Scott
THE SPIRAL STAIRCASE   Warner Bros., 1975, w/Allan G. Scott
JOSEPH ANDREWS   Paramount, 1977, w/Allan G. Scott
THE AWAKENING   Orion/Warner Bros., 1980, w/Clive Exton & Allan G. Scott
MARTIN'S DAY   MGM/UA, 1985, w/Allan G. Scott
LADY JANE   Paramount, 1986, Story
SWORD OF GIDEON (CTF)   Alliance Entertainment/Les Films Ariane/HBO Premiere Films/CTV/Telefilm Canada/Rogers Cablesystems/Radio-Canada, 1986

STEALING HEAVEN   FilmDallas, 1988
YOUNG CATHERINE (CTF)   Consolidate/Primedia/
    Lenfilm, 1991

Screenplays:
THE NINE TIGER MAN w/Allan G. Scott
THE GOKEN RENDEZVOUS w/Allan G. Scott
THE MAN FROM NOWHERE w/Allan G. Scott & G. Tabori
THE PERSIAN RANSOM w/Allan G. Scott
THE YARMAKOV TRANSFER w/Allan G. Scott
THE MAN WHO WAS SHERLOCK HOLMES
    w/Allan G. Scott
THE MURDER LEAGUE w/Allan G. Scott
PLUMB DRILLIN w/Allan G. Scott
ST. PETERSBURG/CANNES EXPRESS
GOODBYE CALIFORNIA
ODD'S END
JEMIMA SHORE
WHISPERS
KLYNT'S LAW
MATA HARI
GEORGIA O'KEEFE

JAMES BRYCE*
Agent: Heacock Literary Agency, Inc. - Los Angeles,
    213/393-6227

TREASURE OF THE FOUR CROWNS   Cannon, 1983,
    w/Lloyd Battista & Jerry Lazarus

BILL BRYDEN*
Agent: William Morris Agency - Beverly Hills, 213/274-7451

THE LONG RIDERS   United Artists, 1980, w/James
    Keach, Stacy Keach & Steven Philip Smith

Screenplays:
A HANDSOME AND CHARMING MAN

JAMES DAVID BUCHANAN*
Agent: CAA - Beverly Hills, 213/288-4545

THE HAPPENING   Columbia, 1967, w/Ronald Austin &
    Frank R. Pierson
MIDAS RUN   1969, w/Ronald Austin & Berne Giler
HARRY IN YOUR POCKET   United Artists, 1973,
    w/Ronald Austin
BRENDA STARR   Triumph, 1991, w/Noreen Stone &
    Jenny Wolkind

Screenplays:
THE MICK
FOOL'S GOLD
DIFFERENT RULES
MIDNIGHT SUN
THE NEW ROSE
RIOTOUS CONDUCT
CURACAO

RONALD L. BUCK*
Contact: WGA - Los Angeles, 213/550-1000

HARRY & SON   Orion, 1984, w/Paul Newman

PETER BUCKMAN
APPOINTMENT WITH DEATH   Cannon, 1988,
    w/Anthony Shaffer & Michael Winner

BRAD BUCKNER*
Contact: WGA - Los Angeles, 213/550-1000
Business: B & E Enterprises, Paramount TV, 213/956-5959

Screenplays:
UFO w/Eugenie Ross-Leming
ROMANTIC FOOLS w/Eugenie Ross-Leming
SVENGALI w/Eugenie Ross-Leming
FOREIGNERS w/Eugenie Ross-Leming
CADETS w/Eugenie Ross-Leming
LOOSE WOMEN w/Eugenie Ross-Leming
LAMB OF GOD w/Eugenie Ross-Leming
THE KID w/Eugenie Ross-Leming
FORGET ME NOT w/Eugenie Ross-Leming

VICTOR BUELL*
Contact: Steven Rose, 213/650-7300

SILHOUETTE (CTF)   MCA Television Network, 1990,
    w/Jay Wolf

JEFF BUHAI*
Agent: United Talent Agency - Beverly Hills, 213/273-6700

REVENGE OF THE NERDS   20th Century-Fox, 1984,
    w/Steve Zacharias
THE WHOOPEE BOYS   Paramount, 1986,
    w/Steve Zacharias & David Obst
LAST RESORT   Concorde/Cinema Group, 1986,
    w/Steve Zacharias
JOCKS   Crown International, 1987, w/David Obst & Steve
    Zacharias as "Mike Lanahan & David Oas"
JOHNNY BE GOOD   Orion, 1988, w/David Obst &
    Steve Zacharias

Screenplays:
BIKERS FROM HELL w/Steve Zacharias
DALLAS DEBS w/Steve Zacharias
GIRLS IN TROUBLE w/Steve Zacharias
DEEP COVER w/Steve Zacharias
HOPELESSNESS & DESPAIR w/Steve Zacharias
MR. VICE PRESIDENT w/Steve Zacharias & Robert Kears
THE TRUTH ABOUT SWEDES w/Steve Zacharias
LOVELINE w/Steve Zacharias
AFTERGLOW w/Steve Zacharias
HARRAD II w/Steve Zacharias
HOSPITAL w/Steve Zacharias
INSIDE THE INQUIRER w/Steve Zacharias
VULGARIANS w/Steve Zacharias
HEAVY METAL WEEKEND w/Steve Zacharias
REVENGE OF THE NUDES w/Steve Zacharias

CHARLES BUKOWSKI
BARFLY   Cannon, 1987

VICANGELO BULLOCK*
Contact: 213/392-4323

OUT OF CONTROL   New World, 1985, w/Sandra
    Weintraub Rolland

ALAN BUNCE
BABAR: THE MOVIE (AF)   New Line Cinema, 1989,
    w/John De Klein, Raymond Jaffelice, Peter Sauder &
    J.D. Smith, directed

EDWARD BUNKER*
Agent: The Artists Agency - Los Angeles, 213/277-7779

STRAIGHT TIME   Warner Bros., 1978, w/Jeffrey Boam & Alvin Sargent
RUNAWAY TRAIN   Cannon, 1985, w/Djordje Milicevic & Paul Zindel

MARK BUNTZMAN
Contact: 818/980-3007

EXTERMINATOR 2   Cannon, 1984, w/William Sachs, directed

JOYCE BUNUEL
Agent: The Marion Rosenberg Office - West Hollywood, 213/653-7383

TATTOO   20th Century-Fox, 1981

JOHN BUNZEL*
Agent: Harris & Goldberg - Los Angeles, 213/553-5200

Screenplays:
DEATH OF A BUICK

ROBERT BURGE
VASECTOMY, A DELICATE MATTER   Seymour Borde & Associates, 1986, w/Robert Hilliard, directed

NEAL R. BURGER*
Agent: APA - Los Angeles, 213/273-0744

Screenplays:
UP THE GARDEN PATH w/George E. Simpson
GHOSTBOAT w/George E. Simpson
DAN HAZARD AND THE LEGION OF EVIL w/George E. Simpson

ANTHONY BURGESS
Agent: Allison & Busby Ltd., 6A Noel St., London W1V 3RB, England

MOSES   Avco Embassy, 1976, w/Vittorio Bonicelli & Gianfranco de Bosio

JOHN BURGESS
SUNDOWN: THE VAMPIRE IN RETREAT   Vestron, 1989, w/Anthony Hickox

DAVID BURKE*
Agent: United Talent Agency - Beverly Hills, 213/273-6700

THE TAKING OF BEVERLY HILLS   Nelson Entertainment, 1991, w/David Fuller & Rick Natkin

MARTYN BURKE*
Agent: CAA - Beverly Hills, 213/288-4545

POWER PLAY   Magnum International Pictures/Cavry Film Productions, 1978, directed
TOP SECRET!   Paramount, 1984, w/Jim Abrahams, David Zucker & Jerry Zucker
THE LAST CHASE   Crown International, 1981, w/Christopher Crowe & Taylor Sutherland

Screenplays:
BIG BAND MUSIC
HOT FOOT
COUP D'ETAT
LAUGHING WAR

JEFF BURKHART*
Agent: ICM - Los Angeles, 213/550-4000

WHERE THE BOYS ARE   Tri-Star, 1984, w/Stu Krieger

Screenplays:
AMERICAN TRAGEDY

STEVE BURKOW*
Contact: WGA - Los Angeles, 213/550-1000

BODY SLAM   DEG, 1987, w/Shel Lytton

TOM BURMAN
MEET THE HOLLOWHEADS   Moviestore Entertainment, 1989, w/Lisa Morton, directed

ALAN BURNETT
DUCKTALES: THE MOVIE - THE TREASURE OF THE LOST LAMP (AF)   Buena Vista, 1990

CHARLES BURNETT*
Agent: Triad Artists, Inc. - Los Angeles, 213/556-2727

SEVERAL FRIENDS   1969, directed
THE HORSE   1973, directed
KILLER OF SHEEP   1977, directed
BLESS THEIR LITTLE HEARTS   1982
MY BROTHER'S WEDDING   1984, directed
I FRESH   1987
TO SLEEP WITH ANGER   Samuel Goldwyn Company, 1990, directed

Screenplays:
BLACKBIRD FLY

ALLAN BURNS*
Agent: CAA - Beverly Hills, 213/288-4545

BUTCH AND SUNDANCE: THE EARLY DAYS   20th Century-Fox, 1979
A LITTLE ROMANCE ★   Orion/Warner Bros., 1979
JUST THE WAY YOU ARE   MGM/UA, 1984
JUST BETWEEN FRIENDS   Orion, 1986, directed

Screenplays:
HOLDING ON DOUBLE FAULT w/James L. Brooks
CHINA BLUES
PARENTAL GUIDANCE
HAPPY ALL THE TIME
HEARTS DESIRE

FRANCIS BURNS
(See Larry Gelbart)

JACK BURNS*
Agent: David Shapira & Associates - Sherman Oaks, 818/906-0322

THE MUPPET MOVIE   ITC, 1979, w/Jerry Juhl

MARK BURNS*
Agent: H. N. Swanson, Inc. - Los Angeles, 213/652-5385

MARRIED TO THE MOB   Orion, 1988, w/Barry Strugatz
SHE-DEVIL   Orion, 1989, w/Barry Strugatz

Screenplays:
ON THE LAM w/Barry Strugatz

STANLEY BURNS*
Agent: Shapiro/Lichtman - Los Angeles, 213/859-8877

CHARLIE CHAN AND THE CURSE OF THE DRAGON QUEEN   American Cinema, 1981, w/David Axelrod

JEFF BURR
Business: Conquest Entertainment, 9417 Wexford Drive, Tujunga, CA 91042, 818/352-4316

DIVIDED WE FALL   Conquest Entertainment/Pegasus Productions, 1982, co-directed
THE OFFSPRING FROM A WHISPER TO A SCREAM   TMS Pictures, 1987, w/C. Courtney Joyner & Darin Scott, co-directed

RICHARD BURRIDGE
Agent: A.D. Peters & Co., Ltd. - London, 011/441/580-9592

ABSOLUTE BEGINNERS   Orion, 1986, w/Don MacPherson & Christopher Wicking

Screenplays:
SUNDAY BEER

GEOFF BURROWES
Agent: InterTalent - Los Angeles, 213/858-6200

RETURN TO SNOWY RIVER   Buena Vista, 1988, w/John Dixon, directed

MICHAEL BURTON*
Agent: ICM - Los Angeles, 213/550-4000

FLIGHT OF THE NAVIGATOR   Buena Vista, 1986, w/Matt MacManus
SHOOT TO KILL   Buena Vista, 1988, w/Daniel Petrie Jr. & Harv Zimmel

Screenplays:
THE BUSH PILOT
WHEN WORLDS COLLIDE

ROD BURTON
Agent: The Wright Concept - Hollywood, 213/461-3844

Screenplays:
ITALIAN BASKETBALL

TIM BURTON
Business: Tim Burton Productions, 1041 N. Formosa Ave., West Hollywood, CA 90046, 213/850-2665

VINCENT (Short), directed
FRANKENWEENIE (Short), directed
EDWARD SCISSORHANDS   20th Century Fox, 1990, Story, directed

JOHN BUSHELMAN
THE IRON TRIANGLE   Scotti Bros., 1989, w/Larry Hilbrand & Eric Weston
VIOLENT ZONE   Arista Films, 1989, w/David Pritchard

DAVID BUTLER
VOYAGE OF THE DAMNED ★   ITC, 1976, w/Steve Shagan
BEAR ISLAND   Taft International, 1980, w/Don Sharp & Murray Smith

MICHAEL BUTLER*
Agent: Jim Preminger Agency - Los Angeles, 213/475-9491

BRANNIGAN   United Artists, 1975, w/William P. McGivern, William Norton & Christopher Trumbo
THE CAR   Universal, 1977, w/Dennis Shryack & Lane Slate
THE GAUNTLET   Warner Bros., 1977, w/Dennis Shryack
MURDER BY PHONE   New World, 1982, w/Dennis Shryack & John Kent Harrison
FLASHPOINT   Tri-Star, 1984, w/Dennis Shryack
PALE RIDER   Warner Bros., 1985, w/Dennis Shryack
CODE OF SILENCE   Orion, 1985, w/Dennis Shryack & Mike Gray

Screenplays:
50-50 w/Dennis Shryack
THE EXECUTIONER w/Dennis Shryack

FLOYD BYARS*
Agent: The Gersh Agency - Beverly Hills, 213/274-6611
Contact: 212/925-8907

MAKING MR. RIGHT   Orion, 1987, w/Laurie Frank
MINDWALK   Triton Pictures, 1991, w/Fritjof Capra

Screenplays:
TATIANA w/Andrei Konchalovsky
SO SUE ME

DAVID BYRNE
Contact: Gary Kurfirst Management - New York, 212/957-0900

TRUE STORIES   Warner Bros., 1986, w/Beth Henley & Stephen Tobolowsky, directed

JOHN BYRUM*
Agent: CAA - Beverly Hills, 213/288-4545

MAHOGANY   Paramount, 1975
INSERTS   United Artists, 1976, directed
HARRY AND WALTER GO TO NEW YORK   Columbia, 1976, w/Robert Kaufman
VALENTINO   United Artists, 1977, w/Ken Russell
HEART BEAT   Orion/Warner Bros., 1979, directed
SPHINX   Orion/Warner Bros., 1981
SCANDALOUS   Orion, 1984, w/Rob Cohen
THE RAZOR'S EDGE   Columbia, 1984, w/Bill Murray, directed

Screenplays:
THE RECOVERY w/Rob Cohen
YOUNG MEN WITH UNLIMITED CAPITAL
BUYOUT

C

MICHAEL CACOYANNIS
Contact: Greek Film Centre, Penepistimiou Street, Athens 134, Greece, o1/618924

A MATTER OF DIGNITY   Finos, 1957, directed
A GIRL IN BLACK   Kingsley International, 1959, directed
ZORBA THE GREEK ★   20th Century-Fox, 1964, directed
THE DAY THE FISH CAME OUT   20th Century-Fox, 1967, directed
THE TROJAN WOMEN   Cinerama Releasing Corporation, 1971, directed

GERARD M. CAHILL*
Agent: ICM - Los Angeles, 213/550-4000

SURVIVAL RUN   *SPREE* Film Ventures, 1978, w/Frederic Shore & Larry Spiegel

BARRY CAILLIER
DAREDREAMER   Lensman Co., 1989, w/Pat Royce, directed

ALAN CAILOU*
Agent: Reece Halsey Agency - Los Angeles, 213/652-2409

CLARENCE THE CROSS-EYED LION   MGM, 1965, w/Art Arthur & Marshall Thompson
EVIL KNIEVAL   MGM, 1971, w/John Milius
KINGDOM OF THE SPIDERS   Dimension, 1977, w/Richard Robinson

CHRISTOPHER CAIN
Agent: ICM - Los Angeles, 213/550-4000

SIXTH AND MAIN   National Cinema, 1977, directed

JOSEPH M. CALA
ANGEL   New World, 1984, w/Robert Vincent O'Neil
AVENGING ANGEL   New World, 1985, w/Robert Vincent O'Neil

ANNE CAMERON
TICKET TO HEAVEN   United Artists Classics, 1981, w/R.L. Thomas

JAMES CAMERON*
Agent: ICM - Los Angeles, 213/550-4000
Business: Lightstorm Entertainment, 3100 Damon Way, Burbank, CA 91505, 818/562-1301

THE TERMINATOR   Orion, 1984, w/Gale Anne Hurd, directed
RAMBO: FIRST BLOOD PART II   Tri-Star, 1985, w/Sylvester Stallone
ALIENS   20th Century Fox, 1986, directed
THE ABYSS   20th Century Fox, 1989, directed
TERMINATOR 2: JUDGMENT DAY   Tri-Star, 1991, w/William Wisher , directed

JULIA CAMERON
PUBLIC LIVES (P)
BLOOD LINES (P)
AMERICAN BOY (FD)   1978
GOD'S WILL   Power and Light Productions, 1989, directed

Screenplays:
THE BEST TABLE
NORMAL MURDER
LUDES
OZARK
THE WORKS
MILE STRAIGHT DOWN
TWINKLE

KEN CAMERON*
Business: Pavilion Films, 117 Blues Point Road, McMahons Point, NSW Australia 2060, 02/92-8358

MONKEY GRIP   Cinecom, 1982, w/Helen Garner, directed
FAST TALKING   Cinecom, 1986, directed

LORNE CAMERON*
Agent: Shorr, Stille & Associates - Los Angeles, 213/659-6160

LIKE FATHER LIKE SON   Tri-Star, 1987, w/Steven Bloom
CLARENCE (CTF)   Atlantis Films/Northstar Entertainment/ South Pacific Pictures, 1990, w/David Hoselton

Screenplays:
CUPID
COURTING

PAUL CAMINI
SILENT NIGHT, DEADLY NIGHT   Tri-Star, 1984, Story

CHINA CAMMELL
WHITE OF THE EYE   Palisades Entertainment, 1987, w/Donald Cammell

DONALD CAMMELL*
Agent: William Morris Agency - Beverly Hills, 213/274-7451

DUFFY   Columbia, 1968, w/Harry Joe Brown Jr.
PERFORMANCE   Warner Bros., 1970, co-directed
TILT   Warner Bros., 1979, w/Rudy Durand
WHITE OF THE EYE   Palisades Entertainment, 1987, w/China Cammell, directed
CENTRIFUGE   Vestron, 1990, w/J.C. Pollack

Screenplays:
THE LAST VIDEO
A COFFIN FOR DIMITRIOS

JOE CAMP*
Business: Mulberry Square Productions, One Glen Lakes, 8140 Walnut Hill Lane - Suite 301, Dallas, TX 75231, 214/369-2430

BENJI   Mulberry Square, 1974, directed
FOR THE LOVE OF BENJI   Mulberry Square, 1978, directed
OH, HEAVENLY DOG!   20th Century-Fox, 1980, w/Rod Browning, directed
BENJI: THE HUNTED   Buena Vista, 1987, directed

Ca

TOM CAMP*
Agent: The Irv Schechter Company - Beverly Hills, 213/278-8070

SHARK (P)

Screenplays:
HASENPFEFFER IN THE TORRID ZONE
DISCREET COMPANY
ANGEL PANGS
WEATHERCHILD

JUAN CAMPANELLA
Agent: William Morris Agency - Beverly Hills, 213/274-7451

Screenplays:
HOT WHISKEY & LEMON

ANNEKE CAMPBELL
Agent: Susan Smith & Associates - Beverly Hills, 213/852-4777

Screenplays:
ANNE HUTCHINSON

CLIFTON CAMPBELL*
Agent: CAA - Beverly Hills, 213/288-4545

CHECKERS (P)
NATIVOS (P)
EMERALD TREE BOA (P)
THE FIGURE (P)
TETHER DISORDER (P)

Screenplays:
PUNTA GORDA
LOVING WIFE
THE ACCORD
POWDER BLUE
OF SOUND MIND AND BODY
A MENTION OF HER FORMER SELF
STROKE OF GENIUS
ACT OF ATTRITION

DOUG CAMPBELL
Agent: Carl Belfor Entertainment Management Company - Sherman Oaks, 818/994-8095

SEASON OF FEAR MGM/UA, 1989, directed

JANE CAMPION
Contact: New Zealand Film Commission, P.O. Box 11546, Wellington, New Zealand, 4/859-754

SWEETIE Avenue Pictures, 1989, w/Gerard Lee, directed

CHRISTOPHER CANAAN*
Agent: Robinson, Weintraub, Gross & Associates - Los Angeles, 213/653-5802

THE TEN MILLION DOLLAR GETAWAY Alvin Cooperman Productions/Wilshire Court Productions, 1991

Screenplays:
CALEXICO
FULL COURT PRESS
OUT

DORAN WILLIAM CANNON*
Contact: WGA - Los Angeles, 213/550-1000

SKIDOO Paramount, 1968
BREWSTER McCLOUD MGM, 1970

DYAN CANNON
Contact: Directors Guild of America - Los Angeles, 213/289-2000

NUMBER ONE (Short) ★ 1976, directed
THE END OF INNOCENCE Skouras Pictures, 1990, directed

DONALD CANTRELL*
Agent: ICM - Los Angeles, 213/550-4000

O.C. AND STIGGS MGM/UA, 1987, w/Ted Mann

LEON CAPETANOS*
Agent: United Talent Agency - Beverly Hills, 213/273-6700

SUMMER RUN Lighthouse, 1974, directed
THE GUMBALL RALLY Warner Bros., 1976
GREASED LIGHTNING Warner Bros., 1977, w/Lawrence Dukone, Melvin Van Peebles & Kenneth Vose
TEMPEST Columbia, 1982, w/Paul Mazursky
MOSCOW ON THE HUDSON Columbia, 1984, w/Paul Mazursky
DOWN AND OUT IN BEVERLY HILLS Buena Vista, 1986, w/Paul Mazursky
MOON OVER PARADOR Universal, 1988, w/Paul Mazursky
FLETCH LIVES Universal, 1989

Screenplays:
MEET THE MORON
LAST MAN AT ARLINGTON
WHITE ON WHITE
LOST CITY
NIAGARA FALLS
MISSING PERSON
SCHOOL DAYS

CARMINE CAPOBIANCO
CEMETARY HIGH Titan Productions, 1989, w/Gorman Bechard

JAMES CAPPE*
Agent: Jim Preminger Agency - Los Angeles, 213/475-9491

THE ADVENTURES OF FORD FAIRLANE 20th Century Fox, 1990, w/David Arnott & Daniel Waters

BERNT CAPRA
Contact: Swiss Film Center, Munstergasse 18, 8001 Zurich, Switzerland, 01/472860

MINDWALK Triton Pictures, 1991, Story, directed

JIM CARABATSOS*
Agent: Shapiro/Lichtman - Los Angeles, 213/859-8877

HEROES Universal, 1977
BEYOND THE REEF Universal, 1981, w/Louis LaRusso II
UNDERGROUND ACES Filmways, 1981, w/Leonore Wright & Andrew Peter Marin
NO MERCY Tri-Star, 1986

HEARTBREAK RIDGE   Warner Bros., 1986
HAMBURGER HILL   Tri-Star, 1987

Screenplays:
CRUISE w/Steven Seagal
UNWANTED ATTENTIONS

STEVEN W. CARABATSOS*
Agent: The Gurian Agency - Los Angeles, 213/550-0400

EL CONDOR   National General, 1970, w/Larry Cohen
TENTACLES   20th Century-Fox, 1977, w/others
THE LAST FLIGHT OF NOAH'S ARK   Buena Vista,
   1980, w/George Arthur Bloom & Sandy Glass
HOT PURSUIT   Paramount, 1987, w/Steven Lisberger

WALTER CARBONE
SOMETHING SPECIAL   *WILLY MILLY/I WAS A TEENAGE BOY*   Cinema Group, 1986,
   w/Carla Reuben

J. S. CARDONE*
(Joseph S. Cardone)
Agent: Circle Talent Associates - Beverly Hills,
   213/281-3765

THE SLAYER   21st Century Distribution, 1982,
   w/William R. Ewing, directed
THUNDER ALLEY   Cannon, 1985, directed
SHADOW ZONE   Paramount, 1990, directed
A ROW OF CROWS   Propaganda Films,
   1991, directed

Screenplays:
UNDER THE WIRE
COLD HEAT
THE MUMMY AND THE ARMADILLO
FALLOUT

MARK PATRICK CARDUCCI*
Agent: William Morris Agency - Beverly Hills,
   213/274-7451

PUMPKINHEAD   MGM/UA, 1988, w/Gary Gerani
BURIED ALIVE   (CTF)   MCA Entertainment, 1990

Screenplays:
LIGHT AT THE END
HOB
LITTLEY ITALY
THE COMIC AND THE CON

TOPPER CAREW
Agent: ICM - Los Angeles, 213/550-4000

D.C. CAB   Universal, 1983, Story w/Joel Schumacher
TALKING DIRTY AFTER DARK   New Line Cinema,
   1991, directed

PETER CAREY
Agent: London Management - London,
   011/441/493-1610

BLISS   New World, 1986, w/Ray Lawrence
UNTIL THE END OF THE WORLD   Road Movies,
   1991, w/Wim Wenders

JOHN CARLEN*
Agent: Shapiro/Lichtman - Los Angeles, 213/859-8877

Screenplays:
FIELDS OF VISION
TABLE DANCING
PARADISE ROAD

CLANCY CARLILE
HONKYTONK MAN   Warner Bros., 1982

ANNE CARLISLE
LIQUID SKY   Cinevista, 1983, w/Slava Tsukerman &
   Nina V. Kerova

LEWIS JOHN CARLINO*
Agent: CAA - Beverly Hills, 213/288-4545

TELEMACHUS (P)
SECONDS   Paramount, 1966
THE BROTHERHOOD   Paramount, 1968
THE FOX   Warner Bros., 1968, w/Howard Koch
THE MECHANIC   United Artists, 1972
A REFLECTION OF FEAR   Columbia, 1973,
   w/Edward Hume
CRAZY JOE   Columbia, 1974
THE SAILOR WHO FELL FROM GRACE WITH THE SEA
   Avco Embassy, 1976, directed
I NEVER PROMISED YOU A ROSE GARDEN ★   New
   World, 1977, w/Gavin Lambert
THE GREAT SANTINI   *THE ACE*   Orion/Warner Bros.,
   1980, directed
RESURRECTION   Universal, 1980
HAUNTED SUMMER   Cannon, 1988

Screenplays:
CENTERFOLD
STRANGER IN A STRANGE LAND
SALINAS
THE ANDREASSON AFFAIR   PHENOMENON
KIN

LEWIS JOHN CARLINO II
Agent: Circle Talent Associates - Beverly Hills,
   213/285-1585

Screenplays:
INHERITENCE
THIS IS THE DAY
THE HEADMASTER'S PRINCIPLE
THE WHITE SPACE

JIM CARLSON*
Agent: Monteiro Rose Agency - Encino,
   818/501-1177

POUND PUPPIES AND THE LEGEND OF BIG PAW(AF)
   Tri-Star, 1988, w/Terrence McDonnell

MATTHEW J. CARLSON*
Contact: WGA - Los Angeles, 213/550-1000

Screenplays:
BUZZ ORBIT

Ca

ROY CARLSON*
Agent: United Talent Agency - Beverly Hills, 213/273-6700

STAND ALONE   New World, 1985

Screenplays:
CHINA MOON
YANKEE WHITE
THE WRONG MAN
DEEP UMBRA
LIME GREEN
COLLISION   (shared)
IN THE HIGH GROUND
THE TENDER
MARTHA HONEY

CLARK CARLTON
VALET GIRLS   Empire Pictures, 1987

DON CARMODY
Agent: Gray/Goodman/Inc. - Beverly Hills, 213/276-7070

WHISPERS   Live Home Video, 1990, Adaptation
THE HIT MAN   Cannon, 1991, w/Robert Geoffrion

MICHAEL CARMODY
SYNGENOR   South Gate Entertainment, 1990, Story

CHARLES ROBERT CARNER*
Agent: CAA - Beverly Hills, 213/288-4545
Business: South Side Films Inc., 8417 Harold Way, Los Angeles, CA 90069, 213/650-7507

GYMKATA   MGM/UA, 1985
LET'S GET HARRY   Tri-Star, 1986
BLIND FURY   Tri-Star, 1990

Screenplays:
THE BATTLING SPUMONTI BROTHERS
THE ADVENTURES OF JONATHAN CABOT
AMERICAN PIE
CRIME OF THE CENTURY
DEAD HEAT OF SUMMER
THE DEFIER OF FATE
THE FOX
HOT CARGO
LION OF IRELAND
THE LONELY ONE
MAZE
MONEY TO BURN
THE PROTECTOR
QUEEN BEE
SILENT SERVICE
SIMON SAYS
WARLORD
YOUNG EVE

ROBERT B. CARNEY*
Agent: William Morris Agency - New York, 212/586-5100

Screenplays:
TUG OF WAR
HOMETOWN
MURDER OF MIDNIGHT
NIGHT FLIGHTS

GLENN GORDON CARON*
Agent: CAA - Beverly Hills, 213/288-4545

CONDORMAN   Buena Vista, 1981, w/Mickey Rose & Marc Stirdivant

Screenplays:
EVITA (directing)
KNOWING DAMON

A.J. CAROTHERS*
Agent: Triad Artists, Inc. - Los Angeles, 213/556-2727

THE MIRACLE OF THE WHITE STALLIONS   Buena Vista, 1963
EMIL AND THE DETECTIVE   Buena Vista, 1964
THE HAPPIEST MILLIONAIRE   Buena Vista, 1967
NEVER A DULL MOMENT   Buena Vista, 1968
HERO AT LARGE   MGM/United Artists, 1980
THE SECRET OF MY SUCCESS   Universal, 1987, w/Jim Cash & Jack Epps Jr.

Screenplays:
MERMAID w/Robert Towne
JAZZ BABIES
THE THIRTEEN CLOCKS
HANSEL & GRETEL
FANCY HARDWARE
PIANO SOLO
WHISKEY MAN
THE GIRL WITH THE GOLDEN HAIR
STAIRWAY TO HEAVEN
ADAM'S RIB
JEFFERSON MCGRAW
FREE SPIRIT
TEMPTING FATE
EXECUTIVE PRIVILEGE

JOHN CARPENTER*
Agent: ICM - Los Angeles, 213/550-4000

DARK STAR   Jack H. Harris Enterprises, 1974, w/Dan O'Bannon, directed
ASSAULT ON PRECINCT 13   Turtle Releasing Corporation, 1976, directed
THE EYES OF LAURA MARS   Columbia, 1978, w/David Z. Goodman
HALLOWEEN   Compass International, 1978, w/Debra Hill, directed
HALLOWEEN II   Universal, 1981, w/Debra Hill
THE FOG   Avco Embassy, 1981, w/Debra Hill, directed
ESCAPE FROM NEW YORK   Avco Embassy, 1981, w/Nick Castle, directed
BLACK MOON RISING   New World, 1986, w/William Gray & Desmond Nakano
PRINCE OF DARKNESS   Universal, 1987, as "Martin Quatermass," directed
THEY LIVE   Universal, 1989, as "Frank Armitage," directed
EL DIABLO (CTF)   Wizan/Black Productions, 1990, w/Bill Philips & Tommy Lee Wallace

STEPHEN W. CARPENTER*
Agent: William Morris Agency - Beverly Hills, 213/274-7451

THE DORM THAT DRIPPED BLOOD   *PRANKS*   Artists Releasing Corporation/Film Ventures International, 1982, w/Jeffrey Obrow & Stacey Giachino, co-directed
THE POWER   Artists Releasing Corporation/Film Ventures International, 1984, w/Jeffrey Obrow, co-directed

THE KINDRED   FM Entertainment, 1987,
  w/others, co-directed
THE SERVANTS OF TWILIGHT   Trimark Pictures,
  1991, w/Jeffrey Obrow

Screenplays:
BUSYBODIES

ALAN CARR*
Business: Allan Carr Enterprises, P.O. Box 691670,
  Los Angeles, CA 90069, 213/278-2490

CAN'T STOP THE MUSIC   AFD, 1980,
  w/Bronte Woodard

RICHARD CARR
MAN FROM DEL RIO   United Artists, 1956
TOO LATE BLUES   Paramount, 1961,
  w/John Cassavetes
HELL IS FOR HEROES   Paramount, 1962,
  w/Robert Pirosh
HEAVEN WITH A GUN   MGM, 1969
AMERICANA   Crown International, 1983

MICHAEL CARRERAS
Contact: British Academy of Film & Television Arts,
  195 Piccadilly, London W1, England, 71/734-0022

THE UNHOLY FOUR   *THE STRANGER CAME HOME*
  Exclusvie, 1954
CURSE OF THE MUMMY'S TOMB   Columbia,
  1964, as "Henry Younger"
PREHISTORIC WOMEN   *SLAVE GIRLS*   Hammer,
  1966, directed
ONE MILLION YEARS B.C.   Hammer, 1966
CREATURES THE WORLD FORGOT   Columbia, 1970

JEAN-CLAUDE CARRIERE*
Contact: WGA - New York, 212/245-6180

THE SUITOR   CAPAC, 1962, w/Pierre Etaix
THE DIARY OF A CHAMBERMAID   Speva, 1964,
  w/Luis Bunuel
VIVA MARIA!   United Artists, 1965, w/Louis Malle
HOTEL PARADISO   MGM, 1966, w/Peter Glenville
THE MILKY WAY   United Artists, 1967, w/Luis Bunuel
BELLE DE JOUR   Allied Artists, 1967, w/Luis Bunuel
BORSALINO   Paramount, 1970, w/Jean Cau, Jacues
  Deray & Claude Sautet
TAKING OFF   Universal, 1971, w/Milos Forman, John
  Guare & John Klein
THE DISCREET CHARM OF THE BOURGEOISIE ★
  20th Century-Fox, 1972, w/Luis Bunuel
THAT OBSCURE OBJECT OF DESIRE ★   First Artists,
  1977, w/Luis Bunuel
A BUTTERFLY ON THE SHOULDER   *UN PAPILLON
  SUR L'EPAULE*   Gaumont, 1978, w/Tonino Guerra
THE TIN DRUM   New World, 1980, w/Franz Seitz &
  Volker Schlondorff
SAUVE QUIE PEUT LA VIE   *EVERY MAN FOR
  HIMSELF IN LIFE*   New Yorker/Zoetrope, 1980,
  w/Anne-Marie Mieville & Jean-Luc Godard
THE ASSOCIATE   Quartet, 1982, w/Rene Gainville
CIRCLE OF DECEIT   United Artists Classics, 1982,
  w/Volker Schlondorff, Margarethe von Trotta &
  Kai Hermann
THE RETURN OF MARTIN GUERRE   European
  International, 1983, w/Daniel Vigne
DANTON   Triumph, 1983

SWANN IN LOVE   Orion Classics, 1984, w/Peter Brook &
  Marie-Helen Estienne
THE UNBEARABLE LIGHTNESS OF BEING ★   Orion,
  1988, w/Philip Kaufman
THE MAHABHARATA   MK2 USA, 1989
VALMONT   Orion, 1989
MAY FOOLS   Orion Classics, 1990, w/Louis Malle
CYRANO DE BERGERAC   Orion Classics, 1990,
  w/Jean-Paul Rappeneau
AT PLAY IN THE FIELDS OF THE LORD   Saul Zaentz Co.,
  1991, w/Hector Babenco

Screenplays:
BLACK ANGEL   w/Philip Kaufman

MATHIEU CARRIERE
BEETHOVEN'S NEPHEW   New World, 1988,
  w/Paul Morrissey

ROBERT B. CARRINGTON*
Agent: Jerome Siegel Associates - Los Angeles,
  213/850-1275

KALEIDOSCOPE   Warner Bros., 1966
WAIT UNTIL DARK   Warner Bros., 1967, w/Jane
  Howard-Carrington
FEAR IS THE KEY   Paramount, 1973
VENOM   Paramount, 1982

Screenplays:
A FESTIVAL OF FEAR
ARE YOU ALONE TONIGHT?
THE PLAYPEN
COLD WAR SWAP
DEATH TRACK
THE DONOR
DEATHWORK

J. LARRY CARROLL*
Contact: WGA - Los Angeles, 213/550-1000

THE DAY TIME ENDED   Compass International, 1979,
  w/Wayne Schmidt & David Schmoeller

ROBERT CARROLL
Agent: Susan Smith & Associates - Beverly Hills,
  213/852-4777

SONNY BOY   Triumph, 1991

TOD CARROLL
Agent: ICM - Los Angeles, 213/550-4000

NATIONAL LAMPOON'S MOVIE MADNESS   United Artists,
  1982, w/Shary Flenniken, Pat Mephitis, Gerald Sussman
  & Ellis Weiner
O.C. AND STIGGS   MGM/UA, 1987, Story
CLEAN AND SOBER   Warner Bros., 1988

Screenplays:
REDEMPTION
WOMEN ON THE VERGE OF A NERVOUS BREAKDOWN
  (remake)
BUTLERS
LA TULIPE
MY GOD THEY'VE GOT BOSCO
LES COMPERES   (remake)

Ca

FILM WRITERS GUIDE

WILLARD CARROLL
Agent: William Morris Agency - Beverly Hills, 213/274-7451

Screenplays:
FULL MOON

RODNEY CARR-SMITH
BARTLEBY   Pantheon, 1970, w/Anthony Friedmann, directed
LOLLY MADONNA XXX   MGM, 1973, w/Sue Grafton

L. M. KIT CARSON*
Agent: The Daniel Ostroff Agency - Los Angeles, 213/278-2020

DAVID HOLZMAN'S DIARY   Grove Press, 1967, w/Jim McBride
THE LEXINGTON EXPERIENCE (FD)   Korda, 1971
THE AMERICAN DREAMER (FD)   EYR, 1971, w/Dennis Hopper & Laurence Schiller
THE LAST WORD   Samuel Goldwyn Company, 1979, w/Greg Smith & Michael Varhol
BREATHLESS   Orion, 1983, w/Jim McBride
PARIS, TEXAS   TLC Films/20th Century-Fox, 1984, Adaptation
CHINESE BOXES   Chris Sievernich Productions/Palace Productions, 1984
THE TEXAS CHAINSAW MASSACRE PART 2   Cannon, 1986

Screenplays:
THE NEGOTIATOR (CTF)
NORIEGA VERDAD (CTF)
SWEETHEARTS
ELEKTRA ASSASSIN w/Jim McBride
THE MOVIEGOER w/Jim McBride
VAMPIRE BLUES

ANGELA CARTER
Agent: London Management - London, 011/441/493-1610

THE COMPANY OF WOLVES   Cannon, 1984, w/Neil Jordan
THE MAGIC TOYSHOP   Skouras Pictures, 1989

RUTH CARTER
COMING UP ROSES   Skouras Pictures, 1987

SARA FLANIGAN CARTER*
Contact: WGA - New York, 212/245-6180

SUDIE AND SIMPSON (CTF)   Freed/Laufer, 1990, w/Ken Koser

Screenplays:
WILDFIRE (CTF)

DEE CARUSO*
Contact: WGA - Los Angeles, 213/550-1000

WHICH WAY TO THE FRONT?   Warner Bros., 1970, w/Gerald Gardner
THE WORLD'S GREATEST ATHLETE   Buena Vista, 1973, w/Gerald Gardner
DOIN' TIME   The Ladd Company/Warner Bros.,1984, w/Franelle Silver & Ron Zwang

STEVE CARVER
BULLETPROOF   CineTel Films, 1987, w/T.L. Lankford, directed

CORT CASADY
Agent: Barry Perelman Agency - Los Angeles, 213/274-5999

Screenplays:
UNDERGROUND

DAVID CASCI*
Agent: Warden & White Associates - Beverly Hills, 213/852-1028

EXTENDEND PLAY (Short), directed

Screenplays:
THE PAGEMASTER
KIDSTUFF
TOM, DICK AND HARRY
TEMPORARY INCONVENIENCE
PANAMANIA

RICHARD CASEY
HELLBENT   Hellbent Productions, 1989, directed

JIM CASH*
Agent: CAA - Beverly Hills, 213/288-4545

TOP GUN   Paramount, 1986, w/Jack Epps Jr.
LEGAL EAGLES   Universal, 1986, w/Jack Epps Jr.
THE SECRET OF MY SUCCESS   Universal, 1987, w/A.J. Carothers & Jack Epps Jr.
TURNER & HOOCH   Buena Vista, 1989, w/JackEpps Jr., Daniel Petrie Jr., Michael Blodgett & Dennis Shryack
DICK TRACY   Buena Vista, 1990, w/Jack Epps Jr.

Screenplays:
SISTER ACT w/Jack Epps Jr.
THE EDDIE COCHRAN STORY w/Jack Epps Jr.
REVENGE OF BLACKTHORN w/Jack Epps Jr.
WHEREABOUTS w/Jack Epps Jr.
DANGEROUSLY w/Jack Epps Jr. & Bennett Tramer
MR. MAYOR w/Jack Epps Jr.
MILWAUKEE CONFIDENTIAL w/Jack Epps Jr.
DIRTY FIVE w/Jack Epps Jr.
DIVIDING LINE w/Jack Epps Jr.

ALAN CASTLE*
Contact: WGA - Los Angeles, 213/550-1000

STRANDED   New Line Cinema, 1987

NICK CASTLE*
Agent: CAA - Beverly Hills, 213/288-4545

SKATETOWN, U.S.A.   Columbia, 1979
PRAY TV   Filmways, 1980
ESCAPE FROM NEW YORK   Avco Embassy, 1981, w/John Carpenter
TAG   New World, 1982, directed
KISS ME KILL ME   New World, 1982
THE BOY WHO COULD FLY   20th Century Fox, 1986, directed
TAP   Tri-Star, 1989, directed
HOOK   Tri-Star, 1991, Story w/Jim Hart

Screenplays:
MY GENERATION

ROBERT CASWELL*
Agent: Triad Artists, Inc. - Los Angeles, 213/556-2727

A CRY IN THE DARK   Warner Bros., 1988,
    w/Fred Schepisi
THE DOCTOR   Buena Vista, 1991

Screenplays:
CHILDREN OF DUST
THUNDER

LILIANI CAVANI
Address: via Filangeri, 4 Rome, Italy, 06/360-1832

THE NIGHT PORTER   Avco Embassy, 1974, w/Italo
    Moscati, directed
THE BERLIN AFFAIR   Cannon, 1985, w/Roberta
    Mazzoni, directed
FRANCESCO   Karol Film/RAI/Royal Film, 1989,
    w/Roberta Mazzoni, directed

MARIA ELENE CELLINO*
Contact: 213/684-1791

NO RETREAT, NO SURRENDER II   Shapiro Glickenhaus,
    1989, w/Roy Horan & Keith W. Strandberg

JANUS CERCONE
Agent: United Talent Agency - Beverly Hills, 213/273-6700

Screenplays:
SENATOR'S WIFE
VIRGINIA REEL
KNOCK OUT
THE RUNAROUND
HOCUS POCUS
NIGHTENGALE
WAYS AND MEANS

GINNY CERRELLA*
Agent: Triad Artists, Inc. - Los Angeles, 213/556-2727

SISTER, SISTER   New World, 1988, w/Joel Cohen &
    Bill Condon

Screenplays:
PETALS IN THE WIND
NOBODY'S PERFECT
RONNIE FINKELHOF, SUPERSTAR
JERSEY SKYLINE
THE PRINCE OF POP
DEAD GIVEAWAY
VOODOO
UNNATURAL ACTS
THIEF OF TIME
GYPSY SWITCH
MARMALADE

CLAUDE CHABROL
Agent: Cineart, 31 Avenue Champs Elysees, 75008 Paris,
    France, 4/256-3574
Contact: French Film Office, 745 Fifth Avenue, New York,
    NY 10151, 212/832-8860

LE BEAU SERGE   United Motion Picture Organization,
    1958, directed
THE COUSINS   Films Around the World, 1959, directed
LES BICHES   VGC, 1968, directed
LA FEMME INFIDEL   Allied Artists, 1968, directed
LE BOUCHER   Cinerama Releasing Corporation,
    1969, directed
STORY OF WOMEN   MK2/New Yorker Films, 1989, w/Colo
    Tavernier O'Hagan, directed
QUIET DAYS IN CLICHY   Pathe, 1990, w/Ugo
    Leonzio, directed
MADAME BOVARY   Samuel Goldwyn Company,
    1991, directed

KITTY CHALMERS
JOURNEY TO THE CENTER OF THE EARTH   Cannon,
    1987, w/Regina Davis, Rusty Lemorande & Debra Ricci
CYBORG   Cannon, 1989

JEAN CHALOPIN
RAINBROW BRITE AND THE STAR STEALER (AF)
    Warner Bros., 1985, Story w/Howard R. Cohen

JOHN CHAMPION
MUSTANG COUNTRY   Universal, 1976, directed

ROBERT CHANDLEE*
Contact: WGA - Los Angeles, 213/550-1000

THE KILLER INSIDE ME   Warner Bros., 1976,
    w/Edward Mann

ELIZABETH CHANDLER*
Agent: ICM - Los Angeles, 213/550-4000

Screenplays:
RENEGADES

WARREN CHANEY
HAUNTED   Sandpiper Productions, 1990
BROKEN SPUR   Sandpiper Productions, 1990, directed

Screenplays:
BEHIND THE MASK

ANDREW CHAPMAN*
Agent: ICM - Los Angeles, 213/550-4000

Screenplays:
THE SEA WOLF
WORLD ON FIRE

LEIGH CHAPMAN*
Agent: ICM - Los Angeles, 213/550-4000

A SWINGIN' SUMMER   United Screen Hearts, 1965
TRUCK TURNER   American International, 1974
DIRTY MARY, CRAZY LARRY   20th Century-Fox, 1974,
    w/Antonio Santean
HOW COME NOBODY'S ON OUR SIDE?   American Films
    Limited, 1975
BOARDWALK   Atlantic Releasing Corporation, 1979,
    w/Stephen Verona
STEEL *LOOK DOWN AND DIE*   World Northal, 1980
THE OCTAGON   American Cinema, 1980
IMPULSE   Warner Bros., 1990, w/John DeMarco
STORM AND SORROW (CTF)   Accent Entertainment/
    Hearst Entertainment, 1990

Screenplays:
CAPTAIN BUTTERFLY
DETROIT

Ch

FILM WRITERS GUIDE

MATTHEW CHAPMAN*
Contact: WGA - Los Angeles, 213/550-1000

HUSSY   Watchgrove Ltd., 1980, directed
STRANGER'S KISS   Orion Classics, 1984, w/Blaine Novak, directed
SLOW BURN (CTF)   Joel Schumacher Productions/Universal Pay TV, 1986, directed
HEART OF MIDNIGHT   Virgin Vision, 1989, directed

PRISCILLA CHAPMAN
Contact: Weissman & Wolff - Los Angeles, 213/858-7888

THE FAN   Paramount, 1981, w/John Hartwell

RICHARD E. CHAPMAN*
Agent: William Morris Agency - Beverly Hills, 213/274-7451

Screenplays:
MY FELLOW AMERICANS w/Jack Kaplan
HOMEWORK
TWENTY-ONE THE HARD WAY
THE MAN WHO GAVE UP HIS NAME
AND NOW MY LOFE
50 FREE AND CLEAR
QUEEN FOR A DAY
THE JET PROPELLED COUCH
BRASS ANGELS
THE POLICEMAN

ROBIN CHAPMAN
TRIPLE ECHO   Hemdale, 1972
FORCE 10 FROM NAVARONE   American International, 1978

TOM CHAPMAN*
Agent: ICM - Los Angeles, 213/550-4000

HANGAR #18   Sunn Classic, 1980, Story w/James L. Conway
THE BOOGENS   Jensen Farley Pictures, 1982, Story w/David O'Malley

DAVID A. CHAPPE*
Agent: United Talent Agency - Beverly Hills, 213/273-6700

Screenplays:
GALE FORCE w/Larry Konner & Mark Rosenthal
MAXWELL TRAIN
TREASURE OF GUNSIGHT BUTTE

ERIC CHAPPELL
RISING DAMP   ITC, 1980

MEHDI CHAREF
Contact: French Film Office, 745 Fifth Avenue, New York, NY 10151, 212/832-8860

TEA IN THE HAREM   Cinecom, 1986, directed

DAVID H. CHASE*
Agent: InterTalent - Los Angeles, 213/858-6200

Screenplays:
TUNA HELL
LIARS
FEMALE SUSPECTS
CHANGING SIDES
NERVOUS SYSTEM

DAVID M. CHASKIN
Agent: APA - Los Angeles, 213/273-0744

A NIGHTMARE ON ELM STREET, PART 2: FREDDY'S REVENGE   New Line Cinema, 1985
THE CURSE   Trans World Entertainment, 1987
I, MADMAN   Trans World Entertainment, 1989

Screenplays:
THE VICTOR w/Richard Kletter (directing)
THE WELL
BOLTS!
HARDCOVER

CYNTHIA A. CHERBAK*
Agent: Dytman & Associates - Beverly Hills, 213/288-1827

THE KISSING PLACE (CTF)   Wilshire Court Productions, 1990, w/Richard Altabef & Michael Wing

JOHN R. CHERRY III
ERNEST GOES TO CAMP   Buena Vista, 1987, w/Coke Sams, directed

STANLEY Z. CHERRY
Agent: Shapiro/Lichtman - Los Angeles, 213/859-8877
Busines Manager: Steven Kattleman, Cooper, Epstein, Hurewitz, 9465 Wilshire Blvd., Beverly Hills, CA 90212, 213/278-1111

BUNNY O'HARE   American International, 1971, w/Coslough Johnson

MARC CHESLER*
Contact: WGA - Los Angeles, 213/550-1000

Screenplays:
AMERICAN LADY w/Gail Fisher
DISTANT RELATIVE w/Gail Fisher
ME, MYSELF AND I w/Gail Fisher
MALE-FEMALE w/Gail Fisher
STIRRUPS w/Gail Fisher

HOWARD M. CHESLEY*
Contact: WGA - Los Angeles, 213/550-1000

Screenplays:
LONGING TO FALL
RESISTING ARREST
LIKE HARRY

LIONEL CHETWYND*
Agent: Barrett, Benson, McCartt & Weston - Los Angeles, 213/247-5500

WE THE PEOPLE...200 (P) shared
BLEEDING GREAT ORCHIDS (P)
MAYBE THAT'S YOUR PROBLEM (P)
THE APPRENTICESHIP OF DUDDY KRAVITZ ★   Paramount, 1974, Adaptation
TWO SOLITUDES   New World-Mutual, 1978, directed
QUINTET   20th Century-Fox, 1979, Story w/Robert Altman & Patricia Resnick
THE HANOI HILTON   Cannon, 1987, directed

ALICE CHILDRESS*
Agent: Flora Roberts, Inc. - New York, 212/355-4165

A HERO AIN'T NOTHING BUT A SANDWICH
   New World, 1977

HELEN CHILDRESS
Agent: United Talent Agency - Beverly Hills, 213/273-6700

Screenplays:
SIGNS OF LIFE

CHARLES CHIODO*
Contact: 818/842-5656

KILLER KLOWNS FROM OUTER SPACE   TransWorld
   Entertainment, 1988, w/Steven Chiodo

STEVEN CHIODO*
Contact: 818/246-3174

KILLER KLOWNS FROM OUTER SPACE   TransWorld
   Entertainment, 1988, w/Charles Chiodo, directed

DAVID CHISOLM*
Agent: CAA - Beverly Hills, 213/288-4545

THE WIZARD   Universal, 1989

Screenplays:
THE DREAM CHILD
STREETWISE
SILENT SERVICES
DEVIL PUPS

THOMAS CHONG*
Agent: The Artists Agency - Los Angeles, 213/277-7779

UP IN SMOKE   Paramount, 1978, w/Richard
   "Cheech" Marin
CHEECH & CHONG'S NEXT MOVIE   Universal, 1980,
   w/Richard "Cheech" Marin, directed
CHEECH & CHONG'S NICE DREAMS   Columbia, 1981,
   w/Richard "Cheech" Marin, directed
THINGS ARE TOUGH ALL OVER   Columbia, 1982,
   w/Richard "Cheech" Marin
CHEECH & CHONG: STILL SMOKIN'   Paramount, 1983,
   w/Richard "Cheech" Marin, directed
CHEECH & CHONG'S THE CORSICAN BROTHERS
   Orion, 1984, w/Richard "Cheech" Marin, directed
FAR OUT MAN   New Line Cinema, 1990, directed

MICHAEL CHOQUETTE
STITCHES   International Film Marketing, 1985,
   w/Michael Paseornek

ELIE CHOURAQUI
Contact: French Film Office, 745 Fifth Avenue,
   New York, NY 10151, 212/832-8860

LOVE SONGS PAROLES ET MUSIQUE   Spectrafilm,
   1984, directed
MAN ON FIRE   Tri-Star, 1987, w/Sergio Donati, directed

RANJIT CHOWDREY
SAM & ME   Sunrise Films Ltd. Toronto/Film Four
   International, 1991

H.R. (ROGER) CHRISTIAN
Agent: ICM - London, 01/629-8080

KING OF THE MOUNTAIN   Universal, 1981

DAVID CHUTE
Contact: 213/739-1682

CLICK: THE CALENDAR GIRL KILLER   Crown
   International, 1989, w/David Reskin, Ross Hagen &
   Hoke Howell

GERARD CICCORITTI
Business: Lightshow Communications, Inc., 19 Tennis
   Crescent - Suite 8, Toronto, Ontario M4K 1J4, Canada,
   416/465-6465

SKULL: A NIGHT OF TERROR   Geonib Properties, 1989,
   w/Robert Bergman
A WHISPER TO A SCREAM   Distant Horizon and
   Lighthouse Communications, 1989, w/Robert Bergman

CYNTHIA CIDRE*
Agent: CAA - Beverly Hills, 213/288-4545

IN COUNTRY   Warner Bros., 1989, w/Frank Pierson
FIRES WITHIN   MGM-Pathe, 1991
THE MAMBO KINGS   Warner Bros., 1991

Screenplays:
DOUBLE EXPOSURE
RAISING HELL
BLUE MOON
FOOLS DIE
NERVE ENDINGS
VOODOO QUEEN

MATT CIMBER
BUTTERFLY   Analysis, 1981, w/John Goff, directed
YELLOW HAIR AND THE FORTRESS OF GOLD   Crown
   Inernational, 1984, w/John Kershaw, directed

MICHAEL CIMINO*
Agent: ICM - Los Angeles, 213/550-4000

SILENT RUNNING   Universal, 1971, w/Steven Bochco &
   Deric Washburn
MAGNUM FORCE   Warner Bros., 1973, w/John Milius
THUNDERBOLT AND LIGHTFOOT   United Artists,
   1974, directed
THE DEER HUNTER ★   Universal, 1978, Story w/Louis
   Garfinkle & Quinn K. Redeker, directed
HEAVEN'S GATE   United Artists, 1980, directed
YEAR OF THE DRAGON   MGM/UA, 1985,
   w/Oliver Stone, directed

TONY CINCIRIPINI
THE LAWLESS LAND   Concorde Pictures, 1989,
   w/Larry Leahy

JIM CIRILE
Agent: Susan Smith & Associates - Beverly Hills,
   213/852-4777

Screenplays:
A CLEAN SWEEP
EARTHSHAKER

DON CIRILLO
Agent: Circle Talent Associates - Beverly Hills, 213/285-1585

Screenplays:
JERSEY TO HEAVEN AND BACK
TWO JOHNNIES
SIX FIGURES
MOLLY
PUMPING GAS

PATRICK CIRILLO*
Agent: Triad Artists, Inc. - Los Angeles, 213/556-2727

HOMER AND EDDIE   Skouras Pictures, 1990

Screenplays:
CITY OF DARKNESS w/Joe Gayton
PSYCHOTIC REACTION
SOJOURN

TOM CITRANO*
Agent: The Sarnoff Co., Inc. - 818/761-4495

NIGHT EYES   Amritraj-Baldwin Entertainment, 1990, w/Andrew Stevens

BOB CLARK*
Business Manager: Harold D. Cohen - Los Angeles, 213/550-0570

PORKY'S   20th Century-Fox, 1982, directed
PORKY'S II: THE NEXT DAY   20th Century-Fox, 1983, w/Alan Ormsby & Roger Swaybill, directed
A CHRISTMAS STORY   MGM/UA, 1983, w/Jean Shepherd & Leigh Brown, directed
FROM THE HIP   DEG, 1987, w/David E. Kelly, directed
LOOSE CANNONS   Tri-Star, 1990, w/Richard Christian Matheson & Richard Matheson, directed

Screenplays:
THE SHE MAN

BRIAN CLARK
Agent: Judy Daish Agency - London, 011/441/486-5405

WHOSE LIFE IS IT ANYWAY?   MGM/UA, 1981, w/Reginald Rose

Screenplays:
COMPUTER PROJECT
MEDICAL SCHOOL

BRUCE CLARK*
Contact: Attorney Kant & Star - 213/394-7642

GALAXY OF TERROR   New World, 1981, w/Marc Siegler, directed

DENNIS LYNTON CLARK*
Agent: The Brandt Company - Studio City, 818/506-7747

COMES A HORSEMAN   United Artists, 1978
THE KEEP   Paramount, 1983, Adaptation
THE COURTMARTIAL OF JACKIE ROBINSON (CTF)   Turner Network Television, 1990, w/L. Travis Clark, Steve Duncan & Clayton Frohman

Screenplays:
FREEWALKERS (directing)
PORT ROYAL
PAUL BUNYAN
CHILDREN'S CRUSADE
AMAZING GRACE
BAND OF BROTHERS
VALLEY BOYS
THIRTEEN
THE LAST CHUCKER
SAVAGE HONOR
TRAILBLAZERS
THAI PIRATES (CTF)
WOUNDED KNEE THE DAY THE SUN DIED (CTF)

DUANE CLARK
SHAKING THE TREE   U.S. Film Trust, 1991, w/Steven Wilde, directed

GREYDON CLARK
ANGELS BRIGADE   Arista, 1980, w/Alvin L. Fast, directed
SKINHEADS   Amazing Movies, 1989, w/David Reskin

Screenplays:
TERROR OF MANHATTAN w/Michael J. Murray (directing)

KAREN CLARK*
Agent: Broder-Kurland-Webb-Uffner - Los Angeles, 213/656-9262

LISA   MGM/UA, 1990, w/Gary A. Sherman

RON CLARK*
Agent: David Shapira & Associates - Sherman Oaks, 818/906-0322

WALLY'S CAFE (P)
MURDER AT THE HOWARD JOHNSON'S (P) w/Sam Bobrick
NO HARD FEELINGS (P)
THE INCOMPARABLE LOULOU (P)
SILENT MOVIE   20th Century-Fox, 1976, w/Mel Brooks & Rudy DeLuca
NORMAN, IS THAT YOU?   MGM/United Artists, 1976, w/Sam Bobrick & George Schlatter, from his play w/Sam Bobrick
HIGH ANXIETY   20th Century-Fox, 1977, w/Mel Brooks, Rudy DeLuca & Barry Levinson
REVENGE OF THE PINK PANTHER   United Artists, 1978, w/Blake Edwards & Frank Waldman
THE FUNNY FARM   New World, 1983, directed
LIFE STINKS   MGM-Pathe, 1991, Story w/Mel Brooks, Rudy DeLuca & Steve Haberman

Screenplays:
BENITO w/Dom DeLuise
THE INCREDIBLE SHRINKING MAN
BUMPERS
BLOOMIES
SELLING SEASON
NOSE JOB
HARDWARE

WOODROW W. CLARK
THE HEALING FORCE   Woody Clark Productions, 1983, w/Joanne Parrent & Jay Miracle

ARTHUR C. CLARKE
Agent: Scott Meredith Agency - New York,
212/245-5500

2001: A SPACE ODYSSEY ★   MGM, 1968,
w/Stanley Kubrick

FRANK CLARKE
Agent: ICM - Los Angeles, 213/550-4000

LETTER TO BREZHNEV   Circle Releasing
Corporation, 1986
WONDERLAND   Vestron, 1989

JOHN CLARKE
LONELY HEARTS   Samuel Goldwyn Company, 1982,
w/Paul Cox

ROY CLARKE*
Contact: 01/828-3528

HAWKS   Skouras Pictures, 1989

WES CLARRIDGE*
Agent: Triad Artists, Inc. - Los Angeles, 213/556-2727

DEADLY GAME (CTF)   Osiris Productions/Wilshire
Court Productions, 1991

Screenplays:
THE AMERICA'S CUP
THE ENCHANTMENT
THE FLYING DUTCHMAN
CIRCUS ROAD
FAR CENTAURI
NIGHTS OF EDEN
WILD WEST SHOW
STORM WARNING
YEAR OF THE TIGER

JAMES CLAVELL*
Contact: Secretary - Marie Lyon, 213/474-8282

THE FLY   20th Century-Fox, 1958
WATUSI   MGM, 1959
FIVE GATES TO HELL   20th Century-Fox,
1959, directed
WALK LIKE A DRAGON   Paramount, 1960,
w/Dan Mainwaring, directed
THE GREAT ESCAPE   United Artists, 1963,
w/W.R. Burnett
633 SQUADRON   United Artists, 1964,
w/Howard Koch
THE SATAN BUG   United Artists, 1965,
w/Edward Anhalt
TO SIR, WITH LOVE   Columbia, 1967, directed
THE LAST VALLEY   Cinerama Releasing Corporation,
1971, directed

TIM CLAWSON*
Contact: 213/464-5808

THEY CALL ME BRUCE? *A FISTFUL OF CHOPSTICKS*
Artists Releasing Corporation/Film Ventures
International, 1982, w/Elliott Hong, David
Randolf & Johnny Yune

ANDREW DICE CLAY
(Andrew Clay Silverstein)
Agent: InterTalent - Los Angeles, 213/858-6200

DICE RULES (FD)   7 Arts/Carolco, 1991, Concert Material
and Story, "A Day in the Life"

THOMAS M. CLEAVER*
Agent: The Coppage Company - North Hollywood,
818/980-1106

THE TERROR WITHIN   Concorde, 1989
HEROES STAND ALONE   Concorde, 1989

Screenplays:
WELCOME HOME
BROTHERS IN ARMS
CRADLE

JOHN CLEESE
Business: Prominent Features, Ltd., 68A Delancey St.,
London NW1 7RY, England, 01/284-1004

THE RISE AND RISE OF MICHAEL RIMMER   Warner
Bros., 1970, w/Graham Chapman, Peter Cook &
Kevin Billington
RENTADICK   Rank/Paradine/Virgin, 1972,
w/Graham Chapman
AND NOW FOR SOMETHING COMPLETELY DIFFERENT
Columbia, 1972, w/Graham Chapman, Terry Gilliam,
Eric Idle, Terry Jones & Michael Palin
MONTY PYTHON AND THE HOLY GRAIL   Cinema 5, 1974,
w/Graham Chapman, Terry Gilliam, Eric Idle, Terry Jones
& Michael Palin
MONTY PYTHON'S LIFE OF BRIAN   Orion/Warner Bros.,
1979, w/Graham Chapman, Terry Gilliam, Eric Idle,
Terry Jones & Michael Palin
MONTY PYTHON LIVE AT THE HOLLYWOOD BOWL
Columbia, 1982, w/Graham Chapman, Terry Gilliam,
Eric Idle, Terry Jones & Michael Palin
MONTY PYTHON'S THE MEANING OF LIFE   Universal,
1983, w/Graham Chapman, Terry Gilliam, Eric Idle,
Terry Jones & Michael Palin
A FISH CALLED WANDA ★   MGM/UA, 1988

TOM CLEGG
Contact: British Academy of Film & Television Arts,
195 Piccadilly, London W1, England, 01/734-0022

McVICAR   Crown International, 1981,
w/JohnMcVicar, directed

BRIAN H. CLEMENS*
Agent: Paul Kohner, Inc. - Los Angeles, 213/550-1060

THE DEPRAVED   Danzigers, 1957
AN HONOURABLE MURDER   Danziger, 1959,
w/Eldon Howard
THE TELL-TALE HEART   1963
STATION SIX - SAHARA   Allied Artists, 1963,
w/Bryan Forbes
THE CORRUPT ONES *THE PEKING MEDALLION*
Warner Bros., 1967
AND SOON THE DARKNESS   Levitt-Pickman, 1971,
w/Terry Nation
SEE NO EVIL   Columbia, 1971
DR. JEKYLL AND SISTER HYDE   Hammer, 1971

Cl

FILM
WRITERS
GUIDE

F
I
L
M

W
R
I
T
E
R
S

CAPTAIN KRONOS, VAMPIRE HUNTER   Hammer/
   Paramount, 1973, directed
THE GOLDEN VOYAGE OF SINBAD   Columbia, 1973,
   w/Ray Harryhausen
THE WATCHER IN THE WOODS   Buena Vista, 1980,
   w/Harry Spalding & Rosemary Anne Sisson

SAM CLEMENS
SLIPSTREAM   Entertainment Film, 1989, Story

DICK CLEMENT*
Agent: Broder-Kurland-Webb-Uffner - Los Angeles,
   213/656-9262

THE JOKERS   Universal, 1967, w/Ian LaFrenais
HANNIBAL BROOKS   United Artists, 1968,
   w/Ian LaFrenais
OTLEY   Columbia, 1969, w/Ian LaFrenais, directed
CATCH ME A SPY   Rank, 1971, w/Ian
   LaFrenais, directed
VILLAIN   EMI, 1971, w/Ian LaFrenais
THE LIKELY LADS   EMI, 1976, w/Ian LaFrenais
PORRIDGE   ITC, 1979, w/Ian LaFrenais, directed
THE PRISONER OF ZENDA   Universal, 1979,
   w/Ian LaFrenais
WATER   Atlantic Releasing Corporation, 1984,
   w/Ian LaFrenais & Bill Persky, directed
VICE VERSA   Columbia, 1988, w/Ian LaFrenais
THE COMMITMENTS   20th Century-Fox, 1991,
   w/Ian LaFrenais & Roddy Doyle

RENE CLEMENT
Contact: French Film Office, 745 Fifth Avenue,
   New York, NY 10151, 212/832-8860

LA BATAILLE DU RAIL   CGCF, 1945, directed
LES MAUDITS (THE DAMNED)   Speva Film, 1947,
   w/Henri Jeanson & Jacques Remy, directed
LOVERS, HAPPY LOVERS!   KNAVE OF HEARTS
   20th Century-Fox, 1954, w/Hugh Mills, directed
JOY HOUSE   THE LOVE CAGE   MGM, 1964,
   w/Pascal Jardin & Charles Williams, directed

DULANY ROSS CLEMENTS
DANGER ZONE II: REAPER'S REVENGE   Skouras
   Pictures, 1989

RON CLEMENTS
Business: Walt Disney Productions, 818/560-1000

THE GREAT MOUSE DETECTIVE (AF)   Buena Vista,
   1989, w/others, co-directed
THE LITTLE MERMAID (AF)   Buena Vista, 1989,
   w/John Musker, co-directed

JAKE CLESI
BURIED ALIVE   21st Century Film Corporation, 1990,
   w/Stuart Lee

GRAEME CLIFFORD
Agent: CAA - Beverly Hills, 213/288-4545

Screenplays:
FLASHER'S MAGIC

EDWARD CLINTON
HONKY TONK FREEWAY   Universal/AFD, 1981

ROBERT CLOUSE
Agent: ICM - Los Angeles, 213/550-4000

THE ULTIMATE WARRIOR   Warner Bros., 1975, directed
THE AMSTERDAM KILL   Columbia, 1978, w/Gregor
   Teifer, directed
THE PACK   Warner Bros., 1977, directed
THE BIG BRAWL   Warner Bros., 1980, directed
FORCE: FIVE   American Cinema, 1981, (based on
   screenplay by Emil Farkas & George Goldsmith), directed

CHRISTOPHER J. CLUESS*
Agent: Broder-Kurland-Webb-Uffner - Los Angeles,
   213/656-9262

Screenplays:
STARWRECK w/Stuart Kreisman
THE LAST HIGH SCHOOL MOVIE w/Stuart Kreisman

RAPHAEL CLUZEL
LIGHT YEARS   Miramax, 1988, w/Blaine Novak

LEWIS COATES
(Luigi Cozzi)
Address: via Cassia 834, pal.F, Rome, Italy, 06/366-8116

STARCRASH   New World, 1979, w/Patrick
   Wachsberger, directed
HERCULES   MGM/UA/Cannon, 1983, directed
THE BLACK CAT   21st Century Film Corp, 1990, directed

JAY COCKS*
Agent: CAA - Beverly Hills, 213/288-4545

Screenplays:
AGE OF INNOCENCE w/Martin Scorsese
AMERICAN REVOLUTION
GANGS OF NEW YORK

WAYNE COE
GRIM PRAIRIE TALES   East/West Film Partners Prods.,
   1990, directed

ETHAN COEN
Agent: United Talent Agency - Beverly Hills, 213/273-6700

CRIMEWAVE   Columbia, 1985, w/Joel Coen & Sam Raimi
BLOOD SIMPLE   Circle Films, 1986, w/Joel Coen
RAISING ARIZONA   20th Century Fox, 1987, w/Joel Coen
MILLER'S CROSSING   20th Century Fox, 1990,
   w/Joel Coen
BARTON FINK   20th Century Fox, 1991, w/Joel Coen

JOEL COEN
Agent: United Talent Agency - Beverly Hills, 213/273-6700

CRIMEWAVE   Columbia, 1985, w/Ethan Coen &
   Sam Raimi
BLOOD SIMPLE   Circle Films, 1986, w/Ethan
   Coen, directed
RAISING ARIZONA   20th Century Fox, 1987, w/Ethan
   Coen, directed
MILLER'S CROSSING   20th Century Fox, 1990, w/Ethan
   Coen, directed
BARTON FINK   20th Century Fox, 1991, w/Ethan
   Coen, directed

CHARLIE COFFEY*
Contact: WGA - Los Angeles, 213/550-1000

EARTH GIRLS ARE EASY   Vestron, 1988, w/Julie Brown
& Terrence E. McNally

MARTIN P. COHAN*
Agent: Robinson, Weintraub, Gross & Associates -
Los Angeles, 213/653-5802

HUMANOIDS FROM THE DEEP   New World, 1980,
Story w/Frank Arnold

BARNEY COHEN
FRIDAY THE 13TH, PART IV: THE FINAL CHAPTER
Paramount, 1984
KILLER PARTY   MGM/UA, 1986

BENNETT COHEN*
Agent: ICM - Los Angeles, 213/550-4000

RAINBOW DRIVE (CTF)   Viacom-Dove-ITC, 1990,
w/Bill Philips

CHARLES ZEV COHEN*
Agent: Triad Artists, Inc. - Los Angeles,
213/556-2727

LADY BEWARE   Scotti Bros., 1987, w/Susan Miller
EDDIE AND THE CRUISERS II: EDDIE LIVES
Scotti Bros., 1989, w/Rick Doehring

Screenplays:
PENKNIFE

CHARLIE COHEN
ERNEST GOES TO JAIL   Buena Vista, 1990

DAVID COHEN*
Contact: WGA - Los Angeles, 213/550-1000

FRIDAY THE 13TH - A NEW BEGINNING   Paramount,
1985, w/Martin Kitrosser & Danny Steinmann
HOLLYWOOD ZAP   Troma, 1986, directed

DAVID AARON COHEN*
Agent: Shorr, Stille & Associates - Los Angeles,
213/659-6160

POINT OF VIEW   Contrast Ltd., 1990
V.I. WARSHAWSKI   Buena Vista, 1991, w/Edward
Taylor & Nick Thiel

Screenplays:
GO DOWN MOSES
BLOOD BROTHERS

HOWARD R. COHEN
SATURDAY THE 14TH   New World, 1981, directed
SPACE RAIDERS   New World, 1983, directed
STRYKER   New World, 1983
DEATHSTALKER   New World, 1984
RAINBOW BRITE AND THE STAR STEALER (AF)
Warner Bros., 1985
DEATHSTALKER II: THE WARRIORS FROM HELL
Concorde, 1988
LORDS OF THE DEEP   Concorde, 1989, w/Daryl Haney

SATURDAY THE 14TH STRIKES BACK   Concorde,
1990, directed
SPACE CASE   Lunar Bynne Limited Productions,
1990, directed

JOEL COHEN*
Contact: 213/876-8663

SISTER, SISTER   New World, 1988, w/Ginny Cerrella &
Bill Condon
PASS THE AMMO   New Century/Vista, 1988,
w/Neil Cohen

KATHY COHEN*
Agent: CAA - Beverly Hills, 213/288-4545

Screenplays:
THE GOSSIP COLULMNIST
SKIRTS AND ZIPPERS
THE RED FERRARI

LARRY COHEN*
Agent: Robert Littman Company - Beverly Hills,
213/278-1572

THE RETURN OF THE SEVEN   United Artists, 1966
DADDY'S GONE A HUNTING   Warner Bros., 1969,
w/Lorenzo Semple Jr.
EL CONDOR   National General, 1970,
w/Steven W. Carabatsos
HELL UP IN HARLEM   American International,
1973, directed
IT'S ALIVE   Warner Bros., 1974, directed
DEMON   GOD TOLD ME TO   New World,
1977, directed
IT LIVES AGAIN   Warner Bros., 1978, directed
THE PRIVATE FILES OF J. EDGAR HOOVER   American
International, 1978, directed
THE AMERICAN SUCCESS CO.   SUCCESS   Columbia,
1979, w/William Richert
FULL MOON HIGH   Filmways, 1981, directed
I, THE JURY   20th Century-Fox, 1982
Q   United Film Distribution, 1982, directed
SCANDALOUS   Orion, 1984, Story w/John Byrum &
Rob Cohen
SPECIAL EFFECTS   New Line Cinema, 1985, directed
PERFECT STRANGERS   New Line Cinema,
1985, directed
THE STUFF   New World, 1985, directed
RETURN TO SALEM'S LOT   Warner Bros., 1987,
w/James Dixon, directed
IT'S ALIVE III: ISLAND OF THE ALIVE   Warner Bros.,
1987, directed
BEST SELLER   Orion, 1987
MANIAC COP   Shapiro/Glickenhaus, 1988
DEADLY ILLUSION   CineTel Films, 1988, directed
WICKED STEPMOTHER   MGM/UA, 1989, directed
INTO THIN AIR   Triumph, 1990
MANIAC COP 2   The Movie House, 1990
THE AMBULANCE   Triumph, 1990, directed

Screenplays:
FEVER OF THE HUNT w/Peter Lenkov
BEST FRIEND
SO HELP ME GOD
CANDIDATE FOR OBLIVION
THE MAN WHO LOVED HITCHCOCK (directing)

Co

FILM WRITERS GUIDE

LAWRENCE D. COHEN*
Agent: William Morris Agency - Beverly Hills, 213/274-7451

CARRIE   United Artists, 1976, play followed
GHOST STORY   Universal, 1981

Screenplays:
A WOMAN OF INDEPENDENT MEANS
MOTHER AND TWO DAUGHTERS
SHARP PRACTICE

LAWRENCE J. COHEN*
Agent: CAA - Beverly Hills, 213/288-4545

START THE REVOLUTION WITHOUT ME   Warner Bros., 1970, w/Fred Freeman
S*P*Y*S   20th Century-Fox, 1974, w/Fred Freeman & Malcolm Marmorstein
THE BIG BUS   Paramount, 1976, w/Fred Freeman
DELIRIOUS   MGM-Pathe, 1991, w/Fred Freeman

Screenplays:
JACK THE BEAR
THE PSYCHIATRIST & THE THIEF   w/Fred Freeman
KARISTAN   w/Fred Freeman

NEIL COHEN*
Agent: William Morris Agency - Beverly Hills, 213/274-7451

PASS THE AMMO   New Century/Vista, 1988, w/Joel Cohen
RICH BOYS   International Film Marketing, 1990, co-directed

Screenplays:
THE FLYING PELICAN
DESPERATE

ROB COHEN*
Business: Badham-Cohen Group, Universal Studios, 818/777-3477

SCANDALOUS   Orion, 1984, w/John Byrum, directed

Screenplays:
THE RECOVERY   w/John Byrum

RONALD M. COHEN*
Agent: The Coppage Company - North Hollywood, 818/980-1106

BLUE   Paramount, 1968, w/Meade Roberts
THE GOOD GUYS AND THE BAD GUYS   Warner Bros., 1969, w/Dennis Shryack
TWILIGHT'S LAST GLEAMING   Allied Artists, 1977, w/Edward Heubsch

HARLEY COKLISS
WARLORDS OF THE 21ST CENTURY   New World, 1982, w/Irviing Austin & John Beech

BRANDON COLE
Agent: The Gersh Agency - Beverly Hills, 213/274-6611

SONS   Pacific Pictures, 1989, w/Alexandre Rockwell

S. MICHAEL COLE
Agent: Warden & White Associates - Beverly Hills, 213/852-1028

Screenplays:
THE PRIOR LIFE OF MICKEY SLATER   w/Jean Ford
IMMACULATE DECEPTION   w/Jean Ford

TOM COLE*
Agent: Harris & Goldberg - Los Angeles, 213/553-5200

MEDAL OF HONOR RAG (P)
ABOUT TIME (P)
THE EIGHTIES (P)
SMOOTH TALK   Spectrafilm, 1985
STREETS OF GOLD   20th Century Fox, 1986, w/Heywood Gould & Richard Price

Screenplays:
CASTLES IN THE AIR

DAVID COLEMAN
Agent: Circle Talent Associates - Beverly Hills, 213/285-1585

ENDLESS DESCENT   DEG, 1989

Screenplays:
HAT TRICK
SNAKE PIT
THE OVERLORD

RUSSELL W. COLGIN
YOUNG WARRIORS   Cannon, 1986, w/Lawrence D. Foldes

LEWIS A. COLICK*
Agent: CAA - Beverly Hills, 213/288-4545

THE DIRT BIKE KID   Concorde/Cinema Group, 1985, w/David Brandes

Screenplays:
UNLAWFUL ENTRY
RADIANT CITY
THE PLUMBER

MICHAEL COLLEARY*
Agent: The Agency - Los Angeles, 213/551-3000

Screenplays:
FACE-OFF   w/Mike Werb
ARCHANGELS

ROBERT COLLECTOR*
Agent: William Morris Agency - Beverly Hills, 213/274-7451

Screenplays:
MEMOIRS OF AN INVISIBLE MAN   w/Dana Olsen
THE VULGARIANS   w/Dana Olsen
MEN ON BASE   w/Dana Olsen
GOLD LUST   w/Dana Olsen
YOUR WISH IS MY COMMAND   w/Dana Olsen

JOHN COLLEE
PAPER MASK   Film Four International, 1991

RONALD COLLIER
CLOSE SHAVE   Tobann International, 1981,
   w/Robert Hendrickson

A.M. COLLINS*
Agent: Irvin Arthur Associates - Beverly Hills,
   213/278-5934

ANGRY HOUSEWIVES (P), also screenplay

Screenplays:
DO IT FOR THE MONEY

JACKIE COLLINS
Agent: Irving Paul Lazar Agency - Beverly Hills,
   213/275-6153

THE STUD   Trans American, 1978
THE WORLD IS FULL OF MARRIED MEN   New
   Realm, 1979
YESTERDAY'S HERO   EMI, 1979

ROBERT COLLINS*
Agent: United Talent Agency - Beverly Hills,
   213/273-6700

SAVAGE HARVEST   20th Century-Fox, 1981,
   w/Robert Blees, directed

ARTHUR COLLIS*
Agent: H.N. Swanson, Inc. - Los Angeles, 213/652-5385

BLUE DESERT   Neo Motion Pictures, 1991,
   w/Bradley Battersby

JENNIFER COLLOPY*
Agent: William Morris Agency - Beverly Hills,
   213/274-7451

Screenplays:
ONE SUMMER, A MIRACLE
PRIVATE WARS
DOUBLE TIME
THE MEASURING WALL
A FEW GOOD WOMEN
LEPRECHAUN

HARRY COLOMBY*
Agent: CAA - Beverly Hills, 213/288-4545

JOHNNY DANGEROUSLY   20th Century Fox, 1987,
   w/Jeff Harris, Bernie Kukoff & Norman Steinberg
TOUCH AND GO   Tri-Star, 1987, w/Alan Ormsby &
   Bob Sand

CARL COLPAERT
DELUSION   I.R.S. Releasing, 1991,
   w/Kurt Voss, directed

CHRIS COLUMBUS*
Agent: CAA - Beverly Hills, 213/288-4545

RECKLESS   MGM/UA, 1984
GREMLINS   Warner Bros., 1984
THE GOONIES   Warner Bros., 1985
YOUNG SHERLOCK HOLMES   Paramount, 1985
HEARTBREAK HOTEL   Buena Vista, 1988, directed

ONLY THE LONELY   20th Century Fox, 1991, directed
LITTLE NEMO (AF)   Hemdale, 1992, w/Richard Outten

Screenplays:
WARPED ARROWS
I THINK I'M GOING TO LIKE IT HERE
STIFFS

BETTY COMDEN*
Agent: ICM - Los Angeles, 213/550-4000

THE BARKLEYS OF BROADWAY   MGM, 1949,
   w/Adolph Green
ON THE TOWN   MGM, 1949, w/Adolph Green
SINGIN' IN THE RAIN   MGM, 1952, w/Adolph Green
THE BAND WAGON ★   MGM, 1953, w/Adolph Green
IT'S ALWAYS FAIR WEATHER ★   MGM, 1955,
   w/Adolph Green
AUNTIE MAME   Warner Bros., 1958, w/Adolph Green
BELLS ARE RINGING   MGM, 1960, w/Adolph Green,
   from their play
WHAT A WAY TO GO   20th Century-Fox, 1963,
   w/Adolph Green

ROBERT J. COMFORT*
Agent: Harris & Goldberg - Los Angeles, 213/553-5200

DOGFIGHT   Warner Bros., 1991

Screenplays:
SPIDER w/Rick Kellard
NICE GIRLS w/Rick Kellard
TOM WEST w/Rick Kellard
GREEN SKY
VINCE AND AL GO TO WAR

LIZ COMICI*
Agent: Shapiro/Lichtman - Los Angeles, 213/859-8877

Screenplays:
LITTLE NAPOLEON w/Lou Comici
THE VISITOR w/Lou Comici
THE CHINESE MURDERS w/Lou Comici
RIVALS w/Lou Comici
NIGHTFALL w/Lou Comici
BLUE w/Lou Comici

LOU COMICI*
Agent: Shapiro/Lichtman - Los Angeles, 213/859-8877

Screenplays:
LITTLE NAPOLEON w/Liz Comici
THE VISITOR w/Liz Comici
THE CHINESE MURDERS w/Liz Comici
RIVALS w/Liz Comici
NIGHTFALL w/Liz Comici
BLUE w/Liz Comici

RICHARD COMPTON
RETURN TO MACON COUNTY   American International,
   1975, directed

RICHARD CONDON*
Agent: Harold Matson Company - New York,
   212/679-4490

PRIZZI'S HONOR ★   20th Century Fox, 1985,
   w/Janet Roach

Co

FILM WRITERS GUIDE

WILLIAM CONDON*
Agent: CAA - Beverly Hills, 213/288-4545

STRANGE BEHAVIOR *DEAD KIDS* World Northal, 1981, w/Michael Laughlin
STRANGE INVADERS Orion, 1983, w/Michael Laughlin
SISTER, SISTER New World, 1988, w/Ginny Cerrella & Joel Cohen, directed
MURDER 101 (CTF) Alan Barnette/MCA Television, 1991, w/Roy Johansen
F/X 2: THE DEADLY ART OF ILLUSION Orion, 1991

Screenplays:
THIRTEENTH DUKE w/Richard Manning
THE KID IN THE GREY FEDORA
BLOOD SECRETS
LAST KISS

CHRIS CONKLING
THE LORD OF THE RINGS (AF) United Artists, 1978, w/Peter S. Beagle

SHANE CONNAUGHTON
Agent: William Morris Agency - Beverly Hills, 213/274-7451

THE DOLLAR BOTTOM Paramount, 1981
MY LEFT FOOT ★ Miramax, 1989, w/Jim Sheridan

Screenplays:
THE PLAYBOYS w/Kerry Crabbe

JON CONNOLLY*
Agent: CAA - Beverly Hills, 213/288-4545

THE DREAM TEAM Universal, 1989, w/David Loucka

Screenplays:
SINGLE AGAIN w/David Loucka
AUGIE

RAY CONNOLLY*
Contact: WGA - Los Angeles, 213/550-1000

THAT'LL BE THE DAY EMI, 1973
STARDUST EMI, 1974
FOREVER YOUNG Cinecom, 1986

Screenplays:
WORKING CLASS HERO
TRICK OR TREAT

PHILLIP D. CONNORS
EVILS OF THE NIGHT Shapiro Entertainment, 1985, w/Mardi Rustam

PAT CONROY*
Agent: CAA - Beverly Hills, 213/288-4545

Screenplays:
THE PRINCE OF TIDES w/Becky Johnston
EX w/Doug Marlette
ATLANTA BURNING

ROBERT CONTE*
Agent: Barrett, Benson, McCartt & Weston - Los Angeles, 213/247-5500

ODD JOBS Tri-Star, 1986, w/Peter Martin Wortmann
WHO'S HARRY CRUMB? Tri-Star, 1988, w/Peter Martin Wortmann

Screenplays:
DAYTIME w/Peter Martin Wortmann
FUGITIVE GUYS w/Peter Martin Wortmann
THE GREAT PRETENDER w/Peter Martin Wortmann

GARY CONWAY*
Contact: WGA - Los Angeles, 213/550-1000

AMERICAN NINJA 2 Cannon, 1987, w/James Booth
OVER THE TOP Cannon, 1987, Story w/David Engelbach
AMERICAN NINJA 3: BLOOD HUNT Cannon, 1989, Story

GERALD F. CONWAY*
Agent: Maggie Field Agency - Studio City, 818/980-2001

FIRE AND ICE (AF) 20th Century-Fox, 1983, w/Roy Thomas
CONAN THE DESTROYER Universal, 1984, Story w/Roy Thomas

JAMES L. CONWAY*
Agent: CAA - Beverly Hills, 213/288-4545

HANGAR #18 Sunn Classic, 1980, Story w/Tom Chapman, directed
THE PRESIDENT MUST DIE Jensen Farley Pictures, 1981, w/Cliff Osmond, directed

TIM CONWAY*
Business Manager: Michael N. Cobin - Los Angeles, 213/461-3344

THEY WENT THAT-A-WAY & THAT-A-WAY International Picture Show, 1978
THE PRIZE FIGHTER New World, 1979, w/John Myhers
THE PRIVATE EYES New World, 1980, w/John Myhers
THE LONGSHOT Orion, 1986

DAVID COOK
WALTER AND JUNE *LOVING WALTER* Film Forum, 1986

DOUGLAS S. COOK*
Agent: Sanford, Skouras, Gross & Associates - Los Angeles, 213/208-2100

PAYOFF (CTF) Viacom, 1991, w/David Weisberg

PETER COOK
BEDAZZLED 20th Century Fox, 1967
THE RISE AND RISE OF MICHAEL RIMMER Warner Bros., 1970, w/Graham Chapman, John Cleese & Kevin Billington
THE HOUND OF THE BASKERVILLES Atlantic Releasing Corporation, 1979, w/Dudley Moore & Paul Morrissey
YELLOWBEARD Orion, 1983, w/Graham Chapman & Bernard McKenna

T. S. COOK*
(Thomas S. Cook)
Agent: Triad Artists, Inc. - Los Angeles, 213/556-2727

THE CHINA SYNDROME ★ Columbia, 1979,
    w/Michael Gray & James Bridges
NIGHTBREAKER (CTF) Turner Network
    Television, 1989

JON COOKSEY
Agent: The Wright Concept - Hollywood, 213/461-3844

Screenplays:
TIL MARRIAGE DO US PART w/Ali Matheson
HIT PARADE w/Ali Matheson
MISS MARLOW w/Ali Matheson

BARRY MICHAEL COOPER*
Agent: William Morris Agency - New York,
    212/586-5100

WRITING ON THE WALL (P), also screenplay
NEW JACK CITY Warner Bros., 1991, w/Thomas
    Lee Wright

Screenplays:
ABOVE THE RIM

MATT COOPER*
Agent: William Morris Agency - Beverly Hills,
    213/274-7451

Screenplays:
A VIEW FROM THE TOP

NATALIE COOPER*
Agent: Sanford, Skouras, Gross & Associates -
    Los Angeles, 213/208-2100

DESERT HEARTS Samuel Goldwyn Company, 1986

Screenplays:
WHITE MAN'S BURDEN
OHIO SHUFFLE
YOUNG LILLY

SUSAN COOPER*
Agent: ICM - New York, 212/556-5600

Screenplays:
DINNER AT THE HOMESICK RESTAURANT
    w/Hume Cronyn

JEFF COPELAND
TALES OF THE UNKNOWN AIP Home Video, 1990,
    "Warped," w/Roger Nygard

MARTIN COPELAND*
Agent: William Morris Agency - Beverly Hills,
    213/274-7451

THE HEAVENLY KID Orion, 1985, w/Cary Medoway

Screenplays:
TOO DEEP FOR TEARS
BEST RIDE FROM NEW YORK

FRANCIS FORD COPPOLA
Agent: CAA - Beverly Hills, 213/288-4545
Business: Zoetrope Studioes, Sentinal Building, 916 Kearny
    Street, San Francisco, CA 94133, 415/789-7500

TONIGHT FOR SURE Premier Pictures, 1961, directed
DEMENTIA 13 American International, 1963, directed
THIS PROPERTY IS CONDEMNED Paramount, 1966,
    w/Fred Coe & Edith Sommer
IS PARIS BURNING? Paramount, 1966, w/Gore Vidal
YOU'RE A BIG BOY NOW 7 Arts, 1966, directed
THE RAIN PEOPLE Warner Bros., 1969, directed
PATTON ★★ 20th Century-Fox, 1970,
    w/Edmund H. North
THE GODFATHER ★ Paramount, 1972, w/Mario
    Puzo, directed
THE CONVERSATION ★ Paramount, 1974, directed
THE GODFATHER, PART II ★★ Paramount, 1974,
    w/Mario Puzo, directed
THE GREAT GATSBY Paramount, 1974
APOCALYPSE NOW ★ United Artists, 1979,
    w/John Milius, directed
ONE FROM THE HEART Columbia, 1982, w/Armyan
    Bernstein, directed
RUMBLE FISH Universal, 1983, w/S.E. Hinton, directed
THE COTTON CLUB Orion, 1984, w/William
    Kennedy, directed
NEW YORK STORIES Buena Vista, 1989, "LifeWithout
    Zoe," w/Sofia Coppola, directed
THE GODFATHER, PART III Paramount, 1990, w/Mario
    Puzo, directed

ROMAN COPPOLA
THE SPIRIT OF '76 Columbia, 1990, Story
    w/Lucas Reiner

SOFIA COPPOLA
NEW YORK STORIES Buena Vista, 1989, "LifeWithout
    Zoe," w/Francis Ford Coppola

BILL CORBETT
Agent: Susan Smith & Associates - Beverly Hills,
    213/852-4777

DOWN THE PIKE (P)
AIRPORT ANGLE (P)
MOTORCADE (P)
WINGED FEET (P)

Screenplays:
THE REPTILE
DONNY QUICK

SERGIO CORBUCCI
Address: via Donatello 15, Rome, Italy, 06/360-7610

SUPER FUZZ Avco Embassy, 1981, w/Sabataino
    Ciuffini, directed

NICK COREA*
Agent: David Shapira & Associates - Sherman Oaks,
    818/906-0322

Screenplays:
R & R
LANEPLAY

Co

JOHN CORK*
Agent: United Talent Agency - Beverly Hills, 213/273-6700

THE LONG WALK HOME   Miramax, 1990

Screenplays:
THE FUNERAL

ROGER CORMAN
Business: Concorde Pictures, 11600 San Vicente Blvd., Los Angeles, CA 90049, 213/826-0978

FRANKENSTEIN UNBOUND   20th Century Fox, 1990, w/F.X. Feeney, directed

JOHN CORNELL
Contact: Australian Film Commission, 9229 Sunset Blvd., Los Angeles, CA 90069, 213/275-7074

"CROCODILE" DUNDEE ★   Paramount, 1986, w/Paul Hogan & Ken Shadie, directed

EUGENE CORR*
Agent: CAA - Beverly Hills, 213/288-4545

WILDROSE   Troma, 1984, w/John Hanson
DESERT BLOOM   Columbia, 1986, directed

AXEL CORTI
Contact: Directors Guild of Austria, Museumstrasse 5/17, A-1070, Vienna, Austria, 0222/938380

THE KING'S WHORE   J&M Entertainment, 1990, w/Frederic Raphael & Daniel Vigne, directed

MICHAEL CORY
LOOSE SCREWS   Concorde, 1985

CHRISTOPHER COSBY*
Contact: 213/839-7209

BLOODSPORT   Cannon, 1988, w/Mel Friedman & Sheldon Lettich

DON COSCARELLI*
Agent: The Agency - Los Angeles, 213/551-3000
Business: Starway International, 8033 Sunset Blvd., Suite 405, Los Angeles, CA 90046, 213/650-6995

PHANTASM   Avco Embassy, 1979, directed
THE BEASTMASTER   MGM/UA, 1982, w/Paul Pepperman, directed
PHANTASM II   Universal, 1988, directed
SURVIVAL QUEST   MGM/UA, 1990, directed

GEORGE PAN COSMATOS
Agent: ICM - Los Angeles, 213/550-4000

THE CASSANDRA CROSSING   Avco Embassy, 1977, w/Robert Katz & Tom Mankiewicz, directed

JAMES COSTIGAN*
Agent: ICM - Los Angeles, 213/550-4000

KING DAVID   Paramount, 1985, w/Andrew Birkin
MR. NORTH   Samuel Goldwyn Company, 1988, w/John Huston & Janet Roach

LANNY COTLER
Agent: Jim Preminger Agency - Los Angeles, 213/475-9491

THE EARTHLING   Filmways, 1981

MANNY COTO*
Agent: Triad Artists, Inc. - Los Angeles, 213/277-5656

Screenplays:
THE TICKING MAN w/Brian Helgeland

JOHN COTTER
CHEETAH   Buena Vista, 1989, w/Griff DuRhone & Erik Tarloff

ALLEN COULTER
Agent: Warden & White Associates - Beverly Hills, 213/852-1028

Screenplays:
TRUE HEARTS

BILL D. COUTURIÉ*
Agent: CAA - Beverly Hills, 213/288-4545

TWICE UPON A TIME (AF)   The Ladd Company/Warner Bros., 1983, w/Suella Kennedy, John Korty & Charles Swenson
DEAR AMERICA: LETTERS FROM VIETNAM (FD)   Taurus Entertainment, 1987, w/Richard Dewhurst, directed

Screenplays:
SPACE BROTHER w/Richard Dewhurst

GIL COWAN
Agent: ICM - Los Angeles, 213/550-1000

OPPOSING FORCES   Orion, 1987

RONALD COWEN*
Agent: William Morris Agency - Beverly Hills, 213/274-7451

Screenplays:
FIREFLY w/Daniel Lipman
FAMILY DANCING w/Daniel Lipman

ALEX COX
Agent: Stephanie Mann Agency - Los Angeles, 213/653-7130

REPO MAN   Universal, 1984, directed
SID & NANCY   Samuel Goldwyn Company, 1986, w/Abbe Wool, directed
STRAIGHT TO HELL   Island Films, 1987, w/Dick Rude, directed

BRIAN COX
Business: Distant Horizon, 52 Crescent Ave., St. George, Staten Island, NY 10301, 718/816-6732

DEADLY OBSESSION   Distant Horizon, 1989, w/Jeno Hodi & Paul Wolansky

JAMES D. COX*
Agent: United Talent Agency - Beverly Hills, 213/273-6700

RITZVILLE (Short), directed
EAT THE SUN (Short), directed
NEPTUNE (Short), directed

OLIVER & CO. (AF)   Buena Vista, 1988, w/Timothy J.
   Disney & James Mangold
THE RESCUERS DOWN UNDER (AF)   Buena Vista,
   1990, w/Karvey Kirkpatrick, Joe Ranft &
   Byron Simpson

Screenplays:
FERNGULLY: THE LAST RAINFOREST (AF)
BEAUTY AND THE BEAST (AF)
GOOD DOG CARL
HOCUS POCUS

PAUL COX
Agent: S.T.E. Representation - Beverly Hills,
   213/550-3982 or Cameron's Management -
   Australia, 02/358/6433

LONELY HEARTS   Samuel Goldwyn Company, 1982,
   w/John Clarke, directed
MAN OF FLOWERS   Spectrafilm, 1983,
   w/Bob Ellis, directed
MY FIRST WIFE   Spectrafilm, 1984, w/Bob
   Ellis, directed
CACTUS   Spectrafilm, 1986, w/Bob Ellis & Norman
   Kaye, directed
GOLDEN BRAID   Australian Film Commission/Film
   Victoria/Ilumination Films, 1990, w/Barry
   Dickins, directed

KERRY CRABBE
MEMOIRS OF A SURVIVOR   EMI, 1981,
   w/David Gladwell

Screenplays:
THE PLAYBOYS w/Shane Connaughton

PETER CRABBE*
Agent: William Morris Agency - Beverly Hills,
   213/274-7451

Screenplays:
SHORE LEAVE
HOME FOR THE HOLIDAYS
HOME BY MIDNIGHT

H.A.L. CRAIG
WATERLOO   Columbia, 1970, w/Sergie Bondarchuk
LION OF THE DESERT   United Film Distribution, 1981

LAURIE CRAIG*
Agent: ICM - Los Angeles, 213/550-4000

MODERN GIRLS   Atlantic Releasing Corporation, 1986

Screenplays:
BAKED ALASKA

WES CRAVEN*
Agent: ICM - Los Angeles, 213/550-4000
Business: Wes Craven Films, 8271 Melrose Ave.,
   Los Angeles, CA 90046, 213/550-4000

THE HILLS HAVE EYES   Vanguard, 1977, directed
DEADLY BLESSING   United Artists/Polygram, 1981,
   w/Glenn M. Benest & Matthew Barr
SWAMP THING   Embassy, 1982
A NIGHTMARE ON ELM STREET   New Line Cinema,
   1984, directed
THE HILLS HAVE EYES II   Castle Hill Productions,
   1985, directed
A NIGHTMARE ON ELM STREET PART 3:
DREAM WARRIORS   New Line Cinema, 1987, w/Bruce
   Wagner, Frank Darabont & Chuck Russell
SHOCKER   Universal, 1989, directed

Screenplays:
THE PEOPLE UNDER THE STAIRS

BOBBY CRAWFORD*
Agent: Richland/Wunsch/Hohman Agency - Los Angeles,
   213/278-1955

A RAGE IN HARLEM   Miramax, 1991, w/John Toles-Bey

JOANNA CRAWFORD*
Agent: Robinson, Weintraub, Gross & Associates -
   Los Angeles, 213/653-5802

THE LITTLE ARK   Cinema Center, 1971
BIRCH INTERVAL   Gamma III, 1976

NANCY VOYLES CRAWFORD*
Contact: WGA - Los Angeles, 213/550-1000

SIDEWINDER 1   Avco Embassy, 1977,
   w/Thomas McMahon
CARAVANS   Universal, 1979, w/Thomas A. McMahon &
   Lorraine Williams

WAYNE CRAWFORD*
Business: Gibraltar Entertainment, 14101 Valleyheart Dr.,
   #205, Sherman Oaks, CA, 91423, 818/501-2076

VALLEY GIRL   Atlantic Releasing Corporation, 1983,
   w/Andrew Lane
JAKE SPEED   New World, 1986, w/Andrew Lane

JAMES CRESSON*
(James Hicks)
Agent: William Morris Agency - Beverly Hills, 213/274-7451

THE MORNING AFTER   20th Century Fox, 1986
CHATAHOOCHEE   Hemdale, 1990

Screenplays:
DEFENSELESS
WIT'S END

CHARLES CRICHTON
Agent: MLR Representation Ltd., 200 Fulham Road,
   London SW10, England

FLOODS OF FEAR   Rank, 1958, directed
THE BOY WHO STOLE A MILLION   Paramount, 1960,
   w/John Eldridge, directed
A FISH CALLED WANDA ★   MGM/UA, 1988, Story
   w/John Cleese, directed

MICHAEL CRICHTON*
Agent: CAA - Beverly Hills, 213/288-4545

EXTREME CLOSEUP   National General, 1973
WESTWORLD   MGM, 1973, directed
COMA   MGM/UA, 1978, directed
THE GREAT TRAIN ROBBERY   United Artists,
   1979, directed
LOOKER   The Ladd Company/Warner Bros., 1981, directed
RUNAWAY   Tri-Star, 1984, directed

Cr

FILM WRITERS GUIDE

FRANK CRISTINA
TERESA CRISTINA
(See Tom Laughlin)

MICHAEL CRISTOFER*
Agent: CAA - Beverly Hills, 213/288-4545

SHADOW BOX (P), also teleplay
LADY AND THE CLARINET (P)
BLACK ANGEL (P)
FALLING IN LOVE   Paramount, 1984
THE WITCHES OF EASTWICK   Warner Bros., 1987
THE BONFIRE OF THE VANITIES   Warner Bros., 1990

Screenplays:
JURASSIC PARK
CC PYLE & THE BUNION DERBY
MODIGLIANI
THE LADY & THE CLARINET
THE GREAT AMERICAN BELLY DANCE
GENTLE VENGENCE
THE MAIN
VANITIES
SILENCE
TRINITY

KEITH CRITCHLOW
VOLUNTEERS   Tri-Star, 1985, Story

DAVID CRONENBERG
Agent: CAA - Beverly Hills, 213/288-4545
Business: 217 Avenue Road, Toronto, Ontario M5R 2J3, Canada, 415/961-3432

STEREO   Emergent Films, 1969, directed
CRIMES OF THE FUTURE   Emergent Films, 1970, directed
THEY CAME FROM WITHIN SHIVERS   Trans-America, 1976, directed
RABID   New World, 1977, directed
FAST COMPANY   Topar, 1979, w/Phil Savath & Courtney Smith, directed
THE BROOD   New World, 1979, directed
SCANNERS   Avco Embassy, 1981, directed
VIDEODROME   Universal, 1983, directed
THE FLY   20th Century Fox, 1986, w/CharlesEdward Pogue, directed
DEAD RINGERS   20th Century Fox, 1988, w/Norman Snider, directed
NAKED LUNCH   20th Century Fox, 1991, directed

KAREN CRONER*
Agent: William Morris Agency - Beverly Hills, 213/274-7451

GAS, FOOD, LODGING (Short), directed

Screenplays:
DUE EAST
DEXTERITY

ISAAC CRONIN
CHAN IS MISSING   New Yorker, 1982, w/Wayne Wang & Terrel Seltzer

HUME CRONYN
Agent: ICM - New York, 212/556-5600

Screenplays:
DINNER AT THE HOMESICK RESTAURANT w/Susan Cooper

ALISON CROSS*
Agent: CAA - Beverly Hills, 213/288-4545

Screenplays:
SPECIAL CIRCUMSTANCES
PALM BEACH
SAIGON
TWO ARE GUILTY

ANDREW CROSS
SHOCK 'EM DEAD   Academy Entertainment, 1991, w/Mark Freed

BEVERLY CROSS
THE LONG SHIPS   Columbia, 1963, w/Berkely Mather
JASON AND THE ARGONAUTS   Columbia, 1963, w/Jan Read
GENGIS KHAN   Columbia, 1964, w/Clarke Reynolds
HALF A SIXPENCE   Paramount, 1967
SINBAD AND THE EYE OF THE TIGER   Columbia, 1977
CLASH OF THE TITANS   United Artists, 1981

AVERY CROUNSE
Business: Elysian Pictures, 650 N. Bronson Ave. - Suite 215, Los Angeles, CA 90004, 213/871-8689

EYES OF FIRE   Aquarius Films, 1986, directed
THE INVISIBLE KID   Taurus Entertainment, 1988, directed

BILL CROUNSE
9 1/2 NINJAS   Republic Pictures, 1991, w/Don Pequignot

CAMERON CROWE*
Agent: CAA - Beverly Hills, 213/288-4545

FAST TIMES AT RIDGEMONT HIGH   Universal, 1982
THE WILD LIFE   Universal, 1984
SAY ANYTHING   20th Century Fox, 1989, directed
SINGLES   Warner Bros., 1991, directed

CHRISTOPHER CROWE*
Agent: United Talent Agency - Beverly Hills, 213/273-6700

THE LAST CHASE   Crown International, 1981, as "C.R. O'Cristopher," w/Martyn Burke & Taylor Sutherland
NIGHTMARES   Universal, 1983, w/Jeffrey Bloom
THE MEAN SEASON   Orion, 1985, as "Leon Piedmont"
OFF LIMITS   20th Century Fox, 1988, w/Jack Thibeau, directed

Screenplays:
THE LAST OF THE MOHICANS w/Michael Mann
SESSIONS (directing)
AC/DC
GOODNIGHT MOON

MART CROWLEY*
Agent: ICM - Los Angeles, 213/550-4000

A BREEZE FROM THE GULF (P)
REMOTE ASYLUM (P)
THE BOYS IN THE BAND   National General, 1970, from his play

JOHN CROWTHER
KILL AND KILL AGAIN   Film Ventures International, 1981
THE EVIL THAT MEN DO   Tri-Star, 1984, w/David Lee Henry
MISSING IN ACTION   Cannon, 1984, Story w/Lance Hool
THE WILD PAIR   Trans World Entertainment, 1987, Story w/Joseph Gunn
DAMNED RIVER   MGM/UA, 1990, w/Bayard Johnson

JIM CRUICKSHANK*
Agent: CAA - Beverly Hills, 213/288-4545

BREAKING ALL THE RULES   New World, 1985, w/James Orr
TOUGH GUYS   Buena Vista, 1986, w/James Orr
THREE MEN AND A BABY   Buena Vista, 1987, w/James Orr
MR. DESTINY   Buena Vista, 1990, w/James Orr

Screenplays:
FUN PARK w/James Orr
BANDIT w/James Orr

TOM CRUISE
Agent: CAA - Beverly Hills, 213/288-4545

DAYS OF THUNDER   Paramount, 1990, Story w/Robert Towne

JIM CRUMLEY*
Agent: William Morris Agency - Beverly Hills, 213/274-7451

Screenplays:
THE DANCING BEAR w/Tim Hunter
THE LAST GOOD KISS
TUNNELS OF CU CHI

CATHERINE CRYAN
A CRY IN THE WILD   Concorde/New Horizons, 1990, w/Gary Paulsen
DEEP SPACE   Califilm, 1991
SLUMBER PARTY MASSACRE 3   Concorde, 1991

BILLY CRYSTAL*
Agent: ICM - Los Angeles, 213/550-4000

MEMORIES OF ME   MGM, 1988, w/Eric Roth

FRANK CUCCI
LILY IN LOVE   New Line Cinema, 1985

FRED CUL CULLEN
THE MAN FROM SNOWY RIVER   20th Century-Fox, 1983 (See John Dixon)

JOSEPHINE CUMMINGS*
Agent: Barrett, Benson, McCartt & Weston - Los Angeles, 213/247-5500

Screenplays:
ALTAR BOUND w/Richard Yalem

RAY CUNNEFF*
Agent: Shorr, Stille & Associates - Los Angeles, 213/659-6160

THE RAIN KILLER   Concorde, 1990

JERE P. CUNNINGHAM*
Agent: ICM - Los Angeles, 213/550-4000
Business: Sky Blue Productions, Inc. - 818/907-9966

THE LAST OF THE FINEST   Orion, 1990, w/George Armitage & Thomas Lee Wright

Screenplays:
CENTURION (directing)
FLAMINGO
SHIVA
BUILDERS

LAURA CUNNINGHAM*
Agent: William Morris Agency - Beverly Hills, 213/274-7451

Screenplays:
SLEEPING ARRANGEMENTS

TIM CURNEN*
Business Manager: Peter Turner, 213/315-4772

FORBIDDEN WORLD   New World, 1982
GHOST WARRIOR SWORDKILL   Empire Pictures, 1986

Screenplays:
SCALAWAGS
BEASTIES
TUNNEL IN THE SKY

LAUREN CURRIER
Contact: Eric Weismann, Esq. - Los Angeles, 213/858-7888

CUJO   Warner Bros., 1983, w/Don Carlos Dunaway

VALERIE CURTIN*
Agent: CAA - Beverly Hills, 213/288-4545

...AND JUSTICE FOR ALL ★   Columbia, 1979, w/Barry Levinson
INSIDE MOVES   AFD, 1980, w/Barry Levinson
BEST FRIENDS   Warner Bros., 1982, w/Barry Levinson
UNFAITHFULLY YOURS   20th Century-Fox, 1984, w/Barry Levinson & Robert Klane

Screenplays:
TOYS w/Barry Levinson
TWO LUCKY PEOPLE

RICHARD CURTIS
THE TALL GUY   Miramax, 1990

Cu

FILM WRITERS GUIDE

STEPHEN J. CURWICK*
Agent: The Wright Concept - Hollywood, 213/461-3844

POLICE ACADEMY 5: ASSIGNMENT MIAMI BEACH Warner Bros., 1988
POLICE ACADEMY 6: CITY UNDER SEIGE Warner Bros., 1989

Screenplays:
WHITE MAGIC

CARLTON CUSE*
Agent: CAA - Beverly Hills, 213/288-4545

Screenplays:
NATIVES
SPACE CASE

HOWARD CUSHNIR*
Agent: Shorr, Stille & Associates - Beverly Hills, 213/659-6160

Screenplays:
FLY AWAY HOME
IDIOT SAINT
NOTHING DOWN
COMING ATTRACTIONS

NEIL CUTHBERT*
Agent: William Morris Agency - New York, 212/586-5100

Screenplays:
SAUCER
PLUTO NASH
GLADIATOR OUTCASTS
SEDUCE AND DESTROY
MIRACLE ON 34TH STREET
CONNECTICUT YANKEE IN KING
    ARTHUR'S COURT

RON CUTLER*
Contact: WGA - Los Angeles, 213/550-1000

ARTICLE 99 Orion, 1991

D

JOHN DAHL*
Agent: United Talent Agency - Beverly Hills, 213/273-6700

PRIVATE INVESTIGATIONS MGM/UA, 1987, w/David Warfield
KILL ME AGAIN MGM/UA, 1990, w/David Warfield, directed

Screenplays:
RED ROCK WEST (Shared) (directing)

BOB DAHLIN
Contact: Directors Guild of America - Los Angeles, 213/289-2000

MONSTER IN THE CLOSET Troma, 1987, directed

ROBERT DALEY
Agent: Sterling Lord Literistic - New York, 212/696-2800

Screenplays:
THE INFORMANT w/Ken Friedman

WALTER DALLENBACH*
Agent: The Irv Schechter Company - Beverly Hills, 213/278-8070

LAS VEGAS LADY Crown International, 1986

DEBORAH DALTON*
Agent: ICM - Los Angeles, 213/550-4000

WHORE Tri-Mark Pictures, 1991, w/Ken Russell

WALTER (WALLY) DALTON*
Contact: WGA - Los Angeles, 213/550-1000

Screenplays:
DOYLE TO DOYLE

GERRY DALY
BLACK MAGIC WOMAN Trimark Pictures, 1991

APRIL DAMMANN
Agent: The Wright Concept - Hollywood, 213/461-3844

ROSE & KATZ (Short)

Screenplays:
UNDER WRAPS
THE COLORS OF CHRISTMAS

BARBARA DANA*
Agent: Rosenstone/Wender - New York, 212/832-8330

CHU CHU AND THE PHILLY FLASH 20th Century-Fox, 1981

BILL DANA*
Contact: WGA - Los Angeles, 213/550-1000

THE NUDE BOMB   Universal, 1980, w/Arne Sultan & Leonard B. Stern

LAWRENCE DANE
Address: P.O. Box 310, Station F, Toronto MHY 2L7, Canada, 416/923-6000

HEAVENLY BODIES   MGM/UA, 1985, w/Ron Base, directed

LOGAN N. DANFORTH
Agent: ICM - Los Angeles, 213/550-4000

CROSS-COUNTRY   New World, 1983, w/William Gray

RODNEY DANGERFIELD*
Business: Paper Clip Productions, 213/282-2754

EASY MONEY   Orion, 1983, w/Dennis Blair, Michael Endler & P.J. O'Rourke
BACK TO SCHOOL   Orion, 1986, Story w/Greg Fields & Dennis Snee
ROVER DANGERFIELD (AF)   Warner Bros., 1991

JOHN R. DANIELS
GETTING OVER   Continental Films, 1981, Story w/Bernie Rollins

STAN DANIELS*
Agent: APA - Los Angeles, 213/273-0744

THE LONELY GUY   Universal, 1984, w/Ed. Weinberger
GLORY! GLORY! (CMS)   Atlantis Films Ltd./Orion TV, 1989
GETTING THERE (CTF)   HBO, 1991

MARIA DANTE
SPACE MUTINY   Action International Pictures, 1989

RICHARD CHRISTIAN DANUS*
Agent: APA - Los Angeles, 213/273-0744

XANADU   Universal, 1980, w/Marc Rubel

FRANK DARABONT*
Agent: United Talent Agency - Beverly Hills, 213/273-6700

A NIGHTMARE ON ELM STREET PART 3: DREAM WARRIORS   New Line Cinema, 1987, w/Chuck Russell, Wes Craven & Bruce Wagner
THE BLOB   Tri-Star, 1988, w/Chuck Russell
THE FLY II   20th Century Fox, 1989, w/Mick Garris, Jim Wheat & Ken Wheat

Screenplays:
THE WOMAN IN THE ROOM *(directing)*
STRANGERS IN LEADVILLE *(Shared)*
COMMANDO II
A STITCH IN TIME
INFINITY CUBE *(Shared)*

JULIE DASH
DAUGHTERS OF THE DUST   Geechee Girls Productions/American Playhouse, 1991, directed

DAVID DASHEV
Agent: The Gersh Agency - Beverly Hills, 213/274-6611
Contact: 213/688-9055

SMOKEY AND THE BANDIT PART 3   Universal, 1983, w/Stuart Birnbaum
THE ZOO GANG   Warner Bros., 1985, Story w/Stuart Birnbaum, Pen Densham & John Watson
SUMMER SCHOOL   Paramount, 1987, Story w/Stuart Birnbaum & Jeff Franklin

Screenplays:
THE SILVER CROSS w/Stuart Birnbaum
CHAMPAGNE FOR CAESAR   CHANCE OF A LIFETIME w/Stuart Birnbaum
SOME OF MY BEST FRIENDS w/Stuart Birnbaum

JULES DASSIN
Business Manager: Leon Kaplan, Mitchell, Silberberg & Knapp, 11377 W. Olympic Blvd., Los Angeles, CA 90064, 213/312-3187

HE WHO MUST DIE   1957, w/Ben Barzman, directed
WHERE THE HOT WIND BLOWS   LA LOI   MGM, 1958, w/Diego Fabbri, directed
NEVER ON SUNDAY ★   Lopert, 1960, directed
PHAEDRA   United Artists, 1961, directed
10:30 P.M. SUMMER   United Artists, 1966, w/Marguerite Duras, directed
UPTIGHT   Paramount, 1968, w/Ruby Dee & Julian Mayfield, directed
PROMISE AT DAWN   Avco Embassy, 1970, directed
A DREAM OF PASSION   Avco Embassy, 1978, directed

LARRY DAVID*
Agent: United Talent Agency - Beverly Hills, 213/273-6700

Screenplays:
PROGNOSIS NEGATIVE
TWO BITS

MARJORIE S. DAVID*
Agent: Triad Artists, Inc. - Los Angeles, 213/556-2727

MARIA'S LOVERS   Cannon, 1984, w/Gerard Brach, Andrei Konchalovsky & Paul Zindel
SHY PEOPLE   Cannon, 1987, w/Gerard Brach & Andrei Konchalovsky

PAUL DAVIDS*
Agent: CAA - Beverly Hills, 213/288-4545

SHE DANCES ALONE   Continental, 1982

ARLENE DAVIDSON*
Agent: The Strick Agency - Los Angeles, 213/273-0919

EDDIE AND THE CRUISERS   Embassy, 1983, w/Martin Davidson

BOAZ DAVIDSON
Contact: Directors Guild of America - Los Angeles, 213/289-2000

IT'S A FUNNY, FUNNY WORLD   Noah Films, 1978, w/Zvi Shissel
LEMON POPSICLE   Noah Films, 1981, w/Eli Tabor, directed
THE LAST AMERICAN VIRGIN   Cannon, 1982, directed
HOT RESORT   Cannon, 1985, w/John Robins & Norman Hudis
SALSA   Cannon, 1988, w/Tomas Benitez & Shepard Goldman, directed
YOUNG COMMANDOS   Cannon, 1991, w/Greg Latter

MARTIN DAVIDSON*
Agent: Harris & Goldberg - Los Angeles, 213/553-5200

IF EVER I SEE YOU AGAIN   Columbia, 1978, w/Joseph Brooks
ALMOST SUMMER   Universal, 1978, w/Judith Berg & Sandra Berg, directed
EDDIE AND THE CRUISERS   Embassy, 1983, w/Arlene Davidson, directed

ANDREW DAVIES
Agent: London Management - London, 011/441/493-1610

CONSUMING PASSIONS   Samuel Goldwyn Company, 1988, w/Paul D. Zimmerman
A PRIVATE LIFE   Totem Productions, 1989

Screenplays:
FOREIGN LANGUAGES

JACK DAVIES*
Agent: Shapiro/Lichtman - Los Angeles, 213/859-8877

CONVICT 99   Gainsborough, 1938, w/Marriott Edgar, Val Guest & Ralph Smart
LAUGHTER IN PARADISE   ABPC, 1951, w/Michael Pertwee
CURTAIN UP   Rank, 1952, w/Michael Pertwee
MR. POTTS GOES TO MOSCOW   TOP SECRET ABP, 1952, w/Michael Pertwee
HAPPY EVER AFTER   TONIGHT'S THE NIGHT   ABP, 1954, w/Michael Pertwee & L.A.F. Strong
JUMPING FOR JOY   Rank, 1955, w/Henry E. Blyth
AN ALLIGATOR NAMED DAISY   Rank, 1955
DOCTOR AT SEA   Rank, 1955, w/Nicholas Phipps
UP IN THE WORLD   Rank, 1956, w/Peter Blackmore & Henry Blyth
TRUE AS A TURTLE   Rank, 1956, w/John Coates & Nicholas Phipps
THE SQUARE PEG   Rank, 1958
DON'T PANIC, CHAPS!   Hammer, 1959
FOLLOW A STAR   Rank, 1959, w/Henry Blyth & Norman Wisdom
THE BULLDOG BREED   Rank, 1960, w/Henry Blyth & Norman Wisdom
A COMING OUT PARTY   VERY IMPORTANT PERSON   Rank, 1961
NEARLY A NASTY ACCIDENT   British Lion, 1961, w/Hugh Woodruff
ON THE BEAT   Rank, 1962
THE FAST LADY   Rank, 1962, w/Henry Blyth
CROOKS ANONYMOUS   Anglo Amalgamated, 1962, w/Henry Blyth
FATHER CAME TOO   Rank, 1963, w/Henry Blyth
A STITCH IN TIME   Rank, 1963
THE EARLY BIRD   Rank, 1965, w/Henry Blyth, Eddie Leslie & Norman Wisdom
THOSE MAGNIFICENT MEN IN THEIR FLYING MACHINES ★   20th Century-Fox, 1965, w/Ken Annakin
DOCTOR IN CLOVER   Rank, 1966
GAMBIT   Universal, 1966, w/Alvin Sargent
THE CAVERN   20th Century-Fox, 1966, w/Michael Pertwee
THOSE DARING YOUNG MEN IN THEIR JAUNTY JALOPIES   Paramount, 1969, w/Ken Annakin
DOCTOR IN TROUBLE   Rank, 1970
PAPER TIGER   Joseph E. Levine Presents, 1976
ffolkes   Universal, 1980

RAY DAVIES
Contact: British Academy of Film & Television Arts, 195 Picadilly, London W1, England, 01/734-0022

RETURN TO WATERLOO   New Line Cinema, 1985, directed

TERENCE DAVIES
Contact: British Academy of Film & Television Arts, 195 Picadilly, London W1, England, 01/734-0022

DISTANT VOICES, STILL LIVES   Alive Films, 1989, directed

Screenplays:
THE LONG DAY CLOSES (directing)

WILLIAM J. DAVIES*
Agent: United Talent Agency - Beverly Hills, 213/273-6700

TWINS   Universal, 1988, w/William Osborne, Timothy Harris & Herschel Weingrod

Screenplays:
THE REAL McCOY w/William Osborne
FOREIGN EXCHANGE w/William Osborne
PRITCHARD COUNTY w/William Osborne
EARTHQUAKE w/William Osborne
MAMA GOT A HANDGUN IN HER BAG w/William Osborne

ALMER JOHN DAVIS
UNDER THE GUN   Marquis Pictures, 1989, w/James Devney & James Sbardellati

ANDREW DAVIS*
Agent: The Agency - Los Angeles, 213/551-3000

STONY ISLAND   World Northal, 1980, w/Tamar Hoffs, directed
ABOVE THE LAW   Warner Bros., 1988, w/Steven Pressfield & Ronald Shusett, directed

ANDY DAVIS
BEAT STREET   Orion, 1984, w/David Gilbert & Paul Golding

BART DAVIS
Agent: William Morris Agency - Beverly Hills, 213/274-7451

IMPULSE   20th Century-Fox, 1984, w/Don Carlos Dunaway
LOVE OR MONEY   Hemdale, 1990, w/ElyseEngland & Michael Zausner

FULL FATHOM FIVE   Concorde, 1990

Screenplays:
ERNEST SAVES CAMELOT w/Michael Zausner

BILL C. DAVIS
DANCING IN THE END ZONE (P)
MASS APPEAL   Universal, 1984, from his play

CARLOS DAVIS
DROP DEAD, FRED   New Line Cinema, 1991,
   w/Anthony Fingleton

CHARLES DAVIS
THUNDER RUN   Cannon, 1986, w/Carol Heyer

DESMOND DAVIS
Agent: Shapiro/Lichtman - Los Angeles, 213/859-8877

AN INSPECTOR CALLS   British Lion, 1954
THE UNCLE   Play-Pix, 1964, w/Margaret
   Abrams, directed
TIME LOST AND TIME REMEMBERED   I WAS HAPPY
   HERE   Continental, 1966, w/Edna O'Brien

GERRY DAVIS*
Agent: David Shapira & Associates - Sherman Oaks,
   818/906-0322

THE FINAL COUNTDOWN   United Artists, 1980,
   w/David Ambrose, Thomas Hunter & Peter Powell

Screenplays:
THE INVISIBLE LIGHT

GREG DAVIS
Agent: United Talent Agency - Beverly Hills, 213/273-6700

Screenplays:
US AND THEM w/Larry Garcia
HARRY SCARRY WANTS TO MARRY w/Larry Garcia
WIND IN THE WILLOWS w/Larry Garcia

IAN DAVIS
THE HUNGER   MGM/UA, 1983, w/Michael Thomas

JEFFERSON DAVIS
THE TICKET OUTTA HERE   Black & White Pictures,
   1990, co-directed

JOEL DAVIS*
Agent: Sheri Mann Agency - Los Angeles, 213/655-6266

Screenplays:
REIGN OF TERROR
CROSSING THE LINE
ONE BY ONE
DIVERSIONS
IT TOOK FIRST PRIZE IN HOUSTON w/Winston A. Howlett

NORTHROP DAVIS*
Agent: ICM - Los Angeles, 213/550-4000

THE BUS (Short), directed
THE WELDER (Short), directed

Screenplays:
MADLANDS

OSSIE DAVIS
Agent: The Artists Agency - Los Angeles,
   213/277-7779

COTTON COMES TO HARLEM   United Artists, 1970,
   w/Arnold Perl, directed

PETER S. DAVIS
Agent: ICM - New York, 212/556-5600
Business: Davis-Panzer Productions, 1438 N. Gower St.,
   Suite 573, Los Angeles, CA 90028, 213/463-2343

STEEL   LOOK DOWN AND DIE   World Northal, 1980,
   Story w/Rob Ewing & William N. Panzer

ROBERT P. DAVIS*
Contact: WGA - New York, 212/245-6180

THE PILOT   Summit Featuers, 1981

TOM DAVIS*
Contact: WGA - Los Angeles, 213/550-1000

ONE MORE SATURDAY NIGHT   Columbia, 1986,
   w/Al Franken

Screenplays:
SIRENS OF TITAN

WALTER HALSEY DAVIS*
Agent: InterTalent - Los Angeles, 213/271-0600

PANHANDLE (P)
TILDEN (P)
THE TAPIOCA MISANTHROPA (P)
SEVEN HOURS TO JUDGMENT   Trans World
   Entertainment, 1988, w/Steven E. DeSouza

ZACH DAVIS
LIQUID DREAMS   Fox/Elwes Corp., 1991,
   w/Mark Manos

ANNABEL DAVIS-GOFF*
Agent: William Morris Agency - Beverly Hills,
   213/274-7451

Screenplays:
NIGHT TENNIS
WOMEN IN JEOPARDY
AS THE WORM TURNS

ANTHONY M. DAWSON
Address: via Appia Antica 184, Rome Italy, 06/782-2367

YOR, THE HUNTER FROM THE FUTURE   Columbia,
   1983, w/Robert Bailey, directed

GERRY DAY
THE BLACK HOLE   Buena Vista, 1979,
   w/Jeb Rosebrook

JONATHAN DAY*
Agent: William Morris Agency - New York, 212/586-5100

Screenplays:
BIG PINK
FOURTH OF JULY

De

FILM WRITERS GUIDE

WILLIAM DEAR*
Agent: InterTalent - Los Angeles, 213/858-6200

THE NORTHVILLE CEMETARY MASSACRE   Cannon, 1976, w/Thomas C. Dyke, co-directed
TIMERIDER   Jensen Farley Pictures, 1983, w/Michael Nesmith, directed
HARRY AND THE HENDERSONS   Universal, 1987, w/William E. Martin & Ezra D. Rappaport, directed
THE ROCKETEER   Buena Vista, 1991, Story w/Danny Bilson & Paul De Meo

Screenplays:
HOME FOR THE HOLIDAYS

JAMES DEARDEN*
Agent: ICM - Los Angeles, 213/550-4000

FATAL ATTRACTION ★   Paramount, 1987, from his teleplay "Diversion"
PASCALI'S ISLAND   Avenue Pictures, 1988, directed
A KISS BEFORE DYING   Universal, 1991, directed

Screenplays:
RANSOM
PHANTOM
MADNESS OF A SEDUCED WOMAN
THE RINGER
SCARAMOUCHE

JOHN DeBELLO
ATTACK OF THE KILLER TOMATOES   1980, directed
HAPPY HOUR   TMS Pictures, 1987, w/Constantine Dillon & J. Stephen Peace, directed
RETURN OF THE KILLER TOMATOES   New World, 1988, directed

ALLEN N. DeBEVOISE
Agent: Triad Artists, Inc. - Los Angeles, 213/556-2727

BREAKIN'   MGM/UA/Cannon, 1984, w/Charles Parker & Gerald Scarfe

PHILLIPE DE BROCA
Contact: French Film Office, 745 Fifth Ave., New York, NY 10151, 212/832-8860

CARTOUCHE   Embassy, 1962, directed
THAT MAN FROM RIO ★   Lopert, 1964, w/others, directed
DEAR DETECTIVE   DEAR INSPECTOR   Cinema 5, 1978, w/Michael Audiard, directed

DENISE DeCLUE*
Agent: CAA - Beverly Hills, 213/288-4545

GRIMM (P)
ABOUT LAST NIGHT   Tri-Star, 1986, w/Tim Kazurinsky
FOR KEEPS   Tri-Star, 1988, w/Tim Kazurinsky

Screenplays:
ABOUT LAST NIGHT 2   w/Tim Kazurinsky
BIG SUCCESS   w/Tim Kazurinsky
WEEKEND WARRIORS

EDWARD DECTER*
Agent: United Talent Agency - Beverly Hills, 213/273-6700

OPTIONS   Vestron, 1989, w/John J. Strauss

Screenplays:
FOREVER MURRAY   w/John J. Strauss
YARD WARS   w/John J. Strauss
THERE'S SOMETHING ABOUT MARY   w/John J. Strauss
LAST CHANCE TO DANCE BEFORE THE FREEWAY
AIRWAVES   w/Paul Reiser

FRANK DEESE*
Agent: William Morris Agency - Beverly Hills, 213/274-7451

THE PRINCIPAL   Tri-Star, 1987

Screenplays:
UNDER THE ROCK PILE
LICENSED TO DRIVE
COMPANY MAN
KILLER SAM

CHRIS DeFARIA*
Agent: The Roberts Company - Los Angeles, 213/552-7800

Screenplays:
COMING ATTRACTIONS
SLAYER
AMITYVILLE 6

J. GREG DeFELICE
OUT OF THE DARK   CineTel Films, 1989, w/Zane W. Levitt

JAMES DeFELICE
WHY SHOOT THE TEACHER?   Quartet, 1977

FRANK DE FELITTA*
Contact: WGA - Los Angeles, 213/550-1000

ZPG   Paramount, 1972, w/Max Ehrlich
AUDREY ROSE   United Artists, 1977
THE ENTITY   20th Century-Fox, 1983
SCISSORS   Vidmark, 1991, directed

RAYMOND DeFELITTA
Agent: CAA - Beverly Hills, 213/288-4545

BRONX CHEERS (Short) ★   1990, directed

Screenplays:
BEGIN THE BEGUINE
THE FABULOUS NOBODIES
CAN'T GET ARRESTED
THE WAR OF CHRISTMAS

FRANK DEFORD*
Agent: Sterling Lord Agency - New York, 212/751-2533

TRADING HEARTS   New Century/Vista, 1988

Screenplays:
PEERS

MICHAEL DeGUZMAN*
Agent: Broder-Kurland-Webb-Uffner - Los Angeles, 213/656-9262

JAWS THE REVENGE   Universal, 1987

STEVE DeJARNATT*
Agent: United Talent Agency - Beverly Hills, 213/273-6700

TARZANA (Short), 1979, directed
STRANGE BREW   MGM/UA, 1983, w/Rick Moranis & Dave Thomas
MIRACLE MILE   Hemdale, 1988, directed

Screenplays:
FUTUREBALL
INSOMNIA
HAIR OF THE DOG

COLMAN DeKAY*
Agent: Broder-Kurland-Webb-Uffner - Los Angeles, 213/656-9262

BLOODHOUNDS OF BROADWAY   Columbia, 1989, w/Howard Brookner

FRED DEKKER*
Agent: InterTalent - Los Angeles, 213/858-6200

HOUSE   New World, 1986, Story
NIGHT OF THE CREEPS   Tri-Star, 1986, directed
THE MONSTER SQUAD   Tri-Star, 1987, w/Shane Black, directed
IF LOOKS COULD KILL   Warner Bros., 1991, Story

Screenplays:
ROBOCOP 3 w/Frank Miller (directing)
THE FOREVER FACTOR
GODZILLA

JOHN DeKLEIN
THE CARE BEARS ADVENTURE IN WONDERLAND (AF)   Cineplex Odeon, 1987, w/Susan Snooks
BABAR: THE MOVIE (AF)   New Line Cinema, 1989, w/Alan Bunce, Raymond Jeffelice, Peter Sauder & Peter Sauder

SHELAGH DELANEY
Agent: Pleshette & Green - Los Angeles, 213/465-0428

A TASTE OF HONEY   Continental, 1962, w/Tony Richardson
CHARLIE BUBBLES   Universal, 1968
DANCE WITH A STRANGER   Samuel Goldwyn Company, 1985

Screenplays:
WIDE SARGASSO SEA
THE RAILWAY STATION MAN

ROBERT De LAURENTIS*
Agent: Barrett, Benson, McCartt & Weston - Los Angeles, 213/247-5500

GREEN ICE   ITC, 1981, w/others
A LITTLE SEX   Universal, 1982

Screenplays:
BLACK TIE

KINGDOM OF DREAMS
TEENAGE GHOST STORY

MARCUS DeLEON
KISS ME A KILLER   Califilm, 1991, w/Christopher Wooden, directed

SEAN DELGADO
ALEXA   Platinum Pictures, 1989, w/Peggy Bruen, directed

FRANCIS DELIA*
Agent: Camden-ITG - Los Angeles, 213/289-2700

FREEWAY   New World, 1988, w/Darrell Fetty

WANDA DELL
Business: Dell Films, 1905 Powers Ferry Rd., Suite 260, Atlanta, GA, 30067, 404/955-6924

MARVIN AND TIGE   LIKE FATHER AND SON   20th Century-Fox International Classics, 1983, w/Eric Weston

JEFFREY DELMAN
VOODOO DAWN   Academy Entertainment, 1990, w/Evan Dunsky, Thomas Rendon & John Russo

PETER DeL MONTE
Address: via Poerio 59/D, Rome, Italy, 06/585451

JULIA AND JULIA   Cinecom, 1987, w/Silvia Napolitano & Sandra Petraglia, directed

LAUREL DELP
Agent: Susan Smith & Associates - Beverly Hills, 213/852-4777

Screenplays:
LUNETTA PARK
HEATWAVE
ONE LOOK

RUDY DeLUCA*
Agent: The Gersh Agency - Beverly Hills, 213/274-6611

SILENT MOVIE   20th Century-Fox, 1976, w/Mel Brooks, Ron Clark & Barry Levinson
HIGH ANXIETY   20th Century-Fox, 1977, w/Mel Brooks, Ron Clark & Barry Levinson
CAVEMAN   United Artists, 1981, w/Carl Gottlieb
TRANSYLVANIA 6-5000   New World, 1985, directed
MILLION DOLLAR MYSTERY   DEG, 1987, w/Tim Metcalfe & Miguel Tejada-Flores
LIFE STINKS   MGM-Pathe, 1991, w/Mel Brooks & Steve Haberman

Screenplays:
LAND OF THE NICE

ROBERT DeMAIO*
Agent: Sanford, Skouras, Gross & Associates - Los Angeles, 213/208-2100

Screenplays:
ANNA OF THE SUBWAY
BEWITCHED, BOTHERED AND BEWILDERED

De

FILM WRITERS GUIDE

JOHN DeMARCO*
Agent: The Agency - Los Angeles, 213/551-3000

IMPULSE   Warner Bros., 1990, w/Leigh Chapman

RICHARD DEMBO
Contact: Swiss Film Center, Munstergasse 18, 8001 Zurich, Switzerland, 01/472860

DANGEROUS MOVES   Arthur Cohn Productions, 1984, directed

PAUL De MEO*
Agent: United Talent Agency - Beverly Hills, 213/273-6700

FUTURE COP   TRANCERS   Empire Pictures, 1985, w/Danny Bilson
ZONE TROOPERS   Empire Pictures, 1986, w/Danny Bilson
ELIMINATORS   Empire Pictures, 1986, w/Danny Bilson
THE WRONG GUYS   New World, 1988, w/Danny Bilson
ARENA   Empire Pictures, 1988, w/Danny Bilson
PULSEPOUNDERS   Empire Pictures, 1988, w/Danny Bilson
THE ROCKETEER   Buena Vista, 1991, w/Danny Bilson

PAUL De MIELCHE*
Agent: The Artists Agency - Los Angeles, 213/277-7779

AMERICAN NINJA   Cannon, 1985

JONATHAN DEMME*
Agent: CAA - Beverly Hills, 213/288-4545

ANGELS HARD AS THEY COME   New World, 1971, w/Joe Viola
THE HOT BOX   1972, w/Joe Viola
BLACK MAMA, WHITE MAMA   1972, w/others
CAGED HEAT   New World, 1974, directed
FIGHTING MAD   20th Century-Fox, 1976, directed

KEN DENBOW
DECEPTIONS (CTF)   Republic Pictures, 1990, Story

SUSANNAH DeNIMES
SURVIVAL GAME   Trans World Entertainment, 1987, w/Herb Freed & P.W. Swann

CLAIRE DENIS
Contact: French Film Office, 745 Fifth Avenue, New York, NY 10151, 212/832-8860

CHOCOLAT   Orion Classics, 1989, w/Jean-Pol Fargeau, directed

CHARLES DENNIS*
Agent: Preferred Artists - Encino, 818/990-0305

DOUBLE NEGATIVE   Best Film and Video, 1980, w/Janis Allen & Thomas Hedley, Jr.
FINDERS KEEPERS   Warner Bros., 1984, w/Ronny Graham & Terence Marsh
COVERGIRL   New World, 1984

Screenplays:
THE BEARD
RENO AND THE DOC (CTF)

PEN DENSHAM*
Agent: ICM - Los Angeles, 213/550-4000
Business: Trilogy Entertainment Group, 1875 Century Park East - Suite 500, Los Angeles, CA 90067, 213/785-3855

THE ZOO GANG   New World, 1985, w/John Watson, co-directed
ROBIN HOOD: PRINCE OF THIEVES   Warner Bros., 1991, w/John Watson

Screenplays:
BLIND LUCK   w/John Watson
FLYING TIGERS   w/John Watson
ACCELERATOR

BRIAN De PALMA
Agent: United Talent Agency - Beverly Hills, 213/273-6700

GREETINGS   Sigman III, 1968, w/Charles S. Hirsch, directed
THE WEDDING PARTY   Powell Productions Plus/Ondine, 1969, directed
HI, MOM!   Sigma III, 1970, directed
SISTERS   American International, 1973, w/Louise Rose, directed
PHANTOM OF THE PARADISE   20th Century-Fox, 1974, directed
HOME MOVIES   United Artists Classics, 1980, w/others, directed
DRESSED TO KILL   Filmways, 1980, directed
BLOW OUT   Filmways, 1981, directed
BODY DOUBLE   Columbia, 1984, w/Robert J. Avrech, directed

Screenplays:
THE DEMOLISHED MAN   w/Oliver Stone
TREASURE

SUZANNE De PASSE
Business: Gordy/De Passe Productions, 5750 Wilshire Blvd. - Suite 610, Los Angeles, CA 90036, 213/965-2580

LADY SINGS THE BLUES ★   Paramount, 1972, w/Chris Clark & Terence McCloy

JOHN DEREK
Contact: Directors Guild of America - Los Angeles, 213/289-2000

FANTASIES   AND ONCE UPON A LOVE   Joseph Brenner Associates, 1981, directed
BOLERO   Cannon, 1984, directed
GHOSTS CAN'T DO IT   Triumph, 1990, directed

EVERETT DeROCHE
THE LONG WEEKEND   1978
PATRICK   Cinema Shares International, 1979
THE DAY AFTER HALLOWEEN   SNAPSHOT   Group 1, 1979, w/Chris DeRoche
HARLEQUIN   Greater Union Film Distributors, 1980
ROAD GAMES   Avco Embassy, 1981
TREASURE OF THE YANKEE ZEPHYR   RACE TO THE YANKEE ZEPHYR   Artists Releasing Corporation/Film Ventures International, 1984
RAZORBACK   Warner Bros., 1985
THE QUEST   Miramax, 1986
LINK   Thorn-EMI, 1986
WINDRIDER   MGM/UA, 1987, w/Bonnie Harris

Screenplays:
FROG
NAKED UNDER CAPRICORN

CLYDE DERRICK
Agent: Susan Smith & Associates - Beverly Hills, 213/852-4777

Screenplays:
AFTERLIFE
THIS SPY'S IN LOVE WITH YOU

DOMINIQUE DeRUDDERE
Contact: National Tourist Office, 61 Rue de Marche Aux Herbs, B1000 Brussels, Belgium, 02/513-8940

LOVE IS A DOG FROM HELL   Cineplex Odeon, 1987, w/Marc Didden, directed
WAIT UNTIL SPRING, BANDINI   Orion Classics, 1990, directed

TOM DeSIMONE*
Agent: APA - Los Angeles, 213/273-0744

REFORM SCHOOL GIRLS   New World, 1986, directed
ANGEL III: THE FINAL CHAPTER   New World, 1988, directed

Screenplays:
WANTED DEAD OR ALIVE II

DICK DESMOND
Agent: ICM - Los Angeles, 213/550-4000

ENTER THE NINJA   Cannon, 1981, w/Menahem Golan & Judd Bernard

STEVEN E. DE SOUZA*
Agent: United Talent Agency - Beverly Hills, 213/273-6700

ARNOLD'S WRECKING COMPANY   Cine-Globe, 1973
48 HRS.   Paramount, 1982, w/Larry Gross, Walter Hill & Roger Spottiswoode
THE RETURN OF CAPTAIN INVINCIBLE   New World, 1983, w/Andrew Gaty
COMMANDO   20th Century Fox, 1985
THE RUNNING MAN   Tri-Star, 1987
SEVEN HOURS TO JUDGEMENT   Trans World, Entertainment, 1988, as "Elliot Stephens," w/Walter Halsey Davis
DIE HARD   20th Century Fox, 1988, w/Jeb Stuart
BAD DREAMS   20th Century Fox, 1988, w/Andrew Fleming
DIE HARD 2: DIE HARDER   20th Century Fox, 1990, w/Doug Richardson
HUDSON HAWK   Tri-Star, 1991, w/Dan Waters

Screenplays:
THIN ICE
CRITICS CHOICE
DEAD RECKONING

ANDREW DETTMAN
Agent: Triad Artists, Inc. - Los Angeles, 213/556-2727

Screenplays:
WARLORD w/Daniel Truly

ANDREW DEUTSCH
Agent: The Chasin Agency - Beverly Hills, 213/278-7505

PLATOON LEADER   Cannon, 1988, w/Rick Marx & David Walker
RIVER OF DEATH   Cannon, 1989, w/Edward Simpson

Screenplays:
ROOT RETURNS
THORNY HAWKINS
THE GLOW

DON DEVLIN
LOVING   Columbia, 1970

JAMES DEVNEY
UNDER THE GUN   Marquis Pictures, 1989, w/Almer John Davis & James Sbardellati

CHRISTOPHER DeVORE*
Agent: The Partos Co. - Los Angeles, 213/876-5500

THE ELEPHANT MAN ★   Paramount, 1980, w/Eric Bergren & David Lynch
FRANCES   Universal/AFD, 1982, w/Eric Bergren & Nicholas Kazan
HAMLET   Warner Bros., 1990, w/Franco Zefferelli

Screenplays:
A WRINKLE IN TIME w/Eric Bergren

GARY M. DeVORE*
Agent: Harris & Goldberg - Los Angeles, 213/553-5200

BACK ROADS   Warner Bros., 1981
THE DOGS OF WAR   United Artists, 1981, w/George Malko
SOLO   Dayton-Stewart Organization, 1984
RAW DEAL   DEG, 1986, w/Norman Wexler
RUNNING SCARED   MGM/UA, 1986, w/Jimmy Huston
TRAXX   DEG, 1988

Screenplays:
BLOODSHOT
HAPPY TRAILS
THE LIGHTS
HARD KNOX
THE SEARCH FOR JOSEPH TULLY

CAREY DEVUONO*
Agent: S.T.E. Representation - Beverly Hills, 213/550-3982

Screenplays:
BAKERTON TC-1
ESCAPE FROM SUMMER CAMP

RICHARD DEWHURST*
Contact: WGA - Los Angeles, 213/550-1000

DEAR AMERICA: LETTERS HOME FROM VIETNAM (FD)   Taurus Entertainment, 1987, w/Bill Couturié

Screenplays:
SPACE BROTHER w/Bill Couturié
KIXI
MOMMY DON'T

De

NICOLE De WILDE
THE RAGGEDY RAWNEY   Four Seasons Entertainment, 1990, w/Bob Hoskins

JACK DeWITT
SITTING BULL   United Artists, 1954, w/Sidney Sheldon
WOLF LARSEN   Allied Artists, 1958, w/Turnley Walker
JACK OF DIAMONDS   MGM, 1967, w/Sandy Howard
A MAN CALLED HORSE   Cinema Center, 1970
MAN IN THE WILDERNESS   Warner Bros., 1971
THE NEPTUNE FACTOR   20th Century-Fox, 1972
THE RETURN OF A MAN CALLED HORSE   United Artists, 1976
SKY RIDERS   20th Century-Fox, 1976, w/Stanley Mann & Garry Michael White
TRIUMPHS OF A MAN CALLED HORSE   Jensen Farley Pictures, 1983, w/Carlos Aured & Ken Blackwell

THOMAS DeWOLFE
MISPLACED   Original Cinema, 1991, w/Louis Vansen

PETE DEXTER*
Agent: ICM - Los Angeles, 213/550-4000

PARIS TROUT (CTF)   Showtime, 1991

Screenplays:
RUSH
DEADWOOD

JANIS DIAMOND*
Agent: Barry Perelman Agency - Los Angeles, 213/274-5999

TAGGET (CTF)   Mirisch-Tagget-MCA, 1991, w/Peter S. Fischer & Richard T. Heffron

Screenplays:
SOUND BARRIER

PAUL DIAMOND*
Agent: Robinson, Weintraub, Gross & Associates - Los Angeles, 213/653-5802

THE CHICKEN CHRONICLES   Avco Embassy, 1977

JOAN DIDION*
Agent: ICM - Los Angeles, 213/550-4000

PANIC IN NEEDLE PARK   20th Century-Fox, 1971, w/John G. Dunne
PLAY IT AS IT LAYS   Universal, 1972, w/John G. Dunne
A STAR IS BORN   Warner Bros., 1976, w/John G. Dunne & Frank R. Pierson
TRUE CONFESSIONS   United Artists, 1981, w/John G. Dunne

Screenplays:
PLAYLAND   w/John G. Dunne
KINGDOM   w/John G. Dunne
DEER PARK   w/John G. Dunne

ANTON DIETHER*
Agent: The Artists Group, Ltd. - Los Angeles, 213/552-1100

NIGHT GAMES   Avco Embassy, 1980, w/Clarke Reynolds

Screenplays:
MOSCOW EXCHANGE
THINGS THAT GO BUMP IN THE NIGHT
ROCK CITY

MICHAEL DIGAETANO*
Agent: CAA - Beverly Hills, 213/288-4545

Screenplays:
BACK TO SCHOOL II   w/Lawrence Gay
MY FAVORITE LIFE   w/Lawrence Gay
THE BIG ONES   w/Lawrence Gay
DOUBLE VISION   w/Lawrence Gay
LOOSE SHOES

ERIN DIGNAM
DENIAL   Filmstar, 1991, directed

RICHARD DiLELLO*
Agent: Robinson, Weintraub, Gross & Associates - Los Angeles, 213/653-5802

BAD BOYS   Universal/AFD, 1983
COLORS   Orion, 1988, Story w/Michael Schiffer

Screenplays:
DARK MOON RISING
ESCAPE

CONSTANTIN DILLON
HAPPY HOUR   TMS Pictures, 1987, w/John De Bello & J. Stephen Peace

ROBERT DILLON*
Agent: CAA - Beverly Hills, 213/288-4545

CITY OF FEAR   Columbia, 1958, w/Steven Ritch
X - THE MAN WITH THE X-RAY EYES   American International, 1963, w/Ray Russell
13 FRIGHTENED GIRLS   Columbia, 1963
THE OLD DARK HOUSE   Columbia, 1963
MUSCLE BEACH PARTY   American International, 1964
PRIME CUT   National General, 1972
99 AND 44/100 % DEAD   20th Century-Fox, 1974
FRENCH CONNECTION II   20th Century-Fox, 1975, w/Laurie Dillon & Alexander Jacobs
THE RIVER   Universal, 1984, w/Julian Barry
REVOLUTION   Warner Bros., 1985
THE SURVIVALIST   Lockstar Productions, 1986
FLIGHT OF THE INTRUDER   Paramount, 1991, w/David Shaber

Screenplays:
RUBY CAIRO   w/Michael Thomas
MICK   w/Eoghan Harris
NORTH STAR

EDWARD DiLORENZO
THE IDOLMAKER   United Artists, 1980

RICHARD DIMITRI*
Agent: The Daniel Ostroff Agency - Los Angeles, 213/278-2020

Screenplays:
HOTEL HAWAII
BIG TOP
PAROLE PETE

MARCIA DINNEEN*
Agent: Susan Smith & Associates - Beverly Hills, 213/852-4777

AN UNREMARKABLE LIFE   SVS, 1989

GREG DINNER
SHIPWRECKED   Buena Vista, 1991, w/Bob Foss, Nils Gaup & Nick Thiel

GERALD Di PEGO*
Contact: George Diskant, Esq. - Los Angeles, 213/824-3773

W   Cinerama Releasing Corporation, 1974, w/James Kelly
SHARKY'S MACHINE   Orion/Warner Bros., 1981
KEEPER OF THE CITY   Viacom Pictures, 1991

Screenplays:
REACH WELL WHERE YOU ARE GOING
WITH A VENGEANCE w/James Kelly
THE INSURANCE COMPANY
CISCO
ANNA LEE
THE OF
RAPTURE
SO LONG MAGGIE LOVE
ROMANCE

MARK DiSALLE
KICKBOXER   Pathe Entertainment, 1989, Story w/Jean-Claude Van Damme, directed

TIMOTHY J. DISNEY
OLIVER & CO. (AF)   Buena Vista, 1988, w/Jim Cox & James Mangold

LARRY DITILLIO*
Agent: Monteiro Rose Agency - Encino, 818/501-1177

THE SECRET OF THE SWORD (AF)   Atlantic Releasing Corporation, 1985, w/Bob Forward

JAMES DIXON*
Contact: WGA - Los Angeles, 213/550-1000

RETURN TO SALEMS LOT   Warner Bros., 1987, w/Larry Cohen

JOHN DIXON
THE MAN FROM SNOWY RIVER   20th Century-Fox, 1983 (from a screenplay by Fred Cul Cullen)
RETURN TO SNOWY RIVER   Buena Vista, 1988, w/Geoff Burrowes

LESLIE DIXON*
Agent: ICM - Los Angeles, 213/550-4000

OUTRAGEOUS FORTUNE   Buena Vista, 1987
OVERBOARD   MGM/UA, 1987
LOVERBOY   Tri-Star, 1989, w/Robin Schiff & Tom Ropelewski

Screenplays:
JUNIOR ACHIEVEMENT
A.K.A.

EDWARD DMYTRYK
Agent: Kurt Frings Agency - Beverly Hills, 213/274-8883

BLUEBEARD   Cinerama Releasing Corporation, 1972, w/Ennio di Concini & Maria Pia Fusco, directed

FRANK Q. DOBBS*
Agent: Contemporary Artists, Ltd. - Beverly Hills, 213/278-8250

UPHILL ALL THE WAY   New World, 1986, directed

LEM DOBBS*
Agent: United Talent Agency - Beverly Hills, 213/273-6700

HIDER IN THE HOUSE   Vestron, 1989
THE HARD WAY   Universal, 1991, w/Daniel Pyne

Screenplays:
KAFKA
THE MARVEL OF THE HAUNTED CASTLE
LONG GONE AND FAR AWAY
EDWARD FORD
DEVIL'S ISLAND
LIVE ROUNDS
WHITE ROSE
DOWNTOWN

JAMES J. DOCHERTY*
Agent: Barry Perelman Agency - Los Angeles, 213/274-5999

HOLLYWOOD VICE SQUAD   Concorde/Cinema Group, 1986
NIGHTSTICK   Production Distribution Co., 1987
STREET JUSTICE   Lorimar, 1989

RUDY DOCHTERMANN*
(Rudolph Carl Dochtermann)
Agent: Herman & Lewis Talent Agency - Los Angeles, 213/550-8913

THE FIENDISH PLOT OF DR. FU MANCHU   United Artists, 1980, w/Jim Moloney

E.L. DOCTOROW*
Agent: ICM - New York, 212/556-5600

DRINKS BEFORE DINNER (P)
DANIEL   Paramount, 1983

ROBERT DODSON
NAKED OBSESSION   Concorde, 1991

Do

FILM WRITERS GUIDE

RICK DOEHRING*
Agent: Preferred Artists - Encino, 818/990-0305

EDDIE AND THE CRUISERS II: EDDIE LIVES   Scotti Bros., 1989, w/Charles Zev Cohen

CHRISTOPHER DOHERTY
ROSALIE GOES SHOPPING   Four Seasons Entertainment, 1990, w/Eleonore Adlon & Percy Adlon

JAMES DOHERTY
NIGHT STICK   Production Distribution Co., 1987

BOB DOLMAN*
Agent: CAA - Beverly Hills, 213/288-4545

WILLOW   MGM/UA, 1988

Screenplays:
UNTITLED RON HOWARD PROJECT
T'S A FAIR WORLD   w/Harry Shearer
MICHAEL BYE FALLDOWN
BRIDGE TO THE MOON
THE TOUR

MARTIN DOLMAN
AFTER THE FALL OF NEW YORK   Almi Pictures, 1985, w/Julian Berry & Gabriel Rossini, directed

HENRY DOMONIC
WATCHERS II   Concorde, 1990
FLIGHT OF BLACK ANGEL (CTF)   Hess-Kallberg Productions, 1991
THE UNBORN   Califilm, 1991

ANN DONAHUE*
Contact: WGA - Los Angeles, 213/550-1000

Screenplays:
THOSE BEAUMONT GIRLS
PALER SHADE OF GREY
THE PROSPECT
THE INVITATION

ROGER DONALDSON
Agent: CAA - Beverly Hills, 213/288-4545

SMASH PALACE   Atlantic Releasing Corporation, 1981, w/Peter Hansard & Bruno Lawrence, directed

SERGIO DONATI
Contact: 06/646-1569 (Italy)

THE BIG GUNDOWN   PEA, 1966, w/Sergio Sollima
ONCE UPON A TIME IN THE WEST   Paramount, 1969, w/Sergio Leone
ORCA   Paramount, 1977, w/Luciano Vincenzoni
HOLOCAUST 2000   THE CHOSEN   Rank, 1977, w/Alberto De Martino & Michael Robson
RAW DEAL   DEG, 1986, Story w/Luciano Vincenzoni
MAN ON FIRE   Tri-Star, 1987, w/Elie Chouraqui

WALTER DONIGER*
Agent: Wile Enterprises, Inc. - Los Angeles, 213/828-9768

ROPE OF SAND   Paramount, 1949
ALONG THE GREAT DIVIDE   Warner Bros., 1950, w/Lewis Meltzer
ALASKA SEAS   Paramount, 1953, w/Geoffrey Homes
DUFFY OF SAN QUENTIN   Warner Bros., 1953, directed
HOLD BACK THE NIGHT   Universal-International, 1956, w/John C. Higgins
THE GUNS OF FORT PETTICOAT   Columbia, 1957
STONE COLD   Columbia, 1991,

RICHARD DONN*
Contact: WGA - Los Angeles, 213/550-1000

DIPLOMATIC IMMUNITY   Fries Distribution, 1991, w/Randall Frakes

BEN DONNELLY
LAST RITES   Cannon, 1980, w/Dominic Paris

THOMAS M. DONNELLY*
Agent: United Talent Agency - Beverly Hills, 213/273-6700

DEFIANCE   American International, 1980
QUICKSILVER   Columbia, 1986, directed
TALENT FOR THE GAME   Paramount, 1991, w/Larry Ferguson & David Himmelstein

Screenplays:
REDEMPTION (directing)
ROUGH JUSTICE
JACK OF HEARTS
TIN MAN
SNAFU
GROWN UPS
THE LIFE OF RAFAELLE GALLO
THE BUFF

MARY AGNES DONOGHUE*
Agent: The Gersh Agency - Beverly Hills, 213/274-6611

THE BUDDY SYSTEM   20th Century Fox, 1984
BEACHES   Buena Vista, 1988
THE MRS.   Buena Vista, 1991

Screenplays:
PARADISE (directing)
THE BEAN TREES
HOT FLASHES
RULES OF ENGAGEMENT

MARTIN DONOVAN*
Agent: APA - Los Angeles, 213/273-0744

LOVING COUPLES   20th Century-Fox, 1980

MARTIN DONOVAN
Agent: United Talent Agency - Beverly Hills, 213/273-6700

APARTMENT ZERO   Skouras Pictures, 1989, w/David Koepp, directed

Screenplays:
DEATH BECOMES HER   w/David Koepp

PAUL DONOVAN
Address: P.O. Box 2261, Station M, Halifax, Nova Scotia B3J 3L8, Canada, 902/420-1577

SELF-DEFENSE   SIEGE   New Line Cinema, 1983, directed
DEF-CON 4   New World, 1985, directed
NORMAN'S AWESOME EXPERIENCE   Norstar Entertainment, 1990

ANITA DOOHAN*
Agent: Robinson, Weintraub, Gross & Associates - Los Angeles, 213/653-5802

WHISPERS   Live Home Video, 1990

PAUL DOOLEY
Agent: ICM - Los Angeles, 213/550-4000

HEALTH   20th Century-Fox, 1980, w/Robert Altman & Frank Barhydt

MARJORIE DOPPELT*
Contact: WGA - Los Angeles, 213/550-1000

TERROR IN THE AISLES (FD)   Universal, 1984

MATTHEW DORFF*
Susan Smith & Associates - Beverly Hills, 213/852-4777

CAMPUS MAN   Paramount, 1987, w/Geoffrey Baere & Alex Horvat

Screenplays:
REDLINES
CRUSADERS
SEX AND THE MARRIED WOMAN
CLASSY KILL
RANDOM ENCOUNTER
I LOVE A VAMPIRE
THE EXAMINER
THE CORONER
PIT BULLS FROM HELL

PHOEBE DORIN*
Agent: Warden & White Associates - Beverly Hills, 213/852-1028

Screenplays:
CONDUIT   w/Christian Stoianovich
THE RUNAWAY WIFE   w/Christian Stoianovich
WITHOUT MERCY   w/Christian Stoianovich
THE 13TH FLOOR   w/Christian Stoianovich

DORIS DÖRRIE
STRAIGHT THROUGH THE HEART   1983, directed
IN THE BELLY OF THE WHALE   1984, directed
MEN...   New Yorker Films, 1986, directed
ME AND HIM   Columbia, 1989, Adaptation w/Michael Juncker, directed

FERNANDO DOTY*
Agent: ICM - Los Angeles, 213/550-4000

Screenplays:
FOOLPROOF
THE KITCHEN CABINET
SEX AND ARCHITECTURE

JOSEPH DOUGHERTY
STEEL & LACE   Friest Distribution, 1990, w/Dave Edison

JOSEPH DOUGHERTY*
Agent: William Morris Agency - New York, 212/586-5100

DIGBY (P)   also screenplay

Screenplays:
LOVECRAFT (CTF)
LADY LAZARUS
SAINT VALENTINE (CTF)
LUNATIC FRINGE
VERY OLD MONEY

MACGREGOR DOUGLAS*
Contact: WGA - Los Angeles, 213/550-1000

TWO MOON JUNCTION   Lorimar, 1988, Story w/Zalman King

PETER VINCENT DOUGLAS*
Agent: CAA - Beverly Hills, 213/288-4545

A TIGER'S TALE   Atlantic Releasing Corporation, 1987, directed

Screenplays:
ROSES ARE RED   w/Merridith Baer & Gary Goldman
A WORK OF ART

NANCY DOWD*
Agent: APA - Los Angeles, 213/273-0744

LOVE (Short), directed
SLAP SHOT   Universal, 1977
COMING HOME ★★   United Artists, 1978, Story
LADIES AND GENTLEMEN, THE FABULOUS STAINS   Paramount, 1982, as "Rob Morton"
SWING SHIFT   Warner Bros., 1983, w/Bo Goldman and Ron Nyswaner, as "Rob Morton"
HAPPY NEW YEAR   Columbia, 1987, as "Warner Lane"
LET IT RIDE   Warner Bros., 1989, as "Ernest Morton"

Screenplays:
SEX IN THE 90'S
CENTERFOLD   w/Ron Shelton
GOOD VIBES
R & R
JUST CRAZY ABOUT

ROBERT DOWNEY
Agent: ICM - Los Angeles, 213/550-4000

CHAFED ELBOWS   Grove Press, 1965, directed
NO MORE EXCUSES   Rogosin, 1968, directed
PUTNEY SWOPE   Cinema 5, 1969, directed
POUND   United Artists, 1970, directed
GREASER'S PALACE   Greaser's Palace, 1972, directed
THE GONG SHOW MOVIE   Universal, 1980, w/Chuck Barris
AMERICA   ASA Communications, 1986, directed
TOO MUCH SUN   New Line Cinema, 1990, w/Laura Ernst & Al Schwartz, directed

RODDY DOYLE
THE COMMITMENTS   20th Century Fox, 1991, w/Dick Clement & Ian La Frenais

BRIAN DOYLE-MURRAY
Contact: Yohalem, Gilman & Co., CPA - 213/371-2000

CADDYSHACK   Orion/Warner Bros., 1980, w/Douglas Kenney & Harold Ramis
CLUB PARADISE   Warner Bros., 1985, w/Harold Ramis

Dr

FILM WRITERS GUIDE

BERT L. DRAGIN
Agent: Solomon Weingarten & Associates - Los Angeles, 213/474-8703

SUMMER CAMP NIGHTMARE *THE BUTTERFLY REVOLUTION* Concorde, 1987, w/Penelope Spheeris, directed
TWICE DEAD Concorde, 1989, w/Robert McDonnell, directed

STAN DRAGOTI
Agent: CAA - Beverly Hills, 213/288-4545

DIRTY LITTLE BILLY Columbia, 1972, w/Charles Moss, directed

T.S. DRAKE*
Agent: Hamilburg Agency - Los Angeles, 213/657-1501

TERROR TRAIN 20th Century-Fox, 1980

ANTHONY DRAZAN
Agent: United Talent Agency - Beverly Hills, 213/273-6700

Screenplays:
ZEBRAHEAD, THE GREY BOY *(directed)*
LIVING WITHOUT YOU
BICYCLE DAYS
BIG BROTHER
THE SOFT TOUCH

HAL DRESNER*
(Harold A. Dresner)
Agent: Richland/Wunsch/Hohman Agency - Los Angeles, 213/278-1955

THE EXTRAORDINARY SEAMAN MGM, 1969, w/Philip Rock
THE APRIL FOOLS National General, 1969
Sssssssss Universal, 1973
THE EIGER SANCTION Universal, 1974, w/Warren B. Murphy & Rod Whitaker
ZORRO, THE GAY BLADE 20th Century-Fox, 1981

Screenplays:
THANKS DAD w/J. Crittendon
BO-PEEP
EASY STREET
THE CHEAT

LORIN H. DREYFUSS*
Agent: The Roberts Company - Los Angeles, 213/552-7800

DETECTIVE SCHOOL DROP OUTS *DUMB DICKS* Cannon, 1986, w/David Landsberg
DUTCH TREAT Cannon, 1987, w/David Landsberg

JOHN A. DRIMMER*
Agent: Susan Smith & Associates - Beverly Hills, 213/852-4777

IMPULSE 20th Century-Fox, 1984, Story
ICEMAN Universal, 1984, w/Chip Proser

Screenplays:
BATTLE IN THE EROGENOUS ZONE

GARY DRUCKER*
Agent: Triad Artists, Inc. - Los Angeles, 213/556-2727

Screenplays:
SOLDIERS OF FORTUNE
NEIGHBORHOOD WATCH
WEEGEE

MICHAEL B. DRUXMAN
KEATON'S COP Cannon, 1990

Screenplays:
DILLINGER AND CAPONE

LEE DRYSDALE
Agent: ICM - Los Angeles, 213/550-4000

LEATHER JACKETS 1991, directed

Screenplays:
DEFENCELESS UNDER THE NIGHT
WASTELAND
NEEDLES (CTF)
LEGAL TENDER
JACK CARTER'S LAW
ROGUE TROOPER

ADAM DUBOV*
Agent: United Talent Agency - Beverly Hills, 213/273-6700

THE GRAND POSEUR (Short), directed

Screenplays:
PURPLE WEST w/Janice Shapiro
WILD RIDE w/Janice Shapiro
UNFORGETTABLE w/Janice Shapiro
TUBESTEAK w/Janice Shapiro

PETER JOHN DUFFELL
Agent: The Artists Agency - Los Angeles, 213/277-7779

ENGLAND MADE ME Cine Globe, 1973, w/Desmond Cory, directed

MICHAEL DUGAN*
Agent: David Shapira & Associates - Sherman Oaks, 818/906-0322

Screenplays:
OBJECT OF DESIRE
SPECIAL FAVORS
RED TAIL SQUADRON

THOMAS C. DUGAN
FATAL SKIES AIP, 1990, Story w/James Eaton & William Zipp, directed

GEORGE DUGDALE
SLAUGHTER HIGH Vestron, 1987, directed

JOHN DUIGAN
Contact: Melinda Jason Company - Burbank, 818/954-2500

MOUTH TO MOUTH Vega Film Productions, 1978, directed
WINTER OF OUR DREAMS Satori, 1981, directed
FAR EAST Filmco Australia, 1983, directed

THE YEAR MY VOICE BROKE   Avenue Pictures, 1987, directed

Screenplays:
WILD SARGASSO SEA (directing)
THE ICE DANCER

DON CARLOS DUNAWAY*
Agent: United Talent Agency - Beverly Hills, 213/273-6700

CUJO   Warner Bros., 1983, w/Lauren Currier
IMPULSE   20th Century-Fox, 1984, w/Bart Davis

ANDREA DUNBAR
RITA, SUE AND BOB TOO!   Orion Classics, 1987, from her play

MICHAEL DUNCAN
Agent: Warden & White Associates - Beverly Hills, 213/852-1028

EXPOSURE (P)

Screenplays:
TIME OUT OF JOINT w/Sam Hamm
SNAKES AND LADDERS
NO HANGUPS
ON THE ROAD AGAIN

PATRICK DUNCAN*
Agent: Preferred Artists - Encino, 818/990-0305

BEACHGIRLS   Crown International, 1982, w/Phil Groves
84 CHARLIE MOPIC   New Century/Vista, 1989, directed

Screenplays:
PRISONER OF THE ROAD
TRUE SPORT
HOME BEFORE MORNING
A MIDNIGHT CLEAR w/W. Horton
ELFIN
THE FINEST KIND
ANGEL'S FLIGHT

STEVE DUNCAN*
Agent: The Agency - Los Angeles, 213/551-3000

THE COURTMARTIAL OF JACKIE ROBINSON (CTF)   Turner Network Television, 1990, w/L. Travis Clark, Dennis L. Clark & Clayton Frohman

Screenplays:
UNDER ONE ROOF

NINIAN DUNETT
RESTLESS NATIVES   Orion Classics, 1985

HARRY DUNN
Agent: Circle Talent Associates - Beverly Hills, 213/285-1585

COYOTE SUMMER (P)

Screenplays:
ON THE AIR
THE HONEYMOON

ROBERT J. DUNN*
Agent: Sanford, Skouras, Gross & Associates - Los Angeles, 213/208-2100

Screenplays:
OZONE
IS YOUR BROTHER BLUE?
SWEET LIES
THE LONG SATURDAY NIGHT

JAMES PATRICK DUNNE
Agent: United Talent Agency - Beverly Hills, 213/273-6700

Screenplays:
I OWE YOU MY LIFE
MOE'S WORLD
CHOICES   THE SIXTH MAN

JOHN GREGORY DUNNE*
Agent: ICM - Los Angeles, 213/550-4000

PANIC IN NEEDLE PARK   20th Century-Fox, 1971, w/Joan Didion
PLAY IT AS IT LAYS   Universal, 1971, w/Joan Didion
A STAR IS BORN   Warner Bros., 1976, w/Joan Didion & Frank R. Pierson
TRUE CONFESSIONS   United Artists, 1981, w/Joan Didion

Screenplays:
PLAYLAND w/Joan Didion
KINGDOM w/Joan Didion
DEER PARK w/Joan Didion

PHILIP DUNNE*
Agent: The Mitchell J. Hamilburg Agency - Los Angeles, 213/657-1501

THE LATE GEORGE APLEY   20th Century-Fox, 1946
THE GHOST AND MRS. MUIR   20th Century-Fox, 1947
ESCAPE   20th Century-Fox, 1948
PINKY   20th Century-Fox, 1949, w/Dudley Nichols
DAVID AND BATHSHEBA   20th Century-Fox, 1951
ANNE OF THE INDIES   20th Century-Fox, 1951, w/Arthur Caesar
WAY OF A GAUCHO   20th Century-Fox, 1952
LYDIA BAILEY   20th Century-Fox, 1952, w/Michael Blankfort
DEMETRIUS AND THE GLADIATORS   20th Century-Fox, 1954
THE EGYPTIAN   20th Century-Fox, 1954, w/Casey Robinson
THE VIEW FROM POMPEY'S HEAD   20th Century-Fox, 1955, directed
THREE BRAVE MEN   20th Century-Fox, 1956, directed
HILDA CRANE   20th Century-Fox, 1956
TEN NORTH FREDERICK   20th Century-Fox, 1958, directed
BLUE DENIM   *BLUE JEANS*   20th Century-Fox, 1959, w/Edith Sommer
BLINDFOLD   Universal, 1965, w/W.H. Menger, directed
THE AGONY AND THE ECSTASY   20th Century-Fox, 1965

Screenplays:
POTTER TAKES FLIGHT w/Perry Howze & Randy Howze

EVAN DUNSKY
VOODOO DAWN   Academy Entertainment, 1990, w/Jeffrey Delman, Thomas Rendon & John Russo

Du
FILM WRITERS GUIDE

CHRISTOPHER DURANG*
Agent: CAA - Beverly Hills, 213/288-4545

SISTER MARY IGNATIUS EXPLAINS IT ALL FOR YOU (P)
THE MARRIAGE OF BETTE AND BOO (P)
LAUGHING WILD (P)
A HISTORY OF THE AMERICAN FILM (P)
BEYOND THERAPY   New World, 1987, w/Robert Altman, from his play

Screenplays:
THE ADVENTURES OF LOLA

MARGUERITE DURAS
Contact: French Film Office, 745 Fifth Avenue, New York, NY 10151, 212/832-8860

HIROSHIMA, MON AMOUR ★   Zenith, 1959
UNE AUSSI LONGUE ABSENCE (THE LONG ABSENCE)   Procinex, 1961, w/Gerald Jarlot
10:30 P.M. SUMMER   United Artists, 1966, w/Jules Dassin

Screenplays:
THE LOVER w/Jean-Jacques Annaud & Gerard Brach

TODD DURHAM*
Agent: William Morris Agency - Beverly Hills, 213/274-7451
Business: Living Hell Productions, P.O. Box 1804, Beverly Hills, CA 90213, 213/851-8540

VISIONS OF SUGAR-PLUMS   Regency Entertainment, 1984, directed
HYPERSPACE   Regency Entertainment, 1986, directed

Screenplays:
TEXAS RANGERS
SIGNED, SEALED, DELIVERED
ANIMAL PASSION
THE LIFE AND ADVENTURES OF SANTA CLAUS
BLACK CREEK
BEAUTY BECOMES THE BEAST
MR. SMITH GOES TO HELL
GOV
WILD BILL BEETHOVEN
POISON APPLES
WIMPS FROM SPACE
PEE-WEE HERMAN VS. THE FLYING SAUCERS

GRIFF DuRHONE
Agent: Broder-Kurland-Webb-Uffner - Los Angeles, 213/656-9262

CHEETAH   Buena Vista, 1989, w/John Cotter & Erik Tarloff

PHILIP DUSENBERRY
Contact: Pinder Lane Productions - New York, 212/489-0880

THE NATURAL   Tri-Star, 1984, w/Roger Towne

ROBERT DUVALL
Agent: ICM - Los Angeles, 213/550-4000

ANGELO, MY LOVE   Cinecom, 1983, directed

LAURENCE DWORET*
Agent: ICM - Los Angeles, 213/550-4000

Screenplays:
ULTIMATUM w/Robert Roy Pool
CROSSING w/Denise DiNovi

H. KAYE DYAL
LONE WOLF McQUADE   Orion, 1983, Story w/B.J. Nelson

DALE DYE*
Agent: Robinson, Weintraub, Gross & Associates - Los Angeles, 213/653-5802

FIRE BIRDS   Buena Vista, 1990, Story w/John K. Swenson & Step Tyner

ANNE DYER
BATTLE BEYOND THE STARS   New World, 1980, Story w/John Sayles

E

MAUREEN EARL
Agent: ICM - Los Angeles, 213/550-4000

Screenplays:
FAMILY ALBUM
BEREAVEMENTS

KENNETH EASTAUGH
MR. LOVE   Warner Bros., 1986

CAROLE EASTMAN*
(Adrien Joyce)
Agent: ICM - Los Angeles, 213/550-4000
Business Manager: Guild Management, 213/277-9711

THE SHOOTING   American International, 1966
THE MODEL SHOP   Columbia, 1969
FIVE EASY PIECES ★   Columbia, 1970
PUZZLE OF A DOWNFALL CHILD   Universal, 1970
THE FORTUNE   Columbia, 1975
MAN TROUBLE   1991

Screenplays:
RUNNING MATES

CHARLES EASTMAN*
Contact: Armstrong, Hendler & Hirsch - Los Angeles, 213/553-0305

LITTLE FAUSS AND BIG HALSY   Paramount, 1970
THE ALL-AMERICAN BOY   Warner Bros., 1973, directed
SECOND-HAND HEARTS   Lorimar/Paramount, 1981

JAMES EATON
FATAL SKIES   AIP, 1990, w/William Zipp

MICHAEL EATON*
Contact: 213/660-9049

THE TRAGEDY OF FLIGHT 103: THE INSIDE STORY (CTF)   HBO Showcase/Granada Films, 1990

FRAN LEWIS EBELING
THE LADIES CLUB   New Line Cinema, 1986, w/Paul Mason

THOMAS EBERHARDT*
Agent: The Daniel Ostroff Agency - Los Angeles, 213/278-2020

NIGHT OF THE COMET   Atlantic Releasing Corporation, 1984, directed
THE NIGHT BEFORE   Kings Road Productions, 1987, w/Gregory Scherick, directed

Screenplays:
HONEY I BLEW UP THE BABY
ALL I WANT FOR CHRISTMAS
WHITE COVER
NOISE IN THE NIGHT w/Marc Stirdivant
CHANCE OF A LIFETIME
ONE FANTASTIC NIGHT
THE MAD MISS MANTON

ROGER EBERT
Contact: Attorney Donald M. Ephraim - Chicago, 312/321-9700

BEYOND THE VALLEY OF THE DOLLS   20th Century-Fox, 1970

MICHAEL ALAN EDDY*
Agent: William Morris Agency - Beverly Hills, 213/274-7451

BEDROOM EYES   Aquarius Releasing, 1984

Screenplays:
STEAL THE NIGHT
COUNSELOR
PEN PAL
GUN SHY
STAR WITNESS
THE GIFT
BLACK ON WHITE
BABY BLUE EYES
LITTLE GIRL LOST
BEVERLY HILLS COP III

RICK EDELSTEIN*
Contact: WGA - Los Angeles, 213/550-1000

Screenplays:
A MATTER OF CHOICE

DAVID EDGAR
Agent: Michael Imison, Playwrights - London, 011/441/354-3274

NICHOLAS NICKLEBY (P)
MARY BARNES (P)
LADY JANE   Paramount, 1986

PATRICK EDGEWORTH
RAW DEAL   Greater Union Film Distributors, 1977
DRIVING FORCE   J&M Entertainment, 1990

DAVE EDISON
STEEL & LACE   Fries Distribution, 1990, w/Joseph Dougherty

DON EDMONDS
BARE KNUCKLES   Intercontinental, 1978, directed

ERIC EDSON*
Agent: United Talent Agency - Beverly Hills, 213/273-6700

THE ROSE AND THE JACKAL (CTF)   Steve White Productions/Spectator Films/PWD Productions, 1990
DIVING IN   Skouras Pictures, 1990

Screenplays:
THE HERO
SOLOMON'S MIND
SCALAWAGS
CHASER
SNOOKUMS

BLAKE EDWARDS*
Agent: Triad Artists, Inc. - Los Angeles, 213/556-2727
Business: Blake Edwards Co., 9336 W. Washington Blvd., Culver City, CA 90232, 213/202-3375

PANHANDLE   Allied Artists, 1948, w/John C. Champion
SOUND OFF   Columbia, 1952, w/Richard Quine
ALL ASHORE   Columbia, 1952, w/Richard Quine
DRIVE A CROOKED ROAD   Columbia, 1954
THE ATOMIC KID   Republic, 1954, Story
MY SISTER EILEEN   Columbia, 1955, w/Richard Quine
BRING YOUR SMILE ALONG   Columbia, 1955, directed
HE LAUGHED LAST   Columbia, 1956, directed
OPERATION MAD BELL   Columbia, 1957, w/Arthur Carter & Jed Harris
MISTER CORY   Universal-International, 1957, directed
THIS HAPPY FEELING   Universal-International, 1958, directed
SOLDIER IN THE RAIN   Allied Artists, 1963, w/Maurice Richlin
THE PINK PANTHER   United Artists, 1964, w/Maurice Richlin, directed
A SHOT IN THE DARK   United Artists, 1964, w/William Peter Blatty, directed
WHAT DID YOU DO IN THE WAR, DADDY?   United Artists, 1966, w/William Peter Blatty, directed
GUNN   Warner Bros., 1967, w/William Peter Blatty, directed
THE PARTY   United Artists, 1968, w/FrankWaldman & Tom Waldman, directed
DARLING LILI   Paramount, 1970, w/William Peter Blatty, directed
WILD ROVERS   MGM, 1971, directed
THE TAMARIND SEED   Avco Embassy, 1974, directed
RETURN OF THE PINK PANTHER   United Artists, 1975, w/Frank Waldman, directed
THE PINK PANTHER STRIKES AGAIN   United Artists, 1976, w/Frank Waldman, directed
REVENGE OF THE PINK PANTHER   United Artists, 1978, w/Ron Clark & Frank Waldman, directed
10   Orion/Warner Bros., 1979, directed
S.O.B.   Paramount, 1981, directed
VICTOR/VICTORIA ★   MGM/United Artists, 1982, directed

Ed

FILM WRITERS GUIDE

TRAIL OF THE PINK PANTHER   MGM/United Artists, 1982, w/Geoffrey Edwards, Tom Waldman & Frank Waldman, directed
CURSE OF THE PINK PANTHER   MGM/UA, 1983, w/Geoffrey Edwards, directed
THE MAN WHO LOVED WOMEN   Columbia, 1983, w/Geoffrey Edwards & Milton Wexler, directed
CITY HEAT   Warner Bros., 1l984, w/Joseph C. Stinson, as "Sam O. Brown"
A FINE MESS   Columbia, 1986, directed
THAT'S LIFE!   Columbia, 1986, w/Milton Wexler, directed
SUNSET   Tri-Star, 1987, directed
SKIN DEEP   20th Century Fox, 1989, directed
SWITCH   Warner Bros., 1991, directed

GEOFFREY B. EDWARDS*
Business Manager: Glass/Rosen/Orkin - 818/907-1600

TRAIL OF THE PINK PANTHER   MGM/United Artists, 1982, w/Blake Edwards, Tom Waldman & Frank Waldman
CURSE OF THE PINK PANTHER   MGM/UA, 1983, w/Blake Edwards
THE MAN WHO LOVED WOMEN   Columbia, 1983, w/Blake Edwards & Milton Wexler
RAD   Tri-Star, 1986, w/Sam Bernard

HENRY EDWARDS
Agent: The Gersh Agency - Beverly Hills, 213/274-6611

SGT. PEPPER'S LONELY HEARTS CLUB BAND   Universal, 1978

PAUL F. EDWARDS*
Agent: ICM - Los Angeles, 213/550-4000

TRACKDOWN   United Artists, 1976
HIGH-BALLIN'   American International, 1978
FIRE BIRDS   Buena Vista, 1990, w/David Taylor & Nick Thiel

Screenplays:
LOOSE CANNON w/Larry Ferguson
TULKU STAR OF TIBET
THE WILD BIG RED
LEONARD PELTIER STORY IN THE SPIRIT OF CRAZY HORSE
STEALING THUNDER

TOM EDWARDS*
Agent: Thal Literary Management - Los Angeles, 213/659-4946

WIZARDS OF THE LOST KINGDOM   Concorde/Cinema Group, 1985

CHRISTINE EDZARD
Contact: British Academy of Film & Television Arts, 195 Picadilly, London W1, England, 01/734-0022

STORIES FROM A FLYING TRUNK   EMI, 1979, directed
LITTLE DORRIT, PART 1: NOBODY'S FAULT ★   Cannon, 1989, directed
LITTLE DORRIT, PART 2: LITTLE DORRIT'S STORY ★   Cannon, 1989, directed

SAM EGAN*
Agent: William Morris Agency - Beverly Hills, 213/274-7451

ELVIRA: MISTRESS OF THE DARK   New World, 1988, w/John Paragon & Cassandra Peterson
IMAGINE: JOHN LENNON (FD)   Warner Bros., 1988, w/Andrew Solt

Screenplays:
THE BORROWER

CHARLES H. EGLEE*
Agent: InterTalent - Los Angeles, 213/271-0600

DEADLY EYES   NIGHT EYES   Warner Bros., 1983

JAN EGLESON
Agent: William Morris Agency - Beverly Hills, 213/274-7451

BILLY IN THE LOWLANDS   Theater Co. of Boston, 1979, directed
THE DARK END OF THE STREET   First Run Features, 1981, directed
THE LITTLE SISTER   American Playhouse, 1985, directed

Screenplays:
MANCHESTER ANGEL

ATOM EGOYAN
Business: Ego Film Arts, 490 Adelaide Street West - Suite 102, Toronto, Ontario M5V 1T3, 416/365-2137

NEXT OF KIN   Ego Film Arts, 1985, directed
FAMILY VIEWING   Ego Film Arts, 1987, directed
SPEAKING PARTS   Cinephile, 1990, directed

ROBERT H. EISELE*
Agent: Ken Sherman & Associates - Beverly Hills, 213/273-8840

Screenplays:
BREACH OF CONTRACT

D. E. EISENBERG
DREAM A LITTLE DREAM   Vestron, 1989, w/Daniel Jay Franklin & Marc Rocco

MAX EISENBERG*
Agent: Monteiro Rose Agency - Encino, 818/501-1177

Screenplays:
THE CROSSING
SMART MONEY
I WAS A TEENAGE BOOKIE
RANGERS
ME, MYSELF AND I

JO EISINGER
NIGHT AND THE CITY   20th Century-Fox, 1950
THE SLEEPING CITY   Universal-International, 1950
THE SYSTEM   Warner Bros., 1953
BEDEVILLED   MGM, 1955
CRIME OF PASSION   United Artists, 1956
THE BIG BOODLE   United Artists, 1957
OSCAR WILDE   Vantage, 1959
HOUSE OF THE SEVEN HAWKS   MGM, 1959
THE BOY WHO STOLE A MILLION   British Lion, 1960, w/Charles Crichton

FILM WRITERS

THEY CAME TO ROB LOS VEGAS   Warner Bros., 1969, w/Antonio Isasi
THE JIGSAW MAN   United Film Distribution, 1984

LONNE ELDER III*
Agent: Preferred Artists - Encino, 818/990-0305

SOUNDER ★   20th Century-Fox, 1972
PART 2 SOUNDER   Gamma III, 1976
BUSTIN' LOOSE   Universal, 1981, Adaptation

KEVIN ELDERS*
Business Manager: Marvin Meyer, Rosenfelt, Meyer, and Susman, 9601 Wilshire Boulevard, Beverly Hills, CA 90210, 213/858-7700

IRON EAGLE   Tri-Star, 1986, w/Sidney J. Furie
IRON EAGLE II   Tri-Star, 1988, w/Sidney J. Furie

Screenplays:
IRON EAGLE III
RAID ON BAGHDAD
ONE NATION INVISIBLE
STREET
MEGASCANNER

LAURICE ELEHWANY*
Agent: InterTalent - Los Angeles, 213/858-6200

MY GIRL   Columbia, 1991

RICHARD ELFMAN
FORBIDDEN ZONE   Sutton Marketing, 1980, w/Matthew Bright, Nick L. Martinson & Nick James

MICHAEL ELIAS*
Agent: CAA - Beverly Hills, 213/288-4545

THE FRISCO KID   Warner Bros., 1979, w/Frank Shaw
THE JERK   Universal, 1979, w/Carl Gottlieb & Steve Martin
SERIAL   Paramount, 1980, w/Richard Eustis
YOUNG DOCTORS IN LOVE   20th Century-Fox, 1982, w/Richard Eustis

Screenplays:
ON THE BRINK w/Richard Eustis
BANDIES (P) w/Richard Eustis
DIRE STRAITS w/Richard Eustis
BLACKJACK & SALTY w/Richard Eustis

JAN ELIASBERG
Agent: InterTalent - Los Angeles, 213/858-6200

Screenplays:
GROWING UP FAST
TRAVELLING LIGHT
CELINA'S WORLD

JOYCE ELIASON*
Agent: ICM - Los Angeles, 213/550-4000

TELL ME A RIDDLE   Filmways, 1980, w/Alev Lyttle

Screenplays:
HEAVEN SCENT w/Ken Friedman
SECOND TIME LUCKY
HEARTS

ROBERT ELLIOT*
Agent: William Morris Agency - New York, 212/586-5100

RICH GIRL   Studio Three Film Corporation, 1991

TED ELLIOTT*
Agent: William Morris Agency - Beverly Hills, 213/274-7451

LITTLE MONSTERS   Vestron, 1989, w/Terry Rossio

Screenplays:
PRINCESS OF MARS w/Terry Rossio
DUNN'S CONUNDRUM w/Terry Rossio

BOB ELLIS
MAN OF FLOWERS   Spectrafilm, 1983, w/Paul Cox
MY FIRST WIFE   Spectrafilm, 1984, w/Paul Cox
CACTUS   Spectrafilm, 1986, w/Paul Cox & Norman Kaye
WARM NIGHTS ON A SLOW MOVING TRAIN   Miramax, 1987, w/Deny Lawrence, directed

GARY ELLIS
TALES OF THE UNKNOWN   AIP Home Video, 1990, "Living on Video"

HARLAN ELLISON*
Agent: Shapiro/Lichtman - Los Angeles, 213/859-8877

THE OSCAR   Paramount, 1966, w/Clarence Greene & Russel Rouse

Screenplays:
WOULD YOU DO IT FOR A PENNY?
STRANGLEHOLD
HARLAN ELLISON'S MOVIE
BLIND VOICES
SEVEN WORLDS, SEVEN WARRIORS
THE WHIMPER OF WHIPPED DOGS
I, ROBOT
NICK THE GREEK
BEST BY FAR
SWING LOW, SWEET HARRIET
THE DREAM MERCHANTS
RUMBLE
KHADIM
BUG JACK BARRON

MAX EMBER*
Agent: Robert Littman Company - Beverly Hills, 213/278-1572

Screenplays:
THE PRINCE OF PARK AVENUE
THE FROG PRINCE
FRATS
HOLLYWOOD HIGH
BIMBO

JOHN EMERY
FREEDOM   Satori, 1985

IAN EMES
Agent: ICM - Los Angeles, 213/550-4000

KNIGHTS AND EMERALDS   Warner Bros., 1986, directed

FILM WRITERS GUIDE

MERVYN EMRYS
MINISTRY OF VENGEANCE Concorde, 1989,
    w/Brian D. Jeffries & Ann Narus

ROBERT ENDERS*
Agent: David Shapira & Associates - Sherman Oaks,
    818/906-0322

VOICES Hemdale, 1973, w/George Kirgo
THE MAIDS American Film Theatre, 1975,
    w/Christopher Miles
CONDUCT UNBECOMING Allied Artists, 1975
NASTY HABITS Brut Productions, 1977

CY ENDFIELD
Contact: British Academy of Film & Television Arts,
    195 Picadilly, London W1, England, 01/734-0022

THE MASTER PLAN Astor, 1954, as
    "Hugh Raker," directed
CHILD IN THE HOUSE Eros, 1956
HELL DRIVERS Rank, 1957, w/John
    Kruse, directed
SEA FURY Rank, 1958, w/John Kruse, directed
JET STORM British Lion, 1959, w/Sigmund
    Miller, directed
ZULU Embassy, 1964, w/John Prebble, directed
SANDS OF THE KALAHARI Paramount,
    1965, directed
UNIVERSAL SOLDIER Appaloosa, 1971, directed
ZULU DAWN New World, 1982, w/Anthony Storey

MICHAEL S. ENDLER*
Contact: 818/783-8110

EASY MONEY Orion, 1983, w/Dennis Blair, Rodney
    Dangerfield & P. J. O'Rourke

DAVID ENGELBACH*
Agent: The Turtle Agency - Studio City, 818/506-6898

DEATH WISH II Filmways, 1982
AMERICA 3000 Cannon, 1986, directed
OVER THE TOP Cannon, 1987, Story w/Gary Conway

ROBERT ENGELS*
Agent: CAA - Beverly Hills, 213/288-4545

Screenplays:
ACTION PHOTOGRAPHY

ELYSE ENGLAND
LOVE OR MONEY Hemdale, 1990, w/Bart Davis &
    Michael Zausner

DIANE ENGLISH*
Agent: William Morris Agency - Beverly Hills,
    213/274-7451
Business: Shukovsky-English Productions, Warner
    Bros. TV, 818/954-3700

Screenplays:
A MARRIED LIFE
DRIVE ME CRAZY
PERFECT TIMING
THREE DAYS, FOUR NIGHTS

DON ENRIGHT*
Agent: David Shapira & Associates - Sherman Oaks,
    818/906-0322

SEARCH AND DESTROY Film Ventures
    International, 1981
SPASMS Producers Distribution Company, 1983

DELIA EPHRON*
Agent: CAA - Beverly Hills, 213/550-4000

Screenplays:
THIS IS YOUR LIFE w/Nora Ephron
FUNNY SAUCE

NORA EPHRON*
Agent: ICM - New York, 212/556-5600

SILKWOOD ★ 20th Century-Fox, 1983, w/Alice Arlen
HEARTBURN Paramount, 1985
WHEN HARRY MET SALLY... ★ Castle Rock/
    Columbia, 1989
COOKIE Warner Bros., 1989, w/Alice Arlen
MY BLUE HEAVEN Warner Bros., 1990

Screenplays:
THIS IS YOUR LIFE w/Delia Ephron (directing)
MODERN BRIDE w/Alice Arlen & Joan Taylor
ENCORE

TOM EPPERSON*
Agent: Triad Artists, Inc. - Los Angeles, 213/556-2727

Screenplays:
THE BOND w/Billy Bob Thornton
THE OTIS REDDING STORY w/Billy Bob Thornton

JACK EPPS, JR.*
Agent: CAA - Beverly Hills, 213/288-4545

TOP GUN Paramount, 1986, w/Jim Cash
LEGAL EAGLES Universal, 1986, w/Jim Cash
THE SECRET OF MY SUCCESS Universal, 1987,
    w/A.J. Carothers & Jim Cash
TURNER & HOOCH Buena Vista, 1989, w/Jim Cash,
    Daniel Petrie Jr., Michael Blodgett & Dennis Shryack
DICK TRACY Buena Vista, 1990, w/Jim Cash

Screenplays:
SISTER ACT w/Jim Cash
THE EDDIE COCHRAN STORY w/Jim Cash
REVENGE OF BLACKTHORN w/Jim Cash
WHEREABOUTS w/Jim Cash
DANGEROUSLY w/Jim Cash & Bennett Tramer
MR. MAYOR w/Jim Cash
MILWAUKEE CONFIDENTIAL w/Jim Cash
DIRTY FIVE w/Jim Cash
DIVIDING LINE w/Jim Cash

MICKEY EPPS
JOYSTICKS Jensen Farley Pictures, 1983, w/Al Gomez

DAVID EPSTEIN
Agent: Triad Artists, Inc. - Los Angeles, 213/556-2727

Screenplays:
DEAD AIR

JULIUS J. EPSTEIN*
Agent: ICM - Los Angeles, 213/550-4000

CONFESSION   Warner Bros., 1937,
   w/Margaret Le Vino
DAUGHTERS COURAGEOUS   Warner Bros., 1939,
   w/Philip G. Epstein
FOUR WIVES   Warner Bros., 1939, w/Philip G.
   Epstein & Maurice Hanline
NO TIME FOR COMEDY   Warner Bros., 1940,
   w/Philip G. Epstein
THE BRIDE CAME C.O.D.   Warner Bros., 1940,
   w/Philip G. Epstein
SATURDAY'S CHILDREN   Warner Bros., 1940,
   w/Philip G. Epstein
THE STRAWBERRY BLONDE   Warner Bros., 1941,
   w/Philip G. Epstein
THE MAN WHO CAME TO DINNER   Warner Bros.,
   1941, w/Philip G. Epstein
ARSENIC AND OLD LACE   Warner Bros., 1942,
   w/Philip G. Epstein
MRS. SKEFFINGTON   Warner Bros., 1944,
   w/Philip G. Epstein
CASABLANCA ★★   Warner Bros., 1943,
   w/Philip G. Epstein & Howard Koch
ONE MORE TOMORROW   Warner Bros., 1946,
   w/Philip G. Epstein, Charles Hoffman &
   Catherine Turney
ROMANCE ON THE HIGH SEAS   Warner Bros., 1948,
   w/Philip G. Epstein & I.A.L. Diamond
MY FOOLISH HEART   Goldwyn, 1949,
   w/Philip G. Epstein
TAKE CARE OF MY LITTLE GIRL   20th Century-Fox,
   1951, w/Philip G. Epstein
FOREVER FEMALE   Paramount, 1953,
   w/Philip G. Epstein
THE LAST TIME I SAW PARIS   MGM, 1954,
   w/Philip G. Epstein & Richard Brooks
YOUNG AT HEART   Warner Bros., 1954,
   w/Leonore Coffee
THE TENDER TRAP   MGM, 1955
KISS THEM FOR ME   20th Century-Fox, 1957
TAKE A GIANT STEP   United Artists, 1958,
   w/Louis S. Peterson
FANNY   Warner Bros., 1960
TALL STORY   Warner Bros., 1960
THE LIGHT IN THE PIAZZA   MGM, 1962
SEND ME NO FLOWERS   Universal
   International, 1964
RETURN FROM THE ASHES   United Artists, 1965
ANY WEDNESDAY   Warner Bros., 1966
PETE'N'TILLIE ★   Universal, 1972
ONCE IS NOT ENOUGH   Paramount, 1975
CROSS OF IRON   EMI-Rapid Film, 1977,
   w/Herbert Asmodi
HOUSE CALLS   Universal, 1978, w/Alan Mandel,
   Max Shulman & Charles Shyer
REUBEN, REUBEN ★   20th Century-Fox, 1983

GORDON ERIKSEN
THE BIG DIS   Pyramid Films, 1989, w/Robert
   Pilotte, co-directed

LAURA ERNST
TOO MUCH SUN   New Line Cinema, 1990, w/Robert
   Downey & Al Schwartz

ELLEN ERWIN
Agent: Circle Talent Associates - Beverly Hills, 213/285-1585

Screenplays:
THE SPRAY w/Jean Barash
THE IMMORTALIST w/Jean Barash

JOHN ESKOW*
Agent: CAA - Beverly Hills, 21/288-4545

PINK CADILLAC   Warner Bros., 1989
AIR AMERICA   Tri-Star, 1990, w/Richard Rush

Screenplays:
NEW CANTERBURY TALES
BLAST FROM THE PAST
SMOKESTACK LIGHTING
THE BRITISH DIPLOMAT
THE GREAT PRETENDER
CIVIL DEFENSE
ROBINSON & CARUSO
MINDREADER

JOHN ESPOSITO
GRAVEYARD SHIFT   Paramount, 1990

ALLEN ESROCK
Agent: The Wright Concept - Hollywood, 213/461-3844

Screenplays:
FLASH

EMILIO ESTEVEZ*
Agent: InterTalent - Los Angeles, 213/271-0600
Business: Euphoria Films, Orion Pictures, 213/282-2862

THAT WAS THEN, THIS IS NOW   Paramount, 1985
WISDOM   20th Century Fox, 1987, directed
MEN AT WORK   Triumph Releasing, 1990, directed

ALLEN ESTRIN*
Contact: WGA - Los Angeles, 213/550-1000

Screenplays:
OUR HOUSE w/Mark Estrin
MODEL COP
HOW TO MURDER YOUR PARENTS

ERIC ESTRIN*
Agent: William Morris Agency - Beverly Hills, 213/274-7451

Screenplays:
TAX MAN w/Michael Berlin
RED BIRD DOWN w/Michael Berlin

MARK G. ESTRIN*
Contact: WGA - Los Angeles, 213/550-1000

Screenplays:
OUR HOUSE w/Allen Estrin

JOE ESZTERHAS*
Agent: ICM - Los Angeles, 213/550-4000

F.I.S.T.   United Artists, 1978, w/Sylvester Stallone
FLASHDANCE   Paramount, 1983, w/Thomas Hedley
JAGGED EDGE   Columbia, 1985

Eu

FILM WRITERS GUIDE

BIG SHOTS   20th Century Fox, 1987
HEARTS OF FIRE   Lorimar, 1988, w/Scott Richardson
BETRAYED   MGM/UA, 1988
CHECKING OUT   Warner Bros., 1989
MUSIC BOX   Tri-Star, 1989
BASIC INSTINCT   Tri-Star, 1991

Screenplays:
ORIGINAL SIN
MAGIC MAN
BEAT THE EAGLE
CITY HALL w/J. Morgan
PALS
DIESHOT
NARC
PLATINUM
FLASHDANCE II
ROWDY

JOHN T. EUBANK
THE FINAL ALLIANCE   RC/Columbia Pictures Home Video, 1991, w/Havel Goldstein

RICHARD D. EUSTIS*
Agent: CAA - Beverly Hills, 213/288-4545

SERIAL   Paramount, 1980, w/Michael Elias
YOUNG DOCTORS IN LOVE   20th Century-Fox, 1982, w/Michael Elias

Screenplays:
ON THE BRINK w/Michael Elias
BANDIES (P) w/Michael Elias
DIRE STRAITS w/Michael Elias
BLACKJACK & SALTY w/Michael Elias

BRUCE A. EVANS*
Agent: CAA - Beverly Hills, 213/288-4545
Business: Evans-Gideon Productions, Universal Studios, 818/777-3121

A MAN, A WOMAN AND A BANK   Avco Embassy, 1979, w/Ray Gideon
STARMAN   Columbia, 1984, w/Ray Gideon
STAND BY ME ★   Columbia, 1986, w/Ray Gideon
MADE IN HEAVEN   Lorimar, 1988, w/Ray Gideon

Screenplays:
KUFFS w/Ray Gideon (directing)
THE DAY BEFORE MIDNIGHT w/Ray Gideon
BLACK RICE w/Ray Gideon
THE BETHUNE w/Ray Gideon
CHRISTMAS IN JULY w/Ray Gideon

DAVID MICKEY EVANS*
Agent: Camden-ITG - Los Angeles, 213/556-2022

RADIO FLYERS   Columbia, 1991

Screenplays:
THE DEVIL'S PLAYGROUND
HIGHWAY TO HELL

LEO EVANS*
Contact: WGA - Los Angeles, 213/550-1000

HELL HIGH   JGM Enterprises, 1989, w/Douglas Grossman

NICK EVANS
MURDER BY THE BOOK (CTF)   TVS International, 1990

ROB EWING
STEEL *LOOK DOWN AND DIE*   World Northal, 1980, Story w/Peter S. Davis & William N. Panzer

WILLIAM R. EWING*
Contact: 818/345-2790

THE SLAYER   21st Century Distribution, 1982, w/J.S. Cardone

CLIVE EXTON*
Business Manager: Teresa C. Deane, CPA, 2516 Via Tejon, Suite 216, Palos Verdes Estates, CA 90274, 213/373-9741

A PLACE TO GO   British Lion, 1963, w/Michael Relph
NIGHT MUST FALL   MGM, 1964
ISADORA *THE LOVES OF ISADORA*   Universal, 1968, w/Melvyn Bragg
ENTERTAINING MR. SLOANE   Pathe, 1969
TEN RILLINGTON PLACE   Columbia, 1970
RUNNING SCARED   Paramount, 1972, w/David Hemmings
DOOMWATCH   Tigon, 1972
THE HOUSE IN NIGHTMARE PARK   EMI, 1973, w/Terry Nation
THE AWAKENING   EMI, 1980, w/Chris Bryant & Allan Scott
RED SONJA   MGM/UA, 1985, w/George Macdonald Fraser

D.M. (DAVID) EYRE JR.*
Agent: The Artists Agency - Los Angeles, 213/277-7779

CATTLE ANNIE AND LITTLE BRITCHES   Universal, 1981, w/Robert S. Ward
WOLFEN   Orion/Warner Bros., 1981, w/Michael Wadleigh
ONE CUP OF COFFEE   Miramax, 1991, w/Robin Armstrong

Screenplays:
HAIL, ALMA MATER

JOHN EZRINE*
Agent: Irvin Arthur Associates - Beverly Hills, 213/278-5934

A DANGEROUS GAME   Hemdale, 1989

Screenplays:
SATAN'S LITTLE SISTER

F

CHRIS FABER
Agent: United Talent Agency - Beverly Hills, 213/273-6700

HANG 'EM REALLY HIGH (Short), 1989, w/Danniel Baron

Screenplays:
ASSAULT ON EMPIRE STATE MOUNTAIN (CTF) w/Danniel Baron
THE BIG PLUNGE w/Danniel Baron
FAT CHANCE w/Danniel Baron
JACKPOT w/Danniel Baron

CHRISTIAN FABER
BAIL JUMPER Angelika Films, 1990, w/Josephine Wallace

RACHEL FABIEN
LA VIE CONTINUE Triumph/Columbia, 1982, w/Moshe Mizrahi
EVERY TIME WE SAY GOODBYE Tri-Star, 1988, w/Leah Appet & Moshe Mizrahi

DAVID FALLON*
Agent: United Talent Agency - Beverly Hills, 213/273-6700

SPLIT DECISIONS New Century/Vista, 1988
WHITE FANG Buena Vista, 1991, w/Jeanne Rosenberg & Nick Thiel

Screenplays:
NEWSIES w/Tom Rickman
SEVEN SUMMITS
HARDBALL
STREETWISE

MICHAEL FALLON*
Agent: William Morris Agency - Beverly Hills, 213/274-7451

Screenplays:
CARVER'S BOX
THE MASK

KEVIN M. FALLS*
Agent: United Talent Agency - Beverly Hills, 213/273-6700

Screenplays:
BREAKING BALLS AND BROKEN HEARTS
LEFT COAST
THE TEMP
DOVE
BACHELOR MOM
BABY IN THE SILO
PUFFS
TENLEY'S MEN
SEPARATE WAYS

JAMAA FANAKA
Business Manager: Saul Rittenberg, Loeb & Loeb, 10100 Santa Monica Boulevard, Suite 2200, Los Angeles, CA 90067, 213/282-2000

EMMA MAE 1976, directed
PENITENTIARY Jerry Gross Organization, 1979, directed
PENITENTIARY II MGM/UA, 1982, directed
PENITENTIARY III Cannon, 1987, directed
STREET WARS Jamaa Fanaka Productions, 1991, directed

HAMPTON FANCHER*
Agent: United Talent Agency - Beverly Hills, 213/273-6700

BLADE RUNNER The Ladd Company/Warner Bros., 1982, w/David Peoples
THE MIGHTY QUINN MGM/UA, 1989

Screenplays:
THE PAINTER
CHINESE BANDITS
MRS. CALIBAN
PRISM
TOUCH
SALVATION

JACQUES FANSTEN
Contact: French Film Office, 745 Fifth Avenue, New York, NY 10151, 212/832-8860

CROSS MY HEART MK2 Productions, 1991, directed

MICHAEL FARGAS
PRIME RISK Almi Pictures, 1985, directed

EMIL FARKAS
FORCE: FIVE American Cinema, 1981, w/George Goldsmith

FRANK FARMER
SLUMBER PARTY '57 Cannon, 1977

GRAEME FARMER
DARLINGS OF THE GODS (CMS) Simpson Le Mesurier Films Production/Australian Broadcasting Corporation/Thames TV, 1990, w/Roger Simpson

RALPH FARQUHAR*
Agent: Triad Artists, Inc. - Los Angeles, 213/556-2727

KRUSH GROOVE Warner Bros., 1985

TREVOR A. FARRANT*
Business: Punchline Pty. Ltd. - 08/512-930 (Australia)

THE PIRATE MOVIE 20th Century-Fox, 1982
STRUCK BY LIGHTNING Beyond International Group, 1990

PETER FARRELLY*
Agent: CAA - Beverly Hills, 213/288-4545

Screenplays:
ADULT EDUCATION w/Bennett Yellin
DUST TO DUST w/Bennett Yellin
YOUNG LOVERS w/Bennett Yellin
FREE SPIRITS w/Bennett Yellin

OUR PLANET TONIGHT w/Bennett Yellin
BLACK TIE w/Bennett Yellin
POISON IVY w/Bennett Yellin

JOHN FARRIS*
Agent: The Agency - Los Angeles, 213/551-3000

DEAR DEAD DELILAH   Southern Star, 1975, directed
THE FURY   20th Century-Fox, 1978

JOHN FASANO*
Agent: ICM - Los Angeles, 213/550-4000

ANOTHER 48 HRS.   Paramount, 1990, w/Larry Gross & Jeb Stuart

Screenplays:
GIRL'S CLUB
BLUE BLOOD

ALVIN L. FAST
DEATHTRAP   Mars, 1976, w/Mardi Rustam
ANGEL'S BRIGADE   Arista, 1980, w/Greydon Clark

LINDA R. FAVILA*
Contact: WGA - Los Angeles, 213/550-1000

BORIS & NATASHA   MCEG, 1990, w/Charles E. Fradin, unreleased

WILLIAM FAY
RISING STORM   Gibraltar Releasing, 1989, w/Gary Rosen

JEFF FAZIO*
Agent: Pleshette & Green - Los Angeles, 213/465-0428

Screenplays:
AL DENTE
AIRBORNE
PARIS AMERICAN
IN THE BAG

JACQUELINE FEATHER*
Agent: Harris & Goldberg - Los Angeles, 213/553-5200

Screenplays:
THE BOXER   w/David Seidler
CLOSE TO HOME   w/David Seidler
GLITTERBUG   w/David Seidler

F.X. FEENEY*
Paul Kohner, Inc. - Los Angeles, 213/550-1060

FRANKENSTEIN UNBOUND   20th Century Fox, 1990, w/Roger Corman

JARRE FEES*
Agent: ICM - Los Angeles, 213/550-4000

PERMANENT RECORD   Paramount, 1988, w/Larry Ketron & Alice Liddle

LINDA FEFERMAN*
Agent: The Gersh Agency - Beverly Hills, 213/274-6611

SEVEN MINUTES IN HEAVEN   Warner Bros., 1986, w/Jane Bernstein, directed

JULES FEIFFER*
Agent: The Roberts Company - Los Angeles, 213/552-7800
& The Lantz Office - New York, 212/586-0200

GROWN-UPS (P)
A THINK PIECE (P)
ELLIOT LOVES (P)
LITTLE MURDERS   20th Century-Fox, 1970
CARNAL KNOWLEDGE   Avco Embassy, 1971
POPEYE   Paramount, 1980
I WANT TO GO HOME   MK2, 1989

Screenplays:
BABY PICTURES
ANSWERS
LITTLE BRUCIE
TERRY & THE PIRATES

J. D. FEIGELSON*
Contact: 213/273-7769

Screenplays:
ASTRONAUTS WIVES
ALMOST HUMAN

JUDITH FEIN*
Agent: Triad Artists, Inc. - Los Angeles, 213/556-2727

Screenplays:
SISTERS
WHAT EVERY WOMAN WANTS
CHANGING TIMES
AFTER JIMMY
DIRTY DANCING II
INTIMATE WRITINGS OF THEODORE HAMMER

STEPHEN J. FEKE*
Agent: Camden-ITG - Los Angeles, 213/289-2700

WHEN A STRANGER CALLS   Columbia, 1979, w/Fred Walton
HADLEY'S REBELLION   American Film Distributors, 1984, w/Fred Walton
PAPA WAS A PREACHER   La Rose Distributors, 1986
MAC & ME   Orion, 1988, w/Stewart Raffill
TRAPPED (CTF)   USA/MCA Television, 1989, w/Fred Walton
KEYS TO FREEDOM   RPB Pictures/Queens Cross Productions, 1990, directed

Screenplays:
AMONG HONORABLE MEN
ST. JOHN'S BREAD
OUT OF THE DARK LOCKERS

NICHOLAS FELACCI
Agent: William Morris Agency - Beverly Hills, 213/274-7451

Screenplays:
THE BRANDENBURG   w/Damon Santostefano

MARK L. FELDBERG*
Agent: The Irv Schechter Company - Beverly Hills, 213/278-8070

LET'S GET HARRY   Tri-Star, 1987, Story w/Samuel Fuller
DISORDERLIES   Warner Bros., 1987, w/Mitchell Klebanoff

Screenplays:
BEVERLY HILLS NINJA   w/Mitchell Klebanoff

DENNIS J. FELDMAN*
Agent: ICM - Los Angeles, 213/550-4000

JUST ONE OF THE GUYS   Columbia, 1985,
   w/Jeff Franklin
THE GOLDEN CHILD   Paramount, 1986
REAL MEN   MGM/UA, 1987, directed

Screenplays:
THE PIRANDELLO FACTOR
BUDDHA OF BRANDENBERG
MONSTER NIGHT
DAYWORLD

JOHN FELDMAN
Agent: InterTalent - Los Angeles, 213/858-6200

ALLIGATOR EYES   Castle Hill, 1990, directed

JOHNATHAN FELDMAN*
Agent: CAA - Beverly Hills, 213/288-4545

Screenplays:
SWING KIDS
BAND OF ANGELS
PROOF POSITIVE (CTF)

RACHEL FELDMAN
Agent: The Irv Schechter Company - Beverly Hills,
   213/278-8070

GIUSTINA (Short), directed

Screenplays:
MAJORITY RULES   HIP TO BE SQUARE
   w/Susan Nanus
SMOTHERED w/Susan Nanus
INTO DARKNESS

RANDY FELDMAN*
Agent: CAA - Beverly Hills, 213/288-4545

HELL NIGHT   Aquarius, 1981
TANGO & CASH   Warner Bros., 1989

Screenplays:
MAN TO MAN
RENEGADE

J. P. FELIX
EDGE OF SANITY   Millimeter Films, 1989, w/Ron Raley

FEDERICO FELLINI
Address: Via Margutta 110, Rome, Italy, 06/6780173

L'AMORE   Tevere Film, 1948, w/Tullio Pinelli &
   Roberto Rosselini
IL CAMMINO DELLA SPERANZA   Lux, 1950,
   w/Tullio Pinelli
VARIETY LIGHTS   Pathe Contemporary, 1950, w/Tullio
   Pinelli, Ennio Flaiano & Alberto Lattuada, co-directed
THE WHITE SHEIK   Pathe Contermporary, 1952,
   w/Tullio Pinelli & Ennio Flaiano, directed
I VITTELONI   API Productions, 1953, w/Ennio
   Flaiano, directed
LOVE IN THE CITY   Italian Films Export, 1953,
   Episode IV: "A Matrimonal Agency" w/Tullio
   Pinelli, directed
LA STRADA   Trans-Lux, 1954, w/Tullio Pinelli & Ennio
   Flaiano, directed
IL BIDONE   Astor, 1955, w/Tullio Pinelli &
   Ennio Flaiano, directed
NIGHTS OF CABIRIA   Lopert, 1957, w/Tullio Pinelli &
   Ennio Flaiano
LA DOLCE VITA ★   Astor, 1960, w/Tullio Pinelli &
   Ennio Flaiano, directed
BOCCACCIO '70   Embasssy, 1962, Part II "The
   Temptations of Doctor Antonio," w/Tullio Pinelli &
   Ennio Flaiano, directed
8-1/2 ★   Embassy, 1963, w/Tullio Pinelli, Ennio Flaiano &
   Brunello Rondi, directed
JULIET OF THE SPIRITS   Rizzoli, 1965, w/Tullio Pinelli,
   Ennio Flaiano & Brunello Rondi, directed
SPIRITS OF THE DEAD   *HISTOIRES EXTRAORDINAIRES*
   American International, 1969, Episode III "Toby Dammit,"
   w/Bernardino Zapponi, directed
FELLINI SATYRICON   United Artists, 1970, w/Bernardino
   Zapponi, directed
FELLINI'S ROMA   United Artists, 1972, w/Bernardino
   Zapponi, directed
AMARCORD ★   New World, 1974, w/Tonino
   Guerra, directed
CASANOVA ★   *IL CASANOVA DI FEDERICO FELLINI*
   Universal, 1977, w/Bernardino Zapponi, directed
ORCHESTRA REHEARSAL   New Yorker, 1979,
   w/Bernardino Zapponi, directed
CITY OF WOMEN   Gaumont/New Yorker, 1981,
   w/Bernardino Zapponi & Brunello Rondi
AND THE SHIP SAILS ON   Triumph/Colulmbia, 1983,
   w/Tonino Guerra, directed
GINGER AND FRED   MGM/UA, 1986, w/Tonino Guerra &
   Tullio Pinelli, directed
L'INTERVISTA   Alijosha Productions/Cinecitta/RAI,
   1987, directed
THE VOICE OF THE MOON   Penta Distribuzione, 1990,
   w/Tullio Pinelli & Ermanno Cavazzoni, directed

ANDREW J. FENADY*
Agent: ICM - Los Angeles, 213/550-4000
Business: Fenady Associates, Inc., 249 N. Larchmont Blvd. -
   Suite 6, Los Angeles, CA 90004, 213/466-6375

STAKEOUT ON DOPE STREET   Warner Bros., 1958,
   w/Irvin Kershner & Irwin Schwartz
RIDE BEYOND VENGEANCE   Columbia, 1966
CHISUM   Warner Bros., 1970
THE MAN WITH BOGART'S FACE   *SAM MARLOW,*
   PRIVATE EYE   20th Century-Fox, 1980

BLAIR FERGUSON*
Agent: Lake & Douroux - Beverly Hills, 213/557-0700

Screenplays:
THE MOVES MAKE THE MAN
STONE WINGS
TUNNEL BOYS
MUD SWEAT AND GEARS
PEACHES POINT

LARRY FERGUSON*
Agent: InterTalent - Los Angeles, 213/271-0600

ST. HELENS   Davis-Panzer Productions, 1981,
   w/Peter Bellwood
HIGHLANDER   20th Century Fox, 1986, w/Peter Bellwood
   & Gregory Widen
BEVERLY HILLS COP II   Paramount, 1987,
   w/Warren Skaaren

THE PRESIDIO   Paramount, 1988
THE HUNT FOR RED OCTOBER   Paramount, 1990, w/Donald Stewart
TALENT FOR THE GAME   Paramount, 1991, w/Tom Donnelly & David Himmelstein

Screenplays:
THE LAST LAUGH w/Peter Bellwood
MALACHI w/Peter Bellwood
BLOOD LEGACY
THE LAWBREAKERS
SID

GEORGE FERNANDEZ
CEASE FIRE   Cineworld, 1985, from his play "Vietnam Trilogy"

BETH FERRIS
HEARTLAND   Levitt-Pickman, 1979

DARRELL FETTY*
Agent: Writers & Artists Agency - Los Angeles, 213/820-2240

FREEWAY   New World, 1988, w/Francis Delia

MANUEL FIDELLO
FRIDAY THE 13TH, PART VII: THE NEW BLOOD   Paramount, 1988, w/Daryl Haney

DAVID M. FIELD*
Agent: William Morris Agency - Beverly Hills, 213/274-7451

AMAZING GRACE AND CHUCK   Tri-Star, 1987

Screenplays:
LIME'S CRISIS w/Ron Bass
HEART'S DESIRE

GREG FIELDS*
Contact: 213/460-5955

BACK TO SCHOOL   Orion, 1986, Story w/Rodney Dangerfield & Dennis Snee

MARIA FIELDS
DEADLY DANCER   Action International Pictures, 1990, w/David Halpern

MICHAEL FIELDS
Agent: William Morris Agency - Beverly Hills, 213/274-7451

Screenplays:
FACE

SCOTT G. FIELDS*
Agent: ICM - Los Angeles, 213/550-4000

DANGEROUSLY CLOSE   Cannon, 1986, w/Marty Ross & John Stockwell
UNDER COVER   Cannon, 1987, w/John Stockwell

HARVEY FIERSTEIN*
Agent: William Morris Agency - New York, 212/586-5100

LA CAGE AUX FOLLES (P)
SPOOKHOUSE (P)

TORCH SONG TRILOGY   New Line Cinema, 1988, from his play
TIDY ENDINGS (CTF)   HBO/Sandollar Productions, 1988

Screenplays:
SINGING SISTERS

MIKE FIGGIS
Agent: ICM - Los Angeles, 213/550-4000

STORMY MONDAY   Atlantic Releasing Corporation, 1986, directed
LIEBESTRAUM   MGM-Pathe, 1991, directed

PETER FILARDI*
Agent: ICM - Los Angeles, 213/550-4000

FLATLINERS   Columbia, 1990

Screenplays:
TOM CAT

JEREMY BERTRAND FINCH*
Agent: Preferred Artists - Encino, 818/990-0305

Screenplays:
THE GIVER
WHIPLASH
OUTCALLS

MARTINA S. FINCH*
Agent: Preferred Artists - Encino, 818/990-0305

Screenplays:
FALSE PAPERS

CARMEN FINESTRA*
Agent: William Morris Agency - Beverly Hills, 213/274-7451

Screenplays:
HARV, THE BARBARIAN

ANTHONY J. FINGLETON*
Agent: Maggie Field Agency - Studio City, 818/980-2001

OVER MY DEAD BODY (P)   shared
DROP DEAD, FRED   New Line Cinema, 1991, w/Carlos Davis

Screenplays:
HOME FOR CHRISTMAS

WILLIAM M. FINKELSTEIN*
Agent: United Talent Agency - Beverly Hills, 213/273-6700

Screenplays:
LONG ODD FROM JERSEY

KENNETH FINKLEMAN*
Agent: CAA - Beverly Hills, 213/288-4545

GREASE 2   Paramount, 1982
AIRPLANE II: THE SEQUEL   Paramount, 1983, directed
ILLEGALLY YOURS   DEG, 1986, w/Michael Kaplan & John Levenstein, as "Max Dickens & M.A. Stewart"

HEAD OFFICE   Tri-Star, 1986, directed
WHO'S THAT GIRL?   Warner Bros., 1987,
   w/Andrew Smith

Screenplays:
NEWS w/Gary Ross
TWO LITTLE RICH GIRLS
COMEBACK
ASSASSINATION ON EMBASSY ROAD
SUNNY WITH RAIN
ALAMAGORDO
DANGEROUSLY

WILLIAM FRANKLIN FINLEY
Agent: Stone Manners Agency - Los Angeles,
   213/275-9599

THE FIRST TIME   New Line Cinema, 1982, w/Charlie
   Loventhal & Susan Weiser-Finley

JOHN FINNEGAN
ALL'S FAIR   Moviestore Entertainment, 1989, w/William
   Pace, Tom Rondinella & Randee Russell

SAM FIRSTENBERG
Agent: CAA - Bevelry Hills, 213/288-4545

ONE MORE CHANCE   Cannon, 1981, directed

MICHAEL FIRTH
Business: P.O. Box 37-177, Parnell, Auckland,
   New Zealand, 09/399-699

SYLVIA   MGM/UA Classics, 1985, w/F. Fairfax &
   Michele Quill, directed

JANICE FISCHER*
Agent: Triad Artists, Inc. - Los Angeles, 213/556-2727

THE LOST BOYS   Warner Bros., 1987, w/Jeffrey
   Boam & James Jeremias

Screenplays:
INTER-GALACTIC HIGH w/James Jeremias
MERLYN w/James Jeremias
HELL OF A DEAL w/J. Tappis
MISSING LINKS w/M. Ganzel
DR. VOODOO

MAX FISCHER
THE LUCKY STAR   Pickman Films, 1981,
   w/Jack Rosenthal

PETER S. FISCHER*
Agent: CAA - Beverly Hills, 213/288-4545

TAGGET (CTF)   Mirisch-Tagget-MCA, 1991, w/Janis
   Diamond & Richard T. Heffron

STEPHEN C. FISCHER*
Contact: WGA - Los Angeles, 213/550-1000

Screenplays:
SOMETHING LINGERS
WHEN A MAN LOVES A WOMAN (THE INSIDE STORY)
PHYSICAL CHEMISTRY

CARRIE FISHER*
Agent: CAA - Beverly Hills, 213/288-4545

POSTCARDS FROM THE EDGE   Columbia, 1990

Screenplays:
CHRISTMAS IN LAS VEGAS
SURRENDER THE PINK

DAVID FISHER
Address: 14144 Dickens, Apt. 115, Sherman Oaks, CA
   91423, 818/907-1368

LIAR'S MOON   Crown International, 1982, directed
TOY SOLDIERS   New World, 1984, w/Walter
   Fox, directed

GAIL FISHER*
Contact: WGA - Los Angeles, 213/550-1000

Screenplays:
AMERICAN LADY w/Marc Chesler
DISTANT RELATIVE w/Marc Chesler
ME, MYSELF AND I w/Marc Chesler
MALE-FEMALE w/Marc Chesler
STIRRUPS w/Marc Chesler

JIM FISHER*
Agent: Writers & Artists Agency - Los Angeles, 213/820-2240

Screenplays:
CHUMP TOWER w/Jim Staahl
UNDER SURVEILLANCE w/Jim Staahl
DUH BOAT S.O.S. w/Jim Staahl

MICHAEL FISHER*
Contact: WGA - Los Angeles, 213/550-1000

EARTHBOUND   Taft International, 1981

ROBERT FISHER*
Contact: WGA - Los Angeles, 213/550-1000

THE IMPOSSIBLE YEARS (P) w/Arthur Marx
A GLOBAL AFFAIR   Seven Arts, 1963, w/Arthur Marx &
   Charles Lederer
I'LL TAKE SWEDEN   United Artists, 1965, w/Arthur Marx &
   Nat Perrin
EIGHT ON THE LAM   United Artists, 1966, w/Arthur Marx,
   Albert E. Lewin & Burt Styler
CANCEL MY RESERVATION   Naho Enterprises, 1972,
   w/Arthur Marx

TERRY LOUISE FISHER*
Agent: ICM - Los Angeles, 213/550-4000

SECOND THOUGHTS   Universal, 1983, Story
   w/Steve Brown

BILL FISHMAN*
Agent: ICM - Los Angeles, 213/550-4000
Business: Fisher & Preachman, 1310 Main Street, Venice,
   CA 90291, 213/392-1896

TAPEHEADS   Avenue Pictures, 1988, w/Peter
   McCarthy, directed

Screenplays:
DREAMING OF BABYLON

Fi

FILM WRITERS GUIDE

JEFFREY ALAN FISKIN*
Agent: CAA - Beverly Hills, 213/288-4545

ANGEL UNCHAINED   American International, 1969
CUTTER'S WAY   United Artists Classics, 1981
THE PURSUIT OF D.B. COOPER   Universal, 1981
CRACKERS   Universal, 1984
REVENGE   Columbia, 1990, w/Jim Harrison

Screenplays:
CRAVAN
FIRST CLASS
A CHRONICLE OF BRIMSTONE
CHANGE OF PLANS
FLASHDANCE II
BASKETBALL DIARIES
THE BOURNE IDENTITY

BENEDICT FITZGERALD
Agentt: Solomon Weingarten & Associates - Los Angeles, 213/474-8703

WISE BLOOD   New Line Cinema, 1979, w/Michael Fitzgerald

ED FITZGERALD
Agent: The Irv Schechter Company - Beverly Hills, 213/278-8070

Screenplays:
HEAVEN SENT w/Paul Koval

MICHAEL FITZGERALD
WISE BLOOD   New Line Cinema, 1979, w/Benedict Fitzgerald

FANNIE FLAGG
Agent: CAA - Beverly Hills, 213/288-4545

Screenplays:
FRIED GREEN TOMATOES AT THE WHISTLE STOP CAFE

JOE FLAHERTY*
Agent: William Morris Agency - Beverly Hills, 213/274-7451

Screenplays:
BIG BROADCAST

FIONNULA FLANAGAN
Agent: The Artists Agency - Los Angeles, 213/277-7779

JAMES JOYCE'S WOMEN   Universal, 1985

GREGORY FLEEMAN*
Contact: WGA - Los Angeles, 213/550-1000

F/X   Orion, 1986, w/Robert Megginson

Screenplays:
TWO COPS w/Robert Megginson

BUD FLEISHER
HARDCASE AND FIST   United Entertainment, 1989, w/Tony Zarindast

ANDREW FLEMING
Agent: InterTalent - Los Angeles, 213/271-0600

BAD DREAMS   20th Century Fox, 1988, w/Steven de Souza, directed

SHARY FLENNIKEN
NATIONAL LAMPOON'S MOVIE MADNESS   United Artists, 1982, w/Tod Carroll, Pat Mephitis, Gerald Sussman & Ellis Weiner

THEODORE J. FLICKER*
Business Manager: Marvin Freedman, Freedman, Kinzelberg & Broder, 1801 Avenue of the Stars, Los Angeles, CA 90067, 213/277-0700

SPINOUT   MGM, 1966, w/George Kirgo
THE PRESIDENT'S ANALYST   Paramount, 1967, directed
UP IN THE CELLAR   American International, 1970, directed

MIGUEL TEJADA-FLORES
(See Miguel TEJADA-FLORES)

JOHN FLYNN
Agent: United Talent Agency - Beverly Hills, 213/273-6700

THE OUTFIT   MGM, 1974, directed

ELLEN L. FOGLE*
Agent: United Talent Agency - Beverly Hills, 213/273-6700

Screenplays:
FILTHY RICH

LAWRENCE D. FOLDES
Contact: Ronald G. Gabler, 9606 Santa Monica Blvd., Beverly Hills, CA 90210, 213/205-8908
Business: Star Cinema Production Group, Inc., 6523 Hollywood Blvd. - Suite 927, Los Angeles, CA 90028, 213/463-2000

YOUNG WARRIORS   Cannon, 1983, w/Russell W. Colgin, directed

PETER FOLDY
Agent: Media Artists Group - Hollywood, 213/463-5610

HOT MOVES   Cardinal Pictures Corp., 1985, w/Larry Anderson
HOMEBOYS   DB Media, 1991

Screenplays:
LUNA PARK
POSTCARD FROM PARADISE
SMOKE SCREEN

PETER FOLEG
THE UNSEEN   World Northal, 1981, Story w/Michael L. Grace, Kim Henkel & Nancy Rifkin

JAMES FOLEY*
Agent: CAA - Beverly Hills, 213/288-4545

AFTER DARK, MY SWEET   Avenue Pictures, 1990, w/Robert Redlin, directed

ALAN R. FOLSOM*
Agent: The Marion Rosenberg Office - West Hollywood, 213/653-7383

Screenplays:
DEADLY FORCE

PETER FONDA
Agent: The Artists Agency - Los Angeles, 213/277-7779

EASY RIDER ★ Columbia, 1969, w/Dennis Hopper & Terry Southern
FATAL MISSION Funahara, 1990, w/others

NAOMI FONER*
Agent: CAA - Beverly Hills, 213/288-4545

VIOLETS ARE BLUE Columbia, 1986
RUNNING ON EMPTY ★ Warner Bros., 1987

Screenplays:
A DANGEROUS WOMAN
THE HOMESMAN
FIRST LIGHT
TRIANGLE
BABY, BABY
LOOKING FOR WORK
VERY GOOD GIRLS
RANDOM HEARTS
ALIBIS

FERNANDO FONSECA
THE UNHOLY Vestron, 1988, w/Philip Yordan

LLOYD FONVIELLE*
Business Manager: Addis-Wechsler & Associates - Los Angeles, 213/954-9000

LORDS OF DISCIPLINE Paramount, 1983, w/Thomas Pope
THE BRIDE Columbia, 1985
CHERRY 2000 Orion, 1986, Story
GOTHAM (CTF) Showtime/Phoenix Entertainment Group/Keith Addis & Associates, 1988, directed

Screenplays:
THE KING LIVES
WOMEN, MONEY & RESTAURANTS
FOOLISH THINGS
EVE'S RIB
ATLANTIS

HORTON FOOTE*
Agent: Lucy Kroll Agency - New York, 212/877-0627

COURTSHIP (P), also teleplay
TALKING PICTURES (P)
STORM FEAR United Artists, 1955
TO KILL A MOCKINGBIRD ★★ Universal, 1962
BABY, THE RAIN MUST FALL Columbia, 1965, from his play "The Travelling Lady"
THE CHASE Columbia, 1966
HURRY, SUNDOWN Paramount, 1967, w/Thomas C. Ryan
FOOLS PARADE Columbia, 1971
TOMORROW Filmgroup, 1972
TENDER MERCIES ★★ Universal/AFD, 1983
1918 Cinecom International, 1985, from his play
THE TRIP TO BOUNTIFUL ★ Island Pictures, 1985, from his play
ON VALENTINES DAY Angelika Films, 1986, from his play "Valentines Day"
CONVICTS MCEG, 1991

Screenplays:
THE WIDOW CLAIRE (from his play)
SPRING MOON
ROOTS IN A PARCHED GROUND
HEART MOUNTAIN
MY FIRST LADY
OF MICE AND MEN

BRYAN FORBES*
Agent: The Marion Rosenberg Office - Los Angeles, 213/653-7383

COCKLESHELL HEROES Columbia, 1955, w/Richard Maibaum
HOUSE OF SECRETS Rank, 1956, w/Robert Buckner
THE BLACK TENT Rank, 1956, w/Robin Maugham
THE BABY AND THE BATTLESHIP British Lion, 1956, w/Jay Lewis & Gilbert Hackforth-Jones
I WAS MONTY'S DOUBLE NTA Pictures, 1958
THE CAPTAIN'S TABLE Rank, 1958, w/Nicholas Phipps & John Whiting
DANGER WITHIN British Lion, 1959, w/Frank Harvey
THE ANGRY SILENCE British Lion, 1960
MAN IN THE MOON Allied Film Makers, 1960, w/Michael Relph
THE LEAGUE OF GENTLEMEN Rank, 1960
ONLY TWO CAN PLAY British Lion, 1962
THE L-SHAPED ROOM British Lion, 1962, directed
STATION SIX-SAHARA Allied Artists, 1963, w/Brian Clemens
SEANCE ON A WET AFTERNOON Rank, 1964, directed
OF HUMAN BONDAGE MGM, 1964
KING RAT Columbia, 1965, directed
THE WHISPERERS United Artists, 1966, directed
DEADFALL 20th Century-Fox, 1968, directed
THE RAGING MOON LONG AGO TOMORROW EMI, 1970, directed
THE SLIPPER AND THE ROSE: THE STORY OF CINDERELLA Universal, 1976, w/Richard M. Sherman & Robert B. Sherman, directed
INTERNATIONAL VELVET MGM/United Artists, 1978, directed
HOPSCOTCH Avco Embassy, 1980
BETTER LATE THAN NEVER Warner Bros., 1983, directed
THE NAKED FACE Cannon, 1985, directed

JEAN FORD*
Agent: Warden & White Associates - Beverly Hills, 213/852-1028

Screenplays:
THE PRIOR LIFE OF MICKEY SLATER w/S. Michael Cole
IMMACULATE DECEPTION w/S. Michael Cole

RICHARD FORD
Agent: ICM - Los Angeles, 213/550-4000

BRIGHT ANGEL Hemdale, 1991

RICHARD FOREMAN
STRONG MEDICINE Film Forum, 1981

STEPHEN H. FOREMAN*
Agent: The Artists Agency - Los Angeles, 213/277-7779

THE JAZZ SINGER   AFD, 1980, Adaptation

Screenplays:
DESPERADO
WOMAN IN THE WILDERNESS
SUPERSTITION
KEY WEST
THE JOURNEY OF AUGUST KING
COUGAR
BEN & JOANNA
PINK MOUNTAIN TINNY

MILOS FORMAN
Agent: The Lantz Office - New York, 212/586-0200

LOVES OF A BLONDE   Prominent, 1966, w/Ivan Passer & Jaroslav Papusek, directed
THE FIREMAN'S BALL   Cinema 5, 1968, w/Ivan Passer & Jaroslav Papousek, directed
TAKING OFF   Universal, 1971, w/jean Claude Carriere, John Guare & John Klein, directed

DOUG FORSMITH
LIBERTY & BASH   Fries Home Video, 1990

BILL FORSYTH
Agent: CAA - Beverly Hills, 213/288-4545

THAT SINKING FEELING   Samuel Goldwyn Company, 1979, directed
GREGORY'S GIRL   Samuel Goldwyn Company, 1982, directed
LOCAL HERO   Warner Bros., 1983, directed
COMFORT AND JOY   Universal, 1984, directed
HOUSEKEEPING   Columbia, 1987, directed

FREDERICK FORSYTH*
Agent: Curtis Brown, Ltd. - New York, 212/473-5400

THE FOURTH PROTOCOL   Lorimar, 1987

ROB FORSYTH
CLEARCUT   Alliance International, 1991

BOB FORWARD
THE SECRET OF THE SWORD (AF)   Atlantic Releasing Corporation, 1985, w/Larry Ditillo

BOB FOSS
SHIPWRECKED   Buena Vista, 1991, w/Greg Dinner, Nils Gaup & Nick Thiel

ROBERT O. FOSTER*
Agent: The Gersh Agency - Beverly Hills, 213/274-6611

CLINTON AND NADINE (CTF)   HBO Pictures/ITC, 1988
DEAD-BANG   Warner Bros., 1989

ROBERT FOWLER*
Agent: Harold R. Greene Inc. - Los Angeles, 213/852-4959

BELOW THE BELT   Atlantic Releasing Corporation, 1980, w/Sherrie Sonnett

ALAN C. FOX
THE PARTY ANIMAL   International Film Marketing, 1985, Story

ERICA FOX
DEAD WOMEN IN LINGERIE   Seagate Films, 1990, w/John Romo, directed

FRED S. FOX*
Agent: The Irv Schechter Company - Beverly Hills, 213/278-8070

OH GOD! BOOK II   Warner Bros., 1980, w/Josh Greenfeld, Hal Goldman, Seaman Jacobs & Melissa Miller

ROBBIE FOX*
Agent: CAA - Beverly Hills, 213/288-4545

THE GREAT O'GRADY (Short), directed

Screenplays:
FOUR MONTHS 12 MINUTES (directing)
SO I MARRIED AN AXE-MURDERER
SLIGHTLY PANICKED
SHOOTING ELIZABETH
JOEY ON THE 31ST FLOOR

TERRY CURTIS FOX*
Agent: United Talent Agency - Beverly Hills, 213/273-6700

COPS (P), also screenplay
JUSTICE (P)
SUMMER GARDEN (P)
THE PORNOGRAPHER'S DAUGHTER (P)
THE PERFECT WITNESS (CTF)   HBO Premiere Films, 1989, w/Ron Hutchinson

Screenplays:
JUNGLELAND
SUNSTROKE
FLASH OF EDEN
THE PROSECUTION
13
THE LIFE OF RAFELLO GALLO

WALTER FOX
Agent: ICM - Los Angeles, 213/550-4000

TOY SOLDIERS   New World, 1984, w/David Fisher

CHARLES E. FRADIN
BORIS & NATASHA   MCEG, 1990, w/Linda R. Favila, unreleased

Screenplays:
DELIVERY BOY

CLAUDIO FRAGASSO
THE SEVEN MAGNIFICENT GLADIATORS   Cannon, 1985

RANDALL FRAKES
ROLLER BLADE   New World, 1986, w/Donald G. Jackson
DIPLOMATIC IMMUNITY   Fries Distribution, 1991, w/Richard Donn

JOSEPH R. FRALEY*
Business Manager: Tim O'Connor, 818/769-1425

SILENT RAGE   Columbia, 1982

RICARDO FRANCO
BLOOD AND SAND   Overseas Film Group, 1989,
   w/Rafael Azcona & Thomas Fucci
BERLIN BLUES   Cannon, 1989, directed

A. SCOTT FRANK*
Agent: CAA - Beverly Hills, 213/288-4545

PLAIN CLOTHES   Paramount, 1988
DEAD AGAIN   Paramount, 1991
LITTLE MAN TATE   Orion, 1991

Screenplays:
GLORY DAYS

CAROL FRANK*
Agent: Shorr, Stille & Associates - Los Angeles,
   213/659-6160

SORORITY HOUSE MASSACRE   Concorde,
   1987, directed

CHRISTOPHER FRANK
THE FRENCH WAY   LOVE AT THE TOP
   Peppercorn-Wormser, 1975
FEMMES DE PERSONNE   European Classics,
   1986, directed
L'ANNEE DES MEDUSES   European Classics,
   1987, directed
MALONE   Orion, 1987

HARRIET FRANK, JR. *
Agent: William Morris Agency - Beverly Hills, 213/274-7451

STEEL RIVER   Warner Bros., 1948,
   w/Stephen Longstreet
WHIPLASH   Warner Bros., 1948, w/Maurice Geraghty
TEN WANTED MEN   Columbia, 1955, Story
   w/Irving Ravetch
THE LONG HOT SUMMER   MGM, 1958,
   w/Irving Ravetch
THE SOUND AND THE FURY   20th Century-Fox,
   1959, w/Irving Ravetch
HOME FROM THE HILL   MGM, 1959, w/Irving Ravetch
THE DARK AT THE TOP OF THE STAIRS   Warner Bros.,
   1960, w/Irving Ravetch
HUD ★   Paramount, 1963, w/Irving Ravetch
HOMBRE   20th Century-Fox, 1967, w/Irving Ravetch
THE REIVERS   National General, 1969,
   w/Irving Ravetch
THE COWBOYS   Warner Bros., 1972, w/Irving Ravetch
THE SPIKES GANG   United Artists, 1974,
   w/Irving Ravetch
CONRACK   20th Century-Fox, 1974, w/Irving Ravetch
NORMA RAE ★   20th Century-Fox, 1979,
   w/Irving Ravetch
MURPHY'S ROMANCE   Columbia, 1985,
   w/Irving Ravetch
STANLEY & IRIS   MGM/UA, 1990, w/Irving Ravetch

Screenplays:
BEGINNERS   w/Barbara Benedek & Irving Ravetch
MIXED FEELINGS   w/Irving Ravetch
SINGLE   w/Irving Ravetch

LAURIE FRANK*
Agent: Susan Smith & Associates - Beverly Hills,
   213/852-4777

MAKING MR. RIGHT   Orion, 1987, w/Floyd Byars

Screenplays:
HARD TO GET
IN DEEP   w/Jocko Potter
BEAUTY AND BRAINS

SCOTT FRANK
(See A. Scott Frank)

DAVID FRANKEL*
Agent: ICM - Los Angeles, 213/550-4000

FUNNY ABOUT LOVE   Paramount, 1990,
   w/Norman Steinberg

Screenplays:
NERVOUS TICKS

DEBRA FRANKEL*
Agent: CNA & Associates - Los Angeles, 213/556-4343

Screenplays:
NANCY NEWTON, R.N.
NO T.V.
DEVIL'S FOOD

AL FRANKEN*
Agent: Harris & Goldberg - Los Angeles, 213/553-5200
Personal Manager: Barry Secunda, 212/247-4790

ONE MORE SATURDAY NIGHT   Columbia, 1986,
   w/Tom Davis

CARL FRANKLIN
Business: Concorde Pictures, 11600 San Vicente Blvd.,
   Los Angeles, CA 90049, 213/826-0978

PUNK (Short), directed
EYE OF THE EAGLE II: INSIDE THE ENEMY   Concorde,
   1989, w/Dan Gagliasso, directed

DANIEL JAY FRANKLIN*
Agent: Harris & Goldberg - Los Angeles, 213/553-5200

DREAM A LITTLE DREAM   Vestron, 1989, w/D.E.
   Eisenberg & Marc Rocco

GEORGE FRANKLIN
Agent: Broder-Kurland-Webb-Uffner - Los Angeles,
   213/656-9262

THE INCUBUS   Film Ventures International, 1982

HOWARD FRANKLIN*
Agent: CAA - Beverly Hills, 213/288-4545

THE NAME OF THE ROSE   20th Century Fox, 1986,
   w/Andrew Birkin, Gerard Brach & Alain Godard
SOMEONE TO WATCH OVER ME   Columbia, 1987
QUICK CHANGE   Warner Bros., 1990, co-directed

Screenplays:
PUBLIC EYE
QUEEN OF KINGDOM

Fr

FILM WRITERS GUIDE

HOOVERVILLE
THE SHADOW
THE MAN WHO SAVED THE WORLD

JEFF FRANKLIN*
Agent: Barrett, Benson, McCartt & Weston - Los Angeles, 213/247-5500
Business: Jeff Franklin Productions, 10202 W. Washington Blvd., Culver City, CA 90232, 213/280-5428

JUST ONE OF THE GUYS   Columbia, 1985, w/Dennis Feldman
SUMMER SCHOOL   Paramount, 1987

DAVID H. FRANZONI*
Contact: WGA - Los Angeles, 213/550-1000

JUMPIN' JACK FLASH   20th Century Fox, 1986, w/Patricia Irving, J.W. Melville & Christopher Thompson

Screenplays:
GOLD w/Bob Swaim
THE 9TH FOX
TORN
THE CLUB
FIRE

GEORGE MACDONALD FRASER
Contact: British Film Institute, 011/441/437-4355

THE THREE MUSKETEERS   20th Century-Fox, 1974
THE FOUR MUSKETEERS   20th Century-Fox, 1975
ROYAL FLASH   20th Century-Fox, 1976
CROSSED SWORDS   THE PRINCE AND THE PAUPER   20th Century-Fox, 1977
OCTOPUSSY   MGM/UA, 1983, w/Richard Maibaum & Michael G. Wilson
RED SONJA   MGM/United Artists, 1985, w/Clive Exton
THE RETURN OF THE MUSKETEERS   Universal, 1990

Screenplays:
STILLWELL w/Calder Willingham
COLOSSUS
THE ICE PEOPLE
OUT OF TIME

MICHAEL FRAYN
Agent: Roberta Pryor, Inc. - New York, 212/245-0420

BENEFACTORS (P)
NOISES OFF (P)
CLOCKWISE   Universal, 1986

BILL FREED
Agent: David Shapira & Associates - Sherman Oaks, 818/906-0322

WATCHERS   Tri-Star, 1988, w/Damian Lee

DONALD FREED*
Agent: ICM - Los Angeles, 213/550-4000

VETERAN'S DAY (P)
INQUEST: THE U.S. VS. JULIUS AND ETHEL ROSENBERG (P)
THE WHITE CROW: EICHMANN IN JERUSALEM (P), also screenplay
ALFRED AND VICTORIA: A LIFE (P)
THE QUARTERED MAN (P), also screenplay
OUR MAN IN NICARAGUA (P)
IS HE STILL DEAD? (P)
CIRCE AND BRAVO (P)
EXECUTIVE ACTION   EA Enterprises, 1973, Story w/Mark Lane
SECRET HONOR   Cinecom International, 1985, w/Arnold M. Stone, from his play "Secret Honor : The Last Testament of Richard M. Nixon"

Screenplays:
OF LOVE AND SHADOW
RICHARDSON w/Mark Lane
SLAY THE DREAMER

HERB FREED*
Contact: Slaff, Mosk & Rudman, 9200 Sunset Blvd., Los Angeles, CA 90069, 213/275-5351

BEYOND EVIL   IFI-Scope III, 1980, w/Paul Ross, directed
GRADUATION DAY   IFI/Scope III, 1981, w/Anne Marisse
SURVIVAL GAME   Trans World Entertainment, 1987, w/Susannah de Nimes & P.W. Swann

Screenplays:
THE DAY THE EARTH STRUCK BACK w/Marion Segal

MARK FREED
SHOCK 'EM DEAD   Academy Entertainment, 1991, w/Andrew Cross, directed

JERROLD FREEDMAN*
Agent: Richland/Wunsch/Hohman Agency - Los Angeles, 213/278-1955

BORDERLINE   AFD, 1980, w/Steve Kline, directed

DAVID FREEMAN*
Agent: ICM - Los Angeles, 213/550-4000

FIRST LOVE   Paramount, 1977, w/Jane Stanton Hitchcock
THE BORDER   Universal, 1982, w/Walon Green & Deric Washburn
STREET SMART   Cannon, 1987

Screenplays:
AMERICAN ROULETTE
MADE IN AMERICA
TOUGH CUSTOMERS
HUMORESQUE
TREASURE ISLAND
PLAY CRAZY
INNER FIRE
CHASER

FRED FREEMAN*
Agent: CAA - Beverly Hills, 213/288-4545

START THE REVOLUTION WITHOUT ME   Warner Bros., 1970, w/Lawrence J. Cohen
S*P*Y*S   20th Century-Fox, 1974, w/Lawrence J. Cohen & Malcolm Marmorstein
THE BIG BUS   Paramount, 1976, w/Lawrence J. Cohen
DELIRIOUS   MGM-Pathe, 1991, w/Lawrence J. Cohen

Screenplays:
THE PSYCHIATRIST AND THE THIEF w/Lawrence J. Cohen
KARISTAN w/Lawrence J. Cohen

110

JOAN FREEMAN*
Contact: WGA - Los Angeles, 213/550-1000 or Directors Guild of America - Los Angeles, 213/289-2000

STREETWALKIN'   Concorde/Cinema Group, 1985, w/Robert Alden & Diane Gonciarz, directed

LYN FREEMAN*
Contact: WGA - Los Angeles, 213/550-1000

WITHOUT WARNING   Filmways, 1980, w/Daniel Grodnick, Ben Nett & Steve Mathis

ROB FRESCO*
Contact: 213/470-7571

INTIMATE STRANGER   South Gate Entertainment, 1991

JUDY FREUDBERG*
Agent: William Morris Agency - New York, 212/586-5100

SESAME STREET PRESENTS FOLLOW THAT BIRD   Warner Bros., 1985, w/Tony Geiss
AN AMERICAN TAIL (AF)   Universal, 1986, w/Tony Geiss
THE LAND BEFORE TIME (AF)   Universal, 1987, Story w/Tony Geiss

Screenplays:
OPERATION AMANDA   NAVY BRATS w/Tony Geiss

RICHARD L. FRIEDENBERG*
Agent: The Daniel Ostroff Agency - Los Angeles, 213/278-2020

THE LIFE AND TIMES OF GRIZZLY ADAMS   Sunn Classic, 1976, directed
FRONTIER FREMONT   Sunn Classic, 1976, Shared story, directed
DYING YOUNG   20th Century Fox, 1991

Screenplays:
A RIVER RUNS THROUGH IT
CITIZEN TOM PAINE
THE MUSIC ROOM
INTO SELMA
RAINBOW WARRIOR
KING OF KINGS

WILLIAM FRIEDKIN*
Agent: ICM - Los Angeles, 213/550-4000

CRUISING   United Artists, 1980, directed
TO LIVE AND DIE IN L.A.   MGM/UA, 1985, w/Gerald Petievich, directed
RAMPAGE   DEG, 1987, unreleased, directed
THE GUARDIAN   Universal, 1990, w/Dan Greenburg & Stephen Volk, directed

ADAM FRIEDMAN
Agent: Circle Talent Associates - Beverly Hills, 213/285-1585

RAPPIN'   Cannon, 1985, w/Robert Litz

Screenplays:
ONE FELL SWOOP
STRAY DANCER

BRENT V. FRIEDMAN
SYNGENOR   South Gate Entertainment, 1990
H.P. LOVECRAFT'S THE RESURRECTED   Scotti Bros., 1991

Screenplays:
SHATTERBRAIN

BRUCE JAY FRIEDMAN*
Agent: CAA - Beverly Hills, 213/288-4545

STIR CRAZY   Columbia, 1980
DOCTOR DETROIT   Universal, 1983, w/Robert Boris & Carl Gottlieb
SPLASH ★   Buena Vista, 1984, w/Lowell Ganz & Babaloo Mandel

Screenplays:
BODY POLITIC
PX
OUR LADY OF THE LOCKERS
DEEP TROUBLE
YOUR BASIC LOUSY MARRIAGE
ABOUT HARRY TOWNS
LIFE ENDS AT FORTY
DETROIT ABE
SCUBA DUBA
LET'S HEAR IT FOR A BEAUTIFUL GUY
TOKYO WOES

KENNETH H. FRIEDMAN*
Agent: Sanford, Skouras, Gross & Associates - Los Angeles, 213/208-2100

DEATH BY INVITATION   1971, directed
WHITE LINE FEVER   Columbia, 1975, w/Jonathan Kaplan
MR. BILLION   20th Century-Fox, 1976, w/Jonathan Kaplan
HEART LIKE A WHEEL   20th Century-Fox, 1983
MADE IN USA   DEG, 1986, directed
JOHNNY HANDSOME   Tri-Star, 1989
CADILLAC MAN   Orion, 1990

Screenplays:
THE INFORMANT w/Robert Daley
ZODIAC
GARBAGE
HEAVEN SCENT w/Joyce Eliason
NIGHTSIDE
KEY WEST DRUG SMUGGLING
THE BOOSTER
IN THE LINE OF FIRE

MEL FRIEDMAN*
Contact: WGA - Los Angeles, 213/550-1000

BLOODSPORT   Cannon, 1988, w/Christopher Cosby & Sheldon Lettich

Screenplays:
ALIEN COP
GOLDEN KNIGHTS
DEADLY METAL

RICHARD FRIEDMAN
SCARED STIFF   International Film Marketing, 1987, w/Daniel F. Bacanar & Mark Frost

RON FRIEDMAN*
Agent: Shapiro/Lichtman - Los Angeles, 213/859-8877

THE TRANSFORMERS: THE MOVIE (AF)   DEG, 1986

STEPHEN FRIEDMAN
LOVIN' MOLLY   Columbia, 1974

TOM FRIEDMAN*
Agent: ICM - New York, 212/556-5600

TIME WALKER   New World, 1982, w/Karen Levitt
DANGER ZONE II: REAPER'S REVENGE   Skouras Pictures, 1989, Story w/Jason Williams

AVA OSTERN FRIES
(See Ava OSTERN-Fries)

BILL FROEHLICH*
Agent: Robinson, Weintraub, Gross & Associates - Los Angeles, 213/653-5802

RETURN TO HORROR HIGH   New World, 1987, w/Mark Lisson, Dana Escalante & Greg H. Sim

CLAYTON S. FROHMAN*
Agent: United Talent Agency - Beverly Hills, 213/273-6700

UNDER FIRE   Orion, 1983, w/Ron Shelton
THE DELINQUENTS   Warner Bros., 1990, w/Mac Gudgeon
THE COURTMARTIAL OF JACKIE ROBINSON (CTF)   Turner Network Television, 1990, w/L. Travis Clark, Dennis Clark & Steve Duncan

Screenplays:
MAKING THUNDERBIRDS
PRECIOUS METAL
SUNBELT
CHEERLEADER OF THE NEW LEFT
GIANT KILLER

MEL FROHMAN*
Agent: APA - Los Angeles, 213/273-0744

...ALL THE MARBLES   MGM/United Artists, 1981

MARK C. FROST*
Agent: CAA - Beverly Hills, 213/288-4545
Business: Lynch/Frost Productions - Van Nuys, 818/909-7900

THE BELIEVERS   Orion, 1987
SCARED STIFF   International Film Marketing, 1987, w/Daniel F. Bacaner & Richard Friedman

Screenplays:
STORYVILLE (directing)
ONE SALIVA BUBBLE w/David Lynch
BLIND LUCK w/R. Lance Hill
GOOD MORNING, CHICAGO
72-HOUR CLUB
THE SECOND EXPEDITION
LUNCH AT FIRST SIGHT
BLIND VOICES
GHOST DIARY
TRUE ROMANCE
GRIDLOCK
TRACES
VENUS DESCENDING

SCOTT FROST*
Agent: Susan Smith & Associates - Beverly Hills, 213/852-4777

Screenplays:
SPUTNICK
SURRENDER DOROTHY
A LITTLE TOUCHED

WILLIAM FRUET
Business: Jaguar Productions Ltd., 51 Olive Avenue, Toronto, Ontario M6G 1T7, Canada, 416/535-3569

GOIN' DOWN THE ROAD   Chevron, 1970
RIP-OFF   Alliance, 1972, directed
WEDDING IN WHITE   Avco Embassy, 1973, directed
SLIPSTREAM   Pacific Rim Films, 1974
THE HOUSE BY THE LAKE   DEATH WEEKEND   American International, 1977, directed

ROY FRUMKES
Business: Bat Track Productions, 166 W. 83rd St., New York, NY 10024, 212/873-6626

STREET TRASH   Lightning Pictures, 1987

RICK FRY
BRIDE OF RE-ANIMATOR   Troma, 1991, Story w/Brian Yuzna

E. MAX FRYE*
Agent: InterTalent - Los Angeles, 213/271-0600
Business Manager: Tom Hansen, Hansen, Jacobsen & Teiter, 335 North Maple Drive, Suite 270, Beverly Hills, CA 90210

SOMETHING WILD   Orion, 1986

Screenplays:
TWISSLEMAN
DEAR JOHNNY POGUE
THE BIG PLUNGE

ROBERT FUEST
Agent: Leading Players, 31 Kings Rd., London SW3, England

JUST LIKE A WOMAN   Monarch, 1966, directed
DR. PHIBES RISES AGAIN   American International, 1972, w/Robert Blees, directed
THE LAST DAYS OF MAN ON EARTH   THE FINAL PROGRAM   New World, 1974, directed

ATHOL FUGARD
Agent: William Morris Agency - New York, 212/586-5100

MASTER HAROLD AND THE BOYS (P)
THE ROAD TO MECCA (P)
A LESSON FROM ALOES (P)
THE ISLAND (P)
SIZWE BANZI IS DEAD (P)
MY CHILDREN! MY AFRICA! (P)
MARIGOLDS IN AUGUST   RM Productions, 1984
THE GUEST   RM Productions, 1984

LEE FULKERSON
FREE RIDE   Galaxy International, 1986, w/Robert Bell & Ronald Zwang

CHARLES H. FULLER*
Agent: William Morris Agency - New York, 212/586-5100

BURNER'S FROLIC (P)
ZOOMAN AND THE SIGN (P)
A SOLDIER'S STORY ★   Columbia, 1984, from his play "A Soldier's Play"

Screenplays:
THE BROWNSVILLE ROAD
SIMPLE JUSTICE
KINGSBLOOD

DAVID FULLER*
Agent: The Daniel Ostroff Agency - Los Angeles, 213/278-2020

THE HEIST (CTF)   HBO Pictures, 1989, w/Rick Natkin
THE TAKING OF BEVERLY HILLS   Nelson Entertainment, 1991, w/Rick Natkin & David Burke

Screenplays:
NECESSARY ROUGHNESS w/Rick Natkin
ALL THAT CAN BE w/Rick Natkin

KIM FULLER*
Contact: WGA - Los Angeles, 213/550-1000

LENNY LIVE AND UNLEASHED   Miramax, 1989, w/Lenny Henry

LESLIE FULLER*
Agent: William Morris Agency - Beverly Hills, 213/274-7451

Screenplays:
SHAMELESS
REC ROOM
BLOOD RELATIONS

SAMUEL FULLER*
Contact: 213/563-7761

CONFIRM OR DENY   20th Century-Fox, 1941, w/Jo Swerling & Henry Wales
I SHOT JESSE JAMES   Screen Guild, 1949, directed
SHOCKPROOF   Columbia, 1949, w/Helen Deutsch
THE BARON OF ARIZONA   Lippert, 1950, directed
FIXED BAYONETS!   20th Century-Fox, 1951, directed
PARK ROW   United Artists, 1952, directed
PICKUP ON SOUTH STREET   20th Century-Fox, 1953, directed
HELL AND HIGH WATER   20th Century-Fox, 1954, directed
RUN OF THE ARROW   Global, 1956, directed
FORTY GUNS   20th Century-Fox, 1957, directed
CHINA GATE   20th Century-Fox, 1957, directed
THE CRIMSON KIMONO   Columbia, 1959, directed
UNDERWORLD USA   Columbia, 1960, directed
MERRILL'S MARAUDERS   Warner Bros., 1962, w/Milton Sperling, directed
SHOCK CORRIDOR   Allied Artists, 1963, directed
CAPETOWN AFFAIR   20th Century-Fox, 1967, w/Harold Medford
SHARK!   Heritage, 1970, w/John Kingsbridge, directed
DEAD PIGEONS ON BEETHOVEN STREET   Emerson, 1972, directed
THE KLANSMAN   Paramount, 1974, w/Millard Kaufman
THE BIG RED ONE   United Artists, 1980, directed
WHITE DOG   Paramount, 1982, w/Curtis Lee Hanson, directed
LET'S GET HARRY   Tri-Star, 1987, Story w/Mark L. Feldberg
STREET OF NO RETURN   Thunder Films International/Animagrafo Producoes/FR3, 1989, directed

CHOSEI FUNAHARA
FATAL MISSION   Funahara, 1990, w/Peter Fonda, Anthony Gentile, John Gentile & George Rowe

SIDNEY J. FURIE
Agent: ICM - Los Angeles, 213/550-4000
Business: Furie Productions Inc., 9169 Sunset Blvd., Los Angeles, CA 90069

DURING ONE NIGHT NIGHT OF PASSION   Astor, 1961, directed
THE LAWYER   Paramount, 1970, w/Harold Buchman, directed
THE BOYS IN COMPANY C   Columbia, 1978, w/Rick Natkin, directed
PURPLE HEARTS   The Laddy Company/Warner Bros., 1984, w/Rick Natkin, directed
IRON EAGLE   Tri-Star, 1986, w/Kevin Elders, directed
IRON EAGLE II   Tri-Star, 1988, w/Kevin Elders, directed
THE TAKING OF BEVERLY HILLS   Nelson Entertainment, 1991, Story w/David Fuller & Rick Natkin, directed

GEORGE FURTH*
Agent: The Roberts Company - Los Angeles, 213/552-7800 & The Lantz Company - New York, 212/586-0200

Screenplays:
AMERICA'S SWEETHEART
PRECIOUS SONS

JOHN FUSCO*
Agent: William Morris Agency - New York, 212/586-5100

CROSSROADS   Columbia, 1986
YOUNG GUNS   20th Century Fox, 1988
YOUNG GUNS II   20th Century Fox, 1990

Screenplays:
THUNDERHEART
THE BABE
BLUES WATER
SMACK IN THE MIDDLE w/L. Craig
FABLECHASE
TOWNIES

G

PAL GABOR
BRADY'S ESCAPE   Satori Releasing, 1984, Story

MITCHELL GABOURI
BUYING TIME   MGM/UA, 1989, w/Richard Gabouri, directed

RICHARD GABOURI
BUYING TIME   MGM/UA, 1989, w/Mitchell Gabouri

GEORGE GAGE
Contact: Directors Guild of America - Los Angeles, 213/289-2000

SKATEBOARD   Universal, 1978, w/Dick Wolf, directed
FLESHBURN   Crown International, 1984, w/Beth Gage, directed

DAN GAGLIASSO
EYE OF THE EAGLE II: INSIDE THE ENEMY   Concorde Pictures, 1989, w/Carl Franklin

CHARLES L. GAINES
Agent: Phoenix Literary Agency - Livingston, Montana, 406/222-2848

STAY HUNGRY   United Artists, 1976, w/Bob Rafelson

FRANK GALATI*
Agent: William Morris Agency - Beverly Hills, 213/274-7451

THE GRAPES OF WRATH (P)
THE ACCIDENTAL TOURIST ★   Warner Bros., 1988, w/Lawrence Kasdan

Screenplays:
A CONFEDERACY OF DUNCES
TRACER
THE LIVING END

BOB GALE*
Agent: CAA - Beverly Hills, 213/288-4545

I WANNA HOLD YOUR HAND   Universal, 1978, w/Robert Zemeckis
1941   Universal/Columbia, 1979, w/Robert Zemeckis
USED CARS   Columbia, 1980, w/Robert Zemeckis
BACK TO THE FUTURE ★   Universal, 1985, w/Robert Zemeckis
BACK TO THE FUTURE II   Universal, 1989
BACK TO THE FUTURE III   Universal, 1990

Screenplays:
GANGLAND w/Robert Zemeckis
JIMBO'S STAND
HENRY STAR, OUTLAW
DIPLOMATIC IMMUNITY
CARPOOL

CHARLES R. GALE*
Agent: CAA - Beverly Hills, 213/288-4545

MAKING THE GRADE   MGM/UA/Cannon, 1984, Story w/Gene Quintano
GUILTY AS CHARGED   I.R.S. Releasing, 1991

Screenplays:
PLASTIC MAN
CAPTAIN NUKE AND THE BOMBER BOYS
HI, I'M FROM HELL
COMMON STOCK
MERGERS AND ACQUISITIONS

TIMOTHY GALFAS*
Agent: The Agency - Los Angeles, 213/551-3000

MATILDA   American International, 1978, w/Albert S. Ruddy
SUNNYSIDE   American International, 1979, w/Jeff King, directed

JOHN A. GALLAGHER
Agent: The Parks Agency - New York, 212/254-9067

BEACH HOUSE   New Line Cinema, 1982, w/Marino Amaruso, directed
POSED FOR MURDER   Double Helix Films, 1988
STREET HUNTER   21st Century, 1990, w/Steven James, directed

Screenplays:
BLUE HIGHWAYS
SCREWDRIVER
THE KILLER INSTINCT
TIME CAPSULE
BLOODY FELLOWS w/Ethan Reiff
FIREWOLF w/Steve James
NIGHT EAGLE w/Steve James
HELL SOLDIER w/Steve James
TRACKDOWN w/Robert Ginty
SOMEWHERE IN THE MEDITERRANEAN w/Denis Leary

GEORGE GALLO*
Agent: CAA - Beverly Hills, 213/288-4545

WISE GUYS   MGM/UA, 1986
MIDNIGHT RUN   Universal, 1988
29TH STREET   20th Century Fox, 1991, directed

Screenplays:
THE PRETENDER (directing)
AMERICAN MELTDOWN w/E. Olsiewicz
PROS & CONS
THE GRASS IS GREENER
MAESTRO & ME   AMERICAN BRASS
003 STOOGES
DEBS
BULLET PROOF HEARTS
STOLEN FLOWER

GUY J. GALLO*
Agent: ICM - New York, 212/556-5600

UNDER THE VOLCANO   Universal, 1984

BRIAN GAMBLE
RED SURF   Arrowhead Entertainment, 1990, Story w/Jason Hoffs & Vincent Roberts

TOM W. GAMMILL*
Agent: William Morris Agency - Beverly Hills,
213/274-7451

Screenplays:
THEY ARE US w/Max Pross

JOSEPH M. GANNON*
Agent: Jim Preminger Agency - Los Angeles,
213/475-9491

SOLAR CRISIS Scochiku-Fuji, 1990, w/Ted Sarafian

LOWELL GANZ*
Agent: CAA - Beverly Hills, 213/288-4545

NIGHTSHIFT The Ladd Company/Warner Bros., 1982,
w/Babaloo Mandel
SPLASH ★ Buena Vista, 1984, w/Bruce Jay Friedman &
Babaloo Mandel
SPIES LIKE US Warner Bros., 1985, w/Dan Aykroyd &
Babaloo Mandel
GUNG HO Paramount, 1986, w/Babaloo Mandel
VIBES Columbia, 1988, w/Babaloo Mandel
PARENTHOOD Univeral, 1989, w/Babaloo Mandel
CITY SLICKERS Castle Rock/Columbia, 1991,
w/Babaloo Mandel

Screenplays:
A LEAGUE OF THEIR OWN w/Babaloo Mandel
MR. SATURDAY NIGHT w/Babaloo Mandel
OVER MY DEAD BODY w/Babaloo Mandel
THE PERFECT COUPLE w/Babaloo Mandel
DANCE SKINS w/Babaloo Mandel
C. DMIAS w/Garry Marshall
HAPPY HOUR
KIAMESHA
THE GREATEST SHOW ON EARTH

LARRY GARCIA
Agent: United Talent Agency - Beverly Hills, 213/273-6700

Screenplays:
US AND THEM w/Greg Davis
HARRY SCARRY WANTS TO MARRY w/Greg Davis
WIND IN THE WILLOWS w/Greg Davis

GERALD GARDNER*
Agent: Shapiro/Lichtman - Los Angeles, 213/859-8877

WHICH WAY TO THE FRONT? Warner Bros., 1970,
w/Dee Caruso
THE WORLD'S GREATEST ATHLETE Buena Vista,
1973, w/Dee Caruso

HERB GARDNER*
Agent: The Roberts Company - Los Angeles, 213/552-7800
& The Lantz Office - New York, 212/586-0200

I'M NOT RAPPAPORT (P)
CONVERSATIONS WITH MY FATHER (P)
A THOUSAND CLOWNS ★ United Artists, 1965,
from his play
WHO IS HARRY KELLERMAN AND WHY IS HE
SAYING ALL THESE TERRIBLE THINGS ABOUT ME?
National General, 1971
THIEVES Paramount, 1977, from his play
THE GOODBYE PEOPLE Embassy, 1984,
from his play, directed

LEONARD C. GARDNER*
Contact: Evarts Ziegler - Los Angeles, 213/278-0070

FAT CITY Columbia, 1972
VALENTINO RETURNS Skouras Pictures, 1989

LEO GAREN*
Agent: Warden & White Associates - Beverly Hills,
213/852-1028

BAND OF THE HAND Tri-Star, 1986, w/Jack Baran

Screenplays:
DON'T HOLD BACK w/Jack Baran
HEX
DOUBLE EAGLE
SNAKEBITE AND TNT

BRIAN GARFIELD*
Agent: Barrett, Benson, McCartt & Weston - Los Angeles,
213/247-5500

THE LAST HARD MEN 20th Century-Fox, 1976
HOPSCOTCH Avco Embassy, 1980, w/Bryan Forbes
THE STEPFATHER New Century/Vista, 1987, Story
w/Caroline Lefcourt & Donald E. Westlake

Screenplays:
THE PERFECT CRIME
NECESSITY

LOUIS A. GARFINKLE*
Agent: Circle Talent Associates - Beverly Hills,
213/281-3765

THE DOBERMAN GANG Dimension, 1973, w/Frank
Ray Perilli
LITTLE CIGARS 1973, w/Frank Ray Perilli
THE DEER HUNTER ★ Universal, 1978, Story w/Michael
Cimino & Quinn K. Redeker

Screenplays:
SHANGHAI TANGO w/Quinn Redeker
VOSA w/Quinn Redeker
THE EEZMO w/Quinn Redeker
BENYA THE KING

GERRY GARIBALDI
Agent: United Talent Agency - Beverly Hills,
213/273-6700

Screenplays:
RAINBOWS

ROBERT GARLAND*
Agent: CAA - Beverly Hills, 213/288-4545

THE ELECTRIC HORSEMAN Columbia, 1979
NO WAY OUT Orion, 1987
THE BIG BLUE Columbia/WEG, 1988, w/Luc Besson

Screenplays:
GIANT
DOUBLE
CAPE DISAPPOINTMENT
LANCELOT
THE GULF OF MOSQUITOS
DELAYED REACTION

HELEN GARNER
MONKEY GRIP   Cinecom, 1982, w/Ken Cameron

TONY GARNETT*
Business Manager: Michael Mesnick, CPA, 213/473-9101

PROSTITUTE   Mainline Films, 1979, directed
DEEP IN THE HEART   *HANDGUN*   Warner Bros., 1981, directed

JOSEPH GAROFALO*
Contact: Walter Teller, 213/278-8622

EVIL SPEAK   The Frank Moreno Co., 1982, w/Eric Weston

MICK GARRIS*
Agent: CAA - Beverly Hills, 213/288-4545

CRITTERS 2   New Line Cinema, 1988, w/D.T. Twohy, directed
COMING SOON (CTD)   Universal Pay TV, 1983, w/John Landis
BATTERIES NOT INCLUDED   Universal, 1987, Story
THE FLY II   20th Century Fox, 1989, w/Frank Darabont, Jim Wheat & Ken Wheat

Screenplays:
ALMOST IRRESISTIBLE
DOUBLE VISION
BLACK SHEEP
BLOODSTONE
UNCLE WILLIE
HALLOWEEN HOUSE
RED SLEEP   w/Richard Matheson

PAUL GARSON
CYCLONE   CineTel Films, 1987, w/T.L. Lankford

KEN GASS
THE SQUAMISH FIVE   CBC Film, 1989, w/Terence McKenna

HAROLD GAST*
Agent: Shapiro/Lichtman - Los Angeles, 213/859-8877

IRONCLADS (CTF)   Rosemont Productions, 1991

JOHN GATLIFF
DEATH BEFORE DISHONOR   New World, 1987, w/Lawrence Kubik

ANDREW GATY
THE RETURN OF CAPTAIN INVINCIBLE   New World, 1983, w/Steven E. De Souza

NILS GAUP
PATHFINDER   International Film Exchange Ltd., 1990, directed
SHIPWRECKED   Buena Vista, 1991, w/Greg Dinner, Bob Foss & Nick Thiel, directed

COSTA - GAVRAS
Agent: CAA - Beverly Hills, 213/288-4545

THE SLEEPING CAR MURDERS   7 Arts, 1966, Adaptation, directed
Z ★   Cinema 5, 1969, w/Jorge Semprun, directed
MISSING ★★   Universal, 1982, w/Donald Stewart, directed
FAMILY BUSINESS   European Classics, 1987

JOHN GAY*
Agent: CAA - Beverly Hills, 213/288-4545

RUN SILENT RUN DEEP   United Artists, 1958
SEPARATE TABLES ★   United Artists, 1958, w/Terence Rattigan
THE FOUR HORSEMEN OF THE APOCALYPSE   MGM, 1961, w/Robert Ardrey
THE HAPPY THEIVES   United Artists, 1962
THE COURTSHIP OF EDDIE'S FATHER   MGM, 1962
THE HALLELUJAH TRAIL   United Artists, 1965
THE LAST SAFARI   Paramount, 1967
THE POWER   MGM, 1967
NO WAY TO TRAT A LADY   Paramount, 1968
SOLDIER BLUE   Avco Embassy, 1970
SOMETIMES A GREAT NOTION   *NEVER GIVE AN INCH*   Universal, 1971
HENNESSY   American International, 1975

LAWRENCE GAY*
Agent: CAA - Beverly Hills, 213/288-4545

Screenplays:
BACK TO SCHOOL II   w/Michael Digaetano
DOUBLE VISION   w/Michael Digaetano
THE BIG ONES   w/Michael Digaetano
ME, MYSELF & I

STEVEN GAYDOS*
Agent: The Lantz Office - New York, 212/586-0200

Screenplays:
ARMED RESPONSE   w/Rene Balcer

MICHAEL GAYLIN*
Agent: ICM - Los Angeles, 213/550-4000

Screenplays:
THE COVER
BABCOCK ON BAKER STREET (CTF)

JOE GAYTON*
Agent: InterTalent - Los Angeles, 213/271-0600

UNCOMMON VALOR   Paramount, 1983
WARM SUMMER RAIN   Trans World Entertainment, 1989, directed
SHOUT   Universal, 1991

Screenplays:
CITY OF DARKNESS   w/Pat Cirillo
CITY KIDS   w/Tony Gayton
CHASING KILROY   w/Tony Gayton
OF PAWNS AND KNIGHTS
KNIGHTLY DREAMS
KID IRISH   SMOKER

DAN GAZZANIGA
SPECIAL DELIVERY   American International, 1976

DAVID GEEVES
AMERICAN NINJA 4: THE ANNIHILATION   Cannon, 1991

PLEASANT GEHMAN
THE RUNNIN' KIND   MGM/UA, 1990, w/Max Tash

THEODORE (TED) GEISEL
(Dr. Suess)
Contact: Publisher-Random House - New York, 212/751-2600

GERALD McBOING BOING (AF)   UPA, 1951
THE FIVE THOUSAND FINGERS OF DOCTOR T
   Columbia, 1953, w/Allan Scott

Screenplays:
OH, THE PLACES YOU'LL GO

TONY GEISS*
Agent: William Morris Agency - New York, 212/586-5100

SESAME STREET PRESENTS FOLLOW THAT BIRD
   Warner Bros., 1985, w/Judy Freudberg
AN AMERICAN TAIL (AF)   Universal, 1986,
   w/Judy Freudberg
THE LAND BEFORE TIME (AF)   Universal, 1987,
   Story w/Judy Freudberg

Screenplays:
OPERATION AMANDA   NAVY BRATS   w/Judy Freudberg

ARNIE GELBART
THE GUNRUNNER   New World, 1989

LARRY GELBART*
Agent: Barry Pollack - Los Angeles, 213/550-4525

SLY FOX (P), also screenplay
POWER FAILURE (P)
MASTERGATE (P)
CITY OF ANGELS (P)
A FUNNY THING HAPPENED ON THE WAY TO THE
   FORUM (P) w/Burt Shevelove
THE NOTORIOUS LANDLADY   Columbia, 1962,
   w/Richard Quine
NOT WITH MY WIFE YOU DON'T   Warner Bros., 1966,
   w/Peter Barnes & Norman Panama
THE WRONG BOX   Columbia, 1966, w/Burt Shevelove
THE CHASTITY BELT   ON THE WAY TO THE
   CRUSADES I MET A GIRL WHO...   Warner Bros.,
   1967, w/Luigi Magri
A FINE PAIR   1968, w/others
OH, GOD! ★   Warner Bros., 1977
MOVIE, MOVIE   Warner Bros., 1978, w/Sheldon Keller
ROUGH CUT   Paramount, 1980, as "Francis Burns"
NEIGHBORS   Columbia, 1981
TOOTSIE ★   Columbia, 1982, w/Murray Schisgal
BLAME IT ON RIO   20th Century Fox, 1984,
   w/Charlie Peters

Screenplays:
BARBARIANS AT THE GATE
JAZZ BABIES
KILL-IN
NOBODY LIKES AN HONEST COP
UNITED STATES
HOTEL ROYALE
MOVIE, MOVIE II
TWO + TWO

STEPHEN GELLER*
Agent: The Gersh Agency - Beverly Hills, 213/274-6611

SLAUGHTERHOUSE FIVE   Universal, 1971
ASHANTI   Columbia, 1970
SEE NO EVIL   Columbia, 1971
THE VALACHI PAPERS   *JOE VALACHI: I SEGRETI DI COSA NOSTRA*   Columbia, 1972

Screenplays:
GOOD AS GOLD

JONATHAN GEMS*
Agent: ICM - Los Angeles, 213/550-4000

WHITE MISCHIEF   Columbia, 1988, w/Michael Radford

PETER GENT*
Contact: 616/382-3784

NORTH DALLAS FORTY   Paramount, 1979, w/Ted
   Kotcheff & Frank Yablans

ANTHONY GENTILE
FATAL MISSION   Funahara, 1990, w/Peter Fonda, Chosei
   Funahara, John Gentile & George Rowe

JOHN GENTILE
FATAL MISSION   Funahara, 1990, w/Peter Fonda,
   Anthony Gentile, Chosei Funahara & George Rowe

ROBERT GEOFFRION
HONEYMOON   International Film Marketing, 1987,
   w/Patrick Jamian & Phillipe Setbon
THE HIT MAN   Cannon, 1991, w/Don Carmody

JIM GEOGHAN*
Agent: David Shapira & Associates - Sherman Oaks,
   818/906-0322

ONLY KIDDING (P)
STOOGEMANIA   Atlantic Releasing Corporation, 1986,
   w/Chuck Workman

JON A. GEORGE*
Contact: WGA - Los Angeles, 213/550-1000

ESCAPE 2000   New World, 1983, w/Neill Hicks
THE FINAL TERROR   Comworld, 1983, w/Neil Hicks &
   Ronald Shusett

GARY GERANI
PUMPKINHEAD   MGM/UA, 1988, w/Mark Patrick Carducci

ANNE GERARD
Agent: Pleshette & Green - Los Angeles, 213/465-0428

LOVE CHILD   The Ladd Company/Warner Bros.,1982,
   w/Katherine Spektor

BILL GERBER*
Agent: The Gersh Agency - Beverly Hills, 213/274-6611

Screenplays:
DADDY'S LITTLE GIRL
HER SIDE OF THE FAMILY

CHRIS GEROLMO*
Agent: CAA - Beverly Hills, 213/288-4545

MILES FROM HOME   Cinecom International, 1988
MISSISSIPPI BURNING   Orion, 1989

Screenplays:
NO EXCUSE

Ge

LEONARD GERSHE*
Agent: ICM - Los Angeles, 213/550-4000

FUNNY FACE ★   Paramount, 1956
SILK STOCKINGS   MGM, 1957, w/Leonard Spiegelgass
BUTTERFLIES ARE FREE   Columbia, 1972, from his play
FORTY CARATS   Columbia, 1973, from his play

TED GERSHUN
FAR FROM HOME   Vestron, 1989, Story

NICHOLAS GESSNER
QUICKER THAN THE EYE   Eural Films/FR3/Condor Films, 1988, w/Joseph Morhaim, directed

ROBERT GETCHELL*
Agent: CAA - Beverly Hills, 213/288-4545

ALICE DOESN'T LIVE HERE ANY MORE ★   Warner Bros., 1974
BOUND FOR GLORY ★   United Artists, 1976
MOMMIE DEAREST   Paramount, 1981, w/Frank Perry, Tracy Hotchner & Frank Yablans
SWEET DREAMS   Tri-Star, 1985
STELLA   Buena Vista, 1990

Screenplays:
SHIBUMI
ROADSHOW
THE LIGHT FANTASTIC
CIVIL WARS

ERIC GETHERS*
Agent: APA - Los Angeles, 213/273-0744

Screenplays:
THE MAVEN
HILDY
LIFE UPSIDE DOWN

CRAIG GHOLSON
Agent: William Morris Agency - Beverly Hills, 213/274-7451

ADJUSTABLE POSITIONS (P), also screenplay

STACEY GIACHINO
THE DORM THAT DRIPPED BLOOD   *PRANKS*   Artists Releasing Corporation/Film Ventures International, 1982, w/Jeffrey Obrow & Stephen Carpenter

JOE GIANNONE
MADMAN   Jensen Farley Pictures, 1982, directed

DUNCAN GIBBINS*
Agent: The Brandt Company - Studio City, 818/506-7747

THIRD DEGREE BURN (CTF)   HBO Pictures, 1989, w/Yale Udoff, directed
EVE OF DESTRUCTION   Orion, 1991, w/Yale Udoff, directed

PETER GIBBS
ARTHUR'S HALLOWED GROUND   Cinecom, 1986

BRIAN GIBSON
Agent: ICM - Los Angeles, 213/550-4000

BREAKING GLASS   Paramount, 1980, directed

NELSON GIDDING*
Agent: Wile Enterprises, Inc. - Los Angeles, 213/828-9768

THE HELEN MORGAN STORY   Warner Bros., 1957, w/Oscar Saul, Dean Reisner & Stephen Longstreet
I WANT TO LIVE! ★   United Artists, 1958, w/Don Mankiewicz
ONIONHEAD   Warner Bros., 1958
ODDS AGAINST TOMORROW   United Artists, 1959, w/John O. Killens
THE INSPECTOR   20th Century-Fox, 1961
NINE HOURS TO RAMA   20th Century-Fox, 1962
THE HAUNTING   MGM, 1963
THE LOST COMMAND   Columbia/Red Lion, 1966
SKULLDUGGERY   Universal, 1970
THE ANDROMEDA STRAIN   Universal, 1971
THE HINDENBURG   Universal, 1975
BEYOND THE POSEIDON ADVENTURE   Warner Bros., 1979

RAYNOLD GIDEON*
Agent: CAA - Beverly Hills, 213/288-4545
Business: Evans-Gideon Productions, Universal Studios, 818/777-3121

A MAN, A WOMAN AND A BANK   Avco Embassy, 1979, w/Bruce Evans
STARMAN   Columbia, 1984, w/Bruce Evans
STAND BY ME ★   Columbia, 1986, w/Bruce Evans
MADE IN HEAVEN   Lorimar, 1987, w/Bruce Evans

Screenplays:
KUFFS w/Bruce Evans
BLACK RICE w/Bruce Evans
THE BETHUNE w/Bruce Evans
CHRISTMAS IN JULY w/Bruce Evans
THE DAY BEFORE MIDNIGHT w/Bruce Evans

CAMILLE GIFFORD
DIRTY TRICKS   Avco Embassy, w/Thomas Gifford, Eleanor Elias Norton & William W. Norton Sr.

THOMAS GIFFORD
DIRTY TRICKS   Avco Embassy, w/Camille Gifford, Eleanor Elias Norton & William W. Norton Sr.

BRAD GILBERT
TOUCH OF A STRANGER   Raven-Star Pictures, 1990, w/Joslyn Barnes, directed

BRIAN GILBERT
Agent: CAA - Beverly Hills, 213/288-4545

FRENCH LESSON   *THE FROG PRINCE*   Warner Bros., 1984, Adaptation, directed
SHARMA AND BEYOND   Cinecom, 1986, directed

BRUCE GILBERT
BY DAWN'S EARLY LIGHT (CTF)   HBO/Panavision International, 1990

HUGO GILBERT
Contact: Ziffren, Brittenham & Branca - Los Angeles, 213/552-3388

HOT TO TROT   Warner Bros., 1988, w/Stephen Neigher & Charlie Peters

LEWIS GILBERT
Contact: Gang, Tyre & Brown - Los Angeles, 213/463-4863

HUNDRED HOUR HUNT   *EMERGENCY CALL* Greshler, 1952, w/Vernon Harris, directed
THE GOOD DIE YOUNG   United Artists, 1954, w/Vernon Harris, directed
THE SEA SHALL NOT HAVE THEM   Eros, 1954, w/Vernon Harris, directed
REACH FOR THE SKY   Rank, 1956, directed
CARVE HER NAME WITH PRIDE   Lopert, 1958, w/Vernon Harris, directed
FERRY TO HONG KONG   20th Century-Fox, 1958, w/Vernon Harris, directed
THE ADVENTURERS   Paramount, 1970, w/Michael Hastings, directed

DAVID K. GILER*
Agent: ICM - Los Angeles, 213/550-4000

MYRA BRECKINRIDGE   20th Century-Fox, 1970, w/Mike Sarne
THE PARALLAX VIEW   Paramount, 1974, w/Lorenzo Semple Jr.
THE BLACK BIRD   Columbia, 1975, directed
FUN WITH DICK AND JANE   Columbia, 1977, w/Jerry Belson & Mordecai Richler
SOUTHERN COMFORT   20th Century-Fox, 1981, w/Walter Hill & Michael Kane
THE MONEY PIT   Universal, 1986
ALIENS   20th Century Fox, 1986, Story w/James Cameron & Walter Hill

Screenplays:
ALIEN III w/Walter Hill
RICH PEOPLE HAVING FUN w/Lynne Giler
LA CAGE AUX FOLLES, USA w/Reinhold Weege
SPIRITS

LYNNE D. GILER*
Agent: ICM - Los Angeles, 213/550-4000

Screenplays:
RICH PEOPLE HAVING FUN w/David Giler
TALKING DIRTY
SILHOUETTES
SEX TIPS FOR GIRLS
KRIPPENDORF'S TRIBE

STUART GILLARD*
Agent: The Agency - Los Angeles, 213/551-3000

PARADISE   Avco Embassy, 1982, directed
IF YOU COULD SEE WHAT I HEAR   Jensen FarleyPictures, 1982
SPRING FEVER   Comworld, 1983, w/Fred Stefan
A MAN CALLED SARGE   Cannon, 1990, directed

TERRY GILLIAM
Agent: CAA - Beverly Hills, 213/288-4545

AND NOW FOR SOMETHING COMPLETELY DIFFERENT   Columbia, 1972, w/Graham Chapman, John Cleese, Eric Idle, Terry Jones & Michael Palin
MONTY PYTHON AND THE HOLY GRAIL   Cinema 5, 1974, w/Graham Chapman, John Cleese, Eric Idle, Terry Jones & Michael Palin, directed
JABBERWOCKY   Cinema 5, 1977, w/Charles Alverson, directed
MONTY PYTHON'S LIFE OF BRIAN   Orion/Warner Bros., 1979, w/Graham Chapman, John Cleese, Eric Idle, Terry Jones & Michael Palin
TIME BANDITS   Avco Embassy, 1981, w/Michael Palin, directed
MONTY PYTHON LIVE AT THE HOLLYWOOD BOWL   Columbia, 1982, w/Graham Chapman, John Cleese, Eric Idle, Terry Jones & Michael Palin
MONTY PYTHON'S THE MEANING OF LIFE   Universal, 1983, w/Graham Chapman, John Cleese, Eric Idle, Terry Jones & Michael Palin, directed
BRAZIL ★   Universal, 1985, w/Charles McKeown & Tom Stoppard, directed
THE ADVENTURES OF BARON MUNCHAUSEN   Columbia, 1988, w/Charles McKeown, directed

VINCE GILLIGAN*
Agent: Triad Artists, Inc. - Los Angeles, 213/556-2727

Screenplays:
WILDER NAPALM

FRANK D. GILROY*
Agent: William Morris Agency - New York, 212/586-5100

THE FASTEST GUN ALIVE   MGM, 1956, w/Russel Rouse
THE GALLANT HOURS   United Artists, 1959, w/Beirne Lay Jr.
THE SUBJECT WAS ROSES   MGM, 1968, from his play
THE ONLY GAME IN TOWN   20th Century-Fox, 1969, from his play
DESPERATE CHARACTERS   ITC, 1971, directed
FROM NOON TIL THREE   United Artists, 1976, directed
ONCE IN PARIS...   Atlantic Releasing Corporation, 1978, directed
JINXED   MGM/UA, 1982, as "Bert Blessing," w/David Newman
THE GIG   Castle Hill Productions, 1985, directed
THE LUCKIEST MAN IN THE WORLD   Co-Star Entertainment, 1989, directed

Screenplays:
WHAT I DID THAT SUMMER

TONY GILROY*
Agent: ICM - Los Angeles, 213/550-4000

Screenplays:
PRAY FOR RAIN
R.S.V.P.

BRYAN GINDOFF*
Agent: The Irv Schechter Company - Beverly Hills, 213/278-8070

LOSIN' IT   Embassy, 1983, Story w/B.W.L. Norton

Gi

ROBERT GINTY
Agent: APA - Los Angeles, 213/273-0744

Screenplays:
DEVIL AND THE DEAP BLUE SEA w/Tony Palmer
TRACKDOWN w/John A. Gallagher

UGO GIORGETTI
FESTA NDR Films, 1990, directed

BUDDY GIOVINAZZO
SHE'S BACK Vestron, 1989

GEORGE GIPE
Agent: APA - Los Angeles, 213/273-0744

THE LIVING END (P)
DEAD MEN DON'T WEAR PLAID Universal, 1982, w/Steve Martin & Carl Reiner
THE MAN WITH TWO BRAINS Warner Bros., 1983, w/Steve Martin & Carl Reiner

Screenplays:
HOT SHEET
THE PICTURE OF GORIAN DAY
DOMINANT GENES
BULL
PRINCE CHARMING
MANHATTAN STAGECOACH
ROAD TO RUIN
THE ADVENTURES OF WILLIE & MADELINE
OPUS ONE
ACES

BERNARD GIRARD
THE BIG PUNCH Warner Bros., 1948
BREAKTHROUGH Warner Bros., 1950, w/Joseph L. Breen Jr. & Ted Sherdeman
DEAD HEAT ON A MERRY-GO-ROUND Paramount, 1966, directed
THE MAD ROOM Columbia, 1969, w/A.Z. Martin, directed

MICHAEL PAUL GIRARD
GETTING LUCKY Vista Street Productions, 1990, directed

GILBERT GIRION
AMERICAN BLUE NOTE Panorama Entertainment, 1991

ROBERT GITTLER
THE BUDDY HOLLY STORY Columbia, 1978

ANTHONY H. GITTLESON
Agent: William Morris Agency - Beverly Hills, 213/274-7451

Screenplays:
WITCHCRAFT w/Celia Gittleson
DAYS OF AWE KABALAH w/Celia Gittleson

CELIA GITTLESON
Agent: William Morris Agency - Beverly Hills, 213/274-7451

Screenplays:
WITCHCRAFT w/Tony Gittleson
DAYS OF AWE KABALAH w/Tony Gittleson

RICHARD N. GLADSTEIN
SILENT NIGHT, DEADLY NIGHT III: YOU BETTER WATCH OUT! Quiet Fims, 1989, Story w/Monte Hellman & Carlos Lazlo

JOANNA McCLELLAND GLASS
(See Joanna McCLELLAND - Glass)

ROBERT GLASS*
Agent: William Morris Agency - Beverly Hills, 213/274-7451

RUNNING AGAINST TIME (CTF) Finnegun-Pinchuk Productions, 1990, w/Stanley Shapiro
DEATH DREAMS (CTF) Ultra Entertainment/Dick Clark Film Group Inc., 1991

Screenplays:
NIGHT VISIONS
ACTS OF GOD (CTF)

SANDY GLASS*
Contact: WGA - Los Angeles, 213/550-1000

THE LAST FLIGHT OF NOAH'S ARK Buena Vista, 1980, w/Steve Carabatsos & George Arthur Bloom

HOWARD GLASSER
OUT COLD Hemdale, 1989, w/George Malko

MITCH GLAZER*
(Mitchell Aram Glazer)
Agent: CAA - Beverly Hills, 213/288-4545

MR. MIKE'S MONDO VIDEO New Line Cinema, 1979, w/Michael O'Donoghue, Emily Prager & Dirk Wittenborn
SCROOGED Paramount, 1988, w/Michael O'Donoghue

Screenplays:
MOON OVER MIAMI
ARRIVE ALIVE w/Michael O'Donoghue
LOLA w/Michael O'Donoghue
THE HOUSE GUEST w/Michael O'Donoghue
A FISH STORY
KINGPIN
BUNCO

MICHAEL GLEASON*
Agent: ICM - Los Angeles, 213/550-4000

FAST CHARLIE...THE MOONBEAM RIDER Universal, 1979

MICHIE GLEASON
SUMMER HEAT Atlantic Releasing Corporation, 1987, directed

JAMES GLICKENHAUS
Business: Shapiro Glickenhaus Entertainment, 12001 Ventura Place - Suite 404, Studio City, CA 91604, 818/766-8500

THE ASTROLOGER Interstar, 1977, directed
THE EXTERMINATOR Avco Embassy, 1980, directed
THE SOLDIER Embassy, 1982, directed
THE PROTECTOR Warner Bros., 1985, directed
SHAKEDOWN Universal, 1988, directed
ROOM AT THE END OF THE UNIVERSE Shapiro-Glickenhaus, 1989, directed

ALAN JAY GLUECKMAN*
Agent: Shapiro/Lichtman - Los Angeles, 213/859-8877

NIGHT WARNING   Comworld, 1983, w/Stephen Breimer & Boom Collins
RUSSKIES   New Century Entertainment, 1988, w/Sheldon Lettich & Michael Nankin
GROSS ANATOMY   Buena Vista, 1990, Story w/Stanley Isaacs, Howard Rosenman & Mark Spragg

Screenplays:
THE WORST MOVIE EVER MADE
THE DICK AND THE DOC
DAREDEVILS OF THE GOLDEN LEGION
THE NEXT PRESIDENT OF THE U.S.A.
BRIDE AND GROOM
IT ALMOST WASN'T CHRISTMAS
SAVAGE RED
PEEL MY BANANA

JEAN-LUC GODARD
Contact: French Film Office, 745 Fifth Avenue, New York, NY 10151, 212/832-8860

BAND OF OUTSIDERS   Royal Films International, 1964, directed
THE MARRIED WOMAN   Royal Films International, 1964, directed
ALPHAVILLE   Pathe Contemporary, 1965, directed
THE OLDEST PROFESSION   Goldstone, 1967, Shared, directed
SAUVE QUI PEUT LA VIE   *EVERY MAN FOR HIMSELF IN LIFE*   New Yorker/Zoetrope, 1980, w/Jean-Claude Carriere & Anne-Marie Mieville, directed
PASSION   United Artists Classics, 1983, directed
DETECTIVE   Spectrafilm, 1985, w/Anne-Marie Mieville, Alain Sarde & Philippe Setbon
NOUVELLE VOGUE (NEW WAVE)   Vega Film SA, 1990, directed

GARY W. GODDARD*
Agent: CAA - Beverly Hills, 213/288-4545

TARZAN, THE APE MAN   MGM/United Artists, 1981, w/Tom Rowe

Screenplays:
MAJOR, MAJOR
SPACE COMMANDS

IVAN GOFF*
Contact: WGA - Los Angeles, 213/550-1000

BACKFIRE   Warner Bros., 1949, w/Larry Marcus & Ben Roberts
GOODBYE MY FANCY   Warner Bros., 1951, w/Ben Roberts
CAPTAIN HORATIO HORNBLOWER   Warner Bros., 1951, w/Aeneas Mackenzie & Ben Roberts
COME FILL THE CUP   Warner Bros., 1951, w/Ben Roberts
GREEN FIRE   MGM, 1954, w/Ben Roberts
KING OF THE KYBER RIFLES   20th Century-Fox, 1954, w/Ben Roberts
SERENADE   Warner Bros., 1956, w/Ben Roberts & John Twist
MAN OF A THOUSAND FACES   Universal-International, 1957, w/Ben Roberts & R. Wright Campbell
BAND OF ANGELS   Warner Bros., 1957, w/Ben Roberts & John Twist
SHAKE HANDS WITH THE DEVIL   United Artists, 1959, w/Ben Roberts
PORTRAIT IN BLACK   Universal-International, 1960, w/Ben Roberts
MIDNIGHT LACE   Universal, 1960, w/Ben Roberts
THE LEGEND OF THE LONE RANGER   Universal/AFD, 1981, w/Michael Kane, Ben Roberts & William Roberts

JOHN GOFF*
Contact: WGA - Los Angeles, 213/550-1000

BUTTERFLY   Analysis, 1981, w/Matt Cimber
THE NIGHT STALKER   Almi Pictures, 1987, w/Don Edmonds
DEADLY INTENT   Fries Entertainment, 1988
HIT LIST   New Line Cinema, 1989, w/Peter Brosnan

MENAHEM GOLAN*
Business: 21st Century Film Corporation, 7000 W. 3rd St., Los Angeles, CA 90048, 213/658-3000

DIAMONDS   Avco Embassy, 1975, w/David Paulsen, directed
THE MAGICIAN OF LUBLIN   Cannon, 1979, w/Irving S. White, directed
THE APPLE   Cannon, 1980, directed
ENTER THE NINJA   Cannon, 1981, w/Dick Desmond & Judd Bernard, directed
SAHARA   MGM/UA, 1984, Story
HOT CHILI   Cannon, 1985, w/William Sachs
THE DELTA FORCE   Cannon, 1986, w/James Bruner, directed
HANNA'S WAR   Cannon, 1988, w/Stanley Mann, directed
THE FORBIDDEN DANCE   Columbia, 1990, Story as "Joseph Goldman"
MACK THE KNIFE   21st Century Film Corp, 1990, directed

AVRAM DEAN GOLD
Agent: The Wright Concept - Hollywood, 213/461-3844

Screenplays:
DREAMS
DATABANK
SHADOW OF FEAR
KEEPER OF THE GATE
THE INSIDERS

LEE GOLD*
Contact: WGA - Los Angeles, 213/550-1000

A CAPTIVE IN THE LAND   Vision International, 1991

DAN GOLDBERG*
Agent: CAA - Beverly Hills, 213/288-4545

MEATBALLS   Paramount, 1979, w/Janis Allen, Len Blum & Harold Ramis
STRIPES   Columbia, 1981, w/Len Blum & Harold Ramis
HEAVY METAL (AF)   Columbia, 1981, w/Len Blum
SPACEHUNTER: ADVENTURES IN THE FORBIDDEN ZONE   Columbia, 1983, w/Len Blum, Edith Rey & David Preston
FEDS   Warner Bros., 1988, w/Len Blum, directed

Screenplays:
RABBIT BOY   w/Len Blum
WIDOWS   w/Len Blum

Go

DICK GOLDBERG*
Agent: Bret Adams, Ltd. - New York, 212/765-5630

THE IMAGEMAKER   Castle Hill Productions, 1986, w/Hal Weiner

GARY DAVID GOLDBERG*
Agent: Jim Preminger Agency - Los Angeles, 213/475-9491

DAD   Universal, 1989, directed

Screenplays:
COMING OF AGE IN NEW YORK CITY   MARVIN AND SARA
SON OF GREASE   GREASIER
SILKY
REEL TO REEL

HARRIS GOLDBERG*
Agent: William Morris Agency - Beverly Hills, 213/274-7451

Screenplays:
ESCAPE FROM WANNA WANNA   w/Tom Nursall
GETTING EVEN   w/Tom Nursall

HOWARD GOLDBERG*
Agent: Monteiro Rose Agency - Encino, 818/501-1177

SPONTANEOUS COMBUSTION   Taurus Entertainment, 1990, w/Tobe Hooper

LEE GOLDBERG*
Agent: William Morris Agency - Beverly Hills, 213/274-7451

Screenplays:
.357 VIGILANTE   w/Bill Rabkin
BLADE   w/Bill Rabkin

MARSHALL GOLDBERG*
Agent: William Morris Agency - Beverly Hills, 213/274-7451

Screenplays:
HOLY WARS

DAN GOLDEN
NAKED OBSESSION   Concorde, 1991, Story w/Roger Dodson, directed

MARTHA GOLDHIRSH*
Agent: William Morris Agency - Beverly Hills, 213/274-7451

SIBLING RIVALRY   Castle Rock/Columbia, 1990

Screenplays:
MY TWO HUSBANDS
FAMILY MAN
AUGUST IN MANHATTAN

DANIEL GOLDIN*
Agent: Writers & Artists Agency - Los Angeles, 213/820-2240

DARKMAN   Universal, 1990, w/Josh Goldin, Chuck Pfarrer, Ivan Raimi & Sam Raimi
WELCOME TO BUZZSAW   Universal, 1991, w/Josh Goldin

Screenplays:
JEFFREY OF ARABIA   w/Josh Goldin
LIFE AFTER LIFE   w/Josh Goldin
MATES   w/Josh Goldin

JOSHUA P. GOLDIN*
Agent: Writers & Artists Agency - Los Angeles, 213/820-2240

DARKMAN   Universal, 1990, w/Daniel Goldin, Chuck Pfarrer, Ivan Raimi & Sam Raimi
WELCOME TO BUZZSAW   Universal, 1991, w/Daniel Goldin

Screenplays:
JEFFREY OF ARABIA   w/Dan Goldin
LIFE AFTER LIFE   w/Dan Goldin
MATES   w/Daniel Goldin

MARILYN GOLDIN
Contact: French Film Office, 745 Fifth Avenue, New York, NY 10151, 212/832-8860

BAROCCO   1976
CAMILLE CLAUDEL   Orion Classics, 1989, w/Bruno Nuytten

PAUL GOLDING*
Contact: WGA - Los Angeles, 213/550-1000

BEAT STREET   Orion, 1984, w/Andy Davis & David Gilbert
PULSE   Columbia, 1988, directed

Screenplays:
BREAKFAST OF CHAMPIONS

B.J. GOLDMAN
TRIPWIRE   CineTel Films, 1989, w/James Lemmo

BO GOLDMAN*
Agent: CAA - Beverly Hills, 213/288-4545

ONE FLEW OVER THE CUCKOO'S NEST ★★   United Artists, 1976, w/Lawrence Hauben
THE ROSE   20th Century-Fox, 1979, w/Bill Kerby
MELVIN AND HOWARD ★★   Universal, 1980
SHOOT THE MOON   MGM/UA, 1982
SWING SHIFT   Warner Bros., 1983, w/Nancy Dowd & Ron Nyswaner as "Rob Morton"
LITTLE NIKITA   Columbia, 1988, w/John Hill

Screenplays:
SCENT OF A WOMAN
HOT SHOT   w/Neal Marshall
TIME STEPS
SWITCHING
PEARL
THE OLD NEIGHBORHOOD
THE FOUR HUNDRED
YOU FOR ME
ANITA FACTOR
MONKEYS
MURDER ON THE BRIDGE

GARY GOLDMAN
Agent: ICM - Los Angeles, 213/550-4000

BIG TROUBLE IN LITTLE CHINA   20th Century Fox, 1986, w/David Weinstein

TOTAL RECALL   Tri-Star, 1990, w/Dan O'Bannon & Ronald Shusettt
NAVY SEALS   Orion, 1990, w/Chuck Pfarrer

Screenplays:
NEW ORLEANS MUSICAL
HALLELUJAH
WARRIORS
ROSES ARE RED

GARY L. GOLDMAN*
Business Manager: Meyer, Benadon & Shapiro, 213/857-7300
Business: Sullivan/Bluth Studios, 2501 W. Burbank Blvd., Suite 201, Burbank, CA, 91505, 818/840-9446

THE SECRET OF NIMH (AF)   MGM/UA, 1982, Story Adaptation w/Don Bluth, Will Finn & John Pomeroy
ALL DOGS GO TO HEAVEN (AF)   MGM/UA, 1989, Story w/others

HAL GOLDMAN*
Contact: WGA - Los Angeles, 213/550-1000

OH GOD! BOOK II   Warner Bros., 1980, w/Fred Fox, Josh Greenfeld, Seaman Jacobs & Melissa Miller

JAMES A. GOLDMAN*
Agent: William Morris Agency - Beverly Hills, 213/274-7451

A FAMILY AFFAIR (P) w/William Goldman & John Kander
FOLLIES (P)
BLOOD, SWEAT AND STANLEY POOLE (P) w/William Goldman
THE LION IN WINTER ★★   Avco Embassy, 1968, from his play
THEY MIGHT BE GIANTS   Universal, 1971, from his play
NICHOLAS AND ALEXANDRA   Columbia, 1971
ROBIN AND MARIAN   Columbia, 1976
WHITE NIGHTS   Columbia, 1985, w/Eric Hughes

Screenplays:
CHINA HAND
GONE WITH THE WIND - PART II
MAN FROM GREEK AND ROMAN   w/C. Forman
BANNER BUSINESS

JOSEPH GOLDMAN
(See Menahem Golan)

SHEPARD GOLDMAN
SALSA   Cannon, 1988, w/Tomas Benitez & Boaz Davidson

Screenplays:
THE MERRY WIVES OF BEVERLY HILLS

WENDY GOLDMAN*
Agent: United Talent Agency - Beverly Hills, 213/273-6700

CASUAL SEX?   Universal, 1988, w/Judy Toll, from their play

Screenplays:
THE SECRET LIFE OF GIRLS   w/Judy Toll

WILLIAM GOLDMAN*
Agent: CAA - Beverly Hills, 213/288-4545

A FAMILY AFFAIR (P) w/James A. Goldman & John Kander
BLOOD, SWEAT AND STANLEY POOLE (P) w/James A. Goldman
MASQUERADE   United Artists, 1965, w/Michael Relph
HARPER   Warner Bros., 1966
BUTCH CASSIDY AND THE SUNDANCE KID ★★   20th Century-Fox, 1969
THE HOT ROCK   20th Century-Fox, 1972
THE GREAT WALDO PEPPER   Universal, 1975
THE STEPFORD WIVES   Columbia, 1975
ALL THE PRESIDENT'S MEN ★★   Warner Bros., 1976
MARATHON MAN   Paramount, 1976
A BRIDGE TOO FAR   United Artists, 1977
MAGIC   20th Century-Fox, 1978
THE PRINCESS BRIDE   20th Century Fox, 1987
HEAT   Paramount, 1987
MISERY   Castle Rock/Columbia, 1990

Screenplays:
THE YEAR OF THE COMET
THE GHOST AND THE DARKNESS
NATIONAL PASTTIME
RESCUE
THE SEA KINGS
THE SKI BUM

RAY GOLDRUP
Agent: Jack Scagnetti Agency - North Hollywood, 818/762-3871

WINDWALKER   Pacific International, 1980

AKIVRA GOLDSMAN*
Agent: ICM - Los Angeles, 213/550-4000

Screenplays:
INDIAN SUMMER

BRUCE L. GOLDSMITH*
Contact: WGA - Los Angeles, 213/550-1000

Screenplays:
KID STUFF

GEORGE H. GOLDSMITH*
Agent: Shapiro/Lichtman - Los Angeles, 213/859-8877

FORCE: FIVE   American Cinema, 1981, w/Emil Farkas
CHILDREN OF THE CORN   New World, 1984
BLUE MONKEY   Spectrafilm, 1987
NOWHERE TO HIDE   New Century/Vista, 1987, w/Alex Rebar

ALLAN S. GOLDSTEIN*
Contact: 818/766-8628

ROOFTOPS   New Century/Vista, 1989, Story w/Tony Mark

HAVEL GOLDSTEIN
THE FINAL ALLIANCE   RCA/Columbia Pictures Home Video, 1991, w/John T. Eubank

JOSHUA GOLDSTEIN*
Contact: WGA - Los Angeles, 213/550-1000

18 AGAIN!   New World, 1988, w/Jonathan Prince

Screenplays:
THE FINE TOUCH w/Jonathan Prince
THE SKY$ THE LIMIT w/Jonathan Prince

BOBCAT GOLDTHWAIT*
Agent: ICM - Los Angeles, 213/550-4000

SHAKES THE CLOWN   I.R.S. Releasing, 1991, directed

STEVE GOMER
Contact: Directors Guild of America - Los Angeles, 213/289-2000

SWEET LORRAINE   Angelika Films, 1987, Story w/Shelly Altman, George Malko & Michael Zettler, directed

AL GOMEZ
JOYSTICKS   Jensen Farley Pictures, 1983, w/Mickey Epps

DIANE GONCIARZ
STREETWALKIN'   Concorde/Cinema Group, 1985, w/Robert Alden & Joan Freeman

WILLIAM GOODHART*
Contact: Ronald S. Konecky, Esq., 485 Madison Avenue, New York, NY 10022, 212/980-0120

GENERATION   Avco Embassy, 1969, from his play
THE HERETIC: EXORCIST II   Warner Bros., 1977
CLOUD DANCER   Blossom, 1980

Screenplays:
THE MOVIEGOER
CONJUNCTION
TOO FAR TO WALK
LOOKING OUT
THE TOUR
WARRIOR OF THE RAINBOW
NO TRANSFER
SOME KIND OF PROGRESS
THE DEATHBIRTH OF HOUDINI
THE SANDMAN
THE SIXTH COMMANDMENT

DAVID ZELAG GOODMAN*
Contact: WGA - Los Angeles, 213/550-1000

THE STRANGLERS OF BOMBAY   Columbia, 1959
LOVERS AND OTHER STRANGERS ★   Cinerama Releasing Corporation, 1970, w/Joseph Bologna & Renee Taylor
MONTE WALSH   National General, 1970, w/Lukas Heller
STRAW DOGS   Cinerama Releasing Corporation, 1972, w/Sam Peckinpah
MAN ON A SWING   Paramount, 1975
FAREWELL, MY LOVELY   Avco Embassy, 1975
LOGAN'S RUN   MGM/UA, 1976
MARCH OR DIE   Columbia, 1977
THE EYES OF LAURA MARS   Columbia, 1978, w/John Carpenter
FIGHTING BACK   Paramount, 1982, w/Thomas Hedley
MAN, WOMAN AND CHILD   Paramount, 1983, w/Erich Segal

Screenplays:
IN A LONELY PLACE w/Michael Grais & Mark Victor
BEYOND THE LAW
THE DEEP (Sequel)
THE RELIGION
HOLLOW POINT

MICHAEL PATRICK GOODMAN*
Agent: Gray/Goodman, Inc. - Beverly Hills, 213/276-7070

WANTED DEAD OR ALIVE   New World, 1987, w/Gary A. Sherman & Brian Taggart

Screenplays:
FALLING OF ANGELS
FIREPOWER

ALEX GORBY
Agent: Barrett, Benson, McCartt & Weston - Los Angeles, 213/247-5500

Screenplays:
PLAY MONEY   FUNNY MONEY w/Andy Rose

BERT I. GORDON*
Agent: Contemporary Artists - Beverly Hills, 213/278-8250

CYCLOPS   American International, 1957, directed
THE AMAZING COLOSSAL MAN   American International, 1957, w/Mark Hanna, directed
THE MAD BOMBER   Cinemation, 1973, directed
NECROMANCY   Cinerama Releasing Corporation, 1973, directed
THE FOOD OF THE GODS   American International, 1976, directed
FOOD OF THE GODS II   Concorde-Centaur, 1989, as "Richard Bennett," w/E. Kim Brewster

BOB GORDON*
Agent: The Gersh Agency - Beverly Hills, 213/274-6611

Screenplays:
ADDICTED TO LOVE

BRYAN GORDON*
Agent: United Talent Agency - Beverly Hills, 213/273-6700

RAY'S MALE HETEROSEXUAL DANCE HALL (Short) ★★ 1987, directed

Screenplays:
PIE IN THE SKY
KISS THE BABY
URIAH
WORTH WINNING
MARY WANTS TO HAVE AN AFFAIR

DAN GORDON*
Agent: The Agency - Los Angeles, 213/551-3000

TRAIN RIDE TO HOLLYWOOD   Taylor-Laughlin, 1975
TANK   Universal, 1984
GOTCHA!   Universal, 1985
GULAG (CTF)   Lorimar Productions/HBO Premiere Films, 1985

Screenplays:
MURDER IN THE FIRST w/Michael Schiffer
A MATTER OF HONOR

EDWIN GORDON*
Contact: WGA - Los Angeles, 213/550-1000

THE CHOSEN   20th Century-Fox International Classics, 1982

FRITZ GORDON
SLEEPAWAY CAMP 3: TEENAGE WASTELAND   Double Helix Films, 1989

KEITH GORDON*
Agent: ICM - Los Angeles, 213/550-4000

THE CHOCOLATE WAR   MCEG, 1988, directed
STATIC   Sandstar Releasing, 1989, w/Mark Romanek

Screenplays:
A MIDNIGHT CLEAR (directing)

STUART GORDON*
Agent: United Talent Agency - Beverly Hills, 213/273-6700

H.P. LOVECRAFT'S RE-ANIMATOR   Empire Pictures, 1985, w/William J. Norris & Dennis Paoli, directed
FROM BEYOND   Empire Pictures, 1986, Adaptation w/Dennis Paoli & Brian Yuzma, directed
HONEY, I SHRUNK THE KIDS   Buena Vista, 1989, Story w/Ed Naha & Brian Yuzna
ROBOTJOX   Triumph Releasing, 1990, Story, directed

NICK GORE*
Agent: David Shapira & Associates - Sherman Oaks, 818/906-0322

Screenplays:
THE NOMINATION w/Jerry Jacobius
BLOOMER GIRLS w/Jerry Jacobius
WISHFUL THINKING w/Jerry Jacobius

CLAUDE GORETTA
Contact: Swiss Film Center, Munstergasse 18, 8001 Zurich, Switzerland, 01/472860

THE LACEMAKER   New Yorker, 1977, w/Pascal Laine, directed
THE DEATH OF MARIO RICCI   New Line Showcase, 1983, w/Georges Haldasdirected

KATHY GORI*
Agent: APA - Los Angeles, 213/273-0744

SAVE THE LAST DANCE FOR ME   Swann American Pictures, 1981, w/Alan Berger

Screenplays:
THE BUFF w/Alan Berger
THE GOLD COAST w/Alan Berger
MERCY GIRLS w/Alan Berger
I'M NOT CHARLIE w/Alan Berger
THE MAN SHE KNEW w/Alan Berger
HER SAINTED HUSBAND w/Alan Berger
GOODBYE FOREVER w/Alan Berger
RICH LITTLE POOR GIRLS w/Alan Berger & Joan Rivers
FOR BETTER OR FOR WORSE w/Alan Berger

ROCKET MAN LIFE ON EARTH w/Alan Berger
NATIONAL PARK w/Alan Berger
LADIES DAY w/Alan Berger
UNDER WRAPS w/Alan Berger
SHAGGY w/Alan Berger

JIM GORMAN*
Contact: Bloom, Dekom & Hergott - Los Angeles, 213/278-8622
Business: Beckner-Gorman Productions, Hollywood Pictures, 818/567-5180

Screenplays:
TEXAS LEAD AND GOLD w/Michael Beckner
CUTTHROATE ISLAND (Story w/Michael Beckner)
HOSTILE TAKEOVER w/Michael Beckner

CHARLES GORMLEY
Contact: British Academy of Film & Television Arts, 195 Piccadilly, London W1, England, 01/734-0022

GOSPEL ACCORDING TO VIC   Skouras Pictures, 1987, directed

EDDIE GORODETSKY*
Agent: William Morris Agency - New York, 212/586-5100

Screenplays:
MY MOTHER CAN FLY

ROBERT E. GOSNELL*
Agent: Thal Literary Management - Los Angeles, 213/659-4946

FIREWALKER   Cannon, 1986

PHILIP KAN GOTANDA*
Agent: Helen Merrill - New York, 212/591-5326

THE WASH   Skouras Pictures, 1988, from his play

CARL GOTTLIEB*
Agent: ICM - Los Angeles, 213/550-4000

JAWS   Universal, 1975, w/Peter Benchley
WHICH WAY IS UP?   Universal, 1978, w/Cecil Brown
JAWS II   Universal, 1978, w/Howard Sackler
THE JERK   Universal, 1979, w/Michael Elias & Steve Martin
CAVEMAN   United Artists, 1981, w/Rudy DeLuca, directed
DOCTOR DETROIT   Universal, 1983, w/Robert Boris & Bruce Jay Friedman
JAWS 3-D   Universal, 1983, w/Richard Matheson

Screenplays:
PAUL BUNYAN
HIGHWAY PATROL

MICHAEL GOTTLIEB*
Business: Harmony Pictures, 2921 W. Alameda Avenue, Burbank, CA 91505, 818/846-6700

MANNEQUIN   20th Century Fox, 1987, w/Ed Rugoff, directed

Screenplays:
WHOPPER w/Ed Rugoff

Go
FILM WRITERS GUIDE

PAUL GOTTLIEB
IN PRAISE OF OLDER WOMEN   Avco Embassy, 1978

HEYWOOD GOULD*
Agent: CAA - Beverly Hills, 213/288-4545

ROLLING THUNDER   American International, 1978, w/Paul Schrader
THE BOYS FROM BRAZIL   20th Century-Fox, 1978
FORT APACHE, THE BRONX   20th Century-Fox, 1981
STREETS OF GOLD   20th Century Fox, 1986, w/Tom Cole & Richard Price
COCKTAIL   Buena Vista, 1988
ONE GOOD COP   Buena Vista, 1991, directed

Screenplays:
DIPLOMATIC IMMUNITY
DOUBLE BANG
ANGELS IN THE OUTFIELD

DAVID S. GOYER*
Agent: United Talent Agency - Beverly Hills, 213/273-6700

DEATH WARRANT   MGM/UA, 1990
KICKBOXER 2   Trimark Pictures, 1991

Screenplays:
LIBERATOR
ARCADE
ALIAS
JACK OF HEARTS
ICE AGE

MICHAEL L. GRACE*
Agent: Maggie Field Agency - Studio City, 818/980-2001

THE UNSEEN   World Northal, 1981

ED GRACZYK
COME BACK TO THE 5 & DIME, JIMMY DEAN, JIMMY DEAN   Cinecom, 1982, from his play

WENDY GRAF*
Contact: WGA - Los Angeles, 213/550-1000

Screenplays:
LIFESAVERS   w/Lisa Stotsky
ALL MINE   w/Lisa Stotsky
FINAL ARGUMENTS   w/Lisa Stotsky

TODD GRAFF
Agent: Susan Smith & Associates - Beverly Hills, 213/852-4777

Screenplays:
USED PEOPLE

SUE GRAFTON*
Agent: Sanford, Skouras, Gross & Associates - Los Angeles, 213/208-2100

LOLLY MADONNA XXX   MGM, 1973, w/Rodney Carr-Smith

JANICE LEE GRAHAM*
Contact: WGA - Los Angeles, 213/550-1000

UNTIL SEPTEMBER   MGM/UA, 1984

Screenplays:
ALEXANDER & NEIL

JESSE GRAHAM
OUT OF TIME   Motion Pictures International, 1989

MELANIE GRAHAM*
Agent: Favored Artists Agency - Los Angeles, 213/653-3191

A SINFUL LIFE   New Line Cinema, 1989, from her play "Just Like the Pom-Pom Girls"

MICHAEL AXEL GRAHAM*
Agent: Jim Preminger Agency - Los Angeles, 213/475-9491

Screenplays:
THE POLICEMAN

RONNY GRAHAM*
Agent: Robinson, Weintraub, Gross & Associates - Los Angeles, 213/653-5802

TO BE OR NOT TO BE   20th Century-Fox, 1983, w/Thomas Meehan
FINDERS KEEPERS   Warner Bros., 1984, w/Terence Marsh & Charles Dennis
SPACEBALLS   MGM/UA, 1987, w/Mel Brooks & Thomas Meehan

MICHAEL GRAIS*
Agent: CAA - Beverly Hills, 213/288-4545

THE THIN LINE   New Yorker, 1980, w/Mark Victor
DEATH HUNT   20th Century-Fox, 1981, w/Mark Victor
POLTERGEIST   MGM/UA, 1980, w/Steven Spielberg & Mark Victor
POLTERGEIST II: THE OTHER SIDE   MGM/UA, 1986, w/Mark Victor
MARKED FOR DEATH   20th Century Fox, 1990, w/Mark Victor

Screenplays:
WARP   w/Mark Victor
TRUEST SPORT   w/Mark Victor
IN A LONELY PLACE   w/Mark Victor & David Z. Goodman
BRAIN   w/Mark Victor
TURN LEFT OR DIE   w/Mark Victor
OCTOBER CIRCLE   w/Mark Victor

DEREK GRANGER
A HANDFUL OF DUST   New Line Cinema, 1988, w/Charles Sturridge & Tim Sullivan

PERCY GRANGER
Agent: ICM - Los Angeles, 213/550-4000

Screenplays:
BLIND LOVE

BARRA GRANT*
Agent: ICM - Los Angeles, 213/550-4000

SLOW DANCING IN THE BIG CITY   United Artists, 1978
MISUNDERSTOOD   MGM/UA, 1984

Screenplays:
HEY MR. FANTASY
INTENSIVE CARE

GARY GRAVER
TEXAS LIGHTNING   Film Ventures International, 1981, directed
TRICK OR TREAT   Lone Star, 1983, directed

JOHN GRAY
Agent: CAA - Beverly Hills, 213/288-4545

BILLY GALVIN   Vestron, 1986, directed
THE LOST CAPONE (CTF)   Patchett-Kaufman Entertainment, 1990

MIKE GRAY*
Agent: William Morris Agency - Beverly Hills, 213/274-7451

THE CHINA SYNDROME ★   Columbia, 1979, w/T.S. Cook & James Bridges
WAVELENGTH   New World, 1983, directed
CODE OF SILENCE   Orion, 1985, w/Michael Blodgett & Dennis Shyrack

SIMON GRAY
Agent: Judy Daish Agency - London, 011/441/486-5405

OTHERWISE ENGAGED (P)
QUARTERMAINE'S TERMS (P)
BUTLEY   American Film Theatre, 1974, from his play
A MONTH IN THE COUNTRY   Orion Classics, 1987

SPALDING GRAY
Agent: ICM - Los Angeles, 213/550-4000

Plays/Monologues include: *Sex and Death to the Age of 14, Booze Cars and College Girls, A Personal History of the American Theater, Terrors of Pleasure, Three Places in Rhode Island (trilogy), Monster in a Box*

SWIMMING TO CAMBODIA   Cinecom, 1987, from his play

WILLIAM GRAY*
Agent: Barry Perelman Agency - Los Angeles, 213/274-5999

PROM NIGHT   Avco Embassy, 1980
THE CHANGELING   AFD, 1980, w/Diana Maddox
AN EYE FOR AN EYE   Avco Embassy, 1981, w/James Bruner
HUMONGOUS   Embassy, 1982
CROSS-COUNTRY   New World, 1983, w/Logan N. Danforth
THE PHILADELPHIA EXPERIMENT   New World, 1984, w/Michael Janover
BLACK MOON RISING   New World, 1986, w/John Carpenter & Desmond Nakano

BRIAN GRAZER
Agent: CAA - Beverly Hills, 213/288-4545
Business: Imagine Films Entertainment, Inc., 1925 Century Park East, Los Angeles, CA 90067, 213/277-1665

SPLASH ★   Buena Vista, 1984, Story
ARMED AND DANGEROUS   Columbia, 1986, Story w/James Keach & Harold Ramis

MIKE GRECO
ALOHA SUMMER   Spectrafilm, 1988, w/Bob Benedetto

ADOLPH GREEN*
Agent: ICM - Los Angeles, 213/550-4000

THE BARKLEYS OF BROADWAY   MGM, 1949, w/Betty Comden
ON THE TOWN   MGM, 1949, w/Betty Comden
SINGIN' IN THE RAIN   MGM, 1952, w/Betty Comden
THE BAND WAGON ★   MGM, 1953, w/Betty Comden
IT'S ALWAYS FAIR WEATHER ★   MGM, 1955, w/Betty Comden
AUNTIE MAME   Warner Bros., 1958, w/Betty Comden
BELLS ARE RINGING   MGM, 1960, w/Betty Comden, from their play
WHAT A WAY TO GO   20th Century-Fox, 1963, w/Betty Comden

CLIFF GREEN
PICNIC AT HANGING ROCK   Atlantic Releasing Corporation, 1975
SUMMERFIELD   Greater Union Film Distributors, 1977

CLIFFORD GREEN*
Agent: William Morris Agency - Beverly Hills, 213/274-7451

BABY - SECRET OF THE LOST LEGEND   Buena Vista, 1985, w/Ellen Green
SPACECAMP   20th Century Fox, 1986, w/Ellen Green & Casey T. Mitchell, as "W.W. Wicket"
THE SEVENTH SIGN   Tri-Star, 1988, w/Ellen Green as "George Kaplan & W.W. Wicket"

Screenplays:
THE PRESIDENT STEPS OUT   *w/Ellen Green*
MAGIC HOUR   ORPHEUS PROJECT   *w/Ellen Green*
WHITE ANGEL   *w/Ellen Green*

ELLEN GREEN*
Agent: William Morris Agency - Beverly Hills, 213/274-7451

BABY - SECRET OF THE LOST LEGEND   Buena Vista, 1985, w/Cliff Green
SPACECAMP   20th Century Fox, 1986, w/Cliff Green & Casey T. Mitchell, as "W.W. Wicket"
THE SEVENTH SIGN   Tri-Star, 1988, w/Cliff Green as "George Kaplan & W.W. Wicket"

Screenplays:
THE PRESIDENT STEPS OUT   *w/Cliff Green*
MAGIC HOUR   ORPHEUS PROJECT   *w/Cliff Green*
WHITE ANGEL   *w/Cliff Green*

GERALD GREEN*
Agent: William Morris Agency - New York, 212/586-5100

THE LAST ANGRY MAN   Columbia, 1959

Gr — Film Writers Guide

Screenplays:
O JERUSALEM
THE PLOT TO MURDER THE POPE
EL PUEBLO

WALON GREEN*
Agent: William Morris Agency - Beverly Hills, 213/274-7451

THE WILD BUNCH ★   Warner Bros., 1969,
   w/Sam Peckinpah
SORCERER   *WAGES OF FEAR*   Universal/
   Paramount, 1977
THE BRINK'S JOB   Universal, 1978
THE SECRET LIFE OF PLANTS (FD)   Paramount, 1978,
   w/Michael Braun & Peter Thompson, directed
THE BORDER   Universal, 1982, w/David Freeman &
   Deric Washburn
SOLARBABIES   MGM/UA, 1986, w/Douglas
   Anthony Metrov
CRUSOE   Island Pictures, 1988, w/Christopher Logue
ROBOCOP 2   Orion, 1990, w/Frank Miller

Screenplays:
RED DRAGON
CENTERFOLD
L.A. WOMAN
PARLOR GAMES
THE DUPLICATED MAN
WASTED
DINOSAUR (AF)
DUE PROCESS

PETER GREENAWAY
Contact: British Academy of Film & Television Arts,
   195 Piccadilly, London W1, England, 01/734-0022

THE DRAUGHTSMAN'S CONTRACT   United Artists
   Classics, 1983, directed
A ZED AND TWO NOUGHTS   Skouras Pictures,
   1985, directed
THE BELLY OF AN ARCHITECT   Skouras Pictures,
   1987, directed
DROWNING BY NUMBERS   Galaxy International,
   1988, directed
THE COOK, THE THIEF, HIS WIFE AND HER LOVER
   Miramax, 1990, directed
PROSPERO'S BOOK   Miramax, 1991, directed

BOB GREENBERG
LOBSTER MAN FROM MARS   Electric Pictures, 1989

DAN GREENBURG*
Agent: Susan Smith & Associates - Beverly Hills,
   213/852-4777

I COULD NEVER HAVE SEX WITH ANY MAN WHO
   HAS SO LITTLE RESPECT FOR MY HUSBAND
   Cinema 5, 1973
FOREPLAY   Cinema National, 1975, w/David Odell &
   Jack Richardson
PRIVATE LESSONS   Jensen Farley Pictures, 1981
PRIVATE SCHOOL   Universal, 1983,
   w/Suzanne O'Malley
THE GUARDIAN   Universal, 1990, w/William Friedkin &
   Stephen Volk

Screenplays:
SHELLY
EXES

STEVE GREENBERG
Agent: Shapiro/Lichtman - Los Angeles, 213/859-8877

DEFENSE PLAY   Trans World Entertainment, 1988,
   w/Aubrey Solomon

CLARENCE GREENE*
Contact: WGA - Los Angeles, 213/550-1000

D.O.A.   Buena Vista, 1988, Story w/Charles Edward Pogue
   & Russell Rouse

DAVID GREENE
Agent: CAA - Beverly Hills, 213/288-4545

GODSPELL   Columbia, 1973, w/John Michael
   Tebelak, directed

SPARKY GREENE
Agent: Circle Talent Associates - Beverly Hills, 213/285-1585

AMERICAN SHOESHINE (Short), w/Jillian
   Palethorpe, directed

Screenplays:
AMAZING BUT TRUE w/Jillian Palethorpe
DIRTY TRICKS w/Jillian Palethorpe
CROOKED HOUSE w/Jillian Palethorpe
MY AMERICAN FORTUNE w/Jillian Palethorpe

STEVEN S. GREENE*
Contact: WGA - Los Angeles, 213/550-1000

HARDBODIES   Columbia, 1984, w/Eric Alter &
   Mark Griffiths
THE EXPERTS   Paramount, 1988, w/Eric Alter &
   Nick Thiel

Screenplays:
MARRYING UP w/Eric Alter
NOSEJOB w/Stan Sheff
SLEEPING BEAUTY

JOSH GREENFELD*
Agent: Shapiro/Lichtman - Los Angeles, 213/859-8877

HARRY AND TONTO ★   20th Century-Fox, 1974,
   w/Paul Mazursky
OH GOD! BOOK II   Warner Bros., 1980, w/Fred Fox, Hal
   Goldman, Seaman Jacobs & Melissa Miller (from his story)

ADAM GREENMAN*
Agent: William Morris Agency - Beverly Hills, 213/274-7451

Screenplays:
THREE OF HEARTS
SOME KIND OF LOVE
JEOPARDY
BAILING OUT
ANNE FLETCHER
BURIED ALIVE
SEX ADDICTS (CTF)

MAGGIE GREENWALD
Agent: InterTalent - Los Angeles, 213/271-0600

HOME REMEDY   Xerox Productions, 1988, directed
THE KILL OFF   Films Around the World, 1990, directed

Screenplays:
SAVAGE NIGHT

NANCY GREENWALD
Agent: S.T.E. Representation - Beverly Hills,
213/550-3982

Screenplays:
LADY CAT

DAVID GREENWALT*
Agent: ICM - Los Angeles, 213/550-4000

UTILITIES *GETTING EVEN* New World, 1983,
w/James Kouf
WACKO Jensen Farley Pictures, 1983, w/James Kouf,
Dana Olsen & Michael Spound
CLASS Orion, 1983, w/James Kouf
AMERICAN DREAMER Warner Bros., 1984,
w/James Kouf
SECRET ADMIRER Orion, 1985, w/James
Kouf, directed
SHAKER RUN Challenge Film Corp., 1985,
w/James Kouf

Screenplays:
GREED w/James Kouf
AIRPLANE III w/James Kouf
BIGAMY w/James Kouf
THE LAKE w/James Kouf
HONEYMOON w/James Kouf

DAN GREER
BAKER'S HAWK Doyt-Dayton, 1976

ANDRE GREGORY
MY DINNER WITH ANDRE New Yorker, 1981,
w/Wallace Shawn

RICHARD GREGSON*
Agent: ICM - Los Angeles, 213/550-4000

EMINENT DOMAIN Triumph, 1991,
w/Andrzej Krakowski

GORDON GREISMAN*
Agent: CAA - Beverly Hills, 213/288-4545

Screenplays:
LOST
PRELUDE
A LIVING WAGE
SILENCES
CASTAWAYS
FELLOW TRAVELERS
AGAINST THE WIND

TOM GRIFFIN
Agent: William Morris Agency - Beverly Hills,
213/274-7451

THE BOYS NEXT DOOR (P)
EINSTEIN AND THE POLAR BEAR (P)
DINNER AT EIGHT (CTF) Think Entertainment, 1989

Screenplays:
FIDELITY
MR. AMBASSADOR

CHARLES B. GRIFFITH
Agent: Jim Preminger Agency - Los Angeles,
213/475-9491

A BUCKET OF BLOOD American International, 1957
ATTACK OF THE CRAB MONSTERS Allied Artists, 1957
NOT OF THIS EARTH Allied Artists, 1957, w/Mark Hanna
THE WILD ANGELS American International, 1966
EAT MY DUST New World, 1976, directed
DR. HECKYL AND MR. HYPE Cannon, 1980, directed

MARK L. GRIFFITHS*
Agent: The Turtle Agency - Studio City, 818/506-6898

RUNNING HOT New Line Cinema, 1984, directed
HARDBODIES Columbia, 1984, w/Steven Greene &
Eric Alter, directed
HARDBODIES 2 CineTel Films, 1986, w/Eric
Alter, directed

THOMAS IAN GRIFFITH*
Agent: CAA - Beverly Hills, 213/288-4545

NIGHT OF THE WARRIOR Trimark, 1991

TREVOR GRIFFITHS*
Agent: CAA - Beverly Hills, 213/288-4545

COMEDIANS (P)
THE PARTY (P)
SAM (P)
OCCUPATIONS (P)
THE WAGES OF THIN (P)
REDS ★ Paramount, 1981, w/Warren Beatty
SINGING THE BLUES IN RED Angelika Films, 1988

TONY GRISONI
DARK WATER ITC, 1980, w/Andrew Bogle
QUEEN OF HEARTS Cinecom, 1989

KENNETH W. GRISWOLD
CHAMPIONS FOREVER (FD) Ion Pictures, 1989

RAJKO GRLIC
THAT SUMMER OF WHITE ROSES Amy International/
Jadran Film, 1989, w/Simon MacCorkindale & Borislav
Pekic, directed

TINUS GROBLER
BRUTAL GLORY Quintex Entertainment, 1991

GEOFF GRODE*
Agent: Warden & White Associates - Beverly Hills,
213/852-1028

Screenplays:
TWO GUYS FROM ITALY
SINGLE FILE
SANTA CRUZ
THE FOURTH DICK

CHARLES GRODIN*
Agent: ICM - New York, 212/556-5600

PRICE OF FAME (P)
MOVERS & SHAKERS MGM/UA, 1985

Gr

DANIEL GRODNIK
Business: Paragon Entertainment, 2211 Corinth Ave. - Suite 305, Los Angeles, CA 90064, 213/478-7272

WITHOUT WARNING   Filmways, 1980, w/Lyn Freeman, Ben Nett & Steve Mathis

FERDE GROFE JR.*
Contact: Sal Lawrence, 213/275-5114

JUDGMENT DAY   Rockport/Ferde Grofe Films, 1989, directed

SALLIE GROO
Agent: APA - Los Angeles, 213/273-0744

Screenplays:
DAUGHTERS OF MUSIC

ALAN GROSS*
Agent: Warden & White Associates - Beverly Hills, 213/852-1028

THE MAN IN 605 (P)
LUNCHING (P)

Screenplays:
THE LOVE SONG OF RUDY KAZOO
AMERICAN GOTHIC

JOEL GROSS
Agent: William Morris Agency - New York, 212/586-5100

MESMER (P)

Screenplays:
WIDOW (CTF)

LARRY GROSS*
Agent: CAA - Beverly Hills, 213/288-4545

HEADIN' FOR BROADWAY   20th Century-Fox, 1980, w/Joseph Brooks & Hilary Henkin
48 HRS.   Paramount, 1982, w/Walter Hill, Steven De Souza & Roger Spottiswoode
STREETS OF FIRE   Universal, 1984, w/Walter Hill
ANOTHER 48 HRS.   Paramount, 1990, w/John Fasano & Jeb Stuart
BODY PARTS   Paramount, 1991, w/Eric Red & Norman Snider

Screenplays:
SUCCESS w/Mary Robison
NOT A THROUGH STREET
SNOW BLIND
MAD LOVE
THE BARTENDER
SMALL COLLEGE IN THE WOODS
LIFE LINE
BROADWAY
ADULTERY
NEON
QUEEN OF MIDNIGHT
L.A. AT NIGHT
THROB
THE EXECUTIONER

MARJORIE L. GROSS*
Agent: William Morris Agency - Beverly Hills, 213/274-7451

Screenplays:
HAPPILY EVER AFTER
SPOOKY

DOUGLAS GROSSMAN
Contact: Andrew Rigrod, Esq. - 213/858-0682

UP THE CREEK   Orion, 1984, Story w/Jim Kouf & Jeffrey Sherman
HELL HIGH   JGM Enterprises, 1989, w/Leo Evans, directed

LYNN GROSSMAN*
Agent: United Talent Agency - Beverly Hills, 213/273-6700

TOKYO POP   Spectrafilm, 1988, w/Fran Rubel Kuzui

Screenplays:
HOME FOR THE HOLIDAYS
WANTED (Shared)
GROWING UP
CLEAR CUT
MARRIED LIFE

JOHN P. GROVES*
Contact: WGA - Los Angeles, 213/550-1000

THE GOLDEN SEAL   Samuel Goldwyn Company, 1983
AMERICAN GLADIATOR   Buena Vista, 1985
BIGGLES   New Century/Vista, 1988, w/Kent Walwin

Screenplays:
DEATH PROBE
SQUAW MAN
KLUDGE

PHIL GROVES
BEACHGIRLS   Crown International, 1982, w/Patrick Duncan

JEAN GRUAULT
Contact: French Film Office, 745 Fifth Avenue, New York, NY 10151, 212/832-8860

JULES ET JIM   Janus, 1961, w/Francois Truffaut
THE WILD CHILD   United Artists, 1970, w/Francois Truffaut
THE STORY OF ADELE H.   New World, 1975, w/Suzanne Schiffman & Francois Truffaut
MON ONCLE D'AMERIQUE ★   New World, 1980
L'AMOUR A MORT   Roissy Film, 1984
LIFE IS A BED OF ROSES   Spectrafilm, 1984
LES ANNEES 80S   World Artists, 1985, w/Chantal Akerman
THE MYSTERY OF ALEXINA   European Classics, 1985, w/Rene Feret

LARRY M. GRUSIN*
Contact: WGA - Los Angeles, 213/550-1000

GARBO TALKS   MGM/UA, 1984

Screenplays:
IRREPLACEABLE KID
CHROMIUM BLUE
EARTHLY DELIGHTS

LIVING ARROWS
ADAM & EVE THE SECOND
BACKWARDS ON A HORSE
ONE IN A MILLION
IVAN

JOHN GUARE*
Agent: ICM - New York, 212/556-5600

LYDIE BREEZE (P)
THE HOUSE OF BLUE LEAVES (P)
LANDSCAPE OF THE BODY (P)
BOSOMS AND NEGLECT (P)
RICH AND FAMOUS (P)
GARDENIA (P)
SIX DEGREES OF SEPARATION (P)
MOON OVER MIAMI (P) also screenplay
TAKING OFF   Universal, 1971, w/Jean-Claude Carriere, Milos Forman & John Klein
ATLANTIC CITY ★   Paramount, 1981

Screenplays:
STARK TRUTH
GERSHWIN
SALUTE THE ARTIST
THE BIG KISS
BAMBOOZLE
STEPPENWOLF
EYE CONTACT

PAUL GUAY*
Agent: The Roberts Company - Los Angeles, 213/552-7800

Screenplays:
THE C NOTE w/Steve Mazur
ABRA CADAVER w/Steve Mazur

RICHARD GUAY
Business: Forward Films, 2445 Herring Avenue, Bronx, NY 10469

TRUE LOVE   MGM/UA, 1989, w/Nancy Savoca

MAC GUDGEON
GROUND ZERO   Avenue Pictures, 1988, w/Jan Sardi
THE DELINQUENTS   Warner Bros., 1990, w/Clayton Frohman

ANN GUEDES
BEARSKIN: AN URBAN FAIRYTALE   Film Four International/British Screen/Cinema Action IPC/RPT, 1989, w/Eduardo Guedes, co-directed

EDUARDO GUEDES
BEARSKIN: AN URBAN FAIRYTALE   Film Four International/British Screen/Cinema Action IPC/RPT, 1989, w/Ann Guedes, co-directed

ROBERT GUENETTE*
Agent: ICM - Los Angeles, 213/550-4000

THE MYSTERIOUS MONSTERS (FD)   Sunn Classic, 1976, directed
THE MAN WHO SAW TOMORROW (FD)   Warner Bros., 1981, w/Alan Hopgood, directed

ANDREW GUERDAT*
Agent: CAA - Beverly Hills, 213/288-4545

FOURTH STORY (CTF)   Viacom Pictures Inc./Konigsberg-Sanitsky Co., 1991

TONINO GUERRA
LA NOTTE   Lopert, 1961, w/Michelangelo Antonioni & Ennio Flaiano
L'AVVENTURA   Janus, 1961, w/Michelangelo Antonioni & Elio Bertolini
L'ECLISSE (THE ECLIPSE)   Paris Film, 1952, w/others
LA NOIA (THE EMPTY CANCAS)   CC Chapion, 1964, w/others
RED DESERT   Rizzoli, 1965, w/Michelangelo Antonioni
CASANOVA '70 ★   Embassy, 1965, w/others
THE TENTH VICTIM   Avco Embassy, 1965, w/others
BLOW-UP ★   Premier, 1966, w/Michelangelo Antonioni & Edward Bond
IN SEARCH OF GREGORY   Universal, 1969, w/Lucile Laks
ZABRISKIE POINT   MGM, 1970, w/Michelangelo Antonioni, Fred Gardner, Clare Peploe & Sam Shepard
AMARCORD ★   New World, 1974, w/Federico Fellini
CADAVERIA ECCELLENTI (ILLUSTRIOUS CORPSES)   United Artists, 1975, w/Francesco Rosi & Lino Jannuzzi
A BUTTERFLY ON THE SHOULDER   UN PAPILLON SUR L'EPAULE   Gaumont, 1978, w/Jean-Claude Carriere
EBOLI   CHRIST STOPPED AT EBOLI 1979, w/Raffaele La Capria & Francesco Rosi   Franklin Media, 1980
THE NIGHT OF THE SHOOTING STARS   LA NOTTE DI SANS LORENZO   United Artists Classics, 1982, w/Paolo Taviani, Vittorio Taviani & Guiliana G. DeNegri
AND THE SHIP SAILS ON   Triumph/Columbia, 1983, w/Federico Fellini
NOSTALGHIA   Grange Communications, 1984, w/Andre Tarkovsky
HENRY IV   Orion Classics, 1985, w/Marco Bellocchio
GINGER AND FRED   MGM/UA, 1986, w/Federico Fellini & Tullio Pinelli
NIGHT SUN   1990, co-scriptor
JOURNEY OF LOVE   Centaur Releasing, 1990
EVERYBODY'S FINE   Miramax, 1991, w/Giuseppe Tornatore

CHRISTOPHER GUEST*
Agent: CAA - Beverly Hills, 213/288-4545

THIS IS SPINAL TAP   Embassy, 1984, w/Michael McKean, Harry Shearer & Rob Reiner
THE BIG PICTURE   Columbia, 1989, w/Michael McKean & Michael Varhol, directed

JUDITH A. GUEST*
Agent: Patricia Karlan Agency - Burbank, 818/846-8666

RACHEL RIVER   Taurus Entertainment, 1989

VAL GUEST
Agent: ICM - London, 71/629-8080

CONVICT 99   Gainsborough, 1938, w/Jack Davies, Marriott Edgar & Ralph Smart
ASK A POLICEMAN   Gainsborough, 1938, w/Marriott Edgar & J.O.C. Orton
BAND WAGON   Gainsborough, 1939, w/Marriott Edgar
CHARLEY'S BIG-HEARTED AUNT   Gainsborough, 1940, w/Marriott Edgar

BACK ROOM BOY General Film Distributors, 1942, w/Marriott Edgar
MISS LONDON LTD. General Film Distributors, 1943, w/Marriott Edgar, directed
GIVE US THE MOON General Film Distributors, 1944, directed
BEES IN PARADISE General Film Distributors, 1944, w/Marriott Edgar, directed
I'LL BE YOUR SWEETHEART General Film Distributors, 1945, w/Val Valentine, directed
MURDER AT THE WINDMILL Grand National, 1949, directed
PAPER ORCHARD Columbia, 1949
HAPPY GO LOVELY ABP, 1950
MISS PILGRIM'S PROGRESS Grand National, 1950, directed
MISTER DRAKE'S DUCK United Artists, 1951, directed
ANOTHER MAN'S POISON United Artists, 1952
PENNY PRINCESS Rank, 1952, directed
THE RUNAWAY BUS Eros, 1954, directed
DANCE LITTLE LADY Renown, 1954, w/Doreen Montgomery, directed
BREAK IN THE CIRCLE 20th Century-Fox, 1955, directed
THE CREEPING UNKNOWN *THE QUARTERMASS EXPERIMENT* Hammer, 1955, w/Richard Landau, directed
ENEMY FROM SPACE *QUATERMASS II* Hammer, 1957, w/Nigel Kneale, directed
UP THE CREEK Byron, 1958, directed
THE CAMP ON BLOOD ISLAND Columbia, 1958, w/Jon Manchip White, directed
HELL IS A CITY Columbia, 1960, directed
STOP ME BEFORE I KILL *THE FULL TREATMENT* Columbia, 1961, w/R.S. Thorn, directed
THE DAY THE EARTH CAUGHT FIRE Universal, 1962, w/Wolf Mankowitz, directed
JIGSAW British Lion, 1962, directed
EIGHTY THOUSAND SUSPECTS Rank, 1963, directed
CONTEST GIRL *THE BEAUTY JUNGLE* Continental, 1964, w/Robert Muller, directed
WHERE THE SPIES ARE MGM, 1965, w/Wolf Mankowitz, directed
ASSIGNMENT K Columbia, 1968, w/Maurice Foster & Bill Strutton, directed
WHEN DINOSAURS RULED THE EARTH Hammer, 1969, directed
THE BOYS IN BLUE MAM Ltd./Apollo Leisure Group, 1983, directed

PAUL JOSEPH GULINO
MURDEROUS VISION (CTF) Gary Sherman/Wilshire Court Productions, 1991

JOSEPH A. GUNN*
Agent: Shapiro/Lichtman - Los Angeles, 213/859-8877

THE WILD PAIR Trans World Entertainment, 1987

ROBERT GUNTER
Agent: Circle Talent Associates - Beverly Hills, 213/285-1585

Screenplays:
MAYHEM
THE DREAD BOYS
FALSE PROFIT
MOMMA'S BOY
THE LEMON

DANIEL J. GUNTZELMAN*
Agent: CAA - Beverly Hills, 213/288-4545

REVENGE OF THE NERDS II 20th Century Fox, 1987, w/Steve Marshall

Screenplays:
HOT WATER w/Steve Marshall
PAPARAZZI w/Steve Marshall

A.R. "PETE" GURNEY*
Agent: William Morris Agency - New York, 212/586-5100

THE DAVID SHOW (P)
SCENES FROM AMERICAN LIFE (P)
RICHARD CORY (P)
THE WAYSIDE MOTOR INN (P)
WHAT I DID LAST SUMMER (P)
THE GOLDEN AGE (P)
THE PERFECT PARTY (P)
SWEET SUE (P)
THE DINING ROOM (P)
THE COCKTAIL HOUR (P)
THE MIDDLE AGES (P)
ANOTHER ANTIGONE (P)
LOVE LETTERS (P), also screenplay
SNOW BALL (P)
THE OLD BOY)S)

Screenplays:
HURDLES
THE HOUSE OF MIRTH

DAN GURSKIS*
Agent: APA - Los Angeles, 213/273-0744

CIVIL WARS (P)
PATER NOSTER (P)
THE STRANGER Columbia, 1987

BETH R. GUTCHEON*
Agent: CAA - Beverly Hills, 213/288-4545

WITHOUT A TRACE 20th Century-Fox, 1983

Screenplays:
THE MARRIAGE STORY
MATINEE

VINCENT GUTIERREZ*
Agent: Warden & White Associates - Beverly Hills, 213/852-1028

Screenplays:
BLESS ME ULTIMA
WELCOME HOME
WOMAN OF THE RING
A FLAG TO FLY
THE JOURNEY OF MARIA LOPEZ

RICHARD A. GUTTMAN*
Agent: The Cooper Agency - Los Angeles, 213/277-8422

HIGHPOINT New World, 1984, w/Ian Sutherland
THE LAST ELEPHANT (CTF) RHI Entertainment/Quintex Entertainment, 1990, w/Bill Bozzone

Screenplays:
MOST WANTED

ROBERT GUZA JR.*
Agent: The Morton Agency - Los Angeles, 213/824-4089

PROM NIGHT   Avco Embassy, 1980, Story
CURTAINS   Jensen Farley Pictures, 1983

STEPHEN R. GYLLENHAAL*
Agent: CAA - Beverly Hills, 213/288-4545

THE NEW KIDS   Columbia, 1985

H

CHARLIE S. HAAS*
Agent: CAA - Beverly Hills, 213/288-4545

OVER THE EDGE   Orion/Warner Bros., 1979,
    w/Tim Hunter
TEX   Buena Vista, 1982, w/Tim Hunter
RECKLESS DISREGARD (CTF)   Telecom Entertainment/
    Polar Film Corporation/Fremantle of Canada Ltd., 1985
MARTIANS GO HOME   Taurus Entertainment, 1990
GREMLINS 2 THE NEW BATCH   Warner Bros., 1990

Screenplays:
TRAP DOOR w/Tim Hunter
HOMELANDS
DEATH MAKES THE CHART
BACK ON TOP

STEVE HABERMAN*
Agent: The Gersh Agency - Beverly Hills, 213/274-6611

LIFE STINKS   MGM-Pathe, 1991, w/Mel Brooks &
    Rudy DeLuca

TOD HACKETT
(See Alan Ormsby)

DENNIS E. HACKIN*
Agent: The Artists Agency - Los Angeles, 213/277-7779

WANDA NEVADA   United Artists, 1979
BRONCO BILLY   Warner Bros., 1980
NO HOLDS BARRED   New Line Cinema, 1989

Screenplays:
SHOWDOWN IN LITTLE TOKYO w/Jonathan Lemkin
THUNDERBOAT w/Stuart Birnbaum

MOSHE HADAR
CARTEL   Shapiro Glickenhaus, 1990

HORATIUS HAEBERLE
THE LAST WORD   Samuel Goldwyn Company,
    1979, Story

ROLF HAEDRICH
AMONG THE CINDERS   New World, 1985, w/John
    O'Shea, directed

ZION HAEN
TRIUMPH OF THE SPIRIT   Nova International Films, 1989,
    Story w/Shimon Arama

GEORGE HAGEN
Agent: United Talent Agency - Beverly Hills,
    213/273-6700

Screenplays:
STIFFS
SMALL FEARS
PAJAMA PRINCESS

ROSS HAGEN*
Agent: Barry Perelman Agency - Los Angeles,
    213/274-5999

CLICK: THE CALENDAR GIRL KILLER   Crown
    International, 1991, w/Hoke Howell, David Chute &
    David Reskin, co-directed

STEVEN HAGER*
Contact: WGA - New York, 212/245-6180

BEAT STREET   Orion, 1984, Story

PAUL HAGGIS*
Contact: 818/247-1007

Screenplays:
RED HOT w/Michael Maurer

OLIVER D. HAILEY*
Agent: ICM - Los Angeles, 213/550-4000

FOR THE USE OF THE HALL (P)
JUST YOU AND ME KID   Columbia, 1979,
    w/Leonard B. Stern

RICHARD HAINES
SPACE AVENGER   Manley Productions, 1990, w/Lynwood
    Sawyer, directed

MERVYN HAISMAN
JANE AND THE LOST CITY   New World, 1987

JOE HALDEMAN
ROBOTJOX   Triumph Releasing, 1990

JONATHAN HALES
LOOPHOLE   MGM/United Artists, 1980
THE MIRROR CRACK'D   EMI, 1980, w/Barry Sandler

JOHN HALFPENNY
ROCK & RULE (AF)   MGM/UA, 1985, w/Peter Sauder

KENNETH J. HALL
THE TOMB   Trans World Entertainment, 1986
DR. ALIEN   Phantom Productions, 1989
PUPPET MASTER   Full Moon, 1989, Story
    w/Charles Band

PARNELL HALL
C.H.U.D.   New World, 1984

LASSE HALLSTROM
Agent: Sanford, Skouras, Gross & Associates - Los Angeles, 213/208-2100

MY LIFE AS A DOG ★   Skouras Pictures, 1987, w/Reidar Jonsson, Brasse Brannstrom & Per Berglund, directed

Screenplays:
PETER PAN

DAVID HALPERN
DEADLY DANCER   Action International Pictures, 1990, w/Maria Fields

DENIS M. HAMILL*
Agent: ICM - Los Angeles, 213/550-4000

TURK 182   20th Century Fox, 1985, w/John Hamill & James Gregory Kingston
CRITICAL CONDITION   Paramount, 1987, w/John Hamill

Screenplays:
STOMPING GROUND w/John Hamill
A KILLING FOR CHRIST w/John Hamill
REFORM SCHOOL PROJECT w/John Hamill
DIPLOMATIC IMMUNITY w/John Hamill
ENCORE w/John Hamill
WHERE THERE'S A WILL w/John Hamill
DIVERSIONS w/John Hamill

JOHN P. HAMILL*
Contact: 914/876-2794

TURK 182   20th Century Fox, 1985, w/Denis Hamill & James Gregory Kingston
CRITICAL CONDITION   Paramount, 1987, w/Denis Hamill

Screenplays:
STOMPING GROUND w/Denis Hamill
A KILLING FOR CHRIST w/Denis Hamill
REFORM SCHOOL PROJECT w/Denis Hamill
DIPLOMATIC IMMUNITY w/Denis Hamill
ENCORE w/Denis Hamill
WHERE THERE'S A WILL w/Denis Hamill
DIVERSIONS w/Denis Hamill

PETE HAMILL*
Agent: CAA - Beverly Hills, 213/288-4545

DOC   United Artists, 1971
BADGE 373   Paramount, 1973
THE NEON EMPIRE (CTF)   Fries Entertainment/Richard Maynard Productions, 1989

Screenplays:
CAR RACING STORY
HORSE RACING
DIRTY LAUNDRY
JACK THE RIPPER
JUDGMENT DAY

ANN LEWIS HAMILTON*
Agent: Pleshette & Green - Los Angeles, 213/465-0428

Screenplays:
THE GIRLS OF SUMMER

GUY HAMILTON
Agent: ICM - Los Angeles, 213/550-4000

THE COLDITZ STORY   Republic, 1955, w/Ivan Foxwell, directed
A TOUCH OF LARCENY   Paramount, 1959, w/Ivan Foxwell & Roger MacDougall, directed

SAM HAMM*
Agent: Warden & White Associates - Beverly Hills, 213/852-1028

NEVER CRY WOLF   Buena Vista, 1983, w/Curtis Lee Hanson & Richard Kletter
BATMAN   Warner Bros., 1989, w/Warren Skaaren

Screenplays:
TIME OUT OF JOINT w/Michael Duncan
WATCHMEN
THE AVENGERS
RENEGADE
PULITZER PRIZE
DUMBLUCK
HANG TIME
WHITE WEDDING

DIANA HAMMOND*
Contact: Weissman & Wolf - Los Angeles, 213/858-7888

Screenplays:
SHADOW OF GOD
FATHER'S DAY
ARE YOU OUT OF MY MIND?
HOLY BLOOD, HOLY GRAIL
MOUSE PACKS
WILDCARD
VIRGIN

JEFFREY HAMMOND*
Agent: Triad Artists, Inc. - Los Angeles, 213/556-2727

Screenplays:
COLD EYE w/Mark Kruger

CHRISTOPHER HAMPTON
Agent: William Morris Agency - Beverly Hills, 213/274-7451

THE PHILANTHROPIST (P)
WHITE CAMELEON (P)
A DOLL'S HOUSE   Elkins, 1973
TALES FROM THE VIENNA WOODS   Cinema 5, 1981, w/Maximilian Schell
BEYOND THE LIMIT   Paramount, 1983
THE WOLF AT THE DOOR   International Film Marketing, 1986
THE GOOD FATHER   Skouras Pictures, 1987
DANGEROUS LIAISONS ★★   Warner Bros., 1988, from his play

Screenplays:
NOSTROMO w/Robert Bolt
IMAGINING ARGENTINA
THE LAST SECRET
THE MOON & SIXPENCE
RUSSIAN STORY
THE PORTAGE TO SAN CRISTOBAL
CARRINGTON
THE FLORENTINES

BLANCHE HANALIS*
Agent: Preferred Artists - Encino, 818/990-0305

THE TROUBLE WITH ANGELS   Columbia, 1966
WHERE ANGELS GO, TROUBLE FOLLOWS
   Columbia, 1968
FISH HAWK   Avco Embassy, 1981

JOHN HANCOCK*
Agent: Camden-ITG - Los Angeles, 213/289-2700

WEEDS   DEG, 1987, w/Dorothy Tristan, directed

CHIP HAND*
Agent: The Irv Schechter Company - Beverly Hills,
   213/278-8070

LOVELINES   Tri-Star, 1984, w/William Hillman

PETER HANDKE
THE GOALIE'S ANXIETY AT THE PENALTY KICK
   Bauer International, 1972
THE WRONG MOVE   New Yorker, 1975
THE LEFT-HANDED WOMAN   1978, directed
WINGS OF DESIRE   DER HIMMEL UBER BERLIN
   Orion Classics, 1987, w/Wim Wenders

KEN HANDLER
DELIVERY BOYS   New World, 1985, directed

DARYL HANEY
DADDY'S BOYS   Concorde, 1988
FRIDAY THE 13TH, PART VII: THE NEW BLOOD
   Paramount, 1988, w/Manuel Fidello
LORDS OF THE DEEP   Concorde, 1989,
   w/Howard Cohen
CRIME ZONE   Concorde, 1989
MASQUE OF THE RED DEATH   Concorde, 1989,
   w/Larry Brand
CRACKDOWN   Concorde, 1991, w/Ross Bell

PETER J. HANKOFF*
Agent: Abrams Artists & Associates - Los Angeles,
   213/859-0625

Screenplays:
SANTERIA w/David Madsen
RED CAR w/David Madsen
INSIDE JOB w/David Madsen
RHYTHM & BLUES w/David Madsen
BORROWED TIME w/David Madsen
NIGHTFALL w/Brian Grant
HELL SPA
BREAKTHROUGH
THE CHAINLETTER
THE CRIMINAL MIND OF J. C. LOOMIS
MR. HAPPY

WILLIAM HANLEY*
Agent: Susan Smith & Associates - Beverly Hills,
   213/852-4777

Screenplays:
CODE BLUE
BLUE CHIP

BRIAN HANNANT
Contact: Australian Film Commission, 9229 Sunset Blvd.,
   Los Angeles, CA 90069, 213/275-7074

THE ROAD WARRIOR   MAD MAX II   Warner Bros., 1982,
   w/Terry Hayes

ROB HANNING
Agent: United Talent Agency - Beverly Hills, 213/273-6700

CLUB XII I(P) w/Randy Weiner

Screenplays:
YO' JULIETTE w/Randy Weiner

ERIC HANSEN*
Agent: The Roberts Company - Los Angeles, 213/552-7800

Screenplays:
THE PROMOTER w/Gregory Hansen
MUM'S THE WORD w/Gregory Hansen
SEVEN SOULS w/Gregory Hansen

GREGORY HANSEN*
Agent: The Roberts Company - Los Angeles, 213/552-7800

Screenplays:
THE PROMOTER w/Eric Hansen
MUM'S THE WORD w/Eric Hansen
SEVEN SOULS w/Eric Hansen

CURTIS LEE HANSON*
Agent: United Talent Agency - Beverly Hills, 213/273-6700

A BULLET FOR PRETTY BOY   American
   International, 1970
THE DUNWICH HORROR   American International, 1970,
   w/Henry Rosenbaum & Ronald Silkowsky
THE AROUSERS   SWEET KILL   New World, 1976
THE SILENT PARTNER   EMC Films/Aurora, 1979
WHITE DOG   Paramount, 1982, w/Samuel Fuller
NEVER CRY WOLF   Buena Vista, 1983, w/Sam Hamm &
   Richard Kletter
THE BEDROOM WINDOW   DEG, 1987, directed

Screenplays:
THE BROTHERHOOD OF THE GRAPE (directing)

JOHN HANSON
Business: New Front Films, 125 W. Richmond Avenue, Point
   Richmond, CA 94801, 415/231-0225

NORTHERN LIGHTS   Cinemanifest/New Front Films, 1978,
   w/Rob Nilsson, co-directed
WILDROSE   Troma, 1984, w/Eugene Corr, directed

STEWART HARDING
SPACEHUNTER: ADVENTURES IN THE FORBIDDEN
   ZONE   Columbia, 1983, Story w/Jean LaFleur

EVA HARDY
SHE'LL BE WEARING PINK PAJAMAS   Film Forum, 1986

JONATHAN HARDY
BREAKER MORANT ★   New World/Quartet, 1980,
   w/Bruce Beresford & David Stevens

ROBIN HARDY
Address: c/o Robert Lasky, 1150 Fifth Avenue, New York, NY 10128

THE FANTASIST   ITC, 1986, directed
FORBIDDEN SUN   Academy Entertainment, 1989

DAVID HARE
Agent: ICM - Los Angeles, 213/550-4000

SAIGON - YEAR OF THE CAT (P), also teleplay
SLAG (P)
THE GREAT EXHIBITION (P)
A MAP OF THE WORLD (P)
RACING DEMON (P)
THE KNIFE (P)
BRASSNECK (P) w/Howard Brenton
KNUCKLE (P)
FANSHEN (P)
LICKING HITLER (P)
DREAMS OF LEAVING (P)
PRAVDA (P) w/Howard Brenton
THE SECRET RAPTURE (P)
PLENTY   20th Century Fox, 1985, from his play, directed
WETHERBY   MGM/UA Classics, 1985, directed
STRAPLESS   Miramax, 1990, directed
PARIS BY NIGHT   Cineplex Odeon, 1990, directed

DEAN HARGROVE*
Agent: Broder-Kurland-Webb-Uffner - Los Angeles, 213/656-9262

THE MANCHU EAGLE MURDER MYSTERY   United Artists, 1975, w/Gabriel Dell, directed

RENNY HARLIN
Agent: ICM - Los Angeles, 213/550-4000

BORN AMERICAN   Cinema Group, 1986, w/Markus Selin, directed

ROBERT M. HARLING*
Agent: CAA - Beverly Hills, 213/288-4545

STEEL MAGNOLIAS   Tri-Star, 1989, from his play
SOAPDISH   Paramount, 1991, w/Andrew Bergman

SAMUEL H. HARPER*
Agent: Triad Artists, Inc. - Los Angeles, 213/556-2727

Screenplays:
SCHOOL SPIRIT
FUNNY BUSINESS
LATER
STANDUP
BLAST FROM THE PAST

MICHAEL HARRESCHOU*
Contact: WGA - Los Angeles, 213/550-1000

SAFARI 3000   MGM/United Artists, 1982

BONNIE HARRIS
WINDRIDER   MGM/UA, 1987, w/Everett DeRoche

DAMIAN HARRIS
Business Manager: Addis-Wechsler & Associates - Los Angeles, 213/954-9000

THE RACHEL PAPERS   MGM/UA, 1989, directed

FRANK HARRIS
KILLPOINT   Crown International, 1984, directed

HAL HARRIS*
Agent: CAA - Beverly Hills, 213/288-4545

Screenplays:
GREYSTOKE II
CORONADO'S GOLD
SPORTSMAN OF THE YEAR

JAMES B. HARRIS*
Agent: ICM - Los Angeles, 213/550-4000
Business: James B. Harris Productions, 248-1/2 Lasky Drive, Beverly Hills, CA 900212, 213/273-4270

SOME CALL IT LOVING   CineGlobe, 1973, directed
FAST-WALKING   Pickman Films, 1982, directed
COP   Atlantic Releasing Corporation, 1988, directed

MARK HARRIS*
Agent: ICM - Los Angeles, 213/550-4000

BANG THE DRUM SLOWLY   Paramount, 1973

PAUL HARRIS
NICE GIRLS DON'T EXPLODE   New World, 1987

SUSAN HARRIS*
Agent: CAA - Beverly Hills, 213/288-4545

Screenplays:
FATHER'S DAY

TIMOTHY H. HARRIS*
Agent: APA - Los Angeles, 213/273-0744
Business: Myrtos Productions, Universal Studios, 818/777-1000

CHEAPER TO KEEP HER   American Cinema, 1980, w/Herschel Weingrod
TRADING PLACES   Paramount, 1983, w/Herschel Weingrod
BREWSTER'S MILLIONS   Universal, 1985, w/Herschel Weingrod
MY STEPMOTHER IS AN ALIEN   WEG, 1988, Jonathan Reynolds, Herschel Weingrod & Jericho Stone
TWINS   Universal, 1988, w/Herschel Weingrod, William Davies & William Osborne
KINDERGARTEN COP   Universal, 1990, w/Herschel Weingrod & Murray Salem
PURE LUCK   Universal, 1991, w/Herschel Weingrod

Screenplays:
DUMMIES w/Herschel Weingrod
SIBERIAN EXPRESS w/Herschel Weingrod
THE FRENCH KISS w/Herschel Weingrod
THE PIED PIPER w/Herschel Weingrod
THE FUGITIVE PIGEON w/Herschel Weingrod
BIGFINGER w/Herschel Weingrod
MICKEY w/Herschel Weingrod
BEAUTY SCHOOL w/Herschel Weingrod

WENDELL B. HARRIS, JR.
Agent: United Talent Agency - Beverly Hills,
   213/273-6700

CHAMELEON STREET   Films Around the World,
   1990, directed

Screenplays:
JOE LOUIS

JIM HARRISON*
Agent: Phoenix Literary Agency - Livingston, Montana,
   406/222-2848

A FAR EDGE (P)
COLD FEET   Avenue Pictures, 1989, w/Tom McGuane
REVENGE   Columbia, 1990, w/Jeffrey Fiskin

Screenplays:
BETWEEN WARS

JOHN KENT HARRISON*
Agent: CAA - Beverly Hills, 213/288-4545

MURDER BY PHONE   New World, 1982, w/Michael
   Butler & Dennis Shryack
BEAUTIFUL DREAMERS   Cinexus/Famous Players/
   CF/P Distribution, 1990, directed
MEMORIES OF MURDER (CTF)   Houston Lady
   Co./Viacom, 1990, w/Nevin Schreiner

Screenplays:
IN DEEP
ROAST BEEF ON SUNDAY
FUR TRADING IN AMERICA

LINDSAY HARRISON*
Agent: William Morris Agency - Beverly Hills,
   213/274-7451

FRATERNITY VACATION   New World, 1985

Screenplays:
AT 17 w/Kathleen Rowell
COMING OF AGE
HOLIDAY ADVENTURE
CUSTODY
WOMEN OF BEVERLY HILLS

PAUL CARTER HARRISON
YOUNGBLOOD   American International, 1978

WILLIAM HARRISON*
Agent: William Morris Agency - New York, 212/586-5100

ROLLERBALL   United Artists, 1975
MOUNTAINS OF THE MOON   Tri-Star, 1990,
   w/Bob Rafelson

DON MICHAEL HARRY
HARLEY DAVIDSON AND THE MARLBORO MAN
   MGM-Pathe, 1991

LEE HARRY
SILENT NIGHT, DEADLY NIGHT PART II   Ascot
   Entertainment Group, 1987, w/Joseph H.
   Earle, directed

T. MICHAEL HARRY
IN THE SHADOW OF KILIMANJARO   Scotti Bros., 1986,
   w/Jeffrey M. Sneller

CHRISTOPHER HART*
Agent: The Artists Agency - Los Angeles, 213/277-7779

EAT AND RUN   New World, 1987, w/Stan Hart, directed

JIM V. HART*
Agent: CAA - Beverly Hills, 213/288-4545

GIMME AN F   20th Century Fox, 1985
HOOK   Tri-Star, 1991, w/Malia Scotch Marmo

Screenplays:
DRACULA - THE UNTOLD STORY
FRAT RATS
STILL CRAZY w/Bill Kerby
TROUBLE IN BIG D
HOSE JOB
BLOOD MAN
PROTEKTOR
WINTER
HONEYMOON
OLD FRIEND OF THE FAMILY
DRAGONS
WARRIOR BLUE

JOE HART
REPO JAKE   PM Home Video, 1991

KENNETH HARTFORD
HELL SQUAD   Cannon, 1987

HAL HARTLEY
Business: True Fiction Pictures, 12 W. 27th St. 10th Floor,
   New York, NY 10001, 212/684-4284

THE UNBELIEVABLE TRUTH   Miramax, 1990, directed
TRUST   Fine Line Features, 1991, directed

Screenplays:
SIMPLE MEN

PHIL HARTMAN*
Agent: William Morris Agency - Beverly Hills, 213/274-7451

PEE WEE'S BIG ADVENTURE   Warner Bros., 1985,
   w/Paul Reubens & Michael Varhol

Screenplays:
THE CASE OF THE PURPLE TERROR: A CHICK
HAZARD MYSTERY
MR. FIX-IT
THE LIAR MOVIE

RAYMOND C. HARTUNG*
Contact: WGA - Los Angeles, 213/550-1000

SNOW KILL (CTF)   Wilshire Court Productions, 1990,
   w/Harv Zimmel
FATAL EXPOSURE (CTF)   GC Group/Wilshire Court
   Productions, 1991

Screenplays:
TEMPTING FATE
TRASH PATROL
SCREENPLAY
SMART MONEY

JOHN HARTWELL
Agent: Barrett, Benson, McCartt & Weston - Los Angeles, 213/247-5500

THE FAN   Paramount, 1981, w/Priscilla Chapman

RON HARVEY
FIST OF FEAR TOUCH OF DEATH   Aquarius, 1980

JENNY A. HARWELL
Agent: Triad Artists, Inc. - Los Angeles, 213/556-2727

Screenplays:
THE MAN IN THE MOON

RONALD HARWOOD
Agent: The Artists Agency - Los Angeles, 213/277-7779

ANOTHER TIME (P)
PRIVATE POTTER   MGM, 1962, from his play
A HIGH WIND IN JAMAICA   20th Century-Fox, 1965, w/Dennis Cannan & Stanley Mann
DIAMONDS FOR BREAKFAST   Paramount, 1968, w/Pierre Rouve & N.F. Simpson
EYEWITNESS   ITC, 1970
ONE DAY IN THE LIFE OF IVAN DENISOVICH   Group W, 1971
OPERATION DAYBREAK   Warner Bros., 1975
THE DRESSER ★   Columbia, 1983, from his play
THE DOCTOR AND THE DEVILS   20th Century Fox, 1985
TCHIN-TCHIN   Silvio Berlusconi Communications/Produzioni Cinematografiche, 1991

PATRICK B. HASBURGH*
Agent: CAA - Beverly Hills, 213/288-4545

Screenplays:
SLOEHAND HOLIDAY

GUSTAV HASFORD
Contact: Publisher-Bantam Books - New York, 212/765-6500

FULL METAL JACKET ★   Warner Bros., 1987, w/Michael Herr & Stanley Kubrick

CHARLIE HAUCK*
Agent: United Talent Agency - Beverly Hills, 213/273-6700

Screenplays:
ENGAGED TO BE MARRIED
OFFICE ROMANCE

JEFF HAUSE*
Agent: Warden & White Associates - Beverly Hills, 213/852-1028

ONCE BITTEN   Samuel Goldwyn Company, 1985, w/Dave Hines & Jonathan Roberts

Screenplays:
THE RIGHT HAND MEN w/Dave Hines
NUCLEAR REACTIONS w/Dave Hines

MICHAEL HAWES
ONE DARK NIGHT   Comworld, 1983, w/Tom McLoughlin

CHRISTOPHER HAWTHORNE*
Agent: William Morris Agency - New York, 212/586-5100

PARENTS   Vestron, 1989

Screenplays:
PROWLER

DAVID HAY
Agent: Warden & White Associates - Beverly Hills, 213/852-1028

Screenplays:
SUSPICIOUS MINDS

JIM HAYDEN
Agent: William Morris Agency - Beverly Hills, 213/274-7451

Screenplays:
THE RECOVERY

JOHN MICHAEL HAYES*
Agent: Ned Brown Agency - West Los Angeles, 213/456-8068

RED-BALL EXPRESS   Universal-International, 1952
THUNDER BAY   Universal-International, 1953, w/Gil Doud
TORCH SONG   MGM, 1953, w/Jan Lustig
REAR WINDOW ★   Paramount, 1954
TO CATCH A THIEF   Paramount, 1955
THE TROUBLE WITH HARRY   Paramount, 1955
THE BAR SINISTER   MGM, 1955
THE ROSE TATTOO   Paramount, 1955
PEYTON PLACE   20th Century-Fox, 1957
BUT NOT FOR ME   Paramount, 1959
BUTTERFIELD EIGHT   MGM, 1960, w/Charles Schnee
THE CARPETBAGGERS   Paramount, 1964
THE CHALK GARDEN   Universal-International, 1964
WHERE LOVE HAS GONE   Paramount, 1964
HARLOW   Paramount, 1965
JUDITH   Paramount, 1965

JOSEPH HAYES*
Agent: Curtis Brown, Ltd. - Los Angeles 213/461-0148

THE DESPERATE HOURS   Paramount, 1955, from his play
THE YOUNG DOCTORS   United Artists, 1961
DESPERATE HOURS   MGM/UA, 1990, w/Lawrence Konner & Mark Rosenthal

STEVEN HAYES*
Agent: Stone Manners Agency - Los Angeles, 213/275-9599

Screenplays:
THE WHITE SHERPA

TERRY HAYES
Business: Kennedy Miller Productions, 30 Orwell St., Kings Cross, Sydney, Australia

THE ROAD WARRIOR MAD MAX II   Warner Bros., 1982, w/George Miller & Brian Hannant
MAD MAX BEYOND THUNDERDOME   Warner Bros., 1985, w/George Miller
DEAD CALM   Warner Bros., 1989
BANGKOK HILTON (CTF)   Kennedy Miller Productions, 1990

Screenplays:
THE SAINT

BRIAN HAYLES
NOTHING BUT THE NIGHT   Rank, 1972
WARLORDS OF ATLANTIS   Columbia, 1978
ARABIAN ADVENTURE   Badger Films, 1979

TODD HAYNES
SUPERSTAR: THE KAREN CARPENTER STORY
   (Short), directed
POISON   Zeitgeist Films, 1991, directed

JACK HAZAN
Contact: British Academy of Film & Television Arts, 195
   Piccadilly, London W1, England, 01/734-0022

RUDE BOY   Atlantic Releasing Corporation, 1980,
   w/David Mingay & Ray Gange, directed

BARRY HEALEY
ONE MAGIC CHRISTMAS   Buena Vista, 1985,
   Story w/Phillip Borsos & Thomas Meehan

MICHAEL P. HEALY
Contact: 818/907-7843

VAMPING   Atlantic Releasing Corporation, 1984

JANET HEANEY*
Agent: The Roberts Company - Los Angeles,
   213/552-7800

POWWOW HIGHWAY   Warner Bros., 1989,
   w/Jean Stawarz

Screenplays:
RUNNING OUT

JONATHAN HEAP
Agent: Thal Literary Management - Los Angeles,
   213/659-4946

12:01 (Short) ★ 1990, w/Stephen Tolkin, directed

Screenplays:
HONOR BOUND   w/Philip Morton
WHAT NICK SAW   w/Philip Morton
THE SUN   w/Philip Morton & Tom Read

DALE HEARD
Business Manger: Addis-Wechsler & Associates -
   Los Angeles, 213/954-9000

Screenplays:
WARRIOR

LAURENCE HEATH*
Agent: The Irv Schechter Company - Beverly Hills,
   213/278-8070

TRIUMPH OF THE SPIRIT   Nova International Films,
   1989, w/Andrzej Krakowski

MERRILL HEATTER*
Contact: WGA - Los Angeles, 213/550-1000

SNAPSHOT   Group 1, 1979

DAVID HEAVENER
TWISTED JUSTICE   Seymour Borde & Associates,
   1990, directed
KILL CRAZY   Media Home Entertainment,
   1991, directed

Screenplays:
PRIME TARGET   (directing)

AMY HECKERLING*
Agent: The Gersh Agency - Beverly Hills, 213/274-6611

LOOK WHO'S TALKING   Tri-Star, 1989, directed
LOOK WHO'S TALKING TOO   Tri-Star, 1990, w/Neal
   Israel, directed

JOHN BRYANT HEDBERG
Agent: Circle Talent Associates - Beverly Hills,
   213/285-1585

Screenplays:
AMERICAN NINJA V LITTLE NINJA MAN
   w/George Saunders
LONE JUSTICE CUSTODY   w/George Saunders
BOMB SQUAD   w/George Saunders
MAGIC BUS   w/George Saunders
TEEN GENIE   w/George Saunders
MARSHALL LAW III   w/George Saunders

ROB HEDDEN*
Agent: S.T.E. Representation, Ltd. - Beverly Hills,
   213/550-3982

FRIDAY THE 13TH PART VIII: JASON TAKES
   MANHATTAN   Paramount, 1989, directed

THOMAS HEDLEY, JR.*
Agent: ICM - Los Angeles, 213/550-4000

MR. PATMAN   Film Consortium, 1980
DOUBLE NEGATIVE   Best Film and Video, 1980, w/Janis
   Allen & Charles Dennis
CIRCLE OF TWO   World Northal, 1981
FIGHTING BACK   Paramount, 1982,
   w/David Z. Goodman
FLASHDANCE   Paramount, 1983, w/Joe Eszterhas
HARD TO HOLD   Universal, 1984

Screenplays:
TOUGH TANGO
STREET DANDY
VALENTINO PLACE
BLOOD MAN
PROTEKTOR
WINTER

TERRANCE HEFFERNAN
HEARTACHES   MPM, 1982

RICHARD T. HEFFRON
Agent: CAA - Beverly Hills, 213/288-4545

TAGGET (CTF)   Mirisch-Tagget-MCA, 1991, w/Janis
   Diamond & Peter S. Fischer, directed

He

FILM WRITERS GUIDE

RICHARD HEFT
Agent: Circle Talent Associates - Beverly Hills, 213/285-1585

LASER MISSION   Bavaria Filmworks, 1989

Screenplays:
THE STINGER
THE SWIMMING POOL
ZONE TWO

DAVID HEISLER
PRIVATE COLLECTIONS   Red Wing Productions, 1990, w/Bruce Williams

MATS HELGE
RUSSIAN TERMINATOR   Arena Home Video, 1991, directed

BRIAN HELGELAND*
Agent: Triad Artists, Inc. - Los Angeles, 213/556-2727

A NIGHTMARE ON ELM STREET 4: THE DREAM MASTER   New Line Cinema, 1988, w/Scott Pierce
976-EVIL   New Line Cinema, 1989, w/Rhet Topham

Screenplays:
THE TICKING MAN w/Manny Coto
DUKE STEAMER: WORLD'S GREATEST BODYGUARD

CRAIG HELLER*
Agent: Robinson, Weintraub, Gross & Associates - Los Angeles, 213/653-5802

Screenplays:
READY OR NOT w/Guy Schulman
SEPARATE WAYS w/Guy Schulman

GREGORY HELLER
ALPHABET CITY   Atlantic Releasing Corporation, 1984, w/Amos Poe

JOSEPH HELLER
Contact: Publisher-Dell Books - New York, 212/765-6500

SEX AND THE SINGLE GIRL   Warner Bros., 1964, w/David R. Schwartz
DIRTY DINGUS MAGEE   MGM, 1970, w/Frank Waldman & Tom Waldman

Screenplays:
GOOD AS GOLD

ZOE HELLER
TWENTY-ONE   Anglo International Films Ltd., 1991, w/Don Boyd

MONTE HELLMAN
Agent: Susan Smith & Associates - Beverly Hills, 213/852-4777

SILENT NIGHT, DEADLY NIGHT III: YOU BETTER WATCH OUT!   Quiet Fims, 1989, Story w/Richard N. Gladstein & Carlos Lazlo, directed

ROBERT HENDRICKSON
CLOSE SHAVE   Tobann International, 1981, w/Ronald Collier

ALEX HENDRIE
Agent: Circle Talent Associates - Beverly Hills, 213/285-1585

Screenplays:
TEXAS JACK
McFEE'S LAST CASE
THE RIDE

SHIRL HENDRYX*
Agent: Media Artists Group - Hollywood, 213/463-5610

RUNNING BRAVE   Buena Vista, 1983, w/Henry Bean

FRANK HENENLOTTER
Business: Lievins/Henenlotter, 443 West 43rd Street #1, New York, NY 10036, 212/265-2166

BASKET CASE   Analysis, 1982, directed
BASKET CASE 2   Shapiro Glickenhaus, 1990, directed
FRANKENHOOKER   Shapiro Glickenhaus, 1990, w/Robert Martin, directed

KIM HENKEL*
Contact: WGA - Los Angeles, 213/550-1000

THE TEXAS CHAINSAW MASSACRE   Bryanston, 1974, w/Tobe Hooper
THE UNSEEN   World Northal, 1981, Story w/Peter Foleg, Michael L. Grace & Nancy Rifkin
LAST NIGHT AT THE ALAMO   Cinecom, 1983

HILARY HENKIN*
Agent: CAA - Beverly Hills, 213/288-4545

HEADIN' FOR BROADWAY   20th Century-Fox, 1980, w/Joseph Brooks & Larry Gross
FATAL BEAUTY   MGM/UA, 1987, w/Dean Reisner
ROAD HOUSE   MGM/UA, 1989, w/David Lee Henry

Screenplays:
EXECUTIONER
STOLEN FLOWER
ROMEO IS BLEEDING
ANNA & JAKE
FOREIGN BODIES
DIVINE COMEDY

BETH HENLEY*
Agent: William Morris Agency - Beverly Hills, 213/274-7451

THE WAKE OF JAMIE FOSTER (P)
THE DEBUTANTE BALL (P)
THE LUCKY SPOT (P)
ABUNDANCE (P)
TRUE STORIES   Warner Bros., 1986, w/David Byrne & Stephen Tobolowsky
CRIMES OF THE HEART ★   DEG, 1986, from her play
NOBODY'S FOOL   Island Pictures, 1986
MISS FIRECRACKER   Corsair, 1989, from her play "The Miss Firecracker Contest"

Screenplays:
STRAWBERRY
LONG & HAPPY LIFE

PAUL W. HENNING*
Contact: Norman Tyre - Los Angeles, 213/463-4863

LOVER COME BACK ★   Universal International, 1961, w/Stanley Shapiro
BEDTIME STORY   Universal International, 1964, w/Stanley Shapiro
DIRTY ROTTEN SCOUNDRELS   Orion, 1989, w/Stanley Shapiro & Dale Launer

BUCK HENRY*
Agent: William Morris Agency - Beverly Hills, 213/274-7451

THE TROUBLEMAKER   Janus, 1964
THE GRADUATE ★   Avco Embassy, 1967, w/Calder Willingham
CANDY   Selmor, 1968
CATCH-22   Paramount, 1970
THE OWL AND THE PUSSYCAT   Columbia, 1970
WHAT'S UP DOC?   Warner Bros., 1972, w/Robert Benton & David Newman
THE DAY OF THE DOLPHIN   Avco Embassy, 1973
FIRST FAMILY   Warner Bros., 1980, directed
PROTOCOL   Warner Bros., 1984

Screenplays:
GUSHER
BABE WEST
AMERICAN ROULETTE
APE
COMRADES

DAVID LEE HENRY
(See R. Lance Hill)

LENNY HENRY
LENNY LIVE AND UNLEASHED   Miramax, 1989, w/Kim Fuller

PAUL G. HENSLER*
Agent: Lake & Douroux - Beverly Hills, 213/557-0700

DON'T CRY, IT'S ONLY THUNDER   Sanrio, 1982
GOTCHA!   Universal, 1985, Story w/Dan Gordon

J. MIYOKO HENSLEY*
Agent: Preferred Artists - Encino, 818/990-0305

Screenplays:
THE DANCING BANDIT   w/Steven Hensley
NEON DREAMS   w/Steven Hensley

STEVEN HENSLEY*
Agent: Preferred Artists - Encino, 818/990-0305

Screenplays:
THE DANCING BANDIT   w/J. Miyoko Hensley
NEON DREAMS   w/J. Miyoko Hensley

PAUL HENUGGE
THE ROSE GARDEN   Cannon, 1989

BOBBY HERBECK*
Agent: APA - Los Angeles, 213/273-0744

TEENAGE MUTANT NINJA TURTLES   New Line Cinema, 1990, w/Todd W. Langen

BOB HERBERT
REBEL   Vestron, 1986, w/Michael Jenkins, from his play "No Names...No Pack Drill"

STEPHEN HEREK
Agent: United Talent Agency - Beverly Hills, 213/273-6700

CRITTERS   New Line Cinema, 1985, w/Domonic Muir, directed

MAXINE HERMAN*
Agent: APA - Los Angeles, 213/273-0744

Screenplays:
BLUE HEAVEN

PEE-WEE HERMAN
(See Paul Reubens)

LEONARD HERMES
STRYKER   New World, 1983, Story

JAIME HUMBERTO HERMOSILLO
Agent: Rene Fuentes-Chao, Cinevista, Inc., 353 West 39th St., New York, NY 10018, 212/947-4373

MATINEE   Azteca Films, 1978, directed
DONA HERLINDA AND HER TWO SONS   Cinevista, 1985, directed

MICHAEL HERR
FULL METAL JACKET ★   Warner Bros., 1987, w/Gustav Hasford & Stanley Kubrick

ROWDY HERRINGTON*
Agent: Triad Artists, Inc. - Los Angeles, 213/556-2727

JACK'S BACK   Cinema Group, 1988, directed

Screenplays:
THREE RIVERS   (directing)
OCEAN BOULEVARD   w/Greg Taylor

MARSHALL HERSKOVITZ*
Agent: CAA - Beverly Hills, 213/288-4545

Screenplays:
BABY GENIUS   w/Ed Zwick
DRAWING FIRE
SECRET SEVENTEEN (CTF)

JIM HERZFELD*
Agent: InterTalent - Los Angeles, 213/858-6200

TAPEHEADS   Avenue Pictures, 1988, Story w/Bill Fishman, Peter McCarthy & Ryan Rowe

JOHN M. HERZFELD*
Agent: William Morris Agency - Beverly Hills, 213/274-7451

VOICES   MGM/UA, 1979
HARD FEELINGS   Astral Bellevue, 1981
TWO OF A KIND   20th Century Fox, 1983, directed
THE LAST WINTER   Tri-Star, 1984
HANG TOUGH   Moviestore Entertainment, 1990, w/W.D. Richter, filmed in 1980

He
FILM WRITERS GUIDE

Screenplays:
THE MIDNIGHT CLUB
SECOND CHANCE
TAILS, I DIE
ON EASY STREET
RESCUE
SEASIDE HEIGHTS
JAMAICA

WERNER HERZOG
Contact: German Film & TV Academy, Pommernallee 1, 1 Berlin 19, West Germany, 0311/302-6096

SIGNS OF LIFE   Werner Herzog Filmproduction, 1968, directed
AGUIRRE THE WRATH OF GOD   New Yorker, 1973, directed
HEART OF GLASS   New Yorker, 1976, directed
NOSFERATU THE VAMPYRE   20th Century-Fox, 1979, directed
FITZCARRALDO   New World, 1982, directed
WHERE THE GREEN ANTS DREAM   Orion Classics, 1984, directed

KIT HESKETH-HARVEY
MAURICE   Cinecom, 1987, w/James Ivory

GORDON HESSLER
Agent: Triad Artists, Inc. - Los Angeles, 213/556-2727

THE GIRL IN A SWING   Millimeter Films, 1989, directed

CHARLTON HESTON
Agent: ICM - Los Angeles, 213/550-4000

ANTONY AND CLEOPATRA   Rank, 1973, directed

FRASER CLARKE HESTON*
Agent: Sanford, Skouras, Gross & Associates - Los Angeles, 213/208-2100
Business: Agamemnon Films, Inc., 2730 La Cuesta Drive, Los Angeles, CA 90046, 213/851-0211

THE MOUNTAIN MEN   Columbia, 1980
MOTHER LODE   Agamemnon Films, 1982, w/Peter Snell
TREASURE ISLAND (CTF)   Agamemnon Films/ British Lion, 1990, directed

Screenplays:
THE STRANDING
SEE YOU LATER, ALLIGATOR

CAROL HEYER
THUNDER RUN   Cannon, 1986, w/Charles Davis

DOUGLAS HEYES*
Business Manager: Clarke Lilly Associates, 333 Apolena Ave., Balboa Island, CA 92662, 714/833-3347

DRUMS OF TAHITI   Columbia, 1953, w/Robert E. Kent
THE BATTLE OF ROGUE RIVER   Columbia, 1954
THE IRON GLOVE   Columbia, 1954, w/Jesse L. Lasky Jr. & De Vallon Scott
KITTEN WITH A WHIP   Universal, 1964, directed
BEAU GESTE   Universal, 1966, directed
ICE STATION ZEBRA   MGM, 1968, w/Harry Julian Fink

LOUIS M. HEYWARD*
Contact: WGA - Los Angeles, 213/550-1000

SERGEANT DEADHEAD   American International, 1965
CITY UNDER THE SEA   WAR GODS OF THE DEEP   American International, 1965, w/Charles Bennett
DR. GOLDFOOT AND THE GIRL BOMBS   American International, 1966, w/Robert Kaufman
THE GHOST IN THE INVISIBLE BIKINI   American International, 1966, w/Elwood Ellman
THE GLASS SPHINX   American International, 1968, w/Adriano Bolsoni

BRUCE HICKEY
NECROPOLIS   Empire Pictures, 1987, directed

MICHAEL HICKEY
SILENT NIGHT, DEADLY NIGHT   Tri-Star, 1984

PAMELA HICKEY*
Agent: H. N. Swanson, Inc. - Los Angeles, 213/652-5385

Screenplays:
ACE OF THE NEWSREELS   w/Dennys McCoy
HARRY THE LION   w/Dennys McCoy
FULL RECOVERY   w/Dennys McCoy

GAIL MORGAN HICKMAN*
Contact: WGA - Los Angeles, 213/550-1000

THE BIG SCORE   Almi Pictures, 1983
THE ENFORCER   1986
MURPHY'S LAW   Cannon, 1987
NUMBER ONE WITH A BULLET   Cannon, 1987, w/Andrew Kurtzman, James Belushi & Rob Riley
DEATHWISH 4: THE CRACKDOWN   Cannon, 1987

ANTHONY HICKOX
Business: Hickox Films - Los Angeles, 213/876-8423

WAXWORK   Vestron, 1988, directed
SUNDOWN: THE VAMPIRE IN RETREAT   Vestron, 1989, w/John Burgess, directed
WAXWORK II: LOST IN TIME   Electric Pictures, 1991, directed

JAMES HICKS
(See James Cresson)

NEILL D. HICKS*
Contact: WGA - Los Angeles, 213/550-1000

ESCAPE 2000   New World, 1983, w/Jon George
THE FINAL TERROR   Comworld, 1983, w/Jon George & Ronald Shusett
DEAD RECKONING (CTF)   MCA Entertainment, 1990, w/Andie McCuaig

JULIE HICKSON*
Agent: United Talent Agency - Beverly Hills, 213/273-6700

Screenplays:
TRUE LOVE
TUNNELS OF LOVE
MEMOIRS OF A MIDGET
CLEO FROM NINE TO FIVE
CONFESSIONS OF AN EX-SECRET SERVICE AGENT

LARRY HILBRAND
THE IRON TRIANGLE   Scotti Bros., 1989, w/John
   Bushelman & Eric Weston

DEBRA HILL*
Agent: The Gersh Agency - Beverly Hills, 213/274-6611
Business: Debra Hill Productions, Walt Disney Studios,
   818/560-1951

HALLOWEEN   Compass International, 1978,
   w/John Carpenter
HALLOWEEN II   Universal, 1981, w/John Carpenter
THE FOG   Avco Embassy, 1981, w/John Carpenter

JACKSON HILL*
Contact: WGA - Los Angeles, 213/550-1000

DEATH SHIP   Avco Embassy, 1980, Story
   w/David P. Lewis

JAMES HILL
Agent: London Management - London,
   011/441/493-1610

HIS MAJESTY O'KEEFE   Warner Bros., 1954,
   w/Borden Chase
GIUSEPPINA (Short), 1960, directed
THE BELSTONE FOX   *FREE SPIRIT*   Cine III,
   1973, directed

JOHN HILL*
Agent: Broder-Kurland-Webb-Uffner - Los Angeles,
   213/656-9262

HEARTBEEPS   Universal, 1981
LITTLE NIKITA   Columbia, 1988, w/Bo Goldman
QUIGLEY DOWN UNDER   Warner Bros., 1990

Screenplays:
RICH KID
MRS. MERLIN
GOOD LUCK
THIN ICE
CHOPPER & THE FLASH
FAR AS THE EYE CAN SEE
HIGHWAYMAN OF CONCORD
THOSE OF US WITHOUT KEYS
VICTOR'S BIG SCORE
HARD-BOILED
WORLD'S GREATEST HUMAN FLY

R. LANCE HILL*
(David Lee Henry)
Agent: The Gersh Agency - Beverly Hills,
   213/274-6611

HARRY TRACY   Quartet Films Inc., 1983
THE EVIL THAT MEN DO   Tri-Star, 1984,
   w/John Crowther
8 MILLION WAYS TO DIE   Tri-Star, 1986,
   w/Oliver Stone
ROAD HOUSE   MGM/UA, 1989, w/Hilary Henkin
OUT FOR JUSTICE   Warner Bros., 1991

Screenplays:
BLIND LUCK w/Mark Frost

WALTER HILL*
Agent: ICM - Los Angeles, 213/550-4000

THE GETAWAY   National General, 1972
HICKEY AND BOGGS   United Artists, 1972
THE MACKINTOSH MAN   Warner Bros., 1973
THE THIEF WHO CAME TO DINNER   Warner Bros., 1973
HARD TIMES   Columbia, 1975, w/Bryan Gindorff & Bruce
   Henstell, directed
THE DROWNING POOL   Warner Bros., 1975, w/Lorenzo
   Semple & Tracy Keenan Wynn
THE DRIVER   20th Century-Fox, 1978, directed
THE WARRIORS   Paramount, 1979, w/David
   Shaber, directed
SOUTHERN COMFORT   20th Century-Fox, 1981, w/David
   Giler & Michael Kane, directed
48 HRS.   Paramount, 1982, w/Steven De Souza, Larry
   Gross & Roger Spottiswoode, directed
STREETS OF FIRE   Universal, 1984, w/Larry
   Gross, directed
BLUE CITY   Paramount, 1986, w/Lukas Heller
ALIENS   20th Century Fox, 1986, Story w/James Cameron
   & David Giler
RED HEAT   Tri-Star, 1988, w/Harry Kleiner & Troy
   Kennedy Martin, directed

Screenplays:
ALIEN III w/David Giler
THE LAST GOOD KISS

ROBERT HILLIARD*
Agent: Sutter-Walls & Associates - Los Angeles,
   213/658-8200

VASECTOMY, A DELICATE MATTER   Seymour Borde &
   Associates, 1986, w/Robert Burge

WILLIAM BYRON HILLMAN*
Agent: The Brustein Company - Los Angeles, 213/286-0990

DOUBLE EXPOSURE   Crown International, 1982, directed
LOVE LINES   Tri-Star, 1984, w/Chip Hand

DAVID J. HIMMELSTEIN*
Agent: CAA - Beverly Hills, 213/288-4545

POWER   20th Century Fox, 1986
TALENT FOR THE GAME   20th Century Fox, 1991,
   w/Tom Donnelly & Larry Ferguson

Screenplays:
VILLAGE OF THE DAMNED
U.S. MARSHALL
SPECIAL ELECTION
SILENT SERVICE

GRANT HINDEN-MILLER
STARLIGHT HOTEL   Republic Pictures, 1987

ALAN HINES
Agent: ICM - Los Angeles, 213/550-4000

SQUARE DANCE   Island Pictures, 1987

BARRY HINES
KES   United Artists, 1969, w/Tony Garnett & Ken Loach
THE GAMEKEEPER   ATV, 1980

Hi

FILM WRITERS GUIDE

DAVID S. HINES*
Agent: Warden & White Associates - Beverly Hills, 213/852-1028

ONCE BITTEN   Samuel Goldwyn Company, 1985, w/Jeff Hause & Jonathan Roberts

Screenplays:
THE RIGHT HAND MEN w/Jeff Hause
NUCLEAR REACTIONS w/Jeff Hause

S. E. HINTON*
Agent: Curtis Brown, Ltd. - New York, 212/755-4200

RUMBLE FISH   Universal, 1983, w/Francis Coppola

CHARLES S. HIRSCH*
Business Manager: Carol Akiyama, Personal Manager - Sherman Oaks, 818/906-3639

GREETINGS   Sigma III, 1968, w/Brian DePalma
HI, MOM!   Sigma III, 1970, Story w/Brian DePalma

ROGER O. HIRSON
Agent: William Morris Agency - Beverly Hills, 213/274-7451

PIPPIN (P)
DEMON SEED   MGM/UA, 1977, w/Robert J. Jaffe

MICHAEL HIRST
Agent: Linda Siefert & Associates - London, 011/441/229-5163

THE DECEIVERS   Cinecom, 1988
FOOLS OF FORTUNE   New Line Cinema, 1990
THE BALLAD OF THE SAD CAFE   Angelika Films, 1991

Screenplays:
MEETING VENUS w/Istvan Szabo

KEN HIXON*
Agent: United Talent Agency - Beverly Hills, 213/273-6700

GRANDVIEW, U.S.A.   Warner Bros., 1984
MORGAN STEWART'S COMING HOME   New Century/Vista, 1987, w/David Titcher

Screenplays:
SPICE OF LIFE
MY SILENT PARTNER
HARD SELL

WILLIAM HJORTSBERG*
Agent: Phoenix Literary Agency - Livingston, Montana, 406/222-2848

THUNDER AND LIGHTNING   20th Century-Fox, 1977
LEGEND   Universal, 1986

Screenplays:
FALLING ANGEL
SIX WHITE HORSES

FREDERICA HOBIN*
Agent: Monteiro Rose Agency - Encino, 818/501-1177

Screenplays:
BIMBOS
THE BATTLE OF MAPLE GLEN

VICKI HOCHBERG*
(Victoria G. Hochberg)
Agent: ICM - Los Angeles, 213/550-4000

CRUMBS (Short), directed
'57 CAD (Short), directed

Screenplays:
FRIES w/Danny Opatoshu
SAM AND YETTA

ADRIAN HODGES
THE BRIDGE   British Screen/Film Four International, 1991

MIKE HODGES
Agent: Hatton & Baker - London, 011/441/439-2971

GET CARTER   MGM, 1971, directed
PULP   United Artists, 1972, directed
THE TERMINAL MAN   Warner Bros., 1974, directed
DAMIEN - OMEN II   20th Century-Fox, 1978, w/Stanley Mann
BLACK RAINBOW   Goldcrest Film & Television, 1990, directed

HELEN HODGMAN
THE RIGHT HAND MAN   FilmDallas, 1987

JENO HODI
DEADLY OBSESSION   Distant Horizon, 1989, w/Brian Cox & Paul Wolansky, directed

ALICE S. HOFFMAN
Agent: The Gersh Agency - Beverly Hills, 213/274-6611

INDEPENDENCE DAY   Warner Bros., 1983

MICHAEL HOFFMAN*
Agent: ICM - Los Angeles, 213/550-4000

PRIVILEGED   New Yorker, 1982, w/Rupert Walters & David Woolcambe, directed
RESTLESS NATIVES   Orion Classics, 1985, directed
PROMISED LAND   Vestron, 1987, directed

JASON HOFFS
RED SURF   Arrowhead Entertainment, 1990, Story w/Brian Gamble & Vincent Roberts

TAMAR SIMON HOFFS*
Agent: The Gersh Agency - Beverly Hills, 213/274-6611

LEPKE   Warner Bros., 1974, w/Wesley Lau
STONEY ISLAND   World Northal, 1980, w/Andrew Davis
THE ALLNIGHTER   Universal, 1987, w/Margot L. Kessler, directed

BRETT HOGAN
"CROCODILE" DUNDEE II   Paramount, 1988, w/Paul Hogan

PAUL HOGAN
Agent: CAA - Beverly Hills, 213/288-4545
Business: Paramount Pictures, 5555 Melrose Ave., Hollywood, CA 90067, 213/468-5796

"CROCODILE" DUNDEE ★   Paramount, 1986, w/John Cornell & Ken Shadie

"CROCODILE" DUNDEE II   Paramount, 1988,
  w/Brett Hogan
ALMOST AN ANGEL   Paramount, 1990

LAWRENCE R. HOLBEN*
Agent: Solomon Weingarten & Associates - Los Angeles,
  213/474-8703

THE HIDING PLACE   World Wide, 1974
NO LONGER ALONE   World Wide, 1978

BRIAN HOHLFELD*
Agent: Sanford, Skouras, Gross & Associates -
  Los Angeles, 213/208-2100

HE SAID SHE SAID   Paramount, 1991

Screenplays:
CLONE

AGNIESZKA HOLLAND
Agent: Triad Artists, Inc. - Los Angeles,
  213/556-2727

ROUGH TREATMENT   Film Polski, 1980,
  w/Andrzej Wajda
A WOMAN ALONE   WOMAN ON HER OWN   1981,
  w/Maciej Karpinsk, directed
DANTON   Triumph/Columbia, 1983
A LOVE IN GERMANY   Triumph/Columbia, 1983,
  w/Boleslaw Michalek & Andrzej Wajda
ANGRY HARVEST   European Classics, 1986, w/Paul
  Hengge, directed
ANNA   Vestron, 1987
TO KILL A PRIEST   Columbia, 1990, w/Jean-Yves
  Pitoun, directed
KORCZAK   New Yorker Films, 1991
EUROPA, EUROPA   Orion Classics, 1991, directed

GERRY HOLLAND
JAWS OF SATAN   United Artists, 1984

SAVAGE STEVE HOLLAND*
Agent: CAA - Beverly Hills, 213/288-4545

BETTER OFF DEAD   Warner Bros., 1985, directed
ONE CRAZY SUMMER   Warner Bros.,
  1986, directed

TOM HOLLAND*
Agent: United Talent Agency - Beverly Hills,
  213/273-6700

THE BEAST WITHIN   MGM/United Artists, 1982
PSYCHO II   Universal, 1983
CLASS OF '84   United Film Distribution, 1984, w/Mark
  Lester & John Saxton
CLOAK AND DAGGER   Universal, 1984
SCREAM FOR HELP   Lorimar, 1984
FRIGHT NIGHT   Columbia, 1985, directed
CHILD'S PLAY   MGM/UA, 1988, w/Don Mancini &
  John Lafia, directed

Screenplays:
EVERYBODY CHARLESTON

ALLEN HOLLEB*
Agent: William Morris Agency - Beverly Hills, 213/274-7451

CANDY STRIPE NURSES   New World, 1974, directed

Screenplays:
CITY HALL
FOOLS PARADISE
DEADWOOD
THE STRETCH
FREESTYLE

MERRIN HOLT*
Agent: Camden-ITG - Los Angeles, 213/289-2700

BUY AND CELL   Empire Pictures, 1988, w/Ken Kraus

ROGER S. HOLZBERG*
Agent: APA - Los Angeles, 213/273-0744

MIDNIGHT CROSSING   Vestron, 1988, w/Doug
  Weiser, directed

Screenplays:
WHALESONG

ELLIOTT HONG
THEY CALL ME BRUCE?   A FISTFUL OF CHOPSTICKS
  Artists Releasing Corporation/Film Ventures
  International, 1982, w/Tim Clawson, David
  Randolf & Johnny Yune, directed

HARRY HOOK
Agent: CAA - Beverly Hills, 213/288-4545

THE KITCHEN TOTO   Cannon, 1987, directed

TOBE HOOPER
Agent: Triad Artists, Inc. - Los Angeles, 213/556-2727

THE TEXAS CHAINSAW MASSACRE   Bryanston, 1974,
  w/Kim Henkel, directed
SPONTANEOUS COMBUSTION   Taurus Entertainment,
  1990, w/Howard Goldberg, directed

ARTHUR HOPCRAFT
AGATHA   Warner Bros., 1979, w/Kathleen Tynan

JOHN HOPKINS*
Agent: William Morris Agency - New York, 212/586-5100

TWO LEFT FEET   British Lion, 1963, w/Roy Baker
THUNDERBALL   United Artists, 1964, w/Richard Maibaum
VIRGIN SOLDIERS   Columbia, 1969
THE OFFENCE   United Artists, 1973, from his play "This
  Story of Yours:
MURDER BY DECREE   Avco Embassy, 1979
THE POWER   Artists Releasing Corporation/Film Ventures
  International, 1984, Story w/Stephen Carpenter, Jeffrey
  Obrow & John Penny
THE HOLCROFT COVENANT   Universal, 1985,
  w/Edward Anhalt & Richard Maibaum
TORMENT   New World, 1986, w/Samson
  Aslanian, directed

Screenplays:
JOURNEY TO OHM
ALLARD LOWENSTEIN STORY (CTF)
A VIEW FROM THE SQUARE

KAREN LEIGH HOPKINS*
Agent: InterTalent - Los Angeles, 213/858-6200

WELCOME HOME, ROXY CARMICHAEL
   Paramount, 1990

Screenplays:
SEPARATE CHECKS w/Donald Wrye

DENNIS HOPPER
Agent: CAA - Beverly Hills, 213/288-4545

EASY RIDER ★ Columbia, 1969, w/Peter Fonda &
   Terry Southern, directed
THE AMERICAN DREAMER (FD) EYR, 1971,
   w/L.M. Kit Carson & Laurence Schiller
THE LAST MOVIE Universal, 1971, Story w/Stewart
   Stern, directed

ROY HORAN
NO RETREAT, NO SURRENDER II Shapiro
   Glickenhaus, 1989, w/Maria Elen Cellino &
   Keith W. Strandberg

LANNY HORN
FAST FOOD Fries Entertainment, 1989,
   w/Clark Brandon

ISRAEL HOROVITZ*
Agent: William Morris Agency - Beverly Hills,
   213/274-7451

THE INDIAN WANTS THE BRONX (P)
LINE (P)
IT'S CALLED THE SUGAR PLUM (P)
MORNING (P)
DR. HERO (P)
THE PRIMARY ENGLISH CLASS (P)
SHOOTING GALLERY RATS (P)
THE REASON WE EAT (P)
MACKEREL (P)
THE WIDOW'S BLIND DATE (P)
SUNDAY RUNNERS IN THE RAIN (P)
SCROOGE & MARLEY (P)
RATS (P)
THE WAKEFIELD TRILOGY (P)
THE STRAWBERRY STATEMENT MGM, 1970
BELIEVE IN ME MGM, 1971
AUTHOR! AUTHOR! 20th Century-Fox, 1982
A MAN IN LOVE Cinecom, 1987, w/Diane Kurys

Screenplays:
ASTOR HAIR
LETTERS TO IRIS
FELL
HOW TO GET MARRIED
DADDY'S BOY
THE BOOTH
PAYOFSKY'S DISCOVERY
THE BIG QUESTION

ANTHONY HOROWITZ
DIAMOND'S EDGE Castle Hill Productions, 1990

MARK HOROWITZ*
Agent: Robinson, Weintraub, Gross & Associates -
   Los Angeles, 213/653-5802

ALMOST YOU 20th Century-Fox, 1984

Screenplays:
DARK WIND
GALATEA
AMERICAN SPIRIT

CRAIG HORRALL
SEX APPEAL Platinum Pictures, 1986, w/Chuck Vincent
BAD BLOOD Platinum Pictures, 1989
WILDEST DREAMS Platinum Pictures, 1990

ALEX HORVAT*
Agent: ICM - Los Angeles, 213/550-4000
Business: Sulaco Bay Films - Los Angeles, 213/208-2515

CAMPUS MAN Paramount, 1987, w/Geoffrey Baere &
   Matt Dorff

DAVID HOSELTON*
Agent: Shorr, Stille & Associates - Los Angeles,
   213/659-6160

CLARENCE (CTF) Atlantis Films/Northstar Entertainment/
   South Pacific Pictures, 1990, w/Lorne Cameron

BOB HOSKINS
Agent: CAA - Beverly Hills, 213/288-4545

THE RAGGEDY RAWNEY Four Seasons Entertainment,
   1990, w/Nicole De Wilde, directed

DAN HOSKINS
PRETTY SMART New World, 1987
CHROME HEARTS Image Organization, 1990
CHOPPER CHICKS IN ZOMBIE TOWN Troma,
   1991, directed

A.E. HOTCHNER
Business: Newman's Own, Westport, CT

HEMINGWAY'S ADVENTURES OF A YOUNG MAN
   20th Century-Fox, 1962

TRACY HOTCHNER*
Contact: WGA - Los Angeles, 213/550-1000

MOMMIE DEAREST Paramount, 1981, w/Frank Perry,
   Frank Yablans & Robert Getchell

RON HOUSE*
Contact: WGA - Los Angeles, 213/550-1000

BULLSHOT! Island Alive, 1983, w/Alan Shearman &
   Diz White
THE SHRIMP ON THE BARBIE Unity Pictures Corp.,
   1990, w/Alan Shearman & Grant Morris

DIANNE HOUSTON*
Agent: CAA - Beverly Hills, 213/288-4545

Screenplays:
EM
THE FISHERMAN

ROBERT (BOBBY) HOUSTON*
Agent: Harris & Goldberg - Los Angeles, 213/553-5200

BAD MANNERS *GROWING PAINS* New World, 1984,
   w/Joseph Kwong, directed

TRUST ME   Cinecom, 1989, w/Gary Rigdon, directed
HOTEL OKLAHOMA   European American Entertainment, 1991, w/Lisa Sutton, directed

CY HOWARD
EVERY LITTLE CROOK AND NANNY   MGM, 1972, w/Jon Axelrod & Robert Klane, directed

ELIZABETH JANE HOWARD
GETTING IT RIGHT   MCEG, 1989

KARIN HOWARD
Agent: Ken Sherman & Associates - Beverly Hills, 213/273-8840
Business: Distant Diesel Productions, Inc., 3541 Landa Street, Los Angeles, CA 90039, 213/662-1409 & 213/662-9411

THE NEVERENDING STORY II: THE NEXT CHAPTER   Warner Bros., 1990

Screenplays:
THE NEVERENDING STORY III
THE TIGRESS
WOMAN IN THE DARK

KEN HOWARD
CHALLENGE THE WIND   Sell Entertainment, 1990, w/William Blackburn & Marla Young

RALPH HOWARD
Agent: William Morris Agency - Beverly Hills, 213/274-7451

Screenplays:
RADIO ZERO

RANCE HOWARD*
Business: Major H Studios, 213/468-5000

GRAND THEFT AUTO   New World, 1978, w/Ron Howard

Screenplays:
WOMAN WARRIOR (CTF)

RON HOWARD*
Agent: CAA - Beverly Hills, 213/288-4545
Business: Imagine Films Entertainment, Inc., 1925 Century Park East, Los Angeles, CA 90067, 213/277-1665

GRAND THEFT AUTO   New World, 1978, w/Rance Howard, directed
LEO AND LOREE   United Artists, 1980, Story w/James Ritz
PARENTHOOD   Universal, 1989, Story w/Lowell Ganz & Babaloo Mandel, directed

SANDY HOWARD*
Business: World Entertainment & Business Network, Inc., 7060 Hollywood Blvd. - Suite 1024, Los Angeles, CA 90028, 213/467-4151

JACK OF DIAMONDS   MGM, 1967, w/Jack DeWitt
VICE SQUAD   Avco Embassy, 1982, w/Kenneth Peters & Robert Vincent O'Neill

HOKE HOWELL
CLICK: THE CALENDAR GIRL KILLER   Crown International, 1991, w/Ross Hagen, David Chute & David Reskin

FRANK HOWSON
HEAVEN TONIGHT   Boulevard Films, 1990, w/Alister Webb

PERRY HOWZE*
Contact: WGA - Los Angeles, 213/550-1000

MAID TO ORDER   New Century/Vista, 1987, w/Randy Howze & Amy Jones
MYSTIC PIZZA   Samuel Goldwyn Company, 1988, w/Randy Howze, Amy Jones & Alfred Uhry
CHANCES ARE   Tri-Star, 1988, w/Randy Howze

Screenplays:
POTTER TAKES FLIGHT w/Randy Howze & Philip Dunne
QUEEN OF N.Y. w/Randy Howze

RANDY HOWZE*
Contact: WGA - Los Angeles, 213/550-1000

MAID TO ORDER   New Century/Vista, 1987, w/Perry Howze & Amy Jones
MYSTIC PIZZA   Samuel Goldwyn Company, 1988, w/Perry Howze, Amy Jones & Alfred Uhry
CHANCES ARE   Tri-Star, 1988, w/Perry Howze

Screenplays:
POTTER TAKES FLIGHT w/Perry Howze & Philip Dunne
QUEEN OF N.Y. w/Perry Howze

NORMAN HUDIS*
Agent: Triad Artists, Inc. - Los Angeles, 213/556-2727

THE HIGH TERRACE   CIPA, 1956, w/Alfred Shaughnessy
PASSPORT TO TREASON   Eros, 1956, w/Kenneth Hales
THE HOUR OF DECISION   Eros, 1957
CARRY ON SERGEANT   Anglo Amalgamated, 1958
THE DUKE WORE JEANS   Insignia, 1958
PLEASE TURN OVER   Anglo Amalgamated, 1959
BEWARE OF THE CHILDREN   NO KIDDING   American International, 1960, w/Robin Estridge
TWICE AROUND THE DAFFODILS   Anglo-Amalgamated, 1962
CARRY ON CRUISING   Governor, 1962
NURSE OF WHEELS   Anglo Amalgamated, 1963
HOT RESORT   Cannon, 1985, w/Boaz Davidson & John Robins

REGINALD HUDLIN
Agent: Triad Artists, Inc. - Los Angeles, 213/556-2727

THE KOLD WAVES (Short), directed
REGGIE'S WORLD OF SOUL (Short), directed
HOUSE PARTY   New Line Cinema, 1990, directed

ROY HUGGINS*
Agent: Triad Artists, Inc. - Los Angeles, 213/556-2727

TOO LATE FOR TEARS   United Artists, 1949
HANGMAN'S KNOT   Columbia, 1952, directed
GUN FURY   Columbia, 1953, w/Irving Wallace
PUSHOVER   Columbia, 1954
A FEVER IN THE BLOOD   Warner Bros., 1960, w/Harry Kleiner

Hu

CAROL HUGHES*
Contact: WGA - Los Angeles, 213/550-1000

MISSING LINK   Universal, 1989, w/David Hughes, co-directed

DAVID HUGHES*
Contact: WGA - Los Angeles, 213/550-1000

MISSING LINK   Universal, 1989, w/Carol Hughes, co-directed

ERIC HUGHES*
Contact: 213/652-0222

RAISE THE TITANIC   AFD, 1980, w/Adam Kennedy
AGAINST ALL ODDS   Columbia, 1984
WHITE NIGHTS   Columbia, 1985, w/James Goldman

Screenplays:
NOCTURNE
WAR DANCE
A LOUSY KILLING

GERALD VAUGHN HUGHES
Agent: ICM - Los Angeles, 213/550-4000

SEBASTIAN   Paramount, 1968
THE DUELLISTS   Paramount, 1978

JOHN HUGHES*
Agent: CAA - Beverly Hills, 213/288-4545
Business: Hughes Entertainment, 254 Market Street, Lake Forest, IL 60045, 708/615-0030

NATIONAL LAMPOON'S CLASS REUNION   20th Century-Fox, 1982
NATIONAL LAMPOON'S VACATION   Warner Bros., 1983
MR. MOM   20th Century-Fox, 1983
NATE AND HAYES   Paramount, 1983, w/David Odell
SIXTEEN CANDLES   Universal, 1984, directed
THE BREAKFAST CLUB   Universal, 1985, directed
WEIRD SCIENCE   Universal, 1985, directed
NATIONAL LAMPOON'S EUROPEAN VACATION   Warner Bros., 1985, w/Robert Klane
PRETTY IN PINK   Paramount, 1986
FERRIS BUELLER'S DAY OFF   Paramount, 1986, directed
SOME KIND OF WONDERFUL   Paramount, 1987
PLANES, TRAINS AND AUTOMOBILES   Paramount, 1987, directed
SHE'S HAVING A BABY   Paramount, 1988, directed
THE GREAT OUTDOORS   Universal, 1988
UNCLE BUCK   Universal, 1989, directed
NATIONAL LAMPOON'S CHRISTMAS VACATION   Warner Bros., 1989
HOME ALONE   20th Century Fox, 1990
CAREER OPPORTUNITIES   Universal, 1990
DUTCH   20th Century Fox, 1991
CURLY SUE   Warner Bros., 1991

Screenplays:
HOME ALONE, AGAIN
OIL & VINEGAR
MOTORHEADS VS. SPORTOS
PRISON PLANET   KHAN
SPY VS. SPY
MUSCLE CARS
DALLAS DEBUTANTE
SCHOOL SPIRIT
THREE SECRETARIES
THE DANCE
THE NANNY
BALL AND CHAIN
THE BUGSTER
LARRY'S LATE FOR LIFE

KEN HUGHES
Agent: Robert Eisenbach Agency - Los Angeles, 213/962-5809
Contact: 213/851-6323

THE BRAIN MACHINE   RKO Radio, 1955, directed
THE DEADLIEST SIN   CONFESSION   Allied Artists, 1955, directed
PORTRAIT IN SMOKE   WICKED AS THEY COME   Columbia, 1956, directed
TOWN ON TRIAL   Columbia, 1956, w/Robert Westerby
HIGH FLIGHT   Columbia, 1957, w/Joseph Landon
JAZZBOAT   Columbia, 1959, w/John Antrobus, directed
THE MAN WITH THE GREEN CARNATION   POSTMARK FOR DANGER   Anglo-Amalgamated, 1955, w/Guy Green
THE SMALL WORLD OF SAMMY LEE   Bryanston, 1962, diected
ARRIVEDERCI, BABY!   DROP DEAD, DARLING   Paramount, 1966, directed
CHITTY CHITTY BANG BANG   United Artists, 1968, w/Roald Dahl, directed
CROMWELL   Columbia, 1970, directed
ALFIE DARLING   OH! ALFIE   EMI, 1975, directed

RON HUGO
Agent: William Morris Agency - Beverly Hills, 213/274-7451

Screenplays:
THIN WALLS
THE ADVERTISER
REVENGE OF THE POTATO
DREAMLAND
TINGLER

EDWARD C. HUME*
Agent: Triad Artists, Inc. - Los Angeles, 213/556-2727

SUMMERTREE   Columbia, 1971, w/Stephen Yafa
A REFLECTION OF FEAR   Columbia, 1973, w/Lewis John Carlino
TWO-MINUTE WARNING   Universal, 1976
THE TERRY FOX STORY (CTF)   HBO Premiere Films/Robert Cooper Films II, 1983

Screenplays:
DEPARTMENT STORE
POWER OF THE DOG
THE EAGLE AND THE IRON CROSS

JOEL DON HUMPHREYS*
Agent: The Gersh Agency - Beverly Hills, 213/274-6611

MY HEROES HAVE ALWAYS BEEN COWBOYS   Samuel Goldwyn Company, 1991

DAVID HUMPHRIES
QUADROPHENIA   World Northal, 1979, w/Franc Roddam & Martin Stellman
THE HAUNTING OF JULIA   Discovery, 1981

PETER HUNE
Agent: Camden-ITG - Los Angeles, 213/289-2700

Screenplays:
STEPMOTHER

JACKSON HUNSIKER
TEN LITTLE INDIANS   Cannon, 1989, w/Gerry O'Hara

BOB HUNT
Agent: ICM - Los Angeles, 213/550-4000

THE BOOGENS   Jensen Farley Pictures, 1982,
  w/David O'Malley
THE HIDDEN   New Line Cinema, 1987

ED HUNT
STARSHIP INVASIONS   Warner Bros., 1977, directed
KING OF THE STREETS   Shapiro Entertainment,
  1986, w/Ruben Gordon, Barry Pearson &
  Steven Shoenberg
BLOODY BIRTHDAY   Judica Productions, 1986,
  w/Barry Pearson, directed

EVAN HUNTER*
(Ed McBain)
Agent: Paul Kohner, Inc. - Los Angeles, 213/555-1060

STRANGERS WHEN WE MEET   Columbia, 1960
THE BIRDS   Universal, 1963
FUZZ   United Artists, 1972
WALK PROUD   Universal, 1979

FREDERIC HUNTER*
Agent: Warden & White Associates - Beverly Hills,
  213/852-1028

Screenplays:
SOMEONE SPECIAL
ACCOMPLICE
FOREVER

JAMES GRANBY HUNTER
CABO BLANCO   Avco Embassy, 1981, Story
  w/Milton Gelman

JOHN HUNTER*
Agent: ICM - Los Angeles, 213/550-4000

THE GREY FOX   United Artists Classics, 1983

RUSSELL HUNTER
THE CHANGELING   AFD, 1980, Story

THOMAS HUNTER
Agent: The Strick Agency - Los Angeles, 213/273-0919

THE FINAL COUNTDOWN   United Artists, 1980,
  w/David Ambrose, Gerry Davis & Peter Powell

TIM HUNTER*
Agent: United Talent Agency - Beverly Hills, 213/273-6700

OVER THE EDGE   Orion/Warner Bros., 1979,
  w/Charlie Haas
TEX   Buena Vista, 1982, w/Charlie Haas, directed

Screenplays:
LIVES OF THE TWINS   (directing)
TRAP DOOR   w/Charlie Haas
THE DANCING BEAR   w/James Crumely
JUDGE DREDD

CAROLINE HUPPERT
Contact: French Film Office, 745 Fifth Avenue, New York,
  NY 10151, 212/832-8860

SINCERELY CHARLOTTE   New Line Cinema, 1986,
  w/Luc Beraud & Joelle Gordon, directed

GALE ANNE HURD
Business: Pacific Western Productions, 270 N. Canon
  Drive - Suite 1195, Beverly Hills, CA 90210

THE TERMINATOR   Orion, 1984, w/James Cameron

MAURICE E. HURLEY*
Agent: Shapiro/Lichtman - Los Angeles, 213/859-8877

Screenplays:
THE PATRIOT'S GAME
THE WAY OUT
THE MOE BURG STORY

DAVID M. HURWITZ*
Agent: United Talent Agency - Beverly Hills, 213/273-6700

Screenplays:
MULTIPLE CHOICES   w/Larry Arnstein

HARRY HURWITZ*
Business: RSM Productions, Inc., 42 West End Avenue,
  New York, NY 10024, 212/496-1357

THE PROJECTIONIST   Maron Films Ltd., 1971, directed
THE COMEBACK TRAIL   Dynamite Entertainment/
  Rearguard Productions, 1971, directed
RICHARD   Billings, 1972, w/Lovees Yerby, directed
UNDER THE RAINBOW   Orion/Warner Bros., 1981, w/Pat
  McCormick, Martin Smith, Pat Bradley & Fred Bauer
THAT'S ADEQUATE   South Gate Entertainment,
  1989, directed

JIMMY HUSTON*
Agent: Triad Artists, Inc. - Los Angeles, 213/556-2727

FINAL EXAM   MPM, 1981, directed
RUNNING SCARED   MGM/UA, 1986, w/Gary DeVore

Screenplays:
MOT
THE BIG PLAYER
BAD BLOOD

TONY HUSTON
Agent: Paul Kohner, Inc. - Los Angeles, 213/550-1060

THE DEAD ★   Vestron, 1987

RON HUTCHINSON*
Agent: The Artists Agency - Los Angeles, 213/277-7779

RAT IN THE SKULL (P)
THE PERFECT WITNESS (CTF)   HBO Premiere Films,
  1989, w/Terry Curtis Fox

RED KING, WHITE KNIGHT (CTF)   Entertainment
   Productions/Zenith, 1989
THE JOSEPHINE BAKER STORY (CTF)   HBO Pictures/
   RHI Entertainment/Anglia Television Ltd., 1991

Screenplays:
PRISONER OF HONOR (CTF)
THE HOSTAGE
BODIES

WILLARD M. HUYCK*
Agent: CAA - Beverly Hills, 213/288-4545

THE DEVIL'S EIGHT   American International, 1968,
   w/John Milius & James Gordon White
AMERICAN GRAFFITI ★   Universal, 1973, w/Gloria
   Katz & George Lucas
MESSIAH OF EVIL   International Cinefilm, 1975,
   w/Gloria Katz, directed
LUCKY LADY   20th Century-Fox, 1975, w/Gloria Katz
FRENCH POSTCARDS   Paramount, 1979, w/Gloria
   Katz, directed
INDIANA JONES AND THE TEMPLE OF DOOM
   Paramount, 1984, w/Gloria Katz
BEST DEFENSE   Paramount, 1984, w/Gloria
   Katz, directed
HOWARD THE DUCK   Universal, 1986, w/Gloria
   Katz, directed

Screenplays:
NIGHT RIDE DOWN   w/Gloria Katz
THE AIR-CONDITIONED DREAM   w/Gloria Katz
NIAGRA FALLS   w/Gloria Katz
RADIOLAND MURDERS   w/Gloria Katz
A YELLOW RAFT IN BLUE WATER   w/Gloria Katz

DAVID HENRY HWANG*
Agent: CAA - Beverly Hills, 213/288-4545

RICH RELATIONS (P)
FAMILY DEVOTIONS (P)
THE DANCE AND THE RAILROAD (P)
M. BUTTERFLY (P), also screenplay

Screenplays:
THE IDIOT
GOLDEN GATE
SEVEN YEARS IN TIBET
IGO ONO

PETER HYAMS*
Agent: ICM - Los Angeles, 213/550-4000

T.R. BASKIN   Paramount, 1971
BUSTING   United Artists, 1973, directed
TELEFON   MGM/UA, 1977, w/Stirling Silliphant
CAPRICORN ONE   20th Century-Fox, 1978, directed
HANOVER STREET   Columbia, 1979, directed
THE HUNTER   Paramount, 1980, w/Ted Leighton
OUTLAND   The Ladd Company/Warner Bros.,
   1981, directed
THE STAR CHAMBER   20th Century-Fox, 1983,
   w/Roderick Taylor, directed
2010   MGM/UA, 1984, directed
NARROW MARGIN   Tri-Star, 1990, directed

NOEL HYND*
Contact: WGA - New York, 212/245-6180

AGENCY   Jensen Farley Pictures, 1981

I

JEREMY IACONE
Agent: CAA - Beverly Hills, 213/288-4545

Screenplays:
BLOOD IN BLOOD OUT   (Shared)
MAN OF DESTINY
WILLIE THE HAT'S KID
TOMMY SWIFT
PRIMO
DANGEROUS RELATIONS
WINTER CHILDREN
DANCING QUEEN

LEON ICHASO
Agent: CAA - Beverly Hills, 213/288-4545

EL SUPER   Columbia, 1979, w/Manuel Arce, directed
CROSSOVER DREAMS   Miramax, 1985, w/Manuel
   Arce & Ruben Blades, directed

JOE IDE*
Agent: United Talent Agency - Beverly Hills,
   213/273-6700

Screenplays:
WEDLOCK
PAYBACK

ERIC IDLE*
Agent: ICM - Los Angeles, 213/550-4000

AND NOW FOR SOMETHING COMPLETELY
   DIFFERENT Columbia, 1972, w/Graham Chapman,
   John Cleese, Terry Gilliam, Terry Jones &
   Michael Palin
MONTY PYTHON AND THE HOLY GRAIL   Cinema 5,
   1974, w/Graham Chapman, John Cleese, Terry Gilliam,
   Terry Jones & Michael Palin
ALL YOU NEED IS CASH   THE RUTLES   Rutles Corps
   Productions, 1978, co-directed
MONTY PYTHON'S LIFE OF BRIAN   Orion/Warner Bros.,
   1979, w/Graham Chapman, John Cleese,Terry Gilliam,
   Terry Jones & Michael Palin
MONTY PYTHON LIVE AT THE HOLLYWOOD BOWL
   Columbia, 1982, w/Graham Chapman, John Cleese,
   Terry Gilliam, Terry Jones & Michael Palin
MONTY PYTHON'S THE MEANING OF LIFE   Universal,
   1983, w/Graham Chapman, John Cleese, Terry Gilliam,
   Terry Jones & Michael Palin

Screenplays:
HOW I WON THE LOTTERY
ROAD TO MARS
RUTLAND ISLES   THE RUTLAND TRIANGLE

MICHAEL IGNATIEFF
1919 Spectrafilm, 1986, w/Hugh Brody

HASSAN ILDARI
FACE OF THE ENEMY   Tri-Culture Pictures, 1989, Story, directed

Screenplays:
FLOWERMAN

W. PETER ILIFF*
Agent: United Talent Agency - Beverly Hills, 213/273-6700

POINT BREAK   20th Century Fox, 1991
PRAYER OF THE ROLLERBOYS   Castle Hill Productions, 1991

Screenplays:
CAGE
ROCKET'S RED GLARE
HACKSAW

NEIL ILLINGSWORTH
HEART OF THE STAG   New World, 1984

SHOHEI IMAMURA
Contact: Directors Guild of Japan, Tsukada Building, 8-33 Udagawa-cho, Shibuya-ku, Tokyo 150, Japan, 3/461-4411

THE BALLAD OF NARAYAMA   Kino International/Janus, 1983, directed

DON INGALLS*
Agent: Shapiro/Lichtman - Los Angeles, 213/859-8877

Screenplays:
CHRYSANTHEMUM COVENANT

ALBERT INNAURATO*
Agent: William Morris Agency - New York, 212/586-5100

GEMINI (P)
EARTHWORMS (P)
MAGDA AND CALLAS (P)
THE RETURN OF MAGDA DA SILVA (P) also screenplay

MARKUS INNOCENTI
MURDER STORY   Contracts International/Elsevier-Vendex Film, 1989, w/Eddie Arno, co-directed

TINO INSANA*
Contact: WGA - Los Angeles, 213/550-1000

MASTERS OF MENACE   CineTel Films/New Line Cinema, 1990

Screenplays:
HIGH HOPES
THE BIG BANG (CTF)
THE MONARCHS OF MANHATTAN
MOTLEY'S CREW

DAVID IRVING
Agent: Triad Artists, Inc. - Los Angeles, 213/556-2727

RUMPELSTILTSKIN   Cannon, 1987, directed
THE EMPEROR'S NEW CLOTHES   Cannon, 1988, directed

JOHN IRVING
Agent: Sterling Lord Literistic - New York, 212/696-2800

Screenplays:
CIDER HOUSE RULES

PATRICIA IRVING*
Agent: ICM - Los Angeles, 213/550-4000

JUMPIN' JACK FLASH   20th Century Fox, 1986, w/David H. Franzoni, J.W. Melville & Christopher Thompson

DAVID A. ISAACS*
Agent: Broder-Kurland-Webb-Uffner - Los Angeles, 213/656-9262

VOLUNTEERS   Tri-Star, 1985, w/Ken Levine
MANNEQUIN TWO: ON THE MOVE   20th Century Fox, 1991, w/Ken Levine, Betsy Israel & Ed Rugoff

Screenplays:
GETTING AWAY *w/Ken Levine*
HOME FRONT *w/Ken Levine*
STAR SPANGLED ADVENTURE *w/Ken Levine*
THE LIVING LEGEND *w/Ken Levine*

JILL ISAACS
Agent: CAA - Beverly Hills, 213/288-4545

Screenplays:
THE ENTERPRISE
ANGEL'S FLIGHT

STANLEY ISAACS*
Contact: Attorney Keith Fleer, 213/285-6222

GROSS ANATOMY   Buena Vista, 1990, Story w/Alan Jay Glueckman, Howard Rosenman & Mark Spragg

SUSAN ISAACS*
Agent: William Morris Agency - New York, 212/586-5100

COMPROMISING POSITIONS   Paramount, 1985
HELLO AGAIN   Buena Vista, 1987

TARA ISON*
Agent: CAA - Beverly Hills, 213/288-4545

DON'T TELL MOM THE BABYSITTER'S DEAD   Warner Bros., 1991, w/Neil Landau

Screenplays:
TRUE TO LIFE *w/Neil Landau*
BELOVED SON *w/Neil Landau*
INSIDE OUT *w/Neil Landau*
TRANSYLVANIA-PENNSYLVANIA *w/Neil Landau*

BETSY ISRAEL
Agent: Melanie Jackson Agency - New York, 212/582-8585

MANNEQUIN TWO: ON THE MOVE   20th Century Fox, 1991, w/David Isaacs, Ken Levine & Ed Rugoff

BOB ISRAEL
BACHELOR PARTY   20th Century Fox, 1984, Story

Is

CHARLES E. ISRAEL
ANGELA   Embassy, 1984

NEAL ISRAEL*
Agent: ICM - Los Angeles, 213/550-4000

TUNNEL VISION   Worldwide, 1976, w/Michael Mislove, directed
BACHELOR PARTY   20th Century-Fox, 1984, w/Pat Proft, directed
POLICE ACADEMY   The Ladd Company/Warner Bros., 1984, w/Pat Proft & Hugh Wilson
MOVING VIOLATIONS   20th Century Fox, 1985, w/Pat Proft, directed
REAL GENIUS   Tri-Star, 1985, w/Pat Proft & Peter Torokvei
LOOL WHO'S TALKING TOO   Tri-Star, 1990, w/Amy Heckerling
SKETCHES   New Line Cinema, 1991, diected

Screenplays:
UP FOR GRABS w/Pat Proft
THE CHILDREN'S CRUSADE w/F. Abatemarco & J. Roth
OPERATION U.F.O.

JUZO ITAMI
Agent: ICM - Los Angeles, 213/550-4000

THE FUNERAL   New Yorker, 1987, directed
TAMPOPO   New Yorker, 1987, directed
A TAXING WOMAN   New Yorker, 1988, directed
A TAXING WOMAN RETURNS   New Yorker, 1989, directed

JAMES IVORY
Agent: CAA - Beverly Hills, 213/288-4545
Business: Merchant Ivory Productions, 250 W. 57th St. - Suite 1913 A, New York, NY 10019, 212/582-8049

SHAKESPEARE WALLAH   Continental, 1966, w/Ruth Prawer-Jhabvala, directed
THE GURU   20th Century-Fox, 1969, w/Ruth Prawer-Jhabvala, directed
BOMBAY TALKIE   Dia Films, 1970, w/Ruth Prawer-Jhabvala, directed
MAURICE   Cinecom, 1987, w/Kit Hesketh-Harvey, directed

STEVEN IYAMA
LAST CALL   Prism Entertainment, 1990

J

ARNALDO JABAR
I LOVE YOU   Atlantic Releasing Corporation, 1982, directed

MAX JACK
Agent: Barrett, Benson, McCartt & Weston - Los Angeles, 213/247-5500

THE AMBASSADOR   MGM/UA/Cannon, 1985

DONALD G. JACKSON
ROLLER BLADE   New World, 1986, w/Randall Frakes, directed

LEWIS JACKSON*
Contact: WGA - New York, 212/245-6180

YOU BETTER WATCH OUT   CHRISTMAS EVIL   Edward R. Pressman Productions, 1980, directed

MARK JACKSON*
Contact: WGA - Los Angeles, 213/550-1000

EYES OF A STRANGER   Warner Bros., 1981, w/Eric L. Bloom

TRACEY JACKSON
Agent: United Talent Agency - Beverly Hills, 213/273-6700

Screenplays:
THE ROSENBERGS & JULIETTE

JERRY JACOBIUS*
Agent: David Shapira & Associates - Sherman Oaks, 818/906-0322

Screenplays:
THE NOMINATION w/Nick Gore
BLOOMER GIRLS w/Nick Gore
WISHFUL THINKING w/Nick Gore

BARRY A. JACOBS*
Agent: Contemporary Artists, Ltd. - Beverly Hills, 213/278-8250

THE FURTHER ADVENTURES OF TENNESSEE BUCK   Trans World Entertainment, 1988, w/Stuart Jacobs

JACK JACOBS*
Business Manager: Arthur Dreifuss/G. Michaud, 818/981-6680

IN SEARCH OF HISTORIC JESUS   Sunn Classic, 1979, w/Melvin Wald

LAWRENCE-HILTON JACOBS
ANGELS OF THE CITY   Raedon Home Video, 1989,
   w/Raymond Martino & Joseph Merhi, directed

MICHAEL JACOBS*
Agent: Triad Artists, Inc. - Los Angeles,
   213/556-2727

CERTAIN FURY   New World, 1985
3:15   Dakota Entertainment, 1986, w/Sam Bernard
HALLOWEEN 5: THE REVENGE OF MICHAEL MYERS
   Galaxy International, 1989, w/Shem Bitterman &
   Dominique Othenin-Girard

SEAMAN JACOBS*
Agent: The Cooper Agency - Los Angeles,
   213/277-8422

IT HAPPENED AT THE WORLD'S FAIR   MGM, 1962,
   w/Si Rose
OH GOD! BOOK II   Warner Bros., 1980, w/Fred Fox,
   Josh Greenfeld, Hal Goldman & Melissa Miller

STUART JACOBS*
Agent: Contemporary Artists, Ltd. - Beverly Hills,
   213/278-8250

THE FURTHER ADVENTURES OF TENNESSEE
   BUCK   Trans World Entertainment, 1988,
   w/Barrry Jacobs

WILL JACOBS
Agent: Susan Smith & Associates - Beverly Hills,
   213/852-4777

Screenplays:
THE TROUBLE WITH GIRLS

JOHN JACOBSEN
Agent: William Morris Agency - Beverly Hills,
   213/274-7451

Screenplays:
THIRTEENTH STEP
CALLING OUT

JOSEPH JACOBY
THE GREAT BANK HOAX   SHENANIGANS   Warner
   Bros., 1978, directed

JUST JAECKIN
Contact: Directors Guild of America - Los Angeles,
   213/289-2000

LADY CHATTERLEY'S LOVER   Cannon, 1982,
   w/Christopher Wicking, directed
THE PERILS OF GWENDOLINE IN THE LAND OF
   THE YIK YAK   GWENDOLINE   Samuel Goldwyn
   Company, 1984, directed

RICK JAFFA*
Agent: William Morris Agency - Beverly Hills,
   213/274-7451

Screenplays:
HELL BENT - AND BACK   w/Doug Richardson

ROBERT J. JAFFE*
Agent: Camden-ITG - Los Angeles, 213/289-2700

DEMON SEED   MGM/UA, 1977, w/Roger O. Hirson
MOTEL HELL   United Artists, 1980,
   w/Steven-Charles Jaffe
NIGHTFLYERS   New Century/Vista, 1987

STEVEN-CHARLES JAFFE*
Agent: Camden-ITG - Los Angeles, 213/289-2700
Business: Pari Passu Productions, Paramount Pictures,
   213/956-5841

MOTEL HELL   United Artists, 1980, w/Robert Jaffe

HENRY JAGLOM
Business: International Rainbow Pictures, The Penthouse,
   9165 Sunset Blvd., Los Angeles, CA 90069, 213/271-0202

A SAFE PLACE   Columbia, 1971, directed
TRACKS   Castle Hill Productions, 1976, directed
SITTING DUCKS   Specialty Films, 1979, directed
CAN SHE BAKE A CHERRY PIE?   Castle Hill Productions/
   Quartet Films, 1983, directed
ALWAYS   Samuel Goldwyn Company, 1985, directed
SOMEONE TO LOVE   Rainbow/Castle Hill Productions,
   1987, directed
NEW YEAR'S DAY   International Rainbow Pictures,
   1989, directed
EATING   International Rainbow Pictures, 1990, directed

DON JAKOBY*
Agent: ICM - Los Angeles, 213/550-4000

BLUE THUNDER   Columbia, 1983, w/Dan O'Bannon
THE PHILADELPHIA EXPERIMENT   New World, 1984,
   Story w/Wallace Bennett
LIFEFORCE   Tri-Star, 1985, w/Dan O'Bannon
INVADERS FROM MARS   Cannon, 1986,
   w/Dan O'Bannon
ARACHNOPHOBIA   Buena Vista, 1990, w/Wesley Strick

Screenplays:
D.C. THRILLER w/Jeb Stuart & Gary Thompson
TELEKINETIC MAN w/Dan O'Bannon
THE PRIMITIVE w/Dan O'Bannon
HEAVY ARMOR

PATRICK JAMAIN
Contact: Academy of Canadian Cinema & Television, 633
   Yonge Street - 2nd Floor, Toronto, Ontario M4Y 1Z9,
   Canada, 416/967-0315

HONEYMOON   International Film Marketing, 1987,
   w/Robert Geoffrion & Philippe Setbon, directed

DARIUS JAMES
Agent: William Morris Agency - Beverly Hills, 213/274-7451

Screenplays:
MIGHTY JACKS

FREDERICK JAMES
Agent: William Morris Agency - Beverly Hills, 213/274-7451

HUMANOIDS FROM THE DEEP   New World, 1980

Ja

FILM WRITERS GUIDE

NICK JAMES
FORBIDDEN ZONE   Sutton Marketing, 1980,
   w/Matthew Bright, Richard Elfman & Nick L. Martinson

STEVE JAMES
STREET HUNTER   21st Century, 1990,
   w/John A. Gallagher

Screenplays:
FIREWOLF   w/John A. Gallagher
NIGHT EAGLE   w/John A. Gallagher
HELL SOLDIER   w/John A. Gallagher

ALAN JANES
WINTER FLIGHT   Cinecom, 1984

MICHAEL JANOVER*
Contact: Philip Gross - 213/552-7823

HARDLY WORKING   20th Century-Fox, 1981,
   w/Jerry Lewis
THE PHILADELPHIA EXPERIMENT   New World, 1984,
   w/William Gray

TAMA JANOWITZ
Agent: ICM - Los Angeles, 213/550-4000

SLAVES OF NEW YORK   Tri-Star, 1989

DEREK JARMAN
Contact: c/o Mundy Ellis, British Film Institute, 81 Dean
   Street, London W1, England

JUBILEE   Libra, 1979, w/others, directed
THE TEMPEST   World Northal, 1980, directed
CARAVAGGIO   Cinevista, 1986, directed
WAR REQUIEM   Movie Visions, 1990, directed
THE GARDEN   (no distributor), 1991, directed

JIM JARMUSCH
Contact: Frankfurt, Garbus, Klein & Selz - New York,
   212/980-0120
Business: Black Snake Productions, Inc., 24 Prince
   Street - Suite 7, New York, NY 10012, 212/226-1341

PERMANENT VACATION   Gray City,
   1982, directed
STRANGER THAN PARADISE   Samuel Goldwyn
   Company, 1984, directed
DOWN BY LAW   Island Pictures, 1986, directed
MYSTERY TRAIN   Orion, 1989, directed

KEVIN JARRE*
Agent: William Morris Agency - Beverly Hills,
   213/274-7451

RAMBO: FIRST BLOOD PART II   Tri-Star,
   1985, Story
GLORY   Tri-Star, 1989

Screenplays:
FATHER AND SON   VALHALLA'S WAKE
DEAD OR ALIVE   (CTF)
JUDGEMENT NIGHT
MAGNIFICENT SEVEN
GOLDEN GATE IRON
THE DEVIL'S OWN

PAUL JARRICO*
Contact: WGA - Los Angeles, 213/550-1000

MESSENGER OF DEATH   Cannon, 1988

BRIAN D. JEFFRIES
MINISTRY OF VENGEANCE   Concorde, 1989, w/Mervyn
   Emrys & Ann Narus
HANGFIRE   Motion Picture Corporation, 1991

LIONEL JEFFRIES
Agent: ICM - London, 01/629-8080

THE RAILWAY CHILDREN   EMI, 1970, directed
THE AMAZING MR. BLUNDEN   Goldstone,
   1973, directed
WOMBLING FREE   Rank, 1977, directed

RICHARD JEFFERIES
Agent: William Morris Agency - Beverly Hills, 213/274-7451

BLOOD TIDE   21s Century, 1982, w/Donald Langdon &
   Nico Mastorakis, directed

Screenplays:
THE VAGRANT
PETER'S EARTH
THE REAL ROMEO
JUST MET
PALS FOREVER

LEN JENKIN*
Agent: Flora Roberts, Inc. - New York, 212/355-4165

AMERICAN NOTES (P)
POOR FOLKS' PLEASURE (P)
BLAME IT ON THE NIGHT   Tri-Star, 1984

DAN JENKINS*
Agent: ICM - New York, 212/556-5600

BAJA OKLAHOMA   HBO Pictures/Rastar Productions,
   1988, w/Bobby Roth
DEAD SOLID PERFECT (CTF)   HBO Pictures/David
   Merrick Productions, 1988, w/Bobby Roth

Screenplays:
FLAT OUT SPEED   w/Edwin Shrake
SLIM AND NONE   w/Edwin Shrake
LOOSE WOMEN   w/Edwin Shrake
DAMN YANKEES   w/Edwin Shrake
DINOSAUR WINE   w/Edwin Shrake
LIMO   w/Edwin Shrake
DEATH DEFYING T.S. BABCOCK   w/R. Biheller
LIFE ITS OWN SELF
GREAT AMERICA

ERIC JENKINS
Agent: William Morris Agency - Beverly Hills,
   213/274-7451

Screenplays:
RUSTY

JOHN JENKINS
PATTI ROCKS   FilmDallas, 1988, w/David Burton Morris,
   Chris Mulkey & Karen Landry

MICHAEL JENKINS
Contact: Australian Film Commission, 9229 Sunset Blvd.,
  Los Angeles, CA 90069, 213/275-7074

CAREFUL HE MIGHT HEAR YOU   TLC Films/20th
  Century-Fox, 1984
REBEL   Vestron, 1986, w/Bob Herbert, directed

VICTORIA JENKINS*
Agent: Shapiro/Lichtman - Los Angeles, 213/859-8877

STACKING   Spectrafilm, 1987

JIM JENNEWEIN*
Agent: United Talent Agency - Beverly Hills, 213/273-6700

Screenplays:
STAY TUNED   w/Tom S. Parker
THE FAMILY MAN   w/Tom S. Parker

MICHAEL JENNING*
Agent: William Morris Agency - Beverly Hills, 213/274-7451

NEXT OF KIN   Warner Bros., 1989

Screenplays:
CAPONE IN LAREDO   w/John Norville
LEWD CONDUCT
STREET SMARTS
CINDERELLA UNIVERSE
LETHAL GAS
DEADBEATS
ACT OF LOVE
DARKNESS AT PEMBERLY
DARK CITY
LAST GOOD KISS

PETER JENSEN
Agent: Warden & White Associates - Beverly Hills,
  213/852-1028

Screenplays:
SNUGGLEFOOT   w/Mikel Anderson
KISS KISS, KILL KILL   w/Mikel Anderson
CRASH AND BURN   w/Mikel Anderson

JAMES JEREMIAS*
Agent: CAA - Beverly Hills, 213/288-4545

THE LOST BOYS   Warner Bros., 1987, w/Jeffrey
  Boam & Janice Fischer

Screenplays:
INTER-GALACTIC HIGH   w/Janice Fischer
MERLYN   w/Janice Fischer

JERICO
(See Jerico STONE)

BILL JESSE
RIFF-RAFF   Parallax Pictures, 1991

SUE JETT*
Agent: CAA - Beverly Hills, 213/288-4545

Screenplays:
FIRST, LAST & ALWAYS
LOOKING FOR LOVE

BOB JEWSON
STIR   Hoyts, 1980

RUTH PRAWER JHABVALA*
Agent: CAA - Beverly Hills, 213/288-4545

THE HOUSEHOLDER   Royal Films International, 1963
SHAKESPEARE WALLAH   Continental, 1966,
  w/James Ivory
THE GURU   20th Century-Fox, 1969,
  w/James Ivory
BOMBAY TALKIE   Dia Films, 1970, w/James Ivory
SWEET SOUNDS   Merchant-Ivory Productions, 1976
ROSELAND   Cinema Shares International, 1977
THE EUROPEANS   Levitt-Pickman, 1979
HULLABALOO OVER GEORGIE & BONNIE'S PICTURES
  Corinth, 1979
JANE AUSTEN IN MANHATTAN   Contemporary, 1980
QUARTET   New World, 1981
HEAT & DUST   Universal Classics, 1983
THE BOSTONIANS   Almi Pictures, 1984
A ROOM WITH A VIEW ★★   Cinecom International, 1986
MADAME SOUSATZKA   Universal, 1988,
  w/John Schlesinger
MR. AND MRS. BRIDGE   Miramax, 1990

Screenplays:
HOWARD'S END

PENN JILLETTE*
Agent: ICM - Los Angeles, 213/550-4000
Business Manager: Mike Wills, Buggs & Rudy Discount
  Corporation, 142 West 49th Street #1214, New York,
  NY 10019

PENN & TELLER GET KILLED   Warner Bros.,
  1989, w/Teller

NEAL JIMENEZ*
Agent: Richland/Wunsch/Hohman Agency - Los Angeles,
  213/278-1955

WHERE THE RIVER RUNS BLACK   MGM/UA, 1986,
  w/Peter Silverman
RIVER'S EDGE   Hemdale, 1987
FOR THE BOYS   20th Century Fox, 1991, w/Marshall
  Brickman & Lindy Laub
THE WATER DANCE   Pacific Western Productions,
  1991, co-directed

Screenplays:
DARK WIND
CHILDREN WITH EMERALD EYES
THE VIRGIN
LAZARO
BLUE ANGEL
SON OF ELVIS

ROBERT E. JIRAS
I AM THE CHEESE   Libra Cinema 5, 1983,
  w/David Lange

PETER JOBIN*
Contact: WGA - New York, 212/245-6180

HAPPY BIRTHDAY TO ME   Columbia, 1981, w/John
  Saxton & Timothy Bond

ALEXANDRO JODOROWSKY
EL TOPO   ABKCO, 1971, directed
SANTA SANGRE   Expanded Entertainment, 1989, w/Claudio Argento & Roberto Leoni, directed

ARTHUR JOFFE
Contact: French Film Office, 745 Fifth Avenue, New York, NY 10151, 212/832-8860

HAREM   Sara Films, 1985, w/Richard Prieur & Tom Rayfiel, directed

ROLAND JOFFÉ*
Business: Lightmotive, 662 N. Robertson Blvd., Los Angeles, CA 90069, 213/659-6200

FAT MAN AND LITTLE BOY   Paramount, 1989, w/Bruce Robinson, directed

ROY JOHANSEN*
Agent: Patricia Karlan Agency - Burbank, 818/846-8666

BACK TO HANNIBAL: THE RETURN OF TOM SAWYER AND HUCKLEBERRY FINN (CTF)   Gay-Jay Productions/The Disney Channel, 1990
MURDER 101 (CTF)   Alan Barnette/MCA Television, 1991, w/William Condon

BAYARD JOHNSON
DAMNED RIVER   MGM/UA, 1990, w/John Crowther

CHARLES JOHNSON*
Agent: Shapiro/Lichtman - Los Angeles, 213/859-8877

THE MONKEY HUSTLE   American International, 1976

DIANE JOHNSON
Agent: Flora Roberts, Inc. - New York, 212/355-4165

THE SHINING   Warner Bros., 1980, w/Stanley Kubrick

GEORGE CLAYTON JOHNSON*
Contact: WGA - Los Angeles, 213/550-1000

TWILIGHT ZONE - THE MOVIE   Warner Bros, 1983, Segment 2, w/Richard Matheson & Josh Rogan

J. RANDAL JOHNSON*
(Randy Johnson)
Agent: ICM - Los Angeles, 213/550-4000

DUDES   New Century/Vista, 1987
THE DOORS   Tri-Star, 1991, w/Oliver Stone

Screenplays:
TESLA
SLAUGHTER ALLEY
SENIOR YEARS
URBAN LEGENDS   w/Gregory Widen, Ethan Wiley, William Judkins & Donald Knowlton

KENNETH JOHNSON*
Agent: United Talent Agency - Beverly Hills, 213/273-6700

Screenplays:
THE MADWOMAN OF NEW YORK (directing)
THE FIRSTBORN (directing)

MONICA JOHNSON*
Agent: Harris & Goldberg - Los Angeles, 213/553-5200

AMERICATHON   United Artists, 1979, w/Michael Mislove
REAL LIFE   Paramount, 1979, w/Albert Brooks & Harry Shearer
MODERN ROMANCE   Columbia, 1981, w/Albert Brooks
JEKYLL AND HYDE...TOGETHER AGAIN   Paramount, 1982, w/Jerry Belson, Michael Leeson & Harvey Miller
LOST IN AMERICA   Warner Bros./The Geffen Company, 1985, w/Albert Brooks

Screenplays:
THE CLINIC
BATTLE FOR PALM SPRINGS
THANK GOD THERE'S A ROOF

PAT JOHNSON
Agent: The Irv Schechter Company - Beverly Hills, 213/278-8070

A FORCE OF ONE   American Cinema, 1979, Story w/Ernest Tidyman

PATRICK READ JOHNSON
Agent: CAA - Beverly Hills, 213/288-4545

SPACED INVADERS   Buena Vista, 1990, w/Scott Lawrence Alexander, directed

Screenplays:
STAR SAILOR
DRAGONHEART
SUMMERTIME
SANTIAGO

RANDY JOHNSON
(See J. Randal Johnson)

STEPHEN JOHNSON*
Agent: Jim Preminger Agency - Los Angeles, 213/475-9491

STOP AT NOTHING (CTF)   Empty Chair Productions, 1991

TERRY JOHNSON
INSIGNIFICANCE   Island Alive, 1985, from his play

TODD JOHNSON*
Agent: Warden & White Associates - Beverly Hills, 213/852-1028

Screenplays:
EUGENE AND HIS SEAMLESS PANTS   w/Patrick Ranahan
HEAD DOWN TILT   w/Patrick Ranahan

BECKY JOHNSTON*
Agent: ICM - Los Angeles, 213/550-4000

UNDER THE CHERRY MOON   Warner Bros., 1986

Screenplays:
THE PRINCE OF TIDES   w/Pat Conroy

AARON KIM JOHNSTON
THE LAST WINTER   Rode Pictures Inc., 1989, directed

Screenplays:
GIRLS TOWN
HARDBOILED

TONY JOHNSTON
THE SIEGE OF FIREBASE GLORIA   Fries Entertainment, 1989, w/William Nagle

TUCKER JOHNSTON
BLOOD SALVAGE   Paragon Arts International, 1990, w/Ken Sanders, directed

AMY JONES*
Agent: ICM - Los Angeles, 213/550-4000

LOVE LETTERS   New World, 1983, directed
MAID TO ORDER   New Century/Vista, 1987, w/Perry Howze & Randy Howze, directed
MYSTIC PIZZA   Samuel Goldwyn Company, 1988, w/Perry Howze, Randy Howze & Alfred Uhry

Screenplays:
IT HAD TO BE STEVE   w/Holly Goldberg Sloan & Tracy Keenan Wynn

BRIAN THOMAS JONES
OCEAN DRIVE WEEKEND   Troma, 1985, directed
ESCAPE FROM SAFEHAVEN   SVS Films, 1989, w/James McCalmont, directed

EVAN JONES*
Contact: Writers Guild of Great Britain - London, 011/441/723-8074

THESE ARE THE DAMNED   Columbia, 1962
EVA   Times, 1962, w/Hugo Butler
KING AND COUNTRY   Allied Artists, 1965
MODESTY BLAISE   20th Century-Fox, 1966
FUNERAL IN BERLIN   Paramount, 1967
OUTBACK *WAKE IN FRIGHT*   United Artists, 1971
VICTORY   Lorimar/Paramount, 1981, w/Yabo Yablonsky
THE KILLING OF ANGEL STREET   Forest Home Films, 1981, w/Michael Craig & Cecil Holmes
CHAMPIONS   Embassy, 1984
KANGAROO   Cineplex Odeon, 1987
A SHOW OF FORCE   Paramount, 1990, w/John Strong

IAN JONES
NED KELLY   United Artists, 1970, w/Tony Richardson
THE LIGHTHORSEMEN   Cinecom, 1988

JANET DULIN JONES
Agent: Warden & White Associates - Beverly Hills, 213/852-1028

Screenplays:
AVENGING ANGEL
NO OTHER LOVE
FADE AWAY

LAURA JONES
HIGH TIDE   Tri-Star, 1987
AN ANGEL AT MY TABLE   Fine Line Features, 1991

LAURIE JONES
IN THE SPIRIT   Castle Hill Productions, 1990, w/Jeannie Berlin

MARTIN JONES*
Contact: WGA - New York, 212/245-6180

PRISON STORIES: WOMEN ON THE INSIDE (CTF)   Francine LeFrak Productions/HBO Showcase, 1991, "Esperanza"; "New Chicks" w/Dick Beebe & Jule Selbo

ROBERT C. JONES*
Agent: The Marion Rosenberg Office - Los Angeles, 213/653-7383

COMING HOME ★★   United Artists, 1978, w/Waldo Salt

Screenplays:
GOD BLESS YOU, MR. ROSEWATER

TERRY JONES
Contact: Anne James, Monty Python Office - London, 011/441/487-4485

CONSUMING PASSIONS (P) w/Michael Palin
AND NOW FOR SOMETHING COMPLETELY DIFFERENT   Columbia, 1972, w/Graham Chapman, John Cleese, Terry Gilliam, Eric Idle & Michael Palin
MONTY PYTHON AND THE HOLY GRAIL   Cinema 5, 1974, w/Graham Chapman, John Cleese, Terry Gilliam, Eric Idle & Michael Palin, directed
MONTY PYTHON'S LIFE OF BRIAN   Orion/Warner Bros., 1979, w/Graham Chapman, John Cleese, Terry Gilliam, Eric Idle & Michael Palin, directed
MONTY PYTHON LIVE AT THE HOLLYWOOD BOWL   Columbia, 1982, w/Graham Chapman, John Cleese, Terry Gilliam, Eric Idle & Michael Palin
MONTY PYTHON'S THE MEANING OF LIFE   Universal, 1983, w/Graham Chapman, John Cleese, Terry Gilliam, Eric Idle & Michael Palin, directed
LABYRINTH   Tri-Star, 1986
ERIK THE VIKING   Orion, 1989, directed

NEIL JORDAN
Agent: Casaratto Company - London, 01/287-4450

DANNY BOY *ANGEL*   Triumph/Columbia, 1983, directed
THE COMPANY OF WOLVES   Cannon, 1984, w/Angela Carter, directed
MONA LISA   Island Pictures, 1986, w/David Leland, directed
HIGH SPIRITS   Tri-Star, 1988, directed
THE MIRACLE   Miramax, 1991, directed

Screenplays:
BROKEN DREAMS   w/John Boorman

ROBERT L. JOSEPH*
Agent: CAA - Beverly Hills, 213/288-4545

ECHOES OF A SUMMER   CineArtists, 1976

WALTER JOSTEN
Business: Paragon Arts International, 6777 Hollywood Blvd. - Suite 520, Hollywood, CA 90028, 213/465-5355

NIGHT ANGEL   Fries Entertainment, 1990, w/Joe Augustyn

ADRIEN JOYCE
(See Carole Eastman)

Jo
FILM WRITERS GUIDE

C. COURTNEY JOYNER
THE OFFSPRING   TMS Pictures, 1987, w/Jeff Burr & Darin Scott
PRISON   Empire Pictures, 1988
CATACOMBS   Empire Pictures, 1988
VIETNAM, TEXAS   Epic Productions, 1990, w/Tom Badal
CLASS OF 1999   Taurus Entertainment, 1990

Screenplays:
PUPPETMASTER III
DOCTOR MORDRID   w/Charles Band
THE GYPSY ANGELS   EAST OF THE SUN   w/Virgil W. Vogel
SCORPION   w/Kevin Meyer
DARK STREET   w/Warren Peters
DOUBLE ACTION MAN
A DELICATE LINK
THE WHITE ZONE
THE PENALTY BOX
FAMILY REUNION

JERRY R. JUHL*
Contact: Paul J. White, CPA, 213/462-2885

THE MUPPET MOVIE   AFD, 1979, w/Jack Burns
THE GREAT MUPPET CAPER   Universal/AFD, 1981, w/Tom Patchett, Jack Rose & Jay Tarses

K

KEITH KACZOREK
LADY AVENGER   Marco Colombo, 1989, w/Will Schmitz

TERRY KAHN
FOX   Eagle Entertainment, 1991, directed

CONSTANCE KAISERMAN
Business: Merchant Ivory Productions, 250 West 57th St., Suite 1913, New York, NY 10023, 212/582-8049

MY LITTLE GIRL   Hemdale, 1987, w/Nan Mason, directed

LEE KALCHEIM
Agent: Triad Artists, Inc. - Los Angeles, 213/556-2727

Screenplays:
ATOMIC FOLLIES

REBECCA KALIN
Agent: William Morris Agency - Beverly Hills, 213/274-7451

Screenplays:
FIRE PRINCESS
TELLING TIME

JAY KAMEN*
Agent: Warden & White Associates - Beverly Hills, 213/852-1028

Screenplays:
THE JEWELER   w/Robert Kizer
S.W.M.

ROBERT MARK KAMEN*
Agent: CAA - Beverly Hills, 213/288-4545

TAPS   20th Century-Fox, 1981, w/Darryl Ponicsan
SPLIT IMAGE   Orion, 1982, w/Robert Kaufman & Scott Spencer
THE KARATE KID   Columbia, 1984
THE KARATE KID PART II   Columbia, 1986
THE KARATE KID PART III   Columbia, 1989

Screenplays:
THE POWER OF ONE
CROSSINGS
RYOMA
AFGHAN PROJECT

STUART KAMINSKY
ENEMY TERRITORY   Empire Pictures, 1987, w/Bobby Liddell

STEVEN W. KAMPMANN*
Agent: The Gersh Agency - Beverly Hills, 213/274-6611

BACK TO SCHOOL   Orion, 1986, w/Will Aldis, Harold Ramis & Peter Torokvei
THE COUCH TRIP   Orion, 1988, w/Will Aldis & Sean Stein
STEALING HOME   Warner Bros., 1988, w/Will Aldis, directed
CLIFFORD   Orion, 1992, w/Will Aldis, directed

STEPHEN KANDEL*
Agent: Shapiro/Lichtman - Los Angeles, 213/859-8877

BATTLE OF THE CORAL SEA   Columbia, 1959, w/Dan Ullman
CHAMBER OF HORRORS   Warner Bros., 1966
CANNON FOR CORDOBA   United Artists, 1970

MICHAEL KANE*
Agent: Monteiro Rose Agency - Encino, 818/501-1177

SMOKEY AND THE BANDIT II   Universal, 1977
FOOLIN' AROUND   Columbia, 1978, w/David Swift
HOT STUFF   Columbia, 1979, w/Donald E. Westlake
THE LEGEND OF THE LONE RANGER   Universal/AFD, 1981, w/Ben Roberts, William Roberts & Ivan Goff
HARD COUNTRY   Universal, 1981
SOUTHERN COMFORT   20th Century-Fox, 1981, w/Walter Hill & David Giler
ALL THE RIGHT MOVES   20th Century-Fox, 1983
THE BEAR   Embassy, 1984

Screenplays:
LONG DAN
GHOST TOWN
SATURDAY'S CHILD
THE DEEP II
THE CISCO KID
DEEP TROUBLE

SARATOGA
STRIKE THREE CALLED
SEVEN THE HARD WAY
JAYWALKING
ESCROW
BANDMAN

ROBERT G. KANE*
Contact: WGA - Los Angeles, 213/550-1000

KISSES FOR MY PRESIDENT   Warner Bros., 1964,
    w/Claude Binyon
THE VILLAIN   Columbia, 1979

JEFF KANEW
Contact: Directors Guild of America - Los Angeles,
    213/289-2000

NATURAL ENEMIES   Cinema 5, 1979, directed
EDDIE MACON'S RUN   Universal, 1983, directed

CHARLES T. KANGANIS
L.A. HEAT   PM Entertainment, 1989

FAY KANIN*
Agent: William Morris Agency - Beverly Hills, 213/274-7451

GOODBYE MY FANCY (P), w/Michael Kanin
BLONDIE FOR VICTORY   Columbia, 1942
MY PAL GUS   20th Century-Fox, 1952, w/Michael Kanin
RHAPSODY   MGM, 1954, w/Michael Kanin
THE OPPOSITE SEX   MGM, 1956, w/Michael Kanin
TEACHER'S PET ★   Paramount, 1958, w/Michael Kanin
THE RIGHT APPROACH   20th Century-Fox, 1961,
    w/Michael Kanin
SWORDMAN OF SIENA   MGM, 1962, w/Michael Kanin

Screenplays:
THE SURROGATE
THE SOURCE

MICHAEL KANIN*
Business Manager: Henry Bamberger, 213/466-2780

GOODBYE MY FANCY (P) w/Fay Kanin
WOMAN OF THE YEAR ★★   MGM, 1942,
    w/Ring Lardner Jr.
THE CROSS OF LORRAINE   MGM, 1944, w/Robert
    Andrews, Alexander Esway & Ring Lardner Jr.
CENTENNIAL SUMMER   20th Century-Fox, 1946
WHEN I GROW UP   Horizon, 1950, directed
MY PAL GUS   20th Century-Fox, 1952, w/Fay Kanin
RHAPSODY   MGM, 1954, w/FayKanin
THE OPPOSITE SEX   MGM, 1956, w/Fay Kanin
TEACHER'S PET ★   Paramount, 1958, w/Fay Kanin
THE RIGHT APPROACH   20th Century-Fox, 1961,
    w/Fay Kanin
SWORDMAN OF SIENA   MGM, 1962, w/Fay Kanin
THE OUTRAGE   MGM, 1964
HOW TO COMMIT MARRIAGE   Cinerama Releasing
    Corporation, 1969, w/Ben Starr

HAL KANTER
Business Manager: James Harper & Associates, 13063
    Ventura Blvd., Studio City, CA 91604, 818/788-8683

HERE COME THE GIRLS   Paramount, 1953,
    w/Edmund Hartmann
ABOUT MRS. LESLIE   Paramount, 1954, w/Ketti Frings
CASANOVA'S BIG NIGHT   Paramount, 1954,
    w/Edmund Hartmann
LOVING YOU   Paramount, 1957, w/Herbert
    Baker, directed
ONCE UPON A HORSE   Universal, 1958, directed
BACHELOR IN PARADISE   MGM, 1961,
    w/Valentine Davies
BLUE HAWAII   Paramount, 1961
MOVE OVER DARLING   20th Century-Fox, 1963,
    w/Jack Sher
DEAR BRIGITTE   20th Century-Fox, 1965

ED KAPLAN*
Agent: ICM - Los Angeles, 213/550-4000

ALL IN A SUMMER'S DAY (Short), directed

Screenplays:
SUMMERHOUSE
SUGAR & SPIKE

GEORGE KAPLAN
(See Clifford Green & Ellen Green)

JACK KAPLAN*
Agent: CAA - Beverly Hills, 213/288-4545

Screenplays:
MY FELLOW AMERICANS w/Richard Chapman
WHISTLING DIXIE
LAND OF OPPORTUNITY w/Jonathan Lynn

JAMES KAPLAN*
Agent: ICM - Los Angeles, 213/550-4000

Screenplays:
NATIVE GENIUS w/Peter Kaplan
BLACK WALLS

JONATHAN KAPLAN*
Agent: CAA - Beverly Hills, 213/288-4545

WHITE LINE FEVER   Columbia, 1975, w/Ken
    Friedman, directed
MR. BILLION   20th Century-Fox, 1976, w/Ken
    Friedman, directed

MARTY KAPLAN*
Business: Walt Disney Studios, 818/972-3590

Screenplays:
NOISES OFF

MICHAEL A. KAPLAN*
Agent: ICM - Los Angeles, 213/550-4000

ILLEGALLY YOURS   DEG, 1986, w/Ken Finkelman & John
    Levenstein, as "Max Dickens & M.A. Stewart"

Screenplays:
CARLESS w/John Levenstein
TALES OF THE NEW DEPRESSION

LARRY KARASZEWSKI*
Agent: InterTalent - Los Angeles, 213/858-6200

PROBLEM CHILD   Universal, 1990, w/Scott Alexander
PROBLEM CHILD 2   Universal, 1991, w/Scott Alexander

Ka

FILM WRITERS GUIDE

JANICE KARMAN
THE CHIPMUNK ADVENTURE (AF)   Samuel Goldwyn Company, 1986, w/Ross Bagdasarian, directed

THOMAS KARNOWSKI
THE SWORD AND THE SORCERER   Group 1, 1982, w/Albert Pyun & John Stuckmeyer

LAWRENCE KASDAN*
Agent: United Talent Agency - Beverly Hills, 213/273-6700

THE EMPIRE STRIKES BACK   20th Century-Fox, 1980, w/Leigh Brackett
CONTINENTAL DIVIDE   Universal, 1981
RAIDERS OF THE LOST ARK   Paramount, 1981
BODY HEAT   Warner Bros., 1981, directed
RETURN OF THE JEDI   20th Century-Fox, 1983, w/George Lucas
THE BIG CHILL ★   Columbia, 1983, w/Barbara Benedek, directed
SILVERADO   Columbia, 1985, w/Mark Kasdan, directed
THE ACCIDENTAL TOURIST ★   Warner Bros., 1988, w/Frank Galati, directed
GRAND CANYON   20th Century Fox, 1991, directed

Screenplays:
THE BODYGUARD

MARK KASDAN*
Agent: CAA - Beverly Hills, 213/288-4545

SILVERADO   Columbia, 1985, w/Lawrence Kasdan
CRIMINAL LAW   Hemdale, 1989

MARY ANNE KASICA*
Agent: Shapiro/Lichtman - Los Angeles, 213/859-8877

Screenplays:
BUZZARDS LUCK   w/Michael Scheff

JEROME A. KASS*
Agent: Richland/Wunsch/Hohman Agency - Los Angeles, 213/278-1955

THE BLACK STALLION RETURNS   MGM/UA, 1983, w/Richard Kletter

LEONARD KASTLE
THE HONEYMOON KILLERS   Cinerama Releasing Corporation, 1969, directed

DAPHNA KASTNER
JULIA HAS TWO LOVERS   South Gate Entertainment, 1991, w/Bashar Shbib

MITCHEL L. KATLIN*
Agent: United Talent Agency - Beverly Hills, 213/273-6700

OPPORTUNITY KNOCKS   Universal, 1990, w/Nat Bernstein

Screenplays:
ON THE AIR   w/Nat Bernstein
WHEN THE WIFE'S AWAY   w/Nat Bernstein
LORD OF THE MANOR   w/Nat Bernstein

ALLAN D. KATZ*
Agent: CAA - Beverly Hills, 213/288-4545

BIG MAN ON CAMPUS   Vestron, 1989

EVAN KATZ
Agent: InterTalent - Beverly Hills, 213/858-6200

Screenplays:
COUNTERFEIT FATHER w/Tom Ropelewski

GLORIA KATZ*
Agent: CAA - Beverly Hills, 213/288-4545

AMERICAN GRAFFITI ★   Universal, 1973, w/Willard Huyck & George Lucas
MESSIAH OF EVIL   International Cinefilm, 1975, w/Willard Huyck
LUCKY LADY   20th Century-Fox, 1975, w/Willard Huyck
FRENCH POSTCARDS   Paramount, 1979, w/Willard Huyck
INDIANA JONES AND THE TEMPLE OF DOOM   Paramount, 1984, w/Willard Huyck
BEST DEFENSE   Paramount, 1984, w/Willard Huyck
HOWARD THE DUCK   Universal, 1986, w/Willard Huyck

Screenplays:
NIGHT RIDE DOWN   w/Willard Huyck
THE AIR-CONDITIONED DREAM   w/Willard Huyck
NIAGRA FALLS   w/Willard Huyck
RADIOLAND MURDERS   w/Willard Huyck
A YELLOW RAFT IN BLUE WATER   w/Willard Huyck

JONATHAN KATZ*
Contact: WGA - New York, 212/245-6180

HOUSE OF GAMES   Orion, 1987, Story w/David Mamet

JORDAN KATZ
Agent: United Talent Agency - Beverly Hills, 213/273-6700

Screenplays:
TRIAL BY JURY

ROBERT KATZ
THE CASSANDRA CROSSING   Avco Embassy, 1977, w/George Pan Cosmatos & Tom Mankiewicz
THE SALAMANDER   ITC, 1983
HOTEL COLONIAL   Columbia, 1987, w/Ira Barmak, Enzo Monteleone & Cinzia Torrini

STEPHEN KATZ*
Agent: Warden & White Associates - Beverly Hills, 213/852-1028

SATAN'S PRINCESS   Paramount Home Video/Sun Heat Pictures, 1991

Screenplays:
DESIGNATED HITTER
KNEE DEEP IN ALLIGATORS

JONATHAN KAUFER*
Agent: ICM - Los Angeles, 213/550-4000

SOUP FOR ONE   Warner Bros., 1982, directed

Screenplays:
WAR BABIES
ALL CONQUERS LOVE
HORROR HOLIDAY
COMPUTER
THE EDUCATION OF LINUS DOOLEY
SLEEPWALKER

CHARLES KAUFMAN
Business: Troma, Inc., 733 Ninth Avenue, New York, NY 10019, 212/757-4555

MOTHER'S DAY   United Film Distribution, 1980, w/Warren D. Leight, directed
WAITRESS!   Troma, 1982, w/Michael Stone
WHEN NATURE CALLS   Troma, 1985, directed

Screenplays:
ELVES w/Larry B. Williams
WENDELL WILCOX AND THE MONSTER MAKERS w/Larry B. Williams

LLOYD KAUFMAN
Business: Troma, Inc., 733 Ninth Avenue, New York, NY 10019, 212/757-4555

STUCK ON YOU!   Troma, 1983, w/others, co-directed
THE TOXIC AVENGER, PART III: THE LAST TEMPTATION OF TOXIE   Troma, 1989, w/Gay Partington Terry, co-directed
CLASS OF NUKE 'EM HIGH PART 2: SUBHUMANOID MELTDOWN   Troma, 1991, w/Eric Louzil, Carl Morano, Marcus Rolling, Jeffrey W. Sass & Matt Unger

MILLARD KAUFMAN*
Agent: Jim Preminger Agency - Los Angeles, 213/475-9491

TAKE THE HIGH GROUND ★   MGM, 1953
BAD DAY AT BLACK ROCK ★   MGM, 1954
RAINTREE COUNTRY   MGM, 1958
NEVER SO FEW   MGM, 1959
CONVICTS FOUR   REPRIEVE   Allied Artists, 1962, directed
THE WAR LORD   Universal, 1965, w/John Collier
THE KLANSMAN   Paramount, 1974, w/Samuel Fuller

PHILIP KAUFMAN*
Agent: CAA - Beverly Hills, 213/288-4545

GOLDSTEIN   Altura, 1965, co-directed
FEARLESS FRANK   American International, 1969, directed
THE GREAT NORTHFIELD, MINNESOTA RAID   Universal, 1972, directed
THE OUTLAW JOSEY WALES   Warner Bros., 1976, w/Sonia Chernus
THE WANDERERS   Orion/Warner Bros., 1979, w/Rose Kaufman, directed
RAIDERS OF THE LOST ARK   Paramount, 1981, Story w/George Lucas
THE RIGHT STUFF   The Ladd Company/Warner Bros., 1983, directed
THE UNBEARABLE LIGHTNESS OF BEING ★   Orion, 1988, w/Jean-Claude Carriere, directed
HENRY & JUNE   Universal, 1990, w/Rose Kaufman, directed

Screenplays:
BLACK ANGEL w/Jean-Claude Carriere

ROBERT KAUFMAN*
Contact: WGA - Los Angeles, 213/550-1000

DR. GOLDFOOT AND THE BIKINI MACHINE   American International, 1965, w/Elwood Ullman
SKI PARTY   American International, 1965
DR. GOLDFOOT AND THE GIRL BOMBS   American International, 1966, w/Lewis M. Heyward
THE COOL ONES   Warner Bros., 1967
I LOVE MY WIFE   Universal, 1970
GETTING STRAIGHT   Columbia, 1970
FREEBIE AND THE BEAN   Warner Bros., 1974
HARRY AND WALTER GO TO NEW YORK   Columbia, 1976, w/John Byrum
THE HAPPY HOOKER GOES TO WASHINGTON   Cannon, 1977
LOVE AT FIRST BITE   American International, 1979
NOTHING PERSONAL   American International, 1980
HOW TO BEAT THE HIGH COST OF LIVING   American International, 1980
SPLIT IMAGE   Orion, 1982, w/Robert Mark Kamen & Scott Spencer
THE CHECK IS IN THE MAIL   Ascot Entertainment Group, 1986
SEPARATE VACATIONS   RSK Entertainment, 1986

Screenplays:
LOVE AT SECOND BITE
MAJOR BIRNBAUM
GIRLSTOWN
REVOLTING
TREVOR
P.O.W.
THE ONE HUNDRED DOLLAR MISUNDERSTANDING
FU MANCHU
SPAGHETTI
LOOPHOLE
WEEKENDS
THE ITALIANS
THE FAME GAME
MIGHTY MOUSE
THE BULLIES
ONE DAY AT A TIME

ROSE L. KAUFMAN*
Contact: 415/421-3374

THE WANDERERS   Orion/Warner Bros., 1979, w/Philip Kaufman
HENRY & JUNE   Universal, 1990, w/Philip Kaufman

AKI KAURISMAKI
Busines: Villealfa Film Productions, Minna Canthinkatu 20, SF-00250, Helsinki, Finland, 0/41-37-88

CRIME AND PUNISHMENT   Villealfa Film Productions, 1983, directed
CALAMARI UNION   Villealfa Film Productions, 1985, directed
SHADOWS IN PARADISE   Villealfa Film Productions, 1986, directed

Ka

FILM WRITERS GUIDE

HAMLET GOES BUSINESS   Villealfa Film Productions, 1987, directed
ARIEL   Villealfa Film Productions, 1989, directed
LENINGRAD COWBOYS GO AMERICA   Orion Classics, 1990, directed
I HIRED A CONTRACT KILLER   Villealfa Film Productions/Swedish Film Institute, 1990, directed
THE MATCH FACTORY GIRL   Villealfa Film Productions/Swedish Film Institute, 1990, directed

LAURA KAVANAU
Agent: H. N. Swanson, Inc. - Los Angeles, 213/652-5385

Screenplays:
DOWN FOR BLOOD w/Michael Levine

DUSTY KAY*
Agent: William Morris Agency - Beverly Hills, 213/274-7451

Screenplays:
WANTED

KAREN KAY
CALL ME   Vestron, 1988

TONY KAYDEN*
Agent: Barrett, Benson, McCartt & Weston - Los Angeles, 213/247-5500

OUT OF BOUNDS   Columbia, 1986
SLIPSTREAM   Entertainment Film, 1989

Screenplays:
DON'T THINK TWICE
THE AVENGER
POLICE PYTHON .357
MIDNIGHT BLUE
NOVEMBER MAN
HOUSE DETECTIVE
DIRE STRAITS

JOHN KAYE*
Agent: The Daniel Ostroff Agency - Los Angeles, 213/278-2020

CHERRY TERRY, THE ROCKIN' ROBIN (P)
RAFFERTY AND THE GOLD DUST TWINS   Warner Bros., 1975
AMERICAN HOT WAX   Paramount, 1978
WHERE THE BUFFALO ROAM   Universal, 1980

Screenplays:
MERCY SPRINGS
MAGNETIC NORTH
TELEPHONE JACK

NORMAN KAYE
CACTUS   Spectrafilm, 1986, w/Paul Cox & Bob Ellis

PHOEBE KAYLOR
CARNY   United Artists, 1980, Story w/Robert Kaylor & Robbie Robertson

ROBERT KAYLOR
CARNY   United Artists, 1980, Story w/Phoebe Kaylor & Robbie Robertson, directed

ELIA KAZAN*
Business: 174 East 95th St., New York, NY 10128

AMERICA, AMERICA ★   Warner Bros., 1963, directed
THE VISITORS   United Artists, 1972, directed
THE ARRANGEMENT   Warner Bros., 1969, directed

NICHOLAS KAZAN*
Agent: Sanford, Skouras, Gross & Associates - Los Angeles, 213/208-2100

FAMILY LIFE (P)
SOUTHERN COMFORT (P)
SAFE HOUSE (P)
FRANCES   Universal/AFD, 1982, w/Eric Bergren & Christopher DeVore
AT CLOSE RANGE   Orion, 1986
PATTY HEARST   Atlantic Releasing Corporation, 1988
REVERSAL OF FORTUNE ★   Warner Bros., 1990
MOBSTERS   Universal, 1991, w/Mike Mahern
GLADIATOR   Columbia, 1991, w/Lyle Kessler

Screenplays:
DREAM LOVER (directing)
CORTES
ANIMALS w/D. Dunaway
THE RIDE-ALONG
GETTING IT
VIRGIN
TIME & AGAIN
OUTLAWS
GRACE
GRAY MATTERS
SINGLE WOMEN
THE SURVIVALIST
PUNK DADDY
THE BEARD
BEACH
SHOOT FOR THE STARS
HOME GROWN

TIM KAZURINSKY*
Agent: CAA - Beverly Hills, 213/288-4545

ABOUT LAST NIGHT   Tri-Star, 1986, w/Denise De Clue
FOR KEEPS   Tri-Star, 1988, w/Denise De Clue

Screenplays:
ABOUT LAST NIGHT 2 w/Denise DeClue
BIG SUCCESS w/Denise De Clue

JAMES KEACH*
Agent: The Gersh Agency - Beverly Hills, 213/274-6611

THE LONG RIDERS   United Artists, 1980, w/Bill Bryden, Stacy Keach & Steven Philip Smith
ARMED AND DANGEROUS   Columbia, 1986, w/Brian Grazer & Harold Ramis

STACY KEACH
Agent: Triad Artists, Inc. - Los Angeles, 213/556-2727

THE LONG RIDERS   United Artists, 1980, w/Bill Bryden, James Keach & Steven Philip Smith

LAURENCE KEANE
BIG MEAT EATER   New Line Cinema, 1984, w/Phil Savath & Chris Windsor

ROBERT KEATS*
Agent: Writers & Artists Agency - Los Angeles, 213/820-2240

THE CLOSER   Ion Pictures, 1991, w/Louis La Russo II

Screenplays:
FLEX
NANETTE OF THE NORTH

BARRY KEEFFE
Agent: London Management - London, 011/441/493-1610

THE LONG GOOD FRIDAY   Embassy, 1982

Screenplays:
THE TIGHTROPE MAN
THE BLUNDERER (CTF)

HARVEY KEITH
Contact: Directors Guild of America - Los Angeles, 213/289-2000

JEZEBEL'S KISS   Shapiro Glickenhaus, 1990, directed

WOODY KEITH
INITIATION: SILENT NIGHT, DEADLY NIGHT 4   Silent Films, 1990
BRIDE OF RE-ANIMATOR   Troma, 1991, w/Rick Fry

JOHN KELLEHER
Business: Liberty Films, The Forum, 74-80 Camden St., London NW1 0JL, England, 01/387-5733

EAT THE PEACH   Skouras, 1987, w/Peter Ormrod

FREDERICK KING KELLER
Agent: David Shapira & Associates - Sherman Oaks, 818/906-0322

TUCK EVERLASTING   Coe Films, 1981, directed
VAMPING   Atlantic Releasing Corporation, 1984, Story, directed

DAVID E. KELLEY*
Agent: United Talent Agency - Beverly Hills, 213/273-6700

FROM THE HIP   DEG, 1987, w/Bob Clark

Screenplays:
EDDIE'S BACK

HUGH KELLEY
CAGE   New Century/Vista, 1989

WILLIAM KELLEY*
Agent: Reece Halsey Agency - Los Angeles, 213/652-2409

WITNESS ★★   Paramount, 1985, w/Earl Wallace

Screenplays:
CALLED HOME w/Earl Wallace

D.A. KELLOGG
BITTERSWEET LOVE   Avco Embassy, 1976, w/Adrian Morrall

MARJORIE KELLOGG*
Agent: The Lantz Office - New York, 212/586-0200

TELL ME THAT YOU LOVE ME, JUNIE MOON   Paramount, 1969
THE BELL JAR   Avco Embassy, 1979

CASEY KELLY
Agent: Triad Artists, Inc. - Los Angeles, 213/556-2727

DADDY LONG LEGS (P)
ERRAND OF MERCY (P)
THE OTHER WOMAN (P)

Screenplays:
SOMEPLACE ELSE
GREENER PASTURES
LETTERS TO SCHWARTZY
BURNING TIME

CHRIS KELLY
ANY MAN'S DEATH   INI Entertainment, 1990, w/Iain Roy

MARGARET KELLY
PUBERTY BLUES   Universal Classics, 1983

THOMAS KELSEY
PURPLE HAZE   Triumph/Columbia, 1983, Story w/David Burton Morris & Victoria Wozniak

KEVIN KELTON*
Agent: ICM - Los Angeles, 213/550-4000

Screenplays:
DEVIL'S ADVOCATE

PAUL KEMBER
NOT QUITE PARADISE   New World, 1985

TOM (ZBIGNIEW) KEMPINSKI
Agent: Sanford, Skouras, Gross & Associates - Los Angeles, 213/208-2100

SEPARATION (P), also teleplay
TIMBUCTOO (P)
PAPER MARRIAGES (P)
DUET FOR ONE   Cannon, 1987, w/Andrei Konchalovsky & Jeremy Lipp, from his play

THOMAS KENEALLY
THE CHANT OF JIMMIE BLACKSMITH   New Yorker, 1978, Story
SILVER CITY   Samuel Goldwyn Company, 1985, w/Sophia Turkiewicz

PETER KENNA
THE GOOD WIFE   Atlantic Releasing Corporation, 1986

ADAM KENNEDY
THE DOVE   Paramount, 1974, w/Peter Beagle
THE DOMINO PRINCIPLE   Avco Embassy, 1977
RAISE THE TITANIC   AFD, 1980, w/Eric Hughes

BURT KENNEDY*
Agent: Sanford, Skouras, Gross & Associates - Los Angeles, 213/208-2100

SEVEN MEN FROM NOW   Batjac, 1956
FORT DOBBS   Warner Bros., 1957,
    w/George W. George
THE TALL T   Columbia, 1957
RIDE LONESOME   Columbia, 1959
YELLOWSTONE KELLY   Warner Bros., 1959
COMANCHE STATION   Columbia, 1960
THE CANADIANS   20th Century-Fox, 1961, directed
SIX BLACK HORSES   Universal-International, 1962
MAIL ORDER BRIDE   MGM, 1963, directed
THE ROUNDERS   MGM, 1965, directed
WELCOME TO HARD TIMES   MGM, 1967, directed
YOUNG BILLY YOUNG   United Artists, 1969, directed
HANNIE CAULDER   Paramount, 1971, w/David Haft as
    "Z.X. Jones," directed
THE TRAIN ROBBERS   Warner Bros., 1973, directed
THE TROUBLE WITH SPIES   DEG, 1987, directed
WHITE HUNTER, BLACK HEART   Warner Bros.,
    1990, w/James Bridges & Peter Viertel

JAMES KENNEDY
Agent: Joseph/Knight Agency - Los Angeles, 213/465-5474

THE WINNERS CIRCLE (P)
STATEN ISLAND FERRY (P)
THE GANDY DANCER (P)
SWIFTY (P)
MAD VINCENT (P)
PERFUME (P)
THE HOLDING COMPANY (P)
DOGFIGHT (P)
HIT AND RUN (P)
CEREMONY FOR THE MIDGET (Short)

Screenplays:
SUCCESS
KEY WEST
JIMMY JONES
BABY BABY BABY
BULLETPROOF
BODIE
HEARTLAND U.S.A.

LEON ISAAC KENNEDY
BODY AND SOUL   Cannon, 1981 (from a screenplay
    by Abraham Polonsky)
KNIGHTS OF THE CITY   New World, 1986

SUELLA KENNEDY
TWICE UPON A TIME (AF)   The Ladd Company/
    Warner Bros., 1983, w/Bill Couterie, John Korty &
    Charles Swenson

WILLIAM KENNEDY*
Agent: Pleshette & Green - Los Angeles, 213/465-0428

THE COTTON CLUB   Orion, 1984, w/Francis Coppola
IRONWEED   Tri-Star, 1987

Screenplays:
BILLY PHELAN'S GREATEST GAME
LEGS

TONY KENRICK*
Agent: William Morris Agency - Beverly Hills, 213/274-7451

NOBODY'S PERFEKT   Columbia, 1981

Screenplays:
MOMMA KNOWS BEST
DEAD END

BILL KERBY*
Agent: CAA - Beverly Hills, 213/288-4545

THE LAST AMERICAN HERO   20th Century-Fox, 1973
THE GRAVY TRAIN   Columbia, 1974, w/David Whitney
FIREPOWER   ITC, 1977, Story w/Michael Winner
HOOPER   Warner Bros., 1978, w/Thomas Rickman
THE ROSE   20th Century-Fox, 1979, w/Bo Goldman

Screenplays:
THE ANYTHING GUYS
STILL CRAZY w/Jim Hart
THE TOWER
MOONTRAP
TRAP DOOR
OUT OF BODY
THE WAR HORSE

RONNI KERN*
Agent: Harris & Goldberg - Los Angeles, 213/553-5200

A CHANGE OF SEASONS   20th Century-Fox, 1980,
    w/Erich Segal & Fred Segal
AMERICAN POP (AF)   Columbia, 1981

Screenplays:
REUNION
THE BUST OUT KING
FAST COMPANY
FISHTAIL
SOLD
RAISING TWAIN
SHIP MOVEMENTS
PRINCESS OF PAROLE
THE TROUBLE WITH LARRY
LOVE STORY '78

SARAH M. KERNOCHAN*
Contact: WGA - Los Angeles, 213/550-1000

9 1/2 WEEKS   MGM/UA, 1986, w/Zalman King &
    Patricia L. Knop
DANCERS   Cannon, 1987
IMPROMPTU   Hemdale, 1991

Screenplays:
DELTA OF VENUS w/Colo Tavernier O'Hagan
THE PSYCHIC

NINA V. KEROVA
LIQUID SKY   Cinevista, 1983, w/Slava Tsukerman &
    Anne Carlisle

FRANK KERR*
Contact: WGA - Los Angeles, 213/550-1000

TRUE BLOOD   Fries Entertainment, 1989, directed

Screenplays:
THE CHILDREN OF THE EARTH
THE SECOND COMING
UNDERGROUND
WAR BABY

JOHN KERSHAW
THE LONELY LADY   Universal, 1983,
   w/Shawn Randall
YELLOWHAIR AND THE FORTRESS OF GOLD
   Crown International, 1984, w/Matt Cimber

CLAUDE KERVEN
CANDY STORE   (Short)
MORTAL THOUGHTS   Columbia, 1991,
   w/William Reilly

BRADLEY KESDEN
MEATBALLS III   TMS Pictures, 1986,
   w/Michael Paseornek

ELLEN KESEND*
Agent: Lake & Douroux - Beverly Hills, 213/557-0700

Screenplays:
IN 'N' OUT
SPACE CASE
CONVICTIONS

LYLE D. KESSLER*
Agent: United Talent Agency - Beverly Hills,
   213/273-6700

ROBBERS (P)
THE WATERING PLACE (P)
POSSESSION (P)
THE VIEWING (P)
TOUCHED   Lorimar Productions/Wildwood
   Partners, 1983
ORPHANS   Lorimar, 1987, from his play
GLADIATOR   Columbia, 1991, w/Nick Kazan

Screenplays:
THE SAINT OF FORT WASHINGTON
WAYWARD ANGEL

MARGOT L. KESSLER
THE ALLNIGHTER   Universal, 1987,
   w/Tamar S. Hoffs

MERLE KESSLER
(Ian Shoales)
ZADAR! COW FROM HELL   Stone Peach
   Productions, 1989

MARCI KETCHEL
Agent: Warden & White Associates - Beverly Hills,
   213/852-1028

Screenplays:
DEAD EVEN   w/Mike Ketchel
THE DEVIL'S PLAYGROUND   w/Mike Ketchel

MIKE KETCHEL
Agent: Warden & White Associates - Beverly Hills,
   213/852-1028

Screenplays:
DEAD EVEN   w/Miarci Ketchel
THE DEVIL'S PLAYGROUND   w/Miarci Ketchel

LARRY KETRON*
Agent: United Talent Agency - Beverly Hills,
   213/273-6700

PERMANENT RECORD   Paramount, 1988, w/Jarre Fees
   & Alice Liddle
FRESH HORSES   Weintraub Entertainment, 1988,
   from his play
VITAL SIGNS   20th Century Fox, 1990,
   w/Jeb Stuart

Screenplays:
AFRICAN FACTOR
SUN BEARING DOWN
RACHEL FATE
ASIAN SHADE
DEATH OF A DIRTY BLONDE
CAPTAIN AMANDA

CHRIS KEYSER*
Agent: United Talent Agency - Beverly Hills,
   213/273-6700

Screenplays:
SISTER
THE POINT
SOUTHERN CROSS
DEAD OF SUMMER
JAG
OUT OF CHARACTER
MANHATTAN ISLAND

EDWARD KHMARA*
Agent: ICM - Los Angeles, 213/550-4000

LADYHAWKE   Warner Bros., 1985, w/Tom Mankiewicz &
   Michael Thomas
ENEMY MINE   20th Century Fox, 1985
NECROPOLIS   Empire Pictures, 1986

Screenplays:
ROLLER DISCO
THE INVITATION   w/R. Eisele
DRAGON

CALLIE KHOURI*
Agent: ICM - Los Angeles, 213/550-4000

THELMA AND LOUISE   MGM-Pathe, 1991

BRUCE KIMMEL
Agent: Stone Manners Agency - Los Angeles,
   213/275-9599

THE FIRST NUDIE MUSICAL   Paramount,
   1976, co-directed
SPACESHIP   THE CREATURE WASN'T NICE   Almi
   Cinema 5, 1982, directed

TIM KINCAID
ESCAPE FROM BAD GIRLS DORMITORY   Films Around
   the World, 1985, directed
BREEDERS   Empire Pictures, 1986, directed
MUTANT HUNT   Empire Pictures, 1986, directed
ROBOT HOLOCAUST   Empire Pictures, 1987, directed
THE OCCULTIST   Empire Pictures, 1987, directed

Ki

JEFFREY KINDLEY*
Contact: WGA - Los Angeles, 213/550-1000

THE HITCHHIKERS (P)

Screenplays:
WESTLANDER
IS THERE LIFE AFTER HIGH SCHOOL?
FIRST OFFENDER (CTF)

LARRY L. KING
THE BEST LITTLE WHOREHOUSE IN TEXAS
   Universal, 1982, w/Peter Masterson, from their play

LAURA KING*
Agent: United Talent Agency - Beverly Hills, 213/273-6700

Screenplays:
BLESSING IN DISGUISE
CHEEK TO CHEEK

LESLIE KING*
Agent: William Morris Agency - Beverly Hills, 213/274-7451

SON OF DARKNESS: TO DIE FOR II   Trimark Pictures, 1991

RICK KING
Agent: Writers & Artists Agency - Los Angeles, 213/820-2240

HARD CHOICES   Lorimar, 1986, directed
HOTSHOT   International Film Marketing, 1987, w/Joe Sauter, directed
POINT BREAK   20th Century Fox, 1991, Story w/Peter Iliff

Screenplays:
WATCHING THE DETECTIVE

ROBERT KING*
Agent: Shorr, Stille & Associates - Los Angeles, 213/659-6160

THE NEST   Concorde, 1987
UNDER THE BOARDWALK   New World, 1989
BLOODFIST   Concorde, 1989
PHANTOM OF THE MALL: ERIC'S REVENGE
   Fries Entertainment, 1989, w/Tony Michelman & Scott J. Schneid

Screenplays:
EL DORADO

STEPHEN KING*
Agent: CAA - Beverly Hills, 213/288-4545

CREEPSHOW   Warner Bros., 1982
STEPHEN KING'S CAT'S EYE   MGM/UA, 1985
SILVER BULLET   Paramount, 1985
MAXIMUM OVERDRIVE   DEG, 1986, directed
CREEPSHOW 2   New World, 1987, Story
PET SEMATARY   Paramount, 1989

Screenplays:
SLEEPWALKERS

ZALMAN KING*
Agent: Triad Artists, Inc. - Los Angeles, 213/556-2727

ROADIE   United Artists, 1980, Story w/Big Boy Medlin, Alan Rudolph & Michael Ventura
9 1/2 WEEKS   MGM/UA, 1986, w/Sarah Kernochan & Patricia L. Knop
WILDFIRE   Cinema Group, 1988, w/Matthew Bright
TWO MOON JUNCTION   Lorimar, 1988, directed
WILD ORCHID   Triumph, 1990, w/Patricia L. Knop, directed
WILD ORCHID II: BLUE MOVIE BLUE   Vision International, 1991, directed

Screenplays:
HOT w/Patricia L. Knop
BAKERSFIELD BLUES
ANGELS FLIGHT
GUITAR DOLLS
STREET HEAT
FIRST AMERICAN REBEL
COMPOSURE
GOD'S HEAD
PULL THE TRIGGER
GOOD-BYE

JAMES GREGORY KINGSTON*
Contact: WGA - Los Angeles, 213/550-1000

TURK 182   20th Century Fox, 1985, w/Denis Hamill & John Hamill

ERNEST KINOY*
Agent: William Morris Agency - New York, 212/586-5100

BROTHER JOHN   Columbia, 1970
BUCK AND THE PREACHER   Columbia, 1971
LEADBELLY   Paramount, 1976
MURROW (CTF)   HBO Premiere Films/Titus Productions/TVS Ltd. Productions, 1986
WHITE WATER SUMMER   Columbia, 1987, w/Mayna Starr
CHERNOBYL: THE FINAL WARNING (CTF)   Roger Gimbel Productions/Carolco Television, 1991

WILLIAM KINSOLVING*
Agent: ICM - Los Angeles, 213/550-4000

Screenplays:
BORN WITH THE CENTURY
JADE

GEORGE KIRGO*
Agent: CAA - Beverly Hills, 213/288-4545

RED LINE 7000   Paramount, 1965
SPINOUT   MGM, 1966, w/Theodore J. Flicker
DON'T MAKE WAVES   MGM, 1967, w/Ira Wallach
VOICES   Hemdale, 1973, w/Robert Enders

D. SHONE KIRKPATRICK
Agent: United Talent Agency - Beverly Hills, 213/273-6700

BROTHERS IN ARMS   Ablo, 1989

Screenplays:
HATTERAS
WHITER SHADE OF PALE
SMITH AND WESSON

BRUCE KIRSCHBAUM*
Agent: Writers & Artists Agency - Los Angeles, 213/820-2240

BACK TO THE BEACH   Paramount, 1987, Story
   w/James Komack & B.W.L. Norton

Screenplays:
MISTY BLUE RIVER
PIGSKINS (shared)

DAVID KIRSCHNER*
Agent: William Morris Agency - Beverly Hills, 213/274-7451

AN AMERICAN TAIL (AF)   Universal, 1986, Story
   w/Judy Freudberg & Tony Geiss

ROY KISSIN
ON THE EDGE   Skouras Pictures, 1986, Story
   w/Rob Nilsson

MARTIN KITROSSER
FRIDAY THE 13TH PART 3   Paramount, 1982,
   w/Carol Watson
MEATBALLS PART II   Tri-Star, 1984, Story
   w/Carol Watson
FRIDAY THE 13TH - A NEW BEGINNING   Paramount,
   1985, w/David Cohen & Danny Steinmann

ROBERT KLANE*
Agent: ICM - Los Angeles, 213/550-4000

WHERE'S POPPA?   United Artists, 1970
EVERY LITTLE CROOK AND NANNY   MGM, 1972,
   w/Jonathan Axelrod & Cy Howard
FIRE SALE   20th Century-Fox, 1977
THANK GOD IT'S FRIDAY   Columbia, 1978, directed
UNFAITHFULLY YOURS   20th Century Fox, 1984,
   w/Valerie Curtin & Barry Levinson
THE MAN WITH ONE RED SHOE   20th Century
   Fox, 1985
NATIONAL LAMPOON'S EUROPEAN VACATION
   Warner Bros., 1985, w/John Hughes
WALK LIKE A MAN   MGM/UA, 1987
WEEKEND AT BERNIE'S   20th Century Fox, 1989

Screenplays:
FOLKS
JURY DUTY
POST OFFICE
TRANSYLVANIA MUSICAL
LA CAGE AUX FOLLES, U.S.A.
THE HORSE IS DEAD
RUBY RED
GREASIER
PLAY MONEY

RIC KLASS
ELLIOT FAUMAN, PH.D.   Taurus Entertainment,
   1990, directed

ANDREW KLAVAN
Agent: Harris & Goldberg - Los Angeles, 213/553-5200

A SHOCK TO THE SYSTEM   Corsair Pictures, 1990

Screenplays:
ROUGH JUSTICE
DON'T SAY A WORD

MITCHELL S. KLEBANOFF*
Agent: The Irv Schechter Company - Beverly Hills, 213/278-8070

DISORDERLIES   Warner Bros., 1987, w/Mark Feldberg

Screenplays:
BEVERLY HILLS NINJA   w/Mark Feldberg

DENNIS KLEIN*
Agent: United Talent Agency - Beverly Hills, 213/273-6700

Screenplays:
SEX & VIOLENCE
THE GOOD DOCTOR   (directing)
LAST DANCE OF THE GOLDEN WEST (CTF)

JAIME B. KLEIN
PANDEMONIUM   MGM/UA, 1982, w/Richard Whitley

Screenplays:
ROAD TO RUIN   w/Richard Whitley
REGATTA   w/Richard Whitley
MR. NICE GUY
760 NO. MAPLE
MILLION DOLLAR TOWN
THINGS INVISIBLE TO SEE

RICHERD KLEINBERG
Contact: Bloom, Dekom & Hergott - Los Angeles, 213/859-6820

Screenplays:
SLEIGHT OF HAND
DEAD GIVEAWAY
PILOT ERROR

AVI KLEINBERGER*
Contact: WGA - Los Angeles, 213/550-1000

AMERICAN NINJA   Cannon, 1985, Story w/Gideon Amir
P.O.W. THE ESCAPE   Cannon, 1986, Story
   w/Gideon Amir

HARRY KLEINER*
Business Manager: Joel Gotler, 213/275-6330

FALLEN ANGEL   20th Century-Fox, 1945
THE STREET WITH NO NAME   20th Century-Fox, 1948
RED SKIES OF MONTANA   20th Century-Fox, 1952
KANGAROO   20th Century-Fox, 1952
SALOME   Columbia, 1953, w/Jesse Lasky Jr.
CARMEN JONES   20th Century-Fox, 1954
THE VIOLENT MEN   ROUGH COMPANY
   Columbia, 1955
THE GARMENT JUNGLE   Columbia, 1957
ICE PALACE   Warner Bros., 1960
A FEVER IN THE BLOOD   Warner Bros., 1960,
   w/Roy Huggins
FANTASTIC VOYAGE   20th Century-Fox, 1966
BULLITT   Warner Bros., 1968, w/Alan R. Trustman
LE MANS   National General, 1970
EXTREME PREJUDICE   Tri-Star, 1987,
   w/Deric Washburn
RED HEAT   Tri-Star, 1988, w/Walter Hill & Troy
   Kennedy Martin

KI

MAGGIE KLEINMAN*
Agent: Susan Smith & Associates - Beverly Hills, 213/852-4777

WELCOME HOME   Columbia, 1989

Screenplays:
WHITE HUNTERS
CAUGHT DEAD   w/Diane Wagner
FINAL BALLOT
SLUMLORD
PRINCE CHARMING

CARL D. KLEINSCHMIDT*
Agent: ICM - Los Angeles, 213/550-4000

MIDDLE AGE CRAZY   20th Century-Fox, 1980

RANDAL KLEISER*
Contact: Schneider/Shannon, Manager - 818/509-0844
Business: Randal Kleiser Productions, 3050 Runyan Canyon Road, Los Angeles, CA, 90046, 213/851-5224

STREET PEOPLE   American International, 1976, w/others
SUMMER LOVERS   Filmways, 1982, directed
NORTH SHORE   Universal, 1987, Story w/William Phelps

WALTER KLENHARD*
Agent: David Shapira & Associates - Sherman Oaks, 818/906-0322

SWEET POISON (CTF)   Smart Money Productions Inc./MTE, 1991

Screenplays:
GOODNIGHT MOON
DANCER'S TOUCH

RICHARD C. KLETTER*
Agent: CAA - Beverly Hills, 213/288-4545

TEACH 109 (Short), directed
NEVER CRY WOLF   Buena Vista, 1983, w/Sam Hamm & Curtis Lee Hanson
THE BLACK STALLION RETURNS   MGM/UA, 1983, w/Jerome Kass

Screenplays:
THE VICTOR   w/David Chaskin
AMERICAN EXPRESS   w/Craig Bolotin
QUINT'S LAST CASE   w/E. Ellison, R.Nilsson & S. Wax
FLYING
DIAMONDS

MAX KLEVEN*
Contact: WGA - Los Angeles, 213/550-1000

RUCKUS   *THE LONER*   New World, 1981, directed

STEVEN E. KLINE*
Contact: WGA - Los Angeles, 213/550-1000

BORDERLINE   AFD, 1980, w/Jerrold Freedman

WOODY KLING
HERE COME THE LITTLES   Atlantic Releasing Corporation, 1985

JUDSON KLINGER*
Agent: Stone Manners Agency - Los Angeles, 213/275-9599

ENDANGERED SPECIES   MGM/UA, 1982, Story w/Richard Woods

STEVEN KLOVES*
Agent: United Talent Agency - Beverly Hills, 213/273-6700

RACING WITH THE MOON   Paramount, 1984
THE FABULOUS BAKER BOYS ★   20th Century Fox, 1989, directed

Screenplays:
SWINGS
SANTEE

NIGEL KNEALE
Contact: British Academy of Film & Television Arts, 195 Piccadilly, London W1, England, 71/734-0022

THE ABOMINABLE SNOWMAN   20th Century-Fox, 1957
ENEMY FROM SPACE   *QUATERMASS II*   Hammer, 1957, w/Val Guest
LOOK BACK IN ANGER   Warner Bros., 1958
THE ENTERTAINER   British Lion, 1960, w/John Osborne
HMS DEFIANT   *DAMN THE DEFIANT*   Columbia, 1962, w/Edmund H. North
FIRST MEN IN THE MOON   Columbia, 1964, w/Jan Read
THE DEVIL'S OWN   *THE WITCHES*   Hammer, 1966
FIVE MILLION YEARS TO EARTH   *QUATERMASS AND THE PIT*   Hammer, 1967

CHRISTOPHER KNIGHT
Business: Knight-Tyson Productions, 127 Broadway - Suite 220, Santa Monica, CA 90401, 213/395-7100

WINNERS TAKE ALL   Apollo Pictures, 1987, Story w/Tom Tatum

PATRICIA LOUISIANNA KNOP*
Agent: Triad Artists, Inc. - Los Angeles, 213/556-2727

THE PASSOVER PLOT   Atlas, 1977, w/Millard Cohan
LADY OSCAR   Toho, 1978
SILENCE OF THE NORTH   Universal, 1982
9 1/2 WEEKS   MGM/UA, 1986, w/Sarah Kernochan & Zalman King
SIESTA   Lorimar, 1987
WILD ORCHID   Triumph, 1990, w/Zalman King

Screenplays:
FOUR DAYS IN FEBRUARY
HOT   w/Zalman King
THE TOURIST   w/Clair Noto
FOR THE FIRST TIME

CHRISTOPHER E. KNOPF*
Agent: William Morris Agency - Beverly Hills, 213/274-7451

THE TALL STRANGER   Allied Artists, 1957
TWENTY MILLION MILES TO EARTH   Columbia, 1957, w/Bob Williams

EMPEROR OF THE NORTH POLE *SHACK!* 20th
   Century-Fox, 1973
POSSE Paramount, 1975, w/William Roberts
THE CHOIRBOYS Universal, 1977
SCOTT JOPLIN Universal, 1977

Screenplays:
SCARLET & THE BLACK

C. J. KOCH
THE YEAR OF LIVING DANGEROUSLY MGM/UA,
   1983, w/David Williamson & Peter Weir

HERMAN KOCH
WINGS OF FAME First Floor Features, 1990,
   w/Otakar Votocek

HOWARD KOCH*
Contact: WGA - Los Angeles, 213/550-1000

THE SEA HAWK Warner Bros., 1940, w/Seton I. Miller
CASABLANCA ★ Warner Bros., 1943, w/Julius J.
   Epstein & Philip G. Epstein
RHAPSODY IN BLUE Warner Bros., 1945,
   w/Elliot Paul
THREE STRANGERS Warner Bros., 1946,
   w/John Huston
NO SAD SONGS FOR ME Columbia, 1950
THE THIRTEENTH LETTER 20th Century-Fox, 1951
THE GREENGAGE SUMMER *LOSS OF INNOCENCE*
   Columbia, 1961
THE WAR LOVER Columbia, 1962
633 SQUADRON United Artists, 1964,
   w/James Clavell
THE FOX Claridge, 1968, w/Lewis John Carlino

LAIRD KOENIG*
Agent: Paul Kohner, Inc. - Los Angeles, 213/550-1060

SCENE OF THE CRIME (P)
RED SUN National General, 1972, w/Denne Bart
   Petitclerc, William Roberts & Lawrence Roman
THE LITTLE GIRL WHO LIVES DOWN THE LANE
   American International, 1977
SIDNEY SHELDON'S BLOODLINE Paramount, 1979
INCHON! MGM/UA, 1982, w/Robin Moore
TWIST OF FATE Condor Productions/Nelson
   Entertainment, 1991

Screenplays:
TENNESSEE NIGHTS w/Nicholas Gessner
RISING SUN

DAVID KOEPP*
Agent: United Talent Agency - Beverly Hills,
   213/273-6700

APARTMENT ZERO Skouras Pictures, 1989,
   w/Martin Donovan
BAD INFLUENCE Trans World Entertainment, 1990
TOY SOLDIERS Tri-Star, 1991, w/Daniel Petrie Jr.

Screenplays:
DEATH BECOMES HER w/Martin Donovan
ADVENTURE I w/John Kamps
DARK ANGEL w/John Kamps & Jonathan Tydor
CARLITO'S WAY

HOWARD KOHN*
Agent: Thal Literary Management - Los Angeles,
   213/659-4946

ROLLOVER Orion/Warner Bros., 1981, Story w/David
   Shaber & David Weir

JOHN KOHN*
Contact: WGA - Los Angeles, 213/550-1000

THE SIEGE OF THE SAXONS Columbia, 1963,
   w/Jud Kinberg
THE COLLECTOR ★ Columbia, 1965, w/Stanley Mann
GOLDEN GIRL Avco Embassy, 1979
SHANGHAI SURPRISE MGM/UA, 1986, w/Robert Bentley

AMOS KOLLEK
Contact: Israel Film Centre, Ministry of Industry & Trade, 30
   Agron Street, P.O. Box 299, Jerusalem, Israel, 02/210297

GOODBYE NEW YORK Castle Hill Productions,
   1985, directed
FOREVER, LULU Tri-Star, 1987, directed
HIGH STAKES Vestron, 1990, directed

XAVIER KOLLER
Agent: ICM - Los Angeles, 213/550-4000

JOURNEY OF HOPE Miramax, 1990, directed

JAMES KOMACK*
Agent: ICM - Los Angeles, 213/550-4000

BACK TO THE BEACH Paramount, 1987, Story w/Bruce
   Kirschbaum & B.W.L. Norton

ANDREI KONCHALOVSKY*
Agent: CAA - Beverly Hills, 213/288-4545

ANDREI RUBLEV Mosfilm, 1966, w/Andrei Tarkovsky
A NEST OF GENTRY Corinth, 1969, w/Valentin
   Yezhov, directed
MARIA'S LOVERS Cannon, 1984, w/Gerard Brach,
   Marjorie David & Paul Zindel, directed
DUET FOR ONE Cannon, 1987, w/Tom Kempinski &
   Jeremy Lipp, directed
SHY PEOPLE Cannon, 1987, w/Gerard Brach & Marjorie
   David, directed
THE INNER CIRCLE Columbia, 1991, w/Anatoli
   Usov, directed

Screenplays:
TATIANA w/Floyd Byars

HARRY KONDOLEON
Agent: William Morris Agency - Beverly Hills, 213/274-7451

ZERO POSITIVE (P)

Screenplays:
IT AND EVERYTHING ELSE

JACKIE KONG
Contact: Bob Brenner, Esq. - Los Angeles, 213/553-2525

THE BEING BFV Films, 1983, directed
NIGHT PATROL New World, 1984, w/Murray Langston &
   Bill Osco, directed

Ko

LAWRENCE KONNER*
Agent: CAA - Beverly Hills, 213/288-4545
Business: Konner-Rosenthal, Paramount Pictures, 213/956-5909

THE LEGEND OF BILLIE JEAN   Tri-Star, 1985, w/Mark Rosenthal
THE JEWEL OF THE NILE   20th Century Fox, 1985, w/Mark Rosenthal
SUPERMAN IV: THE QUEST FOR PEACE   Warner Bros., 1987, w/Mark Rosenthal
THE IN CROWD   Orion, 1988, w/Mark Rosenthal
DESPERATE HOURS   Warner Bros., 1990, w/Mark Rosenthal & Joseph Hayes

Screenplays:
GALE FORCE w/Mark Rosenthal & David A. Chappe
FORTRESS w/Mark Rosenthal
THE HIT w/Mark Rosenthal

JEFFREY S. KONVITZ*
Contact: WGA - Los Angeles, 213/550-1000

THE SENTINEL   Universal, 1976, w/Michael Winner
GORP   Filmways, 1980

HOWARD R. KORDER*
Agent: The Tantleff Office - New York, 212/941-3939

BOYS' LIFE (P)   also screenplay
SEARCH AND DESTROY (P)
LIP SERVICE (CTF)   Cinehaus, 1988, from his play

Screenplays:
MRS. & MR. KELLY

MARI KORNHAUSER
Agent: William Morris Agency - Beverly Hills, 213/274-7451

ZANDALEE   New Line Cinema, 1991

Screenplays:
THEY DON'T DANCE MUCH
HEART AND SOUL
THE TORRID ZONE
SCORPIONS
BURMA

JOHN V. KORTY*
Agent: Richland/Wunsch/Hohman Agency - Los Angeles, 213/278-1955

CRAZY QUILT   Farallon, 1965, directed
FUNNYMAN   New Yorker, 1967, w/Peter Bonerz, directed
OLIVER'S STORY   Paramount, 1978, w/Erich Segal, directed
TWICE UPON A TIME (AF)   The Ladd Company/Warner Bros., 1983, w/Charles Swenson, Suella Kennedy & Bill Couturie, co-directed

ANNIE KORZEN
NOBODY'S PERFECT   Moviestore Entertainment, 1990, w/Joel Block

BOB KOSBERG*
Business: Robert Kosberg Productions, Tri-Star Pictures, 213/280-4774

IN THE MOOD   Lorimar, 1987, Story w/Phil Alden Robinson & David Simon

KEN KOSER*
Contact: WGA - New York, 212/245-6180

SUDIE AND SIMPSON (CTF)   Freed/Laufer, 1990, w/Sara Flanigan Carter

RON KOSLOW*
Agent: CAA - Beverly Hills, 213/288-4545

LIFEGUARD   Paramount, 1976
FIRSTBORN   Paramount, 1984
INTO THE NIGHT   Universal, 1985

Screenplays:
WOLF & ROSE
THE GLORY BOYS
TAPPING THE SOURCE

JOHN H. KOSTMAYER*
Agent: InterTalent - Los Angeles, 213/858-6200

WHERE'S THE BODY (P)
ON THE MONEY (P)
I LOVE YOU TO DEATH   Tri-Star, 1990

Screenplays:
BRITTLE INNINGS

TED KOTCHEFF
Agent: CAA - Beverly Hills, 213/288-4545

NORTH DALLAS FORTY   Paramount, 1979, w/Peter Gent & Frank Yablans, directed

WILLIAM KOTZWINKLE
Agent: The Gersh Agency - Beverly Hills, 213/274-6611

A NIGHTMARE ON ELM STREET PART IV: THE DREAM MASTER   New Line Cinema, 1988, Story w/Brian Helgeland
BOOK OF LOVE   New Line Cinema, 1991

Screenplays:
NIGHTINGALE AND THE SATIN WOMAN

JIM KOUF*
Agent: ICM - Los Angeles, 213/550-4000
Business: Kouf-Bigelow Productions, Walt Disney Pictures, 818/560-5103

PINK MOTEL   New Image, 1982
UTILITIES *GETTING EVEN* New World, 1983, w/David Greenwalt
WACKO   Jensen Farley Pictures, 1983, w/David Greenwalt, Dana Olsen & Michael Spound
CLASS   Orion, 1983, w/David Greenwalt
UP THE CREEK   Orion, 1983
AMERICAN DREAMER   Warner Bros., 1984, w/David Greenwalt
SECRET ADMIRER   Orion, 1985, w/David Greenwalt

SHAKER RUN   Challenge Film Corporation, 1985,
    w/David Greenwalt
MIRACLES   Orion, 1986, directed
STAKEOUT   Buena Vista, 1987
DISORGANIZED CRIME   Buena Vista, 1989, directed

Screenplays:
GREED w/David Greenwalt
AIRPLANE III w/David Greenwalt
BIGAMY w/David Greenwalt
THE LAKE w/David Greenwalt
HONEYMOON w/David Greenwalt

EDWARD KOVACH
THINK BIG   Concorde, 1990, w/David Tausik &
    Jon Turtletaub

PAUL KOVAL
Agent: The Irv Schechter Company - Beverly Hills,
    213/278-8070

Screenplays:
HEAVEN SENT w/Ed Fitzgerald

JANET KOVALCIK
Agent: Triad Artists, Inc. - Los Angeles, 213/556-2727

Screenplays:
DEAR DIGBY
THE WORLD'S OLDEST LIVING BRIDESMAID
AMERICAN BEAUTY
THE SHOWER
AFTER ALL THESE YEARS
DURNER'S SPRING
THE JAMAICAN AND THE RAISIN
SENIOR YEAR
STANDING IN THE SHADOWS OF LOVE
A WOMAN'S PLACE

RON KOVIC
Agent: ICM - Los Angeles, 213/550-4000

BORN ON THE FOURTH OF JULY ★   Universal,
    1989, w/Oliver Stone

MICHAEL KOZOLL*
Contact: 213/202-3377

FIRST BLOOD   Orion, 1982, w/William Sackheim &
    Sylvester Stallone
THE HARD WAY   Universal, 1991, Story
    w/Lem Dobbs

Screenplays:
NATURAL ACTS

ROBERT KRAFT
HUDSON HAWK   Tri-Star, 1991, Story w/Bruce Willis

ROBERT KRAFT*
Agent: Writers & Artists Agency - Los Angeles,
    213/820-2240

Screenplays:
AS YOUNG AS YOU FEEL w/Ted Pushinsky
MAKING MONEY w/Ted Pushinsky

ANDRZEJ KRAKOWSKI
Agent: The Brandt Company - Studio City, 818/506-7747

THE CALIFORNIA REICH (FD) ★   Yasny Talking
    Pictures, 1975
TRIUMPH OF THE SPIRIT   Nova International Films,
    1989, w/Laurence Heath
EMINENT DOMAIN   Triumph Releasing, 1991,
    w/Richard Gregson

Screenplays:
THE WEDDING WAS BEAUTIFUL, PEOPLE WERE CRYING
LANTON MILLS

MARK KRAM*
Contact: WGA - Los Angeles, 213/550-1000

Screenplays:
BLOW AWAY w/David Loucka & Dean Selmier
JOEY FAMOUS w/David Loucka
THE DREAM CASE w/David Loucka
WEEKEND WARRIORS w/David Loucka
MARATHON

LARRY KRAMER*
Agent: William Morris Agency - New York, 212/586-5100

THE NORMAL HEART (P)
WOMEN IN LOVE ★   United Artists, 1969
LOST HORIZON   Columbia, 1972

RICHARD L. KRAMER*
Agent: CAA - Beverly Hills, 213/288-4545

Screenplays:
LIBBY
PETTING ZOO
SECOND HEAVEN
ALUMNI
SAVING GRACE
BEST IS YET TO BE

SUSAN KRAMER*
Agent: William Morris Agency - Beverly Hills, 213/274-7451

Screenplays:
ISN'T IT ROMANTIC

SARA KRANE*
Agent: The Roberts Company - Los Angeles, 213/552-7800

Screenplays:
THE RED FERRARI
*SHE SAID SHE LIKED THE WAY SHE HELD THE
    MICROPHONE*
DIRTY DANCING II

KEN KRAUSS*
Agent: Camden-ITG - Los Angeles, 213/289-2700

BUY AND CELL   Empire Pictures, 1988, w/Merrin Holt

STEVEN M. KRAUZER*
Contact: WGA - Los Angeles, 213/550-1000

COCAINE WARS   Concorde/Cinema Group, 1985
SWEET REVENGE   Concorde, 1987, w/Tim McCoy

Kr
FILM WRITERS GUIDE

STUART G. KREISMAN*
Agent: Broder-Kurland-Webb-Uffner - Los Angeles, 213/656-9262

Screenplays:
STARWRECK w/Chris Cluess
THE LAST HIGH SCHOOL MOVIE w/Chris Cluess

EDDIE KRELL
DELIRIUM   Odyssey Pictures, 1980, Story w/Jim Loew

STU KRIEGER*
Agent: The Daniel Ostroff Agency - Los Angeles, 213/278-2020

WHERE THE BOYS ARE   Tri-Star, 1984, w/Jeff Burkhart
THE LAND BEFORE TIME (AF)   Universal, 1988

Screenplays:
BE TRUE TO YOUR SCHOOL
MAPLE & ELM
KINFOLK
SHOOT THE DEGROOTS
ONCE UPON A MARRIAGE
A TROLL IN CENTRAL PARK (AF)

PETER A. KRIKES*
Agent: William Morris Agency - Beverly Hills, 213/274-7451

STAR TREK IV: THE VOYAGE HOME   Paramount, 1986, w/Harve Bennett, Steve Meerson & Nicholas Meyer
BACK TO THE BEACH   Paramount, 1987, w/Steve Meerson & Christopher Thompson
DOUBLE IMPACT   Columbia, 1991, Story w/Steve Meerson, Sheldon Lettich & Jean-Claude Van Damme

Screenplays:
THAT'S LIFE, 1986 w/Steve Meerson
A NEW KIND OF LOVE w/Steve Meerson
RIVER OAKS w/Steve Meerson
THE LONG WAY HOME w/Steve Meerson
ON GUARD w/Steve Meerson
19 PURCHASE STREET w/Steve Meerson
PLANET OF THE TEENAGERS w/Steve Meerson
MONEY FROM THE SKY w/Steve Meerson

R. TIMOTHY KRING*
Agent: ICM - Los Angeles, 213/550-4000

TEEN WOLF TOO   Atlantic Releasing Corporation, 1987

Screenplays:
SUBLET
SLIPPED DISC

MARC KRISTAL
TORN APART   Castle Hill Productions, 1990

MICHAEL H. KROHN*
Agent: William Morris Agency - Beverly Hills, 213/274-7451

Screenplays
GREEN LANTERN
GUNSLINGER

STEPHEN D. KRONISH*
Agent: Lake & Douroux - Beverly Hills, 213/557-0700

Screenplays:
DEADLY HONEYMOON

JEREMY JOE KRONSBERG*
Business Manager: Leonard Granger, 213/858-1573

EVERY WHICH WAY BUT LOOSE   Warner Bros., 1978
GOING APE!   Paramount, 1981, directed

Screenplays:
POINT AFTER
LOVE LUCK

SANDY KROOPF*
Agent: William Morris Agency - Beverly Hills, 213/274-7451

BIRDY   Tri-Star, 1984, w/Jack Behr

Screenplays:
B STREET w/Jack Behr
PUBLIC SECRETS w/Jack Behr
MATINEE w/Jack Behr
RUNAWAY w/Jack Behr
ALIAS EDDIE SHERBERT w/Jack Behr
WITNESS TO WAR w/Jack Behr
BOOK OF EPPE w/Jack Behr
THE MONKEY WRENCH GANG w/Jack Behr
PERFECT COUNTERFEIT w/Jack Behr
SPEECHLESS w/Jack Behr
SERIOUS LIVING w/Jack Behr
IT HAPPENED TOMORROW w/Jack Behr

MARK KRUGER*
Agent: Richland/Wunsch/Hohman Agency - Los Angeles, 213/278-1955

Screenplays:
COLD EYE w/Jeffrey Hammond

LAWRENCE KUBIK*
Business: The Kubik Company - Los Angeles, 213/859-9777

DEATH BEFORE DISHONOR   New World, 1987, w/John Gatliff

STANLEY KUBRICK*
Contact: Loeb & Loeb - Los Angeles, 213/552-7774

FEAR AND DESIRE   Joseph Burstyn, Inc., 1954, directed
KILLER'S KISS   United Artists, 1955, directed
THE KILLING   United Artists, 1956, directed
PATHS OF GLORY   United Artists, 1957, w/Calder Willingham & Jim Thompson, directed
DR. STRANGELOVE, OR: HOW I LEARNED TO STOP WORRYING AND LOVE THE BOMB ★   Columbia, 1964, w/Peter George & Terry Southern, directed
2001: A SPACE ODYSSEY ★   MGM, 1968, w/Arthur C. Clarke, directed
A CLOCKWORK ORANGE ★   Warner Bros., 1971, directed
BARRY LYNDON ★   Warner Bros., 1975, directed
THE SHINING   Warner Bros., 1980, w/Diane Johnson, directed
FULL METAL JACKET ★   Warner Bros., 1987, w/Gustav Hasford & Michael Herr, directed

NORBERT KUCKELMANN
MAN UNDER SUSPICION   Spectrafilm, 1985, directed

ROBERT KUHN
Agent: The Wright Concept - Hollywood, 213/461-3844

Screenplays:
ROYAL COACH TAXI

BERNIE KUKOFF*
Agent: Robinson, Weintraub, Gross & Associates -
    Los Angeles, 213/653-5802

JOHNNY DANGEROUSLY   20th Century Fox, 1984,
    w/Harry Colomby, Jeff Harris & Norman Steinberg

STEVEN M. KUNES*
Agent: Shapiro/Lichtman - Los Angeles, 213/859-8877

Screenplays:
RUM RUNNERS
DINNER AT THE HOMESICK RESTAURANT
LOOK HOMEWARD ANGEL
A CONFEDERACY OF DUNCES
LOVE, ROGER

DARRYL KUNTZ
DAKOTA   Miramax, 1988, w/Lynn Kuntz

LYNN KUNTZ
DAKOTA   Miramax, 1988, w/Darryl Kuntz

HANIF KUREISHI
Agent: The Artists Agency - Los Angeles, 213/277-7779

MY BEAUTIFUL LAUNDRETTE ★   Orion Classics, 1986
SAMMY AND ROSIE GET LAID   Cinecom, 1987

Screenplays:
LONDON KILLS ME (directing)

JOHN A. KURI
Business: Sheffield Entertainment Corporation, 16133
    Ventura Blvd., Suite 700, Encino, CA, 91436,
    818/501-8471

CAPTIVE HEARTS   MGM/UA, 1987, w/Pat Morita

CARL L. KURLANDER*
Agent: William Morris Agency - Beverly Hills, 213/274-7451

ST. ELMO'S FIRE   Columbia, 1985, w/Joel Schumacher

Screenplays:
BABY TALK
HANDSOME DEVILS

AKIRA KUROSAWA
Contact: Directors Guild of Japan, Tsukada Building,
    8-33 Udagawa-cho, Shibuya-ku, Tokyo 150,
    Japan, 3/461-4411

UMA   1941, shared
SEISHUN NO KIRYU   1942
TSUBA NO GAIKA   1942
SANSHIRO SUGATA   Toho, 1943, shared, directed
THE MOST BEAUTIFUL   Toho, 1944, directed
DOHYO-MATSURI   1944
SANSHIRO SUGATA - PART TWO   Toho, 1945, directed
THE MEN WHO TREAD ON THE TIGER'S TAIL   Toho,
    1945, directed
APPARE ISSHIN TASUKE   1945, shared
NO REGRETS FOR OUR YOUTH   Toho, 1946,
    shared, directed
ONE WONDERFUL SUNDAY   Toho, 1947,
    shared, directed
TO THE END OF THE SILVER MOUNTAINS   1947, shared
FOUR LOVE STORIES   1947, "First Love"
THE PORTRAIT   1948
DRUNKEN ANGEL   Toho, 1948, shared, directed
THE QUIET DUEL   Daiei, 1949, shared, directed
STRAY DOG   Toho, 1949, shared, directed
YAKOMAN AND TETSU   1949
THE LADY FROM HELL   1949
SCANDAL   Shochiku, 1959, shared, directed
RASHOMON   RKO Radio, 1950, shared, directed
ESCAPE AT DAWN   1950
TETSU "JIBA"   1950
FENCING MASTER   1950
THE IDIOT   Schochiku, 1951, shared, directed
BEYOND LOVE AND HATE   1951
THE DEN OF BEASTS   1951
THE DUEL AT KAGIYA CORNER   1951
IKIRU   Brandon, 1952, w/Hideo Oguni & Shinobu
    Hashimoto, directed
SEVEN SAMURAI   Landmark Releasing, 1954, Hideo
    Oguni & Shinobu Hashimoto, directed
I LIVE IN FEAR   Brandon, 1955, shared, directed
THRONE OF BLOOD *THE CASTLE OF THE SPIDER'S
    WEB*   Brandon, 1957, w/others, directed
THE LOWER DEPTHS   Brandon, 1957, shared, directed
300 MILES THROUGH ENEMY LINES   1957
THE HIDDEN FORTRESS *THREE BAD MEN IN A HIDDEN
    FORTRESS*   Toho, 1958, shared, directed
THE BAD SLEEP WELL   Toho, 1960, shared, directed
THE SAGA OF THE VAGABOND   1690, shared
YOJIMBO   Seneca International, 1961, shared, directed
SANJURO   Toho, 1962, shared, directed
HIGH AND LOW   East West Classics, 1963, w/Hideo
    Oguni, Ryuzo Kikushima & Ejiro Hisaito, directed
RED BEARD   Toho, 1965, w/Masato Ide & Hideo
    Oguni, directed
DODES 'KA'DEN   Janus, 1970, shared, directed
DERSU UZALA   New World, 1975, shared, directed
KAGEMUSHA: THE SHADOW WARRIOR   20th Century-
    Fox, 1980, w/Masato Ide, directed
RAN   Orion Classics, 1985, w/Hideo Oguni &
    Masato Ide, directed
HORSE   R5/S8, 1986, w/Kajiro Yamamoto
AKIRA KUROSAWA'S DREAMS   Warner Bros.,
    1990, directed
RHAPSODY IN AUGUST   Odyssey Entertainment,
    1991, directed

PAUL KURTA
Contact: Creative Group Productions, 6126 Rhodes Avenue,
    North Hollywood, CA 91606, 818/508-8212

KEY EXCHANGE   20th Century Fox, 1985,
    w/John Romano

ANDREW KURTZMAN
Agent: InterTalent - Los Angeles, 213/858-6200

NUMBER ONE WITH A BULLET   Cannon, 1987, w/Gail
    Morgan Hickman, Rob Riley & James Belushi
SEE NO EVIL, HEAR NO EVIL   Tri-Star, 1989, w/Earl
    Barret, Arne Sultan, Eliot Wald & Gene Wilder

DIANE KURYS
Agent: Triad Artists, Inc. - Los Angeles, 213/556-2727

PEPPERMINT SODA *DIABOLO MENTHE* New Yorker, 1977, directed
COCKTAIL MOLOTOV Putnam Square, 1980, directed
ENTRE NOUS *COUP DE FOUDRE* United Artists Classics, 1983, directed
A MAN IN LOVE Cinecom, 1987, w/Israel Horovitz, directed
C'EST LA VIE Samuel Goldwyn Company, 1990, w/Alain le Henry, directed

RON KURZ*
Contact: WGA - Los Angeles, 213/550-1000

FRIDAY THE 13TH PART 2 Paramount, 1981

FRAN RUBEL KUZUI
Agent: CAA - Beverly Hills, 213/288-4545

TOKYO POP Spectrafilm, 1988, w/Lynn Grossman, directed

L

CLAIRE LABINE*
Agent: William Morris Agency - New York, 212/586-5100

Screenplays:
SUMMER OF THE FALCON

RICHARD LABRIE
BLOOD AND CONCRETE: A LOVE STORY I.R.S. Media, 1991, w/Jeff Reiner

DANY LaFERRIERE
HOW TO MAKE LOVE TO A NEGRO WITHOUT GETTING TIRED Angelika Films, 1990, w/Richard Sadler

GEORGE LAFIA
DEADLY WEAPON Empire Pictures, 1989, Story w/Michael Miner

JOHN J. LAFIA*
Agent: CAA - Beverly Hills, 213/288-4545

THE BLUE IGUANA Paramount, 1988, directed
CHILDS PLAY MGM/UA, 1989, w/Tom Holland & Don Mancini

Screenplays:
THE BLACK GLASS
DAGGER, INC.
SOB'S

JEAN LaFLEUR
SPACEHUNTER: ADVENTURES IN THE FORBIDDEN ZONE Columbia, 1983, Story w/Stewart Harding

IAN LaFRENAIS*
Agent: Broder-Kurland-Webb-Uffner - Los Angeles, 213/656-9262

THE JOKERS Universal, 1967, w/Dick Clement
HANNIBAL BROOKS United Artists, 1968, w/Dick Clement
OTLEY Columbia, 1969, w/Dick Clement
CATCH ME A SPY Rank, 1971, w/Dick Clement
VILLAIN EMI, 1971, w/Dick Clement
THE LIKELY LADS EMI, 1976, w/Dick Clement
PORRIDGE ITC, 1979, w/Dick Clement
THE PRISONER OF ZENDA Universa, 1979, w/Dick Clement
WATER Atlantic Releasing Corporation, 1984, w/Dick Clement & Bill Persky
VICE VERSA Columbia, 1988, w/Dick Clement
THE COMMITMENTS 20th Century-Fox, 1991, w/Dick Clement & Roddy Doyle

CELINE La FRIENERE
CITY ON FIRE Astral-Bellevue, 1979, w/Jack Hill & David P. Lewis
FOREIGN BODY Orion, 1986

RICHARD LaGRAVENESE*
Agent: United Talent Agency - Beverly Hills, 213/273-6700

RUDE AWAKENING Orion, 1989, w/Neil Levy
THE FISHER KING Tri-Star, 1991

Screenplays:
SKIRTS
WIDOWS
THE REF
LITTLE PRINCESS
A MIRROR HAS TWO FACES
CATS
THE TALISMAN

MURDO LAIRD
Agent: Warden & White Associates - Beverly Hills, 213/852-1028

Screenplays:
YOSHIKO
DANIELLA
PANAMA
PROLOGUES
RUBY RED

RITA LAKIN*
Agent: Camden-ITG - Los Angeles, 213/289-2700

VOICE OF THE HEART (CTF) Worldvision, 1990

FRANK LaLOGGIA
Business: LaLoggia Productions - Los Angeles, 213/462-3055

FEAR NO EVIL Avco Embassy, 1981, directed
LADY IN WHITE New Century/Vista, 1988, directed

ROSS La MANNA*
Agent: William Morris Agency - Beverly Hills, 213/274-7451

Screenplays:
DNA w/John McCormick
TORPEDOS w/John McCormick
CHOPPERS w/John McCormick
PRIDE AND JOY w/John McCormick

GAVIN LAMBERT
BITTER VICTORY   Columbia, 1957, w/Nicholas Ray & Rene Hardy
SONS AND LOVERS ★   20th Century-Fox, 1960, w/T.E.B. Clarke
THE ROMAN SPRING OF MRS. STONE   Warner Bros., 1961
INSIDE DAISY CLOVER   Warner Bros., 1965
I NEVER PROMISED YOU A ROSE GARDEN ★   New World, 1977, w/Lewis John Carlino
DEAD ON THE MONEY (CTF)   Perfect Circle Corp./Voyage Productions Inc., 1991

BILL LAMOND*
Agent: Bennett Agency - Los Angeles, 213/471-2251

THIS TIME FOREVER   (Canadian), 1985

Screenplays:
WILD BLUE YONDER w/Jo LaMond
THE EX-MR. WINFIELD w/Jo LaMond

JO LAMOND*
Agent: Bennett Agency - Los Angeles, 213/471-2251

Screenplays:
WILD BLUE YONDER w/Bill LaMond
THE EX-MR. WINFIELD w/Bill LaMond

LAURA LAMSON
Agent: ICM - Los Angeles, 213/550-4000

Screenplays:
BY GRAND CENTRAL STATION I SAT DOWN AND WEPT
LORNA DOON

MIKE LANAHAN
(See Jeff Buhai, David Obst & Steve Zacharias)

BILL LANCASTER*
Agent: ICM - Los Angeles, 213/550-4000

THE BAD NEWS BEARS   Paramount, 1976
THE BAD NEWS BEARS GO TO JAPAN   Paramount, 1978
THE THING   Universal, 1982

Screenplays:
MONKEY KING
THE BAD NEWS BEARS GO TO CUBA
CALIFORNIA ROUGH AND TUMBLE
VIDA

PETER LANCE*
Contact: WGA - Los Angeles, 213/550-1000

Screenplays:
ANGELS OF DEATH
THE COVER UP

NEIL LANDAU*
Agent: CAA - Beverly Hills, 213/288-4545

MAPS FOR DROWSINESS (P)
DON'T TELL MOM THE BABYSITTER'S DEAD   Warner Bros., 1991, w/Tara Ison

Screenplays:
TRUE TO LIFE w/Tara Ison
BELOVED SON w/Tara Ison
INSIDE OUT w/Tara Ison
TRANSYLVANIA-PENNSYLVANIA w/Tara Ison

JOHN LANDIS*
Agent: CAA - Beverly Hills, 213/288-4545

SCHLOCK   Jack H. Harris Enterprises, 1973, directed
THE BLUES BROTHERS   Universal, 1980, w/Dan Aykroyd, directed
AN AMERICAN WEREWOLF IN LONDON   Universal, 1981, directed
COMING SOON (CTD)   Universal Pay TV, 1983, w/Mick Garris, directed
TWILIGHT ZONE - THE MOVIE   Warner Bros., 1983, Prologue & Segment 1, directed
CLUE   Paramount, 1985, Story w/Jonathan Lynn

KAREN LANDRY
Agent: Susan Smith & Associates - Beverly Hills, 213/852-4777

PATTI ROCKS   FilmDallas, 1988, w/John Jenkins, David Burton Morris & Chris Mulkey

DAVID LANDSBERG*
Agent: The Roberts Company - Los Angeles, 213/552-7800

DETECTIVE SCHOOL DROPOUTS   DUMB DICKS   Cannon, 1986, w/Lorin Dreyfuss
DUTCH TREAT   Cannon, 1987, w/Lorin Dreyfuss

ANDREW J. LANE*
Business: Gibraltar Entertainment, 14101 Valleyheart Dr., #205, Sherman Oaks, CA, 91423, 818/501-2076

VALLEY GIRL   Atlantic Releasing Corporation, 1983, w/Wayne Crawford
JAKE SPEED   New World, 1986, w/Wayne Crawford

Screenplays:
LONELY HEARTS (directing)

BRIAN ALAN LANE*
Contact: Attorney Dixon Dern, 213/557-0417

THE GIRL FROM MARS (CTF)   Atlantis Films Ltd., 1991

CHARLES LANE
Agent: William Morris Agency - Beverly Hills, 213/274-7451

A PLACE IN TIME (Short), directed
SIDEWALK STORIES   Island Pictures, 1989, directed

Screenplays:
SKINS

WARNER LANE
(See Nancy Dowd)

LANIER LANEY*
Contact: Hansen, Jacobson & Teller - Los Angeles, 213/271-8777

LOVE AT STAKE *BURNIN' LOVE* Tri-Star, 1988, w/Terry Sweeney
SHAG: THE MOVIE Hemdale, 1989, w/Terry Sweeney & Robin Swicord

MICHEL LANG
THE GIFT Samuel Goldwyn Company, 1983, directed

PERRY LANG*
Agent: ICM - Los Angeles, 213/550-4000

LITTLE VEGAS I.R.S. Releasing, 1990, directed

DONALD LANGDON
BLOOD TIDE 21st Century, 1982, w/Richard Jeffries & Nico Mastorakis

DAVID LANGE
I AM THE CHEESE Almi, 1983, w/Robert Jiras

MONIQUE LANGE
THE TROUT Triumph, 1982, w/Joseph Losey

TODD W. LANGEN*
Agent: The Wright Concept - Hollywood, 213/461-3844

TEENAGE MUTANT NINJA TURTLES New Line Cinema, 1990, w/Bobby Herbeck
TEENAGE MUTANT NINJA TURTLES II: THE SECRET OF THE OOZE New Line Cinema, 1991

Screenplays:
I...DO
IN NO PARTICULAR ORDER

JOHN LANGLEY
P.O.W. THE ESCAPE Cannon, 1986, w/James Bruner, Malcolm Barbour & Jeremy Lipp

BRUCE LANSBURY*
Agent: Rogers & Associates - North Hollywood, 818/509-1010

I'M DANGEROUS TONIGHT (CTF) MCA Television, 1990, w/Philip John Taylor

ROY LANGSDON
THE FORBIDDEN DANCE Columbia, 1990, w/John Platt
OUT OF SIGHT, OUT OF MIND Spectrum Entertainment Group, 1990, w/John Platt

MURRAY LANGSTON
NIGHT PATROL New World, 1984, w/Jackie Kong & Bill Osco

T. L. LANKFORD
ARMED RESPONSE CineTel Films, 1986
CYCLONE CineTel Films, 1987, w/Paul Garson
BULLETPROOF CineTel Films, 1987, w/Steve Carver
DEEP SPACE Trans World Entertainment, 1988, w/Fred Olen Ray
SOUTH OF RENO Castle Hill Productions, 1988, w/Mark Rezyka
MOB BOSS Vidmark Entertainment, 1990

JEFF LANTOS
Agent: Warden & White Associates - Beverly Hills, 213/852-1028

Screenplays:
LATE BLOOMERS w/Leann Lantos & Jeff Levin
TIGHT QUARTERS w/Leann Lantos & Jeff Levin
EVERYTHING COUNTS w/Leann Lantos & Jeff Levin

LEANN LANTOS
Agent: Warden & White Associates - Beverly Hills, 213/852-1028

Screenplays:
LATE BLOOMERS w/Jeff Lantos & Jeff Levin
TIGHT QUARTERS w/Jeff Lantos & Jeff Levin
EVERYTHING COUNTS w/Jeff Lantos & Jeff Levin

RING LARDNER, JR.*
Agent: Jim Preminger Agency - Los Angeles, 213/475-9491

TOMORROW THE WORLD United Artists, 1944, w/Leopold Atlas
WOMAN OF THE YEAR ★★ MGM, 1942, w/Michael Kanin
THE CROSS OF LORRAINE MGM, 1944, w/Robert Andrews, Alexander Esway & Michael Kanin
CLOACK AND DAGGER U.S. Pictures, 1946, w/Albert Matz
THE FORBIDDEN STREET *BRITTANIA MEWS* 20th Century-Fox, 1948
THE CINCINNATI KID MGM, 1965, w/Terry Southern
M*A*S*H ★★ 20th Century-Fox, 1970
THE GREATEST Columbia, 1977

JEREMY LARNER*
Contact: George Diskant, Esq. - Los Angeles, 213/824-3773

DRIVE, HE SAID Columbia, 1971, w/Jack Nicholson
THE CANDIDATE ★★ Warner Bros., 1972

Screenplays:
WATER DANCER
JOSHUA MACHINE

NANCY LARSON*
Agent: H.N. Swanson, Inc. - Los Angeles, 213/652-5385

COACH Crown International, 1978, w/Stephen Bruce Rose
THE WIZARD OF LONELINESS Skouras Pictures, 1988

Screenplays:
ZORRO
ISABEL EBERHARDT
MOTHERLOAD
LEGEND OF THE GRAIL

LOUIS La RUSSO II*
Agent: The Artists Agency - Los Angeles, 213/277-7779

LAMPPOST REUNION (P)
BEYOND THE REEF Universal, 1981, w/Jim Carabatsos
THE CLOSER Ion Pictures, 1991, w/Robert Keats, from his play "Wheelbarrow Closers"

Screenplays:
TIME FOR WEDDING CAKE

ALEX LASKER
Agent: ICM - Los Angeles, 213/550-4000

FIREFOX Warner Bros., 1982, w/Wendell Wellman
DOUBLECROSSED (CTF) Green/Epstein Productions/
  Lorimar TV, 1991, Story w/Roger Young

LAWRENCE LASKER*
Agent: InterTalent - Los Angeles, 213/858-6200
Business: Lasker-Parkes, 10202 W. Washington Blvd.,
  Producers Bldg. - Suite 142, Culver City, CA 90232,
  213/280-4267

WARGAMES ★ MGM/UA, 1983, w/Walter F. Parkes
PROJECT X 20th Century Fox, 1987, Story
  w/Stanley Weiser

Screenplays:
SNEAKERS w/Walter F. Parkes & Phil Alden Robinson
THE GENIUS w/Walter F. Parkes
PETER PAN w/Walter F. Parkes

AARON LATHAM*
Agent: CAA - Beverly Hills, 213/288-4545

URBAN COWBOY Paramount, 1980, w/Jim Bridges
PERFECT Columbia, 1985, w/Jim Bridges

Screenplays:
THE ZERO CLUB

LYNN MARIE LATHAM*
Agent: Pleshette & Green - Los Angeles, 213/465-0428

Screenplays:
COMING OUT

GREGG LATTER
JOBMAN Blue Rock Films, 1990, w/Darrell Roodt

LINDY LAUB*
Contact: WGA - Los Angeles, 213/550-1000

SHIKSE (Short) , directed
FOR THE BOYS 20th Century Fox, 1991, w/Marshall
  Brickman & Neal Jimenez

Screenplays:
LUDLOW, 1914
TWO VIRGINS
REFUGE

MICHAEL LAUGHLIN
STRANGE BEHAVIOR *DEAD KIDS* World Northal,
  1981, w/William Condon, directed
STRANGE INVADERS Orion, 1983, w/William
  Condon, directed
MESMERIZED RKO/Challenge Corporation Services,
  1984, directed

TOM LAUGHLIN
Contact: Directors Guild of America - Los Angeles,
  213/289-2000

BORN LOSERS American International, 1967, directed
BILLY JACK Warner Bros., 1973, as "Frank & Teresa
  Cristina," directed
BILLY JACK GOES TO WASHINGTON Taylor-Laughlin,
  1978, as "Frank & Teresa Cristina," directed

DALE LAUNER*
Business: 20th Century Fox, 10201 W. Pico Blvd., Bldg. 1 -
  Suite 146, Los Angeles, CA 90035, 213/203-2081

RUTHLESS PEOPLE Buena Vista, 1986
BLIND DATE Tri-Star, 1987
DIRTY ROTTEN SCOUNDRELS Orion, 1988, w/Paul
  Henning & Stanley Shapiro
LOVE POTION :#9 20th Century Fox, 1991, directed

Screenplays:
MY COUSIN VINNY
BEVERLY HILLBILLIES

MICHAEL LAURENCE*
Contact: WGA - New York, 212/245-6180

WHICH WAY HOME (CTF) TNT/McElroy & McElroy, 1991

ARTHUR LAURENTS
SCREAM (P)
THE TIME OF THE CUCKOO (P)
CAUGHT Enterprise, 1948
ROPE Warner Bros., 1948
ANNA LUCASTA Columbia, 1949, w/Philip Yordan
ANASTASIA Fox, 1956
BONJOUR TRISTESSE Columbia, 1957
GYPSY Warner Bros., 1962, from his play
THE WAY WE WERE Columbia, 1973
THE TURNING POINT ★ 20th Century-Fox, 1977

BRUNO LAWRENCE
SMASH PALACE Atlantic Releasing Corporation, 1981,
  w/Roger Donaldson & Peter Hansard
THE QUIET EARTH Skouras Pictures, 1985, w/Bill Baer &
  Sam Pillsbury

DAVID LAWRENCE*
Agent: The Agency - Los Angeles, 213/551-3000

ESCAPE 2000 New World, 1983, Story w/George
  Schenck & Robert Williams

JEROME LAWRENCE*
Agent: ICM - Los Angeles, 213/550-4000

TOAST OF THE TOWN (P) w/Robert E. Lee
AUNTIE MAME (P) w/Robert E. Lee
THE GANG'S ALL HERE (P) w/Robert E. Lee
THE NIGHT THOREAU SPENT IN JAIL (P) w/Robert E. Lee
INHERIT THE WIND (P) w/Robert E. Lee
FIRST MONDAY IN OCTOBER Paramount, 1981,
  w/Robert E. Lee, from their play

Screenplays:
THE CLOCK STRUCK ONE w/Robert E. Lee

MARC LAWRENCE*
Agent: United Talent Agency - Beverly Hills,
  213/273-6700

Screenplays:
PARADISE MISPLACED

PETER LAWRENCE
THE BURNING Filmways/Orion, 1982, w/Bob Weinstein
TERMINAL CHOICE Almi Pictures, 1985, w/Neal Bell

La

FILM WRITERS GUIDE

RAY LAWRENCE
Contact: Australian Film Commission, 9229 Sunset Blvd., Los Angeles, CA 90069, 213/275-7074

BLISS   New World, 1986, w/Peter Carey, directed

J. F. LAWTON*
Agent: ICM - Los Angeles, 213/550-4000

THE ARTIST (Short)
RENESANCE (Short)
CANNIBAL WOMEN IN THE AVOCADO JUNGLE OF DEATH   Megalomania Productions, 1989, as "J.D. Athens," directed
PIZZA MAN   Megalomania Productions (no distributor), 1991, as "J.D. Athens," directed
PRETTY WOMAN   Buena Vista, 1990
MISTRESS   Tribeca Productions, 1991, w/Barry Primus

Screenplays:
RED SNEAKERS (directing)
DREADNOUGHT
SLEEPLESS NIGHTS

RICHARD LAWTON*
Agent: Warden & White Associates - Beverly Hills, 213/852-1028

Screenplays:
I, TINA
REVENGE ROMANCE
IN THE SHADOW OF THE BIG CHEESE
WHITE MAN'S BURDEN

MICHAEL LAZAROU*
Agent: United Talent Agency - Beverly Hills, 213/273-6700

HEAT WAVE (CTF)   Avnet/Kerner Co., 1990

Screenplays:
RAZZMATAZZ

JERRY LAZARUS*
Contact: 213/464-8381

TREASURE OF THE FOUR CROWNS   Cannon, 1983, w/Lloyd Battista & Jim Bryce
HONEYMOON ACADEMY   Triumph, 1990, w/Gene Quintano

CARLOS LAZLO
SILENT NIGHT, DEADLY NIGHT III: YOU BETTER WATCH OUT!   Quiet Films, 1989

PAUL LEADON
AROUND THE WORLD IN 80 WAYS   Alive Films, 1987, w/Stephen MacLean

LARRY LEAHY
THE LAWLESS LAND   Concorde Pictures, 1989, w/Tony Cinciripini

NORMAN LEAR *
Business: Act III Communications, Sunset-Gower Studios, 1438 N. Gower St. - Bldg. 35, Los Angeles, CA 90028, 213/460-7240

COME BLOW YOUR HORN   Paramount, 1962
DIVORCE AMERICAN STYLE ★   Columbia, 1967
THE NIGHT THEY RAIDED MINSKY'S   United Artists, 1968, w/Sidney Michaels & Arnold Schulman
COLD TURKEY   United Artists, 1971, directed

FRED LEBOW
Agent: The Goldstein Company - Los Angeles, 213/659-9511

Screenplays:
FATHER AND SON w/Daniel Sullivan
SANTA'S DAUGHTER w/Daniel Sullivan
NEW YEAR'S EVE w/Daniel Sullivan
SNOW FLAKES w/Daniel Sullivan
ECHO OF VALOR
MEMORIAL
GRAN PRIX 2000
UNEMPLOYMENT BLUES

PAUL LEDER*
Agent: The Irv Schechter Company - Beverly Hills, 213/278-8070

GOIN' TO CHICAGO   Poor Robert Productions, 1990, directed
MURDER BY NUMBERS   Burnhill Productions, 1990, directed

RICHARD LEDERER
THE HOLLYWOOD KNIGHTS   Columbia, 1980, Story w/Floyd Mutrux & William Tennant

DAMIAN LEE
Business: Rose & Ruby Productions, Inc., 33 Howard St., Toronto, Ontario M4X 1J6, Canada, 416/961-0555

BUSTED UP   Shapiro Entertainment, 1987
WATCHERS   Tri-Star, 1988, w/Bill Freed

GALEN LEE*
Agent: ICM - New York, 212/556-5600

ROADHOUSE 66   Atlantic Releasing Corporation, 1984, w/George Simpson

GERARD LEE
SWEETIE   Avenue Pictures, 1989, w/Jane Campion

MARK W. LEE*
Agent: Circle Talent Associates - Beverly Hills, 213/285-1585

REBEL ARMIES DEEP INTO CHAD (P)
PIRATES (P)
CALIFORNIA DOGFIGHT (P)
PARADISE (P)

Screenplays:
CRAZY FOR KATE
SPARE PARTS
KAMPALA
FINAL VOWS

PATRICK LEE
PERFUME OF THE CYCLONE   Movie Group, 1990

ROBERT E. LEE*
Agent: ICM - Los Angeles, 213/550-4000

TOAST OF THE TOWN (P) w/Jerome Lawrence
AUNTIE MAME (P) w/Jerome Lawrence

THE GANG'S ALL HERE (P) w/Jerome Lawrence
THE NIGHT THOREAU SPENT IN JAIL (P)
    w/Jerome Lawrence
INHERIT THE WIND (P) w/Jerome Lawrence
FIRST MONDAY IN OCTOBER   Paramount, 1981,
    w/Jerome Lawrence, from their play

Screenplays:
THE CLOCK STRUCK ONE w/Jerome Lawrence

SPIKE LEE
(Shelton Jackson Lee)
Contact: Frankfurt, Garbus, Klein & Selz - New York,
    212/980-0120
Business: Forty Acres & A Mule Filmworks, 124 DeKalb
    Ave., Brooklyn, NY 11217, 718/624-3703

JOE'S BED-STUY BARBERSHOP: WE CUT HEADS
    First Run Features, 1983, directed
SHE'S GOTTA HAVE IT   Island Pictures,
    1986, directed
SCHOOL DAZE   Columbia, 1988, directed
DO THE RIGHT THING ★ Universal, 1989, directed
MO' BETTER BLUES   Universal, 1990, directed
JUNGLE FEVER   Universal, 1991, directed

STUART LEE
BURIED ALIVE   21st Century Film, 1990, w/Jake Clesi

MICHAEL J. LEESON*
Agent: CAA - Beverly Hills, 213/288-4545

JEKYLL AND HYDE...TOGETHER AGAIN   Paramount,
    1982, w/Jerry Belson, Monica Johnson & Harvey Miller
THE SURVIVORS   Columbia, 1983
NO SMALL AFFAIR   Columbia, 1984, w/Craig Bolotin,
    as "Terence Mulcahy"
THE WAR OF THE ROSES   20th Century Fox, 1989

Screenplays:
LES COMPERES
A YEAR AND A DAY
THE MAN WHO COULD WORK MIRACLES

CAROLINE LEFCOURT
THE STEPFATHER   New Century/Vista, 1987,
    Story w/Brian Garfield & Donald E. Westlake

PETER LEFCOURT*
Agent: Robinson, Weintraub, Gross & Associates -
    Los Angeles, 213/653-5802

Screenplays:
INHERIT THE MOB

GEORGE LEFFERTS
Agent: The Artists Agency - Los Angeles,
    213/277-7779

MEAN DOG BLUES   American International, 1978

DOUGLAS A. LEFLER*
Agent: Stephanie Rogers & Associates - North Hollywood,
    818/509-1010

STEEL DAWN   Vestron, 1987

ERNEST LEHMAN*
Agent: The Gersh Agency - Beverly Hills, 213/274-6611

EXECUTIVE SUITE   MGM, 1954
SABRINA ★   Paramount, 1954, w/Samuel Taylor &
    Billy Wilder
THE KING AND I   20th Century-Fox, 1956
SOMEBODY UP THERE LIKES ME   MGM, 1956
SWEET SMELL OF SUCCESS   United Artists, 1957,
    w/Clifford Odets
NORTH BY NORTHWEST ★   MGM, 1959
FROM THE TERRACE   20th Century-Fox, 1960
WEST SIDE STORY ★   United Artists, 1961
THE PRIZE   MGM, 1963
THE SOUND OF MUSIC   20th Century-Fox, 1965
WHO'S AFRAID OF VIRGINIA WOOLF? ★   Warner
    Bros., 1966
HELLO DOLLY   20th Century-Fox, 1969
PORTNOY'S COMPLAINT   Warner Bros., 1972, directed
BLACK SUNDAY   Paramount, 1976, w/Ivan Moffat &
    Kenneth Ross
FAMILY PLOT   Universal, 1976

MICHAEL LEHMANN
Agent: CAA - Beverly Hills, 213/288-4545

MEET THE APPLEGATES *THE APPLEGATES* Triton
    Pictures, 1991, w/Redbeard Simmons, directed

Screenplays:
LE SURF HOT w/Redbeard Simmons
DREAMDATE

JERRY LEICHTLING*
Agent: CAA - Beverly Hills, 213/288-4545

PEGGY SUE GOT MARRIED   Tri-Star, 1986,
    w/Arlene Sarner

Screenplays:
THE TALISMAN w/Arlene Sarner
HONKY TONK SUE w/Arlene Sarner

MIKE LEIGH
Agent: Peters, Fraser & Dunlop - London, 71/376-7676

BLEAK MOMENTS   Autumn/Memorial/BFI, 1971, directed
HIGH HOPES   Skouras Pictures, 1989, directed
LIFE IS SWEET   October Films, 1991, directed

WARREN D. LEIGHT*
Agent: William Morris Agency - Beverly Hills, 213/274-7451

MOTHER'S DAY   United Film Distribution, 1980,
    w/Charles Kaufman
STUCK ON YOU!   Troma, 1983, w/others
BEFORE THE NICKELODEON   First Run Features, 1983,
    w/Charles Musser
ME AND HIM   Columbia, 1989

Screenplays:
POOR LITTLE LAMBS
THE NIGHT WE NEVER MET

MICHAEL W. LEIGHTON*
Contact: 213/390-1000

RUSH WEEK   RCA/Columbia Home Video, 1991,
    w/Russell Y. Manzatt

Le

FILM WRITERS GUIDE

TED LEIGHTON
Agent: CAA - Beverly Hills, 213/288-4545

THE HUNTER   Paramount, 1980, w/Peter Hyams

MOLLY-ANN LEIKIN*
Contact: Attorney Nancy Hammerstein - Los Angeles, 213/828-8378

Screenplays:
ABBY & SOCKS
FRENCH DRESSING
DOOLITTLE & STICK
LEFTY'S PIANO

MATT LEIPZIG
HOUR OF THE ASSASSIN   Concorde, 1987

DAVID LELAND
Agent: Casaratto Company - London, 01/287-4450

MONA LISA   Island Pictures, 1986, w/Neil Jordan
PERSONAL SERVICES   Vestron, 1987
WISH YOU WERE HERE   Atlantic Releasing Corporation, 1987, directed

CLAUDE LELOUCH
Contact: French Film Office, 745 Fifth Avenue, New York, NY 10151, 212/832-8860

A MAN AND A WOMAN ★ Allied Artists, 1966, w/Pierre Uytterhoeven, directed
LIVE FOR LIFE   United Artists, 1967, w/Pierre Uytterhoeven, directed
HAPPY NEW YEAR   *LA BONNE ANNEE*   Avco Embassy, 1973, directed
AND NOW MY LOVE   *TOUTE UNE VIE* ★ Avco Embassy, 1975, w/Pierre Uytterhoeven, directed
SECOND CHANCE   *SI C'ETAIT A REFAIR*   United Artists Classics, 1976, directed
ANOTHER MAN, ANOTHER CHANCE   United Artists, 1977, directed
ROBERT ET ROBERT   Quartet, 1978, directed
BOLERO   *LES UNS ET LES AUTRES/ WITHIN MEMORY*   Double 13/Sharp Features, 1982, directed
A MAN AND A WOMAN: 20 YEARS LATER   Warner Bros., 1986, directed

JONATHAN LEMKIN*
Agent: United Talent Agency - Beverly Hills, 213/273-6700

Screenplays:
SHOWDOWN IN LITTLE TOKYO w/Dennis Hackin
RED SUN RISING
DRUG WARS THE SIEGE
NO DEPOSIT, NO RETURN

JAMES LEMMO
HEART   New World, 1987, w/Randy Jurgenson, directed
TRIPWIRE   CineTel Films, 1989, w/B.J. Goldman, directed

Screenplays:
THE RETREAT (Shared, directing)

RUSTY LEMORANDE*
Contact: Hansen, Jacobson & Teller - Los Angeles, 213/271-8777

ELECTRIC DREAMS   MGM/UA, 1984
JOURNEY TO THE CENTER OF THE EARTH   Cannon, 1987, w/Kitty Chalmers, Regina Davis & Debra Ricci, directed
THE TURN OF THE SCREW   Electric Pictures, 1991, directed

Screenplays:
THE FRIENDLY
GHOST TOWN U.S.A.

PETER LENKOV*
Agent: Triad Artists, Inc. - Los Angeles, 213/556-2727

Screenplays:
TOUGH LUCK
DEMOLITION MAN
FEVER OF THE HUNT w/Larry Cohen
MAN OF THE FUTURE

ROBERT W. LENSKI*
Agent: William Morris Agency - Beverly Hills, 213/274-7451

Screenplays:
BEVERLY HILLS BOX 33
WANDERLUST
MILITARY MAN

DEAN LENT
BORDER RADIO   International Film Marketing, w/Allison Anders & Kurt Voss, co-directed

NORM LENZER*
Business: 7471 Melrose Ave. - Suite 8, Los Angeles, 213/653-1011

THE ADVENTURES OF THE AMERICAN RABBIT (AF)   Atlantic Releasing Corporation, 1986

MALCOLM LEO*
Agent: APA - Los Angeles, 213/273-0744
Business: Malcolm Leo Productions, 6536 Sunset Blvd., Hollywood, CA 90028, 213/464-4448

THIS IS ELVIS (FD)   Warner Bros., 1981, w/Andrew Solt

ELMORE LEONARD*
Agent: H.N. Swanson, Inc. - Los Angeles, 213/652-5385

THE MOONSHINE WAR   MGM, 1970
JOE KIDD   Universal, 1972
MR. MAJESTYK   United Artists, 1974
STICK   Universal, 1985, w/Joseph Stinson
52 PICK-UP   Cannon, 1986, w/John Steppling
THE ROSARY MURDERS   New Line Cinema, 1987, w/Fred Walton
CAT CHASER   Vestron, 1990, w/Jim Borrelli & Alan Sharp

Screenplays:
JUVENILE

HUGH LEONARD*
Agent: William Morris Agency - New York, 212/586-5100

BROTH OF A BOY (P)
INTERLUDE Columbia, 1968, w/Lee Langley
GREAT CATHERINE Warner Bros., 1968
PERCY MGM, 1971
OUR MISS FRED EMI, 1972
DA FilmDallas Pictures, 1988, from his play

Screenplays:
O'NEIL
THE PATRICK PIERCE MOTEL
STEPHEN "D"

JOHN LEONE
Agent: Camden-ITG - Los Angeles, 213/289-2700

TOUGH ENOUGH 20th Century-Fox, 1983

GLENN LEOPOLD*
Contact: Wayne Alexander, Esq, - Los Angeles, 213/312-4104

THE PROWLER Sandhurst Corporation, 1982, w/Neal F. Barbera
TOO SCARED TO SCREAM Moviestore Entertainment, 1985, w/Neal F. Barbera

TOM LEOPOLD*
Agent: Triad Artists, Inc. - Los Angeles, 213/556-2727

CLUB PARADISE Warner Bros., 1986, Story w/Chris Miller, Ed Roboto & David Standish

ERIC LERNER*
Contact: 413/585-8986

BIRD ON A WIRE Universal, 1990, w/David Seltzer & Louis Venosta

MICHAEL LERNER
Agent: William Morris Agency - Beverly Hills, 213/274-7451

Screenplays:
PANIC

GEN LeROY
Agent: William Morris Agency - Beverly Hills, 213/274-7451

Screenplays:
BEAUTY AND THE BEAST (AF)
THE THIN MAN'S LAST CASE
IT'S A CRIME
GREASEPAINT

DENNIS LESS
LABYRINTH Tri-Star, 1986, Story w/Jim Henson

MICHAEL LESSAC*
Contact: WGA - Los Angeles, 213/550-1000

Screenplays:
HOUSE OF CARDS (directing)

MARK L. LESTER
Contact: Directors Guild of America - Los Angeles, 213/289-2000

STEEL ARENA L.-T. Films, 1973, directed
CLASS OF '84 United Film Distribution, 1982, w/John Saxton & Tom Holland, directed
CLASS OF 1999 Taurus Entertainment, 1990, Story, directed

MICHAEL LESTER
CODENAME: WILDGEESE New World, 1986

SHELDON B. LETTICH*
Agent: ICM - Los Angeles, 213/550-4000

TRACERS (P), shared
FIREFIGHT (Short), 1986, directed
RUSSKIES New Century Entertainment, 1987, w/Alan Glueckman & Michael Nankin
RAMBO III Tri-Star, 1988, w/Sylvester Stallone
BLOODSPORT Cannon, 1988, w/Chris Cosby & Mel Friedman
LIONHEART Universal, 1991, w/Jean-Claude Van Damme, directed
DOUBLE IMPACT Columbia, 1991, w/Jean-Claude Van Damme, directed

BRIAN LEVANT*
Agent: United Talent Agency - Beverly Hills, 213/273-6700

Screenplays:
THAT'S ALL FOLKS
HONEY, THE DOG ATE THE KIDS

JEREMY LEVEN*
Agent: The Agency - Los Angeles, 213/551-3000

CREATOR Universal, 1985
PLAYING FOR KEEPS Universal, 1986, w/Bob Weinstein & Harvey Weinstein

Screenplays:
SATAN, CRAZY AS HELL
ACE TRUCKING CO.

JOHN LEVENSTEIN*
Agent: ICM - Los Angeles, 213/550-4000

ILLEGALLY YOURS DEG, 1986, w/Ken Finkelman & Michael Kaplan, as "Max Dickens & M.A. Stewart"

Screenplays:
CARLESS w/Michael Kaplan

A. A. LEVER
PRIMO BABY Victory Film, 1990

FRANK LEVERING
PARASITE Embassy, 1982, w/Alan J. Adler & Michael Shoob

JAY LEVEY
U.H.F. Orion, 1989, w/Al Yankovic, directed

JEFF LEVIN*
Agent: Warden & White Associates - Beverly Hills, 213/852-1028

Screenplays:
LATE BLOOMERS w/Leann Lantos & Jeff Lantos
TIGHT QUARTERS w/Leann Lantos & Jeff Lantos
EVERYTHING COUNTS w/Leann Lantos & Jeff Lantos

SHIRA LEVIN
Agent: Susan Smith & Associates - Beverly Hills, 213/852-4777

Screenplays:
IF MORNING EVER COMES w/Gary Weiner

EMILY B. LEVINE*
Agent: William Morris Agency - Beverly Hills, 213/274-7451

Screenplays:
THE FLING

KEN LEVINE*
Agent: Broder-Kurland-Webb-Uffner - Los Angeles, 213/656-9262

VOLUNTEERS Tri-Star, 1985, w/David Isaacs
MANNEQUIN TWO: ON THE MOVE 20th Century Fox, 1991, w/David Isaacs, Betsy Israel & Ed Rugoff

Screenplays:
GETTING AWAY w/David Isaacs
HOME FRONT w/David Isaacs
STAR SPANGLED ADVENTURE w/David Isaacs
LIVING LEGEND w/David Isaacs

LAURA LEVINE
Agent: The Wright Concept - Hollywood, 213/461-3844

Screenplays:
DUMPED

MICHAEL LEVINE
Agent: H. N. Swanson - Los Angeles, 213/652-5385

Screenplays:
DOWN FOR BLOOD w/Laura Kavanau

PAUL LEVINE
BEST OF THE BEST Taurus Entertainment, 1989

BARRY LEVINSON
THE INTERNECINE PROJECT Allied Artists, 1974, w/Jonathan Lynn
STREET GIRLS New World, 1975, w/Michael Miller

BARRY LEVINSON*
Agent: CAA - Beverly Hills, 213/288-4545
Business: Baltimore Pictures, Culver Studios, 213/202-3535

SILENT MOVIE 20th Century-Fox, 1976, w/Mel Brooks, Ron Clark & Rudy DeLuca
HIGH ANXIETY 20th Century-Fox, 1977, w/Mel Brooks, Ron Clark & Rudy DeLuca
...AND JUSTICE FOR ALL ★ Columbia, 1979, w/Valerie Curtin
INSIDE MOVES AFD, 1980, w/Valerie Curtin
BEST FRIENDS Warner Bros., 1982, w/Valerie Curtin
DINER ★ MGM/United Artists, 1982, directed
UNFAITHFULLY YOURS 20th Century–Fox, 1984, w/Valerie Curtin & Robert Klane
TIN MEN Buena Vista, 1987, directed
AVALON ★ Tri-Star, 1990, directed

Screenplays:
TOYS w/Valerie Curtin

DAVID LEVINSON*
Agent: Warden & White Associates - Beverly Hills, 213/852-1028

Screenplays:
SEEING STARS
SHOULDER TO SHOULDER
SOME KIDS ARE REALLY WEIRD
SHAKE RATTLE 'N' ROLL
JANE Q. PUBLIC

LARRY LEVINSON
MISSING IN ACTION 2: THE BEGINNING Cannon, 1985, w/Arthur Silver & Steve Bing

KAREN LEVITT
TIME WALKER New World, 1982, w/Tom Friedman

ZANE W. LEVITT
Business: Zeta Entertainment, Ltd., 6565 Sunset Blvd., #321, Hollywood, CA 90028, 213/461-7332

OUT OF THE DARK CineTel Films, 1989, w/J. Greg DeFelice

JEFERY LEVY*
Contact: WGA - Los Angeles, 213/550-1000

GHOULIES Empire Pictures, 1986, w/Luca Bercovici
ROCKULA Cannon, 1989, w/Luca Bercovici & Christopher Verwiel

NEIL A. LEVY*
Agent: ICM - Los Angeles, 213/550-4000

RUDE AWAKENING Orion, 1989, w/Richard LaGravenese

JEREMY LEW*
Contact: WGA - Los Angeles, 213/550-1000

Screenplays:
SESSIONS

ANDY LEWIS*
Contact: WGA - Los Angeles, 213/550-1000

UNDERGROUND United Artists, 1970, w/Ron Bishop
KLUTE ★ Warner Bros., 1971, w/Dave Lewis

Screenplays:
THE TRIUMPH OF LINCOLN CLUN w/Dave Lewis
PANAMA
THEO
ZANDE
PANIC
BRANT

FILM WRITERS GUIDE

THE ARMS MERCHANT
BINARY PROJECT
MARCO
ALLIE
NINA

DAVID P. LEWIS*
Contact: WGA - Los Angeles, 213/550-1000

KLUTE ★   Warner Bros., 1971, w/Andy Lewis
CITY ON FIRE   Astral-Bellevue, 1979, w/Jack Hill & Celine La Freniere
DEATH SHIP   Avco Embassy, 1980, Story w/Jack Hill

Screenplays:
THE TRIUMPH OF LINCOLN CLUN w/Andy Lewis

EDWARD LEWIS*
Business Manager: Melvin A. Singer, 818/783-9500

BROTHERS   Warner Bros., 1977, w/Mildred Lewis

EVERETT LEWIS
THE NATURAL HISTORY OF PARKING LOTS   Little Deer Productions, 1989, directed

Screenplays:
SUZI AND THE MECHANIC (directing)

FIONA LEWIS*
Agent: William Morris Agency - Beverly Hills, 213/274-7451

Screenplays:
EASY VIRTUE
WHITE GOLD
AMERICAN RHAPSODY
ABOVE SUSPICION
LAST WEEKEND
GOING FOR BROKE
REALM 7
IN GOOD HANDS
LIBELED LADY
DIPLOMATIC IMMUNITY
HARDBALL
AMATEURS
CLASS CONFLICT

JEFF LEWIS
Agent: Circle Talent Associates - Beverly Hills, 213/285-1585

Screenplays:
VAN GOGH'S LAST PORTRAIT
DEATH IN THE DANCING LIGHTS

JERRY LEWIS*
Agent: William Morris Agency - Beverly Hills, 213/274-7451

THE BELLBOY   Paramount, 1960, directed
THE LADIES' MAN   Paramount, 1961, w/Bill Richmond, directed
THE ERRAND BOY   Paramount, 1962, directed
THE NUTTY PROFESSOR   Paramount, 1963, w/Bill Richmond, directed
THE PATSY   Paramount, 1964, directed
THE FAMILY JEWELS   Paramount, 1965, w/Bill Richmond, directed
THE BIG MOUTH   Columbia, 1967, w/Bill Richmond, directed
THE DAY THE CLOWN CRIED   directed, unreleased
HARDLY WORKING   20th Century-Fox, 1981, w/Michael Janover, directed
SMORGASBORD   Warner Bros., 1985, w/Bill Richmond, directed

MILDRED LEWIS
BROTHERS   Warner Bros., 1977, w/Edward Lewis

WARREN LEWIS*
Agent: Shorr, Stille & Associates - Los Angeles, 213/659-6160

BLACK RAIN   Paramount, 1989, w/Craig Bolotin

WILLIAM W. LEWIS
Agent: Rosenstone/Wender - New York, 212/832-8330

BRADY'S ESCAPE   Satori Releasing, 1984

DENIS LEWISTON
HOT TARGET   Crown International, 1985, directed

ELLIOTT LEWITT
AT CLOSE RANGE   Orion, 1986, Story w/Nicholas Kazan

ALICE LIDDLE*
Contact: WGA - Los Angeles, 213/550-1000

PERMANENT RECORD   Paramount, 1988, w/Jarre Fees & Larry Ketron

BOBBY LIDELL
ENEMY TERROR   Empire Pictures, 1987, Story w/Stuart Kaminsky

JEFF LIEBERMAN*
Agent: Barrett, Benson, McCartt & Weston - Los Angeles, 213/247-5500

SQUIRM   American International, 1976, directed
BLUE SUNSHINE   Cinema Shares International, 1979, directed

JOHN LINDE
AFTER SCHOOL   Moviestore Entertainment, 1989, w/Rod McBrien, Hugh Parks & Joe Tankersley

MARK LINDQUIST*
Agent: ICM - Los Angeles, 213/550-4000

Screenplays:
AFTER THE PEEPSHOW

MICHAEL LINDSAY-HOGG
Contact: Directors Guild of America - Los Angeles, 213/289-2000

THE OBJECT OF BEAUTY   Avenue Pictures, 1991, directed

JIM LINDSAY*
Contact: WGA - Los Angeles, 213/550-1000

Screenplays:
CONVICT COWBOY w/Rick Way
MY MOTHER WEARS ARMY BOOTS w/Rick Way

Li

FILM WRITERS GUIDE

WILLIAM LINK*
Agent: CAA - Beverly Hills, 213/288-4545
Business: Foxcroft Productions, Universal Studios, 818/777-1000

ROLLERCOASTER   Universal, 1977, w/Richard Levinson

RICHARD LINKLATER
SLACKER   Orion Classics, 1991, directed

EUGENE LIPINSKI
Contact: Academy of Canadian Cinema & Television, 633 Yonge Street - 2nd Floor, Toronto, Ontario M4Y 1Z9, Canada, 416/967-0315

PERFECTLY NORMAL   Four Seasons Entertainment, 1991, w/Paul Quarrington

DANIEL LIPMAN*
Agent: William Morris Agency - Beverly Hills, 213/274-7451

Screenplays:
FIREFLY w/Ron Cowen
FAMILY DANCING   w/Ron Cowen

JEREMY D. LIPP*
Contact: Attorney Samantha Shad, 213/276-7017

P.O.W. THE ESCAPE   Cannon, 1986, w/Malcolm Barbour, James Bruner & John Langley
DUET FOR ONE   Cannon, 1987, w/Andrei Konchalovsky & Tom Kempinski

Screenplays:
THE SIMULATOR

DHANI LIPSIUS*
Contact: WGA - Los Angeles, 213/550-1000

HALLOWEEN 4   Galaxy International, 1988, Story w/Alan McElroy, Benjamin Ruffner & Larry Rattner

AARON LIPSTADT
Agent: CAA - Beverly Hills, 213/288-4545

CITY LIMITS   Atlantic Releasing Corporation, 1985, w/Don Opper & James Reigle, directed

STEVEN LISBERGER*
Agent: ICM - Los Angeles, 213/550-4000

ANIMALYMPICS (AF)   Lisberger Studios, 1980, directed
TRON   Buena Vista, 1982, directed
HOT PURSUIT   Paramount, 1987, w/Steve Carabatsos, directed

MARK L. LISSON*
Agent: Robinson, Weintraub, Gross & Associates - Los Angeles, 213/653-5802

RETURN TO HORROR HIGH   New World, 1987, w/Dana Escalanta & Bill Froehlich

SHELLEY P. LIST*
Agent: CAA - Beverly Hills, 213/288-4545

Screenplays:
ASYLUM

ROBERT LITTELL
THE AMATEUR   20th Century-Fox, 1982, w/Diana Maddox

Screenplays:
OUCH!

EZRA LITWAK*
Agent: United Talent Agency - Beverly Hills, 213/273-6700

THE BUTCHER'S WIFE   Paramount, 1991, w/Marjorie Schwartz

Screenplays:
WINGS w/Marjori Schwartz

ROBERT LITZ
Agent: APA - Los Angeles, 213/273-0744

RAPPIN'   Cannon, 1985, w/Adam Friedman

Screenplays:
IMPOSSIBLE FROM HERE

JERRY LIU
PING PONG   Samuel Goldwyn Company, 1987

HAROLD LIVINGSTON*
Agent: Preferred Artists - Encino, 818/990-0305

THE HELL WITH HEROS   Universal, 1968, w/Halstead Welles
STAR TREK - THE MOTION PICTURE   Paramount, 1979

DANIEL W. LJOKA*
Contact: 213/654-7909

Screenplays:
FIND AMANDA A HUSBAND

JEREMY LLOYD
VAMPIRA   Columbia, 1974
THE BAWDY ADVENTURES OF TOM JONES   Universal, 1975
ARE YOU BEING SERVED?   EMI, 1977, w/David Croft

MICHAEL LLOYD
LOVELINES   Tri-Star, 1984, Story w/Chip Hand & William Hillman

KENNETH LOACH
Agent: Judy Daish Agency - London, 011/441/486-5405

POOR COW   Anglo Amalgamated, 1967l, w/Nell Dunn, directed
KES   United Artists, 1970, w/Tony Garnet & Barry Hines, directed

JOSEPH LOEB III*
Agent: CAA - Beverly Hills, 213/288-4545

TEEN WOLF   Atlantic Releasing Corporation, 1985, w/Matthew Weisman
COMMANDO   20th Century Fox, 1975, Story w/Steven deSouza & Matthew Weisman
TEEN WOLF TOO   Atlantic Releasing Corporaiton, 1987, Story w/Matthew Weisman
BURGLAR   Warner Bros., 1987, w/Matthew Weisman & Hugh Wilson

Screenplays:
SILENT PARTNERS w/Matthew Weisman
NIGHTTIME GUY w/Matthew Weisman
VALLEY GIRL II

JIM LOEW
DELIRIUM   Odyssey Pictures, 1980, Story w/Eddie Krell

NORMAN LOFTIS
SMALL TIME   Norman Loftis Productions, 1990, directed

ROBERT LOGAN
REPOSSESSED   7 Arts/New Line Cinema, 1990, directed

CHRISTOPHER LOGUE
SAVAGE MESSIAH   MGM, 1972
CRUSOE   Island Pictures, 1988, w/Walon Green

ULLI LOMMEL
Business: Horizons Productions, 1134 N. Ogden Drive, West Hollywood, CA 90046, 213/654-6911

A TASTE OF SIN   Ambassador, 1983, w/John P. Marsh & Ron Norman, directed
BRAINWAVES   MPM, 1983, directed
THE DEVONSVILLE TERROR   MPM, 1983, w/George T. Lindsey & Suzanna Love, directed
WARBIRDS   Vidmark Entertainment, 1989, w/Clifford B. Wellman, directed

BRITT LOMOND
SWORDS OF HEAVEN   Trans World Entertainment, 1985, w/James Bruner, William P. O'Hagan & Joseph Randazzo

RICHARD LONCRAINE
Agent: Triad Artists, Inc. - Los Angeles, 213/556-2727

BELLMAN AND TRUE   Island Pictures, 1987, w/Desmond Lowden & Michael Wearing

ROBBY LONDON*
Contact: 818/995-3800

PINOCCHIO AND THE EMPEROR OF THE NIGHT (AF)   New World, 1987, w/Barry O'Brien & Dennis O'Flaherty
HAPPILY EVER AFTER   Kel-Air Entertainment, 1990, w/Martha Moran

ROY LONDON*
Contact: Michael H. Lester, Esq. - Los Angeles, 213/395-1704

TIGER WARSAW   Sony Pictures, 1988

Screenplays:
HIT MAN w/Kenneth Pressman

JOAN LONG
THE PICTURE SHOW MAN   Roadshow Distributors, 1977
CADDIE   Atlantic Releasing Corporation, 1981

MARTIN LOPEZ
MUTANT ON THE BOUNTY   Skouras Pictures, 1989

STEPHEN LORD*
Agent: Shapiro/Lichtman - Los Angeles, 213/859-8877

BEYOND AND BACK   Sunn Classic, 1978
THE BERMUDA TRIANGLE   Sunn Classic, 1979

LIDDY LOREE
Agent: Warden & White Associates - Beverly Hills, 213/852-1028

Screenplays:
THE BRIDE OF FRANK w/Jackie Rabinowitz
BUSYBODIES w/Jackie Rabinowitz

ALEC LORIMORE*
Contact: WGA - Los Angeles, 213/550-1000

Screenplays:
FIVE CAR STUD w/Terry Winkless
SEQUENCE w/Terry Winkless
FAST LANE w/Terry Winkless
OUT OF THE BOX w/Terry Winkless
TOO GOOD TO BE TRUE w/Terry Winkless
THE GREAT CAPE GIRARDEAU LEAP   w/Terry Winkless
WASHINGTON PAGES w/Terry Winkless
THE JETSONS w/Terry Winkless
VODONE w/Terry Winkless
THE RUNNER w/Terry Winkless
PARTNERS IN TIME w/Terry Winkless

PATRICIA LOSEY
STEAMING   New World, 1984

EMIL LOTEANU
Contact: Union of Soviet Filmmakers, Vassilievskaya 13, Moscow, U.S.S.R., tel.: 250-4114

THE SHOOTING PARTY   Mosfilm, 1978, directed

DAVID LOUCKA*
Agent: ICM - Los Angeles, 213/550-4000

THE DREAM TEAM   Universal, 1989, w/Jon Connolly

Screenplays:
BLOW AWAY w/Mark Kram & Dean Selmier
JOEY FAMOUS w/Mark Kram
THE DREAM CASE w/Mark Kram
WEEKEND WARRIORS w/Mark Kram
HIGH FIDELITY (Shared)
THE TRUTH (Shared)
THE ASSOCIATE (Shared)
"M" (Shared)
COP AND A HALF
THEY'VE LANDED
AMEROSA PLACE
A GOOD MAN
BEVERLY HILLS NINJA

DAVID LOUGHERY*
Agent: United Talent Agency - Beverly Hills, 213/273-6700

DREAMSCAPE   20th Century-Fox, 1984, w/Joe Ruben & Chuck Russell
STAR TREK V: THE FINAL FRONTIER   Paramount, 1989
FLASHBACK   Paramount, 1990

Screenplays:
JUICE

Lo

NIGHT ON THE TOWN
PASSENGER 57
THE MAN WITH NINE LIVES
MAD MISS MANTON
SON OF A GUN

ERIC LOUZIL
CLASS OF NUKE E'M HIGH PART 2: SUBHUMANOID
  MELTDOWN Troma, 1991, w/Lloyd Kaufman,
  Carl Morano, Marcus Rolling, Jeffrey W. Sass &
  Matt Unger, directed

Screenplays:
LUKAS' CHILD (directing)

MICHAEL JAMES LOVE*
Agent: The Gersh Agency - Beverly Hills, 213/274-6611

GABY - A TRUE STORY Tri-Star, 1987,
  w/Martin Salinas

Screenplays:
FLY AWAY HOME w/Martin Salinas

CHARLES LOVENTHAL
Agent: APA - Los Angeles, 213/273-0744

HOME MOVIES United Artists Classics, 1980, w/others
THE FIRST TIME New Line Cinema, 1982, w/Susan
  Wieser-Finley & W. Franklin Finley, directed
HIGHER EDUCATION Sicom Productions, 1987

Screenplays:
THE REAL WORLD

BERT LOVITT
PRINCE JACK Castle Hill Productions, 1984, directed

ROBERT LOVY
Agent: Triad Artists, Inc. - Los Angeles, 213/556-2727

CIRCUITRY MAN Skouras Pictures, 1990,
  w/Steven Lovy

STEVEN LOVY
Agent: Triad Artists, Inc. - Los Angeles, 213/556-2727

CIRCUITRY MAN Skouras Pictures, 1990, w/Robert
  Lovy, directed

DESMOND LOWDEN
Agent: Lemon, Unna & Durbridge - London,
  011/441/727-1346

BELLMAN AND TRUE Island Pictures, 1987,
  w/Richard Loncraine & Michael Wearing

RICHARD LOWENSTEIN
Agent: Triad Artists, Inc. - Los Angeles, 213/556-2727

STRIKEBOUND TRM Productions, 1985, directed
DOGS IN SPACE Skouras Pictures, 1987, directed

WOLF LOWENTHAL
COMIN' AT YA! Filmways, 1981, w/Lloyd Battista &
  Eugene Quintano

CRAIG LUCAS*
Agent: William Morris Agency - New York, 212/586-5100

RECKLESS (P), also screenplay
THREE POSTCARDS (P)
BLUE WINDOW (P)
MARRY ME A LITTLE (P)
PRELUDE TO A KISS (P), also screenplay
LONGTIME COMPANION Samuel Goldwyn
  Company, 1990

GEORGE LUCAS
Business: Lucasfilm Ltd., P.O. Box 668, San Anselmo, CA
  94960, 415/662-1800 or 453-7700??

THX 1138 Warner Bros., 1971, w/Walter Murch, directed
AMERICAN GRAFFITI ★ Universal, 1973, w/Willard Huyck
  & Gloria Katz, directed
STAR WARS ★ 20th Century-Fox, 1977, directed
RAIDERS OF THE LOST ARK Paramount, 1981, Story
  w/Philip Kaufman
RETURN OF THE JEDI 20th Century-Fox, 1983,
  w/Lawrence Kasdan
INDIANA JONES AND THE TEMPLE OF DOOM
  Paramount, 1984, Story
WILLOW MGM/UA, 1988, Story
INDIANA JONES AND THE LAST CRUSADE Paramount,
  1989, Story w/Menno Meyjes

WILLIAM LUCE*
Agent: William Morris Agency - Beverly Hills, 213/274-7451

Screenplays:
CURRER BELL, ESQ.

JERRY LUDWIG*
Agent: United Talent Agency - Beverly Hills, 213/273-6700

DEADLY DESIRE (CTF) Skylark Films/Wilshire Court
  Productions, 1991

TOBY LUDWIG*
Agent: United Talent Agency - Beverly Hills, 213/273-6700

DEADLY DESIRE (CTF) Skylark Films/Wilshire Court
  Productions, 1991, Story w/Jerry Ludwig

KURT LUEDTKE*
Agent: CAA - Beverly Hills, 213/288-4545

ABSENCE OF MALICE ★ Columbia, 1981
OUT OF AFRICA ★★ Universal, 1985

Screenplays:
THE DISTANT SHORE
HEARTS
WALLS
SILENCE WILL SPEAK
SCHINDLER'S LIST

ERIC LUKE*
Agent: Sanford, Skouras, Gross & Associates - Los Angeles,
  213/208-2100

EXPLORERS Paramount, 1985

Screenplays:
ATTACK FROM OUTER SPACE
NIGHTMARE

HARRY
THE JETSONS
THE WITCH   THE GUESTS

SIDNEY LUMET
Agent: ICM - Los Angeles, 213/550-4000

PRINCE OF THE CITY ★   Orion/Warner Bros., 1981,
    w/Jay Presson Allen, directed
Q & A   Tri-Star, 1990, directed

STEVEN LUOTTO
IRON WARRIOR   Tri-Star, 1987, w/Al Bradley

TONY LURASCHI
THE OUTSIDER   Paramount, 1980, directed

BRAD LYNCH
MR. FROST   Triumph, 1990, w/Philippe Setbon

DAVID LYNCH*
Agent: CAA - Beverly Hills, 213/288-4545
Business: Lynch/Frost Productions, 7700 Balboa Blvd.,
    Van Nuys, CA 91406, 818/909-7900

ERASERHEAD   Libra, 1978, directed
THE ELEPHANT MAN ★   Paramount, 1980, w/Eric
    Bergren & Christopher DeVore, directed
DUNE   Universal, 1984, directed
BLUE VELVET   DEG, 1986, directed
WILD AT HEART   Samuel Goldwyn Company,
    1990, directed

Screenplays:
ONE SALIVA BUBBLE   w/Mark Frost
RONNIE ROCKET

JENNIFER LYNCH*
Agent: CAA - Beverly Hills, 213/288-4545

Screenplays:
BOXING HELENA   (directing)

MARTIN LYNCH
A PRAYER FOR THE DYING   Samuel Goldwyn
    Company, 1987, w/Edmund Ward

CAROL LYNN
CLICK: THE CALENDAR GIRL KILLER   Crown
    International, 1991, Story w/John Stewart

JONATHAN LYNN*
Agent: CAA - Beverly Hills, 213/288-4545

GINGERBREAD MAN (P)
ARMS & THE MAN (P)
TONIGHT AT 8:30 (P)
SONGBOOK (P)
PASS THE BUTLER (P)
HOTEL PARADISE (P)
MICK'S PEOPLE   (Short)
THE INTERNECINE PROJECT   Allied Artists, 1974,
    w/Barry Levinson
CLUE   Paramount, 1985, directed
NUNS ON THE RUN   20th Century Fox, 1990, directed

Screenplays:
LAND OF OPPORTUNITY   w/Jack Kaplan
ROCKITS
BIG DEAL

ALEV LYTLE
TELL ME A RIDDLE   Filmways, 1980, w/Joyce Eliason

SHEL LYTTON
BODY SLAM   DEG, 1987, w/Steve Burkow

M

DICK MAAS
Agent: Triad Artists, Inc. - Los Angeles, 213/556-2727

THE LIFT   Island Alive/Media Home Entertainment,
    1983, directed
FLODDER   Concorde Films, 1986, directed
AMSTERDAMNED   Vestron, 1987, directed

LEONARD MAAS JR.
WHY ME?   Triumph, 1989, w/Donald E. Westlake
I COME IN PEACE   Triumph, 1990, w/Jonathan Tydor

EDUARDO MACHADO*
Agent: Warden & White Associates - Beverly Hills,
    213/852-1028

MODERN LADIES OF GUANABACOA (P)
BROKEN EGGS (P)
SECOND GENERATION (P)
FABIOLA (P)
WHEN IT'S OVER (P)   w/Geraldine Sherman
WHY TO REFUSE (P)
ONCE REMOVED (P)
DON JUAN IN NEW YORK (P)
BURNING BEACH (P)
STEVIE WANTS TO PLAY THE BLUES (P)

Screenplays:
CHINA RIOS (CTF)
FIELDER'S CHOICE

SIMON MacCORKINDALE
Contact: Screen Actors Guild - Los Angeles, 213/465-4600

THAT SUMMER OF WHITE ROSES   Amy International/
    Jadran Film, 1989, w/Rajko Grlic & Borislav Pekic

BERNARD MacLAVERTY
CAL   Warner Bros., 1984
LAMB   Film Forum, 1986

STEPHEN J. MacLEAN*
Contact: WGA - Los Angeles, 213/550-1000

STARSTRUCK   Cinecom International, 1982
AROUND THE WORLD IN 80 WAYS   Alive Films, 1987,
    w/Paul Leadon, directed

Screenplays:
THE TROPICS

ALISTAIR MacLEAN
WHERE EAGLES DARE MGM, 1969
WHEN EIGHT BELLS TOLL Winkast, 1971
PUPPET ON A CHAIN Cinerama Releasing Company, 1972, w/Don Sharp & Paul Wheeler
BREAKHEART PASS United Artists, 1976

ANDREW MacLEAR
DEALERS Skouras Pictures, 1989

MATT MacMANUS*
Agent: CAA - Beverly Hills, 213/288-4545

FLIGHT OF THE NAVIGATOR Buena Vista, 1986, w/Michael Burton

DON MacPHERSON
Agent: Casaratto Company - London, 01/287-4450

ABSOLUTE BEGINNERS Orion, 1986, w/Richard Burridge & Christopher Wicking
THE BIG MAN Miramax, 1991

Screenplays:
DARK ANGEL

BRENT MADDOCK*
Agent: The Roberts Company - Los Angeles, 213/552-7800

SHORT CIRCUIT Tri-Star, 1986, w/S.S. Wilson
BATTERIES NOT INCLUDED Universal, 1986, w/Brad Bird, Matthew Robbins & S.S. Wilson
SHORT CIRCUIT II Tri-Star, 1988, w/S.S. Wilson
TREMORS Universal, 1990, w/S.S. Wilson
GHOST DAD Universal, 1990, w/S.S. Wilson & Chris Reese

DIANA MADDOX*
Agent: Larry Grossman & Associates - Beverly Hills, 213/550-8127

THE CHANGELING AFD, 1980, w/William Gray
THE AMATEUR 20th Century-Fox, 1982, w/Robert Littell

GUY MAGAR
Contact: Directors Guild of America - Los Angeles, 213/289-2000
Business: Renegade Films, 8033 Sunset Blvd. - Suite 1102, Los Angeles, CA, 90046, 213/466-0786

RETRIBUTION Taurus Entertainment, 1988, w/Lee Wasserman

DOUG MAGEE*
Agent: APA - Los Angeles, 213/273-0744

SOMEBODY HAS TO SHOOT THE PICTURE (CTF) Alan Barnette Productions, 1990

MARK MAGILL
WAITING FOR THE MOON Skouras Pictures, 1987

ALBERT MAGNOLI*
Agent: ICM - Los Angeles, 213/550-4000

PURPLE RAIN Warner Bros., 1984, w/William Blinn, directed

JEFFREY P. MAGUIRE*
Contact: WGA - Los Angeles, 213/550-1000

VAMPIRE LUST Demos Films, 1975, w/Djordje Milicevic
RECKLESS Can-America Productions, 1979, w/Djordje Milicevic
VICTORY Lorimar/Paramount, 1981, Story w/Djordje Milicevic
TOBY MCTEAGUE Spectrafilm, 1986, w/Jamie Brown & Djordje Milicevic

Screenplays:
LAST KISS w/Djordje Millicevic

DEZSO MAGYAR*
Agent: William Morris Agency - Beverly Hills, 213/274-7451

OFF BEAT Buena Vista, 1986, Story
STREETS OF GOLD 20th Century Fox, 1986, Story
NO SECRETS I.R.S. Releasing, 1991, w/Ken Selden, directed

ANTHONY MAHARJ
CROSS FIRE Silvertree Pictures, 1989, w/Noah Blough, directed
FUTURE HUNTERS Lightning Pictures, 1989, Story

Screenplays:
RAGE (directing)

MIKE MAHERN*
Agent: United Talent Agency - Beverly Hills, 213/273-6700

MOBSTERS Universal, 1991, w/Nick Kazan

Screenplays:
TRUST
FREEDOM SUMMER

WILLIAM MAI*
Contact: WGA - Los Angeles, 213/550-1000

THE LIGHTSHIP Castle Hill Productions, 1986, w/David C. Taylor

NORMAN MAILER
Contact: Directors Guild of America - Los Angeles, 213/289-2000

WILD 90 Supreme Mix, 1968, directed
BEYOND THE LAW Grove Press, 1968, directed
MAIDSTONE Supreme Mix, 1971, directed
TOUGH GUYS DON'T DANCE Cannon, 1985, directed

DUSAN MAKAVEJEV
MAN IS NOT A BIRD Grove Press, 1965, directed
LOVE AFFAIR: OR THE CASE OF THE MISSING SWITCHBOARD OPERATOR Brandon, 1966, directed
INNOCENCE UNPROTECTED Grove Press, 1968, directed
WR - MYSTERIES OF THE ORGANISM Cinema 5, 1971, directed
SWEET MOVIE Biograph, 1975, directed
MONTENEGRO *MONTENEGRO, OR PIGS AND PEARLS* Atlantic Releasing Corporation, 1981, directed
MANIFESTO Cannon, 1989, directed

BOB MAKELA
Agent: Susan Smith & Associates - Beverly Hills, 213/852-4777

Screenplays:
ADVENTURES IN BACHELORHOOD

ANNE MAKEPEACE
THOUSAND PIECES OF GOLD   American Playhouse/Maverick Films/Kelly/Yamamoto/Film Four International, 1991

TERENCE MALICK*
Contact: WGA - Los Angeles, 213/550-1000

DEADHEAD MILES   Paramount, 1971
POCKET MONEY   National General, 1972
BADLANDS   Warner Bros., 1974, directed
GRAVY TRAIN THE DION BROTHERS   Columbia, 1974
DAYS OF HEAVEN   Paramount, 1978, directed

Screenplays:
COUNTRYMAN
THE JERRY LEE LEWIS PROJECT

GEORGE MALKO*
Agent: Robinson, Weintraub, Gross & Associates - Los Angeles, 213/653-5802

THE DOGS OF WAR   United Artists, 1981, w/Gary M. DeVore
SWEET LORRAINE   Angelika Films, 1987, Story w/Shelly Altman, Steve Gomer & Michael Zettler
OUT COLD   Hemdale, 1989, w/Howard Glasser

Screenplays:
SLOW BURN
KISS OFF
SOB SISTERS
ROGUE FROM MOTOR CITY

LOUIS MALLE*
Agent: ICM - New York, 212/556-5600

FRANTIC ASCENSEUR POUR L'ECHAFAUD/ELEVATOR TO THE GALLOWS/LIFT TO THE SCAFFOLD   Times, 1957, w/Roger Nimier, directed
THE LOVERS   Zenith International, 1958, directed
ZAZIE ZAZIE DANS DE METRO   Astor, 1960, directed
THE FIRE WITHIN (LE FEU FOLLET)   Governor, 1963, directed
VIVA MARIA!   United Artists, 1965, w/Jean-Claude Carriere, directed
MURMUR OF THE HEART LE SOUFFLE AU COEUR ★   Palomar, 1972, directed
LACOMBE LUCIEN   20th Century-Fox, 1974, directed
BLACK MOON   20th Century-Fox, 1975, directed
AU REVOIR, LES ENFANTS ★   Orion Classics, 1987, directed
MAY FOOLS   Orion Classics, 1990, w/Jean-Claude Carriere, directed

BRUCE MALMUTH*
Agent: The Irv Schechter Company - Beverly Hills, 213/278-8070

Screenplays:
MAMA'S BOY
JUDGEMENT DAY

MARK MALONE*
Agent: United Talent Agency - Beverly Hills, 213/273-6700

DEAD OF WINTER   MGM/UA, 1987, w/Marc Shmuger
SIGNS OF LIFE   Avenue Pictures, 1989

Screenplays:
HOODS
THE WRIGHT BROS.

WILLIAM MALONE
Agent: CAA - Beverly Hills, 213/288-4545

CREATURE   Cardinal Releasing, 1985, w/Allan Reed, directed

DAVID MAMET*
Agent: Rosenstone/Wender - New York, 212/832-8330

AMERICAN BUFFALO (P)
EDMOND (P), also screenplay
GLENGARRY GLEN ROSS (P), also screenplay
LAKEBOAT (P)
A LIFE IN THE THEATER (P)
REUNION (P)
DARK PONY (P)
SEXUAL PERVERSITY IN CHICAGO (P)
THE DUCK VARIATIONS (P)
THE SHAWL (P)
PRAIRIE DU CHIEN (P)
THE WATER ENGINE (P)
MR. HAPPINESS (P)
THE WOODS (P)
SPEED-THE-PLOW (P)
THE POSTMAN ALWAYS RINGS TWICE   Paramount, 1981
THE VERDICT ★   20th Century-Fox, 1982
THE UNTOUCHABLES   Paramount, 1987
HOUSE OF GAMES   Orion, 1987, directed
THINGS CHANGE   Columbia, 1988, w/Shel Silverstein, directed
WE'RE NO ANGELS   Paramount, 1989
HOMICIDE   Triumph, 1991, directed

Screenplays:
HOFFA
ACE IN THE HOLE
MALCOLM X
KINGDOM
STATE & MAIN
DEERSLAYER

DON MANCINI*
Agent: Writers & Artists Agency - Los Angeles, 213/820-2240

CHILD'S PLAY   MGM/UA, 1989, w/Tom Holland & John Lafia
CHILD'S PLAY 2   Universal, 1990
CHILD'S PLAY 3   Universal, 1991

Screenplays:
DOG WHO CRIED WOLF
GREEN HORNET

ALAN R. MANDEL*
Agent: ICM - Los Angeles, 213/550-4000

SMOKEY AND THE BANDIT   Universal, 1977, w/James Lee Barrett & Charles Shyer
HOUSE CALLS   Universal, 1978, w/Julius J. Epstein, Max Shulman & Charles Shyer

GOIN' SOUTH   Paramount, 1979, w/Al Ramrus, John Herman Shaner & Charles Shyer

Screenplays:
BREAKFAST ON BEDFORD DRIVE w/Charles Shyer
THE LONG RAINBOW w/Charles Shyer
BIG DEAL ON MACARTHUR BOULEVARD w/Charles Shyer
TICKETS w/Charles Shyer
LADIES DAY
MOTHER NATURE'S DAUGHTER
DOMESTIC RELATIONS
JAKE'S THING
JUST ONE OF THOSE THINGS
JOE COLLEGE

BABALOO MANDEL*
Agent: CAA - Beverly Hills, 213/288-4545

NIGHT SHIFT   The Ladd Company/Warner Bros., 1982, w/Bruce Jay Friedman & Lowell Ganz
SPLASH ★   Buena Vista, 1984, w/Bruce Jay Friedman & Lowell Ganz
SPIES LIKE US   Warner Bros., 1985, w/Dan Aykroyd & Lowell Ganz
GUNG HO   Paramount, 1986, w/Lowell Ganz
VIBES   Columbia, 1988, w/Lowell Ganz
PARENTHOOD   Universal, 1989, w/Lowell Ganz
CITY SLICKERS   Castle Rock/Columbia, 1991, w/Lowell Ganz

Screenplays:
A LEAGUE OF THEIR OWN w/Lowell Ganz
MR. SATURDAY NIGHT w/Lowell Ganz
OVER MY DEAD BODY w/Lowell Ganz
DANCE SKINS w/Lowell Ganz
PERFECT COUPLE w/Lowell Ganz

LORING MANDEL*
Agent: Rosenstone/Wender - New York, 212/832-8330

ALL THE WAY HOME (P)
TOO CONFUSED, THE ANGEL (P)
COUNTDOWN   Warner Bros., 1968
PROMISES IN THE DARK   Orion/Warner Bros., 1979
THE LITTLE DRUMMER GIRL   Warner Bros., 1984

Screenplays:
REBELLION
CLOSING TIME

JEFF MANDELL
FIREHEAD   A.I.P. Studios, 1991, w/Peter Vuval

JAMES MANGOLD
OLIVER & CO. (AF)   Buena Vista, 1988, w/James Cox & Timothy J. Disney

JOHN MANKIEWICZ*
Contact: WGA - Los Angeles, 213/550-1000

Screenplays:
THE PRIDE AND THE JOY

JOSEPH L. MANKIEWICZ
Business Manager: Arthur B. Greene - New York, 212/661-8200

DIPLOMANIACS   RKO, 1933, w/Henry Meyers
DRAGONWYCK   20th Century-Fox, 1946, directed
SOMEWHERE IN THE NIGHT   20th Century-Fox, 1946, w/Howard Dimsdale, directed
A LETTER TO THREE WIVES ★★   20th Century-Fox, 1949
NO WAY OUT   20th Century-Fox, 1950, w/Lesser Samuels, directed
ALL ABOUT EVE ★   20th Century-Fox, 1950, directed
PEOPLE WILL TALK   20th Century-Fox, 1951, directed
JULIUS CAESAR   MGM, 1953, directed
THE BAREFOOT CONTESSA ★   United Artists, 1954, directed
GUYS AND DOLLS   Goldwyn, 1955
THE QUIET AMERICAN   United Artists, 1957, directed
CLEOPATRA   20th Century-Fox, 1963, w/Sidney Buchman & Ranald MacDougall & others, directed
THE HONEY POT   United Artists, 1966, directed

TOM MANKIEWICZ*
Agent: ICM - Los Angeles, 213/550-4000

THE SWEET RIDE   20th Century-Fox, 1968
DIAMONDS ARE FOREVER   United Artists, 1971, w/Richard Maibaum
LIVE AND LET DIE   United Artists, 1973
THE MAN WITH THE GOLDEN GUN   United Artists, 1974, w/Richard Maibaum
MOTHER, JUGS & SPEED   20th Century-Fox, 1976
THE EAGLE HAS LANDED   Columbia, 1977
THE CASSANDRA CROSSING   Avco Embassy, 1977, w/George Pan Cosmatos & Robert Katz
LADYHAWKE   Warner Bros., 1985, w/Edward Khmara & Michael Thomas
DRAGNET   Universal, 1987, w/Dan Aykroyd & Alan Zweibel, directed

Screenplays:
WASHINGTON GIRLS w/Colin Higgins
THE PRACTICE

WOLF MANKOWITZ
A KID FOR TWO FARTHINGS   London Films, 1955
THE BESPOKE OVERCOAT   Remus, 1956
EXPRESSO BONGO   British Lion, 1959, from his play
THE MILLIONAIRESS   20th Century-Fox, 1960
HOUSE OF FRIGHT   THE TWO FACES OF DR. JEKYLL   Hammer, 1960
THE DAY THE EARTH CAUGHT FIRE   British Lion, 1961, w/Val Guest
THE WALTZ OF THE TOREADORS   Rank, 1962
WHERE THE SPIES ARE   MGM, 1965, w/Val Guest
THE TWENTY-FIFTH HOUR   Concordia, 1967, w/Francois Boyer & Henri Verneuil
CASINO ROYALE   Columbia, 1967, w/John Law & Michael Sayers
BLOOMFIELD   THE HERO   World Film Services, 1969
TEASURE ISLAND   Massfilms, 1971, w/Orson Welles
BLACK BEAUTY   Tigon, 1971
THE HIRELING   Columbia, 1973
ALMONDS AND RAISINS (FD)   Brook Productions, 1983

ABBY MANN*
Agent: ICM - Los Angeles, 213/550-4000

JUDGMENT AT NUREMBERG ★★   United Artists, 1961, from his play
THE CONDEMNED OF ALTONA   20th Century-Fox, 1962, w/Cesare Zavattini
A CHILD IS WAITING   United Artists, 1963
SHIP OF FOOLS ★   Columbia, 1965
THE DETECTIVE   20th Century-Fox, 1968

REPORT TO THE COMMISSIONER   United Artists, 1974, w/Ernest Tidyman
WAR AND LOVE   Cannon, 1985
MURDERERS AMONG US: THE SIMON WIESENTHAL STORY (CTF)   HBO Pictures/Robert Cooper Productions/TVS Films, 1989, w/Ron Hutchinson & Robin Vote

EDWARD MANN*
Agent: The Cooper Agency - Los Angeles, 213/277-8422

THE KILLER INSIDE ME   Warner Bros., 1976, w/Robert Chandlee

EMILY MANN*
Agent: William Morris Agency - New York, 212/586-5100

STILL LIFE (P)

Screenplays:
WINNIE

MICHAEL MANN*
Agent: ICM - Los Angeles, 213/550-4205

THIEF   United Artists, 1981, directed
THE KEEP   Paramount, 1983, directed
MANHUNTER   DEG, 1986, directed

Screenplays:
THE LAST OF THE MOHICANS
   w/Chris Crowe (directing)

STANLEY MANN*
Agent: The Agency - Los Angeles, 213/551-3000

ANOTHER TIME, ANOTHER PLACE   Paramount, 1958
THE MOUSE THAT ROARED   Columbia, 1959, w/Roger Macdougall
HIS AND HERS   Eros, 1960, w/Jan Lowell & Mark Lowell
THE MARK   20th Century-Fox, 1961, w/Sidney Buchman
WOMAN OF STRAW   United Artists, 1964, w/Robert Muller & Michael Relph
RAPTURE   20th Century-Fox International Classics, 1965
UP FROM THE BEACH   20th Century-Fox, 1965, w/Claude Brule
A HIGH WIND IN JAMAICA   20th Century-Fox, 1965, w/Denis Cannan & Ronald Harwood
THE COLLECTOR ★   Columbia, 1965, w/John Kohn
THE NAKED RUNNER   Warner Bros., 1967
THE STRANGE AFFAIR   Paramount, 1968
FRAULEIN DOKTOR   Paramount, 1968, w/others
RUSSIAN ROULETTE   Avco Embassy, 1975, w/Tom Ardies & Arnold Margolin
SKY RIDERS   20th Century-Fox, 1976, w/Jack DeWitt & Garry Michael White
BREAKING POINT   20th Century-Fox, 1976, w/Roger Swaybill
THE SILENT FLUTE   Volare, 1978, w/Stirling Silliphant
DAMIEN - OMEN II   20th Century-Fox, 1978, w/Michael Hodges
METEOR   American International, 1979, w/Edmund H. North
CIRCLE OF IRON   Avco Embassy, 1979, w/Stirling Silliphant
EYE OF THE NEEDLE   United Artists, 1981

FIRESTARTER   Universal, 1984
CONAN THE DESTROYER   Universal, 1984
TAI-PAN   DEG, 1986, w/John Briley
HANNA'S WAR   Cannon, 1988, w/Menahem Golan

Screenplays:
POWELL
THIRD TIME LUCKY
EVENING FLIGHT

TED MANN*
Agent: Warden & White Associates - Beverly Hills, 213/852-1028

O.C. AND STIGGS   MGM/UA, 1987, w/Donald Cantrell

Screenplays:
THE BUTLER SCHOOL
CAMPUS COPS
THE VULGARIANS
BLOWN OFF THE MAP
MALIBU BUZZARDS
DRIVE AWAY

RICHARD MANNING*
Agent: APA - Los Angeles, 213/273-0744

Screenplays:
THE THIRTEENTH DUKE w/Richard Condon

ROGER D. MANNING
GRUNT! THE WRESTLING MOVIE   New World, 1985

MARK MANOS
LIQUID DREAMS   Fox/Elwes Corp., 1991, w/Zach Davis, directed

RUSSELL V. MANZATT*
Contact: 213/455-1617

RUSH WEEK   RCA/Columbia Home Video, 1991, w/Michael W. Leighton

LINDSAY MARACOTTA*
Contact: WGA - Los Angeles, 213/550-1000

Screenplays:
UNRAVELLED
PARALLEL WORLDS

TERRY MARCEL
Agent: London Management - London, 71/493-1610

HAWK THE SLAYER   ITC, 1976, w/Harry Robertson
THERE GOES THE BRIDE   Lonsdale, 1980, w/Ray Cooney, directed

TIMOTHY MARCH
Agent: CAA - Beverly Hills, 213/288-4545

A PIECE OF THE ACTION   Warner Bros., 1977, Story
FAST FORWARD   Columbia, 1985, Story

JAMES MARCUS
TANK MALLING   Pointlane Films, 1989, w/Mick Southworth, directed

Ma

LAWRENCE B. MARCUS*
Agent: ICM - Los Angeles, 213/550-4000

BACKFIRE   Warner Bros., 1949, w/Ivan Goff & Ben Roberts
DARK CITY   Paramount, 1950, w/John Meredyth Lucas
THE UNGUARDED MOMENT   Universal-International, 1956, w/Herb Meadow
THE VOICE IN THE MIRROR   Universal-International, 1958
A COVENANT WITH DEATH   Warner Bros., 1966, w/Saul Levitt
PETULIA   Warner Bros., 1968
JUSTINE   20th Century-Fox, 1969
GOING HOME   MGM, 1971
ALEX & THE GYPSY   20th Century-Fox, 1976
THE STUNT MAN ★   20th Century-Fox, 1980

EVE ROSE MAREMONT
Agent: InterTalent - Los Angeles, 213/858-6200

Screenplays:
HOMESICK

PAUL B. MARGOLIS*
Agent: Triad Artists, Inc. - Los Angeles, 213/556-2727

Screenplays:
CHROMIUM YELLOW
MISSING WIVES

ANDREW PETER MARIN*
Agent: CAA - Beverly Hills, 213/288-4545

HOG WILD   Avco Embassy, 1980
UNDERGROUND ACES   Filmways, 1981, w/Jim Carabatsos & Lenore Wright

RICHARD "CHEECH" MARIN*
Agent: CAA - Beverly Hills, 213/288-4545

UP IN SMOKE   Paramount, 1978, w/Tommy Chong
CHEECH & CHONG'S NEXT MOVIE   Universal, 1980, w/Tommy Chong
CHEECH & CHONG'S NICE DREAMS   Columbia, 1981, w/Tommy Chong
THINGS ARE TOUGH ALL OVER   Columbia, 1982, w/Tommy Chong
CHEECH & CHONG: STILL SMOKIN'   Paramount, 1983, w/Tommy Chong
CHEECH & CHONG'S THE CORSICAN BROTHERS   Orion, 1984, w/Tommy Chong
BORN IN EAST L.A.   Universal, 1987, directed

ANNE MARISSE
GRADUATION DAY   IFI-Scope III, 1981, w/Herb Freed

TONY MARK*
Business Manager: Jeffrey M. Fryer & Co. - Los Angeles, 213/473-5040

ROOFTOPS   New Century/Vista, 1989, Story w/Allan Goldstein

PETER MARKLE*
Agent: CAA - Beverly Hills, 213/288-4545

THE PERSONALS   New World, 1982, directed
YOUNGBLOOD   MGM/UA, 1986, directed

Screenplays:
SKULL & BONES

MERRILL MARKOE*
Business Manager: Nigro, Karlen & Segal - Los Angeles, 213/277-4657

Screenplays:
JUST ANOTHER LOVE STORY
LIVING THE ALTERNATIVE LIFE

MITCH MARKOWITZ*
Agent: Larry Grossman & Associates - Beverly Hills, 213/550-8127

GOOD MORNING VIETNAM   Buena Vista, 1987
CRAZY PEOPLE   Paramount, 1990

Screenplays:
FALSE LABOR
GETTING GIRLS
BREAKING UP IS HARD TO DO
THE LAST HASIDIC COMIC
ROBBERS

ARTHUR R. MARKS*
Agent: Contemporary Artists - Beverly Hills, 213/278-8250

BONNIE'S KIDS   General Film Corporation, 1974, directed
THE ROOM MATES   General Film Corporation, 1973, directed

DENNIS MARKS*
Contact: WGA - Los Angeles, 213/550-1000

THE JETSONS (AF)   Universal, 1990

NEAL MARLENS*
Agent: United Talent Agency - Beverly Hills, 213/273-6700
Business: The Black/Marlens Company, 1440 S. Sepulveda Blvd., Los Angeles, CA, 90025, 213/444-8100

Screenplays:
THE JUMPING OFF POINT w/Carol Black

DOUG MARLETTE*
Agent: ICM - Los Angeles, 213/550-4000

Screenplays:
EX w/Pat Conroy

MALIA SCOTCH MARMO
Agent: InterTalent - Los Angeles, 213/858-6200

ONCE AROUND   Universal, 1991
HOOK   Tri-Star, 1991, w/Jim V. Hart

Screenplays:
SIGHTINGS

MALCOLM MARMORSTEIN*
Agent: Preferred Artists - Encino, 818/990-0305

S*P*Y*S 20th Century-Fox, 1974, w/Lawrence J.
  Cohen & Fred Freeman
WHIFFS 20th Century-Fox, 1975
PETE'S DRAGON Buena Vista, 1977
RETURN FROM WITCH MOUNTAIN BuenaVista, 1978
DEAD MEN DON'T DIE TransAtlantic Pictures,
  1990, directed

EUGENE MARNER
Contact: Directors Guild of America - Los Angeles,
  213/289-2000

BEAUTY AND THE BEAST Cannon, 1987, directed

LEON MARR
Agent: William Morris Agency - Beverly Hills, 213/274-7451

DANCING IN THE DARK New World, 1986, directed

TERENCE MARSH*
Agent: Sandra Marsh Management - Sherman Oaks,
  818/905-6961

FINDERS KEEPERS Warner Bros., 1984, w/Charles
  Dennis & Ronny Graham
HAUNTED HONEYMOON Orion, 1986, w/Gene Wilder

ANDREW MARSHALL
Contact: 011/441-8056

THE MISDAVENTURES OF MR. WILT Samuel Goldwyn
  Company, 1990, Adaptation w/David Renwick

Screenplays:
MUSHROOM BUTTON w/David Renwick
JINGLE BELLS w/David Renwick

GARRY MARSHALL*
Agent: ICM - New York, 212/556-5600
Business Manager: Diane Frazen, Henderson
  Productions, 10067 Riverside Drive, North
  Hollywood, CA 91602, 818/985-6417

WRONG TURN AT LUNGFISH (P)
HOW SWEET IT IS National General, 1968,
  w/Jerry Belson
THE GRASSHOPPER National General, 1979,
  w/Jerry Belson
THE FLAMINGO KID 20th Century Fox, 1984, w/Neal
  Marshall, directed

Screenplays:
LOVE, ROGER w/Jerry Belson
C. DMIAS w/Lowell Ganz

NEAL MARSHALL*
Agent: William Morris Agency - Beverly Hills, 213/274-7451

THE FLAMINGO KID 20th Century Fox, 1984,
  w/Garry Marshall

Screenplays:
G.I. JONES
THE CAB DRIVER
PAJAMA PRINCESS
WIFE MISTRESS

STEVE K. MARSHALL*
Agent: CAA - Beverly Hills, 213/288-4545

REVENGE OF THE NERDS II 20th Century Fox, 1987,
  w/Dan Guntzelman

Screenplays:
HOT WATER w/Dan Guntzelman
PAPARAZZI w/Dan Guntzelman

MARDIK MARTIN*
Agent: The Partos Company - Los Angeles,
  213/876-5500

MEAN STREETS Warner Bros., 1973,
  w/Martin Scorsese
NEW YORK, NEW YORK United Artists, 1977,
  w/Earl Mac Rauch
RAGING BULL United Artists, 1978, w/Paul Schrader

Screenplays:
CARLITO'S WAY w/Earl Mac Rauch
ROCK 'N' ROLL STORY
WEEGIE

PAMELA SUE MARTIN
Agent: APA - Los Angeles, 213/273-0744

TORCHLIGHT International Film Marketing, 1984,
  w/Eliza Moorman

RICHARD WAYNE MARTIN
NO JUSTICE Richfield's Releasing, 1989, co-directed

ROBERT MARTIN
FRANKENHOOKER Shapiro Glickenhaus, 1990,
  w/Frank Henenlotter

STEVE MARTIN*
Agent: APA - Los Angeles, 213/273-0744

THE JERK Universal, 1979, w/Michael Elias &
  Carl Gottlieb
DEAD MEN DON'T WEAR PLAID Universal, 1982,
  w/George Gipe & Carl Reiner
THE MAN WITH TWO BRAINS Warner Bros., 1983,
  w/George Gipe & Carl Reiner
THREE AMIGOS Orion, 1986, w/Lorne Michaels &
  Randy Newman
ROXANNE Columbia, 1987
L.A. STORY Tri-Star, 1991

Screenplays:
THE TOUCH

TROY KENNEDY MARTIN*
Agent: Sanford, Skouras, Gross & Associates - Los Angeles,
  213/208-2100

THE ITALIAN JOB Paramount, 1969
KELLY'S HEROES MGM, 1970
THE JERUSALEM FILE MGM, 1971
SWEENEY 2 EMI, 1978
RED HEAT Tri-Star, 1988, w/Walter Hill & Harry Kleiner

Screenplays:
TROPPO

Ma

FILM WRITERS GUIDE

WILLIAM E. MARTIN*
Contact: WGA - Los Angeles, 213/550-1000

HARRY AND THE HENDERSONS   Universal, 1987,
w/William Dear & Ezra D. Rappaport

RICHARD MARTINI*
Agent: The Gersh Agency - Beverly Hills, 213/274-6611

THREE FOR THE ROAD   New Century/Vista, 1987,
w/Miguel Tejada-Flores & Tim Metcalfe
YOU CAN'T HURRY LOVE   MCEG, 1988, directed
LIMIT UP   MCEG, 1990, w/Lu Anders, directed

RAYMOND MARTINO
ANGELS OF THE CITY   Raedon Home Video, 1989,
w/Lawrence-Hilton Jacobs & Joseph Merhi
AMERICAN BORN   PM Home Video, 1990, w/Addison
Randall, directed

NICK L. MARTINSON
FORBIDDEN ZONE   Sutton Marketing, 1980,
w/Matthew Bright, Richard Elfman & Nick James

MIKE MARVIN*
Agent: The Irv Schechter Company - Beverly Hills,
213/278-8070

SIX PACK   20th Century-Fox, 1982, w/Alex Matter
HOT DOG - THE MOVIE   MGM/UA, 1984
THE WRAITH   New Century/Vista, 1986, directed

Screenplays:
BED & BREAKFAST w/Andy Tennant
HALF BAKED! w/Andy Tennant

ARTHUR MARX*
Contact: WGA - Los Angeles, 213/550-1000

THE IMPOSSIBLE YEARS (P) w/Robert Fisher
A GLOBAL AFFAIR   Seven Arts, 1963, w/Robert
Fisher & Charles Lederer
I'LL TAKE SWEDEN   United Artists, 1965, w/Robert
Fisher & Nat Perrin
EIGHT ON THE LAM   United Artists, 1966, w/Robert
Fisher, Albert E. Lewin & Burt Styler
CANCEL MY RESERVATION   Naho Enterprises,
1972, w/Robert Fisher

RICK (R.J.) MARX
Contact: 213/285-8077

C.O.D.   Lone Star, 1982
PREPPIES   Platinum, 1984, w/Chuck Vincent
POMPEII WARRIOR QUEEN   Seymour Borde &
Associates, 1987
DRAGONARD   Cannon, 1987
GOR   Cannon, 1988
DEAD MAN WALKING   Metropolis Productions/Hit Films,
1988, w/John Weidner
PLATOON LEADER   Cannon, 1988, w/Andrew
Deutsch & David Walker
OUTLAW OF GOR   Cannon, 1989, w/Harry Alan Towers
MASTER OF DRAGONARD HILL   Cannon, 1990,
w/Harry Alan Towers

Screenplays:
LAMBADAMY: THE OPERATION (Shared)
THE HELL CHANNEL

JACK MASON
A MATTER OF DEGREES   Backbeat Productions, 1989,
w/W.T. Morgan & Randall Poster

NAN MASON
MY LITTLE GIRL   Hemdale, 1987, w/Connie Kaiserman

PAUL MASON*
Agent: ICM - Los Angeles, 213/550-4000

THE LADIES CLUB   New Line Cinema, 1986,
w/FranLewis Ebeling
THE FURTHER ADVENTURES OF TENNESSEE BUCK
Trans World Entertainment, 1988, Story

ED MAST
BOMBS AWAY   Shapiro Entertainment, 1985,
w/Bruce Wilson

BILL MASTERS
Agent: United Talent Agency - Beverly Hills, 213/273-6700

Screenplays:
GOOD NEWS/BAD NEWS
THE MONEY TRAIN

PETER MASTERSON
Business: Tejas Productions, 1165 Fifth Avenue - Apt. 15A,
New York, NY, 10029, 212/427-4055

THE BEST LITTLE WHOREHOUSE IN TEXAS   Universal,
1982, w/Larry L. King, from their play

NICO MASTORAKIS
Agent: The Artists Group - Los Angeles, 213/552-1100
Business: Omega Pictures, 8760 Shoreham Drive -
Suite 501, Los Angeles, CA 90069, 213/855-0516

BLOOD TIDE   21st Century, 1982, w/Richard Jeffries &
Donald Langdon
BLIND DATE   New Line Cinema, 1984, w/Fred C.
Perry, directed
GLITCH!   Omega Pictures, 1988, directed
BLOODSTONE   Omega Pictures, 1989, w/Curt Allen

ARMAND MASTROIANNI
Agent: William Morris Agency - Beverly Hills,
213/274-7451

Screenplays:
SKINS (directing)
RAPALLO & SONS

WILLIAM MASTROSIMONE*
Agent: William Morris Agency - New York, 212/586-5100

SUNSHINE (P)
CAT'S PAW (P)
TAMER OF HORSES (P), also screenplay
EXTREMITIES   Atlantic Releasing Corporation, 1986,
from his play
THE BEAST   Columbia, 1988, from his play "Nanawatai"

Screenplays:
THE CHICO MENDEZ STORY
DAMON
IN FROM THE COLD

ALI MATHESON
Agent: The Wright Concept - Hollywood, 213/461-3844

Screenplays:
TIL MARRIAGE DO US PART w/Jon Cooksey
HIT PARADE w/Jon Cooksey
MISS MARLOW w/Jon Cooksey
BEAUTY SLEEP

CHRISTIAN L. MATHESON*
Agent: InterTalent - Los Angeles, 213/858-6200

BILL & TED'S EXCELLENT ADVENTURE   Orion, 1989, w/Ed Solomon
BILL & TED'S BOGUS JOURNEY   Orion, 1991, w/Ed Solomon

Screenplays:
KILLER BEACH BABES (directing)

RICHARD CHRISTIAN MATHESON*
Contact: WGA - Los Angeles, 213/550-1000

THREE O'CLOCK HIGH   Universal, 1987, w/Tom Szollosi
IT TAKES TWO   MGM/UA, 1989, w/Tom Szollosi
LOOSE CANNONS   Tri-Star, 1990, w/Richard Matheson & Bob Clark

Screenplays:
SLUM LORD w/Tom Szollosi
BLOOD PRESSURE w/Tom Szollosi
WHOSE WOODS THESE ARE w/Tom Szollosi
SHIFTER w/Richard Matheson
RED SLEEP w/Mick Garris
MAN'S BEST FRIEND

RICHARD MATHESON*
Agent: InterTalent - Los Angeles, 213/858-6200

NOW YOU SEE IT (P)
RANSOM   MGM, 1955, w/Cyril Hume
INCREDIBLE SHRINKING MAN   Universal, 1957
THE BEAT GENERATION   Albert Zugsmith, 1959, w/Lewis Meltzer
HOUSE OF USHER   American International, 1960
MASTER OF THE WORLD   American International, 1961
TALES OF TERROR   American International, 1961
THE PIT AND THE PENDULUM   American International, 1961
BURN, WITCH, BURN NIGHT OF THE EAGLE   American International, 1962, w/Charles Beaumont & George Baxt
THE COMEDY OF TERRORS   American International, 1963
THE RAVEN   American International, 1963
DIE, DIE, MY DARLING FANATIC   Columbia, 1965
THE YOUNG WARRIORS   Universal, 1967
THE DEVIL'S BRIDE   Hammer, 1968
DE SADE   American International, 1969
THE LEGEND OF HELL HOUSE   20th Century-Fox, 1974
SOMEWHERE IN TIME   Universal, 1980
TWILIGHT ZONE- THE MOVIE   Warner Bros., 1983, Segments 3 & 4
JAWS 3-D   Universal, 1983, w/Carl Gottlieb
DUEL   Universal, 1983
LOOSE CANNONS   Tri-Star, 1990, w/Richard C. Matheson & Bob Clark

Screenplays:
SHIFTER w/Richard C. Matheson
FACE-OFF
WHAT DREAMS MAY COME
BIG TIME RETURN
IMPLOSION
FORBIDDEN LAND
DEDMAN
SKEDADDLE
THE LAST REVOLUTION
NOVUM
CREATURE
RED SLEEP w/Mick Garris

STEVE MATHIS
WITHOUT WARNING   Filmways, 1980, w/Lyn Freeman, Dan Grodnick & Ben Nett

MELISSA MATHISON*
Agent: CAA - Beverly Hills, 213/288-4545

THE BLACK STALLION   United Artists, 1979, w/Jeanne Rosenberg & William Wittliff
THE ESCAPE ARTIST   Orion/Warner Bros., 1982, w/Stephen Zito
E.T.: THE EXTRATERRESTRIAL ★   Universal, 1982

Screenplays:
E.T. II
WINTER'S TALE
TINTIN

MICHAEL MATLOCK
TALES OF THE UNKNOWN   AIP Home Video, 1990, "Jack Falls Down"

ALEX MATTER
SIX PACK   20th Century-Fox, 1982, w/Mike Marvin

BURNY MATTISON
Business: Walt Disney Co., 500 S. Buena Vista St., Burbank, CA 91521, 818/560-1000

THE FOX AND THE HOUND (AF)   Buena Vista, 1981, Story w/others
THE GREAT MOUSE DETECTIVE (AF)   Buena Vista, 1986, w/others, directed

NAT MAULDIN*
Agent: Dytman & Associates - Beverly Hills, 213/288-1827

DOWNTOWN   20th Century Fox, 1990

Screenplays:
ROGER RABBIT II

RICHARD MAXWELL*
Agent: United Talent Agency - Beverly Hills, 213/273-6700

THE CHALLENGE   Embassy, 1982, w/John Sayles
THE SERPENT AND THE RAINBOW   Universal, 1988, w/Adam Rodman
SHADOW OF CHINA   New Line Cinema, 1991, w/Mitsuo Yanagimachi

Screenplays:
SHEET LIGHTNINGS
DOUBLE SUNRISE
HANDCARVED COFFINS

SNAKEHEAD
INTRUDERS
FALSE FLAG

ELAINE MAY*
(Elaine Berlin)
Business Manager: Scott Bercu - New York, 212/391-4900

MR. GOGOL AND MR. PREEN (P)
SUCH GOOD FRIENDS   Paramount, 1971
A NEW LEAF   Paramount, 1971, directed
MIKEY AND NICKY   Paramount, 1977, directed
HEAVEN CAN WAIT ★   Paramount, 1978,
  w/Warren Beatty
ISHTAR   Columbia, 1987, directed

Screenplays:
MEN *(remake)*
THE ONE-HUNDRED DOLLAR MISUNDERSTANDING

PAUL MAYERSBERG
Agent: William Morris Agency - Beverly Hills, 213/274-7451

THE MAN WHO FELL TO EARTH   Cinema 5, 1976
THE DISAPPEARANCE   Levitt-Pickman, 1977
MERRY CHRISTMAS, MR. LAWRENCE   Universal,
  1983, w/Nagisa Oshima
EUREKA   United Artists Classics, 1984
CAPTIVE *HEROINE*   CineTel Films, 1986, directed
NIGHTFALL   Concorde, 1988, directed

WENDELL MAYES*
Contact: George Diskant, Esq. - 213/824-3773

THE WAY TO THE GOLD   20th Century-Fox, 1957
THE SPIRIT OF ST. LOUIS   Warner Bros., 1957,
  w/Billy Wilder
THE HUNTERS   20th Century-Fox, 1958
FROM HELL TO TEXAS   *MANHUNT*   20th Century-Fox,
  1958, w/Robert Buckner
THE HANGING TREE   Warner Bros., 1958,
  w/Halstead Welles
ANATOMY OF A MURDER ★   Columbia, 1959
ADVISE AND CONSENT   Columbia, 1962
IN HARMS WAY   Paramount, 1965
VON RYAN'S EXPRESS   20th Century-Fox, 1965,
  w/Joseph Landon
HOTEL   Warner Bros., 1967
THE POSEIDON ADVENTURE   20th Century-Fox,
  1972, w/Stirling Silliphant
THE REVENGERS   Cinema Center, 1972
THE BANK SHOT   United Artists, 1974
DEATH WISH   Paramount, 1974
THE ENEMY BELOW   20th Century-Fox, 1976
GO TELL THE SPARTANS   Avco Embassy, 1978
LOVE AND BULLETS   ITC, 1979, w/John Melson
MONSIGNOR   20th Century-Fox, 1982,
  w/Abraham Polonsky

TONY MAYLAM
Contact: Directors Guild of America - Los Angeles,
  213/289-2000
Business: Worldwide Productions, 303-315 Cricklewood
  Broadway, London NW2, England, 011/452/809-0214

WHITE ROCK (FD)   EMI, 1977, directed
THE RIDDLE OF THE SANDS   Satori, 1979,
  w/John Bailey, directed

MELANIE MAYRON*
Agent: Triad Artists, Inc. - Los Angeles, 213/556-2727

STICKY FINGERS   Spectrafilm, 1988,
  w/Catlin Adams

MICHAEL MAYSON
Contact: Frankfurt, Garbus, Klein & Selz - New York,
  212/980-0120

BILLY TURNER'S SECRET   (Short), directed

Screenplays:
THROWIN' BASS

STEVE MAZUR*
Agent: The Roberts Company - Los Angeles,
  213/552-7800

Screenplays:
THE C NOTE w/Paul Guay
ABRA CADAVER w/Paul Guay

JILL MAZURSKY*
Agent: ICM - Los Angeles, 213/550-4000

TAKING CARE OF BUSINESS   Buena Vista, 1990,
  w/Jeffrey Abrams

Screenplays:
UNDER THE GUN w/Jeffrey Abrams
GONE FISHIN' w/Jeffrey Abrams

PAUL MAZURSKY*
Agent: ICM - Los Angeles, 213/550-4000

I LOVE YOU, ALICE B. TOKLAS   Warner Bros., 1968,
  w/Larry Tucker
BOB & CAROL & TED & ALICE ★   Columbia, 1969,
  w/Larry Tucker, directed
ALEX IN WONDERLAND   MGM, 1970, w/Larry
  Tucker, directed
BLUME IN LOVE   Warner Bros., 1973, directed
HARRY AND TONTO ★   20th Century-Fox, 1974,
  w/Josh Greenfeld, directed
NEXT STOP, GREENWICH VILLAGE   20th Century-Fox,
  1976, directed
AN UNMARRIED WOMAN ★   20th Century-Fox,
  1978, directed
WILLIE AND PHIL   20th Century-Fox, 1980, directed
TEMPEST   Columbia, 1982, w/Leon
  Capetanos, directed
MOSCOW ON THE HUDSON   Columbia, 1984, w/Leon
  Capetanos, directed
DOWN AND OUT IN BEVERLY HILLS   Buena Vista,
  1986, w/Leon Capetanos, directed
MOON OVER PARADOR   Univeral, 1988, w/Leon
  Capetanos, directed
ENEMIES, A LOVE STORY ★   20th Century Fox, 1989,
  w/Roger L. Simon, directed
SCENES FROM A MALL   Buena Vista, 1991, w/Roger L.
  Simon, directed

ED McBAIN
(See Evan Hunter)

JIM McBRIDE*
Agent: The Daniel Ostroff Agency - Los Angeles, 213/278-2020

DAVID HOLZMAN'S DIARY   Grove Press, 1967, w/L.M. Kit Carson, directed
MY GIRLFRIEND'S WEDDING   1968, directed
GLEN AND RANDA   UMC, 1971, w/Lorenzo Mars & Rudy Wurlitzer
HOT TIMES *A HARD DAY FOR ARCHIE*   1973, directed
BREATHLESS   Orion, 1983, w/L.M. Kit Carson, directed
GREAT BALLS OF FIRE!   Orion, 1989, w/Jack Baran, directed

Screenplays:
ELEKTRA ASSASSIN   w/L.M. Kit Carson
THE MOVIEGOER   w/L.M. Kit Carson
CONFESSIONS OF A DANGEROUS MIND   w/Jack Baran
CHALLENGER

PETER McBRIDE
Agent: The Wright Concept - Hollywood, 213/461-3844

Screenplays:
SEE NO EVIL
THREE DAYS IN HELL
THE ACTOR

ROD McBRIEN
AFTER SCHOOL   Moviestore Entertainment, 1989, w/John Linde, Hugh Parks & Joe Tankersley

ROD McCALL
Agent: The Chasin Agency - Beverly Hills, 213/278-7505

SALLY & BUDDY & LORETTA (Short), directed
EARLY WINTER   1976, unreleased, directed

Screenplays:
WITH OPEN ARMS   w/Luis Puenzo
HOT MOON   w/Suzanne Blum
BIRTHDAY
CABOOSE
HENRY LEAVES HOME
JO AND THE LIZARDS
ROADWAY
KOHCHEE
NINO
RADIO KILLERS FROM OUTER SPACE

JAMES McCALMONT
ESCAPE FROM SAFEHAVEN   SVS Films, 1989, w/Brian Thomas Jones

TIMOTHY B. McCANLIES*
Agent: InterTalent - Los Angeles, 213/858-6200

NORTH SHORE   Universal, 1987, w/William Phelps

Screenplays:
SECOND TO NONE   FLY BY aka THAI PIRATES
HARLEM
DEVIL'S BARGAIN
LOUISIANA RUN
MONTE CARLO COPS

BRYAN McCANN
BULLIES   Universal, 1986, w/John Sheppard

PETER McCARTHY
TAPEHEADS   Avenue Pictures, 1988, w/Bill Fishman

TODD McCARTHY
PRESTON STURGES: THE RISE AND FALL OF AN AMERICAN DREAMER (FD)   Barking Dog Productions, 1989
HOLLYWOOD MAVERICKS (FD)   American Film Institute/NHK Enterprises, Inc., 1989, w/Michael Henry Wilson

PAUL McCARTNEY
Agent: ICM - Los Angeles, 213/550-4000

GIVE MY REGARDS TO BROAD STREET   20th Century-Fox, 1984

SEAN McCARVER*
Contact: WGA - Los Angeles, 213/550-1000

Screenplays:
NIKKI & ME
BRIGADOON
STIR IT UP
SHOOT THE DEGROODTS

JOANNA McCLELLAND-GLASS
Agent: ICM - Los Angeles, 213/550-4000

Screenplays:
TIES THAT BIND
WOMAN WANTED

BILL McCLOSKEY
Agent: Circle Talent Associates - Beverly Hills, 213/285-1585

Screenplays:
BAD SPORTS   w/Eric Williams
ONE NIGHT ONLY   w/Eric Williams

JONAS McCORD*
Agent: CAA - Beverly Hills, 213/288-4545

Screenplays:
DAMAGES

JOHN McCORMICK*
Agent: William Morris Agency - Beverly Hills, 213/274-7451

LIVING ON TOKYO TIME   Skouras Pictures, 1987, w/Steven Okazaki

Screenplays:
DNA   w/Ross La Manna
TORPEDOS   w/Ross La Manna
CHOPPERS   w/Ross La Manna
PRIDE AND JOY   w/Ross La Manna

PATRICK B. McCORMICK*
Agent: Shapiro/Lichtman - Los Angeles, 213/859-8877

UNDER THE RAINBOW   Orion/Warner Bros., 1981, w/Harry Hurwitz, Martin Smith, Pat Bradley & Fred Bauer

TOM McCOWN*
Contact: WGA - Los Angeles, 213/550-1000

HEART OF DIXIE   Orion, 1989

Screenplays:
BRIDGE TO TERABITHIA
THE ROSE OF SHARON
LIGHT YEARS

ARCH McCOY
HERE COME THE TIGERS   American
   International, 1978

DENNYS McCOY*
Agent: H. N. Swanson, Inc. - Los Angeles, 213/652-5385

Screenplays:
ACE OF THE NEWSREELS w/Pamela Hickey
HARRY THE LION w/Pamela Hickey
FULL RECOVERY wPamela Hickey

TIM McCOY
SWEET REVENGE   Concorde, 1987,
   w/Steven M. Krauzer

ANDIE McCUAIG
DEAD RECKONING (CTF)   Houston Lady Co./MCA
   Entertainment, 1990, w/Neill D. Hicks

JIM McCULLOUGH, JR.
MOUNTAINTOP MOTEL MASSACRE   New World, 1986

ROBERT McDONNELL
TWICE DEAD   Concorde, 1989, w/Bert L. Dragin

TERRANCE McDONNELL*
Agent: Monteiro Rose Agency - Encino, 818/501-1177

POUND PUPPIES AND THE LEGEND OF BIG PAW (AF)
   Tri-Star, 1988, w/Jim Carlson

MICHAEL M. McDOWELL*
Agent: William Morris Agency - Beverly Hills, 213/274-7451

BEETLEJUICE   The Geffen Company/Warner Bros.,
   1988, w/Warren Skaaren
TALES FROM THE DARKSIDE: THE MOVIE
   Paramount, 1990, "Lot 249" & "Lover's Vow"

Screenplays:
TALES FROM THE DARKSIDE: THE MOVIE II
   w/Gahan Wilson
PET PEOPLE
WOMEN BEHIND BARS
NIGHTCLUB CONFIDENTIAL
ESP MCGREE
MUMMIES
THINNER

MATTHEW McDUFFIE
Agent: United Talent Agency - Beverly Hills, 213/273-6700

Screenplays:
BILLY HELL
ANGELS ON HORSEBACK
KISS THE GROUND
WISHBONES

ALAN B. McELROY*
Agent: CAA - Beverly Hills, 213/288-4545

HALLOWEEN 4   Galaxy International, 1989
WHEELS OF TERROR (CTF)   Once Upon a Time, 1990

IAN McEWAN
Agent: CAA - Beverly Hills, 213/288-4545

THE PLOUGHMAN'S LUNCH   Samuel Goldwyn
   Company, 1984

Screenplays:
THE INNOCENT
THE GOOD SHOW
SOURSWEET

REX McGEE*
Agent: CAA - Beverly Hills, 213/288-4545
Business: 9507 Santa Monica Blvd. - Suite 206, Beverly Hills,
   CA 90210, 213/859-8156

Screenplays:
COMMUNITY STANDARDS
PAL SMURCH
UNTYING THE KNOT
THE LIFE OF THE PARTY
THE HONEYMOON
WALTZ IN MARATHON
MEET MR. BRINK
EASY LIVING
DECEPTION
THE HARDY BOYS

JOSANN McGIBBON*
Agent: The Daniel Ostroff Agency - Los Angeles,
   213/278-2020

WORTH WINNING   20th Century Fox, 1989,
   w/Sara Parriott
THREE MEN AND A LITTLE LADY   Buena Vista, 1990,
   Story w/Sara Parriott
THE FAVOR   Orion, 1992, w/Sara Parriott

Screenplays:
MRS. CALIFORNIA w/Sara Parriott
RUNAWAY BRIDE w/Sara Parriott

DAVID McGILLIVRAY
TERROR   Crown International, 1979

DOUGLAS McGRATH*
Agent: APA - New York, 212/852-1500

THE BIG DAY (P)

Screenplays:
JUST MARRIED
BORN YESTERDAY

GEORGE McGRATH*
Contact: WGA - Los Angeles, 213/550-1000

BIG-TOP PEE WEE   Paramount, 1988, w/Paul Reubens

JOHN McGRATH
Agent: Margaret Ramsay Ltd. - London, 011/441/240-0691

BILLION DOLLAR BRAIN   United Artists, 1967
THE BOFORS GUN   Rank, 1968

THE RECKONING   Columbia, 1969
THE DRESSMAKER   Euro-American, 1988

THOMAS McGRATH
INDEPENDENCE   20th Century-Fox, 1976, w/Joyce
 Ritter & Lloyd Ritter

JOHN McGREEVY*
Agent: Preferred Artists - Encino, 818/990-0305

HOT ROD GIRL   American International, 1956
DEATH IN SMALL DOSES   1957
CAST A LONG SHADOW   United Artists, 1959,
 w/Martin H. Goldsmith
HELLO DOWN THERE   Paramount, 1969,
 w/Frank Telford
NIGHT CROSSING   Buena Vista, 1982

THOMAS McGUANE*
Agent: ICM - Los Angeles, 213/550-4000

92 IN THE SHADE   United Artists, 1975, directed
RANCHO DELUXE   United Artists, 1975
THE MISSOURI BREAKS   United Artists, 1976
TOM HORN   Warner Bros., 1980, w/Edwin Shrake
COLD FEET   Avenue Pictures, 1989, w/Jim Harrison

Screenplays:
SOLDIERS OF MISFORTUNE
NOBODY'S ANGEL
BOULEVARD WEST
TROPICAL WHOLESALE
TOKYO BAY
FLYING COLORS
THE EL WESTERN

DON McGUIRE*
Contact: WGA - Los Angeles, 213/550-1000

MEET DANNY WILSON   Universal-International, 1951
WALKING MY BABY BACK HOME   Universal-
 International, 1953, w/Oscar Brodney
THREE RING CIRCUS   Paramount, 1954,
 w/Joseph Pevney
ARTISTS AND MODELS   Paramount, 1955,
 w/Frank Tashlin
JOHNNY CONCHO   United Artists, 1956, w/David P.
 Harmon, directed
HEAR ME GOOD   Paramount, 1957, directed
THE DELICATED DELINQUENT   Paramount,
 1957, directed
SUPPOSE THEY GAVE A WAR AND NOBODY CAME?
 Cinerama Releasing Corporationa, 1970, w/Hal Captain
TOOTSIE ★   Columbia, 1982, Story w/Larry Gelbart

JAY McINERNEY*
Agent: ICM - Los Angeles, 213/550-4000

BRIGHT LIGHTS, BIG CITY   MGM/UA, 1988

DOUGLAS LLOYD McINTOSH*
Agent: Camden-ITG - Los Angeles, 213/289-2700

Screenplays:
BAD WOMAN BLUES
THE LAUGHING MAN

DOUG McINTYRE*
Agent: The Wright Concept - Hollywood, 213/461-3844

Screenplays:
RIDE THE WIND

ELIZABETH McKAY
AN UNSUITABLE JOB FOR A WOMAN   Castle Hill
 Productions, 1985

STEVEN McKAY*
Agent: Triad Artists, Inc. - Los Angeles, 213/556-2727

HARD TO KILL   Warner Bros., 1990

Screenplays:
BODY HUNTER

MICHAEL McKEAN*
Agent: Triad Artists, Inc. - Los Angeles, 213/556-2727

THIS IS SPINAL TAP   Embassy, 1984, w/Christopher
 Guest, Harry Shearer & Rob Reiner
THE BIG PICTURE   Columbia, 1989, w/Christopher Guest
 & Michael Varhol

BERNARD McKENNA
THE ODD JOB   Columbia, 1978, w/Graham Chapman
YELLOWBEARD   Orion, 1983, w/Graham Chapman &
 Peter Cook

TERENCE McKENNA
THE SQUAMISH FIVE   CBC Film, 1989, w/Ken Gass

BLEU McKENZIE
KING OF THE CITY   CLUB LIFE   Troma, 1986, Story
 w/Norman Thaddeus Vane

CHARLES McKEOWN
BRAZIL ★   Universal, 1985, w/Terry Gilliam &
 Tom Stoppard
THE ADVENTURES OF BARON MUNCHAUSEN
 Columbia, 1988, w/Terry Gilliam

W.R. (BILL) McKINNEY, JR.*
Agent: Stephanie Mann Agency - Los Angeles, 213/653-7130

TEACHERS   MGM/UA, 1984

Screenplays:
PRIDE AND JOY
BAREHUNTIN'
CHINA
WINSTON COME HOME, YOUR DOG DIED TUESDAY
THE PHENOM
THE BUTLER

DON McLENNAN
Agent: Barrett, Benson, McCartt & Weston - Los Angeles,
 213/247-5500

HARD KNOCKS   Andromeda Productions, 1980, w/Hilton
 Bonner, directed
SLATE, WYN & ME   Hemdale, 1987, directed

Screenplays:
BEFORE YOUR VERY EYES   w/Hilton Bonner
KING ISLAND   w/Zbigniew Friedrich

Mc

MOST WANTED MAN w/Larry Held
JAILBAIT w/Tom Burstall
WHITE HEAT
UNFINISHED BUSINESS
COMEDY OF ERRORS

TOM McLOUGHLIN*
Contact: WGA - Los Angeles, 213/550-1000

ONE DARK NIGHT   Comworld, 1983, w/Michael Hawes, directed
FRIDAY THE 13TH, PART VI: JASON LIVES   Paramount, 1986, directed
DATE WITH AN ANGEL   DEG, 1987, directed

THOMAS McMAHON
SIDEWINDER 1   Avco Embassy, 1977, w/Nancy Voyles Crawford

LARRY McMURTRY*
Agent: Irving Paul Lazar Agency - Beverly Hills, 213/275-6153

THE LAST PICTURE SHOW ★   Columbia, 1971, w/Peter Bogdanovich
MONTANA (CTF)   Turner Network TV, 1989
MEMPHIS (CTF)   Turner Network TV, 1991, w/Cybill Shepherd
FALLING FROM GRACE   Columbia, 1992

Screenplays:
DANCE WITH ME OUTSIDE   w/L. Silko
DESERT ROSE
SOMEBODY'S DARLING
ALL MY FRIENDS ARE GOING TO BE STRANGERS
JUBILEE
HONKY TONK SUE
CROSSING NIAGARA

KEITH McNALLY
END OF THE NIGHT   In Absentia Productions, 1991, directed

TERRENCE McNALLY
Agent: William Morris Agency - New York, 212/586-5100

WHERE HAS TOMMY FLOWERS GONE? (P)
BAD HABITS (P)
IT'S ONLY A PLAY (P)
THE LISBON TRAVIATA (P)
AND THINGS THAT GO BUMP IN THE NIGHT (P)
NEXT (P)
LIPS TOGETHER, TEETH APART (P)
THE RITZ   Warner Bros., 1976, from his play
FRANKIE AND JOHNNY   Paramount, 1991, from his play "Frankie and Johnny in the Clair De Lune"

TERRENCE E. McNALLY
EARTH GIRLS ARE EASY   Vestron, 1988, w/Julie Brown & Charlie Coffey

JOHN McNAUGHTON
Agent: ICM - Los Angeles, 213/550-4000

HENRY...PORTRAIT OF A SERIAL KILLER   Greycat, 1989, w/Richard Fire, directed

Screenplays:
STEP RIGHT UP

JERRY McNEELY*
Agent: Triad Artists, Inc. - Los Angeles, 213/556-2727

BLIND VENGEANCE (CTF)   Spanish Trail Productions, 1990, Story w/Howard Rodman

STEPHEN F. McPHERSON*
Agent: United Talent Agency - Beverly Hills, 213/273-6700

COCOON: THE RETURN   20th Century Fox, 1987

Screenplays:
GOING HOME w/Elizabeth Bradley
OUTWARD BOUND w/Elizabeth Bradley
MAD DASH w/Elizabeth Bradley
TO THE MANOR BORN w/Elizabeth Bradley
THE GRAY GHOST MIDNIGHT FLYER w/Elizabeth Bradley

JOHN McTIERNAN*
Agent: William Morris Agency - Beverly Hills, 213/274-7451

NOMADS   Atlantic Releasing Corporation, 1985, directed

Screenplays:
QUEST OF ST. JAMES ELK
TREASURE HUNT

KATHY McWORTER*
Agent: Preferred Artists - Encino, 818/990-0305

Screenplays:
THE CHEESE STANDS ALONE
BATS
THE BOY WHO EATS ROCKS

BIG BOY MEDLIN*
Agent: ICM - Los Angeles, 213/550-4000

ROADIE   United Artists, 1981, w/Michael Ventura

Screenplays:
MEANWHILE BACK AT THE KREMLIN w/Michael Ventura
HOWLING AT THE MOON w/Michael Ventura
MONTREAUX
THE JOKER AND THE DEALER
SHOT NIGHT
BEACH PARTY '85
LOW POWER

MURRAY MEDNICK*
Agent: Camden-ITG - Los Angeles, 213/289-2700

SHATTER'N'WADE (P)

Screenplays:
SCAR

MARK MEDOFF*
Agent: William Morris Agency - New York, 212/586-5100

THE TURNAROUND (P)
THE MAGESTIC KID (P)
THE HANDS OF ITS ENEMY (P)
THE HEART OUTRIGHT (P)
THE BAD BOYS (P)   also screenplay
FREE (P)   also screenplay
CAPTAIN SUNTAN RIDES AGAIN (P)   also screenplay
GOOD GUYS WEAR BLACK   American Cinema, 1978, w/Bruce Cohn

WHEN YOU COMIN' BACK RED RYDER?   Columbia, 1979, from his play
CHILDREN OF A LESSER GOD ★   Paramount, 1986, w/Hesper Anderson, from his play
OFF BEAT   Buena Vista, 1986
APOLOGY (CTF)   Roger Gimbel Productions/Peregrine Entertainment/ASAP Productions/HBO, 1986
CLARA'S HEART   Warner Bros., 1988
CITY OF JOY   Tri-Star, 1991

Screenplays:
FOURTH FURY
BULLY
LAST WISH
MISS ONE THOUSAND SPRING BLOSSOMS
DECEPTION

CARY MEDOWAY
Agent: Shapiro/Lichtman - Los Angeles, 213/859-8877

THE HEAVENLY KID   Orion, 1985, w/Martin Copeland, directed

THOMAS MEEHAN*
Agent: Camden-ITG - Los Angeles, 213/289-2700

ANNIE (P)
TO BE OR NOT TO BE   20th Century-Fox, 1983, w/Ronny Graham
ONE MAGIC CHRISTMAS   Buena Vista, 1985
SPACEBALLS   MGM/UA, 1987, w/Mel Brooks & Ronny Graham

STEVE MEERSON*
Agent: William Morris Agency - Beverly Hills, 213/274-7451

STAR TREK IV: THE VOYAGE HOME   Paramount, 1986, w/Harve Bennett, Peter Krikes & Nicholas Meyer
BACK TO THE BEACH   Paramount, 1987, w/Peter Krikes & Christopher Thompson
DOUBLE IMPACT   Columbia, 1991, Story w/Peter Krikes, Sheldon Lettich & Jean-Claude Van Damme

Screenplays:
THAT'S LIFE, 1986 w/Peter Krikes
A NEW KIND OF LOVE w/Peter Krikes
RIVER OAKS w/Peter Krikes
THE LONG WAY HOME w/Peter Krikes
ON GUARD w/Peter Krikes
19 PURCHASE STREET w/Peter Krikes
PLANET OF THE TEENAGERS w/Peter Krikes
MONEY FROM THE SKY w/Peter Krikes

ROBERT T. MEGGINSON*
Agent: APA - Los Angeles, 213/273-0744

F/X   Orion, 1986, w/Gregory Fleeman

Screenplays:
TWO COPS w/Gregory Fleeman
DOUBTING THOMAS
FLAWLESS

GEORGE MENDELUK
Agent: The Irv Schechter Company - Beverly Hills, 213/278-8070
Business: World Classic Pictures, 6263 Tapia Drive, Malibu, CA 90265, 213/457-9911

STONE COLD DEAD   Dimension, 1979, directed

RAMON MENENDEZ*
Agent: ICM - Los Angeles, 213/550-4000

STAND AND DELIVER   Warner Bros., 1988, w/Tom Musca

ROBIN MENKEN
YOUNG LUST   RSO Films, 1982, w/Bruce Wagner
TEEN WITCH   Trans World Entertainment, 1989, w/Vernon Zimmerman

NINA MENKES
MAGDALENA VIRAGA   Menkes Film Productions, 1986, directed
QUEEN OF DIAMONDS   Menkes Film Productions, 1991, directed

JOE MENOSKY*
Agent: Writers & Artists Agency - Los Angeles, 213/820-2240

HIDING OUT   DEG, 1987, w/Jeff Rothberg

JIRI MENZEL
Contact: Czechoslovak Filmexport, Department of Coproductions & Service Facilities, Vaclavske Names ti 28, 111-45 Prague 1, Czechoslovakia, tel.: 268412

CLOSELY WATCHED TRAINS   Sigma III, 1966, directed
CAPRICIOUS SUMMER   Sigma III, 1968, directed
THOSE WONDERFUL MOVIE CRANKS   *MAGICIANS OF THE SILVER SCREEN*   1979, w/Oldrich Vicek, directed

PAT MEPHITIS
Agent: Phoenix Literary Agency - Livingston, Montana, 406/222-2848

NATIONAL LAMPOON'S MOVIE MADNESS   United Artists, 1982, w/Tod Carroll, Shary Flenniken, Gerald Sussman & Ellis Weiner

JOSEPH MERHI
ANGELS OF THE CITY   Raedon Home Video, 1989, w/Lawrence Hilton-Jacobs & Raymond Martino

MONTE MERRICK*
Agent: Writers & Artists Agency - Los Angeles, 213/820-2240

HELL OF A TOWN (P)
PRIDE AND JOY (P)
STAYING TOGETHER   Hemdale, 1989
MEMPHIS BELLE   Warner Bros., 1990

Screenplays:
TOKYO DIAMOND
ALIVE
LANE FROST STORY
STARRY EYED
TENDERFOOT

BOB MERRILL*
Agent: Shapiro/Lichtman - Los Angeles, 213/859-8877

W.C. FIELDS AND ME   Universal, 1976

KEITH MERRILL
Contact: Directors Guild of America - Los Angeles, 213/289-2000

TAKE DOWN   Buena Vista, 1979, w/Eric Herdershot, directed
HARRY'S WAR   Taft International, 1981, directed

PHILIP FRANK MESSINA*
Agent: Robinson, Weintraub, Gross & Associates - Los Angeles, 213/653-5802

BRAINSTORM   MGM/UA, 1983, w/Robert Stitzel

KEN METCALFE
FIRECRACKER   New World, 1981, w/Cirio Santiago

STEPHEN B. METCALFE*
Agent: United Talent Agency - Beverly Hills, 213/273-6700

PILGRIM (P)
EMILY (P)
VIKINGS (P), also screenplay
FLORIDA STRAITS (CTF)   HBO Premiere Films/Robert Cooper Productions, 1986
JACKNIFE   Cineplex Odeon, 1989, from his play "Strange Snow"
COUSINS   Paramount, 1989

Screenplays:
MACHINE GUN KELLY
HALF A LIFETIME (CTF)
EVERLOVIN' BROWN
THE TIME BETWEEN
BOYS FROM GALILEE
LAST SEPTEMBER
THE BIG NOISE
TIME FLIES
COMMENCEMENT

TIMOTHY J. METCALFE*
Agent: InterTalent - Los Angeles, 213/858-6200

REVENGE OF THE NERDS   20th Century Fox, 1984, Story w/Jeff Buhai, Miguel Tejada-Flores & Steve Zacharias
THREE FOR THE ROAD   New Century/Vista, 1987, w/Richard Martini & Miguel Tejada-Flores
MILLION DOLLAR MYSTERY   DEG, 1987, w/Miguel Tejada-Flores & Rudy DeLuca
FRIGHT NIGHT PART 2   New Century/Vista, 1989, w/Miguel Tejada-Flores & Tommy Lee Wallace
IRON MAZE   Iron Maze Productions, 1991

Screenplays:
CALIFORNIA

DOUGLAS ANTHONY METROV*
Agent: CAA - Beverly Hills, 213/288-4545

SOLARBABIES   MGM/UA, 1986, w/Walon Green

RADLEY METZGER
THE LICKERISH QUARTET   Audobon, 1970, directed
THE CAT AND THE CANARY   Quartet, 1982, directed

JOHN MEYER*
Contact: WGA - New York, 212/245-6180

NOT FOR PUBLICATION   Samuel Goldwyn Company, 1984, w/Paul Bartel

MARLANE MEYER*
Agent: Triad Artists, Inc. - Los Angeles, 213/556-2727

PRISON STORIES: WOMEN ON THE INSIDE (CTF)   Francine LeFrak Productions/HBO Showcase, 1991, "Parole Board"

NICHOLAS MEYER*
Agent: CAA - Beverly Hills, 213/288-4545
Business: Pari Passu Productions, Paramount Pictures, 213/956-5841

INVASION OF THE BEE GIRLS   1973
THE SEVEN-PERCENT SOLUTION ★   Universal, 1976
TIME AFTER TIME   Orion/Warner Bros., 1977, directed
STAR TREK IV: THE VOYAGE HOME   Paramount, 1986, w/Harve Bennett, Peter Krikes & Steve Meerson

Screenplays:
STAR TREK VI : THE UNDISCOVERED COUNTRY
   w/Denny Martin Flynn (directing)
BLACK ORCHID
CHARMED LIVES
CONJURING
THE FRAME-UP
UNDERSTUDY

RUSS MEYER
Business: RM Films International Inc., P.O. Box 3748, Hollywood, CA 90028, 213/466-7791

THE IMMORAL MR. TEAS   Pedram, 1959, directed
EVE AND THE HANDYMAN   Eve, 1961, directed
EROTICA   Eve, 1961, directed
THE IMMORTAL WEST AND HOW IT WAS LOST   Eve, 1961, directed
LORNA   Eve, 1965, directed
MOTOR PSYCHO   Eve, 1965, shared, directed
FASTER, PUSSYCAT! KILL! KILL!   Eve, 1965, shared, directed
GOOD MORNING...AND GOODBYE   Eve, 1967, directed
FINDERS KEEPERS, LOVERS WEEPERS   Eve, 1968, directed
CHERRY, HARRY AND RAQUEL   Eve, 1969, shared, directed
BEYOND THE VALLEY OF THE DOLLS   20th Century-Fox, 1970, Story, shared, directed
SWEET SUZY! *BLACKSNAKE*   Signal 166, 1975, shared, directed
SUPERVIXENS   RM Films, 1975, shared, directed
RUSS MEYER'S UP!   RM Films, 1976, directed
BENEATH THE VALLEY OF THE ULTRAVIXENS   RM Films, 1979, directed

NANCY J. MEYERS*
Agent: ICM - Los Angeles, 213/550-4000

PRIVATE BENJAMIN ★   Warner Bros., 1980, w/Harvey Miller & Charles Shyer
IRRECONCILABLE DIFFERENCES   Warner Bros., 1984, w/Charles Shyer

PROTOCOL   Warner Bros., 1984, Story w/Harvey
   Miller & Charles Shyer
BABY BOOM   MGM/UA, 1987, w/Charles Shyer

Screenplays:
FATHER OF THE BRIDE w/Charles Shyer
CRIMINALS w/Charles Shyer

MENNO MEYJES*
Agent: CAA - Beverly Hills, 213/288-4545

THE COLOR PURPLE ★   Warner Bros., 1985
LIONHEART   Orion, 1987, w/Richard Outten
INDIANA JONES AND THE LAST CRUSADE   Paramount, 1989, Story w/George Lucas

Screenplays:
CAPA
RACING IN THE STREETS
DEATH OF ROCK & ROLL
THE SECRET GARDEN
LORENZO DEMICI

LEONARD MICHAELS*
Agent: ICM - Los Angeles, 213/550-4000
Contact: 415/642-3467

THE MEN'S CLUB   Atlantic Releasing
   Corporation, 1986

LORNE MICHAELS
Business: Broadway Video, 1619 Broadway, 9th Floor, New York, NY, 10019, 212/265-7621

THREE AMIGOS   Orion, 1986, w/Steve Martin & Randy Newman

MURRAY MICHAELS
TUFF TURF   New World, 1985, Story w/Gregg Collins O'Neill

TONY MICHELMAN*
Agent: David Shapira & Associates - Sherman Oaks, 818/906-0322

PHANTOM OF THE MALL: ERIC'S REVENGE
   Fries Entertainment, 1989, w/Robert King & Scott J. Schneid

Screenplays:
DOWNFALL w/Scott J. Schneid
THE RED HOUR w/Scott J. Schneid
INVASION OF THE BODY BUILDERS
   w/Scott J. Schneid

DAVID MICHENER
THE FOX AND THE HOUND (AF)   Buena Vista, 1981, Story w/others
THE GREAT MOUSE DETECTIVE (AF)   Buena Vista, 1986, w/others, co-directed

BETTE MIDLER
Business: All-Girl Pictures, Walt Disney Pictures, 500 S. Buena Vista St., Burbank, CA 91521, 818/560-5000

DIVINE MADNESS   Warner Bros., 1980, w/Jerry Blatt & Bruce Vilanch

ANNE-MARIE MIEVILLE
Contact: French Film Office, 745 Fifth Avenue, New York, NY 10151, 212/832-8860

SAUVE QUI PEUT LA VIE *EVERY MAN FOR HIMSELF N LIFE*   New Yorker/Zoetrope, 1980, w/Jean-Luc Godard & Jean-Claude Carriere
FIRST NAME: CARMEN   Spectrafilm, 1984
DETECTIVE   Spectrafilm, 1985, w/Jean-Luc Godard, Alain Sarde & Philippe Setbon

NIKITA MIKHALKOV
Contact: Union of Soviet Filmmakers, Vassilievskaya 13, Moscow, U.S.S.R., tel: 250-4114

DARK EYES   Island Pictures, 1987, w/Alexander Adabachian, directed

DJORDJE MILICEVIC*
Business Manager: Singer, Lewak, Greenbaum - Los Angeles, 213/477-3924

WET RAINBOW   Demos Films, 1974, w/Paul Baerwold, directed
VAMPIRE LUST   Demos Films, 1975, w/Jeff Maguire, directed
RECKLESS   Can-America Productions, 1979, w/Jeff Maguire, directed
VICTORY   Lorimar/Paramount, 1981, Story w/Jeff Maguire
RUNAWAY TRAIN   Cannon, 1985, w/Edward Bunker & Paul Zindel
TOBY McTEAGUE   Spectrafilm, 1986, w/JamieBrown & Jeff Maguire

Screenplays:
ABOVE SUSPICION
DEATH OF A STOCKBROKER
ENTERPRISE w/David Wheeler
FLAG FOR SUNRISE
GIRL ON A GOLDEN LEASH
HAMMER HAND
HIGHWAY ONE
LAST KISS w/Jeff Maguire
REMORA
ROCK AND GOAL
SECOND CHANCE
SHADOW 81
SHOOTER
SIEGE OF SILENCE
WOUNDED KNEE

FRANK MILITARY, JR.*
Agent: William Morris Agency - New York, 212/586-5100

Screenplays:
THE LOTTERY ROSE (directing)
BIRDS OF PREY
THE SILENCE
ANATOMY OF A JURY
THE PIECE
BEYOND A REASONABLE DOUBT

JOHN MILIUS*
Agent: ICM - Los Angeles, 213/550-4000

THE DEVIL'S EIGHT   American International, 1968, w/James Gordon White & Willard Hyuck
EVEL KNIEVEL   MGM, 1971, w/Alan Caillou

Mi
FILM WRITERS GUIDE

THE LIFE AND TIMES OF JUDGE ROY BEAN National General, 1972
JEREMIAH JOHNSON Warner Bros., 1972, w/Edward Anhalt
MAGNUM FORCE Warner Bros., 1973, w/Michael Cimino
DILLINGER American International, 1973, directed
THE WIND AND THE LION MGM/United Artists, 1975, directed
BIG WEDNESDAY Warner Bros., 1978, w/Dennis Aaberg, directed
1941 Universal/Columbia, 1979, Story
APOCALYPSE NOW ★ United Artists, 1979, w/Francis Coppola
CONAN THE BARBARIAN Universal, 1982, w/Oliver Stone, directed
RED DAWN MGM/UA, 1984, w/Kevin Reynolds, directed
EXTREME PREJUDICE Tri-Star, 1987, Story w/Fred Rexer
FAREWELL TO THE KING Orion, 1989, directed

Screenplays:
THE SIEGE OF LENINGRAD
THE VIKING

JEFF MILLAR*
Contact: WGA - Los Angeles, 213/550-1000

DEAD AND BURIED Avco Embassy, 1981, Story w/Alex Stern

ANNIE MILLER
Contact: French Film Office, 745 Fifth Avenue, New York, NY 10151, 212/832-8860

THE LITTLE THIEF Miramax, 1989

ARTHUR MILLER*
Agent: ICM - New York, 212/556-5600

ALL MY SONS (P)
DEATH OF A SALESMAN (P)
THE CRUCIBLE (P)
A MEMORY OF TWO MONDAYS (P)
A VIEW FROM THE BRIDGE (P)
AFTER THE FALL (P)
INCIDENT AT VICHY (P)
THE PRICE (P)
THE CREATION OF THE WORLD AND OTHER BUSINESS (P)
THE ARCHBISHOP'S CEILING (P)
THE AMERICAN CLOCK (P)
DANGER: MEMORY! (P)
THE RIDE DOWN TO MOUNT MORGAN (P)
CLARA (P)
THE MISFITS United Artists, 1961
EVERYBODY WINS Orion, 1990

BRUCE MILLER*
Agent: William Morris Agency - Beverly Hills, 213/274-7451

Screenplays:
CRAZY FOR YOU

CHRIS MILLER*
Agent: Harris & Goldberg - Los Angeles, 213/553-5200

NATIONAL LAMPOON'S ANIMAL HOUSE Universal, 1978, Douglas Kenney & Harold Ramis
CLUB PARADISE Warner Bros., 1986, Story w/Tom Leopold, Ed Roboto & David Standish

Screenplays:
THE CO-EDS w/Michael Sutton
THE TECHNICOLOR TIME MACHINE w/Michael Sutton
ANIMAL HOUSE NOW w/Michael Sutton
NO SUCH LUCK w/Michael Sutton
WITCHCRAFT w/Michael Sutton
BEL-AIR BUTLER w/Michael Sutton
JUST LIKE A WOMAN w/Michael Sutton

CLAUDE MILLER
Contact: French Film Office, 745 Fifth Avenue, New York, NY 10151, 212/832-8860

GARDE A VUE Ariane, 1981, w/Jean Herman, directed

FRANK MILLER*
Agent: Shapiro/Lichtman - Los Angeles, 213/859-8877

ROBOCOP 2 Orion, 1990, w/Walon Green

Screenplays:
ROBOCOP 3 w/Fred Dekker

GEOF MILLER*
Contact: WGA - Los Angeles, 213/550-1000

DEEPSTAR SIX Tri-Star, 1989, w/Lewis Abernathy

GEORGE MILLER
Business Manager: Arnold Burk, Gang, Tyre & Brown, Inc., 6400 Sunset Blvd., Los Angeles, CA 90028, 213/463-4863
Business: Kennedy Miller Productions, 30 Orwell Street, Kings Cross, Sydney, Australia

MAD MAX American International, 1979, w/James McCausland, directed
THE ROAD WARRIOR *MAD MAX II* Warner Bros., 1982, w/Brian Hannant & Terry Hayes, directed
MAD MAX BEYOND THUNDERDOME Warner Bros., 1985, w/Terry Hayes, directed

Screenplays:
LORENZO'S OIL w/Nick Enright (directing)

HARVEY MILLER*
Agent: ICM - Los Angeles, 213/550-4000
Business Manager: Jess S. Morgan & Co., Inc. - Los Angeles, 213/937-1552

PRIVATE BENJAMIN ★ Warner Bros., 1980, w/Nancy Meyers & Charles Shyer
JEKYLL AND HYDE...TOGETHER AGAIN Paramount, 1982, w/Jerry Belson, Monica Johnson & Michael Leeson
CANNONBALL RUN II Warner Bros., 1984, w/Hal Needham & Albert Ruddy
PROTOCOL Warner Bros., 1984, Story w/Nancy Meyers & Charles Shyer
BAD MEDICINE 20th Century Fox, 1985, directed

JASON MILLER*
Agent: The Artists Agency - Los Angeles, 213/277-7779

LOU GEHRIG DID NOT DIE OF CANCER (P)
THAT CHAMPIONSHIP SEASON   Cannon, 1982, from his play, directed

Screenplays:
SHAKE DOWN THE THUNDER

MARK MILLER
Agent: The Irv Schechter Company - Beverly Hills, 213/278-8070

SAVANNAH SMILES   Embassy, 1982

MELISSA MILLER
OH GOD! BOOK II   Warner Bros., 1980, w/Fred S. Fox, Josh Greenfeld, Hal Goldman & Seaman Jacobs

MICHAEL MILLER*
Agent: Warden & White Associates - Beverly Hills, 213/852-1028

Screenplays:
ORION POKER
HELLBENT
LAWYERS, GUNS AND MONEY

MOLLIE D. MILLER*
Agent: CAA - Beverly Hills, 213/288-4545

Screenplays:
GIRL CRAZY
SOLO
MODERN DOLLS

SUSAN MILLER
Agent: United Talent Agency - Beverly Hills, 213/273-6700

LADY BEWARE   Scotti Bros., 1987, w/Charles Zev Smith

VICTOR MILLER
Agent: Rick Hashagen & Associates - New York, 212/315-3130

FRIDAY THE 13TH   Paramount, 1980
A STRANGER IS WATCHING   MGM/UA, 1982, w/Earl Mac Rauch

GREG MILLIN
THE CLINIC   Satori, 1985

WILLIAM P. MILLING
Agent: Solomon Weingarten & Associates - Los Angeles, 213/474-8703

FORBIDDEN AMERICA   1982
SILENT MADNESS   Almi Pictures, 1984, Shared
SAVAGE DAWN   MAG Enterprises/Gregory Earls Productions, 1985
WOLFPACK   JER, 1986
CAGED FURY   21st Century Film Corporation, 1989, directed

RON MILNER*
Agent: William Morris Agency - Beverly Hills, 213/274-7451

CHECKMATES (P)

Screenplays:
THE JAMES BROWN STORY

MICHAEL MINER*
Agent: United Talent Agency - Beverly Hills, 213/273-6700

ROBOCOP   Orion, 1987, w/Edward Neumeier
DEADLY WEAPON   Empire Pictures, 1989, directed

Screenplays:
STRAT w/Edward Neumeier
THE EXECUTIONER w/Edward Neumeier
COMPANY MAN w/Edward Neumeier
HITMAN w/Edward Neumeier
WHITE TRASH w/Edward Neumeier (co-directing)
UPSIDE-DOWN
IRONMAN
BEAT THE DEVIL

ANTHONY MINGHELLA*
Agent: William Morris Agency - Beverly Hills, 213/274-7451

MADE IN BANGKOK (P)   also screenplay
TRULY, MADLY, DEEPLY   Samuel Goldwyn Company, 1991, directed

JOSEPH MINION*
Agent: William Morris Agency - Beverly Hills, 213/274-7451

AFTER HOURS   The Geffen Company/Warner Bros., 1985
VAMPIRE'S KISS   Hemdale, 1989

Screenplays:
MRS. DUKE'S MILLIONS
MOTORAMA

ROY MINTON
SCUM   Berwick Street Films, 1979
SCRUBBERS   Orion Classics, 1984, w/Jeremy Watt & Mai Zetterling

MELANIE I. MINTZ*
Contact: WGA - Los Angeles, 213/550-1000

LEADER OF THE PACK (P)
JUST ONCE (P)

Screenplays:
POWER: THE PHIL SPECTOR STORY
IN SUBMISSION

MURRAY MINTZ*
Agent: David Shapira & Associates - Sherman Oaks, 818/906-0322

Screenplays:
RED SCARE w/Joshua Smith
COLD CASH w/Joshua Smith
HIGH MOON
HEIR APPARENT
CARDIAC ARREST

Mi — FILM WRITERS GUIDE

JAY MIRACLE
THE HEALING FORCE   Woody Clark Productions, 1983, w/Woodrow W. Clark & Joanne Parrent

DAVID MIRKIN*
Agent: United Talent Agency - Beverly Hills, 213/273-6700

THE LAST RESORT   Concorde/Cinema Group, 1986

Screenplays:
GUERILLA VIDEO
TRIMMING THE FAMILY TREE
THE LAST RESORT

BRAD A. MIRMAN*
Agent: Writers & Artists - Los Angeles, 213/820-2240

Screenplays:
KNIGHT MOVES
PARTNERS IN CRIME
THE SET-UP
G.I. JILL

DAVID A. MISCH*
Agent: William Morris Agency - Beverly Hills, 213/274-7451

Screenplays:
DISTURBING THE PEACE
CONVENTIONS
GIRLGRABBERS FROM VENUS

RENEE MISSEL*
Agent: ICM - Los Angeles, 213/550-4000
Business: Renee Missel Productions, Samuel Goldwyn Company, 213/464-8560

MY MAN ADAM   Tri-Star, 1985, w/Roger L. Simon

JULIAN MITCHELL
Agent: The Lantz Office - New York, 212/586-0200

ARABESQUE   Universal, 1966, w/Stanley Price & Pierre Marton
ANOTHER COUNTRY   20th Century-Fox, 1984, from his play
VINCENT AND THEO   Hemdale, 1990

SOLLACE MITCHELL
Agent: CAA - Beverly Hills, 213/288-4545

Screenplays:
DOUBLE TAKE
PRESENT LAUGHTER
COLLEGE BOWL
THE WEDDING
SHELTER ISLAND
HATCHECK
HELLUVA DEAL
PG

STEVE MITCHELL
CHOPPING MALL   KILLBOTS   Concorde, 1986, w/Jim Wynorski

STEVEN LONG MITCHELL*
Agent: The Wright Concept - Hollywood, 213/451-3844

SKI PATROL   Triumph, 1990 w/Craig Van Sickle

Screenplays:
THE RAVAGER   w/Craig Van Sickle
LEGACY   w/Craig Van Sickle

MOSHE MIZRAHI
Agent: The Gersh Agency - Beverly Hills, 213/274-6611
Business: Rosa Productions, 5 rue D'Artois, 75008 Paris, France, 04/359-4704

MADAME ROSA   Lira Films, 1977, directed
I SENT A LETTER TO MY LOVE   CHERE INCONNUE   Atlantic Releasing Corporation, 1980, w/Gerard Brach, directed
LA VIE CONTINUE   Triumph/Columbia, 1982, w/Rachel Fabien, directed
EVERY TIME WE SAY GOODBYE   Tri-Star, 1986, w/Rachel Fabien & Leah Appet, directed

JORDAN H. MOFFET*
Agent: United Talent Agency - Beverly Hills, 213/273-6700

Screenplays:
ROCK BOTTOM
FAMILY ROYALTY

JIM MOLONEY*
Agent: CAA - Beverly Hills, 213/288-4545

THE FIENDISH PLOT OF DR. FU MANCHU   United Artists, 1980, w/Rudy Dochtermann

ROBERT MOLONEY*
Contact: WGA - Los Angeles, 213/550-1000

Screenplays:
NEED TO KNOW
JAKE'S TOMATOES
THE ID & I
HALLEY'S CONNECTION
BACK NINE
FOR ONE NIGHT ONLY

PAUL MONASH*
Agent: Triad Artists, Inc. - Los Angeles, 213/556-2727

BAIL OUT AT 43,000   United Artists, 1957
THE SAFECRACKER   MGM, 1958
THE SCARFACE MOB   Desilu, 1958
THE GUN RUNNERS   United Artists, 1958, w/Daniel Mainwaring
THE FRIENDS OF EDDIE COYLE   Paramount, 1973

PAUL S. MONES
Business Manager: Addis-Wechsler & Associates - Los Angeles, 213/954-9000

THE BEAT   Vestron, 1987, directed

Screenplays:
FATHERS AND SONS   (directing)

CHRISTOPHER MONGER*
Agent: Sanford, Skouras, Gross & Associates - Los Angeles, 213/208-2100

WAITING FOR THE LIGHT   Triumph, 1990, directed

Screenplays:
JANE ANNE
IF WISHES WERE HORSES

VINCENT MONGOL
CHAINED HEAT   Jensen Farley Pictures, 1983, w/Paul Nicolas
WARD B   *HELLHOLE*   Arkoff International Pictures, 1985

MEREDITH MONK
BOOK OF DAYS   The Stutz Company, 1991, w/Tone Blevins

CAROL MonPERE*
Agent: William Morris Agency - Beverly Hills, 213/274-7451

THE MOUSE AND HIS CHILD (AF)   Sanrio, 1977

Screenplays:
MIDNIGHT SOLDIER
THE LIMIT
UNFINISHED BUSINESS
COMBAT ZONE

MARCEL MONTECINO*
Agent: CAA - Beverly Hills, 213/288-4545

Screenplays:
IMPROPER CONDUCT
THE CROSS-KILLER
BIG TIME
TUSKE GI ARMEN RED TAILS

CLAIRE MONATGOMERY
THE PERFECT BRIDE (CTF)   Image Organization, 1991, w/Monty Montgomery

MICHAEL T. MONTGOMERY*
Agent: The Adler Agency - Studio City, 818/769-5003

EYE OF THE TIGER   Scotti Bros., 1986
ROLLING VENGEANCE   Apollo Pictures, 1987

MONTY MONTGOMERY*
Contact: WGA - Los Angeles, 213/550-1000

THE LOVELESS   Atlantic Releasing Corporation, 1981, w/Kathryn Bigelow, co-directed
THE PERFECT BRIDE (CTF)   Image Organization, 1991, w/Claire Montgomery

PAUL MOONEY*
Business Manager: Helen Shaw - Los Angeles, 213/474-8032

JO JO DANCER, YOUR LIFE IS CALLING   Columbia, 1986, w/Richard Pryor & Rocco Urbisci

BRIAN MOORE*
Agent: ICM - Los Angeles, 213/550-4000

THE LUCK OF GINGER COFFEY   Continental, 1964
TORN CURTAIN   Universal, 1966
THE BLOOD OF OTHERS (CMS)   HBO Premiere Films/ICC/Filmax Productions, 1984
CONTROL (CTF)   HBO Showcase/Alliance Entertainment Corp/Cristaldifilm/Les Films Ariane, 1987

Screenplays:
BLACK ROBE

DONOVAN MOORE*
Contact: WGA - Los Angeles, 213/550-1000

Screenplays:
ROBOT
IN TROUBLE
DAYWORLD

DUDLEY MOORE*
Agent: ICM - Los Angeles, 213/550-4000

THIRTY IS A DANGEROUS AGE, CYNTHIA   Columbia, 1967, w/Joe McGrath & John Wells
BEDAZZLED   20th Century-Fox, 1967, Story w/Peter Cook
THE HOUND OF THE BASKERVILLES   Atlantic Releasing Corporation, 1979, w/Peter Cook & Paul Morrissey

MICHAEL MOORE
Business: Center for Alternative Media, 2025 Pennsylvania Ave. - Suite 918, Washington, D.C. 20006, 202/287-4974

ROGER & ME (FD)   Warner Bros., 1989, directed

ROBIN MOORE
INCHON!   MGM/UA, 1982, w/Laird Koenig

SIMON MOORE*
Contact: WGA - Los Angeles, 213/550-1000

UP ON THE ROOF (P)

Screenplays:
THE OTHER WOMAN (directing)
THE DARK HORIZON
THE TENTH KINGDOM
THE BIG BREAK
REBEL MAGIC

TERRY MOORE
Contact: Screen Actors Guild - Los Angeles, 213/465-4600

BEVERLY HILLS BRATS   Taurus Entertainment, 1989, Story w/Jerry Rivers

WESLEY MOORE
Agent: William Morris Agency - Beverly Hills, 213/274-7451

SWIM VISIT (P)
APPRENTICE TO MURDER   New World, 1988, w/Alan Scott

Screenplays:
DOUBLE TAKE
TELEGRAPH HILL

WILLIAM MOORE
FIVE DAYS FROM HOME   Universal, 1978

JOCELYN MOOREHOUSE
PROOF   House & Moorehouse Films/Film Victoria, 1991, directed

FRANK MOORHOUSE
THE COCA COLA KID   Cinecom/Film Gallery, 1985
BETWEEN WARS   Satori, 1985
THE EVERLASTING SECRET FAMILY   International Film Exchange, 1989

ELIZA MOORMAN
TORCHLIGHT   International Film Marketing, 1984, w/Pamela Sue Martin

PHILLIPPE MORA
Agent: The Marion Rosenberg Office - West Hollywood, 213/653-7383

BROTHER, CAN YOU SPARE A DIME? (FD)   Dimension, 1975, directed
MAD DOG MAD DOG MORGAN   Cinema Shares International, 1976, directed
HOWLING III THE MARSUPIALS: THE HOWLING III   Square Pictures, 1987, directed

Screenplays:
PTERODACTYL WOMAN OF BRENTWOOD (directing)

MARTHA MORAN
HAPPILY EVER AFTER   Kel-Air Entertainment, 1990, w/Robby London

RICK MORANIS*
Agent: APA - Los Angeles, 213/273-0744

STRANGE BREW   MGM/UA, 1983, w/Dave Thomas & Steve DeJarnatt, directed

Screenplays:
KILLER CHARLIE FIVE (Shared)

CARL MORANO
CLASS OF NUKE E'M HIGH PART 2: SUBHUMANOID MELTDOWN   Troma, 1991, w/Lloyd Kaufman, Eric Louzil, Marcus Rolling, Jeffrey W. Sass & Matt Unger, directed

ANDRE MORGAN*
Business: Ruddy-Morgan Productions, 120 El Camino Dr. - Suite 112, Beverly Hills, CA, 90212, 213/271-7698

MEGAFORCE   20th Century-Fox, 1982, w/James Whittaker, Albert S. Ruddy & Hal Needham

DARIN MORGAN*
Agent: Warden & White Associates - Beverly Hills, 213/852-1028

Screenplays:
BEL AIR PATROL
HELLBOUND

GLEN MORGAN*
Agent: United Talent Agency - Beverly Hills, 213/273-6700

THE BOYS NEXT DOOR   New World, 1985, w/James Wong

Screenplays:
HANGMAN w/James Wong

SCOTT MORGAN
Agent: Susan Smith & Associates - Beverly Hills, 213/852-4777

Screenplays:
SUPERTANKER
ADDICTED TO LOVE   CASEY JONES
COLD FEET

W.T. MORGAN
A MATTER OF DEGREES   Backbeat Productions, 1989, w/Jack Mason & Randall Poster, directed

JOSEPH MORHAIM
QUICKER THAN THE EYE   Eural Films/FR3/Condor Films, 1988, w/Nicholas Gessner

DON MORIARTY
ZORRO, THE GAY BLADE   20th Century-Fox, 1981, Story w/Greg Alt, Hal Dresner & Bob Randall

PAT MORITA
Contact: 213/552-2020

CAPTIVE HEARTS   MGM/UA, 1987, w/John A. Kuri

TONY MORPHETT
THE LAST WAVE   United Artists, 1977, w/Petru Popescu
SWEET TALKER   New Visions, 1991

MICHAEL MORPUGO
WHEN THE WHALES CAME   20th Century Fox, 1989

ADRIAN MORRALL
BITTERSWEET LOVE   Avco Embassy, 1976, w/D.A. Kellogg

DAVID BURTON MORRIS*
Agent: William Morris Agency - Beverly Hills, 213/274-7451

PURPLE HAZE   Triumph/Columbia, 1983, Story w/Thomas Kelsey & Victoria Wozniak, directed
PATTI ROCKS   FilmDallas, 1988, w/John Jenkins, Karen Landry & Chris Mulkey, directed

Screenplays:
ASSUMING ROOM TEMPERATURE (directing)

GRANT MORRIS*
Agent: The Irv Schechter Company - Beverly Hills, 213/278-8070

THE RETURN OF SWAMP THING   Lightyear Entertainment, 1989, w/Derek Spencer
THE SHRIMP ON THE BARBIE   Unity Pictures Corp., 1990, w/Ron House & Alan Shearman

Screenplays:
THE AMERICAN WAY w/Louis Venosta

JUDY MORRIS
Contact: Australian Film Comission, 9229 Sunset Blvd., Los Angeles, CA 90069, 213/275-7074

LUIGI'S LADIES   TraLaLa Films Ltd., 1989, w/Ranald Allan, Jennifer Claire & Wendy Hughes, directed

STEVE MORRIS
Agent: The Wright Concept - Hollywood, 213/461-3844

Screenplays:
UNNATURAL HISTORY w/Robin Shephard

JOHN MORRISEY
9 1/2 NINJAS   Republic Pictures, 1991, Story w/Bill Crounse & Don Pequignot

PAUL MORRISSEY
ANDY WARHOL'S DRACULA   BLOOD FOR DRACULA   Bryanston, 1974, directed
ANDY WARHOL'S FRANKENSTEIN   FLESH FOR FRANKENSTEIN   Bryanston, 1974, directed
THE HOUND OF THE BASKERVILLES   Atlantic Releasing Corporation, 1979, w/Peter Cook & Dudley Moore, directed
MIXED BLOOD   Sara Films, 1984, directed
BEETHOVEN'S NEPHEW   New World, 1988, w/Mathieu Carriere, directed
SPIKE OF BENSONHURST   FilmDallas, 1988, w/Alan Bowne, directed

Screenplays:
STRAY DOG w/Jule Selbo

BARRY MORROW*
Agent: William Morris Agency - Beverly Hills, 213/274-7451

RAIN MAN ★★   MGM/UA, 1987, w/Ron Bass

Screenplays:
SUPER MARIO BROTHERS: THE MOVIE
BELLY UP
BLOOD ON THE TRACKS
DELICATE ARRANGEMENTS
TREVOR

JOHN MORTIMER*
Agent: CAA - Beverly Hills, 213/288-4545

GUNS OF DARKNESS   ABP, 1962
THE DOCK BRIEF   MGM, 1962, w/Pierre Rouve, from his play
THE RUNNING MAN   Columbia, 1963
BUNNY LAKE IS MISSING   Columbia, 1965, w/Penelope Mortimer
A FLEA IN HER EAR   20th Century-Fox, 1968
JOHN AND MARY   20th Century-Fox, 1969
NO SEX PLEASE, WE'RE BRITISH   Columbia, 1973, w/Brian Cooke & Anthony Marriott

Screenplays:
THE MAN WHO WAS THURSDAY
THE STAND IN
AMOK
CAUSE CELEBRE
DR. FISCHER OF GENEVA
PARADISE POSTPONED

PENELOPE MORTIMER
BUNNY LAKE IS MISSING   Columbia, 1965, w/John Mortimer
A SUMMER STORY   Atlantic Releasing Corporation, 1988

ERNEST MORTON
(See Nancy Dowd)

LISA MORTON
MEET THE HOLLOWHEADS   Moviestore Entertainment, 1989, w/Tom Burman

PHILIP MORTON*
Agent: Thal Literary Management - Los Angeles, 213/659-4946

WHO'S WRITING THIS (P) w/Bruce Paddock
IN THE WINGS (P) w/Bruce Paddock

Screenplays:
THE SUN w/Jonathan Heap & Tom Reed
HONOR BOUND w/Jonathan Heap
CAUGHT w/Jonathan Heap
WHAT NICK SAW w/Jonathan Heap
PARENTAL DISCRETION ADVISED w/Tommy Blaze
ROCK THUNDER w/Tommy Blaze
HARRY'S LOT
ROUGH JUSTICE
TELEPATH

ROB MORTON
(See Nancy Dowd, Bo Goldman & Ron Nyswaner)

RICHARD MOSES
ON THE RIGHT TRACK   20th Century-Fox, 1981, w/Avery Buddy & Tina Pina

ALAN MOSKOWITZ*
Agent: APA - Los Angeles, 213/273-0744

MORTAL PASSIONS   Gibraltar Releasing, 1990

MARC MOSS
Agent: Susan Smith & Associates - Beverly Hills, 213/852-4777

Screenplays:
FAIR GAME
RED JACKET

CAROLINE MOURIS
BEGINNER'S LUCK   New World, 1986, w/Frank Mouris

FRANK MOURIS
FRANK FILM (Short) ★   directed
BEGINNER'S LUCK   New World, 1986, w/Caroline Mouris, co-directed

MALCOLM MOWBRAY
Agent: Bennett Agency - Los Angeles, 213/471-2251

A PRIVATE FUNCTION   Island Alive, 1985, Story w/Allan Bennett, directed

Mo

FILM WRITERS GUIDE

ALLAN MOYLE*
Agent: William Morris Agency - Beverly Hills, 213/274-7451

THE RUBBER GUN   Schuman-Katzka, 1978, directed
EAST END HUSTLE   Troma, 1979, as "Alan Bozo Moyle," w/Frank Vitale
TIMES SQUARE   AFD, 1980, Story w/Leanne Unger, directed
PUMP UP THE VOLUME   New Line Cinema, 1990, directed
LOVE CRIMES   Miramax, 1991

Screenplays:
HEAD HUNTER

ELAINE MUELLER*
Agent: Warden & White Associates - Beverly Hills, 213/852-1028

Screenplays:
SPACES IN THE DARK
GARDENA MIRACLE
LEAD STORY
BLOWIN' IN THE WIND

TERENCE MULCAHY
(See Michael Leeson)

JIM MULHOLLAND*
Agent: APA - Los Angeles, 213/273-0744

AMAZON WOMEN ON THE MOON   Universal, 1987, w/Michael Barrie
OSCAR   Buena Vista, 1991, w/Michael Barrie

Screenplays:
AFTER THE FOX   w/Michael Barrie
THE CATCH   w/Michael Barrie

CHRIS MULKEY
Agent: S.T.E. Representation - Beverly Hills, 213/550-3982

PATTI ROCKS   FilmDallas, 1988, w/John Jenkins, Karen Landry & David Burton Morris

MARTIN MULL*
Agent: APA - Los Angeles, 213/273-0744

RENTED LIPS   Cineworld Enterprises, 1988

KEVIN MULLIGAN*
Agent: Shorr, Stille & Associates - Los Angeles, 213/659-6160

Screenplays
KID BROTHER

MARK MULLIN*
Agent: Pleshette & Green - Los Angeles, 213/465-0428

COOL BLUE   Cinema Corp of America, 1990, w/Richard Shepard, co-directed

ROBERT MUNDY*
Agent: Susan Smith & Associates - Beverly Hills, 213/852-4777

THE VISITOR   International Picture Show, 1980, w/Luciano Comici
CHATTANOOGA CHOO CHOO   April Fools, 1984, w/Steven Philip Smith

Screenplays:
21
SERVANT'S ENTRANCE
BLACK PANTHER
CASANOVA SLEPT HERE

IAN MUNE
Business: Mirage Entertainment Ltd., P.O.Box 1113, Auckland, New Zealand, 09/790-097

SLEEPING DOGS   Aardvark Films, 1977, w/Arthur Baysting
GOODBYE PORK PIE   Samuel Goldwyn Company, 1980, w/Geoff Murphy
CAME A HOT FRIDAY   Orion Classics, 1985, w/Dean Parker, directed

WALTER MURCH*
Contact: Bloom, Dekom & Hergott - Los Angeles, 213/278-8622

THX 1138   Warner Bros., 1971, w/George Lucas
RETURN TO OZ   Buena Vista, 1985, w/Gill Dennis, directed

FREDI M. MURER
Contact: Swiss Film Center, Munstergasse 18, 8001 Zurich, Switzerland, 01/472-860

ALPINE FIRE   Vestron, 1987, directed

MICHAEL MURPHEY*
Contact: WGA - Los Angeles, 213/550-1000

HARD COUNTRY   Universal, 1981, Story w/Michael Kane

MICHAEL S. MURPHEY
Business: Soisson Murphey Productions, 9060 Santa Monica Blvd. - Suite 210, Los Angeles, CA, 90069, 213/273-3157

HAMBONE AND HILLIE   New World, 1984, w/Sandra K. Bailey & Joel Soisson
THE SUPERNATURALS   Republic Entertainment/Sandy Howard Productions, 1985, w/Joel Soisson
TRICK OR TREAT   DEG, 1986, w/Joel Soisson & Rhet Topham

COLLEEN MURPHY
TERMINI STATION   Northern Arts Entertainment, 1991

EDDIE MURPHY
Agent: ICM - Los Angeles, 213/550-4000

EDDIE MURPHY RAW   Paramount, 1987, w/Keenen Ivory Wayans
BEVERLY HILLS COP II   Paramount, 1987, Story w/Robert D. Wachs
COMING TO AMERICA   Paramount, 1988, Story
HARLEM NIGHTS   Paramount, 1989, directed

GARY MURPHY*
Agent: William Morris Agency - Beverly Hills, 213/274-7451

WITHOUT A CLUE   Orion, 1989, w/Larry Strawther

Screenplays:
8:24 TO HEAVEN w/Larry Strawther

GEOFF MURPHY
Agent: InterTalent - Los Angeles, 213/858-6200

GOODBYE PORK PIE   Samuel Goldwyn Company, 1980, w/Ian Mune, directed
UTU   Pickman Films, 1983, w/Keith Aberdein, directed

RICHARD MURPHY*
Agent: Sanford, Skouras, Gross & Associates - Los Angeles, 213/208-2100

Screenplays:
RADIO MAN w/Stan Seidel
STORMY WEATHER

RICHARD T. MURPHY*
Agent: Vanguard - Los Angeles, 213/829-5000

CRY OF THE CITY   20th Century-Fox, 1948
DEEP WATERS   20th Century-Fox, 1948
SLATTERY'S HURRICANE   20th Century-Fox, 1949, w/Herman Wolk
PANIC IN THE STREETS ★   20th Century-Fox, 1950, w/Edna Anhalt & Edward Anhalt
YOU'RE IN THE ARMY NOW   USS TEAKETTLE   20th Century-Fox, 1951
THE DESERT RATS   20th Century-Fox, 1953
THREE STRIPES IN THE SUN   THE GENTLE SERGEANT   Columbia, 1955, directed
COMPULSION   20th Century-Fox, 1959
THE WACKIEST SHIP IN THE ARMY   Columbia, 1960, directed
THE KIDNAPPING OF THE PRESIDENT   Crown, 1980

TAB MURPHY*
Contact: WGA - Los Angeles, 213/550-1000

MY BEST FRIEND IS A VAMPIRE   Kings Road Entertainment, 1988
GORILLAS IN THE MIST ★   Universal, 1988, Story w/Anna Hamilton Phelan

Screenplays:
M.I.A.
ECLIPSE OF THE BEAST
BLACK MASK
KING FOR A DAY
DUTCH HARBOR
HEAVEN & EARTH
QUEEN OF ST. JAMES ELK
TREASURE HUNT
A FAR OFF PLACE

WARREN MURPHY*
Agent: Barry Perelman Agency - Los Angeles, 213/274-5999

THE EIGER SANCTION   Universal, 1975, w/Hal Dresner & Rod Whitaker
LETHAL WEAPON 2   Warner Bros., 1989, Story w/Shane Black

BILL MURRAY
Agent: CAA - Beverly Hills, 213/288-4545

THE RAZOR'S EDGE   Columbia, 1984, w/John Byrum

MICHAEL J. MURRAY*
Agent: Writers & Artists Agency - Los Angeles, 213/820-2240

Screenplays:
TERROR OF MANHATTAN w/Greydon Clark
THE LIGHTNING FIELD (CTF)
THE PARROT
THE FALL OF THE HOUSE OF USHER
MASK OF THE RED DEATH
THE RAVEN
THE MUMMY

TOM MUSCA*
Agent: ICM - Los Angeles, 213/550-4000

STAND AND DELIVER   Warner Bros., 1988, w/Ramon Menendez
LITTLE NIKITA   Columbia, 1988, Story w/Terry Schwartz

STEVE MUSCARELLA*
Agent: Circle Talent Associates - Beverly Hills, 213/285-1585

ECHOES (Short), directed

Screenplays:
COLD STORAGE
CLUB DEAD

JOHN MUSKER
Business: Walt Disney Studios, 818/560-1000

THE GREAT MOUSE DETECTIVE (AF)   Buena Vista, 1989, w/others, co-directed
THE LITTLE MERMAID (AF)   Buena Vista, 1989, w/Ron Clements, co-directed

FLOYD MUTRUX*
Agent: CAA - Beverly Hills, 213/288-4545

THE CHRISTIAN LICORICE STORE   National General, 1971
DUSTY AND SWEETS McGEE   Warner Bros., 1971, directed
FREEBIE AND THE BEAN   Warner Bros., 1974, Story
ALOHA, BOBBY AND ROSE   Columbia, 1975, directed
THE HOLLYWOOD KNIGHTS   Columbia, 1980, directed
THERE GOES MY BABY   Orion, 1991, directed

Screenplays:
AMERICAN ME
BANK JOB w/H. Matofsky
GO TO WORK
HILLSIDE STRANGLER
SKYLINE DRIVE
MAX THE FOX
HAPPY HOUR   SANTA ANA WIND
HEAT WAVE
ALONG CAME JONES

NANCYLEE MYATT
little secrets   Cinecom, 1991, from her play "Slumber Party"

CINDY MYERS*
Agent: Harris & Goldberg - Los Angeles, 213/553-5200

FORGOTTEN PRISONERS: THE AMNESTY FILES (CTF)
  Turner Pictures, 1990, w/Rex Weiner

Screenplays:
PEACOCK RAG
TELLING TALES
SNAKES

MIKE MYERS*
Agent: United Talent Agency - Beverly Hills, 213/273-6700

Screenplays:
WAYNE'S WORLD: THE MOVIE (Shared)

SCOTT MYERS*
Contact: WGA - Los Angeles, 213/550-1000

K-9   Universal, 1989, w/Steven Siegel

JOHN MYHERS*
Agent: Sheri Mann Agency - Los Angeles, 213/850-1777

THE PRIZE FIGHTER   New World, 1979, w/Tim Conway
THE PRIVATE EYES   New World, 1980, w/Tim Conway

N

WILLIAM NAGLE
DEATH OF A SOLDIER   Scotti Bros., 1986
THE SIEGE OF FIREBASE GLORIA   Fries
  Entertainment, 1989, w/Tony Johnston

ED NAHA*
Agent: ICM - Los Angeles, 213/550-4000

TROLL   Empire Pictures, 1986
DOLLS   Empire Pictures, 1987
HONEY, I SHRUNK THE KIDS   Buena Vista, 1989,
  w/Tom Schulman
CHUD II: BUD THE CHUD   Vestron, 1989,
  as "M. Kane Jeeves"

Screenplays:
THE UNKNOWN SOLDIER
ERNEST SPACED OUT
BREAKDOWN
HEX

DESMOND NAKANO*
Agent: William Morris Agency - Beverly Hills,
  213/274-7451

BOULEVARD NIGHTS   Warner Bros., 1979
BODY ROCK   New World, 1984
BLACK MOON RISING   New World, 1986, w/John
  Carpenter & William Gray
LAST EXIT TO BROOKLYN   Constantin Films, 1990

SPENSER NAKASAKO
LIFE IS CHEAP...BUT TOILET PAPER IS EXPENSIVE
  Silverlight Entertainment, 1990, co-directed

STEVEN NALEVANSKY
BLOOD BEACH   Jerry Gross Organization, 1981, Story
  w/Jeffrey Bloom

FRANK NAMEI*
Agent: Barrett, Benson, McCartt & Weston - Los Angeles,
  213/247-5500

COLLISION COURSE   DEG, 1987, w/Robert Resnikoff

MICHAEL NANKIN*
Agent: ICM - Los Angeles, 213/550-4000

MIDNIGHT MADNESS   Buena Vista, 1980, w/David
  Wechter, co-directed
THE GATE   New Century/Vista, 1987
RUSSKIES   New Century, 1987, w/Alan Glueckman &
  Sheldon Lettich

Screenplays:
THE GATE II

SUSAN NANUS*
Agent: William Morris Agency - New York, 212/586-5100

THE SURVIVOR (S)

Screenplays:
MAJORITY RULES HIP TO BE SQUARE
  w/Rachel Feldman
SMOTHERED w/Rachel Feldman
AMERICAN HARVEST
THE MOST ELIGIBLE MAN IN NEW YORK
BEAT THE EAGLE

JO NAPOLEON*
Agent: William Morris Agency - Beverly Hills, 213/274-7451

Screenplays:
AFTER THE BEAR HUNT
JAGUAR
THE SMASHBOX

ANN NARUS
Business: Motion Picture Corp. of America, 1401 Ocean
  Ave. - 3rd Floor, Santa Monica, CA 90401,
  213/319-9500

MINISTRY OF VENGEANCE   Concorde, 1989, w/Brian D.
  Jeffries & Mervyn Emrys

JAMES NASALLA
O'HARA'S WIFE   Davis-Panzer Productions, 1982,
  w/William S. Bartman

N. RICHARD NASH*
Contact: WGA - Los Angeles, 213/550-1000

THE RAINMAKER   Paramount, 1956, from his play
PORGY AND BESS   Goldwyn, 1959
ONE SUMMER LOVE *DRAGONFLY*   American
  International, 1976

JAMES NATHAN*
Agent: Stone Manners Agency - Los Angeles, 213/275-9599

THE KILLING TIME   New World, 1987, w/Don Bohlinger & Bruce Franklin Singer

Screenplays:
SMOKESCREEN w/Dan Bohlinger

STEVE NATHAN*
Agent: ICM - Los Angeles, 213/550-4000

Screenplays:
THE ENGAGEMENT w/Paul Price
LOOSE WOMEN w/Paul Price
IN THE PROCESS w/Paul Price
THE AILEEN QUINN STORY w/Paul Price
UTILITIES w/Paul Price

MICHAEL J. NATHANSON*
Busines Manager: Matt Sauer, Rosenfield, Meyer & Susman, 9601 Wilshire Blvd., Beverly Hills, CA 90210, 213/858-7700

SHE'S OUT OF CONTROL   Columbia, 1989, w/Seth Winston

TERRY NATION
Agent: Triad Artists, Inc. - Los Angeles, 213/556-2727

AND SOON THE DARKNESS   Associated British, 1970, w/Brian Clemens
THE HOUSE IN NIGHTMARE PARK   EMI, 1973, w/Clive Exton

RICK NATKIN*
Agent: The Daniel Ostroff Agency - Los Angeles, 213/278-2020

THE BOYS IN COMPANY C   Columbia, 1978, w/Sidney Furie
NIGHT OF THE JUGGLER   Columbia, 1980, w/Bill Norton Sr.
PURPLE HEARTS   The Ladd Company/Warner Bros., 1984, w/Sidney Furie
THE HEIST (CTF)   HBO Pictures, 1989, w/David Fuller
THE TAKING OF BEVERLY HILLS   Nelson Entertainment, 1991, w/David Fuller & David Burke

Screenplays:
NECESSARY ROUGHNESS w/David Fuller
ALL THAT CAN BE w/David Fuller

BILL NAUD
NECROMANCER   Bonnaire Films & Spectrum Entertainment, 1989

GREGORY NAVA*
Agent: ICM - Los Angeles, 213/550-4000

THE CONFESSIONS OF AMANS   Bauer International, 1977, w/Anna Thomas, directed
THE END OF AUGUST   Quartet, 1982, w/Anna Thomas, Eula Seaton & Leon Heller
EL NORTE ★   Cinecom/Island Alive, 1984, w/Anna Thomas, directed
A TIME OF DESTINY   Columbia, 1988, w/Anna Thomas, directed

JEFFREY W. NEAL*
Agent: ICM - Los Angeles, 213/550-4000

Screenplays:
LONE JUSTICE
BACKSTREETS

HAROLD NEBENZAL*
Agent: CAA - Beverly Hills, 213/288-4545

THE WILBY CONSPIRACY   United Artists, 1975, w/Rod Amateau
KINJITE: FORBIDDEN SUBJECTS   Cannon, 1989

Screenplays:
PURSUIT MANUMIT w/Rod Amateu

HAL NEEDHAM*
Agent: ICM - Los Angeles, 213/550-4000
Business: Bandit Productions, 3518 Cahuenga Blvd West - Suite 110, Los Angeles, CA 90068, 213/876-8052

MEGAFORCE   20th Century-Fox, 1982, w/James Whittaker, Albert S. Ruddy & Andre Morgan, directed
STROKER ACE   Universal, 1983, w/Hugh Wilson, directed
CANONBALL RUN II   Warner Bros., 1984, w/Harvey Miller & Albert S. Ruddy, directed

STEPHEN C. NEIGHER*
Agent: United Talent Agency - Beverly Hills, 213/273-6700

HOT TO TROT   Warner Bros., 1988, w/Hugo Gilbert & Charlie Peters

Screenplays:
KING OF THE USA
STAYING ON TOP

STEVEN NEILL
THE DAY TIME ENDED   Compass International, 1979, Story

B.J. NELSON
Agent: Circle Talent Associates - Beverly Hills, 213/281-3765

LONE WOLF McQUADE   Orion, 1983
APT PUPIL   New Century/Vista, 1989
SCANNERS II: THE NEW ORDER   Triton Pictures, 1991

Screenplays:
SCANNERS 3
BUDDY COPS w/David O'Malley

DONALD R. NELSON*
Agent: Wile Enterprises, Inc. - Los Angeles, 213/828-9768

ONE MORE TRAIN TO ROB   Universal, 1971, w/Don Tait
NO DEPOSIT, NO RETURN   Buena Vista, 1976, w/Arthur Alsberg
GUS   Buena Vista, 1976, w/Arthur Alsberg
HERBIE GOES TO MONTE CARLO   Buena Vista, 1977, w/Arthur Alsberg
HOT LEAD AND COLD FEET   Buena Vista, 1978, w/Arthur Alsberg & Joe McEveety

PETER NELSON*
Agent: APA - Los Angeles, 213/273-0744

THE LONELY PASSION OF JUDITH HEARNE   Island Pictures, 1987

ROGERS NELSON
(See Prince)

JOE NEOLA*
Contact: WGA - Los Angeles, 213/550-1000

Screenplays:
FIVE O'CLOCK FOXTROT   w/Mary Neola

MARY NEOLA*
Contact: WGA - Los Angeles, 213/550-1000

Screenplays:
FIVE O'CLOCK FOXTROT   w/Joe Neola

MICHAEL NESMITH*
Business: Pacific Arts, 50 N. La Cienega Blvd. - Suite 210, Beverly Hills, CA, 90211, 213/657-2233

TIMERIDER   Jensen Farley Pictures, 1983, w/William Dear

LEONARD NEUBAUER*
Contact: WGA - Los Angeles, 213/550-1000

NEW YEAR'S EVIL   Cannon, 1981

CHRIS NEUFELD
THE BIG PLUNGE   Embassy International, 1985

EDWARD NEUMEIER*
Agent: United Talent Agency - Beverly Hills, 213/273-6700

ROBOCOP   Orion, 1987, w/Michael Miner

Screenplays:
STRAT   w/Michael Miner
THE EXECUTIONER   w/Michael Miner
COMPANY MAN   w/Michael Miner
HITMAN   w/Michael Miner (co-directing)
WHITE TRASH   w/Michael Miner

CRAIG J. NEVIUS*
Agent: Shorr, Stille & Associates - Los Angeles, 213/659-6160

HAPPY TOGETHER   Borde Releasing Corp., 1990

ROBERT NEWCOMBE
Agent: The Agency - Los Angeles, 213/551-3000

Screenplays:
YOU SHOULD SEE THE CONKLIN'S LIVING ROOM

ANTHONY NEWLEY*
Agent: ICM - Los Angeles, 213/550-4000

ROAR OF THE GREASEPAINT, SMELL OF THE CROWD (S)   w/Leslie Bricusse
STOP THE WORLD - I WANT TO GET OFF   Warner Bros., 1966, w/Leslie Bricusse
CAN HIERONYMUS MERKIN EVER FORGET MERCY HUMPPE & FIND TRUE HAPPINESS?   Universal, 1969, w/Herman Raucher, directed

DAVID NEWMAN*
Agent: United Talent Agency - Beverly Hills, 213/273-6700

BONNIE AND CLYDE ★   Warner Bros., 1967, w/Robert Benton
THERE WAS A CROOKED MAN...   United Artists, 1970, w/Robert Benton
WHAT'S UP DOC?   Warner Bros., 1972, w/Robert Benton & Buck Henry
BAD COMPANY   Paramount, 1972, w/Robert Benton
SUPERMAN   Warner Bros., 1978, w/Robert Benton, Leslie Newman & Mario Puzo
SUPERMAN II   Warner Bros., 1980, w/Leslie Newman & Mario Puzo
JINXED   MGM/UA, 1982, w/Frank Gilroy
STILL OF THE NIGHT   MGM/UA, 1982, Story w/Robert Benton
SUPERMAN III   Warner Bros., 1983, w/Leslie Newman
SHEENA   Columbia, 1984, w/Lorenzo Semple
SANTA CLAUS: THE MOVIE   Tri-Star, 1985

Screenplays:
THE VISITORS
THE FUGITIVE
SMOOTH CRIMINAL
CAPTAIN ZAP AND THE BRUTE (CTF)

LESLIE NEWMAN*
Agent: ICM - New York, 212/556-5600

SUPERMAN   Warner Bros., 1978, w/Robert Benton, David Newman & Mario Puzo
SUPERMAN II   Warner Bros., 1980, w/David Newman & Mario Puzo
SUPERMAN III   Warner Bros., 1983, w/David Newman

Screenplays:
THE SHADOW
GATHERING FORCE
HAPPILY EVER AFTER

PAUL NEWMAN*
Agent: CAA - Beverly Hills, 213/288-4545

HARRY & SON   Orion, 1984, w/Ronald L. Buck, directed

RANDY NEWMAN*
Business Manager: Gelfand, Rennert & Feldman - Los Angeles, 213/553-1707

THREE AMIGOS   Orion, 1986, w/Steve Martin & Lorne Michaels

WALTER NEWMAN*
Agent: The Gurian Agency - Los Angeles, 213/550-0400

ACE IN THE HOLE ★   Paramount, 1951, w/Billy Wilder
THE MAN WITH THE GOLDEN ARM   1955, w/Lewis Meltzer
UNDERWATER   RKO, 1955, w/Robert B. Bailey & Hugh King
THE TRUE STORY OF JESSE JAMES   Fox, 1956

CRIME AND PUNISHMENT USA   Allied Artists, 1958
THE INTERNS   Columbia, 1962, w/David Swift
CAT BALLOU ★   Columbia, 1965, w/Frank Pierson
BLOODBROTHERS ★   Warner Bros., 1978
THE CHAMP   MGM/UA, 1979, w/Spencer Eastman
SAINT JACK   New World, 1979

Screenplays:
JOAQUIN
HARROW ALLEY
RIDE THE WILD RED
SULLIVAN'S STATION
HIGH-RISE WEEKEND
MOOSH

MAURIZIO NICHETTI
THE ICICLE THIEF   Aries Releasing, 1990, w/Mauro Monti, directed

PAUL NICHOLAS
Contact: Directors Guild of America - Los Angeles, 213/289-2000

CHAINED HEAT   Jensen Farley Pictures, 1983, w/Vincent Mongol, directed
THE NAKED CAGE   Cannon, 1986, directed

ALLAN F. NICHOLLS*
Business: P.O. Box 165, New York, NY 10014, 212/664-2458

A WEDDING   20th Century-Fox, 1978, w/Robert Altman, John Considine & Patricia Resnick
A PERFECT COUPLE   20th Century-Fox, 1979, w/Robert Altman

JOHN NICHOLS*
Agent: Curtis Brown, Ltd. - New York, 212/473-5400

THE MILAGRO BEANFIELD WAR   Universal, 1988, w/David S. Ward

PETER NICHOLS
Agent: Margaret Ramsay Ltd. - London, 011/441/240-0691

HAVING A WILD WEEKEND   *CATCH US IF YOU CAN*   Warner Bros., 1965
GEORGY GIRL   Columbia, 1966, w/Margaret Forster
A DAY IN THE DEATH OF JOE EGG   Columbia, 1971, from his play
THE NATIONAL HEALTH   Columbia, 1973, from his play
PRIVATES ON PARADE   Orion Classics, 1984, from his play

JACK NICHOLSON
Contact: Sandy Bresler, Bresler, Kelly & Kipperman - Encino, 818/905-1155

THUNDER ISLAND   1963, shared
RIDE IN THE WHIRLWIND   American International, 1966
FLIGHT TO FURY   Harold Goldman Associates, 1966
THE TRIP   American Internation, 1967
HEAD   Columbia, 1968, w/Bob Rafelson
DRIVE, HE SAID   Columbia, 1970, w/Jeremy Larner, directed

WILLIAM NICHOLSON
Contact: British Academy of Film & Television Arts, 195 Piccadilly, London W1, England, 71/734-0022

SHADOWLANDS (S), also screenplay

Screenplays:
SARAFINA!
MISS SHERRI

NICHOLAS NICIPHOR*
Agent: Barry Perelman Agency - Los Angeles, 213/274-5999

OUR WINNING SEASON   American International, 1978
FATAL CHARM   MCEG, 1990

DARYL G. NICKENS*
Agent: APA - Los Angeles, 213/273-0744

Screenplays:
AT YOUR SERVICE

TED NICOLAOU
Agent: David Shapira & Associates - Sherman Oaks, 818/906-0322

SOUTHERN HOSPITALITY (Short), directed
TERRORVISION   Empire Pictures, 1986, directed
ASSAULT OF THE KILLER BIMBOS   Empire Pictures, 1988

BRUCE NICOLAYSEN
THE PASSAGE   United Artists, 1979

HARRY NILSSON
THE TELEPHONE   New World, 1988, w/Terry Southern

ROB NILSSON
Agent: Sanford, Skouras, Gross & Associates - Los Angeles, 213/208-2100

NORTHERN LIGHTS   Cinemanifest/New Front Films, 1978, w/John Hanson, co-directed
ON THE EDGE   Skouras Pictures, 1986, directed
SIGNAL SEVEN   One Pass Pictures, 1986, directed
HEAT AND SUNLIGHT   New Front Alliance/Snowball Productions, 1987, directed

LEONARD NIMOY*
Agent: The Gersh Agency - Los Angeles, 213/274-6611
Business Manager: Richard B. Francis, 213/277-7351

STAR TREK IV: THE VOYAGE HOME   Paramount, 1986, Story w/Harve Bennett, directed

MICKEY NIVELLI
HEAVEN BECOMES HELL   Taurus Entertainment, 1989, directed

TIM NOAH
DAREDREAMER   Lensman Co., 1989, Story w/Barry Cailllier & Pat Royce

No

FILM WRITERS GUIDE

JUDY NOGG
Agent: Susan Smith & Associates - Beverly Hills, 213/852-4777

Screenplays:
THE ALTERNATE
THE SMUGGLER

CHRIS NOLAN
Agent: Jim Preminger Agency - Los Angeles, 213/475-9491

Screenplays:
FLOATING BRIDGE w/Laurie Scholnick

DIANE NOOMIN*
Contact: WGA - Los Angeles, 213/550-1000

Screenplays:
ZIPPYVISION w/Bill Griffith

TOM NOONAN
RED WIND (CTF)   MCA Television, 1991

MICHAEL NORELL*
Agent: William Morris Agency - Beverly Hills, 213/274-7451

LONG GONE (CTF)   HBO Pictures/The Landsburg Company, 1987

Screenplays:
THE INCIDENT
CALL ME A COP
BARNUM
PALS

MARC NORMAN*
Agent: ICM - Los Angeles, 213/550-4000

OKLAHOMA CRUDE   Columbia, 1973
ZANDY'S BRIDE   Warner Bros., 1974
THE KILLER ELITE   United Artists, 1975, w/ Stirling Silliphant
THE AVIATOR   MGM/UA, 1985
BAT-21   Tri-Star, 1988, as "George Gordon," w/William C. Anderson

Screenplays:
MAHAD
2 GOOD 2 BE FORGOTTEN
SHADOW CATCHER
THE LOCK NESS MONSTER
FAHAD & LENA
HERZOG
STATION CHIEF

MARSHA NORMAN*
Agent: United Talent Agency - Beverly Hills, 213/273-6700

GETTING OUT (S)
THE SECRET GARDEN (S)
THE LAUNDROMAT (CTF)   Byck-Lancaster Productions/Sandcastle 5 Productions, 1985
'NIGHT, MOTHER   Universal, 1986, from her play
THIRD AND OAK: THE POOL HALL (CTF)   Nederlander Television and Film, 1989

Screenplays:
MEDICINE WOMAN
CHILDREN WITH EMERALD EYES
MY SHADOW

AARON NORRIS
Business Manager: Jim Rogers and Associates, 8285 Sunset Blvd. - Suite 1, Los Angeles, CA 90046

INVASION U.S.A.   Cannon, 1985, Story w/James Bruner

CHUCK NORRIS*
Agent: ICM - Los Angeles, 213/550-4000

INVASION U.S.A.   Cannon, 1985, w/James Bruner
BRADDOCK: MISSING IN ACTION III   Cannon, 1988, w/James Bruner

PAMELA R. NORRIS
Agent: Triad Artists, Inc. - Los Angeles, 213/556-2727

TROOP BEVERLY HILLS   WEG, 1989, w/Margaret Grieco Oberman

WILLIAM H. NORRIS
H.P. LOVECRAFT'S RE-ANIMATOR   Empire Pictures, 1985, w/Stuart Gordon & Dennis Paoli

B.W.L. NORTON, JR.*
Contact: WGA - Los Angeles, 213/550-1000

CISCO PIKE   Columbia, 1971, directed
OUTLAW BLUES   Warner Bros., 1977
CONVOY   United Artists, 1978
MORE AMERICAN GRAFFITI   Universal, 1979, directed
LOSIN' IT   Embassy, 1983
BACK TO THE BEACH   Paramount, 1987, Story w/Bruce Kirschbaum & James Komack

Screenplays:
LOCKDOWN
BULL
KITELINE
BULLROAR

ELEANOR ELIAS NORTON*
Contact: WGA - Los Angeles, 213/550-1000

THE DAY OF THE ANIMALS   Film Ventures International, 1976, w/William Norton
DIRTY TRICKS   Avco Embassy, 1981, w/William Norton, Thomas Gifford & Camille Gifford

WILLIAM W. NORTON, SR.*
Agent: The Irv Schechter Company - Beverly Hills, 213/278-8070

THE SCALPHUNTERS   United Artists, 1968
SAM WHISKEY   United Artists, 1969
THE MACKENZIE BREAK   United Artists, 1970
THE HUNTING PARTY   United Artists, 1971, w/Gilbert Alexander & Lou Morheim
WHITE LIGHTNING   United Artists, 1973
TRADER HORN   MGM, 1973, w/Edward Harper
BIG BAD MAMA   New World, 1974, w/Frances Doel
BRANNIGAN   United Artists, 1975, w/Michael Butler, William P. McGivern & Christopher Trumbo

THE DAY OF THE ANIMALS   Film Ventures International, 1976, w/Eleanor Norton
MOVING VIOLATION   20th Century-Fox, 1976, w/David R. Osterhout
GATOR   United Artists, 1976
A SMALL TOWN IN TEXAS   American International, 1976
NIGHT OF THE JUGGLER   Columbia, 1980, w/Rick Natkin
DIRTY TRICKS   Avco Embassy, 1981, w/Eleanor Elias Norton, Thomas Gifford & Camille Gifford

JOHN NORVILLE*
Agent: William Morris Agency - Beverly Hills, 213/274-7451

Screenplays:
CAPONE IN LAREDO w/Michael Jenning
THE AMERICAN SPORTSMAN
AN EXILE'S BAGGAGE
LOUIE LOUIE

FRANK NORWOOD*
Agent: Writers & Artists Agency - Los Angeles, 213/820-2240

PAST MIDNIGHT   Cinetel Films, 1991

Screenplays:
PEACEMAKER
WALKING ON GLASS
BLIND SIDE

CLAIRE NOTO*
Agent: Triad Artists, Inc. - Los Angeles, 213/556-2727

Screenplays:
THE TOURIST w/Patricia Knop
SLAVE, A TRUE STORY
THE HEAVENLY
BLONDES
PAPARAZZI

BLAINE NOVAK*
Contact: WGA - New York, 212/245-6180

STRANGER'S KISS   Orion Classics, 1984, w/Matthew Chapman
GOOD TO GO   Island Pictures, 1986, directed
LIGHT YEARS   Miramax, 1988, w/Raphael Cluzel

Screenplays:
BEAUTIFUL ENEMIES
THE DRIFT
SUNSET UNLIMITED
BEAT THE BURDEN

PHILLIP NOYCE
Agent: Writers & Artists Agency - Los Angeles, 213/820-2240

NEWSFRONT   New Yorker, 1979, directed
HEATWAVE   New Line Cinema, 1982, w/Marc Rosenberg, directed

VICTOR NUNEZ
Agent: Paul Kohner, Inc. - Los Angeles, 213/550-1060

A FLASH OF GREEN   Spectrafilm, 1985, directed

KEM NUNN*
Agent: United Talent Agency - Beverly Hills, 213/273-6700

Screenplays:
STREEETRACERS
TAPPING THE SOURCE
UNASSIGNED TERRITORY

TREVOR NUNN
Contact: Attorney Bill Fournier, Campbell Hooper, 35 Old Queen St., London SW1H 9JD, England, 71/222-9070

HEDDA   Brut Productions, 1975, directed

TOM NURSALL*
Agent: William Morris Agency - Beverly Hills, 213/274-7451

Screenplays:
ESCAPE FROM WANNA WANNA w/Harris Goldberg
GETTING EVEN w/Harris Goldberg

BRUNO NUYTTEN
Contact: French Film Office, 745 Fifth Avenue, New York, NY 10151, 212/832-8860

CAMILLE CLAUDEL   Orion Classics, 1989, w/Marilyn Goldin, directed

RICHARD NYGARD
TALES OF THE UNKNOWN   AIP Home Video, 1990, "Warped" w/Jeff Copeland

RON NYSWANER*
Agent: Sanford, Skouras, Gross & Associates - Los Angeles, 213/208-2100

F/10 SPLIT (S)
SURVIVING DAUGHTER (S)
THE F WORD (S)
SMITHEREENS   New Line Cinema, 1982, w/Susan Seidelman
SWING SHIFT   Warner Bros., 1983, w/Nancy Dowd & Bo Goldman, as "Rob Morton"
PURPLE HEARTS   Warner Bros., 1984
MRS. SOFFEL   MGM/UA, 1984
THE PRINCE OF PENNSYLVANIA   New Line Cinema, 1988, directed
GROSS ANATOMY   Buena Vista, 1989, w/Mark Spragg
LOVE HURTS   Vestron, 1991

Screenplays:
THE WINNER
SHELLEY'S LEG
HEARTACHES INTO THE FIRE

O

DAVID OAS
(See Jeff Buhai, David Obst & Steve Zacharias)

DAN O'BANNON*
Agent: Morton Agency - Los Angeles, 213/824-4089

DARK STAR   Jack H. Harris Enterprises, 1974,
    w/John Carpenter
ALIEN   20th Century-Fox, 1979
DEAD AND BURIED   Avco Embassy, 1981,
    w/ Ronald Shusett
BLUE THUNDER   Columbia, 1983, w/Don Jakoby
LIFEFORCE   Tri-Star, 1985, w/Don Jakoby
THE RETURN OF THE LIVING DEAD   Orion,
    1985, directed
INVADERS FROM MARS   Cannon, 1986, w/Don Jakoby
TOTAL RECALL   Tri-Star, 1990, w/Gary Goldman &
    Ronald Shusett

Screenplays:
TELEKINETIC MAN w/Don Jakoby
THE PRIMITIVE w/Don Jakoby
HEMOGOBLIN

ROCKNE S. O'BANNON*
Agent: InterTalent - Los Angeles, 213/858-6200

ALIEN NATION   20th Century Fox, 1988
FEAR (CTF)   Vestron, 1989

MARGARET GRIECO OBERMAN*
Agent: Richland/Wunsch/Hohman Agency - Los Angeles,
    213/278-1955

TROOP BEVERLY HILLS   WEG, 1989, w/Pamela Norris

Screenplays:
MR. DARLING w/Rosie Shuster
THE BROTHER-IN-LAW
THE STAND-UP GUY

BARRY O'BRIEN*
Contact: 213/201-0892

PINOCCHIO AND THE EMPEROR OF THE NIGHT (AF)
    New World, 1987, w/Robby London &
    Dennis O'Flaherty

RICHARD O'BRIEN
THE ROCKY HORROR PICTURE SHOW   20th
    Century-Fox, 1976, w/Jim Sharman, from his play
SHOCK TREATMENT   20th Century-Fox, 1981,
    w/Jim Sharman

JEFFREY OBROW
THE POWER   Artists Releasing Corporation/Film Ventures
    Internatioal, 1982, w/Stephen Carpenter, co-directed
THE DORM THAT DRIPPED BLOOD   *PRANKS*   Artists
    Releasing Corporation/Film Ventures International, 1983,
    w/Stephen Carpenter & Stacey Giachino, co-directed
THE KINDRED   FM Entertainment, 1987,
    w/others, co-directed
THE SERVANTS OF TWILIGHT   Trimark Pictures, 1991,
    w/Stephen Carpenter, directed

DAVID OBST*
Contact: WGA - Los Angeles, 213/550-1000

THE WHOOPEE BOYS   Paramount, 1986, w/Jeff Buhai &
    Steve Zacharias
JOCKS   Crown International, 1987, w/Jeff Buhai & Steve
    Zacharias, as "Mike Lanahan & David Oas"
JOHNNY BE GOOD   Orion, 1988, w/Jeff Buhai &
    Steve Zacharias
PERFECT HARMONY (CTF)   Sea Breeze
    Productions, 1991

C.R. O'CHRISTOPHER
(See Christopher Crowe)

DAVID ODELL*
Contact: Bloom, Dekom & Hergott - Los Angeles,
    213/278-8622

CRY UNCLE   Cambist, 1971
DEALING: OR THE BERKELEY-TO-BOSTON-FORTY-
    BRICK-LOST-BAG BLUES   Warner Bros., 1972
FOREPLAY   Cinema National, 1975, w/Dan Greenberg &
    Jack Richardson
THE PRESIDENT'S WOMEN   Krona, 1981
THE DARK CRYSTAL   Universal, 1982
NATE AND HAYES   Paramount, 1983, w/John Hughes
SUPERGIRL   Warner Bros., 1984
MASTERS OF THE UNIVERSE   Cannon, 1987

Screenplays:
VOODOO w/Petru Popescu
THE STORK
DIRTY EDDIE
SWAMPOUT
NOVEL LIFE
MARIE LAVEAU
THE CATHODE MONSTER

MICHAEL O'DONOGHUE*
Agent: William Morris Agency - New York, 212/586-5100

MR. MIKE'S MONDO VIDEO   New Line Cinema, 1979,
    w/Mitch Glazer, Emily Prager & Dirk Wittenborn, directed
SCROOGED   Paramount, 1988, w/Mitch Glazer

Screenplays:
ARRIVE ALIVE w/Mitch Glazer
LOLA w/Mitch Glazer
THE HOUSE GUEST w/Mitch Glazer
DROP DEAD
SLAMMER

DENNIS O'FLAHERTY*
Agent: Camden-ITG - Los Angeles, 213/289-2700

HAMMETT   Orion/Warner Bros., 1982, w/ Ross Thomas
PINOCCHIO AND THE EMPEROR OF THE NIGHT (AF)
    New World, 1987, w/Robby London & Barry O'Brien

Screenplays:
SOUND OFF
FEVER
LACKAWANNA
MOST LIKELY TO SUCCEED
HIGH STEEL
RINO
SUNSHINE FLYER
BROTHERHOOD OF THE GRAPE

COLO TAVERNIER O'HAGAN
Contact: French Film Office, 745 Fifth Avenue, New York, NY 10151, 212/832-8860

A WEEK'S VACATION *UNE SEMAINE DE VACANCES* Biograph, 1982, w/Marie-Francois Hans & Bertrand Tavernier
A SUNDAY IN THE COUNTRY MGM/UA Classics, 1984, w/Bertrand Tavernier
BEATRICE *LA PASSION BEATRICE* Samuel Goldwyn Company, 1987
SUMMER INTERLUDE *COMEDIE D'ETE* Ariel/Zeitan, 1989, w/Daniel Vigne
STORY OF WOMEN MK2/New Yorker Film, 1989, w/Claude Chabrol
DADDY NOSTALGIA Avenue Pictures, 1991

Screenplays:
DELTA OF VENUS w/Sarah Kernochan

WILLIAM P. O'HAGAN
SWORDS OF HEAVEN Trans World Entertainment, 1989, w/James Bruner, Britt Lomond & Joseph Randazzo

GERRY O'HARA
THE PLEASURE GIRLS Times, 1965, directed
ALL THE RIGHT NOISES 20th Century-Fox, 1971, directed
THE BITCH Brent Walker Productions, 1979, directed
TEN LITTLE INDIANS Cannon, 1989, w/Jackson Hunsicker
THE PHANTOM OF THE OPERA 21st Century Film Corp., 1989, Story

STEVEN OKAZAKI
LIVING ON TOKYO TIME Skouras Pictures, 1987, w/John McCormick, directed

ENRICO OLDOINI
BYE BYE BABY Seymour Borde & Associates, 1989, w/Liliana Betti & Paolo Costella, directed

HENRY OLEK*
Agent: Shorr, Stille & Associates - Los Angeles, 213/659-6160

A DIFFERENT STORY Avco, 1978
TULIPS Avco Embassy, 1981
ALL OF ME Universal, 1984, Adaptation

Screenplays:
WAVES
HEAVEN SCENT
A FEW MURDERS IN THE NEIGHBORHOOD
PARTY BALL
ENTICE & CONSENT
FRIEND OF THE COURT

JOEL OLIANSKY*
Agent: ICM - Los Angeles, 213/550-4000

COUNTERPOINT Universal, 1967, w/James Lee
THE TODD KILLINGS National General, 1971, w/Dennis Murphy
THE COMPETITION Columbia, 1980, directed
BIRD Warner Bros., 1988
THE SILENCE AT BETHANY Keener Productions/American Playhouse Theatrical Films, 1988, directed

Screenplays:
SALERNO & FINNEGAN
FREE JOANIE LITTLE
THE ANTAGONISTS
THE CHILL
THE BIG BROKERS
THE BELLS

DAVID OLIVER
CAVEGIRL Crown International, 1985, directed

RON OLIVER
HELLO MARY LOU: PROM NIGHT II Samuel Goldwyn Company, 1987
THE LAST KISS: PROM NIGHT III Norstar Entertainment, 1990, co-directed

Screenplays:
DELUSIONS (directing)

MARTY OLLSTEIN*
Agent: CNA & Associates - Los Angeles, 213/556-4343

DANGEROUS LOVE Concorde, 1988, directed

ARNE OLSEN*
Agent: Shorr, Stille & Associates - Los Angeles, 213/659-6160

RED SCORPION Shapiro Glickenhaus, 1989

Screenplays:
COP AND A HALF
SHOOTING STARS
BRAINDAZZLED
RAPID FIRE

DANA R. OLSEN*
Agent: InterTalent - Los Angeles, 213/858-6200

IT CAME FROM HOLLYWOOD Paramount, 1982
WACKO Jensen Farley Pictures, 1983, w/James Kouf, David Greenwalt & Michael Spound
GOING BERSERK Universal, 1983, w/David Steinberg
THE 'BURBS Universal, 1989

Screenplays:
MEMOIRS OF AN INVISIBLE MAN w/Robert Collector
THE VULGARIANS w/Robert Collector
MEN ON BASE w/Robert Collector
GOLD LUST w/Robert Collector
YOUR WISH IS MY COMMAND w/Robert Collector
TRAFFIC SCHOOL
HALLS OF SHAME

DOUG OLSEN
THE AMITYVILLE CURSE Allegro Films, 1990, Adaptatioan w/Michael Krueger & Norvell Rose

FILM WRITERS GUIDE

WILLIAM OLSEN
Agent: Abrams Artists & Associates - New York, 212/935-8980

GETTING IT ON   Comworld, 1983, directed

MARTIN OLSON
Agent: H. N. Swanson, Inc. - Los Angeles, 213/652-5385

Screenplays:
JEFF
DIMENSION OF MIRACLES
IT'S A WONDERFUL WORLD
LITTLE DRACULA

DAVID O'MALLEY*
Agent: The Daniel Ostroff Agency - Los Angeles, 213/278-2020

THE BOOGENS   Jensen Farley Pictures, 1982, w/Bob Hunt
KID COLTER   TMS Pictures, 1985, directed
EASY WHEELS   Fries Entertainment, 1989, w/Celia Abrams & Ivan Raimi, directed
EDGE OF HONOR   Academy Entertainment, 1991

Screenplays:
BUDDY COPS w/B.J. Nelson

JASON O'MALLEY
BACKSTREET DREAMS   Vidmark Ent., 1990

Screenplays:
BOARDWALK

SUZANNE O'MALLEY
Agent: APA - Los Angeles, 213/273-0744

PRIVATE SCHOOL   Universal, 1983, w/Dan Greenburg

Screenplays:
LADY BODYGUARDS
THE WORST PERSON IN N.Y.
THE DUMBBELL

BRADFORD O'NEIL
Agent: Warden & White Associates - Beverly Hills, 213/852-1028

Screenplays:
CUTTHROAT AND ZEBRA

DENIS O'NEIL
Agent: Susan Smith & Associates - Beverly Hills, 213/852-4777

Screenplays:
SPY HOTEL
CALL ME BOB
UNFINISHED BUSINESS
JOE HOUSE

ROBERT VINCENT O'NEIL*
Agent: Preferred Artists - Encino, 818/990-0305

THE BALTIMORE BULLET   Avco Embassy, 1980, w/John F. Brascia
VICE SQUAD   Avco Embassy, 1982, w/Sandy Howard & Kenneth Peters
DEADLY FORCE   Embassy, 1983, w/Ken Blackwell & Barry Schneider
ANGEL   New World, 1984, w/Joseph M. Cala, directed
AVENGING ANGEL   New World, 1985, w/Joseph M.Cala, directed

GENE O'NEILL*
Agent: The Irv Schechter Company - Beverly Hills, 213/278-8070

DOWN TWISTED   Cannon, 1987, w/Noreen Tobin

GREG COLLINS O'NEILL*
Contact: 213/651-1075

TUFF TURF   New World, 1985, Story w/Murray Michaels
THE SLEEPING CAR   Triax Entertainment, 1990

DANNY OPATOSHU*
Agent: Sanford, Skouras, Gross & Associates - Los Angeles, 213/208-2100

THE STUDENT TEACHERS   New World, 1973
GET CRAZY   Embassy, 1983, w/Henry Rosenbaum & David Taylor

Screenplays:
FRIES w/Vicki Hochburg

DON OPPER*
Contact: 213/962-2380

ANDROID   New World, 1982, w/James Reigle
CITY LIMITS   Atlantic Releasing Corporation, 1985, w/Aaron Lipstadt & James Reigle
SLAM DANCE   Island Pictures, 1987

RENEE ORIN*
Agent: Sutter/Walls Associates - Los Angeles, 213/658-8200

Screenplays:
TIL DEATH DO US PART
UNFINISHED BUSINESS

HARIS ORKIN*
Agent: United Talent Agency - Beverly Hills, 213/273-6700

Screenplays:
JOE AND ROSALIA
THE PASADENA KID
TAKING CHANCES
ANOTHER FINE MESS
THE LAVENDAR HILL MOB
MOST WANTED
SIN CITY
BIGMALEON
ADOPT-A-CON
HARD TO MISS

PETER ORMROD
EAT THE PEACH   Skouras Pictures, 1986, w/John Kelleher, directed

ALAN ORMSBY*
Agent: United Talent Agency - Beverly Hills, 213/273-6700

CHILDREN SHOULDN'T PLAY WITH DEAD THINGS
   Gemini Film, 1972
DEATHDREAM 1972
DERANGED 1974, directed
MY BODYGUARD 20th Century-Fox, 1980
THE LITTLE DRAGONS Aurora, 1980, w/Harvey
   Applebaum, Louis G. Atlee & Rudolph Borchert
CAT PEOPLE Universal, 1982
PORKY'S II: THE NEXT DAY 20th Century-Fox, 1983,
   w/Bob Clark & Roger Swaybill
TOUCH AND GO Tri-Star, 1986, w/Harry Colomby &
   Bob Sand
POPCORN Studio Three Film Corp., 1991,
   as "Tod Hackett"

Screenplays:
FAMILY PORTRAIT
NORTHEAST KINGDOM
CONDUCT UNBECOMING
MEMORY BOY (Shared)
HUMBOLDT COUNTY
TWISTED!

P.J. O'ROURKE
Agent: Phoenix Literary Agency - Livingston,
   Montana, 406/222-2848

EASY MONEY Orion, 1983, w/Dennis Blair, Rodney
   Dangerfield & Michael Endler

Screenplays:
MARGARITAVILLE

JAMES ORR*
Agent: CAA - Beverly Hills, 213/288-4545

BREAKING ALL THE RULES New World, 1985,
   w/Jim Cruickshank, directed
TOUGH GUYS Buena Vista, 1986, w/Jim Cruickshank
THREE MEN AND A BABY Buena Vista, 1987,
   w/ Jim Cruickshank
MR. DESTINY Buena Vista, 1990, w/Jim
   Cruickshank, directed

Screenplays:
FUN PARK w/Jim Cruickshank
BANDIT w/Jim Cruickshank

JOHN OSBORNE
Contact: British Academy of Film & Television Arts,
   195 Piccadilly, London W1, England, 71/734-0022

LOOK BACK IN ANGER (S)
LUTHER (S)
THE ENTERTAINER British Lion, 1960, w/Nigel Kneale,
   from his play
TOM JONES ★★ United Artists, 1963
INADMISSABLE EVIDENCE Paramount, 1968,
   from his play

WILLIAM H. OSBORNE*
Agent: United Talent Agency - Beverly Hills, 213/273-6700

TWINS Universal, 1988, w/William Davies, Timothy
   Harris & Herschel Weingrod

Screenplays:
THE REAL McCOY w/William Davies

FOREIGN EXCHANGE
EARTHQUAKE
PRITCHARD COUNTY
MAMA GOT A HUNDGUN IN HER BAG

WILLIAM OSCO
NIGHT PATROL New World, 1981, w/Jackie Kong &
   Murray Langston

JOHN O'SHEA
AMONG THE CINDERS New World, 1985,
   w/Rolf Haedrich

SUZANNE OSHRY*
Agent: CAA - Beverly Hills, 213/288-4545

Screenplays:
DOING BUSINESS

CLIFF OSMOND*
Contact: Directors Guild of America - Los Angeles,
   213/289-2000

THE PRESIDENT MUST DIE Jensen Farley Pictures,
   1981, w/James L. Conway
THE PENITENT Cineworld, 1988, directed

SUZANNE OSTEN
THE GUARDIAN ANGEL Sandrew Film, 1990, w/Etienne
   Glaser & Madeleine Gustafsson, directed

AVA OSTERN-FRIES
Business: Avanti Enterprises, c/o Fries Entertainment,
   6922 Hollywood Blvd., Los Angeles, CA 90028-6133,
   213/468-8306

TROOP BEVERLY HILLS WEG, 1989, Story

DOMINIQUE OTHENIN-GIRARD
HALLOWEEN 5: THE REVENGE OF MICHAEL MYERS
   Galaxy International, 1989, w/Shem Bitterman &
   Michael Jacobs, directed

JEAN-PAUL OULLETTE
Business: Yankee Classic Pictures, 4072 Inglewood Blvd. -
   Suite 2, Los Angeles, CA 90066, 213/397-0587

THE UNNAMEABLE Vidmark Entertainment, 1988

DARRIN OURA
Agent: The Wright Concept - Hollywood, 213/461-3844

Screenplays:
DIVORCE PENDING
LIVE WIRE
MUSIC HALL
BURIED
DEMON
THE DEAD OF NIGHT

GERARD OURY
Contact: French Film Office, 745 Fifth Avenue,
   New York, NY 10151, 212/832-8860

DON'T LOOK NOW...WE'RE BEING SHOT AT *LA
   GRANDE VADROVILLE* Cinepix, 1966, directed
THE BRAIN Paramount, 1969, w/Marcel Julian & Daniel
   Thompson, directed

RICHARD OUTTEN*
Agent: Harris & Goldberg - Los Angeles, 213/553-5200

LIONHEART   Orion, 1987, w/Menno Meyjes
LITTLE NEMO (AF)   Hemdale, 1992, w/Chris Columbus

Screenplays:
THE ENCHANTING
GLOBAL P.D.
SPACE CASE
ON MY HONOR
TRANSYLVANIA-PENNSYLVANIA
GOONIES 2
PET SEMATARY 2

WILLIAM OVERGARD
THE LAST DINOSAUR (AF)   Rankin & Bass
   Productions, 1977
THE BUSHIDO BLADE   Trident, 1981

ALUN OWEN
Contact: British Academy of Film & Television Arts,
   195 Piccadilly, London W1, England, 71/734-0022

THE CONCRETE JUNGLE   *THE CRIMINAL*   Merton
   Park, 1960, w/Jimmy Sangster
A HARD DAY'S NIGHT ★   United Artists, 1964

FRANK OZ*
Agent: CAA - Beverly Hills, 213/288-4545

THE MUPPETS TAKE MANHATTAN   Tri-Star, 1984,
   w/Tom Patchett & Jay Tarses, directed

P

WILLIAM PACE
ALL'S FAIR   Moviestore Entertainment, 1989, w/John
   Finnegan, Tom Rondinella & Randee Russell

TOM PAGE*
Agent: Warden & White Associates - Beverly Hills,
   213/852-1028

Screenplays:
HOUSE OF CHROME
MASK OF MICHAEL
HITTING CHARLOTTE

MARNIE PAIGE
HYPER SAPIEN   Tri-Star, 1986, w/Richard Adcock &
   Christopher Blue

ALAN J. PAKULA
Agent: ICM - Los Angeles, 213/550-4000
Business: The Pakula Company, 330 West 58th Street -
   Suite 5H, New York, NY 10019, 212/664-0640

SOPHIE'S CHOICE ★   Universal/AFD, 1982, directed
SEE YOU IN THE MORNING   Lorimar, 1988, directed
PRESUMED INNOCENT   Warner Bros., 1990,
   w/Frank Pierson, directed

DOUG PALAU*
Agent: CAA - Beverly Hills, 213/288-4545

Screenplays:
PRINCE CHARMING
FIXIN' TO DIE

EUZHAN PALCY
Agent: William Morris Agency - Beverly Hills, 213/274-7451

SUGAR CANE ALLEY   Orion, 1983, directed
A DRY WHITE SEASON   MGM/UA, 1989, w/Colin
   Welland, directed

SARAH C. PALEY*
Agent: William Morris Agency - New York, 212/586-5100

Screenplays:
IT CAME FROM POLAND
FAIRY GODMOTHER
WHAT HAPPENED TO HARRY
ALMOST HUMAN
MISTER MAGOO

JILLIAN PALETHORPE
Agent: Circle Talent Associates - Beverly Hills, 213/285-1585

AMERICAN SHOESHINE (Short), w/Sparky Greene

Screenplays:
AMAZING BUT TRUE w/Sparky Greene
DIRTY TRICKS w/Sparky Greene
CROOKED HOUSE w/Sparky Greene
MY AMERICAN FORTUNE w/Sparky Greene

MICHAEL PALIN
Business: Prominent Features Ltd., 68A Delancey St.,
   London NW1 7RY, England, 01/284-1004

CONSUMING PASSIONS (S) w/Terry Jones
AND NOW FOR SOMETHING COMPLETELY DIFFERENT
   Columbia, 1972, w/ Graham Chapman, John Cleese,
   Terry Gilliam, Eric Idle & Terry Jones
MONTY PYTHON AND THE HOLY GRAIL   Cinema 5,
   1974, w/Graham Chapman, John Cleese, Terry Gilliam,
   Eric Idle & Terry Jones
MONTY PYTHON'S LIFE OF BRIAN   Orion/Warner Bros.,
   1979, w/Graham Chapman, John Cleese, Terry Gilliam,
   Eric Idle & Terry Jones
TIME BANDITS   Avco Embassy, 1981, w/Terry Gilliam
MONTY PYTHON LIVE AT THE HOLLYWOOD BOWL
   Columbia, 1982, w/Graham Chapman, John Cleese,
   Terry Gilliam, Eric Idle & Terry Jones
THE MISSIONARY   Columbia, 1982
THE SECRET POLICEMAN'S OTHER BALL   Miramax,
   1982, w/Marty Feldman & Martin Lewis
MONTY PYTHON'S THE MEANING OF LIFE   Universal,
   1983, w/Graham Chapman, John Cleese, Terry Gilliam,
   Eric Idle & Terry Jones

ROSPO PALLENBERG*
Agent: ICM - Los Angeles, 213/550-4000

EXCALIBUR   Orion/Warner Bros., 1981
THE EMERALD FOREST   20th Century Fox, 1985

Screenplays:
THE STAND
ROBOTS RULE

ANDERS PALM
MURDER ON LINE ONE   Academy Entertainment, 1990, directed

ANTHONY PALMER*
Agent: Pleshette & Green - Los Angeles, 213/465-0428

NIGHT GAME   Trans World Entertainment, 1989, w/Spencer Eastman

MELINDA PALMER
Agent: Janklow & Associates - Los Angeles, 213/785-9550

THE GARBAGE PAIL KIDS MOVIE   Atlantic Releasing Corporation, 1987, w/Rod Amateau

TONY PALMER
Business: Isolde Film Productions - London, 71/323-4050

TESTIMONY   Isolde Films, 1988, w/David Rudkin, directed

CHAZZ PALMINTERI*
Agent: William Morris Agency - Beverly Hills, 213/274-7451

A BRONX TALE (S)   also screenplay
FAITHFUL (S)

DENNIS J. PALUMBO*
Agent: William Morris Agency - Beverly Hills, 213/274-7451

ALL THE PLEASURES PROVE (S)
MY FAVORITE YEAR   MGM/UA, 1982, w/Norman Steinberg

Screenplays:
KIDD
THE MAN WHO GAVE UP HIS NAME
THE GHOST OF HELL'S KITCHEN
DOUBLES
THE WORKS
POE
THE GRAND GAME
WORKING TRASH
RITES OF SUMMER
THURSDAY'S CHILD

NORMAN PANAMA*
Agent: Kaplan-Stahler - Beverly Hills, 213/653-4483

AND THE ANGELS SING   Paramount, 1943, w/Melvin Frank & Claude Binyon
THANK YOUR LUCKY STARS   Warner Bros., 1943, w/Melvin Frank & James V. Kern
DUFFY'S TAVERN   Paramount, 1945, w/Melvin Frank
MONSIEUR BEAUCAIRE   Paramount, 1945, w/Melvin Frank
THE ROAD TO UTOPIA ★   Paramount, 1945, w/Melvin Frank
OUR HEARTS WERE GROWING UP   Paramount, 1946, w/Melvin Frank
THE RETURN OF OCTOBER   Columbia, 1948, w/Melvin Frank
MR. BLANDINGS BUILDS HIS DREAM HOUSE   RKO, 1948, w/Melvin Frank
THE REFORMER AND THE REDHEAD   MGM, 1950, w/Melvin Frank, co-directed
STRICTLY DISHONORABLE   MGM, 1951, w/Melvin Frank, co-directed
CALLAWAY WENT THATAWAY   MGM, 1951, w/Melvin Frank
ABOVE AND BEYOND   MGM, 1952, w/Melvin Frank, co-directed
KNOCK ON WOOD ★   Paramount, 1954, w/Melvin Frank, co-directed
WHITE CHRISTMAS   Paramount, 1954, w/Melvin Frank & Norman Krasna
THE COURT JESTER   Paramount, 1955, w/Melvin Frank, co-directed
THAT CERTAIN FEELING   Paramount, 1956, w/Melvin Frank, William Altman & I.A.L. Diamond, co-directed
THE TRAP   THE BAITED TRAP   Paramount, 1958, w/Richard Alan Simmons, directed
L'IL ABNER   Paramount, 1959, w/Melvin Frank
THE FACTS OF LIFE ★   United Artists, 1960, w/Melvin Frank
ROAD TO HONG KONG   United Artists, 1962, w/Melvin Frank, co-directed
NOT WITH MY WIFE, YOU DON'T!   Warner Bros., 1966, w/Peter Barnes & Larry Gelbart, directed
I WILL, I WILL...FOR NOW   20th Century-Fox, 1976, w/Albert E. Lewin

WILLIAM N. PANZER
Business: Davis-Panzer Productions, 1438 N. Gover St., Suite 573, Los Angeles, CA 90028, 213/463-2343

STEEL   LOOK DOWN AND DIE   World Northal, 1980, Story w/Peter S. Davis & Rob Ewing

DENNIS PAOLI
H.P. LOVECRAFT'S RE-ANIMATOR   Empire Pictures, 1985, w/Stuart Gordon & William H. Norris
FROM BEYOND   Empire Pictures, 1986
THE PIT AND THE PENDULUM   Full Moon Entertainment, 1991

Screenplays:
CRASH AND BURN

MICHAEL J. PARADISE
(Giulio Paradisi)
THE VISITOR   International Picture Show, 1980, Story w/Ovidio Assontis

JOHN PARAGON*
Agent: William Morris Agency - Beverly Hills, 213/274-7451

ELVIRA: MISTRESS OF THE DARK   New World, 1988, w/Sam Egan & Cassandra Peterson

Screenplays:
BORN TO SUFFER
BUZZWORD

GAIL PARENT*
Agent: CAA - Beverly Hills, 213/288-4545

SHEILA LEVINE IS DEAD AND LIVING IN NEW YORK   Paramount, 1975, w/Kenny Solms
THE MAIN EVENT   Warner Bros., 1979, w/ Andrew Smith
CROSS MY HEART   Universal, 1987, w/Armyan Bernstein

Screenplays:
SLAVES OF LOVE
DOCTORS IN HOLLYWOOD

Pa

FILM WRITERS GUIDE

DOMINIC PARIS
LAST RITES   Cannon, 1980, w/Ben Donnelly

HENRY C. PARKE*
Agent: Warden & White Associates - Beverly Hills, 213/852-1028

Screenplays:
WHITE LIES
ROAR OF THE PRESS
ON THE LAM
STRAWBERRY FIELDS
UNFINISHED BUSINESS
HONEYMOON
DEADLY ERNEST

ALAN PARKER
Agent: CAA - Beverly Hills, 213/288-4545
Business: 7720 Sunset Blvd., Los Angeles, CA 90046, 213/969-0969

MELODY   Hemdale, 1971
BUGSY MALONE   Paramount, 1976, directed
ANGEL HEART   Tri-Star, 1987, directed
COME SEE THE PARADISE   20th Century Fox, 1990, directed

CARY PARKER
THE GIRL IN THE PICTURE   Samuel Goldwyn Company, 1986, directed

CHARLES PARKER
BREAKIN'   MGM/UA/Cannon, 1984, w/Allen DeBevoise & Gerald Scalfe

DAVID PARKER
Agent: CAA - Beverly Hills, 213/288-4545

MALCOLM   Vestron, 1986
RIKKY AND PETE   MGM/UA, 1988
THE BIG STEAL   Overseas Film Group, 1991

G. ROSS PARKER*
Agent: ICM - New York, 212/556-5600

Screenplays:
HIGH HEELED SNEAKERS
DOLL FACE
KNOCK WOOD

MONICA PARKER*
Agent: Broder-Kurland-Webb-Uffner - Los Angeles, 213/656-9262

ALL DOGS GO TO HEAVEN (AF)   MGM/UA, 1989, Story w/others

SCOTT PARKER*
Agent: The Coppage Company - North Hollywood, 818/980-1106

DIE LAUGHING   Orion/Warner Bros., 1980, w/Robby Benson & Jerry Segal
HE KNOWS YOU'RE ALONE   MGM/UA, 1980

Screenplays:
SATURDAY AFTERNOON   w/Eric Bloom
THE WRONG DOOR

BEMS
CAREER MOVE
GO TO HELL
MUSHROOM
IF YOU BELIEVE
FLATBUSH GAS
GROWN-UPS
GRIMOIRE

TOM S. PARKER*
Agent: United Talent Agency - Beverly Hills, 213/273-6700

Screenplays:
STAY TUNED   w/Jim Jennewein
THE FAMILY MAN   w/Jim Jennewein

WALTER F. PARKES*
Agent: CAA - Beverly Hills, 213/288-4545
Business: Lasker-Parkes, 10202 W. Washington Blvd., Producers Bldg. - Suite 142, Culver City, CA 90232, 213/280-4267

WARGAMES ★   MGM/UA, 1983, w/Lawrence Lasker

Screenplays:
SNEAKERS   w/Lawrence Lasker & Phil Alden Robinson
THE GENIUS   w/Lawrence Lasker
PETER PAN   w/Lawrence Lasker

ERIC PARKINSON
SOULTAKER   Taurus Entertainment, 1990, Story w/Vivian Schilling

HUGH PARKS
AFTER SCHOOL   Moviestore Entertainment, 1989, w/John Linde, Rod McBrien & Joe Tankersley

JOANNE PARRENT
Agent: The Artists Group - Los Angeles, 213/552-1100

THE HEALING FORCE   Woody Clark Productions, 1983, w/Woodrow W. Clark & Jay Miracle

JAMES D. PARRIOTT*
Agent: United Talent Agency - Beverly Hills, 213/273-6700

HEART CONDITION   New Line Cinema, 1990, directed

SARA PARRIOTT*
Agent: The Daniel Ostroff Agency - Los Angeles, 213/278-2020

WORTH WINNING   20th Century Fox, 1989, w/Josan McGibbon
THREE MEN AND A LITTLE LADY   Buena Vista, 1990, Story w/Josan McGibbon
THE FAVOR   Orion, 1992, w/Josan McGibbon

Screenplays:
MRS. CALIFORNIA   w/Josan McGibbon
RUNAWAY BRIDE   w/Josan McGibbon

MICHAEL PART*
Agent: Harris & Goldberg - Los Angeles, 213/553-5200

Screenplays:
DOORNAIL

MICHAEL PASEORNEK
Agent: Ned Brown Agency - Los Angeles, 213/276-1131

STITCHES   International Film Marketing, 1985,
   w/Michael Coquette
MEATBALLS III   TMS Pictures, 1986, w/Bradley Kesden
SNAKEEATER'S REVENGE   Image Organization,
   1990, w/Don Carmody & John Dunning

ELIZABETH PASSERELLI
Agent: Circle Talent Associates - Beverly Hills,
   213/285-1585

Screenplays:
PRODIGAL SON
OTHERWISE ENGAGED

IVAN PASSER
Agent: The Agency - Los Angeles, 213/551-3000

LOVES OF A BLONDE   Prominent, 1966, w/Milos
   Forman & Jaroslav Papousek
THE FIREMAN'S BALL   Cinema 5, 1968, w/Milos
   Forman & Jaroslav Papousek
LAW AND DISORDER   Columbia, 1974, w/Ken Harris
   Fishman & William Richert, directed

JAMES PASTERNAK
Agent: Warden & White Associates - Beverly Hills,
   213/852-1028

Screenplays:
LIGHTNING BENDER
SHOOTING STARS
GREAT HANDS
TEACH ME TONIGHT

TOM PATCHETT*
Agent: CAA - Beverly Hills, 213/288-4545

WOLVERINES (S)
MAD MAGAZINE PRESENTS UP THE ACADEMY
   Warner Bros., 1980, w/Jay Tarses
THE GREAT MUPPET CAPER   Universal/AFD, 1981,
   w/ Jay Tarses, Jerry Juhl & Jack Rose
THE MUPPETS TAKE MANHATTAN   Tri-Star, 1984,
   w/Frank Oz & Jay Tarses

Screenplays:
THE BRAVE YOUNG MEN OF WEINBERG
   w/Jay Tarses
THE KID WHO COULD GO TO HIS LEFT
   w/Jay Tarses
CROOKS   w/Jay Tarses

MICHAEL PATE
Business: Pisces Productions, 21 Bundarra Road,
   Bellevue Hill, NSW, 2023, Australia, 02/30-4208

TIM   Satori, 1979, directed
THE MANGO TREE   Satori, 1982

JOHN PATERSON
ANNIE'S COMING OUT   Film Australia, 1984,
   w/Chris Borthwick
A TEST OF LOVE   Universal, 1985,
   w/Chris Borthwick

VICKIE PATIK*
Agent: ICM - Los Angeles, 213/550-4000

Screenplays:
FAMILY MELODRAMA
INTERSLOPE

VINCENT PATRICK*
Agent: United Talent Agency - Beverly Hills, 213/273-6700

THE POPE OF GREENWICH VILLAGE   MGM/UA, 1984
FAMILY BUSINESS   Tri-Star, 1989

Screenplays:
IN FROM THE COLD
OF THE LORD
JOE II
MY NEW PARTNER
HARLEM UNIVERSITY
AT PLAY

JAMES BRENDAN PATTERSON
Agent: Warden & White Associates - Beverly Hills,
   213/852-1028

Screenplays:
MAJIC SHOW
STEEPLECHASE
HONEYMOON
POP!

DOROTHY KOSTER PAUL
Business: Paul Entertainment, Inc., 517A Wilshire Blvd.,
   Santa Monica, CA ,90401, 213/319-3562

ETERNITY   Paul Entertainment, 1990, w/Steven Paul &
   Jon Voight

HENRY PAUL
Business: Paul Entertainment, Inc., 517A Wilshire Blvd.,
   Santa Monica, CA ,90401, 213/319-3562

FALLING IN LOVE AGAIN   International Picture Show,
   1980, Story w/Steven Paul

STEVEN PAUL
Business: Paul Entertainment, Inc., 517A Wilshire Blvd.,
   Santa Monica, CA ,90401, 213/319-3562

FALLING IN LOVE AGAIN   International Picture Show,
   1980, w/Ted Allan & Susannah York, directed
SLAPSTICK OF ANOTHER KIND   *SLAPSTICK*
   Entertainment Releasing Corporation/International
   FilmMarketing, 1983, directed
NEVER TOO YOUNG TO DIE   Paul Releasing, 1986,
   w/Gil Bettman & Anton Fitz
ETERNITY   Paul Entertainment, 1990, w/Dorothy Koster
   Paul & Jon Voight, directed

DAVID PAULSEN*
Agent: Richland/Wunsch/Hohman Agency - Los Angeles,
   213/278-1955

DIAMONDS   Avco Embassy, 1975, w/Menahem Golan
SAVAGE WEEKEND   *THE UPSTATE MURDERS*
   Cannon, 1976, directed
THE URANIUM CONSPIRACY   Noah Films, 1978
SCHIZOID   Cannon, 1980, directed

Pa

FILM WRITERS GUIDE

GARY PAULSEN
A CRY IN THE WILD   Concorde/New Horizons, 1990, w/Catherine Cryan

Screenplays:
HATCHET

ANDREW PAYNE
SPACED OUT   Miramax, 1981

Screenplays:
THE PASSION OF MARTIN (directing)

WILLIAM MOSLEY PAYNE*
Agent: Triad Artists, Inc. - Los Angeles, 213/556-2727

LIVIN' LARGE   Samuel Goldwyn Company, 1991

J. STEPHEN PEACE
HAPPY HOUR   The Movie Store, 1987, w/John De Bello & Constantine Dillon

GREG PEAD
(See Yahoo Serious)

BARRY PEARSON
KING OF THE STREETS   Shapiro Entertainment, 1986, w/Ed Hunt, Ruben Gordon & Steven Shoenberg
BLOODY BIRTHDAY   Judica Productions, 1986, w/Ed Hunt

DURK PEARSON*
Contact: WGA - Los Angeles, 213/550-1000

THE DEAD POOL   Warner Bros., 1988, Story w/Steve Sharon & Sandy Shaw

KIMI PECK*
Agent: The Gersh Agency - Beverly Hills, 213/274-6611

LITTLE DARLINGS   Paramount, 1980, w/Dalene Young

Screenplays:
HOW TO MARRY A MILLIONAIRE

DAVID E. PECKINPAH*
Agent: Broder-Kurland-Webb-Uffner - Los Angeles, 213/656-9262

Screenplays:
PALS FOREVER
OUTLAW SKIES

ROBERT L. PEETE*
Contact: WGA - Los Angeles, 213/550-1000

IT'S CALLED SURVIVAL (S)
THE CENTERFOLD GIRLS   Dimension, 1974
DRIVE-IN   Columbia, 1976

HANAN PELED
DEADLINE   Skouras Pictures, 1987

HOWARD C. PEN
SWORD OF THE VALIANT   Cannon, 1984, w/Stephen Weeks & Philip M. Breen

ARTHUR PENN
Agent: ICM - New York, 212/556-6810

ALICE'S RESTAURANT   United Artists, 1969, w/Venable Herndon, directed

LEO PENN*
Agent: Sanford, Skouras, Gross & Associates - Los Angeles, 213/208-2100

JUDGMENT IN BERLIN   New Line Cinema, 1988, w/Joshua Sinclair, directed

SEAN PENN
Agent: CAA - Beverly Hills, 213/288-4545

INDIAN RUNNER   Universal, 1991, directed

VAL PENN*
Contact: WGA - Los Angeles, 213/550-1000

Screenplays:
JUST DESERTS

JOHN V. PENNEY*
Agent: H.N. Swanson, Inc. - Los Angeles, 213/652-5385

THE POWER   Artists Releasing Corporation/Film Ventuers International, 1982, Story w/Stephen Carpenter, John Hopkins & Jeffrey Obrow
THE KINDRED   FM Entertainment, 1987, w/others

DAVID PEOPLES*
Agent: Shapiro/Lichtman - Los Angeles, 213/859-8877

BLADE RUNNER   The Ladd Company/Warner Bros., 1982, w/Hampton Fancher
LEVIATHAN   MGM/UA, 1989, w/Jeb Stuart
THE BLOOD OF HEROES   New Line Cinema, 1990, directed
DEADFALL   ITC, 1990

Screenplays:
HERO AND A HALF
SGT. ROCK
LADY HAWKS
VINDICATORS
TIME BOMB
JOURNEY OF THE 14 PRESIDENTS
TAXI TO GLORY
CUT WHORE KILLINGS
GRABBERS
CHINESE BANDIT
GUATEMALA
WHORES GOLD
JOINT ACCOUNT

CLARE PEPLOE
Agent: ICM, Ltd. - London, 01/629-8080

ZABRISKIE POINT   MGM, 1970, w/Michelangelo Antonioni, Fred Gardner, Tonino Guerra & Sam Shepard
LUNA   20th Century-Fox, 1979, w/Bernardo Bertolucci & Giuseppe Bertolucci
HIGH SEASON   Hemdale, 1988, w/Mark Peploe, directed

MARK PEPLOE*
Agent: ICM - Los Angeles, 213/550-4000

THE PIED PIPER   Paramount, 1972, w/Andrew Birkin & Jacques Demy
THE PASSENGER *PROFESSIONE: REPORTER* MGM/United Artsits, 1975, w/Michelangelo Antonioni & Peter Wollen
THE LAST EMPEROR ★ Columbia, 1987, w/Bernardo Bertolucci
HIGH SEASON   Hemdale, 1988, w/Clare Peploe
THE SHELTERING SKY   Warner Bros., 1990, w/Bernardo Bertolucci

Screenplays:
THE CREW w/Michelangelo Antonioni
OUT OF THE BLUE
VICTORY
CATFISH TANGLE

PAUL PEPPERMAN
THE BEASTMASTER   MGM/UA, 1982, w/Don Coscarelli

DON PEQUIGNOT
9 1/2 NINJAS   Republic Pictures, 1991, w/Bill Crounse

MIGUEL PEREIRA
VERONICO CRUZ   Cinevista, 1990, directed

FRANK RAY PERILLI*
Contact: 213/850-5160

LITTLE CIGARS   1973 w/Louis Garfinkle
THE DOBERMAN GANG   Dimension, 1973, w/Louis Garfinkle
DRACULA'S DOG   Crown International, 1978
ALLIGATOR   Group 1, 1980, Story w/John Sayles
THE LAND OF NO RETURN   International Picture Show, 1981, w/Kent Bateman
JOEY TAKES A CAB   Bandwagon Productions, 1991

Screenplays:
THE GODMOTHER w/Louis Garfinkle
TIJUANA DONKEY w/Louis Garfinkle

ANTHONY PERKINS
Agent: The Gersh Agency - Beverly Hills, 213/274-6611

THE LAST OF SHIELA   Warner Bros., 1973, w/Stephen Sondheim

HEIDE PERLMAN*
Agent: CAA - Beverly Hills, 213/288-4545

Screenplays:
THE SHOWER

FRANK PERRY
Agent: ICM - New York, 212/556-5600

MOMMIE DEAREST   Paramount, 1981, w/Robert Getchell, Tracy Hotchner & Frank Yablans, directed

FRED C. PERRY
BLIND DATE   New Line Cinema, 1984, w/Nico Mastorakis

BILL PERSKY*
Agent: CAA - Beverly Hills, 213/288-4545

WATER   Atlantic Releasing Corporation, 1984, w/Dick Clement & Ian La Frenais

P.J. PESCE
Agent: United Talent Agency - Beverly Hills, 213/273-6700

THE AFTERLIFE OF GRANDPA (Short), directed

Screenplays:
LEO'S MISERABLE AFFLICTIONS AND UNFORTUNATE MISHAPS
CASEY SPEAKS w/Adam Belanoff

CHARLIE PETERS*
Agent: CAA - Beverly Hills, 213/288-4545

PATERNITY   Paramount, 1981
KISS ME GOODBYE   20th Century-Fox, 1982
BLAME IT ON RIO   20th Century-Fox, 1984, w/Larry Gelbart
HOT TO TROT   Warner Bros., 1988, w/Hugo Gilbert & Stephen Neigher
HER ALIBI   Warner Bros., 1989
THREE MEN AND A LITTLE LADY   Buena Vista, 1990

Screenplays:
EXPECTING MIRACLES
THE JUGGLER
HONEYCHILD
HOPELESS ROMANTIC

KENNETH PETERS
Agent: Barry Perelman Agency - Los Angeles, 213/274-5999

VICE SQUAD   Avco Embassy, 1982, w/Sandy Howard & Robert Vincent O'Neil

STEPHEN PETERS
Agent: The Chasin Agency - Beverly Hills, 213/278-7505

THE PARK IS MINE (CTF)   HBO Premiere Films/Astral Film Productions/ICC, 1985
THE FOURTH WAR   Cannon, 1990, w/Kenneth Ross

Screenplays:
HIGH SPEED
THE STAND OUT
THE BINGE
AMERICAN COUP

WOLFGANG PETERSEN
Agent: The Chasin Agency - Beverly Hills, 213/274-7451

DAS BOOT (THE BOAT) ★   Triumph/Columbia, 1981, directed
THE NEVERENDING STORY   Warner Bros., 1984, w/Herman Weigel, directed
SHATTERED   MGM-Pathe, 1991, directed

Screenplays:
FIELDS OF HONOR w/Andrew Birkin (directing)

CASSANDRA PETERSON
Contact: Screen Actors Guild - Los Angeles, 213/465-4600

ELVIRA: MISTRESS OF THE DARK   New World, 1988, w/Sam Egan & John Paragon

DANIEL M. PETERSON
GIRLFRIEND FROM HELL   IVE, 1990, directed

DON PETERSON
AN ALMOST PERFECT AFFAIR   Paramount, 1979, w/Walter Bernstein
TARGET   Warner Bros., 1985, w/Howard Berk

MAURICE PETERSON
Agent: ICM - New York, 212/556-5600

HOMEWORK   Jensen Farley Pictures, 1982, w/Don Saffran

GERALD D. PETIEVICH*
Agent: ICM - Los Angeles, 213/550-4000

TO LIVE AND DIE IN L.A.   MGM/UA, 1985, w/William Friedkin

DENNE BART PETITCLERC*
Agent: The Gersh Agency - Beverly Hills, 213/274-6611

RED SUN   National General, 1972, w/Laird Koenig, William Roberts & Lawrence Roman
AN OPEN SEASON   Impala/Arpa, 1974
ISLANDS IN THE STREAM   Paramount, 1977

Screenplays:
WINTER SONG
LANCERS
DESTINIES
DOUBLE EAGLE
MEN OF THE DRAGON
PIECES OF SEVEN
PROMETHEUS
A FAREWELL TO ARMS
SILENT NIGHT
LORD OF THE AMAZON

DANIEL PETRIE
Agent: CAA - Beverly Hills, 213/288-4545
Business: 13201 Haney Place, Los Angeles, CA, 90049, 213/451-9157

THE BAY BOY   Orion, 1984, directed

Screenplays:
THE SECOND COMING

DANIEL PETRIE, JR.*
Agent: Richland/Wunsch/Hohman Agency - Los Angeles, 213/278-1955

BEVERLY HILLS COP ★   Paramount, 1984
THE BIG EASY   Columbia, 1987
SHOOT TO KILL   Buena Vista, 1988, w/Michael Burton & Harv Zimmel
TURNER & HOOCH   Buena Vista, 1989, w/Michael Blodgett, Dennis Shryack, Jim Cash & Jack Epps
TOY SOLDIERS   Tri-Star, 1991, w/David Koepp, directed

Screenplays:
FIRESTAR
OUT OF TIME

P.J. PETTIETTE
BAD DREAMS   20th Century Fox, 1988, Story w/Michael Dick, Andrew Fleming & Yuri Zeltser

PEYO
THE SMURFS AND THE MAGIC FLUTE (AF)   Atlantic Releasing Corporation, 1983

HARLEY PEYTON*
Agent: CAA - Beverly Hills, 213/288-4545

LESS THAN ZERO   20th Century Fox, 1987

Screenplays:
WILD BOYS
HOT WIRE
LIFE DURING WARTIME

CHUCK PFAFFER*
Agent: Vanguard Associates - Santa Monica, 213/829-5000

NAVY SEALS   Orion, 1990, w/Gary Goldman
DARK MAN   Universal, 1990, w/Daniel Goldin, Joshua Goldin, Ivan Raimi & Sam Raimi

Screenplays:
MEDAL OF VALOR

ANNA HAMILTON PHELAN*
Agent: CAA - Beverly Hills, 213/288-4545

MASK   Universal, 1985
GORILLAS IN THE MIST ★   Universal, 1988

Screenplays:
MACHINE GUN KELLY
ONE MORE TIME
THE HOME FRONT

WILLIAM W. PHELPS*
Agent: ICM - Los Angeles, 213/550-4000

NORTH SHORE   Universal, 1987, w/Tim McCanlies, directed

Screenplays:
BROTHER TO BROTHER
ETHICAL CHOICE

BILL PHILLIPS*
Agent: The Gersh Agency - Beverly Hills, 213/274-6611

CHRISTINE   Columbia, 1983
FIRE WITH FIRE   *CAPTIVE HEARTS*   Paramount, 1986, w/Paul Boorstin, Sharon Boorstin & Warren Skaaren
PHYSICAL EVIDENCE   Columbia, 1989
RISING SON (CTF)   Sarabande Productions, 1990

EL DIABLO (CTF)   Wizan/Black Productions, 1990,
    w/John Carpenter & Tommy Lee Wallace
RAINBOW DRIVE (CTF)   Viacom-Dove-ITC, 1990,
    w/Bennett Cohen

Screenplays:
PAY DIRT   (directing)

LOU DIAMOND PHILLIPS
Agent: Harris & Goldberg - Los Angeles, 213/553-5200

AMBITION   Miramax, 1991

MAURICE PHILLIPS
Contact: Directors Guild of America - Los Angeles,
    213/289-2000

ENID IS SLEEPING   Vestron, 1991, w/A.J. Tipping &
    James Whaley, directed

MAURICE PIALAT
Contact: French Film Office, 745 Fifth Avenue, New York,
    NY, 10151, 213/832-8860

UNDER THE SUN OF SATAN   Alive Films, 1987,
    w/Sylvie Danton, directed
VAN GOGH   (no distributor), 1991, directed

REX PICKETT*
Agent: Susan Smith & Associates - Beverly Hills,
    213/852-4777

CALIFORNIA WITHOUT END   Nightfilm Productions,
    1983, directed
FROM HOLLYWOOD TO DEADWOOD   Island Pictures,
    1989, directed

Screenplays:
BAJA HIDEAWAY
KNIFE IN THE HEART
DECOY
THE ROAD BACK
LILY
RED WIND
WHO SHOT SAMUEL RAY?
OPERATION CULIACAN
CRITICAL MASS   w/Howard Cohen

LEON PIEDMONT
(See Christopher Crowe)

JOHN PIELMEIER*
Agent: E.M.A. - Los Angeles, 213/461-0148

SLEIGHT OF HAND (S)
HAUNTED LIVES (S)
THE BOYS OF WINTER (S)
EVENING (S)
JASS (S)
AGNES OF GOD   Columbia, 1985, from his play

Screenplays:
SERENADE
ASCENT

CHARLES B. PIERCE
THE LEGEND OF BOGGY CREEK   Howco International,
    1973, directed
WINTERHAWK   Howco International, 1975, directed
THE WINDS OF AUTUMN   Howco International,
    1976, directed
GREYEAGLE   American International, 1977, directed
THE NORSEMEN   American International, 1978, directed
THE EVICTORS   American International, 1979, w/Paul
    Fisk & Gary Rusoff, directed
SACRED GROUND   Pacific International, 1983, directed
SUDDEN IMPACT   Warner Bros., 1983, Story
    w/Earl E. Smith
BOGGY CREEK II   Howco International, 1985, directed

SCOTT PIERCE*
Contact: WGA - Los Angeles, 213/550-1000

A NIGHTMARE ON ELM STREET 4: THE DREAM MASTER
    New Line Cinema, 1988, w/Brian Helgeland

DORI PIERSON*
Contact: 818/540-1941

SPOT MARKS THE X (CTF)   Catalina Production
    Group, 1986
BIG BUSINESS   Buena Vista, 1988, w/Marc Rubel

Screenplays:
ONE FINE DAY
EXCESS BAGGAGE
RETURN ENGAGEMENT
FRIENDLY RELATIONS
HIGH AND LONESOME
CONTINENTAL CIRCUS

FRANK R. PIERSON*
Agent: United Talent Agency - Beverly Hills, 213/273-6700

CAT BALLOU ★   Columbia, 1965, w/Walter Newman
COOL HAND LUKE ★   Warner Bros., 1967,
    w/Donn Pearce
THE HAPPENING   Columbia, 1967, w/Ronald Austin &
    James D. Buchanan
THE LOOKING GLASS WAR   Columbia, 1969, directed
THE ANDERSON TAPES   Columbia, 1971
DOG DAY AFTERNOON ★★   Warner Bros., 1975
A STAR IS BORN   Warner Bros., 1976, w/Joan Didion &
    John Gregory Dunne, directed
KING OF THE GYPSIES   Paramount, 1978, directed
IN COUNTRY   Warner Bros., 1989, w/Cynthia Cidre
PRESUMED INNOCENT   Warner Bros., 1990,
    w/Alan J. Pakula

Screenplays:
AIN'T THAT AMERICA
HANDCARVED COFFINS
THE EVANGELIST
MEN OF BRONZE
DESIRE
BOYLE

JEREMY PIKSER*
Contact: WGA - New York, 212/245-6180

THE LEMON SISTERS   Miramax, 1990

NICHOLAS PILEGGI*
Agent: CAA - Beverly Hills, 213/288-4545

GOOD FELLAS ★   Warner Bros., 1990, w/Martin Scorsese

Screenplays:
THE COP WHO CAME IN FROM THE HEAT

Pi

SAM PILLSBURY
Agent: ICM - Los Angeles, 213/550-4000

THE SCARECROW   Oasis, 1981, w/Michael Heath, directed
THE QUIET EARTH   Skouras Pictures, 1985, w/Bill Baer & Bruno Lawrence

ROBERT PILOTTE
THE BIG DIS   Pyramid Films, 1989, w/Gordon Eriksen

TINA PINE*
Contact: 516/654-5045

ON THE RIGHT TRACK   20th Century-Fox, 1981, w/Buddy Avery & Richard Moses

MIGUEL PINERO
SHORT EYES   The Film League, 1978, from his play

JOHN PINKNEY
THIRST   Greater Union Film Distributors, 1979

HAROLD PINTER
Agent: Judy Daish Agency - London, 011/441/486-5405
Business: c/o ACTAC Ltd., 16 Cadogan Lane, London SW1, England, 01/235-2797

THE HOTHOUSE (S)
OLD TIMES (S)
NO MAN'S LAND (S)
THE DUMB WAITER (S), also teleplay
A SLIGHT ACHE (S)
THE ROOM (S), also teleplay
THE COLLECTION (S)
THE LOVER (S)
LANDSCAPE (S)
MOUNTAIN LANGUAGE (S)
ONE FOR THE ROAD (S)
THE SERVANT   Landau, 1964
THE CARETAKER   *THE GUEST*   Caretaker Films, 1964, from his play
THE PUMPKIN EATER   Columbia, 1964
THE QUILLER MEMORANDUM   Rank, 1966
ACCIDENT   Cinema 5, 1967
THE BIRTHDAY PARTY   Palomar, 1968, from his play
THE GO-BETWEEN   EMI, 1970
THE HOMECOMING   American Express, 1973, from his play
THE LAST TYCOON   Paramount, 1976
THE FRENCH LIEUTENANT'S WOMAN ★   United Artists, 1981
BETRAYAL ★   20th Century-Fox International Classics, 1983, from his play
TURTLE DIARY   Samuel Goldwyn Company, 1985
THE HANDMAID'S TALE   Cinecom, 1990
THE COMFORT OF STRANGERS   Skouras Pictures, 1991
REUNION   Les Films Ariane/FR3 Films, 1991

Screenplays:
REMEMBRANCE OF THINGS PAST
REMAINS OF THE DAY

DAVID PIRIE
Agent: London Management - London, 011/441/493-1610

Screenplays:
DREAM DEMONS
LOVE ACT
TOTAL ECLIPSE OF THE HEART

MARK PIRRO
DEATHROW GAMESHOW   Crown International, 1987
MY MOM'S A WEREWOLF   Crown International, 1988

DEAN PITCHFORD*
Agent: Richland/Wunsch/Hohman Agency - Los Angeles, 213/278-1955

FOOTLOOSE   Paramount, 1984
SING   Tri-Star, 1989

Screenplays:
PARALLELS
ELSEWHERE

JEAN-YVES PITOUN*
Agent: CAA - Beverly Hills, 213/288-4545

TO KILL A PRIEST   Columbia, 1990, w/Agnieszka Holland

Screenplays:
MISTAKEN IDENTITY
DUE PROCESS
LOVE KILLS
THE PARTNER
FRENCH KISS

GLEN PITRE
BELIZAIRE THE CAJUN   Skouras Pictures, 1986, directed

Screenplays:
REDFISH

ANGELO PIZZO*
Agent: ICM - Los Angeles, 213/550-4000

HOOSIERS   Orion, 1986

Screenplays:
KNIGHTS OF TERROR
SATURDAYS HEROS

BRET T. PLATE*
Contact: WGA - Los Angeles, 213/550-1000

Screenplays:
DOWN EAST

ALAN PLATER
Agent: Margaret Ramsay Ltd. - London, 011/441/240-0691

THE VIRGIN AND THE GYPSY   Chevron, 1970
IT SHOULDN'T HAPPEN TO A VET   EMI, 1976
PRIEST OF LOVE   Filmways, 1981

JOHN PLATT
THE FORBIDDEN DANCE   Columbia, 1990, w/Roy Langsdon
OUT OF SIGHT, OUT OF MIND   Spectrum Entertainment Group, 1990, w/Roy Langsdon

POLLY PLATT*
Business: Gracie Films, 20th Century-Fox, 213/203-3770

TARGETS   Paramount, 1968, Story w/Peter Bogdanovich
GOOD LUCK, MISS WYCOFF   Bel Air-Gradison, 1972
PRETTY BABY   Paramount, 1978

Screenplays:
THE ASSISTANT

JOHN PLEFFER
THE SINGER AND THE DANCER   Columbia, 1977,
    w/Gillian Armstrong

RICK PODELL*
Agent: Sutter/Walls Associates - Los Angeles,
    213/658-8200

NOTHING IN COMMON   Tri-Star, 1986,
    w/ Michael Preminger

Screenplays:
HIGHER EDUCATION w/Michael Preminger
TUXEDO TERRACE w/Michael Preminger
LAWRENCE MANOR w/Michael Preminger
LIES AND MORE LIES
THE LAST VIRGIN IN AMERICA
AMERICAN COUPLE

AMOS POE*
Agent: William Morris Agency - New York, 212/586-5100

THE FOREIGNER   Amos Poe Visions, 1978, directed
SUBWAY RIDERS   Hep Pictures, 1981, directed
ALPHABET CITY   Atlantic Releasing Corporation,
    1984, w/Gregory Heller, directed
ROCKET GIBRALTAR   Columbia, 1988

Screenplays:
THE TIDES
PORT OF CALL
BEACH HOUSE

S. LEE POGOSTIN*
Agent: Shapiro/Lichtman - Los Angeles,
    213/859-8877

PRESSURE POINT   United Artists, 1962,
    w/Hubert Cornfield
SYNANON GET OFF MY BACK   Columbia, 1965,
    w/Ian Bernard
HARD CONTRACT   20th Century-Fox, 1969, directed
GOLDEN NEEDLES   American International, 1974,
    w/Sylvia Schneble
HIGH ROAD TO CHINA   Warner Bros., 1983, w/Sandra
    Weintraub Roland

CHARLES EDWARD POGUE*
Agent: ICM - Los Angeles, 213/550-4000

WHO DONE IT, DARLING? (S)
SINBAD (S)
THE EBONY APE (S)
DOUBLE-ENTENDRE (S)
VAPOR OF GLORY (S)
PSYCHO III   Universal, 1986
THE FLY   20th Century Fox, 1986, w/David Cronenberg
D.O.A.   Buena Vista, 1988

Screenplays:
SIGN OF THE FOUR
THE HOUND OF THE BASKERVILLES
THE NAPOLEON OF CRIME
BLOOD OF THE GODS
THE GREYSTONE
THE KINGMAKERS
SATAN'S SORROW
BLOOD & SEX
FRANKENSTEIN

WILLIAM POHLAD
OLD EXPLORERS   Taurus Entertainment, 1991, directed

GREGORY POIRIER
DANGER ZONE III: STEEL HORSE WAR   Danger Zone
    Company, 1990, w/Jason Williams

SIDNEY POITIER
Agent: CAA - Los Angeles, 213/288-4545

FOR LOVE OF IVY   Cinerama Releasing Corporation,
    1968, Story

ROMAN POLANSKI
Agent: ICM - Los Angeles, 213/550-4000

KNIFE IN THE WATER   Kanawha, 1963, w/Jakub
    Goldberg & Jerzy Skolimowski, directed
DO YOU LIKE WOMEN?   Francoriz, 1964, w/Gerard Brach
REPULSION   Royal Films International, 1965, w/Gerard
    Brach, directed
CUL-DE-SAC   Sigma III, 1966, w/Gerard Brach, directed
THE FEARLESS VAMPIRE KILLERS, OR PARDON ME BUT
    YOUR TEETH ARE IN MY NECK DANCE OF THE
    VAMPIRES   MGM, 1967, w/Gerard Brach, directed
ROSEMARY'S BABY ★   Paramount, 1968, directed
WHAT?   Avco Embassy, 1973, w/Gerard Brach, directed
THE TENANT   Paramount, 1976, w/Gerard
    Brach, directed
TESS   Columbia, 1980, w/Gerard Brach & John
    Brownjohn, directed
PIRATES   Cannon, 1986, w/Gerard Brach, directed
FRANTIC   Warner Bros., 1988, w/Gerard Brach, directed

STEPHEN POLIAKOFF
Agent: Margaret Ramsay Ltd. - London,
    011/441/240-0691

RUNNERS   Goldcrest, 1983
SHE'S BEEN AWAY   BBC Films, 1989

BARRY POLLACK
COOL BREEZE   MGM, 1972, directed

VICKI POLON*
Agent: Robinson, Weintraub, Gross & Associates -
    Los Angeles, 213/653-5802

GIRLFRIENDS   Warner Bros., 1978

Screenplays:
MR. WONDERFUL w/Amy Schor
MEDALLION w/Joan Micklin Silver
MOUNTAIN CHARLY
HONEYMOON
MOM

ABRAHAM POLONSKY*
Agent: The Gersh Agency - Beverly Hills, 213/274-6611

BODY AND SOUL   Enterprise, 1947
FORCE OF EVIL   MGM, 1948, w/Ira Wolfert, directed
I CAN GET IT FOR YOU WHOLESALE   THIS IS
   MY AFFAIR   20th Century-Fox, 1951
MADIGAN   Universal, 1968, w/Howard Rodman
TELL THEM WILLIE BOY IS HERE   Universal,
   1969, directed
AVALANCHE EXPRESS   20th Century-Fox, 1979
MONSIGNOR   20th Century-Fox, 1982,
   w/Wendell Mayes

JOHN POMEROY
Business: Sullivan/Bluth Studios, 2501 W. Burbank Blvd. -
   Suite 201, Burbank, CA, 91505, 818/840-9446

THE SECRET OF NIMH (AF)   MGM/UA, 1982, Story
   Adaptation w/Don Bluth, Will Finn & Gary Goldman
ALL DOGS GO TO HEAVEN (AF)   MGM/UA, 1989,
   Story w/others

DARRYL PONICSAN*
Agent: CAA - Beverly Hills, 213/288-4545

CINDERELLA LIBERTY   20th Century-Fox, 1974
TAPS   20th Century-Fox, 1981, w/Robert Mark Kamen
VISION QUEST   Warner Bros., 1985
NUTS   Warner Bros., 1987, w/Alvin Sargent & Tom Topor
THE BOOST   Hemdale, 1988

Screenplays:
SCHOOL TIES
WHISPERS IN BEDLAM
MATARESE CIRCLE   w/R. Dupont & K. Hughes
LETHAL GAS
REAL PROPERTY
THE TRUEST SPORT
THE RINGER

ROBERT ROY POOL*
Agent: ICM - Los Angeles, 213/550-4000

THE BIG TOWN   Columbia, 1987

Screenplays:
ULTIMATUM   w/Laurence Dworet
THE PRACTICE
THE SECOND RECKONING
UNDERGROUND
GOLD COAST

THOMAS POPE*
Agent: William Morris Agency - Beverly Hills, 213/274-7451

THE MANITOU   Herman Weist Productions, 1978,
   w/Jon Cedar & William Girdler
A GREAT RIDE   Mason International, 1979,
   w/ Walter Dallenbach
THE BLACK HOLE   Buena Vista, 1979
THE LORDS OF DISCIPLINE   Paramount, 1983,
   w/Lloyd Fonvielle
HAMMETT   Orion/Warner Bros., 1983, Story Adaptation

Screenplays:
COLD DOG SOUP
THE CURIOUS CASE OF BENJAMIN BUTTON
THE EAGLE OF BROADWAY
YOUNG TEDDY ROOSEVELT

EINSTEIN
ASCENT
TOM MIX AND PANCHO VILLA
CROSSING NIAGARA
PEERS
JEDEDIAH SMITH
CONTACT
PROHIBITION STORY
WOMAN NEXT DOOR
PROVIDENCE
WORD OF HONOR

PETRU S. POPESCU*
Agent: APA - Los Angeles, 213/273-0744

THE LAST WAVE   United Artists, 1977, w/Tony Morphett &
   Peter Weir
DEATH OF AN ANGEL   20th Century Fox, 1985, directed

Screenplays:
VOODOO   w/David Odell
BEFORE & AFTER EDITH

DANNY PORFIRO
Agent: Writers & Artists Agency - Los Angeles, 213/820-2240

DOMINICK & EUGENE   Orion, 1988, Story

LON PORTER
Agent: Writers & Artists Agency - Los Angeles, 213/820-2240

URTH/BONE/MORT (S)
TWO DOLLAR ROMANCE (S)

Screenplays:
A REASONABLE MADNESS
DEADLINE AT DAWN
ALTER EGO
SUMMER JOB
THE TREASURE OF BOCA MACAVA

WILL PORTER
(See Will Aldis)

RANDALL POSTER
A MATTER OF DEGREES   Backbeat Productions, 1989,
   w/Jack Mason & W.T. Morgan

DENNIS POTTER*
Contact: 213/277-7779

PENNIES FROM HEAVEN ★   MGM/United Artists, 1981
BRIMSTONE & TREACLE   United Artists Classics, 1982
GORKY PARK   Orion, 1983
DREAMCHILD   Universal, 1985
TENDER IS THE NIGHT (CMS)   Showtime/BBC/Seven
   Network, 1985
THE SINGING DETECTIVE (TF)   BBC/ABC Australia,
   1987, also theatrical release
TRACK 29   Island Pictures, 1988
BLACKEYES   BBC/Paravision/Blackeyes Ltd,
   1990, directed

Screenplays:
SECRET FRIENDS   (directing)
WHITE HOTEL
DOUBLE DARE
THE MAN WHO WOULD NOT DIE
OPIUM BLUE

MICHEL POTTS
SCHWEITZER   Sugar Entertainment, 1990

JON POVILL*
Agent: Barry Perelman Agency - Los Angeles,
   213/274-5999

TOTAL RECALL   Tri-Star, 1990, Story w/Dan
   O'Bannon & Ronald Shusett

Screenplays:
DREAM GIRL   w/Deke Simon
BROKEN PROMISES, MENDED DREAMS
A SPANGLE IN DARKNESS

REINALDO POVOD*
Agent: William Morris Agency - New York, 212/586-5100

CUBA AND HIS TEDDY BEAR (S)
LA PUTA VIDA (S)

Screenplays:
NO PLACE TO BE SOMEBODY

ANN POWELL*
Contact: 213/393-5345

Screenplays:
LUCKY STRIKE   w/Rose Schacht
NIGHT OWL   w/Rose Schacht

CHARLES PRATT, JR.
Agent: The Irv Schechter Company - Beverly Hills,
   213/278-8070

THE INITIATION   New World, 1984

DENNIS A. PRATT
AMERICAN JUSTICE   The Movie Store, 1986

RUTH PRAWER JHABVALA
(See Ruth Prawer JHABVALA)

JANEY PREGER
THAT SUMMER   Columbia, 1979

BURT PRELUTSKY*
Agent: Robinson, Weintraub, Gross & Associates -
   Los Angeles, 213/653-5802

Screenplays:
FOR SINGLES ONLY
NOT GUILTY
A ROYAL MESS

MICHAEL A. PREMINGER*
Agent: The Irv Schecter Company - Beverly Hills,
   213/278-8070

NOTHING IN COMMON   Tri-Star, 1986,
   w/ Rick Podell

Screenplays:
HIGHER EDUCATION   w/Rick Podell
TUXEDO TERRACE   w/Rick Podell
LAWRENCE MANOR   w/Rick Podell

STEVEN PRESSFIELD*
Agent: Harris & Goldberg - Los Angeles, 213/553-5200

KING KONG LIVES   DEG, 1986, w/Ronald Shusett
ABOVE THE LAW   Warner Bros., 1988, w/Andrew Davis &
   Ronald Shusett

Screenplays:
FREEJACK   w/Ronald Shusett
BORN TO RUN

KENNETH PRESSMAN*
Business Manager: Scott Hudson - New York, 212/570-9645

Screenplays:
HITMAN   w/Roy London

JAY PRESSON ALLEN
(See Jay Presson ALLEN)

DAVID PRESTON
SPACEHUNTER: ADVENTURES IN THE FORBIDDEN
   ZONE   Columbia, 1983, w/Len Blum, Dan Goldberg &
   Edith Rey

Screenplays:
TWIN SISTERS

GAYLENE PRESTON
Contact: New Zealand Film Commission, P.O. Box 11546,
   Wellington, NZ, 4/859-754

DARK OF THE NIGHT   MR. WRONG   Quartet, 1985,
   w/Geoff Murphy & Graham Tetley, directed

TREVOR PRESTON
SLAYGROUND   Universal, 1984
BILLY THE KID AND THE GREEN BAIZE VAMPIRE
   ITC, 1985
PARKER   Birgin Films, 1985

JEFFREY PRICE*
Agent: CAA - Beverly Hills, 213/288-4545

TRENCHCOAT   Buena Vista, 1983, w/Peter Seaman
WHO FRAMED ROGER RABBIT   Buena Vista, 1988, w/
   Peter Seaman
DOC HOLLYWOOD   Buena Vista, 1991, w/Peter Seaman
   & Daniel Pyne

Screenplays:
MR. WHISTLE   w/Peter Seaman
SPEND, SPEND, SPEND   w/Peter Seaman
LAST HOLIDAY   w/Peter Seaman
GOOD KING HARRY   w/Peter Seaman
MISS MOTHERWELL   w/Peter Seaman

PAUL PRICE*
Agent: The Turtle Agency - Studio City, 818/506-6898

Screenplays:
THE ENGAGEMENT   w/Steve Nathan
LOOSE WOMEN   w/Steve Nathan
IN THE PROCESS   w/Steve Nathan
THE AILEEN QUINN STORY   w/Steve Nathan
UTILITIES   w/Steve Nathan

R. BARKER PRICE*
Agent: Barrett, Benson, McCartt & Weston - Los Angeles, 213/247-5500

Screenplays:
CATACOMBS
CAFE RACER
THE GROTTO

RICHARD PRICE*
Agent: Sanford, Skouras, Gross & Associates - Los Angeles, 213/208-2100

STREETS OF GOLD   20th Century Fox, 1986, w/Tom Cole & Heywood Gould
THE COLOR OF MONEY ★   Buena Vista, 1986
NEW YORK STORIES   Buena Vista, 1989, "Life Lessons"
SEA OF LOVE   Universal, 1989

Screenplays:
MAD DOG AND GLORY
NIGHT AND THE CITY
EAST COAST HIGH
DREAMSTREET
EMPIRE   STEEL ANGEL
COLOR WAR
WINGO

STANLEY PRICE
CLOSE RELATIONS (CTF)   Lionheart Television, 1990

TIM ROSE PRICE
Agent: Casaratto Company - London, 01/287-4450

DARK OBSESSION   DIAMOND SKULLS   Circle Releasing, 1991

Screenplays:
INCIDENT AT BARROW CREEK

BARRY PRIMUS
MISTRESS   Tribeca Productions, 1991, w/J.F. Lawton, directed

PRINCE
(Rogers Nelson)
Agent: CAA - Beverly Hills, 213/288-4545

GRAFFITI BRIDGE   Warner Bros., 1990, directed

JONATHAN PRINCE*
Contact: WGA - Los Angeles, 213/550-1000

18 AGAIN!   New World, 1988, w/Josh Goldstein

Screenplays:
THE FINE TOUCH w/Josh Goldstein
THE SKY$ THE LIMIT w/Josh Goldstein

PETER PRINCE
Agent: Casaratto Company - London, 01/287-4450

THE HIT   Island Alive, 1984

Screenplays:
OPPENHEIMER

DAVID A. PRIOR
Business: Action International Pictures, 10726 McCune Ave., Los Angeles, CA 90034, 213/559-8805

HELL ON THE BATTLEGROUND   Action International Pictures, 1989, directed
DEADLY DANCER   Action International Pictures, 1990, Story
THE FINAL SANCTION   Action International Pictures, 1990, directed
RAW NERVE   Action International Pictures, 1991, w/Lawrence L. Simeone, directed

DAVID PRITCHARD
VIOLENT ZONE   Arista Films, 1989, w/John Bushelman

PAT PROFT*
Agent: InterTalent - Los Angeles, 213/858-6200

BACHELOR PARTY   20th Century Fox, 1984, w/ Neal Israel
POLICE ACADEMY   The Ladd Company/Warner Bros., 1984, w/ Neal Israel & Hugh Wilson
MOVING VIOLATIONS   20th Century Fox, 1985, w/Neal Israel
REAL GENIUS   Tri-Star, 1985, w/Neal Israel & Peter Torokvei
THE NAKED GUN   Paramount, 1988, w/Jim Abrahams, David Zucker & Jerry Zucker
LUCKY STIFF   New Line Cinema, 1989
NAKED GUN 2 1/2: THE SMELL OF FEAR   Paramount, 1991, w/David Zucker
HOT SHOTS!   20th Century Fox, 1991, w/Jim Abrahams
LAME DUCKS   Paramount, 1991

Screenplays:
UP FOR GRABS w/Neil Israel
THE GOSSIP COLUMNIST
HUSTLE BUNS
ROLLIN' STONED...A ROADIE'S RIOTOUS REVELATIONS
SUMMIT KILL

CHIP PROSER*
Agent: William Morris Agency - Beverly Hills, 213/274-7451

ICEMAN   Universal, 1984, w/John Drimmer
INNERSPACE   Warner Bros., 1987, w/Jeffrey Boam

Screenplays:
ZODIAC (directing)
INTERFACE

FEDERICO PROSPERI
CURSE II: THE BITE   Trans World Entertainment, 1989, w/Susan Zelouf

MAX PROSS*
Agent: William Morris Agency - Beverly Hills, 213/274-7451

Screenplays:
THEY ARE US w/Tom Gammill

GREG PRUSS*
Agent: InterTalent - Los Angeles, 213/858-6200

Screenplays:
BODY HUNTER
NICK FURY

RICHARD PRYOR*
Agent: ICM - Los Angeles, 213/550-4000

BUSTIN' LOOSE   Universal, 1981, Story
RICHARD PRYOR LIVE ON THE SUNSET STRIP (FD)
   Columbia, 1982
RICHARD PRYOR HERE AND NOW (FD)   Columbia,
   1983, directed
JO JO DANCER, YOUR LIFE IS CALLING   Columbia,
   1986, w/Paul Mooney & Rocco Urbisci, directed

LUIS PUENZO
Agent: Triad Artists, Inc. - Los Angeles, 213/556-2727

THE OFFICIAL STORY ★   Historias Cinematograficas,
   1985, w/Aida Bortnik, directed
OLD GRINGO   Columbia, 1989, w/Aida Bortnik, directed

Screenplays:
THE PLAGUE (directing)

FRANK PUGLIESE*
Agent: United Talent Agency - Beverly Hills, 213/273-6700

AVEN'U BOYS (S)
KING OF CONNECTICUT (S)
DEM BUMS (S)

Screenplays:
DA BOYS
YO OLIVER
THE QUARTER MILE
FRANKY'S STREETS
GEORGE MILLER ADRESS UNKNOWN (Shared)

CHARLES G. PURPURA*
Agent: CAA - Beverly Hills, 213/288-4545

HEAVEN HELP US   Tri-Star, 1984
SATISFACTION   20th Century Fox, 1988

Screenplays:
REPLAY

DAVID PURSALL
COUNT FIVE AND DIE   20th Century-Fox, 1957,
   w/Jack Seddon
VILLAGE OF DAUGHTERS   MGM, 1961,
   w/Jack Seddon
THE SECRET PARTNER   MGM, 1961, w/Jack Seddon
MURDER SHE SAID   MGM, 1961, w/Jack Seddon
KILL OR CURE   MGM, 1962, w/Jack Seddon
THE LONGEST DAY   20th Century-Fox, 1962,
   w/Jack Seddon, Romain Gary, James Jones &
   Cornelius Ryan
MURDER AHOY   MGM, 1964, w/Jack Seddon
MURDER MOST FOUL   MGM, 1964, w/Jack Seddon
THE ALPHABET MURDERS   MGM, 1965,
   w/Jack Seddon
THE BLUE MAX   20th Century-Fox, 1966,
   w/Jack Seddon
THE SOUTHERN STAR   Columbia, 1968,
   w/Jack Seddon
WHAT CHANGED CHARLEY FARTHING
   Patina-Hildago, 1975, w/Jack Seddon
TOMORROW NEVER COMES   Rank, 1978, w/Jack
   Seddon & Sydney Banks

TED PUSHINSKY*
Agent: Writers & Artists Agency - Los Angeles, 213/820-2240

Screenplays:
AS YOUNG AS YOU FEEL w/Robert Kraft
MAKING MONEY w/Robert Kraft

MARIO PUZO*
Contact: Bert Fields, Greenberg, Glusker, Fields, Claman &
   Machtinger - Los Angeles, 213/553-3610

THE GODFATHER ★★   Paramount, 1972, w/Francis
   Ford Coppola
THE GODFATHER, PART II ★★   Paramount, 1974,
   w/Francis Ford Coppola
EARTHQUAKE   Universal, 1974, w/George Fox
SUPERMAN   Warner Bros., 1978, w/Robert Benton,
   David Newman & Leslie Newman
SUPERMAN II   Warner Bros., 1980, w/David Newman &
   Leslie Newman
THE COTTON CLUB   Orion, 1984, Story w/Francis Ford
   Coppola & William Kennedy
THE GODFATHER, PART III   Paramount, 1990, w/Francis
   Ford Coppola

Screenplays:
CHRISTOPHER COLUMBUS: THE MOVIE

DANIEL PYNE*
Agent: United Talent Agency - Beverly Hills, 213/273-6700

PACIFIC HEIGHTS   20th Century Fox, 1990
THE HARD WAY   Universal, 1991, w/Lem Dobbs
DOC HOLLYWOOD   Buena Vista, 1991, w/Jeffrey Price &
   Peter Seaman

Screenplays:
WHITE SANDS
SEVEN
WINNING UGLY
AMERICAN IRON

ALBERT PYUN*
Agent: United Talent Agency - Beverly Hills, 213/273-6700

THE SWORD AND THE SORCERER   Group 1, 1982,
   w/Tom Karnowski & John Stuckmeyer, directed
RADIOACTIVE DREAMS   DEG, 1986, directed
VICIOUS LIPS   Empire Pictures, 1987, directed
DOWN TWISTED   Cannon, 1987, Story, directed
ALIEN FROM L.A.   Cannon, 1988, w/Regina Davis &
   Debra Ricci

Q

PAUL QUARRINGTON
PERFECTLY NORMAL   Four Seasons Entertainment, 1991, w/Eugene Lipinski

MARTIN QUATERMASS
(See John Carpenter)

FLORENCE QUENTIN
Contact: French Film Office, 745 Fifth Avenue, New York, NY 10151, 212/832-8860

TATIE DANIELLE   Prestige Films, 1991

MOE QUIGLEY
COLD STEEL   CineTel Films, 1987, w/Michael D. Sonye

MICHELE QUILL
SYLVIA   MGM/UA Classics, 1985, w/F. Fairfax & Michael Firth

KEVIN QUINN *
Contact: WGA - Los Angeles, 213/550-1000

Screenplays:
PRESSURE
OPHELIA
WAY OUT WEST
FUNERAL PARTY
THE DAY THE EARTH STOOD STILL
LEGMAN
DEPUTY
MIDSUMMER MOON

EUGENE QUINTANO *
Agent: ICM - Los Angeles, 213/550-4000
Business: Trans World Entertainment, 3330 W. Cahuenga Blvd. - Suite 500, Los Angeles, CA, 90068, 213/969-2800

COMIN' AT YA!   Filmways, 1981, w/Wolf Lowenthal & Lloyd Battista
MAKING THE GRADE   MGM/UA/Cannon, 1984
KING SOLOMON'S MINES   Cannon, 1985, w/James R. Silke
ALLAN QUATERMAIN AND THE LOST CITY OF GOLD   Cannon, 1987, w/Lee Reynolds
POLICE ACADEMY 3: BACK IN TRAINING   Warner Bros., 1986
POLICE ACADEMY 4: CITIZENS ON PATROL   Warner Bros., 1987
HONEYMOON ACADEMY   Triumph, 1989, w/Jerry Lazarus, directed

Screenplays:
BAR STARS
THE LONG HILL
HOUSESITTING IN BEVERLY HILLS
COMMANDO SCHOOL

R

DAVID RABE *
Agent: United Talent Agency - Beverly Hills, 213/273-6700

HURLY BURLY (S)
STICKS AND BONES (S)
THE BASIC TRAINING OF PAVLO HUMMEL (S)
THE ORPHAN (S)
IN THE BOOM BOOM ROOM (S)
GOOSE AND TOM TOM (S)
THOSE THE RIVER KEEPS (S)
I'M DANCING AS FAST AS I CAN   Paramount, 1982
STREAMERS   United Artists Classics, 1983, from his play
CASUALTIES OF WAR   Columbia, 1989

Screenplays:
THE FIRM

JACKIE RABINOWITZ
Agent: Warden & White Associates - Beverly Hills, 213/852-1028

Screenplays:
THE BRIDE OF FRANK w/Liddy Loree
BUSYBODIES w/Liddy Loree

WILLIAM RABKIN *
Agent: William Morris Agency - Beverly Hills, 213/274-7451

Screenplays:
.357 VIGILANTE w/Lee Goldberg
BLADE w/Lee Goldberg
SHATTERDOLL

PETER RADER *
Agent: CAA - Beverly Hills, 213/288-4545

Screenplays:
WATERWORLD

MICHAEL RADFORD
Agent: Triad Artists, Inc. - Los Angeles, 213/556-2727

ANOTHER TIME, ANOTHER PLACE   Samuel Goldwyn Company, 1983, directed
1984   Atlantic Releasing Corporation, 1984, directed
WHITE MISCHIEF   Columbia, 1987, w/Jonathan Gems, directed

BOB RAFELSON *
Agent: ICM - Los Angeles, 213/550-4000
Business: Marmont Productions, 8439 Sunset Blvd. - Suite 108, Los Angeles, CA 90069, 213/650-3195

HEAD   Columbia, 1968, w/Jack Nicholson, directed
FIVE EASY PIECES ★   Columbia, 1970, Story w/Carole Eastman, directed
STAY HUNGRY   United Artists, 1976, w/Charles Gaines, directed
MOUNTAINS OF THE MOON   Tri-Star, 1990, w/William Harrison, directed

PICCIO RAFFANINI
OBSESSION: A TASTE FOR FEAR   Titanus Produzione, 1989, w/Lidia Ravera, directed

STEWART RAFFILL
Agent: The Adler Agency - Studio City, 818/769-5003

NAPOLEON AND SAMANTHA   Buena Vista, 1972
THE ADVENTURES OF THE WILDERNESS FAMILY   Pacific International, 1975, directed
ACROSS THE GREAT DIVIDE   Pacific International, 1976, directed
THE SEA GYPSIES   Warner Bros., 1978, directed
HIGH RISK   American Cinema, 1981, directed
THE ICE PIRATES   MGM/UA, 1983, w/Stanford Sherman, directed
MAC AND ME   Orion, 1988, w/Stephen Feke, directed

Screenplays:
PASSENGER 57

JOHN RAFFO*
Agent: United Talent Agency - Beverly Hills, 213/273-6700

Screenplays:
PINCUSHION
DAYBREAKER
WARRIOR

TEX RAGSDALE
MOONTRAP   Shapiro-Glickenhaus, 1989

PHILIP W. RAILSBACK*
Agent: Sanford, Skouras, Gross & Associates - Los Angeles, 213/208-2100

Screenplays:
LUCK
GARDEN OF THORNS

IVAN RAIMI
Contact: c/o Renaissance Motion Pictures, Inc., 6381 Hollywood Blvd. - Suite 680, Los Angeles, CA 90028, 213/463-9965

EASY WHEELS   Fries Entertainment, 1989, w/Celia Adams & David O'Malley
DARK MAN   Universal, 1990, w/Daniel Goldin, Josh Goldin, Chuck Pfarrer & Sam Raimi

Screenplays:
ARMY OF DARKNESS w/Sam Raimi

SAM RAIMI*
Agent: InterTalent - Los Angeles, 213/271-0600
Business: Renaissance Motion Pictures, Inc., 6381 Hollywood Blvd. - Suite 680, Los Angeles, CA 90028, 213/463-9965

THE EVIL DEAD   New Line Cinema, 1983, directed
CRIMEWAVE   Columbia, 1985, w/Ethan Coen & Joel Coen, directed
EVIL DEAD 2   DEG, 1987, w/Scott Spiegel, directed
DARK MAN   Universal, 1990, w/Daniel Goldin, Josh Goldin, Chuck Pfarrer & Ivan Raimi, directed

Screenplays:
ARMY OF DARKNESS w/Ivan Raimi (directing)

YVONNE RAINER
PRIVILEGE   Zeitgeist Films, 1991, directed

RONALD L. RALEY
EDGE OF SANITY   Millimeter Films, 1989, w/J.P. Felix

ALEXANDER D. RAMATI*
Contact: WGA - Los Angeles, 213/550-1000

THE ASSISI UNDERGROUND   Cannon, 1985, directed

HAROLD A. RAMIS*
Agent: CAA - Beverly Hills, 2123/288-4545
Business: Ocean Pictures, 2821 Main St., Santa Monica, CA 90405, 213/399-9271

NATIONAL LAMPOON'S ANIMAL HOUSE   Universal, 1978, w/Douglas Kenney & Chris Miller
MEATBALLS   Paramount, 1979, w/Janis Allen, Len Blum & Dan Goldberg
CADDYSHACK   Orion/Warner Bros., 1980, w/Douglas Kenney & Brian Doyle Murray, directed
STRIPES   Columbia, 1981, w/Len Blum & Dan Goldberg
NATIONAL LAMPOON'S VACATION   Warner Bros., 1983, w/Chevy Chase & John Hughes, directed
GHOSTBUSTERS   Columbia, 1984, w/Dan Aykroyd
CLUB PARADISE   Warner Bros., 1986, w/Brian Doyle Murray, directed
BACK TO SCHOOL   Orion, 1986, w/Steven Kampmann, Will Aldis & Peter Torokvei
ARMED AND DANGEROUS   Columbia, 1987, w/Peter Torokvei
CADDYSHACK II   Warner Bros., 1988, w/PeterTorokvei
GHOSTBUSTERS II   Columbia, 1989, w/Dan Aykroyd
ROVER DANGERFIELD (AF)   Warner Bros., 1991, Story w/ Rodney Dangerfield

Screenplays:
CHAMPAGNE NIGHTS w/Peter Torokvei
CLUBHOUSE

AL RAMRUS*
Agent: Preferred Artists - Encino, 818/990-0305

HALLS OF ANGER   United Artists, 1970, w/John Herman Shaner
THE ISLAND OF DR. MOREAU   American International, 1977, w/John Herman Shaner
GOIN' SOUTH   Paramount, 1978, w/Alan Mandel, John Herman Shaner & Charles Shyer

PATRICK RANAHAN*
Agent: Warden & White Associates - Beverly Hills, 213/852-1028

Screenplays:
EUGENE AND HIS SEAMLESS PANTS w/Todd Johnson
HEAD DOWN TILT w/Todd Johnson

ADDISON RANDALL
AMERICAN BORN   PM Home Video, 1990, w/Raymond Martino

BOB RANDALL
Agent: E.M.A. - Los Angeles, 213/461-0148

ZORRO, THE GAY BLADE   20th Century-Fox, 1981, Story w/Greg Alt, Hal Dresner, & Don Moriarty

SHAWN RANDALL
THE LONELY LADY   Universal, 1983, w/John Kershaw

JOHN RANDAZZO
SWORDS OF HEAVEN   Trans World Entertainment, 1985, w/James Bruner, Britt Lomond & William P. O'Hagan

DAVID RANDOLF
THEY CALL ME BRUCE? A FISTFUL OF CHOPSTICKS   Artists Releasing Corporation/Film Ventures International, 1982, w/Tim Clawson, Elliott Hong & Johnny Yune

TIMNA RANON*
Contact: Dorn & Donaldson - Los Angeles, 213/557-0417

Screenplays:
THE EAGLE
HOLD FAST MY WORLDS   REBEKAH

MORT RANSEN
FALLING OVER BACKWARDS   Astral Films, 1990, directed

MARTIN RANSOHOFF*
Business: Albacore Films, 9350 Wilshire Blvd. - Suite 219, Beverly Hills, CA 90212, 213/274-4585, 213/274-4585

A CHANGE OF SEASONS   20th Century-Fox, 1980, Story w/Erich Segal

STEVE RANSOHOFF
PHYSICAL EVIDENCE   Columbia, 1989, Story w/Bill Phillips

FREDERIC RAPHAEL*
Agent: William Morris Agency - Beverly Hills, 213/274-7451

BACHELOR OF HEARTS   Rank, 1958, w/Leslie Bricusse
WHY BOTHER TO KNOCK   ABP, 1961, w/Dennis Cannan & Frederick Gotfurt
NOTHING BUT THE BEST   Anglo Amalgamated, 1964
DARLING ★★   Anglo Amalgamated, 1965
TWO FOR THE ROAD ★   20th Century-Fox, 1966
FAR FROM THE MADDING CROWD   EMI, 1967
A SEVERED HEAD   Columbia, 1970
DAISY MILLER   Paramount, 1974
RICHARD'S THINGS   New World, 1981
THE KING'S WHORE   J & M Entertainment, 1990, w/Axel Corti & Daniel Vigne

Screenplays:
DESIRE w/Henry Bean & Leora Barish
THE RIGHT MAN
WE THREE   CAESAR AND ROSALIE
A NEW WIFE
LIBBY HOLMAN
SONG BIRD
IN THOSE DAYS
LOVE AFFAIR
THE BIG ONE
ROSES, ROSES
THE CURSE OF GENIUS

JERRY RAPP*
Agent: William Morris Agency - Beverly Hills, 213/274-7451

Screenplays:
THE TOURISTS w/Jeff Berman
ON THE AIR w/Jeff Begman

DON RAPPAPORT*
Agent: The Roberts Company - Los Angeles, 213/552-7800

Screenplays:
THE END ZONE

EZRA D. RAPPAPORT*
Agent: Shapiro/Lichtman - Los Angeles, 213/859-8877

DEJA VU   Cannon, 1985, w/Anthony Richmond & Arnold Schmidt
HARRY AND THE HENDERSONS   Universal, 1987, w/William Dear & William E. Martin

MARK RAPPAPORT
IMPOSTORS   First Run Features, 1981

JEAN-PAUL RAPPENEAU
Contact: French Film Office, 745 Fifth Avenue, New York, NY 10151, 212/832-8860

THAT MAN FROM RIO ★   Lopert, 1964, w/others
LE SAUVAGE   1978, w/Elisabeth Rappeneau & Jean-Loup Dabadie, directed
CYRANO DE BERGERAC   Orion Classics, 1990, w/Jean-Claude Carriere, directed

JUDITH RASCOE*
Agent: William Morris Agency - Beverly Hills, 213/274-7451

ROAD MOVIE   Grove Press, 1974
WHO'LL STOP THE RAIN   United Artists, 1978
A PORTRAIT OF THE ARTIST AS A YOUNG MAN   Howard Mahler Films, 1979
ENDLESS LOVE   Universal, 1981
EAT A BOWL OF TEA   Columbia, 1989
HAVANA   Universal, 1990, w/David Rayfiel

Screenplays:
THE FORTUNE TELLER
HANDCARVED COFFINS
PICTURES FROM THE WATER TRADE

TINA RATHBORNE
Agent: ICM - Los Angeles, 213/550-4000

ZELLY & ME   Columbia, 1988, directed

LARRY RATTNER*
Contact: Attorney Shelly Browning, 213/858-7700

HALLOWEEN 4   Galaxy International, 1988, Story w/Dhani Lipsius, Alan McElroy & Benjamin Ruffner
THE HORSEPLAYER   Relentless Entertainment, 1989, w/Kurt Voss
GENUINE RISK   I.R.S. Releasing, 1990, Story w/Kurt Voss

EARL MAC RAUCH*
Agent: Sanford, Skouras, Gross & Associates - Los Angeles, 213/208-2100

NEW YORK, NEW YORK   United Artists, 1977, w/Mardik Martin
A STRANGER IS WATCHING   MGM/UA, 1982, w/Victor Miller
THE ADVENTURES OF BUCKAROO BANZAI ACROSS THE 8TH DIMENSION   20th Century-Fox, 1984
WIRED   Taurus Entertainment, 1989

Screenplays:
NATIVE TONGUE
CARLITO'S WAY   w/Mardik Martin
SCI-FI HIGH
TAPPING THE SOURCE
GRASS ROOTS
NOBLE ENEMIES
BIG BAND OF BLUES
THE LAST RIDE
JET CAR
WILD SANCTUARY
BOYS IN BLUES

HERMAN RAUCHER*
Business Manager: A.B. Greene, 101 Park Avenue, New York, NY 10178, 212/661-8200

SWEET NOVEMBER   Warner Bros., 1968
CAN HIERONYMUS MERKIN EVER FORGET MERCY HUMPPE & FIND TRUE HAPPINESS?   Universal, 1969, w/Anthony Newley
WATERMELON MAN   Columbia, 1970
SUMMER OF '42 ★   Warner Bros., 1971
CLASS OF '44   Warner Bros., 1973
ODE TO BILLY JOE   Warner Bros., 1976
THE OTHER SIDE OF MIDNIGHT   20th Century-Fox, 1977, w/Daniel Taradash

Screenplays:
THERE SHOULD HAVE BEEN CASTLES
GLORY DAY
CHARLIE IS MY DARLING
CRY GORF
IT'S ME AGAIN
HIT ME EASY
MAYNARD'S HOUSE
THREE FEET TO GERMANY
TUTTO E. FINITO
TWO WAYS TO GO

IRVING RAVETCH*
Agent: William Morris Agency - Beverly Hills, 213/274-7451

THE OUTRIDERS   MGM, 1950
VENGEANCE VALLEY   MGM, 1951
TEN WANTED MEN   Columbia, 1955, Story w/Harriet Frank Jr.
THE LONG HOT SUMMER   MGM, 1958, w/Harriet Frank Jr.
THE SOUND AND THE FURY   20th Century-Fox, 1959, w/Harriet Frank Jr.
HOME FROM THE HILL   MGM, 1959, w/Irving Ravetch
THE DARK AT THE TOP OF THE STAIRS   Warner Bros., 1960, w/Harriet Frank, Jr.
HUD ★   Paramount, 1963, w/Harriet Frank, Jr.
HOMBRE   20th Century-Fox, 1967, w/Harriet Frank, Jr.
THE REIVERS   National General, 1969, w/Harriet Frank, Jr.
THE COWBOYS   Warner Bros., 1972, w/Harriet Frank, Jr.
THE SPIKES GANG   United Artists, 1974, w/Harriet Frank, Jr.
CONRACK   20th Century-Fox, 1974, w/Harriet Frank, Jr.
NORMA RAE ★   20th Century-Fox, 1979, w/Harriet Frank, Jr.
MURPHY'S ROMANCE   Columbia, 1985, w/Harriet Frank, Jr.
STANLEY & IRIS   MGM/UA, 1990, w/Harriet Frank, Jr.

Screenplays:
BEGINNERS   w/Barbara Benedek & Harriet Frank, Jr.
MIXED FEELINGS   w/Harriet Frank, Jr.
SINGLE   w/Harriet Frank, Jr.

RAND RAVICH*
Agent: Susan Smith & Associates - Beverly Hills, 213/852-4777

CRIME LORDS   Image Organization, 1991

Screenplays:
GRANDFATHER

WENDELL RAWLS
Agent: CAA - Beverly Hills, 213/288-4545

Screenplays:
ABOVE THE FOLD

MARC RAY*
Contact: 213/550-0570

Screenplays:
STEPFATHER III
BOOK OF THE CHILD

BILLY RAY*
Agent: Triad Artists, Inc. - Los Angeles, 213/556-2727

Screenplays:
THE COLOR OF NIGHT
HONG KONG THRILLER
KISS THE BRIDE
MODEL COP

FRED OLEN RAY
Business: American-Independent Productions, Inc., 6515 Sunset Blvd. - Suite 402, Hollywood, CA 90028, 213/856-9369

BIOHAZARD   21st Century, 1985, directed
BULLETPROOF   CineTel Films, 1987, Story w/T.L. Lankford
DEEP SPACE   Trans World Entertainment, 1988, w/T.L. Lankford, directed

LESLIE A. RAY*
Agent: ICM - Los Angeles, 213/550-4000

MY DEMON LOVER   New Line Cinema, 1987

Screenplays:
MORGAN   w/Michael Taav
STREET HEARTS
MAKING WAVES

Ra

FILM WRITERS GUIDE

DAVID RAYFIEL*
Contact: 212/772-2221

CASTLE KEEP   Columbia, 1969, w/Daniel Taradash
VALDEZ IS COMING   United Artists, 1970,
  w/Roland Kibbee
THREE DAYS OF THE CONDOR   Paramount, 1975,
  w/Lorenzo Semple
LIPSTICK   Paramount, 1976
DEATH WATCH   Quartet, 1980, w/Bertrand Tavernier
ROUND MIDNIGHT   Warner Bros., 1986,
  w/Bertrand Tavernier
HAVANA   Universal, 1990, w/Judith Rascoe

Screenplays:
THE TRIANGLE FACTORY
BOYS & GIRLS TOGETHER
WELCOME HOME, WELL DONE
SILENCE

KATHERINE J. REBACK*
Business Manager: Oberman, Tivoli, Miller & Lou,
  213/471-9300

Screenplays:
THE RECEPTIONIST

ALEX REBAR
NOWHERE TO HIDE   New Century/Vista, 1987,
  w/George Goldsmith

ERIC RED*
Agent: United Talent Agency - Beverly Hills, 213/273-6700

THE HITCHER   Tri-Star, 1986
NEAR DARK   DEG, 1987, w/Kathryn Bigelow
COHEN & TATE   Nelson Entertainment, 1988, directed
BLUE STEEL   MGM/UA, 1990, w/Kathryn Bigelow
BODY PARTS   Paramount, 1991, w/Larry Gross &
  Norman Snider, directed

Screenplays:
UNDERTOW   w/Kathryn Bigelow
CANAL STREET
LOST BOYS II

JAY A. REDACK*
Agent: ICM - Los Angeles, 213/550-4000

RABBIT TEST   Avco Embassy, 1978, w/Joan Rivers

QUINN K. REDEKER*
Agent: Circle Talent Associates - Beverly Hills,
  213/281-3765

THE DEER HUNTER ★   United Artists, 1978, Story
  w/Michael Cimino & Louis Garfinkle

Screenplays:
SHANGHAI TANGO   w/Louis Garfinkle
VOSA   w/Louis Garfinkle
THE EEZMO   w/Louis Garfinkle

JAMES REDFORD*
Agent: William Morris Agency - Beverly Hills, 213/274-7451

Screenplays:
ROCKY ROAD

ROBERT REDLIN*
Agent: Camden-ITG - Los Angeles, 213/289-2700

AFTER DARK, MY SWEET   Avenue Pictures, 1990,
  w/James Foley

ALLAN REED
CREATURE   Cardinal Releasing, 1985, w/William Malone

JOEL M. REED
NIGHT OF THE ZOMBIES   NMD, 1981

CHRISTOPHER REEVE
Agent: ICM - Los Angeles, 213/550-4000

SUPERMAN IV: THE QUEST FOR PEACE   Warner Bros.,
  1987, Story w/Lawrence Konner & Mark Rosenthal

BRIAN REHAK*
Agent: The Roberts Company - Los Angeles, 213/552-7800

THE IMAGE (CTF)   Citadel Entertainment
  Productions, 1990

Screenplays:
1968
TRAFFIC SCHOOL

JULIE REICHERT*
Agent: Monteiro Rose Agency - Encino, 818/501-1177

BREAKIN' 2: ELECTRIC BOOGALOO   Tri-Star, 1984,
  w/Jan Ventura

MARK REICHERT
UNION CITY   Kinesis Ltd., 1980, directed

ALASTAIR REID
Agent: PTA, Bugle House, 21a Noel St., London W1V 3PD,
  England, 71/434-9513

BABY LOVE   Avco Embassy, 1969, w/Guido Coen &
  Michael Klinger, directed
SOMETHING TO HIDE   Avton, 1971, directed

JAMES REIGLE
ANDROID   New World, 1982, w/Don Opper
CITY LIMITS   Atlantic Releasing Corporation, 1985, w/
  Aaron Lipstadt & Don Opper

WILLIAM REILLY*
Agent: Triad Artists, Inc. - Los Angeles, 213/556-2727

THE BROAD COALITION   WHAT DO I TELL THE BOYS AT
  THE STATION?   August, 1972
MEN OF RESPECT   Columbia, 1991, directed
MORTAL THOUGHTS   Columbia, 1991, w/Claude Kerven

CARL REINER*
Agent: William Morris Agency - Beverly Hills, 213/274-7451

THE THRILL OF IT ALL   Universal-International, 1963
THE ART OF LOVE   Universal, 1965
ENTER LAUGHING   Columbia, 1967, w/Joseph Stein,
  from his play, directed
THE COMIC   Columbia, 1969, w/Aaron Rubin, directed

DEAD MEN DON'T WEAR PLAID   Universal, 1979,
    w/George Gipe & Steve Martin, directed
THE MAN WITH TWO BRAINS   Warner Bros., 1983,
    w/George Gipe & Steve Martin, directed
BERT RIGBY, YOU'RE A FOOL   Warner Bros.,
    1989, directed

JEFF REINER
BLOOD AND CONCRETE: A LOVE STORY   I.R.S. Media,
    1991, w/Richard LaBrie, directed

LUCAS REINER
THE SPIRIT OF '76   Caste Rock/Columbia,
    1990, directed

ROB REINER*
Agent: CAA - Beverly Hills, 213/288-4545
Business: Castle Rock Entertainment, 335 N. Maple Drive -
    Suite 135, Beverly Hills, CA, 90210, 213/285-2300

THIS IS SPINAL TAP   Embassy, 1984, w/Christopher
    Guest, Michael McKean & Harry Shearer, directed

GUSTAVE V. REININGER*
Agent: Camden-ITG - Los Angeles, 213/289-2700

Screenplays:
WALK WITH ANGELS
GULF COAST
TEN TENTHS

MARK A. REISMAN*
Agent: The Irv Schechter Company - Beverly Hills,
    213/278-8070

SUMMER RENTAL   Paramount, 1985,
    w/Jeremy Stevens

Screenplays:
BIG HOSPITAL   w/Jeremy Stevens
NINETY MINUTES   w/Jeremy Stevens

IVAN REITMAN
Agent: CAA - Beverly Hills, 213/288-4545

LEGAL EAGLES   Universal, 1986, Story w/Jim Cash &
    Jack Epps Jr., directed

LINDA REMY*
Contact: 415/381-0390

DESERT BLOOM   Columbia, 1986, Story
    w/Eugene Corr

SHELDON RENAN
LAMBADA   Warner Bros., 1990, w/Joel Silberg

THOMAS RENDON
VOODOO DAWN   Academy Entertainment, 1990,
    w/Jeffrey Delman, Evan Dunsky & John Russo

ROBERT SCOTT RENEAU*
Agent: William Morris Agency - Beverly Hills,
    213/274-7451

ACTION JACKSON   Lorimar, 1988

DAVID RENWICK
Contact: 011/441-8056

THE MISADVENTURES OF MR. WILT   Samuel Goldwyn
    Company, 1990, Adaptation w/Andrew Marshall

Screenplays:
MUSHROOM BUTTON   w/Andrew Marshall
JINGLE BELLS   w/Andrew Marshall

DAVID RESKIN
Contact: 213/462-2275

ACTION U.S.A.   Stewart & Berger Inc., 1989
SKINHEADS   Amazing Movies, 1989, w/Greydon Clark
CLICK: THE CALENDAR GIRL KILLER   Crown
    International, 1989, w/David Chute, Ross Hagen &
    Hoke Howell

PATRICIA RESNICK*
Agent: William Morris Agency - Beverly Hills, 213/274-7451

LADIES IN WAITING (S)
A WEDDING   20th Century-Fox, 1978, w/Robert Altman,
    John Considine & Allan Nichols
QUINTET   20th Century-Fox, 1979, w/Robert Altman &
    Frank Barhydt
NINE TO FIVE   20th Century-Fox, 1980, w/Colin Higgins
MAXIE   Orion, 1985
SECOND SIGHT   Warner Bros., 1989, w/Tom Schulman

Screenplays:
STRAIGHT TALK
SORORITY
THREE AFTER THIRTY
FIRST BOOK OF EPPIE
FAMILY SECRETS
CROSSTOWN
HELL CAN WAIT
WRONG PLANET   (Story w/Lee Rose)
ROUGH TRADE   (Story w/Lee Rose)

ROBERT D. RESNIKOFF*
Agent: United Talent Agency - Beverly Hills, 213/273-6700

THE JOGGER   (Short), directed
COLLISION COURSE   DEG, 1987, w/Frank Namei
THE FIRST POWER   Orion, 1990, directed

Screenplays:
SHADOW DEAL   (directing)
THE 400

CARLA REUBEN
SOMETHING SPECIAL   WILLY MILLY/I WAS A TEENAGE
    BOY   Cinema Group, 1986, w/Walter Carbone

PAUL REUBENS*
(Pee-Wee Herman)
Business Manager: Philbot & Co., 818/905-9500

PEE-WEE'S BIG ADVENTURE   Warner Bros., 1985,
    w/Phil Hartman & Michael Varhol
BIG TOP PEE-WEE   Paramount, 1988, w/George McGrath

FRED REXER
EXTREME PREJUDICE   Tri-Star, 1987, Story
    w/John Milius

EDITH REY
SPACEHUNTER: ADVENTURES IN THE FORBIDDEN ZONE   Columbia, 1983, w/Len Blum, Dan Goldberg & David Preston
BREAKING ALL THE RULES   New World, 1985, Story w/Rafal Zielinski

CHRISTOPHER REYNOLDS
OFFERINGS   Arista Films, 1989, directed

CLARKE REYNOLDS
Contact: Tucker, Morgan & Martindale -Los Angeles, 213/474-0810

SON OF A GUNFIGHTER   MGM, 1964
THE VIKING QUEEN   Warner Bros., 1967
OPERATION THUNDERBOLT   Cinema Shares International, 1978
NIGHT GAMES   Avco Embassy, 1980, w/Anton Diether

JONATHAN REYNOLDS*
Agent: ICM - Los Angeles, 213/550-4000

GENIUSES (S)
MICKI AND MAUDE   Columbia, 1984
LEONARD PART 6   Columbia, 1987
SWITCHING CHANNELS   Tri-Star, 1988
MY STEPMOTHER IS AN ALIEN   WEG, 1988, w/Timothy Harris, Herschel Weingrod & Jericho Stone

Screenplays:
THE SURVIVALISTS
KATE
WHEREABOUTS
HAR'LD

KEVIN H. REYNOLDS
Agent: William Morris Agency - Beverly Hills, 213/274-7451
Business: Windmill Films Inc., 248 Westminster Ave., Venice, CA 90291, 213/399-1448

RED DAWN   MGM/UA, 1984, w/John Milius
FANDANGO   Warner Bros., 1985, directed

Screenplays:
LITTLE THINGS
THE FIRE

LEE D. REYNOLDS*
Agent: ICM - Los Angeles, 213/550-4000

ALLAN QUATERMAIN AND THE LOST CITY OF GOLD   Cannon, 1987, w/Gene Quintano
DELTA FORCE 2   MGM/UA, 1990

Screenplays:
SHERLOCK HOLMES ON THE ORIENT EXPRESS
STRANGER IN A STRANGE LAND
HOT OFF THE WIRE
TWO OF THE MISSING
BALEFIRE
HANG ON TIGHT
WISHFUL THINKING
PIGEON BOY

REBECCA REYNOLDS
OVEREXPOSED   Concorde, 1990, w/Larry Brand

MARK REZYKA
SOUTH OF RENO   Castle Hill Productions, 1988, w/T.L. Lankford, directed

PHILLIP RHEE
BEST OF THE BEST   Taurus Entertainment, 1989, Story w/Paul Levine

GRIFF RHYS-JONES
MORONS FROM OUTER SPACE   Universal, 1985, w/Mel Smith

RONALD RIBMAN*
Agent: William Morris Agency - New York, 212/586-5100

THE RUG MERCHANTS OF CHAOS (S)
THE ANGEL LEVINE   United Artists, 1970, w/Bill Gunn

RUDY RICCI
THE RETURN OF THE LIVING DEAD   Orion, 1985, Story w/John Russo & Russell Streiner

JOHN RICE*
Agent: The Gersh Agency - Beverly Hills, 213/274-6611

CURIOSITY KILLS (CTF)   MCA Television Entertainment, 1990, w/Joe Batteer

SUSAN C. RICE*
Agent: CAA - Beverly Hills, 213/288-4545

ENORMOUS CHANGES AT THE LAST MINUTE   TC Films International, 1985, w/John Sayles
ANIMAL BEHAVIOR   Millimeter Films, 1989

Screenplays:
LOVE THIRTY
GOOD SPORTS
FAT CHANCE
ENOUGH ROPE

DAVID N. RICH*
Agent: Barrett, Benson, McCartt & Weston - Los Angeles, 213/247-5500

RENEGADES   Universal, 1989

MATTY RICH
Agent: William Morris Agency - Beverly Hills, 213/274-7451

STRAIGHT OUT OF BROOKLYN   Samuel Goldwyn Company, 1991, directed

RICHARD RICH
THE BLACK CAULDRON (AF)   Buena Vista, 1985, w/others, directed

RON RICH
GHOST FEVER   Miramax, 1987, w/Oscar Brodney

DOUG RICHARDSON*
Agent: CAA - Beverly Hills, 213/288-4545

DIE HARD 2: DIE HARDER   20th Century Fox, 1990, w/Steven E. deSouza

Screenplays:
HELL BENT - AND BACK w/Rick Jaffa
TELEGRAPH ROAD
PRAVDA
HONOR BRIGHT
LAWYERS, GUNS AND MONEY

PETER RICHARDSON
Contact: British Academy of Film & Television Arts, 195 Piccadilly, London W1, England, 01/734-0022

THE SUPERGRASS   Hemdale, 1986, w/Peter Richens, directed
EAT THE RICH   New Line Cinema, 1987, w/Peter Richens, directed

SCOTT RICHARDSON
Agent: ICM - Los Angeles, 213/550-4000

HEARTS OF FIRE   Lorimar, 1988, w/Joe Eszterhas

Screenplays:
LOST WEEKEND

TONY RICHARDSON
Business: 1478 N. Kings Road, Los Angeles, CA 90069, 213/656-5314

A TASTE OF HONEY   Continental, 1962, w/Shelagh Delaney, directed
NED KELLY   United Artists, 1970, w/Ian Jones, directed
THE HOTEL NEW HAMPSHIRE   Orion, 1984, directed

WILLIAM RICHERT*
Agent: ICM - Los Angeles, 213/550-4000

LAW AND DISORDER   Columbia, 1974, w/Kenneth Harris Fishman & Ivan Passer
THE HAPPY HOOKER   Double H, 1975
WINTER KILLS   Avco Embassy, 1979, directed
THE AMERICAN SUCCESS CO.   SUCCESS Columbia, 1979, w/Larry Cohen, directed
A NIGHT IN THE LIFE OF JIMMY REARDON   20th Century Fox, 1988, directed

Screenplays:
PRIZZI'S FAMILY
THE PRESIDENT ELOPES
SUGARPUSS

MORDECAI RICHLER*
Agent: ICM - Los Angeles, 213/550-4000

NO LOVE FOR JOHNNIE   Rank, 1960, w/Nicholas Phipps
YOUNG AND WILLING   THE WILD AND THE WILLING Rank, 1962, w/Nicholas Phipps
LIFE AT THE TOP   Columbia, 1965
THE APPRENTICESHIP OF DUDDY KRAVITZ ★   Paramount, 1974
FUN WITH DICK AND JANE   Columbia, 1977, w/Jerry Belson & David Giler
JACOB TWO-TWO MEETS THE HOODED FANG   Cinema Shares International, 1978
JOSHUA THEN AND NOW   20th Century Fox, 1985

Screenplays:
THE BOYS
ST. URBAIN'S HORSEMAN

MEG RICHMAN
Agent: Shorr, Stille & Associates - Los Angeles, 213/659-6160

Screenplays:
SHOUTED FIRE

ANTHONY RICHMOND
Business Manager: Harry Schaffer, Guild Management, 9911 W. Pico Blvd., Los Angeles, CA, 90036, 213/277-9711

DEJA VU   Cannon, 1985, w/Ezra D. Rappaport & Arnold Schmidt, directed

BILL RICHMOND*
Agent: Robinson, Weintraub, Gross & Associates - Los Angeles, 213/653-5802

THE LADIES' MAN   Paramount, 1961, w/Jerry Lewis
THE NUTTY PROFESSOR   Paramount, 1963, w/Jerry Lewis
THE FAMILY JEWELS   Paramount, 1965, w/Jerry Lewis
THE BIG MOUTH   Columbia, 1967, w/Jerry Lewis
SMORGASBORD   Warner Bros., 1985, w/Jerry Lewis

Screenplays:
OFF AND RUNNING
THE NUTTY PROFESSOR II

ERIC A. RICHTER
THE INHERITORS   Island Alive, 1985, w/Walter Bannert

W.D. RICHTER*
Agent: Shapiro/Lichtman - Los Angeles, 213/859-8877

SLITHER   MGM, 1972
PEEPER   *FAT CHANCE*   20th Century-Fox, 1975
NICKELODEON   Columbia, 1976, w/Peter Bogdanovich
INVASION OF THE BODY SNATCHERS   United Artists, 1978
DRACULA   Universal, 1979
BRUBAKER ★   20th Century-Fox, 1980, w/Arthur Ross
ALL NIGHT LONG   Universal, 1981
HARD FEELINGS   Astral Bellvue, 1981
BIG TROUBLE IN LITTLE CHINA   20th Century Fox, 1986, Adaptation
HANG TOUGH   Moviestore Entertainment, 1990, w/John Herzfeld, filmed in 1980

Screenplays:
JUST LIKE NEW YORK
WORDS AND MUSIC
LES REPOUX
SECOND MARRIAGE
THE CHRIS LUKAS PROJECT
ROBOTO
ALLEY OOP
THE BUSINESS STORY
THE NINJA
HOME OF THE BRAVE
PURSUIT
TERROR SHIP
WINGING IT
BEFORE WE SAY GOODBYE
NIGHT PEOPLE
SUDDEN TURNS
GYROSCOPE
JUMBO MURDERS
DEADLY HONEYMOON

Ri

FILM WRITERS GUIDE

TERROR ON DUNCAN ISLAND
THE MASTER
SILENT NIGHT
RIOTOUS ASSEMBLY
MANIAC SLAYS BLONDE
RUBY RED
ROCKY MOUNTAIN TIME
STARLIGHT PARADE
TERATOMA

WILLIAM HARLAN RICHTER
Agent: CAA - Beverly Hills, 213/288-4545

Screenplays:
REVOLVER
BURNING DAYLIGHT

THOMAS RICKMAN*
Agent: CAA - Beverly Hills, 213/288-4545

KANSAS CITY BOMBER   MGM, 1972,
   w/Calvin Clements
THE LAUGHING POLICEMAN   20th Century-Fox, 1973
THE WHITE DAWN   Paramount, 1976,
   w/James Houston
W.W. AND THE DIXIE DANCEKINGS   20th
   Century-Fox, 1975
HOOPER   Warner Bros., 1978, w/Bill Kerby
COAL MINER'S DAUGHTER ★   Universal, 1980
THE RIVER RAT   Paramount, 1984, directed
EVERYBODY'S ALL-AMERICAN   Warner Bros., 1988

Screenplays:
NEWSIES w/David Fallon
STARS FELL ON ALABAMA w/Billy Field
TWO-PENNY SPARROW
THE LEAVINGS OF B.T. WOMECK
WORLDBEATER
COLOR MAN
THE ZIG-ZAG MAN
UNION STORY

PHILIP RIDLEY
Contact: British Academy of Film & Television Arts,
   195 Piccadilly, London W1, England, 71/734-0022

THE KRAYS   Miramax, 1990
THE REFLECTING SKIN   Prestige Films, 1991, directed

WILLIAM RIEAD
SCORPION   Crown International, 1986, directed

DEAN F. RIESNER*
Agent: InterTalent - Los Angeles, 213/858-6200

THE HELEN MORGAN STORY   Warner Bros., 1957,
   w/Nelson Gidding, Stephen Longstreet & Oscar Saul
COOGAN'S BLUFF   Universal, 1968, w/Herman
   Miller & Howard Rodman
PLAY MISTY FOR ME   Universal, 1971, w/Jo Heims
DIRTY HARRY   Warner Bros., 1971, w/Harry Julian
   Fink & Rita M. Fink
CHARLEY VARRICK   Universal, 1973,
   w/Howard Rodman
THE TAKE   1974
THE ENFORCER   Warner Bros., 1976,
   w/Stirling Silliphant
FATAL BEAUTY   MGM/UA, 1987, w/Hilary Henkin

Screenplays:
HIGH COUNTRY
I LOVE YOU

ADAM RIFKIN*
Agent: William Morris Agency - Beverly Hills, 213/274-7451

NEVER ON TUESDAY   Palisades Entertainment,
   1990, directed
THE DARK BACKWARD   Elwes/Wyman-Talmadge/L.A.
   Dreams, 1991, directed

Screenplays:
PICKLE ON MY TONGUE

NANCY RIFKIN
THE UNSEEN   World Northal, 1981, Story w/Peter Foleg,
   Michael L. Grace & Kim Henkel

GARY RIGDON
TRUST ME   Cinecom, 1989, w/Bobby Houston

ROB RILEY
NUMBER ONE WITH A BULLET   Cannon, 1987, w/Gail
   Morgan Hickman, Andrew Kurtzman & James Belushi

JETTE RINCK
TUFF TURF   New World, 1985

Screenplays:
TRIBES
GLASS HOUSE

DAVID W. RINTELS*
Agent: CAA - Beverly Hills, 213/288-4545

SCORPIO   United Artists, 1972, w/Gerald Wilson
NOT WITHOUT MY DAUGHTER   MGM-Pathe, 1991

ROB RITCHIE
THE INVESTIGATION: INSIDE A TERRORIST
   BOMBING (CTF)   Granada Television, 1990

JOE RITTER
THE TOXIC AVENGER   Troma, 1985

JOYCE RITTER
INDEPENDENCE   20th Century-Fox, 1976, w/Thomas
   McGrath & Lloyd Ritter

LLOYD RITTER
INDEPENDENCE   20th Century-Fox, 1976, w/Thomas
   McGrath & Joyce Ritter

JAMES J. RITZ*
Agent: Shapiro/Lichtman - Los Angeles, 213/859-8877

LEO AND LOREE   United Artists, 1980

THOMAS RITZ
Business: Maverick Productions, 6056 Morella Ave.,
   North Hollywood, CA 91606, 818/766-9984

Screenplays:
GOOD MORNING HEARTACHE
10 DEGREES SOUTHWEST
ON THE LINE
DOG'S LIFE

JERRY RIVERS
BEVERLY HILLS BRATS   Taurus Entertainment, 1989,
   Story w/Terry Moore

JOAN RIVERS*
Business Manager: Nigro, Karlen & Segal, 213/277-4657

RABBIT TEST   Avco Embassy, 1978, w/Jay A.
   Reback, directed

DAVID ROACH
YOUNG EINSTEIN   Warner Bros., 1989,
   w/Yahoo Serious

JANET ROACH*
Agent: United Talent Agency - Beverly Hills, 213/273-6700

PRIZZI'S HONOR ★   20th Century Fox, 1985,
   w/Richard Condon
MR. NORTH   Samuel Goldwyn Company, 1988,
   w/John Huston & James Costigan

Screenplays:
FIRST WIVE'S CLUB
BUCK ISLAND
FREUD'S HAT
CAPER
IN HER OWN IMAGE

MATTHEW L. ROBBINS*
Agent: ICM - Los Angeles, 213/550-4000

THE SUGARLAND EXPRESS   Universal, 1974,
   w/Hal Barwood & Steven Spielberg
THE BINGO LONG TRAVELING ALL-STARS & MOTOR
   KINGS   Universal, 1976, w/Hal Barwood
MACARTHUR   Universal, 1977, w/HalBarwood
CORVETTE SUMMER   MGM/United Artists, 1978,
   w/Hal Barwood, directed
DRAGONSLAYER   Paramount, 1981, w/Hal
   Barwood, directed
WARNING SIGN   20th Century Fox, 1985,
   w/Hal Barwood
BATTERIES NOT INCLUDED   Universal, 1987,
   w/Brad Bird, Brent Maddock & S.S. Wilson, directed

Screenplays:
THE GRID w/Hal Barwood
NEWSREEL w/Hal Barwood
WITNESSES w/Hal Barwood
HOME FREE w/Hal Barwood
NIGHT SHADE w/Hal Barwood

TIM ROBBINS
Agent: ICM - Los Angeles, 213/550-4000

CARNAGE (S)

Screenplays:
BOB ROBERTS,TIMES ARE CHANGING
   BACK (directing)

JOE ROBERTS
MY TUTOR   Crown International, 1983

JONATHAN ROBERTS*
Agent: William Morris Agency - Beverly Hills, 213/274-7451

ONCE BITTEN   Samuel Goldwyn Company, 1985, w/Jeff
   Hause & David Hines
THE SURE THING   Embassy, 1985, w/Steven Bloom

Screenplays:
FRANKENSTEIN GOES TO HARLEM
DREAMDATE

JUNE ROBERTS*
Agent: CAA - Beverly Hills, 213/288-4545

EXPERIENCE PREFERRED BUT NOT ESSENTIAL
   Samuel Goldwyn Company, 1983
MERMAIDS   Orion, 1990

Screenplays:
TWO BIT ROMANCE w/Randi Mayem Singer
RIDING THE DOLPHIN
KICK

SCOTT ROBERTS
THE AMERICAN WAY   RIDERS OF THE STORM
   Miramax, 1987

Screenplays:
K-2

VINCENT ROBERTS
RED SURF   Arrowhead Entertainment, 1990

WILLIAM ROBERTS*
Contact: WGA - Los Angeles, 213/550-1000

YOU FOR ME   MGM, 1952
EASY TO LOVE   MGM, 1953, w/Laslo Vadnay
FAST COMPANY   MGM, 1953
HER TWELVE MEN   MGM, 1954, w/Laura Z. Hobson
THE MATING GAME   MGM , 1959
THE MAGNIFICENT SEVEN   United Artists, 1960
COME FLY WITH ME   MGM, 1962
THE WONDERFUL WORLD OF THE BROTHERS GRIMM
   MGM, 1962, w/Charles Beaumont & David P. Herman
THE BRIDGE AT REMAGEN   United Artists, 1968,
   w/Richard Yates
DEVIL'S BRIGADE   United Artists, 1968
ONE MORE TRAIN TO ROB   Universal, 1971
RED SUN   National General, 1972, w/Laird Koenig, Denne
   Bart Petitclerc & Lawrence Roman
THE LAST AMERICAN HERO   20th Century-Fox, 1973
POSSE   Paramount, 1975, w/Christopher Knopf
THE LEGEND OF THE LONE RANGER   Universal/AFD,
   1981, w/Ivan Goff, Michael Kane & Ben Roberts
10 TO MIDNIGHT   Cannon, 1983

Screenplays:
THE RETURN OF MAGDA LA SELVA

CLIFF ROBERTSON
Agent: ICM - Los Angeles, 213/550-4000

J.W. COOP   Columbia, 1971, w/Gary Cartwright &
   Bud Shrake, directed

HARRY ROBERTSON
HAWK THE SLAYER   ITC, 1976, w/Terry Marcel

Ro

FILM WRITERS GUIDE

R.J. ROBERTSON
Agent: CAA - Beverly Hills, 213/288-4545

FORBIDDEN WORLD   New World, 1982, Story
   w/Jim Wynorski
BIG MAD MOMA II   Concorde, 1988, w/Jim Wynorski
NOT OF THIS EARTH   Concorde, 1988, w/Jim Wynorski
THE HAUNTING OF MORELLA   Concorde, 1990,
   w/Jim Wynorski
TRANSYLVANIA TWIST   Concorde, 1990
THINK BIG   Concorde, 1990, Story w/Jim Wynorski

Screenplays:
FINAL EMBRACE w/Jim Wynorski
MUNCHIES II w/Jim Wynorski

ROBBIE ROBERTSON*
Business Manager: Addis-Wechsler & Associates -
   Los Angeles, 213/954-9000

CARNY   United Artists, 1980, Story w/Phoebe Kaylor &
   Robert Kaylor

JOHN M. ROBINS*
Contact: WGA - Los Angeles, 213/550-1000

DEATH SHIP   Avco Embassy, 1980
HOT RESORT   Cannon, 1985, w/Boaz Davidson &
   Norman Hudis, directed

BRUCE C. ROBINSON*
Agent: CAA - Beverly Hills, 213/288-4545

THE KILLING FIELDS ★   Warner Bros., 1984
WITHNAIL AND I   Cineplex Odeon, 1987, directed
HOW TO GET AHEAD IN ADVERTISING   Warner Bros.,
   1989, directed
FAT MAN AND LITTLE BOY   Paramount, 1989,
   w/Roland Joffe

Screenplays:
AN ACT OF LOVE
JENNIFER EIGHT

LEE ROBINSON
THE HIGHEST HONOR   New World, 1984

PHIL ALDEN ROBINSON*
Business Manager: Peter Turner, 213/315-4772
Business: Universal Studios, 818/777-5055

RHINESTONE   20th Century Fox, 1984,
   w/Sylvester Stallone
ALL OF ME   Universal, 1984
IN THE MOOD   THE WOO WOO KID   Lorimar,
   1987, directed
FIELD OF DREAMS ★   Universal, 1989, directed
RELENTLESS   New Line Cinema, 1989,
   as "Jack T.D. Robinson"

Screenplays:
SNEAKERS w/Lawrence Lasker &
   Walter Parkes (directing)

RICHARD ROBINSON
KINGDOM OF THE SPIDERS   Dimension, 1977,
   w/Alan Cailou

TODD ROBINSON*
Agent: Shorr, Stille & Associates - Los Angeles,
   213/659-6160

Screenplays:
A PASSAGE HOME

TOM ROBINSON
SALVATION!   Circle Releasing, 1987, w/Beth B & Scott B

MARY ROBISON*
Agent: William Morris Agency - Beverly Hills, 213/274-7451

Screenplays:
SUCCESS w/Larry Gross

ED ROBOTO
Agent: APA - Los Angeles, 213/273-0744

CLUB PARADISE   Warner Bros., 1986, Story w/Tom
   Leopold, Chris Miller & David Standish

MICHAEL ROBSON
HOLOCAUST 2000   THE CHOSEN   Rank, 1977,
   w/Alberto De Martino & Sergio Donati
THE 39 STEPS   International Picture Show, 1978
THE WATER BABIES   Pethurst International/Film
   Polski, 1978

MARC ROCCO
Business: Yankee Entertainment Group, 2919 Burbank
   Blvd. - Suite C, Burbank, CA 91505, 818/954-0780

DREAM A LITTLE DREAM   Vestron, 1989, w/D.E.
   Eisenberg & Daniel Jay Franklin, directed

ERIC ROCHANT
Contact: French Film Office, 745 Fifth Avenue, New York,
   NY 10151, 212/832-8860

TOO MUCH   Cannon, 1987, directed
THE 5TH MONKEY   21st Century Film Corporation,
   1990, directed
LOVE WITHOUT PITY   (no distributor), 1991, directed

ALEXANDRE ROCKWELL
SONS   Pacific Pictures, 1989, w/Brandon Cole, directed

ROBERT RODAT*
Agent: Maggie Field Agency - Studio City, 818/980-2001

Screenplays:
DISTORTION
THE CHRISTMAS CONSPIRACY

GENE RODDENBERRY
Contact: Star Trek-The Next Generation, Paramount
   Television, 5555 Melrose Ave., Los Angeles, CA 90038,
   213/956-5000

PRETTY MAIDS ALL IN A ROW   MGM, 1971

MARY RODGERS*
Agent: The Cooper Agency - Los Angeles, 213/277-8422

FREAKY FRIDAY   Buena Vista, 1977
THE DEVIL AND MAX DEVLIN   Buena Vista, 1981

ADAM D. RODMAN*
Agent: United Talent Agency - Beverly Hills, 213/273-6700

THE SERPENT AND THE RAINBOW   Universal, 1987,
    w/Richard Maxwell, as "A.R. Simoun"

Screenplays:
THE SILENT MAN
CONNECTIONS
ACT OF FAITH
BUG JACK BARRON

HOWARD A. RODMAN*
Agent: United Talent Agency - Beverly Hills, 213/273-6700

Screenplays:
SOUTH OF HEAVEN
DADDY EMPIRE
DESTINY EXPRESS
SOMEBODY ELSE

MICHAEL ROEMER
Contact: Yale School of Art, Box 1605A, Yale Station,
    New Haven, CT 06520, 203/432-2600

NOTHING BUT A MAN   Cinema 5, 1965, co-directed
THE PLOT AGAINST HARRY   New Yorker, 1990,
    directed, filmed in 1968

Screenplays:
FAMOUS LONG AGO

JOSH ROGAN
Agent: CAA - Beverly Hills, 213/288-4545

TWILIGHT ZONE - THE MOVIE   Warner Bros.,
    1983, Segment 2 w/George Clayton Johnson &
    Richard Matheson

ROY ROGOSIN*
Contact: 603/433-4472

WEEKEND WARRIORS   The Movie Store, 1986,
    w/Bruce Belland

ERIC ROHMER
Contact: French Film Office, 745 Fifth Avenue, New York,
    NY, 10151, 212/832-8860
Business: 26 Avenue Pierre-ler-de-Serbie, 75008
    Paris, France

LA COLLECTIONNEUSE   Pathe Contemporary,
    1967, directed
MY NIGHT AT MAUD'S ★   Pathe Contemporary,
    1970, directed
CLAIRE'S KNEE   *L'AMOUR, L'APRES-MIDI*   Columbia,
    1971, directed
CHLOE IN THE AFTERNOON   Columbia, 1972, directed
THE MARQUISE OF O...   New Line Cinema,
    1976, directed
PERCEVAL   *PERCEVAL LE GALLOIS*   New Yorker,
    1978, directed
THE AVIATOR'S WIFE   New Yorker, 1981, directed
LE BEAU MARRIAGE   United Artists Classics, 1982,
    directed
PAULINE AT THE BEACH   Orion Classics,
    1983, directed
FULL MOON IN PARIS   *LES NUITS DE LA
    PLEINE LUNE*   Orion Classics, 1984, directed

SUMMER   *LE RAYON VERT*   Orion Classics,
    1985, directed
FOUR ADVENTURES OF REINETTE AND
    MIRABELLE   New Yorker, 1987, directed
BOYFRIENDS AND GIRLFRIENDS   *L'AMI DE MON AMIE*
    Orion Classics, 1987, directed
A TALE OF SPRINGTIME   Orion Classics, 1991, diected

SANDRA WEINTRAUB ROLAND
(formerly Sandra Weintraub)
Agent: J. Michael Bloom, Ltd. - Los Angeles, 213/275-6800

HIGH ROAD TO CHINA   Warner Bros., 1983,
    w/S. Lee Pogostin
OUT OF CONTROL   New World, 1985,
    w/Vicangelo Bullock
THE PRINCESS ACADEMY   Empire Pictures,
    1987, directed
THE WOMEN'S CLUB   Lightning Pictures, 1987, directed

MARCUS ROLLING
CLASS OF NUKE 'EM HIGH 2: SUBHUMANOID
    MELTDOWN   Troma, 1991, w/Lloyd Kaufman, Eric
    Louzil, Carl Morano, Jeffrey W. Sass & Matt Unger

BERNIE ROLLINS
Agent: Sheri Mann Agency - Los Angeles, 213/850-1777

GETTING OVER   Continental Films, 1981

LAWRENCE ROMAN*
Agent: Robinson, Weintraub, Gross & Associates - Los
    Angeles, 213/653-5802

ALONE TOGETHER (S)
P.S. I LOVE YOU (S)
VICE SQUAD   United Artists, 1953
DRUMS ACROSS THE RIVER   Universal-International,
    1954, w/John K. Butler
NAKED ALIBI   Universal-International, 1954
ONE DESIRE   Universal-International, 1955,
    w/Robert Blees
THE MAN FROM BITTER RIDGE   Universal-
    International, 1955
A KISS BEFORE DYING   United Artists, 1956
THE SHARK FIGHTERS   United Artists, 1956,
    w/John Robinson
SLAUGHTER ON TENTH AVENUE   Universal-
    International, 1957
UNDER THE YUM YUM TREE   Columbia, 1963, w/David
    Swift, from his play
THE SWINGER   Paramount, 1966
PAPER LION   United Artists, 1968
RED SUN   National General, 1972, w/Laird Koenig,
    DenneBart Petitclerc & William Roberts
A WARM DECEMBER   National General, 1973
McQ   Warner Bros., 1974

MARK ROMANEK
Contact: 213/462-6400

STATIC   Sandstar Releasing, 1989, w/Keith
    Gordon, directed

Screenplays:
CRASH
GHOST BOY MOON

Ro

FILM WRITERS GUIDE

JOHN ROMANO*
Agent: CAA - Beverly Hills, 213/288-4545

KEY EXCHANGE   20th Century Fox, 1985, under pseudonym, w/Paul Kurta

Screenplays:
TRAIL OF THE FOX
A WOMAN'S PLACE
ACTS
MARRIAGE OR BUST
PERFUME

GEORGE A. ROMERO
Agent: The Gersh Agency - Beverly Hills, 213/274-6611

THE CRAZIES   CODE NAME: TRIXIE   Cambist, 1972, directed
HUNGRY WIVES   Jack H. Harris Enterprises, 1973, directed
MARTIN   Libra, 1978, directed
DAWN OF THE DEAD   United Film Distribution, 1979, directed
KNIGHTRIDERS   United Film Distribution, 1981
DAY OF THE DEAD   United Film Distribution, 1985, directed
CREEPSHOW 2   New World, 1987
MONKEY SHINES   Orion, 1988, directed
TALES FROM THE DARKSIDE   Paramount, 1990, "Cat From Hell"
NIGHT OF THE LIVING DEAD   21st Century Film Corporation, 1990
THE DARK HALF   Orion, 1992, directed

JOHN ROMO
DEAD WOMEN IN LINGERIE   Seagate Films, 1990, w/Erica Fox

TOM RONDINELLA
ALL'S FAIR   Moviestore Entertainment, 1989, w/John Finnegan, William Pace & Randee Russell

DARRELL ROODT
Contact: Department of Interior, Civitas Building, Struben Street, Pretoria 0002, South Africa, 12/48-2551

PLACE OF WEEPING   New World, 1986, directed
JOBMAN   Blue Rock Films, 1990, w/Gregg Latter, directed

DONALD P. ROOS*
Agent: Patricia Karlan Agency - Burbank, 818/846-8666

LOVE FIELD   Orion, 1991

Screenplays:
SINGLE WHITE FEMALE

TOM ROPELEWSKI*
Agent: ICM - Los Angeles, 213/550-4000

THE KISS   Tri-Star, 1988, w/Stephen Volk
LOVERBOY   Tri-Star, 1989, w/Leslie Dixon & Robin Schiff
MADHOUSE   Orion, 1990, directed

Screenplays:
COUNTERFEIT FATHER   w/Eva Katz

ANDY ROSE*
Agent: David Shapira & Associates - Sherman Oaks, 818/906-0322

Screenplays:
PLAY MONEY   FUNNY MONEY   w/Alex Gorby
SPAGHETTI MEN
McHALE'S NAVY

JACK ROSE*
Contact: WGA - Los Angeles, 213/550-1000

ROAD TO RIO   Paramount, 1947, w/Edmund Beloin
SORROWFUL JONES   Paramount, 1949, w/Mel Shavelson & Edmund Hartmann
ALWAYS LEAVE THEM LAUGHING   Warner Bros., 1949, w/Mel Shavelson
THE DAUGHTER OF ROSIE O'GRADY   Warner Bros., 1950, w/Peter Milne & Mel Shavelson
ON MOONLIGHT BAY   Warner Bros., 1951, w/Mel Shavelson
ROOM FOR ONE MORE   Warner Bros., 1952, w/Mel Shavelson
APRIL IN PARIS   Warner Bros., 1952, w/Mel Shavelson
I'LL SEE YOU IN MY DREAMS   Warner Bros., 1952, w/Mel Shavelson
TROUBLE ALONG THE WAY   Warner Bros., 1953, w/Mel Shavelson
LIVING IT UP   Paramount, 1954, w/Mel Shavelson
THE SEVEN LITTLE FOYS ★   Paramount, 1955, w/Mel Shavelson
BEAU JAMES   Paramount, 1957, w/Mel Shavelson
HOUSEBOAT   Paramount, 1958, w/Mel Shavelson
THE FIVE PENNIES   Paramount, 1959, w/Mel Shavelson
IT STARTED IN NAPLES   Paramount, 1960, w/Mel Shavelson & Susi Cecchi d'Amico
ON THE DOUBLE   Paramount, 1961, w/MelShavelson
WHO'S GOT THE ACTION?   Paramount, 1962
PAPA'S DELICATE CONDITION   Paramount, 1963
WHO'S BEEN SLEEPING IN MY BED?   Paramount, 1963
A TOUCH OF CLASS ★   Avco Embassy, 1973, w/Melvin Frank
LOST AND FOUND   Columbia, 1979, w/Melvin Frank
THE GREAT MUPPET CAPER   Universal/AFD, 1981, w/Jerry Juhl, Tom Patchett & Jay Tarses

JOEL ROSE
Agent: William Morris Agency - Beverly Hills, 213/274-7451

Screenplays:
IT'S NOT SUPERSTITION

LEE ROSE
Agent: The Irv Schechter Company - Beverly Hills, 213/278-8070

Screenplays:
WRONG PLANET
ROUGH TRADE
BACK BY 10
LEAVE OF ABSENCE

MICKEY ROSE*
Agent: Larry Grossman & Associates - Beverly Hills, 213/550-8127

TAKE THE MONEY AND RUN   Cinerama Releasing Corporation, 1969, w/Woody Allen
BANANAS   United Artists, 1971, w/Woody Allen

STUDENT BODIES   Paramount, 1981, directed
CONDORMAN   Buena Vista, 1981, w/Glenn Gordon
    Caron & Marc Stirdivant

NORVELL ROSE
THE AMITYVILLE CURSE   Allegro Films, 1990,
    w/Michael Krueger

REGINALD ROSE*
Agent: Preferred Artists - Encino, 818/990-0305

CRIME IN THE STREETS   Allied Artists, 1956,
    from his teleplay
TWELVE ANGRY MEN ★   United Artists, 1957,
    from his play
THE MAN IN THE NET   United Artists, 1958
MAN OF THE WEST   United Artists, 1958
BAXTER   EMI, 1972
THE WILD GEESE   Rank, 1978
SOMEBODY KILLED HER HUSBAND   Columbia, 1978
WHOSE LIFE IS IT ANYWAY?   MGM/United Artists,
    1981, w/Brian Clark
THE SEA WOLVES   Paramount/Lorimar, 1981
WHO DARES WINS   Rank, 1982
THE FINAL OPTION   MGM/UA, 1983
WILD GEESE II   Universal, 1986

JEB ROSEBROOK*
Agent: Broder-Kurland-Webb-Uffner - Los Angeles,
    213/656-9262

JUNIOR BONNER   ABC Films, 1972
THE BLACK HOLE   Buena Vista, 1979, w/Gerry Day

GARY ROSEN*
Agent: The Irv Schechter Company - Beverly Hills,
    213/278-8070

RISING STORM   Gibraltar Releasing, 1989,
    w/William Fay
FRAMED (CTF)   HBO Pictures, 1990

HERBERT H. ROSEN
COASTER   Atlantic Film Group, 1981

MARTIN ROSEN
WATERSHIP DOWN (AF)   Avco Embassy,
    1978, directed
THE PLAGUE DOGS (AF)   Nepenthe Productions,
    1982, directed

HENRY ROSENBAUM*
Agent: CAA - Beverly Hills, 213/288-4545

A BULLET FOR PRETTY BOY   American
    International, 1970
THE DUNWICH HORROR   American International,
    1970, w/Curtis Lee Hanson & Ronald Silkowsky
BLACK MAMA, WHITE MAMA   American
    International, 1973
HANKY PANKY   Columbia, 1982, w/David Taylor
GET CRAZY   Embassy, 1983, w/Danny Opatoshu &
    David Taylor
LOCK UP   Tri-Star, 1989, w/Richard Smith & Jeb Stuart

Screenplays:
KNOCKOUT
MR. MAUI

JEFFREY ROSENBAUM
FIREWALKER   Cannon, 1986, Story w/Norman Aladjem &
    Robert Gosnell

ANITA ROSENBERG*
Agent: Barrett, Benson, McCartt & Weston - Los Angeles,
    213/247-5500

MODERN GIRLS   Atlantic Releasing Corporation, 1986,
    Story w/Laurie Craig
ASSAULT OF THE KILLER BIMBOS   Empire Pictures,
    1988, Story w/Patti Astor & Ted Nicolau, directed

JEANNE ROSENBERG*
Contact: WGA - Los Angeles, 213/550-1000

THE BLACK STALLION   United Artists, 1979, w/Melissa
    Mathison & William D. Witliff
THE JOURNEY OF NATTY GANN   Buena Vista, 1985
WHITE FANG   Buena Vista, 1991, w/David Fallon &
    Nick Thiel

MARC ROSENBERG
HEATWAVE   New Line Cinema, 1983, w/Phillip Noyce
DINGO   August Entertainment, 1991

DALE ROSENBLOOM*
Contact: WGA - Los Angeles, 213/550-1000

INSTANT KARMA   MGM/UA, 1990, w/Bruce A. Taylor

HOWARD ROSENMAN
Business: Sandollar Productions, 8730 Sunset Blvd. -
    Bldg. 50, Los Angeles, CA 90069, 213/659-5933

GROSS ANATOMY   Buena Vista, 1990, Story w/Alan Jay
    Glueckman, Stanley Isaacs & Mark Spragg

JACK ROSENTHAL*
Agent: William Morris Agency - Beverly Hills, 213/274-7451

THE KNOWLEDGE (S), also screenplay
ANOTHER SUNDAY & SWEET PEA (S)
SMASH (S)
THE LOVERS!   British Lion, 1973
THE LUCKY STAR   Pickman Films, 1981, w/Max Fischer
YENTL   MGM/UA, 1983, w/Barbra Streisand
KIPPERBANG   P'TANG, YANG, KIPPERBANG   MGM/UA
    Classics, 1984
THE CHAIN   Rank, 1985

Screenplays:
FAMILY MATTERS
THE BEST
GABRIELA
NON-WHITE COMEDY
AND A NIGHTINGALE SANG....
CONVENTIONS

MARK D. ROSENTHAL*
Agent: CAA - Beverly Hills, 213/288-4545
Business: Konner-Rosenthal Productions, Paramount,
    213/956-5909

THE JEWEL OF THE NILE   20th Century Fox, 1985,
    w/Larry Konner
THE LEGEND OF BILLIE JEAN   Tri-Star, 1985,
    w/Larry Konner

SUPERMAN IV: THE QUEST FOR PEACE   Warner Bros., 1987, w/Larry Konner
THE IN CROWD   Orion, 1988, w/Larry Konner, directed
DESPERATE HOURS   Warner Bros., 1990, w/Larry Konner & Joseph Hayes

Screenplays:
GALE FORCE   w/Larry Konner & David A. Chappe
FORTRESS   w/Larry Konner
THE HIT   w/Larry Konner

ROBERT J. ROSENTHAL
Business: Apple-Rose Productions, 3961 Landmark St., Culver City, CA 90232, 213/204-1000

MALIBU BEACH   Crown International, 1978, w/Celia Susan Cotelo
ZAPPED!   Embassy, 1982, w/Bruce Rubin, directed

FRANCESCO ROSI
BELLISSIMA   1951, w/Suso Cecchi D'Amico, Luciano Visconti & Cesare Zavattini, directed
THE BIGAMIST   Royal, 1957, w/Sergio Amidei, Age Scarpelli & Elio Talarico
SALVATORE GIULIANO   Lux, 1961, w/others, directed
LE MANI SULLA CITTA (HANDS OVER THE CITY)   Galatea Film, 1963, w/others, directed
CADAVERI ECCELLENTI (ILLUSTRIOUS CORPSES)   United Artists, 1976, w/Tonnino Guerra, Lino Jannuzzi, directed
EBOLI   CHRIST STOPPED AT EBOLI   Franklin Media, 1980, w/Tonino Guerra & Raffaele La Capria, directed
THREE BROTHERS   New World, 1981, directed
BIZET'S CARMEN   CARMEN   Triumph/Columbia, 1984, directed

MARK ROSMAN*
Agent: CAA - Beverly Hills, 213/288-4545

THE HOUSE ON SORORITY ROW   Film Ventures, 1983, directed

MARK ROSNER*
Agent: CAA - Beverly Hills, 213/288-4545

SAVE THE LAST DANCE FOR ME (Short), directed
ON OCEAN FRONT WALK (FD)   1977, directed

Screenplays:
RIVALS
STRANGLEHOLD   COACH
COMBAT ZONE

ALAN DUNCAN ROSS
Agent: William Morris Agency - Beverly Hills, 213/274-7451

Screenplays:
CALIFORNIA DREAMIN
DOUBLE BLIND

ARTHUR ROSS*
Contact: WGA - Los Angeles, 213/550-1000

THE STAND AT APACHE RIVER   Universal-International, 1953
THE CREATURE FROM THE BLACK LAGOON   Universal-International, 1954, w/Harry Essex
THE THREE WORLDS OF GULLIVER   Columbia, 1959, w/Jack Sher
BRUBAKER ★   20th Century-Fox, 1980, Story w/W.D. Richter

DONALD H. ROSS*
Agent: The Cooper Agency - Los Angeles, 213/277-8422

HAMBURGER...THE MOTION PICTURE   FM Entertainment, 1986

GARY A. ROSS*
Agent: CAA - Beverly Hills, 213/288-4545

BIG ★   20th Century Fox, 1988, w/Anne Spielberg

Screenplays:
NEWS   w/Ken Finkelman
DAVE

JUDITH ROSS*
Agent: ICM - Los Angeles, 213/550-4000

AN ALMOST PERFECT PERSON (S)
RICH KIDS   United Artists, 1979

Screenplays:
THE OTHER MAN
JANE'S HOUSE
PARADISE

KENNETH ROSS*
Agent: ICM - Los Angeles, 213/550-4000

THE DAY OF THE JACKAL   Universal, 1973
THE ODESSA FILE   Columbia, 1974, w/George Markstein
BLACK SUNDAY   Paramount, 1977, w/Ernest Lehman & Ivan Moffatt
THE FOURTH WAR   Cannon, 1990, w/Stephen Peters

MARTIN K. (MARTY) ROSS*
Agent: The Gersh Agency - New York, 212/997-1818

DANGEROUSLY CLOSE   Cannon, 1986, w/Scott Fields & John Stockwell
THE IMPOSSIBLE SPY (CTF)   BBC TV/Quartet International/IMGC, 1987, w/Douglas Livingstone

PAUL ROSS
BEYOND EVIL   IFI-Scope III, 1980, w/Herb Freed

TERRY P. ROSSIO*
Agent: William Morris Agency - Beverly Hills, 213/274-7451

LITTLE MONSTERS   Vestron, 1989, w/Ted Elliott

Screenplays:
PRINCESS OF MARS   w/Ted Elliott
DUNN'S CONUNDRUM   w/Ted Elliott

EUGENIE ROSS-LEMING*
Contact: WGA - Los Angeles, 213/550-1000
Business: B & E Enterprises, Paramount TV, 213/956-5959

Screenplays:
CADETS   w/Brad Buckner
LOOSE WOMEN   w/Brad Buckner
UFO   w/Brad Buckner

ROMANTIC FOOLS w/Brad Buckner
SVENGALI w/Brad Buckner
FOREIGNERS w/Brad Buckner
LAMB OF GOD w/Brad Buckner
THE KID w/Brad Buckner
FORGET ME NOT w/Brad Buckner

BOBBY ROTH*
Agent: Triad Artists, Inc. - Los Angeles,
  213/556-2727

INDEPENDENCE DAY Unifilm, 1977, directed
THE BOSS' SON Circle Associates, 1980, directed
HEARTBREAKERS Orion, 1984, directed
BAJA OKLAHOMA HBO Pictures/Rastar Productions,
  w/Dan Jenkins, directed
DEAD SOLID PERFECT (CTF) HBO Pictures/David
  Merrick Prodcuctions, 1988, w/Dan Jenkins, directed
THE MAN INSIDE New Line Cinema, 1990, directed

Screenplays:
WALLRAFF
NATIVES

ERIC ROTH*
Agent: CAA - Beverly Hills, 213/288-4545

THE NICKEL RIDE 20th Century-Fox, 1975
THE CONCORDE - AIRPORT '79 Universal, 1979
SUSPECT Tri-Star, 1987
MEMORIES OF ME MGM/UA, 1988, w/Billy Crystal

Screenplays:
MR. JONES
THE POSTMAN
THE BOP
CHEEK TO CHEEK
NICK THE GREEK
MA BELL
LOVERS
MURDER AT THE MOVIES
US
WONDER BOY
INTENSIVE CARE
BODIE
LOUIE
WILLIE
GOODNIGHT MOON
NERVE ENDING
THE DANGER
GOSPEL

TAMARA LYNN ROTH*
Contact: 818/841-8484

Screenplays:
THE COLOR OF EVENING

JEFF ROTHBERG*
Agent: William Morris Agency - Beverly Hills,
  213/274-7451

HIDING OUT DEG, 1987, w/Joe Menosky

Screenplays:
MR. WRONG
ANNIE II
THE INSIDER

RICHARD ROTHSTEIN*
Agent: ICM - Los Angeles, 213/550-4000

DEATH VALLEY Universal, 1982
HARD TO HOLD Universal, 1984, Story w/Tom Hedley

Screenplays:
UNIVERSAL SOLDIER w/Leslie Bohem

ERLINDA QUILAOIT ROWE
FATAL MISSION Funahara, 1990, Story

FREDDIE ROWE
HOWLING IV...THE ORIGINAL NIGHTMARE Allied
  Entertainment, 1988, w/Clive Turner

GEORGE ROWE
FATAL MISSION Funahara, 1990, w/Peter Fonda, Chosei
  Funahara, Anthony Gentile & John Gentile, directed

RYAN ROWE*
Agent: CAA - Beverly Hills, 213/288-4545

TAPEHEADS Avenue Pictures, 1988, Story w/Bill
  Fishman, Jim Herzfeld & Peter McCarthy

Screenplays:
KILLER BEACH BABES (Story w/Chris Matheson)
THE MAN WITH 9 LIVES
BESIDE MYSELF
LOSERS
GENIE BOB

THOMAS L. ROWE*
Contact: WGA - Los Angeles, 213/550-1000

TARZAN, THE APE MAN MGM/United Artists, 1981,
  w/Gary Goddard

Screenplays:
NO LAUGHING MATTER

KATHLEEN K. ROWELL*
Agent: The Gersh Agency - Beverly Hills, 213/274-6611

THE OUTSIDERS Warner Bros., 1983
JOY OF SEX Paramount, 1984, w/J.J. Salter

MARK ROWEN*
Contact: WGA - Los Angeles, 213/550-1000

Screenplays:
NO ONE TO KISS AT MIDNIGHT

IAIN ROY
ANY MAN'S DEATH INI Entertainment, 1990,
  w/Chris Kelly

PAT ROYCE
DAREDREAMER Lensman Co., 1989, w/Barry Caillier

ROBB ROYER*
Agent: APA - Los Angeles, 213/273-0744

Screenplays:
LOCKED OUT w/Sean Finnegan

PATRICIA ROZEMA*
Business: Vos Productions, Inc., 152 John St., Suite 502, Toronto M5V 2T2, Canada, 416/971-9401

I'VE HEARD THE MERMAIDS SINGING   Miramax, 1987, directed
WHITE ROOM   Alliance Releasing, 1990, directed

JOHN RUANE
DEATH IN BRUNSWICK   Overseas Film Group, 1990, w/Boyd Oxlade, directed

MARC R. RUBEL*
Agent: William Morris Agency - Beverly Hills, 213/274-7451

XANADU   Universal, 1980, w/Richard Christian Danus
BIG BUSINESS   Buena Vista, 1988, w/Dori Pierson

ALBERT RUBEN
Agent: CAA - Beverly Hills, 213/288-4545

THE SEVEN-UPS   20th Century-Fox, 1973, w/Alexander Jacobs
VISIT TO A CHIEF'S SON   United Artists, 1974

ANDY RUBEN*
Agent: ICM - Los Angeles, 213/550-4000
Business: Concorde Films, 11600 San Vicente Blvd., Los Angeles, CA, 90049, 213/820-6733

THE PATRIOT   Crown International, 1986, w/Katt Shea Ruben
STRIPPED TO KILL   Concorde, 1987, w/Katt Shea Ruben
DANCE OF THE DAMNED   Concorde, 1989, w/Katt Shea Ruben
STREETS   Concorde, 1990, w/Katt Shea Ruben

Screenplays:
POISON IVY w/Katt Shea Ruben

JOSEPH RUBEN*
Agent: United Talent Agency - Beverly Hills, 213/273-6700

THE POM-POM GIRLS   Crown International, 1976, directed
JOYRIDE   American International, 1977, w/Peter Rainer, directed
DREAMSCAPE   20th Century Fox, 1984, w/David Loughery & Chuck Russell, directed

Screenplays:
JUICE
NIGHT ON THE TOWN

KATT SHEA RUBEN
Business: Concorde Films, 11600 San Vicente Blvd., Los Angeles, CA, 90049, 213/820-6733

THE PATRIOT   Crown International, 1986, w/Andy Ruben, directed
STRIPPED TO KILL   Concorde, 1987, w/Andy Ruben, directed
DANCE OF THE DAMNED   Concorde, 1989, w/Andy Ruben, directed
STRIPPED TO KILL 2   Concorde, 1990, directed
STREETS   Concorde, 1990, w/Andy Ruben, directed

Screenplays:
POISON IVY w/Andy Ruben (directing)

BRUCE RUBIN*
Contact: WGA - Los Angeles, 213/550-1000

ZAPPED!   Embassy, 1982, w/Robert J. Rosenthal

BRUCE JOEL RUBIN*
Agent: Sanford, Skouras, Gross & Associates - Los Angeles, 213/208-2100

BRAINSTORM   MGM/UA, 1983, Story
DEADLY FRIEND   Warner Bros., 1986
GHOST ★★   Paramount, 1990
JACOB'S LADDER   Tri-Star, 1990

MANN RUBIN*
Agent: The Coppage Company - North Hollywood, 818/980-1106
Contact: 213/271-5398

THE BEST OF EVERYTHING   20th Century-Fox, 1959, w/Edith Sommer
BRAINSTORM   Warner Bros., 1965
AN AMERICAN DREAM   Warner Bros., 1966
WARNING SHOT   Paramount, 1966
THE FIRST DEADLY SIN   Filmways, 1980
THE HUMAN SHIELD   Cannon, 1991

RICHARD RUBIN
NEVER FORGET (CTF)   Turner Network Television, 1991

ALAN RUCKER*
Agent: William Morris Agency - Beverly Hills, 213/274-7451

HOMETOWN BOY MAKES GOOD (CTF)   HBO Television, 1990

ALBERT S. RUDDY*
Business: Ruddy-Morgan Productions, 120 El Camino Dr. - Suite 112, Beverly Hills, CA, 90212, 213/271-7698

MATILDA   American International, 1978, w/Timothy Galfas
MEGAFORCE   20th Century-Fox, 1982, w/James Whittaker, Hal Needham & Andre Morgan
CANONBALL RUN II   Warner Bros., 1984, w/Harvey Miller & Hal Needham

DAVID RUDKIN
Agent: Margaret Ramsay Ltd. - London, 011/441/240-0691

TESTIMONY   Isolde Films, 1988, w/Tony Palmer
DECEMBER BRIDE   Film Four Productions, 1991

PAUL RUDNICK*
Agent: CAA - Beverly Hills, 213/288-4545

I HATE HAMLET (S)
THE ADDAMS FAMILY   Paramount, 1991, w/Caroline Thompson & Larry Wilson

Screenplays:
POOR LITTLE LAMBS
MAGIC TIME
GOSSIP COLUMNIST

ALAN S. RUDOLPH*
Agent: CAA - Beverly Hills, 213/288-4545

PREMONITION   Transvue, 1972, directed
BUFFALO BILL AND THE INDIANS, or SITTING
  BULL'S HISTORY LESSON   United Artists, 1976,
  w/Robert Altman
WELCOME TO L.A.   United Artists/Lions Gate,
  1977, directed
REMEMBER MY NAME   Columbia/Lagoon Associates,
  1979, directed
ROADIE   United Artists, 1980, Story w/Zalman King,
  Big Boy Medlin & Michael Ventura, directed
ENDANGERED SPECIES   MGM/UA, 1982, w/John
  Binder, directed
CHOOSE ME   Island Alive/New Cinema, 1984, directed
TROUBLE IN MIND   Alive Films, 1985, directed
THE MODERNS   Alive Films, 1988, w/Jon
  Bradshaw, directed
LOVE AT LARGE   Orion, 1990, directed

Screenplays:
THE FAR SIDE

BENJAMIN RUFFNER*
Contact: Ilan Bialer, Esq. - 213/550-4515

HALLOWEEN 4   Galaxy International, 1988,
  Story w/Dhani Lipsius, Alan McElroy & Larry Rattner

ED RUGOFF*
Agent: Jim Preminger Agency - Los Angeles,
  213/475-9491

MANNEQUIN   20th Century Fox, 1987,
  w/Michael Gottlieb
MANANEQUIN TWO: ON THE MOVE   20th
  Century Fox, 1991, w/David Isaacs, Betsy Israel &
  Ken Levine

Screenplays:
WHOPPER   w/Michael Gottlieb

TERRY RUNTE*
Agent: Triad Artists, Inc. - Los Angeles, 213/556-2727

MYSTERY DATE   Orion, 1991, w/Parker Bennett

CHRIS RUPPENTHAL*
Agent: CAA - Beverly Hills, 213/288-4545

VIOLENT DEATH, A MUSICAL (Short), directed,
  based on his play (Shared)

Screenplays:
WE'RE IN THE MONEY
FIREDOGS   w/Ira Besserman
MAN OF GOD

CHRISTOPHER RUSH
VENUS PETER   British Film Institute, 1989, w/Ian Sellar

RICHARD RUSH*
Agent: CAA - Beverly Hills, 213/288-4545

OF LOVE AND DESIRE   New World, 1963, w/Laslo
  Gorag, directed
PSYCH-OUT   American International, 1968, directed

THE STUNT MAN ★   20th Century-Fox, 1980, Story,
  directed
AIR AMERICA   Tri-Star, 1990, w/John Eskow

Screenplays:
THE FAT LADY (directing)
THE LONG DARK TEATIME OF THE SOUL

BRIAN RUSSELL*
Contact: WGA - Los Angeles, 213/550-1000

THE ANNIHILATORS   New World, 1985

CHUCK RUSSELL*
Agent: United Talent Agency - Beverly Hills, 213/273-6700

DREAMSCAPE   20th Century Fox, 1984, w/David
  Loughery & Joe Ruben
A NIGHTMARE ON ELM STREET PART 3: DREAM
WARRIORS   New Line Cinema, 1987, w/Wes Craven,
  Frank Darabont & Bruce Wagner, directed
THE BLOB   Tri-Star, 1988, w/Frank Darabont, directed

Screenplays:
SHADOW OF DEATH (directing)

JAY W. RUSSELL
Agent: The Gersh Agency - Beverly Hills, 213/274-6611

END OF THE LINE   Orion Classics, 1988,
  w/John Wohlbruck, directed

KEN RUSSELL
Agent: ICM - Los Angeles, 213/550-4000

THE DEVILS   Warner Bros., 1971, directed
THE BOY FRIEND   MGM, 1971, directed
MAHLER   Mayfair, 1974, directed
TOMMY   Columbia, 1975, directed
LISZTOMANIA   Warner Bros., 1975, directed
VALENTINO   United Artists, 1977, w/John Byrum, directed
SALOME'S LAST DANCE   Vestron, 1988, directed
THE LAIR OF THE WHITE WORM   Vestron,
  1988, directed
THE RAINBOW   Vestron, 1989, w/Vivian Russell, directed
WHORE   Trimark Pictures, 1991, w/Deborah
  Dalton, directed

RANDEE Y. RUSSELL*
Agent: Broder-Kurland-Webb-Uffner - Los Angeles,
  213/656-9262

ALL'S FAIR   Moviestore Entertainment, 1989, w/John
  Finnegan, William Pace & Tom Rondinella

VIVIAN RUSSELL
THE RAINBOW   Vestron, 1989, w/Ken Russell

WILLY RUSSELL
Agent: Margaret Ramsay Ltd. - London, 011/441/240-0691

JOHN PAUL GEORGE RINGO AND BURT (S)
EDUCATING RITA ★   Columbia, 1983, from his play
SHIRLEY VALENTINE   Paramount, 1989, from his play
DANCIN' THRU THE DARK   Palace Pictures/British Screen/
  BBC Films/Formost Films, 1990

JOHN A. RUSSO
NIGHT OF THE LIVING DEAD   Continental, 1968
THE RETURN OF THE LIVING DEAD   Orion, 1985,
  Story w/Rudy Ricci & Russell Streiner
VOODOO DAWN   AIP, 1990, w/Jeffrey Delman, Evan
  Dunsky & Thomas Rendon

MARDI RUSTAM
DEATHTRAP   Mars, 1976, w/Alvin L. Fast
EVILS OF THE NIGHT   Shapiro Entertainment, 1985,
  w/Phillip D. Connors, directed

NEIL RUTTENBERG
Agent: David Shapira & Associates - Sherman Oaks,
  818/906-0322

THE MASK OF SARNATH (Short), directed
DEATHSTALKERS II: NECROPOLIS   Concorde, 1986

Screenplays:
MAD DOG COLL
SPIDER MAN
MISTER TWISTER
ANT MAN
DEATHCATHALON

MORRIE RUVINSKY*
Agent: Robinson, Weintraub, Gross & Associates -
  Los Angeles, 213/653-5802

IMPROPER CHANNELS   Crown International, 1981,
  w/Adam Arkin & Ian Sutherland

Screenplays:
CHEAP PARTS
RAINY DAYS, RAINY NIGHTS
DISTANT SHORES
THE PLASTIC MILE
THE FINISHING TOUCH

S

MARC SACHNOFF
PENNY ANTE   Andrew Solt Productions, 1990

WILLIAM SACHS*
Agent: The Artists Group - Los Angeles, 213/552-1100

THERE IS NO THIRTEEN   Film Ventures International,
  1977, directed
THE INCREDIBLE MELTING MAN   American
  International, 1978, directed
VAN NUYS BLVD.   Crown International, 1979, directed
GALAXINA   Crown International, 1980, directed
EXTERMINATOR II   Cannon, 1984, w/Mark Buntzman
HOT CHILI   Cannon, 1985, w/Menahem
  Golan, directed
JUDGMENT   Promark, 1991, directed

WILLIAM B. SACKHEIM*
Business Manager: E V Associates - 213/274-8565

BARRICADE   Warner Bros., 1949
PAULA   *THE SILENT VOICE*   Columbia, 1952,
  w/James Poe
FORBIDDEN   Universal-International, 1953, w/Gil Doud
BORDER RIVER   Universal-International, 1953
THE HUMAN JUNGLE   Allied Artists, 1954,
  w/Daniel Fuchs
THE COMPETITION   Columbia, 1980, Story
  w/Joel Oliansky
FIRST BLOOD   Orion, 1982, w/Michael Kozoll &
  Sylvester Stallone

HOWARD SACKLER
THE GREAT WHITE HOPE   20th Century-Fox, 1970,
  from his play
GRAY LADY DOWN   Universal, 1978, w/James Whitaker
SAINT JACK   New World, 1979, w/Peter Bogdanovich &
  Paul Theroux

ALAN SACKS*
Business: Heritage Entertainment, 7920 Sunset Blvd. -
  Suite 200, Los Angeles, CA 90046, 213/850-5858

THRASHIN'   Fries Entertainment, 1986, w/Paul Brown

EZRA M. SACKS*
Agent: CAA - Beverly Hills, 213/288-4545

FM   Universal, 1978
A SMALL CIRCLE OF FRIENDS   United Artists, 1980
WILDCATS   Warner Bros., 1986

Screenplays:
CONEY ISLAND COWBOYS

RICHARD SADLER
HOW TO MAKE LOVE TO A NEGRO WITHOUT GETTING
  TIRED   Angelika Films, 1990, w/Dany LaFerriere

JAMES SADWITH*
Agent: InterTalent - Los Angeles, 213/858-6200

Screenplays:
THE MATCH
IN THE EYE OF THE STORM
MALIBU WARS

DON SAFRAN*
Contact: 818/954-3851

HOMEWORK   Jensen Farley Pictures, 1982,
  w/Maurice Peterson

HENRI SAFRAN
Contact: Mitch Consultancy, 98 Bay Road, Waverton,
  NSW, 2060, Australia, 02/922-6566

NORMAN LOVES ROSE   Atlantic Releasing Corporation,
  1981, directed
THE WILD DUCK   RKR Releasing, 1983, w/Peter Smalley
  & John Lind, directed

BRUCE HIDEMI SAKOU
FRIDAY THE 13TH, PART IV: THE FINAL CHAPTER
  Paramount, 1984, Story

C. L. SALASKI
Agent: Jack Scagnetti Agency - North Hollywood, 818/762-3871

Screenplays:
WITHIN REACH
THROUGH MY EYES

RICHARD SALE*
Agent: H.N. Swanson, Inc. - Los Angeles, 213/652-5385

NORTHWEST OUTPOST   Republic, 1947, w/Elizabeth Meehan
CALENDAR GIRL   Republic, 1947, w/Mary Loos & Lee Loeb
DRIFTWOOD   Republic, 1947, w/Mary Loos
WHEN WILLIE COMES MARCHING HOME   20th Century-Fox, 1949, w/Mary Loos
MR. BELVEDERE GOES TO COLLEGE   20th Century-Fox, 1949, w/Mary Loos & Mary McCall Jr.
MEET ME AFTER THE SHOW   20th Century-Fox, 1951, w/Mary Loos
LET'S DO IT AGAIN   Columbia, 1953, w/Mary Loos
THE FRENCH LINE   RKO, 1953, w/Mary Loos
WOMAN'S WORLD   20th Century-Fox, 1954, w/Mary Loos & Claude Binyon
SUDDENLY   United Artists, 1954
GENTLEMEN MARRY BRUNETTES   United Artists, 1955, w/Mary Loos, directed
SEVEN WAVES AWAY   ABANDON SHIP   Columbia, 1956, directed
TORPEDO RUN   MGM, 1958, w/William Wister Haines
THE WHITE BUFFALO   United Artists, 1977
ASSASSINATION   Cannon, 1987

MURRAY SALEM*
Agent: Camden-ITG - Los Angeles, 213/556-2022

KINDERGARTEN COP   Universal, 1990, w/Timothy Harris & Herschel Weingrod

MARTIN SALINAS
Agent: The Gersh Agency - Beverly Hills, 213/274-6611

GABY - A TRUE STORY   Tri-Star, 1987, w/Michael Love

Screenplays:
FLY AWAY HOME w/Michael Love

JAMES SALTER*
Agent: Sterling Lord Literistic - New York, 212/696-2800

THREE   United Artists, 1969, directed
THE APPOINTMENT   MGM, 1969
DOWNHILL RACER   Paramount, 1969
THRESHOLD   20th Century-Fox International Classics, 1983

JOEL S. SALTZMAN*
Agent: The Agency - Los Angeles, 213/551-3000 or

Screenplays:
THE WIZARD FROM FLATBUSH w/Harv Zimmel
ROMANCE ARTIST

MARK SALTZMAN*
Agent: William Morris Agency - New York, 212/586-5100

THE ADVENTURES OF MILO AND OTIS   Columbia, 1989

Screenplays:
SINBAD (AF)
THE GUARDIANS OF GOOD

VICTOR SALVA
CLOWNHOUSE   Commercial Pictures, 1989, directed

HAROLD SALWEN*
Contact: WGA - Los Angeles, 213/550-1000

Screenplays:
GIRLS TALK
SO LONG, NEW JERSEY

MARK SALZMAN
IRON AND SILK   Sun Productions, 1990, w/Shirley Sun

Screenplays:
GHOST STORY

JEANNE SALZMANN
MEETINGS WITH REMARKABLE MEN   Libra, 1979

COKE SAMS
ERNEST GOES TO CAMP   Buena Vista, 1987, w/John R. Cherry III

ROBERT L. SAND*
Agent: Broder-Kurland-Webb-Uffner - Los Angeles, 213/656-9262

TOUCH AND GO   Tri-Star, 1987, w/Harry Colomby & Alan Ormsby

DUKE SANDEFUR*
(Donald D. Sandefur)
Agent: Barrett, Benson, McCartt & Weston - Los Angeles, 213/247-5500

GHOST TOWN   Trans World Entertainment, 1988
THE PHANTOM OF THE OPERA   21st Century Film Corporation, 1989
PHANTOM OF MANHATTAN   21st Century Film Corporation, 1990

KEN SANDERS
BLOOD SALVAGE   Paragon Arts International, 1990, w/Tucker Johnston

LAMAR SANDERS
Contact: New York University, 212/998-1780

THE KIRLIAN WITNESS   Sarno, 1981, w/Jonathan Sarno

BARRY SANDLER*
Agent: Triad Artists, Inc. - Los Angeles, 213/556-2727

THE LONERS   Fanfare, 1972, w/J. Lawrence
GABLE AND LOMBARD   Universal, 1976
THE DUCHESS AND THE DIRTWATER FOX   20th Century-Fox, 1976, w/Melvin Frank
THE MIRROR CRACK'D   EMI, 1980, w/Jonathan Hales

MAKING LOVE   20th Century-Fox, 1982
CRIMES OF PASSION   New World, 1984

Screenplays:
STAR LADIES   w/J. Rivers
ALL-AMERICAN MURDERS
JULIO AND STEIN

SUSAN SANDLER*
Agent: ICM - Los Angeles, 213/550-4000

CROSSING DELANCEY   Warner Bros., 1988, from her play

Screenplays:
I SLEPT FOR SCIENCE
LONELYVILLE

DONALD S. SANFORD*
Agent: H.N. Swanson, Inc. - Los Angeles, 213/652-5385
Contact: 818/782-4206

SUBMARINE X-1   United Artists, 1967, w/Guy Elmes
MOSQUITO SQUADRON   United Artists, 1968, w/Joyce Perry
MIDWAY   Universal, 1976
RAVAGERS   Columbia, 1979

JIMMY SANGSTER*
Agent: Shapiro/Lichtman - Los Angeles, 213/859-8877

X THE UNKNOWN   Hammer, 1956
THE CURSE OF FRANKENSTEIN   Warner Bros., 1957
THE CRAWLING EYE   *THE TROLLENBERG TERROR*   Eros, 1958
THE SNORKEL   Columbia, 1958, w/Anthony Dawson & Peter Myers
THE REVENGE OF FRANKENSTEIN   Columbia, 1958, w/Hurford Janes
BLOOD OF THE VAMPIRE   Artists Alliance, 1958
HORROR OF DRACULA   *DRACULA*   Universal, 1958
INTENT TO KILL   20th Century-Fox, 1958
JACK THE RIPPER   Mid Century, 1958
THE MAN WHO COULD CHEAT DEATH   Paramount, 1959
THE MUMMY   Hammer, 1959
BRIDE OF DRACULA   Universal-International, 1960, w/Peter Bryan & Edward Percy
THE TERROR OF THE TONGS   Hammer, 1960
THE SIEGE OF SIDNEY STREET   Midcentury, 1960, w/Alexander Baron
THE HELLFIRE CLUB   New World, 1960, w/Leon Griffiths
THE CONCRETE JUNGLE   *THE CRIMINAL*   Fanfare, 1960, w/Alun Owen
SCREAM OF FEAR   *TASTE OF FEAR*   Columbia, 1961
DEVIL SHIP PIRATES   ABP, 1963
MANIAC   Columbia, 1963
PARANOIAC   Universal-International, 1963
NIGHTMARE   Universal-International, 1964
HYSTERIA   MGM, 1964
THE NANNY   ABP, 1965
DEADLIER THAN THE MALE   Rank, 1967, w/Liz Charles-Williams & Dvaid Osborn
THE ANNIVERSARY   Hammer, 1968
CRESCENDO   Warner Bros., 1969, w/Alfred Shaughnessy
THE HORROR OF FRANKENSTEIN   EMI, 1970, directed

FEAR IN THE NIGHT   Hammer, 1972, w/Michael Syson, directed
WHO SLEW AUNTIE ROO?   United Artists, 1978, w/Robert Blees
THE LEGACY   Columbia, 1978, w/Patrick Tilley & Paul Wheeler
THE DEVIL AND MAX DEVLIN   Buena Vista, 1981, Story w/Mary Rodgers
PHOBIA   Paramount, 1981, w/Peter Bellwood, Lew Lehman, Gary A. Sherman & Ronald Shusett

DAMON SANTOSTEFANO*
Agent: William Morris Agency - New York, 212/586-5100

Screenplays:
THE BRANDENBURG   w/Nicholas Felacci

DAVID SAPERSTEIN*
Agent: Susan Schulman Literary Agency - New York, 212/713-1633
Business: Ebbets Field Productions, 16 Carlton Lane, New Rochelle, NY, 10804, 914/636-1281

COCOON   20th Century-Fox, 1984, Story
A KILLING AFFAIR   Hemdale, 1988, directed
PERSONAL CHOICE   Moviestore Entertainment, 1989, directed

DERAN SARAFIAN
Agent: Triad Artists, Inc. - Los Angeles, 213/556-2727

ALIEN PREDATOR   Trans World Entertainment, 1987, directed
INTERZONE   Trans World Entertainment, 1987, directed

TED SARAFIAN*
Agent: Triad Artists, Inc. - Los Angeles, 213/556-2727

SOLAR CRISIS   Scochiku-Fuji, 1990, w/Joe Gannon

JAN SARDI
Agent: A.A. Williams Management - in association w/William Morris Agency - Beverly Hills, 213/274-7451
Business: Victorian International Pictures Pty. Ltd., 30 Lalor Street, Port Melbourne, 3207 Victoria, Australia, 03/646-4777

STREET HERO   1983
MOVING OUT   Satori, 1985
GROUND ZERO   Avenue Pictures, 1988, w/Mac Gudgeon

Screenplays:
SECRETS

ALVIN SARGENT*
Agent: Triad Artists, Inc. - Los Angeles, 213/556-2727

GAMBIT   Universal, 1966, w/Jack Davies
THE STALKING MOON   National General, 1968
THE STERILE CUCKOO   Paramount, 1969
I WALK THE LINE   Columbia, 1970
THE EFFECT OF GAMMA RAYS ON MAN-IN-THE-MOON MARIGOLDS   20th Century-Fox, 1972
PAPER MOON ★   Paramount, 1973
LOVE AND PAIN AND THE WHOLE DAMNED THING   Columbia, 1973
BOBBY DEERFIELD   Columbia, 1977
JULIA ★★   20th Century-Fox, 1977

STRAIGHT TIME   Warner Bros., 1978, w/Jeffrey
  Boam & Edward Bunker
ORDINARY PEOPLE ★★   Paramount, 1980
NUTS   Warner Bros., 1987, w/DarrylPonicsan &
  Tom Topor
DOMINICK & EUGENE   Orion, 1988, w/Corey Blechman
WHITE PALACE   Universal, 1990, w/Ted Tally
WHAT ABOUT BOB?   Buena Vista, 1991, Story
  w/Laura Ziskin

Screenplays:
EVERYTHING MUST CHANGE   w/ R. Voller
SECOND WIND   w/R. Gould
SILENT VOWS
TWO LIVES
JOSHUA
ANYWHERE BUT HERE
MADLY IN LOVE

ARLENE SARNER*
Agent: CAA - Beverly Hills, 213/288-4545

PEGGY SUE GOT MARRIED   Tri-Star, 1986,
  w/Jerry Leichtling

Screenplays:
THE TALISMAN   w/Jerry Leichtling
THE MAN WHO COULD WORK MIRACLES
  w/Jerry Leichtling
HONKY TONK SUE   w/Jerry Leichtling

JONATHAN SARNO
THE KIRLIAN WITNESS   Sarno, 1981, w/Lamar Sanders
RAMONA   (no distributor), 1991, directed

ROBERT SARNO*
Agent: Shapiro/Lichtman - Los Angeles, 213/859-8877

HOWLING II...YOUR SISTER IS A WEREWOLF
  Thorn-EMI, 1986, w/Gary Brandner

Screenplays:
HARDWIRED
AFTERNOON SESSIONS   w/Billy Brown
GETTING DOWN   w/Billy Brown

PETER SASDY
Agent: Shapiro/Lichtman - Los Angeles, 213/859-8877

COUNTESS DRACULA   20th Century-Fox, 1972,
  w/Alexander Paul, Jeremy Paul & Gabriel
  Ronay, directed

JEFFREY W. SASS
Business: Troma Inc., 733 Ninth Ave., New York,
  NY 10019, 212/757-4555

CLASS OF NUKE 'EM HIGH 2: SUBHUMANOID MELT-
  DOWN   Troma, 1991, w/Lloyd Kaufman, Eric Louzil,
  Carl Morano, Marcus Rolling & Matt Unger

OLEY SASSONE
WILD HEARTS CAN'T BE BROKEN   Buena Vista,
  1991, w/Matt Williams

CAROLE LUCIA SATRINA
PUSS IN BOOTS   Cannon, 1989

PETER SAUDER
ROCK & RULE (AF)   MGM/UA, 1985, w/John Halfpenny
THE CARE BEARS MOVIE (AF)   Samuel Goldwyn
  Company, 1985
CARE BEARS MOVIE II: A NEW GENERATION (AF)
  Columbia, 1986
BABAR: THE MOVIE (AF)   New Line Cinema, 1989,
  w/Alan Bunce, John DeKlein, Raymond Jaffelice &
  J.D. Smith

OSCAR SAUL*
Contact: WGA - Los Angeles, 213/550-1000

ONCE UPON A TIME   Columbia, 1944, w/Lewis Meltzer
THE DARK PAST   Columbia, 1948, w/Philip Macdonald &
  Malvin Wald
WOMAN IN HIDING   Universal-International, 1949
THUNDER ON THE HILL   *BONAVENTURE*   Universal-
  International, 1951, w/Andre Solt
AFFAIR IN TRINIDAD   Columbia, 1952, w/James Gunn
THE JOKER IS WILD   Paramount, 1957
THE HELEN MORGAN STORY   Warner Bros., 1957,
  w/Nelson Gidding, Stephen Longstreet & Dean Reisner
THE NAKED MAJA   MGM, 1959, w/otghers
THE SECOND TIME AROUND   20th Century-Fox, 1961,
  w/Cecil Van Heusen
MAJOR DUNDEE   Columbia, 1965, w/Harry Julian Fink &
  Sam Peckinpah
THE SILENCERS   Columbia, 1966

GEORGE SAUNDERS
Agent: Circle Talent Associates - Beverly Hills,
  213/285-1585

Screenplays:
AMERICAN NINJA V LITTLE NINJA MAN
  w/John Bryant Hedberg
LONE JUSTICE CUSTODY   w/John Bryant Hedberg
BOMB SQUAD   w/John Bryant Hedberg
MAGIC BUS   w/John Bryant Hedberg
TEEN GENIE   w/John Bryant Hedberg
MARSHALL LAW III   w/John Bryant Hedberg
CONCRETE COWBOY

JAMES SAUNDERS
Agent: Margaret Ramsay Ltd. - London,
  011/441/240-0691

THE SAILOR'S RETURN   Euston Films Ltd., 1980

CARLOS SAURA
Contact: Ministry of Culture, Motion Picture Division,
  Avenida de Burgos 5, 28036, Madrid, Spain,
  341/202-5351

SWEET HOURS   New Yorker, 1982, directed
CARMEN   Orion Classics, 1983, w/Antonio
  Gades, directed
EL AMOR BRUJO (LOVE, THE MAGICIAN)   Orion Classics,
  1986, w/Antonio Gades, directed
LA NOCHE OSCURA (THE DARK NIGHT)   Iberoamericana,
  1989, directed

JOE SAUTER*
Contact: WGA - New York, 212/245-6180

HOTSHOT   International Film Marketing, 1987,
  w/Rick King

CLAUDE SAUTET
Contact: French Film Office, 745 Fifth Avenue, New York, NY 10151, 212/832-8860

THE THINGS OF LIFE   Columbia, 1970, w/Jean-Loup Dabadie & Paul Guimard, directed
CESAR AND ROSALIE   Cinema 5, 1972, w/Jean-Loup Dabadie, directed
A FEW DAYS WITH ME   Galaxy International, 1988, w/Jacques Fieschi & Jerome Tonnerre, directed

CARL G. SAUTTER*
Agent: Triad Artists, Inc. - Los Angeles, 213/556-2727

Screenplays:
WILD WOMEN DON'T HAVE NO BLUES
A FEW GOOD MEN
TOUGH COOKIES

PAUL SAVAGE*
Agent: APA - Los Angeles, 213/273-0744

INCHON   MGM/UA, 1982, Story w/Robin Moore

PHILIP S. SAVATH*
Contact: WGA - Los Angeles, 213/550-1000

FAST COMPANY   Topar, 1979, w/David Cronenberg & Courtney Smith
BIG MEAT EATER   New Line Cinema, 1984, w/Laurence Keane & Chris Windsor
THE OUTSIDE CHANCE OF MAXIMILIAN GLICK   Southgate Entertainment, 1989

JOSEPH SAVINO*
Agent: Sanford, Skouras, Gross & Associates - Los Angeles, 213/208-2100

DETROIT ROLL (Short), also screenplay
QUEEN'S LOGIC   7 Arts/New Line Cinema, 1991, Story w/Tony Spiridakis

NANCY SAVOCA
Business: Forward Films, 2445 Herring Avenue, Bronx, NY 10469

TRUE LOVE   MGM/UA, 1989, w/Richard Guay, directed

LYNWOOD SAWYER
SPACE AVENGER   Manley Productions, 1990, w/Richard Haines

JOHN T. SAYLES*
Agent: Robinson, Weintraub, Gross & Associates - Los Angeles, 213/653-5802

PIRANHA   New World, 1978
THE LADY IN RED   New World, 1979
BATTLE BEYOND THE STARS   New World, 1979
ALLIGATOR   Group 1, 1980
RETURN OF THE SECAUCUS SEVEN   Libra/Specialty Films, 1980, directed
THE HOWLING   Avco Embassy, 1981, w/Terry Winkless
THE CHALLENGE   Embassy, 1982, w/Richard Maxwell
LIANNA   United Artists Classics, 1983, directed
BABY IT'S YOU   Paramount, 1983, directed
THE BROTHER FROM ANOTHER PLANET   Cinecom, 1984, directed
ENORMOUS CHANGES AT THE LAST MINUTE   TC Films International, 1985, w/Susan Rice
THE CLAN OF THE CAVE BEAR   Warner Bros., 1986
WILD THING   Atlantic Releasing Corporation, 1987
MATEWAN   Cinecom International, 1987, directed
EIGHT MEN OUT   Orion, 1988, directed
BREAKING IN   Samuel Goldwyn Company, 1989
CITY OF HOPE   Samuel Goldwyn Company, 1991, directed

Screenplays:
COMMANDER

JAMES SBARDELLATI
UNDER THE GUN   Marquis Pictures, 1989, w/Almer John Davis & James Devney, directed

GERALD SCALFE
BREAKIN'   MGM/UA/Cannon, 1984, w/Allen DeBevoise & Charles Parker

ROMANO SCAVOLINI
NIGHTMARE   21st Century Distribution, 1981
DOG TAGS   Cinevest Entertainment Group, 1989, directed

ROSE A. SCHACHT*
Contact: WGA - Los Angeles, 213/550-1000

Screenplays:
LUCKY STRIKE w/Ann Powell
NIGHT OWL w/Ann Powell

BLAKE SCHAEFER
CRACK HOUSE   Cannon, 1989

ERIC SCHAEFFER
Agent: Irvin Arthur Associates - Beverly Hills, 213/278-5934

Screenplays:
IF LUCY FELL
DAD'S THE NEW SAVIOR
LIKE AL AND ME
MAY I SEE YOU AGAIN
METER MADNESS
SAL'S PIZZA MOVIE
WHAT ABOUT LOVE
WHAT EVER HAPPENED TO LOVE AT FIRST SIGHT

KEN SCHAFER
Agent: Irvin Arthur Associates - Beverly Hills, 213/278-5934

Screenplays:
A DEATH WITH BRUSH
SHATTER GAME

JOHN J. SCHALTER
Agent: CAA - Beverly Hills, 213/288-4545

Screenplays:
THE GAME
DALLAS TEXANS
NIGHTCALLER
PROFESSOR HOLMES
COACH MOM
BEATING THE ODDS
ESCAPE
OVERTIME
DREAM LOVERS
THE QUID PRO QUO

BLOOD GAMES
PEACEKEEPERS AT WAR
AUTUMN DANCE
DOWN MEXICO WAY

MICHAEL B. SCHEFF*
Agent: Shapiro/Lichtman - Los Angeles, 213/859-8877

AIRPORT '77   Universal, 1977, w/David Spector

Screenplays:
BUZZARDS LUCK w/Mary Anne Kasica

MAXMILLIAN SCHELL
Agent: ICM - Los Angeles, 213/550-4000

END OF THE GAME   20th Century-Fox, 1976, w/Friedrich Durrenmatt, directed

GEORGE W. SCHENCK*
Agent: Barrett, Benson, McCartt & Weston - Los Angeles, 213/247-5500

MORE DEAD THAN ALIVE   United Artists, 1968
BARQUERO   United Artists, 1970, w/William Marks
FUTUREWORLD   American International, 1976, w/Mayo Simon
ESCAPE 2000   New World, 1983, Story w/David Lawrence & Robert Williams

CARL SCHENKEL
SILENCE LIKE GLASS   Bavaria/Lisa Roxy, 1989, w/Bea Hellman, directed

FRED SCHEPISI*
Agent: ICM - New York, 212/556-5600

THE DEVIL'S PLAYGROUND   Entertainment Marketing, 1976, directed
THE CHANT OF JIMMIE BLACKSMITH   New Yorker, 1978, directed
A CRY IN THE DARK   Warner Bros., 1988, w/Robert Caswell

J. NOYES SCHER
Business: Northwinds Entertainment, 3 Sheridan Square - Apt. 8A, New York, NY 10014

PRISONERS OF INERTIA   Northwinds Entertainment, 1989, directed

GREGORY SCHERICK*
Contact: WGA - Los Angeles, 213/550-1000

THE NIGHT BEFORE   Kings Road Productions, 1987, w/Thom Eberhardt

ROBIN L. SCHIFF*
Agent: Broder-Kurland-Webb-Uffner - Los Angeles, 213/656-9262

LOVERBOY   Tri-Star, 1989, w/Leslie Dixon & Tom Ropelewski

Screenplays:
LET'S CALL THE WHOLE THING OFF
VENUS IN BLUE JEANS
RSVP

MICHAEL SCHIFFER*
Agent: CAA - Beverly Hills, 213/277-4545

COLORS   Orion, 1988
LEAN ON ME   Warner Bros., 1989

Screenplays:
MURDER IN THE FIRST w/Dan Gordon
ASCENT   LONGING TO FALL
JOURNEY

SUZANNE SCHIFFMAN
Contact: French Film Office, 745 Fifth Avenue, New York, NY, 10151, 212/832-8860

DAY FOR NIGHT ★   Warner Bros., 1974, w/Jean-Louis Richard & Francois Truffaut
THE STORY OF ADELE H.   New World, 1975, w/Jean Gruault & Francois Truffaut
SMALL CHANGE   L'ARGENT DE POCHE   New World, 1976, w/Francois Truffaut
THE MAN WHO LOVED WOMEN   Cinema 5, 1977, w/Michel Fermaud & Francois Truffaut
THE LAST METRO   United Artists, 1981, w/Francois Truffaut
THE WOMAN NEXT DOOR   United Artists Classics, 1981, w/Jean Aurel & Francois Truffaut
VIVEMENT DIMANCHE   Spectrafilm, 1983, w/Jean Aurel & Francois Truffaut
CONFIDENTIALLY YOURS   Spectrafilm, 1984, w/Jean Aurel & Francois Truffaut
LOVE ON THE GROUND   Spectrafilm, 1986, w/others
SORCERESS   LA MOINE ET LA SORCIERE   European Classics, 1987, directed

TOM SCHILLER*
Contact: Attorney Mark Champlin, 212/692-4855

NOTHING LASTS FOREVER   MGM/UA Classics, 1984, directed

Screenplays:
SAFARI w/Sandy Krinski

VIVIAN SCHILLING
Agent: The Artists Group - Los Angeles, 213/552-1100

SOULTAKER   Taurus Entertainment, 1990

Screenplays:
BLACK CREEK

MURRAY SCHISGAL*
Agent: Arthur B. Greene - New York, 212/661-8200
Business: Punch Productions Inc., 75 Rockefeller Plaza, New York, NY, 10019, 212/484-6900

LUV (S)
ALL OVER TOWN (S)
JIMMY SHINE (S)
TWICE AROUND THE PARK (S)
THE TIGER MAKES OUT   Columbia, 1967, from his play "The Typists & The Tiger"
TOOTSIE ★   Columbia, 1982, w/Larry Gelbart

Screenplays:
THE STAND IN
DAYS AND NIGHTS OF A FRENCH HORN PLAYER
CHEAP LAUGHS

GEORGE SCHLATTER*
Business: George Schlatter Productions, 8321 Beverly Blvd., Los Angeles, CA 90048, 213/655-1400

FIRE AND ICE   Concorde, 1987, w/Digby Wolfe

JOHN SCHLESINGER
Agent: ICM - Los Angeles, 213/550-4000

TERMINUS (FD)   British Transport Films, 1961, directed
MADAME SOUSATZKA   Universal, 1988, w/Ruth Prawer Jhabvala, directed

VOLKER SCHLONDORFF
Agent: ICM - New York, 212/556-5600

THE TIN DRUM   United Artists, 1979, w/Jean-Claude Carriere & Franz Seitz
CIRCLE OF DECEIT   DIE FALSCHUNG   United Artists Classics, 1982, w/Jean-Claude Carriere, Margarethe von Trotta & Kai Hermann, directed
VOYAGER   Bioskop Films/Action Films, 1991, w/Rudy Wurlitzer, directed

RANDY B. SCHLOSSMAN*
Agent: APA - Los Angeles, 213/273-0744

Screenplays:
STUCK IN THE MIDDLE

ARNOLD SCHMIDT
DEJA VU   Cannon, 1985, w/Ezra D. Rappaport & Anthony Richmond

MARLENE SCHMIDT
THEY'RE PLAYING WITH FIRE   New World, 1984, w/Hikmet Avedis
THE FIFTH FLOOR   Film Ventures International, 1980, Story w/Hikmet Avedis
MORTUARY   Artists Releasing Corporation/Film Ventures International, 1983, w/Hikmet Avedis

RICK SCHMIDT
MORGAN'S CAKE   L.L. Productions, 1989, directed

WAYNE SCHMIDT
THE DAY TIME ENDED   Compass International, 1979, w/J. Larry Carroll & David L. Schmoeller

WILL SCHMITZ
LADY AVENGER   Marco Colombo, 1989, w/Keith Kaczorek

DAVID L. SCHMOELLER*
Agent: Shapiro/Lichtman - Los Angeles, 213/859-8877
Business: The Schmoeller Corporation, 2244 Stanley Hills Drive, Los Angeles, CA, 90046, 213/654-0748

THE TOURIST TRAP   Compass International, 1979, w/J. Larry Carroll, directed
THE DAY TIME ENDED   Compass International, 1979, w/J. Larry Carroll & Wayne Schmidt
THE SEDUCTION   Avco Embassy, 1982, directed
CRAWLSPACE   Empire Pictures, 1986, directed
GHOST TOWN   Empire Pictures, 1988, Story, directed

STEPHEN SCHNECK*
Agent: Stone Manners Agency - Los Angeles, 213/275-9599

WELCOME TO BLOOD CITY   EMI, 1977, w/Michael Winder

SCOTT J. SCHNEID*
Agent: David Shapira & Associates - Sherman Oaks, 818/906-0322

PHANTOM OF THE MALL: ERIC'S REVENGE   Fries Entertainment, 1989, w/Robert King & Tony Michelman

Screenplays:
DOWNFALL w/Tony Michelman
THE RED HOUR w/Tony Michelman
INVASION OF THE BODY BUILDERS w/Tony Michelman

BARRY SCHNEIDER
Agent: Preferred Artists - Encino, 818/990-0305

RUBY   Dimension, 1977, w/George Edwards
HARPER VALLEY P.T.A.   April Fools, 1978, w/George Edwards
ROLLER BOOGIE   United Artists, 1979
TAKE THIS JOB AND SHOVE IT   Avco Embassy, 1981
DEADLY FORCE   Embassy, 1983, w/Ken Blackwell & Robert Vincent O'Neil

LAURIE SCHOLNICK
Agent: Jim Preminger Agency - Los Angeles, 213/475-9491

Screenplays:
FLOATING BRIDGE w/Chris Nolan

AMY SCHOR*
Contact: 213/653-7130

Screenplays:
MR. WONDERFUL w/Vicki Polon

DAVID J. SCHOW*
Contact: WGA - Los Angeles, 213/550-1000

LEATHERFACE: TEXAS CHAINSAW MASSACRE III   New Line Cinema, 1990

Screenplays:
CRITTERS 3
CRITTERS 4

LEONARD SCHRADER*
Contact: Henry Holmes, Esq. - Los Angeles, 213/278-1111

THE YAKUZA   Warner Bros., 1975, Story
BLUE COLLAR   Universal, 1978, w/Paul Schrader
OLD BOYFRIENDS   Avco Embassy, 1978, w/Paul Schrader
THE MAN WHO STOLE THE SUN   Kitty, 1982, w/Kazuhiko Hasegawa
MISHIMA: A LIFE IN FOUR CHAPTERS   Warner Bros., 1985, w/Paul Schrader
KISS OF THE SPIDER WOMAN ★   New Yorker Films, 1985
NAKED TANGO   August Entertainment, 1990, directed

PAUL SCHRADER*
Agent: ICM - Los Angeles, 213/550-4000

THE YAKUZA   Warner Bros., 1975, w/Robert Towne
TAXI DRIVER   Columbia, 1976
OBSESSION   Columbia, 1976
ROLLING THUNDER   Universal, 1978,
　w/Heywood Gould
BLUE COLLAR   Universal, 1978, w/Leonard
　Schrader, directed
OLD BOYFRIENDS   Avco Embassy, 1978,
　w/Leonard Schrader
HARDCORE   Columbia, 1979, directed
AMERICAN GIGOLO   Paramount, 1980, directed
RAGING BULL   United Artists, 1980, w/Mardik Martin
MISHIMA: A LIFE IN FOUR CHAPTERS   Warner Bros.,
　1985, w/Leonard Schader, directed
THE MOSQUITO COAST   Warner Bros., 1986
LIGHT OF DAY   Tri-Star, 1987, directed
THE LAST TEMPTATION OF CHRIST   Universal, 1988

Screenplays:
LIGHT SLEEPER (directing)
INVESTIGATION
HEAVEN BELOW w/H. Miller
FOREVER MINE
8 SCENES FROM THE LIFE OF HANK WILLIAMS
COVERT PURPLE
HOLY BLOOD, HOLY GRAIL
GERSHWIN
QUEBECOIS
PIPELINER

NEVIN D. SCHREINER*
Contact: WGA - Los Angeles, 213/550-1000

MEMORIES OF MURDER (CTF)   Houston Lady Co./
　Viacom, 1990, w/John Harrison
THIS GUN FOR HIRE (CTF)   BBK Productions/
　MTE, 1991
MISSING PARENTS (Short), 1991 (on Showtime
　30-Minute Movies)

Screenplays:
KEEPERS
CHINA LAKE
GARCIA
BOOKWORM
THE NEWCOMER
NEW MOON

BARBET SCHROEDER
Agent: CAA - Beverly Hills, 213/288-4545

THE VALLEY obscured by clouds   Lagoon Associates,
　1972, directed
MAITRESSE   Gaumont, 1976, w/Paul
　Voujargol, directed
LES TRICHEURS   Filmsan Galatee, 1983, w/Pascal
　Bonitzer & Steve Baes, directed

BUDD SCHULBERG
Agent: ICM - Los Angeles, 213/550-4000

WINTER CARNIVAL   United Artists, 1939, w/Lester Cole
ON THE WATERFRONT ★★   Columbia, 1954
A FACE IN THE CROWD   Warner Bros., 1957
WIND ACROSS THE EVERGLADES   Warner
　Bros., 1958

Screenplays:
WHAT MAKES SAMMY RUN?

SANDRA SCHULBERG
WILDROSE   Troma, 1985, Story w/John Hansen

ARNOLD SCHULMAN*
Business Manager: Starr & Co., 350 Park Ave., New York,
NY 10022, 212/759-6556

WILD IS THE WIND   Paramount, 1957
A HOLE IN THE HEAD   United Artists, 1959, from his play
CIMARRON   MGM, 1960
LOVE WITH THE PROPER STRANGER ★
　Paramount, 1964
THE NIGHT THEY RAIDED MINSKY'S   United Artists,
　1968, w/Norman Lear & Sidney Michaels
GOODBYE, COLUMBUS ★   Paramount, 1969
TO FIND A MAN   Columbia, 1971
FUNNY LADY   Columbia, 1975, w/Jay Presson Allen
WON TON TON, THE DOG WHO SAVED HOLLYWOOD
　Paramount, 1976, w/Cy Howard
PLAYERS   Paramount, 1979
A CHORUS LINE   Columbia, 1985
TUCKER: THE MAN AND HIS DREAM   Paramount, 1988,
　w/David Seidler

GUY SCHULMAN*
Agent: Robinson, Weintraub, Gross & Associates -
　Los Angeles, 213/653-5802

Screenplays:
READY OR NOT w/Craig Heller
SEPARATE WAYS w/Craig Heller

TOM SCHULMAN*
Agent: CAA - Beverly Hills, 213/288-4545

DEAD POETS SOCIETY ★★   Buena Vista, 1989
HONEY, I SHRUNK THE KIDS   Buena Vista, 1989,
　w/Ed Naha
SECOND SIGHT   Warner Bros., 1989, w/Patricia Resnick
WHAT ABOUT BOB?   Buena Vista, 1991

Screenplays:
THE LAST DAYS OF EDEN

CHARLES M. SCHULZ
Contact: United Features Syndicate

A BOY NAMED CHARLIE BROWN (AF)   National
　General, 1968
SNOOPY, COME HOME (AF)   National General, 1972
RACE FOR YOUR LIFE, CHARLIE BROWN (AF)
　Paramount, 1978
BOY VOYAGE CHARLIE BROWN (AND DON'T
　COME BACK) (AF)   Paramount, 1980

JOEL SCHUMACHER*
Agent: CAA - Beverly Hills, 213/288-4545

SPARKLE   Warner Bros., 1976
CAR WASH   Universal, 1976
THE WIZ   Universal, 1978
D.C. CAB   Universal, 1983, directed
ST. ELMO'S FIRE   Columbia, 1985, w/Carl
　Kurlander, directed

Screenplays:
EXPENSIVE SHOES
HOBGOBLINS

AL SCHWARTZ
Contact: Ronald Lederman & Associates - Los Angeles, 213/277-0334

LOOKIN' TO GET OUT   Paramount, 1982, w/Jon Voight
TOO MUCH SUN   New Line Cinema, 1990, w/Robert Downey & Laura Ernst

MARJORIE SCHWARTZ*
Agent: United Talent Agency - Beverly Hills, 213/273-6700

THE BUTCHER'S WIFE   Paramount, 1991, w/Ezra Litwak

Screenplays:
WINGS w/Ezra Litwak

TERRY SCHWARTZ
LITTLE NIKITA   Columbia, 1988, Story w/Tom Musca

ETTORE SCOLA
Address: via Bertoloni, 1/E, Rome, Italy, 06/875-174

ADUA E LE COMPAGNE   Zebra Film, 1960, w/Ruggero Maccari, Antonio Pietrangeli & Tullio Pinelli
DOWN AND DIRTY   *BRUTTI, SPORCHI E CATTIVI*   New Line Cinema, 1976, directed
A SPECIAL DAY   Cinema 5, 1977, w/Ruggero Maccari, directed
PASSIONE D'AMORE   Putnam Square, 1982, w/Ruggero Maccari, directed
LA NUIT DE VARENNES   Triumph/Columbia, 1982, w/Sergio Amidei, directed
LE BAL   Almi Classics, 1983, w/Ruggero Maccari, Jean-Claude Penchenat & Furio Scarpelli, directed
MACARONI   Paramount, 1985, w/Furio Scarpelli & Ruggero Maccari
THE FAMILY   Vestron, 1987, directed

MARTIN SCORSESE*
Agent: CAA - Beverly Hills, 213/288-4545
Business: Tribeca Film Center, 375 Greenwich St., New York, NY 10013, 212/941-4000

MEAN STREETS   Warner Bros., 1973, w/Mardik Martin, directed
GOOD FELLAS ★   Warner Bros., 1990, w/Nicholas Pileggi, directed

Screenplays:
AGE OF INNOCENCE w/Jay Cocks

ALLAN G. SCOTT*
Agent: Robert Littman Company - Beverly Hills, 213/278-1572

THE MAN WHO HAD POWER OVER WOMEN   Avco Embassy, 1971, w/Chris Bryant
DON'T LOOK NOW   Paramount, 1974, w/Chris Bryant
THE GIRL FROM PETROVKA   Universal, 1974, w/Chris Bryant
THE SPIRAL STAIRCASE   Warner Bros., 1975, w/Chris Bryant
JOSEPH ANDREWS   Paramount, 1977, w/Chris Bryant
THE AWAKENING   Orion/Warner Bros., 1980, w/Chris Bryant & Clive Exton
MARTIN'S DAY   MGM/UA, 1985, w/Chris Bryant
D.A.R.Y.L.   Paramount, 1985, w/David Ambrose & Jeffrey Ellis
CASTAWAY   Cannon, 1987
APPRENTICE TO MURDER   New World, 1988, w/Wesley Moore
THE WITCHES   Warner Bros., 1990
COLD HEAVEN   MCEG, 1991

Screenplays:
THE MATING BIRDS
NINE TIGER MAN w/Chris Bryant
THE MAN FROM NOWHERE w/Chris Bryant & G. Tabori
PLUMB DRILLIN w/Chris Bryant
THE MURDER LEAGUE w/Chris Bryant
THE GOLDEN RENDEZVOUS w/Chris Bryant
THE PERSIAN RANSOM w/Chris Bryant
THE CORMORANT w/Chris Bryant
SOMETHING MOVES w/Chris Bryant
THE YERMAKOV TRANSFER w/Chris Bryant
THE MAN WHO WAS SHERLOCK HOLMES w/Chris Bryant
LIFELINE w/Chris Bryant
THE CHALLENGER
ACROSS THE RIVER AND INTO THE TREES
DON COYOTE
ABRACADAVER
ALEXANDRA

DARIN SCOTT
THE OFFSPRING   TMS Pictures, 1987, w/Jeff Burr & C. Courtney Joyner

Screenplays:
PEE WEES

JAMES SCOTT*
Business: Flamingo Pictures, 47 Lonsdale Avenue - 16th Floor, London N1 1EW, England

STRIKE IT RICH   Miillimeter Films, 1990, directed

JEFFREY SCOTT*
Agent: The Irv Schechter Company - Beverly Hills, 213/278-8070

STARCHASER: THE LEGEND OF ORIN   Atlantic Releasing Corporation, 1985

SUSAN SCRANTON
GAS   Paramount, 1981, Story w/Dick Wolf

STEVEN SEAGAL*
Agent: CAA - Beverly Hills, 213/288-4545
Business: Steamroller Productions, Warner Bros. Pictures, 818/954-4267

ABOVE THE LAW   Warner Bros., 1988, Story w/Andrew Davis

Screenplays:
CRUISE w/Jim Carabatsos

PETER S. SEAMAN*
Agent: CAA - Beverly Hills, 213/288-4545

TRENCHCOAT   Buena Vista, 1983, w/Jeffrey Price
WHO FRAMED ROGER RABBIT   Buena Vista, 1988, w/Jeffrey Price
DOC HOLLYWOOD   Buena Vista, 1991, w/Jeffrey Price & Daniel Pyne

Screenplays:
MR. WHISTLE w/Jeffrey Price
SPEND, SPEND, SPEND w/Jeffrey Price
LAST HOLIDAY w/Jeffrey Price
GOOD KING HARRY w/Jeffrey Price
MISS MOTHERWELL w/Jeffrey Price

DAVIN SEAY*
Agent: William Morris Agency - Beverly Hills, 213/274-7451

Screenplays:
THE WANDERER
HOME FREE

JOHN WILLIAM SEE
FEAR OF ACTING (S)
THE LADY CRIES MURDER (S)
GETTING EVEN   New World, 1983

Screenplays:
REVENGE ROMANCE
BODYGUARD

IAN SEEBERG*
Agent: United Talent Agency - Beverly Hills, 213/273-6700

Screenplays:
TIMERS w/Valerie Bennett
HIGHER GROUND w/Valerie Bennett
MORT w/Valerie Bennett

ERICH SEGAL*
Business Manager: Albert Rettig, Esq., 11777 San Vicente Blvd. - Suite 601, Los Angeles, CA, 90049, 213/826-6330

YELLOW SUBMARINE (AF)   King Features, 1968, w/others
RPM   Columbia, 1970
THE GAMES   20th Century-Fox, 1970
LOVE STORY ★   Paramount, 1970
JENNIFER ON MY MIND   United Artists, 1971
OLIVER'S STORY   Paramount, 1978, w/John Korty
A CHANGE OF SEASONS   20th Century-Fox, 1980, w/Fred Segal & Ronni Kern
MAN, WOMAN AND CHILD   Paramount, 1983, w/David Z. Goodman

JERRY SEGAL*
Contact: WGA - Los Angeles, 213/550-1000

ONE ON ONE   Warner Bros., 1977, w/Robby Benson
DIE LAUGHING   Orion/Warner Bros., 1980, w/Robby Benson & Scott Parker

LINDA A. SEGALL*
Agent: Stephanie Mann Agency - Los Angeles, 213/653-7130

Screenplays:
TROUBLE IN TARZANA
CUBBIE

STAN SEIDEL*
Agent: Sanford, Skouras, Gross & Associates - Los Angeles, 213/208-2100

Screenplays:
RADIO MAN w/Richard Murphy
HIGH RESOLUTION

THE HONEYMOON
DIRECT TO THE TOP
ROOT OF ALL EVIL

SUSAN SEIDELMAN
Agent: ICM - New York, 212/556-6810

Screenplays:
OZONE

DAVID SEIDLER*
Agent: Harris & Goldberg - Los Angeles, 213/553-5200

TUCKER: THE MAN AND HIS DREAM   Paramount, 1988, w/Arnold Schulman

Screenplays:
THE BOXER w/Jacqueline Feather
CLOSE TO HOME w/Jacqueline Feather
GLITTERBUG w/Jacqueline Feather

JULE SELBO*
Agent: United Talent Agency - Beverly Hills, 213/273-6700

PRISON STORIES: WOMEN ON THE INSIDE (CTF)   Francine Letvak Productions/HBO Showcase, 1991, "New Chicks" w/Dick Beebe & Martin Jones

Screenplays:
STRAY DOG w/Paul Morrissey
MRS. CALIBAN
HARD PROMISES
AGGIE
CHEERS
BIG SKY ROMANCE

KEN SELDEN
NO SECRETS   I.R.S. Releasing, 1991, w/Dezso Magyar

HENRY SELICK
Agent: Warden & White Associates - Beverly Hills, 213/852-1028

Screenplays:
NIGHTGAMES w/Michael Shea

MARKUS SELIN
BORN AMERICAN   Cinema Group, 1986, w/Renny Harlin

IAN SELLAR
VENUS PETER   British Film Institute, 1989, w/Christopher Rush, directed

PETER SELLARS
THE CABINET OF DR. RAMIREZ   Capital Entertainment, 1991, directed

ARTHUR D. SELLERS*
Agent: Shapiro/Lichtman - Los Angeles, 213/859-8877

MODERN PROBLEMS   20th Century-Fox, 1981, w/Ken Shapiro & Tom Sherohman

KEVIN S. SELLERS*
Contact: WGA - Los Angeles, 213/550-1000

BLUE SKIES AGAIN   Warner Bros., 1983

DAVID SELTZER*
Agent: CAA - Beverly Hills, 213/288-4545

THE HELLSTROM CHRONICLE (FD)   Cinema 5, 1971
KING, QUEEN, KNAVE   Avco Embassy, 1972,
   w/David Shaw
ONE IS A LONELY NUMBER   MGM, 1972
THE OTHER SIDE OF THE MOUNTAIN   Universal, 1975
THE OMEN   20th Century-Fox, 1976
PROPHECY   Paramount, 1979
TABLE FOR FIVE   Warner Bros., 1983
SIX WEEKS   Polygram, 1985
LUCAS   20th Century Fox, 1986, directed
PUNCHLINE   Columbia, 1988, directed
BIRD ON A WIRE   Universal, 1990, w/Eric Lerner &
   Louis Venosta
SHINING THROUGH   20th Century Fox, 1991, directed

Screenplays:
A PERFECT DAY FOR RASPBERRY RIPPLE
THE CAMEL DRIVE OF 1890
MEGGIDO
OTHER MEN'S DAUGHTERS
HOME AQUATICUS
KILLERS
EQUAL TIME
COOL, CLEAR WATER
ASHES
WHISTLIN' DIXIE

TERREL SELTZER*
Agent: United Talent Agency - Beverly Hills, 213/273-6700

CHAN IS MISSING   New Yorker, 1982, w/Isaac
   Cronin & Wayne Wang
DIM SUM: A LITTLE BIT OF HEART   Orion
   Classics, 1985
HOW I GOT INTO COLLEGE   20th Century Fox, 1989

Screenplays:
ALIEN TIMES
DEFENDANT
TAKING LUCY
THE BEAUTY OF IT
THE GAME SHOW SCANDAL

LORENZO SEMPLE, JR.*
Agent: CAA - Beverly Hills, 213/288-4545

BATMAN   20th Century-Fox, 1966
FATHOM   20th Century-Fox, 1967
PRETTY POISON   20th Century-Fox, 1968
DADDY'S GONE A-HUNTING   Warner Bros., 1969,
   w/Larry Cohen
THE SPORTING CLUB   Avco Embassy, 1971
THE MARRIAGE OF A YOUNG STOCKBROKER
   20th Century-Fox, 1971
PAPILLON   Allied Artists, 1973, w/Dalton Trumbo
THE SUPERCOPS   United Artists, 1974
THE PARALLAX VIEW   Paramount, 1974, w/David Giler
THE DROWNING POOL   Warner Bros., 1975,
   w/Walter Hill & Tracy Keenan Wynn
THREE DAYS OF THE CONDOR   Paramount, 1975,
   w/David Rayfiel
KING KONG   Paramount, 1976
HURRICANE   Paramount, 1979
FLASH GORDON   Universal, 1980
NEVER SAY NEVER AGAIN   Warner Bros., 1983
SHEENA   Columbia, 1984, w/David Newman

Screenplays:
THE DESTROYER
MANDRAKE
MILE HIGH
GOOD RIDDANCE
THE BENGAL LANCERS
WHERE THE SUN NEVER SETS
THE STARS MY DESTINATION
MUTATION
IMPATIENT

JORGE SEMPRUN
LA GUERRE EST FRIE (THE WAR IS OVER)
   Bramlon, 1966
Z ★   Cinerama 5, 1969, w/Costa-Gavras
THE CONFESSION   Paramount, 1970
STAVISKY   Cinemation, 1974

MICHAEL SERAFIN*
Agent: Warden & White Associates - Beverly Hills,
   213/852-1028

Screenplays:
MIND YOUR OWN BUSINESS
TWO ON THE AISLE
THE TENDER HEART
AMERICAN BOY

YAHOO SERIOUS
(Greg Pead)
Contact: Australian Film Commission, 9229 Sunset Blvd.,
   Los Angeles, CA 90069, 213/275-7074

YOUNG EINSTEIN   Warner Bros., 1989, w/David
   Roach, directed

Screenplays:
NED KELLY (directing)

COLINE SERREAU*
Agent: Triad Artists, Inc. - Los Angeles, 213/556-2727

3 MEN AND A CRADLE   Samuel Goldwyn Company,
   1985, directed
MAMA, THERE'S A MAN IN YOUR BED   ROUMALD ET
   JULIETTE   Miramax, 1990, directed

Screenplays:
RANDALL AND JULIET (directing, remake of MAMA..)
JOVA

PHILIPPE SETBON
Contact: French Film Office, 745 Fifth Ave., New York, NY
   10151, 212/832-8860

DETECTIVE   Spectrafilm, 1985, w/Jean-Luc Godard,
   Anne-Marie Mieville & Alain Sarde
HONEYMOON   International Film Marketing, 1987,
   w/Robert Geoffrion & Patrick Jamain
MR. FROST   Triumph, 1990, w/Brad Lynch, directed

DAVID SHABER*
Agent: CAA - Beverly Hills, 213/288-4545

LAST EMBRACE   United Artists, 1979
THE WARRIORS   Paramount, 1979, w/Walter Hill
THOSE LIPS, THOSE EYES   United Artists, 1980
ROLLOVER   Orion/Warner Bros., 1981

NIGHTHAWKS   Universal, 1981
FLIGHT OF THE INTRUDER   Paramount, 1991,
  w/Robert Dillon

Screenplays:
THE LIMEY
LUCY
SCOTCH SOUR
CHINESE BANDIT
GROWING MAN
RIGHTS OF PASSAGE
THE PRINCE OF 47TH STREET
FREEDOM SONG
THE CLOWN
HIGH RISE
WHEELS
VERNA, THE USC GIRL
POLYGAMIST HEAVEN SENT
STROKES
PROPATIA

SAMANTHA SHAD*
Agent: William Morris Agency - Beverly Hills, 213/274-7451

CLASS ACTION   20th Century Fox, 1991, w/Christopher
  Ames & Carolyn Shelby

SUSAN SHADBURNE
Business: Millenium Pictures, Inc., 2580 N.W. Upshur,
  Portland, OR, 97210, 503/227-7041

THE ADVENTURES OF MARK TWAIN (AF)   Atlantic
  Releasing Corporation, 1986
SHADOW PLAY   New World, 1986, directed

KEN SHADIE
"CROCODILE" DUNDEE ★   Paramount, 1980,
  w/John Cornell & Paul Hogan

ANTHONY SHAFFER*
Agent: The Roberts Company - Los Angeles, 213/552-7800
  & The Lantz Office - New York, 212/586-0200

WHODUNNIT (S)
MR. FORBUSH AND THE PENGUINS   CRY OF
  THEPENGUINS   EMI, 1971
FRENZY   Universal, 1972
SLEUTH   20th Century-Fox, 1972
THE WICKER MAN   Warner Bros., 1975
DEATH ON THE NILE   Paramount, 1978
EVIL UNDER THE SUN   Universal/AFD, 1982
ABSOLUTION   Trans World Entertainment, 1988
APPOINTMENT WITH DEATH   Cannon, 1988, w/Peter
  Buckman & Michael Winner

Screenplays:
DEATH COMES AS THE END
BO-PEEP

PETER SHAFFER
Agent: The Roberts Company - Los Angeles,
  213/552-7800

SHRIVINGS (S)
BLACK COMEDY (S)
THE ROYAL HUNT OF THE SUN (S)
THE PRIVATE EAR AND THE PUBLIC EYE (S)
LETTICE & LOVAGE (S)
YONADAB (S)
FIVE FINGER EXERCISE (S)
FOLLOW ME   Universal, 1971, from his play "
  The Public Eye"
EQUUS ★   United Artists, 1977, from his play
AMADEUS ★★   Orion, 1984, from his play

STEVE SHAGAN*
Contact: WGA - Los Angeles, 213/550-1000

TERRIFIC...TERRIFIC! (S)
SAVE THE TIGER ★   Paramount, 1972
HUSTLE   Paramount, 1975
VOYAGE OF THE DAMNED ★   ITC, 1976, w/David Butler
NIGHTWING   Columbia, 1979, w/Edwin Shrake
THE FORMULA   MGM/UA, 1980
THE SICILIAN   20th Century Fox, 1987

Screenplays:
HOLY MEN
TRICKS
THE ELECTRIC COTILLION
FIELDS OF EDEN
RICOCHET
THEY SHALL NOT PASS

JOHN HERMAN SHANER*
Agent: Robinson, Weintraub, Gross & Associates -
  Los Angeles, 213/653-5802

HALLS OF ANGER   United Artists, 1970, w/Al Ramrus
THE ISLAND OF DR. MOREAU   American International,
  1977, w/Al Ramrus
GOIN' SOUTH   Paramount, 1979, w/Alan Mandel,
  Al Ramrus & Charles Shyer
THE LAST MARRIED COUPLE IN AMERICA
  Universal, 1979

Screenplays:
SPARK
BEVERLY HILLS DOCTOR
CASHFLOW
AMERICAN NONSENSE

JOHN PATRICK SHANLEY*
Agent: William Morris Agency - New York, 212/586-5100

DANNY AND THE DEEP BLUE SEA (S)
SAVAGE IN LIMBO (S)
the dreamer examines his pillow (S)
ITALIAN AMERICAN RECONCILIATION (S)
WOMEN OF MANHATTAN (S)
FIVE CORNERS   Handmade Films, 1987
MOONSTRUCK ★★   MGM, 1987
THE JANUARY MAN   MGM/UA, 1989
JOE VERSUS THE VOLCANO   Warner Bros.,
  1990, directed

ALAN M. SHAPIRO*
Agent: The Brandt Company - Studio City,
  818/506-7747

TIGERTOWN (CTF)   Buena Vista, 1984, directed

Screenplays:
STONYBROOK
BUT WHAT ABOUT ME
MY FAMILY
HAUNTED GUITAR
3 TO GET READY

Sh

FILM WRITERS GUIDE

JANICE SHAPIRO*
Agent: Sanford, Skouras, Gross & Associates - Los Angeles, 213/208-2100

THIS YEAR'S MODEL (Short), directed
NIGHT DADDY (Short), directed

Screenplays:
PURPLE WEST w/Adam Dubov
THE CADILLAC KID
WILD RIDE w/Adam Dubov
TUBESTEAK w/Adam Dubov
UNFORGETTABLE w/Adam Dubov

KEN S. SHAPIRO*
Contact: WGA - Los Angeles, 213/550-1000 or Directors Guild of America - Los Angeles, 213/289-2000

THE GROOVE TUBE   Levitt-Pickman, 1974, directed
MODERN PROBLEMS   20th Century-Fox, 1981, w/Tom Sherohman & Arthur Sellers, directed

RICHARD SHAPIRO*
Agent: ICM - Los Angeles, 213/550-4000

THE GREAT SCOUT AND CATHOUSE THURSDAY   American International, 1976

JOHN SHARKEY
OMEGA SYNDROME   New World, 1987
DOUBLE REVENGE   Smart Egg Releasing, 1988, w/Brian Tobin

JIM SHARMAN
Contact: M & L Casting Consultants, 49 Darlinghurst Road, Kings Cross, NSW, 2100, Australia, 02/358-3111

THE ROCKY HORROR PICTURE SHOW   20th Century-Fox, 1976, w/Richard O'Brien, directed
SHOCK TREATMENT   20th Century-Fox, 1981, w/Richard O'Brien, directed

STEVE SHARON*
Agent: Writers & Artists Agency - Los Angeles, 213/820-2240

THE DEAD POOL   Warner Bros., 1988

Screenplays:
LITTLE SHOWDOWN IN TOKYO
SARGEANT K.

ALAN SHARP*
Agent: Paul Kohner, Inc. - Los Angeles, 213/550-1060

THE LAST RUN   MGM, 1971
THE HIRED HAND   Universal, 1971
ULZANA'S RAID   Universal, 1972
BILLY TWO HATS   United Artists, 1973
NIGHT MOVES   Warner Bros., 1975
DAMNATION ALLEY   20th Century-Fox, 1977, w/Lukas Heller
THE OSTERMAN WEEKEND   20th Century-Fox, 1983, w/Ian Masters
LITTLE TREASURE   Tri-Star, 1985, directed
CAT CHASER   Vestron, 1990, w/Jim Borrelli & Elmore Leonard
DESCENDING ANGEL (CTF)   Fredya Rothstein, 1990, w/Robert Siegel & Grace Woodards

Screenplays:
HARD KNOX

CHRISTOPHER W. SHARP
Agent: William Morris Agency - Beverly Hills, 213/274-7451

Screenplays:
MOONCHASER
SHOOTING THE BREEZE

DON SHARP
Agent: ICM - London, 71/629-8080

BACKGROUND   EDGE OF DIVORCE   Group Three, 1953, w/Warren Cheatham Strode
CONFLICT OF WINGS   FUSS OVER FEATHERS   Group Three, 1953, w/John Pudney
THE BLUE PETER   British Lion, 1955, w/John Pudney
A TASTE OF EXCITEMENT   Trio Films, 1964, w/Brian Carton, directed
PUPPET ON A CHAIN   Cinerama Releasing Corporation, 1972, w/Alistair Maclean & Paul Wheeler, directed
BEAR ISLAND   Taft International, 1980, w/David Butler & Murray Smith, directed

KRISCHNA SHAS
HARD ROCK ZOMBIES   Cannon, 1985, w/David Ball, directed

WILLIAM SHATNER
Business Contact: 213/288-0700

STAR TREK V: THE FINAL FRONTIER   Paramount, 1989, Story w/Harve Bennett & David Loughery, directed

MELVILLE SHAVELSON*
Contact: WGA - Los Angeles, 213/550-1000

WHERE THERE'S LIFE   Paramount, 1947, w/Allen Boretz
SORROWFUL JONES   Paramount, 1949, w/Jack Rose & Edmund Hartmann
ALWAYS LEAVE THEM LAUGHING   Warner Bros., 1949, w/Jack Rose
THE DAUGHTER OF ROSIE O'GRADY   Warner Bros., 1950, w/Peter Milne & Jack Rose
DOUBLE DYNAMITE   RKO, 1951, w/Harry Crane & Leo Rosten
ON MOONLIGHT BAY   Warner Bros., 1951, w/Jack Rose
APRIL IN PARIS   Warner Bros., 1952, w/Jack Rose
ROOM FOR ONE MORE   Warner Bros., 1952, w/Jack Rose
I'LL SEE YOU IN MY DREAMS   Warner Bros., 1952, w/Jack Rose
TROUBLE ALONG THE WAY   Warner Bros., 1953, w/Jack Rose
LIVING IT UP   Paramount, 1954, w/Jack Rose
THE SEVEN LITTLE FOYS ★   Paramount, 1955, w/Jack Rose, directed
BEAU JAMES   Paramount, 1957, w/Jack Rose, directed
HOUSEBOAT   Paramount, 1958, w/Jack Rose, directed
THE FIVE PENNIES   Paramount, 1959, w/Jack Rose, directed
IT STARTED IN NAPLES   Paramount, 1960, w/Jack Rose & Susi Cecchi d'Amico, directed

ON THE DOUBLE   Paramount, 1961, w/Jack Rose, directed
THE PIGEON THAT TOOK ROME   Paramount, 1962, directed
A NEW KIND OF LOVE   Paramount, 1963, directed
CAST A GIANT SHADOW   United Artists, 1966, directed
YOURS, MINE AND OURS   United Artists, 1968, w/Mort Lachman, directed
THE WAR BETWEEN MEN AND WOMEN   National General, 1972, w/Danny Arnold, directed
MIXED COMPANY   United Artists, 1974, w/Mort Lachman, directed

SANDY SHAW

THE DEAD POOL   Warner Bros., 1988, Story w/Durk Pearson & Steve Sharon

WALLACE SHAWN
Agent: Triad Artists, Inc. - Los Angeles, 213/556-2727

MARIE AND BRUCE (S)
THE HOTEL PLAY (S)
AUNT DAN AND LEMON (S)
THE FEVER (S)
MY DINNER WITH ANDRE   New Yorker, 1981, w/Andre Gregory

LINDA SHAYNE*
Business Manager: L. Miller Management - 213/392-5802

SCREWBALLS   New World, 1983, w/Jim Wynorski
CRYSTAL HEART   New World, 1987
PURPLE PEOPLE EATERS   Concorde, 1988, directed

BASHAR SHBIB

JULIA HAS TWO LOVERS   South Gate Entertainment, 1991, w/Dapha Kastner, directed

Screenplays:
SWIFT AND NATURAL   w/Gabor Zsigovics (directing)

MICHAEL SHEA
Agent: Warden & White Associates - Beverly Hills, 213/852-1028

Screenplays:
NIGHTGAMES   w/Henry Selick

HARRY SHEARER*
Agent: Triad Artists, Inc. - Los Angeles, 213/556-2727

REAL LIFE   Paramount, 1979, w/Albert Brooks & Monica Johnson
THIS IS SPINAL TAP   Embassy, 1984, w/Christopher Guest, Michael McKean & Rob Reiner

Screenplays:
IT'S A FAIR WORLD   w/Bob Dolman
BOHEMIAN GROVE

ALAN SHEARMAN*
Contact: WGA - Los Angeles, 213/550-1000

THE SHRIMP ON THE BARBIE   Unity Pictures Corp., 1990, w/Ron House & Grant Morris

MARTIN SHEEN
(Ramon Estevez)
Agent: The Liberty Agency - Los Angeles, 213/824-7937
Business: Symphony Pictures, 5711 W. Slauson Blvd. #226, Culver City, CA 90230, 213/649-3668

CADENCE   New Line Cinema, 1990, w/Dennis Shryack, directed

DAVID SHEFFIELD*
Agent: APA - Los Angeles, 213/273-0744

POLICE ACADEMY 2: THEIR FIRST ASSIGNMENT   Warner Bros., 1983, w/Barry Blaustein
COMING TO AMERICA   Paramount, 1988, w/Barry Blaustein

Screenplays:
BOOMERANG   w/Barry Blaustein
THE GELFAN   w/Barry Blaustein
OPTIMUM   w/Barry Blaustein
BUTTERSCOTCH KID   w/Barry Blaustein
LAST HOLIDAY   w/Barry Blaustein
BROTHERS KEEPERS   w/Barry Blaustein

CAROLYN J. SHELBY*
Agent: United Talent Agency - Beverly Hills, 213/273-6700
Business: North Beach Productions, 818/591-2222

CLASS ACTION   20th Century Fox, 1991, w/Christopher Ames & Samantha Shad

Screenplays:
THE MAGIC COTTAGE   w/Christopher Ames
CHAPEL OF LOVE   w/Christopher Ames
BLACK AND BLUE   w/Christopher Ames
IT'S NOT THE MONEY   w/Christopher Ames
LEADER OF THE PACK   w/Christopher Ames

SIDNEY SHELDON*
Agent: CAA - Beverly Hills, 213/288-4545

THE BACHELOR AND THE BOBBY SOXER ★★   RKO, 1947
EASTER PARADE   MGM, 1948, w/Frances Goodrich & Albert Hackett
ANNIE GET YOUR GUN   MGM, 1950
NANCY GOES TO RIO   MGM, 1950
NO QUESTIONS ASKED   MGM, 1951
THREE GUYS NAMED MIKE   MGM, 1951
RICH, YOUNG AND PRETTY   MGM, 1951, w/Dorothy Cooper
REMAINS TO BE SEEN   MGM, 1953
DREAM WIFE   MGM, 1953, w/Herbert Baker & Alfred L. Levitt, directed
YOU'RE NEVER TOO YOUNG   Paramount, 1955
PARDNERS   Paramount, 1956
THE BIRDS AND THE BEES   Paramount, 1956, after Preston Sturges
ANYTHING GOES   Paramount, 1956
THE BUSTER KEATON STORY   Paramount, 1957, w/Robert Smith, directed
ALL IN A NIGHT'S WORK   Paramount, 1961, w/Edmund Beloin & Maurice Richlin
JUMBO   BILLY ROSE'S JUMBO   MGM, 1962

RON SHELTON*
Agent: Sanford, Skouras, Gross & Associates - Los Angeles, 213/208-2100
Business: Raleigh Studios, 650 N. Bronson, Los Angeles, CA 90004, 213/462-5095

UNDER FIRE   Orion, 1983, w/Clayton Frohman
THE BEST OF TIMES   Universal, 1986
BULL DURHAM ★   Orion, 1988, directed
BLAZE   Buena Vista, 1989, directed

Screenplays:
WHITE MEN CAN'T JUMP (directing)
CENTERFOLD w/Nancy Dowd
BLUE CHIPS
ANTELOPE VALLEY
THE BUTTON
THE BOXER & THE BLONDE
TROPICANA

NINA SHENGOLD*
Agent: APA - New York, 212/582-1500

HOMESTEADERS (S)   also screenplay

Screenplays:
FREE LUNCH

RICHARD SHEPARD
COOL BLUE   Cinema Corp of America, 1990, w/Mark Mullin, co-directed

Screenplays:
THE LINGUINE INCIDENT w/Tamar Brott

SAM SHEPARD*
Agent: ICM - Los Angeles, 213/550-4000

RED CROSS (S)
A LIE OF THE MIND (S)
TRUE WEST (S)
BURIED CHILD (S)
CURSE OF THE STARVING CLASS (S)
SHAVED SPLITS (S)
MAD DOG BLUES (S)
THE UNSEEN HAND (S)
4-H CLUB (S)
SUICIDE IN B FLAT (S)
OPERATION: SIDEWINDER (S)
TOOTH OF CRIME (S)
MELODRAMA PLAY (S)
FORENSIC & THE NAVIGATOR (S)
LA TURISTA (S)
COWBOYS (S)
ROCK GARDEN (S)
SEDUCED (S)
STATES OF SHOCK (S)
ZABRISKIE POINT   MGM, 1970, w/Michelangelo Antonioni, Fred Gardner, Tonino Guerra & Clare Peploe
PARIS, TEXAS   TLC Films/20th Century-Fox, 1984
FOOL FOR LOVE   Cannon, 1985, from his play
FAR NORTH   Alive Films, 1988, directed

ROBIN SHEPHARD
Agent: The Wright Concept - Hollywood, 213/461-3844

Screenplays:
UNNATURAL HISTORY w/Steve Morris

CYBILL SHEPHERD
Agent: InterTalent - Los Angeles, 213/858-6200

MEMPHIS (CTF)   Turner Network Television, 1991, w/Larry McMurtry

JEAN P. SHEPHERD
A CHRISTMAS STORY   MGM/UA, 1983, w/Bob Clark & Leigh Brown

JOHN SHEPPARD*
Agent: Barry Perelman Agency - Los Angeles, 213/274-5999

BULLIES   Universal, 1986, w/Bryan McCann

Screenplays:
HIGHER EDUCATION w/H. Lieberman

JIM SHERIDAN
Agent: CAA - Beverly Hills, 213/288-4545
Business: Ferndale Films, Universal Pictures, 818/777-5851

MY LEFT FOOT ★   Miramax, 1989, w/Shane Connaughton, directed
THE FIELD   Avenue Pictures, 1990, directed

GARY A. SHERMAN*
Agent: Broder-Kurland-Webb-Uffner - Los Angeles, 213/656-9262

PHOBIA   Paramount, 1981, w/Peter Bellwood, Lew Lehman, James Sangster & Ronald Shusett
WANTED DEAD OR ALIVE   New World, 1986, w/Michael Patrick Goodman & Brian Taggert, directed
POLTERGEIST III   MGM/UA, 1988, w/Brian Taggert, directed
LISA   MGM/UA, 1990, w/Karen Clark, directed
AFTER THE SHOCK (CTF)   Wilshire Court Productions, 1990, directed

JEFFREY C. SHERMAN*
Agent: CAA - Beverly Hills, 213/288-4545

UP THE CREEK   Orion, 1983, Story w/Jim Kouf & Douglas Grossman

Screenplays:
CUT OUT
HOT DELIVERIES
SUMMER JOB
TEEN TOUR
REVERSE ANGEL

ROBERT SHERMAN*
Contact: WGA - Los Angeles, 213/550-1000

PICTURE MOMMY DEAD   Embassy, 1966

STANFORD L. SHERMAN*
Agent: Shapiro/Lichtman - Los Angeles, 213/859-8877

ANY WHICH WAY YOU CAN   Warner Bros., 1980
KRULL   Columbia, 1983
THE MAN WHO WASN'T THERE   Paramount, 1983
THE ICE PIRATES   MGM/UA, 1983, w/Stewart Raffill

Screenplays:
SEVENTH WORLD
SURPRISE OF THE DEEP

SWEETER THAN HONEY
KID KONG
TOM, NICK & MARY
UNDER PRESSURE
THE DISAPPEARANCE OF THE USS MAKO
SEPTEMBER RUN
THE NIGHT THAT REVEREND CLANCY'S HOME
ONE MORE SONG FOR JESUS
JAKE
THE SHEIKS OF ARABY
THE SABERS OF KANDAHAR
EMPIRES OF THE DEEP

TOM SHEROHMAN
MODERN PROBLEMS   20th Century-Fox, 1981,
   w/Arthur Sellers & Ken Shapiro

SUSAN SHILLIDAY*
Agent: United Talent Agency - Beverly Hills, 213/273-6700

Screenplays:
A WRINKLE IN TIME

COLIN SHINDLER
Agent: ICM - Los Angeles, 213/550-4000

BUSTER   Hemdale, 1988

MARC I. SHMUGER
DEAD OF WINTER   MGM/UA, 1987, w/Mark Malone

Screenplays:
KING OF AMERICA

JACK SHOLDER*
Agent: ICM - Los Angeles, 213/550-4000

THE TATTOOED HITMAN   New Line Cinema, 1977
ALONE IN THE DARK   New Line Cinema, 1982, directed
WHERE ARE THE CHILDREN   Columbia, 1986

MICHAEL SHOOB*
Contact: WGA - Los Angeles, 213/550-1000

PARASITE   Embassy, 1982, w/Alan J. Adler & Frank Levering

FREDERIC SHORE*
Agent: ICM - Los Angeles, 213/550-4000

SURVIVAL RUN   *SPREE*   Film Ventures, 1978,
   w/G.M. Cahill & Larry Spiegel

SIG SHORE*
Contact: WGA - New York, 212/245-6180

SUDDEN DEATH   Marvin Films, 1985, directed

DEL SHORES*
Agent: Artists Circle Entertainment - Los Angeles, 213/275-6330
Business: Warner Bros. TV, 818/954-3135

CHEATIN' (S)
DADDY'S DYIN'...WHO'S GOT THE WILL   MGM/UA, 1990, from his play

MICHAEL J. SHORT*
Contact: WGA - Los Angeles, 213/550-1000

SPEED ZONE   Orion, 1989

ROBERT SHORT*
Agent: Barry Perelman Agency - Los Angeles, 213/274-5999
Business: Robert Short Productions, 4228 Glencoe Avenue, Marina del Rey, CA, 90292, 213/306-6842

RAGE OF HONOR   Trans World Entertainment, 1987, w/Wallace Bennet
PROGRAMMED TO KILL   Trans World Entertainment, 1987, co-directed

Screenplays:
A.I.

EDWIN (BUD) SHRAKE*
Agent: ICM - Los Angeles, 213/550-4000

J.W. COOP   Columbia, 1972, w/Gary Cartwright & Cliff Robertson
KID BLUE   20th Century-Fox, 1973
NIGHTWING   Columbia, 1979, w/Steve Shagan
TOM HORN   Warner Bros., 1980, w/Thomas McGuane
SONGWRITER   Tri-Star, 1984

Screenplays:
FLAT OUT SPEED w/Dan Jenkins
SLIM & NONE w/Dan Jenkins
LOOSE WOMEN w/Dan Jenkins
DAMN YANKEES w/Dan Jenkins
DINOSAUR WINE w/Dan Jenkins
LIMO w/Dan Jenkins
RIP w/G. Cartwright
THE BIG MAMOO
FIRST AMONG THE BEST

DON SHROLL*
Agent: Susan Smith & Associates - Beverly Hills, 213/852-4777

Screenplays:
THE BLUE TRAIN
AN ECLIPSE OF MEN
THE GIFT

DENNIS SHRYACK*
Agent: Harold R. Greene, Inc. - Los Angeles, 213/852-4959

THE GOOD GUYS AND THE BAD GUYS   Warner Bros., 1969, w/Ronald M. Cohen
THE CAR   Universal, 1977, w/Michael Butler & Lane Slate
THE GAUNTLET   Warner Bros., 1977, w/Michael Butler
MURDER BY PHONE   New World, 1982, w/Michael Butler & John Kent Harrison
FLASHPOINT   Tri-Star, 1984, w/Michael Butler
PALE RIDER   Warner Bros., 1985, w/Michael Butler
CODE OF SILENCE   Orion, 1985, w/Michael Butler & Mike Gray
RENT-A-COP   Kings Road, 1988, w/Michael Blodgett
HERO AND THE TERROR   Cannon, 1988, w/Michael Blodgett
TURNER & HOOCH   Buena Vista, 1989, w/Michael Blodgett, Jim Cash & Jack Epps

Sh

FILM WRITERS GUIDE

CADENCE   New Line Cinema, 1990, w/Martin Sheen
RUN   Buena Vista, 1991, w/Michael Blodgett

Screenplays:
50-50 w/Michael Blodgett
THE EXECUTIONER w/Michael Blodgett
THE DOC AND DONNA w/Bill Peterson

RONALD SHUSETT*
Agent: ICM - Los Angeles, 213/550-4000

W   Cinerama Releasing Corporation, 1974, Story w/James Kelly
ALIEN   20th Century-Fox, 1979, Story
DEAD AND BURIED   Avco Embassy, 1981, w/Dan O'Bannon
PHOBIA   Paramount, 1981, w/Peter Bellwood, Lew Lehman, James Sangster & Gary Sherman
THE FINAL TERROR   Comworld, 1983, w/Jon George & Neill Hicks
KING KONG LIVES   DEG, 1986, w/Steven Pressfield
ABOVE THE LAW   Warner Bros., 1988, w/Andrew Davis & Steven Pressfield
TOTAL RECALL   Tri-Star, 1990, w/Gary Goldman & Dan O'Bannon

Screenplays:
FREEJACK w/Steven Pressfield
JANUARY HOUR
THE BIG SCORE

ROSIE SHUSTER
Agent: The Gersh Agency - Beverly Hills, 213/274-6611

GILDA LIVE (FD)   Warner Bros., 1980, w/others

Screenplays:
THE DISAPPEARANCE w/Richard Maxwell
MR. DARLING w/Margaret Oberman
BAD GIRLS w/Nell Cox
JUST IN TIME
MY GIRLFRIEND'S BOYFRIEND
WHAT I DID WITH THE PRESIDENT'S DAUGHTER

NEAL D. SHUSTERMAN*
Agent: Irvin Arthur Associates - Beverly Hills, 213/278-5934

TIME SCAVENGERS   New Line Cinema, 1990

Screenplays:
DISSIDENTS
PILGRIMAGE
EYES OF KID MIDAS
SHADOW CLUB
BRIDGES BURNED
HIDE AND SEEK

CHARLES SHYER*
Agent: ICM - Los Angeles, 213/550-4000

SMOKEY AND THE BANDIT   Universal, 1977, w/James Lee Barrett & Alan Mandel
GOIN' SOUTH   Paramount, 1978, w/Alan Mandel, John Herman Shaner & Al Ramrus
HOUSE CALLS   Universal, 1978, w/ Alan Mandel & Max Shulman
PRIVATE BENJAMIN ★   Warner Bros., 1980, w/Harvey Miller & Nancy Myers
IRRECONCILABLE DIFFERENCES   Warner Bros., 1984, w/Nancy Myers, directed
PROTOCOL   Warner Bros., 1984, Story w/Harvey Miller & Nancy Myers
BABY BOOM   MGM/UA, 1987, w/Nancy Myers, directed

Screenplays:
FATHER OF THE BRIDE w/Nancy Myers (directing)
CRIMINALS w/Nancy Myers
BREAKFAST ON BEDFORD DRIVE w/Alan Mandel
THE LONG RAINBOW w/Alan Mandel
BIG DEAL ON MACARTHUR BOULEVARD w/Alan Mandel
TICKETS w/Alan Mandel

ANDY SIDARIS*
Business: The Sidaris Company, 9229 Sunset Boulevard, Suite 208, Los Angeles, CA, 90069, 213/278-5056

STACEY   New World, 1973, directed
SEVEN   American International, 1979, directed
MALIBU EXPRESS   Malibu Bay Films, 1984, directed
HARD TICKET TO HAWAII   Malibu Bay Films, 1987, directed
PICASSO TRIGGER   Malibu Bay Films, 1988, directed
SAVAGE BEACH   Malibu Bay Films, 1989, directed
GUNS   Malibu Bay Films, 1990, directed
DO OR DIE   Malibu Bay Films, 1991, directed

ABDULAH SIDRAN
WHEN FATHER WAS AWAY ON BUSINESS   Cannon, 1985

LYNN SIEFERT*
Agent: CAA - Beverly Hills, 213/288-4545

Screenplays:
BLUE MAAGA
PLUTO BY JOEY
SYLVIE

ROBERT SIEGAL*
Contact: WGA - New York, 212/245-6180

DESCENDING ANGEL (CTF)   Fredya Rothstein, 1990, w/Alan Sharp & Grace Woodard

BARRY SIEGEL
WINDOWS   United Artists, 1980

GERALD KAY SIEGEL*
Agent: David Shapira & Associates - Sherman Oaks, 818/906-0322

Screenplays:
FUTBOL

STEVE SIEGEL*
Agent: United Talent Agency - Beverly Hills, 213/273-6700

Screenplays:
THE MAN WHO KILLED SHERLOCK HOLMES

STEVEN JAY SIEGEL*
Contact: 213/558-6360

K-9   Universal, 1989, w/Scott Myers

MARC SIEGLER
GALAXY OF TERROR   New World, 1981, w/Bruce Clark

JOEL SILBERG*
Agent: The Gersh Agency - Beverly Hills, 213/274-6611

LAMBADA   Warner Bros., 1990, w/Sheldon
   Renan, directed

JAMES R. SILKE*
Agent: The Morton Agency - Los Angeles, 213/824-4089

REVENGE OF THE NINJA   MGM/UA/Cannon, 1983
SAHARA   MGM/UA, 1984
NINJA III: THE DOMINATION   Cannon, 1984
KING SOLOMON'S MINES   Cannon, 1985,
   w/Eugene Quintano
THE BARBARIANS   Cannon, 1987

STIRLING SILLIPHANT*
Agent: CAA - Beverly Hills, 213/288-4545

FIVE AGAINST THE HOUSE   Columbia, 1955,
   w/John Barnwell
HUK!   United Artists, 1956
NIGHTFALL   Columbia, 1956
THE LINEUP   Columbia, 1958
VILLAGE OF THE DAMNED   MGM, 1960, w/Geoffrey
   Barclay & Wolf Rilla
THE SLENDER THREAD   Paramount, 1966
IN THE HEAT OF THE NIGHT ★★   United Artists, 1967
CHARLY   Cinerama Releasing Corporation, 1968
MARLOWE   MGM, 1969
THE LIBERATION OF L.B. JONES   Columbia, 1970,
   w/Jesse Hill Ford
A WALK IN THE SPRING RAIN   Columbia, 1970
MURPHY'S WAR   Paramount, 1971
THE NEW CENTURIONS   Columbia, 1972
THE POSEIDON ADVENTURE   20th Century-Fox,
   1972, w/Wendell Mayes
SHAFT IN AFRICA   MGM, 1973
THE TOWERING INFERNO   20th Century-Fox, 1974
THE KILLER ELITE   United Artists, 1975,
   w/Marc Norman
THE ENFORCER   Warner Bros., 1976, w/Dean Reisner
TELEFON   MGM/UA, 1977, w/Peter Hyams
THE SWARM   Warner Bros., 1978
THE SILENT FLUTE   Volare, 1978, w/Stanley Mann
CIRCLE OF IRON   Avco Embassy, 1979,
   w/Stanley Mann
WHEN TIME RAN OUT   Warner Bros., 1980,
   w/Carl Foreman
OVER THE TOP   Cannon, 1987, w/Sylvester Stallone
CATCH THE HEAT   Trans World Entertainment, 1987

Screenplays:
SOJOURNERS
HIERO'S JOURNEY
PUMA
WEATHER WAR
THE GREAT COLORADO RIVER MARATHON
PUZZLE

ALAN SILLITOE
Contact: British Academy of Film & Television Arts,
   195 Piccadilly, London W1, England, 71/734-0022

SATURDAY NIGHT AND SUNDAY MORNING
   Bryanston, 1960
THE LONELINESS OF THE LONG DISTANCE RUNNER
   British Lion, 1962
THE RAGMAN'S DAUGHTER   Independent, 1974

AMANDA SILVER*
Agent: William Morris Agency - Beverly Hills,
   213/274-7451

Screenplays:
THE HAND THAT ROCKS THE CRADLE

ARTHUR SILVER*
Agent: ICM - Los Angeles, 213/550-4000

MISSING IN ACTION 2: THE BEGINNING   Cannon,
   1985, w/Larry Levinson & Steve Bing

Screenplays:
THE BUST OUT KING

FRANELLE SILVER*
Agent: The Parness Agency - Los Angeles,
   213/273-2233

DOIN' TIME   The Ladd Company/Warner Bros., 1984,
   w/Dee Caruso & Ron Zwang

Screenplays:
SOLDIERS OF MISFORTUNE

JOAN MICKLIN SILVER*
Agent: Broder-Kurland-Webb-Uffner - Los Angeles,
   213/656-9262
Business: Midwest Film Productions, 600 Madison Avenue,
   New York, NY 10022, 212/355-0282

LIMBO   Universal, 1972, w/James Bridges
HESTER STREET   Midwest Film Productions,
   1975, directed
HEAD OVER HEELS   CHILLY SCENES OF WINTER
   United Artists, 1979, directed

Screenplays:
FUN WHILE IT LASTED w/Fred Barron
MEDALLION w/Vicki Polon

MARISA SILVER*
Agent: ICM - Los Angeles, 213/550-4000

OLD ENOUGH   Orion Classics, 1984, directed

STU SILVER*
Agent: CAA - Beverly Hills, 213/288-4545

THROW MOMMA FROM THE TRAIN   Orion, 1987

Screenplays:
NIGHT ON THE TOWN
NUTTY PROFESSOR II

DAVID A. SILVERMAN*
Agent: Robinson, Weintraub, Gross & Associates -
   Los Angeles, 213/653-5802

Screenplays:
STEPPING OUT

JACK SILVERMAN
CRACK HOUSE   Cannon, 1989, Story

PETER SILVERMAN*
Contact: WGA - Los Angeles, 213/550-1000

WHERE THE RIVER RUNS BLACK   MGM/UA, 1986, w/Neal Jimenez

Screenplays:
AMERICAN HEART

SHEL SILVERSTEIN
Agent: Sheldon Zididor, 2553 N. Atlantic Ave. - Suite 10, Daytona Beach, FL

THINGS CHANGE   Columbia, 1988, w/David Mamet

LINDA SILVERTHORN
BEVERLY HILLS BRATS   Taurus Entertainment, 1989

DAVID SIMKINS*
Agent: Triad Artists, Inc. - Los Angeles, 213/556-2727

ADVENTURES IN BABYSITTING   Buena Vista, 1987

Screenplays:
GRAVITY GUY
SUSPECT BEHAVIOR

ANTHONY SIMMONS
Agent: Hatton and Baker - London, 71/439-2971
Business: West One Film Producers Ltd., c/o Robert Rosner, Palladium House, 1-4 Argyll St., London W1, England

FOUR IN THE MORNING   West One, 1965, directed
THE OPTIMISTS   *THE OPTIMISTS OF NINE ELMS*   Paramount, 1973, directed
BLACK JOY   Hemdale, 1977, w/Jamal Ali, directed

GARNER SIMMONS*
Agent: Wile Enterprises, Inc. - Los Angeles, 213/828-9768

RARE BREED   New World, 1984

Screenplays:
A WITNESS TO MURDER
STRIKER
THE LAST WESTERN
TITAN
THE ORACLE OF MERMAID AVENUE

REDBEARD SIMMONS
Agent: William Morris Agency - Beverly Hills, 213/274-7451

MEET THE APPLEGATES   *THE APPLEGATES*   Triton Pictures, 1990, w/Michael Lehmann

Screenplays:
LE SURF HOT   w/Michael Lehmann
OUT OF THE BOX

ADAM SIMON
Agent: ICM - Los Angeles, 213/550-4000

BRAIN DEAD   Concorde, 1989, w/Charles Beaumont, directed

DAVID SIMON*
Agent: CAA - Beverly Hills, 213/288-4545

IN THE MOOD   Lorimar, 1987, Story w/Bob Kosberg & Phil Alden Robinson

MAYO SIMON*
Agent: Barrett, Benson, McCartt & Weston - Los Angeles, 213/247-5500

DOUBLE MURDER AND SUICIDE (S)
THESE MEN (S)
L.A. UNDER SIEGE (S)
WALKING TO WALDHEIM (S)
ELAINE'S DAUGHTER (S)
ANGEL (S)
I COULD GO ON SINGING   United Artists, 1963
MAROONED   Columbia, 1969
PHASE IV   Paramount, 1973
FUTUREWORLD   American International, 1976, w/George Schenck

NEIL SIMON*
Agent: CAA - Beverly Hills, 213/288-4545
Personal Manager: Albert DaSilva - New York, 212/752-9323

COME BLOW YOUR HORN (S)
FOOLS (S)
THE STAR SPANGLED GIRL (S)
SWEET CHARITY (S)
LITTLE ME (S)
PROMISES, PROMISES (S)
BROADWAY BOUND (S)
JAKE'S WOMEN (S)
LOST IN YONKERS (S), also screenplay
AFTER THE FOX   United Artists, 1966, w/Cesare Zavattini
BAREFOOT IN THE PARK   Paramount, 1967, from his play
THE ODD COUPLE ★   Paramount, 1968, from his play
THE OUT-OF-TOWNERS   Paramount, 1970
PLAZA SUITE   Paramount, 1971, from his play, also teleplay
LAST OF THE RED HOT LOVERS   Paramount, 1972, from his play
THE HEARTBREAK KID   20th Century-Fox, 1972
THE PRISONER OF SECOND AVENUE   Warner Bros., 1975, from his play
THE SUNSHINE BOYS ★   MGM/UA, 1975, from his play
MURDER BY DEATH   Columbia, 1976
THE GOODBYE GIRL ★   Warner Bros., 1977
CALIFORNIA SUITE ★   Columbia, 1978, from his play
THE CHEAP DETECTIVE   Columbia, 1978
CHAPTER TWO   Columbia, 1979, from his play
SEEMS LIKE OLD TIMES   20th Century-Fox, 1980
ONLY WHEN I LAUGH   Columbia, 1981, from his play "The Gingerbread Lady"
I OUGHT TO BE IN PICTURES   20th Century-Fox, 1982
MAX DUGAN RETURNS   20th Century-Fox, 1983
THE SLUGGER'S WIFE   Columbia, 1985
BRIGHTON BEACH MEMOIRS   Universal, 1986, from his play
BILOXI BLUES   Universal, 1988, from his play
THE MARRYING MAN   Buena Vista, 1991

Screenplays:
MY SON'S BROTHER
MR. BAD NEWS

PAUL SIMON*
Contact: WGA - New York, 212/245-6180

ONE TRICK PONY   Warner Bros., 1980

ROGER L. SIMON*
Agent: United Talent Agency - Beverly Hills, 213/273-6700

THE BIG FIX   Universal, 1978
BUSTIN' LOOSE   Universal, 1981
MY MAN ADAM   Tri-Star, 1985, w/Renee Missel, directed
ENEMIES, A LOVE STORY ★   20th Century Fox, 1989, w/Paul Mazursky
SCENES FROM A MALL   Buena Vista, 1991, w/Paul Mazursky

Screenplays:
GOLDEN GATE w/Dyanne Assimow
IN A WILD SANCTUARY w/Dyanne Assimow
BLOOD TIES
THE MENTAL CASE
BAD DEATH
FINAL ANALYSIS
PICTURES OF FIDELMAN
THE GARDNER
THE STRAIGHT MAN
JENNIFER ON MY MIND
MOSES WINE
CAFE LUXEMBOURG

SAM SIMON*
Agent: InterTalent - Los Angeles, 213/858-6200
Business: Gracie Films, 20th Century Fox, 213/203-3770

THE SUPER   20th Century-Fox, 1991,

Screenplays:
BEETLE BAILEY

P.K. SIMONDS*
Agent: United Talent Agency - Beverly Hills, 213/273-6700

Screenplays:
BEVERLY HILLS BODY SNATCHERS

A.R. SIMOUN
(See Adam Rodman)

EDWARD SIMPSON
Agent: The Agency - Los Angeles, 213/551-3000

RIVER OF DEATH   Cannon, 1989, w/Andrew Deutsch

GEORGE E. SIMPSON*
Agent: APA - Los Angeles, 213/273-0744

ROADHOUSE 66   Atlantic Releasing Corporation, 1984, w/Galen Lee

Screenplays:
UP THE GARDEN PATH w/Neal Burger
GHOSTBOAT w/Neal Burger
DAN HAZARD AND THE LEGEND OF EVIL w/Neal Burger
SPIDER BOY
THE CRIMSON KISS
A TOUCH OF THE COWBOY
NO HIGHWAY ON EARTH

ROGER SIMPSON
SQUIZZY TAYLOR   Satori, 1984
DARLINGS OF THE GODS (CMS)   Simpson LeMesurier Films/Australian Broadcasting Corporation/Thames Television, 1991, w/Graeme Farmer

ANDREW SINCLAIR
Contact: British Academy of Film & Television Arts, 195 Piccadilly, London W1, England, 71/732-0022

BEFORE WINTER COMES   Columbia, 1968
UNDER MILK WOOD   Altura, 1973, directed
BLUE BLOOD   Mallard Productions, 1975, directed

JOSHUA SINCLAIR
JUST A GIGOLO   United Artists Classics, 1981
LILI MARLEEN   United Artists Classics, 1981, w/Manfred Purzer
JUDGMENT IN BERLIN   New Line Cinema, 1988, w/Leo Penn

BRUCE FRANKLIN SINGER*
Agent: Broder-Kurland-Webb-Uffner - Los Angeles, 213/656-9262

MEATBALLS PART II   Tri-Star, 1984
THE KILLING TIME   New World, 1987, w/Don Bohlinger & James Nathan

RANDI MAYEM SINGER*
Agent: Triad Artists, Inc. - Los Angeles, 213/556-2727

Screenplays:
TWO BIT ROMANCE w/June Roberts

JOHN SINGLETON
Agent: CAA - Beverly Hills, 213/288-4545

BOYZ N THE HOOD   Columbia, 1991, directed

Screenplays:
THE CHAMP (CTF) (directing)
TWILIGHT TIME

CURT SIODMAK*
Contact: WGA - Los Angeles, 213/550-1000

THE WOLF MAN   Universal, 1940
THE APE   Monogram, 1940, w/Richard Carroll
BLACK FRIDAY   Universal, 1940, w/Eric Taylor
THE CLIMAX   Universal, 1944, w/Lynn Starling
THE BEAST WITH FIVE FINGERS   Warner Bros., 1946
BRIDE OF THE GORILLA   Jack Broder Productions, 1953, directed
RIDERS TO THE STARS   United Artists, 1954
THE CREATURE WITH THE ATOM BRAIN   Columbia, 1955
CURUCU, BEAST OF THE AMAZON   Universal, 1956
EARTH VERSUS THE FLYING SAUCERS   Columbia, 1956, Story

ROSEMARY ANNE SISSON*
Contact: Andrew Mann, 01/734-4751

ESCAPE FROM THE DARK   Buena Vista, 1976
CANDLESHOE   Buena Vista, 1977, w/David Swift
THE WATCHER IN THE WOODS   Buena Vista, 1980, w/Brian Clemens & Harry Spalding

Si

HAL SITOWITZ*
Agent: Triad Artists, Inc. - Los Angeles, 213/556-2727

Screenplays:
BENNY'S HEIR

JOHN SKIPP
A NIGHTMARE ON ELM STREET, PART V: THE DREAM CHILD   New Line Cinema, 1989, Story w/Leslie Bohem & Craig Spector

JERZY SKOLIMOWSKI
Agent: ICM - Los Angeles, 213/550-4000

KNIFE IN THE WATER   Kanuala, 1963, w/Jakub Goldberg & Roman Polanski
DEEP END   Paramount, 1971, w/Jerzy Gruza & Boleslaw Sulik, directed
THE SHOUT   Films Inc., 1979, w/Michael Austin, directed
MOONLIGHTING   Universal Classics, 1982, directed
MESMERIZED   RKO/Challenge Corp., 1984, Story
SUCCESS IS THE BEST REVENGE   Triumph/Columbia, 1984, w/Michael Lyndon, directed
TORRENTS OF SPRING   Millimeter Films, 1990, w/Arcangelo Bonaccorso, directed

Screenplays:
FERDYDURKE
ANGEL FACE

ROBERT F. SKOTAK*
Agent: The Chasin Agency - Beverly Hills, 213/278-7505

Screenplays:
RESURRECTUS w/Lynn Barker
CYCLOPS w/Nicholas Seldon

GEORGE FRANCIS SKROW
BACK TO BACK   Concorde, 1990

BERNARD SLADE*
Agent: APA - Los Angeles, 213/273-0744

FATAL ATTRACTION (S)
STAND UP AND BE COUNTED   Columbia, 1971
SAME TIME, NEXT YEAR ★   Universal, 1978, from his play
TRIBUTE   20th Century-Fox, 1980, from his play
ROMANTIC COMEDY   MGM/UA, 1983, from his play

STEVEN D. SLAVKIN*
Agent: William Morris Agency - Beverly Hills, 213/274-7451

Screenplays:
TALKING TO THE MOOSE
CUTTING CLASS

EVAN SLAWSON
A HOLLYWOOD STORY   Double Helix Films, 1991, w/Tony Zarindast

HOLLY GOLDBERG SLOAN*
Agent: Sanford, Skouras, Gross & Associates - Los Angeles, 213/208-2100

Screenplays:
IT HAD TO BE STEVE w/Amy Jones & Tracy Keenan Wynn
CHANGE OF HEART
BUMPTIOUS

MICHAEL SLOAN*
Agent: ICM - Los Angeles, 213/550-4000

Screenplays:
THE CALLER

RICK SLOANE
VICE ACADEMY   Rick Sloane Productions, 1989, directed

JAMES SLOCUM
AN AMERICAN SUMMER   Boss Entertainment Group, 1991, directed

SHAWN SLOVO
Agent: United Talent Agency - Beverly Hills, 213/273-6700

A WORLD APART   Atlantic Releasing Corporation, 1988

Screenplays:
JAMIE
ORPHAN TRAIN

ERIC SMALL
Agent: Writers & Artists Agency - Los Angeles, 213/820-2240

Screenplays:
RUBICON
HOURGLASS
PURPLE KNIGHT RANGERS
DUAL FORCE

PETER SMALLEY
DEAD END DRIVE-IN   New World, 1986

DAVID H. SMILOW*
Agent: Warden & White Associates - Beverly Hills, 213/852-1028

SPRING BREAK   Columbia, 1983

Screenplays:
DIRTY SECRETS
DREAM TIME
END OF THE LINE
LOST VEGAS
UPWARD BOUND
SMALL WORLD

ANDREW SMITH*
Agent: Richland/Wunsch/Hohman Agency - Los Angeles, 213/278-1955

ANYTHING, ANYTHING (S)
THE MAIN EVENT   Warner Bros., 1979, w/Gail Parent
WHO'S THAT GIRL   Warner Bros., 1987, w/Ken Finkelman

Screenplays:
40 REGULAR
ACE BANDAGE

APRIL SMITH*
Agent: InterTalent - Los Angeles, 213/858-6200

Screenplays:
VIETNAM NURSES

BRADLEY RAND SMITH
Agent: Circle Talent Associates - Beverly Hills, 213/285-1585

MOJAVE (S)

Screenplays:
IN A WORKMANLIKE MANNER
THE DESCENT
THE BLUES
THE QUIET

DAVID SMITH*
Contact: WGA - Los Angeles, 213/550-1000

Screenplays:
TUXEDO PARK
SAVAGES
AGAINST THE WIND

EBBE ROE SMITH*
Agent: Circle Talent Associates - Beverly Hills, 213/285-1585

HOW MUCH WOULD CHUCK (S) also screenplay

Screenplays:
CAR 54, WHERE ARE YOU?
DREAMING OF BABYLON
THE START OVER
FALLING DOWN
THE MIDDLE PEOPLE

GREG P. SMITH
THE LAST WORD   Samuel Goldwyn Company, 1979, w/L.M. Kit Carson & Michael Varhol

HUBERT SMITH
MOONSHINE COUNTY EXPRESS   New World, 1977, w/Daniel Ansley
OUT OF THE DARKNESS   NIGHT CREATURES   Dimension, 1978
THE GLOVE   Pro International, 1981, w/Julian Roffman

JOSHUA SMITH*
Contact: WGA - Los Angeles, 213/550-1000

Screenplays:
RED SCARE w/Murray Mintz

LANCE SMITH
MUNCHIES   Concorde, 1987

MARK ALLEN SMITH*
Agent: William Morris Agency - New York, 212/586-5100

Screenplays:
COLD AS ICE
ROCK AND A HARD PLACE
BLACK AND WHITE
PLAYIN' IN THE BAND
SLOW BURN

MARTIN J. SMITH*
Agent: Kaplan-Stahler Agency - Beverly Hills, 213/653-4483

UNDER THE RAINBOW   Orion/Warner Bros., 1981, w/Pat McCormick, Harry Hurwitz, Pat Bradley & Fred Bauer

MEL SMITH
Contact: British Academy of Film & Television Arts, 195 Piccadilly, London W1, England, 01/734-0022

MORONS FROM OUTER SPACE   Universal, 1985, w/Griff Rhys-Jones

MURRAY SMITH
BEAR ISLAND   Taft Inernational, 1980, w/David Butler & Don Sharp

NOELLA SMITH
SECRETS   Samuel Goldwyn Company, 1984

RICHARD B. SMITH*
Agent: ICM - Los Angeles, 213/550-4000

LOCK UP   Tri-Star, 1989, w/Henry Rosenbaum & Jeb Stuart

Screenplays:
THE BEST OF THE FINEST
WILD BLUE

ROBERT SMITH*
Agent: Paul Kohner, Inc. - Los Angeles, 213/550-1060

XTRO   New Line Cinema, 1983, w/Iain Cassie

STEVEN PHILIP SMITH*
Agent: ICM - Los Angeles, 213/550-4000

THE LONG RIDERS   United Artists, 1980, w/Bill Bryden, James Keach & Stacy Keach
CHATTANOOGA CHOO CHOO   April Fools, 1984, w/Robert Mundy

WILBUR SMITH
SHOUT AT THE DEVIL   American International, 1976, w/Stanley Price & Alistair Reid

STEPHEN SMOKE
Agent: Circle Talent Associates - Beverly Hills, 213/285-1585

LIVING TO DIE   PM Entertainment, 1990

Screenplays:
SHADE
DELIVER US FROM EVIL
VOICES IN THE NIGHT

DENNIS SNEE*
Agent: Shapiro/Lichtman - Los Angeles, 213/859-8877

BACK TO SCHOOL   Orion, 1986, Story w/Rodney Dangerfield & Greg Fields

JEFFREY M. SNELLER
IN THE SHADOW OF KILIMANJARO   Scotti Bros., 1986, w/T. Michael Harry

NORMAN SNIDER*
Agent: Thal Literary Management - Los Angeles, 213/659-4946

PARTNERS   Astral Films, 1976, w/Dan Owen
DEAD RINGERS   20th Century Fox, 1989, w/David Cronenberg
BODY PARTS   Paramount, 1991, w/Larry Gross & Eric Red

SUSAN SNOOKS
THE CARE BEARS ADVENTURE IN WONDERLAND (AF)
    Cineplex Odeon, 1987, w/John DeKlein

BLAKE SNYDER*
Agent: Writers & Artists Agency - Los Angeles,
    213/820-2240

Screenplays:
STOP OR MY MOM WILL SHOOT

STEVEN SODERBERGH*
Agent: United Talent Agency - Beverly Hills, 213/273-6700

OCTOBER 16, 1977 (Short), directed
PASSAGES (Short), directed
JANITOR (Short), directed
SKOAL (Short), directed
RAPID EYE MOVEMENT (Short), directed
WINSTON (Short), directed
sex, lies and videotape ★   Miramax, 1989, directed

Screenplays:
THE LAST SHIP
REVOLVER
DEAD FROM THE NECK UP
CROSSTALK
STATE OF MIND
PROOF POSITIVE

GERARD SOETEMAN*
Agent: The Marion Rosenberg Office - Los Angeles,
    213/653-7383

MAX HAVELAAR   1976
SOLDIER OF ORANGE   Samuel Goldwyn Company,
    1977, w/Kees Holierhoek & Paul Verhoeven
SPETTERS   Samuel Goldwyn Company, 1981
THE FOURTH MAN   Spectrafilm, 1984
FLESH + BLOOD   Orion, 1985, w/Paul Verhoeven
THE ASSAULT   Cannon, 1986

Screenplays:
JUDGE DEE

JOEL SOISSON*
Business: Soisson Murphey Productions, 9060 Santa
    Monica Blvd. - Suite 210, Los Angeles, CA, 90069,
    213/273-3157

HAMBONE AND HILLIE   New World, 1984, w/Sandra K.
    Bailey & Michael S. Murphey
THE SUPERNATURALS   Republic Entertainment/Sandy
    Howard Productions, 1985, w/Michael S. Murphey
TRICK OR TREAT   DEG, 1986, w/Michael S. Murphey &
    Rhet Topham

FERNANDO E. SOLANAS
Contact: French Film Office, 745 Fifth Avenue, New York,
    NY, 10151, 212/832-8860

TANGOS: THE EXILE OF GARDEL   New Yorker,
    1986, directed

FRANCO SOLINAS
KAPO   Vides, 1960, w/Gillo Pontecorvo
SALVATORE GIULIANO   Lux, 1961, w/others
BURN! *QUELMADA!*   PEA, 1968, w/Giorgio Arlorio

THE BATTLE OF ALGIERS ★   Allied Artists, 1968,
    w/Gillo Pontecorvo
MR. KLEIN   Quartet, 1977
HANNA K.   Universal, 1983

KENNY A. SOLMS*
Agent: ICM - Los Angeles, 213/550-4000

SHEILA LEVINE IS DEAD AND LIVING IN NEW YORK
    Paramount, 1975, w/Gail Parent

Screenplays:
TEARJERKER
OH SISTER

AUBREY SOLOMON*
Agent: Shapiro/Lichtman - Los Angeles, 213/859-8877

DEFENSE PLAY   Trans World Entertainment, 1988,
    w/Steven Greenberg

ED SOLOMON*
Agent: CAA - Beverly Hills, 213/288-4545

BILL & TED'S EXCELLENT ADVENTURE   Orion, 1989,
    w/Chris Matheson
BILL & TED'S BOGUS JOURNEY   Orion, 1991,
    w/Chris Matheson

Screenplays:
LEAVING NORMAL
THE UNBELIEVABLES

TODD SOLONDZ
Contact: Frankfurt, Garbus, Klein & Selz - New York,
    212/980-0120

FEAR, ANXIETY AND DEPRESSION   Samuel Goldwyn
    Company, 1989, directed

ANDREW SOLT*
Business: Andrew Solt Productions, 9121 Sunset Blvd.,
    Los Angeles, CA, 90069, 213/276-9522

THIS IS ELVIS (FD)   Warner Bros., 1981, w/Malcolm Leo,
    co-directed
IMAGINE: JOHN LENNON (FD)   Warner Bros., 1988,
    w/Sam Egan, directed

ARNOLD SOMKIN
OVER THE BROOKLYN BRIDGE   MGM/UA/Cannon, 1984

STEPHEN SOMMERS*
Agent: United Talent Agency - Beverly Hills, 213/273-6700

CATCH ME IF YOU CAN   MCEG, 1989, directed

STEPHEN SONDHEIM
Contact: ASCAP - Los Angeles, 213/466-7681

THE LAST OF SHIELA   Warner Bros., 1973,
    w/Anthony Perkins

SHERRIE SONNETT
BELOW THE BELT   Atlantic Releasing Corporation, 1980,
    w/Robert Fowler

MICHAEL D. SONYE
COMMANDO SQUAD   Trans World Entertainment, 1987
BLOOD DINER   Lightning Pictures, 1987
COLD STEEL   CineTel Films, 1987, w/Moe Quigley
OUT ON BAIL   Trans World Entertainment, 1989,
    w/Jason Booth & Tom Badal

TRISH B. SOODIK*
Agent: William Morris Agency - Beverly Hills, 213/274-7451

Screenplays:
THE BLUE PARROT
MARRYING UP
HOME IN ROME (CTF)
CAN'T GET ENOUGH
SHADES

AARON SORKIN
Agent: CAA - Beverly Hills, 213/288-4545

A FEW GOOD MEN (S), also screenplay
MAKING MOVIES (S)

Screenplays:
DAMAGES
LIP STATE

MARC D. SOTKIN*
Agent: ICM - Los Angeles, 213/550-4000

Screenplays:
WITCH DOCTOR

TERRY SOUTHERN*
Contact: WGA - Los Angeles, 213/550-1000

DR. STRANGELOVE OR; HOW I LEARNED TO STOP
    WORRYING AND LOVE THE BOMB ★   Columbia,
    1964, w/Peter George & Stanley Kubrick
THE CINCINNATI KID   MGM, 1965, w/Ring Lardner, Jr.
THE LOVED ONE   MGM, 1965,
    w/Christopher Isherwood
BARBARELLA   Paramount, 1968
EASY RIDER ★   Columbia, 1969, w/Peter Fonda &
    Dennis Hopper
END OF THE ROAD   Allied Artists, 1970, w/Avram
    Avakian & D. MacGuire
THE MAGIC CHRISTIAN   Commonwealth United,
    1970, w/Joseph McGrath & Peter Sellers
THE TELEPHONE   New World, 1988, w/Harry Nilsson

Screenplays:
OBITS w/Harry Nilsson
EASY RIDER 2   BIKER HEAVEN
BLUE MOVIE
FLOATERS
GROSSING OUT

MICK SOUTHWORTH
TANK MALLING   Pointlane Films, 1989,
    w/James Marcus

JACK B. SOWARDS*
Agent: Barrett, Benson, McCartt & Weston - Los Angeles,
    213/247-5500

STAR TREK II: THE WRATH OF KHAN
    Paramount, 1982

HARRY SPALDING*
Contact: WGA - Los Angeles, 213/550-1000

HOUSE OF THE DAMNED   20th Century-Fox, 1963
WITCHCRAFT   20th Century-Fox, 1l964
ONE LITTLE INDIAN   Buena Vista, 1973
THE WATCHER IN THE WOODS   Buena Vista, 1980,
    w/Brian Clemens & Rosemary Anne Sisson

JAN SPEARS
GAME OF DEATH   Columbia, 1979

KATHERINE SPECKTOR
Agent: Richland/Wunsch/Hohman Agency - Los Angeles,
    213/278-1955

LOVE CHILD   The Ladd Company/Warner Bros., 1982,
    w/Anne Gerard

CRAIG SPECTOR
A NIGHTMARE ON ELM STREET, PART V: THE DREAM
    CHILD   New Line Cinema, 1989, Story w/Leslie Bohem
    & John Skipp

DAVID SPECTOR
AIRPORT '77   Universal, 1977, w/Michael Scheff

AARON SPELLING
Business: Spelling Entertainment, 5700 Wilshire Blvd. -
    Suite 575, Los Angeles, CA 90036, 213/965-5700

GUNS OF THE TIMBERLAND   Jaguar, 1960,
    w/Joseph Petracca
ONE FOOT IN HELL   20th Century-Fox, 1960,
    w/Sydney Boehm

DEREK SPENCER
THE RETURN OF SWAMP THING   Lightyear
    Entertainment, 1989, w/Grant Morris

JANE SPENCER
LITTLE NOISES   Monument Pictures, 1991, w/Jon
    Zeiderman, directed

SCOTT SPENCER
Contact: CAA - Beverly Hills, 213/288-4545

SPLIT IMAGE   Orion, 1982, w/Robert Mark Kamen &
    Robert Kaufman

Screenplays:
ACT OF VENGEANCE (CTF)
ASSASSINATION ON EMBASSY ROW
RAPTIVE
LOVEHUNTER
SWEETZER

PENELOPE SPHEERIS*
Agent: The Gersh Agency - Beverly Hills, 213/274-6611

SUBURBIA   THE WILD SIDE   New World, 1984, directed
SUMMER CAMP NIGHTMARE   THE BUTTERFLY REVO-
    LUTION   Concorde, 1987, w/Bert L. Dragin

Screenplays:
BOY CHILD w/Caroline Thompson

Sp

FILM WRITERS GUIDE

LARRY SPIEGEL*
Contact: 213/651-4977

HAIL TO THE CHIEF   20th Century-Fox, 1973, w/others
BOOK OF NUMBERS   Embassy, 1974
SURVIVAL RUN   *SPREE*   Film Ventures, 1978, directed

SCOTT SPIEGEL*
Agent: United Talent Agency - Beverly Hills, 213/273-6700

EVIL DEAD 2   DEG, 1987, w/Sam Raimi
INTRUDER   Phantom Productions, 1989, w/Lawrence Bender, directed
THE ROOKIE   Warner Bros., 1990, w/Boaz Yakin

Screenplays:
WITCHES

ANNE SPIELBERG*
Agent: CAA - Beverly Hills, 213/288-4545

BIG ★   20th Century Fox, 1988, w/Gary Ross

STEVEN SPIELBERG*
Agent: CAA - Beverly Hills, 213/288-4545
Business: Amblin Entertainment, Universal Studios, 818/777-4600

ACE ELI AND ROGER OF THE SKIES   20th Century-Fox, 1973, Story
THE SUGARLAND EXPRESS   Universal, 1974, w/Matthew Robbins & Hal Barwood, directed
CLOSE ENCOUNTERS OF THE THIRD KIND   Columbia, 1977, directed
POLTERGEIST   MGM/UA, 1980, w/Michael Grais & Mark Victor
THE GOONIES   Warner Bros., 1985, Story

AMY SPIES*
Agent: ICM - Los Angeles, 213/550-4000

GIRLS JUST WANT TO HAVE FUN   New World, 1985

Screenplays:
TOO SMART FOR LOVE
BANDSTAND
WHO'S WHO

TONY SPIRIDAKIS*
Agent: ICM - Los Angeles, 213/550-4000

SELF STORAGE (S) w/Shem Bitterman
QUEENS LOGIC   7 Arts/New Line Cinema, 1990

ROGER SPOTTISWOODE
Agent: InterTalent - Los Angeles, 213/858-6200

48 HRS.   Paramount, 1982, w/Steven E. De Souza, Larry Gross & Walter Hill

MARK SPRAGG*
Agent: ICM - Los Angeles, 213/550-4000

GROSS ANATOMY   Buena Vista, 1989, w/Ron Nyswaner

Screenplays:
THE ASSOCIATE
SOUTH OF PICASSO

MARC SPRINGER
BLACK MAGIC WOMAN   Trimark Pictures, 1991, Story w/Gerry Daly & Deryn Warren

NICHOLAS ST. JOHN*
Agent: William Morris Agency - New York, 212/586-5100

MS. 45   Navaron, 1981
FEAR CITY   Chevy Chase Distribution, 1985
CHINA GIRL   Vestron, 1987
KING OF NEW YORK   Miramax, 1990

Screenplays:
TUMBLIN' DICE
SARAH
UNEMPLOYED

JIM STAAHL*
Agent: Writers & Artists Agency - Los Angeles, 213/820-2240

Screenplays:
CHUMP TOWER w/Jim Fisher
UNDER SURVEILLANCE w/Jim Fisher
DUH BOAT   S.O.S. w/Jim Fisher

RAMA LAURIE STAGNER*
Agent: Writers & Artists Agency - Los Angeles, 213/820-2240

BLUE SKY   Orion, 1991

Screenplays:
OTHER WOMEN'S CHILDREN
CLEAR CUT
A WOMAN'S GUIDE TO ADULTRY
ATOMIC ROMANCE
BUILDERS

SYLVESTER STALLONE*
Agent: CAA - Beverly Hills, 213/288-4545
Business: White Eagle Enterprises, 2308 Broadway, Santa Monica, CA, 90404, 213/828-8988

ROCKY ★   United Artists, 1976
PARADISE ALLEY   Universal, 1978, directed
F.I.S.T.   United Artists, 1978, w/Joe Eszterhas
ROCKY II   United Artists, 1979, directed
FIRST BLOOD   Orion, 1982, w/Michael Kozoll & William Sackheim
ROCKY III   MGM/UA, 1982, directed
STAYING ALIVE   Paramount, 1983, w/Norman Wexler, directed
RHINESTONE   20th Century-Fox, 1984, w/Phil Alden Robinson
ROCKY IV   MGM/UA, 1985, directed
RAMBO: FIRST BLOOD PART II   Tri-Star, 1985, w/James Cameron
COBRA   Warner Bros., 1986
OVER THE TOP   Cannon, 1987, w/Stirling Silliphant
RAMBO III   Tri-Star, 1988, w/Shelton Lettich
ROCKY V   MGM/UA, 1990

LARRY STAMPER
WILD THING   Atlantic Releasing Corporation, 1987, Story w/John Sayles

DAVID STANDISH
CLUB PARADISE   Warner Bros., 1986, Story w/Tom Leopold, Chris Miller & Ed Roboto

RICHARD STANLEY*
Agent: Casaratto Company - London, 01/287-4450

HARDWARE   Millimeter Films, 1990, directed

Screenplays:
DUST DEVIL   (directing)

DARREN STAR*
Agent: ICM - Los Angeles, 213/550-4000

DOIN' TIME ON PLANET EARTH   Cannon, 1989
IF LOOKS COULD KILL   Warner Bros., 1991

JAISON STARKES
J.D.'S REVENGE   American International, 1976
THE FISH THAT SAVED PITTSBURGH   United Artists, 1979, w/Edmond Stevens

MANYA STARR*
Contact: WGA - New York, 212/245-6180

WHITE WATER SUMMER   Columbia, 1987, w/Ernest Kinoy

JEAN STAWARZ
POWWOW HIGHWAY   Warner Bros., 1989, w/Janet Heaney

FRED STEFAN
SPRING FEVER   Comworld, 1983, w/Stuart Gillard

JOSEPH STEFANO*
Agent: APA - Los Angeles, 213/273-0744
Business Manager: Leslie Bettis, 213/477-6678

THE BLACK ORCHID   Paramount, 1958
PSYCHO   Paramount, 1960
THE NAKED EDGE   United Artists, 1961
EYE OF THE CAT   Universal, 1969
THE KINDRED   FM Entertainment, 1987, w/others
BLACKOUT   Overseas Film Group, 1989
PSYCHO IV: THE BEGINNING (CTF)   Smart Money/MCA, 1990

Screenplays:
TWO BITS

JOSEPH STEIN*
Contact: WGA - New York, 212/245-6180

ENTER LAUGHING   Columbia, 1967, w/Carl Reiner
FIDDLER ON THE ROOF   United Artists, 1971, from his play

MARK STEIN
Agent: Triad Artists, Inc. - Los Angeles, 213/556-2727

Screenplays:
HOMESITTER
MILWAUKEE CONFIDENTIAL

MICHAEL ERIC STEIN*
Agent: Triad Artists, Inc. - Los Angeles, 213/556-2727

Screenplays:
MONEY RIVER
THE CYCLE

MOROCCAN HAZE
CAT
THE HEIGHTH OF FASHION
LIGHTNING ROD
PUBLIC DREAMING
BERLIN SHADOW

SEAN STEIN*
Contact: WGA - Los Angeles, 213/550-1000

THE COUCH TRIP   Orion, 1988, w/Steven J. Kampmann & Will Aldis

DAVID STEINBERG*
Agent: William Morris Agency - Beverly Hills, 213/274-7451

GOING BERSERK   Universal, 1983, w/Dana Olsen, directed
ALL DOGS GO TO HEAVEN (AF)   MGM/UA, 1989, Story w/others

NORMAN STEINBERG*
Agent: CAA - Beverly Hills, 213/288-4545

BLAZING SADDLES   Warner Bros., 1973, w/Andrew Bergman, Mel Brooks, Richard Pryor & Alan Uger
YES, GIORGIO   MGM/UA, 1982
MY FAVORITE YEAR   MGM/UA, 1982, w/Dennis Palumbo
JOHNNY DANGEROUSLY   20th Century Fox, 1984, w/Harry Columby, Jeff Harris & Bernie Kukoff
FUNNY ABOUT LOVE   Paramount, 1990, w/David Frankel

Screenplays:
HOTEL HAWAII   w/Richard Dimitri
MY SUMMER WITH MOM
CHARLES AND LUCY
MURDER AT PREP SCHOOL
SEX IN AMERICA
ATLANTIC CROSSING
HELP, I'M BEING HELD A PRISONER
THE POPCORN CAPER
THE MAN FROM ST. PAUL

ZIGGY STEINBERG*
Contact: Ted Steinberg, Esq. - Los Angeles, 213/553-4070

PORKY'S REVENGE   20th Century Fox, 1985
THE BOSS' WIFE   Tri-Star, 1986, directed
ANOTHER YOU   Tri-Star, 1991

REED STEINER*
Agent: United Talent Agency - Beverly Hills, 213/273-6700
Business: Bearflag Rebellion Pictures, 110 S. Sweetzer, Los Angeles, CA 90048, 213/655-0461

DISCOVERY BAY   Westwind Pictures/Image Organization, 1988

Screenplays:
STEALING THUNDER
POINT-BLANK
ASSIGNED RISK
CAPT. NUKE AND THE BOMBER BOYS
MR. MOTO

DANNY STEINMANN
SAVAGE STREETS   Entermark, 1985, w/Norman Yonemoto
FRIDAY THE 13TH - A NEW BEGINNING   Paramount, 1985, w/Martin Kitrosser, directed

MARTIN STELLMAN
Agent: Casaratto Company - London, 01/287-4450

QUADROPHENIA   World Northal, 1979, w/Dave Humphries & Franc Roddam
DEFENSE OF THE REALM   Hemdale, 1985
FOR QUEEN AND COUNTRY   Atlantic Releasing Corporation, 1988, w/Trix Worrell, directed

DAVID STENN*
Agent: William Morris Agency - Beverly Hills, 213/274-7451

Screenplays:
COOL AS ICE
BAD LITTLE GIRL
DUMB BLONDE
THE IT GIRL

ELLIOT STEPHENS
(See Steven DeSouza)

JOHN A. STEPPLING*
Agent: William Morris Agency - Beverly Hills, 213/274-7451

PLEDGING MY LOVE (S)
EDDIE COTTREL AT THE PIANO (S)
CHILDREN OF HERAKLES (S)
EXHALING ZERO (S)
TEENAGE WEDDING (S)
MY CRUMMY JOB (S)
THE THRILL (S)
THE SHAPER (S)
THE DREAM COAST (S)
CLOSE (S)
NECK (S)
STANDARD OF THE BREED (S)
A DEEP TROPICAL TAN (S)
52 PICK-UP   Cannon, 1986, w/Elmore Leonard

Screenplays:
THE ANATOMY LESSON
IN THE LIFE

ALEX STERN
DEAD AND BURIED   Avco Embassy, 1981, Story w/Jeff Miller

ELLIOT M. STERN*
Agent: The Agency - Los Angeles, 213/551-3000

Screenplays:
VALET PARKING
THE APPRENTICE
POT OF GOLD
MURPHY'S LAW
TWO GUYS FROM SPACE
SONNY
MY SECRET IDENTITY

LEONARD B. STERN*
Contact: 213/652-0222

THE MILKMAN   Universal-International, 1950, w/Albert Beich, James O'Hanlon & Martin Ragaway
THE JAZZ SINGER   Warner Bros., 1953, w/Frank Davis & Lewis Meltzer
THREE FOR THE SHOW   Columbia, 1955, w/Edward Hope
JUST YOU AND ME, KID   Columbia, 1979, w/Oliver Hailey, diected
THE NUDE BOMB   Universal, 1980, w/Bill Dana & Arne Sultan
TEEN WOLF   Atlantic Releasing Corporation, 1985, Story
TARGET   Warner Bros., 1985, Story
MISSING PIECES   Orion, 1991, directed

NOAH STERN*
Agent: ICM - Los Angeles, 213/550-4000

PYRATES   Live America Inc., 1991, directed

Screenplays:
THE RULES OF THE GAME
RULES OF ATTRACTION

SANDOR STERN*
Agent: Broder-Kurland-Webb-Uffner - Los Angeles, 213/656-9262

THE AMITYVILLE HORROR   American International, 1979
FAST BREAK   Columbia, 1979
PIN   New World, 1989, directed
WEB OF DECEIT (CTF)   Sankan-Wilshire Court, 1990, directed

STEVEN HILLIARD STERN*
Agent: Broder-Kurland-Webb-Uffner - Los Angeles, 213/656-9262

B.S. I LOVE YOU   20th Century-Fox, 1971, directed
NEITHER BY DAY NOR BY NIGHT   Motion Pictures International, 1972, directed
RUNNING   Universal, 1979, directed
LOVE & MURDER   Norstar Entertainment, 1990, directed

STEWART STERN*
Contact: WGA - Los Angeles, 213/550-1000

TERESA ★   MGM, 1951
REBEL WITHOUT A CAUSE   Warner Bros., 1955
THE RACK   MGM, 1956
THUNDER IN THE SUN   Paramount, 1959
THE OUTSIDER   Universal, 1961
THE UGLY AMERICAN   Universal, 1963
RACHEL, RACHEL ★   Warner Bros., 1968
THE LAST MOVIE   Universal, 1971
SUMMER WISHES, WINTER DREAMS   Columbia, 1973

Screenplays:
AN INFINITY OF MIRRORS w/G. Green
VALDEZ HORSES
THE DEATH OF THE SNOW QUEEN

TOM STERN*
Agent: ICM - Los Angeles, 213/550-4000

SQUEAL OF DEATH (Short) w/Alex Winter, co-directed

Screenplays:
WONDERLAND w/Alex Winter
MILO RIGBY ON WHEELS w/Alex Winter
HOWIE'S REVENGE w/Alex Winter

JEFF STETSON*
Agent: William Morris Agency - Beverly Hills, 213/274-7451

THE MEETING (S)
FRATERNITY (S)

Screenplays:
CIVIL WARS

ANDREW STEVENS*
Contact: Screen Actors Guild - Los Angeles, 213/465-4600

NIGHT EYES   Armitraj-Baldwin Entertainment, 1990, w/Tom Citrano
THE TERROR WITHIN II   Concorde, 1991, directed

DAVID STEVENS*
Agent: Barrett, Benson, McCartt & Weston - Los Angeles, 213/247-5500

THE SUM OF US (S)
BREAKER MORANT ★   New World/Quartet, 1980, w/Bruce Beresford & Jonathan Hardy

EDMOND STEVENS*
Agent: Broder-Kurland-Webb-Uffner - Los Angeles, 213/656-9262

THE FISH THAT SAVED PITTSBURGH   United Artists, 1979, w/Jaison Starkes

JEREMY STEVENS*
Agent: The Irv Schechter Company - Beverly Hills, 213/278-8070

SUMMER RENTAL   Paramount, 1985, w/Mark Reisman

Screenplays:
BIG HOSPITAL w/Mark Reisman
NINETY MINUTES w/Mark Reisman

LESLIE C. STEVENS*
Agent: CAA - Beverly Hills, 213/288-4545

THE LEFT HANDED GUN   Warner Bros., 1958
THE MARRIAGE GO ROUND   20th Century-Fox, 1961
HERO'S ISLAND   United Artists, 1962, directed
BUCK ROGERS   Universal, 1979, w/Glen A. Larson
SHEENA   Columbia, 1984, Story w/David Newman
THREE KINDS OF HEAT   Cannon, 1987, directed
RETURN TO BLUE LAGOON   Columbia, 1991

RICK STEVENSON*
Contact: WGA - Los Angeles, 213/550-1000

Screenplays:
ART OF COURTLY LOVE

BILL STEWART
Agent: Cinema Talent International - Los Angeles, 213/656-1937
Business: Stewart Products Co., 2461 Fairbrook Dr., Nashville, TN 37214, 615/883-3333

Screenplays:
UNHEARD MELODIES
PAPER DART
WALLS w/Barbara Holder

DONALD L. STEWART*
Agent: William Morris Agency - Beverly Hills, 213/274-7451

JACKSON COUNTY JAIL   New World, 1976
DEATHSPORT   New World, 1978, w/Henry Suso
MISSING ★★   Universal, 1982, w/Costa-Gavras
THE HUNT FOR RED OCTOBER   Paramount, 1990, w/Larry Ferguson

Screenplays:
UNDER COVER OF DAYLIGHT
FIRST STRIKE
MRS. REDDEN
FIRE MAN
CABO RIO
KEY WEST
KILLING ZONE
FREEZE OUT
CAPA
DEAD SECTOR

DOUGLAS DAY STEWART*
Agent: ICM - Los Angeles, 213/550-4000

WHERE THE RED FERN GROWS   1974, w/E. Lamb
SEVEN ALONE   Doty-Dayton, 1975, w/E. Lamb
AGAINST A CROOKED SKY   Doty-Dayton, 1975
THE OTHER SIDE OF THE MOUNTAIN - PART 2   Universal, 1978
BLUE LAGOON   Columbia, 1980
AN OFFICER AND A GENTLEMAN ★   Paramount, 1982
THIEF OF HEARTS   Paramount, 1984, directed
LISTEN TO ME   WEG, 1989, directed

Screenplays:
ESCAPE FROM BV-JAY
TOO LATE FOR HEROES

JOHN STEWART
ACTION U.S.A.   Stewart & Berger Inc., 1989, Story w/David Reskin, directed
CLICK: THE CALENDAR GIRL KILLER   Crown International, 1991, Story w/Carol Lynn, co-directed

R.J. STEWART*
Agent: ICM - Los Angeles, 213/550-4000

AND GOD CREATED WOMAN   Vestron, 1988

Screenplays:
THE END OF ETERNITY
FIRE HOUSE
GOOD COMPANY
MAGIC FIVE

ROBERT STIGLIANO
FUN DOWN THERE   Frameline, 1990, w/Michael Waite, directed

BEN STILLER*
Agent: William Morris Agency - Beverly Hills, 213/274-7451

Screenplays:
THE WEATHERMEN

WHIT STILLMAN
(J. Whitney Stillman)
Agent: William Morris Agency - Beverly Hills, 213/274-7451

METROPOLITAN ★   New Line Cinema, 1990, directed

Screenplays:
BARCELONA

JOSEPH C. STINSON*
Agent: ICM - Los Angeles, 213/550-4000

SUDDEN IMPACT   Warner Bros., 1983
CITY HEAT   Warner Bros., 1984, w/Blake Edwards
STICK   Universal, 1985, w/Elmore Leonard

Screenplays:
WILDERNESS
KIDD
WINNING STREAK
BANDITS
RECOIL

MARC STIRDIVANT*
Contact: 818/840-5488

CONDORMAN   Buena Vista, 1981, w/Glenn Gordon Caron & Mickey Rose

Screenplays:
NOISE IN THE NIGHT   w/Thom Eberhardt

MILAN STITT*
Agent: Writers & Artists Agency - New York, 212/947-8765

THE RUNNER STUMBLES   20th Century-Fox, 1979, from his play

ROBERT D. STITZEL*
Agent: ICM - Los Angeles, 213/550-4000

BRAINSTORM   MGM/UA, 1983, w/Philip Frank Messina
DISTANT THUNDER   Paramount, 1988
THE TENDER   Paramount, 1989

JOHN STOCKWELL*
Agent: ICM - Los Angeles, 213/550-4000

DANGEROUSLY CLOSE   Cannon, 1986, w/Scott Fields & Marty Ross
UNDER COVER   Cannon, 1987, w/Scott Fields, directed

HUGH STODDART
Contact: British Academy of Film & Television Arts, 195 Piccadilly, London W1, England, 71/734-0022

REMEMBRANCE   Channel Four/Film on Four, 1982
WE THINK THE WORLD OF YOU   Cinecom, 1988

Screenplays:
BURMESE DAYS   w/Julian Bond

CHRISTIAN STOIANOVICH*
Agent: Warden & White Associates - Beverly Hills, 213/852-1028

Screenplays:
CONDUIT   w/Phoebe Dorin
THE RUNAWAY WIFE   w/Phoebe Dorin
WITHOUT MERCY   w/Phoebe Dorin
THE 13TH FLOOR   w/Phoebe Dorin

BRYAN MICHAEL STOLLER
Personal Manager: Russ Blum, The Antares Group, 818/980-8880

UNDERSHORTS: THE MOVIE   Paramount, 1990, directed, unreleased

Screenplays:
LIGHT YEARS AWAY
REX

ANDREW L. STONE*
Agent: Harry Gold & Associates - Studio City, 818/769-5003

STOLEN HEAVEN   Paramount, 1938, w/Eve Greene & Frederick Jackson, directed
THERE'S MAGIC IN MUSIC   Paramount, 1941, directed
THE BACHELOR'S DAUGHTER   United Artists, 1946, directed
FUN ON A WEEKEND   United Artists, 1947, directed
HIGHWAY 301   Warner Bros., 1950, directed
CONFIDENCE GIRL   United Artists, 1951, directed
THE STEEL TRAP   20th Century-Fox, 1952, directed
A BLUEPRINT FOR MURDER   20th Century-Fox, 1953, directed
THE NIGHT HOLDS TERROR   Columbia, 1955, directed
JULIE   MGM, 1956, directed
CRY TERROR!   MGM, 1958, directed
THE DECKS RAN RED   MGM, 1958, w/Virginia Stone, directed
THE LAST VOYAGE   MGM, 1960, directed
RING OF FIRE   MGM, 1961, directed
THE PASSWORD IS COURAGE   MGM, 1963, directed
NEVER PUT IT IN WRITING   Allied Artists, 1964, directed
THE SECRET OF MY SUCCESS   MGM, 1965, directed
SONG OF NORWAY   Cinerama Releasing Corporation, 1970, directed
THE GREAT WALTZ   MGM, 1972, directed

ARNOLD M. STONE
SECRET HONOR   Cinecom International, 1985, w/Donald Freed

JERICO STONE*
Agent: Agency for Creative Talent - Los Angeles, 213/277-4909

MY STEPMOTHER IS AN ALIEN   WEG, 1989, w/Timothy Harris, Herschel Weingrod & Jonathan Reynolds

Screenplays:
MATINEE

MICHAEL STONE*
Contact: WGA - New York, 212/245-6180

WAITRESS!   Troma, 1982, w/Charles Kaufman

NOREEN STONE*
Agent: Shapiro/Lichtman - Los Angeles, 213/859-8877

AMY   Buena Vista, 1981
BRENDA STARR   Triumph, 1991, w/James David Buchanan & Jenny Wolkind

OLIVER STONE*
Agent: CAA - Beverly Hills, 213/288-4545
Business: Ixtlan, Inc., 321 Hampton - Suite 105, Venice, CA 90291, 213/399-2550

SEIZURE   Cinerama Releasing Corporation, 1974, w/E. Mann, directed
MIDNIGHT EXPRESS ★★   Columbia, 1978
THE HAND   Orion/Warner Bros., 1981, directed
CONAN THE BARBARIAN   Universal, 1982, w/John Milius
SCARFACE   Universal, 1983
YEAR OF THE DRAGON   MGM/UA, 1985, w/Michael Cimino
8 MILLION WAYS TO DIE   Tri-Star, 1986, w/R. Lance Hill
SALVADOR ★   Hemdale, 1986, w/Richard Boyle, directed
PLATOON ★   Orion, 1986, directed
WALL STREET   20th Century Fox, 1987, w/Stanley Weiser, directed
TALK RADIO   Universal, 1988, w/Eric Bogosian, directed
BORN ON THE FOURTH OF JULY ★   Universal, 1989, w/Ron Kovic, directed
THE DOORS   Tri-Star, 1991, w/Randy Johnson, directed

Screenplays:
JFK w/Zachary Sklar (directing)
THE DEMOLISHED MAN w/Brian De Palma
THE BRAZIL RUN w/K. Roberts
THE COVER-UP
THE UNGODLY
WILDERNESS
INNOCENT BLOOD

PETER H. STONE*
Agent: ICM - New York, 212/556-5600

WOMAN OF THE YEAR (S)
SUGAR (S)
MY ONE AND ONLY (S) w/T. Mayer
THE WILL ROGERS FOLLIES (S)
CHARADE   Universal, 1964
FATHER GOOSE ★★   Universal, 1964, w/Frank Tarloff
MIRAGE   Universal, 1965
ARABESQUE   Universal, 1966
THE SECRET WAR OF HARRY FRIGG   Universal, 1967, w/Frank Tarloff
SWEET CHARITY   Universal, 1969
SKIN GAME   Warner Bros., 1971, as "Pierre Marton," w/Richard Alan Simmons
1776   Columbia, 1972, from his play
THE TAKING OF PELHAM 1-2-3   United Artists, 1974
SILVER BEARS   Columbia, 1977
WHO IS KILLING THE GREAT CHEFS OF EUROPE?   Warner Bros., 1978
WHY WOULD I LIE?   MGM/United Artists, 1980

Screenplays:
THE FABRICATOR
THE WANTING OF LEVINE   HOLLYWOOD AND LEVINE

ROBERT STONE
Contact: Publisher-Penguin USA - New York, 212/366-2000

WUSA   Paramount, 1970

TOM STOPPARD*
Agent: Fraser & Dunlop - London, 011/441/734-7311

TRAVESTIES (S)
JUMPERS (S)
GALILEO (S)
ARTIST DESCENDING A STAIRCASE (S)
EVERY GOOD BOY DESERVES FAVOR (S)
THE REAL INSPECTOR HOUND (S)
THE REAL THING (S)
HAPGOOD (S)
THE ENGAGEMENT   Memorial, 1970
THE ROMANTIC ENGLISHWOMAN   New World, 1975, w/Thomas Wiseman
DESPAIR   New Line Cinema, 1978
THE HUMAN FACTOR   MGM/UA, 1979
BRAZIL ★   Universal, 1985, w/Terry Gilliam & Charles McKeown
EMPIRE OF THE SUN   Warner Bros., 1987
THE RUSSIA HOUSE   MGM/Pathe Entertainment, 1990
ROSENCRANTZ & GUILDENSTERN ARE DEAD   Cinecom, 1991, from his play, directed
BILLY BATHGATE   Buena Vista, 1991

Screenplays:
A NOVEL LIFE

ANTHONY STOREY
ZULU DAWN   New World, 1982, w/Cy Endfield

LISA B. STOTSKY*
Contact: WGA - Los Angeles, 213/550-1000

Screenplays:
LIFESAVERS w/Wendy Graf
ALL MINE w/Wendy Graf
FINAL ARGUMENTS w/Wendy Graf

WILLIAM STOUT*
Contact: Henry Holmes, Esq. - Los Angeles, 213/278-1111

THE WARRIOR AND THE SORCERESS   New Horizons, 1984, Story w/John Broderick

JIM STRAIN*
Agent: Writers & Artists Agency - Los Angeles, 213/820-2240

BINGO!   Tri-Star, 1991

Screenplays:
BABE & ME
WINSLOW'S MUSE
THE FLASH
SOLDIERS OF FORTUNE
THE LOVER PRINCE
THE BYTES

KEITH W. STRANDBERG
NO RETREAT, NO SURRENDER   New World, 1986
NO RETREAT, NO SURRENDER II   Shapiro Glickenhaus, 1989, w/Marie Elene Cellino & Roy Horan

BRIAN STRASMANN*
Agent: Warden & White Associates - Beverly Hills, 213/852-1028

Screenplays:
CYCLONE
THE BUTTONMEN

WARLOCK HOLMES
ABSTRACT ART
MY SOUL TO KEEP
ON MY HONOR

JEAN-MARIE STRAUB
Contact: French Film Office, 745 Fifth Avenue, New York, NY 10151, 212/832-8860

CLASS RELATIONS   KLASSENVERHALF-NISSE
New Yorker, 1987, directed

JOHN J. STRAUSS*
Agent: United Talent Agency - Beverly Hills, 213/273-6700

OPTIONS   Vestron, 1989, w/Ed Decter

Screenplays:
FOREVER MURRAY w/Ed Decter
YARD WARS w/Ed Decter
THERE'S SOMETHING ABOUT MARY w/Ed Decter

LARRY STRAWTHER*
Agent: William Morris Agency - Beverly Hills, 213/274-7451

WITHOUT A CLUE   Orion, 1989, w/Gary Murphy

Screenplays:
8:24 TO HEAVEN w/Gary Murphy

BILL STREIB*
Agent: The Agency - Los Angeles, 213/551-3000

Screenplays:
AMERICAN PIE

RUSSELL STREINER
THE RETURN OF THE LIVING DEAD   Orion, 1985, Story w/Rudy Ricci & John Russo

BARBRA STREISAND
Agent: CAA - Beverly Hills, 213/288-4545
Business: Barwood Films, 75 Rockefeller Plaza - 18th Floor, New York, NY, 10019, 212/484-7300

YENTL   MGM/UA, 1983, w/Jack Rosenthal, directed

WESLEY E. STRICK*
Agent: CAA - Beverly Hills, 213/288-4545

TRUE BELIEVER   Columbia, 1989
ARACHNOPHOBIA   Buena Vista, 1990, w/Don Jakoby

Screenplays:
FINAL ANALYSIS
BEAUTIFUL NOISE
SNEAKERS
MADE IN JAPAN

WHITLEY STRIEBER
Agent: CAA - Beverly Hills, 213/288-4545

COMMUNION   New Line Cinema, 1989

JOHN STRONG
A SHOW OF FORCE   Paramount, 1990, w/Evan Jones

DANIELE STROPPA
WITCHERY   Filmirage, 1989

BARRY STRUGATZ*
Agent: H. N. Swanson, Inc. - Los Angeles, 213/652-5385

MARRIED TO THE MOB   Orion, 1988, w/Mark Burns
SHE-DEVIL   Orion, 1989, w/Mark Burns

Screenplays:
ON THE LAM w/Mark Burns

ALEXANDER STUART
ORDEAL BY INNOCENCE   MGM/UA, 1984

IAN A. STUART
THE PIT   New World, 1984

JEB STUART*
Agent: United Talent Agency - Beverly Hills, 213/273-6700

DIE HARD   20th Century Fox, 1988, w/Steven De Souza
LEVIATHAN   MGM/UA, 1989, w/David Peoples
LOCK UP   Tri-Star, 1989, w/Henry Rosenbaum & Richard Smith
VITAL SIGNS   20th Century Fox, 1990, w/Larry Ketron
ANOTHER 48 HRS.   Paramount, 1990, w/Larry Gross & John Fasano

Screenplays:
D.C. THRILLER w/Don Jakoby & Gary Thompson
FIRE DOWN BELOW
JURY DUTY
MAXWELL'S TRAIN
JUST CAUSE
PINCUSHION
GOING WEST AMERICA
MIDNIGHT CLUB
IN THE NIGHT
IN EXTREMIS
COUTNERFEIT
ESCAPE

JOHN STUCKMEYER
THE SWORD AND THE SORCERER   Group 1, 1982, w/Thomas Karnowski & Albert Pyun

CHARLES STURRIDGE
Agent: ICM - Los Angeles, 213/550-4000

A HANDFUL OF DUST   New Line Cinema, 1988, w/Derek Granger & Tim Sullivan, directed

ELISEO SUBIELA
Contact: Instituto Nacional de Cinematografica, Lima 319,1073 Buenos Aires, Argentina, tel.: 370-028

MAN FACING SOUTHEAST   FilmDallas, 1987, directed

MILTON SUBOTSKY
THE LAST MILE   United Artists, 1959, w/Seton I. Miller
DR. TERROR'S HOUSE OF HORRORS   Amicus, 1965
DR. WHO AND THE DALEKS   British Lion, 1965
THE SKULL   Paramount, 1965
I, MONSTER   Amicus, 1970
TALES FROM THE CRYPT   Metromedia, 1972
VAULT OF HORROR   Metromedia, 1973
AT THE EARTH'S CORE   Amicus, 1976

ROBERT A. SUHOVSKY*
Contact: 213/278-1255

THE HOUSE WHERE EVIL DWELLS   MGM/UA, 1982

BETH SULLIVAN*
Agent: Favored Artists Agency - Los Angeles, 213/653-3191

CIRCLE OF POWER *MYSTIQUE/BRAINWASH/THE NAKED WEEKEND* Televicine, 1983, w/Stephen Bello

DANIEL SULLIVAN
Agent: The Goldstein Company - Los Angeles, 213/659-9511

Screenplays:
FATHER AND SON w/Fred Lebow
SANTA'S DAUGHTER w/Fred Lebow
NEW YEAR'S EVE w/Fred Lebow
SNOW FLAKES w/Fred Lebow
TERROR RANCH
BAR SONG

FRED G. SULLIVAN
COLD RIVER   Pacific International, 1982, directed
THE BEER DRINKER'S GUIDE TO FITNESS AND FILMMAKING *SULLIVAN'S PAVILLION* Circle Releasing, 1987, directed

KEVIN SULLIVAN*
Agent: Triad Artists, Inc. - Los Angeles, 213/556-2727

Screenplays:
RED TAILS
GREEN CARD BLUES
GHETTO BLASTERS

PATTI SULLIVAN*
Agent: Triad Artists, Inc. - Los Angeles, 213/556-2727

Screenplays:
FAMILY SECRETS

TIM SULLIVAN
Agent: Fraser & Dunlop - London, 011/441/734-7311

A HANDFUL OF DUST   New Line Cinema, 1988, w/Derek Granger & Charles Sturridge

PETER SUMMERS
Contact: Mickey Mayerson, Loeb & Loeb, 10100 Santa Monica Blvd. - Suite 2200, Los Angeles, CA, 90067, 213/282-2165
Business: PDP Productions, 3310 Keystone Ave., Suite One, Los Angeles, CA, 90034, 213/558-4221

THE GAME   Cobra Entertainment Group, 1989

Screenplays:
DEVIL ON THE RUN

SHIRLEY SUN
Business: Sun Productions, 110 Greene St. - Suite 12G, New York, NY 10012

A GREAT WALL   Orion Classics, 1986, w/Peter Wang
IRON AND SILK   Sun Productions, 1990, w/Mark Salzman, directed

CEDRIC SUNDSTROM
Agent: Twentieth Century Artists - Los Angeles, 213/850-5516

AMERICAN NINJA 3: BLOOD HUNT   Cannon, 1989, directed

RONALD A. SUPPA*
Business: Suppa Productions, 3737 Ventura Canyon Ave., Sherman Oaks, CA 91423, 818/784-6369

RIDING THE EDGE   Trans World Entertainment, 1989

BARTH JULES SUSSMAN
NIGHT GAMES   Avco Embassy, 1980, Story w/Anton Diether

TAYLOR SUTHERLAND
THE LAST CHASE   Crown International, 1981, w/Martyn Burke & Christopher Crowe

MICHAEL D. SUTTON*
Agent: Harris & Goldberg - Los Angeles, 213/553-5200

Screenplays:
THE CO-EDS w/Chris Miller
THE TECHNICOLOR TIME MACHINE w/Chris Miller
ANIMAL HOUSE NOW w/Chris Miller
NO SUCH LUCK w/Chris Miller
WITCHCRAFT w/Chris Miller
JUST LIKE A WOMAN w/Chris Miller
BEL-AIR BUTLER w/Chris Miller

BILL SVANOE*
Agent: Barrett, Benson, McCartt & Weston - Los Angeles, 213/247-5500

WALTZ ACROSS TEXAS   Atlantic Releasing Corporation, 1982
FATAL BEAUTY   MGM/UA, 1987, Story

BOB SWAIM*
Agent: ICM - Los Angeles, 213/550-4000

LA BALANCE   Spectrafilm, 1982, w/M. Fabiani, directed
HALF MOON STREET   20th Century Fox, 1986, w/Edward Behr, directed

Screenplays:
THE PARIS PROJECT (directing)
GOLD w/David H. Franzoni

P. W. SWANN
Agent: ICM - Los Angeles, 213/550-4000

SURVIVAL GAME   Trans World Entertainment, 1987, w/Susannah deNimes & Herb Freed

SCOTT J. SWANTON*
Agent: CAA - Beverly Hills, 213/288-4545

RACE FOR GLORY   New Century/Vista, 1989

MILES HOOD SWARTHOUT*
Agent: William Morris Agency - Beverly Hills, 213/274-7451

THE SHOOTIST   Paramount, 1976, w/Scott Hale

Screenplays:
THE TIN LIZZIE TROOP
JOHN WESLEY HARDIN

STEVE SWARTZ
NEVER LEAVE NEVADA   Cabriolet Films, 1989, directed

ALFRED SWEENEY
UP FROM THE DEPTHS   New World, 1979

TERRY SWEENEY*
Contact: Hansen, Jacobson & Teller - Los Angeles, 213/271-8777

LOVE AT STAKE   *BURNIN' LOVE*   Tri-Star, 1988, w/Lanier Laney
SHAG: THE MOVIE   Hemdale, 1989, w/Lanier Laney & Robin Swicord

CHARLES SWENSON
Business: Marukami/Wolf/Swenson, Inc., 1463 Tamarind Ave., Hollywood, CAI 90028, 213/462-6473

DIRTY DUCK (AF)   New World, 1977, shared, directed
TWICE UPON A TIME (AF)   The Ladd Company/Warner Bros., 1983, w/Bill Couterie, Suella Kennedy & John Korty, co-directed

JOHN K. SWENSSON
FIRE BIRDS   Buena Vista, 1990, Story w/Dale Dye & Step Tyner

MICHAEL SWERDLICK*
Agent: ICM - Los Angeles, 213/550-4000

CAN'T BUY ME LOVE   Buena Vista, 1987

ROBIN SWICORD*
Agent: The Artists Agency - Los Angeles, 213/277-7779

CRIMINAL MINDS (S)
SHAG: THE MOVIE   Hemdale, 1989, w/Lanier Laney & Terry Sweeney

Screenplays:
BENJAMIN BUTTON
STOCK CARS FOR CHRIST

DAVID SWIFT*
Contact: Bloom, Dekom & Hergott, 213/278-8622

POLLYANNA   Buena Vista, 1960, directed
THE PARENT TRAP   Buena Vista, 1961, directed
THE INTERNS   Columbia, 1962, w/Walter Newman, directed
LOVE IS A BALL   United Artists, 1962, w/Frank Waldman & Tom Waldman, directed
UNDER THE YUM YUM TREE   Columbia, 1963, w/Lawrence Roman, directed
GOOD NEIGHBOR SAM   Columbia, 1964, w/James Fritzell & Everett Greenbaum, directed
HOW TO SUCCEED IN BUSINESS WITHOUT REALLY TRYING   United Artists, 1967, directed
FOOLIN' AROUND   Columbia, 1978, w/Michael Kane

ALAN SWYER*
Agent: Camden-ITG - Los Angeles, 213/289-2700

THE BUDDY HOLLY STORY   Columbia, 1978, Story
CRITICAL CONDITION   Paramount, 1987, Story w/Denis Hamill & John Hamill

PAUL SYLBERT*
Contact: Sydney Cohen, Esq. - New York, 212/757-4000

THE STEAGLE   Avco Embassy, 1971, directed
NIGHT HAWKS   Universal, 1981, Story w/David Shaber

ISTVAN SZABO
Contact: Hungarofilm, Bathory utca 10, H-1054 Budapest, Hungary, tel.: 116650

MEPHISTO   Analysis, 1980, w/Peter Dobai, directed
COLONEL REDL   Orion Classics, 1985, w/Peter Dobai, directed
HANUSSEN   Hungarofilm, 1988, w/Peter Dobai, directed

Screenplays:
MEETING VENUS   w/Michael Hirst   (directing)

THOMAS E. SZOLLOSI*
Agent: United Talent Agency - Beverly Hills, 213/273-6700

THREE O'CLOCK HIGH   Universal, 1987, w/Richard Christian Matheson
IT TAKES TWO   MGM/UA, 1988, w/Richard Christian Matheson

Screenplays:
SLUM LORD   w/Richard Christian Matheson
BLOOD PRESSURE   w/Richard Christian Matheson
WHOSE WOODS ARE THESE   w/Richard Christian Matheson
ICED
TRUST ME ON THIS
SECOND WIND
HOME PIE

T

MICHAEL TAAV
Agent: ICM - Los Angeles, 213/550-4000

FRIENDS, LOVERS & LUNATICS   Fries Entertainment, 1989

Screenplays:
THE PAINT JOB   (directing)
MORGAN   w/Leslie Ray

JORDAN S. TABAT*
Agent: APA - Los Angeles, 213/273-0744

Screenplays:
THE BELLHOP'S DAUGHTER

BRIAN W. TAGGERT*
Agent: The Agency - Los Angeles, 213/551-3000

VISITING HOURS 20th Century-Fox, 1982
OF UNKNOWN ORIGIN Warner Bros., 1983
THE NEW KIDS Columbia, 1985, Story
   w/Stephen Gyllenhaal
WANTED DEAD OR ALIVE New World, 1987,
   w/Michael Patrick Goodman & Gary Sherman
POLTERGEIST III MGM/UA, 1988, w/Gary Sherman
CHILDREN OF DARKNESS, CHILDREN OF LIGHT (CTF)
   G.C. Group/Wilshire Court, 1991

MARTIN TAHSE*
Business: Martin Tahse Productions, 1364 Palisades
   Beach Rd., Santa Monica, CA ;90401, 213/451-5164

THE LOOKALIKE (CTF) Gallo Entertainment Inc.,
   1990, w/Linda Bergman
MATTERS OF THE HEART (CTF) Tahse-Bergman/
   MCA, 1990, w/Linda Bergman

DON TAIT*
Contact: WGA - Los Angeles, 213/550-1000

ONE MORE TRAIN TO ROB Universal, 1971,
   w/Donald Nelson
SNOWBALL EXPRESS Buena Vista, 1972, w/Arnold
   Margolin & Jim Parker
THE CASTAWAY COWBOY Buena Vista, 1974
THE APPLE DUMPLING GANG Buena Vista, 1974
THE SHAGGY D.A. Buena Vista, 1976
TREASURE OF MATECUMBE Buena Vista, 1976
THE NORTH AVENUE IRREGULARS Buena Vista, 1979
THE APPLE DUMPLING GANG RIDES AGAIN
   Buena Vista, 1979
UNIDENTIFIED FLYING ODDBALL THE SPACEMAN
   AND KING ARTHUR Buena Vista, 1979
HERBIE GOES BANANAS Buena Vista, 1980

TED TALLY*
Agent: ICM - New York, 212/556-5600

TERRA NOVA (S)
HOOTERS (S)
WHITE PALACE Universal, 1990, w/Alvin Sargent
THE SILENCE OF THE LAMBS Orion, 1991

Screenplays:
NICE WORK

ALEXANDER TANA
Agent: Warden & White Associates - Beverly Hills,
   213/852-1028

Screenplays:
MAD FOR MIMA
EARTHSHAKE
MEMORIES IN DRAG
"AFTER ALL" EXPRESS
THE SECRET OF THE MOSAIC
UNDER THE SIGN OF CANCER
THE ZIGZAG MAN
NEW KIND IN TOWN

JOE TANKERSLEY
AFTER SCHOOL Moviestore Entertainment, 1989,
   w/John Linde, Rod McBrien & Hugh Parks

TERRELL M. TANNEN*
Agent: CAA - Beverly Hills, 213/288-4545

Screenplays:
SUNDOG
A GOOD DAY TO DIE
THE MAN WHO GAVE UP HIS NAME

RICHARD H. TANNENBAUM*
Agent: Abrams Artists & Associates - Los Angeles,
   213/859-0625

Screenplays:
CONNECTIONS
NIGHTRUNNER

DANIEL B. TAPLITZ
Agent: ICM - Los Angeles, 213/550-4000

FIVE OUT OF SIX (Short), directed
THE SQUEEZE Tri-Star, 1987

Screenplays:
RANDOM

DANIEL TARADASH*
Contact: WGA - Los Angeles, 213/550-1000

GOLDEN BOY Columbia, 1939, w/Lewis Meltzer,
   Sarah Y. Mason & Victer Heerman
KNOCK ON ANY DOOR Columbia, 1949,
   w/John Monks Jr.
DON'T BOTHER TO KNOCK 20th Century-Fox, 1952
RANCHO NOTORIOUS RKO, 1952
FROM HERE TO ETERNITY ★★ Columbia, 1953
DESIREE 20th Century-Fox, 1954
PICNIC Columbia, 1956
STORM CENTER Columbia, 1956, w/Elick Moll, directed
BELL, BOOK AND CANDLE Columbia, 1958
THE SABOTEUR CODE NAME MORITURI 20th
   Century-Fox, 1965
HAWAII United Artists, 1966, w/Dalton Trumbo
CASTLE KEEP Columbia, 1969, w/David Rayfiel
DOCTOR'S WIVES Columbia, 1970
THE OTHER SIDE OF MIDNIGHT 20th Century-Fox,
   1977, w/Herman Raucher

ERIK S. TARLOFF*
Agent: Shapiro/Lichtman - Los Angeles, 213/859-8877

CHEETAH Buena Vista, 1989, w/John Cotter &
   Griff DuRhone

JAY TARSES*
Agent: United Talent Agency - Beverly Hills, 213/273-6700

MAD MAGAZINE PRESENTS UP THE ACADEMY Warner
   Bros., 1980, w/Tom Patchett
THE GREAT MUPPET CAPER Universal/AFD, 1981,
   w/Tom Patchett, Jerry Juhl & Jack Rose
THE MUPPETS TAKE MANHATTAN Tri-Star, 1984,
   w/Tom Patchett & Frank Oz

Screenplays:
THE BRAVE YOUNG MEN OF WEINBERG w/Tom Patchett
CROOKS w/Tom Patchett
THE KID WHO COULD GO TO HIS LEFT w/Tom Patchett
DANCING IN THE DARK
IT LOOKED LIKE FOREVER

MAX TASH*
Agent: CAA - Beverly Hills, 213/288-4545

THE RUNNIN' KIND   MGM/UA, 1990, w/Pleasant Gehman, directed

TOM TATUM
WINNERS TAKE ALL   Apollo Pictures, 1987, Story w/Christopher Knight

ALEX TAUB*
Agent: William Morris Agency - Beverly Hills, 213/274-7451

Screenplays:
SAVING FACE
HOME GROWN

DAVID TAUSIK
Business: Motion Picture Corp. of America, 1401 Ocean Ave. - 3rd Floor, Santa Monica, CA 90401, 213/319-9500

THINK BIG   Concorde, 1990, w/Edward Kovach & Jon Turtletaub

BERTRAND TAVERNIER
Agent: ICM - Los Angeles, 213/550-4000

THE CLOCKMAKER OF ST. PAUL   Joseph Green Pictures, 1974, w/Jean Aurenche & Pierre Bost, directed
THE JUDGE AND THE ASSASSIN   Libra, 1976, w/Jean Aurenche, directed
SPOILED CHILDREN   Corinth, 1977, w/Charlotte Dubreuil & Christine Pascal, directed
DEATH WATCH   Quartet, 1980, w/David Rayfiel, directed
COUP DE TORCHON   CLEAN SLATE   Biograph/Quartet/Films Inc./The Frank Moreno Company, 1982, w/Jean Aurenche, directed
A WEEK'S VACATION   UNE SEMAINE DE VACANCES   Biograph, 1982, w/Colo Tavernier & Marie-Francoise Hans, directed
A SUNDAY IN THE COUNTRY   MGM/UA Classics, 1984, w/Colo Tavernier, directed
ROUND MIDNIGHT   Warner Bros., 1986, w/David Rayfiel, directed
LIFE AND NOTHING BUT   LA VIE ET RIEN D'AUTRE   UGC, 1989, w/Jean Cosmos, directed

PAOLO TAVIANI
Address: via dell'Ongaro 41, Rome, Italy, 06/5817231

PADRE PADRONE   New Yorker, 1977, w/Vittorio Taviani, co-directed
THE MEADOW   New Yorker, 1979, w/Vittorio Taviani, co-directed
THE NIGHT OF THE SHOOTING STARS   LA NOTTE DI SANS LORENZO   United Artists Classics, 1981, w/Vittorio Taviani, co-directed
KAOS   MGM/UA Classics, 1985, w/Vittorio Taviani, co-directed
GOOD MORNING, BABYLON   Vestron, 1987, w/Vittorio Taviani, co-directed
NIGHT SUN   Filmtre/Raiuno/Capoul/Inerpool/Sara Film/Direkt Film, 1991, w/Vittorio Taviani & Tonino Guerra, co-directed

VITTORIO TAVIANI
Address: via Orti D'Albert 4, Rome, Italy, 06/6541834

PADRE PADRONE   New Yorker, 1977, w/PaoloTaviani, co-directed
THE MEADOW   New Yorker, 1979, w/Paolo Taviania, co-directed
THE NIGHT OF THE SHOOTING STARS   LA NOTTE DI SANS LORENZO   United Artists Classics, 1981, w/Paolo Taviania, co-directed
KAOS   MGM/UA Classics, 1985, w/Paolo Taviani, co-directed
GOOD MORNING, BABYLON   Vestron, 1987, w/Paolo Taviani, co-directed
NIGHT SUN   Filmtre/Raiuno/Capoul/Inerpool/Sara Film/Direkt Film, 1991, w/Paolo Taviani & Tonino Guerra, co-directed

BRUCE A. TAYLOR*
Agent: Gorfaine/Schwartz - Los Angeles, 213/969-1011

INSTANT KARMA   MGM/UA, 1990, w/Dale Rosenbloom

DAVID C. TAYLOR*
Agent: Triad Artists, Inc. - Los Angeles, 213/556-2727

HANKY PANKY   Columbia, 1982, w/Henry Rosenbaum
GET CRAZY   Embassy, 1983, w/Danny Opatoshu & Henry Rosenbaum
LASSITER   Warner Bros., 1984
THE LIGHTSHIP   Castle Hill Productions, 1986, w/William Mai
TRAVELING MAN (CTF)   Irvin Kershner Films, 1989
FIRE BIRDS   Buena Vista, 1990, w/Paul Edwards & Nick Thiel

Screenplays:
NIGHT WORK
ANIMAL FACTORY
PRIVATE SCREENING
TICKET TO RIDE
MAN WITH A GUN
MOVING VIOLATIONS

EDWARD TAYLOR
V.I. WARSHAWSKI   Buena Vista, 1991, w/David Aaron Cohen & Nick Thiel

GREG TAYLOR*
Agent: Writers & Artists Agency - Los Angeles, 213/820-2240

PRANCER   Orion, 1989

Screenplays:
OCEAN BOULEVARD w/Rowdy Herrington
HARRIET THE SPY
FAMILY MAN w/Mike Petzold
PSYCHICS
HI FI

JOAN TAYLOR*
Contact: WGA - Los Angeles, 213/550-1000

Screenplays:
MODERN BRIDE w/Alice Arlen & Nora Ephron
WOMEN'S WORK
MONEY HONEY
BLACK TIE
NIGHT AND DAY

PHILIP JOHN TAYLOR*
Agent: William Morris Agency - Beverly Hills, 213/274-7451

LUST IN THE DUST   New World, 1984
I'M DANGEROUS TONIGHT (CTF)   MCA TV, 1990, w/Bruce Lansbury

RENEE TAYLOR*
Business Manager: Zipperstein & Kantor - Los Angeles, 213/986-4640

LOVERS AND OTHER STRANGERS ★   Cinerama Releasing Corporation, 1970, w/Joseph Bologna & David Z. Goodman
MADE FOR EACH OTHER   20th Century-Fox, 1971, w/Joseph Bologna
MIXED COMPANY   United Artists, 1974, w/Joseph Bologna
IT HAD TO BE YOU   Limelite Studios, 1989, w/Joseph Bologna, from their play

RICHARD TAYLOR*
Contact: WGA - Los Angeles, 213/550-1000

DECEPTIONS (CTF)   Republic Pictures, 1990

ROBERT TAYLOR
HEIDI'S SONG (AF)   Paramount, 1982, w/Joseph Barbera & Jameson Brewer, directed

RODERICK L. TAYLOR*
Agent: ICM - Los Angeles, 213/550-4000

THE STAR CHAMBER   20th Century-Fox, 1983, w/Peter Hyams

Screenplays:
EMPIRE MAN

ALEC TEAGUE
Agent: Warden & White Associates - Beverly Hills, 213/852-1028

Screenplays:
NOP
SMASHBAND
TROIKA

JOHN MICHAEL TEBELAK
GODSPELL   Columbia, 1973, w/David Greene, from his play

ANDRE TECHINE
Contact: French Film Office, 745 Fifth Avenue, New York, NY 10151, 212/832-8860

SCENE OF THE CRIME   1986, w/Pascal Bonitzer & Olivier Assayas, directed
RENDEZ-VOUS   Spectrafilm, 1987, w/Olivier Assayas, directed

HENRY TEFAY
WEEKEND WITH KATE   Phillip Emanuel Productions, 1990, w/Kee Young

ROY G. TEICHER*
Agent: William Morris Agency - Beverly Hills, 213/274-7451

INSIDE OUT   Hemdale, 1986, w/Kevin Bartelme, directed

Screenplays:
MEN WITHOUT BASES

MIGUEL TEJADA-FLORES*
Agent: Harris & Goldberg - Los Angeles, 213/553-5200

REVENGE OF THE NERDS   20th Century Fox, 1984, Story w/Jeff Buhai, Tim Metcalfe & Steve Zacharias
THREE FOR THE ROAD   New Century/Vista, 1987, w/Richard Martini & Tim Metcalfe
MILLION DOLLAR MYSTERY   DEG, 1987, w/Tim Metcalfe & Rudy DeLuca
FRIGHT NIGHT PART 2   New Century/Vista, 1989, w/Tim Metcalfe & Tommy Lee Wallace

Screenplays:
WITH DEADLY INTENT

TELLER*
Agent: ICM - Los Angeles, 213/550-4000

PENN & TELLER GET KILLED   Warner Bros., 1989, w/Penn Jilette

ANDY TENNANT*
Agent: Triad Artists, Inc. - Los Angeles, 213/556-2727

Screenplays:
BED & BREAKFAST w/Mike Marvin
HALF BAKED! w/Mike Marvin
CAMP ESCAPE
HALF IN - FULL OUT
DANCIN' MAN
WANDERLUST
FLIPS
BLACK 'N BLUE
LONG WAY HOME
HOME FOR THE HOLIDAYS

WILLIAM TENNANT
Contact: 213/315-7800

THE HOLLYWOOD KNIGHTS   Columbia, 1980, Story w/Floyd Mutrux & Richard Lederer

KEVIN S. TENNEY
THE BOOK OF JOE (Short), also screenplay
WITCHBOARD   Cinema Group, 1986, directed
PEACEMAKER   Fries Entertainment, 1990, directed

Screenplays:
PARDON MY NINJA

CRAIG M. TEPPER*
Contact: WGA - Los Angeles, 213/550-1000

Screenplays:
DOUBLE JEOPARDY
MAN OF STEEL
IN THE DEEP WOODS

WILLIAM TEPPER
Agent: Circle Talent Associates - Beverly Hills, 213/285-1585

Screenplays:
MONEY TALKS
THE GREAT AND THE NEAR GREAT
UN-MAN PINK & BLUE
MEN WHO DON'T QUIT

GAY PARTINGTON TERRY
Contact: Troma, Inc., 733 Ninth Ave., New York, NY 10019, 212/757-4555

THE TOXIC AVENGER, PART II Troma, 1988
THE TOXIC AVENGER, PART III: THE LAST TEMPTATION OF TOXIE Troma, 1989, w/Lloyd Kaufman

STEVE TESICH*
Agent: ICM - New York, 212/556-5600

NOURISH THE BEAST (S)
THE PASSING GAME (S)
DIVISION STREET (S)
GORKY (S)
BABA GOYA (S)
LAKE OF THE WOODS (S)
THE CARPENTERS (S)
KING OF HEARTS (S)
SQUARE ONE (S)
THE SPEED OF DARKNESS (S)
BREAKING AWAY ★★ 20th Century-Fox, 1979
EYEWITNESS 20th Century-Fox, 1981
FOUR FRIENDS Filmways, 1981
THE WORLD ACCORDING TO GARP Warner Bros., 1982
AMERICAN FLYERS Warner Bros., 1985
ELENI Warner Bros., 1985

Screenplays:
WEATHERMAN
LOVE BUSINESS
BROTHERS
CINDERELLA CITY
CANNES GAMES
OFF THE RECORD
ANYWHERE BUT HERE

ABRAHAM TETENBAUM*
Agent: APA - Los Angeles, 213/273-0744

Screenplays:
SH-BOOM

JOAN TEWKESBURY*
Agent: CAA - Beverly Hills, 213/288-4545

THIEVES LIKE US United Artists, 1974, w/Robert Altman & Calder Willingham
NASHVILLE Paramount, 1976
A NIGHT IN HEAVEN 20th Century-Fox, 1983
COLD SASSY TREE (CTF) Faye Dunaway/Don Ohlmeyer Productions, 1989, directed

Screenplays:
BLUE HIGHWAYS
LADIES NIGHT
INTIMATE RELATIONS

PAUL THEROUX
Agent: H.N. Swanson - Los Angeles, 213/652-5385

SAINT JACK New World, 1979, w/Peter Bogdonavich & Howard Sackler

Screenplays:
CHICAGO LOOP
DEAD GIRLS
THE TOM DOOLEY PROJECT

JACK THIBEAU*
Agent: Barry Perelman Agency - Los Angeles, 213/274-5999

OFF LIMITS 20th Century Fox, 1988, w/Christopher Crowe

NICK W. THIEL*
Agent: United Talent Agency - Beverly Hills, 213/273-6700

THE EXPERTS Paramount, 1988, w/Eric Alter & Steven Greene
FIRE BIRDS Buena Vista, 1990, w/Paul Edwards & David Taylor
WHITE FANG Buena Vista, 1991, w/David Fallon & Jeanne Rosenberg
SHIPWRECKED Buena Vista, 1991, w/Greg Dinner, Bob Foss & Nils Gaup
V.I. WARSHAWSKI Buena Vista, 1991, w/David Aaron Cohen & Edward Taylor

Screenplays:
THE MICK
DOG ROBBERS
HOP
RIDICULOUS MAN
LUCKY STIFF
TRIALS AND TRIBULATIONS OF CHINAMEN
UGLY DUCKLING

ANNA I. THOMAS*
Agent: ICM - Los Angeles, 213/550-4000

THE CONFESSIONS OF AMANS Bauer International, 1977, w/Gregory Nava
THE HAUNTING OF M Independent Productions, 1981, directed
THE END OF AUGUST Quartet, 1982, w/Gregory Nava, Eula Seaton & Leon Heller
EL NORTE ★ Cinecom/Island Alive, 1984, w/Gregory Nava
A TIME OF DESTINY Columbia, 1988, w/Gregory Nava

DAVE THOMAS*
Agent: ICM - Los Angeles, 213/550-4000

STRANGE BREW MGM/UA, 1983, w/Rick Moranis & Steve DeJarnatt, directed

GUY THOMAS*
Agent: Warden & White Associates - Beverly Hills, 213/852-1028

WHOLLY MOSES! Columbia, 1980

Screenplays:
FAST TALKERS

THE GHOST GOES WEST
SHIPMATES
JUNGLE BOY

JIM THOMAS*
Agent: InterTalent - Los Angeles, 213/858-6200

PREDATOR   20th Century Fox, 1987, w/John Thomas
THE RESCUE   Buena Vista, 1988, w/John Thomas
PREDATOR 2   20th Century Fox, 1990, w/John Thomas

Screenplays:
THE DOOMSDAY CONSPIRACY w/John Thomas

JOHN THOMAS*
Agent: InterTalent - Los Angeles, 213/858-6200

PREDATOR   20th Century Fox, 1987, w/Jim Thomas
THE RESCUE   Buena Vista, 1988, w/Jim Thomas
PREDATOR 2   20th Century Fox, 1990, w/Jim Thomas

Screenplays:
THE DOOMSDAY CONSPIRACY w/Jim Thomas

LESLIE E. THOMAS*
Agent: William Morris Agency - New York, 212/586-5100

STAND UP VIRGIN SOLDIERS   Warner Bros., 1977

MICHAEL THOMAS
Agent: United Talent Agency - Beverly Hills, 213/273-6700

THE HUNGER   MGM/UA, 1983, w/Ian Davis
LADYHAWKE   Warner Bros., 1985, w/Edward
  Khmara & Tom Mankiewicz
BURKE AND WILLS   Hemdale, 1987
SCANDAL   Miramax, 1989

Screenplays:
RUBY CAIRO w/Robert Dillon
FIRE ON THE MOUNTAIN
DROP DEAD
QUARTERMAIN
TIL THERE WAS YOU
SUCKERS
THE McGUFFIN
MAN ON FIRE
FIREFALL
GRAVE FOR A DOLPHIN
BROKEN ENGLISH
COMPANY MAN
RUBY KILLS
THE LADY OF SAIGON
OUT OF THE SILENCE
OFFSHORE
CULLA AND RINTHY
DICK TURPIN
HALFWAY TO SHANGHAI
SEVEN YEARS IN TIBET
BERYL MARKHAM
OH VIENNA
LORD ROCHESTER'S MONKEY
TUPAC AMARU
THE DIVA
HEAVENLY BODIES
INFIDEL
TIGER RAG
THE DANGEROUS EDGE (CTF)

RAMZI THOMAS
APPOINTMENT WITH FEAR   Galaxy, 1985, directed

RALPH L. THOMAS*
Agent: Camden-ITG - Los Angeles, 213/289-2700

TICKET TO HEAVEN   United Artists Classics, 1981,
  w/Anne Cameron, directed

ROSS THOMAS*
Agent: S.T.E. Representation - Beverly Hills, 213/550-3982

HAMMETT   Orion/Warner Bros., 1982,
  w/Dennis O'Flaherty

ROY THOMAS
FIRE AND ICE (AF)   20th Century-Fox, 1983,
  w/Gerry Conway
CONAN THE DESTROYER   Universal, 1984, Story
  w/Gerry Conway

CAMILLE THOMASSON
Agent: CAA - Beverly Hills, 213/288-4545

HEROES (Short), 1985, directed
THE BLUE SERGE SUIT (Short), 1986, directed

Screenplays:
TWILIGHT
HARTMAN
SIMPLE GIFTS
AVE MARIA

CAROLINE W. THOMPSON*
Agent: William Morris Agency - Beverly Hills, 213/274-7451

EDWARD SCISSORHANDS   Orion, 1990
THE ADDAMS FAMILY   Paramount, 1991, w/Larry Wilson
  & Paul Rudnick

Screenplays:
ROUGE w/Larry Wilson (directing)
MAI, THE PSYCHIC GIRL w/Larry Wilson
BOY CHILD w/Penelope Spheeris
THE GEEK
DISTANT MUSIC
THE INCREDIBLE JOURNEY
FIRST BURN

CHRISTOPHER N. THOMPSON*
Agent: CAA - Beverly Hills, 213/288-4545

JUMPIN' JACK FLASH   20th Century Fox, 1986, w/David
  H. Franzoni, Patricia Irving & J.W. Melville
BACK TO THE BEACH   Paramount, 1987, w/Peter
  Krikes & Steve Meerson

Screenplays:
RIP VAN HIPPIE
JETSONS

ERNEST THOMPSON*
Agent: InterTalent - Los Angeles, 213/858-6200

A SENSE OF HUMOR (S)
WEST SIDE WALTZ (S), also screenplay
ANSWERS (S)
HUMAN BEINGS (S)

PLAYWRIGHT'S DOG (S)
ON GOLDEN POND ★★   Universal/AFD, 1981,
    from his play
SWEET HEARTS DANCE   Tri-Star, 1988
1969   Atlantic Releasing Corporation, 1988, directed

Screenplays:
THE SAVIOR
CONTACT
KID STUFF
BEAUTY

FRANKLIN THOMPSON*
Agent: S.T.E. Representation - Beverly Hills, 213/550-3982

FORCED VENGEANCE   MGM/UA, 1982

GARY THOMPSON*
Agent: Warden & White Associates - Beverly Hills,
    213/852-1028

Screenplays:
SAFE HOUSE
PUBLIC ENEMY NO. 1
D.C. THRILLER (THE INVISIBLE MAN) w/Don
    Jakoby & Jeb Stuart
KOSHER COPS
THE ULTIMATE GAME
SMALL TOWN SYNDROME
MANHUNT
SPLIT SECOND

J.L. THOMPSON*
Contact: 213/820-7609

FUTURE HUNTERS   Lightning Pictures, 1989

ROB THOMPSON*
Agent: Broder-Kurland-Webb-Uffner - Los Angeles,
    213/656-9262

HEARTS OF THE WEST   MGM/United Artists, 1975
RATBOY   Warner Bros., 1986

Screenplays:
WARRIOR
ALIVE
STARS
SWEET PEA
KEN WARD ENTERS THE JUNGLE
KILLERS DON'T KISS
THE LAST AMERICAN COWBOY
PISTOLEERS

ROBERT E. THOMPSON*
Agent: Wile Enterprises, Inc. - Los Angeles, 213/828-9768

THEY SHOOT HORSES, DON'T THEY? ★   Cinerama
    Releasing Corporation, 1969, w/James Poe

THOMAS THONSON*
Agent: Sanford, Skouras, Gross & Associates -
    Los Angeles, 213/208-2100

Screenplays:
HORIZONTAL MEN
SHOOT FRANK MILLER
YOU DON'T DIE OF LOVE

DAVID C. THOREAU*
Agent: Paul Kohner, Inc. - Los Angeles, 213/550-1060

SIDE OUT   Tri-Star, 1990

STEVEN THORNLEY*
Contact: WGA - Los Angeles, 213/550-1000

HANGAR #18   Sunn Classic, 1980

BILLY BOB THORNTON*
Agent: Triad Artists, Inc. - Los Angeles, 213/556-2727

Screenplays:
THE BOND w/Tom Epperson
THE OTIS REDDING STORY w/Tom Epperson

PATRICK TILLEY
WUTHERING HEIGHTS   American International, 1970
THE PEOPLE THAT TIME FORGOT   American
    International, 1977
THE LEGACY   Columbia, 1978, w/Jimmy Sangster &
    Paul Wheeler

A.J. TIPPING
CAR TROUBLE   Thorn-EMI, 1986, w/James Whaley
ENID IS SLEEPING   Vestron, 1991, w/Maurice Phillips &
    James Whaley

DAVID N. TITCHER*
Agent: Paul Kohner, Inc. - Los Angeles, 213/550-1060

MORGAN STEWART'S COMING HOME   New Century/
    Vista, 1987, w/Ken Hixon

JAMES TOBACK*
Agent: ICM - Los Angeles, 213/550-4000

THE GAMBLER   Parmount, 1974
FINGERS   Brut Productions, 1978, directed
LOVE AND MONEY   Paramount, 1982, directed
EXPOSED   MGM/UA, 1983, directed
THE PICK-UP ARTIST   20th Century Fox, 1987, directed
BUGSY   Tri-Star, 1991

BRIAN TOBIN
DOUBLE REVENGE   Smart Egg Releasing, 1988,
    w/John Sharkey

NOREEN V. TOBIN*
Agent: The Irv Schechter Company - Beverly Hills,
    213/278-8070

DOWN TWISTED   Cannon, 1987, w/Gene O'Neill

STEPHEN TOBOLOWSKY
Agent: Triad Artists, Inc. - Los Angeles, 213/556-2727

TRUE STORIES   Warner Bros., 1986, w/David Byrne &
    Beth Henley
TWO IDIOTS IN HOLLYWOOD   FilmDallas,
    1989, directed

Screenplays:
THE FORTUNE TELLER
RULES OF THE ROAD

DONALD TODD*
Agent: United Talent Agency - Beverly Hills, 213/273-6700

Screenplays:
MANNY
THE ALF MOVIE
I OWE YOU MY LIFE

SERGIO TOLEDO
ONE MAN'S WAR (CTF)   TVS Limited, 1991,
    w/Mike Carter, directed

JOHN TOLES-BEY
Agent: Paul Kohner, Inc. - Los Angeles, 213/550-1060

A RAGE IN HARLEM   Miramax, 1991, w/Bobby Crawford

MICHAEL L. TOLKIN*
Business Manager: Addis-Wechsler & Associates -
    Los Angeles, 213/954-9000

GLEAMING THE CUBE   20th Century Fox, 1989

Screenplays:
THE RAPTURE (directing)
THE PLAYER
DEEP COVER w/Henry Bean
IT LOOKS ALIVE TO ME
WANTED
COWBOY HEAVEN
POWER OF AN ATTORNEY
IPANEMA (CTF)

NEIL TOLKIN*
Agent: ICM - New York, 212/556-5600

LICENSE TO DRIVE   20th Century Fox, 1988

Screenplays:
BURGERVILLE

STEPHEN M. TOLKIN*
Agent: Richland/Wunsch/Hohman Agency - Los Angeles,
    213/278-1955

12:01 P.M. (Short) ★   1990, w/Jonathan Heap
CAPTAIN AMERICA   21st Century Film
    Corporation, 1990
THE PRICE OF LIFE (Short), 1991, directed
    (Showtime 30-Minute Film)

Screenplays:
DAYBREAK
GOLDDIGGERS
THE LAST MARDI GRAS
ASK THE DUST
NOWHERE TO HIDE

JUDY TOLL*
Agent: David Shapira & Associates - Sherman Oaks,
    818/906-0322

CASUAL SEX?   Universal, 1988, w/Wendy Goldman,
    from their play

Screenplays:
THE SECRET LIFE OF GIRLS w/Wendy Goldman

MICHELLE TOMSKI
SAVAGE ISLAND   Empire Pictures, 1985,
    w/Nicholas Beardsly

WILLIAM TONNER*
Agent: The Roberts Company - Los Angeles, 213/552-7800

Screenplays:
NEON LIGHTS
MY KNIGHT IN SHINING ARMOR
HELL OF AN ANGEL
RENT A FAMILY

RHET E. TOPHAM*
Agent: Abrams Artists & Associates - Los Angeles,
    213/859-0625

TRICK OR TREAT   DEG, 1986, w/Michael S. Murphey &
    Joel Soisson
976-EVIL   New Line Cinema, 1989, w/Brian Helgeland

TOM TOPOR*
Agent: Rosenstone/Wender - New York, 212/832-8330

CHEAP (S)
ROMANCE (S)
BUT NOT FOR ME (S)
NUTS   Warner Bros., 1987, w/Darryl Ponicsan & Alvin
    Sargent, from his play
THE ACCUSED   Paramount, 1988
JUDGMENT (CTF)   Tisch/Wightow/Hershman Productions,
    1990, directed

Screenplays:
HERE TO STAY
BLOOD SPORT
THE LAST HONEYMOON
CRASHING
COURTROOM DRAMA: THE PEOPLE VS. JAMESTRUMAN

TRACY TORME*
Agent: ICM - Los Angeles, 213/550-4000

SPELLBINDER   MGM/UA, 1988

GIUSEPPE TORNATORE
IL CAMORRISTA   Aria Cinematografica/Titanus/Reteitalia,
    1986, directed
CINEMA PARADISO   Miramax, 1990, directed
EVERYBODY'S FINE   Miramax, 1991, w/Tonino
    Guerra, directed

PETER J. TOROKVEI*
Agent: William Morris Agency - Beverly Hills,
    213/274-7451

REAL GENIUS   Tri-Star, 1985, w/Neal Israel &
    Pat Proft
ARMED AND DANGEROUS   Columbia, 1986,
    w/Harold Ramis
BACK TO SCHOOL   Orion, 1986, w/Will Aldis,Steven
    Kampmann & Harold Ramis
CADDYSHACK II   Warner Bros., 1988, w/Harold Ramis

Screenplays:
CHAMPAGNE NIGHTS w/Harold Ramis
BEL AIR BUTLER

ROBERT TORRANCE
MUTANT ON THE BOUNTY   Skouras Pictures, 1989, Story w/Martin Lopez, directed

GABE TORRES*
Agent: Broder-Kurland-Webb-Uffner - Los Angeles, 213/656-9262

Screenplays:
DECEMBER (directing)

CINZIA TORRINI
HOTEL COLONIAL   Columbia, 1987, w/Ira Barmak, Robert Katz & Enzo Monteleone, directed

HARRY ALAN TOWERS
(Peter Welbeck)
Business: 21st Century Film Corporation, 8200 Wilshire Blvd., Beverly Hills, CA 90211, 213/658-3000

THE FACE OF FU MANCHU   7 Arts, 1965
FIVE GOLDEN DRAGONS   Towers, 1965
THE BRIDES OF FU MANCHU   Anglo Amalgamated, 1966, directed
TEN LITTLE INDIANS   Tenlit, 1966, w/Peter Yeldham
THE VENGEANCE OF FU MANCHU   Anglo Amalgamated, 1967
AND THEN THERE WERE NONE   EMI, 1974
CALL OF THE WILD   Constantin, 1975, w/Wyn Wells & Peter Yeldham
LIGHTNING: THE WHITE STALLION   Cannon, 1986
POMPEII *WARRIOR QUEEN*   Seymour Borde & Associates, 1987, Story
OUTLAW OF GOR   Cannon, 1989, w/Rick Marx, directed
MASTER OF DRAGONARD HILL   Cannon, 1990, w/Rick Marx

ROBERT TOWNE*
Agent: CAA - Beverly Hills, 213/288-4545

THE LAST WOMAN ON EARTH   Filmgroup, 1960
THE TOMB OF LIGEIA   American International, 1965
VILLA RIDES   Paramount, 1968, w/Sam Peckinpah
THE LAST DETAIL ★   Columbia, 1973
CHINATOWN ★★   Paramount, 1974
SHAMPOO ★   Columbia, 1975, w/Warren Beatty
THE YAKUZA   Warner Bros., 1975, w/Paul Schrader
PERSONAL BEST   Warner Bros., 1982, directed
TEQUILA SUNRISE   Warner Bros., 1988, directed
DAYS OF THUNDER   Paramount, 1990
THE TWO JAKES   Paramount, 1990

Screenplays:
MERMAID w/A.J. Carothers

ROGER TOWNE*
Agent: ICM - Los Angeles, 213/550-4000
Business: Rolling Hills Productions, 204 South Beverly Dr., #166, Beverly Hills, CA 90212, 213/275-0872

THE NATURAL   Tri-Star, 1984, w/Phil Dusenberry

Screenplays:
POODLE SPRINGS
BUBBA SKYLAR

BUD TOWNSEND
THE HIGH COUNTRY   Crown International, 1981

ROBERT TOWNSEND
Agent: Irvin Arhtur Associates - Beverly Hills, 213/278-5934

HOLLYWOOD SHUFFLE   Samuel Goldwyn Company, 1987, w/Keenen Ivory Wayans, directed
THE FIVE HEARTBEATS   20th Century Fox, 1991, w/Keenen Ivory Wayans, directed

BENNETT TRAMER*
Agent: William Morris Agency - Beverly Hills, 213/274-7451

KIDCO   20th Century-Fox, 1984

Screenplays:
DANGEROUSLY w/Jim Cash & Jack Epps Jr.
TOUR '85
HELLO THERE AMERICA
HOTSHOT

JEAN-CLAUDE TRAMONT*
Agent: ICM - Los Angeles, 213/550-4000

ASH WEDNESDAY   Paramount, 1973

THOMAS TRAVERS
A TIME TO REMEMBER   Filmworld Distributors, 1990, directed

DALE TREVILLION*
Agent: ICM - Los Angeles, 213/550-4000

ONE MAN FORCE   Shapiro Glickenhaus, 1989, directed

NADINE TRINTIGANT
NEXT SUMMER   European Classics, 1986, directed

DOROTHY TRISTAN*
Contact: WGA - Los Angeles, 213/550-1000

WEEDS   DEG, 1987, w/John Hancock
STEAL THE SKY (CTF)   HBO Pictures/Yoram Ben Ami Productions/Paramount TV, 1988, w/Christopher Wood

FERNANDO TRUEBA
Contact: Ministry of Culture, Montion Picture Division, Avenida de Burgos 5, 28036 Madrid, Spain, tel.: 91/202-5351

TWISTED OBSESSION   IVE, 1990, w/Manolo Matji, directed

GARRY TRUDEAU*
Agent: Broder-Kurland-Webb-Uffner - Los Angeles, 213/656-9262

DOONESBURY, A MUSICAL COMEDY (S)
TANNER '88 (CMS)   Zenith Productions/Darkhorse Productions, 1988

Screenplays:
ZOO PLANE

GUERDON TRUEBLOOD*
Agent: Broder-Kurland-Webb-Uffner - Los Angeles, 213/656-9262

WELCOME HOME SOLDIER BOYS   20th Century-Fox, 1972

THE LAST HARD MEN   20th Century-Fox, 1976
JAWS 3-D   Universal, 1983, Story

DANIEL TRULY
Agent: Triad Artists, Inc. - Los Angeles, 213/556-2727

Screenplays:
WARLORD   w/Andrew Dettman

CHRISTOPHER TRUMBO
Agent: Harry Gold & Associates - Studio City, 818/769-5003

BRANNIGAN   United Artists, 1975, w/Michael Butler, William P. McGivern & William Norton

ALAN R. TRUSTMAN*
Contact: WGA - Los Angeles, 213/550-1000

BULLITT   Warner Bros., 1968, w/Harry Kleiner
THE THOMAS CROWN AFFAIR   United Artists, 1968
THEY CALL ME MISTER TIBBS!   United Artists, 1970, w/James R. Webb
HIT!   Paramount, 1973, w/David M. Wolf
LADY ICE   Tomorrow Entertainment, 1973, w/Harold Clemins
THE NEXT MAN   Artists Entertainment, 1976, w/Michael Chapman, Mort Fine & David M. Wolf

Screenplays:
S & L
BOSTON GANG WARS

THOMAS L. TRYON*
Agent: ICM - Los Angeles, 213/550-4000

THE OTHER   20th Century-Fox, 1972

SLAVA TSUKERMAN
Contact: 212/620-0110

LIQUID SKY   Cinevista, 1983, w/Anne Carlisle & Nina V. Kerova, directed

RICHARD A. TUGGLE*
Agent: United Talent Agency - Beverly Hills, 213/273-6700

ESCAPE FROM ALCATRAZ   Paramount, 1979
TIGHTROPE   Warner Bros., 1984, directed

SANDY TUNG
Agent: Solomon Weingarten & Associates - Los Angeles, 213/474-8703

BROKEN PROMISE *A MARRIAGE*   Cinecom, 1983, directed
ACROSS THE TRACKS   Rosenbloom Entertainment, 1990, directed

RON TURBEVILLE*
Contact: WGA - Los Angeles, 213/550-1000

BUSTER & BILLIE   Columbia, 1974

SOPHIA TURKIEWICZ
Contact: Australian Film Commission, 9229 Sunset Blvd., Los Angeles, CA 90069, 213/275-7074

SILVER CITY   Samuel Goldwyn Company, 1984, w/Thomas Keneally, directed

ANNE TURNER
CELIA   Hoyts, 1989, directed

Screenplays:
TURTLE BEACH

CLIVE TURNER
HOWLING IV: THE ORIGINAL NIGHTMARE   Allied Entertainment, 1988, w/Freddie Rowe

EDWARD S. TURNER, JR.
Contact: WGA - Los Angeles, 213/550-1000

WINNERS TAKE ALL   Apollo Pictures, 1987
ERNEST SAVES CHRISTMAS   Buena Vista, 1988, w/B. Kline

JON TURTLETAUB
THINK BIG   Concorde, 1990, w/Edward Kovach & David Tausik

D.T. TWOHY*
(David N. Twohy)
Agent: William Morris Agency - Beverly Hills, 213/274-7451

CRITTERS 2   New Line Cinema, 1988, w/Mick Garris
WARLOCK   Trimark Pictures, 1991
THE GRAND TOUR   Wildstreet Productions, 1991, directed

Screenplays:
ALIENS III
TERMINAL VELOCITY   (directing)
THE FUGITIVE
THE LAST GASP

JONATHAN TYDOR*
Agent: United Talent Agency - Los Angeles,

I COME IN PEACE   Triumph, 1990, w/Leonard Maas Jr.

Screenplays:
THE UNINVITED
FROZEN
BODY COUNT

WATT TYLER
Agent: ICM - Los Angeles, 213/550-4000

ALL'S FAIR   Moviestore Entertainment, 1989, Story w/John Finnegan

KATHLEEN TYNAN
Agent: ICM - Los Angeles, 213/550-4000

AGATHA   Warner Bros., 1979, w/Arthur Hopcraft

STEP TYNER
FIRE BIRDS   Buena Vista, 1990, Story w/Dale Dye & John K. Swensson

BOB TZUDIKER*
Agent: Triad Artists, Inc. - Los Angeles, 213/556-2727

Screenplays:
MRS. FAUST w/Noni White

U

YALE M. UDOFF*
Agent: Shapiro/Lichtman - Los Angeles, 213/859-8877

A GUN PLAY (S)
MAGRITTE SKIES (S)
THE EXAMPLE (S)
FIRST DRAFT (S)
THE LITTLE GENTLEMAN L(S)
THE CLUB (S)
FAULT LINE (S)
SHADE (S)
THE ACADEMY OF DESIRE (S)
BAD TIMING/A SENSUAL OBSESSION   World Northal, 1980
THIRD DEGREE BURN (CTF)   HBO Pictures, 1989, w/Duncan Gibbins
EVE OF DESTRUCTION   Orion, 1991, w/Duncan Gibbins

ALAN UGER*
Agent: William Morris Agency - Beverly Hills, 213/274-7451

BLAZING SADDLES   Warner Bros., 1973, w/Andrew Bergman, Mel Brooks, Richard Pryor & Norman Steinberg
LEADER OF THE BAND   New Century/Vista, 1988

Screenplays:
FROST BITE

JIM UHLS*
Agent: InterTalent - Los Angeles, 213/858-6200

Screenplays:
DEAD RECKONING

ALFRED F. UHRY*
Agent: Flora Roberts, Inc. - New York, 212/355-4165

THE ROBBER BRIDEGROOM (S)
MYSTIC PIZZA   Samuel Goldwyn Company, 1988, w/Amy Jones, Perry Howze & Randy Howze
DRIVING MISS DAISY ★★   Warner Bros., 1989, from his play

Screenplays:
RICH IN LOVE

ROBERT M. ULIN*
Agent: United Talent Agency - Beverly Hills, 213/273-6700

Screenplays:
COPY BOYS
CONVENTION
SOUL MATE
C.I.T.
DORIS

FREDERICK R. ULRICH
PHANTOM OF THE MALL: ERIC'S REVENGE   Fries Entertainment, 1989, Story w/Scott J. Schneid

LEANNE UNGER
TIMES SQUARE   AFD, 1980, Story w/Alan Moyle

MATT UNGER
CLASS OF NUKE 'EM HIGH PART 2: SUBHUMANOID MELTDOWN   Troma, 1991, w/Lloyd Kaufman, Eric Louzil, Carl Morano, Marcus Rolling & Jeffrey W. Sass

ROCCO URBISCI*
Agent: William Morris Agency - Beverly Hills, 213/274-7451

JO JO DANCER, YOUR LIFE IS CALLING   Columbia, 1986, w/Paul Mooney & Richard Pryor

PETER USTINOV
Agent: William Morris Agency - Beverly Hills, 213/274-7451

THE WAY AHEAD   THE IMMORTAL BATTALIO   20th Century-Fox, 1944, w/Eric Ambler
SCHOOL FOR SECRETS   General Film Distributors, 1946, directed
VICE VERSA   GFD, 1948, directed
PRIVATE ANGELO   Pilgrim, 1949, w/Michael Anderson, directed
ROMANOFF AND JULIET   Universal, 1961, from his play, directed
BILLY BUDD   Allied Artists, 1962, w/Robert Rossen, directed
LADY L   Concordia, 1965, directed
HOT MILLIONS ★   MGM, 1968, w/Ira Wallach
MEMED, MY HAWK   Filmworld Distribution, 1984, directed

JAMIE UYS
Contact: Department of Interior, Civitas Building, Struben Street, Pretoria 0002, South Africa, 12/48-2551

DINGAKA   Embassy, 1965, directed
THE GODS MUST BE CRAZY   TLC Films/20th Century-Fox, 1979, directed
THE GODS MUST BE CRAZY 2   WEG/Columbia, 1990, directed

V

ROGER VADIM
Business Manager: Addis-Wechsler & Associates - Los Angeles, 213/954-9000

BLACKMAILED   Greater Film Distributors, 1950, w/Hugh Mills
AND GOD CREATED WOMAN   Kingsley International, 1956, directed
THE NIGHT HEAVEN FELL *LES BIJOUTIERS DU CLAIR DE LUNES*   Kingsley International, 1957, Peter Viertel, directed
LES LIAISONS DANGEREUSES *DANGEROUS LIAISONS 1960*   Astor, 1959, w/Claude Brule & Roger Vailland, directed
BLOOD AND ROSES *ET MOURIR DE PLAISIR*   Paramount, 1960, w/Claude Brule & Claude Martin, directed

STEVEN A. VAIL
SCAVENGER HUNT   20th Century-Fox, 1979, w/Henry Harper

LUIS VALDEZ*
Agent: Writers & Artists Agency - Los Angeles, 213/820-2240

I DON'T HAVE TO SHOW YOU NO STINKING BADGES (S)
CORRIDOS (S)
ZOOT SUIT   Universal, 1982, directed, from his play
LA BAMBA   Columbia, 1987, directed

TOR VALENZA
Agent: United Talent Agency - Beverly Hills, 213/273-6700

Screenplays:
RULES OF THE ROAD
NECROPOLIS
MATZGER'S DOG

JEAN VALLELY*
Agent: Triad Artists, Inc. - Los Angeles, 213/556-2727

Screenplays:
DIVORCED WOMEN
FAIR PLAY
TRAVELING LIGHT

SAM VANCE
RIVERBEND   Intercontinental Releasing, 1989

JEAN-CLAUDE VAN DAMME*
Agent: ICM - Los Angeles, 213/550-4000

KICKBOXER   Pathe Entertainment, 1989, Story w/Mark DiSalle
LIONHEART   Universal, 1991, w/Sheldon Lettich
DOUBLE IMPACT   Columbia, 1991, w/Sheldon Lettich

BRUCE VAN DUSEN
COLD FEET   Cinecom, 1984, directed

NORMAN THADDEUS VANE*
Agent: Artists Directions - Los Angeles, 213/273-0600
Business: Screen Writers Productions, 1411 N. Harper Ave., Los Angeles, CA 90046, 213/656-9260

LOLA *TWINKY*   American International, 1970
SHADOW OF THE HAWK   Columbia, 1976, w/Herbert J. Wright
FRIGHTMARE   Saturn International, 1983, directed
THE BLACK ROOM   CI Films, 1984, co-directed
KING OF THE CITY *CLUB LIFE*   Troma, 1986, directed
MIDNIGHT   Sony, 1989, directed

MARIO VAN PEEBLES
Agent: ICM - Los Angeles, 213/550-4000

IDENTITY CRISIS   Block & Chip Productions, 1989

Screenplays:
JULIET

MELVIN VAN PEEBLES
THE STORY OF A THREE-DAY PASS   Sigma III, 1968, directed
SWEET SWEETBACK'S BAADASSSSSS SONG   Cinemation, 1971, directed
GREASED LIGHTNING   Third World, 1977, w/Leon Capetanos, Lawrence DuKore & Kenneth Vose

GUS VAN SANT JR.*
Agent: William Morris Agency - Beverly Hills, 213/274-7451

MALA NOCHE   Frameline, 1987, directed, rereleased 1989
DRUGSTORE COWBOY   Avenue Pictures, 1989, w/Daniel Yost, directed
MY OWN PRIVATE IDAHO   Fine Line Features, 1991, directed

CRAIG VAN SICKLE*
Agent: The Wright Concept - Hollywood, 213/461-3844

SKI PATROL   Triumph, 1990 w/Steven Long Mitchell

Screenplays:
THE RAVAGER w/Steven Long Mitchell
LEGACY w/Steven Long Mitchell

JOSEPH VAN WINKLE
THE WOMAN INSIDE   20th Century-Fox, 1981, directed

AGNES VARDA
Contact: French Film Office, 745 Fifth Ave., New York, NY 10151, 212/832-8860

CLEO FROM 5 TO 7   Zenith, 1962, directed
LE BONHEUR   Clover, 1965, directed
ONE SINGS, THE OTHER DOESN'T   Cinema 5, 1977, directed
MURS MURS (FD)   Cine-Tamaris, 1981, directed
DOCUMENTEUR: AN EMOTION PICTURE   Cine-Tamaris, 1981, directed
VAGABOND *SANS TOIT NI LOI*   International Film Exchange, 1986, directed
JACQUOT OF NANTES   (no distributor), 1991, directed

Va

FILM WRITERS GUIDE

MICHAEL C. VARHOL*
Agent: ICM - Los Angeles, 213/550-4000

THE LAST WORD   Samuel Goldwyn Company, 1979, w/Greg Smith & Kit Carson
PEE-WEE'S BIG ADVENTURE   Warner Bros., 1985, w/Paul Reubens & Phil Hartman
THE BIG PICTURE   Columbia, 1989, w/Christopher Guest & Michael McKean

Screenplays:
TWO GUYS IN TUXEDOS

JOHN VARLEY*
Agent: CAA - Beverly Hills, 213/288-4545

MILLENNIUM   20th Century Fox, 1989

Screenplays:
GALAXY
HAVE SPACE SUIT WILL TRAVEL

CARLOS VASALLO
FISTFIGHTER   Taurus Entertainment, 1989, Story

JOSEPH P. VASQUEZ
Agent: William Morris Agency - Beverly Hills, 213/274-7451

HANGIN' WITH THE HOMEBOYS   New Line Cinema, 1991, directed

Screenplays:
HOMEGIRLS (directing)

FRANCIS VEBER*
Agent: CAA - Beverly Hills, 213/288-4545

DU COTE DE CHEZ L'AUTRE (S)
THE CONTRACT (S)
THE ABDUCTION (S)
CAUSE TOJOURS (S)
ON AURA TOUT VU (S)
THE TROUBLEMAKER (S)
THE TALL BLOND MAN WITH ONE BLACK SHOE   Cinema 5, 1972, w/Yves Robert
A PAIN IN THE A   L'EMMERDEUR   Corwin-Mahler, 1973, w/Edouard Molinaro
LE MAGNIFIQUE   Cine III, 1973
RETURN OF THE TALL BLOND MAN WITH ONE BLACK SHOE   Lanir Releasing, 1974
PEUR SUR LA VILLE   Columbia, 1975
LA CAGE AUX FOLLES ★   United Artists, 1979, w/others
COUP D'ETETE   HOTHEAD   Quartet, 1980
SUNDAY LOVERS   MGM/United Artists, 1981, w/Leslie Bricusse & Gene Wilder
LE CHEVRE   European International, 1981, directed
LA CAGE AUX FOLLES II   United Artists, 1981, w/others
PARTNERS   Paramount, 1982
LES COMPERES   European International, 1983, directed
LES FUGITIFS   Gaumont, 1986, directed
THE LOVER   Cannon, 1986
THREE FUGITIVES   Buena Vista, 1989, directed

Screenplays:
UNDER MY THUMB
KING FOR A DAY

LOUIS VENOSTA
Agent: United Talent Agency - Beverly Hills, 213/273-6700

BERRY GORDY'S THE LAST DRAGON   Tri-Star, 1985
BIRD ON A WIRE   Universal, 1990, w/Eric Lerner & David Seltzer

Screenplays:
THE AMERICAN WAY w/Grant Morris
FORTUNA
THE TOP

JAN F. VENTURA*
Contact: WGA - Los Angeles, 213/550-1000

BREAKIN' 2: ELECTRIC BOOGALOO   Tri-Star, 1984, w/Julie Reichert

MICHAEL VENTURA*
Agent: Sanford, Skouras, Gross & Associates - Los Angeles, 213/208-2100

ROADIE   United Artists, 1981, w/Big Boy Medlin
ECHO PARK   Atlantic Releasing Corporation, 1986

Screenplays:
HOWLING AT THE MOON w/Big Boy Medlin
MEANWHILE BACK AT THE KREMLIN w/Big Boy Medlin
THE GIANT CLAW
HOMAGE TO BARCELONA

SUSAN VERCELLINO
QUIET COOL   New Line Cinema, 1986, w/Clay Borris

MICHAEL VERHOEVEN
THE NASTY GIRL   Miramax, 1990, directed

PAUL VERHOEVEN
Agent: The Marion Rosenberg Office - Los Angeles, 213/653-7383
Business: Riverside Pictures B.V., Koningslaan 17, 1075 AA Amsterdam, Netherlands, 20/640-401

SOLDIER OF ORANGE   Samuel Goldwyn Company, 1977, w/Gerard Soeteman & Kees Molierhoek, directed
FLESH + BLOOD   Orion, 1985, w/Gerard Soeteman, directed

STEPHEN F. VERONA*
Contact: WGA - Los Angeles, 213/550-1000

PIPE DREAMS   Avco Embassy, 1976, directed
BOARDWALK   Atlantic Releasing Corporation, 1979, w/Leigh Chapman, directed

Screenplays:
DECEPTION
PRIMARY COLORS

CHRISTOPHER VERWIEL*
Agent: The Gage Group - Los Angeles, 213/859-8777

ROCKULA   Cannon, 1989, w/Luca Bercovici & Jefery Levy

MARK VICTOR*
Agent: CAA - Beverly Hills, 213/288-4545

THE THIN LINE   New Yorker, 1980, w/Michael Grais
POLTERGEIST   MGM/UA, 1980, w/Michael Grais & Steven Spielberg
DEATH HUNT   20th Century-Fox, 1981, w/Michael Grais
POLTERGEIST II: THE OTHER SIDE   MGM/UA, 1986, w/Michael Grais
MARKED FOR DEATH   20th Century Fox, 1990, w/Michael Grais

Screenplays:
WARP   w/Michael Grais
TRUEST SPORT   w/Michael Grais
IN A LONELY PLACE   w/Michael Grais & David Z. Goodman
BRAIN   w/Michael Grais
TURN LEFT OR DIE   w/Michael Grais
OCTOBER CIRCLE   w/Michael Grais

GORE VIDAL*
Agent: CAA - Beverly Hills, 213/288-4545

VISIT TO A SMALL PLANET   (S)
THE BEST MAN   United Artists, 1946, from his play
THE CATERED AFFAIR   MGM, 1956
I ACCUSE   MGM, 1958
THE SCAPEGOAT   MGM, 1959, w/Robert Hamer
SUDDENLY LAST SUMMER   Columbia, 1960
THE BEST MAN   United Artists, 1964, from his play
IS PARIS BURNING?   Paramount, 1966, w/Francis Ford Coppola
LAST OF THE MOBILE HOT-SHOTS   Warner Bros., 1970
CALIGULA   Analysis Film, 1980

Screenplays:
HUEY
ACTING PRESIDENT
THE BEVERLY WILSHIRE
REUNION
KALKI

JACK VIERTEL
DELUSION   New Line Cinema, 1981

PETER VIERTEL*
Business Manager: Jess Morgan, 213/937-1552

SABOTEUR   Universal, 1942, w/Joan Harrison & Dorothy Parker
WE WERE STRANGERS   Columbia, 1949, w/John Huston
DECISION BEFORE DAWN   20th Century-Fox, 1951
THE NIGHT HEAVEN FELL   LES BIJOUTIERS DU CLAIR DE LUNES   Kingsley International, 1957, Roger Vadim
THE SUN ALSO RISES   20th Century-Fox, 1957
FIVE MILES TO MIDNIGHT   United Artists, 1962, w/Hugh Wheeler
WHITE HUNTER, BLACK HEART   Warner Bros., 1990, w/James Bridges & Burt Kennedy

DANIEL VIGNE
Agent: CAA - Beverly Hills, 213/288-4545

THE RETURN OF MARTIN GUERRE   European International, 1983, w/Jean-Claude Carriere, directed
ONE WOMAN OR TWO   Orion Classics, 1985, w/Elisabeth Rappeneau, directed
SUMMER INTERLUDE   COMEDIE D'ETE   Partners Productions, 1989, w/Colo Tavernier O'Hagan, directed
THE KING'S WHORE   J & M Entertainment, 1990, w/Axel Corti & Frederic Raphael

STEPHEN VIKSTEN*
Agent: ICM - Los Angeles, 213/550-4000

Screenplays:
SURFIN' CIA   w/Joe Ansolabehere
EXTERMINATORS   w/Joe Ansolabehere
THEY WENT WEST

BRUCE VILANCH*
Agent: William Morris Agency - Beverly Hills, 213/274-7451

DIVINE MADNESS   Warner Bros., 1980, w/Jerry Blatt & Bette Midler

Screenplays:
MONOPOLY THE MOVIE   w/Jeff Silverman
PLATINUM SUNSET
FRUITS AND NUTS
CLARA
BENNY AND THE JETS
SAY GOODNIGHT, LILLIAN
SOUR GRAPES
BLAKE AND BREAK
MY FAT FRIEND
SHEET MUSIC

DIMITRI VILLARD
Business: New Star Entertainment, 260 S. Beverly Dr. #200, Beverly Hills, CA 90212, 213/205-0666

ONCE BITTEN   Samuel Goldwyn Company, 1985, Story

VICTOR E. VILLASENOR*
Contact: WGA - Los Angeles, 213/550-1000

THE BALLAD OF GREGORIO CORTEZ   Embassy, 1983, w/Robert M. Young

DAVID VINAS
COCAINE WARS   Concorde, 1986, Story

CHUCK VINCENT
Business: Platinum Pictures, 11-12 44th Avenue, Long Island City, NY 11101, 718/766-3701

PREPPIES   Platinum Pictures, 1984, w/Rick Marx, directed
SEX APPEAL   Platinum Pictures, 1986, w/Craig Horrall, directed
WILDEST DREAMS   Platinum Pictures, 1989, Story, directed

LUCIANO VINCENZONI*
Contact: WGA - Los Angeles, 213/550-1000

RAW DEAL   DEG, 1986, Story w/Sergio Donati

DANIEL H. VINING*
Contact: WGA - Los Angeles, 213/550-1000

PLAIN CLOTHES   Paramount, 1988, Story w/A. Scott Frank

Screenplays:
GOSPEL SINGER
SNAKE EYES
RUBY
DEAD OF NIGHT
IT'S ONLY MONEY
FIRST LOVE
SEMPER FI
BRAWLERS

RANDAL VISCOVICH
NIGHT VISITOR   MGM/UA, 1988

JON VOIGHT
Agent: ICM - Los Angeles, 213/550-4000

LOOKIN' TO GET OUT   Paramount, 1982, w/Al Schwartz
ETERNITY   Paul Entertainment, 1990, w/Steven Paul & Dorothy Koster Paul

STEPHEN VOLK
GOTHIC   Atlantic Releasing Corporation, 1987
THE KISS   Tri-Star, 1988, w/Tom Ropelewski
THE GUARDIAN   Universal, 1990, w/William Friedkin & Dan Greenburg

Screenplays:
LOST SOUL   w/Jeffrey Bell
TELEPATHY
THE HOST
MIRROR IMAGE

MARGARETHE VON TROTTA
Contact: German Film & TV Academy, Pommernallee 1, 1 Berlin 19, West Germany, 0311/302-6096

SISTERS OR THE BALANCE OF HAPPINESS *SCHWESTERN ODER DIE BALANCE DES GLUCKS*   Bioskop Film/First City Films/Blue Dolphin Films, 1979, w/Luisa Francia, directed
MARIANNE AND JULIANNE   *DIE BLEIRNE ZEIT*   New Yorker, 1981, directed
CIRCLE OF DECEIT   United Artists Classics, 1982, w/Jean-Claude Carriere, Kai Hermann & Volker Schlondorff
SHEER MADNESS   RS/58, 1983, directed
ROSA LUXEMBURG   New Yorker, 1987, directed
THE RETURN (L'AFRICAN)   Weltvertrieb Filmverlag dev Antonen, 1990, directed

KURT VONNEGUT, JR.
HAPPY BIRTHDAY, WANDA JUNE   Columbia, 1971, from his play

KURT VOSS
BORDER RADIO   International Film Marketing, 1988, w/Allison Anders & Dean Lent, co-directed
THE HORSEPLAYER   Relentless Entertainment, 1989, w/Larry Rattner, directed
GENUINE RISK   I.R.S. Releasing, 1990, directed
DELUSION   I.R.S. Releasing, 1991, w/Carl Copaert

Screenplays:
WHERE THE DAY TAKES YOU

OTAKAR VOTOCEK
WINGS OF FAME   First Floor Productions, 1990, w/Herman Koch, directed

W

ROBERT D. WACHS*
Business: The Robert D. Wachs Company, 345 N. Maple Dr. - Suite 179, Beverly Hills, CA 90210, 213/276-1123

BEVERLY HILLS COP II   Paramount, 1987, Story w/Eddie Murphy

KEVIN WADE*
Agent: ICM - Los Angeles, 213/550-4000

KEY EXCHANGE (S)
CRUISE CONTROL (S)
WORKING GIRL   20th Century Fox, 1988
TRUE COLORS   Paramount, 1991

Screenplays:
GOOD BEHAVIOR

MICHAEL F. WADLEIGH*
Agent: Harris & Goldberg - Los Angeles, 213/553-5200

WOLFEN   Orion/Warner Bros., 1981, w/David Eyre, directed

AMY WAGNER
Agent: United Talent Agency - Beverly Hills, 213/273-6700

Screenplays:
SHERLOCK SQUIRREL
DAKOTA JACK

BRUCE WAGNER*
Agent: CAA - Beverly Hills, 213/288-4545

YOUNG LUST   RSO Films, 1982, w/Robin Menken
A NIGHTMARE ON ELM STREET 3: DREAM WARRIORS   New Line Cinema, 1987, w/Wes Craven, Frank Darabont & Chuck Russell
SCENES FROM THE CLASS STRUGGLE IN BEVERLY HILLS   Cinecom, 1989

Screenplays:
FORCE MAJEURE
THEY SLEEP BY NIGHT
THE GRAVITY OF STARS

JANE WAGNER*
Agent: ICM - Los Angeles, 213/550-4000

MOMENT BY MOMENT   Universal, 1978, directed
THE INCREDIBLE SHRINKING WOMAN   Universal, 1981
THE SEARCH FOR SIGNS OF INTELLIGENT LIFE IN THE UNIVERSE   Orion Classics, 1991, from her play

ELAINE WAISGLASS
THE HOUSEKEEPER   Castle Hill Productions, 1987

MICHAEL WAITE
FUN DOWN THERE   Frameline, 1990, w/Roger Stigliano

RALPH WAITE
Business Manager: Global Business Management, 9000 Sunset Blvd. - Suite 1115, Los Angeles, CA 90069, 213/278-4141

ON THE NICKEL   Rose's Park, 1980, directed

ELLIOT WALD
Agent: InterTalent - Los Angeles, 213/858-6200

SEE NO EVIL, HEAR NO EVIL   Tri-Star, 1989, w/Earl Barret, Andrew Kurtzman, Arne Sulton & Gene Wilder

MALVIN WALD*
Contact: Laya Gelff & Associates - 818/342-7247

THE DARK PAST   Columbia, 1948, w/Philip Macdonald & Oscar Saul
THE NAKED CITY   Universal, 1948, w/Albert Matz
UNDERCOVER MAN   Columbia, 1949, w/Sydney Boehm
IN SEARCH OF HISTORIC JESUS   Sunn Classic, 1979, w/Jack Jacobs

WILLIAM WALES
(see David E. Ambrose)

DAVID WALKER
PLATOON LEADER   Cannon, 1988, w/Andrew Deutsch & Rick Marx

KEITH A. WALKER*
Agent: Wile Enterprises, Inc. - Los Angeles, 213/828-9768

Screenplays:
FREE WILLY

GARY WALKOW*
Contact: Attorney Frank Gruber, 213/274-5638

THE TROUBLE WITH DICK   Fever Dream Production Company, 1987, directed

Screenplays:
NOON
THIRTY SIX EXPOSURES

ART WALLACE*
Agent: William Morris Agency - New York, 212/586-5100

Screenplays:
THE TELLTALE HEART

EARL W. WALLACE*
Agent: William Morris Agency - Beverly Hills, 213/274-7451

WITNESS ★★   Paramount, 1985, w/William Kelley

Screenplays:
CHOICE OF ARMS
THE RAID ON 330 PARK

JOSEPHINE WALLACE
BAIL JUMPER   Angelika Films, 1990, w/Christian Faber

PAMELA D. WALLACE*
Agent: William Morris Agency - Beverly Hills, 213/274-7451

WITNESS ★★   Paramount, 1985, Story w/William Kelley & Earl W. Wallace

Screenplays:
DREAMS LOST, DREAMS FOUND (CTF)
LOVE WITH A PERFECT STRANGER (CTF)

TOMMY LEE WALLACE*
Agent: Harris & Goldberg - Los Angeles, 213/553-5200

AMITYVILLE II: THE POSSESSION   Orion, 1982
HALLOWEEN III: THE SEASON OF THE WITCH   Universal, 1982, directed
FRIGHT NIGHT PART 2   New Century/Vista, 1989, w/Miguel Tejada-Flores & Tim Metcalfe, directed
FAR FROM HOME   Cinecom, 1989
EL DIABLO (CTF)   Wizan/Black Productions, 1990, w/John Carpenter & Bill Phillips

JOSEPH WALSH
CALIFORNIA SPLIT   Columbia, 1974

RUPERT WALTERS
Agent: William Morris Agency - Beverly Hills, 213/274-7451

PRIVILEGED   New Yorker, 1982, w/Michael Hoffman & David Woolcambe
SOME GIRLS   MGM/UA, 1989

Screenplays:
THE DAY OF THE SUNS

FRED WALTON*
Agent: The Brandt Company - Studio City, 818/506-7747

WHEN A STRANGER CALLS   Columbia, 1979, w/Stephen Feke, directed
HADLEY'S REBELLION   American Film Distribution, 1984, w/Stephen Feke, directed
THE ROSARY MURDERS   New Line Cinema, 1987, w/Elmore Leonard, directed
TRAPPED (CTF)   USA/MCA Television, 1989, w/Stephen Feke, directed

Screenplays:
IN BROAD DAYLIGHT
WHEN A STRANGER CALLS BACK

KENT WALWIN
BIGGLES   New Century/Vista, 1988, w/John P. Groves

JOSEPH WAMBAUGH*
Agent: H.N. Swanson - Los Angeles, 213/652-5385

THE ONION FIELD   Avco Embassy, 1979
THE BLACK MARBLE   Avco Embassy, 1980

PETER WANG
Agent: Stephanie Mann Agency - Los Angeles, 213/653-7130
Business: Peter Wang Films, Inc., 594 Broadway - Suite 906, New York, NY 10012

A GREAT WALL   Orion Classics, 1986, w/Shirley Sun, directed
THE LASERMAN   Original Cinema, 1990, directed

Wa

FILM WRITERS GUIDE

WAYNE WANG*
Agent: William Morris Agency - Beverly Hills, 213/274-7451
Business: C.I.M. Productions, 665 Bush Street, San Francisco, CA 94108, 415/433-2342

CHAN IS MISSING   New Yorker, 1982, w/Isaac Cronin & Terrel Seltzer, directed
DIM SUM: A LITTLE BIT OF HEART   Orion Classics, 1985, Idea w/Lauren Chew & Terrel Seltzer, directed
LIFE IS CHEAP...BUT TOILET PAPER IS EXPENSIVE   Silverlight Entertainment, 1990, Story w/Amir M. Mokri & Spenser Nakasako, co-directed

JEFF WANSHEL*
Agent: ICM - New York, 212/556-5600

Screenplays:
666

DAVID S. WARD*
Agent: CAA - Beverly Hills, 213/288-4545

THE STING ★★   Universal, 1973
CANNERY ROW   MGM/United Artists, 1981, directed
STEELYARD BLUES   Warner Bros., 1983
THE STING II   Universal, 1983
SAVING GRACE   Embassy, 1986, w/Richard Kramer
THE MILAGRO BEANFIELD WAR   Universal, 1988, w/John Nichols
MAJOR LEAGUE   Paramount, 1989, directed
KING RALPH   Universal, 1991, directed

Screenplays:
DIAL TONE
SAN JOAQUIN
HANDLING SIN

EDMUND WARD
THE VIOLENT ENEMY   Trio, 1968
AMSTERDAM AFFAIR   Lippert, 1968
GOODBYE GEMINI   Cinerama Releasing Corporation, 1970
A PRAYER FOR THE DYING   Samuel Goldwyn Company, 1987, w/Martin Lynch

ROBERT M. WARD*
Agent: United Talent Agency - Beverly Hills, 213/273-6700

CATTLE ANNIE AND LITTLE BRITCHES   Universal, 1981, w/David Eyre

Screenplays:
RED BAKER

VINCENT WARD
Agent: CAA - Beverly Hills, 213/288-4545

VIGIL   John Maynard Productions/Film Investment Corporation of New Zealand/New Zealand Film Commission, 1984, w/Graeme Tetley, directed
THE NAVIGATOR: AN ODYSSEY ACROSS TIME
THE NAVIGATOR - A MEDIEVAL ODYSSEY   Circle Releasing, 1988, w/Geoff Chapple & Kely Lyons, directed

Screenplays:
MAP OF THE HUMAN HEART   w/Louis Naura (directing)

CLYDE WARE*
Agent: Shapiro/Lichtman - Los Angeles, 213/859-8877

BAD JIM   21st Century Film Corporation, 1990, directed

Screenplays:
BOJANGLES: THE BILL ROBINSON STORY

DAVID WARFIELD*
Agent: ICM - Los Angeles, 213/550-4000

PRIVATE INVESTIGATIONS   MGM/UA, 1987, w/John Dahl
KILL ME AGAIN   MGM/UA, 1990, w/John Dahl

ALLYN WARNER*
Agent: Abrams Artists & Associates - Los Angeles, 213/859-0625

HOUSE III: THE HORROR SHOW   MGM/UA, 1989, as "Alan Smithee," w/Leslie Bohem

Screenplays:
WHERE THE RAIN IS BORN
RAISING HELL
HAVANA DANCY
RAGGEDY HEARTS CLUB
TRUE CRIME MAGAZINE
GHOST RIDERS IN THE SKY
CURSE OF THE BLACK ROSE
TOP STORY

DERYN WARREN
BLACK MAGIC WOMAN   Trimark Pictures, 1991, Story w/Gerry Daly & Marc Springer, directed

HARRY WARREN*
Agent: The Roberts Company - Los Angeles, 213/552-7800

Screenplays:
WILL TO KILL   w/Joy Warren
SHOOTERS   w/Joy Warren
SHANNA   w/Joy Warren
LITTLE EAGLE   w/Joy Warren

JOHN WARREN*
Agent: CAA - Beverly Hills, 213/288-4545

GET CHARLIE TULLY   OOH, YOU ARE AWFUL   TBS, 1977, w/John Singer

Screenplays:
TRIMMING THE FAMILY TREE
SNEAKY PEOPLE
THE BODY POLITIC
AUGUST FIRE
GIRL IN THE CADILLAC CONVERTIBLE

JOY WARREN*
Agent: The Roberts Company - Los Angeles, 213/552-7800

Screenplays:
WILL TO KILL   w/Harry Warren
SHOOTERS   w/Harry Warren
SHANNA   w/Harry Warren
LITTLE EAGLE   w/Harry Warren

MICHAEL WARREN*
Agent: The Irv Schechter Company - Beverly Hills, 213/278-8070

HAWMPS   Mulberry Square, 1976, w/William Bickley

DERIC WASHBURN*
Agent: United Talent Agency - Beverly Hills, 213/273-6700

SILENT RUNNING   Universal, 1972, w/Steven Bochco & Michael Cimino
THE DEER HUNTER ★   Universal, 1978
THE BORDER   Universal, 1982, w/David Freeman & Walon Green
EXTREME PREJUDICE   Tri-Star, 1987, w/Harry Kleiner

Screenplays:
MURDER OF NAPOLEON
HEAVY DUST
YAMASHITA'S GOLD
TOM MIX & PANCHO VILLA

LEE WASSERMAN
RETRIBUTION   Taurus Entertainment, 1988, w/Guy Magar

STEVEN MARK WASSERMAN*
Agent: Broder-Kurland-Webb-Uffner - Los Angeles, 213/656-9262

Screenplays:
MARK MY WORDS

WENDY J. WASSERSTEIN*
Agent: ICM - Los Angeles, 213/550-4000

ISN'T IT ROMANTIC? (S)
UNCOMMON WOMEN AND OTHERS (S)
THE HEIDI CHRONICLES (S)

Screenplays:
THE OBJECT OF MY AFFECTION
LOCAL TALENT

DANIEL B. WATERS*
Agent: William Morris Agency - Beverly Hills, 213/274-7451

HEATHERS   New World, 1989
THE ADVENTURES OF FORD FAIRLANE   20th Century Fox, 1990, w/David Arnott & James Cappe
HUDSON HAWKE   Tri-Star, 1991, w/Steven deSouza

Screenplays:
BATMAN 2

JOHN WATERS
Agent: InterTalent - Los Angeles, 213/858-6200

MONDO TRASHO   Film-Makers, 1970, directed
PINK FLAMINGOS   Saliva Films, 1974, directed
FEMALE TROUBLE   New Line Cinema, 1975, directed
DESPERATE LIVING   New Line Cinema, 1977, directed
POLYESTER   New Line Cinema, 1981, directed
HAIRSPRAY   New Line Cinema, 1988, directed
CRY-BABY   Universal, 1990, directed

ROBERT E. WATERS
ALLEY CAT   Film Ventures International, 1984

ROGER WATERS
PINK FLOYD - THE WALL   MGM/UA, 1982

GREG WATKINS
A LITTLE STIFF   Just Above the Ground Productions, 1991, w/Caveh Zahedi, co-directed

CAROL A. WATSON*
Agent: Monteiro Rose Agency - Encino, 818/501-1177

FRIDAY THE 13TH PART 3   Paramount, 1982, w/Martin Kitrosser
MEATBALLS PART II   Tri-Star, 1984, Story w/Martin Kitrosser

Screenplays:
STRANGE HEARTS
SEE JANE RUN

JOHN WATSON*
Agent: ICM - Los Angeles, 213/550-4000
Business: Trilogy Entertaiment Group, 1875 Century Park East - Suite 500, Los Angeles, CA 90067, 213/785-3855

THE ZOO GANG   New World, 1985, w/Pen Densham, co-directed
ROBIN HOOD: PRINCE OF THIEVES   Warner Bros., 1991, w/Pen Densham

Screenplays:
BLIND LUCK w/Pen Densham
FLYING TIGERS w/Pen Densham
UPWORLD

PATRICIA WATSON
WHO HAS SEEN THE WIND?   Astral Bellevue, 1977
THE NUTCRACKER PRINCE (AF)   Warner Bros., 1990

JEREMY WATT
SCRUBBERS   Orion Classics, 1984, w/Roy Minton & Mai Zetterling

RICK WAY*
Agent: William Morris Agency - Beverly Hills, 213/274-7451

Screenplays:
CONVICT COWBOY w/Jim Lindsay
MY MOTHER WEARS ARMY BOOTS w/Jim Lindsay

DAMON WAYANS*
Business: Ivory Way Productions/In Living Color, 5746 Sunset Blvd., Hollywood, CA 90028, 213/856-1190

Screenplays:
MO' MONEY
BLANKMAN (directing)

KEENEN IVORY WAYANS*
Agent: InterTalent - Los Angeles, 213/858-6200
Contact: Belinkoff-London-Lichtenberg - Los Angeles, 213/470-2484
Business: Ivory Way Productions/In Living Color, 5746 Sunset Blvd., Hollywood, CA 90028, 213/856-1190

HOLLYWOOD SHUFFLE   Samuel Goldwyn Company, 1987, w/Robert Townsend
EDDIE MURPHY RAW   Paramount, 1987, w/Eddie Murphy

I'M GONNA GIT YOU SUCKA   MGM/UA,
   1989, directed
THE FIVE HEARTBEATS   20th Century Fox, 1991,
   w/Robert Townsend

MICHAEL WEARING
Contact: British Broadcasting Corp., Woodlands,
   80 Wood Lane, London W12 7RJ, England,
   081/743-8000

BELLMAN AND TRUE   Island Pictures, 1987,
   w/Richard Loncraine & Desmond Lowden
FELLOW TRAVELLER (CTF)   British Film Institute/BBC/
   HBO Showcase, 1990

ALISTER WEBB
HEAVEN TONIGHT   Boulevard Films, 1990,
   w/Frank Howson

JAMES WEBB
Agent: CAA - Beverly Hills, 213/288-4545

Screenplays:
RULES OF ENGAGEMENT

LEN WECHSLER*
Agent: Sanford, Skouras, Gross & Associates -
   Los Angeles, 213/208-2100

Screenplays:
CALIFORNIA DREAMING   w/Jeff Smith

DAVID J. WECHTER*
Agent: William Morris Agency - Beverly Hills,
   213/274-7451

MIDNIGHT MADNESS   Buena Vista, 1980, w/Michael
   Nankin, co-directed
MALIBU BIKINI SHOP   THE BIKINI SHOP   International
   Film Marketing, 1987, directed

Screenplays:
MURPHY'S LAW OF GOLF   (co-directing)
BE TRUE TO YOUR SCHOOL
JUNIOR HIGH SCHOOL

STEPHEN WEEKS
GAWAIN AND THE GREEN KNIGHT   United Artists,
   1973, w/Philip Green, directed
GHOST STORY   Weeks, 1974, w/Rosemary
   Sutcliff, directed
SWORD OF THE VALIANT   Cannon, 1984, w/Phillip M.
   Breen & Howard C. Pen, directed

DEEDEE WEHLE
DISTANT THUNDER   Paramount, 1988, Story
   w/Robert Stitzel

HERMAN WEIGEL
Business: Neue Constantin Film, GmbH & Co
   Verleih KG, Kaiserstraße 39, D-8000 München 40,
   West Germany, 38-60-90

CHRISTIANE F.   New World, 1982
THE NEVERENDING STORY   Warner Bros., 1984,
   w/Wolfgang Petersen

ED. WEINBERGER*
Business Manager: Friedman, Kinzelberg, Broder,
   213/277-0700

THE LONELY GUY   Universal, 1984, w/Stan Daniels

Screenplays:
SKETCHLIFE

JAKE WEINBERGER*
Agent: David Shapira & Associates - Sherman Oaks,
   818/906-0322

Screenplays:
COYOTE LOVE   w/Mike Weinberger
ESCAPEES   w/Mike Weinberger

MIKE WEINBERGER*
Agent: David Shapira & Associates - Sherman Oaks,
   818/906-0322

Screenplays:
COYOTE LOVE   w/Jake Weinberger
ESCAPEES   w/Jake Weinberger

WILLIAM DREW WEINBRENNER
Agent: Circle Talent Associates - Beverly Hills,
   213/285-1585

Screenplays:
MY BLUE LADY
THE BURNING COLD

ELLIS WEINER
Business: Spy Magazine, The SPY Building, 5 Union
   Square West, New York, NY 10003

NATIONAL LAMPOON'S MOVIE MADNESS   United Artists,
   1982, w/Tod Carroll, Shary Flenniken, Pat Mephitis &
   Gerald Sussman

GARY WEINER
Agent: Susan Smith & Associates - Beverly Hills,
   213/852-4777

Screenplays:
IF MORNING EVER COMES   w/Shira Levin

HAL WEINER
THE IMAGEMAKER   Castle Hill Productios, 1986, w/Dick
   Goldberg, directed

RANDY WEINER
Agent: United Talent Agency - Beverly Hills,
   213/273-6700

CLUB XII (S)   w/Rob Hanning

Screenplays:
YO' JULIETTE   w/Rob Hanning

REX WEINER*
Agent: The Gersh Agency - Beverly Hills, 213/274-6611

FORGOTTEN PRISONERS: THE AMNESTY FILES (CTF)
   Turner Pictures, 1990, w/Cindy Myers

HERSCHEL A. WEINGROD*
Agent: APA - Los Angeles, 213/273-0744
Business: Myrtos Productions, Universal Studios, 818/777-1000

CHEAPER TO KEEP HER   American Cinema, 1980, w/Timothy Harris
TRADING PLACES   Paramount, 1983, w/Timothy Harris
BREWSTER'S MILLIONS   Universal, 1985, w/Timothy Harris
MY STEPMOTHER IS AN ALIEN   WEG, 1988, w/Timothy Harris, Jonathan Reynolds & Jericho Stone
TWINS   Universal, 1989, w/Timothy Harris, William Davies & William Osborne
KINDERGARTEN COP   Universal, 1990, w/Timothy Harris & Murray Salem
PURE LUCK   Universal, 1991, w/Timothy Harris

Screenplays:
DUMMIES   w/Timothy Harris
SIBERIAN EXPRESS   w/Timothy Harris
THE FRENCH KISS   w/Timothy Harris
THE PIED PIPER   w/Timothy Harris
THE FUGITIVE PIGEON   w/Timothy Harris
BIGFINGER   w/Timothy Harris
MICKEY   w/Timothy Harris
BEAUTY SCHOOL   w/Timothy Harris

BOB WEINSTEIN
Business: Miramax Films, Tribeca Film Center, 375 Greenwich St., New York, NY 10013, 212/941-4000

THE BURNING   Filmways/Orion, 1982, w/Peter Lawrence
PLAYING FOR KEEPS   Universal, 1986, w/Harvey Weinstein & Jeremy Leven, co-directed

DAVID Z. WEINSTEIN*
Agent: Irvin Arthur Associates - Beverly Hills, 213/278-5934

BIG TROUBLE IN LITTLE CHINA   20th Century Fox, 1986, w/Gary Goldman

Screenplays:
RAISING CANE

HARVEY WEINSTEIN
Business: Miramax Films, Tribeca Film Center, 375 Greenwich St., New York, NY 10013, 212/941-4000

PLAYING FOR KEEPS   Universal, 1986, w/Bob Weinstein & Jeremy Leven, co-directed

FRED WEINTRAUB
Business: Fred Weintraub Productions, 1923 1/2 Westwood Blvd. #2, Los Angeles, CA 90025, 213/470-8787

THE BIG BRAWL   Warner Bros., 1980, Story w/Robert Clouse

SANDRA WEINTRAUB ROLAND
(See Sandra Weintraub ROLAND)

DAVID WEIR*
Contact: 415/986-5196

ROLLOVER   Orion/Warner Bros., 1981, Story w/Howard Kohn & David Shaber

PETER WEIR
Agent: CAA - Beverly Hills, 213/288-4545

THREE TO GO   Commonwealth Film Unit Productions, 1971, "Michael," directed
THE CARS THAT ATE PEOPLE   THE CARS THAT ATE PARIS   New Line Cinema, 1974, directed
THE PLUMBER   Barbary Coast, 1978, directed
THE LAST WAVE   World Northal, 1978, w/Tony Morphett & Petru Popescu, directed
GALLIPOLI   Paramount, 1981, Story, directed
THE YEAR OF LIVING DANGEROUSLY   MGM/UA, 1983, w/David Williamson & C.J. Koch, directed
GREEN CARD ★   Buena Vista, 1990, directed

ALLAN C. WEISBECKER*
Agent: The Artists Agency - Los Angeles, 213/277-7779

BEER   Orion, 1985

Screenplays:
STOLEN THUNDER
AN ISLAND IN WINTER
FOREIGN POLICY
DRUMS ALONG THE HUDSON

DAVID WEISBERG*
Agent: Sanford, Skouras, Gross & Associates - Los Angeles, 213/208-2100

PAYOFF (CTF)   Viacom Pictures, 1991, w/Douglas S. Cook

DOUGLAS J. WEISER
MIDNIGHT CROSSING   Vestron, 1988, w/Roger Holzberg

STANLEY G. WEISER*
Agent: ICM - Los Angeles, 213/550-4000

COAST TO COAST   Paramount, 1980
PROJECT X   20th Century Fox, 1987
WALL STREET   20th Century Fox, 1987, w/Oliver Stone

Screenplays:
INSIDE WARS
SERVE AND PROTECT
GOLDEN LEGS

SUSAN WEISER-FINLEY
Agent: Stone Manners Agency - Los Angeles, 213/275-9599

THE FIRST TIME   New Line Cinema, 1982, w/Charlie Loventhal & William Finley

MATTHEW WEISMAN*
Agent: CAA - Beverly Hills, 213/288-4545

TEEN WOLF   Atlantic Releasing Corporation, 1985, w/Joseph Loeb III
COMMANDO   20th Century Fox, 1985, Story w/Steven de Souza & Joseph Loeb III
TEEN WOLF TOO   Atlantic Releasing Corporation, 1987, Story w/Joseph Loeb III
BURGLAR   Warner Bros., 1987, w/Joseph Loeb III & Hugh Wilson

Screenplays:
NIGHTTIME GUY   w/Joseph Loeb III
SILENT PARTNERS   w/Joseph Loeb III

We

DAVID N. WEISS*
Agent: The Irv Schechter Company - Beverly Hills, 213/278-8070

ALL DOGS GO TO HEAVEN (AF) MGM/UA, 1989
ROCK-A-DOODLE (AF) Samuel Goldwyn Company, 1990

PETER WELBECK
(See Harry Alan Towers)

JULIE WELCH
THOSE GLORY, GLORY DAYS Cinecom, 1983

COLIN WELLAND*
Agent: CAA - Beverly Hills, 213/288-4545

YANKS Universal, 1979, w/Walter Bernstein
CHARIOTS OF FIRE ★★ The Ladd Company/Warner Bros., 1981
TWICE IN A LIFETIME The Yorkin Company, 1985
A DRY WHITE SEASON MGM/UA, 1989, w/Euzhan Palcy

Screenplays:
CHARLIE CHAPLIN
LECH WALESA
YELLOW JERSEY
SHACKLETOWN

MICHAEL WELLER*
Agent: Rosenstone/Wender - New York, 212/932-8330

MOONCHILDREN (S)
FISHING (S)
LOOSE ENDS (S), also screenplay
WARFMAN MASTER OF A MILLION SHAPES (S)
THE BALLAD OF SOAPY SMITH (S)
SPOILS OF WAR (S)
HAIR United Artists, 1979
RAGTIME ★ Paramount, 1981
LOST ANGELS Orion, 1989

Screenplays:
DEATH OF AN AMERICAN
THE FIFTH HORSEMAN
AND NOW THERE'S JUST THE THREE OF US
BREAKING THROUGH

WENDELL E. WELLMAN*
Business Manager: Fred Amsel & Associates - Los Angeles, 213/939-1188

FIREFOX Warner Bros., 1982, w/Alex Lasker

AUDREY WELLS
Agent: United Talent Agency - Beverly Hills, 213/273-6700

Screenplays:
RADIO FREE ALASKA

WIM WENDERS
Agent: Paul Kohner, Inc. - Los Angeles, 213/550-1060
Business: Gray City Inc., 853 Broadway, New York, NY 10007, 212/473-3600

ALICE IN THE CITIES New Yorker, 1974, directed
KINGS OF THE ROAD Bauer International, 1976, directed
THE AMERICAN FRIEND New Yorker, 1977, directed
LIGHTNING OVER WATER *NICK'S MOVIE* Pari Films, 1980, w/Nicholas Ray, co-directed
TOKYO-GA (FD) Wim Wenders Produktion/Gray City/Chris Sievernich Produktion, 1985, directed
WINGS OF DESIRE *DER HIMMEL UBER BERLIN* Orion Classics, 1987, w/Peter Handke, directed
UNTIL THE END OF THE WORLD Road Movies, 1991, w/Peter Carey, directed

GINA WENDKOS*
Agent: United Talent Agency - Beverly Hills, 213/273-6700

PERSONALITY (S)
BOYS AND GIRLS/MEN AND WOMEN (S)
FOUR CORNERS (S)
GINGER ALE AFTERNOON Skouras Pictures, 1989, from her play

Screenplays:
JERSEY GIRLS
DINOSAURS
CARRY ME THROUGH
BEAT OF THE NEW WORLD

RICHARD WENK*
Agent: The Gersh Agency - Beverly Hills, 213/274-6611

VAMP New World, 1986, directed

Screenplays:
SCALPER

RONNIE WENKER-KONNER*
Agent: ICM - Los Angeles, 213/550-4000

Screenplays:
THE BIG ROOM

MIKE WERB*
Agent: United Talent Agency - Beverly Hills, 213/273-6700

Screenplays:
MACHINE GUN KELLY
FACE-OFF w/Michel Colleary
CURIOUS GEORGE

LINA WERTMULLER
Address: Piazza Coltilde 5, Rome, Italy, 05/360-7501

THE SEDUCTION OF MIMI *MIMI METALLURGICO FERITO NELL'ONORE* New Line Cinema, 1972, directed
LOVE AND ANARCHY *FILM D'AMORE E D'ANARCHIA* Peppercorn-Wormser, 1973, directed
ALL SCREWED UP *TUTTO A POSTE E NIENTE IN ORDINE* New Line Cinema, 1974, directed
SWEPT AWAY BY AN UNUSUAL DESTINY IN THE BLUE SEA OF AUGUST Cinema 5, 1974, directed
SEVEN BEAUTIES *PASQUALINO SETTEBELLEZZE* ★ Cinema 5, 1976, directed
THE END OF THE WORLD IN OUR USUAL BED IN A NIGHT FULL OF RAIN Warner Bros., 1978, directed
BLOOD FEUD *FATTO DI SANGUE FRA DUE UOMINI PER CAUSA DI UNA VEDOVA (SI SOSPETTANO MOVENTI POLITICI)* AFD, 1980, directed
A JOKE OF DESTINY lying in wait around the corner like a street bandit Samuel Goldwyn Company, 1983, directed
SOTTO, SOTTO Triumph/Columbia, 1984, directed

CAMORRA *UN COMPLICATO INTRIGO DI DONNE, VICOLI E DELITTI* Cannon, 1986, directed
SUMMER NIGHT WITH GREEK PROFILE, ALMOND EYES AND SCENT OF BASIL New Line Cinema, 1986, directed
CRYSTAL OR ASH, FIRE OR WIND, AS LONG AS IT'S LOVE Italian International Films/RAI/Istituto Luce/Italnoleggio, 1989, directed
SATURDAY, SUNDAY AND MONDAY Silvio Berlusconi Communications, 1990, directed

RICHARD WESLEY*
Agent: The Gersh Agency - Beverly Hills, 213/274-6611

THE MIGHTY GENTS (S)
UPTOWN SATURDAY NIGHT Warner Bros., 1974
LET'S DO IT AGAIN Warner Bros., 1975
FAST FORWARD Columbia, 1985
NATIVE SON Cinecom International, 1986

PETER WEST
FISTS OF BLOOD Virgo Productions/TVM Studios, 1989

VALERIE D. WEST*
Agent: Maggie Field Agency - Studio City, 818/980-2001

Screenplays:
GOOD LUCK TO A SWELL KID
CHOICES
MOTHER'S & SON

DONALD E. WESTLAKE*
Agent: Paul Kohner, Inc. - Los Angeles, 213/550-1060

COPS AND ROBBERS United Artists, 1973
HOT STUFF Columbia, 1979, w/Michael Kane
THE STEPFATHER New Century/Vista, 1987
WHY ME? Triumph, 1990, w/Leonard Maas Jr.
THE GRIFTERS ★ Cineplex Odeon/Miramax, 1990

Screenplays:
LOVE IN THE ATTIC

ERIC WESTON
Agent: ICM - Los Angeles, 213/550-4000

EVILSPEAK The Frank Moreno Co., 1982, w/Joseph Garfalo, directed
MARVIN AND TIGE *LIKE FATHER AND SON* 20th Century-Fox International Classics, 1983, w/Wanda Dell, directed
THE IRON TRIANGLE Scotti Bros., 1989, w/John Bushelman & Larry Hilbrand, directed

Screenplays:
DANGEROUS PLACES

HASKELL WEXLER
Agent: Sanford, Skouras, Gross & Associates - Los Angeles, 213/208-2100
Business: Perigro Productions, Inc., 3659 Las Flores Canyon Road, Malibu, CA 90265, 213/456-3438

MEDIUM COOL Paramount, 1969, directed
LATINO Cinecom, 1985, directed

MILTON WEXLER*
Agent: ICM - Los Angeles, 213/550-4000

THE MAN WHO LOVED WOMEN Columbia, 1983, w/Blake Edwards & Geoffrey Edwards
THAT'S LIFE! Columbia, 1986, w/Blake Edwards

NORMAN WEXLER*
Agent: Barrett, Benson, McCartt & Weston - Los Angeles, 213/247-5500

PRIVATE OPENING (S)
JOE ★ Cannon, 1970
SERPICO ★ Paramount, 1973, w/Waldo Salt
MANDINGO Paramount, 1975
DRUM United Artists, 1976
SATURDAY NIGHT FEVER Paramount, 1977
STAYING ALIVE Paramount, 1983, w/Sylvester Stallone
RAW DEAL DEG, 1986, w/Gary DeVore

Screenplays:
LETHAL GAS
ONE JUST MAN
POWER TRIP
LUNATICS
ANATOMY OF A BURGLARY
GROWING SEASON
BOYD

JAMES WHALEY
CAR TROUBLE Thorn-EMI, 1986, w/A.J. Tipping
ENID IS SLEEPING Vestron, 1991, w/A.J. Tipping & Maurice Phillips

JIM WHEAT*
Agent: The Gersh Agency - Beverly Hills, 213/274-6611

SILENT SCREAM American Cinema, 1980, w/Ken Wheat & Wallace Bennett
LIES International Film Marketing, 1983, w/Ken Wheat, co-directed
THE FLY II 20th Century Fox, 1989, w/Frank Darabont, Mick Garris & w/Ken Wheat
AFTER MIDNIGHT MGM/UA, 1989, w/Ken Wheat, co-directed

Screenplays:
MUTATION

KEN WHEAT*
Agent: The Gersh Agency - Beverly Hills, 213/274-6611

SILENT SCREAM American Cinema, 1980, w/Jim Wheat & Wallace Bennett
LIES International Film Marketing, 1983, w/Jim Wheat, co-directed
THE FLY II 20th Century Fox, 1989, w/Frank Darabont, Mick Garris & w/Jim Wheat
AFTER MIDNIGHT MGM/UA, 1989, w/Jim Wheat, co-directed

Screenplays:
MUTATION

ANNE WHEELER
BYE BYE BLUES Circle Releasing, 1989, directed

DOUGLAS N. WHEELER*
Contact: George Diskant, Esq. - Los Angeles,
213/824-3773

Screenplays:
TOOTS IN SOLITUDE
ONLY YOU
LONG DAY BEFORE DARK

PAUL WHEELER
PUPPET ON A CHAIN   Cinerama Releasing Corporation,
   1972, w/Alistair MacLean & Don Sharp
CARAVAN TO VACCARES   Crowndale, 1974
THE LEGACY   Columbia, 1978, w/Jimmy Sangster &
   Patrick Tilley
A BREED APART   Orion, 1984

DIZ WHITE
BULLSHOT!   Island Alive, 1983, w/Ron House &
   Alan Shearman

GARRY MICHAEL WHITE*
Agent: Broder-Kurland-Webb-Uffner - Los Angeles,
   213/656-9262

SCARECROW   Warner Bros., 1973
SKY RIDERS   20th Century-Fox, 1976, w/Jack DeWitt &
   Stanley Mann
THE PROMISE   Universal, 1979

KIMBERLY LYNN WHITE
BODY ROCK   New World, 1984, Story
   w/Desmond Nakano

NONI WHITE*
Agent: Richland/Wunsch/Hohman Agency - Los Angeles,
   213/278-1955

Screenplays:
MRS. FAUST   w/Bob Tzudiker

HUGH J. WHITEMORE*
Agent: Rosenstone/Wender - New York, 212/832-8330

BREAKING THE CODE (S)
PACK OF LIES (S), also teleplay
ALL NEAT IN BLACK STOCKINGS   National General,
   1969, w/Jane Gaskell
ALL CREATURES GREAT AND SMALL   EMI, 1974
MAN AT THE TOP   Anglo-EMI, 1975
THE BLUE BIRD   20th Century-Fox, 1976, w/Alfred
   Hayes & Alexei Kapler
STEVIE   First Artists, 1978, from his play
THE RETURN OF THE SOLDIER   European
   Classics, 1985
84 CHARING CROSS ROAD   Columbia, 1987

Screenplays:
UTZ

RICHARD F. WHITLEY
Agent: Favored Artists Agency - Los Angeles, 213/653-3191

ROCK'N'ROLL HIGH SCHOOL   New World, 1979,
   w/Russ Dvonch & Joseph McBride
PANDEMONIUM   MGM/UA, 1982, w/Jaime Klein

Screenplays:
CHARLIE & MORRY
ESKIMO SUMMER
GETTING IT OVER WITH   w/Russ Dvonch & Amy Heckerling
UNTITLED A-GO-GO   w/Amy Heckerling
ROAD TO RUIN   w/Jaime Klein
THE PERFECT MAN
RED HERRING
REGATTA   w/Jaime Klein
THE CHICAGO KID
BLUD BLOOD
SOMETHING IN THE PARK
DREAM CHASERS
CAT & MOUSE
PRACTICALLY A JOKE
UNDER THE GUN
LIFE STORY
DEATH OF ME YET
HERO SHOT

JOHN WHITMAN*
Contact: WGA - Los Angeles, 213/550-1000

YOUNGBLOOD   MGM/UA, 1986, Story w/Peter Markle

STANFORD C. WHITMORE*
Agent: Robinson, Weintraub, Gross & Associates -
   Los Angeles, 213/653-5802

WAR HUNT   TD Enterprises, 1961
HAMMERSMITH IS OUT   Cinerama, 1972
BABY BLUE MARINE   Columbia, 1976
THE DARK   Film Ventures International, 1979

JAMES WHITTAKER
MEGAFORCE   20th Century-Fox, 1982, w/Albert S. Ruddy,
   Hal Needham & Andre Morgan

Screenplays:
MUSIC CITY BLUES

DAVID WICKES
Agent: ICM - Los Angeles, 213/550-4000

SILVER DREAM RACER   Almi Cinema 5, 1980, directed

W.W. WICKET
(See Clifford & Ellen Green)

CHRISTOPHER WICKING
SCREAM AND SCREAM AGAIN   American
   International, 1969
CRY OF THE BANSHEE   American International, 1970,
   w/Tim Kelly
BLOOD FROM THE MUMMY'S TOMB   Hammer, 1971
TO THE DEVIL A DAUGHTER   EMI, 1976
LADY CHATTERLEY'S LOVER   Cannon, 1982,
   w/Just Jaeckin
ABSOLUTE BEGINNERS   Orion, 1986, w/Richard
   Burridge & Don MacPherson

GREGORY C. WIDEN*
Agent: Writers & Artists Agency - Los Angeles, 213/820-2240

HIGHLANDER   20th Century Fox, 1986, w/Peter Bellwood
   & Larry Ferguson
BACKDRAFT   Universal, 1991

Screenplays:
URBAN LEGENDS   w/Randy Johnson, William Judkins,
   Donald Knowlton & Ethan Wiley

SHOOTERS
DELERIUM 237
O.S.S.
CLAN OF ONE
SHADOW WARRIORS

KEN WIEDERHORN*
Agent: The Gersh Agency - Beverly Hills, 213/274-6611

SHOCK WAVES   Joseph Brenner Associates, 1977, w/John Harrison, directed
RETURN OF THE LIVING DEAD PART II   Lorimar, 1988, directed
DARK TOWER   Spectrafilm, 1989, w/Robert J. Avrech & Ken Blackwell

CHARLES WIENER
RECRUITS   Concorde, 1986, w/B.K. Roderick

JOE WIESENFELD
PRINCES IN EXILE   Cinepix/National Film Board, 1991

BILLY WILDER*
Agent: Paul Kohner, Inc. - Los Angeles, 213/550-1060

MAUVAISE GRAINE   1933, Shared, directed
MUSIC IN THE AIR   20th Century-Fox, 1934, w/Howard Young
CHAMPAGNE WALTZ   Paramount, 1937, w/Story w/H.S. Kraft & Vienna Hall
BLUEBEARD'S EIGHTH WIFE   Paramount, 1938, w/Charles Brackett
MIDNIGHT   Paramount, 1939, w/Charles Brackett
NINOTCHKA ★   MGM, 1939, w/Charles Brackett & Walter Reisch
HOLD BACK THE DAWN ★   Paramount, 1941, w/Charles Brackett
ARISE MY LOVE   Paramount, 1940, w/Charles Brackett
THE MAJOR AND THE MINOR   Paramount, 1942, w/Charles Brackett
BALL OF FIRE   Goldwyn, 1942, w/Charles Brackett
FIVE GRAVES TO CAIRO   Paramount, 1943, w/Charles Brackett, directed
DOUBLE INDEMNITY ★   Paramount, 1944, w/Raymond Chandler, directed
THE LOST WEEKEND   Paramount, 1945, w/Charles Brackett, directed
THE EMPEROR WALTZ   Paramount, 1948, w/Charles Brackett, directed
A FOREIGN AFFAIR ★   Paramount, 1948, w/Charles Brackett & Richard Breen, directed
SUNSET BOULEVARD ★★   Paramount, 1950, w/Charles Brackett & D.M. Marshman Jr., directed
ACE IN THE HOLE ★★   Paramount, 1951, w/Walter Newman & Leslie Samuels, directed
STALAG 17   Paramount, 1953, w/Edwin Blum, directed
SABRINA   Paramount, 1954, w/Ernest Lehman & Samuel Taylor, directed
THE SEVEN YEAR ITCH   20th Century-Fox, 1955, w/George Axelrod, directed
THE SPIRIT OF ST. LOUIS   Warner Bros., 1957, w/Wendell Mayes, directed
LOVE IN THE AFTERNOON   Allied Artists, 1957, w/I.A.L. Diamond, directed
WITNESS FOR THE PROSECUTION   United Artists, 1957, w/Harry Kurnitz, directed
SOME LIKE IT HOT   United Artists, 1959, w/I.A.L. Diamond, directed
THE APARTMENT ★★   United Artists, 1960, w/I.A.L. Diamond, directed
ONE, TWO, THREE   United Artists, 1961, w/I.A.L. Diamond, directed
IRMA LA DOUCE   United Artists, 1963, w/I.A.L. Diamond, directed
KISS ME, STUPID   United Artists, 1964, w/I.A.L. Diamond, directed
THE FORTUNE COOKIE ★   United Artists, 1966, w/I.A.L. Diamond, directed
THE PRIVATE LIFE OF SHERLOCK HOLMES   United Artists, 1970, w/I.A.L. Diamond, directed
AVANTI!   United Artists, 1972, w/I.A.L. Diamond, directed
THE FRONT PAGE   Universal, 1974, w/I.A.L. Diamond, directed
FEDORA   United Artists, 1979, w/I.A.L. Diamond, directed
BUDDY BUDDY   MGM/United Artists, 1981, w/I.A.L. Diamond, directed

DAVID WILDER
KNIGHTS OF THE CITY   New World, 1986, Story w/Leon Isaac Kennedy

GENE WILDER*
Agent: CAA - Beverly Hills, 213/288-4545

THE ADVENTURE OF SHERLOCK HOLMES' SMARTER BROTHER   20th Century-Fox, 1975, directed
YOUNG FRANKENSTEIN ★   20th Century-Fox, 1974, w/Mel Brooks
THE WORLD'S GREATEST LOVER   20th Century-Fox, 1977, directed
SUNDAY LOVERS   MGM/UA, 1981, w/Leslie Bricusse & Francis Veber
THE WOMAN IN RED   Orion, 1984, directed
HAUNTED HONEYMOON   Orion, 1986, w/Terence Marsh, directed
SEE NO EVIL, HEAR NO EVIL   Tri-Star, 1989, w/Earl Barret, Andrew Kurtzman, Arne Sultan & Elliot Wald

JOHN KEITH WILDER*
Agent: CAA - Beverly Hills, 213/288-4545

Screenplays:
THE RIFLEMAN
NEVER SAY DIE
THE LAST OF THE BREED

ETHAN J. WILEY*
Agent: Triad Artists, Inc. - Los Angeles, 213/556-2727

HOUSE   New World, 1986
HOUSE II: THE SECOND STORY   New World, 1987, directed

Screenplays:
A STRANGER IN LEADVILLE
DEVIL'S HIGHWAY
URBAN LEGENDS w/Randy Johnson, Gregory Widen, William Judkins & Donald Knowlton
SPIDERMAN

JEFF WILHELM
Agent: APA - Los Angeles, 213/273-0744

Screenplays:
CAREER MOVES
THE BIG RASCALS
NO PLACE FOR A DAME

KATE WILHELM
THE LOOKALIKE (CTF)   Gallo Entertainment Inc., 1990, Story

DIANE E. WILK*
Agent: Broder-Kurland-Webb-Uffner - Los Angeles, 213/656-9262

Screenplays:
TWO LITTLE RICH GIRLS

AL WILLIAMS
ARACHNOPHOBIA   Buena Vista, 1990, Story w/Don Jakoby

BRIAN WILLIAMS
SMOKEY BITES THE DUST   New World, 1981, Story

BRUCE WILLIAMS
PRIVATE COLLECTIONS   Red Wing Productions, 1990, w/David Heisler, directed

ERIC WILLIAMS
Agent: Circle Talent Associates - Beverly Hills, 213/285-1585

Screenplays:
BAD SPORTS   w/Bill McCloskey
ONE NIGHT ONLY   w/Bill McCloskey

JASON WILLIAMS
DANGER ZONE II: REAPER'S REVENGE   Skouras Pictures, 1989, Story w/Tom Friedman
DANGER ZONE III: STEEL HORSE WAR   Dead Zone Company, 1990, w/Gregory Poirier

LARRY B. WILLIAMS*
Agent: The Gersh Agency - Beverly Hills, 213/274-6611

SPACECAMP   20th Century Fox, 1986, Story w/Patrick Bailey

Screenplays:
ELVES   w/Charles Kaufman
WENDELL WILCOX AND THE MONTER MAKERS   w/Charles Kaufman
THE MAN WHO COULD WORK MIRACLES
GIZMERELDA
PENNY TO THE FERRYMAN
IFFY
ROADS
SPIRIT MOVES
PRESTIDIGITATION
EDISON

MATT WILLIAMS*
Agent: APA - Los Angeles, 213/273-0744

WILD HEARTS CAN'T BE BROKEN   Buena Vista, 1991, w/Oley Sassone

NIGEL WILLIAMS
Agent: Judy Daish Agency - London, 011/441/486-5405

COUNTRY DANCING (S)

OSCAR WILLIAMS*
Contact: Shelly Surpin, Esq., 213/858-0682

FIVE ON THE BLACK HAND SIDE   United Artists, 1973, directed
HOT POTATO   Warner Bros., 1976, directed

ROBERT F. WILLIAMS*
Contact: WGA - Los Angeles, 213/550-1000

ESCAPE 2000   New World, 1983, Story w/David Lawrence & George Schenck

SUSAN WILLIAMS
AMERICAN ANTHEM   Columbia, 1986, Story w/Evan Archerd & Jeff Benjamin

DAVID WILLIAMSON*
Agent: William Morris Agency - Beverly Hills, 213/274-7451

"JOCK" PETERSEN   Avco Embassy, 1975
ELIZA FRASER   Hexagon, 1976
DON'S PARTY   Satori, 1976, from his play
GALLIPOLI   Paramount, 1981
THE CLUB   Roadshow Distributors, 1982
THE YEAR OF LIVING DANGEROUSLY   MGM/UA, 1983, w/Peter Weir & C.J. Koch
PHAR LAP   20th Century-Fox, 1984
TRAVELLING NORTH   Cineplex Odeon, 1987, from his play
A DANGEROUS LIFE (CMS)   HBO/McElroy & McElroy/FilmAccord Corp./Australian Broadcasting Corp./Zenith Productions, 1988
EMERALD CITY   Limelight Production Pty Ltd., 1989, from his play

Screenplays:
THE JANET HARDUVAL STORY
BRADVIK
TURTLE BEACH
PAY THE WIDOW

JEFF WILLIAMSON
ONE DOWN TWO TO GO   Almi Pictures, 1982

TONY WILLIAMSON
NIGHT WATCH   Avco Embassy, 1973
SERGEANT STEINER   Palladium, 1979
BREAKTHROUGH   Maverick Pictures International, 1981

CALDER WILLINGHAM*
Agent: ICM - Los Angeles, 213/550-4000

PATHS OF GLORY   United Artists, 1957, w/Stanley Kubrick & Jim Thompson
THE STRANGE ONE   Columbia, 1957
THE VIKINGS   United Artists, 1958
ONE-EYED JACKS   Paramount, 1961, w/Guy Trosper
THE GRADUATE ★   Avco Embassy, 1967, w/Buck Henry
LITTLE BIG MAN   National General, 1970
THIEVES LIKE US   United Artists, 1974, w/Robert Altman & Joan Tewkesbury

Screenplays:
RAMBLING ROSE
STILLWELL   w/George MacDonald Fraser
THE LUTHER PROJECT
APRIL FOOLS

BRUCE WILLIS
Agent: Triad Artists, Inc. - Los Angeles, 213/556-2727

HUDSON HAWK   Tri-Star, 1991, Story w/Robert Kraft & Steven de Souza

BRUCE WILSON
BOMBS AWAY   Shapiro Entertainment, 1985, w/Ed Mast, directed

DAVID CAMPBELL WILSON*
Agent: William Morris Agency - Beverly Hills, 213/274-7451

THE PERFECT WEAPON   Paramount, 1991

GAHAN WILSON
THE FREEWAY MANIAC   Cannon, 1989, w/Paul Winters

Screenplays:
TALES FROM THE DARKSIDE: THE MOVIE II
   w/Michael McDowell

HUGH WILSON*
Agent: CAA - Beverly Hills, 213/288-4545

STROKER ACE   Universal, 1983, w/Hal Needham
POLICE ACADEMY   The Ladd Company/Warner Bros., 1984, w/Neal Israel & Pat Proft, directed
RUSTLERS' RHAPSODY   Paramount, 1985, directed
BURGLAR   Warner Bros., 1987, w/Joseph Loeb III & Matthew Weisman

Screenplays:
ARRIVE ALIVE
TEXANS
COLOR MAN
BROTHERS-IN-LAW

JULIA WILSON
THE GAME   Visual Perspectives, 1989, w/Curtis Brown

KEVIN WILSON
WILD HORSE   Satori, 1984

LARRY WILSON*
Agent: William Morris Agency - Beverly Hills, 213/274-7451

BEETLEJUICE   Warner Bros., 1988, Story
   w/Michael McDowell
THE ADDAMS FAMILY   Paramount, 1991, w/Caroline Thompson & Paul Rudnick

Screenplays:
ROUGE w/Caroline Thompson
MAI, THE PSYCHIC GIRL w/Caroline Thompson

MICHAEL G. WILSON*
Contact: 213/460-5888

FOR YOUR EYES ONLY   MGM/United Artists, 1981, w/Richard Maibaum
OCTOPUSSY   MGM/UA, 1983 w/George MacDonald Fraser & Richard Maibaum
A VIEW TO A KILL   MGM/UA, 1985, w/Richard Maibaum
THE LIVING DAYLIGHTS   MGM/UA, 1987, w/Richard Maibaum
LICENCE TO KILL   MGM/UA, 1989, w/Richard Maibaum

SANDY WILSON
Agent: Writers & Artists Agency - Los Angeles, 213/820-2240

MY AMERICAN COUSIN   Spectrafilm, 1985, directed
AMERICAN BOYFRIENDS   Alliance Entertainment, 1989, directed

SNOO WILSON
Agent: Casaratto Company - London, 01/287-4450

SHADEY   Skouras Pictures, 1986

Screenplays:
THE GRASS WIDOW
ZODIAC
ORPHEUS IN THE UNDERWORLD

S.S. WILSON*
Agent: The Roberts Company - Los Angeles, 213/552-7800

SHORT CIRCUIT, Tri-Star, 1986, w/Brent Maddock
BATTERIES NOT INCLUDED   Universal, 1987, w/Brad Bird, Brent Maddock & Matthew Robbins
SHORT CIRCUIT II   Tri-Star, 1988, w/Brent Maddock
TREMORS   Universal, 1990, w/Brent Maddock
GHOST DAD   Universal, 1990, w/Brent Maddock & Chris Reese

DAVID G. WILTSE
Agent: William Morris Agency - New York, 212/586-5100

Screenplays:
HURRY UP OR I'LL BE THIRTY
UNDERGROUND

DARRYL WIMBERLY
Agent: Media Artists Group - Hollywood, 213/463-5610

Screenplays:
THE LINE
THICKER THAN WATER
DEAD MAN'S BAY
A TINKER'S DAMN
FAIR HAIR
JACK-MAN
LOVE THY FATHER
WHITEWATER

CHRIS WINDSOR
BIG MEAT EATER   New Line Cinema, 1984, w/Laurence Keane & Phil Savath, directed

MICHAEL WING
THE KISSING PLACE (CTF)   Wilshire Court Productions, 1990, w/Richard Altabef & Cynthia A. Cherbak

CHARLES WINKLER
Agent: The Gersh Agency - Los Angeles, 213/274-6611

YOU TALKIN' TO ME?   MGM/UA, 1987, directed
DISTURBED   Odyssey-Cinecom, 1990, w/Emerson Bixby, directed

IRWIN WINKLER*
Business: Winkler Films, 10125 W. Washington Blvd., Culver City, CA 90230, 213/204-0474

GUILTY BY SUSPICION   Warner Bros., 1991, directed

TERENCE H. WINKLESS*
Agent: William Morris Agency - Beverly Hills, 213/274-7451

THE HOWLING   Avco Embassy, 1981, w/John Sayles
HE'S MY GIRL   Scotti Bros., 1987, Story w/Taylor Ames & Peter Bergman
CORPORATE AFFAIRS   Concorde, 1990, w/Geoffrey Baere, directed

Screenplays:
RAGE AND HONOR   (directing)
FIVE CAR STUD   w/Alec Lorimore
SEQUENCE   w/Alec Lorimore
FAST LANE   w/Alec Lorimore
OUT OF THE BOX   w/Alec Lorimore
TOO GOOD TO BE TRUE   w/Alec Lorimore
THE GREAT CAPE GIRARDEAU LEAP   w/ Alec Lorimore
WASHINGTON PAGES   w/Alec Lorimore
THE JETSONS   w/Alec Lorimore
VODONE   w/Alec Lorimore
THE RUNNER   w/Alec Lorimore
BORN TOO COOL
BLOODFIST

MICHAEL WINNER*
Agent: ICM - Los Angeles, 213/550-4000
Business: Scimitar Films, Ltd., 6-8 Sackville St., London, W1X 1DD, England, 01/734-8385

FIREPOWER   ITC, 1977, Story w/Bill Kerby, directed
THE SENTINEL   Universal, 1977, w/Jeffrey Konvitz, directed
THE BIG SLEEP   United Artists, 1978, directed
THE WICKED LADY   MGM/UA, 1983, w/Leslie Arliss, directed
APPOINTMENT WITH DEATH   Cannon, 1988, w/Peter Buckman & Anthony Shaffer, directed
A CHORUS OF DISAPPROVAL   South Gate Entertainment, 1989, w/Alan Ayckbourn, directed
BULLSEYE!   21st Century Film Corporation, 1991, Story w/Leslie Bricusse & Nick Mead, directed

JERRY WINNICK*
Contact: 6117 Reseda Blvd. #209, 818/342-0221

Screenplays:
WELCOME TO ZIMM'S

SETH WINSTON*
Agent: Stone Manners Agency - Los Angeles, 213/275-9599

SHE'S OUT OF CONTROL   Columbia, 1989, w/Michael J. Nathanson

ALEX WINTER*
Agent: ICM - Los Angeles, 213/550-4000

SQUEAL OF DEATH   (Short) w/Tom Stern, co-directed

Screenplays:
WONDERLAND   w/Tom Stern
MILO RIGBY ON WHEELS   w/Tom Stern
HOWIE'S REVENGE   w/Tom Stern

BRADLEY T. WINTER*
Agent: Lake & Douroux - Beverly Hills, 213/557-0700

THE LAST ELEPHANT (CTF)   RHI Entertainment Inc./Quintex Entertainment Inc., 1990, Story

PAUL WINTERS
THE FREEWAY MANIAC   Cannon, 1989, w/Gahan Wilson, directed

ANTHONY WISDOM
THE RETURN OF SUPERFLY   Triton Pictures, 1990

WILLIAM WISHER*
Agent: The Brandt Company - Studio City, 818/506-7747

TERMINATOR 2: JUDGMENT DAY   Tri-Star, 1991, w/James Cameron

Screenplays:
DAY WORLD
SKIMMER

ELEANOR WITCOMBE*
Contact: WGA - Los Angeles, 213/550-1000

THE GETTING OF WISDOM   Southern Cross, 1977
MY BRILLIANT CAREER   Analysis, 1980

Screenplays:
OVER THE HILL

WILLIAM D. WITTLIFF*
Agent: ICM - Los Angeles, 213/550-4000
Business: 510 Baylor, Austin TX, 78703, 512/476-6821

THE BLACK STALLION   United Artists, 1979, w/Melissa Mathison & Jeanne Rosenberg
HONEYSUCKLE ROSE   Warner Bros., 1980, w/John Binder & Carol Sobieski
RAGGEDY MAN   Universal, 1981
BARBAROSA   Universal/AFD, 1982
COUNTRY   Buena Vista, 1984
RED HEADED STRANGER   Alive Films, 1987, directed
LONESOME DOVE (TF)   Motown Productions, 1989

Screenplays:
THE COWBOY WAY
WHIRLIGIG
NIGHT IN OLD MEXICO
DEEP ELLUM

STEFAN WODOSLAWSKY
CRAZY MOON   Miramax, 1987, w/Tom Berry

IRA WOHL
BEST BOY (FD)   International Film Exchange, 1980, directed

JOHN WOHLBRUCK
END OF THE LINE   Orion Classics, 1988, w/Jay Russell

PAUL WOLANSKY
DEADLY OBSESSION   Distant Horizon, 1989, w/Brian Cox & Jeno Hodi

DICK WOLF*
Business: Wolf Films, Universal Studios, 818/777-3131

SKATEBOARD   Universal, 1978, w/George Gage
GAS   Paramount, 1981
NO MAN'S LAND   Orion, 1987
MASQUERADE   MGM/UA, 1988

Screenplays:
SCHOOL TIES
ACCUSED
THE LAST RIDE

GARY K. WOLF*
Contact: WGA - New York, 212/245-6180

Screenplays:
TYPHOON LAGOON
FLYING TIGERFISH
GENIE MAN

JAY WOLF*
Contact: 213/650-7300

SILHOUETTE (CTF)   MCA Television Network, 1990, w/Victor Buell

DIGBY WOLFE*
Contact: 213/653-2895

FIRE AND ICE   Concorde, 1987, w/George Schlatter

GEORGE C. WOLFE*
Agent: ICM - Los Angeles, 213/550-4000

QUEENIE PIE (S)
THE COLORED MUSEUM (S)
MR. JELLY LORD (S)
SPUNK (S)
BLACKOUT (S)

Screenplays:
FIRE

MICHELE WOLFF
Agent: The Wright Concept - Hollywood, 213/461-3844

Screenplays:
THE WHITE HOUSE

RUTH WOLFF*
Agent: The Lantz Office - New York, 212/586-0200

THE INCREDIBLE SARAH   Avco Embassy, 1976

JUDITH SHERMAN WOLIN
WELCOME TO 18   American Distribution Group, 1986, w/Terry Carr

ANDY WOLK
Agent: CAA - Beverly Hills, 213/288-4545

WINTER'S TALE (S)
RIBCAGE (S)
QUAIL SOUTHWEST (S)
CRIMINAL JUSTICE (CTF)   Elysian Films, 1990, directed

Screenplays:
CAMPAIGN w/Paul Attansio
HEROIC MEASURE
I MARRIED A DEAD MAN
MEASURE OF DEVOTION
THE 13TH FLOOR   THE LEFT

MICHAEL WOLK
Agent: Triad Artists, Inc. - Los Angeles, 213/277-5656

HEART STOPPER (S)
FEMME FATALE (S)

Screenplays:
INNOCENT BLOOD

JENNY WOLKIND
Agent: CAA - Beverly Hills, 213/288-4545

BRENDA STARR   Triumph, 1991, w/James David Buchanan & Noreen Stone

JAMES WONG*
Agent: United Talent Agency - Beverly Hills, 213/273-6700

THE BOYS NEXT DOOR   New World, 1985, w/Glen Morgan

Screenplays:
HANGMAN w/Glen Morgan

JOHN WOO
THE KILLER   Film Work Shop/Circle Releasing, 1991, directed

CHARLES WOOD
Agent: William Morris Agency - Beverly Hills, 213/274-7451

THE KNACK   United Artists, 1965
HELP!   United Artists, 1965, w/Marc Behm
HOW I WON THE WAR   United Artists, 1967
THE CHARGE OF THE LIGHT BRIGADE   United Artists, 1968
THE LONG DAYS DYING   Paramount, 1968
CUBA   United Artists, 1979
RED MONARCH   Enigma Films/Goldcrest Films & Television Ltd., 1983
TUMBLEDOWN (CTF)   BBC Lionheart Productions, 1990

CHRISTOPHER WOOD
Agent: The Gersh Agency - Beverly Hills, 213/274-6611

CONFESSIONS OF A WINDOW CLEANER   Columbia, 1974, w/Val Guest
SEVEN NIGHTS IN JAPAN   EMI, 1976
THE SPY WHO LOVED ME   United Artists, 1977, w/Richard Maibaum
MOONRAKER   United Artists, 1979
REMO WILLIAMS: THE ADVENTURE BEGINS   Orion, 1985
STEAL THE SKY (CTF)   HBO Pictures/Voram Ben Ami Productions/Paramount TV, 1988, w/Dorothy Tristan

DAVID WOOD*
Agent: William Morris Agency - New York, 212/586-5100

BACK HOME (CTF)   TVS Films/Verronmead Productions/ Citadel Entertainment, 1990

GRACE WOODARD*
Contact: WGA - New York, 212/245-6180

DESCENDING ANGEL (CTF)   Fredya Rothstein, 1990, w/Alan Sharp & Robert Siegel

CHRISTOPHER WOODEN
KISS ME A KILLER   Califilm, 1991,
   w/Marcus DeLeon

Screenplays:
VOICE OF A STRANGER w/Jackson Barr

RICHARD WOODS*
Agent: Stone Manners Agency - Los Angeles,
   213/275-9599

ENDANGERED SPECIES   MGM/UA, 1982, Story
   w/Judson Kliner

ABBE WOOL
SID & NANCY   Samuel Goldwyn Company, 1986,
   w/Alex Cox
ROADSIDE PROPETS   Fine Line Features,
   1991, directed

Screenplays:
BUFFALO GIRLS w/Chloe Webb
MELMO MEETS ARLO

TUDY WOOLFE
Agent: William Morris Agency - Beverly Hills, 213/274-7451

MUSTANGS (S)

Screenplays:
RIDE ME DOWN EASY
SOLSTICE

CARL (CHUCK) WORKMAN*
Business: Calliope Films, 195 S. Beverly Dr., #414,
   Beverly Hills, CA 90212, 213/396-5937

WORDS (Short), directed
PRECIOUS IMAGES (Short), directed
THE MONEY   Coliseum, 1977, directed
SWEET DIRTY TONY   Marvin Films, 1981
STOOGEMANIA   Atlantic Releasing Corporation,
   1986, w/Jim Geoghan, directed
MEATBALLS III   TMS Pictures, 1986, Story
SUPERSTAR (FD)   Aries Film Releasing,
   1990, directed

TRIX WORRELL
Contact: Writers Guild of Great Britain - London,
   011/441/723-8074

FOR QUEEN AND COUNTRY   Atlantic Releasing
   Corporation, 1988, w/Martin Stellman

MARVIN WORTH*
Contact: Segal, Goldman & Macnow - Los Angeles,
   213/278-9200

THREE ON A COUCH   Columbia, 1966, w/Arne Sultan,
   Bob Ross & Samuel A. Taylor
SEE NO EVIL, HEAR NO EVIL   Tri-Star, 1989, Story
   w/Arne Sultan & Earl Barrett

MICHAEL WORTH
HEART OF THE STAG   New World, 1984, Story

PETER MARTIN WORTMANN
Agent: Barrett, Benson, McCartt & Weston - Los Angeles,
   213/247-5500

ODD JOBS   Tri-Star, 1986, w/Robert Conte
WHO'S HARRY CRUMB?   Tri-Star, 1988, w/Robert Conte

Screenplays:
DAYTIME w/Robert Conte
FUGITIVE GUYS w/Robert Conte
THE GREAT PRETENDER w/Robert Conte
DOUBLE VISION

VICTORIA WOZNIAK-MORRIS*
Contact: WGA - Los Angeles, 213/550-1000

PURPLE HAZE   Triumph/Columbia, 1983

LENORE A. WRIGHT*
Agent: The Gersh Agency - Beverly Hills, 213/274-6611

UNDERGROUND ACES   Filmways, 1981, w/Jim
   Carabatsos & Andrew Peter Marin

THOMAS LEE WRIGHT*
Agent: United Talent Agency - Beverly Hills, 213/273-6700

THE LAST OF THE FINEST   Orion, 1990, w/George
   Armitage & Jere Cunningham
NEW JACK CITY   Warner Bros., 1991, w/Barry
   Michael Cooper

Screenplays:
DO OR DIE
ONE HEARTBEAT
TRACKER EAST
SOUL OF HONOR
SIXTH FAMILY
STREET LEGAL
FLASHOVER
NICKY
YOUNG MAFIA
THE BIRDCAGE
TORCHLIGHT
TRAINING EXERCISE
GENERAL HOMO
DEAD GROUND
FIREFIGHTER
UNDERCURRENTS

DONALD WRYE*
Agent: ICM - Los Angeles, 213/550-4000

ICE CASTLES   Columbia, 1979, w/Gary L. Baim, directed
THE HOUSE OF GOD   H.O.G.   United Artists,
   1981, directed

Screenplays:
SEPARATE CHECKS w/Karen Leigh Hopkins

ROBERT WUHL*
Agent: ICM - Los Angeles, 213/550-4000

Screenplays:
BIG TOP
TEENAGE KILLER ZOMBIES
OPEN SEASON
CHEAPSHOT
S.O.S.

RUDOLPH G. WURLITZER*
Agent: Favored Artists Agency - Los Angeles, 213/653-3191

GLEN AND RANDA   UMC, 1971, w/Lorenzo Mars & Jim McBride
TWO LANE BLACKTOP   Universal, 1971, w/Will Corry
PAT GARRETT AND BILLY THE KID   MGM, 1973
WALKER   Universal, 1987
CANDY MOUNTAIN   Metropolis Film, 1987, co-directed
VOYAGER   Bioskop Film/Action Films, 1991, w/Volker Schlondorff

Screenplays:
WIND
BEYOND THE MOUNTAIN
ZEBVLON
BAKE AND SHAKE
MAD DOG LAKE
FLATS
MEXICAN JAILBREAK

NED WYNN*
Contact: WGA - Los Angeles, 213/550-1000

CALIFORNIA DREAMING   American International, 1979

TRACY KEENAN WYNN*
Agent: CAA - Beverly Hills, 213/288-4545

THE LONGEST YARD   Paramount, 1974
THE DROWNING POOL   Warner Bros., 1975, w/Walter Hill & Lorenzo Semple
THE DEEP   Columbia, 1977, w/Peter Benchley

Screenplays:
IT HAD TO BE STEVE w/Amy Jones & Holly Goldberg Sloan
END ZONE
THE GAME
ENDANGERED
CADILLAC JACK

JIM WYNORSKI
Personal Manager: L. Miller Management - Los Angeles, 213/392-5802

FORBIDDEN WORLD   New World, 1982, Story w/R.J. Robertson
SORCERESS   New World, 1983
SCREWBALLS   New World, 1983, w/Linda Shayne
THE LOST EMPIRE   JGM Enterprises, 1985, directed
CHOPPING MALL KILLBOTS Concorde, 1986, w/Steve Mitchell, directed
DEATHSTALKER II: NECROPOLIS   Concorde, 1986, Story, directed
BIG BAD MAMA II   Concorde, 1987, w/R.J. Robertson, directed
NOT OF THIS EARTH   Concorde, 1988, w/R.J. Robertson
THE HAUNTING OF MORELLA   Concore, 1990, w/R.J. Robertson, directed
THINK BIG   Concorde, 1990, Story w/R.J. Robertson

Screenplays:
MUNCHIES II w/R.J. Robertson (directing)
FINAL EMBRACE w/R.J. Robertson

FRANK YABLANS*
Business Manager: Kaufman & Bernstein - Los Angeles, 213/277-1900

NORTH DALLAS FORTY   Paramount, 1979, w/Peter Gent & Ted Kotcheff
MOMMIE DEAREST   Paramount, 1981, w/Frank Perry, Tracy Hotchner & Robert Getchell

YABO YABLONSKY*
Agent: Paul Kohner, Inc. - Los Angeles, 213/550-1060

JAGUAR LIVES!   American International, 1979
VICTORY   Lorimar/Paramount, 1981, w/Evan Jones
PORTRAIT OF A HITMAN   Wildfire, 1984

JULIETTE YAGER*
Contact: WGA - Los Angeles, 213/550-1000

Screenplays:
MY WAY OR THE HIGHWAY w/Rip Murray

BOAZ I. YAKIN*
Agent: United Talent Agency - Beverly Hills, 213/273-6700

THE PUNISHER   Castle Premier, 1990
THE ROOKIE   Warner Bros., 1990, w/Scott Spiegel

Screenplays:
COLD FIRE
MADELEINE
AFRIKANER
BROTHER DA SILVA
COAST GUARD PROJECT
THE LINE

LEONARD YAKIR
OUT OF THE BLUE   Discovery, 1982, w/Brenda Nielson

RICHARD YALEM*
Agent: Barrett, Benson, McCartt & Weston - Los Angeles, 213/247-5500

DELIRIUM   Odyssey Pictures, 1989

Screenplays:
ALTAR BOUND w/Josephine Cummings

DAVID YALLOP
Agent: Casaratto Company - London, 01/287-4450

BEYOND REASONABLE DOUBT   Satori Releasing, 1984
CHICAGO JOE AND THE SHOWGIRL   New Line Cinema, 1990

"WEIRD" AL YANKOVIC
Contact: Spotlight Enterprises - Los Angeles, 213/657-8004

U.H.F.   Orion, 1989, w/Jay Levey

Ya

LOUIS YANSEN
MISPLACED   Original Cinema, 1991, w/Thomas DeWolfe, directed

BROCK YATES*
Agent: ICM - Los Angeles, 213/550-4000

SMOKEY AND THE BANDIT, PART II   Universal, 1980, w/Jerry Belson
THE CANNONBALL RUN   20th Century-Fox, 1981

PETER YELDHAM
Contact: British Academy of Film & Television Arts, 195 Piccadilly, London W1, England, 71/734-0022

THE COMEDY MAN   British Lion, 1964
THE LIQUIDATOR   MGM, 1965
TEN LITTLE INDIANS   Tenlit, 1966, w/Harry Alan Towers
THE LONG DUEL   Rank, 1967
AGE OF CONSENT   Columbia, 1969
CALL OF THE WILD   Constantin, 1975, w/Harry Alan Towers & Wyn Wells
WEEKEND OF SHADOWS   Roadshow Distributors, 1978
TOUCH AND GO   Greater Union Film Distributors, 1980

LINDA YELLEN
Agent: William Morris Agency - Beverly Hills, 213/274-7451

COME OUT, COME OUT   Beacon Productions, 1969, directed
LOOKING UP   Levitt-Pickman, 1977, directed

Screenplays:
A REASONABLE DOUBT
MAYBERRY VICE
THE STEVE DUNLEAVY STORY

BENNETT M. YELLIN*
Agent: CAA - Beverly Hills, 213/288-4545

Screenplays:
ADULT EDUCATION w/Peter Farrelly
DUST TO DUST w/Peter Farrelly
YOUNG LOVERS w/Peter Farrelly
FREE SPIRITS w/Peter Farrelly
OUR PLANET TONIGHT w/Peter Farrelly
BLACK TIE w/Peter Farrelly
POISON IVY w/Peter Farrelly

ANTHONY H. YERKOVICH*
Agent: CAA - Beverly Hills, 213/288-4545

Screenplays:
SWEETWATER

NORMAN YONEMOTO
SAVAGE STREETS   Entermark, 1985, w/Danny Steinmann

PHILIP YORDAN*
Contact: WGA - Los Angeles, 213/550-1000

SYNCOPATION   RKO, 1942, w/Frank Cavett & Valentine Davies
WHEN STRANGERS MARRY *BETRAYED*   Monogram, 1944, w/Dennis Cooper
DILLINGER ★   Monogram, 1945
SUSPENSE   Monogram, 1946
WHISTLE STOP   United Artists, 1946
THE CHASE   Nero Pictures, 1947
THE BLACK BOOK   Eagle-Lion, 1949, w/Aeneas Mackenzie
HOUSE OF STRANGERS   20th Century-Fox, 1949
ANNA LUCASTA   Columbia, 1949, from his play, w/Arthur Laurents
BAD MEN OF TOMBSTONE   Allied Artists, 1949, w/Arthur Strawn
EDGE OF DOOM   Goldwyn, 1950
DRUMS IN THE DEEP SOUTH   RKO Radio, 1951
DETECTIVE STORY ★★   Paramount, 1951, w/William Wyler
MARU MARU   Warner Bros., 1952, w/others
MUTINY   United Artists, 1952, w/Sydney Harmon
BLOWING WILD   Warner Bros., 1953
JOHNNY GUITAR   Republic, 1953
HOUDINI   Paramount, 1953
BROKEN LANCE ★★   20th Century-Fox, 1954, Story
THE NAKED JUNGLE   Paramount, 1954, w/Ranald MacDougall
THE MAN FROM LARAMIE   Columbia, 1955, w/Frank Burt
THE BIG COMBO   Allied Artists, 1955
JOE MACBETH   Columbia, 1955
SAVAGE WILDERNESS   Columbia, 1956, w/Russell S. Hughes
THE HARDER THEY FALL   Columbia, 1956
NO DOWN PAYMENT   20th Century-Fox, 1957
MEN IN WAR   Security, 1957
THE DAY OF THE OUTLAW   United Artists, 1958
ANNA LUCASTA   United Artists, 1958 (black version)
THE BRAVADOS   20th Century-Fox, 1958
THE FIEND WHO WALKED THE WEST   20th Century-Fox, 1958, w/Harry Brown
GOD'S LITTLE ACRE   Security, 1958
STUDS LONIGAN   United Artists, 1960
THE BRAMBLE BUSH   Warner Bros., 1960, w/Milton Sperling
KING OF KINGS   MGM, 1961
EL CID   Allied Artists, 1961, w/Ben Barzman
55 DAYS AT PEKING   Bronston, 1962, w/Bernard Gordon
THE DAY OF THE TRIFFIDS   Allied Artists, 1963
THE FALL OF THE ROMAN EMPIRE   Paramount, 1964, w/Ben Barzman
BATTLE OF THE BULGE   Warner Bros., 1965, w/John Melson & Milton Sperling
THE ROYAL HUNT OF THE SUN   National General, 1968
CAPTAIN APACHE   Scotia International, 1971, w/Milton Sperling
CRY WILDERNESS   Visto International, 1971
BAD MAN'S RIVER   Zurbano/Apollo/Roitfeld, 1972, w/Eugenio Martin
THE UNHOLY   Vestron, 1988, w/Fernando Fonseca

SUSANNAH YORK
Agent: Casaratto Company - London, 01/287-4450

FALLING IN LOVE AGAIN   International Picture Show, 1980, Story w/Ted Allan & Steven Paul

DANIEL YOST*
Agent: Barrett, Benson, McCartt & Weston - Los Angeles, 213/556-2600

DRUGSTORE COWBOY   Avenue Pictures, 1989, w/Gus Van Sant
CRIMINAL ACT   Independent Networks Inc./Film Ventures International, 1989

Screenplays:
ON THE PROWL
OUR DREAM HOUSE
ESCAPE TO CANADA
STREET WIRED

BURT YOUNG*
Contact: Andrew Giovingo - New York,
212/767-5550

UNCLE JOE SHANNON   United Artists, 1978

DALENE A. YOUNG
Agent: Kopaloff Company - Los Angeles,
213/203-8430

LITTLE DARLINGS   Paramount, 1980, w/Kimi Peck
CROSS CREEK   Universal/AFD, 1983

Screenplays:
THE BLACK ARROW
PHOTOPLAY w/Martha Coolidge
JASMINE AND THE JELLY THIEF
NIGHTENGALE ON AVENUE B
SARAH WILL
GIOVANNI'S RESTAURANT

JOHN SACRET YOUNG*
Agent: ICM - Los Angeles, 213/550-4000
Management: George Diskant - Los Angeles,
213/824-3773

CHANDLER   MGM, 1971
TESTAMENT   Paramount, 1983
ROMERO   Four Seasons Entertainment, 1989

Screenplays:
AFTER EDEN
FIRE ON THE MOUNTAIN
UNDERGROUND
SAN JOAQUIN
SIRENS

KEE YOUNG
WEEKEND WITH KATE   Phillip Emanuel Productions,
1990, w/Henry Tefay

MARLA YOUNG
CHALLENGE THE WIND   Sell Entertainment, 1990,
w/William Blackburn & Ken Howard

ROBERT M. YOUNG*
Agent: ICM - Los Angeles, 213/550-4000

THE BALLAD OF GREGORIO CORTEZ   Embassy,
1983, w/Victor Villasenor, directed

ROGER YOUNG
Agent: CAA - Beverly Hills, 213/288-4545

DOUBLECROSSED (CTF)   Green/Epstein Productions/
Lorimar TV, 1991, directed

COREY YUEN
NO RETREAT, NO SURRENDER   New World,
1986, Story w/Ng See Yuen, directed

JOHNNY YUNE
THEY CALL ME BRUCE? A FISTFUL OF CHOPSTICKS
Artists Releasing Corporation/Film Ventures International,
1982, w/Tim Clawson, Elliott Hong & David Randolf
THEY STILL CALL ME BRUCE   Shapiro Entertainment,
1987, w/James Orr, co-directed

LARRY YUST
Agent: ICM - Los Angeles, 213/550-4000

TRICK BABY   Universal, 1973, directed
HOMEBODIES   Avco Embassy, 1974, directed
"SAY YES"   Cinetel, 1986, directed

PETER YUVAL
Business: Action International Pictures, 10726 McCune
Avenue, Los Angeles, CA 90034, 213/559-8805

DEAD END CITY   Action International Pictures, 1989,
w/Michael Bogert, directed
FIREHEAD   A.I.P. Studios, 1991, Jeff Mandell, directed

BRIAN YUZNA
FROM BEYOND   Empire Pictures, 1986, Adaptation
w/Stuart Gordon & Dennis Paoli
HONEY, I SHRUNK THE KIDS   Buena Vista, 1989, Story
w/Stuart Gordon & Ed Naha
SOCIETY   Wild Street Pictures, 1989, directed
BRIDE OF RE-ANIMATOR   Troma, 1991, Story
w/Rick Fry, directed

Z

BRYCE ZABEL*
Agent: The Irv Schechter Company - Beverly Hills,
213/278-8070

Screenplays:
LABOR OF LOVE w/Jackie Zabel

JACKIE ZABEL*
Agent: The Irv Schechter Company - Beverly Hills,
213/278-8070

Screenplays:
LABOR OF LOVE w/Bryce Zabel

ALFREDO ZACHARIAS
THE BEES   New World, 1978

STEVEN R. ZACHARIAS*
Agent: United Talent Agency - Beverly Hills, 213/273-6700

THE HARRAD SUMMER   Cinerama Releasing
Corporation, 1974
REVENGE OF THE NERDS   20th Century Fox,
1984, w/Jeff Buhai
THE WHOOPEE BOYS   Paramount, 1986,
w/Jeff Buhai & David Obst
LAST RESORT   Concorde/Cinema Group, 1986,
w/Jeff Buhai

Za

JOCKS   Crown International, 1987, w/Jeff Buhai & David Obst as "Mike Lanahan & David Oas"
JOHNNY BE GOOD   1988, w/Jeff Buhai & David Obst

Screenplays:
BIKERS FROM HELL   w/Jeff Buhai
DALLAS DEBS   w/Jeff Buhai
GIRLS IN TROUBLE   w/Jeff Buhai
DEEP COVER   w/Jeff Buhai
HOPELESSNESS AND DESPAIR   w/Jeff Buhai
MR. VICE PRESIDENT   w/Jeff Buhai & Robert Kears
THE TRUTH ABOUT SWEDES   w/Jeff Buhai
LOVELINE   w/Jeff Buhai
AFTERGLOW   w/Jeff Buhai
HARRAD II   w/Jeff Buhai
HOSPITAL   w/Jeff Buhai
INSIDE THE INQUIRER   w/Jeff Buhai
VULGARIANS   w/Jeff Buhai
HEAVY METAL WEEKEND   w/Jeff Buhai
REVENGE OF THE NUDES   w/Jeff Buhai

MICHAEL ZAGOR*
Agent: Richland/Wunsch/Hohman Agency - Los Angeles, 213/278-1955

THE JOSEPHINE BAKER STORY (CTF)   HBO Pictures/RHI Entertainment/Anglia Television Ltd., 1991, Story w/Ron Hutchinson

STEVEN ZAILLIAN*
Agent: Harold R. Greene, Inc.- Los Angeles, 213/852-4959

THE FALCON AND THE SNOWMAN   Orion, 1985
AWAKENINGS ★   Columbia, 1990

Screenplays:
JACK THE BEAR
SEARCHING FOR BOBBY FISCHER (directing)
ALIVE!
BAD MANNERS
SHOE SHINE
SCHINDLER'S LIST

JORGE ZAMACONA*
Agent: United Talent Agency - Beverly Hills, 213/273-6700

WORLD GONE WILD   Lorimar, 1988

Screenplays:
OUTLAWS
BACK IN BLACK

ALEX ZAMM*
Agent: William Morris Agency - Beverly Hills, 213/274-7451

BIRTHDAY FISH (Short), directed
MY FIRST HAIRCUT (Short), directed
MAESTRO (Short), directed

Screenplays:
PAWNSHOP KID

TONY ZARINDAST
HARDCASE AND FIST   United Entertainment, 1989, w/Bud Fleisher, directed
A HOLLYWOOD STORY   Double Helix Films, 1991, directed, w/Evan Slawson

MICHAEL ZAUSNER
Agent: William Morris Agency - Beverly Hills, 213/274-7451

LOVE OR MONEY   Hemdale, 1990, w/Bart Davis & Elyse England

Screenplays:
ERNEST SAVES CAMELOT   w/Bart Davis

FRANCO ZEFFIRELLI
Address: via Lucio Volumnio 37, Rome, Italy, 06/799441

THE TAMING OF THE SHREW   Columbia, 1967, w/Susi Cecchi d'Amico & Paul Dehn, directed
LA TRAVIATA   Universal Classics, 1982, directed
HAMLET   Warner Bros., 1990, w/Christopher DeVore, directed

JON ZEIDERMAN
LITTLE NOISES   Monument Pictures, 1991, w/Jane Spencer

JIMMY ZEILINGER
Agent: Triad Artists, Inc. - Los Angles, 213/556-2727

LITTLE SISTER   1991, directed

Screenplays:
BRENNER'S WORLD

BEN ZELIG
TOMBOY   Crown International, 1985

SUSAN ZELOUF
CURSE II: THE BITE   Trans World Entertainment, 1989, w/Federico Prosperi

YURI ZELTSER
Agent: Stone Manners Agency - Los Angeles, 213/275-9599

BAD DREAMS   20th Century Fox, 1988, Story w/Michael Dick, Andrew Fleming & P.J. Pettiette
EYE OF THE STORM   Odyssey Distributors, 1991, w/Michael Stewart, directed

ROBERT ZEMECKIS*
Agent: CAA - Beverly Hills, 213/288-4545

I WANNA HOLD YOUR HAND   Universal, 1977, w/Bob Gale, directed
1941   Universal/Columbia, 1979, w/Bob Gale
USED CARS   Columbia, 1980, w/Bob Gale, directed
BACK TO THE FUTURE ★   Universal, 1985, w/Bob Gale, directed
BACK TO THE FUTURE II   Universal, 1989, Story w/Bob Gale, directed
BACK TO THE FUTURE III   Universal, 1990, Story w/Bob Gale, directed

Screenplays:
GANGLAND   w/Bob Gale

MAI ZETTERLING
Agent: Douglas Rae Management - London, 01/836-3903

LOVING COUPLES   Prominent, 1964, w/David Hughes, directed
NIGHT GAMES   Mondial, 1966, directed

DOCTOR GLAS   20th Century-Fox, 1968, directed
THE GIRLS   New Line Cinema, 1969, directed
VINCENT THE DUTCHMAN   1972, directed
WE HAVE MANY NAMES   1976, directed
SCRUBBERS   Orion Classics, 1984, w/Roy Minton & Jeremy Watt, directed
AMAROSA   Sandrews/Swedish Film Institute, 1986, directed

MICHAEL ZETTLER*
Agent: The Gersh Agency - New York, 212/997-1818

SWEET LORRAINE   Angelika Films, 1987, w/Shelly Altman

HOWARD ZIEHM
FLESH GORDON MEETS THE COSMIC CHEERLEADERS   Filmvest International, 1991, w/Doug Frisby, directed

RAFAL ZIELINSKI
Agent: The Agency - Los Angeles, 213/551-3000

BREAKING ALL THE RULES   New World, 1985, Story w/Edith Rey

HARV ZIMMEL*
Agent: The Artists Agency - Los Angeles, 213/277-7779

SHOOT TO KILL   Buena Vista, 1988, w/Michael Burton & Daniel Petrie Jr.
SNOW KILL (CTF)   Wilshire Court Productions, 1990, w/Raymond Hartung

Screenplays:
THE WIZARD FROM FLATBUSH   w/Joel Saltzman
DEEP WORK
THE AMATEUR HOUR
SOMETHING IN THE PARK

PAUL D. ZIMMERMAN*
Agent: ICM - Los Angeles, 213/550-4000

LOVERS AND LIARS   Levitt-Pickman, 1979
THE KING OF COMEDY   20th Century-Fox, 1983
CONSUMING PASSIONS   Samuel Goldwyn Company, 1988, w/Andrew Davies

Screenplays:
THE CAT
MADONNA MADNESS
THE MOST POWERFUL MAN IN THE WORLD
OTHER PEOPLE'S HUSBANDS, OTHER PEOPLE'S WIVES
200
PINKO

STAN ZIMMERMAN*
Agent: ICM - Los Angeles, 213/550-4000

Screenplays:
THE RUTHIE RUDDICK STORY

VERNON ZIMMERMAN*
Business Manager: Eric Weissmann, Weissmann, Wolff, Bergman, Coleman & Schulman, 9665 Wilshire Blvd. - Suite 900, Beverly Hills, CA 90212, 213/858-7888

BOBBIE JO AND THE OUTLAW   American International, 1976
FADE TO BLACK   American Cinema, 1980, directed
TEEN WITCH   Trans World Entertainment, 1989, w/Robin Menken

PAUL ZINDEL*
Agent: ICM - Los Angeles, 213/550-4000

THE EFFECT OF GAMMA RAYS ON MAN-IN-THE-MOON MARIGOLDS (S)
LET ME HEAR YOU WHISPER (S)
UP THE SANDBOX   National General, 1972
MAME   Warner Bros., 1974
MARIA'S LOVERS   Cannon, 1984, w/Gerard Brach, Marjorie David & Andrei Konchalovsky
RUNAWAY TRAIN   Cannon, 1985, w/Edward Bunker & Djordje Milicevic

Screenplays:
THE AMAZING AND DEATH-DEFYING DIARY OF EUGENE DINGMAN

WILLIAM ZIPP
FATAL SKIES   AIP, 1990, w/James Eaton

JOEL F. ZISKIN*
Agent: The Wright Concept - Hollywood, 213/461-3844

MATA HARI   Cannon, 1985

Screenplays:
DUKE AND THE DIPPER
ECLIPSE

LAURA ZISKIN
Contact: 818/560-5976

WHAT ABOUT BOB?   Buena Vista, 1991, Story w/Alvin Sargent

STEPHEN ZITO*
Contact: WGA - Los Angeles, 213/550-1000

THE ESCAPE ARTIST   Orion/Warner Bros., 1982, w/Melissa Mathison

DAVID ZUCKER*
Agent: CAA - Beverly Hills, 213/288-4545

THE KENTUCKY FRIED MOVIE   United Film Distribution, 1977, w/Jim Abrahams & Jerry Zucker
AIRPLANE!   Paramount, 1980, w/Jim Abrahams & Jerry Zucker, co-directed
TOP SECRET!   Paramount, 1984, w/Martyn Burke, Jim Abrahams & Jerry Zucker, co-directed
THE NAKED GUN: FROM THE FILES OF POLICE SQUAD!   Paramount, 1989, w/Jim Abrahams, Pat Proft & Jerry Zucker, directed
THE NAKED GUN 2 1/2: THE SMELL OF FEAR   Paramount, 1991, w/Pat Proft, directed

JERRY ZUCKER*
Agent: CAA - Beverly Hills, 213/288-4545

THE KENTUCKY FRIED MOVIE   United Film Distribution, 1977, w/Jim Abrahams & David Zucker
AIRPLANE!   Paramount, 1980, w/Jim Abrahams & David Zucker, also co-directed
TOP SECRET!   Paramount, 1984, w/Martyn Burke, Jim Abrahams & David Zucker, co-directed
THE NAKED GUN: FROM THE FILES OF POLICE SQUAD!   Paramount, 1989, w/Jim Abrahams, Pat Proft & David Zucker

ALBERT ZUGSMITH
Business: Famous Players International, 1210 N. Wetherly Dr., Los Angeles, CA 90069, 213/275-8221

DONDI   Allied Artists, 1961, w/Gus Edson, directed
MOVIE STAR AMERICAN STYLE OR LSD - I HATE YOU   Famous Players, 1966, w/Graham Lee Mahn & Lulu Talmadge, directed
ON HER BED OF ROSES   Famous Players International, 1966, directed

RON ZWANG*
Business Manager: The Jaymes Co., 818/761-7832

DOIN' TIME   The Ladd Company/Warner Bros., 1984, w/Dee Caruso & Franelle Silver
FREE RIDE   Galaxy International, 1986, w/Robert Bell & Lee Fulkerson

A. MARTIN ZWEIBACH*
Agent: APA - Los Angeles, 213/273-0744
Contact: 818/906-7565

ME, NATALIE   Cinema Center, 1969
YOU CAN'T HAVE EVERYTHING   CACTUS IN THE SNOW   General Film Corp., 1971, directed
GORP   Filmways, 1980, Story w/Jeffrey Konvitz
GRACE QUIGLEY   THE ULTIMATE SOLUTION OF GRACE QUIGLEY   MGM/UA/Cannon, 1984

Screenplays:
MUMMY OF BEVERLY HILLS
SUNLIGHT AND SHADOWS

ALAN ZWEIBEL*
Contact: Bernie Brillstein - Los Angeles, 213/275-6135

DRAGNET   Universal, 1987, w/Dan Aykroyd & Tom Mankiewicz

Screenplays:
NORTH

EDWARD M. ZWICK*
Agent: ICM - Los Angeles, 213/550-4000

Screenplays:
BABY GENIUS   w/Marshall Herskovitz

★ ★ ★ ★

INDICES

FILM TITLES • AGENTS & MANAGERS
ACADEMY AWARDS & NOMINATIONS

AIDS PROJECT LOS ANGELES

We're Making a Difference...Together

-Human Services
-Education
-Advocacy

213/876-8951

INDEX OF FILM TITLES

NOTE: This is not an index of all film titles, only those listed in this book.

Title	Author
$	RICHARD BROOKS
1 + 1 = 3 (P)	SHEM BITTERMAN
2 GOOD 2 BE FORGOTTEN - S	MARC NORMAN
003 STOOGES - S	GEORGE GALLO
3 DAYS, 4 NIGHTS - S	RALPH BAKSHI
3 MEN AND A CRADLE	COLINE SERREAU
3 TO GET READY - S	ALAN SHAPIRO
3 WOMEN	ROBERT ALTMAN
3:15	MICHAEL JACOBS
3:15	SAM BERNARD
4-H CLUB (P)	SAM SHEPARD
5TH MONKEY, THE	ERIC ROCHANT
5TH MUSKETEER, THE	DAVID AMBROSE
8 1/2	BRUNELLO RONDI†
8 1/2	FEDERICO FELLINI
8 MILLION WAYS TO DIE	OLIVER STONE
8 MILLION WAYS TO DIE	R. LANCE HILL
8 SCENES FROM THE LIFE OF HANK WILLIAMS - S	PAUL SCHRADER
8:24 TO HEAVEN - S	GARY MURPHY
8:24 TO HEAVEN - S	LARRY STRAWTHER
9 1/2 NINJAS	BILL CROUNSE
9 1/2 NINJAS	DON PEQUIGNOT
9 1/2 NINJAS	JOHN MORRISEY
9 1/2 WEEKS	PATRICIA L. KNOP
9 1/2 WEEKS	SARAH KERNOCHAN
9 1/2 WEEKS	ZALMAN KING
9/30/55	JAMES BRIDGES
9TH FOX, THE - S	DAVID H. FRANZONI
10	BLAKE EDWARDS
10:30 P.M. SUMMER	JULES DASSIN
10:30 P.M. SUMMER	MARGUERITE DURAS
10 DEGREES SOUTHWEST	THOMAS RITZ
10 TO MIDNIGHT	WILLIAM ROBERTS
11 HARROWHOUSE	JEFFREY BLOOM
12:01 P.M. (SHORT)	JONATHAN HEAP
12:01 P.M. (SHORT)	STEPHEN M. TOLKIN
13 - S	TERRY CURTIS FOX
13 FRIGHTENED GIRLS	ROBERT DILLON
13TH FLOOR, THE - S	ANDY WOLK
13TH FLOOR, THE - S	CHRISTIAN STOIANOVICH
13TH FLOOR, THE - S	PHOEBE DORIN
18 AGAIN!	JONATHAN PRINCE
18 AGAIN!	JOSHUA GOLDSTEIN
19 PURCHASE STREET - S	PETER KRIKES
19 PURCHASE STREET - S	STEVE MEERSON
21 - S	ROBERT MUNDY
29TH STREET	GEORGE GALLO
37.2 DEGREES LE MATIN	JEAN-JACQUES BEINEIX
39 STEPS, THE	MICHAEL ROBSON
40 REGULAR - U	ANDREW SMITH
48 HRS	LARRY GROSS
48 HRS	STEVEN DE SOUZA
48 HRS	WALTER HILL
48 HRS.	ROGER SPOTTISWOODE
50-50 - S	DENNISSHRYACK
50-50 - S	MICHAEL BUTLER
50 FREE AND CLEAR - S	RICHARD CHAPMAN
52 PICK-UP	ELMORE LEONARD
52 PICK-UP	JOHN STEPPLING
55 DAYS AT PEKING	PHILIP YORDAN
57 CAD (SHORT)	VICKI HOCHBURG
72-HOUR CLUB - S	MARK FROST
84 CHARING CROSS ROAD	HUGH WHITEMORE
84 CHARLIE MOPIC	PATRICK DUNCAN
92 IN THE SHADE	THOMAS MCGUANE
99 AND 44/100% DEAD	ROBERT DILLON
100 RIFLES	CLAIR HUFFAKER†
102 BOULEVARD HAUSSMANN	ALAN BENNETT
200 - S	PAUL D. ZIMMERMAN
300 MILES THROUGH ENEMY LINES	AKIRA KUROSAWA
357 - S	LEE GOLDBERG
357 - S	WILLIAM RABKIN
400, THE - S	ROBERT RESNIKOFF
633 SQUADRON	HOWARD KOCH
633 SQUADRON	JAMES CLAVELL
666 - S	JEFF WANSHEL
760 NO. MAPLE - S	JAIME B. KLEIN
976-EVIL	BRIAN HELGELAND
976-EVIL	RHET TOPHAM
1776	PETER STONE
1900	BERNARDO BERTOLUCCI
1918	HORTON FOOTE
1919	HUGH BRODY
1919	MICHAEL IGNATIEFF
1941	BOB GALE
1941	JOHN MILIUS
1941	ROBERT ZEMECKIS
1968 - S	BRIAN REHAK
1969	ERNEST THOMPSON
1984	MICHAEL RADFORD
2001: A SPACE ODYSSEY	ARTHUR C. CLARKE
2001: A SPACE ODYSSEY	STANLEY KUBRICK
2010	PETER HYAMS

A

Title	Author
A.I. - S	ROBERT SHORT
A.K.A. - S	LESLIE DIXON
ABANDON SHIP	RICHARD SALE
ABBY & SOCKS - S	MOLLY-ANN LEIKIN
ABDUCTION, THE (P)	FRANCIS VEBER
ABLE-BODIED SEAMAN, THE (P)	ALAN BOWNE†
ABOMINABLE SNOWMAN, THE	NIGEL KNEALE
ABOUT HARRY TOWNS - S	BRUCE JAY FRIEDMAN
ABOUT LAST NIGHT	DENISE DE CLUE
ABOUT LAST NIGHT	TIM KAZURINSKY
ABOUT LAST NIGHT 2 - S	DENISE DE CLUE
ABOUT LAST NIGHT 2 - S	TIM KAZURINSKY
ABOUT MRS. LESLIE	HAL KANTER
ABOUT TIME (P)	TOM COLE
ABOVE AND BEYOND	NORMAN PANAMA
ABOVE SUSPICION - S	DJORDJE MILICEVIC
ABOVE SUSPICION - S	FIONA LEWIS
ABOVE THE FOLD - S	WENDELL RAWLS
ABOVE THE LAW	ANDREW DAVIS
ABOVE THE LAW	STEVEN PRESSFIELD
ABOVE THE LAW	STEVEN SEAGAL
ABOVE THE LAW	RONALD SHUSETT
ABOVE THE RIM - S	BARRY MICHAEL COOPER
ABRACADAVER - S	ALLAN G. SCOTT
ABRACADAVER - S	PAUL GUAY
ABRACADAVER - S	STEVE MAZUR
ABSENCE OF MALICE	KURT LUEDTKE
ABSENT FRIENDS (P)	ALAN AYCKBOURN
ABSOLUTE BEGINNERS	CHRISTOPHER WICKING
ABSOLUTE BEGINNERS	DON MACPHERSON
ABSOLUTE BEGINNERS	RICHARD BURRIDGE
ABSOLUTION	ANTHONY SHAFFER
ABSTRACT ART - S	BRIAN STRASMANN
ABSURD PERSON SINGULAR (P)	ALAN AYCKBOURN
ABUNDANCE (P)	BETH HENLEY
ABYSS, THE	JAMES CAMERON
AC/DC - S	CHRISTOPHER CROWE
ACADEMY OF DESIRE, THE (P)	YALE UDOFF
ACCELERATOR - S	PEN DENSHAM
ACCIDENT	HAROLD PINTER
ACCIDENTAL TOURIST, THE	FRANK GALATI
ACCIDENTAL TOURIST, THE	LAWRENCE KASDAN
ACCOMPLICE - S	FREDERIC HUNTER
ACCORD, THE - S	CLIFTON CAMPBELL
ACCUSED - S	DICK WOLF
ACCUSED, THE	TOM TOPOR
ACE BANDAGE - S	ANDREW SMITH
ACE ELI AND ROGER OF THE SKIES	STEVEN SPIELBERG
ACE IN THE HOLE	BILLY WILDER
ACE IN THE HOLE	WALTER NEWMAN
ACE IN THE HOLE	DAVID MAMET
ACE OF THE NEWSREELS - S	DENNYS MCCOY
ACE OF THE NEWSREELS - S	PAMELA HICKEY
ACE TRUCKING CO. - S	JEREMY LEVEN
ACE, THE	LEWIS JOHN CARLINO
ACES - S	GEORGE GIPE
ACES - S	LYNNE BARKER
ACROSS THE GREAT DIVIDE	STEWART RAFFILL
ACROSS THE RIVER AND INTO THE TREES- S	ALLAN G. SCOTT
ACROSS THE TRACKS	SANDY TUNG
ACT OF ATTRITION - S - S	CLIFTON CAMPBELL
ACT OF FAITH - S	ADAM RODMAN
ACT OF LOVE - S	MICHAEL JENNING
ACT OF LOVE, AN - S	BRUCE ROBINSON
ACT OF VENGEANCE (CTF) - S	SCOTT SPENCER
ACTING PRESIDENT - S	GORE VIDAL
ACTION JACKSON	ROBERT RENEAU
ACTION PHOTOGRAPHY - S	ROBERT ENGELS
ACTION U.S.A.	DAVID RESKIN
ACTION U.S.A.	JOHN STEWART
ACTOR, THE - S	PETER MCBRIDE
ACTRESS, THE	RUTH GORDON†
ACTS - S	JOHN ROMANO
ACTS OF GOD (CTF) - S	ROBERT GLASS
ACTS OF GOD - S	THOMAS BAUM
ACTUARY - S	DANILO BACH
ADAM AND EVE THE SECOND - S	LARRY GRUSIN
ADAM'S RIB	RUTH GORDON†
ADAM'S RIB - S	A.J. CAROTHERS
ADAM'S SEED - S	ROBBY BENSON
ADDAMS FAMILY	PAUL RUDNIK
ADDAMS FAMILY, THE	CAROLINE THOMPSON
ADDAMS FAMILY, THE	LARRY WILSON
ADDICTED TO LOVE - S	BOB GORDON
ADDICTED TO LOVE - S	SCOTT MORGAN
ADJUSTABLE POSITIONS (P)	CRAIG GHOLSON
ADOPT-A-CON - S	HARIS ORKIN
ADUA E LE COMPAGNE	ETTORE SCOLA
ADULT EDUCATION - S	BENNETT YELLIN
ADULT EDUCATION - S	PETER FARRELLY
ADULTERY - S	LARRY GROSS
ADVENTURE I - S	DAVID KOEPP
ADVENTURE OF SHERLOCK HOLMES' SMARTER BROTHER, THE	GENE WILDER
ADVENTURERS, THE	LEWIS GILBERT
ADVENTURES IN BABYSITTING	DAVID SIMKINS
ADVENTURES IN BACHELORHOOD - S	BOB MAKELA
ADVENTURES OF BARON MUNCHAUSEN, THE	CHARLES MCKEOWN
ADVENTURES OF BARON MUNCHAUSEN, THE	TERRY GILLIAM
ADVENTURES OF BARRY MCKENZIE, THE	BRUCE BERESFORD
ADVENTURES OF BUCKAROO BANZAI, THE	EARL MAC RAUCH
ADVENTURES OF FORD FAIRLANE, THE	DAVID ARNOTT
ADVENTURES OF FORD FAIRLANE, THE	JAMES CAPPE
ADVENTURES OF FORD FAIRLANE, THE	DANIEL WATERS
ADVENTURES OF JONATHAN CABOT, THE - S	CHARLES ROBERT CARNER
ADVENTURES OF LOLA, THE - S	CHRISTOPHER DURANG
ADVENTURES OF MARK TWAIN, THE (AF)	SUSAN SHADBURNE
ADVENTURES OF MILO AND OTIS, THE	MARK SALTZMAN
ADVENTURES OF THE AMERICAN RABBIT, THE (AF)	NORM LENZER
ADVENTURES OF THE WILDERNESS FAMILY	STEWART RAFFILL
ADVENTURES OF WILLIE & MADELINE,THE - S	GEORGE GIPE
ADVERTISER, THE - S	RON HUGO
ADVISE AND CONSENT	WENDELL MAYES
AFFAIR IN TRINIDAD	OSCAR SAUL
AFGHAN PROJECT - S	ROBERT MARK KAMEN
AFRICAN FACTOR - S	LARRY KETRON
AFRIKANER - S	BOAZ YAKIN
AFTER ALL - S	STEVEN L. BLOOM
AFTER ALL EXPRESS - S	ALEXANDER TANA
AFTER ALL THESE YEARS - S	JANET KOVALCIK
AFTER DARK, MY SWEET	ROBERT REDLIN
AFTER DARK, MY SWEET	JAMES FOLEY
AFTER EDEN - S	JOHN SACRET YOUNG
AFTER HOURS	JOSEPH MINION
AFTER JIMMY - S	JUDITH FEIN
AFTER MIDNIGHT	JIM WHEAT
AFTER MIDNIGHT	KEN WHEAT
AFTER SCHOOL	HUGH PARKS
AFTER SCHOOL	JOE TANKERSLEY
AFTER SCHOOL	JOHN LINDE
AFTER SCHOOL	ROD MCBRIEN
AFTER THE BEAR HUNT - S	JO NAPOLEON
AFTER THE FALL (P)	ARTHUR MILLER

Af-Am
FILM WRITERS GUIDE

INDEX OF FILM TITLES

AFTER THE FALL OF NEW YORK ... JULIAN BERRY
AFTER THE FALL OF NEW YORK ... MARTIN DOLMAN
AFTER THE FOX ... NEIL SIMON
AFTER THE FOX - S ... JIM MULHOLLAND
AFTER THE FOX - S ... MICHAEL BARRIE
AFTER THE PEEPSHOW - S ... MARK LINDQUIST
AFTER THE REHEARSAL ... INGMAR BERGMAN
AFTER THE SHOCK (CTF) ... GARY A. SHERMAN
AFTERGLOW - S ... JEFF BUHAI
AFTERGLOW - S ... STEVE ZACHARIAS
AFTERLIFE - S ... CLYDE DERRICK
AFTERLIFE OF GRANDPA, THE (SHORT) ... P.J. PESCE
AFTERNOON SESSIONS - S ... ROBERT SARNO
AGAINST A CROOKED SKY ... DOUGLAS DAY STEWART
AGAINST ALL ODDS ... ERIC HUGHES
AGAINST THE WIND - S ... DAVID SMITH
AGAINST THE WIND - S ... GORDON GREISMAN
AGE OF CONSENT ... PETER YELDMAN
AGE OF INNOCENCE - S ... JAY COCKS
AGE OF INNOCENCE - S ... MARTIN SCORSESE
AGENCY ... NOEL HYND
AGGIE ... JULE SELBO
AGNES OF GOD ... JOHN PIELMEIER
AGONY AND THE ECSTASY, THE ... PHILIP DUNNE
AGUIRRE THE WRATH OF GOD ... WERNER HERZOG
AILEEN QUINN STORY, THE - S ... PAUL PRICE
AILEEN QUINN STORY, THE - S ... STEVE NATHAN
AIN'T NO HEROES - S ... ROBERT BORIS
AIN'T THAT AMERICA - S ... FRANK R. PIERSON
AIR AMERICA ... JOHN ESKOW
AIR AMERICA ... RICHARD RUSH
AIR PARADISE - S ... ANDREW BERGMAN
AIR-CONDITIONED DREAM, THE - S ... GLORIA KATZ
AIR-CONDITIONED DREAM, THE - S ... WILLARD HUYCK
AIRBORNE - S ... JEFF FAZIO
AIRPLANE II: THE SEQUEL ... KEN FINKLEMAN
AIRPLANE III - S ... DAVID GREENWALT
AIRPLANE III - S ... JIM KOUF
AIRPLANE! ... DAVID ZUCKER
AIRPLANE! ... JERRY ZUCKER
AIRPLANE! ... JIM ABRAHAMS
AIRPORT '77 ... DAVID SPECTOR
AIRPORT '77 ... MICHAEL SCHEFF
AIRPORT ANGLE (P) ... BILL CORBETT
AIRWAVES - S ... EDWARD DECTER
AKIRA KUROSAWA'S DREAMS ... AKIRA KUROSAWA
AL DENTE - S ... JEFF FAZIO
ALAMAGORDO - S ... KEN FINKELMAN
ALAMO BAY ... ALICE ARLEN
ALASKA SEAS ... WALTER DONIGER
ALCHEMIST, THE ... ALAN J. ADLER
ALEX & THE GYPSY ... LAWRENCE B. MARCUS
ALEX IN WONDERLAND ... PAUL MAZURKSY
ALEXA ... PEGGY BRUEN
ALEXA ... SEAN DELGADO
ALEXANDER & NEIL - S ... JANICE LEE GRAHAM
ALEXANDRA - S ... ALLAN G. SCOTT
ALF MOVIE, THE - S ... DONALD TODD
ALFIE DARLING ... KEN HUGHES
ALFRED AND VICTORIA: A LIFE (P) ... DONALD FREED
ALIAS - S ... DAVID S. GOYER
ALIAS EDDIE SHERBERT - S ... JACK BEHR
ALIAS EDDIE SHERBERT - S ... SANDY KROOPF
ALIBIS - S ... NAOMI FONER
ALICE ... WOODY ALLEN
ALICE DOESN'T LIVE HERE ANY MORE ... ROBERT GETCHELL
ALICE IN THE CITIES ... WIM WENDERS
ALICE'S RESTAURANT ... ARTHUR PENN
ALIEN ... DAN O' BANNON
ALIEN ... RONALD SHUSETT
ALIENS ... DAVID GILER
ALIENS ... JAMES CAMERON
ALIENS ... WALTER HILL
ALIENS III - S ... D.T. TWOHY
ALIENS III - S ... DAVID K. GILER
ALIEN COP - S ... MEL FRIEDMAN
ALIEN FROM L.A. ... ALBERT PYUN
ALIEN NATION ... ROCKNE O'BANNON
ALIEN PREDATOR ... DERAN SARAFIAN
ALIEN TIMES - S ... TERREL SELTZER
ALIVE - S ... MONTE MERRICK
ALIVE - S ... ROB THOMPSON
ALIVE! - S ... STEVEN ZAILLIAN
ALL ABOUT EVE ... JOSEPH L. MANKIEWICZ
ALL ASHORE ... BLAKE EDWARDS
ALL CONQUERS LOVE - S ... JONATHAN KAUFER
ALL CREATURES GREAT AND SMALL ... HUGH WHITEMORE
ALL DOGS GO TO HEAVEN (AF) ... DAVID STEINBERG
ALL DOGS GO TO HEAVEN (AF) ... DON BLUTH
ALL DOGS GO TO HEAVEN (AF) ... GARY GOLDMAN
ALL DOGS GO TO HEAVEN (AF) ... JOHN POMEROY
ALL DOGS GO TO HEAVEN (AF) ... MONICA PARKER
ALL DOGS GO TO HEAVEN (AF) ... DAVID N. WEISS
ALL I DESIRE ... ROBERT BLEES
ALL I WANT FOR CHRISTMAS ... TOM EBERHARDT
ALL IN A NIGHT'S WORK ... MAURICE RICHLIN†
ALL IN A NIGHT'S WORK ... SIDNEY SHELDON
ALL IN A SUMMER'S DAY (SHORT) ... ED KAPLAN
ALL MINE - S ... LISA STOTSKY
ALL MINE - S ... WENDY GRAF
ALL MY FRIENDS ARE GOING TO BE STRANGERS - S ... LARRY MCMURTRY
ALL MY SONS (P) ... ARTHUR MILLER
ALL NEAT IN BLACK STOCKINGS ... HUGH WHITEMORE
ALL NIGHT LONG ... W.D. RICHTER
ALL OF ME ... HENRY OLEK
ALL OF ME ... PHIL ALDEN ROBINSON
ALL OVER TOWN (P) ... MURRAY SCHISGAL
ALL SCREWED UP ... LINA WERTMULLER
ALL THAT CAN BE - S ... DAVID FULLER
ALL THAT CAN BE - S ... RICK NATKIN
ALL THAT JAZZ ... BOB FOSSE†
ALL THAT JAZZ ... ROBERT ALAN ARTHUR†
...ALL THE MARBLES ... MEL FROHMAN
ALL THE PLEASURES PROVE (P) ... DENNIS PALUMBO
ALL THE PRESIDENT'S MEN ... WILLIAM GOLDMAN
ALL THE RIGHT MOVES ... MICHAEL KANE
ALL THE RIGHT NOISES ... GERRY O'HARA
ALL THE WAY HOME (P) ... LORING MANDEL
ALL THE YOUNG MEN ... HALL BARTLETT
ALL THESE WOMEN ... INGMAR BERGMAN
ALL YOU NEED IS CASH ... ERIC IDLE
ALL'S FAIR ... WATT TYLER
ALL'S FAIR ... JOHN FINNEGAN
ALL'S FAIR ... RANDEE RUSSELL
ALL'S FAIR ... TOM RONDINELLA
ALL'S FAIR ... WILLIAM PACE
ALL-AMERICAN BOY, THE ... CHARLES EASTMAN
ALL-AMERICAN MURDERS - S ... BARRY SANDLER
ALLAN QUATERMAIN AND THE LOST CITY OF GOLD ... LEE D. REYNOLDS
ALLAN QUATERMAIN AND THE LOST CITY OF GOLD ... EUGENE QUINTANO
ALLARD LOWENSTEIN STORY (CTF) - S ... JOHN HOPKINS
ALLEY CAT ... ROBERT E. WATERS
ALLEY OOP - S ... W.D. RICHTER
ALLIE - S ... ANDY LEWIS
ALLIGATOR ... FRANK RAY PERILLI
ALLIGATOR ... JOHN SAYLES
ALLIGATOR EYES ... JOHN FELDMAN
ALLIGATOR NAMED DAISY, AN ... JACK DAVIES
ALLNIGHTER, THE ... MARGOT L. KESSLER
ALLNIGHTER, THE ... TAMAR SIMON HOFFS
ALMONDS AND RAISINS (FD) ... WOLF MANKOWITZ
ALMOST AN ANGEL ... PAUL HOGAN
ALMOST HUMAN - S ... J. D. FEIGELSON
ALMOST HUMAN - S ... SARAH C. PALEY
ALMOST IRRESISTIBLE - S ... MICK GARRIS
ALMOST PERFECT AFFAIR, AN ... DON PETERSON
ALMOST PERFECT AFFAIR, AN ... WALTER BERNSTEIN
ALMOST PERFECT PERSON, AN (P) ... JUDITH ROSS
ALMOST SUMMER ... JUDITH BERG
ALMOST SUMMER ... MARTIN DAVIDSON
ALMOST SUMMER ... SANDRA BERG
ALMOST YOU ... ADAM BROOKS
ALMOST YOU ... MARK HOROWITZ
ALOHA SUMMER ... ROBERT BENEDETTO
ALOHA SUMMER ... MIKE GRECO
ALOHA, BOBBY AND ROSE ... FLOYD MUTRUX
ALONE IN THE DARK ... JACK SHOLDER
ALONE TOGETHER (P) ... LARRY ROMAN
ALONG CAME JONES - S ... FLOYD MUTRUX
ALONG THE GREAT DIVIDE ... WALTER DONIGER
ALPHABET CITY ... AMOS POE
ALPHABET CITY ... GREGORY HELLER
ALPHABET MURDERS, THE ... DAVID PURSALL
ALPHAVILLE ... JEAN-LUC GODARD
ALPINE FIRE ... FREDI M. MURER
ALTAR BOUND - S ... JOSEPHINE CUMMINGS
ALTAR BOUND - S ... RICHARD YALEM
ALTERED STATES ... PADDY CHAYEVSKY†
ALTERNATE, THE - S ... JUDY NOGG
ALUMNI - S ... RICHARD KRAMER
ALWAYS ... HENRY JAGLOM
ALWAYS (1990) ... JERRY BELSON
ALWAYS LEAVE THEM LAUGHING ... JACK ROSE
ALWAYS LEAVE THEM LAUGHING ... MEL SHAVELSON
ALWAYS REMEMBERED - S ... MICHAEL AUERBACH
AMADEUS ... PETER SHAFFER
AMARCORD ... FEDERICO FELLINI
AMARCORD ... TONINO GUERRA
AMAROSA ... MAI ZETTERLING
AMATEUR HOUR, THE - S ... HARV ZIMMEL
AMATEUR, THE ... DIANA MADDOX
AMATEUR, THE ... ROBERT LITTEL
AMATEURS - S ... FIONA LEWIS
AMAZING AND DEATH-DEFYING DIARY OF EUGENE DINGMAN, THE - S ... PAUL ZINDEL
AMAZING BUT TRUE - S ... JILLIAN PALETHORPE
AMAZING BUT TRUE - S ... SPARKY GREENE
AMAZING COLOSSAL MAN, THE ... BERT I. GORDON
AMAZING GRACE - S ... DENNIS CLARK
AMAZING GRACE AND CHUCK ... DAVID FIELD
AMAZING MR. BLUNDEN, THE ... LIONEL JEFFRIES
AMAZING MR. WILLIAMS, THE ... RICHARD MAIBAUM†
AMAZON RUN - S ... PETER BENCHLEY
AMAZON WOMEN ON THE MOON ... JIM MULHOLLAND
AMAZON WOMEN ON THE MOON ... MICHAEL BARRIE
AMBASSADOR, THE ... MAX JACK
AMBULANCE, THE ... LARRY COHEN
AMERICA ... ROBERT DOWNEY
AMERICA 3000 ... DAVID ENGELBACH
AMERICA ME - S ... FLOYD MUTRUX
AMERICA'S CUP, THE ... WES CLARRIDGE
AMERICA'S SWEETHEART - S ... GEORGE FURTH
AMERICA, AMERICA ... ELIA KAZAN
AMERICAN ANTHEM ... SUSAN WILLIAMS
AMERICAN ANTHEM ... EVAN ARCHERD
AMERICAN ANTHEM ... JEFF BENJAMIN
AMERICAN BEAUTY - S ... JANET KOVALCIK
AMERICAN BLUE NOTE ... GILBERT GIRION
AMERICAN BORN ... ADDISON RANDALL
AMERICAN BORN ... RAYMOND MARTINO
AMERICAN BOY (FD) ... JULIA CAMERON
AMERICAN BOY - S ... MICHAEL SERAFIN
AMERICAN BOYFRIENDS ... SANDY WILSON
AMERICAN BRASS - S ... GEORGE GALLO
AMERICAN BUFFALO (P) ... DAVID MAMET
AMERICAN CLOCK, THE (P) ... ARTHUR MILLER
AMERICAN COUP - S ... STEPHEN PETERS
AMERICAN COUPLE - S ... RICK PODELL
AMERICAN DREAM, AN ... MANN RUBIN
AMERICAN DREAMER ... ANN BIDERMAN
AMERICAN DREAMER ... DAVID GREENWALT
AMERICAN DREAMER ... JIM KOUF
AMERICAN DREAMER, THE (FD) ... DENNIS HOPPER
AMERICAN DREAMER, THE (FD) ... L.M. KIT CARSON
AMERICAN EXPRESS - S ... CRAIG BOLOTIN
AMERICAN EXPRESS - S ... RICHARD KLETTER
AMERICAN FLAG, THE - S ... JAY PRESSON ALLEN
AMERICAN FLYERS ... STEVE TESICH
AMERICAN FRIEND, THE ... WIM WENDERS
AMERICAN GIGOLO ... PAUL SCHRADER
AMERICAN GLADIATOR ... JOHN P. GROVES
AMERICAN GOTHIC - S ... ALAN GROSS
AMERICAN GRAFFITI ... GEORGE LUCAS
AMERICAN GRAFFITI ... GLORIA KATZ
AMERICAN GRAFFITI ... WILLARD HUYCK
AMERICAN HARVEST - S ... SUSAN NANUS
AMERICAN HEART -U ... PETER SILVERMAN
AMERICAN HOT WAX ... JOHN KAYE
AMERICAN IRON - S ... DANIEL PYNE
AMERICAN JUSTICE ... DENNIS A. PRATT
AMERICAN LADY - S ... GAIL FISHER
AMERICAN LADY - S ... MARC CHESLER
AMERICAN ME - S ... FLOYD MUTRUX
AMERICAN MELTDOWN - S ... GEORGE GALLO
AMERICAN NINJA ... AVI KLEINBERGER
AMERICAN NINJA ... GIDEON AMIR
AMERICAN NINJA ... PAUL DEMIELCHE
AMERICAN NINJA 2 ... GARY CONWAY
AMERICAN NINJA 2 ... JAMES BOOTH
AMERICAN NINJA 3 ... GARY CONWAY
AMERICAN NINJA 3 ... CEDRIC SUNDSTROM
AMERICAN NINJA 4 ... DAVID GEEVES
AMERICAN NINJA V - S ... GEORGE SAUNDERS
AMERICAN NINJA V - S ... JOHN BRYANT HEDBERG
AMERICAN NONSENSE - S ... JOHN HERMAN SHANER
AMERICAN NOTES (P) ... LEN JENKIN

Am-Ar
FILM WRITERS GUIDE
INDEX OF FILM TITLES

AMERICAN PIE - S ..... BILL STREIB
AMERICAN PIE - S ..... CHARLES ROBERT CARNER
AMERICAN PLACE, AN - S ..... JULIAN BARRY
AMERICAN POP (AF) ..... RONNI KERN
AMERICAN REVOLUTION - S ..... JAY COCKS
AMERICAN RHAPSODY - S ..... FIONA LEWIS
AMERICAN ROULETTE - S ..... BUCK HENRY
AMERICAN ROULETTE - S ..... DAVID FREEMAN
AMERICAN SHOESHINE (SHORT) ..... JILLIAN PALETHORPE
AMERICAN SHOESHINE (SHORT) ..... SPARKY GREENE
AMERICAN SPIRIT - S ..... MARK HOROWITZ
AMERICAN SPORTSMAN - S ..... JOHN NORVILLE
AMERICAN SUCCESS CO., THE ..... LARRY COHEN
AMERICAN SUCCESS CO., THE ..... WILLIAM RICHERT
AMERICAN SUMMER, AN ..... JAMES SLOCUM
AMERICAN TABOO ..... STEVE LUSTGARTEN
AMERICAN TAIL, AN (AF) ..... JUDY FREUDBERG
AMERICAN TAIL, AN (AF) ..... TONY GEISS
AMERICAN TALE, AN (AF) ..... DAVID KIRSCHNER
AMERICAN TRAGEDY - S ..... JEFF BURKHART
AMERICAN WAY, THE ..... SCOTT ROBERTS
AMERICAN WAY, THE - S ..... GRANT MORRIS
AMERICAN WAY, THE - S ..... LOUIS VENOSTA
AMERICAN WEREWOLF IN LONDON, AN ..... JOHN LANDIS
AMERICAN WIFE - S ..... ANDY BOROWITZ
AMERICANA ..... RICHARD CARR
AMERICANIZATION OF EMILY, THE ..... PADDY CHAYEVSKY†
AMERICATHON ..... MONICA JOHNSON
AMEROSA PLACE - S ..... DAVID LOUCKA
AMITYVILLE 3-D ..... DAVID AMBROSE
AMITYVILLE 6 - S ..... CHRIS DEFARIA
AMITYVILLE CURSE, THE ..... DOUG OLSEN
AMITYVILLE CURSE, THE ..... MICHAEL KRUEGER†
AMITYVILLE CURSE, THE ..... NORVELL ROSE
AMITYVILLE HORROR, THE ..... SANDOR STERN
AMITYVILLE II: THE POSSESSION ..... TOMMY LEE WALLACE
AMOK - S ..... JOHN MORTIMER
AMONG HONORABLE MEN - S ..... STEPHEN FEKE
AMONG THE CINDERS ..... JOHN O'SHEA
AMONG THE CINDERS ..... ROLF HAEDRICH
AMSTERDAM AFFAIR ..... EDMUND WARD
AMSTERDAM KILL, THE ..... ROBERT CLOUSE
AMSTERDAMNED ..... DICK MAAS
AMY ..... NOREEN STONE
ANASTASIA ..... ARTHUR LAURENTS
ANATOMY LESSON, THE - S ..... JOHN STEPPLING
ANATOMY OF A BURGLARY - S ..... NORMAN WEXLER
ANATOMY OF A JURY - S ..... FRANK MILITARY JR.
ANATOMY OF A MURDER ..... WENDELL MAYES
AND A NIGHTINGALE SANG - S ..... JACK ROSENTHAL
AND GOD CREATED WOMAN ..... ROGER VADIM
AND GOD CREATED WOMAN ..... R. J. STEWART
...AND JUSTICE FOR ALL ..... VALERIE CURTIN
...AND JUSTICE FOR ALL ..... BARRY LEVINSON
AND NOW FOR SOMETHING COMPLETELY DIFFERENT ..... GRAHAM CHAPMAN†
AND NOW FOR SOMETHING COMPLETELY DIFFERENT ..... ERIC IDLE
AND NOW FOR SOMETHING COMPLETELY DIFFERENT ..... JOHN CLEESE
AND NOW FOR SOMETHING COMPLETELY DIFFERENT ..... MICHAEL PALIN
AND NOW FOR SOMETHING COMPLETELY DIFFERENT ..... TERRY GILLIAM
AND NOW FOR SOMETHING COMPLETELY DIFFERENT ..... TERRY JONES
AND NOW MY LOVE ..... CLAUDE LELOUCH
AND NOW MY LOVE - S ..... RICHARD CHAPMAN
AND NOW THERE'S JUST THE THREE OF US - S ..... MICHAEL WELLER
AND ONCE UPON A LOVE ..... JOHN DEREK
AND SOON THE DARKNESS ..... BRIAN CLEMENS
AND SOON THE DARKNESS ..... TERRY NATION
AND THE ANGELS SING ..... NORMAN PANAMA
AND THE HOME OF THE BRAVE - S ..... GREGORY BREHM
AND THE SHIP SAILS ON ..... FEDERICO FELLINI
AND THE SHIP SAILS ON ..... TONINO GUERRA
AND THEN THERE WERE NONE ..... HARRY ALAN TOWERS
AND THINGS THAT GO BUMP IN THE NIGHT (P) ..... TERRENCE MCNALLY
ANDERSON TAPES, THE ..... FRANK R. PIERSON
ANDREASSON AFFAIR, THE- S ..... LEWIS JOHN CARLINO
ANDREI RUBLEV ..... ANDREI KONCHALOVSKY
ANDROID ..... DON OPPER
ANDROID ..... JAMES REIGLE
ANDROMEDA II (P) ..... RON WHYTE†
ANDROMEDA STRAIN, THE ..... NELSON GIDDING
ANDROSCOGGIN FUGUE (P) ..... DICK BEEBE
ANDY HARDY MEETS A DEBUTANTE ..... THOMAS SELLER†
ANDY WARHOL'S DRACULA ..... PAUL MORRISSEY
ANDY WARHOL'S FRANKENSTEIN ..... PAUL MORRISSEY
ANGEL ..... JOSEPH M. CALA
ANGEL ..... NEIL JORDAN
ANGEL ..... ROBERT VINCENT O'NEIL
ANGEL (P) ..... MAYO SIMON
ANGEL AT MY TABLE, AN ..... LAURA JONES
ANGEL FACE - S ..... JERZY SKOLIMOWSKI
ANGEL HEART ..... ALAN PARKER
ANGEL III: THE FINAL CHAPTER ..... TOM DESIMONE
ANGEL LEVINE, THE ..... RONALD RIBMAN
ANGEL PANGS - S ..... TOM CAMP
ANGEL UNCHAINED ..... JEFFREY ALAN FISKIN
ANGEL'S BRIGADE ..... ALVIN L. FAST
ANGEL'S FLIGHT - S ..... JILL ISAACS
ANGEL'S FLIGHT - S ..... PATRICK DUNCAN
ANGELA ..... CHARLES ISRAEL
ANGELO, MY LOVE ..... ROBERT DUVALL
ANGELS BRIGADE ..... GREYDON CLARK
ANGELS FLIGHT - S ..... ZALMAN KING
ANGELS HARD AS THEY COME ..... JONATHAN DEMME
ANGELS IN THE OUTFIELD - S ..... HEYWOOD GOULD
ANGELS OF DEATH - S ..... PETER LANCE
ANGELS OF THE CITY ..... JOSEPH MEHRI
ANGELS OF THE CITY ..... LAWRENCE HILTON-JACOBS
ANGELS OF THE CITY ..... RAYMOND MARTINO
ANGELS ON HORSEBACK - S ..... MATTHEW MCDUFFIE
ANGRY HARVEST ..... AGNIESZKA HOLLAND
ANGRY HOUSEWIVES (P) ..... A.M. COLLINS
ANGRY SILENCE, THE ..... BRYAN FORBES
ANIMAL BEHAVIOR ..... SUSAN RICE
ANIMAL FACTORY - S ..... DAVID TAYLOR
ANIMAL HOUSE ..... CHRIS MILLER
ANIMAL HOUSE ..... DOUGLAS KENNEY†
ANIMAL HOUSE ..... HAROLD RAMIS
ANIMAL HOUSE NOW - S ..... CHRIS MILLER
ANIMAL HOUSE NOW - S ..... MICHAEL D. SUTTON
ANIMAL PASSION - S ..... TODD DURHAM
ANIMAL WORLD, THE (FD) ..... IRWIN ALLEN
ANIMALS - S ..... NICHOLAS KAZAN
ANIMALYMPICS (AF) ..... STEVEN LISBERGER
ANITA FACTOR - S ..... BO GOLDMAN
ANNA ..... YUREK BOGAYEVICZ
ANNA ..... AGNIESZKA HOLLAND
ANNA & JAKE - S ..... HILARY HENKIN
ANNA LEE - S ..... GERALD DI PEGO
ANNA LUCASTA ..... ARTHUR LAURENTS
ANNA LUCASTA ..... PHILIP YORDAN
ANNA OF THE SUBWAY - S ..... BOB DEMAIO
ANNE BONNY THE PIRATE WOMAN - S ..... JOHN BEAIRD
ANNE FLETCHER - S ..... ADAM GREENMAN
ANNE HUTCHINSON - S ..... ANNEKE CAMPBELL
ANNE OF THE INDIES ..... PHILIP DUNNE
ANNIE ..... CAROL SOBIESKI†
ANNIE (P) ..... THOMAS MEEHAN
ANNIE GET YOUR GUN ..... SIDNEY SHELDON
ANNIE HALL ..... MARSHALL BRICKMAN
ANNIE HALL ..... WOODY ALLEN
ANNIE II - S ..... HOWARD L. ANDERSON
ANNIE II - S ..... JEFF ROTHBERG
ANNIE'S COMING OUT ..... CHRIS BORTHWICK
ANNIE'S COMING OUT ..... JOHN PATERSON
ANNIHILATORS, THE ..... BRIAN RUSSELL
ANNIVERSARY, THE ..... JIMMY SANGSTER
ANOTHER 48 HRS. ..... FRED BRAUGHTON
ANOTHER 48 HRS. ..... JOHN FASANO
ANOTHER 48 HRS. ..... JEB STUART
ANOTHER 48 HRS. ..... LARRY GROSS
ANOTHER ANTIGONE (P) ..... A.R. GURNEY
ANOTHER COUNTRY ..... JULIAN MITCHELL
ANOTHER FINE MESS - S ..... HARRIS ORKIN
ANOTHER MAN'S POISON ..... VAL GUEST
ANOTHER MAN, ANOTHER CHANCE ..... CLAUDE LELOUCH
ANOTHER SUNDAY AND SWEET PEA (P) ..... JACK ROSENTHAL
ANOTHER TIME (P) ..... RONALD HARWOOD
ANOTHER TIME, ANOTHER PLACE ..... STANLEY MANN
ANOTHER TIME, ANOTHER PLACE ..... MICHAEL RADFORD
ANOTHER WOMAN ..... WOODY ALLEN
ANOTHER YOU ..... ZIGGY STEINBERG
ANSWERS (P) ..... ERNEST THOMPSON
ANSWERS - S ..... JULES FEIFFER
ANT MAN - S ..... NEIL RUTTENBERG
ANTAGONISTS, THE - S ..... JOEL OLIANSKY
ANTELOPE VALLEY - S ..... RON SHELTON
ANTONY AND CLEOPATRA ..... CHARLTON HESTON
ANY MAN'S DEATH ..... CHRIS KELLY
ANY MAN'S DEATH ..... IAIN ROY
ANY NUMBER CAN PLAY ..... RICHARD BROOKS
ANY WEDNESDAY ..... JULIUS J. EPSTEIN
ANY WHICH WAY YOU CAN ..... STANFORD SHERMAN
ANYTHING GUYS, THE - S ..... BILL KERBY
ANYTHING, ANYTHING (P) ..... ANDREW SMITH
ANYWHERE BUT HERE - S ..... ALVIN SARGENT
ANYWHERE BUT HERE - S ..... STEVE TESICH
APARTMENT ZERO ..... DAVID KOEPP
APARTMENT ZERO ..... MARTIN DONOVAN
APARTMENT, THE ..... BILLY WILDER
APARTMENT, THE ..... I.A.L. DIAMOND†
APE - S ..... BUCK HENRY
APE, THE ..... CURT SIODMAK
APOCALYPSE NOW ..... FRANCIS FORD COPPOLA
APOCALYPSE NOW ..... JOHN MILIUS
APOLOGY (CTF) ..... MARK MEDOFF
APPALOOSA, THE ..... JAMES BRIDGES
APPALOOSA, THE ..... ROLAND KIBBEE†
APPARE ISSHIN TASUKE ..... AKIRA KUROSAWA
APPLE DUMPLING GANG RIDES AGAIN, THE ..... DON TAIT
APPLE DUMPLING GANG, THE ..... DON TAIT
APPLE, THE ..... MENAHEM GOLAN
APPLEGATES, THE ..... MICHAEL LEHMANN
APPLEGATES, THE ..... REDBEARD SIMMONS
APPOINTMENT WITH DEATH ..... MICHAEL WINNER
APPOINTMENT WITH DEATH ..... PETER BUCKMAN
APPOINTMENT WITH DEATH ..... ANTHONY SHAFFER
APPOINTMENT WITH FEAR ..... RAMZI THOMAS
APPOINTMENT, THE ..... JAMES SALTER
APPRENTICE TO MURDER ..... ALLAN SCOTT
APPRENTICE TO MURDER ..... WESLEY MOORE
APPRENTICE, THE - S ..... ELLIOT M. STERN
APPRENTICESHIP OF DUDDY KRAVITZ, THE ..... LIONEL CHETWYND
APPRENTICESHIP OF DUDDY KRAVITZ, THE ..... MORDECAI RICHLER
APRIL FOOL'S DAY ..... DANILO BACH
APRIL FOOLS - S ..... CALDER WILLINGHAM
APRIL FOOLS, THE ..... HAL DRESNER
APRIL IN PARIS ..... JACK ROSE
APRIL IN PARIS ..... MEL SHAVELSON
APT PUPIL ..... B.J. NELSON
ARABESQUE ..... JULIAN MITCHELL
ARABESQUE ..... PETER STONE
ARABIAN ADVENTURE ..... BRIAN HAYLES
ARACHNOPHOBIA ..... AL WILLIAMS
ARACHNOPHOBIA ..... DON JAKOBY
ARACHNOPHOBIA ..... WESLEY STRICK
ARCADE - S ..... DAVID S. GOYER
ARCHANGELS - S ..... MICHAEL COLLEARY
ARCHBISHOP'S CEILING, THE (P) ..... ARTHUR MILLER
ARE YOU ALONE TONIGHT? - S ..... ROBERT CARRINGTON
ARE YOU BEING SERVED? ..... JEREMY LLOYD
ARE YOU OUT OF MY MIND? - S ..... DIANA HAMMOND
ARE YOU WITH IT? ..... OSCAR BRODNEY
ARENA ..... DANNY BILSON
ARENA ..... PAUL DE MEO
ARIEL ..... AKI KAURISMAKI
ARISE MY LOVE ..... BILLY WILDER
ARMED AND DANGEROUS ..... BRIAN GRAZER
ARMED AND DANGEROUS ..... HAROLD RAMIS
ARMED AND DANGEROUS ..... JAMES KEACH
ARMED AND DANGEROUS ..... PETER TOROKVEI
ARMED RESPONSE ..... T.L. LANKFORD
ARMED RESPONSE - S ..... RENE BALCER
ARMED RESPONSE - S ..... STEVEN GAYDOS
ARMS & THE MAN (P) ..... JONATHAN LYNN
ARMS MERCHANT, THE - S ..... ANDY LEWIS
ARMY OF DARKNESS - S ..... IVAN RAIMI
ARMY OF DARKNESS - S ..... SAM RAIMI
ARNOLD ..... JAMESON BREWER
ARNOLD'S WRECKING COMPANY ..... STEVEN E. DESOUZA
AROUND THE WORLD IN 80 WAYS ..... PAUL LEADON
AROUND THE WORLD IN 80 WAYS ..... STEPHEN J. MACLEAN
AROUSERS, THE ..... CURTIS LEE HANSON

Title	Writer
ARRANGEMENT, THE	ELIA KAZAN
ARRIVE ALIVE - S	HUGH WILSON
ARRIVE ALIVE - S	MICHAEL O'DONOGHUE
ARRIVE ALIVE - S	MITCH GLAZER
ARRIVEDERCI, BABY	KEN HUGHES
ARROGANT, THE	PHILIPPE BLOT
ARSENIC AND OLD LACE	JULIUS J. EPSTEIN
ARSENIC AND OLD LACE	PHILIP G. EPSTEIN†
ART OF COURTLY LOVE - S	RICK STEVENSON
ART OF LOVE, THE	CARL REINER†
ARTHUR	STEVE GORDON†
ARTHUR 2 ON THE ROCKS	ANDY BRECKMAN
ARTHUR'S HALLOWED GROUND	PETER GIBBS
ARTICLE 99	RON CUTLER
ARTIST DESCENDING A STAIRCASE (P)	TOM STOPPARD
ARTIST, THE (SHORT)	J.F. LAWTON
ARTISTS AND MODELS	DON MCGUIRE
AS THE WORM TURNS - S	ANABEL DAVIS-GOFF
AS YOUNG AS YOU FEEL - S	BOB KRAFT
AS YOUNG AS YOU FEEL - S	TED PUSHINSKY
ASCENSEUR POUR L'ECHAFAUD	LOUIS MALLE
ASCENT - S	JOHN PIELMEIER
ASCENT - S	MICHAEL SCHIFFER
ASCENT - S	THOMAS POPE
ASH WEDNESDAY	JEAN-CLAUDE TRAMONT
ASHANTI	STEPHEN GELLER
ASHES - S	DAVID SELTZER
ASIAN SHADE - S	LARRY KETRON
ASK A POLICEMAN	VAL GUEST
ASK THE DUST - S	STEPHEN TOLKIN
ASSASSINATION	RICHARD SALE
ASSASSINATION ON EMBASSY ROAD	KEN FINKLEMAN
ASSASSINATION ON EMBASSY ROW - S	SCOTT SPENCER
ASSAULT OF THE KILLER BIMBOS	ANITA ROSENBERG
ASSAULT OF THE KILLER BIMBOS	PATTI ASTOR
ASSAULT OF THE KILLER BIMBOS	TED NICOLAOU
ASSAULT ON EMPIRE STATE MOUNTAIN (CTF) - S	CHRIS FABER
ASSAULT ON EMPIRE STATE MOUNTAIN (CTF) - S	DANNIEL BARRON
ASSAULT ON PRECINCT 13	JOHN CARPENTER
ASSAULT, THE	GERARD SOETEMAN
ASSIGNED RISK - S	REED STEINER
ASSIGNMENT K	VAL GUEST
ASSISI UNDERGROUND, THE	ALEXANDER RAMATI
ASSISTANT, THE - S	POLLY PLATT
ASSOCIATE, THE	JEAN-CLAUDE CARRIERE
ASSOCIATE, THE - S	DAVID LOUCKA
ASSOCIATE, THE - S	MARK SPRAGG
ASSUMING ROOM TEMPERATURE - S	DAVID BURTON MORRIS
ASTOR HAIR - S	ISRAEL HOROVITZ
ASTROLOGER, THE	JAMES GLICKENHAUS
ASTRONAUT'S WIVES - S	DAVID AMBROSE
ASTRONAUT'S WIVES - S	J. D. FEIGELSON
ASYLUM	ROBERT BLOCH
ASYLUM - S	SHELLEY LIST
AT 17 - S	KATHLEEN ROWELL
AT 17 - S	LINDSAY HARRISON
AT CLOSE RANGE	ELLIOTT LEWIS
AT CLOSE RANGE	NICHOLAS KAZAN
AT LONG LAST LOVE	PETER BOGDANOVICH
AT PLAY - S	VINCENT PATRICK
AT PLAY IN THE FIELDS OF THE LORD	HECTOR BABENCO
AT PLAY IN THE FIELDS OF THE LORD	JEAN-CLAUDE CARRIERE
AT THE EARTH'S CORE	MILTON SUBOTSKY
AT YOUR SERVICE - S	DARYL G. NICKENS
ATAME!	PEDRO ALMODOVAR
ATLANTA BURNING - S	PAT CONROY
ATLANTIC CITY	JOHN GUARE
ATLANTIC CROSSING- S	NORMAN STEINBERG
ATLANTIS - S	LLOYD FONVIELLE
ATLAS SHRUGGED	JOHN HILL
ATOMIC CITY, THE	SYDNEY BOEHM†
ATOMIC FOLLIES -U	LEE KALCHEIM
ATOMIC KID, THE	BLAKE EDWARDS
ATOMIC ROMANCE - S	RAMA LAURIE STAGNER
ATTACK FROM OUTER SPACE - S	ERIC LUKE
ATTACK OF THE CRAB MONSTERS	CHARLES B. GRIFFITH
ATTACK OF THE KILLER TOMATOES	JOHN DEBELLO
AU HASARD, BALTHAZAR	ROBERT BRESSON
AU REVOIR LES ENFANTS	LOUIS MALLE
AUDREY ROSE	FRANK DEFELITTA
AUGIE - S	JON CONNOLLY
AUGUST FIRE - S	JOHN WARREN
AUGUST IN MANHATTAN - S	MARTHA GOLDHIRSH
AUNT DAN AND LEMON (P)	WALLACE SHAWN
AUNTIE MAME	ADOLPH GREEN
AUNTIE MAME	BETTY COMDEN
AUNTIE MAME (P)	JEROME LAWRENCE
AUNTIE MAME (P)	ROBERT E. LEE
AUTHOR! AUTHOR!	GEORGE E.SIMPSON
AUTHOR! AUTHOR!	ISRAEL HOROVITZ
AUTUMN DANCE - S	JOHN J. SCHALTER
AUTUMN LEAVES	ROBERT BLEES
AUTUMN SONATA	INGMAR BERGMAN
AVALANCE EXPRESS	ABRAHAM POLONSKY
AVALANCHE	COREY ALLEN
AVALON	BARRY LEVINSON
AVANTI!	BILLY WILDER
AVANTI!	I.A.L. DIAMOND†
AVE MARIA - S	CAMILLE THOMASSON
AVEN'U BOYS (P)	FRANK PUGLIESE
AVENGER, THE - S	TONY KAYDEN
AVENGERS, THE - S	SAM HAMM
AVENGING ANGEL	JOSEPH M. CALA
AVENGING ANGEL	ROBERT VINCENT O'NEIL
AVENGING ANGEL - S	JANET DULIN JONES
AVENGING FORCE	JAMES BOOTH
AVIATOR'S WIFE, THE	ERIC ROHMER
AVIATOR, THE	MARC NORMAN
AWAKENING, THE	ALLAN G. SCOTT
AWAKENING, THE	CHRIS BRYANT
AWAKENING, THE	CLIVE EXTON
AWAKENINGS	STEVEN ZAILLIAN
AY, CARMELA!	RAFAEL AZCONA

B

Title	Writer
B STREET - S	JACK BEHR
B STREET - S	SANDY KROOPF
B.S. I LOVE YOU	STEVEN HILLIARD STERN
BABA GOYA (P)	STEVE TESICH
BABAR: THE MOVIE (AF)	ALAN BUNCE
BABAR: THE MOVIE (AF)	JOHN DEKLEIN
BABAR: THE MOVIE (AF)	PETER SAUDER
BABCOCK ON BAKER STREET (CTF) - S	MICHAEL GAYLIN
BABE & ME - S	JIM STRAIN
BABE WEST - S	BUCK HENRY
BABE, THE - S	JOHN FUSCO
BABETTE'S FEAST	GABRIEL AXEL
BABY - SECRET OF THE LOST LEGEND	CLIFFORD GREEN
BABY - SECRET OF THE LOST LEGEND	ELLEN GREEN
BABY AND THE BATTLESHIP, THE	BRYAN FORBES
BABY BABY - S	NAOMI FONER
BABY BABY BABY - S	JAMES KENNEDY
BABY BLUE EYES - S	MICHAEL ALAN EDDY
BABY BLUE MARINE	STANFORD WHITMORE
BABY BOOM	CHARLES SHYER
BABY BOOM	NANCY J. MEYERS
BABY GENIUS - S	ED ZWICK
BABY GENIUS - S	MARSHALL HERSKOVITZ
BABY IN THE SILO - S	KEVIN FALLS
BABY IT'S YOU	JOHN SAYLES
BABY LOVE	ALISTAIR REID
BABY MAKER, THE	JAMES BRIDGES
BABY PICTURES - S	JULES FEIFFER
BABY TALK - S	CARL KURLANDER
BABY, THE RAIN MUST FALL	HORTON FOOTE
BACHELOR AND THE BOBBYSOXER, THE	SIDNEY SHELDON
BACHELOR IN PARADISE	HAL KANTER
BACHELOR MOM - S	KEVIN FALLS
BACHELOR OF HEARTS	FREDERIC RAPHAEL
BACHELOR OF HEARTS	LESLIE BRICUSSE
BACHELOR PARTY	BOB ISRAEL
BACHELOR PARTY	NEAL ISRAEL
BACHELOR PARTY	PAT PROFT
BACHELOR PARTY, THE	PADDY CHAYEVSKY†
BACHELOR'S DAUGHTER	ANDREW STONE
BACK BY 10	LEE ROSE
BACK DOOR TO HEAVEN	JOHN BRIGHT†
BACK HOME (CTF)	DAVID WOOD
BACK IN BLACK - S	JORGE ZAMACONA
BACK NINE - S	ROBERT MOLONEY
BACK ON TOP - S	CHARLIE HAAS
BACK ROADS	GARY DEVORE
BACK ROOM BOY	VAL GUEST
BACK ROOM, THE	NORMAN THADDEUS VANE
BACK TO BACK	GEORGE FRANCIS SKROW
BACK TO BATAAN	BEN BARZMAN†
BACK TO HANNIBAL: THE RETURN OF TOM SAWYER AND HUCKLEBERRY FINN (CTF)	ROY JOHANSEN
BACK TO SCHOOL	DENNIS SNEE
BACK TO SCHOOL	GREG FIELDS
BACK TO SCHOOL	HAROLD RAMIS
BACK TO SCHOOL	PETER TOROKVEI
BACK TO SCHOOL	RODNEY DANGERFIELD
BACK TO SCHOOL	STEVEN W. KAMPMANN
BACK TO SCHOOL	WILL ALDIS
BACK TO SCHOOL II - S	LAWRENCE GAY
BACK TO SCHOOL II - S	MICHAEL DIGAETANO
BACK TO THE BEACH	BRUCE KIRSCHBAUM
BACK TO THE BEACH	JAMES KOMACK
BACK TO THE BEACH	B.W.L. NORTON, JR.
BACK TO THE BEACH	CHRISTOPHER THOMPSON
BACK TO THE BEACH	PETER KRIKES
BACK TO THE BEACH	STEVE MEERSON
BACK TO THE FUTURE	BOB GALE
BACK TO THE FUTURE	ROBERT ZEMECKIS
BACK TO THE FUTURE II	BOB GALE
BACK TO THE FUTURE II	ROBERT ZEMECKIS
BACK TO THE FUTURE III	BOB GALE
BACK TO THE FUTURE III	ROBERT ZEMECKIS
BACKDRAFT	GREGORY C. WIDEN
BACKFIRE	IVAN GOFF
BACKFIRE	LAWRENCE B. MARCUS
BACKFIRE	LARRY BRAND
BACKGROUND	DON SHARP
BACKLASH	BILL BENNETT
BACKSTREET DREAMS	JASON O'MALLEY
BACKSTREETS - S	JEFFREY W. NEAL
BACKTRACK - S	ANN LOUISE BARDACH
BACKWARDS ON A HORSE - S	LARRY GRUSIN
BAD BLOOD	CRAIG HORRALL
BAD BLOOD - S	JIMMY HUSTON
BAD BOYS	RICHARD DILELLO
BAD BOYS, THE (P)	MARK MEDOFF
BAD COMPANY	DAVID NEWMAN
BAD COMPANY	ROBERT BENTON
BAD DAY AT BLACK ROCK	MILLARD KAUFMAN
BAD DEATH - S	ROGER L. SIMON
BAD DREAMS	P.J. PETTIETTE
BAD DREAMS	YURI ZELTSER
BAD DREAMS	ANDREW FLEMING
BAD DREAMS	STEVEN DE SOUZA
BAD GIRLS - S	ROSIE SHUSTER
BAD HABITS (P)	TERRENCE MCNALLY
BAD INFLUENCE	DAVID KOEPP
BAD JIM	CLYDE WARE
BAD LITTLE GIRL - S	DAVID STENN
BAD MAN OF BRIMSTONE	RICHARD MAIBAUM†
BAD MAN'S RIVER	PHILIP YORDAN
BAD MANNERS	BOBBY HOUSTON
BAD MANNERS - S	STEVEN ZAILLIAN
BAD MEDICINE	HARVEY MILLER
BAD MEN OF TOMBSTONE	PHILIP YORDAN
BAD NEWS BEARS GO TO CUBA, THE - S	BILL LANCASTER
BAD NEWS BEARS GO TO JAPAN, THE	BILL LANCASTER
BAD NEWS BEARS IN BREAKING TRAINING, THE	PAUL BRICKMAN
BAD NEWS BEARS, THE	BILL LANCASTER
BAD SLEEP WELL, THE	AKIRA KUROSAWA
BAD SPORTS - S	BILL MCCLOSKEY
BAD SPORTS - S	ERIC WILLIAMS
BAD TIMING/A SENSUAL OBSESSION	YALE UDOFF
BAD WOMAN BLUES - S	DOUGLAS LLOYD MCINTOSH
BADGE 373	PETE HAMILL
BADLANDS	TERENCE MALICK
BAGDAD CAFE	ELEONORE ADLON
BAGDAD CAFE	PERCY ADLON
BAIL JUMPER	CHRISTIAN FABER
BAIL JUMPER	JOSEPHINE WALLACE
BAIL OUT AT 43,000	PAUL MONASH
BAILING OUT - S	ADAM GREENMAN
BAITED TRAP, THE	NORMAN PANAMA
BAJA HIDEAWAY - S	REX PICKETT
BAJA OKLAHOMA	BOBBY ROTH
BAJA OKLAHOMA	DAN JENKINS
BAKE AND SHAKE - S	RUDOLPH G. WURLITZER
BAKED ALASKA - S	LAURIE CRAIG
BAKER AND BERNSTEIN - S	ALVIN BORETZ
BAKER COUNTY, USA	JOHN BEAIRD
BAKER'S HAWK	DAN GREER

BAKERSFIELD BLUES - S	ZALMAN KING	
BAKERTON TC-1 - S	CAREY DEVUONO	
BALEFIRE - S	LEE REYNOLDS	
BALL AND CHAIN - S	JOHN HUGHES	
BALL OF FIRE	BILLY WILDER	
BALLAD OF GREGORIO CORTEZ, THE	ROBERT M. YOUNG	
BALLAD OF GREGORIO CORTEZ, THE	VICTOR VILLASENOR	
BALLAD OF JOE HILL, THE	BO WIDERBERG	
BALLAD OF NARAYAMA, THE	SHOHEI IMAMURA	
BALLAD OF SOAPY SMITH, THE (P)	MICHAEL WELLER	
BALLAD OF THE SAD CAFE, THE	MICHAEL HIRST	
BALONEY BOY - S	ADAM BELANOFF	
BALTIMORE BULLET, THE	JOHN F. BRASCIA	
BALTIMORE BULLET, THE	ROBERT VINCENT O'NEIL	
BAMBOO PRISON, THE	EDWIN BLUM	
BAMBOOZLE - S	JOHN GUARE	
BANANAS	MICKEY ROSE	
BANANAS	WOODY ALLEN	
BAND OF ANGELS	IVAN GOFF	
BAND OF ANGELS - S	JONATHAN FELDMAN	
BAND OF BROTHERS - S	DENNIS CLARK	
BAND OF OUTSIDERS	JEAN-LUC GODARD	
BAND OF THE HAND	JACK BARAN	
BAND OF THE HAND	LEO GAREN	
BAND WAGON	VAL GUEST	
BAND WAGON, THE	ADOLPH GREEN	
BAND WAGON, THE	BETTY COMDEN	
BANDIES (P) - S	MICHAEL ELIAS	
BANDIES (P) - S	RICHARD EUSTIS	
BANDIT - S	JAMES ORR	
BANDIT - S	JIM CRUICKSHANK	
BANDITS - S	JOSEPH C. STINSON	
BANDMAN - S	MICHAEL KANE	
BANDOLERO!	JAMES LEE BARRETT†	
BANDSTAND - S	AMY SPIES	
BANG THE DRUM SLOWLY	MARK HARRIS	
BANGKNOK HILTON (CTF)	TERRY HAYES	
BANK JOB - S	FLOYD MUTRUX	
BANK SHOT, THE	WENDELL MAYES	
BANNER BUSINESS - S	JAMES GOLDMAN	
BAR SINISTER, THE	JOHN MICHAEL HAYES	
BAR SONG - S	DANIEL SULLIVAN	
BAR STARS - S	EUGENE QUINTANO	
BARBARELLA	TERRY SOUTHERN	
BARBARIANS AT THE GATE - S	LARRY GELBART	
BARBARIANS, THE	JAMES R. SILKE	
BARBAROSA	WILLIAM D. WITTLIFF	
BARCELONA - S	WHIT STILLMAN	
BARE KNUCKLES	DON EDMONDS	
BAREFOOT CONTESSA, THE	JOSEPH L. MANKIEWICZ	
BAREFOOT IN THE PARK	NEIL SIMON	
BAREHUNTIN' - S	BILL MCKINNEY, JR.	
BARFLY	CHARLES BUKOWSKI	
BARKLEYS OF BROADWAY, THE	ADOLPH GREEN	
BARKLEYS OF BROADWAY, THE	BETTY COMDEN	
BARNUM - S	MICHAEL NORELL	
BAROCCO	MARILYN GOLDIN	
BARON OF ARIZONA, THE	SAMUEL FULLER	
BARQUERO	GEORGE SCHENCK	
BARRICADE	WILLIAM B. SACKHEIM	
BARRICADE - S	MICHAEL AUSTIN	
BARRY LYNDON	STANLEY KUBRICK	
BARRY MARTIN STORY (CTF) - S	JULIAN BARRY	
BARRY MCKENZIE HOLDS HIS OWN	BRUCE BERESFORD	
BARSALINO	JEAN-CLAUDE CARRIERE	
BARTENDER, THE - S	LARRY GROSS	
BARTENDER, THE - S	PIERS ASHWORTH	
BARTLEBY	RODNEY CARR-SMITH	
BARTON FINK	ETHAN COEN	
BARTON FINK	JOEL COEN	
BASIC INSTINCT	JOE ESZTERHAS	
BASIC TRAINING OF PAVLO HUMMEL, THE (P)	DAVID RABE	
BASKET CASE	FRANK HENENLOTTER	
BASKET CASE 2	FRANK HENENLOTTER	
BASKETBALL DIARIES - S	JEFFREY ALAN FISKIN	
BAT-21	MARC NORMAN	
BAT-21	WILLIAM C. ANDERSON	
BATHING BEAUTY	FRANK WALDMAN†	
BATMAN	LORENZO SEMPLE	
BATMAN	WARREN SKAAREN†	
BATMAN	SAM HAMM	
BATMAN 2 - S	DAN WATERS	
BATS - S	KATHY MCWORTER	
BATTERIES NOT INCLUDED	MICK GARRIS	
BATTERIES NOT INCLUDED	BRAD BIRD	
BATTERIES NOT INCLUDED	BRENT MADDOCK	
BATTERIES NOT INCLUDED	MATTHEW ROBBINS	
BATTERIES NOT INCLUDED	S.S. WILSON	
BATTLE AT BLOODY BEACH, THE	RICHARD MAIBAUM†	
BATTLE BEYOND THE STARS	ANNE DYER	
BATTLE BEYOND THE STARS	JOHN SAYLES	
BATTLE CIRCUS	RICHARD BROOKS	
BATTLE FOR PALM SPRINGS - S	MONICA JOHNSON	
BATTLE FOR ROME	DAVID AMBROSE	
BATTLE IN THE EROGENOUS ZONE - S	JOHN A. DRIMMER	
BATTLE OF ALGIERS, THE	FRANCO SOLINAS	
BATTLE OF MAPLE GLEN, THE - S	FREDERICA HOBIN	
BATTLE OF ROGUE RIVER, THE	DOUGLAS HEYES	
BATTLE OF THE BULGE	PHILIP YORDAN	
BATTLE OF THE CORAL SEA	STEPHEN KANDEL	
BATTLE OF THE PHILLIPPINE SEA - S	BARRY BECKERMAN	
BATTLE OF THE RIVER PLATE, THE	EMERIC PRESSBURGER†	
BATTLE OF THE RIVER PLATE, THE	MICHAEL POWELL†	
BATTLEGROUND	ROBERT PIROSH†	
BATTLING SPUMONTI BROTHERS, THE - S	CHARLES ROBERT CARNER	
BAWDY ADVENTURES OF TOM JONES, THE	JEREMY LLOYD	
BAXTER	JEROME BOIVIN	
BAXTER	REGINALD ROSE	
BAY BOY, THE	DANIEL PETRIE	
BAY OF THE ANGELS	JACQUES DEMY	
BAYOU CONFIDENTIAL (P)	DICK BEEBE	
BE TRUE TO YOUR SCHOOL - S	DAVID WECHTER	
BE TRUE TO YOUR SCHOOL - S	STU KRIEGER	
BEACH - S	NICHOLAS KAZAN	
BEACH HOUSE	JOHN GALLAGHER	
BEACH HOUSE	MARINO AMARUSO	
BEACH HOUSE - S	AMOS POE	
BEACH PARTY '85 - S	BIG BOY MEDLIN	
BEACHES	MARY AGNES DONAGHUE	
BEACHGIRLS	PATRICK DUNCAN	
BEACHGIRLS	PHIL GROVES	
BEAN TREES, THE - S	MARY AGNES DONOGHUE	
BEANY AND CECIL SHOW, THE (P)	ALAN BOWNE†	
BEAR ISLAND	DAVID BUTLER	
BEAR ISLAND	DON SHARP	
BEAR ISLAND	MURRAY SMITH	
BEAR, THE	GERARD BRACH	
BEAR, THE	MICHAEL KANE	
BEARD, THE - S	CHARLES DENNIS	
BEARD, THE - S	NICHOLAS KAZAN	
BEARSKIN: AN URBAN FAIRYTALE	ANN GUEDES	
BEARSKIN: AN URBAN FAIRYTALE	EDUARDO GUEDES	
BEAST - S	ROBERT J. AVRECH	
BEAST WITH FIVE FINGERS, THE	CURT SIODMAK	
BEAST WITHIN, THE	TOM HOLLAND	
BEAST, THE	WILLIAM MASTROSIMONE	
BEASTIES - S	TIM CURNEN	
BEASTMASTER, THE	DON COSCARELLI	
BEASTMASTER, THE	PAUL PEPPERMAN	
BEAT GENERATION, THE	RICHARD MATHESON	
BEAT OF THE NEW WORLD - S	GINA WENDKOS	
BEAT STREET	DAVID GILBERT	
BEAT STREET	PAUL GOLDING	
BEAT STREET	STEVEN HAGER	
BEAT STREET	ANDY DAVIS	
BEAT THE BURDEN - S	BLAINE NOVAK	
BEAT THE DEVIL - S	MICHAEL MINER	
BEAT THE EAGLE - S	JOE ESZTERHAS	
BEAT THE EAGLE - S	SUSAN NANUS	
BEAT, THE	PAUL S. MONES	
BEATING THE ODDS - S	JOHN J. SCHALTER	
BEATRICE	COLO TAVERNIER O'HAGAN	
BEAU GESTE	DOUGLAS HEYES	
BEAU JAMES	JACK ROSE	
BEAU JAMES	MEL SHAVELSON	
BEAU PERE	BERTRAND BLIER	
BEAUTIFUL DREAMERS	JOHN KENT HARRISON	
BEAUTIFUL ENEMIES - S	BLAINE NOVAK	
BEAUTIFUL NOISE - S	WESLEY STRICK	
BEAUTY - S	ERNEST THOMPSON	
BEAUTY AND BRAINS - S	LAURIE FRANK	
BEAUTY AND THE BEAST	EUGENE MARNER	
BEAUTY AND THE BEAST (AF) - S	JAMES D. COX	
BEAUTY AND THE BEAST (AF) - S	GEN LEROY	
BEAUTY BECOMES THE BEAST - S	TODD DURHAM	
BEAUTY JUNGLE, THE	VAL GUEST	
BEAUTY OF IT, THE - S	TERREL SELTZER	
BEAUTY SCHOOL - S	HERSCHEL WEINGROD	
BEAUTY SCHOOL - S	TIMOTHY HARRIS	
BECKET	EDWARD ANHALT	
BECOMING THE BUTLERS - S	HESPER ANDERSON	
BED & BREAKFAST - S	ANDY TENNANT	
BED & BREAKFAST - S	MIKE MARVIN	
BEDAZZLED	DUDLEY MOORE	
BEDAZZLED	PETER COOK	
BEDEVILLED	JO EISINGER	
BEDROOM EYES	MICHAEL ALAN EDDY	
BEDROOM WINDOW, THE	CURTIS LEE HANSON	
BEDTIME STORY	PAUL W. HENNING	
BEDTIME STORY	STANLEY SHAPIRO†	
BEER	ALLAN WEISBECKER	
BEER DRINKER'S GUIDE TO FITNESS AND FILMMAKING, THE	FRED G. SULLIVAN	
BEES IN PARADISE	VAL GUEST	
BEES, THE	ALFREDO ZACHARIAS	
BEETHOVEN'S NEPHEW	MATHIEU CARRIERE	
BEETHOVEN'S NEPHEW	PAUL MORRISSEY	
BEETHOVEN'S TENTH - S	JONATHAN BENAIR	
BEETLE BAILEY - S	SAM SIMON	
BEETLEJUICE	LARRY WILSON	
BEETLEJUICE	MICHAEL MCDOWELL	
BEETLEJUICE	WARREN SKAAREN†	
BEFORE & AFTER EDITH - S	PETRU POPESCU	
BEFORE THE NICKELODEON	WARREN D. LEIGHT	
BEFORE THE REVOLUTION	BERNARDO BERTOLUCCI	
BEFORE WE SAY GOODBYE - S	W.D. RICHTER	
BEFORE WINTER COMES	ANDREW SINCLAIR	
BEFORE YOUR VERY EYES - S	DON MCLENNAN	
BEGIN THE BEGUINE - S	RAY DE FELITTA	
BEGINNER'S LUCK	FRANK MOURIS	
BEGINNERS - S	BARBARA BENEDEK	
BEGINNERS - S	HARRIET FRANK JR.	
BEGINNERS - S	IRVING RAVETCH	
BEHIND THE MASK - S	WARREN CHANEY	
BEIJING LEGENDS (P)	SHEM BITTERMAN	
BEING THERE	JERZY KOSINSKI†	
BEING, THE	JACKIE KONG	
BEIRUT (P)	ALAN BOWNE†	
BEL AIR BUTLER - S	CHRIS MILLER	
BEL AIR BUTLER - S	MICHAEL D. SUTTON	
BEL AIR BUTLER - S	PETER TOROKVEI	
BEL AIR PATROL - S	DARIN MORGAN	
BELA LUGOSI STORY, THE	DYANNE ASSIMOW	
BELIEVE IN ME	ISRAEL HOROVITZ	
BELIEVERS, THE	MARK FROST	
BELIZAIRE THE CAJUN	GLEN PITRE	
BELL JAR, THE	MARJORIE KELLOGG	
BELL TOWER, THE - S	JEFFREY ARCH	
BELL, BOOK AND CANDLE	DANIEL TARADASH	
BELLBOY, THE	JERRY LEWIS	
BELLE DE JOUR	JEAN-CLAUDE CARRIERE	
BELLHOP'S DAUGHTER, THE - S	JORDAN S. TABAT	
BELLISSIMA	FRANCESCO ROSSI	
BELLMAN AND TRUE	MICHAEL WEARING	
BELLMAN AND TRUE	RICHARD LONCRAINE	
BELLMAN AND TRUE	DESMOND LOWDEN	
BELLS ARE RINGING	ADOLPH GREEN	
BELLS ARE RINGING	BETTY COMDEN	
BELLS, THE - S	JOEL OLIANSKY	
BELLY OF AN ARCHITECT, THE	PETER GREENAWAY	
BELLY UP - S	BARRY MORROW	
BELOVED SON - S	NEIL LANDAU	
BELOVED SON - S	TARA ISON	
BELOW THE BELT	ROBERT FOWLER	
BELOW THE BELT	SHERRIE SONNETT	
BELSTONE FOX, THE	JAMES HILL	
BEMS - S	SCOTT PARKER	
BEN & JOANNA - S	STEPHEN H. FOREMAN	
BENEATH THE VALLEY OF THE ULTRAVIXENS	RUSS MEYER	
BENEFACTORS (P)	MICHAEL FRAYN	
BENGAL LANCERS, THE - S	LORENZO SEMPLE	
BENITO - S	RON CLARK	
BENJAMIN BUTTON - S	ROBIN SWICORD	
BENJAMIN'S BABIES - S	HAL ACKERMAN	
BENJI	JOE CAMP	
BENJI: THE HUNTED	JOE CAMP	
BENNY AND THE JETS - S	BRUCE VILANCH	
BENNY'S HEIR - S	HAL SITOWITZ	
BENYA THE KING - S	LOUIS GARFINKLE	

INDEX OF FILM TITLES

BEREAVEMENTS - S ... MAUREEN EARL
BERLIN AFFAIR, THE ... LILIANI CAVANI
BERLIN ALEXANDER-PLATZ ... RAINER WERNER FASSBINDER†
BERLIN BLUES ... RICARDO FRANCO
BERLIN SHADOW - S ... MICHAEL ERIC STEIN
BERMUDA TRIANGLE, THE ... STEPHEN LORD
BERRY GORDY'S THE LAST DRAGON ... LOUIS VENOSTA
BERT RIGBY, YOU'RE A FOOL ... CARL REINER
BERYL MARKHAM - S ... MICHAEL THOMAS
BESIDE MYSELF - S ... RYAN ROWE
BESPOKE OVERCOAT, THE ... WOLF MANKOWITZ
BEST BOY (FD) ... IRA WOHL
BEST BY FAR - S ... HARLAN ELLISON
BEST DEFENSE ... GLORIA KATZ
BEST DEFENSE ... WILLARD HUYCK
BEST FRIEND - S ... LARRY COHEN
BEST FRIENDS ... BARRY LEVINSON
BEST FRIENDS ... VALERIE CURTIN
BEST INTENTIONS ... INGMAR BERGMAN
BEST IS YET TO BE - S ... RICHARD KRAMER
BEST LITTLE WHOREHOUSE IN TEXAS, THE ... LARRY L. KING
BEST LITTLE WHOREHOUSE IN TEXAS, THE ... PETER MASTERSON
BEST MAN, THE ... GORE VIDAL
BEST OF EVERYTHING, THE ... MANN RUBIN
BEST OF THE BEST ... PHILLIP REE
BEST OF THE BEST ... PAUL LEVINE
BEST OF THE FINEST, THE ... RICHARD SMITH
BEST OF TIMES, THE ... RON SHELTON
BEST RIDE FROM NEW YORK - S ... MARTIN COPELAND
BEST SELLER ... LARRY COHEN
BEST TABLE, THE- S ... JULIA CAMERON
BEST, THE - S ... JACK ROSENTHAL
BETHUNE, THE - S ... BRUCE EVANS
BETHUNE, THE - S ... RAY GIDEON
BETHUNE: THE MAKING OF A HERO ... TED ALLAN
BETRAYAL ... HAROLD PINTER
BETRAYED ... JOE ESZTERHAS
BETRAYED (1944) ... PHILIP YORDAN
BETSY'S WEDDING ... ALAN ALDA
BETSY, THE ... WALTER BERNSTEIN
BETSY, THE ... WILLIAM BAST
BETTER LATE THAN NEVER ... BRYAN FORBES
BETTER OFF DEAD ... SAVAGE STEVE HOLLAND
BETTY BLUE ... JEAN-JACQUES BEINEIX
BETWEEN THE LINES ... FRED BARRON
BETWEEN WARS ... FRANK MOORHOUSE
BETWEEN WARS - S ... JIM HARRISON
BEVERLY DRIVE - S ... DANILO BACH
BEVERLY HILLBILLIES - S ... DALE LAUNER
BEVERLY HILLS BODY SNATCHERS - S ... P.K. SIMONDS
BEVERLY HILLS BOX 33 - S ... ROBERT LENSKI
BEVERLY HILLS BRATS ... JERRY RIVERS
BEVERLY HILLS BRATS ... TERRY MOORE
BEVERLY HILLS BRATS ... LINDA SILVERTHORN
BEVERLY HILLS COP ... DANILO BACH
BEVERLY HILLS COP ... DANIEL PETRIE, JR.
BEVERLY HILLS COP II ... EDDIE MURPHY
BEVERLY HILLS COP II ... ROBERT D. WACHS
BEVERLY HILLS COP II ... LARRY FERGUSON
BEVERLY HILLS COP II ... WARREN SKAAREN†
BEVERLY HILLS COP III - S ... MICHAEL ALAN EDDY
BEVERLY HILLS NINJA - S ... DAVID LOUCKA
BEVERLY HILLS NINJA - S ... MARK L. FELDBERG
BEVERLY HILLS NINJA - S ... MITCHELL S. KLEBANOFF
BEVERLY HILLS DOCTOR - S ... JOHN HERMAN SHANER
BEVERLY WILSHIRE, THE - S ... GORE VIDAL
BEWARE OF THE CHILDREN ... NORMAN HUDIS
BEWITCHED, BOTHERED AND BEWILDERED - S ... ROBERT DEMAIO
BEYOND A REASONABLE DOUBT - S ... FRANK MILITARY JR.
BEYOND AND BACK ... STEPHEN LORD
BEYOND EVIL ... DAVID BAUGHN
BEYOND EVIL ... HERB FREED
BEYOND EVIL ... PAUL ROSS
BEYOND LOVE AND HATE ... AKIRA KUROSAWA
BEYOND REASONABLE DOUBT ... DAVID YALLOP
BEYOND THE LAW ... NORMAN MAILER
BEYOND THE LAW - S ... DAVID Z. GOODMAN
BEYOND THE LIMIT ... CHRISTOPHER HAMPTON
BEYOND THE MOUNTAIN - S ... RUDOLPH G. WURLITZER
BEYOND THE POSEIDON ADVENTURE ... NELSON GIDDING
BEYOND THE REEF ... LOUIS LARUSSO II
BEYOND THE REEF ... JIM CARABATSOS
BEYOND THE VALLEY OF THE DOLLS ... ROGER EBERT
BEYOND THE VALLEY OF THE DOLLS ... RUSS MEYER
BEYOND THE WALLS ... BENNY BARBASH
BEYOND THERAPY ... CHRISTOPHER DURANG
BEYOND THERAPY ... ROBERT ALTMAN
BICYCLE DAYS - S ... ANTHONY DRAZAN
BICYCLE THIEF, THE ... CESARE ZAVATTINI†
BIG ... ANNE SPIELBERG
BIG ... GARY ROSS
BIG APPLE, THE - S ... JOHN BRILEY
BIG BAD MAMA ... WILLIAM W. NORTON SR.
BIG BAD MAMA II ... JIM WYNORSKI
BIG BAD MAMA II ... R.J. ROBERTSON
BIG BAND MUSIC - S ... MARTYN BURKE
BIG BAND OF BLUES - S ... EARL MAC RAUCH
BIG BANG, THE (CTF) - S ... TINO INSANA
BIG BLUE, THE ... LUC BESSON
BIG BLUE, THE ... ROBERT GARLAND
BIG BOODLE, THE ... JO EISINGER
BIG BRAWL, THE ... FRED WEINTRAUB
BIG BRAWL, THE ... ROBERT CLOUSE
BIG BREAK, THE - S ... SIMON MOORE
BIG BROADCAST - S ... JOE FLAHERTY
BIG BROTHER - S ... ANTHONY DRAZAN
BIG BUS, THE ... LAWRENCE J. COHEN
BIG BUS,THE ... FRED FREEMAN
BIG BUSINESS ... DORI PIERSON
BIG BUSINESS ... MARC RUBEL
BIG CHILL, THE ... BARBARA BENEDEK
BIG CHILL, THE ... LAWRENCE KASDAN
BIG CIRCUS, THE ... IRWIN ALLEN
BIG CIRCUS, THE ... CHARLES BENNETT
BIG CIRCUS, THE ... IRVING WALLACE†
BIG COMBO, THE ... PHILIP YORDAN
BIG DAY, THE (P) ... DOUGLAS MCGRATH
BIG DEAL - S ... JONATHAN LYNN
BIG DEAL ON MACARTHUR BOULEVARD - S ... ALAN MANDEL
BIG DEAL ON MACARTHUR BOULEVARD - S ... CHARLES SHYER
BIG DIS, THE ... GORDON ERIKSEN
BIG DIS, THE ... ROBERT PILOTTE
BIG EASY, THE ... DANIEL PETRIE, JR.
BIG FIX, THE ... ROGER L. SIMON
BIG GUN DOWN, THE ... SERGIO DONATI
BIG HEAT, THE ... SYDNEY BOEHM†
BIG HOSPITAL - S ... JEREMY STEVENS
BIG HOSPITAL - S ... MARK A. REISMAN
BIG KISS, THE - S ... JOHN GUARE
BIG KISS-OFF OF 1944, THE - S ... ANDREW BERGMAN
BIG MAMOO, THE - S ... BUD SHRAKE
BIG MAN EATER ... LAURENCE KEANE
BIG MAN ON CAMPUS ... ALLAN KATZ
BIG MEAT EATER ... CHRIS WINDSOR
BIG MEAT EATER ... LAURENCE KEANE
BIG MEAT EATER ... PHIL SAVATH
BIG MOUTH, THE ... BILL RICHMOND
BIG MOUTH, THE ... JERRY LEWIS
BIG NOISE, THE - S ... STEPHEN METCALFE
BIG NOWHERE, THE - S ... CLIVE BARKER
BIG ONE, THE - S ... FREDERIC RAPHAEL
BIG ONES, THE - S ... LAWRENCE GAY
BIG ONES, THE - S ... MICHAEL DIGAETANO
BIG PICTURE, THE ... CHRISTOPHER GUEST
BIG PICTURE, THE ... MICHAEL MCKEAN
BIG PICTURE, THE ... MICHAEL VARHOL
BIG PINK - S ... JONATHAN DAY
BIG PLAYER, THE - S ... JIMMY HUSTON
BIG PLUNGE, THE ... CHRIS NEUFELD
BIG PLUNGE, THE - S ... DANNIEL BARRON
BIG PLUNGE, THE - S ... DCHRIS FABER
BIG PLUNGE, THE - S ... E. MAX FRYE
BIG PUNCH, THE ... BERNARD GIRARD
BIG QUESTION, THE - S ... ISRAEL HOROVITZ
BIG RASCALS, THE ... JEFF WILHELM
BIG RED ONE, THE ... SAMUEL FULLER
BIG ROOM, THE - S ... RONNIE WENKER-KONNER
BIG SCORE, THE ... GAIL MORGAN HICKMAN
BIG SCORE, THE - S ... RONALD SHUSETT
BIG SHOTS ... JOE ESZTERHAS
BIG SKY ROMANCE ... JULE SELBO
BIG SLEEP, THE ... MICHAEL WINNER
BIG STEAL, THE ... DAVID PARKER
BIG SUCCESS - S ... DENISE DE CLUE
BIG SUCCESS - S ... TIM KAZURINSKY
BIG TIME - S ... MARCEL MONTECINO
BIG TIME RETURN - S ... RICHARD MATHESON
BIG TOP - S ... RICHARD DIMITRI
BIG TOP - S ... ROBERT WUHL
BIG TOP PEE-WEE ... PAUL REUBENS
BIG TOWN, THE ... ROBERT ROY POOL
BIG TROUBLE ... ANDREW BERGMAN
BIG TROUBLE IN LITTLE CHINA ... DAVID Z. WEINSTEIN
BIG TROUBLE IN LITTLE CHINA ... GARY GOLDMAN
BIG TROUBLE IN LITTLE CHINA ... W.D. RICHTER
BIG U, THE - S ... HENRY BEAN
BIG WEDNESDAY ... JOHN MILIUS
BIG-TOP PEE WEE ... GEORGE MCGRATH
BIGAMIST, THE ... FRANCESCO ROSI
BIGAMY - S ... DAVID GREENWALT
BIGAMY - S ... JIM KOUF
BIGFINGER - S ... HERSCHEL WEINGROD
BIGFINGER - S ... TIMOTHY HARRIS
BIGGER THAN LIFE ... RICHARD MAIBAUM†
BIGGLES ... KENT WALWIN
BIGGLES ... JOHN P. GROVES
BIGMALEON - S ... HARIS ORKIN
BIJOU DREAMS (CTF) - S ... DICK BEEBE
BIKER HEAVEN - S ... TERRY SOUTHERN
BIKERS FROM HELL - S ... JEFF BUHAI
BIKERS FROM HELL - S ... STEVEN R. ZACHARIAS
BIKINI BEACH ... WILLIAM ASHER
BIKINI ISLAND ... EMERSON BIXBY
BIKINI SHOP, THE ... DAVID WECHTER
BILL & TED'S BOGUS JOURNEY ... CHRISTIAN L. MATHESON
BILL & TED'S BOGUS JOURNEY ... ED SOLOMON
BILL & TED'S EXCELLENT ADVENTURE ... CHRISTIAN L. MATHESON
BILL & TED'S EXCELLENT ADVENTURE ... ED SOLOMON
BILLION DOLLAR BRAIN ... JOHN MCGRATH
BILLIONAIRE, THE - S ... ROBERT BORIS
BILLY BATHGATE ... TOM STOPPARD
BILLY BUDD ... PETER USTINOV
BILLY BUDD - S ... HESPER ANDERSON
BILLY GALVIN ... JOHN GRAY
BILLY HELL - S ... MATTHEW MCDUFFIE
BILLY IN THE LOWLANDS ... JAN EGLESON
BILLY IRISH (P) ... THOMAS BABE
BILLY JACK ... TOM LAUGHLIN
BILLY JACK GOES TO WASHINGTON ... TOM LAUGHLIN
BILLY PHELAN'S GREATEST GAME - S ... WILLIAM KENNEDY
BILLY ROSE'S JUMBO ... SIDNEY SHELDON
BILLY THE KID AND THE GREEN BAIZE VAMPIRE ... TREVOR PRESTON
BILLY TURNER'S SECRET (SHORT) ... MICHAEL MAYSON
BILLY TWO HATS ... ALAN SHARP
BILOXI BLUES ... NEIL SIMON
BIMBO - S ... MAX EMBER
BIMBOS - S ... FREDERICA HOBIN
BINARY PROJECT - S ... ANDY LEWIS
BINGE, THE - S ... STEPHEN PETERS
BINGO LONG TRAVELING ALL-STARS & MOTOR KINGS, THE ... HAL BARWOOD
BINGO LONG TRAVELING ALL-STARS & MOTOR KINGS, THE ... MATTHEW ROBBINS
BINGO! ... JIM STRAIN
BIOHAZARD ... FRED OLEN RAY
BIRCH INTERVAL ... JOANNA CRAWFORD
BIRD ... JOEL OLIANSKY
BIRD ON A WIRE ... ERIC LERNER
BIRD ON A WIRE ... DAVID SELTZER
BIRD ON A WIRE ... LOUIS VENOSTA
BIRD WITH THE CRYSTAL PLUMMAGE, THE ... DARIO ARGENTO
BIRDCAGE, THE ... THOMAS LEE WRIGHT
BIRDS AND THE BEES, THE ... SIDNEY SHELDON
BIRDS OF PREY - S ... FRANK MILITARY JR.
BIRDS, THE ... EVAN HUNTER
BIRDY ... JACK BEHR
BIRDY ... SANDY KROOPF
BIRTH OF THE BLUES ... HARRY TUGEND†
BIRTHDAY - S ... ROD MCCALL
BIRTHDAY FISH (SHORT) ... ALEX ZAMM
BIRTHDAY PARTY, THE ... HAROLD PINTER
BIRTHRIGHT (P) ... RICHARD MAIBAUM†
BITCH, THE ... GERRY O'HARA
BITE THE BULLET ... RICHARD BROOKS
BITTER VICTORY ... GAVIN LAMBERT

Title	Writer
BITTERSWEET LOVE	ADRIAN MORRALL
BITTERSWEET LOVE	D.A. KELLOGG
BIZET'S CARMEN	FRANCESCO ROSI
BLACK 'N BLUE - S	ANDY TENNANT
BLACK AND BLUE - S	CAROLYN SHELBY
BLACK AND BLUE - S	CHRISTOPHER AMES
BLACK AND WHITE	ANDY BRECKMAN
BLACK AND WHITE - S	MARK ALLEN SMITH
BLACK AND WHITE IN COLOR	GEORGES CONCHON†
BLACK AND WHITE IN COLOR	JEAN-JACQUES ANNAUD
BLACK ANGEL (P)	MICHAEL CRISTOFER
BLACK ANGEL - S	JEAN-CLAUDE CARRIERE
BLACK ANGEL - S	PHILIP KAUFMAN
BLACK ARROW, THE	THOMAS SELLER†
BLACK ARROW, THE - S	DALENE A. YOUNG
BLACK BEAUTY	WOLF MANKOWITZ
BLACK BIRD, THE	DAVID GILER
BLACK BLOOD - S	DAVID BIRKE
BLACK BOOK, THE	PHILIP YORDAN
BLACK CAT, THE	LEWIS COATES
BLACK CAULDRON, THE (AF)	AL WILSON†
BLACK CAULDRON, THE (AF)	RICHARD RICH
BLACK CAULDRON, THE (AF)	TED BERMAN
BLACK COMEDY (P)	PETER SHAFFER
BLACK CREEK - S	TODD DURHAM
BLACK CREEK - S	VIVIAN SCHILLING
BLACK FRIDAY	CURT SIODMAK
BLACK GLASS - S	JOHN LAFIA
BLACK HOLE, THE	GERRY DAY
BLACK HOLE, THE	JEB ROSEBROOK
BLACK HOLE, THE	THOMAS POPE
BLACK JOY	ANTHONY SIMMONS
BLACK MAGIC	CHARLES BENNETT
BLACK MAGIC WOMAN	DERYN WARREN
BLACK MAGIC WOMAN	GERRY DALY
BLACK MAGIC WOMAN	MARC SPRINGER
BLACK MAMA, WHITE MAMA	HENRY ROSENBAUM
BLACK MAMA, WHITE MAMA	JONATHAN DEMME
BLACK MARBLE, THE	JOSEPH WAMBAUGH
BLACK MASK - S	TAB MURPHY
BLACK MOON	LOUIS MALLE
BLACK MOON RISING	DESMOND NAKANO
BLACK MOON RISING	JOHN CARPENTER
BLACK MOON RISING	WILLIAM GRAY
BLACK NARCISSUS	EMERIC PRESSBURGER†
BLACK NARCISSUS	MICHAEL POWELL†
BLACK ON WHITE - S	MICHAEL ALAN EDDY
BLACK ORCHID - S	NICHOLAS MEYER
BLACK ORCHID, THE	JOSEPH STEFANO
BLACK PANTHER, THE	MICHAEL ARMOSTRONG
BLACK PANTHER - S	ROBERT MUNDY
BLACK RAIN	WARREN LEWIS
BLACK RAIN	CRAIG BOLOTIN
BLACK RAINBOW	MIKE HODGES
BLACK RICE - S	BRUCE EVANS
BLACK RICE - S	RAY GIDEON
BLACK ROBE - S	BRIAN MOORE
BLACK SCORPION, THE	ROBERT BLEES
BLACK SHEEP - S	MICK GARRIS
BLACK SHIELD OF FALWORTH, THE	OSCAR BRODNEY
BLACK STALLION RETURNS, THE	JEROME A. KASS
BLACK STALLION RETURNS, THE	RICHARD KLETTER
BLACK STALLION, THE	JEANNE ROSENBERG
BLACK STALLION, THE	MELISSA MATHISON
BLACK STALLION, THE	WILLIAM D. WITTLIFF
BLACK SUNDAY	KENNETH ROSS
BLACK SUNDAY	ERNEST LEHMAN
BLACK TENT, THE	BRYAN FORBES
BLACK TIE - S	BENNETT YELLIN
BLACK TIE - S	JOAN TAYLOR
BLACK TIE - S	PETER FARRELLY
BLACK TIE - S	ROBERT DELAURENTIS
BLACK WALLS - S	JAMES KAPLAN
BLACK WATCH, THE - S	ERNEST GANN
BLACK WIDOW	RON BASS
BLACKBIRD FLY - S	CHARLES BURNETT
BLACKBOARD JUNGLE, THE	RICHARD BROOKS
BLACKEYES	DENNIS POTTER
BLACKJACK & SALTY - S	MICHAEL ELIAS
BLACKJACK & SALTY - S	RICHARD EUSTIS
BLACKMAIL	CHARLES BENNETT
BLACKMAIL (REMAKE)	CHARLES BENNETT
BLACKMAILED	ROGER VADIM
BLACKOUT	JOSEPH STEFANO
BLACKOUT (CTF)	DAVID AMBROSE
BLACKOUT (P)	GEORGE C. WOLFE
BLACKSNAKE	RUSS MEYER
BLADE - S	WILLIAM RABKIN
BLADE - S	LEE GOLDBERG
BLADE RUNNER	DAVID PEOPLES
BLADE RUNNER	HAMPTON FANCHER
BLAKE - S	RON BASS
BLAKE AND BREAK - S	BRUCE VILANCH
BLAME IT ON RIO	CHARLIE PETERS
BLAME IT ON RIO	LARRY GELBART
BLAND AMBITION - S	PAUL BARTEL
BLAND AMBITION - S	RICHARD BLACKBURN
BLANKMAN - S	DAMON WAYANS
BLAST FROM THE PAST - S	JOHN ESKOW
BLAST FROM THE PAST - S	SAMUEL H. HARPER
BLATNOY - S	TERRY BRENNAN
BLAZE	RON SHELTON
BLAZING SADDLES	ALAN UGER
BLAZING SADDLES	ANDREW BERGMAN
BLAZING SADDLES	MEL BROOKS
BLAZING SADDLES	NORMAN STEINBERG
BLEAK MOMENTS	MIKE LEIGH
BLEDSOE (P)	ARNAUD D'USSEAU†
BLEEDING GREAT ORCHIDS (P)	LIONEL CHETWYND
BLESS ME ULTIMA - S	VINCENT GUTIERREZ
BLESS THEIR LITTLE HEARTS	CHARLES BURNETT
BLESSING IN DISGUISE - S	LAURA KING
BLIND DATE (1987)	DALE LAUNER
BLIND DATE (1984)	FRED C. PERRY
BLIND DATE (1984)	NICO MASTORAKIS
BLIND DATE (1959)	BEN BARZMAN†
BLIND FURY	CHARLES ROBERT CARNER
BLIND FURY - S	MICHAEL MCDOWELL
BLIND LOVE - S	PERCY GRANGER
BLIND LUCK - S	JOHN WATSON
BLIND LUCK - S	MARK FROST
BLIND LUCK - S	PEN DENSHAM
BLIND LUCK - S	R. LANCE HILL
BLIND SIDE - S	FRANK NORWOOD
BLIND VENGEANCE (CTF)	JERRY MCNEELY
BLIND VENGEANCE (CTF)	CURT ALLEN
BLIND VOICES - S	HARLAN ELLISON
BLIND VOICES - S	MARK FROST
BLINDFOLD	PHILIP DUNNE
BLINDFOLD - S	MICHAEL J. AUERBACH
BLISS	PETER CAREY
BLISS	RAY LAWRENCE
BLITHE SPIRIT	DAVID LEAN†
BLOB, THE	CHUCK RUSSELL
BLOB, THE	FRANK DARABONT
BLONDE CRAZY	JOHN BRIGHT†
BLONDE FROM PEKING, THE	MARC BEHM
BLONDES - S	CLAIRE NOTO
BLONDIE FOR VICTORY	FAY KANIN
BLOOD & SEX - S	CHARLES EDWARD POGUE
BLOOD AND CONCRETE	JEFF REINER
BLOOD AND CONCRETE	RICHARD LABRIE
BLOOD AND ROSES	ROGER VADIM
BLOOD AND SAND	RICARDO FRANCO
BLOOD BEACH	STEVEN NALEVANSKY
BLOOD BEACH	JEFFREY BLOOM
BLOOD BROTHERS - S	DAVID AARON COHEN
BLOOD DINER	MICHAEL D. SONYE
BLOOD FEUD	LINA WERTMULLER
BLOOD FOR DRACULA	PAUL MORRISSEY
BLOOD FROM THE MUMMY'S TOMB	CHRISTOPHER WICKING
BLOOD GAMES - S	JOHN J. SCHALTER
BLOOD IN BLOOD OUT - S	JEREMY IACONE
BLOOD LEGACY - S	LARRY FERGUSON
BLOOD LINES (P)	JULIA CAMERON
BLOOD MAN - S	JIM HART
BLOOD MAN - S	THOMAS HEDLEY JR.
BLOOD MONEY - S	DAN BRONSON
BLOOD OF HEROES, THE	DAVID PEOPLES
BLOOD OF OTHERS, THE (CTF)	BRIAN MOORE
BLOOD OF THE VAMPIRE	JIMMY SANGSTER
BLOOD OF THE GODS - S	CHARLES EDWARD POGUE
BLOOD ON THE TRACKS - S	BARRY MORROW
BLOOD PRESSURE - S	RICHARD MATHESON
BLOOD PRESSURE - S	TOM SZOLLOSI
BLOOD RELATIONS (CTF) - S	LESLIE FULLER
BLOOD SALVAGE	KEN SANDERS
BLOOD SALVAGE	TUCKER JOHNSTON
BLOOD SECRETS - S	WILLIAM CONDON
BLOOD SIMPLE	ETHAN COEN
BLOOD SIMPLE	JOEL COEN
BLOOD SPORT - S	TOM TOPOR
BLOOD TIDE	DONALD LANGDON
BLOOD TIDE	NICO MASTORAKIS
BLOOD TIDE	RICHARD JEFFRIES
BLOOD TIES - S	ROGER L. SIMON
BLOOD, SWEAT AND STANLEY POOLE (P)	JAMES GOLDMAN
BLOOD, SWEAT AND STANLEY POOLE (P)	WILLIAM GOLDMAN
BLOODBROTHERS	WALTER NEWMAN
BLOODFIST	ROBERT KING
BLOODFIST - S	TERRY WINKLESS
BLOODHOUNDS OF BROADWAY	COLMAN DEKAY
BLOODHOUNDS OF BROADWAY	HOWARD BROOKNER†
BLOODLINE	LAIRD KOENIG
BLOODSHOT - S	GARY DEVORE
BLOODSPORT	CHRISTOPHER COSBY
BLOODSPORT	MEL FRIEDMAN
BLOODSPORT	SHELDON B. LETTICH
BLOODSTONE	CURT ALLEN
BLOODSTONE	NICO MASTORAKIS
BLOODSTONE - S	MICK GARRIS
BLOODY BIRTHDAY	BARRY PEARSON
BLOODY BIRTHDAY	ED HUNT
BLOODY FELLOWS - S	JOHN A. GALLAGHER
BLOOMER GIRLS - S	JERRY JACOBIUS
BLOOMER GIRLS - S	NICK GORE
BLOOMFIELD	WOLF MANKOWITZ
BLOOMIES - S	RON CLARK
BLOW AWAY - S	DAVID LOUCKA
BLOW AWAY - S	MARK KRAM
BLOW OUT	BRIAN DEPALMA
BLOW-UP	MICHELANGELO ANTONIONI
BLOW-UP	TONINO GUERRA
BLOWIN' IN THE WIND - S	ELAINE MUELLER
BLOWING WILD	PHILIP YORDAN
BLOWN OFF THE MAP - S	TED MANN
BLUE	RONALD M. COHEN
BLUE - S	LIZ COMICI
BLUE - S	LOU COMICI
BLUE ANGEL - S	NEAL JIMENEZ
BLUE BIRD, THE	HUGH WHITEMORE
BLUE BLOOD	ANDREW SINCLAIR
BLUE BLOOD - S	JOHN FASANO
BLUE BLOOD - S	RICHARD WHITLEY
BLUE CHIP - S	WILLIAM HANLEY
BLUE CHIPS - S	RON SHELTON
BLUE CITY	LUKAS HELLER†
BLUE CITY	WALTER HILL
BLUE COLLAR	LEONARD SCHRADER
BLUE COLLAR	PAUL SCHRADER
BLUE DENIM	PHILIP DUNNE
BLUE DESERT	ARTHUR COLLIS
BLUE DESERT	BRADLEY BATTERSBY
BLUE HAWAII	HAL KANTER
BLUE HEAVEN - S	MAXINE HERMAN
BLUE HIGHWAYS - S	JOHN A. GALLAGHER
BLUE HIGHWAYS - S	JOAN TEWKESBURY
BLUE HORIZON - S	LARRY ATLAS
BLUE IGUANA, THE	JOHN LAFIA
BLUE JEANS	PHILIP DUNNE
BLUE LAGOON	DOUGLAS DAY STEWART
BLUE MAGAA - S	LYNN SIEFERT
BLUE MAX, THE	BEN BARZMAN†
BLUE MAX, THE	DAVID PURSALL
BLUE MONKEY	GEORGE GOLDSMITH
BLUE MOON - S	CYNTHIA CIDRE
BLUE MOVIE - S	TERRY SOUTHERN
BLUE MURDER - S	WILLIAM BERRY
BLUE PARROT, THE - S	TRISH SOODIK
BLUE PETER, THE	DON SHARP
BLUE SERGE SUIT, THE (SHORT)	CAMILLE THOMASSON
BLUE SKIES AGAIN	KEVIN SELLARS
BLUE SKY	RAMA LAURIE STAGNER
BLUE SMOKE - S	ERIC BOGOSIAN
BLUE STEEL	ERIC RED
BLUE STEEL	KATHRYN BIGELOW
BLUE STREAK - S	JOHN BLUMENTHAL
BLUE STREAK - S	MICHAEL BERRY
BLUE SUNSHINE	JEFF LIEBERMAN
BLUE TATOO - S	PAUL BROWN
BLUE THUNDER	DAN O' BANNON
BLUE TRAIN, THE - S	DON SHROLL
BLUE VEIL, THE - S	LEAH APPET
BLUE VELVET	DAVID LYNCH
BLUE WINDOW (P)	CRAIG LUCAS
BLUEBEARD	EDWARD DMYTRYK
BLUEBEARD'S EIGHTH WIFE	BILLY WILDER
BLUEPRINT FOR MURDER, A	ANDREW STONE
BLUES BROTHERS, THE	DAN AYKROYD
BLUES BROTHERS, THE	JOHN LANDIS

Bl-Br

BLUES WATER - S .... JOHN FUSCO
BLUES, THE - S .... BRADLEY RAND SMITH
BLUME IN LOVE .... PAUL MAZURSKY
BLUNDERER, THE (CTF) - S ...... BARRY KEEFFE
BLUNDERER, THE - S .... KATHRYN BIGELOW
BO-PEEP - S .... ANTHONY SHAFFER
BO-PEEP - S .... HAL DRESNER
BOARDWALK .... LEIGH CHAPMAN
BOARDWALK .... STEPHEN F. VERONA
BOARDWALK - S .... JASON O'MALLEY
BOAT, THE .... WOLFGANG PETERSEN
BOB & CAROL & TED & ALICE ...... PAUL MAZURSKY
BOB ROBERTS, TIMES ARE
  CHANGING BACK - S .... TIM ROBBINS
BOBBIE JO AND THE
  OUTLAW .... VERNON ZIMMERMAN
BOBBIKINS .... OSCAR BRODNEY
BOBBY DARIN STORY, THE - S ...... PAUL ATTANSIO
BOBBY DEERFIELD .... ALVIN SARGENT
BOCCACCIO .... FEDERICO FELLINI
BODIE - S .... JAMES KENNEDY
BODIE - S .... ERIC ROTH
BODIES - S .... RON HUTCHINSON
BODY AND SOUL .... ABRAHAM POLONSKY
BODY AND SOUL .... LEON ISAAC KENNEDY
BODY CHEMISTRY .... JACKSON BARR
BODY COUNTY - S .... JONATHAN TYDOR
BODY DOUBLE .... BRIAN DEPALMA
BODY DOUBLE .... ROBERT J. AVRECH
BODY HEAT .... LAWRENCE KASDAN
BODY HUNTER - S .... STEVEN MCKAY
BODY HUNTER - S .... GREG PRUSS
BODY PARTS .... ERIC RED
BODY PARTS .... LARRY GROSS
BODY PARTS .... NORMAN SNIDER
BODY POLITIC - S .... BRUCE JAY FRIEDMAN
BODY POLITIC, THE - S .... JOHN WARREN
BODY ROCK .... KIMBERLY LYNN WHITE
BODY ROCK .... DESMOND NAKANO
BODY SLAM .... STEVE BURKOW
BODY SLAM .... SHEL LYTTON
BODYGUARD - S .... JOHN WILLIAM SEE
BODYGUARD, THE - S .... LAWRENCE KASDAN
BOEING-BOEING .... EDWARD ANHALT
BOFORS GUN, THE .... JOHN MCGRATH
BOGGY CREEK II .... CHARLES B. PIERCE
BOJANGLES: THE BILL ROBINSON
  STORY - S .... CLYDE WARE
BOLERO (1982) .... JOHN DEREK
BOLERO .... CLAUDE LELOUCH
BOLT UPRIGHT - S .... DAVID ANDRUS
BOLTS! - S .... DAVID M. CHASKIN
BOMB SQUAD - S .... GEORGE SAUNDERS
BOMB SQUAD - S .... JOHN BRYANT HEDBERG
BOMBAY CROSSING - S .... ROBERT BORIS
BOMBAY TALKIE .... JAMES IVORY
BOMBAY TALKIE .... RUTH PRAWER JHABVALA
BOMBERS B-52 .... IRVING WALLACE†
BOMBS AWAY .... BRUCE WILSON
BOMBS AWAY .... ED MAST
BON VOYAGE CHARLIE
  BROWN (AF) .... CHARLES M. SCHULTZ
BONAVENTURE .... OSCAR SAUL
BOND, THE - S .... BILLY BOB THORNTON
BOND, THE - S .... TOM EPPERSON
BONFIRE OF THE VANITIES,
  THE .... MICHAEL CRISTOFER
BONJOUR TRISTESSE .... ARTHUR LAURENTS
BONNIE AND CLYDE .... DAVID NEWMAN
BONNIE AND CLYDE .... ROBERT BENTON
BONNIE'S KIDS .... ARTHUR R. MARKS
BOOGENS, THE .... TOM CHAPMAN
BOOGENS, THE .... BOB HUNT
BOOGENS, THE .... DAVID O'MALLEY
BOOK OF DAYS .... TONE BLEVINS
BOOK OF DAYS .... MEREDITH MONK
BOOK OF EPPE - S .... JACK BEHR
BOOK OF EPPE - S .... SANDY KROOPF
BOOK OF JOE, THE (SHORT) ...... KEVIN S. TENNEY
BOOK OF LOVE .... WILLIAM KOTZWINKLE
BOOK OF NUMBERS .... LARRY SPIEGEL
BOOK OF THE CHILD - S .... MARC RAY
BOOKBINDER, THE - S .... DAVID AMBROSE
BOOKWORM - S .... NEVIN SCHREINER
BOOMERANG .... BARRY BLAUSTEIN
BOOMERANG - S .... DAVID SHEFFIELD
BOOST, THE .... DARRYL PONICSAN
BOOSTER, THE - S .... KEN FRIEDMAN
BOOTH, THE - S .... ISRAEL HOROVITZ
BOP, THE - S .... ERIC ROTH
BORDER RADIO .... DEAN LENT

BORDER RADIO .... KURT VOSS
BORDER RADIO .... ALLISON ANDERS
BORDER RIVER .... WILLIAM B. SACKHEIM
BORDER TOWN - S .... DAVID BIRKE
BORDER, THE .... DAVID FREEMAN
BORDER, THE .... WALON GREEN
BORDER, THE .... DERIC WASHBURN
BORDERLINE .... JERROLD FREEDMAN
BORDERLINE .... STEVEN E. KLINE
BORDERLINES - S .... JOHN BISHOP
BORIS & NATASHA .... CHARLES FRADIN
BORIS & NATASHA .... LINDA R. FAVILA
BORKEN SPUR .... WARREN CHANEY
BORN AGAIN .... WALTER BLOCH†
BORN AMERICAN .... MARKUS SELIN
BORN AMERICAN .... RENNY HARLIN
BORN EVERY MINUTE (P) .... THOMAS BABE
BORN IN EAST L.A. .... CHEECH MARIN
BORN IN FLAMES .... LIZZIE BORDEN
BORN LOSERS .... TOM LAUGHLIN
BORN ON THE FOURTH OF JULY .... RON KOVIC
BORN ON THE FOURTH OF JULY ...... OLIVER STONE
BORN TO RUN - S .... STEVEN PRESSFIELD
BORN TO SUFFER - S .... JOHN PARAGON
BORN TOO COOL - S .... TERRY WINKLESS
BORN WITH THE
  CENTURY - S .... WILLIAM KINSOLVING
BORN YESTERDAY - S .... DOUGLAS MCGRATH
BORROWED TIME - S .... PETER HANKOFF
BORROWER, THE - S .... SAM EGAN
BOSOMS AND NEGLECT (P) .... JOHN GUARE
BOSS' SON - S .... BOBBY ROTH
BOSS' WIFE, THE .... ZIGGY STEINBERG
BOSTON GANG WARS - S .... ALAN R. TRUSTMAN
BOSTON STRANGLER .... EDWARD ANHALT
BOSTONIANS, THE .... RUTH PRAWER JHABVALA
BOTCH - S .... MICHAEL KALESNIKO
BOULEVARD NIGHTS .... DESMOND NAKANO
BOULEVARD WEST - S .... THOMAS MCGUANE
BOUND FOR GLORY .... ROBERT GETCHELL
BOUNTY, THE .... ROBERT BOLT
BOURNE IDENTITY, THE - S .. JEFFREY ALAN FISKIN
BOXER & THE BLONDE, THE - S .... RON SHELTON
BOXER, THE - S .... DAVID SEIDLER
BOXER, THE - S .... JACQUELINE FEATHER
BOXING HELENA - S .... JENNIFER LYNCH
BOXOFFICE .... JOSEF BOGDANOVICH
BOY CHILD - S .... CAROLINE THOMPSON
BOY CHILD - S .... PENELOPE SPHEERIS
BOY FRIEND, THE .... KEN RUSSELL
BOY IN BLUE, THE .... DOUGLAS BOWIE
BOY NAMED CHARLIE
  BROWN, A (AF) .... CHARLES SCHULZ
BOY WHO COULD FLY, THE .... NICK CASTLE
BOY WHO EATS ROCKS,
  THE - S .... KATHY MCWORTER
BOY WHO STOLE A MILLION,
  THE .... CHARLES CRICHTON
BOY WHO STOLE A MILLION, THE .... JO EISINGER
BOY WITH GREEN HAIR, THE .... BEN BARZMAN†
BOY, DID I GET A WRONG
  NUMBER .... ALBERT E. LEWIN†
BOYD - S .... NORMAN WEXLER
BOYFRIEND SCHOOL, THE .... SARAH BIRD
BOYFRIENDS AND GIRLFRIENDS ...... ERIC ROHMER
BOYLE - S .... FRANK R. PIERSON
BOYS & GIRLS TOGETHER - S .... DAVID RAYFIEL
BOYS AND GIRLS/MEN AND
  WOMEN (P) .... GINA WENDKOS
BOYS FORM GALILEE - S .... STEPHEN METCALFE
BOYS FROM BRAZIL, THE .... HEYWOOD GOULD
BOYS IN BLUE, THE .... VAL GUEST
BOYS IN BLUES - S .... EARL MAC RAUCH
BOYS IN COMPANY C, THE .... RICK NATKIN
BOYS IN COMPANY C, THE .... SIDNEY J. FURIE
BOYS IN THE BAND, THE .... MART CROWLEY
BOYS NEXT DOOR, THE .... GLEN MORGAN
BOYS NEXT DOOR, THE .... JAMES WONG
BOYS NEXT DOOR, THE (P) .... TOM GRIFFIN
BOYS OF WINTER, THE (P) .... JOHN PIELMEIER
BOYS' LIFE (P) .... HOWARD KORDER
BOYS, THE - S .... MORDECAI RICHLER
BOYZ N THE HOOD .... JOHN SINGLETON
BRADDOCK: MISSING IN
  ACTION III .... JAMES BRUNER
BRADDOCK: MISSING IN
  ACTION III .... CHUCK NORRIS
BRADVIK - S .... DAVID WILLIAMSON
BRADY'S ESCAPE .... PAL GABOR
BRADY'S ESCAPE .... WILLIAM W. LEWIS
BRAIN - S .... MARK VICTOR

BRAIN - S .... MICHAEL GRAIS
BRAIN DEAD .... ADAM SIMON
BRAIN MACHINE, THE .... KEN HUGHES
BRAIN, THE .... GERARD OURY
BRAINDAZZLED - S .... ARNE OLSEN
BRAINDEAD .... CHARLES BEAUMONT†
BRAINSTORM .... BRUCE JOEL RUBIN
BRAINSTORM .... MANN RUBIN
BRAINSTORM .... PHILIP FRANK MESSINA
BRAINSTORM .... ROBERT STITZEL
BRAINWAVES .... ULLI LOMMEL
BRAMBLE BUSH, THE .... PHILIP YORDAN
BRANDENBURG, THE - S .. DAMON SANTOSTEFANO
BRANDENBURG, THE - S .... NICHOLAS FELACCI
BRANNIGAN .... CHRISTOPHER TRUMBO
BRANNIGAN .... MICHAEL BUTLER
BRANNIGAN .... WILLIAM P. MCGIVERN†
BRANNIGAN .... WILLIAM W. NORTON SR.
BRANNIGAN .... CHRISTOPHER TRUMBO
BRANT - S .... ANDY LEWIS
BRASS ANGELS - S .... RICHARD CHAPMAN
BRASS BOTTLE, THE .... OSCAR BRODNEY
BRASS TARGET .... ALVIN BORETZ
BRASSNECK (P) .... DAVID HARE
BRAVADOS, THE .... PHILIP YORDAN
BRAVE BULLS, THE .... JOHN BRIGHT†
BRAVE YOUNG MEN OF
  WEINBERG, THE - S .... JAY TARSES
BRAVE YOUNG MEN OF
  WEINBERG, THE - S .... TOM PATCHETT
BRAWLERS - S .... DANIEL H. VINING
BRAZIL .... CHARLES MCKEOWN
BRAZIL .... TERRY GILLIAM
BRAZIL .... TOM STOPPARD
BRAZIL RUN, THE - S .... OLIVER STONE
BREACH OF CONTRACT - S .... ROBERT H. EISELE
BREAD AND CHOCOLATE .... FRANCO BRUSATI
BREAK IN THE CIRCLE .... VAL GUEST
BREAKDOWN .... ED NAHA
BREAKER MORANT .... BRUCE BERESFORD
BREAKER MORANT .... DAVID STEVENS
BREAKER MORANT .... JONATHAN HARDY
BREAKFAST AT TIFFANYS .... GEORGE AXELROD
BREAKFAST CLUB, THE .... JOHN HUGHES
BREAKFAST OF CHAMPIONS - S ...... PAUL GOLDING
BREAKFAST ON BEDFORD
  DRIVE - S .... ALAN MANDEL
BREAKFAST ON BEDFORD
  DRIVE - S .... CHARLES SHYER
BREAKHEART PASS .... ALISTAIR MACLEAN
BREAKIN' .... ALLEN DEBEVOISE
BREAKIN' .... CHARLES PARKER
BREAKIN' .... GERALD SCALFE
BREAKIN' 2 .... JAN VENTURA
BREAKIN' 2 .... JULIE REICHERT
BREAKING ALL THE RULES .... EDITH REY
BREAKING ALL THE RULES .... RAFAL ZIELINSKI
BREAKING ALL THE RULES .... JAMES ORR
BREAKING ALL THE RULES .... JIM CRUICKSHANK
BREAKING AWAY .... STEVE TESICH
BREAKING BALLS AND BROKEN
  HEARTS - S .... KEVIN FALLS
BREAKING GLASS .... BRIAN GIBSON
BREAKING IN .... JOHN SAYLES
BREAKING POINT .... STANLEY MANN
BREAKING THE CODE (P) .... HUGH WHITEMORE
BREAKING THROUGH - S .... MICHAEL WELLER
BREAKING UP IS HARD
  TO DO - S .... MITCH MARKOWITZ
BREAKTHROUGH .... BERNARD GIRARD
BREAKTHROUGH .... TONY WILLIAMSON
BREAKTHROUGH - S .... PETER HANKOFF
BREATHLESS .... JIM MCBRIDE
BREATHLESS .... L.M. KIT CARSON
BREED APART, A .... PAUL WHEELER
BREEDERS .... TIM KINCAID
BREEZE FROM THE GULF, A (P) .... MART CROWLEY
BRENDA STARR .... JAMES DAVID BUCHANAN
BRENDA STARR .... JENNY WOLKIND
BRENDA STARR .... NOREEN STONE
BRENNER'S WORLD - S .... JIMMY ZEILINGER
BREWSTER MCCLOUD ... DORAN WILLIAM CANNON
BREWSTER'S MILLIONS ...... HERSCHEL WEINGROD
BREWSTER'S MILLIONS ...... TIMOTHY HARRIS
BRICK DUST - S .... LESLIE BOHEM
BRIDE AND GROOM - S .... ALAN JAY GLUECKMAN
BRIDE CAME C.O.D., THE ...... JULIUS J. EPSTEIN
BRIDE OF DRACULA .... JIMMY SANGSTER
BRIDE OF FRANK, THE - S .... JACKIE RABINOWITZ
BRIDE OF FRANK, THE - S .... LIDDY LOREE
BRIDE OF RE-ANIMATOR .... BRIAN YUZNA

Title	Writer
BRIDE OF RE-ANIMATOR	RICK FRY
BRIDE OF RE-ANIMATOR	WOODY KEITH
BRIDE OF THE GORILLA	CURT SIODMAK
BRIDE WORE BLACK, THE	FRANCOIS TRUFFAUT†
BRIDE, THE	LLOYD FONVIELLE
BRIDES OF FU MANCHU, THE	HARRY ALAN TOWERS
BRIDGE AT REMAGAN, THE	WILLIAM ROBERTS
BRIDGE ON THE RIVER KWAI, THE	CARL FOREMAN†
BRIDGE TO TERABITHIA - S	TOM MCCOWN
BRIDGE TO THE MOON - S	BOB DOLMAN
BRIDGE TOO FAR, A	WILLIAM GOLDMAN
BRIDGE, THE	ADRIAN HODGES
BRIDGE, THE - S	MIKE BINDER
BRIDGES BURNED - S	NEAL SHUSTERMAN
BRIEF ENCOUNTER - S	JOHN BOWEN
BRIGADOON - S	SEAN MCCARVER
BRIGHT ANGEL	RICHARD FORD
BRIGHT LIGHTS, BIG CITY	JAY MCINERNEY
BRIGHTON BEACH MEMOIRS	NEIL SIMON
BRIMSTONE & TREACLE	DENNIS POTTER
BRING YOUR SMILE ALONG	BLAKE EDWARDS
BRINK'S JOB, THE	WALON GREEN
BRITISH DIPLOMAT, THE - S	JOHN ESKOW
BRITTANIA MEWS	RING LARDNER JR.
BRITTLE INNINGS - S	JOHN KOSTMAYER
BROAD COALITION, THE	WILLIAM REILLY
BROADCAST NEWS	JAMES L. BROOKS
BROADWAY - S	LARRY GROSS
BROADWAY BOUND (P)	NEIL SIMON
BROADWAY DANNY ROSE	WOODY ALLEN
BROKEN DREAMS - S	JOHN BOORMAN
BROKEN DREAMS - S	NEIL JORDAN
BROKEN EGGS (P)	EDUARDO MACHADO
BROKEN ENGLISH - S	MICHAEL THOMAS
BROKEN LANCE	PHILIP YORDAN
BROKEN PROMISE	SANDY TUNG
BROKEN PROMISES, MENDED DREAMS - S	JON POVILL
BRONCO BILLY	DENNIS HACKIN
BRONX CHEERS (SHORT)	RAY DE FELITTA
BRONX TALE, A (P)	CHAZZ PALMINTERI
BROOD, THE	DAVID CRONENBERG
BROOKLYN, USA (P)	JOHN BRIGHT†
BROTH OF A BOY (P)	HUGH LEONARD
BROTHER DA SILVA - S	BOAZ YAKIN
BROTHER FROM ANOTHER PLANET, THE	JOHN SAYLES
BROTHER JOHN	ERNEST KINOY
BROTHER TO BROTHER - S	WILLIAM W. PHELPS
BROTHER, CAN YOU SPARE A DIME? (FD)	PHILLIPPE MORA
BROTHER-IN-LAW, THE - S	MARGARET GREICO OBERMAN
BROTHERHOOD OF THE GRAPE - S	DENNIS O'FLAHERTY
BROTHERHOOD OF THE GRAPE, THE - S	CURTIS LEE HANSON
BROTHERHOOD, THE	LEWIS JOHN CARLINO
BROTHERS	EDWARD LEWIS
BROTHERS	MILDRED LEWIS
BROTHERS - S	STEVE TESICH
BROTHERS IN ARMS	D. SHONE KIRKPATRICK
BROTHERS IN ARMS - S	THOMAS M. CLEAVER
BROTHERS IN LAW	ROY BOULTING
BROTHERS KARAMAZOV, THE	RICHARD BROOKS
BROTHERS KEEPERS - S	BARRY BLAUSTEIN
BROTHERS KEEPERS - S	DAVID SHEFFIELD
BROTHERS-IN-LAW - S	HUGH WILSON
BROWNSVILLE ROAD, THE - S	CHARLES FULLER
BRUBAKER	ARTHUR ROSS
BRUBAKER	W.D. RICHTER
BRUTAL GLORY	TITUS GROBLER
BRUTE FORCE	RICHARD BROOKS
BUBBA SKYLAR - S	ROGER TOWNE
BUCK AND THE PREACHER	ERNEST KINOY
BUCK ISLAND - S	JANET ROACH
BUCK ROGERS	LESLIE C. STEVENS
BUCKET OF BLOOD, A	CHARLES B. GRIFFITH
BUDDHA - S	ROBERT BOLT
BUDDHA OF BRANDENBERG - S	DENNIS FELDMAN
BUDDIES	ARTHUR J. BRESSON JR.
BUDDY BUDDY	BILLY WILDER
BUDDY BUDDY	I.A.L. DIAMOND†
BUDDY COPS - S	B.J. NELSON
BUDDY COPS - S	DAVID O'MALLEY
BUDDY HOLLY STORY, THE	ALAN SWYER
BUDDY HOLLY STORY, THE	ROBERT GITLER
BUDDY SYSTEM, THE	MARY AGNES DONAGHUE
BUFF, THE - S	ALAN BERGER
BUFF, THE - S	KATHY GORI
BUFF, THE - S	THOMAS M. DONNELLY
BUFFALO BILL AND THE INDIANS	ALAN RUDOLPH
BUFFALO BILL AND THE INDIANS	ROBERT ALTMAN
BUFFALO GHOST - S	NANCY DOWD
BUFFALO GIRLS - S	ABBE WOOL
BUFFET FROID	BERTRAND BLIER
BUG JACK BARRON - S	HARLAN ELLISON
BUG JACK BARRON - S	ADAM RODMAN
BUGS BUNNY/ROAD RUNNER MOVIE, THE (AF)	CHUCK JONES
BUGS BUNNY/ROAD RUNNER MOVIE, THE (AF)	MIKE MALTESE†
BUGSTER, THE - S	JOHN HUGHES
BUGSY	JAMES TOBACK
BUGSY MALONE	ALAN PARKER
BUILDERS - S	JERE P. CUNNINGHAM
BUILDERS - S	RAMA LAURIE STAGNER
BULL - S	B.W.L. NORTON, JR.
BULL - S	GEORGE GIPE
BULL DURHAM	RON SHELTON
BULLDOG BREED, THE	JACK DAVIES
BULLET FOR PRETTY BOY, A	CURTIS LEE HANSON
BULLET FOR PRETTY BOY, A	HENRY ROSENBAUM
BULLET PROOF HEARTS - S	GEORGE GALLO
BULLETPROOF	FRED OLEN RAY
BULLETPROOF	STEVE CARVER
BULLETPROOF	T.L. LANKFORD
BULLETPROOF - S	JAMES KENNEDY
BULLIES	BRYAN MCCANN
BULLIES	JOHN SHEPPARD
BULLIES, THE - S	ROBERT KAUFMAN
BULLITT	ALAN R. TRUSTMAN
BULLITT	HARRY KLEINER
BULLROAR - S	B.W.L. NORTON, JR.
BULLSEYE!	LESLIE BRICUSSE
BULLSHOT!	DIZ WHITE
BULLSHOT!	RON HOUSE
BULLY - S	MARK MEDOFF
BUMPERS - S	RON CLARK
BUMPTIOUS - S	HOLLY GOLDBERG SLOAN
BUNCO - S	MITCH GLAZER
BUNNY LAKE IS MISSING	JOHN MORTIMER
BUNNY O'HARE	STANLEY Z. CHERRY
BURBS, THE	DANA OLSEN
BURDEN OF PROOF	RENE BALCER
BURGERVILLE - S	NEIL TOLKIN
BURGLAR	HUGH WILSON
BURGLAR	JOSEPH LOEB III
BURGLAR	MATTHEW WEISMAN
BURIED - S	DARRIN OURA
BURIED ALIVE	STUART LEE
BURIED ALIVE	JAKE CLESI
BURIED ALIVE (CTF)	MARK PATRICK CARDUCCI
BURIED ALIVE - S	ADAM GREENMAN
BURIED CHILD (P)	SAM SHEPARD
BURIED INSIDE EXTRA (P)	THOMAS BABE
BURKE AND WILLS	MICHAEL THOMAS
BURMA - S	MARI KORNHAUSER
BURMESE DAYS - S	HUGH STODDART
BURMESE DAYS - S	JULIAN BOND
BURNI	FRANCO SOLINAS
BURN, WITCH, BURN	RICHARD MATHESON
BURNIN' LOVE	LANIER LANEY
BURNIN' LOVE	TERRY SWEENEY
BURNING BEACH (P)	EDUARDO MACHADO
BURNING COLD, THE - S	WILLIAM DREW WEINBRENNER
BURNING DAYLIGHT - S	WILLIAM HARLAN RICHTER
BURNING HILLS, THE	IRVING WALLACE†
BURNING SECRET	ANDREW BIRKIN
BURNING TIME - S	CASEY KELLY
BURNING, THE	BOB WEINSTEIN
BURNING, THE	PETER LAWRENCE
BUS STOP	GEORGE AXELROD
BUS, THE (SHORT)	NORTHROP DAVIS
BUSH PILOT, THE - S	MICHAEL BURTON
BUSHIDO BLADE, THE	WILLIAM OVERGARD
BUSINESS AS USUAL	LEZLI-AN BARRETT
BUSINESS STORY, THE - S	W.D. RICHTER
BUST OUT KING, THE - S	ARTHUR SILVER
BUST OUT KING, THE - S	RONNI KERN
BUSTED	DAMIAN LEE
BUSTER	COLIN SHINDLER
BUSTER & BILLIE	RON TURBEVILLE
BUSTER KEATON STORY, THE	SIDNEY SHELDON
BUSTIN' LOOSE	LONNE ELDER III
BUSTIN' LOOSE	RICHARD PRYOR
BUSTIN' LOOSE	ROGER L. SIMON
BUSTING	PETER HYAMS
BUSYBODIES - S	JACKIE RABINOWITZ
BUSYBODIES - S	LIDDY LOREE
BUSYBODIES - S	STEPHEN W. CARPENTER
BUT NOT FOR ME	JOHN MICHAEL HAYES
BUT NOT FOR ME (P)	TOM TOPOR
BUT WHAT ABOUT ME? - S	ALAN SHAPIRO
BUTCH AND SUNDANCE: THE EARLY DAYS	ALLAN BURNS
BUTCH CASSIDY AND THE SUNDANCE KID	WILLIAM GOLDMAN
BUTCHER'S WIFE, THE	EZRA LITWAK
BUTCHER'S WIFE, THE	MARJORIE SCHWARTZ
BUTLER SCHOOL, THE - S	TED MANN
BUTLER, THE - S	BILL MCKINNEY, JR.
BUTLERS - S	TOD CARROLL
BUTLEY	SIMON GRAY
BUTTERFIELD EIGHT	JOHN MICHAEL HAYES
BUTTERFLIES ARE FREE	LEONARD GERSHE
BUTTERFLY	JOHN GOFF
BUTTERFLY	MATT CIMBER
BUTTERFLY ON THE SHOULDER, A	JEAN-CLAUDE CARRIERE
BUTTERFLY ON THE SHOULDER, A	TONINO GUERRA
BUTTERFLY REVOLUTION, THE	BERT L. DRAGIN
BUTTERFLY REVOLUTION, THE	PENELOPE SPHEERIS
BUTTERSCOTCH KID - S	BARRY BLAUSTEIN
BUTTERSCOTCH KID - S	DAVID SHEFFIELD
BUTTON, THE - S	RON SHELTON
BUTTONMEN, THE - S	BRIAN STRASMANN
BUY AND CELL	KEN KRAUSS
BUY AND CELL	MERRIN HOLT
BUYING TIME	MITCHELL GABOURIE
BUYING TIME	RICHARD GABOURIE
BUYOUT - S	JOHN BYRUM
BUZZ ORBIT - S	MATTHEW J. CARLSON
BUZZARDS LUCK - S	MARY ANNE KASICA
BUZZARDS LUCK - S	MICHAEL SCHEFF
BUZZWORD - S	JOHN PARAGON
BY DAWN'S EARLY LIGHT (CTF)	BRUCE GILBERT
BY GRAND CENTRAL STATION I SAT DOWN AND WEPT - S	LAURA LAMSON
BYE BYE BABY	ENRICO OLDOINI
BYE BYE BLUES	ANNE WHEELER
BYE BYE MONKEY	GERARD BRACH
BYTES, THE - S	JIM STRAIN

C

Title	Writer
C NOTE, THE - S	PAUL GUAY
C NOTE, THE - S	STEVE MAZUR
C'EST LA VIE	DIANE KURYS
C. DMIAS - S	GARRY MARSHALL
C. DMIAS - S	LOWELL GANZ
C.H.U.D.	SHEPARD ABBOTT
C.H.U.D.	PARNELL HALL
C.I.T. - S	ROBERT M. ULIN
C.O.D.	RICK MARX
CAB DRIVER, THE - S	NEAL MARSHALL
CABARET	JAY PRESSON ALLEN
CABINET OF CALIGARI, THE	ROBERT BLOCH
CABINET OF DR. RAMIREZ, THE	PETER SELLARS
CABO BLANCO	JAMES GRANBY HUNTER
CABO RIO- S	DONALD L. STEWART
CABOBLANCO	LUKAS HELLER†
CABOBLANCO	MILTON S. GELMAN†
CABOBLANCO	MORT FINE†
CABOOSE - S	ROD MCCALL
CACCIA TRAGICA	MICHAELANGELO ANTONIONI
CACTUS	BOB ELLIS
CACTUS	NORMAN KAYE
CACTUS	PAUL COX
CACTUS FLOWER	I.A.L. DIAMOND†
CACTUS IN THE SNOW	A. MARTIN ZWEIBACH
CADAVERI ECCELLENTI	TONINO GUERRA
CADAVERI ECCELLENTI	FRANCESCO ROSI
CADAVERS - S	THOMAS BAUM
CADDIE	JOAN LONG
CADDYSHACK	BRIAN DOYLE-MURRAY
CADDYSHACK	DOUGLAS KENNEY†
CADDYSHACK	HAROLD RAMIS
CADDYSHACK II	HAROLD RAMIS
CADDYSHACK II	PETER TOROKVEI
CADENCE	DENNIS SHRYACK

331

Ca-Ca
FILM WRITERS GUIDE

INDEX OF FILM TITLES

CADENCE ... MARTIN SHEEN
CADETS - S ... BRAD BUCKNER
CADETS - S ... EUGENIE ROSS-LEMING
CADILLAC JACK - S ... TRACY KEENAN WYNN
CADILLAC KID, THE - S ... JANICE SHAPIRO
CADILLAC MAN ... KEN FRIEDMAN
CAESAR AND ROSALIE - S ... FREDERIC RAPHAEL
CAFE LUXEMBOURG - S ... ROGER L. SIMON
CAFE RACER - S ... R. BARKER PRICE
CAGE ... HUGH KELLEY
CAGE - S ... PETER ILIFF
CAGED FURY ... WILLIAM P. MILLING
CAGED HEAT ... JONATHAN DEMME
CAL ... BERNARD MACLAVERTY
CALAMARI UNION ... AKI KAURISMAKI
CALENDAR GIRL ... RICHARD SALE
CALEXICO - S ... CHRISTOPHER CANAAN
CALIFORNIA - S ... TIMOTHY J. METCALFE
CALIFORNIA DOGFIGHT (P) ... MARK W. LEE
CALIFORNIA DREAMIN' - S ... ALAN DUNCAN ROSS
CALIFORNIA DREAMING ... NED WYNN
CALIFORNIA DREAMING - S ... LEN WECHSLER
CALIFORNIA REICH, THE (FD) ... ANDRZEJ KRAKOWSKI
CALIFORNIA ROUGH AND TUMBLE - S ... BILL LANCASTER
CALIFORNIA SPLIT ... JOSEPH WALSH
CALIFORNIA SUITE ... NEIL SIMON
CALIFORNIA WITHOUT END - S ... REX PICKETT
CALIGULA ... GORE VIDAL
CALL ME ... KARYN KAY
CALL ME A COP - S ... MICHAEL NORELL
CALL ME BOB - S ... DENIS O'NEIL
CALL ME BWANA ... NATHAN MONASTER†
CALL ME MISTER ... ALBERT E. LEWIN†
CALL MY BROTHER BACK - S ... DAN ALGRANT
CALL OF THE WILD ... HARRY ALAN TOWERS
CALL OF THE WILD ... PETER YELDMAN
CALLAWAY WENT THATAWAY ... NORMAN PANAMA
CALLED HOME - S ... WILLIAM KELLEY
CALLER, THE - S ... MICHAEL SLOAN
CALMOS ... BERTRAND BLIER
CAME A HOT FRIDAY ... IAN MUNE
CAMEL DRIVE OF 1890, THE - S ... DAVID SELTZER
CAMERON'S CLOSET ... GARY BRANDNER
CAMILLE CLAUDEL ... BRUNO NUYTTEN
CAMILLE CLAUDEL ... MARILYN GOLDIN
CAMORRA ... LINA WERTMULLER
CAMP ESCAPE - S ... ANDY TENNANT
CAMP ON BLOOD ISLAND, THE ... VAL GUEST
CAMPAIGN - S ... ANDY WOLK
CAMPAIGN - S ... PAUL ATTANSIO
CAMPUS COPS - S ... TED MANN
CAMPUS MAN ... ALEX HORVAT
CAMPUS MAN ... GEOFFREY BAERE
CAMPUS MAN ... MATTHEW DORFF
CAN HIERONYMUS MERKIN EVER FORGET MERCY HUMPPE & FIND TRUE HAPPINESS? ... ANTHONY NEWLEY
CAN HIERONYMUS MERKIN EVER FORGET MERCY HUMPPE & FIND TRUE HAPPINESS? ... HERMAN RAUCHER
CAN SHE BAKE A CHERRY PIE? ... HENRY JAGLOM
CAN'T BUY ME LOVE ... MICHAEL SWERDLICK
CAN'T GET ARRESTED ... RAY DEFELITTA
CAN'T GET ENOUGH - S ... TRISH SOODIK
CAN'T STOP THE MUSIC ... ALLAN CARR
CAN'T STOP THE MUSIC ... BRONTE WOODARD†
CANADIANS, THE ... BURT KENNEDY
CANAL STREET - S ... ERIC RED
CANCEL MY RESERVATION ... ARTHUR MARX
CANCEL MY RESERVATION ... ROBERT FISHER
CANDIDATE FOR OBLIVION - S ... LARRY COHEN
CANDIDATE, THE ... JEREMY LARNER
CANDLESHOE ... ROSEMARY ANNE SISSON
CANDY ... BUCK HENRY
CANDY MOUNTAIN ... RUDOLPH G. WURLITZER
CANDY STORE (SHORT) ... CLAUDE KERVEN
CANDY STRIPE NURSES ... ALLEN HOLLEB
CANNERY ROW ... DAVID S. WARD
CANNES GAMES - S ... STEVE TESICH
CANNIBAL WOMEN IN THE AVOCADO JUNGLE OF DEATH ... J.F. LAWTON
CANNON FOR CORDOBA ... STEPHEN KANDEL
CANNONBALL ... PAUL BARTEL
CANNONBALL RUN II ... ALBERT S. RUDDY
CANNONBALL RUN II ... HAL NEEDHAM
CANNONBALL RUN II ... HARVEY MILLER
CANNONBALL RUN, THE ... BROCK YATES
CANTERBURY TALE, A ... EMERIC PRESSBURGER†
CANTERBURY TALE, A ... MICHAEL POWELL†
CANTERVILLE GHOST, THE ... EDWIN BLUM
CANVAS, THE - S ... ANN LOUISE BARDACH
CAPA - S ... MENNO MEYJES
CAPA - S ... DONALD L. STEWART
CAPE DISAPPOINTMENT - S ... ROBERT GARLAND
CAPER - S ... JANET ROACH
CAPETOWN AFFAIR ... SAMUEL FULLER
CAPONE IN LAREDO - S ... JOHN NORVILLE
CAPONE IN LAREDO - S ... MICHAEL JENNING
CAPPUCCINO ... ANTHONY J. BOWMAN
CAPRICIOUS SUMMER ... JIRI MENZEL
CAPRICORN ONE ... PETER HYAMS
CAPT AIN NUKE AND THE BOMBER BOYS - S ... REED STEINER
CAPTAIN AMANDA - S ... LARRY KETRON
CAPTAIN AMERICA ... STEPHEN TOLKIN
CAPTAIN APACHE ... PHILIP YORDAN
CAPTAIN BARNES, LIEUTENANT FARNUM - S ... JOHN BRILEY
CAPTAIN BUTTERFLY - S ... LEIGH CHAPMAN
CAPTAIN JACK AND THE MUFFIN TWINS - S ... DAVID BIRKE
CAPTAIN JANUARY ... HARRY TUGEND†
CAPTAIN KRONOS, VAMPIRE HUNTER ... BRIAN H. CLEMENS
CAPTAIN LIGHTFOOT ... OSCAR BRODNEY
CAPTAIN NUKE AND THE BOMBER BOYS - S ... CHARLES GALE
CAPTAIN SUNTAN RIDES AGAIN (P) ... MARK MEDOFF
CAPTAIN YAWK & THE SILVER STREAK - S ... JERRY BELSON
CAPTAIN ZAP AND THE BRUTE (CTF) - S ... DAVID NEWMAN
CAPTAIN'S BLOOD - S ... MICHAEL BLODGETT
CAPTAIN'S TABLE, THE ... BRYAN FORBES
CAPTIVE ... PAUL MAYERSBERG
CAPTIVE HEARTS ... BILL PHILLIPS
CAPTIVE HEARTS ... JOHN A. KURI
CAPTIVE HEARTS ... PAT MORITA
CAPTIVE HEARTS ... PAUL BOORSTIN
CAPTIVE HEARTS ... SHARON BOORSTIN
CAPTIVE HEARTS ... WARREN SKAAREN†
CAPTIVE IN THE LAND, A ... LEE GOLD
CAR 54, WHERE ARE YOU? - S ... EBBE ROE SMITH
CAR RACING STORY - S ... PETE HAMILL
CAR THIEVES - S ... HENRY BEAN
CAR TROUBLE ... A.J. TIPPING
CAR TROUBLE ... JAMES WHALEY
CAR WASH ... JOEL SCHUMACHER
CAR, THE ... LANE SLATE†
CAR, THE ... DENNIS SHRYACK
CAR, THE ... MICHAEL BUTLER
CARAVAGGIO ... DEREK JARMAN
CARAVAN TO VACCARES ... PAUL WHEELER
CARAVANS ... NANCY VOYLES CRAWFORD
CARBON COPY ... STANLEY SHAPIRO†
CARDIAC ARREST - S ... MURRAY MINTZ
CARE BEARS ADVENTURE IN WONDERLAND, THE (AF) ... JOHN DEKLEIN
CARE BEARS ADVENTURE IN WONDERLAND, THE (AF) ... SUSAN SNOOKS
CARE BEARS MOVIE II (AF) ... PETER SAUDER
CARE BEARS MOVIE, THE (AF) ... PETER SAUDER
CAREER MOVE - S ... SCOTT PARKER
CAREER MOVES ... JEFF WILHELM
CAREER OPPORTUNITIES ... JOHN HUGHES
CAREFUL, HE MIGHT HEAR YOU ... MICHAEL JENKINS
CARETAKER, THE ... HAROLD PINTER
CAREY TREATMENT, THE ... JOHN D.F. BLACK
CARIBBEAN WOMAN - S ... ANNE BEATTS
CARLESS - S ... JOHN LEVENSTEIN
CARLESS - S ... MICHAEL A. KAPLAN
CARLITO'S WAY - S ... DAVID KOEPP
CARLITO'S WAY - S ... EARL MAC RAUCH
CARLITO'S WAY - S ... MARDIK MARTIN
CARLTON-BROWNE OF THE F.O. ... ROY BOULTING
CARMEN ... FRANCESCO ROSI
CARMEN ... CARLOS SAURA
CARMEN JONES ... HARRY KLEINER
CARNAGE (P) ... TIM ROBBINS
CARNAL KNOWLEDGE ... JULES FEIFFER
CARNY ... PHOEBE KAYLOR
CARNY ... ROBBIE ROBERTSON
CARNY ... ROBERT KAYLOR
CARNY ... THOMAS BAUM
CARPENTERS, THE (P) ... STEVE TESICH
CARPETBAGGERS, THE ... JOHN MICHAEL HAYES
CARPOOL - S ... BOB GALE
CARRIE ... LAWRENCE D. COHEN
CARRINGTON - S ... CHRISTOPHER HAMPTON
CARROLL SHELBY - S ... JULIAN BARRY
CARRY ME THROUGH - S ... GINA WENDKOS
CARRY ON CRUISING ... NORMAN HUDIS
CARRY ON SERGEANT ... NORMAN HUDIS
CARS - S ... JERRY BELSON
CARS THAT ATE PARIS, THE ... PETER WEIR
CARS THAT ATE PEOPLE, THE ... PETER WEIR
CARTEL ... MOSHE HADAR
CARTOUCHE ... PHILLIPE DE BROCA
CARVE HER NAME WITH PRIDE ... LEWIS GILBERT
CARVER'S BOX - S ... MICHAEL FALLON
CASABLANCA ... HOWARD KOCH
CASABLANCA ... JULIUS J. EPSTEIN
CASABLANCA ... PHILIP G. EPSTEIN†
CASANOVA ... FEDERICO FELLINI
CASANOVA ... TONINO GUERRA
CASANOVA SLEPT HERE - S ... ROBERT MUNDY
CASANOVA'S BIG NIGHT ... HAL KANTER
CASE OF THE PURPLE TERROR, THE - S ... PHIL HARTMAN
CASEY JONES - S ... SCOTT MORGAN
CASEY SPEAKS - S ... ADAM BELANOFF
CASEY SPEAKS - S ... P.J. PESCE
CASEY'S SHADOW ... CAROL SOBIESKI†
CASHFLOW- S ... JOHN HERMAN SHANER
CASINO ROYALE ... WOLF MANKOWITZ
CASSANDRA CROSSING, THE ... GEORGE PAN COSMATOS
CASSANDRA CROSSING, THE ... ROBERT KATZ
CASSANDRA CROSSING, THE ... TOM MANKIEWICZ
CAST A GIANT SHADOW ... MEL SHAVELSON
CAST A LONG SHADOW ... JOHN MCGREEVY
CASTAWAY ... ALLAN G. SCOTT
CASTAWAY COWBOY, THE ... DON TAIT
CASTAWAYS - S ... GORDON GREISMAN
CASTLE KEEP ... DANIEL TARADASH
CASTLE KEEP ... DAVID RAYFIEL
CASTLE OF THE SPIDER'S WEB, THE ... AKIRA KUROSAWA
CASTLES IN THE AIR - S ... TOM COLE
CASUAL SEX? ... JUDY TOLL
CASUAL SEX? ... WENDY GOLDMAN
CASUALTIES OF WAR ... DAVID RABE
CAT & MOUSE - S ... RICHARD WHITLEY
CAT - S ... MICHAEL ERIC STEIN
CAT AND THE CANARY, THE ... RADLEY METZGER
CAT BALLOU ... FRANK R. PIERSON
CAT BALLOU ... WALTER NEWMAN
CAT CHASER ... JIM BORRELLI
CAT CHASER ... ALAN SHARP
CAT CHASER ... ELMORE LEONARD
CAT O'NINE TAILS ... DARIO ARGENTO
CAT ON A HOT TIN ROOF ... RICHARD BROOKS
CAT PEOPLE ... ALAN ORMSBY
CATS - S ... RICHARD LAGRAVENESE
CAT'S EYE ... STEPHEN KING
CAT'S PAW (P) ... WILLIAM MASTROSIMONE
CAT, THE - S ... PAUL D. ZIMMERMAN
CATACOMBS ... C. COURTNEY JOYNER
CATACOMBS - S ... R. BARKER PRICE
CATCH ME A SPY ... DICK CLEMENT
CATCH ME A SPY ... IAN LAFRENAIS
CATCH ME IF YOU CAN ... STEPHEN SOMMERS
CATCH THE HEAT ... STIRLING SILLIPHANT
CATCH US IF YOU CAN ... PETER NICHOLS
CATCH, THE - S ... JIM MULHOLLAND
CATCH, THE - S ... MICHAEL BARRIE
CATCH-22 ... BUCK HENRY
CATERED AFFAIR, THE ... GORE VIDAL
CATFISH TANGLE - S ... MARK PEPLOE
CATHODE MONSTER, THE - S ... DAVID ODELL
CATHOLIC GIRLS (P) ... DORIS BAIZLEY
CATTLE ANNIE AND LITTLE BRITCHES ... DAVID EYRE
CATTLE ANNIE AND LITTLE BRITCHES ... ROBERT M. WARD
CATTLE QUEEN OF MONTANA ... ROBERT BLEES
CATWALKER - S ... ROBERT BORIS
CAUGHT ... ARTHUR LAURENTS
CAUGHT ... JAMES F. COLLIER†
CAUGHT - S ... PHILIP MORTON
CAUGHT DEAD - S ... MAGGIE KLEINMAN
CAUGHT IN THE DRAFT ... HARRY TUGEND†
CAUSE CELEBRE - S ... JOHN MORTIMER
CAUSE TOJOURS (P) ... FRANCIS VEBER
CAVEGIRL ... DAVID OLIVER
CAVEMAN ... CARL GOTTLIEB
CAVEMAN ... RUDY DELUCA
CAVERN, THE ... JACK DAVIES

Title	Writer
CC PYLE AND THE BUNION DERBY - S	MICHAEL CRISTOFER
CEASE FIRE	GEORGE FERNANDEZ
CELESTE	PERCY ADLON
CELIA	ANNE TURNER
CELINA'S WORLD - S	JAN ELIASBERG
CELLING OUT - S	JOHN JACOBSEN
CEMENT GARDEN, THE - S	ANDREW BIRKIN
CEMETARY HIGH	CARMINE CAPOBIANCO
CEMETARY HIGH	GORMAN BECHARD
CENTENNIAL SUMMER	MICHAEL KANIN
CENTERFOLD - S	LEWIS JOHN CARLINO
CENTERFOLD - S	NANCY DOWD
CENTERFOLD - S	RON SHELTON
CENTERFOLD - S	WALON GREEN
CENTERFOLD GIRLS, THE	ROBERT L. PEETE
CENTRIFUGE	DONALD CAMMELL
CENTURION - S	JERE P. CUNNINGHAM
CEREMONY FOR THE MIDGET (SHORT)	JAMES KENNEDY
CERTAIN FURY	MICHAEL JACOBS
CESAR AND ROSALIE	CLAUDE SAUTET
CHAFED ELBOWS	ROBERT DOWNEY
CHAIN, THE	JACK ROSENTHAL
CHAINED HEAT	PAUL NICHOLAS
CHAINED HEAT	VINCENT MONGOL
CHAINLETTER, THE - S	PETER HANKOFF
CHALK GARDEN, THE	JOHN MICHAEL HAYES
CHALLENGE THE WIND	KEN HOWARD
CHALLENGE THE WIND	MARLA YOUNG
CHALLENGE THE WIND	WILLIAM BLACKBURN
CHALLENGE, THE	JOHN SAYLES
CHALLENGE, THE	RICHARD MAXWELL
CHALLENGER - S	JIM MCBRIDE
CHALLENGER, THE	ALLAN G. SCOTT
CHAMBER OF HORRORS	STEPHEN KANDEL
CHAMELEON STREET	WENDELL B. HARRIS JR.
CHAMP, THE	SPENCER EASTMAN†
CHAMP, THE	WALTER NEWMAN
CHAMP, THE (CTF) - S	JOHN SINGLETON
CHAMPAGNE FOR CAESAR - S	DAVID DASHEV
CHAMPAGNE FOR CAESAR - S	STUART BIRNBAUM
CHAMPAGNE NIGHTS - S	HAROLD A. RAMIS
CHAMPAGNE NIGHTS - S	PETER TOROKVEI
CHAMPAGNE WALTZ	BILLY WILDER
CHAMPIONS	EVAN JONES
CHAMPIONS FOREVER (FD)	KENNETH W. GRISWOLD
CHAN IS MISSING	ISAAC CRONIN
CHAN IS MISSING	TERREL SELTZER
CHAN IS MISSING	WAYNE WANG
CHANCE OF A LIFETIME - S	DAVID DASHEV
CHANCE OF A LIFETIME - S	STUART BIRNBAUM
CHANCE OF A LIFETIME - S	THOM EBERHARDT
CHANCES ARE	PERRY HOWZE
CHANCES ARE	RANDY HOWZE
CHANDLER	JOHN SACRET YOUNG
CHANGE OF HABIT	ERIC BERCOVICI
CHANGE OF HEART - S	HOLLY GOLDBERG SLOAN
CHANGE OF HEART - S	GERALD AYRES
CHANGE OF PLANS - S	JEFFREY ALAN FISKIN
CHANGE OF SEASONS, A	FRED SEGAL
CHANGE OF SEASONS, A	MARTIN RANSOHOFF
CHANGE OF SEASONS, A	ERICH SEGAL
CHANGE OF SEASONS, A	RONNI KERN
CHANGELING, THE	RUSSELL HUNTER
CHANGELING, THE	DIANA MADDOX
CHANGELING, THE	WILLIAM GRAY
CHANGING LABELS - S	RICHARD BRENNE
CHANGING SIDES - S	DAVID CHASE
CHANGING TIMES - S	JUDITH FEIN
CHANT OF JIMMIE BLACKSMITH, THE	THOMAS KENEALLY
CHANT OF JIMMIE BLACKSMITH, THE	FRED SCHEPISI
CHAPEL OF LOVE - S	CAROLYN SHELBY
CHAPEL OF LOVE - S	CHRISTOPHER AMES
CHAPPIE - S	JOHN BISHOP
CHAPTER TWO	NEIL SIMON
CHARADE	PETER STONE
CHARGE OF THE LIGHT BRIGADE, THE	CHARLES WOOD
CHARIOTS OF FIRE	COLIN WELLAND
CHARLES AND LUCY- S	NORMAN STEINBERG
CHARLEY MOON	LESLIE BRICUSSE
CHARLEY VARRICK	DEAN RIESNER
CHARLEY'S BIG-HEARTED AUNT	VAL GUEST
CHARLIE & MORRY - S	RICHARD WHITLEY
CHARLIE & MORRY - S	RICHARD F. WHITLEY
CHARLIE BUBBLES	SHELAGH DELANEY
CHARLIE CHAN AND THE CURSE OF THE DRAGON QUEEN	DAVID AXELROD
CHARLIE CHAN AND THE CURSE OF THE DRAGON QUEEN	STANLEY BURNS
CHARLIE CHAPLIN - S	COLIN WELLAND
CHARLIE IS MY DARLING - S	HERMAN RAUCHER
CHARLIE MOON	LESLIE BRICUSSE
CHARLIE WEDEMYER STORY, THE - S	BARRY MORROW
CHARLY	STIRLING SILLIPHANT
CHARMED LIVES - S	NICHOLAS MEYER
CHASE, THE	PHILIP YORDAN
CHASE, THE	HORTON FOOTE
CHASER - S	ERIC EDSON
CHASER - S	DAVID FREEMAN
CHASING KILROY - S	JOE GAYTON
CHASTITY BELT	LARRY GELBART
CHATTAHOOCHEE	JAMES CRESSON
CHATTANOOGA CHOO CHOO	ROBERT MUNDY
CHATTANOOGA CHOO CHOO	STEVEN PHILIP SMITH
CHEAP (P)	TOM TOPOR
CHEAP DETECTIVE, THE	NEIL SIMON
CHEAP LAUGHS - S	MURRAY SCHISGAL
CHEAP PARTS - S	MORRIE RUVINSKY
CHEAPER TO KEEP HER	HERSCHEL WEINGROD
CHEAPER TO KEEP HER	TIMOTHY HARRIS
CHEAPSHOT - S	ROBERT WUHL
CHEAT, THE - S	HAL DRESNER
CHEATIN' (P)	DEL SHORES
CHECK IS IN THE MAIL, THE	ROBERT KAUFMAN
CHECKERS (P)	CLIFTON CAMPBELL
CHECKING OUT	JOE ESZTERHAS
CHECKMATES (P)	RON MILNER
CHEECH & CHONG'S NEXT MOVIE, THE	CHEECH MARIN
CHEECH & CHONG'S NEXT MOVIE, THE	TOMMY CHONG
CHEECH & CHONG'S NICE DREAMS	CHEECH MARIN
CHEECH & CHONG'S NICE DREAMS	TOMMY CHONG
CHEECH & CHONG'S THE CORSICAN BROTHERS	CHEECH MARIN
CHEECH & CHONG'S THE CORSICAN BROTHERS	TOMMY CHONG
CHEECH & CHONG: STILL SMOKIN'	CHEECH MARIN
CHEECH & CHONG: STILL SMOKIN'	TOMMY CHONG
CHEEK TO CHEEK - S	ERIC ROTH
CHEEK TO CHEEK - S	LAURA KING
CHEEK TO CHEEK - S	MICHAEL BORTMAN
CHEERLEADER OF THE NEW LEFT - S	CLAYTON S. FROHMAN
CHEERS - S	JULE SELBO
CHEESE STANDS ALONE, THE - S	KATHY MCWORTER
CHEETAH	ERIK S. TARLOFF
CHEETAH	GRIFF DURHONE
CHEETAH	JOHN COTTER
CHELSEA, THE - S	ANN BIDERMAN
CHERE INCONNUE	MOSHE MIZRAHI
CHERE INCONNUE	GERARD BRACH
CHERNOBYL: THE FINAL WARNING (CTF)	ERNEST KINOY
CHERRY 2000	LLOYD FONVIELLE
CHERRY 2000	MICHAEL ALMEREYDA
CHERRY TERRY, THE ROCKIN' ROBIN (P)	JOHN KAYE
CHERRY, HARRY AND RAQUEL	RUSS MEYER
CHEYENNE SOCIAL CLUB, THE	JAMES LEE BARRETT†
CHICAGO JOE AND THE SHOWGIRL	DAVID YALLOP
CHICAGO KID, THE - S	RICHARD WHITLEY
CHICAGO LOOP - S	PAUL THEROUX
CHICAGO MASQUERADE	OSCAR BRODNEY
CHICKEN CHRONICLES, THE	PAUL DIAMOND
CHILD IN THE HOUSE	CY ENDFIELD
CHILD IS WAITING, A	ABBY MANN
CHILD'S PLAY	DON MANCINI
CHILD'S PLAY	JOHN LAFIA
CHILD'S PLAY	TOM HOLLAND
CHILD'S PLAY 2	DON MANCINI
CHILD'S PLAY 3	DON MANCINI
CHILDREN OF A LESSER GOD	HESPER ANDERSON
CHILDREN OF A LESSER GOD	MARK MEDOFF
CHILDREN OF DARKNESS, CHILDREN OF LIGHT (CTF)	BRIAN W. TAGGERT
CHILDREN OF DUST - S	ROBERT CASWELL
CHILDREN OF HERAKLES (P)	JOHN STEPPLING
CHILDREN OF RAGE	RICHARD ALFIERI
CHILDREN OF SANCHEZ, THE	HALL BARTLETT
CHILDREN OF THE CORN	GEORGE GOLDSMITH
CHILDREN OF THE DAMNED	JOHN BRILEY
CHILDREN OF THE EARTH, THE - S	FRANK KERR
CHILDREN SHOULDN'T PLAY WITH DEAD THINGS	ALAN ORMSBY
CHILDREN WITH EMERALD EYES - S	MARSHA NORMAN
CHILDREN WITH EMERALD EYES - S	NEAL JIMENEZ
CHILDREN'S CRUSADE, THE - S	DENNIS CLARK
CHILDREN'S CRUSADE, THE - S	NEAL ISRAEL
CHILL, THE - S	JOEL OLIANSKY
CHILLY SCENES OF WINTER	JOAN MICKLIN SILVER
CHINA - S	BILL MCKINNEY, JR.
CHINA BLUES - S	ALLAN BURNS
CHINA CRY	JAMES F. COLLIER†
CHINA GATE	SAMUEL FULLER
CHINA GIRL	NICHOLAS ST. JOHN
CHINA HAND - S	JAMES GOLDMAN
CHINA IS NEAR	MARCO BELLOCCHIO
CHINA LAKE - S	NEVIN SCHREINER
CHINA MOON - S	ROY CARLSON
CHINA RIOS (CTF) - S	EDUARDO MACHADO
CHINA SYNDROME, THE	JAMES BRIDGES
CHINA SYNDROME, THE	MIKE GRAY
CHINA SYNDROME, THE	T.S. COOK
CHINATOWN	ROBERT TOWNE
CHINESE BANDIT	DAVID PEOPLES
CHINESE BANDIT - S	DAVID SHABER
CHINESE BANDITS - S	HAMPTON FANCHER
CHINESE BOXES	L.M. KIT CARSON
CHINESE HANDCUFFS - S	R.M. BADAT
CHINESE MURDERS, THE - S	LIZ COMICI
CHINESE MURDERS, THE - S	LOU COMICI
CHINO	CLAIR HUFFAKER†
CHIPMUNK ADVENTURE, THE (AF)	JANICE KARMAN
CHIPMUNK ADVENTURE, THE (AF)	ROSS BAGDASARIAN
CHISUM	ANDREW J. FENADY
CHITTY CHITTY BANG BANG	RICHARD MAIBAUM†
CHITTY CHITTY BANG BANG	KEN HUGHES
CHITTY CHITTY BANG BANG	ROALD DAHL†
CHLOE IN THE AFTERNOON	ERIC ROHMER
CHOCOLAT	CLAIRE DENIS
CHOCOLATE WAR, THE	KEITH GORDON
CHOICE OF ARMS - S	EARL WALLACE
CHOICE OF WEAPONS	JULIAN BOND
CHOICES - S	JAMES P. DUNNE
CHOICES - S	VALERIE WEST
CHOOSE ME	ALAN RUDOLPH
CHOPPER & THE FLASH - S	JOHN HILL
CHOPPER CHICKS IN ZOMBIE TOWN	DAN HOSKINS
CHOPPERS - S	JOHN MCCORMICK
CHOPPERS - S	ROSS LA MANNA
CHOPPING MALL	STEVE MITCHELL
CHOPPING MALL	JIM WYNORSKI
CHORUS LINE, A	ARNOLD SCHULMAN
CHORUS LINE, A (P)	JAMES KIRKWOOD†
CHORUS OF DISAPPROVAL, A	ALAN AYCKBOURN
CHORUS OF DISAPPROVAL, A	ALAN WINNER
CHOSEN, THE	MICHAEL ROBSON
CHOSEN, THE	SERGIO DONATI
CHOSEN, THE	EDWIN GORDON
CHRIS LUCAS STORY - S	ERIC BERGREN
CHRIS LUKAS PROJECT, THE - S	W.D. RICHTER
CHRIST RECRUCIFIED	BEN BARZMAN†
CHRIST STOPPED AT EBOLI	FRANCESCO ROSI
CHRIST STOPPED AT EBOLI	TONINO GUERRA
CHRISTIAN	GABRIEL AXEL
CHRISTIAN LICORICE STORE, THE	FLOYD MUTRUX
CHRISTIANE F.	HERMAN WEIGEL
CHRISTINE	BILL PHILLIPS
CHRISTMAS CONSPIRACY - S	ROBERT RODAT
CHRISTMAS EVIL	LEWIS JACKSON
CHRISTMAS IN JULY - S	BRUCE EVANS
CHRISTMAS IN JULY - S	RAY GIDEON
CHRISTMAS IN LAS VEGAS - S	CARRIE FISHER
CHRISTMAS STORY, A	BOB CLARK
CHRISTMAS STORY, A	JEAN SHEPHERD
CHRISTMAS STORY, A	LEIGH BROWN
CHRISTMAS VACATION	JOHN HUGHES

INDEX OF FILM TITLES

CHRISTOPHER COLUMBUS: THE MOVIE - S ... MARIO PUZO
CHROMIUM BLUE - S ... LARRY GRUSIN
CHROMIUM YELLOW - S ... PAUL B. MARGOLIS
CHRONICLE OF BRIMSTONE, A - S ... JEFFREY ALAN FISKIN
CHRYSANTHEMUM COVENANT - S ... DON INGALLS
CHU CHU AND THE PHILLY FLASH ... BARBARA DANA
CHUD II: BUD THE CHUD ... ED NAHA
CHUMP TOWER - S ... JIM FISHER
CHUMP TOWER - S ... JIM STAAHL
CHUMPS - S ... JOHN BLUMENTHAL
CHUMPS - S ... MICHAEL BERRY
CIDER HOUSE RULES - S ... JOHN IRVING
CIMARRON ... ARNOLD SCHULMAN
CINCINNATI KID, THE ... RING LARDNER JR.
CINCINNATI KID, THE ... TERRY SOUTHERN
CINDERELLA CITY - S ... STEVE TESICH
CINDERELLA LIBERTY ... DARRYL PONICSAN
CINDERELLA UNIVERSE - S ... MICHAEL JENNING
CINEMA PARADISO ... GIUSEPPE TORNATORE
CIRCE AND BRAVO (P) ... DONALD FREED
CIRCLE OF DECEIT ... JEAN-CLAUDE CARRIERE
CIRCLE OF DECEIT ... MARGARETHE VON TROTTA
CIRCLE OF DECEIT ... VOLKER SCHLONDORFF
CIRCLE OF IRON ... STANLEY MANN
CIRCLE OF IRON ... STIRLING SILLIPHANT
CIRCLE OF POWER ... BETH SULLIVAN
CIRCLE OF POWER ... STEPHEN F. BELLO
CIRCLE OF TWO ... THOMAS HEDLEY JR.
CIRCUITRY MAN ... ROBERT LOVY
CIRCUITRY MAN ... STEVEN LOVY
CIRCUS ROAD - S ... WES CLARRIDGE
CISCO - S ... GERALD DI PEGO
CISCO KID, THE - S ... MICHAEL KANE
CISCO PIKE ... B.W.L. NORTON, JR.
CITIZEN SICK - S ... DICK BEEBE
CITIZEN TOM PAINE - S ... RICHARD FRIEDENBERG
CITIZEN'S BAND ... PAUL BRICKMAN
CITY HALL - S ... ALLEN HOLLEB
CITY HALL - S ... JOE ESZTERHAS
CITY HEAT ... BLAKE EDWARDS
CITY HEAT ... JOSEPH C. STINSON
CITY KIDS - S ... JOE GAYTON
CITY LIMITS ... AARON LIPSTADT
CITY LIMITS ... DON OPPER
CITY LIMITS ... JAMES REIGLE
CITY OF ANGELS (P) ... LARRY GELBART
CITY OF ANGELS (P) ... JOHN BRIGHT†
CITY OF DARKNESS - S ... JOE GAYTON
CITY OF DARKNESS - S ... PATRICK CIRILLO
CITY OF FEAR ... ROBERT DILLON
CITY OF HOPE ... JOHN SAYLES
CITY OF JOY ... MARK MEDOFF
CITY OF WOMEN ... BRUNELLO RONDI†
CITY OF WOMEN ... FEDERICO FELLINI
CITY ON FIRE ... CELINE LA FRENIERE
CITY ON FIRE ... DAVID P. LEWIS
CITY SLICKERS ... BABALOO MANDEL
CITY SLICKERS ... LOWELL GANZ
CITY UNDER THE SEA ... LOUIS M. HEYWARD
CITY UNDER THE SEA, THE ... CHARLES BENNETT
CIVIL DEFENSE - S ... JOHN ESKOW
CIVIL WARS (P) ... DAN GURSKIS
CIVIL WARS - S ... JEFF STETSON
CIVIL WARS - S ... ROBERT GETCHELL
CLAIRE'S KNEE ... ERIC ROHMER
CLAIRVOYANT, THE ... CHARLES BENNETT
CLAN OF ONE - S ... GREGORY WIDEN
CLAN OF THE CAVE BEAR, THE ... JOHN SAYLES
CLARA (P) ... ARTHUR MILLER
CLARA - S ... BRUCE VILANCH
CLARA'S HEART ... MARK MEDOFF
CLARENCE (CTF) ... DAVID HOSELTON
CLARENCE (CTF) ... LORNE CAMERON
CLARENCE THE CROSS-EYED LION ... ALAN CAILOU
CLARKSVILLE - S ... HENRY BROMELL
CLASH OF THE TITANS ... BEVERLY CROSS
CLASS ... DAVID GREENWALT
CLASS ... JIM KOUF
CLASS ACTION ... CAROLYN J. SHELBY
CLASS ACTION ... CHRISTOPHER AMES
CLASS ACTION ... SAMANTHA SHAD
CLASS CONFLICT - S ... FIONA LEWIS
CLASS OF '44 ... HERMAN RAUCHER
CLASS OF '84 ... JOHN SAXTON†
CLASS OF '84 ... MARK L. LESTER
CLASS OF '84 ... TOM HOLLAND
CLASS OF 1999 ... C. COURTNEY JOYNER
CLASS OF 1999 ... MARK L. LESTER
CLASS OF MISS MACMICHAEL, THE ... JUDD BERNARD
CLASS OF NUKE 'EM HIGH PART 2 ... CARL MORANO
CLASS OF NUKE 'EM HIGH PART 2 ... ERIC LOUZIL
CLASS OF NUKE 'EM HIGH PART 2 ... JEFFREY W. SASS
CLASS OF NUKE 'EM HIGH PART 2 ... LLOYD KAUFMAN
CLASS OF NUKE 'EM HIGH PART 2 ... MARCUS ROLLING
CLASS OF NUKE 'EM HIGH PART 2 ... MATT UNGER
CLASS RELATIONS ... JEAN-MARIE STRAUB
CLASS REUNION ... JOHN HUGHES
CLASSY KILL - S ... MATTHEW DORFF
CLEAN AND SOBER ... TOD CARROLL
CLEAN SLATE ... BERTRAND TAVERNIER
CLEAN SWEEP, A - S ... JIM CIRILE
CLEAR CUT - S ... LYNN GROSSMAN
CLEAR CUT - S ... RAMA LAURIE STAGNER
CLEARCUT ... ROB FORSYTH
CLEO FROM 5 TO 7 ... AGNES VARDA
CLEO FROM NINE TO FIVE - S ... JULIE HICKSON
CLEOPATRA ... JOSEPH L. MANKIEWICZ
CLEVELAND ROCKS - S ... ANDY BOROWITZ
CLICK: THE CALENDAR GIRL KILLER ... DAVID CHUTE
CLICK: THE CALENDAR GIRL KILLER ... DAVID RESKIN
CLICK: THE CALENDAR GIRL KILLER ... HOKE HOWELL
CLICK: THE CALENDAR GIRL KILLER ... JOHN STEWART
CLICK: THE CALENDAR GIRL KILLER ... ROSS HAGEN
CLICK: THE CALENDAR GIRL MURDER ... CAROL LYNN
CLIFFORD ... STEVEN W. KAMPMANN
CLIFFORD ... WILL ALDIS
CLIMAX, THE ... CURT SIODMAK
CLINIC, THE ... GREG MILLIN
CLINIC, THE - S ... MONICA JOHNSON
CLINTON AND NADINE (CTF) ... ROBERT O. FOSTER
CLOAK & DIAPER- S ... IAN ABRAMS
CLOAK AND DAGGER ... RING LARDNER JR.
CLOAK AND DAGGER ... TOM HOLLAND
CLOCK MAKER, THE ... BERTRAND TAVERNIER
CLOCK STRUCK ONE, THE - S ... JEROME LAWRENCE
CLOCK STRUCK ONE, THE- S ... ROBERT E. LEE
CLOCKWISE ... MICHAEL FRAYN
CLOCKWORK ORANGE, A ... STANLEY KUBRICK
CLONE - S ... BRIAN HOHLFELD
CLOSE (P) ... JOHN STEPPLING
CLOSE ENCOUNTERS OF THE THIRD KIND ... STEVEN SPIELBERG
CLOSE RELATIONS (CTF) ... STANLEY PRICE
CLOSE SHAVE ... ROBERT HENDRICKSON
CLOSE SHAVE ... RONALD COLLIER
CLOSE TO EDEN - S ... ROBERT J. AVRECH
CLOSE TO HOME - S ... JACQUELINE FEATHER
CLOSE TO HOME - S ... DAVID SEIDLER
CLOSELY WATCHED TRAINS ... JIRI MENZEL
CLOSER, THE ... LOUIS LA RUSSO II
CLOSET LAND ... RADHA BHARADWAJ
CLOSING TIME - S ... LORING MANDEL
CLOUD DANCER ... WILLIAM GOODHART
CLOWN, THE - S ... DAVID SHABER
CLOWNHOUSE ... VICTOR SALVA
CLOWNS, THE ... FEDERICO FELLINI
CLUB XII (P) ... RANDY WEINER
CLUB XII (P) ... ROB HANNING
CLUB DEAD - S ... STEVE MUSCARELLA
CLUB LIFE ... BLEU MCKENZIE
CLUB LIFE ... NORMAN THADDEUS VANE
CLUB PARADISE ... DAVID STANDISH
CLUB PARADISE ... ED ROBOTO
CLUB PARADISE ... TOM LEOPOLD
CLUB PARADISE ... BRIAN DOYLE-MURRAY
CLUB PARADISE ... CHRIS MILLER
CLUB PARADISE ... HAROLD RAMIS
CLUB TABOO - S ... J.T. ALLEN
CLUB, THE ... DAVID WILLIAMSON
CLUB, THE (P) ... YALE UDOFF
CLUB, THE - S ... DAVID H. FRANZONI
CLUBHOUSE - S ... HAROLD RAMIS
CLUE ... JOHN LANDIS
CLUE ... JONATHAN LYNN
CO-EDS, THE - S ... CHRIS MILLER
CO-EDS, THE - S ... MICHAEL D. SUTTON
COACH ... NANCY LARSON
COACH - S ... MARK ROSNER
COACH MOM - S ... JOHN J. SCHALTER
COAL MINER'S DAUGHTER ... THOMAS RICKMAN
COAST GUARD PROJECT - S ... BOAZ YAKIN
COAST TO COAST ... STANLEY WEISER
COASTER ... HERBERT H. ROSEN
COBRA ... SYLVESTER STALLONE
COBRA II - S ... MICHAEL BLODGETT
COBRA WOMAN ... RICHARD BROOKS
COCA COLA KID, THE ... FRANK MOORHOUSE
COCAINE WARS ... DAVID VINAS
COCAINE WARS ... STEVEN M. KRAUZER
COCKLESHELL HEROES ... BRYAN FORBES
COCKLESHELL HEROES ... RICHARD MAIBAUM†
COCKTAIL ... HEYWOOD GOULD
COCKTAIL HOUR, THE (P) ... A.R. GURNEY
COCKTAIL MOLOTOV ... DIANE KURYS
COCOON ... DAVID SAPERSTEIN
COCOON ... TOM BENEDEK
COCOON: THE RETURN ... ELIZABETH BRADLEY
COCOON: THE RETURN ... STEPHEN MCPHERSON
CODE BLUE - S ... WILLIAM HANLEY
CODE NAME: EMERALD ... RON BASS
CODE NAME MORITURI ... DANIEL TARADASH
CODE NAME: TRIXIE ... GEORGE A. ROMERO
CODE OF SILENCE ... DENNIS SHRYACK
CODE OF SILENCE ... MICHAEL BUTLER
CODE OF SILENCE ... MIKE GRAY
CODENAME: WILDGEESE ... MICHAEL LESTER
COFFIN FOR DIMITRIOS, A - S ... DONALD CAMMELL
COHEN & TATE ... ERIC RED
COLD AS ICE - S ... MARK ALLEN SMITH
COLD CASH - S ... MURRAY MINTZ
COLD DOG SOUP - S ... THOMAS POPE
COLD EYE - S ... JEFFREY HAMMOND
COLD EYE - S ... MARK KRUGER
COLD FEET (1989) ... JIM HARRISON
COLD FEET (1989) ... THOMAS MCGUANE
COLD FEET (1984) ... BRUCE VAN DUSEN
COLD FEET - S ... SCOTT MORGAN
COLD FIRE - S ... BOAZ YAKIN
COLD HEAT - S ... J.S. CARDONE
COLD HEAVEN ... ALLAN G. SCOTT
COLD RIVER ... FRED G. SULLIVAN
COLD SASSY TREE (CTF) ... JOAN TEWKESBURY
COLD STEEL ... MICHAEL D. SONYE
COLD STEEL ... MOE QUIGLEY
COLD STORAGE - S ... STEVE MUSCARELLA
COLD SWEAT (P) ... NEAL BELL
COLD TURKEY ... NORMAN LEAR
COLD WAR SWAP - S ... ROBERT CARRINGTON
COLDITZ STORY, THE ... GUY HAMILTON
COLLECTION, THE (P) ... HAROLD PINTER
COLLECTOR, THE ... JOHN KOHN
COLLECTOR, THE ... STANLEY MANN
COLLEGE BOWL - S ... SOLLACE MITCHELL
COLLISION ... ROY CARLSON
COLLISION COURSE ... FRANK NAMEI
COLLISION COURSE ... ROBERT RESNIKOFF
COLONEL REDL ... ISTVAN SZABO
COLOR MAN - S ... HUGH WILSON
COLOR MAN - S ... THOMAS RICKMAN
COLOR OF EVENING, THE - U ... TAMARA LYNN ROTH
COLOR OF EVENING, THE - S ... HESPER ANDERSON
COLOR OF MONEY, THE ... RICHARD PRICE
COLOR OF NIGHT, THE - S ... BILLY RAY
COLOR PURPLE, THE ... MENNO MEYJES
COLOR WAR - S ... RICHARD PRICE
COLORED MUSEUM, THE (P) ... GEORGE WOLFE
COLORS ... MICHAEL SCHIFFER
COLORS ... RICHARD DILELLO
COLORS OF CHRISTMAS, THE - S ... APRIL DAMMANN
COLOSSOS: FORBIN PROJECT, THE ... JAMES BRIDGES
COLOSSUS - S ... GEORGE MACDONALD FRASER
COMA ... MICHAEL CRICHTON
COMANCHE STATION ... BURT KENNEDY
COMANCHE TERRITORY ... OSCAR BRODNEY
COMANCHEROS, THE ... CLAIR HUFFAKER†
COMBAT ZONE - S ... CAROL MONPERE
COMBAT ZONE - S ... MARK ROSNER
COME BACK TO THE 5 & DIME, JIMMY DEAN JIMMY DEAN ... ED GRACZYK
COME BLOW YOUR HORN ... NORMAN LEAR
COME BLOW YOUR HORN (P) ... NEIL SIMON
COME FLY WITH ME ... WILLIAM ROBERTS
COME OUT, COME OUT ... LINDA YELLEN
COME SEE THE PARADISE ... ALAN PARKER
COME SEPTEMBER ... MAURICE RICHLIN†

Title	Writer
COME SEPTEMBER	STANLEY SHAPIRO†
COMEBACK - S	KEN FINKLEMAN
COMEBACK TRAIL, THE	HARRY HURWITZ
COMEDIANS (P)	TREVOR GRIFFITHS
COMEDIE D'ETE	COLO TAVERNIER O'HAGAN
COMEDIE D'ETE	DANIEL VIGNE
COMEDY MAN, THE	PETER YELDMAN
COMEDY OF ERRORS - S	DON MCLENNAN
COMEDY OF TERRORS, THE	RICHARD MATHESON
COMES A HORSEMAN	DENNIS CLARK
COMFORT AND JOY	BILL FORSYTH
COMFORT OF STRANGERS, THE	HAROLD PINTER
COMIC AND THE CON, THE - S	MARK PATRICK CARDUCCI
COMIC, THE	CARL REINER
COMIN' AT YA!	LLOYD BATTISTA
COMIN' AT YA!	EUGENE QUINTANO
COMIN' AT YA!	WOLF LOWENTHAL
COMING ATTRACTIONS - S	HOWARD CUSHNIR
COMING ATTRACTIONS - S	CHRIS DEFARIA
COMING HOME	NANCY DOWD
COMING HOME	ROBERT C. JONES
COMING HOME	WALDO SALT†
COMING OF AGE - S	LINDSAY HARRISON
COMING OF AGE IN NEW YORK CITY - S	GARY DAVID GOLDBERG
COMING OUT - S	LYNN MARIE LATHAM
COMING OUT PARTY, A	JACK DAVIES
COMING SOON (CTD)	JOHN LANDIS
COMING SOON (CTD)	MICK GARRIS
COMING TO AMERICA	BARRY BLAUSTEIN
COMING TO AMERICA	EDDIE MURPHY
COMING TO AMERICA	DAVID SHEFFIELD
COMING UP ROSES	RUTH CARTER
COMMAND DECISION (P)	WILLIAM WISTER HAINES†
COMMANDER - S	JOHN SAYLES
COMMANDO	JOSEPH LOEB III
COMMANDO	MATTHEW WEISMAN
COMMANDO	STEVEN DE SOUZA
COMMANDO II - S	FRANK DARABONT
COMMANDO SCHOOL - S	EUGENE QUINTANO
COMMANDO SQUAD	MICHAEL D. SONYE
COMMENCEMENT - S	STEPHEN METCALFE
COMMITMENTS, THE	DICK CLEMENT
COMMITMENTS, THE	RODDY DOYLE
COMMITMENTS, THE	IAN LAFRENAIS
COMMON STOCK - S	CHARLES GALE
COMMUNION	WHITLEY STRIEBER
COMMUNITY PROPERTY - S	ANNE BEATTS
COMMUNITY STANDARDS - S	REX MCGEE
COMPANY MAN - S	FRANK DEESE
COMPANY MAN - S	ED NEUMEIER
COMPANY MAN - S	MICHAEL MINER
COMPANY MAN - S	MICHAEL THOMAS
COMPANY OF WOLVES, THE	ANGELA CARTER
COMPANY OF WOLVES, THE	NEIL JORDAN
COMPETITION, THE	WILLIAM B. SACKHEIM
COMPETITION, THE	JOEL OLIANSKY
COMPOSURE - S	ANN LOUISE BARDACH
COMPOSURE - S	ZALMAN KING
COMPROMISING POSITIONS	SUSAN ISAACS
COMPULSION	RICHARD MURPHY
COMPUTER - S	JONATHAN KAUFER
COMPUTER PROJECT - S	BRIAN CLARK
COMRADES - S	BUCK HENRY
CONAN THE BARBARIAN	JOHN MILIUS
CONAN THE BARBARIAN	OLIVER STONE
CONAN THE DESTROYER	GERRY CONWAY
CONAN THE DESTROYER	ROY THOMAS
CONAN THE DESTROYER	STANLEY MANN
CONCORDE - AIRPORT '79, THE	ERIC ROTH
CONCRETE COWBOY - S	GEORGE SAUNDERS
CONCRETE JUNGLE, THE	ALUN OWEN
CONCRETE JUNGLE, THE	JIMMY SANGSTER
CONCRETE JUNGLE, THE	ALAN J. ADLER
CONDEMNED OF ALTONA, THE	ABBY MANN
CONDORMAN	GLENN GORDON CARON
CONDORMAN	MICKEY ROSE
CONDORMAN	MARC STIRDIVANT
CONDUCT UNBECOMING	ROBERT ENDERS
CONDUCT UNBECOMING - S	ALAN ORMSBY
CONDUIT - S	CHRISTIAN STOIANOVICH
CONDUIT - S	PHOEBE DORIN
CONEY ISLAND COWBOYS - S	EZRA SACKS
CONFEDERACY OF DUNCES, A - S	FRANK GALATI
CONFEDERACY OF DUNCES, A - S	STEVEN M. KUNES
CONFESSION	JULIUS J. EPSTEIN
CONFESSION	KEN HUGHES
CONFESSION, THE	JORGE SEMPRUN
CONFESSIONS OF A DANGEROUS MIND - S	JACK BARAN
CONFESSIONS OF A DANGEROUS MIND - S	JIM MCBRIDE
CONFESSIONS OF A WINDOW CLEANER	CHRISTOPHER WOOD
CONFESSIONS OF AMANS, THE	ANNA THOMAS
CONFESSIONS OF AMANS, THE	GREGORY NAVA
CONFESSIONS OF AN EX-SECRET SERVICE AGENT - S	JULIE HICKSON
CONFIDENCE GIRL	ANDREW STONE
CONFIDENTIALLY YOURS	FRANCOIS TRUFFAUT†
CONFIDENTIALLY YOURS	SUZANNE SCHIFFMAN
CONFIRM OR DENY	SAMUEL FULLER
CONFLICT OF WINGS	DON SHARP
CONFORMIST, THE	BERNARDO BERTOLUCCI
CONGO - S	ROBERT BORIS
CONJUNCTION - S	WILLIAM GOODHART
CONJURING - S	NICHOLAS MEYER
CONNECTICUT YANKEE IN KING ARTHUR'S COURT - S	NEIL CUTHBERT
CONNECTIONS - S	ADAM RODMAN
CONNECTIONS - S	RICHARD TANNENBAUM
CONRACK	HARRIET FRANK JR.
CONRACK	IRVING RAVETCH
CONSPIRACY, THE - S	ROBERT J. AVRECH
CONSUMING PASSIONS	ANDREW DAVIES
CONSUMING PASSIONS	PAUL D. ZIMMERMAN
CONSUMING PASSIONS (P)	MICHAEL PALIN
CONSUMING PASSIONS (P)	TERRY JONES
CONTACT - S	ERNEST THOMPSON
CONTACT - S	THOMAS POPE
CONTEST GIRL	VAL GUEST
CONTINENTAL CIRCUS - S	DORI PIERSON
CONTINENTAL DIVIDE	LAWRENCE KASDAN
CONTRABAND	EMERIC PRESSBURGER†
CONTRABAND	MICHAEL POWELL†
CONTRACT, THE (P)	FRANCIS VEBER
CONTROL (CTF)	BRIAN MOORE
CONUNDRUM - S	DOUGLAS BARR
CONVENTION - S	ROBERT M. ULIN
CONVENTIONS - S	DAVID MISCH
CONVENTIONS - S	JACK ROSENTHAL
CONVERSATION, THE	FRANCIS FORD COPPOLA
CONVERSATIONS WITH MY FATHER (P)	HERB GARDNER
CONVICT 99	JACK DAVIES
CONVICT 99	VAL GUEST
CONVICT COWBOY - S	JIM LINDSAY
CONVICT COWBOY - S	RICK WAY
CONVICTIONS - S	ELLEN KESEND
CONVICTS	HORTON FOOTE
CONVICTS FOUR	MILLARD KAUFMAN
CONVOY	B.W.L. NORTON, JR.
COOGAN'S BLUFF	DEAN RIESNER
COOK FOR MR. GENERAL, A (P)	STEVEN GETHERS†
COOK, THE THIEF, HIS WIFE AND HER LOVER, THE	PETER GREENAWAY
COOKIE	ALICE ARLEN
COOKIE	NORA EPHRON
COOL AS ICE - S	DAVID STENN
COOL BLUE	MARK MULLIN
COOL BLUE	RICHARD SHEPARD
COOL BREEZE	BARRY POLLACK
COOL HAND LUKE	FRANK R. PIERSON
COOL ONES, THE	ROBERT KAUFMAN
COOL, CLEAR WATER - S	DAVID SELTZER
COONSKIN (AF)	RALPH BAKSHI
COP	JAMES B. HARRIS
COP AND A HALF - S	ARNE OLSON
COP AND A HALF - S	DAVID LOUCKA
COP WHO CAME IN FROM THE COLD, THE - S	NICHOLAS PILEGGI
COPS (P)	TERRY CURTIS FOX
COPS AND ROBBERS	DONALD E. WESTLAKE
COPY BOYS - S	ROBERT M. ULIN
CORMORANT, THE - S	ALLAN G. SCOTT
CORONADO'S GOLD - S	HAL HARRIS
CORONER, THE - S	MATTHEW DORFF
CORPORATE AFFAIRS	GEOFFREY BAERE
CORPORATE AFFAIRS	TERENCE WINKLESS
CORRIDOS (P)	LUIS VALDEZ
CORRUPT ONES, THE	BRIAN H. CLEMENS
CORSICAN BROTHERS, THE	CHEECH MARIN
CORSICAN BROTHERS, THE	TOMMY CHONG
CORTES - S	NICHOLAS KAZAN
CORVETTE SUMMER	HAL BARWOOD
CORVETTE SUMMER	MATTHEW ROBBINS
COSMIC CHARLIE - S	MICHAEL AUSTIN
COTTON CLUB, THE	FRANCIS FORD COPPOLA
COTTON CLUB, THE	MARIO PUZO
COTTON CLUB, THE	WILLIAM KENNEDY
COTTON COMES TO HARLEM	OSSIE DAVIS
COUCH TRIP, THE	SEAN STEIN
COUCH TRIP, THE	STEVEN W. KAMPMANN
COUCH TRIP, THE	WILL ALDIS
COUCH, THE	ROBERT BLOCH
COUGAR - S	STEPHEN H. FOREMAN
COUNSELOR - S	MICHAEL ALAN EDDY
COUNT FIVE AND DIE	DAVID PURSALL
COUNT FROM ONE TO TEN - S	LEORA BARISH
COUNTDOWN	LORING MANDEL
COUNTERFEIT - S	JEB STUART
COUNTERFEIT FATHER - S	EVAN KATZ
COUNTERFEIT FATHER - S	TOM ROPELEWSKI
COUNTERPOINT	JOEL OLIANSKY
COUNTESS DRACULA	PETER SASDY
COUNTRY	WILLIAM D. WITTLIFF
COUNTRY DANCINS (P)	NIGEL WILLIAMS
COUNTRYMAN - S	TERENCE MALICK
COUP D'ETAT - S	MARTYN BURKE
COUP D'ETETE	FRANCIS VEBER
COUP DE FOUDRE	DIANE KURYS
COUP DE TORCHON	BERTRAND TAVERNIER
COUP DE VILLE	MIKE BINDER
COURTSHIP OF EDDIE'S FATHER, THE	JOHN GAY
COURT JESTER, THE	NORMAN PANAMA
COURTMARTIAL OF JACKIE ROBINSON, THE (CTF)	DENNIS L. CLARK
COURTMARTIAL OF JACKIE ROBINSON, THE (CTF)	CLAYTON FROHMAN
COURTMARTIAL OF JACKIE ROBINSON, THE (CTF)	STEVE DUNCAN
COURTING - S	LORNE CAMERON
COURTROOM DRAMA: THE PEOPLE VS. JAMES TRUMAN - S	TOM TOPOR
COURTSHIP (P)	HORTON FOOTE
COUSINES, THE	CLAUDE CHABROL
COUSINS	STEPHEN METCALFE
COVENANT WITH DEATH, A	LAWRENCE B. MARCUS
COVER UP, THE - S	PETER LANCE
COVER, THE - S	MICHAEL GAYLIN
COVER-UP, THE - S	OLIVER STONE
COVERGIRL	CHARLES DENNIS
COVERT PURPLE - S	PAUL SCHRADER
COWBOY HEAVEN - S	MICHAEL TOLKIN
COWBOY WAY, THE - S	WILLIAM D. WITTLIFF
COWBOYS (P)	SAM SHEPARD
COWBOYS, THE	HARRIET FRANK JR.
COWBOYS, THE	IRVING RAVETCH
COYOTE LOVE - S	JAKE WEINBERGER
COYOTE LOVE - S	MIKE WEINBERGER
COYOTE SUMMER (P)	HARRY DUNN
CRACK HOUSE	JACK SILVERMAN
CRACK HOUSE	BLAKE SCHAEFER
CRACK IN THE MIRROR	ROBBY BENSON
CRACKDOWN	DARYL HANEY
CRACKDOWN	ROSS BELL
CRACKERS	JEFFREY ALAN FISKIN
CRADLE - S	THOMAS M. CLEAVER
CRASH - S	MARK ROMANEK
CRASH AND BURN - S	MIKEL ANDERSON
CRASH AND BURN - S	PETER JENSEN
CRASHING - S	TOM TOPOR
CRAVAN - S	JEFFREY ALAN FISKIN
CRAWLING EYE, THE	JIMMY SANGSTER
CRAWLSPACE	DAVID SCHMOELLER
CRAZIES, THE	GEORGE A. ROMERO
CRAZY & DAISY - S	GERARD BRACH
CRAZY FOR KATE - S	MARK W. LEE
CRAZY FOR YOU - S	BRUCE MILLER
CRAZY JOE	LEWIS JOHN CARLINO
CRAZY MOON	STEF WODOSLAWSKY
CRAZY MOON	TOM BERRY
CRAZY PEOPLE	MITCH MARKOWITZ
CRAZY QUILT	JOHN V. KORTY
CREATION OF THE WORLD AND OTHER BUSINESS (P)	ARTHUR MILLER
CREATOR	JEREMY LEVEN
CREATURE	ALLAN REED
CREATURE	WILLIAM MALONE
CREATURE - S	RICHARD MATHESON
CREATURE FROM THE BLACK LAGOON, THE	ARTHUR ROSS
CREATURE WASN'T NICE, THE	BRUCE KIMMEL
CREATURE WITH THE ATOM BRAIN, THE	CURT SIODMAK
CREATURES THE WORLD FORGOT	MICHAEL CARRERAS

Title	Writer
CREEPERS	DARIO ARGENTO
CREEPING UNKNOWN, THE	VAL GUEST
CREEPSHOW	STEPHEN KING
CREEPSHOW 2	STEPHEN KING
CREEPSHOW 2	GEORGE A. ROMERO
CRESCENDO	JIMMY SANGSTER
CREW, THE - S	MARK PEPLOE
CREW, THE - S	MICHELANGELO ANTONIONI
CRIES AND WHISPERS	INGMAR BERGMAN
CRIES OF LAUGHTER - S	WARREN ADLER
CRIME AND PUNISHMENT	AKI KAURISMAKI
CRIME AND PUNISHMENT	WALTER NEWMAN
CRIME IN THE STREETS	REGINALD ROSE
CRIME LORDS	RAND RAVICH
CRIME OF PASSION	JO EISINGER
CRIME OF THE CENTURY - S	CHARLES ROBERT CARNER
CRIME ZONE	DARYL HANEY
CRIMES AND MISDEMEANORS	WOODY ALLEN
CRIMES OF PASSION	BARRY SANDLER
CRIMES OF THE FUTURE	DAVID CRONENBERG
CRIMES OF THE HEART	BETH HENLEY
CRIMEWAVE	ETHAN COEN
CRIMEWAVE	JOEL COEN
CRIMEWAVE	SAM RAIMI
CRIMINAL ACT	DANIEL YOST
CRIMINAL LAW	MARK KASDAN
CRIMINAL MIND OF J.C. LOOMIS, THE - S	PETER HANKOFF
CRIMINAL MINDS (P)	ROBIN SWICORD
CRIMINAL, THE	ALUN OWEN
CRIMINAL, THE	JIMMY SANGSTER
CRIMINALS - S	CHARLES SHYER
CRIMINALS - S	NANCY J. MEYERS
CRIMINCAL JUSTICE (CTF)	ANDY WOLK
CRIMSON KIMONO, THE	SAMUEL FULLER
CRIMSON KISS, THE - S	GEORGE E. SIMPSON
CRISIS	RICHARD BROOKS
CRITICAL CONDITION	ALAN SWYER
CRITICAL CONDITION	DENIS HAMILL
CRITICAL CONDITION	JOHN HAMILL
CRITICAL MASS - S	REX PICKETT
CRITICS CHOICE - S	STEVEN DE SOUZA
CRITTERS	STEPHEN HEREK
CRITTERS 2	D.T. TOWHY
CRITTERS 2	MICK GARRIS
CRITTERS 3 - S	DAVID J. SCHOW
CRITTERS 4 - S	DAVID J. SCHOW
CROCODILE DUNDEE	JOHN CORNELL
CROCODILE DUNDEE	KEN SHADIE
CROCODILE DUNDEE	PAUL HOGAN
CROCODILE DUNDEE II	BRETT HOGAN
CROCODILE DUNDEE II	PAUL HOGAN
CROMWELL	KEN HUGHES
CROOKED HEARTS	MICHAEL BORTMAN
CROOKED HOUSE - S	JILLIAN PALETHORPE
CROOKED HOUSE - S	SPARKY GREENE
CROOKED TREE, THE - S	DAVID BIRKE
CROOKS - S	JAY TARSES
CROOKS - S	TOM PATCHETT
CROOKS ANONYMOUS	JACK DAVIES
CROSS CREEK	DALENE YOUNG
CROSS FIRE	ANTHONY MAHARAJ
CROSS FIRE	NOAH BLOUGH
CROSS MY HEART	(1991)JACQUES FANSTEN
CROSS MY HEART	ARMYAN BERNSTEIN
CROSS MY HEART	GAIL PARENT
CROSS OF IRON	JULIUS J. EPSTEIN
CROSS OF LORRAINE, THE	MICHAEL KANIN
CROSS OF LORRAINE, THE	RING LARDNER JR.
CROSS-COUNTRY	LOGAN N. DANFORTH
CROSS-COUNTRY	WILLIAM GRAY
CROSS-KILLER, THE - S	MARCEL MONTECINO
CROSSED SWORDS	GEORGE MACDONALD FRASER
CROSSING - S	LAURENCE DWORET
CROSSING DELANCEY	SUSAN SANDLER
CROSSING NIAGARA	THOMAS POPE
CROSSING NIAGRA - S	LARRY MCMURTRY
CROSSING THE LINE - S	JOEL DAVIS
CROSSING, THE - S	MAX EISENBERG
CROSSINGS - S	ROBERT MARK KAMEN
CROSSOVER DREAMS	MANUEL ARCE
CROSSOVER DREAMS	LEON ICHASO
CROSSOVER DREAMS	RUBEN BLADES
CROSSROADS	JOHN FUSCO
CROSSTALK - S	STEVEN SODERBERGH
CROSSTOWN - S	PATRICIA RESNICK
CROWD ROARS, THE	JOHN BRIGHT†
CRUCIBLE, THE (P)	ARTHUR MILLER
CRUISE - S	JIM CARABATSOS
CRUISE - S	STEVEN SEAGAL
CRUISE CONTROL (P)	KEVIN WADE
CRUISING	WILLIAM FRIEDKIN
CRUMBS (SHORT)	VICKI HOCHBURG
CRUSADERS - S	MATTHEW DORFF
CRUSOE	CHRISTOPHER LOGUE
CRUSOE	WALON GREEN
CRY FREEDOM	JOHN BRILEY
CRY GORF - S	HERMAN RAUCHER
CRY IN THE DARK, A	FRED SCHEPISI
CRY IN THE DARK, A	ROBERT CASWELL
CRY IN THE WILD, A	CATHERINE CRYAN
CRY IN THE WILD, A	GARY PAULSEN
CRY OF THE BANSHEE	CHRISTOPHER WICKING
CRY OF THE CITY	RICHARD MURPHY
CRY OF THE PENGUINS	ANTHONY SHAFFER
CRY TERROR!	ANDREW STONE
CRY UNCLE	DAVID ODELL
CRY WILDERNESS	PHILIP YORDAN
CRY, THE	MICHELANGELO ANTONIONI
CRY-BABY	JOHN WATERS
CRYSTAL HEART	LINDA SHAYNE
CRYSTAL KNIGHTS - S	LESLIE BOHEM
CRYSTAL OR ASH, FIRE OR WIND...	LINA WERTMULLER
CUBA	CHARLES WOOD
CUBA AND HIS TEDDY BEAR (P)	REINALDO POVOD
CUJO	DON CARLOS DUNAWAY
CUJO	LAUREN CURRIER
CUL-DE-SAC	GERARD BRACH
CUL-DE-SAC	ROMAN POLANSKI
CULLA AND RINTHY - S	MICHAEL THOMAS
CULPEPPER CATTLE CO., THE	ERIC BERCOVICI
CUPID - S	LORNE CAMERON
CURACAO - S	JAMES D. BUCHANAN
CURIOSITY KILLS (CTF)	JOE BATTEER
CURIOUS CASE OF BENJAMIN BUTTON, THE - S	THOMAS POPE
CURIOUS GEORGE - S	MIKE WERB
CURIOUSITY KILLS (CTF)	JOHN RICE
CURLY SUE	JOHN HUGHES
CURRER BELL, ESQ. - S	WILLIAM LUCE
CURSE II: THE BITE	FEDERICO PROSPERI
CURSE II: THE BITE	SUSAN ZELOUF
CURSE OF FRANKENSTEIN, THE	JIMMY SANGSTER
CURSE OF GENIUS, THE - S	FREDERIC RAPHAEL
CURSE OF THE BLACK ROSE - S	ALLYN WARNER
CURSE OF THE MUMMY'S TOMB	MICHAEL CARRERAS
CURSE OF THE PINK PANTHER	BLAKE EDWARDS
CURSE OF THE PINK PANTHER	GEOFFREY EDWARDS
CURSE OF THE STARVING CLASS (P)	SAM SHEPARD
CURSE, THE	DAVID M. CHASKIN
CURTAIN CALL AT CACTUS CREEK	OSCAR BRODNEY
CURTAIN UP	JACK DAVIES
CURTAINS	ROBERT GUZA JR.
CURUCU, BEAST OF THE AMAZON	CURT SIODMAK
CUSTODY - S	GEORGE SAUNDERS
CUSTODY - S	JOHN BRYANT HEDBERG
CUSTODY - S	LINDSAY HARRISON
CUT OUT - S	JEFFREY C. SHERMAN
CUT WHORE KILLINGS	DAVID PEOPLES
CUTTER'S WAY	JEFFREY ALAN FISKIN
CUTTHROAT AND ZEBRA - S	BRADFORD O'NEIL
CUTTHROAT ISLAND - S	JIM GORMAN
CUTTHROAT ISLAND - S	MICHAEL BECKNER
CUTTING CLASS - S	STEVEN SLAVKIN
CUTTING EDGE, THE - S	R.M. BADAT
CYBORG	KITTY CHALMERS
CYCLE, THE - S	MICHAEL ERIC STEIN
CYCLONE	PAUL GARSON
CYCLONE	T.L. LANKFORD
CYCLONE - S	BRIAN STRASMANN
CYCLOPS	BERT I. GORDON
CYCLOPS - S	ROBERT F. SKOTAK
CYRANO DE BERGERAC	JEAN-CLAUDE CARRIERE
CYRANO DE BERGERAC	JEAN-PAUL RAPPENEAU

D

Title	Writer
D.A.R.Y.L.	DAVID AMBROSE
D.A.R.Y.L.	ALLAN G. SCOTT
D.C. CAB	TOPPER CAREW
D.C. CAB	JOEL SCHUMACHER
D.C. THRILLER - S	GARY THOMPSON
D.C. THRILLER - S	DON JAKOBY
D.C. THRILLER - S	JEB STUART
D.I., THE	JAMES LEE BARRETT†
D.O.A. (1988)	CHARLES EDWARD POGUE
D.O.A.	CLARENCE GREENE
D.O.A.	RUSSELL ROUSE†
DA	HUGH LEONARD
DA BOYS - S	FRANK PUGLIESE
DAD	GARY DAVID GOLDBERG
DAD'S THE NEW SAVIOR - S	ERIC SCHAEFFER
DADDY EMPIRE - S	HOWARD RODMAN
DADDY LONG LEGS (P)	CASEY KELLY
DADDY NOSTALGIA	COLO TAVERNIER O'HAGAN
DADDY'S BOY - S	ISRAEL HOROVITZ
DADDY'S BOYS	DARYL HANEY
DADDY'S DYIN', WHO'S GOT THE WILL?	DEL SHORES
DADDY'S GONE A-HUNTING	LARRY COHEN
DADDY'S GONE A-HUNTING	LORENZO SEMPLE
DADDY'S LITTLE GIRL - S	BILL GERBER
DAGGER, INC. - S	JOHN LAFIA
DAISY MILLER	FREDERIC RAPHAEL
DAKOTA	DARRYL KUNTZ
DAKOTA	LYNN KUNTZ
DAKOTA JACK - S	AMY WAGNER
DALLAS DEBS - S	JEFF BUHAI
DALLAS DEBS - S	STEVEN R. ZACHARIAS
DALLAS DEBUTANTE - S	JOHN HUGHES
DALLAS TEXANS - S	JOHN J. SCHALTER
DAMAGES - S	AARON SORKIN
DAMAGES - S	JONAS MCCORD
DAMIEN - OMEN II	MIKE HODGES
DAMIEN - OMEN II	STANLEY MANN
DAMN THE DEFIANT	NIGEL KNEALE
DAMN YANKEES - S	DAN JENKINS
DAMN YANKEES - S	BUD SHRAKE
DAMNATION ALLEY	ALAN SHARP
DAMNATION ALLEY	LUKAS HELLER†
DAMNED RIVER	BAYARD JOHNSON
DAMNED RIVER	JOHN CROWTHER
DAMNED, THE	RENE CLEMENT
DAMON - S	WILLIAM MASTROSIMONE
DAN HAZARD AND THE LEGION OF EVIL - S	GEORGE E. SIMPSON
DAN HAZARD AND THE LEGION OF EVIL - S	NEAL R. BURGER
DANCE AND THE RAILROAD, THE (P)	DAVID HENRY HWANG
DANCE FEVER - S	JOHN BEAIRD
DANCE OF THE DAMNED	ANDY RUBEN
DANCE OF THE DAMNED	KATT SHEA RUBEN
DANCE OF THE VAMPIRES	GERARD BRACH
DANCE OF THE VAMPIRES	ROMAN POLANSKI
DANCE SKINS - S	BABALOO MANDEL
DANCE SKINS - S	LOWELL GANZ
DANCE WITH A STRANGER	SHELAGH DELANEY
DANCE WITH ME OUTSIDE - S	LARRY MCMURTRY
DANCE, THE - S	JOHN HUGHES
DANCERS	SARAH KERNOCHAN
DANCER'S TOUCH - S	WALTER KLENHARD
DANCES WITH WOLVES	MICHAEL BLAKE
DANCIN' MAN - S	ANDY TENNANT
DANCIN' THRU THE DARK	WILLY RUSSELL
DANCING BANDIT, THE - S	J. MIYOKO HENSLEY
DANCING BANDIT, THE - S	STEVEN HENSLEY
DANCING BEAR, THE - S	TIM HUNTER
DANCING BEAR, THE - S	JIM CRUMLEY
DANCING IN THE DARK	LEON MARR
DANCING IN THE DARK - S	JAY TARSES
DANCING IN THE END ZONE (P)	BILL C. DAVIS
DANCING IN THE STREET - S	GEORGE ARMITAGE
DANCING LADY	ALLEN RIVKIN†
DANCING ON WATER	JOVAN ACIN
DANCING QUEEN - S	JEREMY IACONE
DANGER WITHIN	BRYAN FORBES
DANGER ZONE II	DULANY ROSS CLEMENTS
DANGER ZONE II	JASON WILLIAMS
DANGER ZONE II	TOM FRIEDMAN
DANGER ZONE III	GREGORY POIRIER
DANGER ZONE III	JASON WILLIAMS
DANGER, THE - S	ERIC ROTH
DANGER: MEMORY! (P)	ARTHUR MILLER
DANGERFIELD'S SAFARI - S	ROBERT BORIS
DANGEROUS EDGE, THE (CTF) - S	MICHAEL THOMAS
DANGEROUS GAME, A	JOHN EZRINE
DANGEROUS LIAISONS	CHRISTOPHER HAMPTON
DANGEROUS LIAISONS 1960	ROGER VADIM
DANGEROUS LIFE, A (CMS)	DAVID WILLIAMSON

Title	Author
DANGEROUS LOVE	MARTY OLLSTEIN
DANGEROUS MISSION	CHARLES BENNETT
DANGEROUS MOVES	RICHARD DEMBO
DANGEROUS PLACES - S	ERIC WESTON
DANGEROUS RELATIONS - S	JEREMY IACONE
DANGEROUS SUMMER, A - S	DAVID AMBROSE
DANGEROUS WOMAN, A - S	NAOMI FONER
DANGEROUSLY - S	BENNETT TRAMER
DANGEROUSLY - S	JACK EPPS JR.
DANGEROUSLY - S	JIM CASH
DANGEROUSLY - S	KEN FINKELMAN
DANGEROUSLY CLOSE	JOHN STOCKWELL
DANGEROUSLY CLOSE	MARTY ROSS
DANGEROUSLY CLOSE	SCOTT G. FIELDS
DANIEL	E.L. DOCTOROW
DANIELLA - S	MURDO LAIRD
DANNY AND THE DEEP BLUE SEA (P)	JOHN PATRICK SHANLEY
DANNY BOY	NEIL JORDAN
DANTON	AGNIESZKA HOLLAND
DANTON	JEAN-CLAUDE CARRIERE
DAREDEVILS OF THE GOLDEN LEGION - S	ALAN JAY GLUECKMAN
DAREDREAMER	BARRY CAILLIER
DAREDREAMER	PAT ROYCE
DAREDREAMER	TIM NOAH
DARK ANGEL - S	DON MACPHERSON
DARK ANGEL - S	DAVID KOEPP
DARK AT THE TOP OF THE STAIRS, THE	HARRIET FRANK JR.
DARK AT THE TOP OF THE STAIRS, THE	IRVING RAVETCH
DARK BACKWARD, THE	ADAM RIFKIN
DARK CITY	LAWRENCE B. MARCUS
DARK CITY - S	MICHAEL JENNING
DARK CRYSTAL, THE	DAVID ODELL
DARK CRYSTAL, THE (AF)	JIM HENSON†
DARK END OF THE STREET, THE	JAN EGLESON
DARK EYES	NIKITA MIKHALKOV
DARK HABITS	PEDRO ALMODOVAR
DARK HALF, THE	GEORGE A. ROMERO
DARK HORIZON, THE - S	SIMON MOORE
DARK MOON RISING - S	RICHARD DILELLO
DARK NIGHT, THE	CARLOS SAURA
DARK OBSESSION	TIM ROSE PRICE
DARK OF THE NIGHT	GAYLENE PRESTON
DARK PASSION	RENE BALCER
DARK PAST, THE	MALVIN WARD
DARK PAST, THE	OSCAR SAUL
DARK PONY (P)	DAVID MAMET
DARK STAR	DAN O' BANNON
DARK STAR	JOHN CARPENTER
DARK STREET - S	C. COURTNEY JOYNER
DARK TOWER	KEN WIEDERHORN
DARK TOWER	ROBERT J. AVRECH
DARK TOWN STRUTTERS	GEORGE B. ARMITAGE
DARK WATER	TONY GRISONI
DARK WIND - S	NEAL JIMENEZ
DARK WIND - S	MARK HOROWITZ
DARK, THE	STANFORD WHITMORE
DARKMAN	CHUCK PFAFFER
DARKMAN	DANIEL GOLDIN
DARKMAN	JOSHUA GOLDIN
DARKMAN	SAM RAIMI
DARKMAN	IVAN RAIMI
DARKNESS AT PEMBERLY - S	MICHAEL JENNING
DARLING	FREDERIC RAPHAEL
DARLING LILI	BLAKE EDWARDS
DARLING LILI	WILLIAM PETER BLATTY
DARLINGS OF THE GODS (CMS)	GRAEME FARMER
DARLINGS OF THE GODS (CMS)	ROGER SIMPSON
DAS BOOT	WOLFGANG PETERSEN
DATABANK - S	AVRAM DEAN GOLD
DATE WITH AN ANGEL	TOM MCLOUGHLIN
DATELINE: PARIS - S	GEOFFREY BAERE
DAUGHTER OF ROSIE O'GRADY, THE	JACK ROSE
DAUGHTER OF ROSIE O'GRADY, THE	MEL SHAVELSON
DAUGHTERS COURAGEOUS	JULIUS J. EPSTEIN
DAUGHTERS OF MUSIC - S	SALLIE GROO
DAUGHTERS OF THE DUST	JULIE DASH
DAVE - S	GARY ROSS
DAVID AND BATHSHEBA	PHILIP DUNNE
DAVID AND LISA	ELEANOR PERRY†
DAVID HOLZMAN'S DIARY	JIM MCBRIDE
DAVID HOLZMAN'S DIARY	L.M. KIT CARSON
DAVID SHOW, THE (P)	A.R. GURNEY
DAWN OF THE DEAD	GEORGE A. ROMERO
DAY AFTER HALLOWEEN, THE	EVERETT DEROCHE
DAY AT THE RACES, A	ROBERT PIROSH†
DAY BEFORE MIDNIGHT, THE - S	BRUCE EVANS
DAY BEFORE MIDNIGHT, THE - S	RAY GIDEON
DAY FOR NIGHT	SUZANNE SCHIFFMAN
DAY IN THE AFTERLIFE - S	CARL BINDER
DAY IN THE DEATH OF JOE EGG, A	PETER NICHOLS
DAY OF FURY, A	OSCAR BRODNEY
DAY OF THE ANIMALS, THE	ELEANOR NORTON
DAY OF THE ANIMALS, THE	WILLIAM NORTON
DAY OF THE DEAD	GEORGE A. ROMERO
DAY OF THE DOLPHIN, THE	BUCK HENRY
DAY OF THE EVIL GUN, THE	ERIC BERCOVICI
DAY OF THE JACKAL, THE	KENNETH ROSS
DAY OF THE LOCUST, THE	WALDO SALT†
DAY OF THE OUTLAW, THE	PHILIP YORDAN
DAY OF THE SUNS, THE - S	RUPERT WALTERS
DAY OF THE TRIFFIDS, THE	PHILIP YORDAN
DAY THE CLOWN CRIED, THE	JERRY LEWIS
DAY THE EARTH CAUGHT FIRE, THE	VAL GUEST
DAY THE EARTH CAUGHT FIRE, THE	WOLF MANKOWITZ
DAY THE EARTH STOOD STILL, THE - S	KEVIN QUINN
DAY THE EARTH STRUCK BACK, THE - S	HERB FREED
DAY THE FISH CAME OUT, THE	MICHAEL CACOYANNIS
DAY THE INDIANS BEAT ST. LOUIS, THE - S	ROBERT BORIS
DAY THE SUN DIED, THE (CTF) - S	DENNIS L. CLARK
DAY THEY ROBBED THE BANK OF ENGLAND, THE	RICHARD MAIBAUM†
DAY TIME ENDED, THE	J. LARRY CARROLL
DAY TIME ENDED, THE	STEVEN NEILL
DAY TIME ENDED, THE	WAYNE SCHMIDT
DAY TIME ENDED, THE	DAVID SCHMOELLER
DAY WORLD - S	WILLIAM WISHER
DAYBREAK - S	STEPHEN M. TOLKIN
DAYBREAKER - S	JOHN RAFFO
DAYDREAMS - S	LESLIE BOHEM
DAYLIGHTING - S	LEORA BARISH
DAYS AND NIGHTS OF A FRENCH HORN PLAYER - S	MURRAY SCHISGAL
DAYS OF AWE - S	ANTHONY GITTLESON
DAYS OF AWE - S	CELIA GITTLESON
DAYS OF HEAVEN	TERENCE MALICK
DAYS OF THUNDER	TOM CRUISE
DAYS OF THUNDER	ROBERT TOWNE
DAYTIME - S	PETER MARTIN WORTMANN
DAYTIME - S	ROBERT CONTE
DAYWORLD - S	DENNIS FELDMAN
DAYWORLD - S	DONOVAN MOORE
DE SADE	RICHARD MATHESON
DEAD AGAIN	A. SCOTT FRANK
DEAD AIR - S	DAVID EPSTEIN
DEAD AND BURIED	ALEX STERN
DEAD AND BURIED	JEFF MILLAR
DEAD AND BURIED	DAN O' BANNON
DEAD AND BURIED	RONALD SHUSETT
DEAD BANG	ROBERT O. FOSTER
DEAD BEAUTY - S	JULIAN BARRY
DEAD CALM	TERRY HAYES
DEAD END - S	TONY KENRICK
DEAD END CITY	MICHAEL BOGERT
DEAD END CITY	PETER YUVAL
DEAD END DRIVE-IN	PETER SMALLEY
DEAD EVEN - S	MARCI KETCHEL
DEAD EVEN - S	MIKE KETCHEL
DEAD FROM THE NECK UP - S	STEVEN SODERBERGH
DEAD GIRLS - S	PAUL THEROUX
DEAD GIVEAWAY - S	GINNY CERRELLA
DEAD GIVEAWAY - S	RICHERD KLEINBERG
DEAD GROUND - S	THOMAS LEE WRIGHT
DEAD HEAT	TERRY BLACK
DEAD HEAT OF SUMMER - S	CHARLES ROBERT CARNER
DEAD HEAT ON A MERRY-GO-ROUND	BERNARD GIRARD
DEAD KIDS	MICHAEL LAUGHLIN
DEAD KIDS	WILLIAM CONDON
DEAD MAN WALKING	RICK MARX
DEAD MAN'S BAY - S	DARRYL WIMBERLY
DEAD MEN DON'T DIE	MALCOLM MARMORSTEIN
DEAD MEN DON'T WEAR PLAID	CARL REINER
DEAD MEN DON'T WEAR PLAID	GEORGE GIPE
DEAD MEN DON'T WEAR PLAID	STEVE MARTIN
DEAD OF NIGHT - S	DANIEL H. VINING
DEAD OF NIGHT, THE - S	DARRIN OURA
DEAD OF SUMMER - S	CHRIS KEYSER
DEAD OF WINTER	MARK MALONE
DEAD ON THE MONEY (CTF)	GAVIN LAMBERT
DEAD OR ALIVE (CTF) - S	KEVIN JARRE
DEAD PIGEONS ON BEETHOVEN STREET	SAMUEL FULLER
DEAD POETS SOCIETY	TOM SCHULMAN
DEAD POOL, THE	DURK PEARSON
DEAD POOL, THE	SANDY SHAW
DEAD POOL, THE	STEVE SHARON
DEAD RECKONING (CTF)	ANDIE MCCUAIG
DEAD RECKONING (CTF)	NEIL D. HICKS
DEAD RECKONING - S	JIM UHLS
DEAD RECKONING - S	STEVEN E. DESOUZA
DEAD RINGERS	DAVID CRONENBERG
DEAD RINGERS	NORMAN SNIDER
DEAD SECTOR - S	DONALD L. STEWART
DEAD SOLID PERFECT (CTF)	BOBBY ROTH
DEAD SOLID PERFECT (CTF)	DAN JENKINS
DEAD WOMEN IN LINGERIE	JOHN ROMO
DEAD WOMEN IN LINGERIE	ERICA FOX
DEAD ZONE, THE	JEFFREY BOAM
DEAD, THE	JANET ROACH
DEAD, THE	TONY HUSTON
DEADBEATS - S	MICHAEL JENNING
DEADFALL	BRYAN FORBES
DEADHEAD MILES	TERENCE MALICK
DEADLIER THAN THE MALE	JIMMY SANGSTER
DEADLIEST SIN, THE	KEN HUGHES
DEADLINE	HANAN PELED
DEADLINE USA	RICHARD BROOKS
DEADLY BEES, THE	ROBERT BLOCH
DEADLY BLESSING	GLENN M. BENEST
DEADLY BLESSING	MATTHEW F. BARR
DEADLY BLESSING	WES CRAVEN
DEADLY DANCER	DAVID HALPERN
DEADLY DANCER	DAVID HEAVENER
DEADLY DANCER	MARIA FIELDS
DEADLY DESIRE (CTF)	JERRY LUDWIG
DEADLY DESIRE (CTF)	TOBY LUDWIG
DEADLY ERNEST - S	HENRY C. PARKE
DEADLY EYES	CHARLES H. EGLEE
DEADLY FORCE	BARRY SCHNEIDER
DEADLY FORCE	KENNETH G. BLACKWELL
DEADLY FORCE	ROBERT VINCENT O'NEIL
DEADLY FORCE - S	ALLAN R. FOLSOM
DEADLY FRIEND	BRUCE JOEL RUBIN
DEADLY GAME (CTF)	WES CLARRIDGE
DEADLY HONEYMOON - S	STEPHEN KRONISH
DEADLY HONEYMOON - S	W.D. RICHTER
DEADLY ILLUSION	LARRY COHEN
DEADLY INHERITANCE, THE - S	JOHN BRILEY
DEADLY INTENT	JOHN GOFF
DEADLY METAL - S	MEL FRIEDMAN
DEADLY OBSESSION	BRIAN COX
DEADLY OBSESSION	JENO HODI
DEADLY OBSESSION	PAUL WOLANSKY
DEADLY TRACKERS, THE	LUKAS HELLER†
DEADLY WEAPON	GEORGE LAFIA
DEADLY WEAPON	MICHAEL MINER
DEADWOOD - S	PETE DEXTER
DEADWOOD - S	ALLEN HOLLEB
DEAL OF THE CENTURY	PAUL BRICKMAN
DEALERS	ANDREW MACLEAR
DEALING: OR THE BERKELEY-TO-BOSTON FORTY-BRICK LOST-BAG BLUES	DAVID ODELL
DEAR AMERICA: LETTERS HOME FROM VIETNAM (FD)	BILL COUTURIE
DEAR AMERICA: LETTERS HOME FROM VIETNAM (FD)	RICHARD DEWHURST
DEAR BRIGITTE	HAL KANTER
DEAR DEAD DELILAH	JOHN FARRIS
DEAR DETECTIVE	PHILLIPE DE BROCA
DEAR INSPECTOR	PHILLIPE DE BROCA
DEAR JOHNNY POGUE - S	E. MAX FRYE
DEATH BECOMES HER - S	DAVID KOEPP
DEATH BECOMES HER - S	MARTIN DONOVAN
DEATH BEFORE DISHONOR	JOHN GATLIFF
DEATH BEFORE DISHONOR	LAWRENCE KUBIK
DEATH BY INVITATION	KEN FRIEDMAN
DEATH COMES TO THE END - S	ANTHONY SHAFFER
DEATH DEFYING T.S. BABCOCK - S	DAN JENKINS
DEATH DREAMS (CTF)	ROBERT GLASS
DEATH HUNT	MARK VICTOR
DEATH HUNT	MICHAEL GRAIS
DEATH IN BRUNSWICK	JOHN RUANE
DEATH IN SMALL DOSES	JOHN MCGREEVY

Da-De

FILM WRITERS GUIDE

INDEX OF FILM TITLES

337

De-Di

FILM WRITERS GUIDE

INDEX OF FILM TITLES

Title	Writer
DEATH IN THE DANCING LIGHTS - S	JEFF LEWIS
DEATH IN THE DESERT - S	THOMAS BABE
DEATH MAKES THE CHART - S	CHARLIE HAAS
DEATH OF A BUICK - S	JOHN BUNZEL
DEATH OF A DIRTY BLONDE - S	LARRY KETRON
DEATH OF A SALESMAN (P)	ARTHUR MILLER
DEATH OF A SOLDIER	WILLIAM NAGLE
DEATH OF A STOCKBROKER - S	DJORDJE MILICEVIC
DEATH OF AN AMERICAN - S	MICHAEL WELLER
DEATH OF AN ANGEL	PETRU POPESCU
DEATH OF MARIO RICCI, THE	CLAUDE GORETTA
DEATH OF ME YET - S	RICHARD WHITLEY
DEATH OF ROCK & ROLL - S	MENNO MEYJES
DEATH OF THE SNOW QUEEN, THE - S	STEWART STERN
DEATH ON THE NILE	ANTHONY SHAFFER
DEATH PROBE - S	JOHN P. GROVES
DEATH SHIP	DAVID P. LEWIS
DEATH SHIP	JACK HILL
DEATH SHIP	JOHN M. ROBINS
DEATH SHIP, THE - S	MICHAEL AUERBACH
DEATH TRACK - S	ROBERT CARRINGTON
DEATH VALLEY	RICHARD ROTHSTEIN
DEATH WARRANT	DAVID S. GOYER
DEATH WATCH	BERTRAND TAVERNIER
DEATH WEEKEND	WILLIAM FRUET
DEATH WISH	WENDELL MAYES
DEATH WISH II	DAVID ENGELBACH
DEATH WISH 3	MICHAEL EDMONDS
DEATH WISH 4	GAIL MORGAN HICKMAN
DEATH WITH BRUSH, A - S	KEN SCHAFER
DEATHBIRTH OF HOUDINI, THE - S	WILLIAM GOODHART
DEATHCATHALON - S	NEIL RUTTENBERG
DEATHDREAM	ALAN ORMSBY
DEATHROW GAMESHOW	MARK PIRRO
DEATHSPORT	DONALD L. STEWART
DEATHSTALKER	HOWARD R. COHEN
DEATHSTALKER II	HOWARD R. COHEN
DEATHSTALKER II	JIM WYNORSKI
DEATHSTALKER II	NEIL RUTTENBERG
DEATHTRAP (1982)	JAY PRESSON ALLEN
DEATHTRAP (1976)	ALVIN L. FAST
DEATHTRAP (1976)	MARDI RUSTAM
DEATHWATCH	DAVID RAYFIEL
DEATHWORK - S	ROBERT CARRINGTON
DEBS - S	GEORGE GALLO
DEBUTANTE BALL, THE (P)	BETH HENLEY
DECEIVERS, THE	MICHAEL HIRST
DECEMBER - S	GABE TORRES
DECEMBER BRIDE	DAVID RUDKIN
DECEPTION - S	STEPHEN VERONA
DECEPTION - S	MARK MEDOFF
DECEPTION - S	REX MCGEE
DECEPTIONS (CTF)	KEN DENBOW
DECEPTIONS (CTF)	RICHARD TAYLOR
DECISION BEFORE DAWN	PETER VIERTEL
DECKS RAN RED, THE	ANDREW STONE
DECLINE OF THE AMERICAN EMPIRE, THE	DENYS ARCAND
DECOY - S	REX PICKETT
DEDMAN - S	RICHARD MATHESON
DEEP ARE THE ROOTS (P)	ARNAUD D'USSEAU†
DEEP COVER - S	HENRY S. BEAN
DEEP COVER - S	MICHAEL L. TOLKIN
DEEP COVER - S	JEFF BUHAI
DEEP COVER - S	STEVEN R. ZACHARIAS
DEEP ELLUM - S	WILLIAM D. WITTLIFF
DEEP END	JERZY SKOLIMOWSKI
DEEP IN THE HEART	TONY GARNETT
DEEP SPACE	CATHERINE CRYAN
DEEP SPACE	FRED OLEN RAY
DEEP SPACE	T.L. LANKFORD
DEEP TROPICAL TAN, A (P)	JOHN STEPPLING
DEEP TROUBLE - S	BRUCE JAY FRIEDMAN
DEEP TROUBLE - S	MICHAEL KANE
DEEP UMBRA - S	ROY CARLSON
DEEP WATERS	RICHARD MURPHY
DEEP WORK - S	HARV ZIMMEL
DEEP, THE	PETER BENCHLEY
DEEP, THE	TRACY KEENAN WYNN
DEEP II, THE - S	MICHAEL KANE
DEEP, THE (SEQUEL) - S	DAVID Z. GOODMAN
DEEPSTAR SIX	GEOF MILLER
DEEPSTAR SIX	LEWIS ABERNATHY
DEER HUNTER, THE	LOUIS GARFINKLE
DEER HUNTER, THE	MICHAEL CIMINO
DEER HUNTER, THE	QUINN REDEKER
DEER HUNTER, THE	DERIC WASHBURN
DEER PARK - S	JOAN DIDION
DEER PARK - S	JOHN GREGORY DUNNE
DEERSLAYER - S	DAVID MAMET
DEF BY TEMPTATION	JAMES BOND III
DEF-COM 4	PAUL DONOVAN
DEFENCELESS UNDER THE NIGHT - S	LEE DRYSDALE
DEFENDANT - S	TERREL SELTZER
DEFENDING YOUR LIFE	ALBERT BROOKS
DEFENSE OF THE REALM	MARTIN STELLMAN
DEFENSE PLAY	AUBREY SOLOMON
DEFENSE PLAY	STEVE GREENBERG
DEFENSELESS - S	JAMES CRESSON
DEFIANCE	THOMAS M. DONNELLY
DEFIER OF FATE, THE - S	CHARLES ROBERT CARNER
DEJA VU	ANTHONY RICHMOND
DEJA VU	ARNOLD SCHMIDT
DEJA VU	EZRA D. RAPPAPORT
DELAYED REACTION - S	ROBERT GARLAND
DELERIUM - S	GREGORY C. WIDEN
DELICATE ARRANGEMENTS - S	BARRY MORROW
DELICATE BALANCE, A	EDWARD ALBEE
DELICATE DELINQUENT, THE	DON MCGUIRE
DELICATE LINK, A - S	C. COURTNEY JOYNER
DELINQUENTS, THE	CLAYTON S. FROHMAN
DELINQUENTS, THE	MAC GUDGEON
DELIRIOUS	FRED FREEMAN
DELIRIOUS	LAWRENCE J. COHEN
DELIRIUM	EDDIE KRELL
DELIRIUM	JIM LOEW
DELIRIUM	RICHARD YALEM
DELIVERY BOY - S	CHARLES FRADIN
DELIVERY BOYS	KEN HANDLER
DELTA FORCE 2	LEE D. REYNOLDS
DELTA FORCE, THE	JAMES BRUNER
DELTA FORCE, THE	MENAHEM GOLAN
DELTA OF VENUS - S	COLO TAVERNIER O'HAGAN
DELTA OF VENUS - S	SARAH M. KERNOCHAN
DELUSION	CARL COLPAERT
DELUSION	KURT VOSS
DELUSION (1981)	JACK VIERTEL
DEM BUMS (P)	FRANK PUGLIESE
DEMENTIA 13	FRANCIS FORD COPPOLA
DEMETRIUS AND THE GLADIATORS	PHILIP DUNNE
DEMOCRACY - S	ALICE ARLEN
DEMOLISHED MAN, THE - S	BRIAN DEPALMA
DEMOLISHED MAN, THE - S	OLIVER STONE
DEMOLITION MAN - S	PETER LENKOV
DEMON	LARRY COHEN
DEMON - S	DARRIN OURA
DEMON SEED	ROGER O. HIRSON
DEMON SEED	ROBERT JAFFE
DEN OF BEASTS, THE	AKIRA KUROSAWA
DENIAL	ERIN DIGNAM
DEPARTMENT STORE - S	ED HUME
DEPRAVED, THE	BRIAN CLEMENS
DEPUTY - S	KEVIN QUINN
DER HIMMEL UBER BERLIN	PETER HANDKE
DER HIMMEL UBER BERLIN	WIM WENDERS
DERANGED	ALAN ORMSBY
DERSU UZALA	AKIRA KUROSAWA
DESCENDING ANGEL (CTF)	GRACE WOODARD
DESCENDING ANGEL (CTF)	ROBERT SIEGAL
DESCENT, THE - S	BRADLEY RAND SMITH
DESERT BLOOM	LINDA REMY
DESERT BLOOM	EUGENE CORR
DESERT HEARTS	NATALIE COOPER
DESERT LEGION	IRVING WALLACE†
DESERT RATS, THE	RICHARD MURPHY
DESERT ROSE - S	LARRY MCMURTRY
DESERT WARRIOR	FREDERICK BAILEY
DESERTER, THE	CLAIR HUFFAKER†
DESIGNATED HITTER - S	STEPHEN KATZ
DESIRE - S	FRANK R. PIERSON
DESIRE - S	FREDERIC RAPHAEL
DESIRE - S	HENRY BEAN
DESIRE - S	LEORA BARISH
DESIREE	DANIEL TARADASH
DESPAIR	TOM STOPPARD
DESPERADO - S	STEPHEN H. FOREMAN
DESPERATE - S	NEIL COHEN
DESPERATE CHARACTERS	FRANK D. GILROY
DESPERATE HOURS	JOSEPH HAYES
DESPERATE HOURS	LARRY KONNER
DESPERATE HOURS	MARK ROSENTHAL
DESPERATE HOURS, THE	JOSEPH HAYES
DESPERATE LIVING	JOHN WATERS
DESPERATELY SEEKING SUSAN	LEORA BARISH
DESTINIES - S	DENNE BART PETITCLERC
DESTINY EXPRESS - S	HOWARD RODMAN
DESTROYER, THE - S	LORENZO SEMPLE
DETECTIVE	ANNE-MARIE MIEVILLE
DETECTIVE	JEAN-LUC GODARD
DETECTIVE	PHILIPPE SETBON
DETECTIVE SCHOOL DROPOUTS	DAVID LANDSBERG
DETECTIVE SCHOOL DROPOUTS	LORIN H. DREYFUSS
DETECTIVE STORY	PHILIP YORDAN
DETECTIVE, THE	ABBY MANN
DETONATOR - S	MICHAEL J. AUERBACH
DETROIT - S	LEIGH CHAPMAN
DETROIT ABE - S	BRUCE JAY FRIEDMAN
DETROIT ROLL (SHORT)	JOSEPH W. SAVINO
DEVIL AND MAX DEVLIN, THE	JIMMY SANGSTER
DEVIL AND MAX DEVLIN, THE	MARY RODGERS
DEVIL AND THE DEEP BLUE SEA - S	ROBERT GINTY
DEVIL IN THE FLESH	MARCO BELLOCCHIO
DEVIL ON THE RUN - S	PETER SUMMERS
DEVIL PUPS - S	DAVID CHISOLM
DEVIL SHIP PIRATES	JIMMY SANGSTER
DEVIL'S ADVOCATE - S	KEVIN KELTON
DEVIL'S ADVOCATE, THE - S	ALEX AYRES - S
DEVIL'S BARGAIN - S	TIM MCCANLIES
DEVIL'S BRIDE, THE	RICHARD MATHESON
DEVIL'S BRIGADE	WILLIAM ROBERTS
DEVIL'S EIGHT, THE	JOHN MILLIUS
DEVIL'S EIGHT, THE	WILLARD HUYCK
DEVIL'S EYE, THE	INGMAR BERGMAN
DEVIL'S FOOD - S	DEBRA FRANKEL
DEVIL'S HAIRPIN, THE	CORNEL WILDE†
DEVIL'S HIGHWAY - S	ETHAN WILEY
DEVIL'S ISLAND - S	LEM DOBBS
DEVIL'S OWN, THE	NIGEL KNEALE
DEVIL'S OWN, THE - S	KEVIN JARRE
DEVIL'S PLAYGROUND, THE	FRED SCHEPISI
DEVIL'S PLAYGROUND, THE - S	DAVID MICKEY EVANS
DEVIL'S PLAYGROUND - S	MARCI KETCHEL
DEVIL'S PLAYGROUND - S	MIKE KETCHEL
DEVIL'S WANTON, THE	INGMAR BERGMAN
DEVILS EYE, THE - S	R.M. BADAT
DEVILS, THE	KEN RUSSELL
DEVONSVILLE TERROR, THE	ULLI LOMMEL
DEXTERITY - S	KAREN CRONER
DI, THE	JAMES LEE BARRETT†
DIABOLO MENTHE	DIANE KURYS
DIAL TONE - S	DAVID S. WARD
DIAMOND MAN - S	ROBERT BORIS
DIAMOND SKULLS	TIM ROSE PRICE
DIAMOND'S EDGE	ANTHONY HOROWITZ
DIAMONDS	DAVID PAULSEN
DIAMONDS	MENAHEM GOLAN
DIAMONDS - S	RICHARD KLETTER
DIAMONDS ARE FOREVER	RICHARD MAIBAUM†
DIAMONDS ARE FOREVER	TOM MANKIEWICZ
DIAMONDS FOR BREAKFAST	RONALD HARWOOD
DIARY OF A CHAMBERMAID, THE	JEAN-CLAUDE CARRIERE
DIARY OF A COUNTRY PRIEST	ROBERT BRESSON
DIARY OF A MAD HOUSEWIFE, THE	ELEANOR PERRY†
DICE RULES (FD)	ANDREW DICE CLAY
DICK AND THE DOC, THE - S	ALAN JAY GLUECKMAN
DICK TRACY	JACK EPPS JR.
DICK TRACY	JIM CASH
DICK TURPIN - S	MICHAEL THOMAS
DIM SUM: A LITTLE BIT OF HEART	WAYNE WANG
DID SHE LEAVE ME ANY MONEY? - S	WLL ALDIS
DIE BLEIRNE ZEIT	MARGARETHE VON TROTTA
DIE FALSCHUNG	VOLKER SCHLONDORFF
DIE HARD	JEB STUART
DIE HARD	STEVEN DE SOUZA
DIE HARD 2: DIE HARDER	DOUG RICHARDSON
DIE HARD 2: DIE HARDER	STEVEN DE SOUZA
DIE LAUGHING	JERRY SEGAL
DIE LAUGHING	ROBBY BENSON
DIE LAUGHING	SCOTT PARKER
DIE, DIE, MY DARLING	RICHARD MATHESON
DIESHOT - S	JOE ESZTERHAS
DIFFERENT RULES - S	JAMES D. BUCHANAN
DIFFERENT STORY, A	HENRY OLEK
DIGBY (P)	JOSEPH DOUGHERTY
DILLINGER	PHILIP YORDAN
DILLINGER	JOHN MILIUS
DILLINGER & CAPONE - S	MICHAEL B. DRUXMAN

Title	Writer
DIM SUM: A LITTLE BIT OF HEART	TERREL SELTZER
DIMENSION OF MIRACLES - S	MARTIN OLSON
DINER	BARRY LEVINSON
DINGO	MARC ROSENBERG
DINGUS, THE - S	LAWRENCE HAUBEN
DINING ROOM, THE (P)	A.R. GURNEY
DINNER AT EIGHT (CTF)	TOM GRIFFIN
DINNER AT THE HOMESICK RESTAURANT - S	HUME CRONYN
DINNER AT THE HOMESICK RESTAURANT - S	STEVEN M. KUNES
DINNER AT THE HOMESICK RESTAURANT - S	SUSAN COOPER
DINOSAUR (AF) - S	WALON GREEN
DINOSAUR WINE - S	DAN JENKINS
DINOSAUR WINE - S	BUD SHRAKE
DINOSAURS - S	GINA WENDKOS
DION BROTHERS, THE	TERENCE MALICK
DIPLOMANIACS	JOSEPH L. MANKIEWICZ
DIPLOMATIC IMMUNITY	RANDALL FRAKES
DIPLOMATIC IMMUNITY	RICHARD DONN
DIPLOMATIC IMMUNITY - S	BOB GALE
DIPLOMATIC IMMUNITY - S	DENIS HAMILL
DIPLOMATIC IMMUNITY - S	FIONA LEWIS
DIPLOMATIC IMMUNITY - S	HEYWOOD GOULD
DIPLOMATIC IMMUNITY - S	JOHN HAMILL
DIRE STRAITS - S	MICHAEL ELIAS
DIRE STRAITS - S	RICHARD EUSTIS
DIRE STRAITS - S	TONY KAYDEN
DIRECT TO THE TOP - S	STAN SEIDEL
DIRT BIKE KID, THE	DAVID BRANDES
DIRT BIKE KID, THE	LEWIS A. COLICK
DIRTY DANCING	ELEANOR BERGSTEIN
DIRTY DANCING II - S	SARA KRANE
DIRTY DANCING II - S	JUDITH FEIN
DIRTY DINGUS MAGEE	JOSEPH HELLER†
DIRTY DINGUS MAGEE	FRANK WALDMAN†
DIRTY DINGUS MAGEE	TOM WALDMAN†
DIRTY DOZEN	LUKAS HELLER†
DIRTY DUCK (AF)	CHARLES SWENSON
DIRTY EDDIE - S	DAVID ODELL
DIRTY FIVE - S	JACK EPPS JR.
DIRTY FIVE - S	JIM CASH
DIRTY HARRY	DEAN RIESNER
DIRTY LAUNDRY - S	PETE HAMILL
DIRTY LITTLE BILLY	STAN DRAGOTI
DIRTY MARY, CRAZY LARRY	LEIGH CHAPMAN
DIRTY ROTTEN SCOUNDRELS	PAUL W. HENNING
DIRTY ROTTEN SCOUNDRELS	STANLEY SHAPIRO†
DIRTY ROTTEN SCOUNDRELS	DALE LAUNER
DIRTY SECRETS - S	DAVID H. SMILOW
DIRTY TRICKS	CAMILLE GIFFORD
DIRTY TRICKS	ELEANOR ELIAS NORTON
DIRTY TRICKS	THOMAS GIFFORD
DIRTY TRICKS	WILLIAM NORTONSR.
DIRTY TRICKS - S	JILLIAN PALETHORPE
DIRTY TRICKS - S	SPARKY GREENE
DISABILITY: A COMEDY (P)	RON WHYTE†
DISAPPEARANCE OF THE USS MAKO, THE - S	STANFORD SHERMAN
DISAPPEARANCE, THE	PAUL MAYERSBERG
DISAPPEARANCE, THE - S	ROSIE SHUSTER
DISCOVERY BAY	REED STEINER
DISCREET CHARM OF THE BOURGEOISIE	JEAN-CLAUDE CARRIERE
DISCREET COMPANY - S	TOM CAMP
DISORDERLIES	MARK L. FELDBERG
DISORDERLIES	MITCHELL S. KLEBANOFF
DISORGANIZED CRIME	JIM KOUF
DISSENTING NUDE - S	LAWRENCE HAUBEN
DISSIDENTS - S	NEAL SHUSTERMAN
DISTANT MUSIC - S	CAROLINE THOMPSON
DISTANT RELATIVE - S	GAIL FISHER
DISTANT RELATIVE - S	MARC CHESLER
DISTANT SHORE, THE - S	KURT LUEDTKE
DISTANT SHORES - S	MORRIE RUVINSKY
DISTANT THUNDER	DEEDEE WEHLE
DISTANT THUNDER	ROBERT STITZEL
DISTANT VOICES, STILL LIVES	TERENCE DAVIES
DISTORTION - S	ROBERT RODAT
DISTRICT, THE - S	ROBERT BORIS
DISTURBED	CHARLES WINKLER
DISTURBED	EMERSON BIXBY
DISTURBING THE PEACE - S	DAVID MISCH
DIVA	JEAN-JACQUES BEINEIX
DIVA, THE - S	MICHAEL THOMAS
DIVE, THE - S	RON BASS
DIVERSIONS - S	JOEL DAVIS
DIVERSIONS - S	DENIS HAMILL
DIVERSIONS - S	JOHN HAMILL
DIVIDED WE FALL	JEFF BURR
DIVIDING LINE - S	JACK EPPS JR.
DIVIDING LINE - S	JIM CASH
DIVINE COMEDY - S	HILARY HENKIN
DIVINE MADNESS	BETTE MIDLER
DIVINE MADNESS	JERRY BLATT
DIVINE MADNESS	BRUCE VILANCH
DIVING IN	ERIC EDSON
DIVISION STREET (P)	STEVE TESICH
DIVORCE AMERICAN STYLE	NORMAN LEAR
DIVORCE PENDING - S	DARRIN OURA
DIVORCED WOMEN - S	JEAN VALLELY
DNA - S	JOHN MCCORMICK
DNA - S	ROSS LA MANNA
DO IT FOR THE MONEY - S	A.M. COLLINS
DO OR DIE	ANDY SIDARIS
DO OR DIE - S	THOMAS LEE WRIGHT
DO THE RIGHT THING	SPIKE LEE
DO YOU LIKE WOMEN?	GERARD BRACH
DO YOU LIKE WOMEN?	ROMAN POLANSKI
DOBERMAN GANG, THE	FRANK RAY PERILLI
DOBERMAN GANG, THE	LOUIS GARFINKLE
DOC	PETE HAMILL
DOC HOLLYWOOD	DANIEL PYNE
DOC HOLLYWOOD	JEFFREY PRICE
DOC HOLLYWOOD	PETER S. SEAMAN
DOCK BRIEF, THE	JOHN MORTIMER
DOCTOR AND THE DEVILS, THE	RONALD HARWOOD
DOCTOR AT SEA	JACK DAVIES
DOCTOR DETROIT	BRUCE JAY FRIEDMAN
DOCTOR DETROIT	CARL GOTTLIEB
DOCTOR DETROIT	ROBERT BORIS
DOCTOR GLAS	MAI ZETTERLING
DOCTOR IN CLOVER	JACK DAVIES
DOCTOR IN TROUBLE	JACK DAVIES
DOCTOR MORDRED - S	CHARLES BAND
DOCTOR MORDRID - S	C. COURTNEY JOYNER
DOCTOR ZHIVAGO	ROBERT BOLT
DOCTOR'S WIVES	DANIEL TARADASH
DOCTOR, THE	ROBERT CASWELL
DOCTORS IN HOLLYWOOD - S	GAIL PARENT
DOCUMENTEUR: AN EMOTION PICTURE	AGNES VARDA
DODES'KA'DEN	AKIRA KUROSAWA
DOG DAY AFTERNOON	FRANK R. PIERSON
DOG ROBBERS - S	NICK W. THIEL
DOG TAGS	ROMANO SCAVOLINI
DOG WHO CRIED WOLF - S	DON MANCINI
DOGFIGHT	ROBERT J. COMFORT
DOGFIGHT (P)	JAMES KENNEDY
DOGPOUND SHUFFLE	JEFFREY BLOOM
DOGS IN SPACE	RICHARD LOWENSTEIN
DOGS OF WAR, THE	GARY DEVORE
DOGS OF WAR, THE	GEORGE MALKO
DOHYO-MATSURI	AKIRA KUROSAWA
DOIN' TIME	DEE CARUSO
DOIN' TIME	FRANELLE SILVER
DOIN' TIME	RON ZWANG
DOIN' TIME ON PLANET EARTH	DARREN STAR
DOING BUSINESS - S	SUZANNE OSHRY
DOLL FACE - S	G. ROSS PARKER
DOLL'S HOUSE, A	CHRISTOPHER HAMPTON
DOLLAR BOTTOM, THE	SHANE CONNAUGHTON
DOLLARS	RICHARD BROOKS
DOLLS	ED NAHA
DOMENICA D'AGOSTO	FRANCO BRUSATI
DOMESTIC RELATIONS - S	ALAN MANDEL
DOMINANT GENES - S	GEORGE GIPE
DOMINICK AND EUGENE	DANNY PORFIRO
DOMINICK AND EUGENE	ALVIN SARGENT
DOMINICK AND EUGENE	COREY BLECHMAN
DOMINO PRINCIPLE, THE	ADAM KENNEDY
DON COYOTE- S	ALLAN G. SCOTT
DON JUAN IN NEW YORK (P)	EDUARDO MACHADO
DONNIE BRASCO - S	PAUL ATTANSIO
DON'S PARTY	DAVID WILLIAMSON
DON'T BOTHER TO KNOCK	DANIEL TARADASH
DON'T CRY, IT'S ONLY THUNDER	PAL HENSLER
DON'T DRINK THE WATER (P)	WOODY ALLEN
DON'T HOLD BACK - S	JACK BARAN
DON'T HOLD BACK - S	LEO GAREN
DON'T LOOK NOW	CHRIS BRYANT
DON'T LOOK NOW	ALLAN G. SCOTT
DON'T LOOK NOW...WE'RE BEING SHOT AT	GERARD OURY
DON'T MAKE WAVES	GEORGE KIRGO
DON'T PANIC, CHAPS!	JACK DAVIES
DON'T SAY A WORD - S	ANDREW KLAVAN
DON'T TELL MOM THE BABYSITTER'S DEAD	NEIL LANDAU
DON'T TELL MOM THE BABYSITTER'S DEAD	TERA ISON
DON'T THINK TWICE - S	TONY KAYDEN
DONA FLOR AND HER TWO HUSBANDS	BRUNO BARRETO
DONA HERLINDA AND HER TWO SONS	JAIME H. HERMOSILLO
DONDI	ALBERT ZUGSMITH
DONKEY SKIN	JACQUES DEMY†
DONNY QUICK - S	BILL CORBETT
DONOR, THE - S	ROBERT CARRINGTON
DOOLITTLE & STICK - S	MOLLY-ANN LEIKIN
DOOMSDAY CONSPIRACY, THE - S	JIM THOMAS
DOOMSDAY CONSPIRACY, THE - S	JOHN THOMAS
DOOMWATCH	CLIVE EXTON
DOONESBURY, AMUSICAL COMEDY (P)	GARRY TRUDEAU
DOORNAIL - S	MICHAEL PART
DOORS, THE	OLIVER STONE
DOORS, THE	RANDY JOHNSON
DORIS - S	ROBERT M. ULIN
DORM THAT DRIPPED BLOOD, THE	STACEY GIACHINO
DORM THAT DRIPPED BLOOD, THE	STEPHEN W. CARPENTER
DORM THAT DRIPPED BLOOD, THE	JEFFREY OBROW
DOUBLE - S	ROBERT GARLAND
DOUBLE ACTION MAN - S	C. COURTNEY JOYNER
DOUBLE BANG - S	HEYWOOD GOULD
DOUBLE BLIND - S	ALAN DUNCAN ROSS
DOUBLE CROSSBONES	OSCAR BRODNEY
DOUBLECROSSED (CTF)	ALEX LASKER
DOUBLECROSSED (CTF)	ROGER YOUNG
DOUBLE DARE - S	DENNIS POTTER
DOUBLE EAGLE - S	LEO GAREN
DOUBLE EAGLE - S	DENNE BART PETITCLERC
DOUBLE EXPOSURE	WILLIAM BYRON HILLMAN
DOUBLE EXPOSURE - S	CYNTHIA CIDRE
DOUBLE FAULT - S	ALLAN BURNS
DOUBLE FAULT - S	JAMES L. BROOKS
DOUBLE IMPACT	JEAN-CLAUDE VAN DAMME
DOUBLE IMPACT	PETER KRIKES
DOUBLE IMPACT	SHELDON LETTICH
DOUBLE IMPACT	STEVE MEERSON
DOUBLE INDEMNITY	BILLY WILDER
DOUBLE JEOPARDY - S	CRAIG TEPPER
DOUBLE LIFE, A	RUTH GORDON†
DOUBLE MURDER AND SUICIDE (P)	MAYO SIMON
DOUBLE NEGATIVE	CHARLES DENNIS
DOUBLE NEGATIVE	JANIS ALLEN
DOUBLE NEGATIVE	THOMAS HEDLEY JR.
DOUBLE REVENGE	BRIAN TOBIN
DOUBLE REVENGE	JOHN SHARKEY
DOUBLE SUNRISE - S	RICHARD MAXWELL
DOUBLE TAKE - S	WESLEY MOORE
DOUBLE TIME - S	JENNIFER COLLOPY
DOUBLE VISION - S	LAWRENCE GAY
DOUBLE VISION - S	MICHAEL DIGAETANO
DOUBLE VISION - S	MICK GARRIS
DOUBLE VISION - S	PETER MARTIN WORTMANN
DOUBLE WHOOPEE - S	JEFFREY PRICE
DOUBLE-ENTENDRE (P)	CHARLES EDWARD POGUE
DOUBLES - S	ANDREW C.J. BERGMAN
DOUBLES - S	DENNIS PALUMBO
DOUBLETAKE - S	SOLLACE MITCHELL
DOUBTING THOMAS - S	ROBERT MEGGINSON
DOVE - S	KEVIN FALLS
DOVE, THE	ADAM KENNEDY
DOVE, THE	PETER S. BEAGLE
DOWN AMONG THE SHELTERING PALMS	ALBERT E. LEWIN†
DOWN AND DIRTY	ETTORE SCOLA
DOWN AND OUT IN BEVERLY HILLS	LEON CAPETANOS
DOWN AND OUT IN BEVERLY HILLS	PAUL MAZURSKY
DOWN BY LAW	JIM JARMUSCH
DOWN EAST - S	BRET T. PLATE
DOWN FOR BLOOD - S	MICHAEL LEVINE
DOWN MEXICO WAY - S	JOHN J. SCHALTER
DOWN THE PIKE (P)	BILL CORBETT
DOWN TO EARTH	EDWIN BLUM
DOWN TWISTED	GENE O'NEILL
DOWN TWISTED	ALBERT PYUN
DOWN TWISTED	NOREEN TOBIN
DOWNHILL RACER	JAMES SALTER
DOWNFALL - S	SCOTT J. SCHNEID

Di-Do

FILM WRITERS GUIDE

INDEX OF FILM TITLES

339

Do-Ed

FILM WRITERS GUIDE

INDEX OF FILM TITLES

Title	Writer
DOWNFALL - S	TONY MICHELMAN
DOWNTOWN	NAT MAULDIN
DOWNTOWN - S	LEM DOBBS
DOYLE TO DOYLE - S	WALLY DALTON
DR. ALIEN	KENNETH J. HALL
DR. DOOLITTLE	LESLIE BRICUSSE
DR. FISCHER OF GENEVA - S	JOHN MORTIMER
DR. GOLDFOOT AND THE BIKINI MACHINE	ROBERT KAUFMAN
DR. GOLDFOOT AND THE GIRL BOMBS	LOUIS M. HEYWARD
DR. GOLDFOOT AND THE GIRL BOMBS	ROBERT KAUFMAN
DR. HECKYL AND MR. HYPE	CHARLES B. GRIFFITH
DR. HERO (P)	ISRAEL HOROVITZ
DR. JEKYLL AND SISTER HYDE	BRIAN CLEMENS
DR. NO	RICHARD MAIBAUM†
DR. PHIBES RISES AGAIN	ROBERT BLEES
DR. PHIBES RISES AGAIN	ROBERT FUEST
DR. STRANGELOVE	STANLEY KUBRICK
DR. STRANGELOVE	TERRY SOUTHERN
DR. TERROR'S HOUSE OF HORRORS	MILTON SUBOTSKY
DR. VOODOO - S	JANICE FISCHER
DR. WHO AND THE DALEKS	MILTON SUBOTSKY
DRACULA - S	JIM V. HART
DRACULA (P)	DICK BEEBE
DRACULA (1979)	W.D. RICHTER
DRACULA (1974)	PAUL MORRISSEY
DRACULA (1958)	JIMMY SANGSTER
DRACULA'S DOG	FRANK RAY PERILLI
DRAGNET	ALAN ZWEIBEL
DRAGNET	DAN AYKROYD
DRAGNET	TOM MANKIEWICZ
DRAGON - S	EDWARD KHMARA
DRAGONFLY	N. RICHARD NASH
DRAGONHEART - S	PATRICK READ JOHNSON
DRAGONS - S	JIM HART
DRAGONSLAYER	HAL BARWOOD
DRAGONSLAYER	MATTHEW ROBBINS
DRAGONWYCK	JOSEPH L. MANKIEWICZ
DRANGO	HALL BARTLETT
DRAUGHTSMAN'S CONTRACT, THE	PETER GREENAWAY
DRAWING FIRE - S	MARSHALL HERSKOVITZ
DREAD BOYS, THE - S	ROBERT GUNTER
DREADNOUGHT - S	J.F. LAWTON
DREAM A LITTLE DREAM	D.E. EISENBERG
DREAM A LITTLE DREAM	DANIEL JAY FRANKLIN
DREAM A LITTLE DREAM	MARC ROCCO
DREAM CASE, THE - S	DAVID LOUCKA
DREAM CASE, THE - S	MARK KRAM
DREAM CHASERS - S	RICHARD WHITLEY
DREAM CHILD, THE - S	DAVID CHISOLM
DREAM COAST, THE (P)	JOHN STEPPLING
DREAM DEMONS - S	DAVID PIRIE
DREAM GIRL - S	JON POVILL
DREAM LOVER	JON BOORSTIN
DREAM LOVER - S	NICHOLAS KAZAN
DREAM LOVERS - S	JOHN J. SCHALTER
DREAM MERCHANTS, THE - S	HARLAN ELLISON
DREAM OF PASSION, A	JULES DASSIN
DREAM TEAM, THE	DAVID LOUCKA
DREAM TEAM, THE	JON CONNOLLY
DREAM TIME - S	DAVID H. SMILOW
DREAM WIFE	SIDNEY SHELDON
DREAMCHILD	DENNIS POTTER
DREAMDATE - S	JONATHAN ROBERTS
DREAMDATE - S	MICHAEL LEHMANN
DREAMER	LARRY BISCHOFF
DREAMING OF BABYLON - S	BILL FISHMAN
DREAMING OF BABYLON - S	EBBE ROE SMITH
DREAMLAND - S	RON HUGO
DREAMS	AKIRA KUROSAWA
DREAMS	INGMAR BERGMAN
DREAMS - S	AVRAM DEAN GOLD
DREAMS LOST, DREAMS FOUND (CTF) - S	PAMELA WALLACE
DREAMS OF LEAVING (P)	DAVID HARE
DREAMSCAPE	CHUCK RUSSELL
DREAMSCAPE	DAVID LOUGHERY
DREAMSCAPE	JOSEPH RUBEN
DREAMSTREET - S	RICHARD PRICE
DRESSED TO KILL	BRIAN DEPALMA
DRESSER, THE	RONALD HARWOOD
DRESSMAKER, THE	JOHN MCGRATH
DRIFT, THE - S	BLAINE NOVAK
DRIFTER, THE	LARRY BRAND
DRIFTWOOD	RICHARD SALE
DRINKING IN AMERICA (P)	ERIC BOGOSIAN
DRINKS BEFORE DINNER (P)	E.L. DOCTOROW
DRIVE A CROOKED ROAD	BLAKE EDWARDS
DRIVE AWAY - S	TED MANN
DRIVE ME CRAZY - S	DIANE ENGLISH
DRIVE, HE SAID	JACK NICHOLSON
DRIVE, HE SAID	JEREMY LARNER
DRIVE-IN	ROBERT L. PEETE
DRIVER, THE	WALTER HILL
DRIVING FORCE	PATRICK EDGEWORTH
DRIVING MISS DAISY	ALFRED UHRY
DROP DEAD - S	MICHAEL O'DONOGHUE
DROP DEAD DARLING	KEN HUGHES
DROP DEAD, FRED	ANTHONY J. FINGLETON
DROP DEAD, FRED	CARLOS DAVIS
DROWNING BY NUMBERS	PETER GREENAWAY
DROWNING POOL, THE	LORENZO SEMPLE
DROWNING POOL, THE	TRACY KEENAN WYNN
DROWNING POOL, THE	WALTER HILL
DRUG WARS - S	JONATHAN LEMKIN
DRUGSTORE COWBOY	DANIEL YOST
DRUGSTORE COWBOY	GUS VAN SANT
DRUM	NORMAN WEXLER
DRUMS ACROSS THE RIVER	LAWRENCE ROMAN
DRUMS ALONG THE HUDSON - S	ALLAN WEISBECKER
DRUMS IN THE DEEP SOUTH	PHILIP YORDAN
DRUMS OF TAHITI	DOUGLAS HEYES
DRUNKEN ANGEL	AKIRA KUROSAWA
DRY WHITE SEASON, A	COLIN WELLAND
DRY WHITE SEASON, A	EUZHAN PALCY
DU COTE DE CHEZ L'AUTRE (P)	FRANCIS VEBER
DUAL FORCE - S	ERIC SMALL
DUCHESS AND THE DIRTWATER FOX, THE	BARRY SANDLER
DUCK VARIATIONS (P)	DAVID MAMET
DUCKTALES: THE MOVIE (AF)	ALAN BURNETT
DUDES	RANDY JOHNSON
DUE EAST - S	KAREN CRONER
DUE PROCESS - S	JEAN-YVES PITOUN
DUE PROCESS - S	WALON GREEN
DUEL	RICHARD MATHESON
DUEL AT KAGIYA CORNER, THE	AKIRA KUROSAWA
DUELLISTS, THE	GERALD VAUGHN HUGHES
DUET - S	DAN ALGRANT
DUET FOR ONE	ANDREI KONCHALOVSKY
DUET FOR ONE	JEREMY D. LIPP
DUET FOR ONE	TOM KEMPINSKI
DUFFY	DONALD CAMMELL
DUFFY OF SAN QUENTIN	WALTER DONIGER
DUFFY'S TAVERN	NORMAN PANAMA
DUH BOAT - S	JIM FISHER
DUH BOAT - S	JIM STAAHL
DUKE STEAMER: WORLD'S GREATEST BODYGUARD - S	BRIAN HELGELAND
DUKE WORE JEANS, THE	NORMAN HUDIS
DUMB BLONDE - S	DAVID STENN
DUMB DICKS	DAVID LANDSBERG
DUMB DICKS	LORIN H. DREYFUSS
DUMB WAITER, THE (P)	HAROLD PINTER
DUMBBELL, THE - S	SUZANNE O'MALLEY
DUMBLUCK - S	SAM HAMM
DUMMIES - S	HERSCHEL WEINGROD
DUMMIES - S	TIMOTHY HARRIS
DUMPED - S	LAURA LEVINE
DUNE	DAVID LYNCH
DUNGEONMASTER, THE	ALLEN ACTOR
DUNN'S CONUNDRUM - S	ERIC BERCOVICI
DUNN'S CONUNDRUM - S	TED ELLIOTT
DUNN'S CONUNDRUM - S	TERRY P. ROSSIO
DUNWICH HORROR, THE	CURTIS LEE HANSON
DUNWICH HORROR, THE	HENRY ROSENBAUM
DUPLICATED MAN, THE - S	WALON GREEN
DURING ONE NIGHT	SIDNEY J. FURIE
DURNER'S SPRING - S	JANET KOVALCIK
DUST DEVIL - S	RICHARD STANLEY
DUST DEVIL, THE - S	IAN ABRAMS
DUST TO DUST - S	BENNETT YELLIN
DUST TO DUST - S	PETER FARRELLY
DUSTY AND SWEETS MCGEE	FLOYD MUTRUX
DUTCH	JOHN HUGHES
DUTCH HARBOR - S	TAB MURPHY
DUTCH LANDSCAPE (P)	JON ROBIN BAITZ
DUTCH TREAT	DAVID LANDSBERG
DUTCH TREAT	LORIN H. DREYFUSS
DYING YOUNG	RICHARD L. FRIEDENBERG

E

Title	Writer
E.T.	MELISSA MATHISON
E.T. II - S	MELISSA MATHISON
EAGLE AND THE IRON CROSS, THE - S	ED HUME
EAGLE HAS LANDED, THE	TOM MANKIEWICZ
EAGLE OF BROADWAY, THE - S	THOMAS POPE
EAGLE'S WING	JOHN BRILEY
EAGLE, THE - S	TIMNA RANON
EARLY BIRD, THE	JACK DAVIES
EARLY WINTER	ROD MCCALL
EARTH GIRLS ARE EASY	CHARLIE COFFEY
EARTH GIRLS ARE EASY	JULIE BROWN
EARTH GIRLS ARE EASY	TERRENCE E. MCNALLY
EARTH VERSUS THE FLYING SAUCERS	CURT SIODMAK
EARTHBOUND	MICHAEL FISHER
EARTHLING, THE	LANNY COTLER
EARTHLY DELIGHTS - S	LARRY GRUSIN
EARTHQUAKE	MARIO PUZO
EARTHQUAKE - S	WILLIAM J. DAVIES
EARTHQUAKE - S	WILLIAM OSBORNE
EARTHSHAKE - S	ALEXANDER TANA
EARTHSHAKER - S	JIM CIRILE
EARTHWORMS (P)	ALBERT INNAURATO
EAST COAST HIGH - S	RICHARD PRICE
EAST COAST, WEST COAST - S	LESLIE BRICUSSE
EAST END HUSTLE	ALLAN MOYLE
EAST OF ELEPHANT ROCK	DON BOYD
EAST OF THE SUN - S	C. COURTNEY JOYNER
EASTER PARADE	SIDNEY SHELDON
EASY LIVING - S	REX MCGEE
EASY MONEY	DENNIS BLAIR
EASY MONEY	MICHAEL S. ENDLER
EASY MONEY	P.J. O'ROURKE
EASY MONEY	RODNEY DANGERFIELD
EASY RIDER	PETER FONDA
EASY RIDER	DENNIS HOPPER
EASY RIDER	TERRY SOUTHERN
EASY RIDER 2 - S	TERRY SOUTHERN
EASY STREET - S	JACK BEHR
EASY STREET - S	HAL DRESNER
EASY TO LOVE	WILLIAM ROBERTS
EASY VIRTUE - S	FIONA LEWIS
EASY WHEELS	CELIA ABRAMS
EASY WHEELS	DAVID O'MALLEY
EASY WHEELS	IVAN RAIMI
EAT A BOWL OF TEA	JUDITH RASCOE
EAT AND RUN	CHRISTOPHER HART
EAT MY DUST	CHARLES B. GRIFFITH
EAT THE PEACH	JOHN KELLEHER
EAT THE PEACH	PETER ORMROD
EAT THE RICH	PETER RICHENS
EAT THE RICH	PETER RICHARDSON
EAT THE SUN (SHORT)	JAMES D. COX
EATING	HENRY JAGLOM
EATING RAOUL	PAUL BARTEL
EATING RAOUL	RICHARD BLACKBURN
EBOLI	FRANCESCO ROSI
EBOLI	TONINO GUERRA
EBONY APE, THE (P)	CHARLES EDWARD POGUE
ECHO AND VALOR - S	FRED LEBOW
ECHO PARK	MICHAEL VENTURA
ECHOES	RICHARD J. ANTHONY
ECHOES	RICHARD ALFIERI
ECHOES (SHORT)	STEVE MUSCARELLA
ECHOES OF A SUMMER	ROBERT L. JOSEPH
ECLIPSE OF MEN, AN - S	DON SHROLL
ECLIPSE OF THE BEAST - S	TAB MURPHY
EDDIE AND THE CRUISERS	ARLENE DAVIDSON
EDDIE AND THE CRUISERS	MARTIN DAVIDSON
EDDIE AND THE CRUISERS II	CHARLES ZEV COHEN
EDDIE AND THE CRUISERS II	RICK DOEHRING
EDDIE COCHRAN STORY, THE - S	JACK EPPS JR.
EDDIE COCHRAN STORY, THE - S	JIM CASH
EDDIE COTTREL AT THE PIANO (P)	JOHN STEPPLING
EDDIE MACON'S RUN	JEFF KANEW
EDDIE MURPHY RAW	KEENEN IVORY WAYANS
EDDIE MURPHY RAW	EDDIE MURPHY
EDDIE'S BACK - S	DAVID E. KELLEY
EDGE OF DIVORCE	DON SHARP
EDGE OF DOOM	PHILIP YORDAN
EDGE OF HONOR	DAVID O'MALLEY
EDGE OF SANITY	J.P. FELIX
EDGE OF SANITY	RONALD L. RALEY
EDGE OF THE WORLD	MICHAEL POWELL†
EDISON - S	LARRY B. WILLIAMS
EDMOND (P)	DAVID MAMET
EDNA BUCHANAN STORY, THE - S	HENRY BEAN
EDUCATING RITA	WILLY RUSSELL
EDUCATION OF LINUS DOOLEY, THE - S	JONATHAN KAUFER

Title	Writer
EDWARD FORD - S	LEM DOBBS
EDWARD SCISSORHANDS	TIM BURTON
EDWARD SCISSORHANDS	CAROLINE THOMPSON
EEZMO, THE - S	LOUIS GARFINKLE
EEZMO, THE - S	QUINN REDEKER
EFFECT OF GAMMA RAYS ON MAN-IN-THE-MOON MARIGOLDS, THE	ALVIN SARGENT
EFFECT OF GAMMA RAYS ON MAN-IN-THE-MOON MARIGOLDS, THE (P)	PAUL ZINDEL
EGYPTIAN, THE	PHILIP DUNNE
EIGER SANCTION, THE	WARREN B. MURPHY
EIGER SANCTION, THE	HAL DRESNER
EIGHT MEN OUT	JOHN SAYLES
EIGHT ON THE LAM	ALBERT E. LEWIN
EIGHT ON THE LAM	ARTHUR MARX
EIGHT ON THE LAM	ROBERT FISHER
EIGHT WOMEN AND A GOAT (P)	JAMES KIRKWOOD†
EIGHTIES, THE	CHANTAL AKERMAN
EIGHTIES, THE	JEAN GRUAULT
EIGHTIES, THE (P)	TOM COLE
EIGHTY THOUSAND SUSPECTS	VAL GUEST
EINSTEIN - S	THOMAS POPE
EINSTEIN AND THE POLAR BEAR - S	TOM GRIFFIN
EL AMOR BRUJO	CARLOS SAURA
EL CID	BEN BARZMAN†
EL CID	PHILIP YORDAN
EL CONDOR	LARRY COHEN
EL CONDOR	STEVEN W. CARABATSOS
EL DIABLO (CTF)	BILL PHILLIPS
EL DIABLO (CTF)	JOHN CARPENTER
EL DIABLO (CTF)	TOMMY LEE WALLACE
EL DORADO - S	ROBERT KING
EL DORADO - S	HENRY BEAN
EL DORADO - S	LEORA BARISH
EL MOURIR DE PLAISIR	ROGER VADIM
EL NORTE	ANNA THOMAS
EL NORTE	GREGORY NAVA
EL PUEBLO - S	GERALD GREEN
EL SALVADOR - S	DANILO BACH
EL SUPER	MANUEL ARCE
EL SUPER	LEON ICHASO
EL TOPO	ALEXANDRO JODORWSKY
EL WESTERN, THE - S	THOMAS MCGUANE
ELAINE'S DAUGHTER (P)	MAYO SIMON
ELECTRA GLIDE IN BLUE	ROBERT BORIS
ELECTRIC CATILLION, THE - S	STEVE SHAGAN
ELECTRIC DREAMS	RUSTY LEMORANDE
ELECTRIC HORSEMAN, THE	ROBERT GARLAND
ELEKTRA ASSASIN - S	JIM MCBRIDE
ELEKTRA ASSASIN - S	L.M. KIT CARSON
ELENI	STEVE TESICH
ELEPHANT MAN, THE	CHRISTOPHER DEVORE
ELEPHANT MAN, THE	DAVID LYNCH
ELEPHANT MAN, THE	ERIC BERGREN
ELEVATOR TO THE GALLOWS	LOUIS MALLE
ELFIN - S	PATRICK DUNCAN
ELIMINATORS	PAUL DE MEO
ELIZA FRASER	DAVID WILLIAMSON
ELLIOT FAUMAN, PH.D.	RIC KLASS
ELLIOT LOVES (P)	JULES FEIFFER
ELMER GANTRY	RICHARD BROOKS
ELMINATORS	DANNY BILSON
ELSEWHERE - S	DEAN PITCHFORD
ELUSIVE PIMPERNEL, THE	EMERIC PRESSBURGER†
ELUSIVE PIMPERNEL, THE	MICHAEL POWELL†
ELVES - S	CHARLES KAUFMAN
ELVES - S	LARRY B. WILLIAMS
ELVIRA: MISTRESS OF THE DARK	JOHN PARAGON
ELVIRA: MISTRESS OF THE DARK	SAM EGAN
ELVIRA: MISTRESS OF THE DARK	CASSANDRA PETERSON
EM - S	DIANNE HOUSTON
EMERALD CITY	DAVID WILLIAMSON
EMERALD FOREST, THE	ROSPO PALLENBERG
EMERALD TREE BOA (P)	CLIFTON CAMPBELL
EMERGENCY CALL	LEWIS GILBERG
EMIL AND THE DETECTIVE	A.J. CAROTHERS
EMILY (P)	STEPHEN METCALFE
EMINENT DOMAIN	ANDRZEJ KRAKOWSKI
EMINENT DOMAIN	RICHARD GREGSON
EMMA MAE	JAMAA FANAKA
EMPEROR OF THE NORTH POLE	CHRISTOPHER E. KNOPF
EMPEROR WALTZ, THE	BILLY WILDER
EMPEROR'S NEW CLOTHES, THE	DAVID IRVING
EMPIRE - S	RICHARD PRICE
EMPIRE MAN - S	RODERICK TAYLOR
EMPIRE OF THE SUN	TOM STOPPARD
EMPIRE STRIKES BACK, THE	LAWRENCE KASDAN
EMPIRES OF THE DEEP - S	STANFORD SHERMAN
ENCHANTING, THE - S	RICHARD OUTTEN
ENCHANTMENT, THE - S	WES CLARRIDGE
ENCORE - S	DENIS HAMILL
ENCORE - S	JOHN HAMILL
ENCORE - S	NORA EPHRON
END OF AUGUST, THE	ANNA THOMAS
END OF AUGUST, THE	GREGORY NAVA
END OF ETERNITY, THE	R.J. STEWART
END OF INNOCENCE, THE	DYAN CANNON
END OF THE GAME	MAXMILLIAN SCHELL
END OF THE LINE	JAY RUSSELL
END OF THE LINE	JOHN WOHLBRUCK
END OF THE LINE - S	DAVID H. SMILOW
END OF THE NIGHT	KEITH MCNALLY
END OF THE ROAD	TERRY SOUTHERN
END OF THE WORLD IN OUR USUAL BED, THE	LINA WERTMULLER
END ZONE - S	TRACY KEENAN WYNN
END ZONE, THE - S	DON RAPPOPORT
END, THE	JERRY BELSON
ENDANGERED - S	JACK BEHR
ENDANGERED - S	DANILO BACH
ENDANGERED - S	TRACY KEENAN WYNN
ENDANGERED SPECIES	JUDSON KLINGER
ENDANGERED SPECIES	RICHARD WOODS
ENDANGERED SPECIES	ALAN RUDOLPH
ENDANGERED SPECIES	JOHN BINDER
ENDLESS DESCENT	DAVID COLEMAN
ENDLESS LOVE	JUDITH RASCOE
ENEMIES, A LOVE STORY	PAUL MAZURSKY
ENEMIES, A LOVE STORY	ROGER L. SIMON
ENEMY BELOW, THE	WENDELL MAYES
ENEMY FROM SPACE	NIGEL KNEALE
ENEMY FROM SPACE	VAL GUEST
ENEMY MINE	EDWARD KHMARA
ENEMY OF THE PEOPLE, AN	ALEXANDER JACOBS†
ENEMY TERRITORY	STUART KAMINSKY
ENEMY TERROR	BOBBY LIDELL
ENFORCER, THE	DEAN RIESNER
ENFORCER, THE	GAIL MORGAN HICKMAN
ENFORCER, THE	STIRLING SILLIPHANT
ENGAGED TO BE MARRIED - S	CHARLIE HAUCK
ENGAGEMENT BABY, THE (P)	STANLEY SHAPIRO†
ENGAGEMENT, THE	TOM STOPPARD
ENGAGEMENT, THE - S	PAUL PRICE
ENGAGEMENT, THE - S	STEVE NATHAN
ENGLAND MADE ME	PETER JOHN DUFFELL
ENID IS SLEEPING	A.J. TIPPING
ENID IS SLEEPING	JAMES WHALEY
ENID IS SLEEPING	MAURICE PHILLIPS
ENIGMA	JOHN BRILEY
ENORMOUS CHANGES AT THE LAST MINUTE	JOHN SAYLES
ENORMOUS CHANGES AT THE LAST MINUTE	SUSAN RICE
ENOUGH ROPE - S	SUSAN RICE
ENTER LAUGHING	JOSEPH STEIN
ENTER LAUGHING	CARL REINER
ENTER THE NINJA	DICK DESMOND
ENTER THE NINJA	JUDD BERNARD
ENTER THE NINJA	MENAHEM GOLAN
ENTERPRISE - S	DJORDJE MILICEVIC
ENTERPRISE, THE - S	JILL ISAACS
ENTERTAINER, THE	JOHN OSBORNE
ENTERTAINER, THE	NIGEL KNEALE
ENTERTAINING MR. SLOANE	CLIVE EXTON
ENTICE & CONSENT - S	HENRY OLEK
ENTITY, THE	FRANK DEFELITTA
ENTRE NOUS	DIANE KURYS
EQUAL TIME - S	DAVID SELTZER
EQUUS	PETER SHAFFER
ERASERHEAD	DAVID LYNCH
ERIK THE VIKING	TERRY JONES
ERNEST GOES TO CAMP	COKE SAMS
ERNEST GOES TO CAMP	JOHN R. CHERRY III
ERNEST GOES TO JAIL	CHARLIE COHEN
ERNEST SAVES CAMELOT - S	BART DAVIS
ERNEST SAVES CAMELOT - S	MICHAEL ZAUSNER
ERNEST SAVES CHRISTMAS	EDWARD S. TURNER
ERNEST SPACED OUT - S	ED NAHA
ERNIE POPOVICH - S	STEVE BING
EROTICA	RUSS MEYER
ERRAND BOY, THE	JERRY LEWIS
ERRAND OF MERCY (P)	CASEY KELLY
ESCAPE	PHILIP DUNNE
ESCAPE - S	JEB STUART
ESCAPE - S	JOHN J. SCHALTER
ESCAPE - S	RICHARD DILELLO
ESCAPE 2000	DAVID LAWRENCE
ESCAPE 2000	GEORGE W. SCHENCK
ESCAPE 2000	ROBERT F. WILLIAMS
ESCAPE 2000	JON A. GEORGE
ESCAPE 2000	NEILL HICKS
ESCAPE ARTIST, THE	MELISSA MATHISON
ESCAPE ARTIST, THE	STEPHEN ZITO
ESCAPE AT DAWN	AKIRA KUROSAWA
ESCAPE FROM BV-JAY - S	DOUGLAS DAY STEWART
ESCAPE FROM ALCATRAZ	RICHARD TUGGLE
ESCAPE FROM BAD GIRLS DORMITORY	TIM KINCAID
ESCAPE FROM NEW YORK	JOHN CARPENTER
ESCAPE FROM NEW YORK	NICK CASTLE
ESCAPE FROM SAFEHAVEN	BRIAN THOMAS JONES
ESCAPE FROM SAFEHAVEN	JAMES MCCALMONT
ESCAPE FROM SUMMER CAMP - S	CAREY DEVUONO
ESCAPE FROM THE DARK	ROSEMARY ANNE SISSON
ESCAPE FROM WANNA WANNA - S	HARRIS GOLDBERG
ESCAPE FROM WANNA WANNA - S	TOM NURSALL
ESCAPE TO ATHENA	EDWARD ANHALT
ESCAPE TO CANADA - S	DANIEL YOST
ESCAPEES - S	JAKE WEINBERGER
ESCAPEES - S	MIKE WEINBERGER
ESCROW - S	MICHAEL KANE
ESKIMO SUMMER - S	RICHARD WHITLEY
ESP MCGREE - S	MICHAEL MCDOWELL
ESTABLISHED PRICE (P)	DENNIS MCINTYRE†
ETERNITY	DOROTHY KOSTER PAUL
ETERNITY	JON VOIGHT
ETERNITY	STEVEN PAUL
ETHICAL CHOICE - S	WILLIAM W. PHELPS
EUGENE AND HIS SEAMLESS PANTS - S	PATRICK RANAHAN
EUGENE AND HIS SEAMLESS PANTS - S	TODD JOHNSON
EUREKA	PAUL MAYERSBERG
EUROPA, EUROPA	AGNIESZKA HOLLAND
EUROPEAN VACATION	JOHN HUGHES
EUROPEAN VACATION	ROBERT KLANE
EUROPEANS, THE	RUTH PRAWER JHABVALA
EVA	EVAN JONES
EVANGELIST, THE - S	FRANK R. PIERSON
EVE AND THE HANDYMAN	RUSS MEYER
EVE OF DESTRUCTION	DUNCAN GIBBINS
EVE OF DESTRUCTION	YALE UDOFF
EVE'S RIB - S	LLOYD FONVIELLE
EVEL KNIEVAL	JOHN MILLIUS
EVENING (P)	JOHN PIELMEIER
EVENING FLIGHT - S	STANLEY MANN
EVENING WITH BEATRICE LILLIE, AN (P)	LESLIE BRICUSSE
EVERLASTING SECRET FAMILY, THE	FRANK MOORHOUSE
EVERLOVIN' BROWN - S	STEPHEN METCALFE
EVERY BREATH - S	KATHRYN BIGELOW
EVERY GOOD BOY DESERVES FAVOR (P)	TOM STOPPARD
EVERY LITTLE CROOK AND NANNY	CY HOWARD
EVERY LITTLE CROOK AND NANNY	ROBERT KLANE
EVERY MAN FOR HIMSELF IN LIFE	ANNE-MARIE MIEVILLE
EVERY MAN FOR HIMSELF IN LIFE	JEAN-CLAUDE CARRIERE
EVERY MAN FOR HIMSELF IN LIFE	JEAN-LUC GODARD
EVERY TIME WE SAY GOODBYE	LEAH APPET
EVERY TIME WE SAY GOODBYE	MOSHE MIZRAHI
EVERY TIME WE SAY GOODBYE	RACHEL FABIEN
EVERY WHICH WAY BUT LOOSE	JEREMY JOE KRONSBERG
EVERYBODY CHARLESTON - S	TOM HOLLAND
EVERYBODY WINS	ARTHUR MILLER
EVERYBODY'S ALL-AMERICAN	THOMAS RICKMAN
EVERYBODY'S FINE	GIUSEPPE TORNATORE
EVERYBODY'S FINE	TONINO GUERRA
EVERYTHING COUNTS - S	JEFF LANTOS
EVERYTHING COUNTS - S	JEFF LEVIN
EVERYTHING COUNTS - S	LEANN LANTOS
EVERYTHING MUST CHANGE - S	ALVIN SARGENT

EVERYTHING YOU ALWAYS WANTED TO KNOW ABOUT SEX* (*BUT WERE AFRAID TO ASK) ... WOODY ALLEN
EVICTORS, THE ... CHARLES B. PIERCE
EVIL DEAD, THE ... SAM RAIMI
EVIL DEAD 2 ... SAM RAIMI
EVIL DEAD 2 ... SCOTT SPIEGEL
EVIL KNIEVAL ... ALAN CAILOU
EVIL SPEAK ... JOSEPH GAROFALO
EVIL THAT MEN DO, THE ... JOHN CROWTHER
EVIL THAT MEN DO, THE ... R. LANCE HILL
EVIL UNDER THE SUN ... ANTHONY SHAFFER
EVILS OF THE NIGHT ... MARDI RUSTAM
EVILS OF THE NIGHT ... PHILLIP D. CONNORS
EVILSPEAK ... ERIC WESTON
EVITA - S ... GLENN GORDON CARON
EX - S ... DOUG MARLETTE
EX - S ... PAT CONROY
EX-MR. WINFIELD, THE - S ... BILL LAMOND
EX-MR. WINFIELD, THE - S ... JO LAMOND
EXAMINER, THE - S ... MATTHEW DORFF
EXIT WOUNDS - S ... DICK BEEBE
EXAMPLE, THE (P) ... YALE UDOFF
EXCALIBUR ... JOHN BOORMAN
EXCALIBUR ... ROSPO PALLENBERG
EXCESS BAGGAGE - S ... DORI PIERSON
EXECUTIONER - S ... HILARY HENKIN
EXECUTIONER, THE - S ... DENNIS SHRYACK
EXECUTIONER, THE - S ... LARRY GROSS
EXECUTIONER, THE - S ... MICHAEL BUTLER
EXECUTIONER, THE - S ... ED NEUMEIER
EXECUTIONER, THE - S ... MICHAEL MINER
EXECUTIVE ACTION ... DONALD FREED
EXECUTIVE PRIVILEGE - S ... A.J. CAROTHERS
EXECUTIVE SUITE ... ERNEST LEHMANN
EXES - S ... DAN GREENBURG
EXHALING ZERO (P) ... JOHN STEPPLING
EXILE'S BAGGAGE, AN - S ... JOHN NORVILLE
EXORCIST III ... WILLIAM PETER BLATTY
EXORCIST, THE ... WILLIAM PETER BLATTY
EXPECTING MIRACLES - S ... CHARLIE PETERS
EXPENDABLES, THE ... PHILLIP ALDERTON
EXPENSIVE SHOES - S ... JOEL SCHUMACHER
EXPERIENCE - S ... QUINN REDEKER
EXPERIENCE PREFERRED BUT NOT ESSENTIAL ... JUNE ROBERTS
EXPERTS, THE ... ERIC ALTER
EXPERTS, THE ... NICK THIEL
EXPERTS, THE ... STEVEN S. GREENE
EXPLORERS ... ERIC LUKE
EXPOSED ... JAMES TOBACK
EXPOSURE (P) ... MICHAEL DUNCAN
EXPRESSO BONGO ... WOLF MANKOWITZ
EXTENDED PLAY (SHORT) ... DAVID CASCI
EXTERMINATOR II ... MARK BUNTZMAN
EXTERMINATOR II ... WILLIAM SACHS
EXTERMINATOR, THE ... JAMES GLICKENHAUS
EXTERMINATORS - S ... JOE ANSOLABEHERE
EXTERMINATORS - S ... STEPHEN VIKSTEN
EXTRAORDINARY SEAMAN, THE ... HAL DRESNER
EXTREME CLOSEUP ... MICHAEL CRICHTON
EXTREME PREJUDICE ... FRED REXER
EXTREME PREJUDICE ... DERIC WASHBURN
EXTREME PREJUDICE ... HARRY KLEINER
EXTREME PREJUDICE ... JOHN MILIUS
EXTREMETIES ... WILLIAM MASTROSIMONE
EYE CONTACT - S ... JOHN GUARE
EYE FOR AN EYE, AN ... JAMES BRUNER
EYE FOR AN EYE, AN ... WILLIAM GRAY
EYE OF THE CAT ... JOSEPH STEFANO
EYE OF THE NEEDLE ... STANLEY MANN
EYE OF THE NEEDLE II ... CARL FRANKLIN
EYE OF THE NEEDLE II ... DAN GAGLIASSO
EYE OF THE STORM ... YURI ZELTSER
EYE OF THE TIGER ... MICHAEL T. MONTGOMERY
EYES OF A STRANGER ... ERIC L. BLOOM
EYES OF A STRANGER ... MARK JACKSON
EYES OF FIRE ... AVERY CROUNSE
EYES OF KID MIDAS - S ... NEAL SHUSTERMAN
EYES OF LAURA MARS, THE ... DAVID Z. GOODMAN
EYES OF LAURA MARS, THE ... JOHN CARPENTER
EYES, THE MOUTH, THE ... MARCO BELLOCCHIO
EYEWITNESS ... RONALD HARWOOD
EYEWITNESS ... STEVE TESICH

F

F AS IN PHILADELPHIA - S ... HOWARD L. ANDERSON
F WORD, THE (P) ... RON NYSWANER
F.B.I. STING - S ... WALTER BERNSTEIN
F.I.S.T. ... JOE ESZTERHAS
F.I.S.T. ... SYLVESTER STALLONE
F/10 SPLIT (P) ... RON NYSWANER
F/X ... GREGORY FLEEMAN
F/X ... ROBERT MEGGINSON
F/X 2 ... RICHARD CONDON
FABIOLA (P) ... EDUARDO MACHADO
FABLECHASE - S ... JOHN FUSCO
FABRICATOR, THE - S ... PETER STONE
FABULOUS BAKER BOYS, THE ... STEVEN KLOVES
FABULOUS NOBODIES, THE ... RAY DEFELITTA
FACE - S ... MICHAEL FIELDS
FACE IN THE CROWD, A ... BUDD SCHULBERG
FACE OF FU MANCHU, THE ... HARRY ALAN TOWERS
FACE OF THE ENEMY ... HASSAN ILDARI
FACE OF THE ENEMY ... PHILIP ALDERTON
FACE TO FACE ... INGMAR BERGMAN
FACE-OFF - S ... MICHAEL COLLEARY
FACE-OFF - S ... MIKE WERB
FACE-OFF - S ... RICHARD MATHESON
FACES ... JOHN CASSAVETES†
FACTS OF LIFE, THE ... NORMAN PANAMA
FADE AWAY - S ... JANET DULIN JONES
FADE TO BLACK ... VERNON ZIMMERMAN
FADEOUT - S ... AIDA BORTNIK
FAERIE TALE - S ... PAUL BOORSTIN
FAERIE TALE - S ... SHARON BOORSTIN
FAHAD & LENA - S ... MARC NORMAN
FAIL SAFE ... WALTER BERNSTEIN
FAIR GAME - S ... MARC MOSS
FAIR HAIR - S ... DARRYL WIMBERLY
FAIR PLAY - S ... JEAN VALLELY
FAIRY GODMOTHER - S ... SARAH C. PALEY
FAITHFUL (P) ... CHAZZ PALMINTERI
FALCON AND THE SNOWMAN, THE ... STEVEN ZAILLIAN
FALL AND RISE OF GLEN, THE - S ... GREG BROOKER
FALL OF THE HOUSE OF USHER, THE - S ... MICHAEL J. MURRAY
FALL OF THE ROMAN EMPIRE, THE ... BEN BARZMAN†
FALL OF THE ROMAN EMPIRE, THE ... PHILIP YORDAN
FALLEN ANGEL ... HARRY KLEINER
FALLING ANGEL - S ... WILLIAM HJORTSBERG
FALLING DOWN - S ... EBBE ROE SMITH
FALLING FROM GRACE ... LARRY MCMURTRY
FALLING IN LOVE ... MICHAEL CRISTOFER
FALLING IN LOVE AGAIN ... HENRY PAUL
FALLING IN LOVE AGAIN ... SUSANNAH YORK
FALLING IN LOVE AGAIN ... STEVEN PAUL
FALLING IN LOVE AGAIN ... TED ALLAN
FALLING OF ANGELS - S ... MICHAEL PATRICK GOODMAN
FALLING OVER BACKWARDS ... MORT RANSEN
FALLOUT - S ... J.S. CARDONE
FALSE FLAG - S ... RICHARD MAXWELL
FALSE IDENTITY ... SANDRA K. BAILEY
FALSE LABOR - S ... MITCH MARKOWITZ
FALSE PAPERS - S ... MARTINA S. FINCH
FALSE PROFIT - S ... ROBERT GUNTER
FAME ... CHRISTOPHER GORE†
FAME GAME, THE - S ... ROBERT KAUFMAN
FAMILY AFFAIR, A (P) ... JAMES GOLDMAN
FAMILY AFFAIR, A (P) ... WILLIAM GOLDMAN
FAMILY ALBUM - S ... MAUREEN EARL
FAMILY BUSINESS ... COSTA-GAVRAS
FAMILY BUSINESS ... VINCENT PATRICK
FAMILY DANCING - S ... DANIEL LIPMAN
FAMILY DANCING - S ... RONALD COWEN
FAMILY DEVOTIONS (P) ... DAVID HENRY HWANG
FAMILY DIES - S ... PIERS ASHWORTH
FAMILY JEWELS, THE ... BILL RICHMOND
FAMILY JEWELS, THE ... JERRY LEWIS
FAMILY LIFE (P) ... NICHOLAS KAZAN
FAMILY MAN - S ... GREG TAYLOR
FAMILY MAN - S ... MARTHA GOLDHIRSH
FAMILY MAN, THE - S ... JIM JENNEWEIN
FAMILY MAN, THE - S ... TOM S. PARKER
FAMILY MATTERS - S ... JACK ROSENTHAL
FAMILY MELODRAMA - S ... VICKIE PATIK
FAMILY PLOT ... ERNEST LEHMAN
FAMILY PORTRAIT - S ... ALAN ORMSBY
FAMILY REUNION - S ... C. COURTNEY JOYNER
FAMILY ROYALTY - S ... JORDAN MOFFET
FAMILY SECRETS - S ... PATTI SULLIVAN
FAMILY SECRETS - S ... PATRICIA RESNICK
FAMILY VIEWING - S ... ATOM EGOYAN
FAMILY, THE ... ETTORE SCOLA
FAMOUS LONG AGO - S ... MICHAEL ROEMER
FAN, THE ... JOHN HARTWELL
FAN, THE ... PRISCILLA CHAPMAN
FANATIC ... RICHARD MATHESON
FANCY HARDWARE - S ... A.J. CAROTHERS
FANDANGO ... KEVIN REYNOLDS
FANNY ... JULIUS J. EPSTEIN
FANNY AND ALEXANDER ... INGMAR BERGMAN
FANSHEN (P) ... DAVID HARE
FANTASIES ... JOHN DEREK
FANTASIST, THE ... ROBIN HARDY
FANTASTIC FOUR - S ... LAWRENCE J. BLOCK
FANTASTIC VOYAGE ... HARRY KLEINER
FAR AS THE EYE CAN SEE - S ... JOHN HILL
FAR CENTAURI - S ... WES CLARRIDGE
FAR EAST ... JOHN DUIGAN
FAR EDGE, A (P) ... JIM HARRISON
FAR FROM HOME ... TED GERSHUNY
FAR FROM HOME ... TOMMY LEE WALLACE
FAR FROM THE MADDING CROWD ... FREDERIC RAPHAEL
FAR NORTH ... SAM SHEPARD
FAR OFF PLACE, A - S ... TAB MURPHY
FAR OUT MAN ... THOMAS CHONG
FAR SIDE, THE - S ... ALAN RUDOLPH
FARENHEIT 451 ... FRANCOIS TRUFFAUT†
FAREWELL TO ARMS, A - S ... DENNE BART PETITCLERC
FAREWELL TO FLESH (P) ... DICK BEEBE
FAREWELL TO THE KING ... JOHN MILIUS
FAREWELL, MY LOVELY ... DAVID Z. GOODMAN
FARMER'S DAUGHTER, THE ... ALLEN RIVKIN†
FAST BREAK ... SANDOR STERN
FAST CHARLIE...THE MOONBEAM RIDER ... MICHAEL GLEASON
FAST COMPANY ... WILLIAM ROBERTS
FAST COMPANY ... DAVID CRONENBERG
FAST COMPANY ... PHILIP S. SAVATH
FAST COMPANY - S ... RONNI KERN
FAST FOOD ... CLARK BRANDON
FAST FOOD ... LANNY HORN
FAST FORWARD ... TIMOTHY MARCH
FAST FORWARD ... RICHARD WESLEY
FAST LADY, THE ... JACK DAVIES
FAST LANE - S ... ALEC LORIMORE
FAST LANE - S ... TERRY WINKLESS
FAST TALKERS - S ... GUY THOMAS
FAST TALKING ... KEN CAMERON
FAST TIMES AT RIDGEMONT HIGH ... CAMERON CROWE
FAST-WALKING ... JAMES B. HARRIS
FASTER, PUSSYCAT! KILL! KILL! ... RUSS MEYER
FASTEST GUN ALIVE, THE ... FRANK D. GILROY
FAT CHANCE ... W.D. RICHTER
FAT CHANCE - S ... CHRIS FABER
FAT CHANCE - S ... DANNIEL BARRON
FAT CHANCE - S ... SUSAN RICE
FAT CITY ... LEONARD GARDNER
FAT LADY, THE - S ... RICHARD RUSH
FAT MAN AND LITTLE BOY ... BRUCE ROBINSON
FAT MAN AND LITTLE BOY ... ROLAND JOFFE
FATAL ATTRACTION ... JAMES DEARDEN
FATAL ATTRACTION (P) ... BERNARD SLADE
FATAL BEAUTY ... BILL SVANOE
FATAL BEAUTY ... DEAN RIESNER
FATAL BEAUTY ... HILARY HENKIN
FATAL CHARM ... NICHOLAS NICIPHOR
FATAL EXPOSURE (CTF) ... RAY HARTUNG
FATAL MISSION ... ANTHONY GENTILE
FATAL MISSION ... CHOSEI FUNAHARA
FATAL MISSION ... ERLINDA QUILAOIT ROWE
FATAL MISSION ... GEORGE ROWE
FATAL MISSION ... JOHN GENTILE
FATAL MISSION ... PETER FONDA
FATAL SKIES ... JAMES EATON
FATAL SKIES ... THOMAS C. DUGAN
FATAL SKIES ... WILLIAM ZIPP
FATHER AND SON - S ... DANIEL SULLIVAN
FATHER AND SON - S ... FRED LEBOW
FATHER AND SON - S ... HESPER ANDERSON
FATHER AND SON - S ... KEVIN JARRE
FATHER CAME TOO ... JACK DAVIES
FATHER GOOSE ... PETER STONE
FATHER OF THE BRIDE - S ... CHARLES SHYER
FATHER OF THE BRIDE - S ... NANCY J. MEYERS
FATHER'S DAY - S ... SUSAN HARRIS
FATHER'S DAY - S ... DIANA HAMMOND
FATHERS AND SONS (P) ... THOMAS BABE
FATHERS AND SONS - S ... PAUL MONES
FATHOM ... LORENZO SEMPLE JR.
FATSO ... ANNE BANCROFT

Title	Writer
FAULT LINE (P)	YALE UDOFF
FAVOR, THE	JOSAN MCGIBBON
FAVOR, THE	SARA PARRIOTT
FAVORITES OF THE MOON	GERARD BRACH
FEAR (CTF)	ROCKNE O'BANNON
FEAR AND DESIRE	STANLEY KUBRICK
FEAR CITY	NICHOLAS ST. JOHN
FEAR IN THE NIGHT	JIMMY SANGSTER
FEAR IS THE KEY	ROBERT CARRINGTON
FEAR NO EVIL	FRANK LALOGGIA
FEAR OF ACTING (P)	JOHN WILLIAM SEE
FEAR, ANXIETY AND DEPRESSION	TODD SOLONDZ
FEARLESS FRANK	PHILIP KAUFMAN
FEARLESS VAMPIRE KILLERS, THE	GERARD BRACH
FEARLESS VAMPIRE KILLERS, THE	ROMAN POLANSKI
FEDORA	BILLY WILDER
FEDORA	I.A.L. DIAMOND†
FEDS	DAN GOLDBERG
FEDS	LEN BLUM
FELL - S	ISRAEL HOROVITZ
FELLINI SATYRICON	FEDERICO FELLINI
FELLINI'S ROMA	FEDERICO FELLINI
FELLOW TRAVELER (CTF)	MICHAEL WEARING
FELLOW TRAVELERS - S	GORDON GREISMAN
FEMALE SUSPECTS - S	DAVID CHASE
FEMALE TROUBLE	JOHN WATERS
FEMME FATALE (P)	MICHAEL WOLK
FEMMES DE PERSONNE	CHRISTOPHER FRANK
FEMMES FATALES	BERTRAND BLIER
FENCING MASTER	AKIRA KUROSAWA
FERDYDURKE - S	JERZY SKOLIMOWSKI
FERNGULLY: THE LAST RAINFOREST (AF) - S	JIM COX
FERRET, THE - S	TERRY BLACK
FERRIS BUELLER'S DAY OFF	JOHN HUGHES
FERRY TO HONG KONG	LEWIS GILBERG
FESTA	UGO GIORGETTI
FESTIVAL OF FEAR, A - S	ROBERT CARRINGTON
FEVER (CTF)	LARRY BROTHERS
FEVER - S	DENNIS O'FLAHERTY
FEVER IN THE BLOOD, A	ROY HUGGINS
FEVER IN THE BLOOD, A	HARRY KLEINER
FEVER OF THE HUNT - S	PETER LENKOV
FEVER OF THE HUNT - S	LARRY COHEN
FEVER PITCH	RICHARD BROOKS
FEVER, THE (P)	WALLACE SHAWN
FEW DAYS WITH ME, A	CLAUDE SAUTET
FEW GOOD MEN, A (P)	AARON SORKIN
FEW GOOD MEN, A	CARL G. SAUTTER
FEW GOOD WOMEN, A - S	JENNIFER COLLOPY
FEW MURDERS IN THE NEIGHBORHOOD, A - S	HENRY OLEK
FFOLKES	JACK DAVIES
FIDDLER ON THE ROOF	JOSEPH STEIN
FIDELITY - S	TOM GRIFFIN
FIELD OF DREAMS	PHIL ALDEN ROBINSON
FIELD, THE	JIM SHERIDAN
FIELDER'S CHOICE - S	EDUARDO MACHADO
FIELDS OF EDEN - S	STEVE SHAGAN
FIELDS OF HONOR - S	ANDREW BIRKIN
FIELDS OF HONOR - S	WOLFGANG PETERSEN
FIELDS OF VISION - S	JOHN CARLEN
FIEND WHO WALKED THE WEST, THE	PHILIP YORDAN
FIENDISH PLOT OF DR. FU MANCHU, THE	JIM MOLONEY
FIENDISH PLOT OF DR. FU MANCHU, THE	RUDY DOCHTERMANN
FIFTH FLOOR, THE	HIKMET AVEDIS
FIFTH FLOOR, THE	MARLENE SCHMIDT
FIFTH FLOOR, THE	MEYER DOLINSKY†
FIFTH HORSEMAN, THE - S	MICHAEL WELLER
FIGHTING BACK	DAVID Z. GOODMAN
FIGHTING BACK	THOMAS HEDLEY JR.
FIGHTING MAD	JONATHAN DEMME
FIGHTING MAD (1948)	JOHN BRIGHT†
FIGURE, THE (P)	CLIFTON CAMPBELL
FILM D'AMORE E D'ANARCHIA	LINA WERTMULLER
FILM SOCIETY, THE (P)	JON ROBIN BAITZ
FILTHY RICH - S	ELLEN L. FOGLE
FINAL ALLIANCE, THE	HAVEL GOLDSTEIN
FINAL ALLIANCE, THE	JOHN T. EUBANK
FINAL ANALYSIS - S	ROGER L. SIMON
FINAL ANALYSIS - S	WESLEY STRICK
FINAL ARGUMENTS - S	LISA STOTSKY
FINAL ARGUMENTS - S	WENDY GRAF
FINAL BALLOT - S	MAGGIE KLEINMAN
FINAL CONFLICT, THE	ANDREW BIRKIN
FINAL COUNTDOWN, THE	PETER POWELL†
FINAL COUNTDOWN, THE	THOMAS HUNTER
FINAL COUNTDOWN, THE	DAVID AMBROSE
FINAL COUNTDOWN, THE	GERRY DAVIS
FINAL EMBRACE - S	JIM WYNORSKI
FINAL EMBRACE - S	R.J. ROBERTSON
FINAL EXAM	JIMMY HUSTON
FINAL OPTION, THE	REGINALD ROSE
FINAL PROGRAMME, THE	ROBERT FUEST
FINAL SANCTION, THE	DAVID HEAVENER
FINAL TERROR, THE	JON A. GEORGE
FINAL TERROR, THE	NEILL D. HICKS
FINAL TERROR, THE	RONALD SHUSETT
FINAL VOWS - S	MARK W. LEE
FINALE - S	JON ROBIN BAITZ
FIND AMANDA A HUSBAND - S	DANIEL W. LJOKA
FINDERS KEEPERS	CHARLES DENNIS
FINDERS KEEPERS	RONNY GRAHAM
FINDERS KEEPERS	TERENCE MARSH
FINDERS KEEPERS, LOVERS WEEPERS	RUSS MEYER
FINE AND PRIVATE PLACE, A - S	PEWTER S. BEAGLE
FINE MESS, A	BLAKE EDWARDS
FINE PAIR, A	LARRY GELBART
FINE TOUCH, THE - S	JONATHAN PRINCE
FINE TOUCH, THE - S	JOSHUA GOLDSTEIN
FINEST KIND, THE - S	PATRICK DUNCAN
FINGERS	JAMES TOBACK
FINISHING TOUCH, THE - S	MORRIE RUVINSKY
FIRE - S	GEORGE WOLFE
FIRE - S	DAVID H. FRANZONI
FIRE AND ICE (1987)	DIGBY WOLFE
FIRE AND ICE (1987)	GEORGE SCHLATTER
FIRE AND ICE (1983)	WILLY BOGNER
FIRE AND ICE (AF)	GERRY CONWAY
FIRE AND ICE (AF)	ROY THOMAS
FIRE AND ICE (AF)	RALPH BAKSHI
FIRE BIRDS	DALE DYE
FIRE BIRDS	DAVID TAYLOR
FIRE BIRDS	JOHN K. SWENSSON
FIRE BIRDS	NICK THIEL
FIRE BIRDS	PAUL F. EDWARDS
FIRE BIRDS	STEP TYNER
FIRE DOWN BELOW - S	JEB STUART
FIRE HOUSE - S	R. J. STEWART
FIRE MAN- S	DONALD L. STEWART
FIRE ON THE MOUNTAIN - S	JOHN SACRET YOUNG
FIRE ON THE MOUNTAIN - S	MICHAEL THOMAS
FIRE PRINCESS - S	REBECCA KALIN
FIRE SALE	ROBERT KLANE
FIRE WITH FIRE	BILL PHILLIPS
FIRE WITH FIRE	PAUL BOORSTIN
FIRE WITH FIRE	SHARON BOORSTIN
FIRE WITH FIRE	WARREN SKAAREN†
FIRE WITHIN, THE	LOUIS MALLE
FIRE, THE - S	KEVIN REYNOLDS
FIRECRACKER	KEN METCALFE
FIREDOGS - S	CHRIS RUPPENTHAL
FIREFALL - S	MICHAEL THOMAS
FIREFIGHT (SHORT)	SHELDON B. LETTICH
FIREFIGHTER - S	THOMAS LEE WRIGHT
FIREFLY - S	DANIEL LIPMAN
FIREFLY - S	RONALD COWEN
FIREFOX	ALEX LASKER
FIREFOX	WENDELL WELLMAN
FIREHEAD	JEFF MANDELL
FIREHEAD	PETER YUVAL
FIREMEN'S BALL, THE	IVAN PASSER
FIREMEN'S BALL, THE	MILOS FORMAN
FIREPOWER	BILL KERBY
FIREPOWER	MICHAEL WINNER
FIREPOWER - S	MICHAEL PATRICK GOODMAN
FIRES WITHIN	CYNTHIA CIDRE
FIRESTAR - S	DANIEL PETRIE, JR.
FIRESTARTER	STANLEY MANN
FIREWALKER	JEFFREY ROSENBAUM
FIREWALKER	NORMAN ALADJEM
FIREWALKER	ROBERT E. GOSNELL
FIREWOLF - S	JOHN A. GALLAGHER
FIREWOLF - S	STEVE JAMES
FIRM, THE - S	DAVID RABE
FIRST AMERICAN REBEL - S	ZALMAN KING
FIRST AMONG THE BEST - S	BUD SHRAKE
FIRST BLOOD	MICHAEL KOZOLL
FIRST BLOOD	SYLVESTER STALLONE
FIRST BLOOD	WILLIAM SACKHEIM
FIRST BOOK OF EPPIE - S	PATRICIA RESNICK
FIRST BORN - S	CAROLINE THOMPSON
FIRST CLASS - S	JEFFREY ALAN FISKIN
FIRST DEADLY SIN, THE	MANN RUBIN
FIRST DRAFT (P)	YALE UDOFF
FIRST FAMILY	BUCK HENRY
FIRST LIGHT - S	NAOMI FONER
FIRST LOVE	DAVID FREEMAN
FIRST LOVE - S	DANIEL H. VINING
FIRST MEN IN THE MOON	NIGEL KNEALE
FIRST MONDAY IN OCTOBER	JEROME LAWRENCE
FIRST MONDAY IN OCTOBER	ROBERT E. LEE
FIRST NAME: CARMEN	ANNE-MARIE MIEVILLE
FIRST NUDIE MUSICAL, THE	BRUCE KIMMEL
FIRST OFFENDER (CTF) - S	JEFFREY KINDLEY
FIRST STRIKE - S	DONALD L. STEWART
FIRST TIME, THE	CHARLES LOVENTHAL
FIRST TIME, THE	SUSAN WEISER-FINLEY
FIRST TIME, THE	WILLIAM FRANKLIN FINLEY
FIRST WIFE, THE (P)	JAY PRESSON ALLEN
FIRST WIVE'S CLUB - S	JANET ROACH
FIRST, LAST & ALWAYS - S	SUE JETTE
FIRSTBORN	RON KOSLOW
FIRSTBORN, THE - S	KENNETH JOHNSON
FISH CALLED WANDA, A	JOHN CLEESE
FISH HAWK	BLANCHE HANALIS
FISH STORY, A - S	MITCH GLAZER
FISH THAT SAVED PITTSBURGH, THE	JAISON STARKES
FISH THAT SAVED PITTSBURGH, THE	EDMOND STEVENS
FISHER KING, THE	RICHARD LAGRAVENESE
FISHERMAN, THE - S	DIANNE HOUSTON
FISHING (P)	MICHAEL WELLER
FISHTAIL - S	RONNI KERN
FIST IN HIS POCKET	MARCO BELLOCCHIO
FIST OF FEAR TOUCH OF DEATH	RON HARVEY
FISTFIGHTER	CARLOS VASALLO
FISTFIGHTER	MAX BLOOM
FISTFUL OF CHOPSTICKS, A	DAVID RANDOLF
FISTFUL OF CHOPSTICKS, A	ELLIOTT HONG
FISTFUL OF CHOPSTICKS, A	JOHNNY YUNE
FISTFUL OF CHOPSTICKS, A	TIM CLAWSON
FISTS OF BLOOD	PETER WEST
FITZCARRALDO	WERNER HERZOG
FIVE AGAINST THE HOUSE	STIRLING SILLIPHANT
FIVE CAR STUD - S	ALEC LORIMORE
FIVE CAR STUD - S	TERRY WINKLESS
FIVE CORNERS	JOHN PATRICK SHANLEY
FIVE DAYS FROM HOME	WILLIAM MOORE
FIVE DAYS ONE SUMMER	MICHAEL AUSTIN
FIVE EASY PIECES	BOB RAFELSON
FIVE EASY PIECES	CAROLE EASTMAN
FIVE FINGER EXERCISE (P)	PETER SHAFFER
FIVE GATES TO HELL	JAMES CLAVELL
FIVE GOLDEN DRAGONS	HARRY ALAN TOWERS
FIVE GRAVES TO CAIRO	BILLY WILDER
FIVE HEARTBEATS, THE	KEENEN IVORY WAYANS
FIVE HEARTBEATS, THE	ROBERT TOWNSEND
FIVE MILES TO MIDNIGHT	PETER VIERTEL
FIVE MILES TO MIDNIGHT	HUGH WHEELER†
FIVE MILLION YEARS TO EARTH	NIGEL KNEALE
FIVE O'CLOCK FOXTROT - S	JOE NEOLA
FIVE O'CLOCK FOXTROT - S	MARY NEOLA
FIVE ON THE BLACK HAND SIDE	OSCAR WILLIAMS
FIVE OUT OF SIX (SHORT)	DANIEL TAPLITZ
FIVE PENNIES, THE	JACK ROSE
FIVE PENNIES, THE	MEL SHAVELSON
FIVE THOUSAND FINGERS OF DOCTOR T, THE	TED GEISEL
FIVE WEEKS IN A BALLOON	CHARLES BENNETT
FIVE WEEKS IN A BALLOON	IRWIN ALLEN
FIXED BAYONETS	SAMUEL FULLER
FIXIN' TO DIE - S	DOUG PALAU
FLAG FOR SUNRISE - S	DJORDJE MILICEVIC
FLAG TO FLY, A - S	VINCENT GUTIERREZ
FLAME	ANDREW BIRKIN
FLAMING STAR	CLAIR HUFFAKER†
FLAMINGO - S	JERE CUNNINGHAM
FLAMINGO KID, THE	GARRY MARSHALL
FLAMINGO KID, THE	NEAL MARSHALL
FLAP	CLAIR HUFFAKER†
FLASH - S	ALLEN ESROCK
FLASH GORDON	LORENZO SEMPLE
FLASH OF EDEN - S	TERRY CURTIS FOX
FLASH OF GREEN, A	VICTOR NUNEZ
FLASH, THE - S	JIM STRAIN
FLASHBACK	DAVID LOUGHERY
FLASHDANCE	JOE ESZTERHAS
FLASHDANCE	THOMAS HEDLEY JR.
FLASHDANCE II - S	JEFFREY ALAN FISKIN
FLASHDANCE II - S	JOE ESZTERHAS

Fl-Fr

FILM WRITERS GUIDE

Title	Writer
FLASHER'S MAGIC - S	GRAEME CLIFFORD
FLASHOVER - S	THOMAS LEE WRIGHT
FLASHPOINT	DENNIS SHRYACK
FLASHPOINT	MICHAEL BUTLER
FLAT OUT - S	LAWRENCE HAUBEN
FLAT OUT SPEED - S	DAN JENKINS
FLAT OUT SPEED - S	BUD SHRAKE
FLATBUSH GAS - S	SCOTT PARKER
FLATLINERS	PETER FILARDI
FLATS - S	RUDOLPH G. WURLITZER
FLAWLESS - S	ROBERT MEGGINSON
FLEA IN HER EAR, A	JOHN MORTIMER
FLESH + BLOOD	GERARD SOETEMAN
FLESH + BLOOD	PAUL VERHOEVEN
FLESH FOR FRANKENSTEIN	PAUL MORRISSEY
FLESH GORDON MEETS THE COSMIC CHEERLEADERS	HOWARD ZIEHM
FLESHBURN	GEORGE GAGE
FLETCH	ANDREW BERGMAN
FLETCH LIVES	LEON CAPETANOS
FLEX - S	ROBERT KEATS
FLIGHT OF BLACK ANGEL (CTF)	HENRY DOMONIC
FLIGHT OF THE INTRUDER	ROBERT DILLON
FLIGHT OF THE INTRUDER	DAVID SHABER
FLIGHT OF THE NAVIGATOR	MARK H. BAKER
FLIGHT OF THE NAVIGATOR	MATT MACMANUS
FLIGHT OF THE NAVIGATOR	MICHAEL BURTON
FLIGHT OF THE PHOENIX	LUKAS HELLER†
FLING, THE - S	EMILY LEVINE
FLIPS - S	ANDY TENNANT
FLIPSIDE - S	DEBORAH BARON
FLOATERS - S	TERRY SOUTHERN
FLOATING BRIDGE - S	CHRIS NOLAN
FLOATING BRIDGE - S	LAURIE SCHOLNICK
FLOATING LIGHT BULB, THE (P)	WOODY ALLEN
FLODDER	DICK MAAS
FLOODS OF FEAR	CHARLES CRICHTON
FLORENTINES, THE - S	CHRISTOPHER HAMPTON
FLORIDA STRAITS (CTF)	STEPHEN METCALFE
FLOWERMAN - S	HASSAN ILDARI
FLOWERS IN THE ATTIC	JEFFREY BLOOM
FLY AWAY HOME - S	HOWARD CUSHNIR
FLY AWAY HOME - S	MARTIN SALINAS
FLY AWAY HOME - S	MICHAEL JAMES LOVE
FLY BY - S	TIMOTHY B. MCCANLIES
FLY, THE	JAMES CLAVELL
FLY, THE	CHARLES EDWARD POGUE
FLY, THE	DAVID CRONENBERG
FLY II, THE	FRANK DARABONT
FLY II, THE	JIM WHEAT
FLY II, THE	KEN WHEAT
FLY II, THE	MICK GARRIS
FLYING - S	RICHARD KLETTER
FLYING COLORS - S	THOMAS MCGUANE
FLYING DUTCHMAN, THE - S	WES CLARRIDGE
FLYING PELICAN, THE - S	NEIL COHEN
FLYING TIGERFISH - S	GARY K. WOLF
FLYING TIGERS - S	JOHN WATSON
FLYING TIGERS - S	JULIAN BARRY
FLYING TIGERS - S	PEN DENSHAM
FM	EZRA SACKS
FOG, THE	DEBRA HILL
FOG, THE	JOHN CARPENTER
FOLKS - S	ROBERT KLANE
FOLLIES (P)	JAMES GOLDMAN
FOLLOW A STAR	JACK DAVIES
FOLLOW ME	PETER SHAFFER
FOLLOW THAT BIRD	JUDY FREUDBERG
FOLLOW THAT BIRD	TONY GEISS
FOOD OF THE GODS, THE	BERT I. GORDON
FOOD OF THE GODS II	BERT I. GORDON
FOOD OF THE GODS II	E. KIM BREWSTER
FOOL FOR LOVE	SAM SHEPARD
FOOL'S GOLD - S	JAMES D. BUCHANAN
FOOLIN' AROUND	DAVID SWIFT
FOOLIN' AROUND	MICHAEL KANE
FOOLISH THINGS - S	LLOYD FONVIELLE
FOOLPROOF - S	FERNANDO DOTY
FOOLS DIE - S	CYNTHIA CIDRE
FOOLS OF FORTUNE	MICHAEL HIRST
FOOLS PARADE	JAMES LEE BARRETT†
FOOLS PARADE	HORTON FOOTE
FOOLS PARADISE - S	ALLEN HOLLEB
FOOTLOOSE	DEAN PITCHFORD
FOR BETTER OR FOR WORSE - S	ALAN BERGER
FOR BETTER OR FOR WORSE - S	KATHY GORI
FOR KEEPS	DENISE DE CLUE
FOR KEEPS	TIM KAZURINSKY
FOR LOVE OF IVY	SIDNEY POITIER
FOR NORA	HESPER ANDERSON
FOR ONE NIGHT ONLY - S	ROBERT MOLONEY
FOR PETE'S SAKE	STANLEY SHAPIRO†
FOR PETE'S SAKE	MAURICE RICHLIN†
FOR QUEEN AND COUNTRY	MARTIN STELLMAN
FOR QUEEN AND COUNTRY	TRIX WORRELL
FOR SALE (P)	JEFFREY ARCH
FOR SINGLES ONLY - S	BURT PRELUTSKY
FOR THE BOYS	MARSHALL BRICKMAN
FOR THE BOYS	NEAL JIMENEZ
FOR THE BOYS	LINDY LAUB
FOR THE FIRST TIME - S	PATRICIA L. KNOP
FOR THE LOVE OF BENJI	JOE CAMP
FOR THE USE OF THE HALL (P)	OLIVER D. HAILEY
FOR YOUR EYES ONLY	MICHAEL G. WILSON
FOR YOUR EYES ONLY	RICHARD MAIBAUM†
FORBIDDEN	WILLIAM B. SACKHEIM
FORBIDDEN AMERICA	WILLIAM P. MILLING
FORBIDDEN DANCE, THE	JOHN PLATT
FORBIDDEN DANCE, THE	MENAHEM GOLAN
FORBIDDEN DANCE, THE	ROY LANGSDON
FORBIDDEN LAND - S	RICHARD MATHESON
FORBIDDEN STREET, THE	RING LARDNER JR.
FORBIDDEN SUN	ROBIN HARDY
FORBIDDEN WORLD	JIM WYNORSKI
FORBIDDEN WORLD	R.J. ROBERTSON
FORBIDDEN WORLD	TIM CURNEN
FORBIDDEN ZONE	MATTHEW BRIGHT
FORBIDDEN ZONE	NICK JAMES
FORBIDDEN ZONE	NICK L. MARTINSON
FORBIDDEN ZONE	RICHARD ELFMAN
FORCE 10 FROM NAVARONE	ROBIN CHAPMAN
FORCE MAJEURE - S	BRUCE WAGNER
FORCE OF EVIL	ABRAHAM POLONSKY
FORCE OF ONE, A	PAT JOHNSON
FORCE OF ONE, A	ERNEST TIDYMAN†
FORCE: FIVE	ROBERT CLOUSE
FORCE: FIVE	EMIL FARKAS
FORCE: FIVE	GEORGE GOLDSMITH
FORCED VENGEANCE	FRANKLIN THOMPSON
FOREIGN AFFAIR, A	BILLY WILDER
FOREIGN BODIES - S	HILARY HENKIN
FOREIGN BODY	CELINE LA FRIENERE
FOREIGN CORRESPONDENT	CHARLES BENNETT
FOREIGN EXCHANGE - S	WILLIAM J. DAVIES
FOREIGN EXCHANGE - S	WILLIAM OSBORNE
FOREIGN LANGUAGES - S	ANDREW DAVIES
FOREIGN POLICY - S	ALLAN WEISBECKER
FOREIGNER, THE	AMOS POE
FOREIGNERS - S	BRAD BUCKNER
FOREIGNERS - S	EUGENIE ROSS-LEMING
FORENSIC & THE NAVIGATOR (P)	SAM SHEPARD
FOREPLAY	DAN GREENBURG
FOREPLAY	DAVID ODELL
FOREVER - S	FREDERIC HUNTER
FOREVER 17 - S	R.M. BADAT
FOREVER FACTOR, THE - S	FRED DEKKER
FOREVER FEMALE	JULIUS J. EPSTEIN
FOREVER MINE - S	PAUL SCHRADER
FOREVER MURRAY - S	EDWARD DECTER
FOREVER MURRAY - S	JOHN J. STRAUSS
FOREVER YOUNG	RAY CONNOLLY
FOREVER, LULU	AMOS KOLLEK
FORGET ME NOT - S	BRAD BUCKNER
FORGET ME NOT - S	EUGENIE ROSS-LEMING
FORGOTTEN PRISONERS: THE AMNESTY FILES (CTF)	CINDY MYERS
FORGOTTEN PRISONERS: THE AMNESTY FILES (CTF)	REX WEINER
FORMULA, THE	STEVE SHAGAN
FORT APACHE, THE BRONX	HEYWOOD GOULD
FORT DOBBS	BURT KENNEDY
FORTRESS - S	LAWRENCE KONNER
FORTRESS - S	MARK ROSENTHAL
FORTUNA - S	LOUIS VENOSTA
FORTUNE COOKIE, THE	BILLY WILDER
FORTUNE COOKIE, THE	I.A.L. DIAMOND†
FORTUNE TELLER, THE - S	JUDITH RASCOE
FORTUNE TELLER, THE - S	STEPHEN TOBOLOWSKY
FORTUNE, THE	CAROLE EASTMAN
FORTY CARATS	LEONARD GERSHE
FORTY GUNS	SAMUEL FULLER
FORTY-DEUCE	ALAN BOWNE†
FOUL PLAY	COLIN HIGGINS†
FOUR ADVENTURES OF REINETTE AND MIRABELLE	ERIC ROHMER
FOUR CORNERS (P)	GINA WENDKOS
FOUR DAYS IN FEBRUARY - S	PATRICIA L. KNOP
FOUR FRIENDS	STEVE TESICH
FOUR HORSEMEN OF THE APOCALYPSE, THE	JOHN GAY
FOUR HUNDRED, THE - S	BO GOLDMAN
FOUR IN THE MORNING	ANTHONY SIMMONS
FOUR LOVE STORIES	AKIRA KUROSAWA
FOUR MONTHS 12 MINUTES - S	ROBBIE FOX
FOUR MUSKETEERS, THE	GEORGE MACDONALD FRASER
FOUR SEASONS, THE	ALAN ALDA
FOUR WIVES	JULIUS J. EPSTEIN
FOURTH DICK, THE - S	GEOFF GRODE
FOURTH FURY - S	MARK MEDOFF
FOURTH MAN, THE	GERARD SOETEMAN
FOURTH OF JULY - S	JONATHAN DAY
FOURTH PROTOCOL, THE	GEORGE AXELROD
FOURTH PROTOCOL, THE	FREDERICK FORSYTH
FOURTH SEASON, THE - S	JOHN BRILEY
FOURTH STORY (CTF)	ANDREW GUERDAT
FOURTH WAR, THE	KENNETH ROSS
FOURTH WAR, THE	STEPHEN PETERS
FOX	TERRY KAHN
FOX AND THE HOUND, THE (AF)	BURNY MATTISON
FOX AND THE HOUND, THE (AF)	DAVID MICHENER
FOX AND THE HOUND, THE (AF)	TED BERMAN
FOX, THE	HOWARD KOCH
FOX, THE	LEWIS JOHN CARLINO
FOX, THE - S	CHARLES ROBERT CARNER
FOXBAT - S	DANILO BACH
FOXES	GERALD AYRES
FRAGILE LIFE, A - S	JOHN BRILEY
FRAME-UP, THE - S	NICHOLAS MEYER
FRAMED	MORT BRISKIN
FRAMED (CTF)	GARY ROSEN
FRANCES	CHRISTOPHER DEVORE
FRANCES	ERIC BERGREN
FRANCES	NICHOLAS KAZAN
FRANCESCO	LILIANI CAVANI
FRANK FILM (SHORT)	FRANK MOURIS
FRANKENCAR - S	PAUL BARTEL
FRANKENCAR - S	RICHARD BLACKBURN
FRANKENHOOKER	FRANK HENLENLOTTER
FRANKENHOOKER	ROBERT MARTIN
FRANKENSTEIN - S	CHARLES EDWARD POGUE
FRANKENSTEIN GOES TO HARLEM - S	JONATHAN ROBERTS
FRANKENSTEIN UNBOUND	F.X. FEENEY
FRANKENSTEIN UNBOUND	ROGER CORMAN
FRANKENWEENIE (SHORT)	TIM BURTON
FRANKIE AND JOHNNY	TERRENCE MCNALLY
FRANKIE: THE FRANKIE LYMON STORY - S	TINA ANDREWS
FRANKY'S STREETS - S	FRANK PUGLIESE
FRANTIC	GERARD BRACH
FRANTIC	ROMAN POLANSKI
FRANTIC (1957)	LOUIS MALLE
FRAT RATS - S	JIM HART
FRATERNITY (P)	JEFF STETSON
FRATERNITY VACATION	LINDSAY HARRISON
FRATS - S	MAX EMBER
FRAULEIN DOKTOR	STANLEY MANN
FREAKY FRIDAY	MARY RODGERS
FREE (P)	MARK MEDOFF
FREE AGENTS - S	JEFFREY ARCH
FREE AT LAST - S	ALEX AYRES
FREE JOANIE LITTLE - S	JOEL OLIANSKY
FREE LUNCH - S	NINA SHENGOLD
FREE RIDE	LEE FULKERSON
FREE RIDE	ROBERT BELL
FREE RIDE	RONALD ZWANG
FREE SPIRIT	JAMES HILL
FREE SPIRIT - S	A.J. CAROTHERS
FREE SPIRITS - S	BENNETT YELLIN
FREE SPIRITS - S	PETER FARRELLY
FREE WILLY - S	KEITH A. WALKER
FREE WILLY - S	TOM BENEDEK
FREEBIE AND THE BEAN	FLOYD MUTRUX
FREEBIE AND THE BEAN	ROBERT KAUFMAN
FREEDOM	JOHN EMERY
FREEDOM SONG - S	DAVID SHABER
FREEDOM SUMMER - S	MIKE MAHERN
FREEJACK - S	RONALD SHUSETT
FREEJACK - S	STEVEN PRESSFIELD
FREESTYLE - S	ALLEN HOLLEB
FREEWALKERS - S	DENNIS CLARK
FREEWAY	DARRELL FETTY
FREEWAY	FRANCIS DELIA
FREEWAY MANIAC, THE	GAHAN WILSON
FREEWAY MANIAC, THE	PAUL WINTERS
FREEZE OUT - S	DONALD L. STEWART
FRENCH CONNECTION, THE	ERNEST TIDYMAN†
FRENCH CONNECTION II	ALEXANDER JACOBS†
FRENCH CONNECTION II	ROBERT DILLON
FRENCH DRESSING - S	MOLLY-ANN LEIKIN

INDEX OF FILM TITLES

FRENCH KISS - S	JEAN-YVES PITOUN
FRENCH KISS, THE - S	HERSCHEL WEINGROD
FRENCH KISS, THE - S	TIMOTHY HARRIS
FRENCH LESSON	BRIAN GILBERT
FRENCH LIEUTENANT'S WOMAN, THE	HAROLD PINTER
FRENCH LINE, THE	RICHARD SALE
FRENCH MISTRESS, A	ROY BOULTING
FRENCH POSTCARDS	GLORIA KATZ
FRENCH POSTCARDS	WILLARD HUYCK
FRENCH REVOLUTION, THE	DAVID AMBROSE
FRENCH TOAST - S	JEFFREY ARCH
FRENCH WAY, THE	CHRISTOPHER FRANK
FRENCHIE	OSCAR BRODNEY
FRENZY	ANTHONY SHAFFER
FRESH HORSES	LARRY KETRON
FRESHMAN, THE	ANDREW BERGMAN
FREUD'S HAT - S	JANET ROACH
FRIDA AND DIEGO - S	ILANA BAR-DIN
FRIDAY THE 13TH	VICTOR MILLER
FRIDAY THE 13TH PART 2	RON KURZ
FRIDAY THE 13TH PART 3	CAROL WATSON
FRIDAY THE 13TH PART 3	MARTIN KITROSSER
FRIDAY THE 13TH, PART IV	BRUCE HIDEMI SAKOU
FRIDAY THE 13TH, PART IV	BARNEY COHEN
FRIDAY THE 13TH PART V	DANNY STEINMANN
FRIDAY THE 13TH PART V	DAVID COHEN
FRIDAY THE 13TH PART V	MARTIN KITROSSER
FRIDAY THE 13TH PART VI	TOM MCLOUGHLIN
FRIDAY THE 13TH, PART VII	DARYL HANEY
FRIDAY THE 13TH, PART VII	MANUEL FIDELLO
FRIDAY THE 13TH PART VIII	ROB HEDDEN
FRIED GREEN TOMATOES AT THE WHISTLE STOP CAFE - S	FANNIE FLAGG
FRIEND OF THE COURT - S	HENRY OLEK
FRIENDLY RELATIONS - S	DORI PIERSON
FRIENDLY, THE - S	RUSTY LEMORANDE
FRIENDS OF EDDIE COYLE, THE	PAUL MONASH
FRIENDS, LOVERS & LUNATICS	MICHAEL TAAV
FRIES - S	DANNY OPATOSHU
FRIES - S	VICKI HOCHBURG
FRIGHT NIGHT	TOM HOLLAND
FRIGHT NIGHT PART 2	MIGUEL TEJADA-FLORES
FRIGHT NIGHT PART 2	TIM METCALFE
FRIGHT NIGHT PART 2	TOMMY LEE WALLACE
FRIGHTMARE	NORMAN THADDEUS VANE
FRINGE DWELLERS, THE	PHOISON BERESFORD
FRINGE DWELLERS, THE	BRUCE BERESFORD
FRISCO KID, THE	MICHAEL ELIAS
FRITZ THE CAT (AF)	RALPH BAKSHI
FROG - S	EVERETT DEROCHE
FROG PRINCE, THE	BRIAN GILBERT
FROG PRINCE, THE - S	MAX EMBER
FROGS	ROBERT BLEES
FROM A WHISPER TO A SCREAM	JEFF BURR
FROM BEYOND	BRIAN YUZNA
FROM BEYOND	STUART GORDON
FROM BEYOND	DENNIS PAOLI
FROM HELL TO TEXAS	WENDELL MAYES
FROM HERE TO ETERNITY	DANIEL TARADASH
FROM HOLLYWOOD TO DEADWOOD	REX PICKETT
FROM NOON TIL THREE	FRANK D. GILROY
FROM RUSSIA WITH LOVE	RICHARD MAIBAUM†
FROM THE EARTH TO THE MOON	ROBERT BLEES
FROM THE HIP	BOB CLARK
FROM THE HIP	DAVID E. KELLEY
FROM THE LIFE OF THE MARIONETTES	INGMAR BERGMAN
FROM THE TERRACE	ERNEST LEHMAN
FRONT PAGE, THE	BILLY WILDER
FRONT PAGE, THE	I.A.L. DIAMOND†
FRONT, THE	WALTER BERNSTEIN
FRONTIER FREEMONT	RICHARD FRIEDENBERG
FROST BITE - S	ALAN UGER
FROZEN - S	JONATHAN TYDOR
FRUIT PALACE, THE - S	PIERS ASHWORTH
FRUITS AND NUTS - S	BRUCE VILANCH
FU MANCHU - S	ROBERT KAUFMAN
FUGITIVE GUYS - S	PETER MARTIN WORTMANN
FUGITIVE GUYS - S	ROBERT CONTE
FUGITIVE PIGEON, THE - S	HERSCHEL WEINGROD
FUGITIVE PIGEON, THE - S	TIMOTHY HARRIS
FUGITIVE, THE - S	DAVID NEWMAN
FUGITIVE, THE - S	D.T. TWOHY
FULL COURT PRESS - S	CHRISTOPHER CANAAN
FULL FATHOM FIVE	BART DAVIS
FULL METAL JACKET	GUSTAV HASFORD
FULL METAL JACKET	MICHAEL HERR
FULL METAL JACKET	STANLEY KUBRICK
FULL MOON - S	WILLARD CARROLL
FULL MOON HIGH	LARRY COHEN
FULL MOON IN BLUE WATER	BILL BOZZONE
FULL MOON IN PARIS	ERIC ROHMER
FULL RECOVERY - S	DENNYS MCCOY
FULL RECOVERY - S	PAMELA HICKEY
FULL TREATMENT, THE	VAL GUEST
FULLBLOOD - S	LOUIS GARFINKLE
FUN DOWN THERE	MICHAEL WAITE
FUN DOWN THERE	ROBERT STIGLIANO
FUN HOUSE (P)	ERIC BOGOSIAN
FUN ON A WEEKEND	ANDREW STONE
FUN PARK - S	JAMES ORR
FUN PARK - S	JIM CRUICKSHANK
FUN WHILE IT LASTED - S	FRED BARRON
FUN WHILE IT LASTED - S	JOAN MICKLIN SILVER
FUN WITH DICK AND JANE	DAVID GILER
FUN WITH DICK AND JANE	JERRY BELSON
FUN WITH DICK AND JANE	MORDECAI RICHLER
FUNERAL IN BERLIN	EVAN JONES
FUNERAL MARCH FOR A ONE-MAN BAND (P)	RON WHYTE†
FUNERAL PARTY - S	KEVIN QUINN
FUNERAL, THE	JUZO ITAMI
FUNERAL, THE - S	JOHN CORK
FUNHOUSE, THE	LAWRENCE J. BLOCK
FUNNY ABOUT LOVE	DAVID FRANKEL
FUNNY ABOUT LOVE	NORMAN STEINBERG
FUNNY BUSINESS	SAMUEL H. HARPER
FUNNY FACE	LEONARD GERSHE
FUNNY FARM	JEFFREY BOAM
FUNNY FARM, THE	RON CLARK
FUNNY LADY	ARNOLD SCHULMAN
FUNNY LADY	JAY PRESSON ALLEN
FUNNY MONEY - S	ALEX GORBY
FUNNY MONEY - S	ANDY ROSE
FUNNY SAUCE - S	DELIA EPHRON
FUNNY THING HAPPENED ON THE WAY TO THE FORUM, A (P)	LARRY GELBART
FUNNYMAN	JOHN KORTY
FUR TRADING IN AMERICA - S	JOHN KENT HARRISON
FURTHER ADVENTURES OF TENNESSEE BUCK, THE	BARRY JACOBS
FURTHER ADVENTURES OF TENNESSEE BUCK, THE	PAUL MASON
FURTHER ADVENTURES OF TENNESSEE BUCK, THE	STUART JACOBS
FURY, THE	JOHN FARRIS
FUSS OVER FEATHERS	DON SHARP
FUTBOL - S	GERALD K. SIEGEL
FUTUREBALL - S	STEVE DEJARNATT
FUTURE COP	DANNY BILSON
FUTURE COP	PAUL DE MEO
FUTURE HUNTERS	ANTHONY MAHARAJ
FUTURE HUNTERS	J.L. THOMPSON
FUTURE, THE - S	MICHAEL ALMEREYDA
FUTUREWORLD	MAYO SIMON
FUTUREWORLD	GEORGE W. SCHENCK
FUZZ - S	EVAN HUNTER

G

G.I. JILL - S	BRAD A. MIRMAN
G.I. JONES - S	NEAL MARSHALL
GABLE AND LOMBARD	BARRY SANDLER
GABRIELA	BRUNO BARRETTO
GABRIELA - S	JACK ROSENTHAL
GABY - A TRUE STORY	MARTIN SALINAS
GABY - A TRUE STORY	MICHAEL JAMES LOVE
GAITS OF THE FOREST, THE - S	ROBERT J. AVRECH
GALATEA - S	MARK HOROWITZ
GALAXINA	WILLIAM SACHS
GALAXY - S	JOHN VARLEY
GALAXY OF TERROR	BRUCE CLARK
GALAXY OF TERROR	MARC SIEGLER
GALE FORCE - S	DAVID CHAPPE
GALE FORCE - S	LARRY KONNER
GALE FORCE - S	MARK ROSENTHAL
GALILEO (P)	TOM STOPPARD
GALLANT HOURS, THE	FRANK D. GILROY
GALLIPOLI	DAVID WILLIAMSON
GALLIPOLI	PETER WEIR
GAMBIT	JACK DAVIES
GAMBIT	ALVIN SARGENT
GAMBLER, THE	JAMES TOBACK
GAME OF DEATH	JAN SPEARS
GAME SHOW SCANDAL, THE - S	TERREL SELTZER
GAME, THE	CURTIS BROWN
GAME, THE	JULIA WILSON
GAME, THE	PETER SUMMERS
GAME, THE - S	JOHN J. SCHALTER
GAME, THE - S	TRACY KEENAN WYNN
GAMEKEEPER, THE	BARRY HINES
GAMES, THE	ERICH SEGAL
GANDHI	JOHN BRILEY
GANDY DANCER, THE (P)	JAMES KENNEDY
GANG THAT COULDN'T SHOOT STRAIGHT	WALDO SALT†
GANG'S ALL HERE, THE (P)	ROBERT E. LEE
GANG'S ALL HERE, THE (P)	JEROME LAWRENCE
GANGLAND - S	ROBERT ZEMECKIS
GANGLAND - S	BOB GALE
GANGS OF NEW YORK - S	JAY COCKS
GARBAGE - S	KENNETH H. FRIEDMAN
GARBAGE PAIL KIDS MOVIE, THE	MELINDA PALMER
GARBAGE PAIL KIDS MOVIE, THE	ROD AMATEAU
GARBO TALKS	LARRY GRUSIN
GARCIA - S	NEVIN SCHREINER
GARDE A VUE	CLAUDE MILLER
GARDEN OF THE FINZI-CONTINIS, THE	FRANCO BRUSATI
GARDEN OF THORNS - S	PHILIP RAILSBACK
GARDEN, THE	DEREK JARMAN
GARDENA MIRACLE - S	ELAINE MUELLER
GARDENIA (P)	JOHN GUARE
GARDENS OF STONE	RON BASS
GARDNER, THE - S	ROGER L. SIMON
GARMENT JUNGLE, THE	HARRY KLEINER
GAS	SUSAN SCRANTON
GAS	DICK WOLF
GAS, FOOD, LODGING (SHORT)	KAREN CRONER
GAS-S-S-S! OR HOW IT BECAME NECESSARY TO DESTROY THE WORLD IN ORDER TO SAVE IT!	GEORGE ARMITAGE
GATE, THE	MICHAEL NANKIN
GATE II, THE - S	MICHAEL NANKIN
GATHERING FORCE - S	LESLIE NEWMAN
GATHERING OF EAGLES, A	ROBERT PIROSH†
GATORA	WILLIAM NORTONSR.
GAUNTLET, THE	MICHAEL BUTLER
GAUNTLET, THE	DENNIS SHRYACK
GAWAIN AND THE GREEN KNIGHT	STEPHEN WEEKS
GEEK, THE - S	CAROLINE THOMPSON
GELFAN, THE - S	BARRY BLAUSTEIN
GELFAN, THE - S	DAVID SHEFFIELD
GEMINI (P)	ALBERT INNAURATO
GENERAL HOMO - S	THOMAS LEE WRIGHT
GENERATION	WILLIAM GOODHART
GENGHIS KHAN	BEVERLY CROSS
GENGHIS KHAN - S	JOHN BRILEY
GENIE BOB - S	RYAN ROWE
GENIE MAN - S	GARY K. WOLF
GENIUS, THE - S	LAWRENCE LASKER
GENIUS, THE - S	WALTER F. PARKES
GENIUSES (P)	JONATHAN REYNOLDS
GENTLE SERGEANT, THE	RICHARD T. MURPHY
GENTLE VENGENCE - S	MICHAEL CRISTOFER
GENTLEMEN MARRY BRUNETTES	RICHARD SALE
GENUINE RISK	KURT VOSS
GENUINE RISK	LARRY J. RATTNER
GEORGE MILLER ADDRESS UNKNOWN - S	FRANK PUGLIESE
GEORGIA O'KEEFE - S	CHRIS BRYANT
GEORGY GIRL	PETER NICHOLS
GERALD MCBOING BOING (AF)	TED GEISEL
GERSHWIN - S	JOHN GAURE
GERSHWIN - S	PAUL SCHRADER
GET CARTER	MIKE HODGES
GET CHARLIE TULLY	JOHN WARREN
GET CRAZY	DANNY OPATOSHU
GET CRAZY	DAVID TAYLOR
GET CRAZY	HENRY ROSENBAUM
GET OFF MY BACK	S. LEE POGOSTIN
GET OUT YOUR HANDKERCHIEFS	BERTRAND BLIER
GETAWAY, THE	WALTER HILL
GETTING AWAY - S	DAVID ISAACS
GETTING AWAY - S	KEN LEVINE
GETTING DOWN - S	ROBERT SARNO
GETTING EVEN	JOHN WILLIAM SEE
GETTING EVEN - S	HARRIS GOLDBERG
GETTING EVEN - S	TOM NURSALL
GETTING GIRLS - S	MITCH MARKOWITZ

Ge-Go
FILM WRITERS GUIDE

INDEX OF FILM TITLES

GETTING IT - S ... NICHOLAS KAZAN
GETTING IT ON! ... WILLIAM OLSEN
GETTING IT OVER WITH - S ... RICHARD WHITLEY
GETTING IT RIGHT ... ELIZABETH JANE HOWARD
GETTING LUCKY ... MICHAEL PAUL GIRARD
GETTING OF WISDOM, THE ... ELEANOR WITCOMBE
GETTING OUT (P) ... MARSHA NORMAN
GETTING OVER ... BERNIE ROLLINS
GETTING OVER ... JOHN R. DANIELS
GETTING STRAIGHT ... ROBERT KAUFMAN
GHANDI ... JOHN BRILEY
GHETTO BLASTERS - S ... KEVIN SULLIVAN
GHOST ... BRUCE JOEL RUBIN
GHOST AND MRS. MUIR, THE ... PHILIP DUNNE
GHOST AND THE DARKNESS, THE - S ... WILLIAM GOLDMAN
GHOST BOY - S ... DAVID ANDRUS
GHOST BOY MOON - S ... MARK ROMANEK
GHOST DAD ... BRENT MADDOCK
GHOST DAD ... S.S. WILSON
GHOST DIARY - S ... MARK FROST
GHOST FEVER ... OSCAR BRODNEY
GHOST FEVER ... RON RICH
GHOST GOES WEST, THE - S ... GUY THOMAS
GHOST IN THE INVISIBLE BIKINI, THE ... LOUIS M. HEYWARD
GHOST OF HELL'S KITCHEN, THE - S ... DENNIS PALUMBO
GHOST RIDERS IN THE SKY - S ... ALLYN WARNER
GHOST STORY (1981) ... LAWRENCE D. COHEN
GHOST STORY (1974) ... STEPHEN WEEKS
GHOST STORY - S ... MARK SALZMAN
GHOST TOWN ... DAVID SCHMOELLER
GHOST TOWN ... DUKE SANDEFUR
GHOST TOWN (1956) ... JAMESON BREWER
GHOST TOWN - S ... MICHAEL KANE
GHOST TOWN USA - S ... RUSTY LEMORANDE
GHOST WARRIOR ... TIM CURNEN
GHOSTBOAT - S ... GEORGE E. SIMPSON
GHOSTBOAT - S ... NEAL R. BURGER
GHOSTBUSTERS ... DAN AYKROYD
GHOSTBUSTERS ... HAROLD RAMIS
GHOSTBUSTERS II ... DAN AYKROYD
GHOSTBUSTERS II ... HAROLD RAMIS
GHOSTS CAN'T DO IT ... JOHN DEREK
GHOSTS, THE - S ... ERIC LUKE
GHOULIES ... JEFERY LEVY
GHOULIES ... LUCA BERCOVICI
GIANT - S ... ROBERT GARLAND
GIANT CLAW, THE - S ... MICHAEL VENTURA
GIANT KILLER - S ... CLAYTON S. FROHMAN
GIFT, THE ... MICHEL LANG
GIFT, THE - S ... DON SHROLL
GIFT, THE - S ... MICHAEL ALAN EDDY
GIG, THE ... FRANK D. GILROY
GILDA LIVE (FD) ... ANNE BEATTS
GILDA LIVE (FD) ... ROSIE SHUSTER
GIMME AN F ... JIM HART
GINGER ALE AFTERNOON ... GINA WENDKOS
GINGER AND FRED ... FEDERICO FELLINI
GINGER AND FRED ... TONINO GUERRA
GINGERBREAD MAN (P) ... JONATHAN LYNN
GIOVANNI'S RESTAURANT - S ... DALENE YOUNG
GIRL FROM MARS, THE (CTF) ... BRIAN ALAN LANE
GIRL FROM PETROVKA, THE ... ALLAN G. SCOTT
GIRL FROM PETROVKA, THE ... CHRIS BRYANT
GIRL IN A SWING, THE ... GORDON HESSLER
GIRL IN BLACK, A ... MICHAEL CACOYANNIS
GIRL IN THE CADILLAC CONVERTIBLE - S ... JOHN WARREN
GIRL IN THE PICTURE, THE ... CARY PARKER
GIRL NAMED TAMIKO, A ... EDWARD ANHALT
GIRL ON A GOLDEN LEASH - S ... DJORDJE MILICEVIC
GIRL WHO COULDN'T SAY NO, THE ... FRANCO BRUSATI
GIRL WITH THE GOLDEN HAIR, THE - S ... A.J. CAROTHERS
GIRL'S CLUB - S ... JOHN FASANO
GIRLCRAZY - S ... MOLLIE D. MILLER
GIRLFRIEND FROM HELL ... DANIEL M. PETERSON
GIRLFRIENDS ... VICKI POLON
GIRLGRABBERS FROM VENUS - S ... DAVID MISCH
GIRLS IN TROUBLE - S ... JEFF BUHAI
GIRLS IN TROUBLE - S ... STEVEN R. ZACHARIAS
GIRLS JUST WANT TO HAVE FUN ... AMY SPIES
GIRLS OF SUMMER, THE - S ... ANN LEWIS HAMILTON
GIRLS TALK - S ... HAROLD SALWEN
GIRLS TOWN - S ... BECKY JOHNSTON
GIRLS, GIRLS, GIRLS ... EDWARD ANHALT
GIRLS, THE ... MAI ZETTERLING
GIRLSTOWN - S ... ROBERT KAUFMAN
GIUESPPINA ... JAMES HILL
GIUSTINA (SHORT) ... RACHEL FELDMAN
GIVE MY REGARDS TO BROAD STREET ... PAUL MCCARTNEY
GIVE US THE MOON ... VAL GUEST
GIVER, THE - S ... JEREMY BERTRAND FINCH
GIZMERELDA - S ... LARRY B. WILLIAMS
GLADIATOR ... LYLE D. KESSLER
GLADIATOR ... NICHOLAS KAZAN
GLADIATOR OUTCASTS - S ... NEIL CUTHBERT
GLASS HOUSE - S ... JETTE RINCK
GLASS SPHINX, THE ... LOUIS M. HEYWARD
GLASS WEB, THE ... ROBERT BLEES
GLEAMING THE CUBE ... MICHAEL TOLKIN
GLEN AND RANDA ... JIM MCBRIDE
GLEN AND RANDA ... RUDOLPH G. WURLITZER
GLEN OR GLENDA ... EDWARD WOOD†
GLENGARRY GLEN ROSS (P) ... DAVID MAMET
GLENN MILLER STORY, THE ... OSCAR BRODNEY
GLITCH! ... NICO MASTORAKIS
GLITTERBUG - S ... DAVID SEIDLER
GLITTERBUG - S ... JACQUELINE FEATHER
GLOBAL AFFAIR, A ... ARTHUR MARX
GLOBAL AFFAIR, A ... ROBERT FISHER
GLOBAL P.D. - S ... RICHARD OUTTEN
GLORIA ... JOHN CASSAVETES†
GLORY ... KEVIN JARRE
GLORY & THE DREAM, THE - S ... ANDREW BIRKIN
GLORY BOYS, THE - S ... RON KOSLOW
GLORY DAY - S ... HERMAN RAUCHER
GLORY DAYS - S ... A. SCOTT FRANK
GLORY! GLORY! (CMS) ... STAN DANIELS
GLOVE, THE ... HUBERT SMITH
GLOW, THE - S ... ANDREW DEUTSCH
GO DOWN MOSES - S ... DAVID AARON COHEN
GO FOR BROKE ... ROBERT PIROSH†
GO TELL THE SPARTANS ... WENDELL MAYES
GO TO HELL - S ... SCOTT PARKER
GO TO WORK - S ... FLOYD MUTRUX
GO-BETWEEN, THE ... HAROLD PINTER
GOALIE'S ANXIETY AT THE PENALTY KICK, THE ... PETER HANDKE
GOD BLESS YOU, MR. ROSEWATER - S ... ROBERT C. JONES
GOD TOLD ME TO ... LARRY COHEN
GOD'S HEAD - S ... ZALMAN KING
GOD'S LITTLE ACRE ... PHILIP YORDAN
GOD'S WILL ... JULIA CAMERON
GODDESS, THE ... PADDY CHAYEVSKY†
GODFATHER, THE ... FRANCIS FORD COPPOLA
GODFATHER, THE ... MARIO PUZO
GODFATHER, PART II, THE ... FRANCIS FORD COPPOLA
GODFATHER, PART II, THE ... MARIO PUZO
GODFATHER, PART III, THE ... FRANCIS FORD COPPOLA
GODFATHER, PART III, THE ... MARIO PUZO
GODS MUST BE CRAZY, THE ... JAMIE UYS
GODS MUST BE CRAZY 2, THE ... JAMIE UYS
GODSPELL ... DAVID GREENE
GODSPELL ... JOHN MICHAEL TEBELAK
GODZILLA - S ... FRED DEKKER
GOIN' DOWN THE ROAD ... WILLIAM C. FRUET
GOIN' SOUTH ... ALAN MANDEL
GOIN' SOUTH ... AL RAMRUS
GOIN' SOUTH ... CHARLES SHYER
GOIN' SOUTH ... JOHN HERMAN SHANER
GOIN' TO CHICAGO ... PAUL LEDER
GOING ALL THE WAY ... FRED BARRON
GOING APE! ... JEREMY JOE KRONSBERG
GOING BERSERK ... DAVID STEINBERG
GOING BERSERK ... DANA OLSEN
GOING FOR BROKE - S ... FIONA LEWIS
GOING HOME ... LAWRENCE MARCUS
GOING HOME - S ... ELIZABETH BRADLEY
GOING HOME - S ... STEPHEN MCPHERSON
GOING IN STYLE ... MARTIN BREST
GOING PLACES ... BERTRAND BLIER
GOING WEST AMERICA - S ... JEB STUART
GOKEN RENDEZVOUS, THE - S ... CHRIS BRYANT
GOLD - S ... BOB SWAIM
GOLD - S ... DAVID H. FRANZONI
GOLD COAST - S ... ROBERT ROY POOL
GOLD COAST, THE - S ... ALAN BERGER
GOLD COAST, THE - S ... KATHY GORI
GOLD LUST - S ... DANA OLSEN
GOLD LUST - S ... ROBERT COLLECTOR
GOLDDIGGERS - S ... STEPHEN M. TOLKIN
GOLDEN AGE, THE (P) ... A.R. GURNEY
GOLDEN BRAID ... PAUL COX
GOLDEN CHILD, THE ... DENNIS FELDMAN
GOLDEN GATE ... DYANNE ASSIMOW
GOLDEN GATE - S ... DAVID HENRY HWANG
GOLDEN GATE - S ... ROGER L. SIMON
GOLDEN GATE IRON - S ... KEVIN JARRE
GOLDEN GIRL ... JOHN KOHN
GOLDEN KNIGHTS - S ... MEL FRIEDMAN
GOLDEN LEGS - S ... STANLEY WEISER
GOLDEN NEEDLES ... S. LEE POGOSTIN
GOLDEN RENDEZVOUS, THE - S ... ALLAN G. SCOTT
GOLDEN SEAL, THE ... JOHN P. GROVES
GOLDEN VOYAGE OF SINBAD, THE ... BRIAN H. CLEMENS
GOLDFINGER ... RICHARD MAIBAUM†
GOLDSTEIN ... PHILIP KAUFMAN
GONE FISHIN' - S ... JEFFREY ABRAMS
GONE FISHIN' - S ... JILL MAZURSKY
GONE WITH THE WIND - PART II - S ... JAMES GOLDMAN
GONG SHOW MOVIE, THE ... CHUCK BARRIS
GONG SHOW MOVIE, THE ... ROBERT DOWNEY
GOOD AS GOLD - S ... JOSEPH HELLER
GOOD AS GOLD - S ... STEPHEN GELLER
GOOD BEHAVIOR - S ... KEVIN WADE
GOOD COMPANY - S ... R. J. STEWART
GOOD DAY TO DIE, A - S ... TERRELL TANNEN
GOOD DIE YOUNG, THE ... LEWIS GILBERG
GOOD DOCTOR, THE - S ... DENNIS KLEIN
GOOD DOG CARL - S ... JAMES D. COX
GOOD FATHER, THE ... CHRISTOPHER HAMPTON
GOOD FELLAS ... MARTIN SCORCESE
GOOD FELLAS ... NICHOLAS PILEGGI
GOOD GUYS AND THE BAD GUYS, THE ... RONALD M. COHEN
GOOD GUYS AND THE BAD GUYS, THE ... DENNIS SHRYACK
GOOD GUYS WEAR BLACK ... MARK MEDOFF
GOOD KING HARRY - S ... JEFFREY PRICE
GOOD KING HARRY - S ... PETER SEAMAN
GOOD LUCK - S ... JOHN HILL
GOOD LUCK TO A SWELL KID - S ... VALERIE WEST
GOOD LUCK, MISS WYCOFF ... POLLY PLATT
GOOD MAN, A - S ... DAVID LOUCKA
GOOD MORNING VIETNAM ... MITCH MARKOWITZ
GOOD MORNING, BABYLON ... PAOLO TAVIANI
GOOD MORNING, BABYLON ... VITTORIO TAVIANI
GOOD MORNING, CHICAGO - S ... MARK FROST
GOOD MORNING, HE LIED - S ... DAVID AMBROSE
GOOD MORNING HEARTACHE - S ... THOMAS RITZ
GOOD MORNING...AND GOODBYE ... RUSS MEYER
GOOD MOTHER, THE ... MICHAEL BORTMAN
GOOD NEIGHBOR SAM ... DAVID SWIFT
GOOD NEWS/BAD NEWS - S ... BILL MASTERS
GOODNIGHT MOON - S ... CHRISTOPHER CROWE
GOODNIGHT MOON - S ... WALTER KLENHARD
GOOD RIDDANCE - S ... LORENZO SEMPLE
GOOD SHOW, THE - S ... IAN MCEWAN
GOOD SPORTS - S ... SUSAN RICE
GOOD TO GO ... BLAINE NOVAK
GOOD VIBES - S ... NANCY DOWD
GOOD WIFE, THE ... PETER KENNA
GOOD-BYE - S ... ZALMAN KING
GOODBYE CALIFORNIA - S ... CHRIS BRYANT
GOODBYE CHARLIE (P) ... GEORGE AXELROD
GOODBYE FOREVER - S ... ALAN BERGER
GOODBYE FOREVER - S ... KATHY GORI
GOODBYE GEMINI ... EDMUND WARD
GOODBYE GIRL, THE ... NEIL SIMON
GOODBYE MY FANCY ... IVAN GOFF
GOODBYE MY FANCY (P) ... FAY KANIN
GOODBYE MY FANCY (P) ... MICHAEL KANIN
GOODBYE NEW YORK ... AMOS KOLLEK
GOODBYE PEOPLE, THE ... HERB GARDNER
GOODBYE PORK PIE ... GEOFF MURPHY
GOODBYE PORK PIE ... IAN MUNE
GOODBYE, CHILDREN ... LOUIS MALLE
GOODBYE, COLUMBUS ... ARNOLD SCHULMAN
GOODNIGHT MOON - S ... ERIC ROTH
GOONIES, THE ... CHRIS COLUMBUS
GOONIES, THE ... STEVEN SPIELBERG
GOONIES 2 - S ... RICHARD OUTTEN
GOOSE AND TOM TOM (P) ... DAVID RABE
GOR ... RICK MARX
GORILLAS IN THE MIST ... ANNA HAMILTON PHELAN
GORILLAS IN THE MIST ... TAB MURPHY
GORKY (P) ... STEVE TESICH
GORKY PARK ... DENNIS POTTER
GORP ... A. MARTIN ZWEIBACH
GORP ... JEFFREY KONVITZ
GOSPEL - S ... ERIC ROTH
GOSPEL ACCORDING TO VIC ... CHARLES GORMLEY

Title	Writer
GOSPEL SINGER - S	DANIEL H. VINING
GOSSIP COLUMNIST - S	PAUL RUDNICK
GOSSIP COLUMNIST, THE - S	KATHY COHEN
GOSSIP COLUMNIST, THE - S	PAT PROFT
GOTCHA!	PAUL G. HENSLER
GOTCHA!	DAN GORDON
GOTHAM (CTF)	LLOYD FONVIELLE
GOTHIC	STEPHEN VOLK
GOV - S	TODD DURHAM
GRABBERS	DAVID PEOPLES
GRACE - S	NICHOLAS KAZAN
GRACE QUIGLEY	A. MARTIN ZWEIBACH
GRAD WEEK - S	THOMAS BABE
GRADUATE, THE	BUCK HENRY
GRADUATE, THE	CALDER WILLINGHAM
GRADUATION DAY	ANNE MARISSE
GRADUATION DAY	DAVID BAUGHN
GRADUATION DAY	HERB FREED
GRAFFITI BRIDGE	PRINCE
GRAN PRIX 2000 - S	FRED LEBOW
GRAND CANYON	LAWRENCE KASDAN
GRAND GAME, THE - S (SHORT)	DENNIS PALUMBO
GRAND POSEUR, THE (SHORT)	ADAM DUBOV
GRAND PRIX	ROBERT ALAN ARTHUR†
GRAND THEFT AUTO	RANCE HOWARD
GRAND THEFT AUTO	RON HOWARD
GRAND TOUR, THE	D.T. TWOHY
GRANDE ISLE - S	HESPER ANDERSON
GRANDFATHER - S	RAND RAVICH
GRANDVIEW, U.S.A.	KEN HIXON
GRAPES OF WRATH, THE (P)	FRANK GALATI
GRASS IS GREENER, THE - S	GEORGE GALLO
GRASS ROOTS - S	EARL MAC RAUCH
GRASS WIDOW, THE - S	SNOO WILSON
GRASSHOPPER, THE	GARRY MARSHALL
GRASSHOPPER, THE	JERRY BELSON
GRAVE FOR A DOLPHIN - S	MICHAEL THOMAS
GRAVEYARD SHIFT	JOHN ESPOSITO
GRAVITY GUY - S	DAVID SIMKINS
GRAVITY OF STARS, THE - S	BRUCE WAGNER
GRAVY TRAIN	TERENCE MALICK
GRAVY TRAIN, THE	BILL KERBY
GRAY GHOST, THE - S	ELIZABETH BRADLEY
GRAY GHOST, THE - S	STEPHEN MCPHERSON
GRAY LADY DOWN	HOWARD SACKLER
GRAY MATTERS - S	NICHOLAS KAZAN
GREASE	BRONTE WOODARD†
GREASE 2	KEN FINKLEMAN
GREASED LIGHTNING	MELVIN VAN PEEBLES
GREASED LIGHTNING	LEON CAPETANOS
GREASEPAINT - S	GEN LEROY
GREASER'S PALACE	ROBERT DOWNEY
GREASIER - S	GARY DAVID GOLDBERG
GREASIER - S	ROBERT KLANE
GREAT AMERICAN BELLY DANCE - S	MICHAEL CRISTOFER
GREAT AND THE NEAR GREAT, THE - S	WILLIAM TEPPER
GREAT BABY BLUE, THE - S	JOHN BRILEY
GREAT BALLS OF FIRE	JACK BARAN
GREAT BALLS OF FIRE	JIM MCBRIDE
GREAT BANK HOAX, THE	JOSEPH JACOBY
GREAT BANK ROBBERY, THE	WILLIAM PETER BLATTY
GREAT CAPE GIRARDEAU LEAP, THE - S	ALEC LORIMORE
GREAT CAPE GIRARDEAU LEAP, THE - S	JERRY BELSON
GREAT CAPE GIRARDEAU LEAP, THE - S	TERRY WINKLESS
GREAT CATHERINE	HUGH LEONARD
GREAT COLORADO RIVER MARATHON, THE - S	STIRLING SILLIPHANT
GREAT ESCAPE, THE	JAMES CLAVELL
GREAT EXHIBITION, THE (P)	DAVID HARE
GREAT EXPECTATIONS	DAVID LEAN†
GREAT GATSBY, THE	FRANCIS FORD COPPOLA
GREAT HANDS - S	JAMES PASTERNAK
GREAT MOUSE DETECTIVE, THE (AF)	BURNY MATTISON
GREAT MOUSE DETECTIVE, THE (AF)	DAVID MICHENER
GREAT MOUSE DETECTIVE, THE (AF)	JOHN MUSKER
GREAT MOUSE DETECTIVE, THE (AF)	RON CLEMENTS
GREAT MUPPET CAPER, THE	JACK ROSE
GREAT MUPPET CAPER, THE	JAY TARSES
GREAT MUPPET CAPER, THE	JERRY JUHL
GREAT MUPPET CAPER, THE	TOM PATCHETT
GREAT MUSIC CHASE, THE - S	LESLIE BRICUSSE
GREAT NORTHFIELD, MINNESOTA RAID, THE	PHILIP KAUFMAN
GREAT O'GRADY, THE (SHORT)	ROBBIE FOX
GREAT OUTDOORS, THE	JOHN HUGHES
GREAT PRETENDER, THE - S	JOHN ESKOW
GREAT PRETENDER, THE - S	PETER MARTIN WORTMANN
GREAT PRETENDER, THE - S	ROBERT CONTE
GREAT RACE, THE	BLAKE EDWARDS
GREAT RIDE, A	THOMAS POPE
GREAT SANTINI, THE	LEWIS JOHN CARLINO
GREAT SCOUT AND CATHOUSE THURSDAY, THE	RICHARD SHAPIRO
GREAT SOLO TOWN (P)	THOMAS BABE
GREAT TRAIN ROBBERY, THE	MICHAEL CRICHTON
GREAT WALDO PEPPER, THE	WILLIAM GOLDMAN
GREAT WALL, A	SHIRLEY SUN
GREAT WALL, A	PETER WANG
GREAT WALTZ, THE	ANDREW STONE
GREAT WHITE HOPE, THE	HOWARD SACKLER
GREATAMERICA - S	DAN JENKINS
GREATEST SHOW ON EARTH, THE - S	LOWELL GANZ
GREATEST STORY EVER TOLD, THE	JAMES LEE BARRETT†
GREATEST, THE	RING LARDNER JR.
GREED - S	DAVID GREENWALT
GREED - S	JIM KOUF
GREEK TYCOON, THE	MORT FINE†
GREEN BERETS, THE	JAMES LEE BARRETT†
GREEN CARD	PETER WEIR
GREEN CARD BLUES - S	KEVIN SULLIVAN
GREEN FIRE	IVAN GOFF
GREEN GLOVE, THE	CHARLES BENNETT
GREEN ICE	EDWARD ANHALT
GREEN ICE	ROBERT DELAURENTIS
GREEN LANTERN - S	MICHAEL KROHN
GREEN SKY - S	ROBERT J. COMFORT
GREENER PASTURES - S	CASEY KELLY
GREENGAGE SUMMER, THE	HOWARD KOCH
GREETINGS	BRIAN DEPALMA
GREETINGS	CHARLES S. HIRSCH
GREGORY'S GIRL	BILL FORSYTH
GREMLINS	CHRIS COLUMBUS
GREMLINS 2	CHARLIE HAAS
GREY FOX, THE	JOHN HUNTER
GREYEAGLE	CHARLES B. PIERCE
GREYSTOKE: THE LEGEND OF TARZAN, LORD OF THE APES	MICHAEL AUSTIN
GREYSTOKE II - S	HAL HARRIS
GRID, THE - S	HAL BARWOOD
GRID, THE - S	MATTHEW ROBBINS
GRIDLOCK - S	MARK FROST
GRIFTERS, THE	DONALD E. WESTLAKE
GRIM PRAIRIE TALES	WAYNE COE
GRIMM (P)	DENISE DE CLUE
GRIMOIRE - S	SCOTT PARKER
GROOVE TUBE, THE	KEN SHAPIRO
GROSS ANATOMY	ALAN JAY GLUECKMAN
GROSS ANATOMY	HOWARD ROSENMAN
GROSS ANATOMY	STANLEY ISAACS
GROSS ANATOMY	MARK SPRAGG
GROSS ANATOMY	RON NYSWANER
GROSSING OUT - S	TERRY SOUTHERN
GROTTO, THE - S	R. BARKER PRICE
GROUND ZERO	JAN SARDI
GROUND ZERO	MAC GUDGEON
GROWING MAN - S	DAVID SHABER
GROWING PAINS	BOBBY HOUSTON
GROWING SEASON - S	NORMAN WEXLER
GROWING UP - S	LYNN GROSSMAN
GROWING UP FAST - S	JAN ELIASBERG
GROWN UPS - S	TOM DONNELLY
GROWN-UPS (P)	JULES FEIFFER
GROWN-UPS - S	SCOTT PARKER
GRUNTI THE WRESTLING MOVIE	ROGER D. MANNING
GUARDIAN ANGEL, THE	SUZANNE OSTEN
GUARDIAN, THE	DAN GREENBURG
GUARDIAN, THE	STEPHEN VOLK
GUARDIAN, THE	WILLIAM FRIEDKIN
GUARDIANS OF GOOD, THE - S	MARK SALTZMAN
GUATEMALA	DAVID PEOPLES
GUERILLA VIDEO - S	DAVID MIRKIN
GUEST, THE (1984)	ATHOL FUGARD
GUEST, THE (1964)	HAROLD PINTER
GUESTS OF THE HOTEL ASTORIA, THE	REZA ALAMEHZADEH
GUILTY AS CHARGED	CHARLES R. GALE
GUILTY BY SUSPICION	IRWIN WINKLER
GUITAR - S	LESLIE BOHEM
GUITAR DOLLS - S	ZALMAN KING
GUITEAU BURLESQUE, THE (P)	DICK BEEBE
GULAG (CTF)	DAN GORDON
GULF COAST - S	GUSTAVE REININGER
GULF OF MOSQUITOS, THE - S	ROBERT GARLAND
GULLIVER'S TRAVELS	DON BLACK
GUMBALL RALLY, THE	LEON CAPETANOS
GUMSHOE KID, THE	VICTOR BARMAK
GUN FURY	IRVING WALLACE†
GUN FURY	ROY HUGGINS
GUN PLAY, A (P)	YALE UDOFF
GUN RUNNERS, THE	PAUL MONASH
GUN SHY - S	MICHAEL ALAN EDDY
GUNFIGHT TO ABILENE	JOHN D.F. BLACK
GUNG HO	EDWIN BLUM
GUNG HO	BABALOO MANDEL
GUNG HO	LOWELL GANZ
GUNN	BLAKE EDWARDS
GUNN	WILLIAM PETER BLATTY
GUNRUNNER, THE	ARNIE GELBART
GUNS	ANDY SIDARIS
GUNS OF DARKNESS	JOHN MORTIMER
GUNS OF FORT PETTICOAT, THE	WALTER DONIGER
GUNS OF NAVARONE, THE	CARL FOREMAN†
GUNS OF THE TIMBERLAND	AARON SPELLING
GUNSLINGER - S	MICHAEL KROHN
GURU, THE	RUTH PRAWER JHABVALA
GUS	ARHUR ALSBERG
GUS	DON NELSON
GUSHER - S	BUCK HENRY
GUY WHO COULD FIX BIKES, THE - S	JULIAN BARRY
GUYS AND DOLLS	JOSEPH L. MANKIEWICZ
GWENDOLINE	JUST JAECKIN
GYMKATA	CHARLES ROBERT CARNER
GYPSY	ARTHUR LAURENTS
GYPSY - S	ROBERT BORIS
GYPSY ANGELS, THE - S	C. COURTNEY JOYNER
GYPSY SWITCH - S	GINNY CERRELLA
GYROSCOPE - S	W.D. RICHTER

H

Title	Writer
H.O.G.	DONALD WRYE
H.P. LOVECRAFT'S RE-ANIMATOR	DENNIS PAOLI
H.P. LOVECRAFT'S RE-ANIMATOR	STUART GORDON
H.P. LOVECRAFT'S RE-ANIMATOR	WILLIAM H. NORRIS
H.P. LOVECRAFT'S THE RESURRECTED	ADAM FRIEDMAN
HACKSAW - S	PETER ILIFF
HADLEY'S REBELLION	FRED WALTON
HADLEY'S REBELLION	STEPHEN FEKE
HAIL TO THE CHIEF	LARRY SPIEGEL
HAIL, ALMA MATER - S	DAVID EYRE
HAIR	MICHAEL WELLER
HAIR OF THE DOG - S	STEVE DEJARNATT
HAIRSPRAY	JOHN WATERS
HALF A LIFETIME (CTF) - S	STEPHEN METCALFE
HALF A SIXPENCE	BEVERLY CROSS
HALF BAKEDI - S	ANDY TENNANT
HALF BAKEDI - S	MIKE MARVIN
HALF IN - FULL OUT - S	ANDY TENNANT
HALF MOON STREET	BOB SWAIM
HALF MOON STREET	EDWARD BEHR
HALFWAY HOUSE - S	TOM BENEDEK
HALFWAY TO SHANGHAI - S	MICHAEL THOMAS
HALLELUJAH - S	GARY GOLDMAN
HALLELUJAH TRAIL, THE	JOHN GAY
HALLEY'S CONNECTION - S	ROBERT MOLONEY
HALLIBURTON - S	BARRY BECKERMAN
HALLOWEEN	DEBRA HILL
HALLOWEEN	JOHN CARPENTER
HALLOWEEN II	DEBRA HILL
HALLOWEEN II	JOHN CARPENTER
HALLOWEEN III	TOMMY LEE WALLACE
HALLOWEEN 4	ALAN B. MCELROY
HALLOWEEN 4	BENJAMIN RUFFNER
HALLOWEEN 4	DHANI LIPSIUS
HALLOWEEN 4	LARRY RATTNER
HALLOWEEN 5	DOMINIQUE OTHENIN-GIRARD
HALLOWEEN 5	MICHAEL JACOBS
HALLOWEEN 5	SHEM BITTERMAN
HALLOWEEN HOUSE - S	MICK GARRIS
HALLS OF ANGER	AL RAMRUS
HALLS OF ANGER	JOHN HERMAN SHANER

Ha-He
FILM WRITERS GUIDE

INDEX OF FILM TITLES

HALLS OF SHAME - S .... DANA OLSEN
HAMBONE AND HILLIE .... JOEL SOISSON
HAMBONE AND HILLIE .... MICHAEL S. MURPHEY
HAMBONE AND HILLIE .... SANDRA K. BAILEY
HAMBURGER HILL .... JIM CARABATSOS
HAMBURGER...THE MOTION PICTURE .... DONALD H. ROSS
HAMLET .... FRANCO ZEFFIRELLI
HAMLET .... CHRISTOPHER DEVORE
HAMLET GOES BUSINESS .... AKI KAURISMAKI
HAMMER HAND - S .... DJORDJE MILICEVIC
HAMMERHEAD .... HERBERT BAKER†
HAMMERHEAD .... WILLIAM BAST
HAMMERSMITH IS OUT .... STANFORD WHITMORE
HAMMETT .... THOMAS POPE
HAMMETT .... DENNIS O'FLAHERTY
HAMMETT .... ROSS THOMAS
HAND THAT ROCKS THE CRADLE, THE - S .... AMANDA SILVER
HAND, THE .... OLIVER STONE
HANDCARVED COFFINS - S .... JUDITH RASCOE
HANDCARVED COFFINS - S .... FRANK R. PIERSON
HANDCARVED COFFINS - S .... RICHARD MAXWELL
HANDFUL OF DUST, A .... CHARLES STURRIDGE
HANDFUL OF DUST, A .... DEREK GRANGER
HANDFUL OF DUST, A .... TIM SULLIVAN
HANDGUN .... TONY GARNETT
HANDLE WITH CARE .... MORTON FINE†
HANDLE WITH CARE .... PAUL BRICKMAN
HANDLING SIN - S .... DAVID S. WARD
HANDMAID'S TALE, THE .... HAROLD PINTER
HANDS OF ITS ENEMY, THE (P) .... MARK MEDOFF
HANDSOME AND CHARMING MAN, A - S .... BILL BRYDEN
HANDSOME DEVILS - S .... CARL KURLANDER
HANG 'EM REALLY HIGH (SHORT) .... CHRIS FABER
HANG 'EM REALLY HIGH (SHORT) .... DANNIEL BARRON
HANG ON TIGHT - S .... LEE REYNOLDS
HANG TIME - S .... SAM HAMM
HANG TOUGH .... JOHN M. HERZFELD
HANG TOUGH .... W.D. RICHTER
HANGAR #18 .... JAMES L. CONWAY
HANGAR #18 .... STEVEN THORNLEY
HANGAR #18 .... TOM CHAPMAN
HANGFIRE .... BRIAN D. JEFFRIES
HANGIN' WITH THE HOMEBOYS .... JOSEPH P. VASQUEZ
HANGING TREE, THE .... WENDELL MAYES
HANGMAN - S .... GLEN MORGAN
HANGMAN - S .... JAMES WONG
HANGMAN'S KNOT .... ROY HUGGINS
HANKY PANKY .... DAVID TAYLOR
HANKY PANKY .... HENRY ROSENBAUM
HANNA K. .... FRANCO SOLINAS
HANNA'S WAR .... MENAHEM GOLAN
HANNA'S WAR .... STANLEY MANN
HANNAH AND HER SISTERS .... WOODY ALLEN
HANNIBAL BROOKS .... DICK CLEMENT
HANNIBAL BROOKS .... IAN LAFRENAIS
HANNIE CAULDER .... BURT KENNEDY
HANOI HILTON, THE .... LIONEL CHETWYND
HANOVER STREET .... PETER HYAMS
HANSEL AND GRETEL - S .... A.J. CAROTHERS
HANUSSEN .... ISTVAN SZABO
HAPGOOD (P) .... TOM STOPPARD
HAPPENING, THE .... JAMES DAVID BUCHANAN
HAPPENING, THE .... FRANK R. PIERSON
HAPPIEST MILLIONAIRE, THE .... A.J. CAROTHERS
HAPPILY EVER AFTER .... MARTHA MORAN
HAPPILY EVER AFTER .... ROBBY LONDON
HAPPILY EVER AFTER - S .... LESLIE NEWMAN
HAPPILY EVER AFTER - S .... MARJORIE GROSS
HAPPINESS CAGE, THE .... RON WHYTE†
HAPPY ALL THE TIME - S .... ALLAN BURNS
HAPPY BIRTHDAY GEMINI .... DICK BENNER†
HAPPY BIRTHDAY TO ME .... JOHN SAXTON†
HAPPY BIRTHDAY TO ME .... PETER JOBIN
HAPPY BIRTHDAY TO ME .... TIMOTHY BOND
HAPPY BIRTHDAY WANDA JUNE .... KURT VONNEGUT JR.
HAPPY ENDING, THE .... RICHARD BROOKS
HAPPY EVER AFTER .... JACK DAVIES
HAPPY GO LOVELY .... VAL GUEST
HAPPY HOOKER GOES TO WASHINGTON, THE .... ROBERT KAUFMAN
HAPPY HOOKER, THE .... WILLIAM RICHERT
HAPPY HOUR .... CONSTANTINE DILLON
HAPPY HOUR .... J. STEPHEN PEACE
HAPPY HOUR .... JOHN DEBELLO
HAPPY HOUR - S .... FLOYD MUTRUX
HAPPY HOUR - S .... LOWELL GANZ
HAPPY IS THE BRIDE .... ROY BOULTING
HAPPY NEW YEAR .... NANCY DOWD
HAPPY NEW YEAR (1973) .... CLAUDE LELOUCH
HAPPY THEIVES, THE .... JOHN GAY
HAPPY TOGETHER .... CRAIG J. NEVIUS
HAPPY TRAILS - S .... GARY DEVORE
HAR'LD - S .... JONATHAN REYNOLDS
HARD CHOICES .... RICK KING
HARD CONTRACT .... S. LEE POGOSTIN
HARD COUNTRY .... MICHAEL MURPHEY
HARD COUNTRY .... MICHAEL KANE
HARD DAY FOR ARCHIE, A .... JIM MCBRIDE
HARD DAY'S NIGHT, A .... ALUN OWEN
HARD FEELING - S .... DYANNE ASSIMOW
HARD FEELINGS .... JOHN HERZFELD
HARD FEELINGS .... W.D. RICHTER
HARD KNOCKS .... DON MCLENNAN
HARD KNOX - S .... ALAN SHARP
HARD KNOX - S .... GARY DEVORE
HARD PROMISES - S .... JULE SELBO
HARD ROCK ZOMBIES .... DAVID BALL
HARD ROCK ZOMBIES .... KRISCHNA SHAS
HARD SELL - S .... KEN HIXON
HARD TICKET TO HAWAII .... ANDY SIDARIS
HARD TIMES .... WALTER HILL
HARD TO GET - S .... LAURIE FRANK
HARD TO HOLD .... RICHARD ROTHSTEIN
HARD TO HOLD .... THOMAS HEDLEY JR.
HARD TO KILL .... STEVEN MCKAY
HARD TO MISS - S .... HARIS ORKIN
HARD TRAVELING .... DAN BESSIE
HARD WAY, THE .... MICHAEL KOZOLL
HARD WAY, THE .... DANIEL PYNE
HARD WAY, THE .... LEM DOBBS
HARD-BOILED - S .... JOHN HILL
HARDBALL - S .... FIONA LEWIS
HARDBALL - S .... DAVID FALLON
HARDBODIES .... ERIC ALTER
HARDBODIES .... MARK L. GRIFFITHS
HARDBODIES .... STEVEN S. GREENE
HARDBODIES 2 .... ERIC ALTER
HARDBODIES 2 .... MARK L. GRIFFITHS
HARDBOILED - S .... BECKY JOHNSTON
HARDCASE AND FIST .... BUD FLEISHER
HARDCASE AND FIST .... TONY ZARINDAST
HARDCORE .... PAUL SCHRADER
HARDCOVER - S .... DAVID M. CHASKIN
HARDCOVER DREAMS - S .... MARK ANDRUS
HARDER THEY FALL, THE .... PHILIP YORDAN
HARDLY WORKING .... JERRY LEWIS
HARDLY WORKING .... MICHAEL JANOVER
HARDWARE .... RICHARD STANLEY
HARDWARE - S .... RON CLARK
HARDWIRED - S .... ROBERT SARNO
HARDY BOYS, THE - S .... REX MCGEE
HAREM .... ARTHUR JOFFE
HARLAN ELLISON'S MOVIE - S .... HARLAN ELLISON
HARLEM - S .... TIM MCCANLIES
HARLEM NIGHTS .... EDDIE MURPHY
HARLEM UNIVERSITY - S .... VINCENT PATRICK
HARLEQUIN .... EVERETT DEROCHE
HARLEY DAVIDSON AND THE MARLBORO MAN .... DON MICHAEL HARRY
HARLOW .... JOHN MICHAEL HAYES
HAROLD AND MAUDE .... COLIN HIGGINS†
HARPER .... WILLIAM GOLDMAN
HARPER VALLEY P.T.A. .... BARRY SCHNEIDER
HARRAD SUMMER, THE .... STEVEN R. ZACHARIAS
HARRAD II - S .... JEFF BUHAI
HARRAD II - S .... STEVE ZACHARIAS
HARRIET THE SPY - S .... GREG TAYLOR
HARROW ALLEY - S .... WALTER NEWMAN
HARRY & SON .... PAUL NEWMAN
HARRY & SON .... RONALD L. BUCK
HARRY - S .... DAVID ANDRUS
HARRY - S .... ERIC LUKE
HARRY AND THE HENDERSONS .... EZRA D. RAPPAPORT
HARRY AND THE HENDERSONS .... WILLIAM DEAR
HARRY AND THE HENDERSONS .... WILLIAM E. MARTIN
HARRY AND TONTO .... JOSH GREENFELD
HARRY AND TONTO .... PAUL MAZURKSY
HARRY AND WALTER GO TO NEW YORK .... JOHN BYRUM
HARRY AND WALTER GO TO NEW YORK .... ROBERT KAUFMAN
HARRY BLACK AND THE TIGER .... SYDNEY BOEHM†
HARRY IN YOUR POCKET .... JAMES DAVID BUCHANAN
HARRY SCARRY WANTS TO MARRY - S .... GREG DAVIS
HARRY SCARRY WANTS TO MARRY - S .... LARRY GARCIA
HARRY THE LION - S .... DENNYS MCCOY
HARRY THE LION - S .... PAMELA HICKEY
HARRY TRACY .... R. LANCE HILL
HARRY'S LOT - S .... PHILIP MORTON
HARRY'S MACHINE .... CURT ALLEN
HARRY'S WAR .... KEITH MERRILL
HARTMAN - S .... CAMILLE THOMASSON
HARV, THE BARBARIAN - S .... CARMEN FINESTRA
HASENPFEFFER IN THE TORRID ZONE - S .... TOM CAMP
HAT TRICK - S .... DAVID COLEMAN
HATCHECK - S .... SOLLACE MITCHELL
HATCHET - S .... GARY PAULSEN
HATTERAS - S .... D. SHONE KIRKPATRICK
HAUNTED .... WARREN CHANEY
HAUNTED GUITAR - S .... ALAN SHAPIRO
HAUNTED HONEYMOON .... GENE WILDER
HAUNTED HONEYMOON .... TERENCE MARSH
HAUNTED HOUSE OF HORROR, THE .... MICHAEL ARMSTRONG
HAUNTED LIVES (P) .... JOHN PIELMEIER
HAUNTED SUMMER .... LEWIS JOHN CARLINO
HAUNTING OF JULIA, THE .... DAVID HUMPHRIES
HAUNTING OF M, THE .... ANNA THOMAS
HAUNTING OF MORELLA, THE .... JIM WYNORSKI
HAUNTING OF MORELLA, THE .... R.J. ROBERTSON
HAUNTING, THE .... NELSON GIDDING
HAVANA .... DAVID RAYFIEL
HAVANA .... JUDITH RASCOE
HAVANA DANCY - S .... ALLYN WARNER
HAVE SPACE SUIT WILL TRAVEL - S .... JOHN VARLEY
HAVING A WILD WEEKEND .... PETER NICHOLS
HAWAII .... DANIEL TARADASH
HAWK THE SLAYER .... HARRY ROBERTSON
HAWK THE SLAYER .... TERRY MARCEL
HAWKS .... ROY CLARKE
HAWMPS .... MICHAEL WARREN
HAWMPS .... WILLIAM BICKLEY
HE KNOWS YOU'RE ALONE .... SCOTT PARKER
HE LAUGHED LAST .... BLAKE EDWARDS
HE SAID SHE SAID .... BRIAN HOLHFELD
HE WHO MUST DIE .... JULES DASSIN
HE'S ALL MINE - S .... DICK BEEBE
HE'S MY GIRL .... PETER BERGMAN
HE'S MY GIRL .... CHARLES F. BOHL
HE'S MY GIRL .... TAYLOR AMES
HE'S MY GIRL .... TERRY WINKLESS
HEAD .... BOB RAFELSON
HEAD .... JACK NICHOLSON
HEAD DOWN TILT - S .... PATRICK RANAHAN
HEAD DOWN TILT - S .... TODD JOHNSON
HEAD HUNTER - S .... ALLAN MOYLE
HEAD OFFICE .... KEN FINKLEMAN
HEAD OVER HEELS .... JOAN MICKLIN SILVER
HEADIN' FOR BROADWAY .... HILARY HENKIN
HEADIN' FOR BROADWAY .... JOSEPH BROOKS
HEADIN' FOR BROADWAY .... LARRY GROSS
HEADING HOMES - S .... RICHARD BRENNE
HEADING WEST - S .... ANN BIDERMAN
HEADLESS EYES, THE .... KENT BATEMAN
HEALING FORCE, THE .... JAY MIRACLE
HEALING FORCE, THE .... JOANNE PARRENT
HEALING FORCE, THE .... WOODROW W. CLARK
HEALTH .... FRANK BARHYDT
HEALTH .... PAUL DOOLEY
HEALTH .... ROBERT ALTMAN
HEAR ME GOOD .... DON MCGUIRE
HEARSE, THE .... WILLIAM BLEICH
HEART .... JAMES LEMMO
HEART & SOUL - S .... MARI KORNHAUSER
HEART BEAT .... JOHN BYRUM
HEART CONDITION .... JAMES D. PARRIOTT
HEART LIKE A WHEEL .... KEN FRIEDMAN
HEART MOUNTAIN - S .... HORTON FOOTE
HEART OF DESIRE .... LUC BERAUD
HEART OF DIXIE .... TOM MCCOWN
HEART OF GLASS .... WERNER HERZOG
HEART OF MIDNIGHT .... MATTHEW CHAPMAN
HEART OF THE STAG .... MICHAEL WORTH
HEART OF THE STAG .... NEIL ILLINGSWORTH
HEART OUTRIGHT, THE (P) .... MARK MEDOFF
HEART STOPPER (P) .... MICHAEL WOLK
HEART'S DESIRE - S .... DAVID FIELD
HEARTACHES .... TERRANCE HEFFERNAN
HEARTACHES INTO THE FIRE - S .... RON NYSWANER

He-Hi
FILM WRITERS GUIDE

Title	Writer
HEARTBEEPS	JOHN HILL
HEARTBREAK HOTEL	CHRIS COLUMBUS
HEARTBREAK KID, THE	NEIL SIMON
HEARTBREAK RIDGE	JIM CARABATSOS
HEARTBREAKERS	BOBBY ROTH
HEARTBURN	NORA EPHRON
HEARTLAND	BETH FERRIS
HEARTLAND U.S.A. - S	JAMES KENNEDY
HEARTS - S	CRAIG BOLOTIN
HEARTS - S	JAMES BRIDGES
HEARTS - S	JOYCE ELIASON
HEARTS - S	KURT LUEDTKE
HEARTS DESIRE - S	ALLAN BURNS
HEARTS OF FIRE	JOE ESZTERHAS
HEARTS OF FIRE	SCOTT RICHARDSON
HEARTS OF THE WEST	ROB THOMPSON
HEARTS ON FIRE (P)	DORIS BAIZLEY
HEAT	WILLIAM GOLDMAN
HEAT AND DUST	RUTH PRAWER JHABVALA
HEAT AND SUNLIGHT	ROB NILSSON
HEAT WAVE (CTF)	MICHAEL LAZAROU
HEAT WAVE - S	FLOYD MUTRUX
HEATWAVE - S	LAUREL DELP
HEATHERS	DANIEL WATERS
HEATLIGHTNING - S	DANIEL BARTOLINI
HEATWAVE	MARC ROSENBERG
HEATWAVE	PHILLIP NOYCE
HEAVEN & EARTH - S	TAB MURPHY
HEAVEN BECOMES HELL	MICKEY NIVELLI
HEAVEN BELOW - S	PAUL SCHRADER
HEAVEN CAN WAIT	ELAINE MAY
HEAVEN CAN WAIT	WARREN BEATTY
HEAVEN HELP US	CHARLES PURPURA
HEAVEN SCENT - S	HENRY OLEK
HEAVEN SCENT - S	JOYCE ELIASON
HEAVEN SCENT - S	KEN FRIEDMAN
HEAVEN SENT - S	DAVID SHABER
HEAVEN SENT - S	ED FITZGERALD
HEAVEN SENT - S	PAUL KOVAL
HEAVEN TONIGHT	ALISTER WEBB
HEAVEN TONIGHT	FRANK HOWSON
HEAVEN WITH A GUN	RICHARD CARR
HEAVEN'S GATE	MICHAEL CIMINO
HEAVENLY BODIES	RON BASE
HEAVENLY BODIES	LAWRENCE DANE
HEAVENLY BODIES - S	MICHAEL THOMAS
HEAVENLY KID, THE	CARY MEDOWAY
HEAVENLY KID, THE	MARTIN COPELAND
HEAVENLY, THE - S	CLAIRE NOTO
HEAVENZAPOPPIN' (P)	DICK BEEBE
HEAVY ARMOR - S	DON JAKOBY
HEAVY DUST - S	DERIC WASHBURN
HEAVY METAL (AF)	DAN GOLDBERG
HEAVY METAL (AF)	LEN BLUM
HEAVY METAL WEEKEND - S	JEFF BUHAI
HEAVY METAL WEEKEND - S	STEVE ZACHARIAS
HEAVY TRAFFIC (AF)	RALPH BAKSHI
HEDDA	TREVOR NUNN
HEIDI CHRONICLES, THE (P)	WENDY WASSERSTEIN
HEIDI'S SONG (AF)	JAMESON BREWER
HEIDI'S SONG (AF)	JOSEPH BARBERA
HEIDI'S SONG (AF)	ROBERT TAYLOR
HEIGHT OF FASHION, THE - S	MICHAEL ERIC STEIN
HEIR APPARENT - S	MURRAY MINTZ
HEIST, THE (CTF)	DAVID FULLER
HEIST, THE (CTF)	RICK NATKIN
HELEN MORGAN STORY, THE	DEAN RIESNER
HELEN MORGAN STORY, THE	NELSON GIDDING
HELEN MORGAN STORY, THE	OSCAR SAUL
HELL AND HIGH WATER	SAMUEL FULLER
HELL BELOW ZERO	RICHARD MAIBAUM†
HELL BENT - AND BACK - S	DOUG RICHARDSON
HELL BENT - AND BACK - S	RICK JAFFA
HELL CAN WAIT - S	PATRICIA RESNICK
HELL CHANNEL, THE - S	RICK MARX
HELL DRIVERS	CY ENDFIELD
HELL HIGH	DOUGLAS GROSSMAN
HELL HIGH	LEO EVANS
HELL IN THE PACIFIC	ERIC BERCOVICI
HELL IN THE PACIFIC	ALEXANDER JACOBS†
HELL IS A CITY	VAL GUEST
HELL IS FOR HEROES	RICHARD CARR
HELL IS FOR HEROES	ROBERT PIROSH†
HELL NIGHT	RANDY FELDMAN
HELL OF A DEAL - S	JANICE FISCHER
HELL OF A TOWN (P)	MONTE MERRICK
HELL OF AN ANGEL - S	WILLIAM TONNER
HELL ON THE BATTLEGROUND	DAVID A. PRIOR
HELL SOLDIER - S	JOHN A. GALLAGHER
HELL SOLDIER - S	STEVE JAMES
HELL SPA - S	PETER HANKOFF
HELL SQUAD	KENNETH HARTFORD
HELL UP IN HARLEM	LARRY COHEN
HELL WITH HEROS, TO	HAROLD LIVINGSTON
HELL-BENT - S	MICHAEL AUERBACH
HELLBENT	RICHARD CASEY
HELLBENT - S	MICHAEL MILLER
HELLBOUND - S	DARIN MORGAN
HELLBOUND: HELLRAISER 2	PETER ATKINS
HELLER IN PINK TIGHTS	WALTER BERNSTEIN
HELLFIGHTERS	CLAIR HUFFAKER†
HELLFIRE CLUB, THE	JIMMY SANGSTER
HELLHOLE	VINCENT MONGOL
HELLO AGAIN	SUSAN ISAACS
HELLO DOLLY	ERNEST LEHMAN
HELLO DOWN THERE	JOHN MCGREEVY
HELLO MARY LOU: PROM NIGHT II	RON OLIVER
HELLO ON FRISCO BAY	SYDNEY BOEHM†
HELLO THERE AMERICA - S	BENNETT TRAMER
HELLRAISER	CLIVE BARKER
HELLRAISER 3 - S	PETER ATKINS
HELLSTROM CHRONICLE, THE (FD)	DAVID SELTZER
HELLUVA DEAL - S	SOLLACE MITCHELL
HELP!	CHARLES WOOD
HELP!	MARC BEHM
HELP, I'M BEING HELD A PRISONER - S	NORMAN STEINBERG
HEMINGWAY'S ADVENTURES OF A YOUNG MAN	A.E. HOTCHNER
HEMOGOBLIN - S	DAN O'BANNON
HEMOGOBLIN - S	DON JAKOBY
HENCEFORWARD(P)	ALAN AYKBOURN
HENDERSON THE RAIN KING - S	JOHN BRILEY
HENNESSY	JOHN GAY
HENRY & JUNE	PHILIP KAUFMAN
HENRY & JUNE	ROSE L. KAUFMAN
HENRY IV	MARCO BELLOCCHIO
HENRY IV	TONINO GUERRA
HENRY LEAVES HOME - S	ROD MCCALL
HENRY STAR, OUTLAW - S	BOB GALE
HENRY V	KENNETH BRANAGH
HER ALIBI	CHARLIE PETERS
HER SAINTED HUSBAND - S	ALAN BERGER
HER SAINTED HUSBAND - S	KATHY GORI
HER SIDE OF THE FAMILY - S	BILL GERBER
HER TWELVE MEN	WILLIAM ROBERTS
HERBIE GOES BANANAS	DON TAIT
HERBIE GOES TO MONTE CARLO	ARTHUR ALSBERG
HERBIE GOES TO MONTE CARLO	DONALD R. NELSON
HERCULES	LEWIS COATES
HERE COME THE GIRLS	HAL KANTER
HERE COME THE LITTLES	WOODY KLING
HERE COME THE TIGERS	ARCH MCCOY
HERE TO STAY - S	TOM TOPOR
HERETIC: EXORCIST II, THE	WILLIAM GOODHART
HERO AIN'T NOTHING BUT A SANDWICH, A	ALICE CHILDRESS
HERO AND A HALF - S	DAVID PEOPLES
HERO AND THE TERROR	DENNIS SHRYACK
HERO AND THE TERROR	MICHAEL BLODGETT
HERO AT LARGE	A.J. CAROTHERS
HERO SHOT - S	RICHARD WHITLEY
HERO'S ISLAND	LESLIE C. STEVENS
HERO, THE	WOLF MANKOWITZ
HERO, THE - S	ERIC EDSON
HEROES	JIM CARABATSOS
HEROES - S	LYNNE BARKER
HEROES (SHORT)	CAMILLE THOMASSON
HEROES OF TELEMARK, THE	BEN BARZMAN†
HEROES STAND ALONE	THOMAS M. CLEAVER
HEROINE	PAUL MAYERSBERG
HERZOG - S	MARC NORMAN
HESTER STREET	JOAN MICKLIN SILVER
HEX - S	LEO GAREN
HEX - S	ED NAHA
HEY BABU RIBA	JOVAN ACIN
HEY GOOD LOOKIN' (AF)	RALPH BAKSHI
HEY MR. FANTASY - S	BARRA GRANT
HI FI - S	GREG TAYLOR
HI, I'M FROM HELL - S	CHARLES GALE
HI, MOMI	BRIAN DEPALMA
HI, MOMI	CHARLES S. HIRSCH
HICKEY AND BOGGS	WALTER HILL
HICKOCK AND CODY - S	IRA BEHR
HIDDEN FORTRESS, THE	AKIRA KUROSAWA
HIDDEN, THE	BOB HUNT
HIDE AND SEEK - S	NEAL SHUSTERMAN
HIDE IN PLAIN SIGHT	SPENCER EASTMAN†
HIDER IN THE HOUSE	LEM DOBBS
HIDING OUT	JEFF ROTHBERG
HIDING OUT	JOE MENOSKY
HIDING PLACE, THE	LAWRENCE R. HOLBEN
HIERO'S JOURNEY - S	STIRLING SILLIPHANT
HIGH AND LONESOME - S	DORI PIERSON
HIGH AND LOW	AKIRA KUROSAWA
HIGH AND THE MIGHTY, THE	ERNEST K. GANN†
HIGH ANXIETY	BARRY LEVINSON
HIGH ANXIETY	MEL BROOKS
HIGH ANXIETY	RON CLARK
HIGH ANXIETY	RUDY DELUCA
HIGH COUNTRY - S	DEAN RIESNER
HIGH COUNTRY, THE	BUD TOWNSEND
HIGH FIDELITY - S	DAVID LOUCKA
HIGH FLIGHT	KEN HUGHES
HIGH HEELED SNEAKERS - S	G. ROSS PARKER
HIGH HEELS	PEDRO ALMODOVAR
HIGH HOPES	MIKE LEIGH
HIGH HOPES - S	TINO INSANA
HIGH MOON - S	MURRAY MINTZ
HIGH PLAINS DRIFTER	ERNEST TIDYMAN†
HIGH RESOLUTION - S	STAN SEIDEL
HIGH RISE - S	DAVID SHABER
HIGH RISK	STEWART RAFFILL
HIGH ROAD TO CHINA	S. LEE POGOSTIN
HIGH ROAD TO CHINA	SANDRA WEINTRAUB ROLAND
HIGH SEASON	CLARE PEPLOE
HIGH SEASON	MARK PEPLOE
HIGH SPEED - S	STEPHEN PETERS
HIGH SPIRITS	NEIL JORDAN
HIGH STAKES	AMOS KOLLEK
HIGH STEEL - S	DENNIS O'FLAHERTY
HIGH TERRACE, THE	NORMAN HUDIS
HIGH TIDE	LAURA JONES
HIGH TREASON	ROY BOULTING
HIGH WALL	SYDNEY BOEHM†
HIGH WIND IN JAMAICA, A	RONALD HARWOOD
HIGH WIND IN JAMAICA, A	STANLEY MANN
HIGH-BALLIN'	PAUL F. EDWARDS
HIGH-RISE WEEKEND - S	WALTER NEWMAN
HIGHER EDUCATION	CHARLES LOVENTHAL
HIGHER EDUCATION - S	JOHN SHEPPARD
HIGHER EDUCATION - S	MICHAEL PREMINGER
HIGHER EDUCATION - S	RICK PODELL
HIGHER GROUND - S	IAN SEEBERG
HIGHER GROUND - S	VALERIE BENNETT
HIGHEST HONOR, THE	LEE ROBINSON
HIGHLANDER	GREGORY WIDEN
HIGHLANDER	LARRY FERGUSON
HIGHLANDER	PETER BELLWOOD
HIGHLANDER 2	PETER BELLWOOD
HIGHPOINT	RICHARD A. GUTTMAN
HIGHWAY 301	ANDREW STONE
HIGHWAY PATROL - S	CARL GOTTLIEB
HIGHWAY TO HELL - S	DAVID MICKEY EVANS
HIGHWAYMAN OF CONCORD - S	JOHN HILL
HILDA CRANE	PHILIP DUNNE
HILDY - S	ERIC GETHERS
HILLS HAVE EYES II, THE	WES CRAVEN
HILLS HAVE EYES, THE	WES CRAVEN
HILLSIDE STRANGLER - S	FLOYD MUTRUX
HINDENBURG, THE	NELSON GIDDING
HIP TO BE SQUARE - S	RACHEL FELDMAN
HIP TO BE SQUARE - S	SUSAN NANUS
HIRED HAND, THE	ALAN SHARP
HIRED MAN, THE (P)	MELVYN BRAGG
HIRELING, THE	WOLF MANKOWITZ
HIROSHIMA, MON AMOUR	MARGUERITE DURAS
HIS AND HERS	STANLEY MANN
HIS LORDSHIP	MICHAEL POWELL†
HIS MAJESTY O'KEEFE	JAMES HILL
HISTOIRES EXTRAORDINAIRES	FEDERICO FELLINI
HISTORY OF THE AMERICAN FILM, A (P)	CHRISTOPHER DURANG
HISTORY OF THE WORLD - PART 1	MEL BROOKS
HIT AND RUN (P)	JAMES KENNEDY
HIT LIST	JOHN GOFF
HIT LIST	PETER BROSNAN
HIT MAN	GEORGE B. ARMITAGE
HIT MAN - S	KENNETH PRESSMAN
HIT MAN - S	ROY LONDON
HITMAN	ED NEUMEIER
HITMAN - S	MICHAEL MINER
HIT MAN, THE	DON CARMODY
HIT MAN, THE	ROBERT GEOFFRION
HIT ME EASY - S	HERMAN RAUCHER
HIT PARADE - S	ALI MATHESON

349

Hi-Ho

FILM WRITERS GUIDE

Title	Writer
HIT PARADE - S	JON COOKSEY
HITI	ALAN TRUSTMAN
HIT, THE	PETER PRINCE
HIT, THE - S	LAWRENCE KONNER
HIT, THE - S	MARK D. ROSENTHAL
HITCHER, THE	ERIC RED
HITCHHIKERS GUIDE TO THE GALAXY - S	ABBE BERNSTEIN
HITCHHIKERS, THE (P)	JEFFREY KINDLEY
HITLER'S SON & PRIEST	LUKAS HELLER†
HITTING CHARLOTTE - S	TOM PAGE
HMS DEFIANT	NIGEL KNEALE
HOB - S	MARK PATRICK CARDUCCI
HOBGOBLINS - S	JOEL SCHUMACHER
HOCUS POCUS - S	JAMES D. COX
HOCUS POCUS - S	JANUS CERCONE
HOFFA - S	DAVID MAMET
HOG WILD	ANDREW PETER MARIN
HOLCROFT COVENANT, THE	EDWARD ANHALT
HOLCROFT COVENANT, THE	GEORGE AXELROD
HOLCROFT COVENANT, THE	JOHN HOPKINS
HOLD BACK THE DAWN	BILLY WILDER
HOLD BACK THE NIGHT	WALTER DONIGER
HOLD FAST MY WORDS - S	TIMNA RANON
HOLDING COMPANY, THE (P)	JAMES KENNEDY
HOLDING ON	ALLAN BURNS
HOLDING ON - S	JAMES L. BROOKS
HOLE IN THE HEAD, A	ARNOLD SCHULMAN
HOLE IN THE HEAD, A	ARNOLD SCHULMAN
HOLIDAY ADVENTURE - S	LINDSAY HARRISON
HOLLOW POINT - S	DAVID Z. GOODMAN
HOLLYWOOD AND LEVINE - S	ANDREW BERGMAN
HOLLYWOOD AND LEVINE - S	PETER STONE
HOLLYWOOD HIGH - S	MAX EMBER
HOLLYWOOD KNIGHTS, THE	RICHARD LEDERER
HOLLYWOOD KNIGHTS, THE	WILLIAM TENNANT
HOLLYWOOD KNIGHTS, THE	FLOYD MUTRUX
HOLLYWOOD MAVERICKS	TODD MCCARTHY
HOLLYWOOD SCANDAL - S	CURTIS ARMSTRONG
HOLLYWOOD SHUFFLE	KEENEN IVORY WAYANS
HOLLYWOOD SHUFFLE	ROBERT TOWNSEND
HOLLYWOOD STORY, A	EVAN SLAWSON
HOLLYWOOD STORY, A	TONY ZARINDAST
HOLLYWOOD VICE	JAMES J. DOCHERTY
HOLLYWOOD ZAP	DAVID COHEN
HOLMEYER'S BRIDGE - S	HAL ACKERMAN
HOLOCAUST 2000	MICHAEL ROBSON
HOLOCAUST 2000	SERGIO DONATI
HOLY BLOOD, HOLY GRAIL - S	DIANA HAMMOND
HOLY BLOOD, HOLY GRAIL - S	PAUL SCHRADER
HOLY WARS - S	MARSHALL GOLDBERG
HOLYMEN - S	STEVE SHAGAN
HOMAGE TO BARCELONA - S	MICHAEL VENTURA
HOMAGE TO CATALONIA - S	WALTER BERNSTEIN
HOMBRE	HARRIET FRANK JR.
HOMBRE	IRVING RAVETCH
HOME - S	TYLER BENSINGER
HOME AGAIN, KATHLEEN (P)	THOMAS BABE
HOME ALONE	JOHN HUGHES
HOME ALONE, AGAIN - S	JOHN HUGHES
HOME AQUATICUS - S	DAVID SELTZER
HOME BEFORE MORNING - S	PATRICK DUNCAN
HOME BY MIDNIGHT - S	PETER CRABBE
HOME FOR CHRISTMAS - S	ANTHONY J. FINGLETON
HOME FOR STRAY CATS (P)	JAMES KIRKWOOD†
HOME FOR THE HOLIDAYS - S	ANDY TENNANT
HOME FOR THE HOLIDAYS - S	LYNN GROSSMAN
HOME FOR THE HOLIDAYS - S	PETER CRABBE
HOME FOR THE HOLIDAYS - S	WILLIAM DEAR
HOME FREE - S	DAVID SEAY
HOME FREE - S	HAL BARWOOD
HOME FREE - S	MATTHEW ROBBINS
HOME FROM THE HILL	HARRIET FRANK JR.
HOME FROM THE HILL	IRVING RAVETCH
HOME FRONT - S	DAVID ISAACS
HOME FRONT - S	KEN LEVINE
HOME FRONT, THE - S	ANNA HAMILTON PHELAN
HOME GROWN - S	ALEX TAUB
HOME GROWN - S	NICHOLAS KAZAN
HOME IN ROME (CTF) - S	TRISH SOODIK
HOME IS WHERE THE HART IS	REX BROMFIELD
HOME MOVIES	BRIAN DEPALMA
HOME MOVIES	CHARLES LOVENTHAL
HOME OF THE BRAVE - S	W.D. RICHTER
HOME PIE - S	TOM SZOLLOSI
HOME REMEDY	MAGGIE GREENWALD
HOMEBODIES	LARRY YUST
HOMEBOYS	PETER FOLDY
HOMECOMING, THE	HAROLD PINTER
HOMEGIRLS - S	JOSEPH P. VASQUEZ
HOMELANDS - S	CHARLIE HAAS
HOMER AND EDDIE	PATRICK CIRILLO
HOMESICK - S	EVE ROSE MAREMENT
HOMESICK - S	DAVID BIRKE
HOMESITTER - S	MARK STEIN
HOMESMAN, THE - S	NAOMI FONER
HOMESTEADERS (P)	NINA SHENGOLD
HOMETOWN - S	ROBERT CARNEY
HOMETOWN BOY MAKES GOOD (CTF)	ALLEN RUCKER
HOMEWORK	DON SAFRAN
HOMEWORK	MAURICE PETERSON
HOMEWORK - S	RICHARD CHAPMAN
HOMICIDE	DAVID MAMET
HONEY POT, THE	JOSEPH L. MANKIEWICZ
HONEY, I BLEW UP THE BABY - S	THOM EBERHARD
HONEY, I SHRUNK THE KIDS	BRIAN YUZNA
HONEY, I SHRUNK THE KIDS	STUART GORDON
HONEY, I SHRUNK THE KIDS	ED NAHA
HONEY, I SHRUNK THE KIDS	TOM SCHULMAN
HONEY, THE DOG ATE THE KIDS - S	BRIAN LEVANT
HONEYCHILD - S	CHARLIE PETERS
HONEYMOON (1987)	PATRICK JAMAIN
HONEYMOON (1987)	PHILIPPE SETBON
HONEYMOON (1987)	ROBERT GEOFFRION
HONEYMOON	MICHAEL POWELL†
HONEYMOON - S	DAVID GREENWALT
HONEYMOON - S	HENRY C. PARKE
HONEYMOON - S	JAMES BRENDAN PATTERSON
HONEYMOON - S	JIM HART
HONEYMOON - S	JIM KOUF
HONEYMOON - S	VICKI POLON
HONEYMOON ACADEMY	EUGENE QUINTANO
HONEYMOON ACADEMY	JERRY LAZARUS
HONEYMOON IN VEGAS - S	ANDREW BERGMAN
HONEYMOON KILLERS, THE	LEONARD KASTLE
HONEYMOON, THE - S	HARRY DUNN
HONEYMOON, THE - S	REX MCGEE
HONEYMOON, THE - S	STAN SEIDEL
HONEYSUCKLE ROSE	CAROL SOBIESKI†
HONEYSUCKLE ROSE	JOHN BINDER
HONEYSUCKLE ROSE	WILLIAM D. WITTLIFF
HONG KONG THRILLER - S	BILLY RAY
HONKY TONK FREEWAY	EDWARD CLINTON
HONKY TONK SUE - S	ARLENE SARNER
HONKY TONK SUE - S	JERRY LEICHTLING
HONKY TONK SUE - S	LARRY MCMURTRY
HONKYTONK MAN	CLANCY CARLILE
HONOR BOUND - S	JONATHAN HEAP
HONOR BOUND - S	PHILIP MORTON
HONOR BRIGHT - S	DOUG RICHARDSON
HONOURABLE MURDER, AN	BRIAN H. CLEMENS
HOODS - S	MARK MALONE
HOOK	JIM HART
HOOK	MALIA SCOTCH MARMO
HOOK	NICK CASTLE
HOOK, LINE AND SINKER	ROD AMATEAU
HOOLIGANS - S	DJORDJE MILICEVIC
HOOPER	BILL KERBY
HOOPER	THOMAS RICKMAN
HOOSIERS (P)	ANGELO PIZZO
HOOTERS (P)	TED TALLY
HOOVERVILLE - S	HOWARD FRANKLIN
HOP - S	NICK W. THIEL
HOPE AND GLORY	JOHN BOORMAN
HOPELESS ROMANTIC - S	CHARLIE PETERS
HOPELESSNESS & DESPAIR - S	JEFF BUHAI
HOPELESSNESS & DESPAIR - S	STEVEN R. ZACHARIAS
HOPSCOTCH	BRIAN GARFIELD
HOPSCOTCH	BRYAN FORBES
HORATIO (P)	RON WHYTE†
HORIZONTAL MEN - S	THOMAS THONSON
HORROR HOLIDAY - S	JONATHAN KAUFER
HORROR HOUSE	MICHAEL ARMSTRONG
HORROR OF DRACULA	JIMMY SANGSTER
HORROR OF FRANKENSTEIN, THE	JIMMY SANGSTER
HORSE	AKIRA KUROSAWA
HORSE IS DEAD, THE - S	ROBERT KLANE
HORSE OPERA - S	DANILO BACH
HORSE RACING - S	PETE HAMILL
HORSE, THE	CHARLES BURNETT
HORSEMEN OF THE SILVER WALL - S	ROBERT J. AVRECH
HORSEPLAYER, THE	KURT VOSS
HORSEPLAYER, THE	LARRY RATTNER
HOSE JOB - S	JIM HART
HOSPITAL MASSACRE	MARC BEHM
HOSPITAL, THE	PADDY CHAYEVSKY†
HOSPITAL - S	JEFF BUHAI
HOSPITAL - S	STEVE ZACHARIAS
HOST, THE - S	STEPHEN VOLK
HOSTAGE, THE - S	RON HUTCHINSON
HOSTILE TAKEOVER - S	JIM GORMAN
HOSTILE TAKEOVER - S	MICHAEL BECKNER
HOSTILE WITNESS - S	RON BASS
HOT - S	PATRICIA L. KNOP
HOT - S	ZALMAN KING
HOT BOX, THE - S	JONATHAN DEMME
HOT CARGO - S	CHARLES ROBERT CARNER
HOT CHILI	MENAHEM GOLAN
HOT CHILI	WILLIAM SACHS
HOT DELIVERIES - S	JEFFREY C. SHERMAN
HOT DOG - THE MOVIE	MIKE MARVIN
HOT FLASHES - S	MARY AGNES DONAGHUE
HOT FOOT - S	MARTYN BURKE
HOT LEAD AND COLD FEET	ARTHUR ALSBERG
HOT LEAD AND COLD FEET	DONALD R. NELSON
HOT MILLIONS	PETER USTINOV
HOT MINUTE - S	PAUL BOORSTIN
HOT MINUTE - S	SHARON BOORSTIN
HOT MOON - S	ROD MCCALL
HOT MOVES	PETER FOLDY
HOT OFF THE WIRE - S	LEE REYNOLDS
HOT POTATO	OSCAR WILLIAMS
HOT PURSUIT	STEVEN W. CARABATSOS
HOT PURSUIT	STEVEN LISBERGER
HOT RESORT	BOAZ DAVIDSON
HOT RESORT	JOHN M. ROBINS
HOT RESORT	NORMAN HUDIS
HOT ROCK, THE	WILLIAM GOLDMAN
HOT ROD GIRL	JOHN MCGREEVY
HOT SHEET - S	GEORGE GIPE
HOT SHOT - S	BO GOLDMAN
HOT SHOTS!	JIM ABRAHAMS
HOT SHOTS!	PAT PROFT
HOT SPOT	CHARLES WILLIAMS†
HOT SPOT	NONA TYSON†
HOT STUFF	DONALD E. WESTLAKE
HOT STUFF	MICHAEL KANE
HOT SUMMER NIGHT	MORTON FINE†
HOT TARGET	DENIS LEWISTON
HOT TIMES	JIM MCBRIDE
HOT TO TROT	CHARLIE PETERS
HOT TO TROT	HUGO GILBERT
HOT TO TROT	STEPHEN C. NEIGHER
HOT TOMORROWS	MARTIN BREST
HOT WATER - S	DANIEL J. GUNTZELMAN
HOT WATER - S	STEVE K. MARSHALL
HOT WHISKEY & LEMON - S	JUAN CAMPANELLA
HOT WIRE - S	HARLEY PEYTON
HOTEL	WENDELL MAYES
HOTEL COLONIAL	CINZI TORRINI
HOTEL COLONIAL	IRA BARMAK
HOTEL COLONIAL	ROBERT KATZ
HOTEL COLONIAL	ENZO MONTELEONE
HOTEL DO - S	CARL BINDER
HOTEL HAWAII - S	NORMAN STEINBERG
HOTEL HAWAII - S	RICHARD DIMITRI
HOTEL NEW HAMPSHIRE, THE	TONY RICHARDSON
HOTEL OKLAHOMA	BOBBY HOUSTON
HOTEL PARADISE (P)	JONATHAN LYNN
HOTEL PLAY, THE (P)	WALLACE SHAWN
HOTEL ROYALE - S	LARRY GELBART
HOTHEAD	FRANCIS VEBER
HOTHOUSE, THE (P)	HAROLD PINTER
HOTSHOT	JOE SAUTER
HOTSHOT	RICK KING
HOTSHOT - S	BENNETT TRAMER
HOUDINI	PHILIP YORDAN
HOUND OF THE BASKERVILLES, THE	DUDLEY MOORE
HOUND OF THE BASKERVILLES, THE	PAUL MORRISSEY
HOUND OF THE BASKERVILLES, THE	PETER COOK
HOUND OF THE BASKERVILLES, THE - S	CHARLES EDWARD POGUE
HOUR OF DECISION, THE	NORMAN HUDIS
HOUR OF THE ANGEL - S	ROBERT J. AVRECH
HOUR OF THE ASSASSIN - S	MATT LEIPZIG
HOUR OF THE GUN	EDWARD ANHALT
HOUR OF THE WOLF	INGMAR BERGMAN
HOURGLASS - S	ERIC SMALL
HOUSE	FRED DEKKER
HOUSE	ETHAN WILEY
HOUSE II	ETHAN WILEY
HOUSE III	ALLYN WARNER

Title	Writer
HOUSE III	LESLIE BOHEM
HOUSE BY THE LAKE, THE	WILLIAM FRUET
HOUSE CALLS	ALAN MANDEL
HOUSE CALLS	CHARLES SHYER
HOUSE CALLS	JULIUS J. EPSTEIN
HOUSE DETECTIVE - S	TONY KAYDEN
HOUSE GUEST, THE - S	MICHAEL O'DONOGHUE
HOUSE GUEST, THE - S	MITCH GLAZER
HOUSE IN NIGHTMARE PARK, THE	CLIVE EXTON
HOUSE IN NIGHTMARE PARK, THE	TERRY NATION
HOUSE OF BAMBOO	HARRY KLEINER
HOUSE OF BLUE LEAVES, THE (P)	JOHN GUARE
HOUSE OF CARDS - S	MICHAEL LESSAC
HOUSE OF CHROME - S	TOM PAGE
HOUSE OF FRIGHT	WOLF MANKOWITZ
HOUSE OF GAMES	JONATHAN KATZ
HOUSE OF GAMES	DAVID MAMET
HOUSE OF GOD, THE	DONALD WRYE
HOUSE OF LOVE - S	ROSS JOHNSON
HOUSE OF MIRTH, THE - S	A.R. GURNEY
HOUSE OF SECRETS	BRYAN FORBES
HOUSE OF STRANGERS	PHILIP YORDAN
HOUSE OF THE DAMNED	HARRY SPALDING
HOUSE OF THE LONG SHADOWS	MICHAEL ARMSTRONG
HOUSE OF THE SEVEN HAWKS	JO EISINGER
HOUSE OF THE SPIRITS - S	AIDA BORTNIK
HOUSE OF THE SPIRITS - S	BILLE AUGUST
HOUSE OF USHER	RICHARD MATHESON
HOUSE ON CARROLL STREET, THE	WALTER BERNSTEIN
HOUSE ON SORORITY ROW, THE	MARK ROSMAN
HOUSE PARTY	REGINALD HUDLIN
HOUSE SWAP - S	JEFF BARON
HOUSE THAT DRIPPED BLOOD, THE	ROBERT BLOCH
HOUSE WHERE EVIL DWELLS, THE	ROBERT A. SUHOVSKY
HOUSEBOAT	JACK ROSE
HOUSEBOAT	MEL SHAVELSON
HOUSEHOLDER, THE	RUTH PRAWER JHABVALA
HOUSEKEEPER, THE	ELAINE WAISGLASS
HOUSEKEEPING	BILL FORSYTH
HOUSESITTING IN BEVERLY HILLS - S	EUGENE QUINTANO
HOUSEWIVES IN PRISON - S	VALRI BROMFIELD
HOW COME NOBODY'S ON OUR SIDE?	LEIGH CHAPMAN
HOW I GOT INTO COLLEGE	TERREL SELTZER
HOW I WON THE LOTTERY - S	ERIC IDLE
HOW I WON THE WAR	CHARLES WOOD
HOW LIKE AN ANGEL (P)	ARNAUD D'USSEAU†
HOW MUCH WOULD CHUCK - S	EBBE ROE SMITH
HOW SLEEP THE BRAVE - S	JOHN BRILEY
HOW SWEET IT IS	GARRY MARSHALL
HOW SWEET IT IS	JERRY BELSON
HOW TO BEAT THE HIGH COST OF LIVING	ROBERT KAUFMAN
HOW TO COMMIT MARRIAGE	MICHAEL KANIN
HOW TO GET AHEAD IN ADVERTISING	BRUCE ROBINSON
HOW TO GET MARRIED - S	ISRAEL HOROVITZ
HOW TO MAKE LOVE TO A NEGRO WITHOUT GETTING TIRED	DANY LAFERRIERE
HOW TO MAKE LOVE TO A NEGRO WITHOUT GETTING TIRED	RICHARD SADLER
HOW TO MARRY A MILLIONAIRE - S	ANDY BOROWITZ
HOW TO MARRY A MILLIONAIRE - S	KIMI PECK
HOW TO MURDER YOUR PARENTS - S	ALLEN ESTRIN
HOW TO MURDER YOUR WIFE	GEORGE AXELROD
HOW TO SAVE A MARRIAGE AND RUIN YOUR LIFE	NATHAN MONASTER†
HOW TO SAVE A MARRIAGE AND RUIN YOUR LIFE	STANLEY SHAPIRO†
HOW TO SUCCEED IN BUSINESS WITHOUT REALLY TRYING	DAVID SWIFT
HOWARD THE DUCK	GLORIA KATZ
HOWARD THE DUCK	WILLARD HUYCK
HOWARD'S END - S	RUTH PRAWER JHABVALA
HOWIE'S REVENGE - S	ALEX WINTER
HOWIE'S REVENGE - S	TOM STERN
HOWLING AT THE MOON - S	BIG BOY MEDLIN
HOWLING AT THE MOON - S	MICHAEL VENTURA
HOWLING, THE	JOHN SAYLES
HOWLING, THE	TERRY WINKLESS
HOWLING II	GARY BRANDNER
HOWLING II	ROBERT SARNO
HOWLING III	PHILLIPPE MORA
HOWLING IV	FREDDIE ROWE
HOWLING IV	CLIVE TURNER
HUD	HARRIET FRANK JR.
HUD	IRVING RAVETCH
HUDSON HAWK	BRUCE WILLIS
HUDSON HAWK	DANIEL B. WATERS
HUDSON HAWK	ROBERT KRAFT
HUDSON HAWK	STEVEN DE SOUZA
HUEY - S	GORE VIDAL
HUGO THE HIPPO (AF)	THOMAS BAUM
HUKI	STIRLING SILLIPHANT
HULLABALOO OVER GEORGIE & BONNIE'S PICTURES	RUTH PRAWER JHABVALA
HUMAN BEINGS (P)	ERNEST THOMPSON
HUMAN FACTOR, THE	TOM STOPPARD
HUMAN JUNGLE, THE	WILLIAM SACKHEIM
HUMAN SHIELD, THE	MANN RUBIN
HUMANOIDS FROM THE DEEP	FRANK ARNOLD
HUMANOIDS FROM THE DEEP	MARTIN B. COHAN
HUMANOIDS FROM THE DEEP	FREDERICK JAMES
HUMBOLDT COUNTY - S	ALAN ORMSBY
HUMONGOUS	WILLIAM GRAY
HUMORESQUE - S	DAVID FREEMAN
HUNDRED HOUR HUNT, THE	LEWIS GILBERG
HUNGER, THE	IAN DAVIS
HUNGER, THE	MICHAEL THOMAS
HUNGRY WIVES	GEORGE A. ROMERO
HUNK	LAWRENCE BASSOFF
HUNT FOR RED OCTOBER, THE	DONALD L. STEWART
HUNT FOR RED OCTOBER, THE	LARRY FERGUSON
HUNTER'S BLOOD	EMMETT ALSTON
HUNTER, THE	TED LEIGHTON
HUNTER, THE	PETER HYAMS
HUNTERS, THE	WENDELL MAYES
HUNTING PARTY, THE	WILLIAM NORTON SR.
HURDLES - S	A.R. GURNEY
HURLY BURLY (P)	DAVID RABE
HURRICANE	LORENZO SEMPLE
HURRY UP OR I'LL BE THIRTY - S	DAVID WILTSE
HURRY, SUNDOWN	HORTON FOOTE
HUSBANDS	JOHN CASSAVETES†
HUSH, HUSH SWEET CHARLOTTE	LUKAS HELLER†
HUSSY	MATTHEW CHAPMAN
HUSTLE	STEVE SHAGAN
HUSTLE BUNS - S	PAT PROFT
HYMN TIME IN THE LAND OF ABANDON - S	JEFFREY BELL
HYPE - S	GEORGE ARMITAGE
HYPER SAPIEN	CHRISTOPHER BLUE
HYPER SAPIEN	MARNIE PAIGE
HYPER SAPIEN	RICHARD ADCOCK
HYPERSPACE	TODD DURHAM
HYSTERIA	JIMMY SANGSTER

I

Title	Writer
I ACCUSE	GORE VIDAL
I AM NO LEGEND - S	ROBERT BORIS
I AM THE CHEESE	DAVE LANGE
I AM THE CHEESE	ROBERT JIRAS
I CAN GET IT FOR YOU WHOLESALE	ABRAHAM POLONSKY
I COME IN PEACE	JONATHAN TYDOR
I COME IN PEACE	LEONARD MAAS JR.
I COULD GO ON SINGING	MAYO SIMON
I COULD NEVER HAVE SEX WITH ANY MAN WHO HAS SO LITTLE RESPECT FOR MY HUSBAND	DAN GREENBURG
I DON'T HAVE TO SHOW YOU NO STINKING BADGES (P)	LUIS VALDEZ
I FOUGHT THE LAW	RENE BALCER
I FRESH	CHARLES BURNETT
I HIRED A CONTRACT KILLER	AKI KAURISMAKI
I KNOW WHERE I'M GOING	EMERIC PRESSBURGER†
I KNOW WHERE I'M GOING	MICHAEL POWELL†
I LIVE IN FEAR	AKIRA KUROSAWA
I LOVE A VAMPIRE - S	MATTHEW DORFF
I LOVE MY WIFE	ROBERT KAUFMAN
I LOVE YOU	ARNALDO JABAR
I LOVE YOU - S	DEAN RIESNER
I LOVE YOU TO DEATH	JOHN H. KOSTMAYER
I LOVE YOU, ALICE B. TOKLAS	PAUL MAZURSKY
I MARRIED A DEAD MAN - S	ANDY WOLK
I MARRIED A WITCH	ROBERT PIROSH†
I NEVER PROMISED YOU A ROSE GARDEN	GAVIN LAMBERT
I NEVER PROMISED YOU A ROSE GARDEN	LEWIS JOHN CARLINO
I NEVER SANG FOR MY FATHER	ROBERT ANDERSON
I ONLY ASKED	SID COLIN†
I OUGHT TO BE IN PICTURES	NEIL SIMON
I OWE YOU MY LIFE - S	DONALD TODD
I OWE YOU MY LIFE - S	JAMES P. DUNNE
I SENT A LETTER TO MY LOVE	GERARD BRACH
I SENT A LETTER TO MY LOVE	MOSHE MIZRAHI
I SHOT JESSE JAMES	SAMUEL FULLER
I SLEPT FOR SCIENCE - S	SUSAN SANDLER
I THINK I'M GOING TO LIKE IT HERE - S	CHRIS COLUMBUS
I THOUGHT I SAW YOU - S	ALICE ARLEN
I VITTELONI	FEDERICO FELLINI
I WALK ALONE	JOHN BRIGHT†
I WALK THE LINE	ALVIN SARGENT
I WANNA HOLD YOUR HAND	BOB GALE
I WANNA HOLD YOUR HAND	ROBERT ZEMECKIS
I WANT TO GO HOME	JULES FEIFFER
I WANT TO LIVE!	NELSON GIDDING
I WAS A TEENAGE BOOKIE - S	MAX EISENBERG
I WAS A TEENAGE BOY	CARLA REUBENS
I WAS A TEENAGE BOY	WALTER CARBONE
I WAS HAPPY HERE	DESMOND DAVIS
I WAS MONTY'S DOUBLE	BRYAN FORBES
I WILL, I WILL...FOR NOW	ALBERT E. LEWIN†
I WILL, I WILL...FOR NOW	NORMAN PANAMA
I'D RATHER BE RICH	OSCAR BRODNEY
I'LL BE YOUR SWEETHEART	VAL GUEST
I'LL GET THERE, IT BETTER BE WORTH THE TRIP - S	HAL ACKERMAN
I'LL SEE YOU IN MY DREAMS	JACK ROSE
I'LL SEE YOU IN MY DREAMS	MEL SHAVELSON
I'LL TAKE SWEDEN	ARTHUR MARX
I'LL TAKE SWEDEN	ROBERT FISHER
I'M DANCING AS FAST AS I CAN	DAVID RABE
I'M DANGEROUS TONIGHT (CTF)	BRUCE LANSBURY
I'M DANGEROUS TONIGHT (CTF)	PHILIP JOHN TAYLOR
I'M GONNA GIT YOU SUCKA	KEENEN IVORY WAYANS
I'M NOT CHARLIE - S	ALAN BERGER
I'M NOT CHARLIE - S	KATHY GORI
I'M NOT RAPPAPORT (P)	HERB GARDNER
I'VE HEARD THE MERMAIDS SINGING	PATRICIA ROZEMA
I, MADMAN	DAVID M. CHASKIN
I, MONSTER	MILTON SUBOTSKY
I, ROBOT - S	HARLAN ELLISON
I, THE JURY	LARRY COHEN
I, THE WORST OF ALL	MARIA LUISA BEMBERG
I, TINA - S	RICHARD LAWTON
I...DO - S	TODD DURHAM
ICE AGE - S	DAVID S. GOYER
ICE CASTLES	DONALD WRYE
ICE CASTLES	GARY L. BAIN
ICE DANCER, THE - S	JOHN DUIGAN
ICE HOUSE	BO BRINKMAN
ICE MAIDENS - S	JEAN-JACQUES BEINEIX
ICE PALACE	HARRY KLEINER
ICE PEOPLE, THE - S	GEORGE MACDONALD FRASER
ICE PIRATES, THE	STANFORD SHERMAN
ICE PIRATES, THE	STEWART RAFFILL
ICE STATION ZEBRA	DOUGLAS HEYES
ICED - S	TOM SZOLLOSI
ICEMAN	CHIP PROSER
ICEMAN	JOHN A. DRIMMER
ICICLE THIEF, THE	MAURIZIO MICHETTI
ID & I, THE - S	ROBERT MOLONEY
IDENTITY CRISIS	MARIO VAN PEEBLES
IDIOT SAINT - S	HOWARD CUSHNIR
IDIOT, THE	AKIRA KUROSAWA
IDIOT, THE - S	DAVID HENRY HWANG
IDOLMAKER, THE	EDWARD DI LORENZO
IF EVER I SEE YOU AGAIN	JOSEPH BROOKS
IF EVER I SEE YOU AGAIN	MARTIN DAVIDSON
IF I HAD A MILLION	JOHN BRIGHT†
IF I SHOULD DIE IN NO MAN'S LAND - S	DANIEL BARTOLINI
IF LOOKS COULD KILL	DARREN STAR
IF LOOKS COULD KILL	FRED DEKKER
IF LUCY FELL - S	ERIC SCHAEFFER
IF MORNING EVER COMES - S	GARY WEINER
IF MORNING EVER COMES - S	SHIRA LEVIN
IF WISHES WERE HORSES - S	CHRIS MONGER
IF YOU BELIEVE - S	SCOTT PARKER

Title	Writer
IF YOU COULD SEE WHAT I HEAR	STUART GILLARD
IFFY - S	LARRY B. WILLIAMS
IGO ONO - S	DAVID HENRY HWANG
IKIRU	AKIRA KUROSAWA
IL BIDONE	FEDERICO FELLINI
IL CAMMINO DELLA SPERANZA	FEDERICO FELLINI
IL CAMORRISTA	GIUSEPPE TORNATORE
IL CASANOVA DI FEDERICO FELLINI	FEDERICO FELLINI
ILL MET BY MOONLIGHT	EMERIC PRESSBURGER†
ILL MET BY MOONLIGHT	MICHAEL POWELL†
ILLEGALLY YOURS	JOHN LEVENSTEIN
ILLEGALLY YOURS	KEN FINKLEMAN
ILLEGALLY YOURS	MICHAEL A. KAPLAN
ILLICIT INTERLUDE	INGMAR BERGMAN
IMAGE, THE (CTF)	BRIAN REHAK
IMAGEMAKER, THE	DICK GOLDBERG
IMAGEMAKER, THE	HAL WEINER
IMAGES	ROBERT ALTMAN
IMAGINE: JOHN LENNON (FD)	ANDREW SOLT
IMAGINE: JOHN LENNON (FD)	SAM EGAN
IMAGINING ARGENTINA - S	CHRISTOPHER HAMPTON
IMMACULATE DECEPTION - S	S. MICHAEL COLE
IMMEDIATE FAMILY	BARBARA BENEDEK
IMMORTAL BATTALION, THE	PETER USTINOV
IMMORTAL MR. TEAS, THE	RUSS MEYER
IMMORTAL WEST AND HOW IT WAS LOST, THE	RUSS MEYER
IMMORTALISTS, THE - S	ELLEN ERWIN
IMMORTALISTS, THE - S	JEAN BARASH
IMPATIENT - S	LORENZO SEMPLE
IMPLOSION - S	RICHARD MATHESON
IMPORTED BRIDGEROOM, THE	PAMELA BERGER
IMPOSSIBLE FROM HERE - S	ROBERT LITZ
IMPOSSIBLE SPY, THE (CTF)	MARTY ROSS
IMPOSSIBLE YEARS, THE	ROBERT FISHER
IMPOSSIBLE YEARS, THE	ARTHUR MARX
IMPOSTORS	MARK RAPPAPORT
IMPROMPTU	SARAH KERNOCHAN
IMPROPER CHANNELS	ADAM ARKIN
IMPROPER CHANNELS	MORRIE RUVINSKY
IMPROPER CONDUCT (FD)	NESTOR ALMENDROS
IMPROPER CONDUCT - S	MARCEL MONTECINO
IMPULSE	JOHN DEMARCO
IMPULSE	LEIGH CHAPMAN
IMPULSE	BART DAVIS
IMPULSE	DON CARLOS DUNAWAY
IMPULSE	JOHN A. DRIMMER
IN A LONELY PLACE - S	DAVID Z. GOODMAN
IN A LONELY PLACE - S	MARK VICTOR
IN A LONELY PLACE - S	MICHAEL GRAIS
IN A SHALLOW GRAVE	KENNETH BOWSER
IN A WILD SANCTUARY	DYANNE ASSIMOW
IN A WORKMANLIKE MANNER - S	BRADLEY RAND SMITH
IN BROAD DAYLIGHT - S	FRED WALTON
IN COLD BLOOD	RICHARD BROOKS
IN COUNTRY	CYNTHIA CIDRE
IN COUNTRY	FRANK R. PIERSON
IN CROWD, THE	LARRY KONNER
IN CROWD, THE	MARK ROSENTHAL
IN DANGEROUS COMPANY	MITCH BROWN
IN DEEP - S	GEORGE BECKERMAN
IN DEEP - S	JOHN KENT HARRISON
IN DEEP - S	LAURIE FRANK
IN ENEMY COUNTRY	EDWARD ANHALT
IN EXTREMIS - S	JEB STUART
IN FROM THE COLD - S	VINCENT PATRICK
IN FROM THE COLD - S	WILLIAM MASTROSIMONE
IN GOD WE TRUST	CHRIS ALLEN
IN GOD WE TRUST	MARTY FELDMAN†
IN GOOD HANDS - S	FIONA LEWIS
IN HARM'S WAY	WENDELL MAYES
IN HER OWN IMAGE - S	JANET ROACH
IN LOVE AND WAR	EDWARD ANHALT
IN NO PARTICULAR ORDER - S	TODD LANGEN
IN PRAISE OF OLDER WOMEN	PAUL GOTTLIEB
IN SEARCH OF GREGORY	TONINO GUERRA
IN SEARCH OF HISTORIC JESUS	JACK JACOBS
IN SEARCH OF HISTORIC JESUS	MELVIN WALD
IN SUBMISSION - S	MELANIE MINTZ
IN THE BAG - S	JEFF FAZIO
IN THE BELLY OF THE WHALE	DORIS DORRIE
IN THE BOOM BOOM ROOM (P)	DAVID RABE
IN THE DEEP WOODS - S	CRAIG TEPPER
IN THE EYE OF THE STORM - S	JAMES SADWITH
IN THE HEAT OF THE NIGHT	STIRLING SILLIPHANT
IN THE HIGH GROUND	ROY CARLSON
IN THE LIFE - S	JOHN STEPPLING
IN THE LINE OF FIRE - S	KEN FRIEDMAN
IN THE MOOD	BOB KOSBERG
IN THE MOOD	DAVID SIMON
IN THE MOOD	PHIL ALDEN ROBINSON
IN THE N - S	JEB STUART
IN THE PROCESS - S	PAUL PRICE
IN THE PROCESS - S	STEVE NATHAN
IN THE SHADOW OF KILIMANJARO	JEFFREY M. SNELLER
IN THE SHADOW OF KILIMANJARO	T. MICHAEL HARRY
IN THE SHADOW OF THE BIG CHEESE - S	RICHARD LAWTON
IN THE SPIRIT	JEANNIE BERLIN
IN THE SPIRIT	LAURIE JONES
IN THE SPIRIT OF CRAZY HORSE	PAUL F. EDWARDS
IN THE WINGS (P)	PHILIP MORTON
IN THOSE DAYS - S	FREDERIC RAPHAEL
IN TROUBLE - S	DONOVAN MOORE
IN'N'OUT - S	ELLEN KESEND
IN-LAWS, THE	ANDREW BERGMAN
INADMISSIBLE EVIDENCE	JOHN OSBORNE
INCHON	PAUL SAVAGE
INCHON	LAIRD KOENIG
INCHON	ROBIN MOORE
INCIDENT, THE - S	MICHAEL NORELL
INCIDENT AT BARROW CREEK - S	TIM ROSE PRICE
INCIDENT AT VICHY (P)	ARTHUR MILLER
INCOMPARABLE LOULOU, THE (P)	RON CLARK
INCREDIBLE JOURNEY, THE - S	CAROLINE THOMPSON
INCREDIBLE MELTING MAN, THE	WILLIAM SACHS
INCREDIBLE MR. LIMPET, THE	JAMESON BREWER
INCREDIBLE SARAH, THE	RUTH WOLFF
INCREDIBLE SHRINKING MAN	RICHARD MATHESON
INCREDIBLE SHRINKING MAN, THE - S	RON CLARK
INCREDIBLE SHRINKING WOMAN, THE	JANE WAGNER
INCUBUS, THE	GEORGE FRANKLIN
INDEPENDENCE	JOYCE RITTER
INDEPENDENCE	LLOYD RITTER
INDEPENDENCE	THOMAS MCGRATH
INDEPENDENCE DAY	ALICE HOFFMAN
INDEPENDENCE DAY	BOBBY ROTH
INDIAN RUNNER	SEAN PENN
INDIAN SUMER - S	AKIVRA GOLDSMAN
INDIAN WANTS THE BRONX, THE (P)	ISRAEL HOROVITZ
INDIAN WARS - S	STANLEY WEISER
INDIANA JONES AND THE LAST CRUSADE	GEORGE LUCAS
INDIANA JONES AND THE LAST CRUSADE	JEFFREY BOAM
INDIANA JONES AND THE LAST CRUSADE	MENNO MEYJES
INDIANA JONES AND THE TEMPLE OF DOOM	GEORGE LUCAS
INDIANA JONES AND THE TEMPLE OF DOOM	GLORIA KATZ
INDIANA JONES AND THE TEMPLE OF DOOM	WILLARD HUYCK
INFERNO	DARIO ARGENTO
INFIDEL - S	MICHAEL THOMAS
INFINITY CUBE - S	FRANK DARABONT
INFINITY OF MIRRORS, AN - S	STEWART STERN
INFORMANT, THE - S	KEN FRIEDMAN
INFORMANT, THE - S	ROBERT DALEY
INHERIT THE MOB - S	PETER LEFCOURT
INHERIT THE WIND (P)	JEROME LAWRENCE
INHERIT THE WIND (P)	ROBERT E. LEE
INHERITORS, THE	ERIC A. RICHTER
INHERITORS, THE	WALTER BANNERT
INITIATION, THE	CHARLES PRATT, JR.
INITIATION: SILENT NIGHT, DEADLY NIGHT 4	WOODY KEITH
INNER CIRCLE, THE	ANDREI KONCHALOVSKY
INNER FIRE - S	DAVID FREEMAN
INNERSPACE	CHIP PROSER
INNERSPACE	JEFFREY BOAM
INNOCENCE UNPROTECTED	DUSAN MAKAVEJEV
INNOCENT BLOOD - S	MICHAEL WOLK
INNOCENT BLOOD - S	OLIVER STONE
INNOCENT MAN, AN	LARRY BROTHERS
INNOCENT, THE - S	IAN MCEWAN
INQUEST: THE U.S. VS JULIUS AND ETHEL ROSENBERG (P)	DONALD FREED
INSERTS	JOHN BYRUM
INSIDE DAISY CLOVER	GAVIN LAMBERT
INSIDE JOB - S	PETER HANKOFF
INSIDE MONKEY ZETTERLAND - S	STEVE ANTIN
INSIDE MOVES	BARRY LEVINSON
INSIDE MOVES	VALERIE CURTIN
INSIDE OUT	KEVIN BARTELME
INSIDE OUT	ROY G. TEICHER
INSIDE OUT - S	DAVID AMBROSE
INSIDE OUT - S	NEIL LANDAU
INSIDE OUT - S	TARA ISON
INSIDE THE INQUIRER - S	JEFF BUHAI
INSIDE THE THIRD REICH - S	ANDREW BIRKIN
INSIDER, THE - S	JEFF ROTHBERG
INSIDERS, THE - S	AVRAM DEAN GOLD
INSIGHT - S	JOHN SACRET YOUNG
INSOMNIA - S	STEVE DEJARNATT
INSPECTOR CALLS, AN	DESMOND DAVIS
INSPECTOR CLOUSEAU	FRANK WALDMAN†
INSPECTOR CLOUSEAU	TOM WALDMAN†
INSPECTOR, THE	NELSON GIDDING
INSTANT KARMA	BRUCE A. TAYLOR
INSTANT KARMA	DALE ROSENBLOOM
INSURANCE COMPANY, THE - S	GERALD DI PEGO
INTENSIVE CARE - S	BARRA GRANT
INTENSIVE CARE - S	ERIC ROTH
INTENT TO KILL	JIMMY SANGSTER
INTER-GALACTIC HIGH - S	JAMES JEREMIAS
INTER-GALACTIC HIGH - S	JANICE FISCHER
INTERCEPTORS - S	JONATHAN BETUEL
INTERCINE PROJECT, THE	BARRY LEVINSON
INTERFACE - S	CHIP PROSER
INTERIORS	WOODY ALLEN
INTERLUDE	HUGH LEONARD
INTERNAL AFFAIRS	HENRY BEAN
INTERNATIONAL VELVET	BRYAN FORBES
INTERNS, THE	DAVID SWIFT
INTERNS, THE	WALTER NEWMAN
INTERRUPTED LIFE, AN - S	JULIAN BARRY
INTERSLOPE - S	VICKIE PATIK
INTERZONE	DERAN SARAFIAN
INTIMATE RELATIONS - S	JOAN TEWKESBURY
INTIMATE STRANGER	ROB FRESCO
INTIMATE WRITINGS OF THEODORE HAMMER - S	JUDITH FEIN
INTO DARKNESS - S	RACHEL FELDMAN
INTO SELMA - S	RICHARD FRIEDENBERG
INTO THE NIGHT	RON KOSLOW
INTO THIN AIR	LARRY COHEN
INTRUDER	LAWRENCE BENDER
INTRUDER	SCOTT SPIEGEL
INTRUDERS - S	RICHARD MAXWELL
INVADERS FROM MARS	DAN O' BANNON
INVADERS FROM MARS	DON JAKOBY
INVASION OF THE BEE GIRLS	NICHOLAS MEYER
INVASION OF THE BODY BUILDERS - S	SCOTT J. SCHNEID
INVASION OF THE BODY BUILDERS - S	TONY MICHELMAN
INVASION OF THE BODY SNATCHERS	W.D. RICHTER
INVASION QUARTET	JOHN BRILEY
INVASION U.S.A	JAMES BRUNER
INVASION U.S.A	AARON NORRIS
INVASION U.S.A	CHUCK NORRIS
INVESTIGATION - S	PAUL SCHRADER
INVESTIGATION, THE: INSIDE A TERRORIST BOMBING (CTF)	ROB RITCHIE
INVISIBLE KID, THE	AVERY CROUNSE
INVISIBLE LIGHT, THE	GERRY DAVIS
INVISIBLE MAN, THE - S	GARY THOMPSON
INVITATION, THE - S	ANN DONAHUE
INVITATION, THE - S	EDWARD KHMARA
IOWA BOYS (P)	SHEM BITTERMAN
IPANEMA (CTF) - S	MICHAEL TOLKIN
IRMA LA DOUCE	BILLY WILDER
IRMA LA DOUCE	I.A.L. DIAMOND†
IRON AND SILK	MARK SALZMAN
IRON AND SILK	SHIRLEY SUN
IRON EAGLE	KEVIN ELDERS
IRON EAGLE	SIDNEY J. FURIE
IRON EAGLE II	KEVIN ELDERS
IRON EAGLE II	SIDNEY J. FURIE
IRON EAGLE III - S	KEVIN ELDERS
IRON GLOVE, THE	DOUGLAS HEYES
IRON MAIDEN, THE	LESLIE BRICUSSE
IRON MAZE	TIMOTHY J. METCALFE

Title	Writer
IRON TRIANGLE, THE	ERIC WESTON
IRON TRIANGLE, THE	JOHN BUSHELMAN
IRON TRIANGLE, THE	LARRY HILBRAND
IRON WARRIOR	AL BRADLEY
IRON WARRIOR	STEVEN LUOTTO
IRONCLADS (CTF)	HAROLD GAST
IRONMAN - S	MICHAEL MINER
IRONWEED	WILLIAM KENNEDY
IRRECONCILABLE DIFFERENCES	CHARLES SHYER
IRRECONCILABLE DIFFERENCES	NANCY J. MEYERS
IRREPLACEABLE KID - S	LARRY GRUSIN
IS HE STILL DEAD? (P)	DONALD FREED
IS PARIS BURNING?	FRANCIS FORD COPPOLA
IS PARIS BURNING?	GORE VIDAL
IS THERE LIFE AFTER HIGH SCHOOL? - S	JEFFREY KINDLEY
IS YOUR BROTHER BLUE? - S	ROB DUNN
ISABEL EBERHARDT - S	NANCY LARSON
ISADORA	MELVYN BRAGG
ISADORA	CLIVE EXTON
ISHTAR	ELAINE MAY
ISLAND IN WINTER, AN - S	ALLAN WEISBECKER
ISLAND OF DR. MOREAU, THE	AL RAMRUS
ISLAND OF DR. MOREAU, THE	JOHN HERMAN SHANER
ISLAND, THE	PETER BENCHLEY
ISLAND, THE (P)	ATHOL FUGARD
ISLANDS IN THE STREAM	DENNE BART PETITCLERC
ISN'T IT ROMANTIC - S	SUSAN KRAMER
ISN'T IT ROMANTIC? (P)	WENDY WASSERSTEIN
IT ALMOST WASN'T CHRISTMAS - S	ALAN JAY GLUECKMAN
IT AND EVERYTHING ELSE - S	HARRY KONDOLEON
IT CAME FROM HOLLYWOOD	DANA R. OLSEN
IT CAME FROM POLAND - S	SARAH C. PALEY
IT GIRL, THE - S	DAVID STENN
IT HAD TO BE STEVE - S	AMY JONES
IT HAD TO BE STEVE - S	HOLLY GOLDBERG SLOAN
IT HAD TO BE STEVE - S	TRACY KEENAN WYNN
IT HAD TO BE YOU	JOSEPH BOLOGNA
IT HAD TO BE YOU	RENEE TAYLOR
IT HAPPENED AT THE WORLD'S FAIR	SEAMAN JACOBS
IT HAPPENED TOMORROW - S	SANDY KROOPF
IT LOOKED LIKE FOREVER - S	JAY TARSES
IT LOOKS ALIVE TO ME - S	MICHAEL TOLKIN
IT SHOULDN'T HAPPEN TO A VET	ALAN PLATER
IT STARTED IN NAPLES	JACK ROSE
IT STARTED IN NAPLES	MEL SHAVELSON
IT TAKES TWO	RICHARD CHRISTIAN MATHESON
IT TAKES TWO	TOM SZOLLOSI
IT TAKES TWO TO MAKE ONE — THE TOTIE FIELDS STORY - S	HESPER ANDERSON
IT TOOK FIRST PRIZE IN HOUSTON - S	JOEL DAVIS
IT'S A BIG COUNTRY	ALLEN RIVKIN†
IT'S A CRIME - S	GEN LEROY
IT'S A FAIR WORLD - S	BOB DOLMAN
IT'S A FAIR WORLD - S	HARRY SHEARER
IT'S A FUNNY, FUNNY WORLD	BOAZ DAVIDSON
IT'S A WONDERFUL WORLD - S	MARTIN OLSON
IT'S ALIVE	LARRY COHEN
IT'S ALIVE III: ISLAND OF THE ALIVE	LARRY COHEN
IT'S ALWAYS FAIR WEATHER	ADOLPH GREEN
IT'S ALWAYS FAIR WEATHER	BETTY COMDEN
IT'S CALLED SURVIVAL (P)	ROBERT L. PEETE
IT'S CALLED THE SUGAR PLUM (P)	ISRAEL HOROVITZ
IT'S ME AGAIN - S	HERMAN RAUCHER
IT'S MY TURN	ELEANOR BERGSTEIN
IT'S NOT SUPERSTITION - S	JOEL ROSE
IT'S NOT THE MONEY - S	CAROLYN SHELBY
IT'S NOT THE MONEY - S	CHRISTOPHER AMES
IT'S NOT THE SIZE THAT COUNTS	SID COLIN†
IT'S ONLY A PLAY (P)	TERRENCE MCNALLY
IT'S ONLY MONEY - S	DANIEL H. VINING
ITALIAN AMERICAN RECONCILIATION (P)	JOHN PATRICK SHANLEY
ITALIAN BASKETBALL - S	ROD BURTON
ITALIAN JOB, THE	TROY KENNEDY MARTIN
ITALIANS, THE - S	ROBERT KAUFMAN
IVAN - S	LARRY GRUSIN

J

Title	Writer
J.D.'S REVENGE	JAISON STARKES
J.W. COOP	CLIFF ROBERTSON
J.W. COOP	BUD SHRAKE
JABBERWOCKY	TERRY GILLIAM
JACK & JILL (CTF) - S	JON ROBIN BAITZ
JACK CARTER'S LAW - S	LEE DRYSDALE
JACK OF DIAMONDS	JACK DEWITT
JACK OF DIAMONDS	SANDY HOWARD
JACK OF HEARTS - S	DAVID S. GOYER
JACK OF HEARTS - S	TOM DONNELLY
JACK THE BEAR - S	STEVEN ZAILLIAN
JACK THE BEAR - S	LAWRENCE J. COHEN
JACK THE RIPPER - S	JIMMY SANGSTER
JACK THE RIPPER - S	PETE HAMILL
JACK'S BACK	ROWDY HERRINGTON
JACK-MAN - S	DARRYL WIMBERLY
JACKNIFE	STEPHEN METCALFE
JACKPOT - S	CHRIS FABER
JACKPOT - S	DANNIEL BARRON
JACKSON COUNTY JAIL	DONALD L. STEWART
JACOB TWO-TWO MEETS THE HOODED FANG	MORDECAI RICHLER
JACOB'S LADDER	BRUCE JOEL RUBIN
JACQUOT OF NANTES	AGNES VARDA
JADE - S	GREGORY BREHM
JADE - S	WILLIAM KINSOLVING
JAG - S	CHRIS KEYSER
JAGGED EDGE	JOE ESZTERHAS
JAGGED EDGE 2 - S	JONATHAN BENAIR
JAGUAR - S	JO NAPOLEON
JAGUAR LIVES!	YABO YABLONSKY
JAILBAIT - S	DON MCLENNAN
JAKE - S	STANFORD SHERMAN
JAKE SPEED	ANDREW LANE
JAKE SPEED	WAYNE CRAWFORD
JAKE'S THING - S	ALAN MANDEL
JAKE'S TOMATOES - S	ROBERT MOLONEY
JAMAICA - S	JOHN HERZFELD
JAMAICAN AND THE RAISIN, THE - S	JANET KOVALCIK
JAMES BROWN STORY, THE - S	RON MILNER
JAMES JOYCE'S WOMEN	FIONNULA FLANAGAN
JAMIE - S	SHAWN SLOVO
JAMIE FORT STORY, THE (SHORT)	ILANA BAR-DIN
JANE AND THE LOST CITY	MERVYN HAISMAN
JANE ANNE - S	CHRIS MONGER
JANE AUSTEN IN MANHATTAN	RUTH PRAWER JHABVALA
JANE Q. PUBLIC - S	DAVID LEVINSON
JANE'S HOUSE - S	JUDITH ROSS
JANET HARDUVAL STORY, THE - S	DAVID WILLIAMSON
JANITOR (SHORT)	STEVEN SODERBERGH
JANUARY HOUR - S	RONALD SHUSETT
JANUARY MAN, THE	JOHN PATRICK SHANLEY
JASMINE AND THE JELLY THIEF - S	DALENE YOUNG
JASON AND THE ARGONAUTS	BEVERLY CROSS
JASS (P)	JOHN PIELMEIER
JAWS	CARL GOTTLIEB
JAWS	PETER BENCHLEY
JAWS II	CARL GOTTLIEB
JAWS 3-D	CARL GOTTLIEB
JAWS 3-D	GUERDON TRUEBLOOD
JAWS 3-D	RICHARD MATHESON
JAWS OF SATAN	GERRY HOLLAND
JAWS THE REVENGE	MICHAEL DE GUZMAN
JAYWALKING - S	MICHAEL KANE
JAZZ BABIES - S	A.J. CAROTHERS
JAZZ BABIES - S	LARRY GELBART
JAZZ SINGER, THE	LEONARD STERN
JAZZ SINGER, THE	HERBERT BAKER†
JAZZ SINGER, THE	STEPHEN H. FOREMAN
JAZZBOAT	KEN HUGHES
JEAN DE FLORETTE	CLAUDE BERRI
JEAN DE FLORETTE	GERARD BRACH
JEAN SEBERG (P)	JULIAN BARRY
JEDEDIAH SMITH - S	THOMAS POPE
JEFF - S	MARTIN OLSON
JEFFERSON MCGRAW - S	A.J. CAROTHERS
JEFFREY OF ARABIA - S	DANIEL GOLDIN
JEFFREY OF ARABIA - S	JOSH GOLDIN
JEKYLL AND HYDE... TOGETHER AGAIN	HARVEY MILLER
JEKYLL AND HYDE... TOGETHER AGAIN	JERRY BELSON
JEKYLL AND HYDE... TOGETHER AGAIN	MICHAEL LEESON
JEKYLL AND HYDE... TOGETHER AGAIN	MONICA JOHNSON
JEMIMA SHORE - S	CHRIS BRYANT
JENNIFER EIGHT - S	BRUCE ROBINSON
JENNIFER ON MY MIND	ERICH SEGAL
JENNIFER ON MY MIND - S	ROGER L. SIMON
JEOPARDY - S	ADAM GREENMAN
JEREMIAH JOHNSON	EDWARD ANHALT
JEREMIAH JOHNSON	JOHN MILLIUS
JEREMY	ARTHUR BARRON
JERK, THE	CARL GOTTLIEB
JERK, THE	MICHAEL ELIAS
JERK, THE	STEVE MARTIN
JERRY LEE LEWIS PROJECT, THE - S	TERENCE MALICK
JERSEY GIRLS - S	GINA WENDKOS
JERSEY SKYLINE - S	GINNY CERRELLA
JERSEY TO HEAVEN AND BACK - S	DON CIRILLO
JERUSALEM FILE, THE	TROY KENNEDY MARTIN
JESUS CHRIST SUPERSTAR	MELVYN BRAGG
JESUS OF MONTREAL	DENYS ARCAND
JET CAR - S	EARL MAC RAUCH
JET PROPELLED COUCH, THE - S	RICHARD CHAPMAN
JET STORM	CY ENDFIELD
JETSONS, THE (AF)	DENNIS MARKS
JETSONS - S	CHRISTOPHER THOMPSON
JETSONS, THE - S	ALEC LORIMORE
JETSONS, THE - S	ERIC LUKE
JETSONS, THE - S	TERRY WINKLESS
JEWEL OF THE NILE, THE	LARRY KONNER
JEWEL OF THE NILE, THE	MARK ROSENTHAL
JEWELER, THE - S	JAY KAMEN
JEZEBEL'S KISS	HARVEY KEITH
JFK - S	OLIVER STONE
JIGSAW	VAL GUEST
JIGSAW MAN, THE	JO EISINGER
JIMBO'S STAND - S	BOB GALE
JIMMY JONES - S	JAMES KENNEDY
JIMMY SHINE (P)	MURRAY SCHISGAL
JIMMY THE KID	SAM BOBRICK
JINGLE BELLS - S	ANDREW MARSHALL
JINGLE BELLS - S	DAVID RENWICK
JINXED	DAVID NEWMAN
JINXED	FRANK D. GILROY
JIVE JUNCTION	IRVING WALLACE†
JO AND THE LIZARDS - S	ROD MCCALL
JO JO DANCER, YOUR LIFE IS CALLING	PAUL MOONEY
JO JO DANCER, YOUR LIFE IS CALLING	RICHARD PRYOR
JO JO DANCER, YOUR LIFE IS CALLING	ROCCO URBISCI
JOAQUIN - S	WALTER NEWMAN
JOBMAN	DARRELL ROODT
JOBMAN	GREGG LATTER
JOCK PETERSEN	DAVID WILLIAMSON
JOCKS	DAVID OBST
JOCKS	STEVEN R. ZACHARIAS
JOE	NORMAN WEXLER
JOE AND ROSALIA - S	HARRIS ORKIN
JOE COLLEGE - S	ALAN MANDEL
JOE HOUSE - S	DENIS O'NEIL
JOE II - S	VINCENT PATRICK
JOE KIDD	ELMORE LEONARD
JOE LOUIS - S	WENDELL HARRIS JR.
JOE MACBETH	PHILIP YORDAN
JOE VALACHI: I SEGRETI DI COSA NOSTRA	STEPHEN GELLER
JOE VERSUS THE VOLCANO	JOHN PATRICK SHANLEY
JOE'S BED STUY BARBERSHOP: WE CUT HEADS	SPIKE LEE
JOEY FAMOUS - S	DAVID LOUCKA
JOEY FAMOUS - S	MARK KRAM
JOEY ON THE 31ST FLOOR - S	ROBBIE FOX
JOEY TAKES A CAB	FRANK RAY PERELLI
JOGGER, THE (SHORT)	ROBERT RESNIKOFF
JOHN AND MARY	JOHN MORTIMER
JOHN GOLDFARB, PLEASE COME HOME	WILLIAM PETER BLATTY
JOHN MEADE'S WOMAN	JOHN BRIGHT†
JOHN PAUL GEORGE RINGO AND BURT (P)	WILLY RUSSELL
JOHN WESLEY HARDIN - S	MILES HOOD SWARTHOUT
JOHNNY BE GOOD	DAVID OBST
JOHNNY BE GOOD	JEFF BUHAI
JOHNNY BE GOOD	STEVEN R. ZACHARIAS

Jo-Ki
FILM WRITERS GUIDE

JOHNNY BULL - S .... KATHLEEN BETSKO-YALE
JOHNNY CONCHO .... DON MCGUIRE
JOHNNY DANGEROUSLY .... BERNIE KUKOFF
JOHNNY DANGEROUSLY .... HARRY COLOMBY
JOHNNY DANGEROUSLY .... JEFF HARRIS
JOHNNY DANGEROUSLY ...... NORMAN STEINBERG
JOHNNY GUITAR .... PHILIP YORDAN
JOHNNY HANDSOME .... KEN FRIEDMAN
JOINT ACCOUNT .... DAVID PEOPLES
JOKE OF DESTINY, A .... LINA WERTMULLER
JOKER AND THE
  DEALER, THE - S .... BIG BOY MEDLIN
JOKER IS WILD, THE .... OSCAR SAUL
JOKERS .... DICK CLEMENT
JOKERS, THE .... IAN LAFRENAIS
JONI .... JAMES F. COLLIER†
JOSEPH ANDREWS .... ALLAN G. SCOTT
JOSEPH ANDREWS .... CHRIS BRYANT
JOSEPHINE AND MEN .... ROY BOULTING
JOSEPHINE BAKER - S .... JULIAN BARRY
JOSEPHINE BAKER
  STORY, THE (CTF) .... MICHAEL ZAGOR
JOSEPHINE BAKER
  STORY, THE (CTF) .... RON HUTCHINSON
JOSHUA - S .... ALVIN SARGENT
JOSHUA MACHINE - S .... JEREMY LARNER
JOSHUA THEN AND NOW ...... MORDECAI RICHLER
JOURNEY - S .... MICHAEL SCHIFFER
JOURNEY OF AUGUST
  KING, THE - S .... STEPHEN H. FOREMAN
JOURNEY OF HOPE .... XAVIER KOLLER
JOURNEY OF LOVE .... TONINO GUERRA
JOURNEY OF MARIA
  LOPEZ, THE - S .... VINCENT GUTIERREZ
JOURNEY OF NATTY
  GANN, THE .... JEANNE ROSENBERG
JOURNEY OF THE
  14 PRESIDENTS .... DAVID PEOPLES
JOURNEY TO OHM - S .... JOHN HOPKINS
JOURNEY TO THE CENTER
  OF THE EARTH .... KITTY CHALMERS
JOURNEY TO THE CENTER
  OF THE EARTH .... RUSTY LEMORANDE
JOURNEY TO THE FAR SIDE
  OF THE SUN .... GERRY ANDERSON
JOVA - S .... COLINE SERREAU
JOY HOUSE .... RENE CLEMENT
JOY OF SEX .... KATHLEEN ROWELL
JOY- S .... IAN ABRAMS
JOYRIDE .... JOSEPH RUBEN
JOYSTICKS .... AL GOMEZ
JOYSTICKS .... MICKEY EPPS
JUBILEE .... DEREK JARMAN
JUBILEE - S .... LARRY MCMURTRY
JUDGE AND THE
  ASSASSIN, THE .... BERTRAND TAVERNIER
JUDGE DEE - S .... GERARD SOETEMAN
JUDGE DREDD - S .... TIM HUNTER
JUDGEMENT DAY .... FERDE GROFE JR.
JUDGEMENT DAY .... BRUCE MALMUTH
JUDGEMENT NIGHT - S .... KEVIN JARRE
JUDGMENT .... WILLIAM SACHS
JUDGMENT (CTF) .... TOM TOPOR
JUDGMENT AT NUREMBERG .... ABBY MANN
JUDGMENT DAY - S .... PETE HAMILL
JUDGMENT IN BERLIN .... JOSHUA SINCLAIR
JUDGMENT IN BERLIN .... LEO PENN
JUDITH .... JOHN MICHAEL HAYES
JUGGLER, THE - S .... CHARLIE PETERS
JUICE - S .... DAVID LOUGHERY
JUICE - S .... JOSEPH RUBEN
JULES ET JIM .... FRANCOIS TRUFFAUT†
JULES ET JIM .... JEAN GRUAULT
JULIA .... ALVIN SARGENT
JULIA AND JULIA .... PETER DEL MONTE
JULIA AND JULIA .... SANDRA PETRAGLIA
JULIA AND JULIA .... SILVIA NAPOLITANO
JULIA HAS TWO LOVERS .... BASHAR SHBIB
JULIA HAS TWO LOVERS .... DAPHNA KASTNER
JULIE .... ANDREW STONE
JULIET - S .... MARIO VAN PEEBLES
JULIET OF THE SPIRITS .... FEDERICO FELLINI
JULIO AND STEIN - S .... BARRY SANDLER
JULIUS CAESAR .... JOSEPH L. MANKIEWICZ
JUMBO .... SIDNEY SHELDON
JUMBO MURDERS - S .... W.D. RICHTER
JUMPERS (P) .... TOM STOPPARD
JUMPIN' JACK
  FLASH .... CHRISTOPHER N. THOMPSON
JUMPIN' JACK FLASH .... DAVID H. FRANZONI
JUMPIN' JACK FLASH .... PATRICIA IRVING
JUMPING FOR JOY .... JACK DAVIES
JUMPING OFF POINT, THE - S ...... CAROL BLACK
JUMPING OFF POINT, THE - S ...... NEAL MARLENS
JUNE BABY - S .... DAVID NEWMAN
JUNGLE BOY - S .... GUY THOMAS
JUNGLE FEVER .... SPIKE LEE
JUNGLELAND - S .... TERRY CURTIS FOX
JUNIOR ACHIEVEMENT - S .... LESLIE DIXON
JUNIOR BONNER .... JEB ROSEBROOK
JUNIOR HIGH SCHOOL - S .... DAVID WECHTER
JUPITER NEEDS
  PARKING - S .... LARRY KARASZEWSKI
JUPITER NEEDS
  PARKING - S .... SCOTT ALEXANDER
JURASSIC PARK - S .... MICHAEL CRISTOFER
JURY DUTY - S .... JEB STUART
JURY DUTY - S .... ROBERT KLANE
JUST A GIGOLO .... JOSHUA SINCLAIR
JUST ANOTHER
  LOVE STORY - S .... MERRILL MARKOE
JUST ANOTHER NIGHT - S .... PARKER BENNETT
JUST ANOTHER NIGHT - S .... TERRY RUNTE
JUST BETWEEN FRIENDS .... ALLAN BURNS
JUST BETWEEN US - S .... DEBORAH BARON
JUST CAUSE - S .... JEB STUART
JUST CRAZY ABOUT - S .... NANCY DOWD
JUST DESERTS - S .... VAL PENN
JUST IN TIME - S .... ROSIE SHUSTER
JUST LIKE A WOMAN .... ROBERT FUEST
JUST LIKE A WOMAN .... CHRIS MILLER
JUST LIKE A WOMAN - S ...... MICHAEL D. SUTTON
JUST LIKE NEW YORK - S .... W.D. RICHTER
JUST MARRIED - S .... DOUGLAS MCGRATH
JUST MET - S .... RICHARD JEFFERIES
JUST OFF BROADWAY .... ARNAUD D'USSEAU†
JUST ONCE (P) .... MELANIE MINTZ
JUST ONE OF THE GUYS .... DENNIS FELDMAN
JUST ONE OF THE GUYS .... JEFF FRANKLIN
JUST ONE OF THOSE THINGS - S .... ALAN MANDEL
JUST TELL ME WHAT
  YOU WANT .... JAY PRESSON ALLEN
JUST THE WAY YOU ARE .... ALLAN BURNS
JUST YOU AND ME, KID ...... LEONARD B. STERN
JUST YOU AND ME, KID .... OLIVER D. HAILEY
JUSTICE (P) .... TERRY CURTIS FOX
JUSTINE .... LAWRENCE B. MARCUS
JUVENILE - S .... ELMORE LEONARD

K

K-2 - S .... SCOTT ROBERTS
K-9 .... SCOTT MYERS
K-9 .... STEVEN JAY SIEGEL
KABALAH - S .... CELIA GITTLESON
KABALAH - S .... TONY GITTLESON
KABYLIA - S .... MICHAEL AUERBACH
KAFKA - S .... LEM DOBBS
KAGEMUSHA: THE
  SHADOW WARRIOR .... AKIRA KUROSAWA
KALEIDOSCOPE .... ROBERT CARRINGTON
KALKI - S .... GORE VIDAL
KAMPALA - S .... MARK W. LEE
KANGAROO .... EVAN JONES
KANGAROO (1952) .... HARRY KLEINER
KANISTAN - S .... FRED FREEMAN
KANSAS .... SPENCER EASTMAN†
KANSAS CITY BOMBER .... THOMAS RICKMAN
KAOS .... PAOLO TAVIANI
KAOS .... VITTORIO TAVIANI
KAPO .... FRANCO SOLINAS
KARATE KID, THE .... ROBERT MARK KAMEN
KARATE KID PART II, THE .... ROBERT MARK KAMEN
KARATE KID PART III, THE ... ROBERT MARK KAMEN
KARISTAN - S .... LAWRENCE J. COHEN
KATE - S .... JONATHAN REYNOLDS
KEATON'S COP .... MICHAEL B. DRUXMAN
KEEP, THE .... MICHAEL MANN
KEEP, THE .... DENNIS L. CLARK
KEEPER OF THE CITY .... GERALD DIPEGO
KEEPER OF THE GATE - S .... AVRAM DEAN GOLD
KEEPERS - S .... NEVIN SCHREINER
KELLY'S HEROES .... TROY KENNEDY MARTIN
KEN WARD ENTERS
  THE JUNGLE - S .... ROB THOMPSON
KENTUCKY BLUE - S .... FREDERICK BAILEY
KENTUCKY FRIED MOVIE, THE ...... DAVID ZUCKER
KENTUCKY FRIED MOVIE, THE ...... JERRY ZUCKER
KENTUCKY FRIED MOVIE, THE ...... JIM ABRAHAMS
KES .... BARRY HINES
KES .... KEN LOACH
KEY EXCHANGE .... JOHN ROMANO
KEY EXCHANGE .... PAUL KURTA
KEY EXCHANGE (P) .... KEVIN WADE
KEY LARGO .... RICHARD BROOKS
KEY WEST - S .... JAMES KENNEDY
KEY WEST - S .... STEPHEN H. FOREMAN
KEY WEST DRUG
  SMUGGLING - S .... KEN FRIEDMAN
KEY WEST- S .... DONALD L. STEWART
KEY, THE .... CARL FOREMAN†
KEYS TO FREEDOM .... STEPHEN FEKE
KGB: THE SECRET WAR .... SANDRA K. BAILEY
KHADIM - S .... HARLAN ELLISON
KHAN - S .... JOHN HUGHES
KIAMESHA - S .... LOWELL GANZ
KICK - S .... JUNE ROBERTS
KICKBOXER .... JEAN-CLAUDE VAN DAMME
KICKBOXER .... MARK DISALLE
KICKBOXER .... GLENN A. BRUCE
KICKBOXER 2 .... DAVID S. GOYER
KID - S .... LESLIE BOHEM
KID BLUE .... BUD SHRAKE
KID BROTHER - S .... KEVIN MULLIGAN
KID CHAMPION (P) .... THOMAS BABE
KID COLTER .... DAVID O'MALLEY
KID FOR TWO FARTHINGS, A ..... WOLF MANKOWITZ
KID FROM CLEVELAND, THE .... JOHN BRIGHT†
KID IN THE GREY
  FEDORA, THE - S .... WILLIAM CONDON
KID IRISH- S .... JOE GAYTON
KID KONG - S .... STANFORD SHERMAN
KID STUFF - S .... BRUCE GOLDSMITH
KID STUFF - S .... ERNEST THOMPSON
KID WHO ATE HER
  PARENTS, THE - S .... VALRI BROMFIELD
KID WHO COULD GO TO HIS
  LEFT, THE - S .... JAY TARSES
KID WHO COULD GO TO HIS
  LEFT, THE - S .... TOM PATCHETT
KID, THE - S .... BRAD BUCKNER
KID, THE - S .... EUGENIE ROSS-LEMING
KIDCO .... BENNETT TRAMER
KIDD - S .... DENNIS PALUMBO
KIDD - S .... JOSEPH C. STINSON
KIDNAPPED .... HIKMET AVEDIS
KIDNAPPING OF THE
  PRESIDENT, THE .... RICHARD MURPHY
KIDS - S .... JERRY BELSON
KIDSTUFF - S .... DAVID CASCI
KILER INSIDE ME, THE .... ROBERT CHANDLEE
KILL AND KILL AGAIN .... JOHN CROWTHER
KILL CRAZY .... DAVID HEAVENER
KILL IN - S .... LARRY GELBART
KILL ME AGAIN .... DAVID WARFIELD
KILL ME AGAIN .... JOHN DAHL
KILL OFF, THE .... MAGGIE GREENWALD
KILL OR CURE .... DAVID PURSALL
KILLBOTS .... STEVE MITCHELL
KILLBOTS .... JIM WYNORSKI
KILLER BEACH BABES - S .... CHRIS MATHESON
KILLER BEACH BABES - S .... RYAN ROWE
KILLER CHARLIE FIVE - S ...... RICK MORANIS
KILLER ELITE, THE .... MARC NORMAN
KILLER ELITE, THE .... STIRLING SILLIPHANT
KILLER INSIDE ME, THE .... EDWARD MANN
KILLER INSTINCT, THE - S .... JOHN A. GALLAGHER
KILLER KLOWNS FROM
  OUTER SPACE .... CHARLES CHIODO
KILLER KLOWNS FROM
  OUTER SPACE .... STEVEN CHIODO
KILLER OF SHEEP .... CHARLES BURNETT
KILLER PARTY .... BARNEY COHEN
KILLER SAM - S .... FRANK DEESE
KILLER'S KISS .... STANLEY KUBRICK
KILLER, THE .... JOHN WOOD
KILLERS .... DAVID SELTZER
KILLERS DON'T KISS - S .... ROB THOMPSON
KILLERS OF
  KILIMANJARO, THE .... RICHARD MAIBAUM†
KILLING AFFAIR, A .... DAVID SAPERSTEIN
KILLING DAD .... MICHAEL AUSTIN
KILLING FIELDS, THE .... BRUCE ROBINSON
KILLING FOR CHRIST, A - S ...... JOHN HAMILL
KILLING FOR CHRIST, A - S ...... DENIS HAMILL
KILLING OF A CHINESE
  BOOKIE, THE .... JOHN CASSAVETES†
KILLING OF ANGEL STREET, THE ...... EVAN JONES
KILLING OF SISTER
  GEORGE, THE .... LUKAS HELLER†
KILLING TIME, THE .... BRUCE FRANKLIN SINGER

KILLING TIME, THE	DON BOHLINGER	KISSING PLACE, THE (CTF)	CYNTHIA A. CHERBAK
KILLING TIME, THE	JAMES NATHAN	KISSING PLACE, THE (CTF)	MICHAEL WING
KILLING ZONE- S	DONALD L. STEWART	KISSING PLACE, THE (CTF)	RICHARD ALTABEF
KILLING, THE	STANLEY KUBRICK	KITCHEN CABINET, THE - S	FERNANDO DOTY
KILLPOINT	FRANK HARRIS	KITCHEN TOTO, THE	HARRY HOOK
KIN - S	LEWIS JOHN CARLINO	KITELINE - S	B.W.L. NORTON, JR.
KINDERGARTEN COP	HERSCHEL A. WEINGROD	KITTEN WITH A WHIP	DOUGLAS HEYES
KINDERGARTEN COP	MURRAY SALEM	KIXI - S	RICHARD DEWHURST
KINDRED, THE	EARL GHAFFARI	KLANSMAN, THE	MILLARD KAUFMAN
KINDRED, THE	JEFFREY OBROW	KLANSMAN, THE	SAMUEL FULLER
KINDRED, THE	JOHN V. PENNEY	KLASSENVERHALF-NISSE	JEAN-MARIE STRAUB
KINDRED, THE	JOSEPH STEFANO	KLUDGE - S	JOHN P. GROVES
KINDRED, THE	STEPHEN W. CARPENTER	KLUTE	ANDY LEWIS
KINFOLK - S	STU KRIEGER	KLUTE	DAVE LEWIS
KING AND COUNTRY	EVAN JONES	KLYNT'S LAW - S	CHRIS BRYANT
KING AND I, THE	ERNEST LEHMAN	KNACK, THE	CHARLES WOOD
KING DAVID	ANDREW BIRKIN	KNAVE OF HEARTS	RENE CLEMENT
KING DAVID	JAMES COSTIGAN	KNEE DEEP IN ALLIGATORS - S	STEPHEN KATZ
KING FOR A DAY - S	FRANCIS VEBER	KNIFE IN THE HEART - S	REX PICKETT
KING FOR A DAY - S	TAB MURPHY	KNIFE IN THE WATER	JERZY SKOLIMOWSKI
KING ISLAND - S	DON MCLENNAN	KNIFE IN THE WATER	ROMAN POLANSKI
KING KONG	LORENZO SEMPLE	KNIFE, THE (P)	DAVID HARE
KING KONG LIVES	RONALD SHUSETT	KNIGHT MOVES - S	BRAD MIRMAN
KING KONG LIVES	STEVEN PRESSFIELD	KNIGHTLY DREAMS - S	JOE GAYTON
KING LIVES, THE - S	LLOYD FONVIELLE	KNIGHTRIDERS	GEORGE A. ROMERO
KING OF AMERICA - S	MARC SHMUGER	KNIGHTS AND EMERALDS	IAN LEWS
KING OF COMEDY, THE	PAUL D. ZIMMERMAN	KNIGHTS OF TERROR - S	ANGELO PIZZO
KING OF CONNECTICUT (P)	FRANK PUGLIESE	KNIGHTS OF THE CITY	DAVID WILDER
KING OF HEARTS (P)	STEVE TESICH	KNIGHTS OF THE CITY	LEON ISSAC KENNEDY
KING OF KINGS	PHILIP YORDAN	KNOCK ON ANY DOOR	DANIEL TARADASH
KING OF KINGS - S	RICHARD FRIEDENBERG	KNOCK ON WOOD	NORMAN PANAMA
KING OF MARVIN GARDENS, THE	JACOB BRACKMAN	KNOCK ON WOOD (P)	ALLEN RIVKIN†
KING OF NEW YORK	NICHOLAS ST. JOHN	KNOCK OUT - S	JANUS CERCONE
KING OF THE CITY	BLEU MCKENZIE	KNOCK WOOD - S	G. ROSS PARKER
KING OF THE CITY	NORMAN THADDEUS VANE	KNOCKOUT - S	HENRY ROSENBAUM
KING OF THE GYPSIES	FRANK R. PIERSON	KNOWING DAMON - S	GLENN GORDON CARON
KING OF THE KHYBER RIFLES	IVAN GOFF	KNOWLEDGE, THE (P)	JACK ROSENTHAL
KING OF THE MOUNTAIN	ROGER CHRISTIAN	KNUCKLE (P)	DAVID HARE
KING OF THE SHADOWS - S	STUART BIRNBAUM	KOHCHEE - S	ROD MCCALL
KING OF THE STREETS	BARRY PEARSON	KOLD WAVES, THE (SHORT)	REGINALD HUDLIN
KING OF THE STREETS	ED HUNT	KORCZAK	AGNIESZKA HOLLAND
KING OF THE USA - S	STEPHEN C. NEIGHER	KOSHER COPS - S	GARY THOMPSON
KING RALPH	DAVID S. WARD	KRAMER VS. KRAMER	ROBERT BENTON
KING RAT	BRYAN FORBES	KRAYS, THE	PHILIP RIDLEY
KING SOLOMON'S MINES	EUGENE QUINTANO	KRIPPENDORF'S TRIBE - S	LYNNE GILER
KING SOLOMON'S MINES	JAMES R. SILKE	KRULL	STANFORD SHERMAN
KING'S WHORE, THE	AXEL CORTI	KRUSH GROOVE	RALPH FARQUHAR
KING'S WHORE, THE	DANIEL VIGNE	KUFFS - S	BRUCE A. EVANS
KING'S WHORE, THE	FREDERIC RAPHAEL	KUFFS - S	RAY GIDEON
KING, QUEEN, KNAVE	DAVID SELTZER		
KINGDOM - S	DAVID MAMET		
KINGDOM - S	JOAN DIDION		
KINGDOM - S	JOHN GREGORY DUNNE		
KINGDOM OF DREAMS - S	ROBERT DELAURENTIS		
KINGDOM OF THE SPIDERS	ALAN CAILOU		
KINGDOM OF THE SPIDERS	RICHARD ROBINSON		
KINGMAKERS, THE - S	CHARLES EDWARD POGUE		
KINGPIN - S	MITCH GLAZER		
KINGS OF THE ROAD	WIM WENDERS		
KINGSBLOOD - S	CHARLES FULLER		
KINJITE: FORBIDDEN SUBJECTS	HAROLD NEBENZAL		
KIPPERBANG	JACK ROSENTHAL		
KIRLIAN WITNESS, THE	JONATHAN SARNO		
KIRLIAN WITNESS, THE	LAMAR SANDERS		
KISS AND TELL (CTF) - S	DAVID AMBROSE		
KISS BEFORE DYING, A (1991)	JAMES DEARDEN		
KISS BEFORE DYING, A (1956)	LAWRENCE ROMAN		
KISS KISS, KILL KILL - S	MIKEL ANDERSON		
KISS KISS, KILL KILL - S	PETER JENSEN		
KISS ME A KILLER	CHRISTOPHER WOODEN		
KISS ME A KILLER	MARCUS DELEON		
KISS ME GOODBYE	CHARLIE PETERS		
KISS ME KILL ME	NICK CASTLE		
KISS ME, STUPID	BILLY WILDER		
KISS ME, STUPID	I.A.L. DIAMOND†		
KISS OF THE SPIDER WOMAN	LEONARD SCHRADER		
KISS OFF - S	GEORGE MALKO		
KISS THE BABY - S	BRYAN GORDON		
KISS THE BOYS GOODBYE	HARRY TUGEND†		
KISS THE BRIDE - S	BILLY RAY		
KISS THE GROUND - S	MATTHEW MCDUFFIE		
KISS THEM FOR ME	JULIUS J. EPSTEIN		
KISS, THE	STEPHEN VOLK		
KISS, THE	TOM ROPELEWSKI		
KISSES FOR MY PRESIDENT	ROBERT G. KANE		

L

L'AFRICAIN	GERARD BRACH
L'AFRICANA	MARGARETHE VON TROTTA
L'AMI DE MON AMIE	ERIC ROHMER
L'AMI DE MON AMIE	ERIC ROHMER
L'AMORE	FEDERICO FELLINI
L'AMOUR A MORT	JEAN GRUAULT
L'AMOUR, L'APRE MIDI	ERIC ROHMER
L'ANNEE DES MEDUSES	CHRISTOPHER FRANK
L'ARGENT	ROBERT BRESSON
L'ARGENT DE POCHE	SUZANNE SCHIFFMAN
L'AVVENTURA	MICHELANGELO ANTONIONI
L'AVVENTURA	TONINO GUERRA
L'ECLISSE	MICHELANGELO ANTONIONI
L'ECLISSE	TONINO GUERRA
L'EMMERDEUR	FRANCIS VEBER
L'ETAT SAUVAGE	GEORGES CONCHON†
L'EVENEMENT LE PLUS IMPORTANT LE DEPUIS	JACQUES DEMY†
L'IL ABNER	NORMAN PANAMA
L'INTERVISTA	FEDERICO FELLINI
L-SHAPED ROOM, THE	BRYAN FORBES
L.A. AT NIGHT - S	LARRY GROSS
L.A. HEAT	CHARLES T. KANGANIS
L.A. STORY	STEVE MARTIN
L.A. UNDER SIEGE (P)	MAYO SIMON
L.A. WOMAN - S	WALON GREEN
LA BALANCE	BOB SWAIM
LA BAMBA	LUIS VALDEZ
LA BATAILLE DU RAIL	RENE CLEMENT
LA BONNE ANNEE	CLAUDE LELOUCH
LA CAGE AUX FOLLES (P)	HARVEY FIERSTEIN
LA CAGE AUX FOLLES	EDOUARD MOLINARO
LA CAGE AUX FOLLES	FRANCIS VEBER
LA CAGE AUX FOLLES II	FRANCIS VEBER
LA CAGE AUX FOLLES, U.S.A. - S	ROBERT KLANE
LA CAGE AUX FOLLES, U.S.A. - S	DAVID GILER
LA CHEVRE	FRANCIS VEBER
LA COLLECTIONNEUSE	ERIC ROHMER
LA DOLCE VITA	BRUNELLO RONDI†
LA DOLCE VITA	FEDERICO FELLINI
LA FEMME INFIDEL	CLAUDE CHABROL
LA GRANDE VARDOVILLE	GERARD OURY
LA GUERRE EST FRIE	JORGE SEMPRUN
LA LOI	JULES DASSIN
LA MOINE ET LA SORCIERE	SUZANNE SCHIFFMAN
LA NOCHE OSCURA	CARLOS SAURA
LA NOI	TONINO GUERRA
LA NOTTE	MICHELANGELO ANTONIONI
LA NOTTE	TONINO GUERRA
LA NOTTE DI SANS LORENZO	PAOLO TAVIANI
LA NOTTE DI SANS LORENZO	TONINO GUERRA
LA NOTTE DI SANS LORENZO	VITTORIO TAVIANI
LA NUIT DE VARENNES	ETTORE SCOLA
LA PASSION BEATRICE	COLO TAVERNIER O'HAGAN
LA PUTA VIDA (P)	REINALDO POVOD
LA STRADA	FEDERICO FELLINI
LA TABLE TOURNANTE	JACQUES DEMY†
LA TRAVIATA	FRANCO ZEFFERILLI
LA TULIPE - S	TOD CARROLL
LA TURISTA (P)	SAM SHEPARD
LA VICTOIRE EN CHANTANT	JEAN-JACQUES ANNAUD
LA VIE CONTINUE	MOSHE MIZRAHI
LA VIE CONTINUE	RACHEL FABIEN
LA VIE ET RIEN D'AUTRE	BERTRAND TAVERNIER
LABOR OF LOVE - S	BRUCE ZABEL
LABOR OF LOVE - S	JACKIE ZABEL
LABRYINTH	LEWIS JOHN CARLINO
LABYRINTH	DENNIS LESS
LABYRINTH	JIM HENSON†
LABYRINTH	TERRY JONES
LABYRINTH 9 - S	HENRY BEAN
LABYRINTH 9 - S	LEORA BARISH
LABYRINTH OF PASSION	PEDRO ALMODOVAR
LACEMAKER, THE	CLAUDE GORETTA
LACKAWANNA - S	DENNIS O'FLAHERTY
LACOMBE LUCIEN	LOUIS MALLE
LADIES AND GENTLEMEN, THE FABULOUS STAINS	NANCY DOWD
LADIES CLUB, THE	FRAN LEWIS EBELING
LADIES CLUB, THE	PAUL MASON
LADIES DAY - S	ALAN BERGER
LADIES DAY - S	ALAN MANDEL
LADIES DAY - S	KATHY GORI
LADIES IN WAITING (P)	PATRICIA RESNICK
LADIES NIGHT - S	JOAN TEWKESBURY
LADIES OF THE CORRIDOR (P)	ARNAUD D'USSEAU†
LADIES OF THE PARK, THE	ROBERT BRESSON
LADIES' MAN, THE	BILL RICHMOND
LADIES' MAN, THE	JERRY LEWIS
LADY AND THE CLARINET, THE - S	MICHAEL CRISTOFER
LADY AT THE WHEEL (P)	LESLIE BRICUSSE
LADY AVENGER	KEITH KACZOREK
LADY AVENGER	WILL SCHMITZ
LADY BEWARE	CHARLES ZEV COHEN
LADY BEWARE	SUSAN MILLER
LADY BODYGUARDS - S	SUZANNE O'MALLEY
LADY CAROLINE LAMB	ROBERT BOLT
LADY CAT - S	NANCY GREENWALD
LADY CHATTERLEY'S LOVER	CHRISTOPHER WICKING
LADY CHATTERLEY'S LOVER	JUST JAECKIN
LADY CRIES MURDER, THE (P)	JOHN WILLIAM SEE
LADY FINGERS - S	GERALD AYRES
LADY FROM HELL, THE	AKIRA KUROSAWA
LADY GODIVA	OSCAR BRODNEY
LADY HAWKS - S	DAVID PEOPLES
LADY ICE	ALAN R. TRUSTMAN
LADY IN RED, THE	JOHN SAYLES
LADY IN WHITE	FRANK LALOGGIA
LADY JANE	CHRIS BRYANT
LADY JANE	DAVID EDGAR
LADY KILLER, THE - S	ROBERT J. AVRECH
LADY L	PETER USTINOV
LADY LAZARUS - S	JOSEPH DOUGHERTY
LADY OF SAIGON, THE - S	MICHAEL THOMAS
LADY OSCAR (1978)	PATRICIA L. KNOP
LADY OSCAR	JACQUES DEMY†
LADY SCARFACE	ARNAUD D'USSEAU†
LADY SINGS THE BLUES	SUZANNE DE PASSE
LADY VANISHES, THE	GEORGE AXELROD
LADYHAWKE	EDWARD KHMARA
LADYHAWKE	MICHAEL THOMAS

355

La-Le

FILM WRITERS GUIDE

INDEX OF FILM TITLES

Title	Writer
LADYHAWKE	TOM MANKIEWICZ
LAIR OF THE WHITE WORM, THE	KEN RUSSELL
LAKE BOAT (P)	DAVID MAMET
LAKE OF THE WOODS (P)	STEVE TESICH
LAKE, THE - S	DAVID GREENWALT
LAKE, THE - S	JIM KOUF
LAMB	BERNARD MACLAVERTY
LAMB OF GOD - S	BRAD BUCKNER
LAMB OF GOD - S	EUGENIE ROSS-LEMING
LAMBADA	JOEL SILBERG
LAMBADA	SHELDON RENAN
LAMBADAMY: THE OPERATION - S	RICK MARX
LAME DUCKS	PAT PROFT
LAMPPOST REUNION, THE (P)	LOUIS LARUSSO II
LANCELOT - S	ROBERT GARLAND
LANCERS - S	DENNE BART PETITCLERC
LAND BEFORE TIME, THE (AF)	JUDY FREUDBERG
LAND BEFORE TIME, THE (AF)	STU KRIEGER
LAND BEFORE TIME, THE (AF)	TONY GEISS
LAND OF NO RETURN, THE	FRANK RAY PERILLI
LAND OF NO RETURN, THE	KENT BATEMAN
LAND OF OPPORTUNITY - S	JACK KAPLAN
LAND OF OPPORTUNITY - S	JONATHAN LYNN
LAND OF THE NICE - S	RUDY DELUCA
LANDSCAPE (P)	HAROLD PINTER
LANDSCAPE IN THE MIST	THEO ANGELOPOULOS
LANDSCAPE OF THE BODY (P)	JOHN GUARE
LANE FROST STORY - S	MONTE MERRICK
LANEPLAY - S	NICK COREA
LANTON MILLS - S	ANDRZEJ KRAKOWSKI
LARRY'S LATE FOR LIFE - S	JOHN HUGHES
LAS VEGAS LADY	WALTER DALLENBACH
LASER MAN, THE	PETER WANG
LASER MISSION	RICHARD HEFT
LASSITER	DAVID TAYLOR
LAST ACT IS A SOLO, THE (P)	ROBERT ANDERSON
LAST AMERICAN COWBOY, THE - S	ROB THOMPSON
LAST AMERICAN HERO, THE	BILL KERBY
LAST AMERICAN HERO, THE	WILLIAM ROBERTS
LAST AMERICAN VIRGIN, THE	BOAZ DAVIDSON
LAST ANGRY MAN, THE	GERALD GREEN
LAST BOY SCOUT, THE	SHANE BLACK
LAST CALL	STEVEN IYAMA
LAST CHANCE TO DANCE - S	EDWARD DECTER
LAST CHANCE TO DANCE - S	STUART BIRNBAUM
LAST CHASE, THE	CHRISTOPHER CROWE
LAST CHASE, THE	MARTYN BURKE
LAST CHASE, THE	TAYLOR SUTHERLAND
LAST CHUCKER, THE - S	DENNIS L. CLARK
LAST DANCE OF THE GOLDEN WEST (CTF) - S	DENNIS KLEIN
LAST DAYS OF EDEN, THE - S	TOM SCHULMAN
LAST DAYS OF MAN ON EARTH, THE	ROBERT FUEST
LAST DETAIL, THE	ROBERT TOWNE
LAST DINOSAUR, THE (AF)	WILLIAM OVERGARD
LAST DRAGON, THE	LOUIS VENOSTA
LAST ELEPHANT, THE (CTF)	BRADLEY T. WINTER
LAST ELEPHANT, THE (CTF)	BILL BOZZONE
LAST ELEPHANT, THE (CTF)	RICHARD A. GUTTMAN
LAST EMBRACE	DAVID SHABER
LAST EMPEROR, THE	BERNARDO BERTOLUCCI
LAST EMPEROR, THE	MARK PEPLOE
LAST EXIT TO BROOKLYN	DESMOND NAKANO
LAST FLIGHT OF NOAH'S ARK, THE	ERNEST K. GANN†
LAST FLIGHT OF NOAH'S ARK, THE	SANDY GLASS
LAST FLIGHT OF NOAH'S ARK, THE	STEVEN W. CARABATSOS
LAST FLIGHT OF NOAHS ARK, THE	GEORGE ARTHUR BLOOM
LAST GOOD KISS - S	MICHAEL JENNING
LAST GOOD KISS, THE - S	JIM CRUMLEY
LAST GOOD KISS, THE - S	WALTER HILL
LAST HARD MEN, THE	GUERDON TRUEBLOOD
LAST HARD MEN, THE	BRIAN GARFIELD
LAST HASIDIC COMIC, THE - S	MITCH MARKOWITZ
LAST HIGH SCHOOL MOVIE, THE - S	CHRISTOPHER CLUESS
LAST HIGH SCHOOL MOVIE, THE - S	STUART G. KREISMAN
LAST HOLIDAY - S	DAVID SHEFFIELD
LAST HOLIDAY - S	BARRY BLAUSTEIN
LAST HOLIDAY - S	JEFFREY PRICE
LAST HOLIDAY - S	PETER SEAMAN
LAST HONEYMOON, THE - S	TOM TOPOR
LAST HUNT, THE	RICHARD BROOKS
LAST ILLUSION, THE - S	DANIEL BARTOLINI
LAST INNOCENT MAN, THE (CTF)	DAN BRONSON
LAST KISS - S	DJORDJE MILICEVIC
LAST KISS - S	JEFFREY P. MAGUIRE
LAST KISS - S	WILLIAM CONDON
LAST KISS, THE: PROM NIGHT III	RON OLIVER
LAST LAUGH, THE - S	LARRY FERGUSON
LAST LAUGH, THE - S	PETER BELLWOOD
LAST LURID MOMENT - S	JULIAN BARRY
LAST MAN AT ARLINGTON - S	LEON CAPETANOS
LAST MARDI GRAS, THE - S	STEPHEN M. TOLKIN
LAST MARRIED COUPLE IN AMERICA, THE	JOHN HERMAN SHANER
LAST METRO, THE	FRANCOIS TRUFFAUT†
LAST METRO, THE	SUZANNE SCHIFFMAN
LAST MILE, THE	MILTON SUBOTSKY
LAST MOVIE, THE	DENNIS HOPPER
LAST MOVIE, THE	STEWART STERN
LAST NIGHT AT THE ALAMO	KIM HENKEL
LAST OF SHEILA, THE	ANTHONY PERKINS
LAST OF SHEILA, THE	STEPHEN SONDHEIM
LAST OF THE BREED, THE - S	JOHN KEITH WILDER
LAST OF THE FINEST, THE	GEORGE ARMITAGE
LAST OF THE FINEST, THE	JERE CUNNINGHAM
LAST OF THE FINEST, THE	THOMAS LEE WRIGHT
LAST OF THE MOBILE HOT-SHOTS	GORE VIDAL
LAST OF THE MOHICANS, THE - S	CHRISTOPHER CROWE
LAST OF THE MOHICANS, THE - S	MICHAEL MANN
LAST OF THE RED HOT LOVERS	NEIL SIMON
LAST PELT, THE (CTF) - S	DICK BEEBE
LAST PICTURE SHOW, THE	LARRY MCMURTRY
LAST PICTURE SHOW, THE	PETER BOGDONAVICH
LAST PLANE OUT	ERNEST TIDYMAN†
LAST REMAKE OF BEAU GESTE, THE	CHRIS ALLEN
LAST REMAKE OF BEAU GESTE, THE	MARTY FELDMAN†
LAST RESORT	JEFF BUHAI
LAST RESORT	STEVEN R. ZACHARIAS
LAST RESORT, THE - S	DAVID MIRKIN
LAST REVOLUTION, THE - S	RICHARD MATHESON
LAST RIDE, THE - S	EARL MAC RAUCH
LAST RIDE, THE - S	DICK WOLF
LAST RITES (1988)	DONALD BELLISARIO
LAST RITES (1980)	BEN DONNELLY
LAST RITES (1980)	DOMINIC PARIS
LAST RUN, THE	ALAN SHARP
LAST SAFARI, THE - S	JOHN GAY
LAST SAFARI, THE - S	ROBERT BORIS
LAST SECRET, THE - S	CHRISTOPHER HAMPTON
LAST SEPTEMBER - S	STEPHEN METCALFE
LAST SHIP, THE - S	STEVEN SODERBERGH
LAST STARFIGHTER, THE	JONATHAN BETUEL
LAST SUMMER	ELEANOR PERRY†
LAST TANGO IN PARIS	BERNARDO BERTOLUCCI
LAST TEMPTATION OF CHRIST, THE	PAUL SCHRADER
LAST TIME I SAW PARIS, THE	JULIUS J. EPSTEIN
LAST TIME I SAW PARIS, THE	PHILIP G. EPSTEIN†
LAST TIME I SAW PARIS, THE	RICHARD BROOKS
LAST TYCOON, THE	HAROLD PINTER
LAST UNICORN, THE	PETER S. BEAGLE
LAST VALLEY, THE	JAMES CLAVELL
LAST VIDEO, THE - S	DONALD CAMMELL
LAST VIRGIN IN AMERICA, THE - S	RICK PODELL
LAST VOYAGE, THE	ANDREW STONE
LAST WAVE, THE	PETER WEIR
LAST WAVE, THE	PETRU POPESCU
LAST WAVE, THE	TONY MORPHETT
LAST WEEKEND - S	FIONA LEWIS
LAST WESTERN, THE - S	GARNER SIMMONS
LAST WINTER, THE	AARON KIM JOHNSTON
LAST WINTER, THE	JOHN HERZFELD
LAST WISH - S	MARK MEDOFF
LAST WOMAN ON EARTH, THE	ROBERT TOWNE
LAST WORD, THE	GREG P. SMITH
LAST WORD, THE	HORATIUS HAEBERLE
LAST WORD, THE	L.M. KIT CARSON
LAST WORD, THE	MICHAEL VARHOL
LAST, THE - S	ERIC RED
LATE BLOOMERS - S	JEFF LANTOS
LATE BLOOMERS - S	JEFF LEVIN
LATE BLOOMERS - S	LEANN LANTOS
LATE FOR DINNER	MARK ANDRUS
LATE GEORGE APPLEY, THE	PHILIP DUNNE
LATE SHOW, THE	ROBERT BENTON
LATER - S	SAMUEL H. HARPER
LATIN JERRY & HOT HOT TOMATOS - S	JACK BARAN
LATINO	HASKELL WEXLER
LAUGHING MAN, THE - S	DOUGLAS LLOYD MCINTOSH
LAUGHING POLICEMAN, THE	THOMAS RICKMAN
LAUGHING WAR - S	MARTYN BURKE
LAUGHING WILD (P)	CHRISTOPHER DURANG
LAUGHTER IN PARADISE	JACK DAVIES
LAUNDROMAT, THE (CTF)	MARSHA NORMAN
LAVENDER HILL MOB, THE - S	HARIS ORKIN
LAW AND DISORDER	IVAN PASSER
LAW AND DISORDER	WILLIAM RICHERT
LAW OF DESIRE	PEDRO ALMODOVAR
LAW OF THE YUKON - S	DAN AYKROYD
LAWBREAKERS, THE - S	LARRY FERGUSON
LAWLESS LAND, THE	LARRY LEAHY
LAWLESS LAND, THE	TONY CINCIRIPINI
LAWRENCE MANOR - S	MICHAEL PREMINGER
LAWRENCE MANOR - S	RICK PODELL
LAWRENCE OF ARABIA	ROBERT BOLT
LAWYER, THE	SIDNEY J. FURIE
LAWYERS, GUNS AND MONEY - S	DOUG RICHARDSON
LAWYERS, GUNS AND MONEY - S	MICHAEL MILLER
LAZARO - S	NEAL JIMENEZ
LE BAL	ETTORE SCOLA
LE BEAU MARRIAGE	ERIC ROHMER
LE BEAU SERGE	CLAUDE CHABROL
LE BONHEUR	AGNES VARDA
LE BOUCHER	CLAUDE CHABROL
LE DERNIER COMBAT	LUC BESSON
LE DIABLE PROBABLEMENT	ROBERT BRESSON
LE FEU FOLLET	LOUIS MALLE
LE MAGNIFIQUE	FRANCIS VEBER
LE MANI SULLA CITTA	FRANCESCO ROSI
LE MANS	HARRY KLEINER
LE POINT DE MIRE	GERARD BRACH
LE RAYON VERT	ERIC ROHMER
LE SAUVAGE	JEAN-PAUL RAPPENEAU
LE SOUFFLE AU COEUR	LOUIS MALLE
LE SURF HOT - S	MICHAEL LEHMANN
LE SURF HOT - S	REDBEARD SIMMONS
LEAD STORY - S	ELAINE MUELLER
LEADBELLY	ERNEST KINOY
LEADER OF THE BAND	ALAN UGER
LEADER OF THE PACK (P)	MELANIE MINTZ
LEADER OF THE PACK - S	CAROLYN SHELBY
LEADER OF THE PACK - S	CHRISTOPHER AMES
LEAGUE OF GENTLEMEN, THE	BRYAN FORBES
LEAGUE OF THEIR OWN, A - S	BABALOO MANDEL
LEAGUE OF THEIR OWN, A - S	LOWELL GANZ
LEAN ON ME	MICHAEL SCHIFFER
LEAP INTO THE VOID	MARCO BELLOCCHIO
LEATHER JACKETS	LEE DRYSDALE
LEATHERFACE: TEXAS CHAINSAW MASSACRE III	DAVID J. SCHOW
LEAVE OF ABSENCE	LEE ROSE
LEAVING NORMAL - S	ED SOLOMON
LEAVINGS OF B.T. WOMECK, THE - S	THOMAS RICKMAN
LECH WALESA	COLIN WELLAND
LEDA AND SWAN	ROBERT J. AVRECH
LEFT, THE - S	ANDY WOLK
LEFT COAST - S	KEVIN FALLS
LEFT HANDED GUN, THE	LESLIE STEVENS
LEFT-HANDED WOMAN, THE	PETER HANDKE
LEFTY'S PIANO - S	MOLLY-ANN LEIKIN
LEGACY - S	CRAIG VAN SICKLE
LEGACY - S	STEVEN L. MITCHELL
LEGACY, THE	JIMMY SANGSTER
LEGACY, THE	PATRICK TILLEY
LEGACY, THE	PAUL WHEELER
LEGAL EAGLES	IVAN REITMAN
LEGAL EAGLES	JACK EPPS JR.
LEGAL EAGLES	JIM CASH
LEGAL TENDER - S	LEE DRYSDALE
LEGEND	WILLIAM HJORTSBERG
LEGEND OF BILLIE JEAN, THE	LARRY KONNER
LEGEND OF BILLIE JEAN, THE	MARK ROSENTHAL
LEGEND OF BOGGY CREEK, THE	CHARLES B. PIERCE
LEGEND OF HELL HOUSE, THE	RICHARD MATHESON
LEGEND OF SARAH, THE	ARNAUD D'USSEAU†
LEGEND OF THE GRAIL - S	NANCY LARSON
LEGEND OF THE LONE RANGER, THE	BEN ROBERTS†

356

Title	Writer
LEGEND OF THE LONE RANGER, THE	IVAN GOFF
LEGEND OF THE LONE RANGER, THE	MICHAEL KANE
LEGEND OF THE LONE RANGER, THE	WILLIAM ROBERTS
LEGMAN - S	KEVIN QUINN
LEGS - S	WILLIAM KENNEDY
LEMON POPSICLE	BOAZ DAVIDSON
LEMON SISTERS, THE	JEREMY PIKSER
LEMON, THE - S	ROBERT GUNTER
LENINGRAD COWBOYS GO AMERICA	AKI KAURISMAKI
LENNY	JULIAN BARRY
LENNY LIVE AND UNLEASHED	KIM FULLER
LENNY LIVE AND UNLEASHED	LENNY HENRY
LEO AND LOREE	RON HOWARD
LEO AND LOREE	JAMES RITZ
LEO THE LAST	JOHN BOORMAN
LEO'S MISERABLE AFFLICTIONS AND UNFORTUNATE MISHAPS - S	P.J. PESCE
LEONARD PART 6	JONATHAN REYNOLDS
LEONARD PELTIER STORY, THE - S	PAUL F. EDWARDS
LEPKE	TAMAR SIMON HOFFS
LEPRECHAUN - S	JENNIFER COLLOPY
LES BICHES	CLAUDE CHABROL
LES BIJOUTIERS DU CLAIR DE LUNES	PETER VIERTEL
LES BIJOUTIERS DU CLAIR DE LUNES	ROGER VADIM
LES COMPERES	FRANCIS VEBER
LES COMPERES - S	MICHAEL LEESON
LES COMPERES (REMAKE) - S	TOD CARROLL
LES FUGITIFS	FRANCIS VEBER
LES LIAISONS DENGEREUSES	ROGER VADIM
LES MAUDITS	RENE CLEMENT
LES REPOUX - S	W.D. RICHTER
LES TRICHEURS	BARBET SCHROEDER
LES UNS ET LES AUTRES	CLAUDE LELOUCH
LES VALSEUSES	BERTRAND BLIER
LESS THAN ZERO	HARLEY PEYTON
LESSON FROM ALOES, A (P)	ATHOL FUGARD
LESSON IN LOVE, A	INGMAR BERGMAN
LET IT RIDE	NANCY DOWD
LET ME HEAR YOU WHISPER (P)	PAUL ZINDEL
LET'S CALL THE WHOLE THING OFF - S	ROBIN SCHIFF
LET'S DO IT AGAIN	RICHARD WESLEY
LET'S GET HARRY	MARK L. FELDBERG
LET'S GET HARRY	SAMUEL FULLER
LET'S GET HARRY	CHARLES ROBERT CARNER
LET'S HEAR IT FOR A BEAUTIFUL GUY - S	BRUCE JAY FRIEDMAN
LETHAL	SANDRA K. BAILEY
LETHAL GAS - S	DARRYL PONICSAN
LETHAL GAS - S	MICHAEL JENNING
LETHAL GAS - S	NORMAN WEXLER
LETHAL WEAPON	SHANE BLACK
LETHAL WEAPON 2	JEFFREY BOAM
LETHAL WEAPON 2	SHANE BLACK
LETHAL WEAPON 2	WARREN MURPHY
LETTER TO BREZHNEV	FRANK CLARKE
LETTER TO THREE WIVES, A	JOSEPH L. MANKIEWICZ
LETTERS TO IRIS - S	ISRAEL HOROVITZ
LETTERS TO SCHWARTZY - S	CASEY KELLY
LETTICE & LOVAGE (P)	PETER SHAFFER
LEVIATHAN	DAVID PEOPLES
LEVIATHAN	JEB STUART
LEWD CONDUCT - S	MICHAEL JENNING
LEXINGTON EXPERIENCE, THE (FD)	L.M. KIT CARSON
LIANNA	JOHN SAYLES
LIAR MOVIE, THE - S	PHIL HARTMAN
LIAR'S MOON	DAVID FISHER
LIARS - S	DAVID CHASE
LIARS, THE - S	DAVID AMBROSE
LIBBY - S	RICHARD KRAMER
LIBBY HOLMAN - S	FREDERIC RAPHAEL
LIBELED LADY - S	FIONA LEWIS
LIBERATION OF L.B. JONES, THE	STIRLING SILLIPHANT
LIBERATOR - S	DAVID S. GOYER
LIBERTY & BASH	DOUG FORSMITH
LIBERTY CITY - S	ANN BIDERMAN
LICENCE TO KILL	MICHAEL G. WILSON
LICENCE TO KILL	RICHARD MAIBAUM†
LICENSE TO DRIVE	NEIL TOLKIN
LICENSED TO DRIVE - S	FRANK DEESE
LICKERISH QUARTET, THE	RADLEY METZGER
LICKING HITLER (P)	DAVID HARE
LIE OF THE MIND, A (P)	SAM SHEPARD
LIEBESTRAUM	MIKE FIGGIS
LIES	JIM WHEAT
LIES	KEN WHEAT
LIES AND MORE LIES - S	RICK PODELL
LIES MY FATHER TOLD ME	TED ALLAN
LIFE AFTER LIFE - S	DANIEL GOLDIN
LIFE AFTER LIFE - S	JOSH GOLDIN
LIFE AND ADVENTURES OF SANTA CLAUS, THE - S	TODD DURHAM
LIFE AND DEATH OF COLONEL BLIMP, THE	EMERIC PRESSBURGER†
LIFE AND DEATH OF COLONEL BLIMP, THE	MICHAEL POWELL†
LIFE AND NOTHING BUT	BERTRAND TAVERNIER
LIFE AND TIMES OF GRIZZLY ADAMS, THE	RICHARD FRIEDENBERG
LIFE AND TIMES OF JUDGE ROY BEAN, THE	JOHN MILLIUS
LIFE AT THE TOP	MORDECAI RICHLER
LIFE DURING WARTIME - S	HARLEY PEYTON
LIFE ENDS AT FORTY - S	BRUCE JAY FRIEDMAN
LIFE IN THE THEATRE, A (P)	DAVID MAMET
LIFE IS CHEAP...BUT TOILET PAPER IS EXPENSIVE	SPENSER NAKASAKO
LIFE IS CHEAP...BUT TOILET PAPER IS EXPENSIVE	WAYNE WANG
LIFE IS SWEET	MIKE LEIGH
LIFE ITS OWN SELF - S	DAN JENKINS
LIFE LINE - S	LARRY GROSS
LIFE OF BRIAN	ERIC IDLE
LIFE OF BRIAN	GRAHAM CHAPMAN†
LIFE OF BRIAN	MICHAEL PALIN
LIFE OF BRIAN	TERRY GILLIAM
LIFE OF RAFAELLE GALLO, THE - S	TOM DONNELLY
LIFE OF RAFAELLE GALLO, THE - S	TERRY CURTIS FOX
LIFE OF THE PARTY, THE - S	REX MCGEE
LIFE ON EARTH - S	ALAN BERGER
LIFE ON EARTH - S	KATHY GORI
LIFE STINKS	MEL BROOKS
LIFE STINKS	RON CLARK
LIFE STINKS	RUDY DELUCA
LIFE STINKS	STEVE HABERMAN
LIFE STORY - S	RICHARD WHITLEY
LIFE UPSIDE DOWN - S	ERIC GETHERS
LIFEFORCE	DAN O' BANNON
LIFEFORCE	DON JAKOBY
LIFEGUARD	RON KOSLOW
LIFELINE - S	ALLAN G. SCOTT
LIFESAVERS - S	LISA STOTSKY
LIFESAVERS - S	WENDY GRAF
LIFT TO THE SCAFFOLD	LOUIS MALLE
LIFT, THE	DICK MAAS
LIGHT AT THE END - S	MARK PATRICK CARDUCCI
LIGHT BLACK - S	CARL BINDER
LIGHT FANTASTIC, THE - S	ROBERT GETCHELL
LIGHT IN THE PIAZZA, THE	JULIUS J. EPSTEIN
LIGHT OF DAY	PAUL SCHRADER
LIGHT SLEEPER - S	PAUL SCHRADER
LIGHT TOUCH, THE	RICHARD BROOKS
LIGHT YEARS	BLAINE NOVAK
LIGHT YEARS	RAPHAEL CLUZEL
LIGHT YEARS - S	TOM MCCOWN
LIGHT YEARS AWAY - S	BRYAN MICHAEL STOLLER
LIGHTHORSEMEN, THE	IAN JONES
LIGHTNING BENDER - S	JAMES PASTERNAK
LIGHTNING FIELD, THE (CTF) - S	MICHAEL J. MURRAY
LIGHTNING OVER WATER	WIM WENDERS
LIGHTNING ROD - S	MICHAEL ERIC STEIN
LIGHTNING: THE WHITE STALLION	HARRY ALAN TOWERS
LIGHTS, THE - S	GARY DEVORE
LIGHTSHIP, THE	WILLIAM MAI
LIGHTSHIP, THE	DAVID TAYLOR
LIKE A TURTLE ON ITS BACK	LUC BERAUD
LIKE AL AND ME - S	ERIC SCHAEFFER
LIKE ANGELS - S	J.T. ALLEN
LIKE FATHER AND SON	ERIC WESTON
LIKE FATHER AND SON	WANDA DELL
LIKE FATHER, LIKE SON	LORNE CAMERON
LIKE FATHER, LIKE SON	STEVEN L. BLOOM
LIKE HARRY - S	HOWARD CHESLEY
LIKELY LADS, THE	DICK CLEMENT
LIKELY LADS, THE	IAN LAFRENAIS
LILI MARLEEN	JOSHUA SINCLAIR
LILY - S	REX PICKETT
LILY IN LOVE	FRANK CUCCI
LIMBO	JAMES BRIDGES
LIMBO	JOAN MICKLIN SILVER
LIME GREEN - S	ROY CARLSON
LIME'S CRISIS - S	DAVID FIELD
LIME'S CRISIS - S	RON BASS
LIMEY, THE - S	DAVID SHABER
LIMIT UP	RICHARD MARTINI
LIMIT, THE - S	CAROL MONPERE
LIMO - S	DAN JENKINS
LIMO - S	BUD SHRAKE
LINE (P)	ISRAEL HOROVITZ
LINE OF FIRE - S	MICHAEL AUERBACH
LINE, THE - S	BOAZ YAKIN
LINE, THE - S	DARRYL WIMBERLY
LINEUP, THE	STIRLING SILLIPHANT
LINGUINE INCIDENT, THE - S	RICHARD SHEPARD
LINK	EVERETT DEROCHE
LION IN WINTER, THE	JAMES GOLDMAN
LION OF IRELAND - S	CHARLES ROBERT CARNER
LION OF THE DESERT	H.A.L. CRAIG
LIONHEART	JEAN-CLAUDE VAN DAMME
LIONHEART	SHELDON B. LETTICH
LIONHEART	MENNO MEYJES
LIONHEART	RICHARD OUTTEN
LIP SERVICE (CTF)	HOWARD KORDER
LIP STATE - S	AARON SORKIN
LIPS TOGETHER, TEETH APART (P)	TERRENCE MCNALLY
LIPSTICK	DAVID RAYFIEL
LIQUID DREAMS	MARK MANOS
LIQUID DREAMS	ZACH DAVIS
LIQUID SKY	ANNE CARLISLE
LIQUID SKY	NINA V. KEROVA
LIQUID SKY	SLAVA TSUKERMAN
LIQUIDATOR, THE	PETER YELDHAM
LISA	KAREN CLARK
LISA	GARY A. SHERMAN
LISBON TRAVIATA, THE (P)	TERRENCE MCNALLY
LISTEN TO ME	DOUGLAS DAY STEWART
LISZTOMANIA	KEN RUSSELL
LITTLE ARK, THE	JOANNA CRAWFORD
LITTLE BIG MAN	CALDER WILLINGHAM
LITTLE BRUCIE - S	JULES FEIFFER
LITTLE CIGARS	FRANK RAY PERILLI
LITTLE CIGARS	LOUIS GARFINKLE
LITTLE DARLINGS	DALENE YOUNG
LITTLE DARLINGS	KIMI PECK
LITTLE DRACULA - S	MARTIN OLSEN
LITTLE DRAGONS, THE	ALAN ORMSBY
LITTLE DRUMMER GIRL, THE	LORING MANDEL
LITTLE EAGLE - S	HARVEY WARREN
LITTLE EAGLE - S	JOY WARREN
LITTLE EGYPT	OSCAR BRODNEY
LITTLE FAMILY BUSINESS, A (P)	JAY PRESSON ALLEN
LITTLE FAUSS AND BIG HALSY	CHARLES EASTMAN
LITTLE GENTLEMAN, THE (P)	YALE UDOFF
LITTLE GIRL LOST - S	MICHAEL ALAN EDDY
LITTLE GIRL WHO LIVES DOWN THE LANE, THE	LAIRD KOENIG
LITTLE ITALY - S	MARK PATRICK CARDUCCI
LITTLE LORD FAUNTLEROY - S	ANDREW BIRKIN
LITTLE MAN TATE	A. SCOTT FRANK
LITTLE ME (P)	NEIL SIMON
LITTLE MERMAID, THE (AF)	JOHN MUSKER
LITTLE MERMAID, THE (AF)	RON CLEMENTS
LITTLE MISS BROADWAY	HARRY TUGEND†
LITTLE MISS MARKER	WALTER BERNSTEIN
LITTLE MONSTERS	TED ELLIOTT
LITTLE MONSTERS	TERRY P. ROSSIO
LITTLE MURDERS	JULES FEIFFER
LITTLE NAPOLEON - S	LIZ COMICI
LITTLE NAPOLEON - S	LOU COMICI
LITTLE NEMO IN SLUMBERLAND (AF)	CHRIS COLUMBUS
LITTLE NEMO (AF)	RICHARD OUTTEN
LITTLE NIKITA	BO GOLDMAN
LITTLE NIKITA	TERRY SCHWARTZ
LITTLE NIKITA	JOHN HILL
LITTLE NIKITA	TOM MUSCA
LITTLE NINJA MAN - S	GEORGE SAUNDERS
LITTLE NINJA MAN - S	JOHN B. HEDBERG
LITTLE NOISES	JON ZEIDERMAN
LITTLE NOISES	JANE SPENCER
LITTLE OLD NEW YORK	HARRY TUGEND†
LITTLE PRINCESS - S	RICHARD LAGRAVENESE
LITTLE ROMANCE, A	ALLAN BURNS
LITTLE SECRETS	NANCYLEE MYATT
LITTLE SEX, A	ROBERT DELAURENTIS

Li-Lo
FILM WRITERS GUIDE

Title	Writer
LITTLE SHOP OF HORRORS	HOWARD ASHMAN†
LITTLE SISTER	JIMMY ZEILINGER
LITTLE SISTER, THE	JAN EGLESON
LITTLE STIFF, A	CAVEH YAHEDI
LITTLE STIFF, A	GREG WATKINS
LITTLE THIEF, THE	ANNIE MILLER
LITTLE THINGS - S	KEVIN REYNOLDS
LITTLE TOUCHED, A - S	SCOTT FROST
LITTLE TREASURE	ALAN SHARP
LITTLE VEGAS	PERRY LANG
LIVE AND LET DIE	TOM MANKIEWICZ
LIVE FOR LIFE	CLAUDE LELOUCH
LIVE ROUNDS - S	LEM DOBBS
LIVE WIRE - S	BART BAKER
LIVE WIRE - S	DARRIN OURA
LIVE WIRE - S	LESLIE BOHEM
LIVES OF THE TWINS, THE - S	TIM HUNTER
LIVIN' LARGE	WILLIAM MOSELY PAYNE
LIVING ARROWS - S	LARRY GRUSIN
LIVING DAYLIGHTS, THE	MICHAEL G. WILSON
LIVING DAYLIGHTS, THE	RICHARD MAIBAUM†
LIVING END, THE (P)	GEORGE GIPE
LIVING END, THE - S	FRANK GALATI
LIVING IDOL, THE	ALBERT E. LEWIN
LIVING IT UP	JACK ROSE
LIVING IT UP	MEL SHAVELSON
LIVING LARGE - S	LEO GAREN
LIVING LEGEND - S	KEN LEVINE
LIVING LEGEND, THE - S	DAVID ISAACS
LIVING ON TOKYO TIME	JOHN MCCORMICK
LIVING ON TOKYO TIME	STEVEN OKAZAKI
LIVING THE ALTERNATIVE LIFE - S	MERRILL MARKOE
LIVING TO DIE	STEPHEN SMOKE
LIVING WAGE, A - S	GORDON GREISMAN
LIVING WITHOUT YOU - S	ANTHONY DRAZAN
LO ZIO INDEGNO	FRANCO BRUSATI
LOBSTER MAN FROM MARS	BOB GREENBERG
LOCAL HERO	BILL FORSYTH
LOCAL TALENT - S	WENDY WASSERSTEIN
LOCK NESS MONSTER, THE - S	MARC NORMAN
LOCK UP	HENRY ROSENBAUM
LOCK UP	JEB STUART
LOCK UP	RICHARD SMITH
LOCKED OUT - S	ROBB ROYER
LOCKDOWN - S	B.W.L. NORTON, JR.
LOCKET, THE	BEN BARZMAN†
LOGAN'S RUN	DAVID Z. GOODMAN
LOLA	JACQUES DEMY†
LOLA	NORMAN THADDEUS VANE
LOLA	RAINER WERNER FASSBINDER†
LOLA - S	MITCH GLAZER
LOLITA	VLADIMIR NABOKOV†
LOLLY MADONNA XXX	RODNEY CARR-SMITH
LOLLY MADONNA XXX	SUE GRAFTON
LONE JUSTICE - S	GEORGE SAUNDERS
LONE JUSTICE - S	JOHN BRYANT HEDBERG
LONE JUSTICE - S	JEFFREY W. NEAL
LONE WOLF MCQUADE	H. KAYE DYAL
LONE WOLF MCQUADE	B.J. NELSON
LONELINESS OF THE LONG DISTANCE RUNNER, THE	ALAN SILLITOE
LONELY GUY, THE	ED. WEINBERGER
LONELY GUY, THE	STAN DANIELS
LONELY HEARTS	JOHN CLARKE
LONELY HEARTS	PAUL COX
LONELY IN AMERICA	BARRY ALEXANDER BROWN
LONELY LADY, THE	JOHN KERSHAW
LONELY LADY, THE	SHAWN RANDALL
LONELY ONE, THE - S	CHARLES ROBERT CARNER
LONELY PASSION OF JUDITH HEARNE, THE	PETER NELSON
LONELYVILLE - S	SUSAN SANDLER
LONER, THE	MAX KLEVEN
LONERS, THE	BARRY SANDLER
LONG & HAPPY LIFE - S	BETH HENLEY
LONG ABSENCE, THE	MARGUERITE DURAS
LONG AGO TOMORROW	BRYAN FORBES
LONG DAN - S	MICHAEL KANE
LONG DARK TEATIME OF THE SOUL, THE - S	RICHARD RUSH
LONG DAY BEFORE DARK - S	DOUG WHEELER
LONG DAY, THE - S	TERENCE DAVIES
LONG DAYS DYING, THE	CHARLES WOOD
LONG DUEL, THE	PETER YELDMAN
LONG GONE (CTF)	MICHAEL NORELL
LONG GONE AND FAR AWAY - S	LEM DOBBS
LONG GOOD FRIDAY, THE	BARRY KEEFFE
LONG GOODBYE, THE	LEIGH BRACKETT†
LONG HILL, THE - S	EUGENE QUINTANO
LONG HOT SUMMER, THE	HARRIET FRANK JR.
LONG HOT SUMMER, THE	IRVING RAVETCH
LONG ODD FROM JERSEY - S	WILLIAM M. FINKELSTEIN
LONG RAINBOW, THE - S	CHARLES SHYER
LONG RAINBOW, THE - S	ALAN MANDEL
LONG RIDERS, THE	BILL BRYDEN
LONG RIDERS, THE	JAMES KEACH
LONG RIDERS, THE	STACY KEACH
LONG RIDERS, THE	STEVEN PHILIP SMITH
LONG SATURDAY NIGHT, THE - S	ROB DUNN
LONG SHIPS, THE	BEVERLY CROSS
LONG WALK HOME, THE	JOHN CORK
LONG WAY HOME - S	ANDY TENNANT
LONG WAY HOME, THE - S	PETER KRIKES
LONG WAY HOME, THE - S	STEVE MEERSON
LONG WEEKEND, THE	EVERETT DEROCHE
LONGEST DAY, THE	DAVID PURSALL
LONGEST YARD, THE	TRACY KEENAN WYNN
LONGING TO FALL - S	HOWARD CHESLEY
LONGING TO FALL - S	MICHAEL SCHIFFER
LONGSHOT, THE	TIM CONWAY
LONGTIME COMPANION	CRAIG LUCAS
LOOK BACK IN ANGER	NIGEL KNEALE
LOOK BACK IN ANGER (P)	JOHN OSBORNE
LOOK DOWN AND DIE	PETER S. DAVIS
LOOK DOWN AND DIE	ROB EWING
LOOK DOWN AND DIE	WILLIAM N. PANZER
LOOK DOWN AND DIE	LEIGH CHAPMAN
LOOK HOMEWARD ANGEL - S	STEVEN M. KUNES
LOOK WHO'S TALKING	AMY HECKERLING
LOOK WHO'S TALKING, TOO	AMY HECKERLING
LOOK WHO'S TALKING, TOO	NEAL ISRAEL
LOOKALIKE, THE (CTF)	KATE WILHELM
LOOKALIKE, THE (CTF)	LINDA BERGMAN
LOOKALIKE, THE (CTF)	MARTIN TAHSE
LOOKER	MICHAEL CRICHTON
LOOKIN' TO GET OUT	AL SCHWARTZ
LOOKIN' TO GET OUT	JON VOIGHT
LOOKING FOR LOVE - S	SUE JETTE
LOOKING FOR MR. GOODBAR	RICHARD BROOKS
LOOKING FOR WORK - S	NAOMI FONER
LOOKING GLASS WAR, THE	FRANK R. PIERSON
LOOKING OUT - S	WILLIAM GOODHART
LOOKING UP	LINDA YELLEN
LOOPHOLE	JONATHAN HALES
LOOPHOLE - S	ROBERT KAUFMAN
LOOSE CANNON	PAUL F. EDWARDS
LOOSE CANNONS	BOB CLARK
LOOSE CANNONS	RICHARD MATHESON
LOOSE ENDS (P)	MICHAEL WELLER
LOOSE SCREWS	MICHAEL CORY
LOOSE SHOES - S	MICHAEL DIGAETANO
LOOSE WOMEN - S	BRAD BUCKNER
LOOSE WOMEN - S	DAN JENKINS
LOOSE WOMEN - S	BUD SHRAKE
LOOSE WOMEN - S	EUGENIE ROSS-LEMING
LOOSE WOMEN - S	PAUL PRICE
LOOSE WOMEN - S	STEVE NATHAN
LORD JIM	RICHARD BROOKS
LORD LOVE A DUCK	GEORGE AXELROD
LORD OF THE AMAZON - S	DENNE BART PETITCLERC
LORD OF THE FLIES	PETER BROOK
LORD OF THE MANOR - S	MITCHEL KATLIN
LORD OF THE MANOR - S	NAT BERNSTEIN
LORD OF THE RINGS, THE (AF)	CHRIS CONKLING
LORD OF THE RINGS, THE (AF)	PETER S. BEAGLE
LORD ROCHESTER'S MONKEY - S	MICHAEL THOMAS
LORDS OF DISCIPLINE, THE	LLOYD FONVIELLE
LORDS OF DISCIPLINE, THE	THOMAS POPE
LORDS OF THE DEEP	DARYL HANEY
LORDS OF THE DEEP	HOWARD R. COHEN
LORENZO DEMICI - S	MENNO MEYJES
LORENZO'S OIL - S	GEORGE MILLER
LORNA	RUSS MEYER
LORNA DOON - S	LAURA LAMSON
LOSERS - S	RYAN ROWE
LOSIN' IT	BRYAN GINDOFF
LOSIN' IT	B.W.L. NORTON, JR.
LOSS OF INNOCENCE	HOWARD KOCH
LOST - S	GORDON GREISMAN
LOST AND FOUND	JACK ROSE
LOST ANGELS	MICHAEL WELLER
LOST BOYS, THE	JAMES JEREMIAS
LOST BOYS, THE	JANICE FISCHER
LOST BOYS, THE	JEFFREY BOAM
LOST BOYS II - S	ERIC RED
LOST CAPONE, THE (CTF)	JOHN GRAY
LOST CITY - S	LEON CAPETANOS
LOST COMMAND, THE	NELSON GIDDING
LOST EMPIRE, THE	JIM WYNORSKI
LOST HIGHWAY, THE - S	ALLISON ANDERS
LOST HORIZON	LARRY KRAMER
LOST IN AMERICA	ALBERT BROOKS
LOST IN AMERICA	MONICA JOHNSON
LOST IN YONKERS (P)	NEIL SIMON
LOST SOUL - S	JEFFREY BELL
LOST SOUL - S	STEPHEN VOLK
LOST VEGAS - S	DAVID H. SMILOW
LOST WEEKEND - S	SCOTT RICHARDSON
LOST WEEKEND, THE	BILLY WILDER
LOST WORLD, THE	CHARLES BENNETT
LOST WORLD, THE	IRWIN ALLEN
LOTTERY ROSE, THE - S	FRANK MILITARY JR.
LOU GEHRIG DID NOT DIE OF CANCER (P)	JASON MILLER
LOUIE - S	ERIC ROTH
LOUIE, LOUIE - S	JOHN NORVILLE
LOUIE, LOUIE - S	THOMAS BAUM
LOUISIANA RUN - S	TIM MCCANLIES
LOUSY KILLING, A - S	ERIC HUGHES
LOVE	NANCY DOWD
LOVE & MURDER	STEVEN HILLIARD STERN
LOVE ACT - S	DAVID PIRIE
LOVE AFFAIR	FREDERIC RAPHAEL
LOVE AFFAIR: OR THE CASE OF THE MISSING SWITCHBOARD OPERATOR	DUSAN MAKAVEJEV
LOVE AND ANARCHY	LINA WERTMULLER
LOVE AND BULLETS	WENDELL MAYES
LOVE AND DEATH	WOODY ALLEN
LOVE AND MONEY	JAMES TOBACK
LOVE AND PAIN AND THE WHOLE DAMNED THING	ALVIN SARGENT
LOVE AT FIRST BITE	ROBERT KAUFMAN
LOVE AT LARGE	ALAN RUDOLPH
LOVE AT SECOND BITE - S	ROBERT KAUFMAN
LOVE AT STAKE	LANIER LANEY
LOVE AT STAKE	TERRY SWEENEY
LOVE AT THE TOP	CHRISTOPHER FRANK
LOVE BUSINESS - S	STEVE TESICH
LOVE CAGE, THE	RENE CLEMENT
LOVE CHILD	ANNE GERARD
LOVE CHILD	KATHERINE SPECKTOR
LOVE CRIMES	ALLAN MOYLE
LOVE FIELD	DONALD P. ROOS
LOVE HURTS	RON NYSWANER
LOVE IN GERMANY, A	AGNIESZKA HOLLAND
LOVE IN THE AFTERNOON	BILLY WILDER
LOVE IN THE AFTERNOON	I.A.L. DIAMOND†
LOVE IN THE ATTIC - S	DONALD E. WESTLAKE
LOVE IN THE CITY	FEDERICO FELLINI
LOVE IS A BALL	DAVID SWIFT
LOVE IS A BALL	FRANK WALDMAN†
LOVE IS A BALL	TOM WALDMAN†
LOVE IS A DOG FROM HELL	DOMINIQUE DERUDDERE
LOVE KILLS - S	JEAN-YVES PITOUN
LOVE LETTERS	AMY JONES
LOVE LETTERS (P)	A.R. GURNEY
LOVE LUCK - S	JEREMY JOE KRONSBERG
LOVE ON THE GROUND	SUZANNE SCHIFFMAN
LOVE ON THE RUN	FRANCOIS TRUFFAUT†
LOVE OR MONEY	BART DAVIS
LOVE OR MONEY	ELYSE ENGLAND
LOVE OR MONEY	MICHAEL ZAUSNER
LOVE POTION #9	DALE LAUNER
LOVE SONG OF RUDY KAZOO, THE - S	ALAN GROSS
LOVE SONGS	ELIE CHOURAQUI
LOVE STORY	ERICH SEGAL
LOVE STORY '78 - S	RONNI KERN
LOVE STREAMS	JOHN CASSAVETES†
LOVE STREAMS	TED ALLAN
LOVE THIRTY - S	SUSAN RICE
LOVE THY FATHER - S	DARRYL WIMBERLY
LOVE WITH A PERFECT STRANGER (CTF) - S	PAMELA WALLACE
LOVE WITH THE PROPER STRANGER	ARNOLD SCHULMAN
LOVE WITHOUT PITY	ERIC ROCHANT
LOVE, ROGER - S	GARRY MARSHALL
LOVE, ROGER - S	JERRY BELSON
LOVE, ROGER - S	STEVEN M. KUNES
LOVE, THE MAGICIAN	CARLOS SAURA
LOVECRAFT (CTF) - S	JOSEPH DOUGHERTY
LOVED ONE, THE	TERRY SOUTHERN
LOVEHUNTER - S	SCOTT SPENCER
LOVING WIFE - S	CLIFTON CAMPBELL

Title	Writer
LOVELESS, THE	MONTY MONTGOMERY
LOVELESS, THE	KATHRYN BIGELOW
LOVELINE - S	JEFF BUHAI
LOVELINE - S	STEVEN R. ZACHARIAS
LOVELINES	MICHAEL LLOYD
LOVELINES	CHIP HAND
LOVELINES	WILLIAM BYRON HILLMAN
LOVER COME BACK	PAUL W. HENNING
LOVER COME BACK	STANLEY SHAPIRO†
LOVER PRINCE, THE - S	JIM STRAIN
LOVER, THE	FRANCIS VEBER
LOVER, THE (P)	HAROLD PINTER
LOVER, THE - S	JEAN-JACQUES ANNAUD
LOVER, THE - S	GERARD BRACH
LOVER, THE - S	MARGUERITE DURAS
LOVERBOY	LESLIE DIXON
LOVERBOY	ROBIN SCHIFF
LOVERBOY	TOM ROPELEWSKI
LOVERS - S	ERIC ROTH
LOVERS AND LIARS	PAUL D. ZIMMERMAN
LOVERS AND OTHER STRANGERS	DAVID Z. GOODMAN
LOVERS AND OTHER STRANGERS	JOSEPH BOLOGNA
LOVERS AND OTHER STRANGERS	RENEE TAYLOR
LOVERSI, THE	JACK ROSENTHAL
LOVERS, HAPPY LOVERSI	RENE CLEMENT
LOVERS, THE	LOUIS MALLE
LOVES OF A BLONDE	IVAN PASSER
LOVES OF A BLONDE	MILOS FORMAN
LOVES OF ISADORA, THE	CLIVE EXTON
LOVES OF ISADORA, THE	MELVYN BRAGG
LOVES OF KAFKA, THE - S	JOHN BRILEY
LOVESICK	MARSHALL BRICKMAN
LOVIN' MOLLY	STEPHEN FRIEDMAN
LOVING	DON DEVLIN
LOVING COUPLES (1980)	MARTIN DONOVAN
LOVING COUPLES	MAI ZETTERLING
LOVING WALTER	DAVID COOK
LOVING YOU	HAL KANTER
LOVING YOU - S	HERBERT BAKER†
LOW DOWN - S	WALTER BERNSTEIN
LOW POWER - S	BIG BOY MEDLIN
LOWER DEPTHS, THE	AKIRA KUROSAWA
LUCAS	DAVID SELTZER
LUCIFER'S REEF - S	MICHAEL BLODGETT
LUCIO FLAVIO	HECTOR BABENCO
LUCK - S	PHILIP RAILSBACK
LUCK OF GINGER COFFEY, THE	BRIAN MOORE
LUCKIEST MAN IN THE WORLD, THE	FRANK D. GILROY
LUCKY IN LOVE - S	VALRI BROMFIELD
LUCKY LADY	GLORIA KATZ
LUCKY LADY	WILLARD HUYCK
LUCKY SPOT, THE (P)	BETH HENLEY
LUCKY STAR, THE	MAX FISCHER
LUCKY STAR, THE	JACK ROSENTHAL
LUCKY STIFF	PAT PROFT
LUCKY STIFF - S	NICK W. THIEL
LUCKY STRIKE - S	ANN POWELL
LUCKY STRIKE - S	ROSE SCHACHT
LUCY - S	DAVID SHABER
LUDES - S	JULIA CAMERON
LUDLOW, 1914 - S	LINDY LAUB
LUIGI'S LADIES	JUDY MORRIS
LUKAS' CHILD - S	ERIC LOUZIL
LUNA	BERNARDO BERTOLUCCI
LUNA	CLARE PEPLOE
LUNA PARK - S	PETER FOLDY
LUNATIC FRINGE - S	JOSEPH DOUGHERTY
LUNATICS - S	NORMAN WEXLER
LUNCH AT FIRST SIGHT - S	MARK FROST
LUNCHING (P)	ALAN GROSS
LUNETTA PARK - S	LAUREL DELP
LUST IN THE DUST	PHILIP JOHN TAYLOR
LUTHER	EDWARD ANHALT
LUTHER (P)	JOHN OSBORNE
LUTHER PROJECT, THE - S	CALDER WILLINGHAM
LUV (P)	MURRAY SCHISGAL
LYDIA BAILEY	PHILIP DUNNE
LYDIE BREEZE (P)	JOHN GUARE

M

Title	Writer
M (REMAKE) - S	DAVID LOUCKA
M WORD, THE - S	MARK ANDRUS
M*A*S*H	RING LARDNER JR.
M. BUTTERFLY (P)	DAVID HENRY HWANG
M.I.A. - S	TAB MURPHY
MA BELL - S	ERIC ROTH
MABEL - S	ROBERT J. AVRECH
MAC AND ME	STEPHEN FEKE
MAC AND ME	STEWART RAFFILL
MACARONI	ETTORE SCOLA
MACARTHUR	HAL BARWOOD
MACARTHUR	MATTHEW ROBBINS
MACBETH	KENNETH TYNANÉ
MACHINE GUN KELLY - S	ANNA HAMILTON PHELAN
MACHINE GUN KELLY - S	MIKE WERB
MACHINE GUN KELLY - S	STEPHEN METCALFE
MACK THE KNIFE	MENAHEM GOLAN
MACKENZIE BREAK, THE	WILLIAM NORTON SR.
MACKEREL (P)	ISRAEL HOROVITZ
MACKINTOSH MAN, THE	WALTER HILL
MAD BOMBER, THE	BERT I. GORDON
MAD BOMBER, THE	MARC BEHM
MAD DASH - S	ELIZABETH BRADLEY
MAD DASH - S	STEPHEN MCPHERSON
MAD DOG	PHILLIPPE MORA
MAD DOG AND GLORY - S	RICHARD PRICE
MAD DOG BLUES (P)	SAM SHEPARD
MAD DOG COLL - S	NEIL RUTTENBERG
MAD DOG LAKE - S	RUDOLPH G. WURLITZER
MAD DOG MORGAN	PHILLIPE MORA
MAD FOR MIMA - S	ALEXANDER TANA
MAD LOVE - S	LARRY GROSS
MAD MAGAZINE PRESENTS UP THE ACADEMY	JAY TARSES
MAD MAGAZINE PRESENTS UP THE ACADEMY	TOM PATCHETT
MAD MAX	GEORGE MILLER
MAD MAX BEYOND THUNDERDOME	GEORGE MILLER
MAD MAX BEYOND THUNDERDOME	TERRY HAYES
MAD MAX II	BRIAN HANNANT
MAD MAX II	GEORGE MILLER
MAD MAX II	TERRY HAYES
MAD MISS MANTON - S	DAVID LOUGHERY
MAD MISS MANTON, THE - S	THOM EBERHARDT
MAD ROOM, THE	BERNARD GIRARD
MAD VINCENT (P)	JAMES KENNEDY
MADAME BOVARY	CLAUDE CHABROL
MADAME BUTTERFLY - S	TOM BENEDEK
MADAME ROSA	MOSHE MIZRAHI
MADAME SOUSATZKA	JOHN SCHLESINGER
MADAME SOUSATZKA	RUTH PRAWER JHABVALA
MADAME X	JEAN HOLLOWAY†
MADCAP	DYANNE ASSIMOW
MADE FOR EACH OTHER	JOSEPH BOLOGNA
MADE FOR EACH OTHER	RENEE TAYLOR
MADE IN AMERICA (P)	ALVIN BORETZ
MADE IN AMERICA - S	DAVID FREEMAN
MADE IN BANGKOK (P)	ANTHONY MINGHELLA
MADE IN HEAVEN	BRUCE EVANS
MADE IN HEAVEN	RAY GIDEON
MADE IN JAPAN - S	WESLEY STRICK
MADE IN USA	KEN FRIEDMAN
MADELEINE - S	BOAZ YAKIN
MADHOUSE	TOM ROPELEWSKI
MADIGAN	ABRAHAM POLONSKY
MADLANDS - S	NORTHROP DAVIS
MADLY IN LOVE - S	ALVIN SARGENT
MADMAN	JOE GIANNONE
MADNESS OF A SEDUCED WOMAN - S	JAMES DEARDEN
MADNESS OF A SEDUCED WOMAN - S	MICHAEL AUSTIN
MADNESS OF THE HEART	CHARLES BENNETT
MADONNA COMPLEX, THE - S	NORMAN BOGNER
MADONNA MADNESS - S	PAUL D. ZIMMERMAN
MADWOMAN OF CHAILLOT, THE	EDWARD ANHALT
MADWOMAN OF NEW YORK, THE - S	KENNETH JOHNSON
MAESTRO & ME - S	GEORGE GALLO
MAESTRO (SHORT)	ALEX ZAMM
MAGDA AND CALLAS (P)	ALBERT INNAURATO
MAGDALENA VIRAGA	NINA MENKES
MAGESTIC KID, THE (P)	MARK MEDOFF
MAGIC	WILLIAM GOLDMAN
MAGIC BUS - S	GEORGE SAUNDERS
MAGIC BUS - S	JOHN BRYANT HEDBERG
MAGIC CHRISTIAN, THE	TERRY SOUTHERN
MAGIC COTTAGE, THE - S	CAROLYN SHELBY
MAGIC COTTAGE, THE - S	CHRISTOPHER AMES
MAGIC FIVE - S	R. J. STEWART
MAGIC HOUR - S	CLIFFORD GREEN
MAGIC HOUR - S	ELLEN GREEN
MAGIC MAN - S	JOE ESZTERHAS
MAGIC OF LASSIE, THE	JEAN HOLLOWAY†
MAGIC TIME - S	PAUL RUDNICK
MAGIC TOYSHOP, THE	ANGELA CARTER
MAGICIAN OF LUBLIN, THE	MENAHEM GOLAN
MAGICIAN, THE	INGMAR BERGMAN
MAGNETIC NORTH - S	JOHN KAYE
MAGNIFICENT OBSESSION	ROBERT BLEES
MAGNIFICENT SEVEN - S	KEVIN JARRE
MAGNIFICENT SEVEN, THE	WILLIAM ROBERTS
MAGNUM FORCE	JOHN MILLIUS
MAGNUM FORCE	MICHAEL CIMINO
MAHABHARATA, THE	JEAN-CLAUDE CARRIERE
MAHAD - S	MARC NORMAN
MAHLER	KEN RUSSELL
MAHOGANY	JOHN BYRUM
MAI, THE PSYCHIC GIRL - S	CAROLINE W. THOMPSON
MAI, THE PSYCHIC GIRL - S	LARRY WILSON
MAID OF HONOR - S	JEFF BARON
MAID TO ORDER	PERRY HOWZE
MAID TO ORDER	RANDY HOWZE
MAID TO ORDER	AMY JONES
MAIDEN RUN - S	ROBERT J. AVRECH
MAIDS, THE	ROBERT ENDERS
MAIDSTONE	NORMAN MAILER
MAIL ORDER BRIDE	BURT KENNEDY
MAIN EVENT, THE	ANDREW SMITH
MAIN EVENT, THE	GAIL PARENT
MAIN, THE - S	MICHAEL CRISTOFER
MAITRESSE	BARBET SCHROEDER
MAJIC SHOW - S	JAMES BRENDAN PATTERSON
MAJOR AND THE MINOR, THE	BILLY WILDER
MAJOR BIRNBAUM - S	ROBERT KAUFMAN
MAJOR DUNDEE	OSCAR SAUL
MAJOR LEAGUE	DAVID S. WARD
MAJOR, MAJOR - S	GARY GODDARD
MAJORITY RULES - S	RACHEL FELDMAN
MAJORITY RULES - S	SUSAN NANUS
MAKING LOVE	BARRY SANDLER
MAKING LOVE	A. SCOTT BERG
MAKING MONEY - S	BOB KRAFT
MAKING MONEY - S	TED PUSHINSKY
MAKING MOVIES (P)	AARON SORKIN
MAKING MR. RIGHT	FLOYD BYARS
MAKING MR. RIGHT	LAURIE FRANK
MAKING THE GRADE	CHARLES GALE
MAKING THE GRADE	EUGENE QUINTANO
MAKING THUNDERBIRDS - S	CLAYTON S. FROHMAN
MAKING WAVES - S	LESLIE RAY
MALA NOCHE	GUS VAN SANT
MALACHI - S	LARRY FERGUSON
MALACHI - S	PETER BELLWOOD
MALCOLM	DAVID PARKER
MALCOLM X - S	DAVID MAMET
MALE-FEMALE	GAIL FISHER
MALE-FEMALE - S	MARC CHESLER
MALIBU BEACH	ROBERT J. ROSENTHAL
MALIBU BIKINI SHOP	DAVID WECHTER
MALIBU BUZZARDS - S	TED MANN
MALIBU EXPRESS	ANDY SIDARIS
MALIBU WARS - S	JAMES SADWITH
MALONE	CHRISTOPHER FRANK
MAMA GOT A HANDGUN IN HER BAG - S	WILLIAM J. DAVIES
MAMA GOT A HANDGUN IN HER BAG - S	WILLIAM OSBORNE
MAMA'S BOY - S	BRUCE MALMUTH
MAMA, THERE'S A MAN IN YOUR BED	COLINE SERREAU
MAMBO KINGS, THE	CYNTHIA CIDRE
MAME	PAUL ZINDEL
MAN AND A WOMAN, A	CLAUDE LELOUCH
MAN AND A WOMAN, A: 20 YEARS LATER	CLAUDE LELOUCH
MAN AT THE TOP	HUGH J. WHITEMORE
MAN CALLED HORSE, A	JACK DEWITT
MAN CALLED SARGE, A	STUART GILLARD
MAN FACING SOUTHEAST	ELISEO SUBIELA
MAN FOR ALL SEASONS, A	ROBERT BOLT
MAN FROM BITTER RIDGE, THE	LARRY ROMAN

MAN FROM DEL RIO .... RICHARD CARR
MAN FROM DOWN
  UNDER, THE .... THOMAS SELLER†
MAN FROM GREEK
  AND ROMAN - S .... JAMES GOLDMAN
MAN FROM LARAMIE, THE .... PHILIP YORDAN
MAN FROM NOWHERE, THE - S .... ALLAN G. SCOTT
MAN FROM NOWHERE, THE - S .... CHRIS BRYANT
MAN FROM SNOWY
  RIVER, THE .... FRED CUL CULLEN
MAN FROM SNOWY RIVER, THE .... JOHN DIXON
MAN FROM ST.
  PAUL, THE - S .... NORMAN STEINBERG
MAN FROM THE DINERS
  CLUB, THE .... WILLIAM PETER BLATTY
MAN IN 605, THE (P) .... ALAN GROSS
MAN IN A COCKED HAT .... ROY BOULTING
MAN IN LOVE, A .... DIANE KURYS
MAN IN LOVE, A .... ISRAEL HOROVITZ
MAN IN THE GLASS
  BOOTH, THE .... EDWARD ANHALT
MAN IN THE MOON .... BRYAN FORBES
MAN IN THE MOON, THE - S .... JENNY HARWELL
MAN IN THE NET, THE .... REGINALD ROSE
MAN IN THE WILDERNESS .... JACK DEWITT
MAN INSIDE, THE .... BOBBY ROTH
MAN IS NOT A BIRD .... DUSAN MAKAVEJEV
MAN OF A THOUSAND FACES .... IVAN GOFF
MAN OF DESTINY - S .... JEREMY IACONE
MAN OF FLOWERS .... BOB ELLIS
MAN OF FLOWERS .... PAUL COX
MAN OF GOD - S .... CHRIS RUPPENTHAL
MAN OF HONOR - S .... MICHAEL BLODGETT
MAN OF IRON .... WILLIAM WISTER HAINES†
MAN OF STEEL - S .... CRAIG TEPPER
MAN OF THE FUTURE - S .... PETER LENKOV
MAN OF THE WEST .... REGINALD ROSE
MAN ON A SWING .... DAVID Z. GOODMAN
MAN ON FIRE .... ELIE CHOURAQUI
MAN ON FIRE .... SERGIO DONATI
MAN ON FIRE - S .... MICHAEL THOMAS
MAN ON THE ROOF, THE .... BO WIDERBERG
MAN SHE KNEW, THE - S .... ALAN BERGER
MAN SHE KNEW, THE - S .... KATHY GORI
MAN TO MAN - S .... RANDY FELDMAN
MAN TROUBLE .... CAROLE EASTMAN
MAN UNDER
  SUSPICION .... NORBERT KUCKELMANN
MAN WHO CAME TO
  DINNER, THE .... JULIUS J. EPSTEIN
MAN WHO CAME TO
  PLAY, THE - S .... LOUIS GARFINKLE
MAN WHO COULD CHEAT
  DEATH, THE .... JIMMY SANGSTER
MAN WHO COULD WORK
  MIRACLES, THE - S .... ARLENE SARNER
MAN WHO COULD WORK
  MIRACLES, THE - S .... LARRY B. WILLIAMS
MAN WHO COULD WORK
  MIRACLES, THE - S .... MICHAEL LEESON
MAN WHO FELL TO
  EARTH, THE .... PAUL MAYERSBERG
MAN WHO GAVE UP HIS
  NAME, THE - S .... DENNIS PALUMBO
MAN WHO GAVE UP HIS
  NAME, THE - S .... RICHARD CHAPMAN
MAN WHO GAVE UP HIS
  NAME, THE - S .... TERRELL TANNEN
MAN WHO HAD POWER
  OVER WOMEN, THE .... CHRIS BRYANT
MAN WHO HAD POWER OVER
  WOMEN, THE .... ALLAN G. SCOTT
MAN WHO KILLED SHERLOCK
  HOLMES, THE - S .... STEVE SIEGEL
MAN WHO KNEW TOO
  MUCH, THE .... CHARLES BENNETT
MAN WHO LOVED
  HITCHCOCK, THE - S .... LARRY COHEN
MAN WHO LOVED
  HITCHCOCK, THE - S .... MAX EMBER
MAN WHO LOVED
  HITCHCOCK, THE - S .... ALLAN SCOTT
MAN WHO LOVED
  WOMEN, THE (1983) .... BLAKE EDWARDS
MAN WHO LOVED
  WOMEN, THE (1983) .... GEOFFREY EDWARDS
MAN WHO LOVED
  WOMEN, THE (1983) .... MILTON WEXLER
MAN WHO LOVED
  WOMEN, THE (1977) .... SUZANNE SCHIFFMAN
MAN WHO LOVED
  WOMEN, THE (1977) .... FRANCOIS TRUFFAUT†
MAN WHO SAVED THE
  WORLD - S .... HOWARD FRANKLIN
MAN WHO SAW TOMORROW,
  THE (FD) .... ROBERT GUENETTE
MAN WHO STOLE THE
  SUN, THE .... LEONARD SCHRADER
MAN WHO WAS SHERLOCK
  HOLMES, THE - S .... CHRIS BRYANT
MAN WHO WAS SHERLOCK
  HOLMES, THE - S .... ALLAN G. SCOTT
MAN WHO WAS
  THURSDAY, THE - S .... JOHN MORTIMER
MAN WHO WASN'T
  THERE, THE .... STANFORD SHERMAN
MAN WHO WOULD BE KING, THE ... JOHN HUSTON†
MAN WHO WOULD
  NOT DIE, THE - S .... DENNIS POTTER
MAN WITH A GUN - S .... DAVID TAYLOR
MAN WITH BOGART'S
  FACE, THE .... ANDREW J. FENADY
MAN WITH 9 LIVES, THE - S .... RYAN ROWE
MAN WITH NINE
  LIVES, THE - S .... DAVID LOUGHERY
MAN WITH ONE RED SHOE, THE .... ROBERT KLANE
MAN WITH THE GOLDEN
  ARM, THE .... WALTER NEWMAN
MAN WITH THE GOLDEN
  GUN, THE .... RICHARD MAIBAUM†
MAN WITH THE GOLDEN
  GUN, THE .... TOM MANKIEWICZ
MAN WITH THE GREEN
  CARNATION, THE .... KEN HUGHES
MAN WITH TWO BRAINS, THE .... CARL REINER
MAN WITH TWO BRAINS, THE .... GEORGE GIPE
MAN WITH TWO BRAINS, THE .... STEVE MARTIN
MAN'S BEST
  FRIEND - S .... RICHARD CHRISTIAN MATHESON
MAN'S FATE - S .... LAWRENCE HAUBEN
MAN'S FATE - S .... DANIEL BARTOLINI
MAN, A WOMAN AND A BANK, A .... BRUCE EVANS
MAN, A WOMAN AND A BANK, A .... RAY GIDEON
MAN, WOMAN AND CHILD .... DAVID Z. GOODMAN
MAN, WOMAN AND CHILD .... ERICH SEGAL
MANCHESTER ANGEL - S .... JAN EGLESON
MANCHU EAGLE MURDER
  MYSTERY, THE .... DEAN HARGROVE
MANCHURIAN
  CANDIDATE, THE .... GEORGE AXELROD
MANDINGO .... NORMAN WEXLER
MANDRAKE - S .... LORENZO SEMPLE
MANDRAKE THE
  MAGICIAN - S .... MICHAEL ALMEREYDA
MANGO TREE, THE .... MICHAEL PATE
MANHATTAN .... MARSHALL BRICKMAN
MANHATTAN .... WOODY ALLEN
MANHATTAN GHOST STORY - S .... RONALD BASS
MANHATTAN ISLAND - S .... CHRIS KEYSER
MANHATTAN
  PROJECT, THE .... MARSHALL BRICKMAN
MANHATTAN PROJECT, THE .... THOMAS BAUM
MANHATTAN STAGECOACH - S .... GEORGE GIPE
MANHUNT - S .... GARY THOMPSON
MANHUNTER .... MICHAEL MANN
MANIAC .... JIMMY SANGSTER
MANIAC COP .... LARRY COHEN
MANIAC COP 2 .... LARRY COHEN
MANIAC SLAYS BLONDE - S .... W.D. RICHTER
MANIFESTO .... DUSAN MAKAVEJEV
MANITOU, THE .... THOMAS POPE
MANNEQUIN .... ED RUGOFF
MANNEQUIN .... MICHAEL GOTTLIEB
MANNEQUIN TWO .... BETSY ISRAEL
MANNEQUIN TWO .... DAVID A. ISAACS
MANNEQUIN TWO .... ED RUGOFF
MANNEQUIN TWO .... KEN LEVINE
MANNY - S .... DONALD TODD
MANON OF THE SPRING .... CLAUDE BERRI
MANON OF THE SPRING .... GERARD BRACH
MANUMIT - S .... HAROLD NEBENZAL
MANUMIT - S .... ROD AMATEAU
MAP OF THE HUMAN HEART - S ...... VINCENT WARD
MAP OF THE WORLD, A (P) .... DAVID HARE
MAPLE & ELM - S .... STU KRIEGER
MAPS FOR DROWSINESS (P) .... NEIL LANDAU
MARATHON - S .... MARK KRAM
MARATHON MAN .... WILLIAM GOLDMAN
MARCH OR DIE .... DAVID Z. GOODMAN
MARCO - S .... ANDY LEWIS
MARGARITAVILLE - S .... P.J. O'ROURKE
MARGRITTE SKIES (P) .... YALE UDOFF
MARIA'S LOVERS .... ANDREI KONCHALOVSKY
MARIA'S LOVERS .... GERARD BRACH
MARIA'S LOVERS .... MARJORIE DAVID
MARIA'S LOVERS .... PAUL ZINDEL
MARIANNE AND
  JULIANE .... MARGARETHE VON TROTTA
MARIE .... JOHN BRILEY
MARIE AND BRUCE (P) .... WALLACE SHAWN
MARIE LAVEAU - S .... DAVID ODELL
MARIGOLDS .... ATHOL FUGARD
MARK MY
  WORDS - S .... STEVEN MARK WASSERMAN
MARK, THE .... STANLEY MANN
MARKED FOR DEATH .... MARK VICTOR
MARKED FOR DEATH .... MICHAEL GRAIS
MARLOWE .... STIRLING SILLIPHANT
MARMALADE - S .... GINNY CERRELLA
MARNIE .... JAY PRESSON ALLEN
MAROONED .... MAYO SIMON
MARQUIS OF O..., THE .... ERIC ROHMER
MARRIAGE GO ROUND, THE .... LESLIE STEVENS
MARRIAGE OF A YOUNG
  STOCKBROKER, THE .... LORENZO SEMPLE
MARRIAGE OF BETTE AND
  BOO, THE (P) .... CHRISTOPHER DURANG
MARRIAGE OR BUST - S .... JOHN ROMANO
MARRIAGE STORY, THE - S .... BETH GUTCHEON
MARRIAGE, A .... SANDY TUNG
MARRIED LIFE - S .... LYNN GROSSMAN
MARRIED LIFE, A - S .... DIANE ENGLISH
MARRIED TO THE MOB .... BARRY STRUGATZ
MARRIED TO THE MOB .... MARK BURNS
MARRIED WOMAN, THE .... JEAN-LUC GODARD
MARRY ME A LITTLE (P) .... CRAIG LUCAS
MARRYING MAN, THE .... NEIL SIMON
MARRYING UP - S .... ERIC ALTER
MARRYING UP - S .... STEVEN S. GREENE
MARRYING UP - S .... TRISH SOODIK
MARSABA - S .... LOUIS GARFINKLE
MARSEILLE CONTRACT, THE .... JUDD BERNARD
MARSHALL LAW III - S .... GEORGE SAUNDERS
MARSHALL LAW III - S .... JOHN B. HEDBERG
MARSUPIALS: THE
  HOWLING III, THE .... PHLILIPPE MORA
MARTHA HONEY- S .... ROY CARLSON
MARTIAL LAW .... RICHARD BRANDES
MARTIANS GO HOME .... CHARLIE HAAS
MARTIN .... GEORGE A. ROMERO
MARTIN'S DAY .... ALLAN G. SCOTT
MARTIN'S DAY .... CHRIS BRYANT
MARTY .... PADDY CHAYEVSKY†
MARU MARU .... PHILIP YORDAN
MARVEL OF THE HAUNTED
  CASTLE, THE - S .... LEM DOBBS
MARVIN AND SARA - S .... GARY DAVID GOLDBERG
MARVIN AND TIGE .... ERIC WESTON
MARVIN AND TIGE .... WANDA DELL
MARY BARNES (P) .... DAVID EDGAR
MARY WANTS TO HAVE
  AN AFFAIR - S .... BRYAN GORDON
MASK .... ANNA HAMILTON PHELAN
MASK, THE - S .... MICHAEL FALLON
MASK OF MICHAEL - S .... TOM PAGE
MASK OF SARNATH,
  THE (SHORT) .... NEIL RUTTENBERG
MASK OF THE RED
  DEATH - S .... MICHAEL J. MURRAY
MASQUE OF THE RED DEATH .... DARYL HANEY
MASQUE OF THE RED DEATH .... LARRY BRAND
MASQUERADE (1988) .... DICK WOLF
MASQUERADE (1965) .... WILLIAM GOLDMAN
MASS APPEAL .... BILL C. DAVIS
MASTER, THE - S .... W.D. RICHTER
MASTER HAROLD AND
  THE BOYS (P) .... ATHOL FUGARD
MASTER OF DRAGONARD
  HILL .... HARRY ALAN TOWERS
MASTER OF DRAGONARD HILL .... RICK MARX
MASTER OF THE WORLD .... RICHARD MATHESON
MASTERGATE (P) .... LARRY GELBART
MASTERS OF MENACE .... TINO INSANA
MASTERS OF THE UNIVERSE .... DAVID ODELL
MATA HARI .... JOEL ZISKIN
MATA HARI - S .... CHRIS BRYANT
MATA HARI, AGENT H21 .... FRANCOIS TRUFFAUT†
MATADOR .... PEDRO ALMODOVAR
MATARESE CIRCLE - S .... DARRYL PONICSAN
MATCH FACTORY GIRL, THE ...... AKI KAURISMAKI
MATCH, THE - S .... JAMES SADWITH
MATES - S .... DANIEL GOLDIN
MATES - S .... JOSHUA GOLDIN
MATEWAN .... JOHN SAYLES

Title	Writer
MATILDA	ALBERT S. RUDDY
MATILDA	TIMOTHY GALFAS
MATINEE	JAIME H. HERMOSILLO
MATINEE - S	BETH GUTCHEON
MATINEE - S	JACK BEHR
MATINEE - S	JERICHO STONE
MATINEE - S	SANDY KROOPF
MATING BIRDS, THE - S	ALLAN SCOTT
MATING GAME, THE	WILLIAM ROBERTS
MATING SEASON - S	NICHOLAS BOGNER
MATTER OF DEGREES, A	JACK MASON
MATTER OF DEGREES, A	RANDALL POSTER
MATTER OF DEGREES, A	W.T. MORGAN
MATTER OF DIGNITY, A	MICHAEL CACOYANNIS
MATTER OF HONOR, A - S	DAN GORDON
MATTER OF LIFE AND DEATH, A	EMERIC PRESSBURGER†
MATTER OF LIFE AND DEATH, A	MICHAEL POWELL†
MATTERS OF THE HEART (CTF)	LINDA BERGMAN
MATTERS OF THE HEART (CTF)	MARTIN TAHSE
MATZGER'S DOG - S	TOR VALENZA
MAURICE	JAMES IVORY
MAURICE	KIT HESKETH-HARVEY
MAUVAISE GRAINE	BILLY WILDER
MAVEN, THE - S	ERIC GETHERS
MAX AND HELEN (CTF)	COREY BLECHMAN
MAX DUGAN RETURNS	NEIL SIMON
MAX HAVELAAR	GERARD SOETEMAN
MAX THE FOX - S	FLOYD MUTRUX
MAXIE	PATRICIA RESNICK
MAXIMUM OVERDRIVE	STEPHEN KING
MAXWELL'S TRAIN - S	DAVID A. CHAPPE
MAXWELL'S TRAIN - S	JEB STUART
MAY FOOLS	JEAN-CLAUDE CARRIERE
MAY FOOLS	LOUIS MALLE
MAY I SEE YOU AGAIN - S	ERIC SCHAEFFER
MAYBE THAT'S YOUR PROBLEM (P)	LIONEL CHETWYND
MAYBERRY VICE - S	LINDA YELLEN
MAYHEM - S	ROBERT GUNTER
MAYNARD'S HOUSE - S	HERMAN RAUCHER
MAZE - S	CHARLES ROBERT CARNER
MCCABE & MRS. MILLER	ROBERT ALTMAN
MCFEE'S LAST CASE - S	ALEX HENDRIE
MCGUFFIN, THE - S	MICHAEL THOMAS
MCHALE'S NAVY	ANDY ROSE
MCQ	LARRY ROMAN
MCVICAR	TOM CLEGG
ME AND HIM	DORIS DORRIE
ME AND HIM	WARREN D. LEIGHT
ME, MYSELF AND I - S	JULIAN BARRY
ME, MYSELF AND I - S	GAIL FISHER
ME, MYSELF AND I - S	MARC CHESLER
ME, MYSELF AND I - S	MAX EISENBERG
ME, NATALIE	A. MARTIN ZWEIBACH
MEADOW, THE	PAOLO TAVIANI
MEADOW, THE	VITTORIO TAVIANI
MEAN DOG BLUES	GEORGE LEFFERTS
MEAN SEASON, THE	CHRISTOPHER CROWE
MEAN STREETS	MARDIK MARTIN
MEAN STREETS	MARTIN SCORCESE
MEANING OF LIFE, THE	ERIC IDLE
MEANING OF LIFE, THE	GRAHAM CHAPMAN†
MEANING OF LIFE, THE	JOHN CLEESE
MEANING OF LIFE, THE	TERRY GILLIAM
MEANING OF LIFE, THE	TERRY JONES
MEANING OF LIFE, THE	MICHAEL PALIN
MEANWHILE BACK AT THE KREMLIN - S	BIG BOY MEDLIN
MEANWHILE BACK AT THE KREMLIN - S	MICHAEL VENTURA
MEASURE OF DEVOTION - S	ANDY WOLK
MEASURING WALL, THE - S	JENNIFER COLLOPY
MEATBALLS	DAN GOLDBERG
MEATBALLS	HAROLD RAMIS
MEATBALLS	JANIS ALLEN
MEATBALLS	LEN BLUM
MEATBALLS PART II	BRUCE SINGER
MEATBALLS PART II	CAROL WATSON
MEATBALLS PART II	MARTIN KITROSSER
MEATBALLS III	MICHAEL PASEORNEK
MEATBALLS III	BRADLEY KESDEN
MEATBALLS III	CHUCK WORKMAN
MEATING VENUS - S	ISTVAN SZABO
MECHANIC, THE	LEWIS JOHN CARLINO
MEDAL OF HONOR RAG (P)	TOM COLE
MEDAL OF VALOR - S	CHUCK PFAFFER
MEDALLION - S	JOAN MICKLIN SILVER
MEDALLION - S	VICKI POLON
MEDICAL SCHOOL - S	BRIAN CLARK
MEDICINE WOMAN - S	MARSHA NORMAN
MEDIUM COOL	HASKELL WEXLER
MEDUSA TOUCH, THE	JOHN BRILEY
MEET DANNY WILSON	DON MCGUIRE
MEET ME AFTER THE SHOW	RICHARD SALE
MEET ME AT THE FAIR	IRVING WALLACE†
MEET MR. BRINK - S	REX MCGEE
MEET THE APPLEGATES	MICHAEL LEHMANN
MEET THE APPLEGATES	REDBEARD SIMMONS
MEET THE HOLLOWHEADS	LISA MORTON
MEET THE HOLLOWHEADS	TOM BURMAN
MEET THE MORON - S	LEON CAPETANOS
MEETING VENUS - S	MICHAEL HIRST
MEETING, THE (P)	JEFF STETSON
MEETINGS WITH REMARKABLE MEN	JEANNE SALZMANN
MEGAFORCE	ALBERT S. RUDDY
MEGAFORCE	ANDRE MORGAN
MEGAFORCE	HAL NEEDHAM
MEGAFORCE	JAMES WHITTAKER
MEGASCANNER - S	KEVIN ELDERS
MEGGIDO - S	DAVID SELTZER
MELMO MEETS ARLO - S	ABBE WOOL
MELODRAMA PLAY (P)	SAM SHEPARD
MELODY	ALAN PARKER
MELVIN AND HOWARD	BO GOLDMAN
MEMBER OF THE WEDDING, THE	EDWARD ANHALT
MEMED, MY HAWK	PETER USTINOV
MEMOIRS OF A MIDGET - S	JULIE HICKSON
MEMOIRS OF A SURVIVOR	KERRY CRABBE
MEMOIRS OF AN INVISIBLE MAN - S	DANA OLSEN
MEMOIRS OF AN INVISIBLE MAN - S	ROBERT COLLECTOR
MEMORIAL - S	FRED LEBOW
MEMORIES IN DRAG - S	ALEXANDER TANA
MEMORIES OF ME	BILLY CRYSTAL
MEMORIES OF ME	ERIC ROTH
MEMORIES OF MURDER (CTF)	NEVIN D. SCHREINER
MEMORIES OF MURDER (CTF)	JOHN KENT HARRISON
MEMORY BOY - S	ALAN ORMSBY
MEMORY OF TWO MONDAYS, A (P)	ARTHUR MILLER
MEMPHIS (CTF)	CYBILL SHEPHERD
MEMPHIS (CTF)	LARRY MCMURTRY
MEMPHIS BELLE	MONTE MERRICK
MEN	DORIS DORRIE
MEN (REMAKE) - S	ELAINE MAY
MEN AT WORK	EMILIO ESTEVEZ
MEN DON'T LEAVE	BARBARA BENEDEK
MEN DON'T LEAVE	PAUL BRICKMAN
MEN IN WAR	PHILIP YORDAN
MEN OF BRONZE - S	FRANK R. PIERSON
MEN OF RESPECT	WILLIAM REILLY
MEN OF THE DRAGON - S	DENNE BART PETITCLERC
MEN ON BASE - S	DANA OLSEN
MEN ON BASE - S	ROBERT COLLECTOR
MEN WHO DON'T QUIT - S	WILLIAM TEPPER
MEN WHO TREAD ON THE TIGER'S TAIL, THE	AKIRA KUROSAWA
MEN WITHOUT BASES - S	ROY G. TEICHER
MEN'S CLUB, THE	LEONARD MICHAELS
MENAGE	BERTRAND BLIER
MENTAL CASE, THE- S	ROGER L. SIMON
MENTION OF HER FORMER SELF, A - S	CLIFTON CAMPBELL
MEPHISTO	ISTVAN SZABO
MERCY GIRLS - S	ALAN BERGER
MERCY GIRLS - S	KATHY GORI
MERCY MAN - S	JULIAN BARRY
MERCY SPRINGS - S	JOHN KAYE
MERGERS AND ACQUISITIONS - S	CHARLES GALE
MERLYN - S	JAMES JEREMIAS
MERLYN - S	JANICE FISCHER
MERMAID - S	A.J. CAROTHERS
MERMAID - S	ROBERT TOWNE
MERMAIDS	JUNE ROBERTS
MERRILL'S MARAUDERS	SAMUEL FULLER
MERRY CHRISTMAS, MR. LAWRENCE	PAUL MAYERSBERG
MERRY WIVES OF BEVERLY HILLS, THE - S	SHEPARD GOLDMAN
MESMER (P)	JOEL GROSS
MESMERIZED	JERZY SKOLIMOWSKI
MESMERIZED	MICHAEL LAUGHLIN
MESSENGER OF DEATH	PAUL JARRICO
MESSIAH OF EVIL	GLORIA KATZ
MESSIAH OF EVIL	WILLARD HUYCK
METALSTORM: THE DESTRUCTION OF JARED-SYN	ALAN J. ADLER
METEOR	STANLEY MANN
METER MADNESS - S	ERIC SCHAEFFER
METROPOLITAN	WHIT STILLMAN
MEXICAN HAYRIDE	OSCAR BRODNEY
MEXICAN JAILBREAK - S	RUDOLPH G. WURLITZER
MIAMI BLUES	GEORGE ARMITAGE
MIAMI STORY - S	ANN BIDERMAN
MICHAEL BYE FALLDOWN - S	BOB DOLMAN
MICK - S	ROBERT DILLON
MICK, THE - S	JAMES D. BUCHANAN
MICK, THE - S	NICK W. THIEL
MICK'S PEOPLE (SHORT)	JONATHAN LYNN
MICKEY - S	TIMOTHY HARRIS
MICKEY - S	HERSCHEL WEINGROD
MICKI AND MAUDE	JONATHAN REYNOLDS
MIDAS RUN	JAMES DAVID BUCHANAN
MIDDLE AGE CRAZY	CARL KLEINSCHMIDT
MIDDLE AGES, THE (P)	A.R. GURNEY
MIDDLE OF THE NIGHT	PADDY CHAYEVSKY†
MIDDLE PEOPLE, THE - S	EBBE ROE SMITH
MIDNIGHT	NORMAN THADDEUS VANE
MIDNIGHT	BILLY WILDER
MIDNIGHT BLUE - S	TONY KAYDEN
MIDNIGHT CLEAR, A - S	KEITH GORDON
MIDNIGHT CLEAR, A - S	PATRICK DUNCAN
MIDNIGHT CLUB - S	JEB STUART
MIDNIGHT CLUB, THE - S	JOHN M. HERZFELD
MIDNIGHT COWBOY	WALDO SALT†
MIDNIGHT CROSSING	DOUG WEISER
MIDNIGHT CROSSING	ROGER HOLZBERG
MIDNIGHT EXPRESS	OLIVER STONE
MIDNIGHT FLYER - S	ELIZABETH BRADLEY
MIDNIGHT FLYER - S	STEPHEN MCPHERSON
MIDNIGHT LACE	IVAN GOFF
MIDNIGHT MADNESS	DAVID WECHTER
MIDNIGHT MADNESS	MICHAEL NANKIN
MIDNIGHT MAN, THE	ROLAND KIBBEE†
MIDNIGHT RUN	GEORGE GALLO
MIDNIGHT SOLDIER - S	CAROL MONPERE
MIDNIGHT SUN - S	JAMES D. BUCHANAN
MIDSUMMER MOON - S	KEVIN QUINN
MIDSUMMER NIGHT'S SEX COMEDY, A	WOODY ALLEN
MIDWAY	DONALD S. SANFORD
MIDWICH CUCKOOS, THE- S	CHRISTOPHER WOOD
MIGHTY GENTS, THE (P)	RICHARD WESLEY
MIGHTY JACKS - S	DARIUS JAMES
MIGHTY MOUSE - S	ROBERT KAUFMAN
MIGHTY QUINN, THE	HAMPTON FANCHER
MIGHTY, MIGHTY - S	LESLIE BOHEM
MIKE'S MURDER	JAMES BRIDGES
MIKEY AND NICKY	ELAINE MAY
MILAGRO BEANFIELD WAR, THE	JOHN NICHOLS
MILAGRO BEANFIELD WAR, THE	DAVID S. WARD
MILE HIGH - S	LORENZO SEMPLE
MILE STRAIGHT DOWN - S	JULIA CAMERON
MILER, THE	ROBBY BENSON
MILES FROM HOME	CHRIS GEROLMO
MILITARY MAN - S	ROBERT LENSKI
MILKMAN, THE	LEONARD B. STERN
MILKRUN, THE - S	LAWRENCE HAUBEN
MILKY WAY, THE	JEAN-CLAUDE CARRIERE
MILLENNIUM	JOHN VARLEY
MILLER'S CROSSING	ETHAN COEN
MILLER'S CROSSING	JOEL COEN
MILLION DOLLAR MYSTERY	MIGUEL TEJADA-FLORES
MILLION DOLLAR MYSTERY	RUDY DELUCA
MILLION DOLLAR MYSTERY	TIM METCALFE
MILLION DOLLAR TOWN - S	JAIME B. KLEIN
MILLIONAIRESS, THE	WOLF MANKOWITZ
MILO RIGBY ON WHEELS - S	ALEX WINTER
MILO RIGBY ON WHEELS - S	TOM STERN
MILWAUKEE CONFIDENTIAL - S	JACK EPPS JR.
MILWAUKEE CONFIDENTIAL - S	JIM CASH
MILWAUKEE CONFIDENTIAL - S	MARK STEIN
MIMI METALLURGICO FERITO NELL O'NORE	LINA WERTMULLER
MIND GAME	LOU DIAMOND PHILLIPS
MIND YOUR OWN BUSINESS - S	MICHAEL SERAFIN
MINDREADER - S	JOHN ESKOW
MINDWALK	FLOYD BYARS
MINDWALK	BERNT CAPRA
MINISTRY OF VENGEANCE	ANN NARUS
MINISTRY OF VENGEANCE	BRIAN D. JEFFIRES

Title	Writer
MINISTRY OF VENGEANCE	MERVYN EMRYS
MINNIE & MOSKOWITZ	JOHN CASSAVETES†
MIRACLE AT MOOSEHEAD - S	ANDREW C.J. BERGMAN
MIRACLE IN MILAN	CESARE ZAVATTINI†
MIRACLE MILE	STEVE DEJARNATT
MIRACLE OF THE WHITE STALLIONS, THE	A.J. CAROTHERS
MIRACLE ON 34TH STREET - S	NEIL CUTHBERT
MIRACLE, THE	NEIL JORDAN
MIRACLES	JIM KOUF
MIRAGE	PETER STONE
MIRROR CRACK'D, THE	JONATHAN HALES
MIRROR CRACK'D, THE	BARRY SANDLER
MIRROR HAS TWO FACES, A - S	RICHARD LAGRAVENESE
MIRROR IMAGE - S	STEPHEN VOLK
MISADVENTURES OF MR. WILT, THE	ANDREW MARSHALL
MISADVENTURES OF MR. WILT, THE	DAVID RENWICK
MISCHIEF	NOEL BLACK
MISERY	WILLIAM GOLDMAN
MISFITS, THE	ARTHUR MILLER
MISHIMA	PAUL SCHRADER
MISHIMA: A LIFE IN FOUR CHAPTERS	LEONARD SCHRADER
MISPLACED	LOUIS YANSEN
MISPLACED	THOMAS DEWOLFE
MISS FIRECRACKER	BETH HENLEY
MISS LONDON LTD.	VAL GUEST
MISS MARLOW - S	ALI MATHESON
MISS MARLOW - S	JON COOKSEY
MISS MARY	MARIA LUISA BEMBERG
MISS MOTHERWELL - S	PETER SEAMAN
MISS ONE THOUSAND SPRING BLOSSOMS - S	MARK MEDOFF
MISS PILGRIM'S PROGRESS	VAL GUEST
MISS SHERRI - S	WILLIAM NICHOLSON
MISSING	COSTA-GAVRAS
MISSING	DONALD L. STEWART
MISSING IN ACTION	JAMES BRUNER
MISSING IN ACTION	JOHN CROWTHER
MISSING IN ACTION 2	ARTHUR SILVER
MISSING IN ACTION 2	LARRY LEVINSON
MISSING IN ACTION 2	STEVE BING
MISSING LINK	CAROL HUGHES
MISSING LINK	DAVID HUGHES
MISSING LINKS - S	JANICE FISCHER
MISSING PARENTS (SHORT)	NEVIN SCHREINER
MISSING PERSON - S	LEON CAPETANOS
MISSING PIECES	LEONARD B. STERN
MISSING WIVES - S	PAUL B. MARGOLIS
MISSION, THE	ROBERT BOLT
MISSIONARY, THE	MICHAEL PALIN
MISSISSIPPI BURNING	CHRIS GEROLMO
MISSISSIPPI MERMAID, THE	FRANCOIS TRUFFAUT†
MISSOURI BREAKS, THE	THOMAS MCGUANE
MISTAKEN IDENTITY - S	JEAN-YVES PITOUN
MISTER CORY	BLAKE EDWARDS
MISTER DRAKE'S DUCK	VAL GUEST
MISTER GOD, THIS IS ANNA - S	JOHN BRILEY
MISTER JOHNSON	WILLIAM BOYD
MISTER MAGOO - S	SARAH C. PALEY
MISTRESS	BARRY PRIMUS
MISTRESS	J.F. LAWTON
MISTRESS OF MONTICELLO - S	TINA ANDREWS
MISTY BLUE RIVER - S	BRUCE KIRSCHBAUM
MISUNDERSTOOD	BARRA GRANT
MITTY - S	ERIC BOGOSIAN
MIXED BLOOD	PAUL MORRISSEY
MIXED COMPANY	JOSEPH BOLOGNA
MIXED COMPANY	RENEE TAYLOR
MIXED COMPANY	MEL SHAVELSON
MIXED FEELINGS - S	HARRIET FRANK JR.
MIXED FEELINGS - S	IRVING RAVETCH
MIZLANSKY/ZILANSKY (P)	JON ROBIN BAITZ
MO' BETTER BLUES	SPIKE LEE
MO 'M ONEY - S	DAMON WAYANS
MOB BOSS	T.L. LANKFORD
MOBSTERS	MIKE MAHERN
MOBSTERS	NICHOLAS KAZAN
MOBY DICK	RAY BRADBURY
MODEL COP - S	ALLEN ESTRIN
MODEL COP - S	BILLY RAY
MODEL SHOP	JACQUES DEMY†
MODEL SHOP, THE	CAROLE EASTMAN
MODERN BRIDE - S	ALICE ARLEN
MODERN BRIDE - S	JOAN TAYLOR
MODERN BRIDE - S	NORA EPHRON
MODERN DOLLS - S	MOLLIE D. MILLER
MODERN GIRLS	LAURIE CRAIG
MODERN GIRLS	ANITA ROSENBERG
MODERN LADIES OF GUANABACOA (P)	EDUARDO MACHADO
MODERN LOVE	ROBBY BENSON
MODERN PROBLEMS	ARTHUR D. SELLERS
MODERN PROBLEMS	KEN SHAPIRO
MODERN PROBLEMS	TOM SHEROHMAN
MODERN ROMANCE	ALBERT BROOKS
MODERN ROMANCE	MONICA JOHNSON
MODERNS, THE	ALAN RUDOLPH
MODERNS, THE	JON BRANDSHAW†
MODESTY BLAISE	EVAN JONES
MODIGLIANI (P)	DENNIS MCINTYRE†
MODIGLIANI (P)	MICHAEL CRISTOFER
MOE BURG STORY, THE - S	MAURICE E. HURLEY
MOE'S WORLD - S	JAMES P. DUNNE
MOJAVE (P)	BRADLEY RAND SMITH
MOLLY - S	DON CIRILLO
MOLLY MAGUIRES, THE	WALTER BERNSTEIN
MOM - S	VICKI POLON
MOMENT BY MOMENT	JANE WAGNER
MOMMA KNOWS BEST - S	TONY KENRICK
MOMMA'S BOY - S	ROBERT GUNTER
MOMMIE DEAREST	FRANK PERRY
MOMMIE DEAREST	FRANK YABLANS
MOMMIE DEAREST	ROBERT GETCHELL
MOMMIE DEAREST	TRACY HOTCHNER
MOMMY DON'T - S	RICHARD DEWHURST
MON ONCLE D'AMERIQUE	JEAN GRUAULT
MONA LISA	DAVID LELAND
MONA LISA	NEIL JORDAN
MONARCHS OF MANHATTAN, THE - S	TINO INSANA
MONDO TRASHO	JOHN WATERS
MONEY	ROBERT BRESSON
MONEY - S	ANDY BRECKMAN
MONEY FROM THE SKY - S	PETER KRIKES
MONEY FROM THE SKY - S	STEVE MEERSON
MONEY HONEY - S	JOAN TAYLOR
MONEY MOVERS	BRUCE BERESFORD
MONEY PIT, THE	DAVID GILER
MONEY RIVER - S	MICHAEL ERIC STEIN
MONEY TALKS - S	WILLIAM TEPPER
MONEY TO BURN - S	CHARLES ROBERT CARNER
MONEY TRAIN, THE - S	BILL MASTERS
MONEY TRAP, THE	WALTER BERNSTEIN
MONEY, THE	CHUCK WORKMAN
MONIKA	INGMAR BERGMAN
MONIMBO	RENE BALCER
MONKEY GRIP	HELEN GARNER
MONKEY GRIP	KEN CAMERON
MONKEY HUSTLE, THE	CHARLES JOHNSON
MONKEY KING - S	BILL LANCASTER
MONKEY SHINES	GEORGE A. ROMERO
MONKEY WRENCH GANG, THE - S	JACK BEHR
MONKEY WRENCH GANG, THE - S	SANDY KROOPF
MONKEYS - S	BO GOLDMAN
MONOPOLY THE MOVIE - S	BRUCE VILANCH
MONSIEUR BEAUCAIRE	NORMAN PANAMA
MONSIGNOR	ABRAHAM POLONSKY
MONSIGNOR	WENDELL MAYES
MONSOON - S	TOM BENEDEK
MONSTER IN THE CLOSET	BOB DAHLIN
MONSTER NIGHT - S	DENNIS FELDMAN
MONSTER SQUAD, THE	FRED DEKKER
MONSTER SQUAD, THE	SHANE BLACK
MONTANA (CTF)	LARRY MCMURTRY
MONTE CARLO COPS - S	TIM MCCANLIES
MONTE WALSH	DAVID Z. GOODMAN
MONTE WALSH	LUKAS HELLER†
MONTENEGRO	DUSAN MAKAVEJEC
MONTH IN THE COUNTRY, A	SIMON GRAY
MONTREAUX - S	BIG BOY MEDLIN
MONTY PYTHON AND THE HOLY GRAIL	ERIC IDLE
MONTY PYTHON AND THE HOLY GRAIL	GRAHAM CHAPMAN†
MONTY PYTHON AND THE HOLY GRAIL	JOHN CLEESE
MONTY PYTHON AND THE HOLY GRAIL	MICHAEL PALIN
MONTY PYTHON AND THE HOLYGRAIL	TERRY GILLIAM
MONTY PYTHON AND THE HOLYGRAIL	TERRY JONES
MONTY PYTHON LIVE AT THE HOLLYWOOD BOWL	ERIC IDLE
MONTY PYTHON LIVE AT THE HOLLYWOOD BOWL	GRAHAM CHAPMAN†
MONTY PYTHON LIVE AT THE HOLLYWOOD BOWL	JOHN CLEESE
MONTY PYTHON LIVE AT THE HOLLYWOOD BOWL	MICHAEL PALIN
MONTY PYTHON LIVE AT THE HOLLYWOOD BOWL	TERRY GILLIAM
MONTY PYTHON LIVE AT THE HOLLYWOOD BOWL	TERRY JONES
MONTY PYTHON'S LIFE OF BRIAN	ERIC IDLE
MONTY PYTHON'S LIFE OF BRIAN	GRAHAM CHAPMAN†
MONTY PYTHON'S LIFE OF BRIAN	JOHN CLEESE
MONTY PYTHON'S LIFE OF BRIAN	MICHAEL PALIN
MONTY PYTHON'S LIFE OF BRIAN	TERRY GILLIAM
MONTY PYTHON'S LIFE OF BRIAN	TERRY JONES
MONTY PYTHON'S THE MEANING OF LIFE	ERIC IDLE
MONTY PYTHON'S THE MEANING OF LIFE	GRAHAM CHAPMAN†
MONTY PYTHON'S THE MEANING OF LIFE	JOHN CLEESE
MONTY PYTHON'S THE MEANING OF LIFE	MICHAEL PALIN
MONTY PYTHON'S THE MEANING OF LIFE	TERRY GILLIAM
MONTY PYTHON'S THE MEANING OF LIFE	TERRY JONES
MOON & SIXPENCE, THE - S	CHRISTOPHER HAMPTON
MOON AND SIXPENCE, THE	ALBERT E. LEWIN†
MOON IN THE GUTTER, THE	JEAN-JACQUES BEINEIX
MOON OVER MIAMI - S	MITCH GLAZER
MOON OVER MIAMI (P)	JOHN GUARE
MOON OVER PARADOR	LEON CAPETANOS
MOON OVER PARADOR	PAUL MAZURKSY
MOONCHASER - S	CHRISTOPHER SHARP
MOONCHILDREN (P)	MICHAEL WELLER
MOONLIGHTING	JERZY SKOLIMOWSKI
MOONRAKER	CHRISTOPHER WOOD
MOONSHINE COUNTYEXPRESS	HUBERT SMITH
MOONSHINE WAR, THE	ELMORE LEONARD
MOONSTRUCK	JOHN PATRICK SHANLEY
MOONTRAP	TEX RAGSDALE
MOONTRAP - S	BILL KERBY
MOOSH - S	WALTER NEWMAN
MORE AMERICAN GRAFFITI	B.W.L. NORTON, JR.
MORE DEAD THAN ALIVE	GEORGE W. SCHENCK
MORGAN - S	LESLIE A. RAY
MORGAN - S	MICHAEL TAAV
MORGAN STEWART'S COMING HOME	DAVID N. TITCHER
MORGAN STEWART'S COMING HOME	KEN HIXON
MORGAN'S CAKE	RICK SCHMIDT
MORNING (P)	ISRAEL HOROVITZ
MORNING, WINTER AND NIGHT - S	HESPER ANDERSON
MOROCCAN HAZE - S	MICHAEL ERIC STEIN
MORONS FROM OUTER SPACE	GRIFF RHYS-JONES
MORONS FROM OUTER SPACE	MEL SMITH
MORT - S	IAN SEEBERG
MORT - S	VALERIE BENNETT
MORTAL PASSIONS	ALAN MOSKOWITZ
MORTAL THOUGHTS	CLAUDE KERVEN
MORTAL THOUGHTS	WILLIAM REILLY
MORTUARY	HIKMET AVEDIS
MORTUARY	MARLENE SCHMIDT
MOSCOW EXCHANGE - S	ANTON DIETHER
MOSCOW ON THE HUDSON	LEON CAPETANOS
MOSCOW ON THE HUDSON	PAUL MAZURKSY
MOSES	ANTHONY BURGESS
MOSES WINE - S	ROGER L. SIMON
MOSQUITO COAST	PAUL SCHRADER
MOSQUITO SQUADRON	DONALD S. SANFORD
MOST BEAUTIFUL, THE	AKIRA KUROSAWA
MOST ELIGIBLE MAN IN NEW YORK, THE - S	SUSAN NANUS
MOST LIKELY TO SUCCEED - S	DENNIS O'FLAHERTY
MOST WANTED - S	RICHARD A. GUTTMAN
MOST WANTED - S	HARIS ORKIN
MOST WANTED MAN - S	DON MCLENNAN
MOSTERS	NICHOLAS KAZAN
MOT - S	JIMMY HUSTON
MOTEL HELL	ROBERT JAFFE
MOTEL HELL	STEVEN-CHARLES JAFFE

Title	Writer
MOTHER LODE	FRASER CLARKE HESTON
MOTHER AND TWO DAUGHTERS - S	LAWRENCE D. COHEN
MOTHER NATURE'S DAUGHTER - S	ALAN MANDEL
MOTHER'S & SON - S	VALERIE WEST
MOTHER'S DAY	CHARLES KAUFMAN
MOTHER'S DAY	WARREN D. LEIGHT
MOTHER, JUGS & SPEED	TOM MANKIEWICZ
MOTHERLOAD - S	NANCY LARSON
MOTLEY'S CREW - S	TINO INSANA
MOTOR PSYCHO	RUSS MEYER
MOTORAMA - S	JOSEPH MINION
MOTORCADE (P)	BILL CORBETT
MOTORHEADS VS. SPORTOS - S	JOHN HUGHES
MOUNTAIN CHARLY - S	VICKI POLON
MOUNTAIN LANGUAGE (P)	HAROLD PINTER
MOUNTAIN MEN, THE	FRASER CLARKE HESTON
MOUNTAINS OF THE MOON	BOB RAFELSON
MOUNTAINS OF THE MOON	WILLIAM HARRISON
MOUNTAINTOP MOTEL MASSACRE	JIM McCULLOUGH JR.
MOUSE AND HIS CHILD, THE (AF)	CAROL MONPERE
MOUSE PACKS - S	DIANA HAMMOND
MOUSE THAT ROARED, THE	STANLEY MANN
MOUTH TO MOUTH	JOHN DUIGAN
MOVE OVER DARLING	HAL KANTER
MOVERS AND SHAKERS	CHARLES GRODIN
MOVES MAKE THE MAN, THE - S	BLAIR FERGUSON
MOVIE MADNESS	TOD CARROLL
MOVIE MADNESS	ELLIS WEINER
MOVIE MADNESS	GERALD SUSSMAN
MOVIE MADNESS	PAT MEPHITIS
MOVIE MADNESS	SHARY FLENNIKEN
MOVIE STAR AMERICAN STYLE	ALBERT ZUGSMITH
MOVIE, MOVIE	LARRY GELBART
MOVIE, MOVIE II - S	LARRY GELBART
MOVIEGOER, THE - S	JIM McBRIDE
MOVIEGOER, THE - S	L.M. KIT CARSON
MOVIEGOER, THE - S	WILLIAM GOODHART
MOVING	ANDY BRECKMAN
MOVING OUT	JAN SARDI
MOVING TARGET - S	PAUL ATTANSIO
MOVING VIOLATION	WILLIAM NORTON SR.
MOVING VIOLATIONS	NEAL ISRAEL
MOVING VIOLATIONS	PAT PROFT
MOVING VIOLATIONS	PAUL BOORSTIN
MOVING VIOLATIONS	SHARON BOORSTIN
MOVING VIOLATIONS	DAVID TAYLOR
MR. ADVENTURE - S	DAVID BIRKE
MR. AMBASSADOR - S	TOM GRIFFIN
MR. AND MRS. BRIDGE	RUTH PRAWER JHABVALA
MR. BAD NEWS- S	NEIL SIMON
MR. BELVEDERE GOES TO COLLEGE	RICHARD SALE
MR. BILLION	JONATHAN KAPLAN
MR. BILLION	KEN FRIEDMAN
MR. BLANDINGS BUILDS HIS DREAM HOUSE	NORMAN PANAMA
MR. DARLING - S	MARGARET GREICO OBERMAN
MR. DARLING - S	ROSIE SHUSTER
MR. DESTINY	JIM CRUICKSHANK
MR. DESTINY	JAMES ORR
MR. FIX-IT - S	PHIL HARTMAN
MR. FORBUSH AND THE PENGUINS	ANTHONY SHAFFER
MR. FROST	BRAD LYNCH
MR. FROST	PHILIPPE SETBON
MR. GOGOL AND MR. PREEN (P)	ELAINE MAY
MR. HAPPINESS (P)	DAVID MAMET
MR. HAPPY - S	PETER HANKOFF
MR. HORN - S	WILLIAM GOLDMAN
MR. JELLY LORD (P)	GEORGE C. WOLFE
MR. JONES - S	ERIC ROTH
MR. KLEIN	FRANCO SOLINAS
MR. LOVE	KENNETH EASTAUGH
MR. MAJESTYK	ELMORE LEONARD
MR. MAUI - S	HENRY ROSENBAUM
MR. MAYOR - S	JACK EPPS JR.
MR. MAYOR - S	JIM CASH
MR. MIKE'S MONDO VIDEO	MICHAEL O'DONOGHUE
MR. MIKE'S MONDO VIDEO	MITCH GLAZER
MR. MOM	JOHN HUGHES
MR. MOTO - S	REED STEINER
MR. NICE GUY - S	JAIME B. KLEIN
MR. NORTH	JAMES COSTIGAN
MR. NORTH	JANET ROACH
MR. NORTH	JOHN HUSTON†
MR. PATMAN	THOMAS HEDLEY JR.
MR. POTTS GOES TO MOSCOW	JACK DAVIES
MR. RIGHT - S	DORIS BAIZLEY
MR. SATURDAY NIGHT - S	BABALOO MANDEL
MR. SATURDAY NIGHT - S	LOWELL GANZ
MR. SMITH GOES TO HELL - S	TODD DURHAM
MR. TWISTER - S	NEIL RUTTENBERG
MR. VICE PRESIDENT - S	STEVEN R. ZACHARIAS
MR. VICE PRESIDENT - S	JEFF BUHAI
MR. WHISTLE - S	JEFFREY PRICE
MR. WHISTLE - S	PETER SEAMAN
MR. WONDERFUL - S	AMY SCHOR
MR. WONDERFUL - S	VICKI POLON
MR. WONDERFUL - S	IAN ABRAMS
MR. WRONG	GAYLENE PRESTON
MR. WRONG - S	JEFF ROTHBERG
MRS. & MR. KELLY - S	HOWARD KORDER
MRS. CALIBAN - S	HAMPTON FANCHER
MRS. CALIBAN - S	JULE SELBO
MRS. CALIFORNIA (P)	DORIS BAIZLEY
MRS. CALIFORNIA - S	JOSAN McGIBBON
MRS. CALIFORNIA - S	SARA PARRIOTT
MRS. DUKE'S MILLIONS - S	JOSEPH MINION
MRS. FAUST - S	BOB TZUDIKER
MRS. FAUST - S	NONI WHITE
MRS. MERLIN - S	JOHN HILL
MRS. MOTHERWELL - S	JEFFREY PRICE
MRS. REDDEN- S	DONALD L. STEWART
MRS. SKEFFINGTON	JULIUS J. EPSTEIN
MRS. SOFFEL	RON NYSWANER
MRS., THE	MARY AGNES DONAGHUE
MS. 45	NICHOLAS ST. JOHN
MUD SWEAT AND GEARS - S	BLAIR FERGUSON
MULTIPLE CHOICES - S	DAVID HURWITZ
MULTIPLE CHOICES - S	LARRY ARNSTEIN
MUM'S THE WORD - S	ERIC HANSEN
MUM'S THE WORD - S	GREGORY HANSEN
MUMMIES- S	MICHAEL McDOWELL
MUMMY AND THE ARMADILLO, THE - S	J.S. CARDONE
MUMMY OF BEVERLY HILLS - S	A. MARTIN ZWEIBACH
MUMMY, THE	JIMMY SANGSTER
MUMMY, THE - S	MICHAEL J. MURRAY
MUNCHIES	LANCE SMITH
MUNCHIES II - S	JIM WYNORSKI
MUNCHIES II - S	R.J. ROBERTSON
MUPPET MOVIE, THE	JACK BURNS
MUPPET MOVIE, THE	JERRY JUHL
MUPPETS TAKE MANHATTAN, THE	FRANK OZ
MUPPETS TAKE MANHATTAN, THE	JAY TARSES
MUPPETS TAKE MANHATTAN, THE	TOM PATCHETT
MURDER 101 (CTF)	ROY JOHANSEN
MURDER 101 (CTF)	WILLIAM CONDON
MURDER AHOY	DAVID PURSALL
MURDER AT PREP SCHOOL- S	NORMAN STEINBERG
MURDER AT THE HOWARD JOHNSON'S (P)	RON CLARK
MURDER AT THE HOWARD JOHNSON'S (P)	SAM BOBRICK
MURDER AT THE MOVIES - S	ERIC ROTH
MURDER AT THE WINDMIL	VAL GUEST
MURDER BY DEATH	NEIL SIMON
MURDER BY DECREE	JOHN HOPKINS
MURDER BY NUMBERS	PAUL LEDER
MURDER BY PHONE	DENNIS SHRYACK
MURDER BY PHONE	JOHN KENT HARRISON
MURDER BY PHONE	MICHAEL BUTLER
MURDER BY THE BOOK (CTF)	NICK EVANS
MURDER IN THE DESERT (P)	THOMAS BABE
MURDER IN THE FIRST - S	DAN GORDON
MURDER IN THE FIRST - S	MICHAEL SCHIFFER
MURDER LEAGUE, THE - S	ALLAN G. SCOTT
MURDER LEAGUE, THE - S	CHRIS BRYANT
MURDER MOST FOUL	DAVID PURSALL
MURDER OF MIDNIGHT - S	ROBERT CARNEY
MURDER OF NAPOLEON - S	DERIC WASHBURN
MURDER ON LINE ONE	ANDERS PALM
MURDER ON THE BRIDGE - S	BO GOLDMAN
MURDER SHE SAID	DAVID PURSALL
MURDER STORY	EDDIE ARNO
MURDER STORY	MARKUS INNOCENTI
MURDERER'S ROW	HERBERT BAKER†
MURDERERS AMONG US: THE SIMON WIESENTHAL STORY (CTF)	ABBY MANN
MURDEROUS VISION (CTF)	PAUL JOSEPH GULINO
MURMUR OF THE HEART	LOUIS MALLE
MURPHY'S LAW	GAIL MORGAN HICKMAN
MURPHY'S LAW - S	ELLIOT M. STERN
MURPHY'S LAW OF GOLF - S	DAVID WECHTER
MURPHY'S ROMANCE	HARRIET FRANK JR.
MURPHY'S ROMANCE	IRVING RAVETCH
MURPHY'S WAR	STIRLING SILLIPHANT
MURROW (CTF)	ERNEST KINOY
MURS MURS (FD)	AGNES VARDA
MUSCLE BEACH PARTY	ROBERT DILLON
MUSCLE CARS - S	JOHN HUGHES
MUSHROOM - S	SCOTT PARKER
MUSHROOM BUTTON - S	ANDREW MARSHALL
MUSHROOM BUTTON - S	DAVID RENWICK
MUSIC BOX	JOE ESZTERHAS
MUSIC CITY BLUES - S	JAMES WHITTAKER
MUSIC HALL - S	DARRIN OURA
MUSIC IN THE AIR	BILLY WILDER
MUSIC LOVERS, THE	MELVYN BRAGG
MUSIC ROOM, THE - S	RICHARD FRIEDENBERG
MUSICAL CHAIRS - S	LESLIE BRICUSSE
MUSTANG - S	MICHAEL BLAKE
MUSTANG COUNTRY	JOHN CHAMPION
MUSTANGS (P)	TUDY WOOLFE
MUTANT HUNT	TIM KINCAID
MUTANT ON THE BOUNTY	MARTIN LOPEZ
MUTANT ON THE BOUNTY	ROBERT TORRANCE
MUTATION - S	LORENZO SEMPLE
MUTATION - S	JIM WHEAT
MUTATION - S	KEN WHEAT
MUTINY	PHILIP YORDAN
MY AMERICAN COUSIN	SANDY WILSON
MY AMERICAN FORTUNE - S	JILLIAN PALETHORPE
MY AMERICAN FORTUNE - S	SPARKY GREENE
MY BEAUTIFUL LAUNDRETTE	HANIF KUREISHI
MY BEST FRIEND IS A VAMPIRE	TAB MURPHY
MY BEST FRIEND'S GIRL	BERTRAND BLIER
MY BEST FRIEND'S GIRL	GERARD BRACH
MY BLOODY VALENTINE	JOHN BEAIRD
MY BLUE HEAVEN	NORA EPHRON
MY BLUE LADY - S	WILLIAM DREW WEINBRENNER
MY BODYGUARD	ALAN ORMSBY
MY BRILLIANT CAREER	ELEANOR WITCOMBE
MY BROTHER'S WEDDING	CHARLES BURNETT
MY CHAUFFEUR	DAVID BEAIRD
MY CHILDREN! MY AFRICA! (P)	ATHOL FUGARD
MY COUSIN VINNIE - S	DALE LAUNER
MY CRUMMY JOB (P)	JOHN STEPPLING
MY DEMON LOVER	LESLIE RAY
MY DINNER WITH ANDRE	ANDRE GREGORY
MY DINNER WITH ANDRE	WALLACE SHAWN
MY FAMILY - S	ALAN SHAPIRO
MY FAT FRIEND - S	BRUCE VILANCH
MY FAVORITE LIFE - S	LAWRENCE GAY
MY FAVORITE LIFE - S	MICHAEL DIGAETANO
MY FAVORITE YEAR	DENNIS PALUMBO
MY FAVORITE YEAR	NORMAN STEINBERG
MY FELLOW AMERICANS - S	JACK KAPLAN
MY FELLOW AMERICANS - S	RICHARD CHAPMAN
MY FIRST HAIRCUT (SHORT)	ALEX ZAMM
MY FIRST LADY - S	HORTON FOOTE
MY FIRST WIFE	BOB ELLIS
MY FIRST WIFE	PAUL COX
MY FOOLISH HEART	JULIUS J. EPSTEIN
MY GENERATION - S	NICK CASTLE
MY GIRL	LAURICE ELEHWANY
MY GIRLFRIEND'S BOYFRIEND - S	ROSIE SHUSTER
MY GIRLFRIEND'S WEDDING	JIM McBRIDE
MY GOD THEY'VE GOT BOSCO - S	TOD CARROLL
MY HEROS HAVE ALWAYS BEEN COWBOYS	JOEL DON HUMPHREYS
MY ILLEGAL ALIEN - S	CHARLES F. BOHL
MY KNIGHT IN SHINING ARMOR - S	WILLIAM TONNER
MY LEFT FOOT	JIM SHERIDAN
MY LEFT FOOT	SHANE CONNAUGHTON
MY LIFE AS A DOG	LASSE HALLSTROM
MY LITTLE GIRL	CONNIE KAISERMAN
MY LITTLE GIRL	NAN MASON
MY LITTLE PONY (AF)	GEORGE ARTHUR BLOOM
MY MAN ADAM	ROGER L. SIMON
MY MAN ADAM	RENEE MISSEL
MY MOM'S A WEREWOLF	MARK PIRRO
MY MOTHER CAN FLY - S	EDDIE GORODETSKY
MY MOTHER WEARS ARMY BOOTS - S	JIM LINDSAY
MY MOTHER WEARS ARMY BOOTS - S	RICK WAY
MY NEW PARTNER - S	VINCENT PATRICK
MY NIGHT AT MAUD'S	ERIC ROHMER
MY ONE AND ONLY (P)	PETER STONE
MY OWN PRIVATE IDAHO - S	GUS VAN SANT

My-Ni
FILM WRITERS GUIDE

MY PAL GUS ... FAY KANIN
MY PAL GUS ... MICHAEL KANIN
MY SCIENCE PROJECT ... JONATHAN BETUEL
MY SECRET IDENTITY - S ... ELLIOT M. STERN
MY SENIOR YEAR - S ... DEBORAH AMELON
MY SHADOW - S ... MARSHA NORMAN
MY SILENT PARTNER - S ... KEN HIXON
MY SISTER EILEEN ... BLAKE EDWARDS
MY SON'S BROTHER - S ... NEIL SIMON
MY SOUL TO KEEP - S ... BRIAN STRASMAN
MY STEPMOTHER IS AN ALIEN ... JERICHO STONE
MY STEPMOTHER IS AN ALIEN ... JONATHAN REYNOLDS
MY STEPMOTHER IS AN ALIEN ... TIMOTHY HARRIS
MY STEPMOTHER IS AN ALIEN ... HERSCHEL WEINGROD
MY SUMMER WITH MOM - S ... NORMAN STEINBERG
MY TUTOR ... JOE ROBERTS
MY TWO HUSBANDS - S ... MARTHA GOLDHIRSH
MY WAY OR THE HIGHWAY - S ... JULIETTE YAEGER
MYRA BRECKINRIDGE ... DAVID GILER
MYSTERIOUS MONSTERS, THE (FD) ... ROBERT GUENETTE
MYSTERY OF ALEXINA, THE ... JEAN GRUAULT
MYSTERY OF THE ROSE BOUQUET, THE (P) ... MANUEL PUIG†
MYSTERY STREET ... RICHARD BROOKS
MYSTERY TRAIN ... JIM JARMUSCH
MYSTIC PIZZA ... ALFRED UHRY
MYSTIC PIZZA ... AMY JONES
MYSTIC PIZZA ... PERRY HOWZE
MYSTIC PIZZA ... RANDY HOWZE
MYSTIQUE ... STEPHEN F. BELLO

N

NADINE ... ROBERT BENTON
NAKED ALIBI ... LARRY ROMAN
NAKED CAGE, THE ... PAUL NICHOLAS
NAKED CHAMBERS (P) ... DICK BEEBE
NAKED CITY, THE ... MELVIN VALD
NAKED EDGE, THE ... JOSEPH STEFANO
NAKED FACE, THE ... BRYAN FORBES
NAKED GUN, THE ... DAVID ZUCKER
NAKED GUN, THE ... JERRY ZUCKER
NAKED GUN, THE ... JIM ABRAHAMS
NAKED GUN, THE ... PAT PROFT
NAKED GUN 2 1/2 ... DAVID ZUCKER
NAKED GUN 2 1/2 ... PAT PROFT
NAKED JUNGLE, THE ... PHILIP YORDAN
NAKED KNIGHT, THE ... INGMAR BERGMAN
NAKED LUNCH ... DAVID CRONENBERG
NAKED MAJA, THE ... ALBERT E. LEWIN†
NAKED MAJA, THE ... OSCAR SAUL
NAKED OBSESSION ... DAN GOLDEN
NAKED OBSESSION ... ROBERT DODSON
NAKED REVERSE - S ... PAUL BOORSTIN
NAKED REVERSE - S ... SHARON BOORSTIN
NAKED RUNNER, THE ... STANLEY MANN
NAKED TANGO ... LEONARD SCHRADER
NAKED UNDER CAPRICORN - S ... EVERETT DEROCHE
NAME OF THE ROSE, THE ... ANDREW BIRKIN
NAME OF THE ROSE, THE ... GERARD BRACH
NAME OF THE ROSE, THE ... HOWARD FRANKLIN
NANA ... MARC BEHM
NANCY GOES TO RIO ... SIDNEY SHELDON
NANCY NEWTON, R.N. - S ... DEBRA FRANKEL
NANETTE OF THE NORTH - S ... ROBERT KEATS
NANNY, THE ... JIMMY SANGSTER
NANNY, THE - S ... JOHN HUGHES
NAPOLEAN OF CRIME, THE - S ... CHARLES EDWARD POGUE
NAPOLEON AND SAMANTHA ... STEWART RAFFILL
NARC - S ... JOE ESZTERHAS
NARROW MARGIN ... PETER HYAMS
NASHVILLE ... JOAN TEWKESBURY
NASTY GIRL, THE ... MICHAEL VERHOEVEN
NASTY HABITS ... ROBERT ENDERS
NATE AND HAYES ... DAVID ODELL
NATE AND HAYES ... JOHN HUGHES
NATIONAL ANTHEMS (P) ... DENNIS MCINTYRE†
NATIONAL HEALTH, THE ... PETER NICHOLS
NATIONAL LAMPOON'S ANIMAL HOUSE ... CHRIS MILLER
NATIONAL LAMPOON'S ANIMAL HOUSE ... DOUGLAS KENNEY†
NATIONAL LAMPOON'S CHRISTMAS VACATION ... JOHN HUGHES
NATIONAL LAMPOON'S CLASS REUNION ... JOHN HUGHES
NATIONAL LAMPOON'S EUROPEAN VACATION ... JOHN HUGHES
NATIONAL LAMPOON'S EUROPEAN VACATION ... ROBERT KLANE
NATIONAL LAMPOON'S MOVIE MADNESS ... TOD CARROLL
NATIONAL LAMPOON'S MOVIE MADNESS ... ELLIS WEINER
NATIONAL LAMPOON'S MOVIE MADNESS ... GERALD SUSSMAN†
NATIONAL LAMPOON'S MOVIE MADNESS ... PAT MEPHITIS
NATIONAL LAMPOON'S MOVIE MADNESS ... SHARY FLENNIKEN
NATIONAL LAMPOON'S VACATION ... HAROLD RAMIS
NATIONAL LAMPOON'S VACATION ... JOHN HUGHES
NATIONAL PARK - S ... ALAN BERGER
NATIONAL PARK - S ... KATHY GORI
NATIONAL PASTTIME - S ... WILLIAM GOLDMAN
NATIVE GENIUS - S ... JAMES KAPLAN
NATIVE SON ... RICHARD WESLEY
NATIVE TONGUE - S ... EARL MAC ROUCH
NATIVES - S ... CARLTON CUSE
NATIVES - S ... BOBBY ROTH
NATIVOS (P) ... CLIFTON CAMPBELL
NATURAL ACTS - S ... MICHAEL KOZOLL
NATURAL ENEMIES ... JEFF KANEW
NATURAL HISTORY OF PARKING LOTS, THE ... EVERETT LEWIS
NATURAL, THE ... PHILIP DUSENBERRY
NATURAL, THE ... ROGER TOWNE
NAVIGATOR: AN ODYSSEY ACROSS TIME, THE ... VINCENT WARD
NAVY BRATS - S ... JUDY FREUDBERG
NAVY BRATS - S ... TONY GEISS
NAVY LARK, THE ... SID COLIN†
NAVY SEALS ... CHUCK PFAFFER
NAVY SEALS ... GARY GOLDMAN
NEAR DARK ... ERIC RED
NEAR DARK ... KATHRYN BIGELOW
NEARLY A NASTY ACCIDENT ... JACK DAVIES
NECESSARY ROUGHNESS - S ... DAVID FULLER
NECESSARY ROUGHNESS - S ... RICK NATKIN
NECESSITY - S ... BRIAN GARFIELD
NECK (P) ... JOHN STEPPLING
NECROMANCER ... BILL NAUD
NECROMANCY ... BERT I. GORDON
NECROPOLIS ... BRUCE HICKEY
NECROPOLIS ... EDWARD KHMARA
NECROPOLIS - S ... TOR VALENZA
NED KELLY ... IAN JONES
NED KELLY ... TONY RICHARDSON
NED KELLY - S ... YAHOO SERIOUS
NEED TO KNOW - S ... ROBERT MOLONEY
NEEDLES (CTF) - S ... LEE DRYSDALE
NEGOTIATOR, THE (CTF) - S ... L.M. KIT CARSON
NEIGHBORHOOD WATCH - S ... GARY DRUCKER
NEIGHBORHOOD, THE - S ... MARK ANDRUS
NEIGHBORS ... LARRY GELBART
NEITHER BY DAY NOR BY NIGHT ... STEVEN HILLIARD STERN
NEON - S ... LARRY GROSS
NEON DREAMS - S ... J. MIYOKO HENSLEY
NEON DREAMS - S ... STEVEN HENSLEY
NEON EMPIRE, THE (CTF) ... PETE HAMILL
NEON LIGHTS - S ... WILLIAM TONNER
NEON ROSE, THE - S ... JAMES D. BUCHANAN
NEPTUNE (SHORT) ... JAMES D. COX
NEPTUNE FACTOR, THE ... JACK DEWITT
NERVE ENDING - S ... ERIC ROTH
NERVE ENDINGS - S ... CYNTHIA CIDRE
NERVOUS SYSTEM - S ... DAVID CHASE
NERVOUS TICKS - S ... DAVID FRANKEL
NEST OF GENTRY, A ... ANDREI KONCHALOVSKY
NEST, THE ... ROBERT KING
NETWORK ... PADDY CHAYEVSKY†
NEVER A DULL MOMENT ... A.J. CAROTHERS
NEVER CRY WOLF ... CURTIS LEE HANSON
NEVER CRY WOLF ... RICHARD KLETTER
NEVER CRY WOLF ... SAM HAMM
NEVER FORGET (CTF) ... RICHARD RUBIN
NEVER GIVE AN INCH ... JOHN GAY
NEVER LEAVE NEVADA ... STEVE SWARTZ
NEVER ON SUNDAY ... JULES DASSIN
NEVER ON TUESDAY ... ADAM RIFKIN
NEVER PUT IT IN WRITING ... ANDREW STONE
NEVER SAY DIE - S ... ANDY BOROWITZ
NEVER SAY DIE - S ... JOHN KEITH WILDER
NEVER SAY GOODBYE ... BEN BARZMAN†
NEVER SAY NEVER AGAIN ... LORENZO SEMPLE
NEVER SO FEW ... MILLARD KAUFMAN
NEVER TOO YOUNG TO DIE ... GIL BETTMAN
NEVER TOO YOUNG TO DIE ... STEVEN PAUL
NEVERENDING STORY, THE ... HERMAN WEIGEL
NEVERENDING STORY, THE ... WOLFGANG PETERSEN
NEVERENDING STORY II, THE ... KARIN HOWARD
NEVERENDING STORY III, THE - S ... KARIN HOWARD
NEW ADVENTURES OF PIPPI LONGSTOCKING, THE ... KEN ANNAKIN
NEW CANTERBURY TALES - S ... JOHN ESKOW
NEW CENTURIONS, THE ... STIRLING SILLIPHANT
NEW JACK CITY ... BARRY MICHAEL COOPER
NEW JACK CITY ... THOMAS LEE WRIGHT
NEW KID IN TOWN - S ... ALEXANDER TANA
NEW KIDS, THE ... BRIAN TAGGERT
NEW KIDS, THE ... STEPHEN GYLLENHAAL
NEW KIND OF LOVE, A ... MEL SHAVELSON
NEW KIND OF LOVE, A - S ... PETER KRIKES
NEW KIND OF LOVE, A - S ... STEVE MEERSON
NEW LEAF, A ... ELAINE MAY
NEW LIFE, A ... ALAN ALDA
NEW MOON - S ... NEVIN SCHREINER
NEW ORLEANS MUSICAL - S ... GARY GOLDMAN
NEW WAVE ... JEAN-LUC GODARD
NEW WIFE, A - S ... FREDERIC RAPHAEL
NEW YEAR'S EVE - S ... DANIEL SULLIVAN
NEW YEAR'S EVE - S ... FRED LEBOW
NEW YEAR'S EVIL ... LEONARD NEUBAUER
NEW YEAR'S EVIL ... EMMETT ALSTON
NEW YEARS DAY ... HENRY JAGLOM
NEW YORK PROJECT, THE - S ... DAN ALGRANT
NEW YORK STORIES ... FRANCIS FORD COPPOLA
NEW YORK STORIES ... RICHARD PRICE
NEW YORK STORIES ... WOODY ALLEN
NEW YORK STORIES ... SOFIA COPPOLA
NEW YORK, NEW YORK ... EARL MAC RAUCH
NEW YORK, NEW YORK ... MARDIK MARTIN
NEWCOMER, THE- S ... NEVIN SCHREINER
NEWS - S ... GARY ROSS
NEWS - S ... KEN FINKLEMAN
NEWSFRONT ... PHILLIP NOYCE
NEWSIES - S ... DAVID FALLON
NEWSIES - S ... THOMAS RICKMAN
NEWSREEL - S ... HAL BARWOOD
NEWSREEL - S ... MATTHEW ROBBINS
NEXT (P) ... TERRENCE MCNALLY
NEXT BIG THING, THE - S ... SAM HAMM
NEXT MAN, THE ... ALAN R. TRUSTMAN
NEXT MAN, THE ... MORT FINE†
NEXT OF KIN (1989) ... MICHAEL JENNING
NEXT OF KIN ... ATOM EGOYAN
NEXT PRESIDENT OF THE U.S.A., THE - S ... ALAN JAY GLUECKMAN
NEXT STOP, GREENWICH VILLAGE ... PAUL MAZURKSY
NEXT SUMMER ... NADINE TRINTIGANT
NIAGRA FALLS - S ... LEON CAPETANOS
NIAGRA FALLS - S ... GLORIA KATZ
NIAGRA FALLS - S ... WILLARD HUYCK
NICE DREAMS ... CHEECH MARIN
NICE DREAMS ... TOMMY CHONG
NICE GIRLS - S ... ROBERT J. COMFORT
NICE GIRLS DON'T EXPLODE ... PAUL HARRIS
NICE WORK - S ... TED TALLY
NICHOLAS AND ALEXANDRA ... JAMES GOLDMAN
NICHOLAS NICKLEBY (P) ... DAVID EDGAR
NICK FURY - S ... GREG PRUSS
NICK THE GREEK - S ... ERIC ROTH
NICK THE GREEK - S ... HARLAN ELLISON
NICK'S MOVIE ... WIM WENDERS
NICKEL RIDE, THE ... ERIC ROTH
NICKELODEON ... PETER BOGDONAVICH
NICKELODEON ... W.D. RICHTER
NICKY - S ... THOMAS LEE WRIGHT
NIGHT AND DAY - S ... JOAN TAYLOR
NIGHT AND THE CITY ... JO EISENGER
NIGHT AND THE CITY - S ... RICHARD PRICE
NIGHT ANGEL ... JOE AUGUSTYN
NIGHT ANGEL ... WALTER JOSTEN
NIGHT BEFORE, THE ... GREGORY SCHERICK
NIGHT BEFORE, THE ... THOMAS EBERHARDT
NIGHT BY NIGHT - S ... KATHRYN BIGELOW
NIGHT CALL NURSES ... GEORGE B. ARMITAGE
NIGHT CREATURES ... HUBERT SMITH
NIGHT CROSSING ... JOHN MCGREEVY
NIGHT DADDY (SHORT) ... JANICE SHAPIRO

INDEX OF FILM TITLES

Title	Writer
NIGHT EAGLE - S	JOHN A. GALLAGHER
NIGHT EAGLE - S	STEVE JAMES
NIGHT EYES	CHARLES EGLEE
NIGHT EYES	ANDREW STEVENS
NIGHT EYES	TOM CITRANO
NIGHT FLIGHTS - S	ROBERT CARNEY
NIGHT GAME	ANTHONY PALMER
NIGHT GAME	SPENCER EASTMAN†
NIGHT GAMES	ANTON DIETHER
NIGHT GAMES	CLARKE REYNOLDS
NIGHT GAMES	MAI ZETTERLING
NIGHT GAMES	BARTH JULES SUSSMAN
NIGHT HAWKS	PAUL SYLBERT
NIGHT HEAVEN FELL, THE	PETER VIERTEL
NIGHT HEAVEN FELL, THE	ROGER VADIM
NIGHT HOLDS TERROR, THE	ANDREW STONE
NIGHT IN HEAVEN, A	JOAN TEWKESBURY
NIGHT IN OLD MEXICO - S	WILLIAM D. WITTLIFF
NIGHT IN THE LIFE OF JIMMY REARDON, A	WILLIAM RICHERT
NIGHT MOVES	ALAN SHARP
NIGHT MUST FALL	CLIVE EXTON
NIGHT OF PASSION	SIDNEY J. FURIE
NIGHT OF THE COMET	THOM EBERHARDT
NIGHT OF THE CREEPS	FRED DEKKER
NIGHT OF THE DEMON	CHARLES BENNETT
NIGHT OF THE DEMONS	JOE AUGUSTYN
NIGHT OF THE EAGLE	RICHARD MATHESON
NIGHT OF THE JUGGLER	RICK NATKIN
NIGHT OF THE JUGGLER	WILLIAM NORTON SR.
NIGHT OF THE LIVING DEAD	GEORGE A. ROMERO
NIGHT OF THE LIVING DEAD	JOHN A. RUSSO
NIGHT OF THE SHOOTING STARS, THE	PAOLO TAVIANI
NIGHT OF THE SHOOTING STARS, THE	TONINO GUERRA
NIGHT OF THE SHOOTING STARS, THE	VITTORIO TAVIANI
NIGHT OF THE TOY SOLDIERS - S	ANDREW BERGMAN
NIGHT OF THE WARRIOR	THOMAS IAN GRIFFITH
NIGHT OF THE ZOMBIES	JOEL M. REED
NIGHT ON THE TOWN - S	DAVID LOUGHERY
NIGHT ON THE TOWN - S	JOSEPH RUBEN
NIGHT ON THE TOWN - S	STU SILVER
NIGHT OWL - S	ANN POWELL
NIGHT OWL - S	ROSE SCHACHT
NIGHT PATROL	WILLIAM OSCO
NIGHT PATROL	JACKIE KONG
NIGHT PATROL	MURRAY LANGSTON
NIGHT PEOPLE - S	W.D. RICHTER
NIGHT PORTER, THE	LILIANI CAVANI
NIGHT RIDE DOWN - S	GLORIDA KATZ
NIGHT RIDE DOWN - S	WILLARD M. HUYCK
NIGHT SCHOOL	RUTH AVERGON
NIGHT SHADE - S	HAL BARWOOD
NIGHT SHADE - S	MATTHEW ROBBINS
NIGHT SHIFT	BABALOO MANDEL
NIGHT SHIFT	LOWELL GANZ
NIGHT STALKER, THE	JOHN GOFF
NIGHT SUN	PAOLO TAVIANI
NIGHT SUN	TONINO GUERRA
NIGHT SUN	VITTORIO TAVIANI
NIGHT TENNIS - S	ANABEL DAVIS-GOFF
NIGHT THAT REVEREND CLANCY'S HOME, THE - S	STANFORD SHERMAN
NIGHT THE LIGHTS WENT OUT IN GEORGIA, THE	BOB BONNEY
NIGHT THEY RAIDED MINSKY'S, THE	NORMAN LEAR
NIGHT THEY RAIDED MINSKY'S, THE	ARNOLD SCHULMAN
NIGHT THOREAU SPENT IN JAIL, THE (P)	JEROME LAWRENCE
NIGHT THOREAU SPENT IN JAIL, THE (P)	ROBERT E. LEE
NIGHT VISIONS - S	ROBERT GLASS
NIGHT VISITOR	RANDAL VISCOVICH
NIGHT WALKER, THE	ROBERT BLOCH
NIGHT WARNING	ALAN JAY GLUECKMAN
NIGHT WARNING	STEPHEN BREIMER
NIGHT WATCH	TONY WILLIAMSON
NIGHT WE NEVER MET, THE - S	WARREN D. LEIGHT
NIGHT WORK - S	DAVID TAYLOR
NIGHT WORK - S	MICHAEL BERRY
NIGHT, MOTHER	MARSHA NORMAN
NIGHTBREAKER (CTF)	T.S. COOK
NIGHTBREED	CLIVE BARKER
NIGHTCALLER - S	JOHN J. SCHALTER
NIGHTCLUB CONFIDENTIAL - S	MICHAEL MCDOWELL
NIGHTCRAWLER - S	BRIAN STRASMANN
NIGHTENGALE - S	JANUS CERCONE
NIGHTENGALE ON AVENUE B - S	DALENE YOUNG
NIGHTFALL	PAUL MAYERSBERG
NIGHTFALL	STIRLING SILLIPHANT
NIGHTFALL - S	LIZ COMICI
NIGHTFALL - S	LOU COMICI
NIGHTFALL - S	PETER HANKOFF
NIGHTFLYERS	ROBERT JAFFE
NIGHTGAMES - S	HENRY SELICK
NIGHTGAMES - S	MICHAEL SHEA
NIGHTHAWKS	DAVID SHABER
NIGHTINGALE AND THE SATIN WOMAN - S	WILLIAM KOTZWINKLE
NIGHTMARE	ROMANO SCAVOLINI
NIGHTMARE	JIMMY SANGSTER
NIGHTMARE - S	ERIC LUKE
NIGHTMARE ON ELM STREET, A	WES CRAVEN
NIGHTMARE ON ELM STREET, PART 2	DAVID M. CHASKIN
NIGHTMARE ON ELM STREET, PART 2	ROY CARLSON
NIGHTMARE ON ELM STREET, PART 3	BRUCE WAGNER
NIGHTMARE ON ELM STREET, PART 3	CHUCK RUSSELL
NIGHTMARE ON ELM STREET, PART 3	FRANK DARABONT
NIGHTMARE ON ELM STREET, PART 3	WES CRAVEN
NIGHTMARE ON ELM STREET, PART 4	SCOTT PIERCE
NIGHTMARE ON ELM STREET, PART 4	BRIAN HELGELAND
NIGHTMARE ON ELM STREET, PART 5	CRAIG SPECTOR
NIGHTMARE ON ELM STREET, PART 5	JOHN SKIP
NIGHTMARE ON ELM STREET, PART 5	LESLIE BOHEM
NIGHTMARES	CHRISTOPHER CROWE
NIGHTMARES	JEFFREY BLOOM
NIGHTRUNNER - S	RICHARD TANNENBAUM
NIGHTS OF CABIRIA	FEDERICO FELLINI
NIGHTS OF EDEN	WES CLARRIDGE
NIGHTSIDE - S	KEN FRIEDMAN
NIGHTSTICK	JAMES J. DOCHERTY
NIGHTSTICK	JAMES DOHERTY
NIGHTTIME GUY - S	JOSEPH LOEB III
NIGHTTIME GUY - S	MATTHEW WEISMAN
NIGHTWING	STEVE SHAGAN
NIGHTWING	BUD SHRAKE
NIJINSKY	HUGH WHEELER†
NIKITA	LUC BESSON
NIKKI & ME - S	SEAN MCCARVER
NINA - S	ANDY LEWIS
NINE DEATHS OF THE NINJA	EMMET ALSTON
NINE HOURS TO RAMA	NELSON GIDDING
NINE TIGER MAN - S	ALLAN G. SCOTT
NINE TIGER MAN, THE- S	CHRIS BRYANT
NINE TO FIVE	COLIN HIGGINS†
NINE TO FIVE	PATRICIA RESNICK
NINETY MINUTES - S	JEREMY STEVENS
NINETY MINUTES - S	MARK A. REISMAN
NINJA III: THE DOMINATION	JAMES R. SILKE
NINJA, THE - S	W.D. RICHTER
NINO - S	ROD MCCALL
NINOTCHKA	BILLY WILDER
NINTH CONFIGURATION, THE	WILLIAM PETER BLATTY
NO DEPOSIT, NO RETURN	ARTHUR ALSBERG
NO DEPOSIT, NO RETURN	DONALD R. NELSON
NO DEPOSIT, NO RETURN - S	JONATHAN LEMKIN
NO DOWN PAYMENT	PHILIP YORDAN
NO EXCUSE - S	CHRIS GEROLMO
NO HANGUPS - S	MICHAEL DUNCAN
NO HARD FEELINGS (P)	RON CLARK
NO HIGHWAY ON EARTH - S	GEORGE E. SIMPSON
NO HOLDS BARRED	DENNIS E. HACKIN
NO JUSTICE	RICHARD WAYNE MARTIN
NO KIDDING	NORMAN HUDIS
NO LAUGHING MATTER - S	THOMAS L. ROWE
NO LONGER ALONE	LAWRENCE HOLBEN
NO LOVE FOR JOHNNIE	MORDECAI RICHLER
NO MAN'S LAND	DICK WOLF
NO MAN'S LAND (P)	HAROLD PINTER
NO MERCY	JIM CARABATSOS
NO MORE BLUES - S	JULIAN BARRY
NO MORE EXCUSES	ROBERT DOWNEY
NO ONE TO KISS AT MIDNIGHT - S	MARK ROWEN
NO OTHER LOVE - S	JANET DULIN JONES
NO PLACE FOR A DAME	JEFF WILHELM
NO PLACE TO BE SOMEBODY - S	REINALDO POVOD
NO QUESTIONS ASKED	SIDNEY SHELDON
NO REGRETS OF OUR YOUTH	AKIRA KUROSAWA
NO RETREAT, NO SURRENDER	COREY YUEN
NO RETREAT, NO SURRENDER	NG SEE YUEN
NO RETREAT, NO SURRENDER	KEITH W. STRANDBERG
NO RETREAT, NO SURRENDER II	MARIA ELENE CELLINO
NO RETREAT, NO SURRENDER II	ROY HORAN
NO RETREAT, NO SURRENDER II	KEITH W. STRANDBERG
NO SAD SONGS FOR ME	HOWARD KOCH
NO SECRETS	DEZSO MAGYAR
NO SECRETS	KEN SELDEN
NO SEX PLEASE WE'RE BRITISH	JOHN MORTIMER
NO SMALL AFFAIR	CRAIG BOLOTIN
NO SMALL AFFAIR	MICHAEL LEESON
NO SUCH LUCK - S	CHRIS MILLER
NO SUCH LUCK - S	MICHAEL D. SUTTON
NO TIME FOR COMEDY	JULIUS J. EPSTEIN
NO TIME FOR COMEDY	PHILIP G. EPSTEIN†
NO T.V. - S	DEBRA FRANKEL
NO TRANSFER - S	WILLIAM GOODHART
NO WAY OUT	ROBERT GARLAND
NO WAY OUT (1950)	JOSEPH L. MANKIEWICZ
NO WAY TO TREAT A LADY	JOHN GAY
NOBLE ENEMIES - S	EARL MAC RAUCH
NOBODY LIKES AN HONEST COP - S	LARRY GELBART
NOBODY'S ANGEL - S	THOMAS MCGUANE
NOBODY'S FOOL	BETH HENLEY
NOBODY'S PERFECT	JOHN D.F. BLACK
NOBODY'S PERFECT	ANNIE KORZEN
NOBODY'S PERFECT	JOEL BLOCK
NOBODY'S PERFECT - S	GINNY CERRELLA
NOBODY'S PERFEKT	TONY KENRICK
NOCTURNE - S	ERIC HUGHES
NOCTURNUS - S	DAVID BIRKE
NOISE IN THE NIGHT - S	MARC STIRDIVANT
NOISE IN THE NIGHT - S	THOM EBERHARDT
NOISES OFF - S	MARTY KAPLAN
NOISES OFF (P)	MICHAEL FRAYN
NOMADS	JOHN MCTIERNAN
NOMINATION, THE - S	JERRY JACOBIUS
NOMINATION, THE - S	NICK GORE
NON-WHITE COMEDY - S	JACK ROSENTHAL
NOON - S	GARY WALKOW
NOP - S	ALEC TEAGUE
NORIEGA VERDAD (CTF) - S	L.M. KIT CARSON
NORMA RAE	HARRIET FRANK JR.
NORMA RAE	IRVING RAVETCH
NORMAL HEART, THE (P)	LARRY KRAMER
NORMAL MURDER - S	JULIA CAMERON
NORMAN CONQUESTS, THE (P)	ALAN AYCKBOURN
NORMAN LOVES ROSE	HENRI SAFRAN
NORMAN'S AWESOME ADVENTURE	PAUL DONOVAN
NORMAN, IS THAT YOU?	RON CLARK
NORMAN, IS THAT YOU?	SAM BOBRICK
NORSEMAN, THE	CHARLES B. PIERCE
NORTH - S	ALAN ZWEIBEL
NORTH AVENUE IRREGULARS, THE	DON TAIT
NORTH BY NORTHWEST	ERNEST LEHMANN
NORTH BY SOUTH - S	MARSHALL BRICKMAN
NORTH DALLAS FORTY	FRANK YABLANS
NORTH DALLAS FORTY	TED KOTCHEFF
NORTH DALLAS FORTY	PETER GENT
NORTH SHORE	RANDAL KLEISER
NORTH SHORE	TIM MCCANLIES
NORTH SHORE	WILLIAM W. PHELPS
NORTH STAR - S	ROBERT DILLON
NORTHEAST KINGDOM - S	ALAN ORMSBY
NORTHERN LIGHTS	JOHN HANSON
NORTHERN LIGHTS	ROB NILSSON
NORTHERN LIGHTS - S	MIKE BINDER
NORTHVILLE CEMETARY MASSACRE, THE	WILLIAM DEAR
NORTHWEST OUTPOST	RICHARD SALE
NOSE JOB - S	RON CLARK
NOSEJOB - S	STEVEN S. GREENE
NOSFERATU THE VAMPYRE	WERNER HERZOG
NOSTALGHIA	ANDREI TARKOVSKY†
NOSTALGHIA	TONINO GUERRA
NOSTROMO	ROBERT BOLT

NOSTROMO - S ... CHRISTOPHER HAMPTON
NOT A THROUGH STREET - S ... LARRY GROSS
NOT AS A STRANGER ... EDWARD ANHALT
NOT FOR PUBLICATION ... JOHN MEYER
NOT FOR PUBLICATION ... PAUL BARTEL
NOT GUILTY - S ... BURT PRELUTSKY
NOT OF THIS EARTH ... JIM WYNORSKI
NOT OF THIS EARTH ... R.J. ROBERTSON
NOT OF THIS EARTH (1957) ... CHARLES B. GRIFFITH
NOT QUITE PARADISE ... PAUL KEMBER
NOT WITH MY WIFE, YOU DON'T ... LARRY GELBART
NOT WITH MY WIFE, YOU DON'T ... NORMAN PANAMA
NOT WITH MY WIFE, YOU DON'T ... PETER BARNES
NOT WITHOUT MY DAUGHTER ... DAVID W. RINTELS
NOTHING BUT A MAN ... MICHAEL ROEMER
NOTHING BUT THE BEST ... FREDERIC RAPHAEL
NOTHING BUT THE NIGHT ... BRIAN HAYLES
NOTHING BUT TROUBLE ... DAN AYKROYD
NOTHING BUT TROUBLE ... PETER AYKROYD
NOTHING DOWN - S ... HOWARD CUSHNIR
NOTHING HUMAN - S ... ABBE BERNSTEIN
NOTHING IN COMMON ... MICHAEL PREMINGER
NOTHING IN COMMON ... RICK PODELL
NOTHING LASTS FOREVER ... TOM SCHILLER
NOTHING PERSONAL ... ROBERT KAUFMAN
NOTORIOUS LANDLADY, THE ... LARRY GELBART
NOTRE HISTOIRE ... BERTRAND BLIER
NOURISH THE BEAST (P) ... STEVE TESICH
NOUVELLE VAGUE ... JEAN-LUC GODARD
NOVEL LIFE - S ... DAVID ODELL
NOVEL LIFE, A - S ... TOM STOPPARD
NOVEMBER MAN - S ... TONY KAYDEN
NOVICE, THE - S ... DAN ALGRANT
NOVUM - S ... RICHARD MATHESON
NOW ABOUT THESE WOMEN ... INGMAR BERGMAN
NOW YOU SEE IT (P) ... RICHARD MATHESON
NOWHERE TO HIDE ... ALEX REBAR
NOWHERE TO HIDE ... GEORGE GOLDSMITH
NOWHERE TO HIDE - S ... STEPHEN TOLKIN
NUCLEAR REACTIONS - S ... DAVID HINES
NUCLEAR REACTIONS - S ... JEFF HAUSE
NUDE BOMB, THE ... ARNE SULTAN†
NUDE BOMB, THE ... BILL DANA
NUDE BOMB, THE ... LEONARD B. STERN
NUMBER ONE (SHORT) ... DYAN CANNON
NUMBER ONE WITH A BULLET ... ANDREW KURTZMAN
NUMBER ONE WITH A BULLET ... GAIL MORGAN HICKMAN
NUMBER ONE WITH A BULLET ... JAMES A. BELUSHI
NUMBER ONE WITH A BULLET ... ROB RILEY
NUN'S STORY, THE ... ROBERT ANDERSON
NUNS ON THE RUN ... JONATHAN LYNN
NUNZIO ... JAMES ANDRONICA
NURSE ON WHEELS ... NORMAN HUDIS
NUTCRACKER PRINCE, THE (AF) ... PATRICIA WATSON
NUTS ... ALVIN SARGENT
NUTS ... DARRYL PONICSAN
NUTS ... TOM TOPOR
NUTS & BOLTS - S ... RENE BALCER
NUTTY PROFESSOR, THE ... BILL RICHMOND
NUTTY PROFESSOR, THE ... JERRY LEWIS
NUTTY PROFESSOR II, THE - S ... BILL RICHMOND
NUTTY PROFESSOR II - S ... STU SILVER

O

O JERUSALEM - S ... GERALD GREEN
O'HARA'S WIFE ... JAMES NASALLA
O'HARA'S WIFE ... WILLIAM S. BARTMAN
O-NEIL - S ... HUGH LEONARD
O.C. AND STIGGS ... DONALD CANTRELL
O.C. AND STIGGS ... TED MANN
O.C. AND STIGGS ... TOD CARROLL
O.S.S. ... RICHARD MAIBAUM†
O.S.S. - S ... GREGORY WIDEN
OBITS - S ... TERRY SOUTHERN
OBJECT OF BEAUTY, THE ... MICHAELLINDSAY-HOGG
OBJECT OF DESIRE - S ... MICHAEL DUGAN
OBJECT OF MY AFFECTION, THE - S ... WENDY WASSERSTEIN
OBSESSION ... PAUL SCHRADER
OBSESSION: A TASTE OF FEAR ... PICCIO RAFFANINI
OCCULTIST, THE ... TIM KINCAID
OCCUPATIONS (P) ... TREVOR GRIFFITHS
OCEAN BOULEVARD - S ... GREG TAYLOR
OCEAN BOULEVARD - S ... ROWDY HERRINGTON
OCEAN DRIVE WEEKEND ... BRYAN JONES
OCTAGON, THE ... PAUL AARON
OCTAGON, THE ... LEIGH CHAPMAN
OCTAVIA ... DAVID BEAIRD
OCTOBER 16, 1977 (SHORT) ... STEVEN SODERBERGH
OCTOBER CIRCLE - S ... MARK VICTOR
OCTOBER CIRCLE - S ... MICHAEL GRAIS
OCTOPUSSY ... GEORGE MACDONALD FRASER
OCTOPUSSY ... MICHAEL G. WILSON
OCTOPUSSY ... RICHARD MAIBAUM†
ODD COUPLE, THE ... NEIL SIMON
ODD JOB, THE ... BERNARD MCKENNA
ODD JOB, THE ... GRAHAM CHAPMAN†
ODD JOBS ... PETER MARTIN WORTMANN
ODD JOBS ... ROBERT CONTE
ODD'S END - S ... CHRIS BRYANT
ODDS AGAINST TOMORROW ... NELSON GIDDING
ODE TO BILLY JOE ... HERMAN RAUCHER
ODESSA FILE, THE ... KENNETH ROSS
OF LOVE AND DESIRE ... RICHARD RUSH
OF HUMAN BONDAGE ... BRYAN FORBES
OF LOVE AND SHADOW - S ... DONALD FREED
OF MICE AND MEN - S ... HORTON FOOTE
OF PAWNS AND KNIGHTS - S ... JOE GAYTON
OF SOUND MIND AND BODY - S ... CLIFTON CAMPBELL
OF THE LORD - S ... VINCENT PATRICK
OF UNKNOWN ORIGIN ... BRIAN TAGGERT
OF, THE - S ... GERALD DI PEGO
OFF AND RUNNING - S ... BILL RICHMOND
OFF BEAT ... DEZSO MAGYAR
OFF BEAT ... MARK MEDOFF
OFF LIMITS ... CHRISTOPHER CROWE
OFF LIMITS ... JACK THIBEAU
OFF THE RECORD - S ... STEVE TESICH
OFFBEAT ... PETER BARNES
OFFENCE, THE ... JOHN HOPKINS
OFFERING - S ... JOHN BRILEY
OFFERINGS ... CHRISTOPHER REYNOLDS
OFFICE ROMANCE - S ... CHARLIE HAUCK
OFFICER AND A GENTLEMAN, AN ... DOUGLAS DAY STEWART
OFFICIAL STORY, THE ... AIDA BORTNIK
OFFICIAL STORY, THE ... LUIS PUENZO
OFFSHORE - S ... MICHAEL THOMAS
OFFSPRING, THE ... C. COURTNEY JOYNER
OFFSPRING, THE ... JEFF BURR
OFFSPRING, THE ... DARIN SCOTT
OH! ALFIE ... KEN HUGHES
OH, CLORIS (P) ... DICK BEEBE
OH, GOD! ... LARRY GELBART
OH GOD! BOOK II ... FRED S. FOX
OH GOD! BOOK II ... HAL GOLDMAN
OH GOD! BOOK II ... JOSH GREENFELD
OH GOD! BOOK II ... MELISSA MILLER
OH GOD! BOOK II ... SEAMAN JACOBS
OH GOD! YOU DEVIL ... ANDREW BERGMAN
OH, HEAVENLY DOG! ... JOE CAMP
OH, HEAVENLY DOG! ... ROD BROWNING
OH ROSALINDA! ... EMERIC PRESSBURGER†
OH ROSALINDA! ... MICHAEL POWELL†
OH SISTER - S ... KENNY A. SOLMS
OH, THE PLACES YOU'LL GO - S ... TED GEISEL
OH VIENNA - S ... MICHAEL THOMAS
OHIO SHUFFLE - S ... NATALIE COOPER
OIL & VINEGAR - S ... JOHN HUGHES
OKLAHOMA CRUDE ... MARC NORMAN
OLD BOY, THE (P) ... A.R. GURNEY
OLD BOYFRIENDS ... PAUL SCHRADER
OLD BOYFRIENDS ... LEONARD SCHRADER
OLD DARK HOUSE, THE ... ROBERT DILLON
OLD ENOUGH ... MARISA SILVER
OLD EXPLORERS ... WILLIAM POHLAD
OLD FRIEND OF THE FAMILY - S ... JIM HART
OLD GRINGO ... AIDA BORTNIK
OLD GRINGO ... LUIS PUENZO
OLD NEIGHBORHOOD, THE - S ... BO GOLDMAN
OLD TIMES (P) ... HAROLD PINTER
OLDEST PROFESSION, THE ... JEAN-LUC GODARD
OLIVER & CO. (AF) ... JAMES MANGOLD
OLIVER & CO. (AF) ... JIM COX
OLIVER & CO. (AF) ... TIMOTHY J. DISNEY
OLIVER TWIST ... DAVID LEAN†
OLIVER'S STORY ... ERICH SEGAL
OLIVER'S STORY ... JOHN KORTY
OMEGA SYNDROME ... JOHN SHARKEY
OMEN, THE ... DAVID SELTZER
ON AURA TOUT VU (P) ... FRANCIS VEBER
ON EASY STREET - S ... JOHN HERZFELD
ON GOLDEN POND ... ERNEST THOMPSON
ON GUARD - S ... PETER KRIKES
ON GUARD - S ... STEVE MEERSON
ON HER BED OF ROSES ... ALBERT ZUGSMITH
ON HER MAJESTY'S SECRET SERVICE ... RICHARD MAIBAUM†
ON MOONLIGHT BAY ... JACK ROSE
ON MOONLIGHT BAY ... MEL SHAVELSON
ON MY HONOR - S ... BRIAN STRASMAN
ON MY HONOR - S ... RICHARD OUTTEN
ON OCEAN FRONT WALK (FD) ... MARK ROSNER
ON THE AIR - S ... HARRY DUNN
ON THE AIR - S ... JEFF BERMAN
ON THE AIR - S ... JERRY RAPP
ON THE AIR - S ... MITCHEL KATLIN
ON THE AIR - S ... NAT BERNSTEIN
ON THE BEACH ... JAMES LEE BARRETT†
ON THE BEAT ... JACK DAVIES
ON THE BRINK - S ... MICHAEL ELIAS
ON THE BRINK - S ... RICHARD EUSTIS
ON THE DOUBLE ... MEL SHAVELSON
ON THE DOUBLE ... JACK ROSE
ON THE EDGE ... ROB NILSSON
ON THE EDGE ... ROY KISSIN
ON THE LAM - S ... BARRY STRUGATZ
ON THE LAM - S ... HENRY C. PARKE
ON THE LAM - S ... MARK BURNS
ON THE LINE ... JOSE LUIS BORAU
ON THE LINE - S ... LESLIE BOHEM
ON THE LINE - S ... THOMAS RITZ
ON THE MONEY (P) ... JOHN H. KOSTMAYER
ON THE NICKEL ... RALPH WAITE
ON THE PROWL - S ... DANIEL YOST
ON THE RIGHT TRACK ... TINA PINE
ON THE RIGHT TRACK ... RICHARD MOSES
ON THE ROAD AGAIN - S ... MICHAEL DUNCAN
ON THE TOWN ... ADOLPH GREEN
ON THE TOWN ... BETTY COMDEN
ON THE WATERFRONT ... BUDD SCHULBERG
ON THE WAY TO THE CRUSADES ... LARRY GELBART
ON THE YARD ... MALCOLM BRALY
ON VALENTINES DAY ... HORTON FOOTE
ONCE AROUND ... MALIA SCOTCH MARMO
ONCE BITTEN ... DAVID HINES
ONCE BITTEN ... JEFF HAUSE
ONCE BITTEN ... JONATHAN ROBERTS
ONCE BITTEN ... DIMITRI VILLARD
ONCE IN PARIS ... FRANK D. GILROY
ONCE IS NOT ENOUGH ... JULIUS J. EPSTEIN
ONCE REMOVED (P) ... EDUARDO MACHADO
ONCE UPON A HORSE ... HAL KANTER
ONCE UPON A MARRIAGE - S ... STU KRIEGER
ONCE UPON A TIME ... OSCAR SAUL
ONCE UPON A TIME IN AMERICA ... SERGIO LEONE†
ONCE UPON A TIME IN THE WEST ... SERGIO DONATI
ONE AND ONLY, THE ... STEVE GORDON†
ONE BY ONE - S ... JOEL DAVIS
ONE CRAZY SUMMER ... SAVAGE STEVE HOLLAND
ONE CROWDED NIGHT ... ARNAUD D'USSEAU†
ONE CUP OF COFFEE ... D.M. EYRE JR.
ONE CUP OF COFFEE ... ROBIN ARMSTRONG
ONE DARK NIGHT ... MICHAEL HAWES
ONE DARK NIGHT ... TOM MCLOUGHLIN
ONE DAY AT A TIME - S ... ROBERT KAUFMAN
ONE DAY IN THE LIFE OF IVAN DENISOVICH ... RONALD HARWOOD
ONE DESIRE ... LAWRENCE ROMAN
ONE DESIRE ... ROBERT BLEES
ONE DOWN TWO TO GO ... JEFF WILLIAMSON
ONE FANTASTIC NIGHT - S ... THOM EBERHARDT
ONE FELL SWOOP - S ... ADAM FRIEDMAN
ONE FINE DAY - S ... DORI PIERSON
ONE FLEW OVER THE CUCKOO'S NEST ... BO GOLDMAN
ONE FLEW OVER THE CUCKOO'S NEST ... LAWRENCE HAUBEN†
ONE FOOT IN HELL ... AARON SPELLING
ONE FOOT IN HELL ... SYDNEY BOEHM†
ONE FOR THE ROAD (P) ... HAROLD PINTER
ONE FROM THE HEART ... ARMYAN BERNSTEIN
ONE FROM THE HEART ... FRANCIS FORD COPPOLA
ONE GOOD COP ... HEYWOOD GOULD
ONE HEARTBEAT ... THOMAS LEE WRIGHT
ONE HUNDRED DOLLAR MISUNDERSTANDING, THE - S ... ELAINE MAY
ONE HUNDRED DOLLAR MISUNDERSTANDING, THE - S ... ROBERT KAUFMAN

Title	Writer
ONE IN A MILLION - S	LARRY GRUSIN
ONE IS A LONELY NUMBER	DAVID SELTZER
ONE JUST MAN - S	NORMAN WEXLER
ONE LITTLE INDIAN	HARRY SPALDING
ONE LOOK - S	LAUREL DELP
ONE MAGIC CHRISTMAS	THOMAS MEEHAN
ONE MAGIC CHRISTMAS	BARRY HEALEY
ONE MAGIC CHRISTMAS	PHILLIP BORSOS
ONE MAN FORCE	DALE TREVILLION
ONE MAN'S WAR (CTF)	SERGIO TOLEDO
ONE MILLION YEARS B.C.	MICHAEL CARRERAS
ONE MORE CHANCE	SAM FIRSTENBERG
ONE MORE SATURDAY NIGHT	AL FRANKEN
ONE MORE SATURDAY NIGHT	TOM DAVIS
ONE MORE SONG FOR JESUS - S	STANFORD SHERMAN
ONE MORE TIME - S	ANNA HAMILTON PHELAN
ONE MORE TIME - S	JULIAN BARRY
ONE MORE TOMORROW	JULIUS J. EPSTEIN
ONE MORE TOMORROW	PHILIP G. EPSTEIN†
ONE MORE TRAIN TO ROB	DON TAIT
ONE MORE TRAIN TO ROB	DONALD R. NELSON
ONE MORE TRAIN TO ROB	WILLIAM ROBERTS
ONE NATION INVISIBLE - S	KEVIN ELDERS
ONE NIGHT ONLY - S	BILL MCCLOSKEY
ONE NIGHT ONLY - S	ERIC WILLIAMS
ONE OF OUR AIRCRAFT IS MISSING	EMERIC PRESSBURGER†
ONE OF OUR AIRCRAFT IS MISSING	MICHAEL POWELL†
ONE OF US	BENNY BARBASH
ONE ON ONE	JERRY SEGAL
ONE ON ONE	ROBBY BENSON
ONE SALIVA BUBBLE - S	DAVID LYNCH
ONE SALIVA BUBBLE - S	MARK FROST
ONE SHINING MOMENT (P)	LESLIE BRICUSSE
ONE SINGS, THE OTHER DOESN'T	AGNES VARDA
ONE SUMMER LOVE	N. RICHARD NASH
ONE SUMMER, A MIRACLE - S	JENNIFER COLLOPY
ONE TRICK PONY	PAUL SIMON
ONE WILD MOMENT	CLAUDE BERRI
ONE WOMAN OR TWO	DANIEL VIGNE
ONE WONDERFUL SUNDAY	AKIRA KUROSAWA
ONE, TWO, THREE	BILLY WILDER
ONE, TWO, THREE	I.A.L. DIAMOND†
ONE-EYED JACKS	CALDER WILLINGHAM
ONION FIELD, THE	JOSEPH WAMBAUGH
ONIONHEAD	NELSON GIDDING
ONLY GAME IN TOWN, THE	FRANK D. GILROY
ONLY KIDDING (P)	JIM GEOGHAN
ONLY THE LONELY	CHRIS COLUMBUS
ONLY THE LONELY (CTF) - S	DICK BEEBE
ONLY TWO CAN PLAY	BRYAN FORBES
ONLY WHEN I LAUGH	NEIL SIMON
ONLY YOU - S	DOUG WHEELER
OOH, YOU ARE AWFUL	JOHN WARREN
OPEN DOORS	GIANNI AMELIO
OPEN SEASON - S	ROBERT WUHL
OPEN SEASON, AN	DENNE BART PETITCLERC
OPENING NIGHT	JOHN CASSAVETES†
OPERATION AMANDA - S	JUDY FREUDBERG
OPERATION AMANDA - S	TONY GEISS
OPERATION CULIACAN - S	REX PICKETT
OPERATION DAYBREAK	RONALD HARWOOD
OPERATION MAD BELL	BLAKE EDWARDS
OPERATION PETTICOAT	MAURICE RICHLIN†
OPERATION PETTICOAT	STANLEY SHAPIRO†
OPERATION THUNDERBOLT	CLARKE REYNOLDS
OPERATION U.F.O. - S	NEIL ISRAEL
OPERATION: SIDEWINDER (P)	SAM SHEPARD
OPHELIA - S	KEVIN QUINN
OPIUM BLUE - S	DENNIS POTTER
OPPENHEIMER - S	PETER PRINCE
OPPORTUNITY KNOCKS	MITCHEL KATLIN
OPPORTUNITY KNOCKS	NAT BERNSTEIN
OPPOSING FORCES	GIL COWAN
OPPOSITE SEX, THE	FAY KANIN
OPPOSITE SEX	, THE MICHAEL KANIN
OPTIMISTS OF NINE ELMS, THE	ANTHONY SIMMONS
OPTIMUM - S	BARRY BLAUSTEIN
OPTIMUM - S	DAVID SHEFFIELD
OPTIONS	JOHN J. STRAUSS
OPTIONS	EDWARD DECTER
OPUS ONE - S	GEORGE GIPE
ORACLE OF MERMAID AVENUE, THE - S	GARNER SIMMONS
ORANGE COUNTY RED - S	TOM BENEDEK
ORCA	SERGIO DONATI
ORCHESTRA REHEARSAL	BRUNELLO RONDI†
ORCHESTRA REHEARSAL	FEDERICO FELLINI
ORDEAL BY INNOCENCE	ALEXANDER STUART
ORDINARY PEOPLE	ALVIN SARGENT
ORIGINAL SIN - S	JOE ESZTERHAS
ORION POKER - S	MICHAEL MILLER
ORPHAN, THE (P)	DAVID RABE
ORPHAN TRAIN - S	SHAWN SLOVO
ORPHANS	LYLE D. KESSLER
ORPHEUS IN THE UNDERWORLD - S	SNOO WILSON
ORPHEUS PROJECT - S	CLIFFORD GREEN
ORPHEUS PROJECT - S	ELLEN GREEN
OSCAR	JIM MULHOLLAND
OSCAR	MICHAEL BARRIE
OSCAR WILD	JO EISINGER
OSCAR, THE	HARLAN ELLISON
OSTERMAN WEEKEND, THE	ALAN SHARP
OTHER MAN, THE - S	JUDITH ROSS
OTHER MEN'S DAUGHTERS - S	DAVID SELTZER
OTHER PEOPLE'S HUSBANDS, OTHER PEOPLE'S WIVES - S	PAUL D. ZIMMERMAN
OTHER SIDE OF MIDNIGHT, THE	DANIEL TARADASH
OTHER SIDE OF MIDNIGHT, THE	HERMAN RAUCHER
OTHER SIDE OF THE MOUNTAIN, THE	DAVID SELTZER
OTHER SIDE OF THE MOUNTAIN - PART II, THE	DOUGLAS DAY STEWART
OTHER WOMAN, THE (P)	CASEY KELLY
OTHER WOMAN, THE - S	SIMON MOORE
OTHER WOMEN'S CHILDREN - S	RAMA LAURIE STAGNER
OTHER, THE	TOM TRYON
OTHERWHERE - S	HAL BARWOOD
OTHERWISE ENGAGED (P)	SIMON GRAY
OTHERWISE ENGAGED - S	ELIZABETH PASSERELLI
OTIS - S	DAVID BRADLEY
OTIS REDDING STORY, THE - S	BILLY BOB THORNTON
OTIS REDDING STORY, THE - S	TOM EPPERSON
OTLEY	DICK CLEMENT
OTLEY	IAN LAFRENAIS
OUCHI - S	ROBERT LITTEL
OUR DREAM HOUSE - S	DANIEL YOST
OUR HEARTS WERE GROWING UP	NORMAN PANAMA
OUR HOUSE - S	ALLEN ESTRIN
OUR HOUSE - S	MARK G. ESTRIN
OUR LADY OF THE LOCKERS - S	BRUCE JAY FRIEDMAN
OUR MAN IN NICARAGUA (P)	DONALD FREED
OUR MISS FRED	HUGH LEONARD
OUR PLANET TONIGHT - S	BENNETT YELLIN
OUR PLANET TONIGHT - S	PETER FARRELLY
OUR WINNING SEASON	NICHOLAS NICIPHOR
OUT - S	CHRISTOPHER CANAAN
OUT COLD	GEORGE MALKO
OUT COLD	HOWARD GLASSER
OUT FOR JUSTICE	R. LANCE HILL
OUT OF AFRICA	KURT LUEDTKE
OUT OF BODY - S	BILL KERBY
OUT OF BOUNDS	TONY KAYDEN
OUT OF CHARACTER - S	CHRIS KEYSER
OUT OF CONTROL	SANDRA WEINTRAUB ROLAND
OUT OF CONTROL	VICANGELO BULLUCK
OUT OF SIGHT, OUT OF MIND	JOHN PLATT
OUT OF SIGHT, OUT OF MIND	ROY LANGSDON
OUT OF THE BLUE	LEONARD YAKIR
OUT OF THE BLUE (P)	LESLIE BRICUSSE
OUT OF THE BLUE - S	MARK PEPLOE
OUT OF THE BOX - S	ALEC LORIMORE
OUT OF THE BOX - S	REDBEARD SIMMONS
OUT OF THE BOX - S	TERRY WINKLESS
OUT OF THE DARK	J. GREG DE FELICE
OUT OF THE DARK	ZANE W. LEVITT
OUT OF THE DARK LOCKERS - S	STEPHEN FEKE
OUT OF THE DARKNESS	HUBERT SMITH
OUT OF THE DARKNESS - S	TERRY BRENNAN
OUT OF THE RAIN - S	SHEM BITTERMAN
OUT OF THE SILENCE - S	MICHAEL THOMAS
OUT OF TIME	JESSE GRAHAM
OUT OF TIME - S	DANIEL PETRIE, JR.
OUT OF TIME - S	GEORGE MACDONALD FRASER
OUT ON BAIL	JASON BOOTH
OUT ON BAIL	MICHAEL D. SONYE
OUT ON BAIL	TOM BADAL
OUT-OF-TOWNERS, THE	NEIL SIMON
OUTBACK	EVAN JONES
OUTCALLS - S	JEREMY BERTRAND FINCH
OUTFIT, THE	JOHN FLYNN
OUTLAND	PETER HYAMS
OUTLAW BLUES	B.W.L. NORTON, JR.
OUTLAW JOSEY WALES, THE	SONIA CHERNUS†
OUTLAW JOSEY WALES, THE	PHILIP KAUFMAN
OUTLAW OF GOR	HARRY ALAN TOWERS
OUTLAW OF GOR	RICK MARX
OUTLAW SKIES - S	DAVID E. PECKINPAH
OUTLAWS - S	JORGE ZAMACONA
OUTLAWS - S	NICHOLAS KAZAN
OUTRAGE, THE	MICHAEL KANIN
OUTRAGEOUS FORTUNE	LESLIE DIXON
OUTRAGEOUS!	DICK BENNER†
OUTRAGEOUS!	DICK BENNER†
OUTRIDERS, THE	IRVING RAVETCH
OUTSIDE CHANCE OF MAXIMILIAN GLICK, THE	PHILIP S. SAVATH
OUTSIDER, THE	STEWART STERN
OUTSIDER, THE	TONY LURASCHI
OUTWARD BOUND - S	ELIZABETH BRADLEY
OUTWARD BOUND - S	STEPHEN MCPHERSON
OVER MY DEAD BODY (P)	ANTHONY J. FINGLETON
OVER MY DEAD BODY - S	BABALOO MANDEL
OVER MY DEAD BODY - S	LOWELL GANZ
OVER THE BROOKLYN BRIDGE	ARNOLD SOMKIN
OVER THE EDGE	CHARLIE HAAS
OVER THE EDGE	TIM HUNTER
OVER THE HILL - S	ELEANOR WITCOMBE
OVER THE TOP	DAVID ENGELBACH
OVER THE TOP	GARY CONWAY
OVER THE TOP	STIRLING SILLIPHANT
OVER THE TOP	SYLVESTER STALLONE
OVERBOARD	LESLIE DIXON
OVEREXPOSED	LARRY BRAND
OVEREXPOSED	REBECCA REYNOLDS
OVERKILLERS, THE - S	DAVID S. GOYER
OVERLORD, THE - S	DAVID COLEMAN
OWL AND THE PUSSYCAT, THE	BUCK HENRY
OXFORD BLUES	ROBERT BORIS
OZARK - S	JULIA CAMERON
OZONE - S	ROB DUNN
OZONE - S	SUSAN SEIDELMAN

P

Title	Writer
P'TANG, YANG, KIPPERBANG	JACK ROSENTHAL
P.K. AND THE KID	NEAL BARBERA
P.O.W. - S	ROBERT KAUFMAN
P.O.W. THE ESCAPE	JAMES BRUNER
P.O.W. THE ESCAPE	JEREMY D. LIPP
P.O.W. THE ESCAPE	JOHN LANGLEY
P.O.W. THE ESCAPE	MALCOLM BARBOUR
P.O.W. THE ESCAPE	AVI KLEINBERGER
P.O.W. THE ESCAPE	GIDEON AMIR
P.S. I LOVE YOU (P)	LARRY ROMAN
PACIFIC HEIGHTS	DANIEL PYNE
PACK OF LIES (P)	HUGH WHITEMORE
PACK, THE	ROBERT CLOUSE
PACKAGE, THE	JOHN BISHOP
PADRE PADRONE	PAOLO TAVIANI
PADRE PADRONE	VITTORIO TAVIANI
PAGEMASTER, THE - S	DAVID CASCI
PAID IN FULL	ROBERT BLEES
PAIN IN THE A, A	FRANCIS VEBER
PAINT JOB, THE - S	MICHAEL TAAV
PAINT YOUR WAGON	PADDY CHAYEVSKY†
PAINTER, THE - S	HAMPTON FANCHER
PAJAMA PRINCESS - S	GEORGE HAGEN
PAJAMA PRINCESS - S	NEAL MARSHALL
PAL SMURCH - S	REX MCGEE
PALE RIDER	DENNIS SHRYACK
PALE RIDER	MICHAEL BUTLER
PALER SHADE OF GREY - S	ANN DONAHUE
PALM BEACH - S	ALISON CROSS
PALS - S	JOE ESZTERHAS
PALS - S	MICHAEL NORELL
PALS FOREVER - S	DAVID E. PECKINPAH
PALS FOREVER - S	RICHARD JEFFERIES
PANAMA	DYANNE ASSIMOW
PANAMA - S	ANDY LEWIS
PANAMA - S	MURDO LAIRD
PANAMANIA - S	DAVID CASCI
PANDEMONIUM	JAIME B. KLEIN
PANDEMONIUM	RICHARD WHITLEY
PANHANDLE	BLAKE EDWARDS
PANHANDLE (P)	WALTER HALSEY DAVIS
PANIC - S	ANDY LEWIS
PANIC - S	MICHAEL LERNER
PANIC IN NEEDLE PARK	JOAN DIDION

367

Pa-Ph
FILM WRITERS GUIDE

INDEX OF FILM TITLES

PANIC IN NEEDLE PARK .... JOHN GREGORY DUNNE
PANIC IN THE STREETS .... EDWARD ANHALT
PANIC IN THE STREETS .... RICHARD T. MURPHY
PAPA WAS A PREACHER .... STEPHEN J. FEKE
PAPA'S DELICATE CONDITION .... JACK ROSE
PAPARAZZI - S .... CLAIRE NOTO
PAPARAZZI - S .... DANIEL J. GUNTZELMAN
PAPARAZZI - S .... STEVE K. MARSHALL
PAPER CHASE, THE .... JAMES BRIDGES
PAPER DART - S .... BILL STEWART
PAPER LION .... LARRY ROMAN
PAPER MARRIAGE (P) .... TOM KEMPINSKI
PAPER MASK .... JOHN COLLEE
PAPER MOON .... ALVIN SARGENT
PAPER ORCHARD .... VAL GUEST
PAPER TIGER .... JACK DAVIES
PAPILLON .... LORENZO SEMPLE
PARADISE .... STUART GILLARD
PARADISE (P) .... MARK W. LEE
PARADISE - S .... JUDITH ROSS
PARADISE - S .... MARY AGNES DONOGHUE
PARADISE ALLEY .... SYLVESTER STALLONE
PARADISE MISPLACED - S .... MARC LAWRENCE
PARADISE POSTPONED - S .... JOHN MORTIMER
PARADISE ROAD - S .... JOHN CARLEN
PARALLAX VIEW, THE .... DAVID GILER
PARALLAX VIEW, THE .... LORENZO SEMPLE
PARALLEL WORLDS - S .... LINDSAY MARACOTTA
PARALLELS - S .... DEAN PITCHFORD
PARANOIAC .... JIMMY SANGSTER
PARASITE .... ALAN J. ADLER
PARASITE .... FRANK LEVERING
PARASITE .... MICHAEL SHOOB
PARDNERS .... SIDNEY SHELDON
PARDON MY NINJA - S .... KEVIN S. TENNEY
PARENT TRAP, THE .... DAVID SWIFT
PARENTAL DISCRETION ADVISED - S .... PHILIP MORTON
PARENTAL GUIDANCE - S .... ALLAN BURNS
PARENTHOOD .... BABALOO MANDEL
PARENTHOOD .... LOWELL GANZ
PARENTHOOD .... RON HOWARD
PARENTS .... CHRISTOPHER HAWTHORNE
PARIS AMERICAN - S .... JEFF FAZIO
PARIS BLUES .... WALTER BERNSTEIN
PARIS BY NIGHT .... DAVID HARE
PARIS PROJECT, THE - S .... BOB SWAIM
PARIS TROUT (CTF) .... PETE DEXTER
PARIS WHEN IT SIZZLES .... GEORGE AXELROD
PARIS, TEXAS .... L.M. KIT CARSON
PARIS, TEXAS .... SAM SHEPARD
PARK IS MINE, THE (CTF) .... STEPHEN PETERS
PARK ROW .... SAMUEL FULLER
PARKER .... TREVOR PRESTON
PARKING .... JACQUES DEMY†
PARLOR GAMES - S .... WALON GREEN
PAROLE OFFICER - S .... JOEL BLASBERG
PAROLE PETE - S .... RICHARD DIMITRI
PAROLES ET MUOSIQUE .... ELIE CHOURAQUI
PARROT, THE - S .... MICHAEL J. MURRAY
PART 2 SOUNDER .... LONNE ELDER III
PARTING GLANCES .... BILL SHERWOOD†
PARTNER, THE - S .... JEAN-YVES PITOUN
PARTNERS .... FRANCIS VEBER
PARTNERS .... NORMAN SNIDER
PARTNERS IN CRIME - S .... BRAD MIRMAN
PARTNERS IN TIME - S .... ALEC LORIMORE
PARTY ANIMAL, THE .... ALAN C. FOX
PARTY ANIMAL, THE .... DAVID BEAIRD
PARTY BALL - S .... HENRY OLEK
PARTY LINE .... RICHARD BRANDES
PARTY'S OVER, THE .... MARC BEHM
PARTY, THE .... BLAKE EDWARDS
PARTY, THE .... FRANK WALDMAN†
PARTY, THE .... TOM WALDMAN†
PARTY, THE (P) .... TREVOR GRIFFITHS
PASADENA KID, THE - S .... HARRIS ORKIN
PASCALI'S ISLAND .... JAMES DEARDEN
PASQUALINO SETTEBELLEZZE .... LINA WERTMULLER
PASS THE AMMO .... JOEL COHEN
PASS THE AMMO .... NEIL COHEN
PASS THE BUTLER (P) .... JONATHAN LYNN
PASSAGE HOME, A - S .... TODD ROBINSON
PASSAGE TO INDIA, A .... DAVID LEAN†
PASSAGE, THE .... BRUCE NICOLAYSEN
PASSAGES (SHORT) .... STEVEN SODERBERGH
PASSENGER 57 - S .... DAVID LOUGHERY
PASSENGER 57 - S .... STEWART RAFFILL
PASSENGER, THE .... MARK PEPLOE
PASSENGER, THE .... MICHELANGELO ANTONIONI
PASSING GAME, THE (P) .... STEVE TESICH
PASSION .... JEAN-LUC GODARD
PASSION OF ANNA, THE .... INGMAR BERGMAN
PASSION OF MARTIN, THE - S .... ANDREW PAYNE
PASSION OF MIND - S .... RON BASS
PASSION PLAY - S .... CHARLES ROBERT CARNER
PASSIONE D'AMORE .... ETTORE SCOLA
PASSOVER PLOT, THE .... PATRICIA L. KNOP
PASSPORT TO TREASON .... NORMAN HUDIS
PASSWORD IS COURAGE, THE .... ANDREW STONE
PAST MIDNIGHT .... FRANK NORWOOD
PAT GARRETT AND BILLY THE KID .... RUDOLPH G. WURLITZER
PATER NOSTER (P) .... DAN GURSKIS
PATERNITY .... CHARLIE PETERS
PATHFINDER .... NILS GAUP
PATHS OF GLORY .... CALDER WILLINGHAM
PATHS OF GLORY .... STANLEY KUBRICK
PATRICK .... EVERETT DEROCHE
PATRICK PIERCE MOTEL, THE - S .... HUGH LEONARD
PATRIOT'S GAME, THE - S .... MAURICE E. HURLEY
PATRIOT, THE .... ANDY RUBEN
PATRIOT, THE .... KATT SHEA RUBEN
PATSY, THE .... JERRY LEWIS
PATTI ROCKS .... CHRIS MULKEY
PATTI ROCKS .... DAVID BURTON MORRIS
PATTI ROCKS .... JOHN JENKINS
PATTI ROCKS .... KAREN LANDRY
PATTON .... FRANCIS FORD COPPOLA
PATTY HEARST .... NICHOLAS KAZAN
PAUL BUNYAN - S .... CARL GOTTLIEB
PAULA .... WILLIAM B. SACKHEIM
PAULINE AT THE BEACH .... ERIC ROHMER
PAWNBROKER, THE .... MORT FINE†
PAWNSHOP KID - S .... ALEX ZAMM
PAY DIRT - S .... BILL PHILLIPS
PAY THE WIDOW - S .... DAVID WILLIAMSON
PAYBACK - S .... JOE IDE
PAYOFF (CTF) .... DAVID WEISBERG
PAYOFF (CTF) .... DOUGLAS S. COOK
PAYOFSKY'S DISCOVERY - S .... ISRAEL HOROVITZ
PEACEKEEPERS AT WAR - S .... JOHN J. SCHALTER
PEACEMAKER .... KEVIN S. TENNEY
PEACEMAKER - S .... FRANK NORWOOD
PEACHES POINT - S .... BLAIR FERGUSON
PEACOCK RAG - S .... CINDY MYERS
PEARL - S .... BO GOLDMAN
PEARL HART - S .... JAMES KAHN
PEARL OF THE SOUTH PACIFIC .... EDWIN BLUM
PEE WEES .... DARIN SCOTT
PEE-WEE HERMAN VS. THE FLYING SAUCERS - S .... TODD DURHAM
PEE-WEE'S BIG ADVENTURE .... MICHAEL VARHOL
PEE-WEE'S BIG ADVENTURE .... PAUL REUBENS
PEE-WEE'S BIG ADVENTURE .... PHIL HARTMAN
PEEKSKILL - S .... ROBERT BORIS
PEEL MY BANANA - S .... ALAN JAY GLUECKMAN
PEEPER .... W.D. RICHTER
PEERS - S .... FRANK DEFORD
PEERS - S .... THOMAS POPE
PEGGY SUE GOT MARRIED .... ARLENE SARNER
PEGGY SUE GOT MARRIED .... JERRY LEICHTLING
PEKING MEDALLION, THE .... BRIAN H. CLEMENS
PELLE THE CONQUEROR .... BILLE AUGUST
PEN PALS - S .... MICHAEL ALAN EDDY
PENALTY BOX, THE - S .... C. COURTNEY JOYNER
PENITENT, THE .... CLIFF OSMOND
PENITENTIARY .... JAMAA FANAKA
PENITENTIARY II .... JAMAA FANAKA
PENITENTIARY III .... JAMAA FANAKA
PENKNIFE - S .... CHARLES ZEV COHEN
PENN & TELLER GET KILLED .... PENN JILLETTE
PENN & TELLER GET KILLED .... TELLER
PENNIES FROM HEAVEN .... DENNIS POTTER
PENNY ANTE .... MARC SACHNOFF
PENNY FOR THE FERRYMAN - S .... LARRY B. WILLIAMS
PENNY PRINCESS .... VAL GUEST
PEOPLE THAT TIME FORGOT, THE .... PATRICK TILLEY
PEOPLE UNDER THE STAIRS, THE - S .... WES CRAVEN
PEOPLE WILL TALK .... JOSEPH L. MANKIEWICZ
PEPI, LUCI & BOM .... PEDRO ALMODOVAR
PEPPERMINT SODA .... DIANE KURYS
PERCEVAL .... ERIC ROHMER
PERCY .... HUGH LEONARD
PERFECT .... AARON LATHAM
PERFECT .... JAMES BRIDGES
PERFECT BRIDE, THE (CTF) .... CLAIRE MONTGOMERY
PERFECT BRIDE, THE (CTF) .... MONTY MONTGOMERY
PERFECT COUNTERFEIT - S .... JACK BEHR
PERFECT COUNTERFEIT - S .... SANDY KROOPF
PERFECT COUPLE, A .... ALLAN F. NICHOLLS
PERFECT COUPLE, A .... ROBERT ALTMAN
PERFECT COUPLE, THE - S .... BABALOO MANDEL
PERFECT COUPLE, THE - S .... LOWELL GANZ
PERFECT CRIME, THE - S .... BRIAN GARFIELD
PERFECT DAY FOR RASPBERRY RIPPLE, A - S .... DAVID SELTZER
PERFECT FURLOUGH, THE .... STANLEY SHAPIRO†
PERFECT HARMONY (CTF) .... DAVID OBST
PERFECT MAN, THE - S .... RICHARD WHITLEY
PERFECT PARTY, THE (P) .... A.R. GURNEY
PERFECT STRANGERS .... LARRY COHEN
PERFECT TIMING - S .... DIANE ENGLISH
PERFECT WEAPON, THE .... DAVID CAMPBELL WILSON
PERFECT WITNESS, THE (CTF) .... RON HUTCHINSON
PERFECT WITNESS, THE (CTF) .... TERRY CURTIS FOX
PERFECTLY NORMAL .... EUGENE LIPINSKI
PERFECTLY NORMAL .... PAUL QUARRINGTON
PERFORMANCE .... DONALD CAMMELL
PERFUME (P) .... JAMES KENNEDY
PERFUME - S .... JOHN ROMANO
PERFUME OF THE CYCLONE .... PATRICK LEE
PERILS OF GWENDOLINE, THE .... JUST JAECKIN
PERMANENT RECORD .... ALICE LIDDLE
PERMANENT RECORD .... JARRE FEES
PERMANENT RECORD .... LARRY KETRON
PERMANENT VACATION .... JIM JARMUSCH
PERSIAN RANSOM, THE - S .... CHRIS BRYANT
PERSIAN RANSOM, THE - S .... ALLAN G. SCOTT
PERSONA .... INGMAR BERGMAN
PERSONAL BEST .... ROBERT TOWNE
PERSONAL CHOICE .... DAVID SAPERSTEIN
PERSONAL LEAVE .... DYANNE ASSIMOW
PERSONAL SERVICES .... DAVID LELAND
PERSONALITY (P) .... GINA WENDKOS
PERSONALS, THE .... PETER MARKLE
PET PEOPLE - S .... MICHAEL MCDOWELL
PET SEMATARY .... STEPHEN KING
PET SEMATARY 2 - S .... RICHARD OUTTEN
PETALS IN THE WIND - S .... GINNY CERRELLA
PETE'N'TILLIE .... JULIUS J. EPSTEIN
PETE'S DRAGON .... MALCOLM MARMORSTEIN
PETER PAN - S .... ANDREW BIRKIN
PETER PAN - S .... LAWRENCE LASKER
PETER PAN - S .... WALTER F. PARKES
PETER PAN - S .... LASSE HALLSTROM
PETER'S EARTH - S .... RICHARD JEFFERIES
PETTING ZOO - S .... RICHARD KRAMER
PETULIA .... LAWRENCE B. MARCUS
PEUR SUR LA VILLE .... FRANCIS VEBER
PEYTON PLACE .... JOHN MICHAEL HAYES
PG - S .... SOLLACE MITCHELL
PHAEDRA .... JULES DASSIN
PHANTASM .... DON COSCARELLI
PHANTASM II .... DON COSCARELLI
PHANTOM - S .... JAMES DEARDEN
PHANTOM OF MANHATTAN .... DUKE SANDEFUR
PHANTOM OF THE MALL: ERIC'S REVENGE .... ROBERT KING
PHANTOM OF THE MALL: ERIC'S REVENGE .... SCOTT J. SCHNEID
PHANTOM OF THE MALL: ERIC'S REVENGE .... FREDERICK R. ULRICH
PHANTOM OF THE MALL: ERIC'S REVENGE .... TONY MICHELMAN
PHANTOM OF THE OPERA, THE .... GERRY O'HARA
PHANTOM OF THE OPERA, THE .... DUKE SANDEFUR
PHANTOM OF THE PARADISE .... BRIAN DEPALMA
PHAR LAP .... DAVID WILLIAMSON
PHASE IV .... MAYO SIMON
PHENOM - S .... BILL MCKINNEY, JR.
PHENOMENA .... DARIO ARGENTO
PHENOMENON - S .... LEWIS JOHN CARLINO
PHILADELPHIA EXPERIMENT, THE .... DON JAKOBY
PHILADELPHIA EXPERIMENT, THE .... MICHAEL JANOVER
PHILADELPHIA EXPERIMENT, THE .... WALLACE BENNETT
PHILADELPHIA EXPERIMENT, THE .... WILLIAM GRAY
PHILANTHROPIST, THE (P) .... CHRISTOPHER HAMPTON
PHOBIA .... GARY A. SHERMAN
PHOBIA .... PETER BELLWOOD
PHOBIA .... RONALD SHUSETT
PHOBIA .... JIMMY SANGSTER

Title	Writer
PHOTO - S	THOMAS BABE
PHOTOPLAY - S	DALENE YOUNG
PHYSICAL CHEMISTRY - S	STEPHEN FISCHER
PHYSICAL EVIDENCE	BILL PHILLIPS
PHYSICAL EVIDENCE	STEVEN RANSOHOFF
PIANO SOLO - S	A.J. CAROTHERS
PICASSO TRIGGER	ANDY SIDARIS
PICK-UP ARTIST, THE	JAMES TOBACK
PICKUP ON SOUTH STREET	SAMUEL FULLER
PICKLE ON MY TONGUE - S	ADAM RIFKIN
PICNIC	DANIEL TARADASH
PICNIC AT HANGING ROCK	CLIFF GREEN
PICTURE MOMMY DEAD	ROBERT SHERMAN
PICTURE OF GORIAN DAY, THE - S	GEORGE GIPE
PICTURE OF FIDELMAN - S	ROGER L. SIMON
PICTURE SHOW MAN, THE	JOAN LONG
PICTURE SNATCHER, THE	ALLEN RIVKIN†
PICTURES FROM THE WATER TRADE - S	JUDITH RASCOE
PIE IN THE SKY - S	BRYAN GORDON
PIECE, THE - S	FRANK MILITARY JR.
PIECE OF THE ACTION, A	TIMOTHY MARCH
PIECES OF SEVEN - S	DENNE BART PETITCLERC
PIED PIPER, THE	ANDREW BIRKIN
PIED PIPER, THE	JACQUES DEMY†
PIED PIPER, THE	MARK PEPLOE
PIED PIPER, THE - S	HERSCHEL WEINGROD
PIED PIPER, THE - S	TIMOTHY HARRIS
PIGEON BOY - S	LEE REYNOLDS
PIGEON THAT TOOK ROME, THE	MEL SHAVELSON
PIGEONS	RON WHYTE†
PIGSKINS - S	BRUCE KIRSCHBAUM
PILGRIM (P)	STEPHEN METCALFE
PILGRIM - S	DAVID ANDRUS
PILGRIMAGE - S	NEAL SHUSTERMAN
PILLOW TALK	MAURICE RICHLIN†
PILLOW TALK	STANLEY SHAPIRO†
PILOT ERROR - S	RICHARD KLEINBERG
PILOT, THE	ROBERT S. DAVIS
PIN	SANDOR STERN
PINCUSHION - S	JOHN RAFFO
PINCUSHION - S	JEB STUART
PING PONG	JERRY LIU
PINK & BLUE - S	WILLIAM TEPPER
PINK CADILLAC	JOHN ESKOW
PINK FLAMINGOS	JOHN WATERS
PINK FLOYD - THE WALL	ROGER WATERS
PINK MOTEL	JIM KOUF
PINK MOUNTAIN TINNY - S	STEPHEN H. FOREMAN
PINK PANTHER STRIKES AGAIN, THE	BLAKE EDWARDS
PINK PANTHER STRIKES AGAIN, THE	FRANK WALDMAN†
PINK PANTHER, THE	BLAKE EDWARDS
PINK PANTHER, THE	MAURICE RICHLIN†
PINKO - S	PAUL D. ZIMMERMAN
PINKY	PHILIP DUNNE
PINOCCHIO AND THE EMPEROR OF THE NIGHT (AF)	DENNIS O'FLAHERTY
PINOCCHIO AND THE EMPEROR OF THE NIGHT (AF)	BARRY O'BRIEN
PINOCCHIO AND THE EMPEROR OF THE NIGHT (AF)	ROBBY LONDON
PIPE DREAMS	STEPHEN F. VERONA
PIPELINER - S	PAUL SCHRADER
PIPPIN (P)	ROGER O. HIRSON
PIRANDELLO FACTOR, THE - S	DENNIS FELDMAN
PIRANHA	JOHN SAYLES
PIRATE MOVIE, THE	TREVOR FARRANT
PIRATES	GERARD BRACH
PIRATES	ROMAN POLANSKI
PIRATES (P)	MARK W. LEE
PIRATES OF PENZANCE, THE	WILFORD LEACH†
PIROUETTE - S	MICHAEL J. AUERBACH
PISTOLEERS - S	ROB THOMPSON
PIT AND THE PENDULUM, THE	DENNIS PAOLI
PIT AND THE PENDULUM, THE	RICHARD MATHESON
PIT BULLS FROM HELL - S	MATTHEW DORFF
PIT, THE	IAN A. STUART
PITCAIRN ISLAND - S	ROBERT BOLT
PIXOTE	HECTOR BABENCO
PIZZA MAN	J.F. LAWTON
PLACE IN TIME, A (SHORT)	CHARLES LANE
PLACE OF WEEPING	DARRELL ROODT
PLACE TO COME TO, A - S	JULIAN BARRY
PLACE TO CRASH, A - S	LARRY DAVID
PLACE TO GO, A	CLIVE EXTON
PLACES IN THE HEART	ROBERT BENTON
PLAGUE DOGS, THE (AF)	MARTIN ROSEN
PLAGUE, THE - S	LUIS PUENZO
PLAIN CLOTHES	A. SCOTT FRANK
PLAIN CLOTHES	DANIEL H. VINING
PLAISIR D'AMOUR - S	RICKY BLACKWOOD
PLANES, TRAINS AND AUTOMOBILES	JOHN HUGHES
PLANET OF THE TEENAGERS - S	PETER KRIKES
PLANET OF THE TEENAGERS - S	STEVE MEERSON
PLASMA CELL REPORT - S	MICHAEL J. AUERBACH
PLASTIC MAN - S	CHARLES GALE
PLASTIC MILE, THE - S	MORRIE RUVINSKY
PLATINUM SUNSET - S	BRUCE VILANCH
PLATINUM - S	JOE ESZTERHAS
PLATOON	OLIVER STONE
PLATOON LEADER	ANDREW DEUTSCH
PLATOON LEADER	DAVID WALKER
PLATOON LEADER	RICK MARX
PLAY CRAZY - S	DAVID FREEMAN
PLAY DIRTY	MELVYN BRAGG
PLAY IT AGAIN, SAM	WOODY ALLEN
PLAY IT AS IT LAYS	JOAN DIDION
PLAY IT AS IT LAYS	JOHN GREGORY DUNNE
PLAY MISTY FOR ME	DEAN RIESNER
PLAY MONEY - S	ALEX GORBY
PLAY MONEY - S	ANDY ROSE
PLAY MONEY - S	ROBERT KLANE
PLAYBOYS, THE - S	SHANE CONNAUGHTON
PLAYBOYS, THE - S	KERRY CRABBE
PLAYER, THE - S	MICHAEL TOLKIN
PLAYERS	ARNOLD SCHULMAN
PLAYGIRL	ROBERT BLEES
PLAYIN' IN THE BAND - S	MARK ALLEN SMITH
PLAYING FOR KEEPS	BOB WEINSTEIN
PLAYING FOR KEEPS	HARVEY WEINSTEIN
PLAYING FOR KEEPS	JEREMY LEVEN
PLAYING TO WIN - S	JOHN BEAIRD
PLAYLAND - S	JOAN DIDION
PLAYLAND - S	JOHN GREGORY DUNNE
PLAYPEN, THE - S	ROBERT CARRINGTON
PLAYWRIGHT'S DOG (P)	ERNEST THOMPSON
PLAZA SUITE	NEIL SIMON
PLEASE TURN OVER	NORMAN HUDIS
PLEASURE GIRLS, THE	GERRY O'HARA
PLEDGING MY LOVE (P)	JOHN STEPPLING
PLENTY	DAVID HARE
PLOT AGAINST HARRY, THE	MICHAEL ROEMER
PLOT TO MURDER THE POPE, THE - S	GERALD GREEN
PLOUGHMAN'S LUNCH, THE	IAN MCEWAN
PLUMB DRILLIN - S	ALLAN G. SCOTT
PLUMB DRILLIN - S	CHRIS BRYANT
PLUMBER, THE	PETER WEIR
PLUMBER, THE - S	LEWIS A. COLICK
PLUMED SERPENT - S	ROBERT BOLT
PLUTO BY JOEY - S	LYNN SIEFERT
PLUTO NASH - S	NEIL CUTHBERT
POCKET MONEY	TERENCE MALICK
POCKETFUL OF MIRACLES	HARRY TUGEND†
POE - S	DENNIS PALUMBO
POINT, THE - S	CHRIS KEYSER
POINT AFTER - S	JEREMY JOE KRONSBERG
POINT BLACK	ALEXANDER JACOBS†
POINT BLANK - S	REED STEINER
POINT BREAK	PETER ILIFF
POINT BREAK	RICK KING
POINT OF VIEW	DAVID AARON COHEN
POISON	TODD HAYNES
POISON APPLES - S	TODD DURHAM
POISON IVY - S	ANDY RUBEN
POISON IVY - S	KATT SHEA RUBEN
POISON IVY - S	BENNETT YELLIN
POISON IVY - S	PETER FARRELLY
POLICE ACADEMY	HUGH WILSON
POLICE ACADEMY	NEAL ISRAEL
POLICE ACADEMY	PAT PROFT
POLICE ACADEMY 2	BARRY BLAUSTEIN
POLICE ACADEMY 2	DAVID SHEFFIELD
POLICE ACADEMY 3	EUGENE QUINTANO
POLICE ACADEMY 4	EUGENE QUINTANO
POLICE ACADEMY 5	STEPHEN J. CURWICK
POLICE ACADEMY 6	STEPHEN J. CURWICK
POLICE PYTHON .357 - S	TONY KAYDEN
POLICEMAN, THE - S	DAVID BIRKE
POLICEMAN, THE - S	MICHAEL AXEL GRAHAM
POLICEMEN, THE - S	RICHARD CHAPMAN
POLLOSK (P)	JON ROBIN BAITZ
POLLYANNA	DAVID SWIFT
POLTERGEIST	MARK VICTOR
POLTERGEIST	MICHAEL GRAIS
POLTERGEIST	STEVEN SPIELBERG
POLTERGEIST II	MARK VICTOR
POLTERGEIST II	MICHAEL GRAIS
POLTERGEIST III	BRIAN TAGGERT
POLTERGEIST III	GARY A. SHERMAN
POLYESTER	JOHN WATERS
POLYGAMIST - S	DAVID SHABER
POM-POM GIRLS, THE	JOSEPH RUBEN
POMPEII	HARRY ALAN TOWERS
POMPEII	RICK MARX
POODLE SPRINGS - S	ROGER TOWNE
POODLE SPRINGS - S	MICHAEL BLAKE
POOR COW	KENNETH LOACH
POOR FOLKS' PLEASURE (P)	LEN JENKIN
POOR LITTLE LAMBS - S	PAUL RUDNICK
POOR LITTLE LAMBS - S	WARREN D. LEIGHT
POOR LITTLE RICH GIRL	HARRY TUGEND†
POPI - S	JAMES BRENDAN PATTERSON
POPCORN	ALAN ORMSBY
POPCORN CAPER, THE - S	NORMAN STEINBERG
POPE JOAN	JOHN BRILEY
POPE OF GREENWICH VILLAGE, THE	VINCENT PATRICK
POPEYE	JULES FEIFFER
PORGY AND BESS	N. RICHARD NASH
PORKY'S	BOB CLARK
PORKY'S II	ALAN ORMSBY
PORKY'S II	BOB CLARK
PORKY'S II	ROGER SWAYBILL†
PORKY'S REVENGE!	ZIGGY STEINBERG
PORNOGRAPHER'S DAUGHTER, THE (P)	TERRY CURTIS FOX
PORRIDGE	DICK CLEMENT
PORRIDGE	IAN LAFRENAIS
PORT OF CALL - S	AMOS POE
PORT ROYAL - S	DENNIS CLARK
PORTAGE TO SAN CRISTOBAL, THE - S	CHRISTOPHER HAMPTON
PORTNOY'S COMPLAINT	ERNEST LEHMAN
PORTRAIT IN BLACK	IVAN GOFF
PORTRAIT IN SMOKE	KEN HUGHES
PORTRAIT OF A HITMAN	YABO YABLONSKY
PORTRAIT OF ALISON	KEN HUGHES
PORTRAIT OF AN ARTIST AS A YOUNG MAN, A	JUDITH RASCOE
PORTRAIT, THE	AKIRA KUROSAWA
POSED FOR MURDER	JOHN A. GALLAGHER
POSEIDON ADVENTURE, THE	STIRLING SILLIPHANT
POSEIDON ADVENTURE, THE	WENDELL MAYES
POSITIVE I.D.	ANDY ANDERSON
POSSE	CHRISTOPHER E. KNOPF
POSSE	WILLIAM ROBERTS
POSSE FROM HELL	CLAIR HUFFAKER†
POSSESSION (P)	LYLE D. KESSLER
POST OFFICE - S	ROBERT KLANE
POSTCARD FROM PARADISE - S	PETER FOLDY
POSTCARDS FROM THE EDGE	CARRIE FISHER
POSTMAN ALWAYS RINGS TWICE, THE	DAVID MAMET
POSTMAN'S KNOCK	JOHN BRILEY
POSTMAN, THE - S	ERIC ROTH
POSTMARK FOR DANGER	KEN HUGHES
POT OF GOLD - S	ELLIOT M. STERN
POTTER TAKES FLIGHT - S	PHILIP DUNNE
POTTER TAKES FLIGHT - S	PERRY HOWZE
POTTER TAKES FLIGHT - S	RANDY HOWZE
POUND	ROBERT DOWNEY
POUND PUPPIES AND THE LEGEND OF BIG PAW (AF)	JIM CARLSON
POUND PUPPIES AND THE LEGEND OF BIG PAW (AF)	TERRANCE MCDONNELL
POWDER BLUE - S	CLIFTON CAMPBELL
POWELL - S	STANLEY MANN
POWER	DAVID HIMMELSTEIN
POWER FAILURE (P)	LARRY GELBART
POWER OF AN ATTORNEY - S	MICHAEL TOLKIN
POWER OF ONE, THE - S	ROBERT MARK KAMEN
POWER OF THE DOG - S	ED HUME
POWER PLAY	MARTYN BURKE
POWER TRIP - S	NORMAN WEXLER
POWER, THE	JEFFREY OBROW
POWER, THE	JOHN HOPKINS
POWER, THE	JOHN PENNEY
POWER, THE	STEPHEN W. CARPENTER
POWER, THE (1967)	JOHN GAY
POWER: THE PHIL SPECTOR STORY - S	MELANIE MINTZ
POWWOW HIGHWAY	JANET HEANEY
POWWOW HIGHWAY	JEAN STAWARZ
PRACTICALLY A JOKE - S	RICHARD WHITLEY
PRACTICALLY NORMAL - S	BRADFORD O'NEIL
PRACTICE, THE - S	ROBERT ROY POOL

INDEX OF FILM TITLES

PRACTICE, THE - S ... TOM MANKIEWICZ
PRAIRIE DU CHIEN (P) ... DAVID MAMET
PRANCER ... GREG TAYLOR
PRANKS ... JEFFREY OBROW
PRANKS ... STEPHEN W. CARPENTER
PRANKS ... STACEY GIACHINO
PRANKSTER CHRONICLES - S ... STUART BIRNBAUM
PRAVDA (P) ... DAVID HARE
PRAVDA - S ... DOUG RICHARDSON
PRAY FOR DEATH ... JAMES BOOTH
PRAY FOR RAIN - S ... TONY GILROY
PRAY TV ... NICK CASTLE
PRAYER FOR MY DAUGHTER, (P) ... THOMAS BABE
PRAYER FOR THE DYING, A ... MARTIN LYNCH
PRAYER FOR THE DYING, A ... EDMUND WARD
PRAYER OF THE ROLLERBOYS ... PETER ILIFF
PRECIOUS IMAGES (SHORT) ... CHUCK WORKMAN
PRECIOUS METAL - S ... CLAYTON S. FROHMAN
PRECIOUS SONS - S ... GEORGE FURTH
PREDATOR ... JIM THOMAS
PREDATOR ... JOHN THOMAS
PREDATOR 2 ... JIM THOMAS
PREDATOR 2 ... JOHN THOMAS
PREGGERS - S ... PAUL BOORSTIN
PREGGERS - S ... SHARON BOORSTIN
PREHISTORIC WOMEN ... MICHAEL CARRERAS
PRELUDE - S ... GORDON GREISMAN
PRELUDE TO A KISS (P) ... CRAIG LUCAS
PREMONITION ... ALAN S. RUDOLPH
PREPPIES ... CHUCK VINCENT
PREPPIES ... RICK MARX
PRESENT LAUGHTER - S ... SOLLACE MITCHELL
PRESIDENT ELOPES, THE - S ... RON BASS
PRESIDENT ELOPES, THE - S ... WILLIAM RICHERT
PRESIDENT MUST DIE, THE ... CLIFF OSMOND
PRESIDENT MUST DIE, THE ... JAMES L. CONWAY
PRESIDENT STEPS OUT, THE - S ... ELLEN GREEN
PRESIDENT STEPS OUT, THE - S ... CLIFFORD GREEN
PRESIDENT'S ANALYST, THE ... THEODORE J. FLICKER
PRESIDENT'S WOMEN, THE ... DAVID ODELL
PRESIDIO, THE ... LARRY FERGUSON
PRESSURE - S ... KEVIN QUINN
PRESSURE POINT, THE ... S. LEE POGOSTIN
PRESTIDIGITATION - S ... LARRY B. WILLIAMS
PRESTON STURGES: THE RISE AND FALL OF AN AMERICAN DREAMER (FD) ... TODD MCCARTHY
PRESUMED INNOCENT ... FRANK R. PIERSON
PRESUMED INNOCENT ... ALAN J. PAKULA
PRETENDER, THE - S ... GEORGE GALLO
PRETTY BABY ... POLLY PLATT
PRETTY IN PINK ... JOHN HUGHES
PRETTY MAIDS ALL IN A ROW ... GENE RODDENBERRY
PRETTY POISON ... LORENZO SEMPLE
PRETTY SMART ... DAN HOSKINS
PRETTY WOMAN ... J.F. LAWTON
PRETTYKILL ... SANDRA K. BAILEY
PREY, THE ... EDWIN SCOTT BROWN
PREY, THE ... SUMMER BROWN
PRICE OF FAME (P) ... CHARLES GRODIN
PRICE OF LIFE, THE (SHORT) ... STEPHEN M. TOLKIN
PRICE, THE (P) ... ARTHUR MILLER
PRICK UP YOUR EARS ... ALAN BENNETT
PRIDE AND JOY (P) ... MONTE MERRICK
PRIDE AND JOY - S ... JOHN MCCORMICK
PRIDE AND JOY - S ... ROSS LA MANNA
PRIDE AND JOY - S ... BILL MCKINNEY, JR.
PRIDE AND THE JOY, THE - S ... JOHN MANKIEWICZ
PRIDE AND THE PASSION, THE ... EDWARD ANHALT
PRIEST OF LOVE ... ALAN PLATER
PRIMARY COLORS - S ... STEPHEN VERONA
PRIMARY ENGLISH CLASS, THE (P) ... ISRAEL HOROVITZ
PRIME CUT ... ROBERT DILLON
PRIME OF MISS JEAN BRODIE, THE ... JAY PRESSON ALLEN
PRIME RISK ... MICHAEL FARGAS
PRIMITIVE, THE - S ... DAN O'BANNON
PRIMITIVE, THE - S ... DON JAKOBY
PRIMO - S ... JEREMY IACONE
PRIMO BABY ... A.A. LEVER
PRINCE AND THE PAUPER, THE ... GEORGE MACDONALD FRASER
PRINCE CHARMING - S ... DOUG PALAU
PRINCE CHARMING - S ... GEORGE GIPE
PRINCE CHARMING - S ... MAGGIE KLEINMAN
PRINCE JACK ... BERT LOVITT
PRINCE OF 47TH STREET, THE - S ... DAVID SHABER
PRINCE OF DARKNESS ... JOHN CARPENTER
PRINCE OF PARK AVENUE, THE - S ... MAX EMBER
PRINCE OF PENNSYLVANIA, THE ... RON NYSWANER
PRINCE OF POP, THE - S ... GINNY CERRELLA
PRINCE OF THE CITY ... SIDNEY LUMET
PRINCE OF THE CITY ... JAY PRESSON ALLEN
PRINCE OF TIDES, THE - S ... BECKY JOHNSTON
PRINCE OF TIDES, THE - S ... PAT CONROY
PRINCES IN EXILE ... JOE WIESENFELD
PRINCESS ACADEMY, THE ... SANDRA WEINTRAUB ROLAND
PRINCESS BRIDE, THE ... WILLIAM GOLDMAN
PRINCESS DAISY (MS) ... DIANA HAMMOND
PRINCESS OF MARS - S ... TED ELLIOTT
PRINCESS OF MARS - S ... TERRY P. ROSSIO
PRINCESS OF PAROLE - S ... RONNI KERN
PRINCESS OF PLUTO - S ... J.T. ALLEN
PRINCIPAL, THE ... FRANK DEESE
PRIOR LIFE OF MICKEY SLATER, THE - S ... JEAN FORD
PRIOR LIFE OF MICKEY SLATER, THE - S ... S. MICHAEL COLE
PRISM - S ... HAMPTON FANCHER
PRISON ... C. COURTNEY JOYNER
PRISON PLANET - S ... JOHN HUGHES
PRISON STORIES: WOMEN ON THE INSIDE (CTF) ... DICK BEEBE
PRISON STORIES: WOMEN ON THE INSIDE (CTF) ... JULE SELBO
PRISON STORIES: WOMEN ON THE INSIDE (CTF) ... MARLANE MEYER
PRISON STORIES: WOMEN ON THE INSIDE (CTF) ... MARTIN JONES
PRISONER OF HONOR (CTF) - S ... RON HUTCHINSON
PRISONER OF SECOND AVENUE, THE ... NEIL SIMON
PRISONER OF THE ROAD - S ... PATRICK DUNCAN
PRISONER OF WAR ... ALLEN RIVKIN†
PRISONER OF ZENDA, THE ... DICK CLEMENT
PRISONER OF ZENDA, THE ... IAN LAFRENAIS
PRISONERS OF INTERTIA ... J. NOYES SCHER
PRITCHARD COUNTY - S ... WILLIAM J. DAVIES
PRITCHARD COUNTY - S ... WILLIAM OSBORNE
PRIVATE ANGELO ... PETER USTINOV
PRIVATE BENJAMIN ... CHARLES SHYER
PRIVATE BENJAMIN ... HARVEY MILLER
PRIVATE BENJAMIN ... NANCY J. MEYERS
PRIVATE COLLECTIONS ... BRUCE WILLIAMS
PRIVATE COLLECTIONS ... DAVID HEISLER
PRIVATE DUTY NURSES ... GEORGE B. ARMITAGE
PRIVATE EAR AND THE PUBLIC EYE, THE (P) ... PETER SHAFFER
PRIVATE EYES, THE ... JOHN MYHERS
PRIVATE EYES, THE ... TIM CONWAY
PRIVATE FILES OF J. EDGAR HOOVER,. THE ... LARRY COHEN
PRIVATE FUNCTION, A ... MALCOLM MOWBRAY
PRIVATE FUNCTION, A ... ALAN BENNETT
PRIVATE INVESTIGATIONS ... DAVID WARFIELD
PRIVATE INVESTIGATIONS ... JOHN DAHL
PRIVATE LESSONS ... DAN GREENBURG
PRIVATE LIFE OF SHERLOCK HOLMES, THE ... BILLY WILDER
PRIVATE LIFE OF SHERLOCK HOLMES, THE ... I.A.L. DIAMOND†
PRIVATE LIFE, A ... ANDREW DAVIES
PRIVATE OPENING (P) ... NORMAN WEXLER
PRIVATE PICTURES - S ... CRAIG BOLOTIN
PRIVATE POTTER ... RONALD HARWOOD
PRIVATE SCHOOL ... DAN GREENBURG
PRIVATE SCHOOL ... SUZANNE O'MALLEY
PRIVATE SCREENING - S ... DAVID TAYLOR
PRIVATE WAR ... TERRY BORST
PRIVATE WARS - S ... JENNIFER COLLOPY
PRIVATES ON PARADE ... PETER NICHOLS
PRIVILEGE ... YVONNE RAINER
PRIVILEGED ... MICHAEL HOFFMAN
PRIVILEGED ... RUPERT WALTERS
PRIZE FIGHTER, THE ... JOHN MYHERS
PRIZE FIGHTER, THE ... TIM CONWAY
PRIZE, THE ... ERNEST LEHMAN
PRIZZI'S FAMILY - S ... WILLIAM RICHERT
PRIZZI'S HONOR ... JANET ROACH
PRIZZI'S HONOR ... RICHARD CONDON
PROBLEM CHILD ... LARRY KARASZEWSKI
PROBLEM CHILD ... SCOTT ALEXANDER
PROBLEM CHILD 2 ... LARRY KARASZEWSKI
PROBLEM CHILD 2 ... SCOTT ALEXANDER
PRODIGAL SON - S ... ELIZABETH PASSERELLI
PRODIGAL, THE ... JAMES F. COLLIER†
PRODUCERS, THE ... MEL BROOKS
PROFESSIONALS, THE ... RICHARD BROOKS
PROFESSIONE: REPORTER ... MARK PEPLOE
PROFESSIONE: REPORTER ... MICHELANGELO ANTONIONI
PROFESSOR HOLMES - S ... JOHN J. SCHALTER
PROGNOSIS NEGATIVE - S ... LARRY DAVID
PROGRAMMED TO KILL ... ROBERT SHORT
PROHIBITION STORY - S ... THOMAS POPE
PROJECT X ... LAWRENCE LASKER
PROJECT X ... STANLEY WEISER
PROJECTIONIST, THE ... HARRY HURWITZ
PROJECTIONS ... RENE BALCER
PROLOGUES - S ... MURDO LAIRD
PROM NIGHT ... WILLIAM GRAY
PROM NIGHT ... ROBERT GUZA JR.
PROMETHEUS - S ... DENNE BART PETITCLERC
PROMISE AT DAWN ... JULES DASSIN
PROMISE HER ANYTHING ... WILLIAM PETER BLATTY
PROMISE, THE ... GARRY MICHAEL WHITE
PROMISED LAND ... MICHAEL HOFFMAN
PROMISES IN THE DARK ... LORING MANDEL
PROMISES, PROMISES (P) ... NEIL SIMON
PROMOTER, THE - S ... ERIC HANSEN
PROMOTER, THE - S ... GREGORY HANSEN
PROOF ... JOCELYN MOOREHOUSE
PROOF POSITIVE - S ... STEVEN SODERBERGH
PROOF POSITIVE (CTF) - S ... JONATHAN FELDMAN
PROPATIA - S ... DAVID SHABER
PROPHECY ... DAVID SELTZER
PROS & CONS - S ... GEORGE GALLO
PROSECUTION, THE - S ... TERRY CURTIS FOX
PROSPECT, THE - S ... ANN DONAHUE
PROSPERO'S BOOK ... PETER GREENAWAY
PROSTITUTE ... TONY GARNETT
PROTECTOR, THE ... JAMES GLICKENHAUS
PROTECTOR, THE - S ... CHARLES ROBERT CARNER
PROTEKTOR - S ... JIM HART
PROTEKTOR - S ... THOMAS HEDLEY JR.
PROTOCOL ... BUCK HENRY
PROTOCOL ... CHARLES SHYER
PROTOCOL ... HARVEY MILLER
PROTOCOL ... NANCY J. MEYERS
PROVIDENCE - S ... THOMAS POPE
PROWLER - S ... CHRISTOPHER HAWTHORNE
PROWLER, THE ... GLENN LEOPOLD
PROWLER, THE ... NEAL BARBERA
PSYCH-OUT ... RICHARD RUSH
PSYCHIATRIST AND THE THIEF, THE - S ... FRED FREEMAN
PSYCHIATRIST AND THE THIEF, THE - S ... LAWRENCE J. COHEN
PSYCHIC, THE - S ... SARAH KERNOCHAN
PSYCHICS - S ... GREG TAYLOR
PSYCHO ... JOSEPH STEFANO
PSYCHO II ... TOM HOLLAND
PSYCHO III ... CHARLES EDWARD POGUE
PSYCHO IV (CTF) ... JOSEPH STEFANO
PSYCHOPATH, THE ... ROBERT BLOCH
PSYCHOTIC REACTIONS - S ... PATRICK CIRILLO
PTERODACTYL WOMAN OF BRENTWOOD - S ... PHILLIPPE MORA
PUBERTY BLUES ... MARGARET KELLY
PUBLIC DREAMING - S ... MICHAEL ERIC STEIN
PUBLIC ENEMY NO. 1 ... GARY THOMPSON
PUBLIC ENEMY, THE ... JOHN BRIGHT†
PUBLIC EYE - S ... HOWARD FRANKLIN
PUBLIC EYE, THE (P) ... PETER SHAFFER
PUBLIC LIVES (P) ... JULIA CAMERON
PUBLIC PIGEON NO. 1 ... HARRY TUGEND†
PUBLIC SECRETS - S ... JACK BEHR
PUBLIC SECRETS - S ... SANDY KROOPF
PUFFS - S ... KEVIN FALLS
PULITZER PRIZE - S ... SAM HAMM
PULL THE TRIGGER - S ... ZALMAN KING
PULP ... MIKE HODGES
PULSE ... PAUL GOLDING
PULSEPOUNDERS ... DANNY BILSON
PULSEPOUNDERS ... PAUL DE MEO
PUMA - S ... STIRLING SILLIPHANT
PUMPING GAS - S ... DON CIRILLO
PUMPKIN EATER, THE ... HAROLD PINTER
PUMPKINHEAD ... GARY GERANI
PUMPKINHEAD ... MARK PATRICK CARDUCCI

Title	Writer
PUNCHLINE	DAVID SELTZER
PUNISHER, THE	BOAZ YAKIN
PUNK (SHORT)	CARL FRANKLIN
PUNK - S	NICHOLAS KAZAN
PUNTA GORDA - S	CLIFTON CAMPBELL
PUPPET MASTER	CHARLES BAND
PUPPET MASTER	KENNETH J. HALL
PUPPET ON A CHAIN	ALISTAIR MACLEAN
PUPPET ON A CHAIN	DON SHARP
PUPPET ON A CHAIN	PAUL WHEELER
PUPPETMASTER III - S	C. COURTNEY JOYNER
PURE LUCK	HERSCHEL A. WEINGROD
PURE LUCK	TIMOTHY H. HARRIS
PURGATORY	MAX APPLE
PURPLE HAZE	DAVID BURTON MORRIS
PURPLE HAZE	THOMAS KELSEY
PURPLE HAZE	VICTORIA WOZNIAK
PURPLE HEARTS	RICK NATKIN
PURPLE HEARTS	RON NYSWANER
PURPLE HEARTS	SIDNEY J. FURIE
PURPLE KNIGHT RANGERS - S	ERIC SMALL
PURPLE MASK, THE	OSCAR BRODNEY
PURPLE PEOPLE EATERS	LINDA SHAYNE
PURPLE RAIN	WILLIAM BLINN
PURPLE RAIN	ALBERT MAGNOLI
PURPLE ROSE OF CAIRO, THE	WOODY ALLEN
PURPLE WEST - S	ADAM DUBOV
PURPLE WEST - S	JANICE SHAPIRO
PURSUIT - S	HAROLD NEBENZAL
PURSUIT - S	ROD AMATEAU
PURSUIT - S	W.D. RICHTER
PURSUIT OF D.B. COOPER, THE	JEFFREY ALAN FISKIN
PUSHOVER	ROY HUGGINS
PUSS IN BOOTS	CAROLE LUCIA SATRINA
PUTNEY SWOPE	ROBERT DOWNEY
PUZZLE - S	STIRLING SILLIPHANT
PUZZLE OF A DOWNFALL CHILD	CAROLE EASTMAN
PX - S	BRUCE JAY FRIEDMAN
PYRATES	NOAH STERN
Q	LARRY COHEN
Q & A	SIDNEY LUMET
QUADROPHENIA	DAVID HUMPHRIES
QUADROPHENIA	MARTIN STELLMAN
QUAIL SOUTHWEST (P)	ANDY WOLK
QUARTER MILE, THE - S	FRANK PUGLIESE
QUARTER TIME - S	MARK ANDRUS
QUARTERED MAN, THE (P)	DONALD FREED
QUARTERMAIN - S	MICHAEL THOMAS
QUARTERMAINE'S TERMS (P)	SIMON GRAY
QUATERMASS AND THE PIT	NIGEL KNEALE
QUATERMASS EXPERIMENT, THE	VAL GUEST
QUATERMASS II	VAL GUEST
QUATERMASS	NIGEL KNEALE
QUARTET	RUTH PRAWER JHABVALA
QUEBECOIS - S	PAUL SCHRADER
QUEEN BEE - S	CHARLES ROBERT CARNER
QUEEN BEE - S	NICHOLAS BOGNER
QUEEN CHRISTINA - S	DAVID AMBROSE
QUEEN FOR A DAY - S	RICHARD CHAPMAN
QUEEN OF DIAMONDS	NINA MENKES
QUEEN OF HEARTS	TONY GRISONI
QUEEN OF KINGDOM - S	HOWARD FRANKLIN
QUEEN OF MIDNIGHT - S	LARRY GROSS
QUEEN OF N.Y. - S	PERRY HOWZE
QUEEN OF N.Y. - S	RANDY HOWZE
QUEEN OF ST. JAMES ELK - S	TAB MURPHY
QUEENIE PIE (P)	GEORGE WOLFE
QUEENS LOGIC	TONY SPIRIDAKIS
QUEENS LOGIC	JOSEPH W. SAVINO
QUELMADAI	FRANCO SOLINAS
QUEST FOR FIRE	GERARD BRACH
QUEST OF ST. JAMES ELK - S	JOHN MCTIERNAN
QUEST, THE	EVERETT DEROCHE
QUICK - S	FREDERICK BAILEY
QUICK CHANGE	HOWARD FRANKLIN
QUICKER THAN THE EYE	JOSEPH MORHAIM
QUICKER THAN THE EYE	NICHOLAS GESSNER
QUICKSILVER	THOMAS M. DONNELLY
QUID PRO QUO, THE - S	JOHN J. SCHALTER
QUIET AMERICAN, THE	JOSEPH L. MANKIEWICZ
QUIET COOL	CLAY BORRIS
QUIET COOL	SUSAN VERCELLINO
QUIET DAYS IN CLICHY	CLAUDE CHABROL
QUIET DUEL, THE	AKIRA KUROSAWA
QUIET EARTH, THE	BRUNO LAWRENCE
QUIET EARTH, THE	SAM PILLSBURY
QUIET, THE - S	BRADLEY RAND SMITH
QUIGLEY DOWN UNDER	JOHN HILL
QUILLER MEMORANDUM, THE	HAROLD PINTER
QUINT'S LAST CASE - S	RICHARD KLETTER
QUINTET	LIONEL CHETWYND
QUINTET	PATRICIA RESNICK
QUINTET	ROBERT ALTMAN
QUINTET	FRANK BARHYDT
QUIZ SHOW PROJECT, THE - S	PAUL ATTANSIO
R & R - S	NANCY DOWD
R & R - S	NICK COREA
R.S.V.P. - S	TONY GILROY
RABBIT BOY - S	DAN GOLDBERG
RABBIT BOY - S	LEN BLUM
RABBIT TEST	JAY A. REDACK
RABBIT TEST	JOAN RIVERS
RABID	DAVID CRONENBERG
RACE FOR GLORY	SCOTT SWANTON
RACE FOR YOUR LIFE, CHARLIE BROWN (AF)	CHARLES SCHULZ
RACE TO THE YANKEE ZEPHYR	EVERETT DEROCHE
RACHEL FATE - S	LARRY KETRON
RACHEL PAPERS, THE	DAMIAN HARRIS
RACHEL RIVER	JUDITH GUEST
RACHEL, RACHEL	STEWART STERN
RACING DEMON (P)	DAVID HARE
RACING IN THE STREETS - S	MENNO MEYJES
RACING WITH THE MOON	STEVEN KLOVES
RACK, THE	STEWART STERN
RAD	GEOFFREY EDWARDS
RAD	SAM BERNARD
RADIANT CITY - S	LEWIS A. COLICK
RADIO DAYS	WOODY ALLEN
RADIO FLYER	DAVID MICKEY EVANS
RADIO FREE ALASKA - S	AUDREY WELLS
RADIO INSIDE (SHORT)	JEFFREY BELL
RADIO KILLERS FROM OUTER SPACE - S	ROD MCCALL
RADIO MAN - S	RICHARD MURPHY
RADIO MAN - S	STAN SEIDEL
RADIO ZERO - S	RALPH HOWARD
RADIOACTIVE DREAMS	ALBERT PYUN
RADIOLAND MURDERS - S	GLORIA KATZ
RADIOLAND MURDERS - S	WILLARD HUYCK
RAFFERTY AND THE GOLD DUST TWINS	JOHN KAYE
RAGE - S	ANTHONY MAHARJ
RAGE AND HONOR - S	TERENCE H. WINKLESS
RAGE IN HARLEM, A	JOHN TOLES-BEY
RAGE IN HARLEM, A	BOBBY CRAWFORD
RAGE OF HONOR	ROBERT SHORT
RAGE OF HONOR	WALLACE BENNETT
RAGGEDY HEARTS CLUB - S	ALLYN WARNER
RAGGEDY MAN	WILLIAM D. WITTLIFF
RAGGEDY RAWNEY, THE	BOB HOSKINS
RAGGEDY RAWNEY, THE	NICOLE DE WILDE
RAGING BULL	MARDIK MARTIN
RAGING BULL	PAUL SCHRADER
RAGING MOON, THE	BRYAN FORBES
RAGMAN'S DAUGHTER, THE	ALAN SILLITOE
RAGTIME	MICHAEL WELLER
RAID ON 330 PARK, THE - S	EARL WALLACE
RAID ON BAGHDAD - S	KEVIN ELDERS
RAIDERS OF THE LOST ARK	GEORGE LUCAS
RAIDERS OF THE LOST ARK	LAWRENCE KASDAN
RAIDERS OF THE LOST ARK	PHILIP KAUFMAN
RAILWAY CHILDREN, THE	LIONEL JEFFRIES
RAILWAY STATION MAN, THE - S	SHELAGH DELANEY
RAIN CRYSTALS - S	ABBE BERNSTEIN
RAIN KILLER, THE - S	RAY CUNNEFF
RAIN MAN	BARRY MORROW
RAIN MAN	RON BASS
RAIN PEOPLE, THE	FRANCIS FORD COPPOLA
RAINBOW BRITE AND THE STAR STEALER (AF)	HOWARD R. COHEN
RAINBOW BRITE AND THE STAR STEALER (AF)	JEAN CHALOPIN
RAINBOW DRIVE (CTF)	BILL PHILLIPS
RAINBOW DRIVE (CTF)	BENNETT COHEN
RAINBOW WARRIOR - S	RICHARD FRIEDENBERG
RAINBOW'S END - S	ED KAPLAN
RAINBOW, THE	VIVIAN RUSSELL
RAINBOW, THE	KEN RUSSELL
RAINBOWS - S	GERRY GARIBALDI
RAINMAKER, THE	N. RICHARD NASH
RAINTREE COUNTY	MILLARD KAUFMAN
RAINY DAYS, RAINY NIGHTS - S	MORRIE RUVINSKY
RAISE THE TITANIC	ADAM KENNEDY
RAISE THE TITANIC	ERIC HUGHES
RAISING ARIZONA	ETHAN COEN
RAISING ARIZONA	JOEL COEN
RAISING CANE - S	DAVID Z. WEINSTEIN
RAISING HELL	CYNTHIA CIDRE
RAISING HELL - S	ALLYN WARNER
RAISING TWAIN - S	RONNI KERN
RAMBLING ROSE - S	CALDER WILLINGHAM
RAMBO: FIRST BLOOD PART II	JAMES CAMERON
RAMBO: FIRST BLOOD PART II	KEVIN JARRE
RAMBO: FIRST BLOOD PART II	SYLVESTER STALLONE
RAMBO III	SHELDON B. LETTICH
RAMBO III	SYLVESTER STALLONE
RAMONA	JONATHAN SARNO
RAMP, THE (P)	SHEM BITTERMAN
RAMPAGE	WILLIAM FRIEDKIN
RAN	AKIRA KUROSAWA
RANCHO DELUXE	THOMAS MCGUANE
RANCHO NOTORIOUS	DANIEL TARADASH
RANDALL AND JULIET - S	COLINE SERREAU
RANDOM - S	DANIEL TAPLITZ
RANDOM ENCOUNTER - S	MATTHEW DORFF
RANDOM HEARTS - S	NAOMI FONER
RANGERS - S	MAX EISENBERG
RANSOM	PAUL WHEELER
RANSOM	RICHARD MATHESON
RANSOM - S	JAMES DEARDEN
RAPALLO & SONS - S	ARMAND MASTROIANNI
RAPID EYE MOVEMENT (SHORT)	STEVEN SODERBERGH
RAPID FIRE - S	ARNE OLSEN
RAPPIN'	ADAM FRIEDMAN
RAPPIN'	ROBERT LITZ
RAPTIVE - S	SCOTT SPENCER
RAPTURE	STANLEY MANN
RAPTURE - S	GERALD DI PEGO
RAPTURE, THE	MICHAEL TOLKIN
RAPTURE, THE - TWO STEP (P)	DICK BEEBE
RARE BREED	GARNER SIMMONS
RASHOMON	AKIRA KUROSAWA
RAT IN THE SKULL (P)	RON HUTCHINSON
RATBOY	ROB THOMPSON
RATS (P)	ISRAEL HOROVITZ
RAVAGER, THE - S	CRAIG VAN SICKLE
RAVAGER, THE - S	STEVEN L. MITCHELL
RAVAGERS	DONALD S. SANFORD
RAVEN, THE	RICHARD MATHESON
RAVEN, THE - S	MICHAEL J. MURRAY
RAW DEAL	GARY DEVORE
RAW DEAL	NORMAN WEXLER
RAW DEAL	SERGIO DONATI
RAW DEAL	LUCIANO VINCENZONI
RAW DEAL	PATRICK EDGEWORTH
RAW NERVE	DAVID A. PRIOR
RAWHEAD REX	CLIVE BARKER
RAY'S MALE HETEROSEXUAL DANCE HALL (SHORT)	BRYAN GORDON
RAZOR'S EDGE, THE	BILL MURRAY
RAZOR'S EDGE, THE	JOHN BYRUM
RAZORBACK	EVERETT DEROCHE
RAZZAMATAZZ - S	MICHAEL LAZAROU
RE-ANIMATOR	DENNIS PAOLI
RE-ANIMATOR	WILLIAM H. NORRIS
RE-ANIMATOR	STUART GORDON
REACH FOR THE SKY	LEWIS GILBERT
REACH WELL WHERE YOU ARE GOING - S	GERALD DI PEGO
READY FOR THE RIVER (P)	NEAL BELL
READY OR NOT - S	CRAIG HELLER
READY OR NOT - S	GUY SCHULMAN
REAL GENIUS	NEAL ISRAEL
REAL GENIUS	PAT PROFT
REAL GENIUS	PETER TOROKVEI
REAL INSPECTOR HOUND, THE (P)	TOM STOPPARD
REAL LIFE	ALBERT BROOKS
REAL LIFE	HARRY SHEARER
REAL LIFE	MONICA JOHNSON
REAL MCCOY, THE - S	WILLIAM J. DAVIES
REAL MEN	DENNIS FELDMAN
REAL PROPERTY - S	DARRYL PONICSAN
REAL ROMEO, THE - S	RICHARD JEFFERIES
REAL THING, THE (P)	TOM STOPPARD

INDEX OF FILM TITLES

REAL WORLD, THE - S .... CHARLES LOVENTHAL
REALM 7 - S .... FIONA LEWIS
REASON WE EAT, THE (P) .... ISRAEL HOROVITZ
REASONABLE DOUBT, A - S .... LINDA YELLEN
REASONABLE MADNESS, A - S .... LON PORTER
REBEKAH - S .... TIMNA RANON
REBEL .... BOB HERBERT
REBEL .... MICHAEL JENKINS
REBEL ARMIES DEEP INTO CHAD (P) .... MARK W. LEE
REBEL LOVE .... MILTON BAGBY JR.
REBEL MAGIC - S .... SIMON MOORE
REBEL WITHOUT A CAUSE .... STEWART STERN
REBEL WOMEN (P) .... THOMAS BABE
REBELLION - S .... LORING MANDEL
REBELLION OF THE HANGED .... JOHN BRIGHT†
REC ROOM - S .... LESLIE FULLER
RECEPTIONIST, THE - S .... CATHERINE REBACK
RECKLESS .... CHRIS COLUMBUS
RECKLESS .... DJORDJE MILICEVIC
RECKLESS .... JEFFREY P. MAGUIRE
RECKLESS (P) .... CRAIG LUCAS
RECKLESS DISREGARD (CTF) .... CHARLIE HAAS
RECKONING, THE .... JOHN MCGRATH
RECLAIMED - S .... ANN LOUISE BARDACH
RECOIL - S .... JOSEPH C. STINSON
RECOVERY, THE - S .... JIM HAYDEN
RECOVERY, THE - S .... JOHN BYRUM
RECOVERY, THE - S .... ROB COHEN
RECRUITS .... CHARLES WIENER
RED BAKER - S .... ROBERT M. WARD
RED BEARD .... AKIRA KUROSAWA
RED BIRD DOWN - S .... ERIC ESTRIN
RED BIRD DOWN - S .... MICHAEL BERLIN
RED CAR - S .... PETER HANKOFF
RED CROSS (P) .... SAM SHEPARD
RED DAWN .... JOHN MILIUS
RED DAWN .... KEVIN REYNOLDS
RED DESERT .... MICHELANGELO ANTONIONI
RED DESERT, THE .... TONINO GUERRA
RED DRAGON - S .... WALON GREEN
RED FERARRI, THE - S .... KATHY COHEN
RED FERRARI, THE - S .... SARA KRANE
RED HANDS, THE - S .... MICHAEL ALMEREYDA
RED HEAT .... HARRY KLEINER
RED HEAT .... TROY KENNEDY MARTIN
RED HEAT .... WALTER HILL
RED HERRING - S .... RICHARD WHITLEY
RED HOT - S .... PAUL HAGGIS
RED HOUR, THE - S .... SCOTT J. SCHNEID
RED HOUR, THE - S .... TONY MICHELMAN
RED JACKET - S .... MARC MOSS
RED KING, WHITE KNIGHT (CTF) .... RON HUTCHINSON
RED KISS .... VERA BELMONT
RED LINE 7000 .... GEORGE KIRGO
RED MONARCH .... CHARLES WOOD
RED ROCK WEST - S .... JOHN DAHL
RED ROOSTER - S .... TOM BENEDEK
RED SCARE - S .... MURRAY MINTZ
RED SCORPION .... ARNE OLSEN
RED SCORPION .... JACK ABRAMOFF
RED SCORPION .... ROBERT ABRAMOFF
RED SHOES, THE .... EMERIC PRESSBURGER†
RED SHOES, THE .... MICHAEL POWELL†
RED SKIES OF MONTANA .... HARRY KLEINER
RED SLEEP - S .... RICHARD MATHESON
RED SLEEP - S .... MICK GARRIS
RED SNEAKERS - S .... J.F. LAWTON
RED SONJA .... CLIVE EXTON
RED SONJA .... GEORGE MACDONALD FRASER
RED SUN .... DENNE BART PETITCLERC
RED SUN .... LAIRD KOENIG
RED SUN .... LAWRENCE ROMAN
RED SUN .... WILLIAM ROBERTS
RED SUN RISING - S .... JONATHAN LEMKIN
RED SURF .... BRIAN GAMBLE
RED SURF .... JASON HOFFS
RED SURF .... VINCENT ROBERTS
RED TAIL SQUADRON - S .... MICHAEL DUGAN
RED TAILS - S .... KEVIN SULLIVAN
RED TAILS - S .... MARCEL MONTECINO
RED WIND (CTF) .... TOM NOONAN
RED WIND - S .... REX PICKETT
RED-BALL EXPRESS .... JOHN MICHAEL HAYES
RED-HEADED STRANGER .... WILLIAM D. WITTLIFF
REDEMPTION - S .... TOD CARROLL
REDEMPTION - S .... TOM DONNELLY
REDFISH - S .... GLEN PITRE
REDLINES - S .... MATTHEW DORFF
REDS .... TREVOR GRIFFITHS
REDS .... WARREN BEATTY
REEL TO REEL - S .... GARY DAVID GOLDBERG
REF, THE - S .... RICHARD LAGRAVENESE
REFLECTING SKIN, THE .... PHILIP RIDLEY
REFLECTION OF FEAR, A .... ED HUME
REFLECTION OF FEAR, A .... LEWIS JOHN CARLINO
REFORM SCHOOL GIRLS .... TOM DESIMONE
REFORM SCHOOL PROJECT - S .... DENIS HAMILL
REFORM SCHOOL PROJECT - S .... JOHN HAMILL
REFORMER AND THE REDHEAD,THE .... NORMAN PANAMA
REFUGE - S .... LINDY LAUB
REGARDING HENRY .... JEFFREY ABRAMS
REGATTA - S .... JAIME KLEIN
REGATTA - S .... RICHARD WHITLEY
REGGIE'S WORLD OF SOUL (SHORT) .... REGINALD HUDLIN
REIGN OF TERROR - S .... JOEL DAVIS
REIVERS, THE .... HARRIET FRANK JR.
REIVERS, THE .... IRVING RAVETCH
RELATIVELY SPEAKING (P) .... ALAN AYCKBOURN
RELATIVES .... ANTHONY J. BOWMAN
RELAY (P) .... BART BAKER
RELENTLESS .... PHIL ALDEN ROBINSON
RELIGION, THE- S .... DAVID Z. GOODMAN
REMAINS OF THE DAY - S .... HAROLD PINTER
REMAINS TO BE SEEN .... SIDNEY SHELDON
REMEMBER MY NAME .... ALAN RUDOLPH
REMEMBRANCE .... HUGH STODDART
REMEMBRANCE OF THINGS PAST - S .... HAROLD PINTER
REMO WILLIAMS: THE ADVENTURE BEGINS .... CHRISTOPHER WOOD
REMORA - S .... DJORDJE MILICEVIC
REMOTE ASYLUM (P) .... MART CROWLEY
RENDEZ-VOUS .... ANDRE TECHINE
RENDEZ-VOUS .... OLIVIER ASSAYAS
RENEGADE - S .... RANDY FELDMAN
RENEGADE - S .... SAM HAMM
RENEGADES .... DAVID RICH
RENEGADES - S .... ELIZABETH CHANDLER
RENESANCE (SHORT) .... J.F. LAWTON
RENO AND THE DOC (CTF) - S .... CHARLES DENNIS
RENT A FAMILY - S .... WILLIAM TONNER
RENT-A-COP .... DENNIS SHRYACK
RENT-A-COP .... MICHAEL BLODGETT
RENTADICK .... GRAHAM CHAPMAN†
RENTADICK .... JOHN CLEESE
RENTED LIPS .... MARTIN MULL
REPLAY - S .... CHARLES PURPURA
REPO JAKE .... JOE HART
REPO MAN .... ALEX COX
REPORT TO THE COMMISSIONER .... ABBY MANN
REPORT TO THE COMMISSIONER .... ERNEST TIDYMAN†
REPOSSESSED .... BOB LOGAN
REPRIEVE .... MILLARD KAUFMAN
REPTILE, THE - S .... BILL CORBETT
REPULSION .... GERARD BRACH
REPULSION .... ROMAN POLANSKI
RESCUE - S .... JOHN HERZFELD
RESCUE - S .... WILLIAM GOLDMAN
RESCUE OF GENERAL DOZIER, THE - S .... DAVID AMBROSE
RESCUE, THE .... JIM THOMAS
RESCUE, THE .... JOHN THOMAS
RESCUERS DOWN UNDER, THE (AF) .... JIM COX
RESISTING ARREST - S .... HOWARD CHESLEY
REST OF DANIEL, THE - S .... JEFFREY ABRAMS
RESTLESS NATIVES .... MICHAEL HOFFMAN
RESTLESS NATIVES .... NINIAN DUNETT
RESTLESS SWORDS OF SHERWOOD FOREST, THE - S .... STUART BIRNBAUM
RESTLESS YEARS, THE .... EDWARD ANHALT
RESURRECTED, THE .... ADAM FRIEDMAN
RESURRECTION .... LEWIS JOHN CARLINO
RESURRECTIONS - S .... LYNNE BARKER
RESURRECTUS - S .... ROBERT F. SKOTAK
RETREAT, THE - S .... JAMES LEMMO
RETRIBUTION .... GUY MAGAR
RETRIBUTION .... LEE WASSERMAN
RETURN ENGAGEMENT - S .... DORI PIERSON
RETURN FROM THE ASHES .... JULIUS J. EPSTEIN
RETURN FROM WITCH MOUNTAIN .... MALCOLM MARMORSTEIN
RETURN OF A MAN CALLED HORSE, THE .... JACK DE WITT
RETURN OF CAPTAIN INVINCIBLE, THE .... ANDREW GATY
RETURN OF CAPTAIN INVINCIBLE, THE .... STEVEN DE SOUZA
RETURN OF MAGDA LA SELVA, THE - S .... ALBERT INNAURATO
RETURN OF MAGDA LA SELVA, THE - U .... WILLIAM ROBERTS
RETURN OF MARTIN GUERRE, THE .... DANIEL VIGNE
RETURN OF MARTIN GUERRE, THE .... JEAN-CLAUDE CARRIERE
RETURN OF OCTOBER, THE .... NORMAN PANAMA
RETURN OF SUPERFLY, THE .... ANTHONY WISDOM
RETURN OF SWAMP THING, THE .... DEREK SPENCER
RETURN OF SWAMP THING, THE .... GRANT MORRIS
RETURN OF THE JEDI .... GEORGE LUCAS
RETURN OF THE JEDI .... LAWRENCE KASDAN
RETURN OF THE KILLER TOMATOES .... JOHN DEBELLO
RETURN OF THE LIVING DEAD, THE .... JOHN RUSSO
RETURN OF THE LIVING DEAD, THE .... RUDY RICCI
RETURN OF THE LIVING DEAD, THE .... RUSSELL STREINER
RETURN OF THE LIVING DEAD, THE .... DAN O' BANNON
RETURN OF THE LIVING DEAD, PART II .... KEN WIEDERHORN
RETURN OF THE MUSKETEERS, THE .... GEORGE MACDONALD FRASER
RETURN OF THE PINK PANTHER, THE .... BLAKE EDWARDS
RETURN OF THE PINK PANTHER, THE .... FRANK WALDMAN†
RETURN OF THE SECAUCUS SEVEN .... JOHN SAYLES
RETURN OF THE SEVEN, THE .... LARRY COHEN
RETURN OF THE SOLDIER, THE .... HUGH WHITEMORE
RETURN OF THE TALL BLOND MAN WITH ONE BLACK SHOE .... FRANCIS VEBER
RETURN TO BLUE LAGOON .... LESLIE C. STEVENS
RETURN TO HORROR HIGH .... MARK L. LISSON
RETURN TO HORROR HIGH .... BILL FROELICH
RETURN TO MACON COUNTY .... RICHARD COMPTON
RETURN TO OZ .... WALTER MURCH
RETURN TO SALEM'S LOT .... JAMES DIXON
RETURN TO SALEM'S LOT .... LARRY COHEN
RETURN TO SNOWY RIVER .... GEOFF BURROWES
RETURN TO SNOWY RIVER .... JOHN DIXON
RETURN TO WATERLOO .... RAY DAVIES
RETURN, THE .... MARGARETHE VON TROTTA
REUBEN, REUBEN .... JULIUS J. EPSTEIN
REUNION .... HAROLD PINTER
REUNION (P) .... DAVID MAMET
REUNION - S .... GORE VIDAL
REUNION - S .... HESPER ANDERSON
REUNION - S .... RON BASS
REUNION - S .... RONNI KERN
REVENGE .... JEFFREY ALAN FISKIN
REVENGE .... JIM HARRISON
REVENGE OF BLACKTHORN - S .... JACK EPPS JR.
REVENGE OF BLACKTHORN - S .... JIM CASH
REVENGE OF FRANKENSTEIN, THE .... JIMMY SANGSTER
REVENGE OF THE NERDS .... JEFF BUHAI
REVENGE OF THE NERDS .... MIGUEL TEJADA-FLORES
REVENGE OF THE NERDS .... STEVEN R. ZACHARIAS
REVENGE OF THE NERDS .... TIM METCALFE
REVENGE OF THE NERDS II .... DANIEL J. GUNTZELMAN
REVENGE OF THE NERDS II .... STEVE K. MARSHALL
REVENGE OF THE NINJA .... JAMES R. SILKE
REVENGE OF THE NUDES - S .... JEFF BUHAI
REVENGE OF THE NUDES - S .... STEVE ZACHARIAS
REVENGE OF THE PINK PANTHER .... BLAKE EDWARDS
REVENGE OF THE PINK PANTHER .... FRANK WALDMAN†
REVENGE OF THE PINK PANTHER .... RON CLARK
REVENGE OF THE POTATO - S .... RON HUGO
REVENGE ROMANCE - S .... JOHN WILLIAM SEE
REVENGE ROMANCE - S .... RICHARD LAWTON
REVENGERS, THE .... WENDELL MAYES
REVERSAL OF FORTUNE .... NICHOLAS KAZAN
REVERSE ANGEL - S .... JEFFREY C. SHERMAN
REVOLTING - S .... ROBERT KAUFMAN
REVOLUTION .... ROBERT DILLON
REVOLUTIONARY WAR - S .... JOHN BINDER
REVOLVER - S .... STEVEN SODERBERGH
REVOLVER - S .... WILLIAM HARLAN RICHTER

Title	Author
REX - S	BRYAN MICHAEL STOLLER
RHAPSODY	FAY KANIN
RHAPSODY	MICHAEL KANIN
RHAPSODY IN AUGUST	AKIRA KUROSAWA
RHAPSODY IN BLUE	HOWARD KOCH
RHAPSODY IN CRIME - S	ANDREW BERGMAN
RHINESTONE	PHIL ALDEN ROBINSON
RHINESTONE	SYLVESTER STALLONE
RHINOCEROS	JULIAN BARRY
RHYTHM & BLUES - S	BARRY BECKERMAN
RHYTHM & BLUES - S	PETER HANKOFF
RIBCAGE (P)	ANDY WOLK
RICH AND FAMOUS	GERALD AYRES
RICH AND FAMOUS (P)	JOHN GUARE
RICH BOYS	NEIL COHEN
RICH GIRL	ROBERT ELLIOTT
RICH IN LOVE - S	ALFRED F. UHRY
RICH KID - S	JOHN HILL
RICH KIDS	JUDITH ROSS
RICH LITTLE POOR GIRLS - S	ALAN BERGER
RICH LITTLE POOR GIRLS - S	KATHY GORI
RICH PEOPLE HAVING FUN - S	DAVID GILER
RICH PEOPLE HAVING FUN - S	LYNNE GILER
RICH RELATIONS (P)	DAVID HENRY HWANG
RICH, YOUNG AND PRETTY	SIDNEY SHELDON
RICHARD	HARRY HURWITZ
RICHARD CORY (P)	A.R. GURNEY
RICHARD PRYOR HERE AND NOW (FD)	RICHARD PRYOR
RICHARD PRYOR LIVE ON THE SUNSET STRIP (FD)	RICHARD PRYOR
RICHARD'S THINGS	FREDERIC RAPHAEL
RICHARDSON - S	DONALD FREED
RICOCHET - S	STEVE SHAGAN
RIDDLE OF THE SANDS, THE	TONY MAYLAM
RIDE BEYOND VENGEANCE	ANDREW J. FENADY
RIDE DOWN MOUNT MORGAN, THE (P)	ARTHUR MILLER
RIDE IN THE WHIRLWIND	JACK NICHOLSON
RIDE LONESOME	BURT KENNEDY
RIDE ME DOWN EASY - S	TUDY WOOLFE
RIDE THE WILD RED - S	WALTER NEWMAN
RIDE THE WIND - S	DOUG MCINTYRE
RIDE TO HANGMAN'S TREE, THE	JOHN D.F. BLACK
RIDE, THE - S	ALEX HENDRIE
RIDE-ALONG, THE - S	NICHOLAS KAZAN
RIDERS OF THE STORM	SCOTT ROBERTS
RIDERS TO THE STARS	CURT SIODMAK
RIDICULOUS MAN - S	NICK W. THIEL
RIDING THE DOLPHIN - S	JUNE ROBERTS
RIDING THE EDGE	RONALD A. SUPPA
RIFF-RAFF	BILL JESSE
RIFFI	JULES DASSIN
RIFLE MAN, THE - S	JOHN KEITH WILDER
RIGHT APPROACH, THE	MICHAEL KANIN
RIGHT APPROACH, THE	FAY KANIN
RIGHT HAND MAN, THE	HELEN HODGMAN
RIGHT HAND MEN, THE - S	DAVID HINES
RIGHT HAND MEN, THE - S	JEFF HAUSE
RIGHT MAN, THE - S	FREDERIC RAPHAEL
RIGHT STUFF, THE	PHILIP KAUFMAN
RIGHTS OF PASSAGE - S	DAVID SHABER
RIKKY AND PETE	DAVID PARKER
RING OF FIRE	ANDREW STONE
RING OF SPIES	PETER BARNES
RING OF TREASON	PETER BARNES
RINGER, THE - S	DARRYL PONICSAN
RINGER, THE - S	JAMES DEARDON
RINO - S	DENNIS O'FLAHERTY
RIO CONCHOS	CLAIR HUFFAKER†
RIOTOUS ASSEMBLY - S	W.D. RICHTER
RIOTOUS CONDUCT - S	JAMES D. BUCHANAN
RIP - S	BUD SHRAKE
RIP VAN HIPPIE - S	CHRISTOPHER THOMPSON
RIP-FF	WILLIAM C. FRUET
RISE AND RISE OF MICHAEL RIMMER, THE	GRAHAM CHAPMAN†
RISE AND RISE OF MICHAEL RIMMER, THE	JOHN CLEESE
RISE AND RISE OF MICHAEL RIMMER, THE	PETER COOK
RISING DAMP	ERIC CHAPPELL
RISING SON (CTF)	BILL PHILLIPS
RISING STORM	GARY ROSEN
RISING STORM	WILLIAM FAY
RISING SUN - S	LAIRD KOENIG
RISK, THE- S	QUINN REDEKER
RISKY BUSINESS	PAUL BRICKMAN
RITA, SUE AND BOB TOO!	ANDREA DUNBAR
RITES OF SUMMER - S	DENNIS PALUMBO
RITZ, THE	TERRENCE MCNALLY
RITZVILLE (SHORT)	JAMES D. COX
RIVALS - S	LIZ COMICI
RIVALS - S	LOU COMICI
RIVALS - S	MARK ROSNER
RIVER OAKS - S	PETER KRIKES
RIVER OAKS - S	STEVE MEERSON
RIVER OF DEATH	ANDREW DEUTSCH
RIVER OF DEATH	EDWARD SIMPSON
RIVER RAT, THE	THOMAS RICKMAN
RIVER RUNS THROUGH IT, A - S	RICHARD FRIEDENBERG
RIVER RUNS THROUGH IT, A - S	WILLIAM HJORTSBERG
RIVER'S EDGE	NEAL JIMENEZ
RIVER, THE	JULIAN BARRY
RIVER, THE	ROBERT DILLON
RIVERBEND	SAM VANCE
RIVERSEND - S	LAWRENCE HAUBEN
ROAD BACK, THE - S	REX PICKETT
ROAD GAMES	EVERETT DEROCHE
ROAD HOUSE	HILARY HENKIN
ROAD HOUSE	R. LANCE HILL
ROAD MOVIE	JUDITH RASCOE
ROAD TO HONG KONG	NORMAN PANAMA
ROAD TO MARS - S	ERIC IDLE
ROAD TO MECCA, THE (P)	ATHOL FUGARD
ROAD TO RIO	JACK ROSE
ROAD TO RUIN - S	GEORGE GIPE
ROAD TO RUIN - S	JAIME B. KLEIN
ROAD TO RUIN - S	RICHARD WHITLEY
ROAD TO UTOPIA, THE	NORMAN PANAMA
ROAD WARRIOR, THE	BRIAN HANNANT
ROAD WARRIOR, THE	GEORGE MILLER
ROAD WARRIOR, THE	TERRY HAYES
ROADHOUSE 66	GALEN LEE
ROADHOUSE 66	GEORGE E. SIMPSON
ROADIE	BIG BOY MEDLIN
ROADIE	MICHAEL VENTURA
ROADIE	ALAN S. RUDOLPH
ROADIE	ZALMAN KING
ROADS - S	LARRY B. WILLIAMS
ROADSHOW - S	ROBERT GETCHELL
ROADWAY - S	ROD MCCALL
ROAR OF THE GREASEPAINT, SMELL OF THE CROWD (P)	ANTHONY NEWLEY
ROAR OF THE GREASEPAINT, SMELL OF THE CROWD (P)	LESLIE BRICUSSE
ROAR OF THE PRESS - S	HENRY C. PARKE
ROAST BEEF ON SUNDAY - S	JOHN KENT HARRISON
ROBBER (P)	LYLE D. KESSLER
ROBBER BRIDEGROOM, THE (P)	ALFRED UHRY
ROBBERS - S	MITCH MARKOWITZ
ROBERT ET ROBERT	CLAUDE LELOUCH
ROBIN AND MARIAN	JAMES GOLDMAN
ROBIN HOOD: PRINCE OF THEIVES	JOHN WATSON
ROBIN HOOD: PRINCE OF THEIVES	PEN DENSHAM
ROBINSON & CARUSO - S	JOHN ESKOW
ROBOCOP	EDWARD NEUMEIER
ROBOCOP	MICHAEL MINER
ROBOCOP 2	FRANK MILLER
ROBOCOP 2	WALON GREEN
ROBOCOP 3 - S	FRANK MILLER
ROBOCOP 3 - S	FRED DEKKER
ROBOT - S	DONOVAN MOORE
ROBOT HOLOCAUST	TIM KINCAID
ROBOTJOX	JOE HALDEMAN
ROBOTJOX	STUART GORDON
ROBOTO - S	W.D. RICHTER
ROBOTS RULE - S	ROSPO PALLENBERG
ROCK & RULE (AF)	JOHN HALFPENNY
ROCK & RULE (AF)	PETER SAUDER
ROCK AND A HARD PLACE - S	MARK ALLEN SMITH
ROCK AND GOAL - S	DJORDJE MILICEVIC
ROCK BOTTOM - S	JORDAN MOFFET
ROCK CITY - S	ANTON DIETHER
ROCK GARDEN (P)	SAM SHEPARD
ROCK THUNDER - S	PHILIP MORTON
ROCK'N'ROLL HIGH SCHOOL	RICHARD WHITLEY
ROCK'N'ROLL HIGH SCHOOL FOREVER	DEBORAH BROCK
ROCK'N'ROLL STORY - S	MARDIK MARTIN
ROCK-A-DOODLE (AF)	DAVID N. WEISS
ROCKERS	TED BAFALOUKAS
ROCKET GIBRALTAR	AMOS POE
ROCKET MAN - S	ALAN BERGER
ROCKET MAN - S	KATHY GORI
ROCKET'S RED GLARE - S	PETER ILIFF
ROCKETEER, THE	DANNY BILSON
ROCKETEER, THE	PAUL DEMEO
ROCKETEER, THE	WILLIAM DEAR
ROCKITS - S	JONATHAN LYNN
ROCKULA	LUCA BERCOVICI
ROCKULA	CHRISTOPHER VERWIEL
ROCKULA	JEFERY LEVY
ROCKY	SYLVESTER STALLONE
ROCKY II	SYLVESTER STALLONE
ROCKY III	SYLVESTER STALLONE
ROCKY IV	SYLVESTER STALLONE
ROCKY V	SYLVESTER STALLONE
ROCKY HORROR PICTURE SHOW, THE	JIM SHARMAN
ROCKY HORROR PICTURE SHOW, THE	RICHARD O'BRIEN
ROCKY MOUNTAIN TIME - S	W.D. RICHTER
ROCKY ROAD - S	JAMES REDFORD
ROGER & ME (FD)	MICHAEL MOORE
ROGER RABBIT II - S	NAT MAULDIN
ROGUE FROM MOTOR CITY - S	GEORGE MALKO
ROGUE TROOPER - S	LEE DRYSDALE
ROGUES - S	STEVEN L. BLOOM
ROLLER BLADE	DONALD G. JACKSON
ROLLER BLADE	RANDALL FRAKES
ROLLER BOOGIE	BARRY SCHNEIDER
ROLLER DISCO - S	EDWARD KHMARA
ROLLERBALL	WILLIAM HARRISON
ROLLERCOASTER	RICHARD LEVINSON†
ROLLERCOASTER	WILLIAM LINK
ROLLIN' STONED...A ROADIE'S RIOTOUS REVELATIONS - S	PAT PROFT
ROLLING NOWHERE - S	TOM BENEDEK
ROLLING THUNDER	HEYWOOD GOULD
ROLLING THUNDER	PAUL SCHRADER
ROLLING VENGEANCE	MICHAEL T. MONTGOMERY
ROLLOVER	DAVID SHABER
ROLLOVER	DAVID WEIR
ROLLOVER	HOWARD KOHN
ROMA	FEDERICO FELLINI
ROMAN SPRING OF MRS. STONE, THE	GAVIN LAMBERT
ROMANCE (P)	TOM TOPOR
ROMANCE - S	GERALD DI PEGO
ROMANCE ARTIST - S	JOEL SALTZMAN
ROMANCE ON THE HIGH SEAS	I.A.L. DIAMOND†
ROMANCE ON THE HIGH SEAS	JULIUS J. EPSTEIN
ROMANCE ON THE HIGH SEAS	PHILIP G. EPSTEIN†
ROMANCING THE STONE	DIANE THOMAS†
ROMANOFF AND JULIET	PETER USTINOV
ROMANTIC COMEDY	BERNARD SLADE
ROMANTIC ENGLISHWOMAN, THE	TOM STOPPARD
ROMANTIC FOOLS - S	BRAD BUCKNER
ROMANTIC FOOLS - S	EUGENIE ROSS-LEMING
ROMANTIC HERO - S	ANTHONY J. BOWMAN
ROMEO AND JULIET	FRANCO BRUSATI
ROMEO IS BLEEDING - S	HILARY HENKIN
ROMERO	JOHN SACRET YOUNG
RONNIE FINKELHOF, SUPERSTAR - S	GINNY CERRELLA
RONNIE ROCKET - S	DAVID LYNCH
ROOFTOPS	TERRY BRENNAN
ROOFTOPS	ALLAN S. GOLDSTEIN
ROOFTOPS	TONY MARK
ROOKIE, THE	BOAZ YAKIN
ROOKIE, THE	SCOTT SPIEGEL
ROOM AT THE END OF THE UNIVERSE	JAMES GLICKENHAUS
ROOM FOR ONE MORE	JACK ROSE
ROOM FOR ONE MORE	MEL SHAVELSON
ROOM MATES, THE	ARTHUR R. MARKS
ROOM WITH A VIEW, A	RUTH PRAWER JHABVALA
ROOM, THE (P)	HAROLD PINTER
ROOMMATES	JACK BARAN
ROOT OF ALL EVIL - S	STAN SEIDEL
ROOT RETURNS - S	ANDREW DEUTSCH
ROOTS IN A PARCHED GROUND - S	HORTON FOOTE
ROPE	ARTHUR LAURENTS
ROPE OF SAND	WALTER DONIGER
ROSA LUXEMBURG	MARGARETHE VON TROTTA
ROSALIE GOES SHOPPING	ELEONORE ADLON
ROSALIE GOES SHOPPING	PERCY ADLON
ROSALIE GOES SHOPPING	CHRISTOPHER DOHERTY
ROSARY MURDERS, THE	ELMORE LEONARD

373

Title	Writer
ROSARY MURDERS, THE	FRED WALTON
ROSE & KATZ (SHORT)	APRIL DAMMANN
ROSE AND THE JACKAL, THE (CTF)	ERIC EDSON
ROSE GARDEN, THE	PAUL HENUGGE
ROSE OF SHARON, THE - S	TOM MCCOWN
ROSE TATTOO, THE	JOHN MICHAEL HAYES
ROSE, THE	BILL KERBY
ROSE, THE	BO GOLDMAN
ROSELAND	RUTH PRAWER JHABVALA
ROSEMARY'S BABY	ROMAN POLANSKI
ROSENBERGS & JULIETTE, THE - S	TRACEY JACKSON
ROSENCRANTZ AND GUILDENSTERN ARE DEAD	TOM STOPPARD
ROSES ARE RED - S	GARY GOLDMAN
ROSES ARE RED - S	PETER VINCENT DOUGLAS
ROSES, ROSES - S	FREDERIC RAPHAEL
ROUGE	CAROLINE THOMPSON
ROUGE - S	LARRY WILSON
ROUGE BAISER	VERA BELMONT
ROUGH COMPANY	HARRY KLEINER
ROUGH CUT	LARRY GELBART
ROUGH JUSTICE - S	ANDREW KLAVAN
ROUGH JUSTICE - S	PHILIP MORTON
ROUGH JUSTICE - S	TOM DONNELLY
ROUGH NIGHT IN JERICO	SYDNEY BOEHM†
ROUGH TRADE	LEE ROSE
ROUGH TRADE - S	PATRICIA RESNICK
ROUGH TREATMENT	AGNIESZKA HOLLAND
ROUND MIDNIGHT	BERTRAND TAVERNIER
ROUND MIDNIGHT	DAVID RAYFIEL
ROUNDERS, THE	BURT KENNEDY
ROUTE 66 - S	JASON BRETT
ROVER DANGERFIELD (AF)	RODNEY DANGERFIELD
ROW OF CROWS, A	J.S. CARDONE
ROWDY - S	JOE ESZTERHAS
ROXANNE	STEVE MARTIN
ROYAL COACH TAXI - S	ROBERT KUHN
ROYAL FLASH	GEORGE MACDONALD FRASER
ROYAL HUNT OF THE SUN, THE (P)	PETER SHAFFER
ROYAL HUNT OF THE SUN, THE	PHILIP YORDAN
ROYAL MESS, A - S	BURT PRELUTSKY
RPM	ERICH SEGAL
RSVP - S	ROBIN SCHIFF
RUBBER GUN, THE	ALLAN MOYLE
RUBICON - S	ERIC SMALL
RUBY	BARRY SCHNEIDER
RUBY - S	DANIEL H. VINING
RUBY CAIRO - S	MICHAEL THOMAS
RUBY CAIRO - S	ROBERT DILLON
RUBY KILLS - S	MICHAEL THOMAS
RUBY RED - S	MURDO LAIRD
RUBY RED - S	ROBERT KLANE
RUBY RED - S	W.D. RICHTER
RUCKUS	MAX KLEVEN
RUDE AWAKENING	RICHARD LAGRAVENESE
RUDE AWAKENING	NEIL LEVY
RUDE BOY	JACK HAZAN
RUG MERCHANTS OF CHAOS, THE (P)	RONALD RIBMAN
RULES OF ATTRACTION - S	NOAH STERN
RULES OF ENGAGEMENT - S	JAMES WEBB
RULES OF ENGAGEMENT - S	MARY AGNES DONAGHUE
RULES OF THE GAME, THE - S	NOAH STERN
RULES OF THE ROAD - S	STEPHEN TOBOLOWSKY
RULES OF THE ROAD - S	TOR VALENZA
RULING CLASS, THE	PETER BARNES
RUM RUNNERS - S	STEVEN M. KUNES
RUMBLE - S	HARLAN ELLISON
RUMBLE FISH	FRANCIS FORD COPPOLA
RUMBLE FISH	S.E. HINTON
RUMPELSTILTSKIN	DAVID IRVING
RUN	MICHAEL BLODGETT
RUN OF THE ARROW	DENNIS SHRYACK
RUN SILENT RUN DEEP	SAMUEL FULLER
RUN SILENT RUN DEEP	JOHN GAY
RUNAROUND, THE - S	JANUS CERCONE
RUNAWAY	MICHAEL CRICHTON
RUNAWAY - S	ANDREW BIRKIN
RUNAWAY - S	JACK BEHR
RUNAWAY - S	SANDY KROOPF
RUNAWAY BRIDE - S	JOSAN MCGIBBON
RUNAWAY BRIDE - S	SARA PARRIOTT
RUNAWAY BUS, THE	VAL GUEST
RUNAWAY TRAIN	DJORDJE MILICEVIC
RUNAWAY TRAIN	EDWARD BUNKER
RUNAWAY TRAIN	PAUL ZINDEL
RUNAWAY WIFE, THE - S	CHRISTIAN STOIANOVICH
RUNAWAY WIFE, THE - S	PHOEBE DORIN
RUNNER STUMBLES, THE	MILAN STITT
RUNNER, THE - S	ALEC LORIMORE
RUNNER, THE - S	TERRY WINKLESS
RUNNERS	STEPHEN POLIAKOFF
RUNNIN' KIND, THE	MAX TASH
RUNNIN' KIND, THE	PLEASANT GEHMAN
RUNNING	STEVEN HILLIARD STERN
RUNNING AGAINST TIME (CTF)	STANLEY SHAPIRO†
RUNNING AGAINST TIME (CTF)	ROBERT GLASS
RUNNING BRAVE	HENRY BEAN
RUNNING BRAVE	SHIRL HENDRYX
RUNNING HOT	MARK L. GRIFFITHS
RUNNING MAN, THE	STEVEN DE SOUZA
RUNNING MAN, THE (1963)	JOHN MORTIMER
RUNNING MATES - S	CAROLE EASTMAN
RUNNING ON EMPTY	NAOMI FONER
RUNNING SCARED (1986)	GARY DEVORE
RUNNING SCARED (1986)	JIMMY HUSTON
RUNNING SCARED (1972)	CLIVE EXTON
RUSH - S	PETE DEXTER
RUSH WEEK	MICHAEL W. LEIGHTON
RUSH WEEK	RUSSELL V. MANZATT
RUSS MEYER'S UP!	RUSS MEYER
RUSSIA HOUSE, THE	TOM STOPPARD
RUSSIAN ROULETTE	STANLEY MANN
RUSSIAN STORY - S	CHRISTOPHER HAMPTON
RUSSIAN TERMINATOR	MATS HELGE
RUSSKIES	ALAN JAY GLUECKMAN
RUSSKIES	MICHAEL NANKIN
RUSSKIES	SHELDON B. LETTICH
RUSTLERS' RHAPSODY	HUGH WILSON
RUSTY - S	ERIC JENKINS
RUTHIE RUDDICK STORY, THE - S	STAN ZIMMERMAN
RUTHLESS PEOPLE	DALE LAUNER
RUTLAND ISLES - S	ERIC IDLE
RUTLAND TRIANGLE, THE - S	ERIC IDLE
RUTLES, THE	ERIC IDLE
RYAN'S DAUGHTER	ROBERT BOLT
RYOMA - S	ROBERT MARK KAMEN

S

Title	Writer
S & L - S	ALAN R. TRUSTMAN
S*P*Y*S	FRED FREEMAN
S*P*Y*S	LAWRENCE J. COHEN
S*P*Y*S	MALCOLM MARMORSTEIN
S.O.B.	BLAKE EDWARDS
S.O.S. - S	ROBERT WUHL
S.O.S. - S	JIM FISHER
S.O.S. - S	JIM STAAHL
S.W.M. - S	JAY KAMEN
SABERS OF KANDAHAR, THE - S	STANFORD SHERMAN
SABOTAGE	CHARLES BENNETT
SABOTEUR	PETER VIERTEL
SABOTEUR, THE	DANIEL TARADASH
SABRINA	BILLY WILDER
SABRINA	ERNEST LEHMAN
SACRED GROUND	CHARLES B. PIERCE
SACRIFICE, THE	ANDREI TARKOVSKY†
SAD SACK, THE	NATHAN MONASTER†
SAFARI - S	TOM SCHILLER
SAFARI 3000	MICHAEL HARRESCHOU
SAFE AT HOME - S	JAY BECKNER
SAFE HOUSE (P)	NICHOLAS KAZAN
SAFE HOUSE - S	GARY THOMPSON
SAFE PLACE, A	HENRY JAGLOM
SAFECRACKER, THE	PAUL MONASH
SAGA OF THE VAGABOND, THE	AKIRA KUROSAWA
SAGITTARIUS PART 1 - DUBLINERS - S	HOWARD L. ANDERSON
SAHARA	JAMES R. SILKE
SAHARA	MENAHEM GOLAN
SAIGON - S	ALISON CROSS
SAIGON - YEAR OF THE CAT (P)	DAVID HARE
SAILOR WHO FELL FROM GRACE WITH THE SEA, THE	LEWIS JOHN CARLINO
SAILOR'S RETURN, THE	JAMES SAUNDERS
SAINT, THE - S	TERRY HAYES
SAINT HARRY - S	MICHAEL AUSTIN
SAINT JACK	HOWARD SACKLER
SAINT JACK	PAUL THEROUX
SAINT JACK	PETER BOGDONAVICH
SAINT JACK	WALTER NEWMAN
SAINT OF FORT WASHINGTON, THE - S	LYLE D. KESSLER
SAINT VALENTINE (CTF) - S	JOSEPH DOUGHERTY
SAL'S PIZZA MOVIE - S	ERIC SCHAEFFER
SALAMANDER, THE	ROBERT KATZ
SALERNO & FINNEGAN - S	JOEL OLIANSKY
SALINAS - S	LEWIS JOHN CARLINO
SALLY & BUDDY & LORETTA (SHORT)	ROD MCCALL
SALLY, IRENE AND MARY	HARRY TUGEND†
SALOME	HARRY KLEINER
SALOME'S LAST DANCE	KEN RUSSELL
SALSA	BOAZ DAVIDSON
SALSA	SHEPARD GOLDMAN
SALSA	TOMAS BENITEZ
SALT LAKE CITY SKYLINE (P)	THOMAS BABE
SALUTE THE ARTIST - S	JOHN GUARE
SALVADOR	OLIVER STONE
SALVADOR	RICHARD BOYLE
SALVATION!	BETH B
SALVATION!	TOM ROBINSON
SALVATION - S	HAMPTON FANCHER
SALVATORE GIULIANO	FRANCESCO ROSI
SALVATORE GIULIANO	FRANCO SOLINAS
SAM & ME	RANJIT CHOWDREY
SAM (P)	TREVOR GRIFFITHS
SAM AND YETTA - S	VICKI HOCHBURG
SAM WHISKEY	WILLIAM NORTON SR.
SAM'S SON	MICHAEL LANDON†
SAME TIME, NEXT YEAR	BERNARD SLADE
SAMMY AND ROSIE GET LAID	HANIF KUREISHI
SAN JOAQUIN -U	DAVID S. WARD
SAN JOSE MILE - S	ROBERT BORIS
SAN QUENTIN	JOHN BRIGHT†
SAND PEBBLES, THE	ROBERT ANDERSON
SANDMAN, THE - S	WILLIAM GOODHART
SANDS OF THE KALAHARI	CY ENDFIELD
SANDY	DAN ALGRANT
SANJURO	AKIRA KUROSAWA
SANS TOIT NI LOI	AGNES VARDA
SANSHIRO SUGATA	AKIRA KUROSAWA
SANSHIRO SUGATA PART II	AKIRA KUROSAWA
SANTA CLAUS - THE MOVIE	DAVID NEWMAN
SANTA CRUZ - S	GEOFF GRODE
SANTA SANGRE	ALEXONDRO JODOROWSKY
SANTA'S DAUGHTER - S	DANIEL SULLIVAN
SANTA'S DAUGHTER - S	FRED LEBOW
SANTEE - S	STEVEN KLOVES
SANTERIA	PETER HANKOFF
SANTIAGO - S	PATRICK READ JOHNSON
SAPPHIRE MAN (SHORT)	CRAIG BOLOTIN
SARAFINA! - S	WILLIAM NICHOLSON
SARAH - S	NICHOLAS ST. JOHN
SARAH WILL - S	DALENE YOUNG
SARATOGA - S	MICHAEL KANE
SARGEANT K. - S	STEVE SHARON
SATAN AND EVE - S	GERARD BRACH
SATAN BUG, THE	EDWARD ANHALT
SATAN BUG, THE	JAMES CLAVELL
SATAN'S BREW	RAINER WERNER FASSBINDER†
SATAN'S LITTLE SISTER - S	JOHN EZRINE
SATAN'S PRINCESS	STEPHEN KATZ
SATAN'S SORROW - S	CHARLES EDWARD POGUE
SATAN, CRAZY AS HELL - S	JEREMY LEVEN
SATISFACTION	CHARLES PURPURA
SATURDAY AFTERNOON - S	SCOTT PARKER
SATURDAY NIGHT AND SUNDAY MORNING	ALAN SILLITOE
SATURDAY NIGHT FEVER	NORMAN WEXLER
SATURDAY THE 14TH	HOWARD R. COHEN
SATURDAY THE 14TH	JEFF BEGUN
SATURDAY THE 14TH STRIKES BACK	HOWARD R. COHEN
SATURDAY'S CHILD - S	MICHAEL KANE
SATURDAY'S CHILDREN	JULIUS J. EPSTEIN
SATURDAY'S CHILDREN	PHILIP G. EPSTEIN†
SATURDAY, SUNDAY AND MONDAY	LINA WERTMULLER
SATURDAYS HEROS - S	ANGELO PIZZO
SATURN 3	MARTIN AMIS
SATURN 3	JOHN BARRY
SATYRICON	FEDERICO FELLINI
SAUCER - S	NEIL CUTHBERT
SAUVE QUI PEUT LA VIE	ANNE-MARIE MIEVILLE
SAUVE QUI PEUT LA VIE	JEAN-CLAUDE CARRIERE
SAUVE QUI PEUT LA VIE	JEAN-LUC GODARD

Title	Writer
SAVAGE - S	PAUL BOORSTIN
SAVAGE - S	SHARON BOORSTIN
SAVAGE BEACH	ANDY SIDARIS
SAVAGE DAWN	WILLIAM P. MILLING
SAVAGE HARVEST	ROBERT BLEES
SAVAGE HARVEST	ROBERT COLLINS
SAVAGE HONOR - S	DENNIS L. CLARK
SAVAGE IN LIMBO (P)	JOHN PATRICK SHANLEY
SAVAGE ISLAND	MICHELLE TOMSKI
SAVAGE ISLAND	NICHOLAS BEARDSLEY
SAVAGE MESSIAH	CHRISTOPHER LOGUE
SAVAGE NIGHT - S	MAGGIE GREENWALD
SAVAGE RED - S	ALAN JAY GLUECKMAN
SAVAGE STREETS	DANNY STEINMANN
SAVAGE STREETS	NORMAN YONEMOTO
SAVAGE WEEKEND	DAVID PAULSEN
SAVAGE WILDERNESS	PHILIP YORDAN
SAVAGES - S	DAVID SMITH
SAVANNAH SMILES	MARK MILLER
SAVE THE LAST DANCE FOR ME (SHORT)	MARK ROSNER
SAVE THE LAST DANCE FOR ME	KATHY GORI
SAVE THE LAST DANCE FOR ME	ALAN BERGER
SAVE THE TIGER	STEVE SHAGAN
SAVIN A FACE - S	BARRY BLAUSTEIN
SAVING FACE - S	ALEX TAUB
SAVING GRACE	DAVID S. WARD
SAVING GRACE - S	RICHARD KRAMER
SAVIOR, THE - S	ERNEST THOMPSON
SAWDUST AND TINSEL	INGMAR BERGMAN
SAY ANYTHING	CAMERON CROWE
SAY GOODNIGHT, LILLIAN - S	BRUCE VILANCH
SAY YES	LARRY YUST
SCALAWAGS - S	ERIC EDSON
SCALAWAGS - S	TIM CURNEN
SCALPER - S	RICHARD WENK
SCALPHUNTERS, THE	WILLIAM NORTON SR.
SCANDAL	MICHAEL THOMAS
SCANDAL	AKIRA KUROSAWA
SCANDALOUS	JOHN BYRUM
SCANDALOUS	LARRY COHEN
SCANDALOUS	ROB COHEN
SCANNERS	DAVID CRONENBERG
SCANNERS II	B.J. NELSON
SCANNERS 3 - S	B.J. NELSON
SCAPEGOAT, THE	GORE VIDAL
SCAR - S	MURRAY MEDNICK
SCARAMOUCHE - S	JAMES DEARDEN
SCARECROW	GARRY MICHAEL WHITE
SCARECROW, THE	SAM PILLSBURY
SCARED STIFF	DANIEL BACANER
SCARED STIFF	MARK C. FROST
SCARED STIFF	RICHARD FRIEDMAN
SCARED STIFF (1953)	HERBERT BAKER†
SCARFACE	OLIVER STONE
SCARFACE MOB, THE	PAUL MONASH
SCARLET & THE BLACK - S	CHRISTOPHER E. KNOPF
SCARLET ANGEL	OSCAR BRODNEY
SCAVENGER HUNT	STEVEN A. VAIL
SCENE OF THE CRIME	ANDRE TECHINE
SCENE OF THE CRIME	OLIVIER ASSAYAS
SCENE OF THE CRIME (P)	LAIRD KOENIG
SCENES FROM A MALL	PAUL MAZURSKY
SCENES FROM A MALL	ROGER L. SIMON
SCENES FROM A MARRIAGE	INGMAR BERGMAN
SCENES FROM AMERICAN LIFE (P)	A.R. GURNEY
SCENES FROM THE CLASS STRUGGLE IN BEVERLY HILLS	BRUCE WAGNER
SCENT OF A WOMAN - S	BO GOLDMAN
SCHINDLER'S LIST - S	KURT LUEDTKE
SCHINDLER'S LIST - S	STEVEN ZAILLIAN
SCHIZOID	DAVID PAULSEN
SCHLOCK	JOHN LANDIS
SCHOOL DAYS - S	LEON CAPETANOS
SCHOOL DAZE	SPIKE LEE
SCHOOL FOR SECRETS	PETER USTINOV
SCHOOL SPIRIT	GEOFFREY BAERE
SCHOOL SPIRIT - S	JOHN HUGHES
SCHOOL SPIRIT - S	SAMUEL H. HARPER
SCHOOL TIES - S	DARRYL PONICSAN
SCHOOL TIES - S	DICK WOLF
SCHWEITZER	MICHEL POTTS
SCHWESTERN ODER DIE BALANCE DES GLUCKS	MARGARETHE VON TROTTA
SCI-FI HIGH - S	EARL MAC RAUCH
SCISSORS	FRANK DEFELITTA
SCORCHERS	DAVID BEAIRD
SCORCHY	HIKMET AVEDIS
SCORING - S	BRUCE VILANICH
SCORPIO	DAVID W. RINTELS
SCORPION	WILLIAM RIEAD
SCORPION - S	C. COURTNEY JOYNER
SCORPION - S	MARI KORNHAUSER
SCOTCH SOUR - S	DAVID SHABER
SCOTT JOPLIN	CHRISTOPHER E. KNOPF
SCOUT, THE- S	ANDREW BERGMAN
SCOUTMASTER - S	ANDY BOROWITZ
SCREAM (P)	ARTHUR LAURENTS
SCREAM AND SCREAM AGAIN	CHRISTOPHER WICKING
SCREAM FOR HELP	TOM HOLLAND
SCREAM OF FEAR	JIMMY SANGSTER
SCREAMING MIMI	ROBERT BLEES
SCREEN TEST	SAM AUSTER
SCREENPLAY - S	RAYMOND HARTUNG
SCREWBALLS	JIM WYNORSKI
SCREWBALLS	LINDA SHAYNE
SCREWDRIVER - S	JOHN A. GALLAGHER
SCROOGE	LESLIE BRICUSSE
SCROOGE & MARLEY (P)	ISRAEL HOROVITZ
SCROOGED	MICHAEL O'DONOGHUE
SCROOGED	MITCH GLAZER
SCRUBBERS	JEREMY WATT
SCRUBBERS	MAI ZETTERLING
SCRUBBERS	ROY MINTON
SCUBA DUBA - S	BRUCE JAY FRIEDMAN
SCUM	ROY MINTON
SEA FURY	CY ENDFIELD
SEA GYPSIES, THE	STEWART RAFFILL
SEA HAWK, THE	HOWARD KOCH
SEA KINGS, THE- S	WILLIAM GOLDMAN
SEA OF LOVE	RICHARD PRICE
SEA SHALL NOT HAVE THEM, THE	LEWIS GILBERT
SEA WOLF, THE - S	ANDREW CHAPMAN
SEA WOLVES, THE	REGINALD ROSE
SEANCE ON A WET AFTERNOON	BRYAN FORBES
SEARCH AND DESTROY	DON ENRIGHT
SEARCH AND DESTROY (P)	HOWARD KORDER
SEARCH FOR JOSEPH TULLY, THE- S	GARY DEVORE
SEARCH FOR SIGNS OF INTELLIGENT LIFE IN THE UNIVERSE, THE	JANE WAGNER
SEARCH FOR TYPHOID MARY, THE - S	TERRY BRENNAN
SEARCHING FOR BOBBY FISCHER - S	STEVEN ZAILLIAN
SEASIDE HEIGHTS - S	JOHN HERZFELD
SEASON OF FEAR	DOUG CAMPBELL
SEASON OF GIANTS, A (CTF)	JULIAN BOND
SEBASTIAN	GERALD VAUGHN HUGHES
SECOND CHANCE	CLAUDE LELOUCH
SECOND CHANCE	SYDNEY BOEHM†
SECOND CHANCE - S	DJORDJE MILICEVIC
SECOND CHANCE - S	JOHN M. HERZFELD
SECOND COMING, THE - S	FRANK KERR
SECOND COMING, THE - S	DANIEL PETRIE
SECOND EXPEDITION, THE - S	MARK FROST
SECOND FIDDLE	HARRY TUGEND†
SECOND GENERATION (P)	EDUARDO MACHADO
SECOND HEAVEN - S	RICHARD KRAMER
SECOND MARRIAGE - S	W.D. RICHTER
SECOND RECKONING, THE - S	ROBERT ROY POOL
SECOND SIGHT	PATRICIA RESNICK
SECOND SIGHT	TOM SCHULMAN
SECOND SON - S	RON BASS
SECOND THOUGHTS	STEVE BROWN
SECOND THOUGHTS	TERRY LOUISE FISHER
SECOND TIME AROUND, THE	OSCAR SAUL
SECOND TIME LUCKY - S	JOYCE ELIASON
SECOND TO NONE - S	TIMOTHY B. MCCANLIES
SECOND WIND	HAL ACKERMAN
SECOND WIND	ALVIN SARGENT
SECOND WIND - S	TOM SZOLLOSI
SECOND-HAND HEARTS	CHARLES EASTMAN
SECONDS	LEWIS JOHN CARLINO
SECRET ADMIRER	DAVID GREENWALT
SECRET ADMIRER	JIM KOUF
SECRET AGENT	CHARLES BENNETT
SECRET AGENT FIREBALL	JULIAN BARRY
SECRET FRIENDS - S	DENNIS POTTER
SECRET GARDEN, THE (P)	MARSHA NORMAN
SECRET GARDEN, THE - S	MENNO MEYJES
SECRET HONOR	ARNOLD M. STONE
SECRET HONOR	DONALD FREED
SECRET LIFE OF AN AMERICAN WIFE, THE	GEORGE AXELROD
SECRET LIFE OF GIRLS, THE - S	JUDY TOLL
SECRET LIFE OF GIRLS, THE - S	WENDY GOLDMAN
SECRET LIFE OF PLANTS, THE	WALON GREEN
SECRET OF MY SUCCESS, THE	A.J. CAROTHERS
SECRET OF MY SUCCESS, THE	JACK EPPS JR.
SECRET OF MY SUCCESS, THE	JIM CASH
SECRET OF MY SUCCESS, THE (1965)	ANDREW STONE
SECRET OF NIMH, THE (AF)	DON BLUTH
SECRET OF NIMH, THE (AF)	GARY L. GOLDMAN
SECRET OF NIMH, THE (AF)	JOHN POMEROY
SECRET OF THE MOSAIC, THE - S	ALEXANDER TANA
SECRET OF THE SWORD, THE (AF)	BOB FORWARD
SECRET OF THE SWORD, THE (AF)	LARRY DITILLIO
SECRET PARTNER, THE	DAVID PURSALL
SECRET PLACES	ZELDA BARRON
SECRET POLICEMAN'S OTHER BALL, THE	MARTY FELDMAN†
SECRET POLICEMAN'S OTHER BALL, THE	MICHAEL PALIN
SECRET RAPTURE, THE (P)	DAVID HARE
SECRET SEVENTEEN (CTF) - S	MARSHALL HERSKOVITZ
SECRET WAR OF HARRY FRIGG, THE	PETER STONE
SECRET WORLD	GERARD BRACH
SECRETS	NOELLA SMITH
SECRETS - S	JAN SARDI
SECRETS OF WOMEN	INGMAR BERGMAN
SEDUCE AND DESTROY - S	NEIL CUTHBERT
SEDUCED (P)	SAM SHEPARD
SEDUCTION OF JOE TYNAN, THE	ALAN ALDA
SEDUCTION OF MIMI, THE	LINA WERTMULLER
SEDUCTION, THE	DAVID SCHMOELLER
SEDUCTRESS, THE - S	DAVID AMBROSE
SEE JANE RUN - S	CAROL WATSON
SEE NO EVIL	STEPHEN GELLER
SEE NO EVIL	BRIAN CLEMENS
SEE NO EVIL - S	PETER MCBRIDE
SEE NO EVIL, HEAR NO EVIL	ARNE SULTAN†
SEE NO EVIL, HEAR NO EVIL	MARVIN WORTH
SEE NO EVIL, HEAR NO EVIL	ANDREW KURTZMAN
SEE NO EVIL, HEAR NO EVIL	EARL BARRET
SEE NO EVIL, HEAR NO EVIL	ELLIOT WALD
SEE NO EVIL, HEAR NO EVIL	GENE WILDER
SEE YOU IN THE MORNING	ALAN J. PAKULA
SEE YOU LATER, ALLIGATOR - S	FRASER CLARKE HESTON
SEEING STARS - S	DAVID LEVINSON
SEEMS LIKE OLD TIMES	NEIL SIMON
SEISHUN NO KIRYU	AKIRA KUROSAWA
SEIZURE	OLIVER STONE
SELF DEFENSE	PAUL DONOVAN
SELF STORAGE (P)	SHEM BITTERMAN
SELF STORAGE (P)	TONY SPIRIDAKIS
SELLING SEASON - S	RON CLARK
SEMELWEISS PROJECT - S	LOUIS GARFINKLE
SEMI-TOUGH	WALTER BERNSTEIN
SEMPER FI - S	DANIEL H. VINING
SENATOR'S WIFE - S	JANUS CERCONE
SEND ME NO FLOWERS	JULIUS J. EPSTEIN
SENDER, THE	THOMAS BAUM
SENIOR YEAR - S	JANET KOVALCIK
SENIOR YEAR - S	RANDY JOHNSON
SENSE OF HUMOR, A (P)	ERNEST THOMPSON
SENTINEL, THE	JEFFREY KONVITZ
SENTINEL, THE	MICHAEL WINNER
SEPARATE CHECKS - S	DONALD WRYE
SEPARATE CHECKS - S	KAREN LEIGH HOPKINS
SEPARATE ROOMS	BERTRAND BLIER
SEPARATE TABLES	JOHN GAY
SEPARATE VACATIONS	ROBERT KAUFMAN
SEPARATE WAYS - S	CRAIG HELLER
SEPARATE WAYS - S	GUY SCHULMAN
SEPARATE WAYS - S	KEVIN FALLS
SEPARATION (P)	TOM KEMPINSKI
SEPTEMBER	WOODY ALLEN
SEPTEMBER RUN - S	STANFORD SHERMAN
SEQUENCE - S	ALEC LORIMORE
SEQUENCE - S	TERRY WINKLESS
SERENADE	IVAN GOFF
SERENADE - S	JOHN PIELMEIER
SERENADING LOUIE - S	CAITLIN ADAMS
SERGEANT DEADHEAD	LOUIS HEYWARD
SERGEANT STEINER	TONY WILLIAMSON
SERIAL	MICHAEL ELIAS
SERIAL	RICHARD EUSTIS
SERIOUS LIVING - S	JACK BEHR
SERIOUS LIVING - S	SANDY KROOPF

Se-Sh

FILM WRITERS GUIDE

INDEX OF FILM TITLES

Title	Writer
SERPENT AND THE RAINBOW, THE	ADAM RODMAN
SERPENT AND THE RAINBOW, THE	RICHARD MAXWELL
SERPENTS EGG, THE	INGMAR BERGMAN
SERPICO	NORMAN WEXLER
SERPICO	WALDO SALT†
SERVANT'S ENTRANCE - S	ROBERT MUNDY
SERVANT, THE	HAROLD PINTER
SERVANTS OF TWILIGHT, THE	JEFFREY OBROW
SERVANTS OF TWILIGHT, THE	STEPHEN W. CARPENTER
SERVE AND PROTECT - S	STANLEY WEISER
SESAME STREET PRESENTS FOLLOW THAT BIRD	JUDY FREUDBERG
SESAME STREET PRESENTS FOLLOW THAT BIRD	TONY GEISS
SESSIONS - S	CHRISTOPHER CROWE
SESSIONS - S	JEREMY LEW
SET-UP, THE - S	BRAD A. MIRMAN
SEVEN	ANDY SIDARIS
SEVEN - S	DANIEL PYNE
SEVEN ALONE	DOUGLAS DAY STEWART
SEVEN BEAUTIES	LINA WERTMULLER
SEVEN HOURS TO JUDGMENT	STEVEN DE SOUZA
SEVEN HOURS TO JUDGMENT	WALTER HALSEY DAVIS
SEVEN LITTLE FOYS, THE	JACK ROSE
SEVEN LITTLE FOYS, THE	MEL SHAVELSON
SEVEN MAGNIFICENT GLADIATORS, THE	CLAUDIO FRAGASSO
SEVEN MEN FROM NOW	BURT KENNEDY
SEVEN MINUTES IN HEAVEN	JANE BERNSTEIN
SEVEN MINUTES IN HEAVEN	LINDA FEFERMAN
SEVEN NIGHTS IN JAPAN	CHRISTOPHER WOOD
SEVEN SAMURAI	AKIRA KUROSAWA
SEVEN SINNERS	HARRY TUGEND†
SEVEN SOULS - S	ERIC HANSEN
SEVEN SOULS - S	GREGORY HANSEN
SEVEN SUMMITS - S	DAVID FALLON
SEVEN THE HARD WAY - S	MICHAEL KANE
SEVEN THIEVES	SYDNEY BOEHM†
SEVEN WAVES AWAY	RICHARD SALE
SEVEN WAYS FROM SUNDOWN	CLAIR HUFFAKER†
SEVEN WORLDS, SEVEN WARRIORS - S	HARLAN ELLISON
SEVEN YEAR ITCH, THE	BILLY WILDER
SEVEN YEAR ITCH, THE	GEORGE AXELROD
SEVEN YEARS IN TIBET - S	DAVID HENRY HWANG
SEVEN YEARS IN TIBET - S	MICHAEL THOMAS
SEVEN-PERCENT SOLUTION, THE	NICHOLAS MEYER
SEVEN-UPS, THE	ALBERT RUBEN
SEVEN-UPS, THE	ALEXANDER JACOBS†
SEVENTH SEAL, THE	INGMAR BERGMAN
SEVENTH SIGN, THE	CLIFFORD GREEN
SEVENTH SIGN, THE	ELLEN GREEN
SEVENTH WORLD - S	STANFORD SHERMAN
SEVERAL FRIENDS	CHARLES BURNETT
SEVERED HEAD, A	FREDERIC RAPHAEL
SEX & VIOLENCE - S	DENNIS KLEIN
SEX ADDICTS (CTF) - S	ADAM GREENMAN
SEX AND ARCHITECTURE - S	FERNANDO DOTY
SEX AND THE MARRIED WOMAN - S	MATTHEW DORFF
SEX AND THE SINGLE GIRL	JOSEPH HELLER
SEX APPEAL	CHUCK VINCENT
SEX APPEAL	CRAIG HORRALL
SEX IN AMERICA- S	NORMAN STEINBERG
SEX IN THE 90'S - S	NANCY DOWD
SEX TIPS FOR GIRLS - S	LYNNE GILER
SEX, DRUGS, ROCK & ROLL	ERIC BOGOSIAN
sex, lies and videotape	STEVEN SODERBERGH
SEXBOMB	JEFF BROADSTREET
SEXBOMB	ROBERT BENSON
SEXTETTE	HERBERT BAKER†
SEXUAL PERVERSITY IN CHICAGO (P)	DAVID MAMET
SGT. PEPPER'S LONELY HEARTS CLUB BAND	HENRY EDWARDS
SGT. ROCK - S	DAVID PEOPLES
SH-BOOM - S	ABRAHAM TETENBAUM
SHACK!	CHRISTOPHER E. KNOPF
SHACKLETOWN - S	COLIN WELLAND
SHADE (P)	YALE UDOFF
SHADES - S	TRISH SOODIK
SHADEY	SNOO WILSON
SHADOW 81 - S	DJORDJE MILICEVIC
SHADOW BOX (P)	MICHAEL CRISTOFER
SHADOW CATCHER - S	MARC NORMAN
SHADOW CLUB - S	NEAL SHUSTERMAN
SHADOW COMPANY - S	SHANE BLACK
SHADOW DEAL - S	ROBERT RESNIKOFF
SHADOW OF DEATH - S	CHUCK RUSSELL
SHADOW OF ANGELS	RAINER WERNER FASSBINDER†
SHADOW OF CHINA	RICHARD MAXWELL
SHADOW OF FEAR - S	AVRAM DEAN GOLD
SHADOW OF GOD - S	DIANA HAMMOND
SHADOW OF THE HAWK	NORMAN THADDEUS VANE
SHADOW PLAY	SUSAN SHADBURNE
SHADOW WARRIORS - S	GREGORY WIDEN
SHADOW ZONE	J.S. CARDONE
SHADOW, THE - S	HOWARD FRANKLIN
SHADOW, THE - S	LESLIE NEWMAN
SHADOWLANDS (P)	WILLIAM NICHOLSON
SHADOWS AND FOG	WOODY ALLEN
SHADOWS IN PARADISE	AKI KAURISMAKI
SHAFT	ERNEST TIDYMAN†
SHAFT	JOHN D.F. BLACK
SHAFT IN AFRICA	STIRLING SILLIPHANT
SHAFT'S BIG SCORE	ERNEST TIDYMAN†
SHAG: THE MOVIE	LANIER LANEY
SHAG: THE MOVIE	ROBIN SWICORD
SHAG: THE MOVIE	TERRY SWEENEY
SHAGGY - S	ALAN BERGER
SHAGGY - S	KATHY GORI
SHAGGY D.A., THE	DON TAIT
SHAKE DOWN THE THUNDER - S	JASON MILLER
SHAKE HANDS	IVAN GOFF
SHAKE RATTLE'N'ROLL - S	DAVID LEVINSON
SHAKEDOWN	JAMES GLICKENHAUS
SHAKER RUN	DAVID GREENWALT
SHAKER RUN	JIM KOUF
SHAKES THE CLOWN	BOBCAT GOLDTHWAIT
SHAKESPEARE WALLAH	JAMES IVORY
SHAKESPEARE WALLAH	RUTH PRAWER JHABVALA
SHAKING THE TREE	DUANE CLARK
SHAME (1988)	BEVERLY BLAKENSHIP
SHAME (1988)	MICHAEL BRINDLEY
SHAME (1968)	INGMAR BERGMAN
SHAMELESS - S	LESLIE FULLER
SHAMPOO	ROBERT TOWNE
SHAMPOO	WARREN BEATTY
SHAMUS	BARRY BECKERMAN
SHANGHAI SURPRISE	JOHN KOHN
SHANGHAI SURPRISE	ROBERT BENTLEY
SHANGHAI TANGO - S	LOUIS GARFINKLE
SHANGHAI TANGO - S	QUINN REDEKER
SHANNA - S	HARVEY WARREN
SHANNA - S	JOY WARREN
SHAPER, THE (P)	JOHN STEPPLING
SHARKI	SAMUEL FULLER
SHARK - S	TOM CAMP
SHARK FIGHTERS, THE	LAWRENCE ROMAN
SHARK'S TREASURE	CORNEL WILDE†
SHARKY'S MACHINE	GERALD DI PEGO
SHARMA AND BEYOND	BRIAN GILBERT
SHARON AND BILLY (P)	ALAN BOWNE†
SHARP PRACTICE - S	LAWRENCE D. COHEN
SHARUN - S	THOMAS BAUM
SHATTER GAME - S	KEN SCHAFER
SHATTER N'WADE (P)	MURRAY MEDNICK
SHATTERBRAIN - S	BRENT V. FRIEDMAN
SHATTERDOLL - S	WILLIAM RABKIN
SHATTERED	WOLFGANG PETERSEN
SHATTERED MOON - S	ABBE BERNSTEIN
SHATTERED SILENCE - S	TOM BENEDEK
SHAVED SPLITS (P)	SAM SHEPARD
SHAWL, THE (P)	DAVID MAMET
SHE DANCES ALONE	PAUL DAVIDS
SHE DONE HIM WRONG	JOHN BRIGHT†
SHE MAN, THE - S	BOB CLARK
SHE SAID SHE LIKED THE WAY SHE HELD THE MICROPHONE - S	SARA KRANE
SHE WROTE THE BOOK	OSCAR BRODNEY
SHE'LL BE WEARING PINK PAJAMAS	EVA HARDY
SHE'S BACK	BUDDY GIOVINAZZO
SHE'S BEEN AWAY	STEPHEN POLIAKOFF
SHE'S GOTTA HAVE IT	SPIKE LEE
SHE'S HAVING A BABY	JOHN HUGHES
SHE'S OUT OF CONTROL	MICHAEL J. NATHANSON
SHE'S OUT OF CONTROL	SETH WINSTON
SHE-DEVIL	BARRY STRUGATZ
SHE-DEVIL	MARK BURNS
SHEENA	DAVID NEWMAN
SHEENA	LESLIE C. STEVENS
SHEENA	LORENZO SEMPLE
SHEER MADNESS	MARGARETHE VON TROTTA
SHEET LIGHTNINGS - S	RICHARD MAXWELL
SHEET MUSIC - S	BRUCE VILANICH
SHEIKS OF ARABY, THE - S	STANFORD SHERMAN
SHEILA LEVINE IS DEAD AND LIVING IN NEW YORK	GAIL PARENT
SHEILA LEVINE IS DEAD AND LIVING IN NEW YORK	KENNY A. SOLMS
SHELLEY'S LEG - S	RON NYSWANER
SHELLY - S	DAN GREENBERG
SHELTER ISLAND - S	SOLLACE MITCHELL
SHELTERING SKY, THE	BERNARDO BERTOLUCCI
SHELTERING SKY, THE	MARK PEPLOE
SHENANIGANS	JOSEPH JACOBY
SHENENDOAH	JAMES LEE BARRETT†
SHERLOCK HOLMES ON THE ORIENT EXPRESS - S	LEE REYNOLDS
SHERLOCK SQUIRREL - S	AMY WAGNER
SHIBUMI - S	ROBERT GETCHELL
SHIFTER - S	RICHARD MATHESON
SHIKSE (SHORT)	LINDY LAUB
SHINING THROUGH	DAVID SELTZER
SHINING, THE	DIANE JOHNSON
SHINING, THE	STANLEY KUBRICK
SHIP MOVEMENTS - S	RONNI KERN
SHIP OF FOOLS	ABBY MANN
SHIPMATES - S	GUY HAMILTON
SHIPWRECKED	BOB FOSS
SHIPWRECKED	GREG DINNER
SHIPWRECKED	NILS GAUP
SHIRLEY VALENTINE	WILLY RUSSELL
SHIVA - S	JERE P. CUNNINGHAM
SHIVERS	DAVID CRONENBERG
SHOCK CORRIDOR	SAMUEL FULLER
SHOCK 'EM DEAD	ANDREW CROSS
SHOCK 'EM DEAD	MARK FREED
SHOCK TO THE SYSTEM, A	ANDREW KLAVAN
SHOCK TO THE SYSTEM, A	ALICE ARLEN
SHOCK TREATMENT	JIM SHARMAN
SHOCK TREATMENT	RICHARD O'BRIEN
SHOCK TREATMENT (1964)	SYDNEY BOEHM†
SHOCK WAVES	KEN WIEDERHORN
SHOCKER	WES CRAVEN
SHOCKPROOF	SAMUEL FULLER
SHOE SHINE- S	STEVEN ZAILLIAN
SHOESHINE	CESARE ZAVATTINI†
SHOOT	DICK BERG
SHOOT FOR THE STARS - S	NICHOLAS KAZAN
SHOOT FRANK MILLER - S	THOMAS THONSON
SHOOT THE DEGROODTS - S	SEAN MCCARVER
SHOOT THE DEGROOTS - S	STU KRIEGER
SHOOT THE MOON	BO GOLDMAN
SHOOT THE PIANO PLAYER	FRANCOIS TRUFFAUT†
SHOOT TO KILL	DANIEL PETRIE, JR.
SHOOT TO KILL	HARV ZIMMEL
SHOOT TO KILL	MICHAEL BURTON
SHOOTER - S	DJORDJE MILICEVIC
SHOOTERS - S	HARVEY WARREN
SHOOTERS - S	JOY WARREN
SHOOTERS - S	GREGORY C. WIDEN
SHOOTING GALLERY RATS (P)	ISRAEL HOROVITZ
SHOOTING PARTY, THE	JULIAN BOND
SHOOTING STARS - S	ARNE OLSEN
SHOOTING STARS - S	JAMES PASTERNAK
SHOOTING THE BREEZE - S	CHRISTOPHER SHARP
SHOOTING, THE	CAROLE EASTMAN
SHOOTIST, THE	MILES HOOD SWARTHOUT
SHORE LEAVE - S	PETER CRABBE
SHORT CIRCUIT	BRENT MADDOCK
SHORT CIRCUIT	S.S. WILSON
SHORT CIRCUIT II	BRENT MADDOCK
SHORT CIRCUIT II	S.S. WILSON
SHORT CUTS - S	FRANK BARHYDT
SHORT CUTS - S	ROBERT ALTMAN
SHORT EYES	MIGUEL PINERO
SHORT TIME	JOHN BLUMENTHAL
SHORT TIME	MICHAEL BERRY
SHOT IN THE DARK, A	BLAKE EDWARDS
SHOT IN THE DARK, A	WILLIAM PETER BLATTY
SHOT NIGHT - S	BIG BOY MEDLIN
SHOULDER TO SHOULDER - S	DAVID LEVINSON
SHOUT	JOE GAYTON
SHOUT AT THE DEVIL	WILBUR SMITH
SHOUT, THE	JERZY SKOLIMOWSKI
SHOUT, THE	MICHAEL AUSTIN
SHOUTED FIRE - S	MEG RICHMAN

Title	Writer
SHOW OF FORCE, A	EVAN JONES
SHOW OF FORCE, A	JOHN STRONG
SHOWDOWN IN LITTLE TOKYO - S	DENNIS E. HACKIN
SHOWDOWN IN LITTLE TOKYO - S	JONATHAN LEMKIN
SHOWDOWN IN LITTLE TOKYO - S	STEVE SHARON
SHOWER, THE - S	HEIDE PERLMAN
SHOWER, THE - S	JANET KOVALCIK
SHOWTIME - S	JULIAN BARRY
SHRIMP ON THE BARBIE, THE	GRANT MORRIS
SHRIMP ON THE BARBIE, THE	ALAN SHEARMAN
SHRIMP ON THE BARBIE, THE	RON HOUSE
SHRIVING, THE (P)	PETER SHAFFER
SHY PEOPLE	ANDREI KONCHALOVSKY
SHY PEOPLE	GERARD BRACH
SHY PEOPLE	MARJORIE DAVID
SI C'ETAIT A REFAIR	CLAUDE LELOUCH
SIBERIAN EXPRESS - S	HERSCHEL WEINGROD
SIBERIAN EXPRESS - S	TIMOTHY HARRIS
SIBLING RIVALRY	MARTHA GOLDHIRSH
SICILIAN, THE	STEVE SHAGAN
SID & NANCY	ALEX COX
SID & NANCY	ABBE WOOL
SID - S	LARRY FERGUSON
SIDE OUT	DAVID THOREAU
SIDE OUT	DOUGLAS SOESBE
SIDEKICK - S	RICHARD BLASUCCI
SIDEWALK STORIES	CHARLES LANE
SIDEWINDER 1	NANCY VOYLES CRAWFORD
SIDEWINDER 1	THOMAS MCMAHON
SIDNEY SHELDON'S BLOODLINE	LAIRD KOENIG
SIEGE	PAUL DONOVAN
SIEGE AT RED RIVER, THE	SYDNEY BOEHM†
SIEGE OF FIREBASE GLORIA, THE	TONY JOHNSTON
SIEGE OF FIREBASE GLORIA, THE	WILLIAM NAGLE
SIEGE OF LENINGRAD, THE - S	JOHN MILIUS
SIEGE OF SIDNEY STREET, THE	JIMMY SANGSTER
SIEGE OF SILENCE - S	DJORDJE MILICEVIC
SIEGE OF THE SAXONS, THE	JOHN KOHN
SIEGE, THE - S	JONATHAN LEMKIN
SIESTA	PATRICIA L. KNOP
SIGHTINGS - S	MALIA SCOTCH MARMO
SIGHTSEER	DYANNE ASSIMOW
SIGN OF THE FOUR - S	CHARLES EDWARD POGUE
SIGN OF THE PAGAN, THE	OSCAR BRODNEY
SIGN OF THE RAM, THE	CHARLES BENNETT
SIGNAL SEVEN	ROB NILSSON
SIGNED, SEALED, DELIVERED - S	TODD DURHAM
SIGNIFICANT OTHER - S	RON BASS
SIGNS OF LIFE	MARK MALONE
SIGNS OF LIFE (1968)	WERNER HERZOG
SIGNS OF LIFE - S	HELEN CHILDRESS
SILENCE - S	DAVID RAYFIEL
SILENCE - S	MICHAEL CRISTOFER
SILENCE AT BETHANY, THE	JOEL OLIANSKY
SILENCE LIKE GLASS	CARL SCHENKIEL
SILENCE OF THE LAMBS, THE	TED TALLY
SILENCE OF THE NORTH	PATRICIA L. KNOP
SILENCE WILL SPEAK - S	KURT LUEDTKE
SILENCE, THE	INGMAR BERGMAN
SILENCE, THE - S	FRANK MILITARY JR.
SILENCERS, THE	OSCAR SAUL
SILENCES - S	GORDON GREISMAN
SILENT FLUTE, THE	STANLEY MANN
SILENT FLUTE, THE	STIRLING SILLIPHANT
SILENT MADNESS	WILLIAM P. MILLING
SILENT MAN, THE - S	ADAM RODMAN
SILENT MOVIE	BARRY LEVINSON
SILENT MOVIE	MEL BROOKS
SILENT MOVIE	RON CLARK
SILENT MOVIE	RUDY DELUCA
SILENT NIGHT - S	DENNE BART PETITCLERC
SILENT NIGHT - S	W.D. RICHTER
SILENT NIGHT, DEADLY NIGHT	PAUL CAMINI
SILENT NIGHT, DEADLY NIGHT	MICHAEL HICKEY
SILENT NIGHT, DEADLY NIGHT PART II	LEE HARRY
SILENT NIGHT, DEADLY NIGHT III	CARLOS LAZLO
SILENT NIGHT, DEADLY NIGHT III	MONTE HELLMAN
SILENT NIGHT, DEADLY NIGHT III	RICHARD N. GLADSTEIN
SILENT PARTNER, THE	CURTIS LEE HANSON
SILENT PARTNERS - S	MATTHEW WEISMAN
SILENT PARTNERS - S	JOSEPH LOEB III
SILENT RAGE	JOSEPH FRALEY
SILENT RUNNING	DERIC WASHBURN
SILENT RUNNING	MICHAEL CIMINO
SILENT RUNNING	STEVEN BOCHCO
SILENT SCREAM	JIM WHEAT
SILENT SCREAM	KEN WHEAT
SILENT SCREAM	WALLACE BENNETT
SILENT SERVICE - S	CHARLES ROBERT CARNER
SILENT SERVICE - S	DAVID HIMMELSTEIN
SILENT SERVICE - S	JASON BRETT
SILENT SERVICES - S	DAVID CHISOLM
SILENT VOICE, THE	WILLIAM B. SACKHEIM
SILENT VOWS - S	ALVIN SARGENT
SILHOUETTE (CTF)	JAY WOLF
SILHOUETTE (CTF)	VICTOR BUELL
SILHOUETTES - S	LYNNE GILER
SILK STOCKINGS	LEONARD GERSHE
SILKEN SKIN	FRANCOIS TRUFFAUT†
SILKWOOD	ALICE ARLEN
SILKWOOD	NORA EPHRON
SILKY - S	GARY DAVID GOLDBERG
SILVER AND GOLIATH - S	JOHN ROMANO
SILVER BEARS	PETER STONE
SILVER BULLET	STEPHEN KING
SILVER CITY	SOPHIA TURKIEWICZ
SILVER CITY	THOMAS KENEALLY
SILVER CROSS, THE - S	DAVID DASHEV
SILVER CROSS, THE - S	STUART BIRNBAUM
SILVER DREAM RACER	DAVID WICKES
SILVER RIVER	HARRIET FRANK JR.
SILVER STREAK	COLIN HIGGINS†
SILVERADO	LAWRENCE KASDAN
SILVERADO	MARK KASDAN
SIMON	MARSHALL BRICKMAN
SIMON	THOMAS BAUM
SIMON SAYS - S	CHARLES ROBERT CARNER
SIMPLE GIFTS - S	CAMILLE THOMASSON
SIMPLE JUSTICE - S	CHARLES FULLER
SIMULATOR, THE - S	JEREMY D. LIPP
SIN CITY - S	HARIS ORKIN
SINBAD (AF) - S	MARK SALTZMAN
SINBAD (P)	CHARLES EDWARD POGUE
SINBAD AND THE EYE OF THE TIGER	BEVERLY CROSS
SINCERELY CHARLOTTE	CAROLINE HUPPERT
SINCERELY CHARLOTTE	LUC BERAUD
SINFUL LIFE, A	MELANIE GRAHAM
SING	DEAN PITCHFORD
SINGER AND THE DANCER, THE	JOHN PLEFFER
SINGIN' IN THE RAIN	ADOLPH GREEN
SINGIN' IN THE RAIN	BETTY COMDEN
SINGING DETECTIVE, THE	DENNIS POTTER
SINGING SISTERS - S	HARVEY FIERSTEIN
SINGING THE BLUES IN RED	TREVOR GRIFFITHS
SINGLE - S	HARRIET FRANK JR.
SINGLE - S	IRVING RAVETCH
SINGLE AGAIN - S	JON CONNOLLY
SINGLE FILE - S	GEOFF GRODE
SINGLE WHITE FEMALE - S	DONALD P. ROOS
SINGLE WOMEN - S	NICHOLAS KAZAN
SINGLES	CAMERON CROWE
SINGLES WEEKEND - S	JULIAN BARRY
SINS OF RACHEL CADE, THE	EDWARD ANHALT
SIRAMON - S	QUINN REDEKER
SIRENS OF TITAN - S	TOM DAVIS
SISTER - S	CHRIS KEYSER
SISTER ACT - S	JACK EPPS JR.
SISTER ACT - S	JIM CASH
SISTER MARY IGNATIUS EXPLAINS IT ALL TO YOU (P)	CHRISTOPHER DURANG
SISTER, SISTER	GINNY CERRELLA
SISTER, SISTER	JOEL COHEN
SISTER, SISTER	WILLIAM CONDON
SISTERS	BRIAN DEPALMA
SISTERS - S	JUDITH FEIN
SISTERS OR THE BALANCE OF HAPPINESS	MARGARETHE VON TROTTA
SITTING BULL	JACK DEWITT
SITTING DUCKS	HENRY JAGLOM
SIX BLACK HORSES	BURT KENNEDY
SIX DEGREES OF SEPARATION (P)	JOHN GUARE
SIX FIGURES - S	DON CIRILLO
SIX PACK	ALEX MATTER
SIX PACK	MIKE MARVIN
SIX WEEKS	DAVID SELTZER
SIX WHITE HORSES - S	WILLIAM HJORTSBERG
SIXTEEN CANDLES	JOHN HUGHES
SIXTH AND MAIN	CHRISTOPHER CAIN
SIXTH COMMANDMENT, THE - S	WILLIAM GOODHART
SIXTH FAMILY - S	THOMAS LEE WRIGHT
SIXTH MAN, THE - S	JAMES P. DUNNE
SIZWE BANZI IS DEAD (P)	ATHOL FUGARD
SKATEBOARD	GEORGE GAGE
SKATEBOARD	DICK WOLF
SKATETOWN, U.S.A.	NICK CASTLE
SKEDADDLE - S	RICHARD MATHESON
SKETCHES	NEAL ISRAEL
SKETCHLIFE - S	ED. WEINBERGER
SKI BUM, THE - S	WILLIAM GOLDMAN
SKI PARTY	ROBERT KAUFMAN
SKI PATROL	CRAIG VAN SICKLE
SKI PATROL	STEVEN L. MITCHELL
SKIDOO	DORAN WILLIAM CANNON
SKIMMER - S	WILLIAM WISHER
SKIN DEEP	BLAKE EDWARDS
SKIN GAME	PETER STONE
SKINHEADS	DAVID RESKIN
SKINHEADS	GREYDON CLARK
SKINNER - S	ALICE ARLEN
SKINS - S	ARMAND MASTROIANNI
SKINS - S	CHARLES LANE
SKIRTS & ZIPPERS - S	KATHY COHEN
SKIRTS - S	RICHARD LAGRAVENESE
SKOAL (SHORT)	STEVEN SODERBERGH
SKULL, THE	MILTON SUBOTSKY
SKULL & BONES - S	PETER MARKLE
SKULL: A NIGHT OF TERROR	GERARD CICCORITTI
SKULL: A NIGHT OF TERROR	ROBERT BERGMAN
SKULLDUGGERY	NELSON GIDDING
SKY RIDERS	GARRY MICHAEL WHITE
SKY RIDERS	JACK DE WITT
SKY RIDERS	STANLEY MANN
SKY'$ THE LIMIT, THE - S	JONATHAN PRiNCE
SKY'$ THE LIMIT, THE - S	JOSHUA GOLDSTEIN
SKYLINE DRIVE - S	FLOYD MUTRUX
SLACKER	RICHARD LINKLATER
SLAG (P)	DAVID HARE
SLAM DANCE	DON OPPER
SLAMMER - S	MICHAEL O'DONOGHUE
SLAP SHOT	NANCY DOWD
SLAPSTICK	STEVEN PAUL
SLAPSTICK OF ANOTHER KIND	STEVEN PAUL
SLATE, WYN & ME	DON MCLENNAN
SLATTERY'S HURRICANE	RICHARD T. MURPHY
SLAUGHTER ALLEY - S	RANDY JOHNSON
SLAUGHTER HIGH	GEORGE DUGDALE
SLAUGHTER ON TENTH AVENUE	LAWRENCE ROMAN
SLAUGHTERHOUSE FIVE	STEPHEN GELLER
SLAVE, A TRUE STORY - S	CLAIRE NOTO
SLAVE GIRLS	MICHAEL CARRERAS
SLAVES OF LOVE - S	GAIL PARENT
SLAVES OF NEW YORK	TAMA JANOWITZ
SLAY THE DREAMER - S	DONALD FREED
SLAYER - S	CHRIS DEFARIA
SLAYER, THE	J.S. CARDONE
SLAYER, THE	WILLIAM R. EWING
SLAYGROUND	TREVOR PRESTON
SLEAZY UNCLE, THE	FRANCO BRUSATI
SLEEPAWAY CAMP 3: TEENAGE WASTELAND	FRITZ GORDON
SLEEPER	MARSHALL BRICKMAN
SLEEPER	WOODY ALLEN
SLEEPING ARRANGEMENTS - S	LAURA CUNNINGHAM
SLEEPING BEAUTY - S	STEVEN S. GREENE
SLEEPING CAR MURDERS, THE	COSTA-GAVRAS
SLEEPING CAR, THE	GREG O'NEILL
SLEEPING CITY, THE	JO EISINGER
SLEEPING DOGS	IAN MUNE
SLEEPING TIGER, THE	CARL FOREMAN†
SLEEPING WITH THE ENEMY	RON BASS
SLEEPLESS IN SEATTLE - S	JEFFREY ARCH
SLEEPLESS NIGHTS - S	J.F. LAWTON
SLEEPWALKER - S	JONATHAN KAUFER
SLEEPWALKERS - S	STEPHEN KING
SLEIGHT OF HAND (P)	JOHN PIELMEIER
SLEIGHT OF HAND - S	RICHERD KLEINBERG
SLENDER THREAD, THE	STIRLING SILLIPHANT
SLEUTH	ANTHONY SHAFFER
SLIGHT ACHE, A (P)	HAROLD PINTER
SLIGHTLY OUT OF FOCUS - S	JULIAN BARRY
SLIGHTLY PANICKED - S	ROBBIE FOX
SLIGHTLY PREGNANT MAN, A	JACQUES DEMY†
SLIGHTLY SCARLET	ROBERT BLEES
SLIM AND NONE - S	BUD SHRAKE
SLIM AND NONE - S	DAN JENKINS
SLIPPED DISC - S	R. TIMOTHY KRING
SLIPPER AND THE ROSE: THE STORY OF CINDERELLA	BRYAN FORBES

Sl-Sp

FILM WRITERS GUIDE

Title	Writer
SLIPSTREAM	TONY KAYDEN
SLIPSTREAM	SAM CLEMENS
SLIPSTREAM	WILLIAM C. FRUET
SLIPSTREAM - S	CHARLES EDWARD POGUE
SLITHER	W.D. RICHTER
SLOEHAND HOLIDAY - S	PATRICK HASBURGH
SLOW BURN (CTF)	MATTHEW CHAPMAN
SLOW BURN - S	MARK ALLEN SMITH
SLOW BURN - S	ELISA BELL
SLOW BURN - S	GEORGE MALKO
SLOW BURN - S	PAUL ATTANSIO
SLOW DANCING IN THE BIG CITY	BARRA GRANT
SLUGGER'S WIFE, THE	NEIL SIMON
SLUMLORD - S	MAGGIE KLEINMAN
SLUM LORD - S	RICHARD CHRISTIAN MATHESON
SLUM LORD - S	TOM SZOLLOSI
SLUMBER PARTY '57	FRANK FARMER
SLUMBERPARTY MASSACRE	RITA MAE BROWN
SLUMBER PARTY MASSACRE II	DEBORAH BROCK
SLUMBER PARTY MASSACRE 3	CATHERINE CRYAN
SLY FOX (P)	LARRY GELBART
SMACK IN THE MIDDLE - S	JOHN FUSCO
SMALL BACK ROOM, THE	EMERIC PRESSBURGER†
SMALL BACK ROOM, THE	MICHAEL POWELL†
SMALL CHANGE	SUZANNE SCHIFFMAN
SMALL CIRCLE OF FRIENDS, A	EZRA SACKS
SMALL COLLEGE IN THE WOODS - S	LARRY GROSS
SMALL FEARS - S	GEORGE HAGEN
SMALL HOTEL - S	GERALD AYRES
SMALL TIME	NORMAN LOFTIS
SMALL TOWN IN TEXAS, A	WILLIAM NORTON SR.
SMALL TOWN SYNDROME - S	GARY THOMPSON
SMALL WORLD - S	DAVID H. SMILOW
SMALL WORLD OF SAMMY LEE, THE	KEN HUGHES
SMART MONEY	JOHN BRIGHT†
SMART MONEY - S	MAX EISENBERG
SMART MONEY - S	RAYMOND HARTUNG
SMASH (P)	JACK ROSENTHAL
SMASH PALACE	BRUNO LAWRENCE
SMASH PALACE	ROGER DONALDSON
SMASHBAND - S	ALEC TEAGUE
SMASHBOX, THE - S	JO NAPOLEON
SMILE	JERRY BELSON
SMILES OF A SUMMER NIGHT	INGMAR BERGMAN
SMITH AND WESSON - S	D. SHONE KIRKPATRICK
SMITHEREENS	RON NYSWANER
SMOKE SCREEN - S	PETER FOLDY
SMOKER - S	JOE GAYTON
SMOKESCREEN - S	DON BOHLINGER
SMOKESCREEN - S	JAMES NATHAN
SMOKESTACK LIGHTING - S	JOHN ESKOW
SMOKEY AND THE BANDIT	ALAN MANDEL
SMOKEY AND THE BANDIT	JAMES LEE BARRETT†
SMOKEY AND THE BANDIT	CHARLES SHYER
SMOKEY AND THE BANDIT, PART II	JERRY BELSON
SMOKEY AND THE BANDIT, PART II	MICHAEL KANE
SMOKEY AND THE BANDIT, PART II	BROCK YATES
SMOKEY AND THE BANDIT, PART 3	DAVID DASHEV
SMOKEY AND THE BANDIT, PART 3	STUART BIRNBAUM
SMOKEY BITES THE DUST	BRIAN WILLIAMS
SMOKEY BITES THE DUST	MAX APPLE
SMOOTH CRIMINAL - S	DAVID NEWMAN
SMOOTH TALK	TOM COLE
SMORGASBORD	BILL RICHMOND
SMORGASBORD	JERRY LEWIS
SMOTHERED - S	RACHEL FELDMAN
SMOTHERED - S	SUSAN NANUS
SMUGGLER, THE - S	JUDY NOGG
SMURFS AND THE MAGIC FLUTE, THE (AF)	PEYO
SNAFU - S	TOM DONNELLY
SNAKE EYES - S	DANIEL H. VINING
SNAKE PIT - S	DAVID COLEMAN
SNAKEBITE AND TNT - S	LEO GAREN
SNAKEEATER'S REVENGE	MICHAEL PASEORNEK
SNAKEHEAD - S	RICHARD MAXWELL
SNAKES - S	CINDY MYERS
SNAKES AND LADDERS - S	MICHAEL DUNCAN
SNAP SHOT	EVERETT DEROCHE
SNAPSHOT	MERRILL HEATTER
SNAPSHOT	CHRIS DEROCHE
SNATCH, THE - S	ANDREW BERGMAN
SNEAKERS - S	LAWRENCE LASKER
SNEAKERS - S	PHIL ALDEN ROBINSON
SNEAKERS - S	WALTER F. PARKES
SNEAKERS - S	WESLEY STRICK
SNEAKY PEOPLE - S	JOHN WARREN
SNIPER, THE	EDWARD ANHALT
SNOOKUMS - S	ERIC EDSON
SNOOPY, COME HOME (AF)	CHARLES SCHULZ
SNORKEL, THE	JIMMY SANGSTER
SNOW BALL (P)	A.R. GURNEY
SNOW BLIND - S	LARRY GROSS
SNOW FLAKES - S	DANIEL SULLIVAN
SNOW FLAKES - S	FRED LEBOW
SNOW JOB	JEFFREY BLOOM
SNOW KILL (CTF)	HARV ZIMMEL
SNOW KILL (CTF)	RAYMOND HARTUNG
SNOWBALL EXPRESS	DON TAIT
SNOWMAN - S	NORMAN BOGNER
SNUGGLEFOOT - S	MIKEL ANDERSON
SNUGGLEFOOT - S	PETER JENSEN
SO FINE	ANDREW BERGMAN
SO HELP ME GOD - S	LARRY COHEN
SO I MARRIED AN AXE MURDERER - S	ROBBIE FOX
SO LONG MAGGIE LOVE - S	GERALD DI PEGO
SO LONG, NEW JERSEY - S	HAROLD SALWEN
SO SUE ME - S	FLOYD BYARS
SO THIS IS NEW YORK	CARL FOREMAN†
SO THIS IS NEW YORK	HERBERT BAKER†
SOAPDISH	ANDREW BERGMAN
SOAPDISH	ROBERT M. HARLING
SOB SISTERS - S	GEORGE MALKO
SOB'S - S	JOHN LAFIA
SOCIAL SECURITY (P)	ANDREW BERGMAN
SOCIETY	BRIAN YUZNA
SOFT BEDS AND HARD BATTLES	ROY BOULTING
SOFT TOUCH, THE - S	ANTHONY DRAZAN
SOJOURN - S	PATRICK CIRILLO
SOJOURNERS - S	STIRLING SILLIPHANT
SOLAR CRISIS	JOSEPH M. GANNON
SOLAR CRISIS	TED SARAFIAN
SOLARBABIES	WALON GREEN
SOLARBABIES	DOUGLAS ANTHONY METROV
SOLARIS	ANDREI TARKOVSKY†
SOLD - S	RONNI KERN
SOLDIER BLUE	JOHN GAY
SOLDIER IN THE RAIN	BLAKE EDWARDS
SOLDIER IN THE RAIN	MAURICE RICHLIN†
SOLDIER OF ORANGE	PAUL VERHOEVEN
SOLDIER'S STORY, A	CHARLES FULLER
SOLDIER, THE	JAMES GLICKENHAUS
SOLDIERS OF FORTUNE - S	GARY DRUCKER
SOLDIERS OF FORTUNE - S	JIM STRAIN
SOLDIERS OF MISFORTUNE - S	FRANELLE SILVER
SOLDIERS OF MISFORTUNE - S	THOMAS MCGUANE
SOLDIERS OF ORANGE	GERARD SOETEMAN
SOLO	GARY DEVORE
SOLO - S	MOLLIE D. MILLER
SOLOMON'S MIND - S	ERIC EDSON
SOLSTICE - S	TUDY WOOLFE
SOME CALL IT LOVING	JAMES B. HARRIS
SOME GIRLS	RUPERT WALTERS
SOME KIDS ARE REALLY WEIRD - S	DAVID LEVINSON
SOME KIND OF HERO	JAMES KIRKWOOD†
SOME KIND OF HERO	ROBERT BORIS
SOME KIND OF LOVE - S	ADAM GREENMAN
SOME KIND OF PROGRESS - S	WILLIAM GOODHART
SOME KIND OF WONDERFUL	JOHN HUGHES
SOME LIKE IT HOT	BILLY WILDER
SOME LIKE IT HOT	I.A.L. DIAMOND†
SOME OF MY BEST FRIENDS - S	DAVID DASHEV
SOME OF MY BEST FRIENDS - S	STUART BIRNBAUM
SOMEBODY ELSE - S	HOWARD RODMAN
SOMEBODY HAS TO SHOOT THE PICTURE (CTF)	DOUG MAGEE
SOMEBODY KILLED HER HUSBAND	REGINALD ROSE
SOMEBODY UP THERE LIKES ME	ERNEST LEHMANN
SOMEBODY'S DARLING - S	LARRY MCMURTRY
SOMEONE SPECIAL - S	FREDERIC HUNTER
SOMEONE TO LOVE	HENRY JAGLOM
SOMEONE TO WATCH OVER ME	HOWARD FRANKLIN
SOMEPLACE ELSE - S	CASEY KELLY
SOMETHING BIG	JAMES LEE BARRETT†
SOMETHING IN THE PARK - S	HARV ZIMMEL
SOMETHING IN THE PARK - S	RICHARD WHITLEY
SOMETHING LINGERS - S	STEPHEN FISCHER
SOMETHING MOVES - S	ALLAN G. SCOTT
SOMETHING OF VALUE	RICHARD BROOKS
SOMETHING SHORT OF PARADISE	FRED BARRON
SOMETHING SPECIAL	CARLA REUBENS
SOMETHING SPECIAL	WALTER CARBONE
SOMETHING TO HIDE	ALISTAIR REID
SOMETHING WICKED THIS WAY COMES	RAY BRADBURY
SOMETHING WILD	E. MAX FRYE
SOMETIMES A GREAT NOTION	JOHN GAY
SOMEWHERE IN THE MEDITERRANEAN - S	JOHN A. GALLAGHER
SOMEWHERE IN THE NIGHT	JOSEPH L. MANKIEWICZ
SOMEWHERE IN TIME	RICHARD MATHESON
SOMMARLEK	INGMAR BERGMAN
SON OF A GUN - S	DAVID LOUGHERY
SON OF A GUNFIGHTER - S	CLARKE REYNOLDS
SON OF DARKNESS: TO DIE FOR II	LESLIE KING
SON OF ELVIS - S	NEAL JIMENEZ
SON OF GREASE - S	GARY DAVID GOLDBERG
SONG BIRD - S	FREDERIC RAPHAEL
SONG IS BORN, A	HARRY TUGEND†
SONG OF NORWAY	ANDREW STONE
SONG OF SURRENDER	RICHARD MAIBAUM††
SONGBOOK (P)	JONATHAN LYNN
SONGWRITER	BUD SHRAKE
SONNY'S - S	ELLIOT M. STERN
SONNY BOY	ROBERT CARROLL
SONS	ALEXANDRE ROCKWELL
SONS	BRANDON COLE
SONS AND LOVERS	GAVIN LAMBERT
SOPHIE'S CHOICE	ALAN J. PAKULA
SORCERER	WALON GREEN
SORCERESS (1987)	SUZANNE SCHIFFMAN
SORCERESS (1983)	JIM WYNORSKI
SORORITY - S	PATRICIA RESNICK
SORORITY HOUSE MASSACRE	CAROL FRANK
SORRENTO - S	JULIAN BARRY
SORROWFUL JONES	JACK ROSE
SORROWFUL JONES	MEL SHAVELSON
SOTTO, SOTTO	LINA WERTMULLER
SOUL MAN	CAROL BLACK
SOUL MATE - S	ROBERT M. ULIN
SOUL OF HONOR - S	THOMAS LEE WRIGHT
SOULTAKER	ERIC PARKINSON
SOULTAKER	VIVIAN SCHILLING
SOUND AND THE FURY, THE	HARRIET FRANK JR.
SOUND AND THE FURY, THE	IRVING RAVETCH
SOUND OF MUSIC, THE	ERNEST LEHMAN
SOUND OFF	BLAKE EDWARDS
SOUND OFF - S	DENNIS O'FLAHERTY
SOUNDER	LONNE ELDER III
SOUP FOR ONE	JONATHAN KAUFER
SOUR GRAPES - S	BRUCE VILANCH
SOURCE, THE - S	FAY KANIN
SOURSWEET - S	IAN MCEWAN
SOUTH OF HEAVEN - S	HOWARD RODMAN
SOUTH OF HEAVEN - S	TED BAFALOUKAS
SOUTH OF PICASSO - S	MARK SPRAGG
SOUTH OF RENO	MARK REZYKA
SOUTH OF RENO	T.L. LANKFORD
SOUTH SEA SINNER	OSCAR BRODNEY
SOUTH SEA WOMAN	EDWIN BLUM
SOUTHERN COMFORT	DAVID GILER
SOUTHERN COMFORT	MICHAEL KANE
SOUTHERN COMFORT	WALTER HILL
SOUTHERN COMFORT (P)	NICHOLAS KAZAN
SOUTHERN CROSS - S	CHRIS KEYSER
SOUTHERN HOSPITALITY (SHORT)	TED NICOLAOU
SOUTHERN STAR, THE	DAVID PURSALL
SPACE AVENGER	LYNWOOD SAWYER
SPACE BROTHER - S	BILL COUTURIE
SPACE BROTHER - S	RICHARD DEWHURST
SPACE CASE	HOWARD R. COHEN
SPACE CASE - S	CARLTON CUSE
SPACE CASE - S	ELLEN KESEND
SPACE CASE - S	RICHARD OUTTEN
SPACE COMMANDS - S	GARY GODDARD
SPACE RAIDERS	HOWARD R. COHEN
SPACEBALLS	MEL BROOKS
SPACEBALLS	RONNY GRAHAM
SPACEBALLS	THOMAS MEEHAN
SPACECAMP	CLIFFORD GREEN
SPACECAMP	ELLEN GREEN

378

Title	Writer
SPACECAMP	LARRY B. WILLIAMS
SPACECAMP	PATRICK BAILEY
SPACED INVADERS	PATRICK READ JOHNSON
SPACED INVADERS	SCOTT LAWRENCE ALEXANDER
SPACED OUT	ANDREW PAYNE
SPACEHUNTER: ADVENTURES IN THE FORBIDDEN ZONE	DAN GOLDBERG
SPACEHUNTER: ADVENTURES IN THE FORBIDDEN ZONE	LEN BLUM
SPACEHUNTER: ADVENTURES IN THE FORBIDDEN ZONE	DAVID PRESTON
SPACEHUNTER: ADVENTURES IN THE FORBIDDEN ZONE	JEAN LAFLEUR
SPACEHUNTER: ADVENTURES IN THE FORBIDDEN ZONE	STEWART HARDING
SPACEHUNTER: ADVENTURES IN THE FORBIDDEN ZONE	EDITH REY
SPACEMAN AND KING ARTHUR, THE	DON TAIT
SPACES IN THE DARK - S	ELAINE MUELLER
SPACESHIP	BRUCE KIMMEL
SPADE & GRAVE - S	TYLER BENSINGER
SPAGHETTI - S	ROBERT KAUFMAN
SPAGHETTI MEN	ANDY ROSE
SPANGLE IN DARKNESS, A - S	JON POVILL
SPARE PARTS - S	MARK W. LEE
SPARK- S	JOHN HERMAN SHANER
SPARKLE	JOEL SCHUMACHER
SPASMS	DON ENRIGHT
SPAVE AVENGER	RICHARD HAINES
SPEAKING PARTS	ATOM EGOYAN
SPECIAL CIRCUMSTANCES - S	ALISON CROSS
SPECIAL DAY, A	ETTORE SCOLA
SPECIAL DELIVERY	DAN GAZZANIGA
SPECIAL EFFECTS	LARRY COHEN
SPECIAL ELECTION - S	DAVID HIMMELSTEIN
SPECIAL FAVORS - S	MICHAEL DUGAN
SPEECHLESS - S	JACK BEHR
SPEECHLESS - S	SANDY KROOPF
SPEED ZONE	MICHAEL J. SHORT
SPEED-THE-PLOW (P)	DAVID MAMET
SPELLBINDER	TRACY TORME
SPELLS - S	ABBE BERNSTEIN
SPELLS - S	TOM BENEDEK
SPEND, SPEND, SPEND - S	PETER SEAMAN
SPEND, SPEND, SPEND - S	JEFFREY PRICE
SPETTERS	GERARD SOETEMAN
SPHINX	JOHN BYRUM
SPICE OF LIFE - S	KEN HIXON
SPIDER - S	ROBERT J. COMFORT
SPIDER'S STRATAGEM, THE	BERNARDO BERTOLUCCI
SPIDER MAN - S	NEIL RUTTENBERG
SPIDERMAN - S	ETHAN WILEY
SPIES LIKE US	BABALOO MANDEL
SPIES LIKE US	DAN AYKROYD
SPIES LIKE US	LOWELL GANZ
SPIKE OF BENSONHURST	ALAN BOWNE†
SPIKE OF BENSONHURST	PAUL MORRISSEY
SPIKES GANG, THE	HARRIET FRANK JR.
SPIKES GANG, THE	IRVING RAVETCH
SPINOUT	GEORGE KIRGO
SPINOUT	THEODORE J. FLICKER
SPIRAL STAIRCASE, THE	ALLAN G. SCOTT
SPIRAL STAIRCASE, THE	CHRIS BRYANT
SPIRIT MOVES - S	LARRY B. WILLIAMS
SPIRIT OF '76, THE	LUCAS REINER
SPIRIT OF '76, THE	ROMAN COPPOLA
SPIRIT OF ST. LOUIS, THE	BILLY WILDER
SPIRIT OF ST. LOUIS, THE	WENDELL MAYES
SPIRITS - S	DAVID GILER
SPIRITS OF THE DEAD	FEDERICO FELLINI
SPLASH	BABALOO MANDEL
SPLASH	BRUCE JAY FRIEDMAN
SPLASH	LOWELL GANZ
SPLASH	BRIAN GRAZER
SPLIT DECISIONS	DAVID FALLON
SPLIT IMAGE	ROBERT KAUFMAN
SPLIT IMAGE	ROBERT MARK KAMEN
SPLIT IMAGE	SCOTT SPENCER
SPLIT SECOND	IRVING WALLACE†
SPLIT SECOND	GARY THOMPSON
SPLIT SECOND (P)	DENNIS MCINTYRE†
SPOILED CHILDREN	BERTRAND TAVERNIER
SPOILERS, THE	OSCAR BRODNEY
SPOILS OF WAR (P)	MICHAEL WELLER
SPONTANEOUS COMBUSTION	HOWARD GOLDBERG
SPONTANEOUS COMBUSTION	TOBE HOOPER
SPOOKHOUSE (P)	HARVEY FIERSTEIN
SPOOKWAFFE - S	WALTER BERNSTEIN
SPOOKY - S	MARJORIE GROSS
SPORTING CLUB, THE	LORENZO SEMPLE
SPORTSMAN OF THE YEAR - S	HAL HARRIS
SPOT MARKS THE X (CTF)	DORI PIERSON
SPOTTERS - S	LAWRENCE J. BLOCK
SPPED OF DARKNESS, THE (P)	STEVE TESICH
SPRAY, THE - S	ELLEN ERWIN
SPRAY, THE - S	JEAN BARASH
SPREE	LARRY SPIEGEL
SPREE	FREDERIC SHORE
SPREE	G.M. CAHILL
SPRING '61 - S	GREG BROOKER
SPRING BREAK	DAVID H. SMILOW
SPRING FEVER	FRED STEFAN
SPRING FEVER	STUART GILLARD
SPRING MOON - S	HORTON FOOTE
SPRING REUNION	ROBERT PIROSH†
SPUNK (P)	GEORGE C. WOLFE
SPUTNICK - S	SCOTT FROST
SPY HOTEL - S	DENIS O'NEIL
SPY IN BLACK, THE	EMERIC PRESSBURGER†
SPY VS. SPY - S	JOHN HUGHES
SPY WHO LOVED ME, THE	RICHARD MAIBAUM†
SPY WHO LOVED ME, THE	CHRISTOPHER WOOD
SQUAMISH FIVE, THE	KEN GASS
SQUAMISH FIVE, THE	TERENCE MCKENNA
SQUARE DANCE	ALAN HINES
SQUARE ONE (P)	STEVE TESICH
SQUARE PEG, THE	JACK DAVIES
SQUAW MAN - S	JOHN P. GROVES
SQUEAKY CLEAN - S	JAY BERNZWEIG
SQUEAL OF DEATH (SHORT)	ALEX WINTER
SQUEAL OF DEATH (SHORT)	TOM STERN
SQUEEZE, THE	DANIEL TAPLITZ
SQUIRM	JEFF LIEBERMAN
SQUIZZY TAYLOR	ROGER SIMPSON
SSSSSSSSSS	HAL DRESNER
ST. ELMO'S FIRE	CARL KURLANDER
ST. ELMO'S FIRE	JOEL SCHUMACHER
ST. HELENS	LARRY FERGUSON
ST. HELENS	PETER BELLWOOD
ST. IVES	BARRY BECKERMAN
ST. JOHN'S BREAD - S	STEPHEN FEKE
ST. JUDE - S	RICKY BLACKWOOD
ST. PETERSBURG/CANNES EXPRESS - S	CHRIS BRYANT
ST. ROCK - S	STEVEN DE SOUZA
ST. URBAIN'S HORSEMAN - S	MORDECAI RICHLER
STACEY	ANDY SIDARIS
STACKING	VICTORIA JENKINS
STACY'S KNIGHTS	MICHAEL BLAKE
STAIRWAY TO HEAVEN - S	A.J. CAROTHERS
STAKEOUT	JIM KOUF
STAKEOUT ON DOPE STREET	ANDREW J. FENADY
STALAG 17	BILLY WILDER
STALAG 17	EDWIN BLUM
STALKING MOON, THE	ALVIN SARGENT
STAND ALONE	ROY CARLSON
STAND AND DELIVER	RAMON MENENDEZ
STAND AND DELIVER	TOM MUSCA
STAND AT APACHE, THE	ARTHUR ROSS
STAND BY ME	BRUCE EVANS
STAND BY ME	RAY GIDEON
STAND IN, THE - S	JOHN MORTIMER
STAND IN, THE - S	MURRAY SCHISGAL
STAND OUT, THE - S	STEPHEN PETERS
STAND UP - S	ERIC BOGOSIAN
STAND UP AND BE COUNTED	BERNARD SLADE
STAND UP VIRGIN SOLDIERS	LESLIE E. THOMAS
STAND, THE - S	ROSPO PALLENBERG
STAND-UP GUY, THE - S	MARGARET GREICO OBERMAN
STANDARD OF THE BREED (P)	JOHN STEPPLING
STANDING IN THE SHADOWS OF LOVE - S	JANET KOVALCIK
STANDUP	SAMUEL H. HARPER
STANLEY & IRIS	HARRIET FRANK JR.
STANLEY & IRIS	IRVING RAVETCH
STAR 80	BOB FOSSE†
STAR CHAMBER, THE	PETER HYAMS
STAR CHAMBER, THE	RODERICK TAYLOR
STAR IS BORN, A	JOAN DIDION
STAR IS BORN, A	JOHN GREGORY DUNNE
STAR IS BORN, A	FRANK R. PIERSON
STAR LADIES - S	BARRY SANDLER
STAR OF TIBET	PAUL F. EDWARDS
STAR QUALITY - S	WALTER BERNSTEIN
STAR SAILOR - S	PATRICK READ JOHNSON
STAR SPANGLED ADVENTURE	DAVID ISAACS
STAR SPANGLED ADVENTURE - S	KEN LEVINE
STAR SPANGLED GIRL, THE (P)	NEIL SIMON
STAR TREK - THE MOTION PICTURE	HAROLD LIVINGSTON
STAR TREK II	JACK SOWARDS
STAR TREK II	HARVE BENNETT
STAR TREK III	HARVE BENNETT
STAR TREK IV	HARVE BENNETT
STAR TREK IV	NICHOLAS MEYER
STAR TREK IV	PETER KRIKES
STAR TREK IV	STEVE MEERSON
STAR TREK IV	LEONARD NIMOY
STAR TREK V	DAVID LOUGHERY
STAR TREK V	HARVE BENNETT
STAR TREK V	WILLIAM SHATNER
STAR TREK VI - S	NICHOLAS MEYER
STAR WARS	GEORGE LUCAS
STAR WITNESS - S	MICHAEL ALAN EDDY
STAR-SPANGLED RHYTHM	HARRY TUGEND†
STARCHASER: THE LEGEND OF ORIN	JEFFREY SCOTT
STARCRASH	LEWIS COATES
STARDUST	RAY CONNOLLY
STARDUST MEMORIES	WOODY ALLEN
STARK TRUTH - S	JOHN GUARE
STARLIGHT HOTEL	GRANT HINDEN-MILLER
STARLIGHT PARADE - S	W.D. RICHTER
STARMAN	BRUCE EVANS
STARMAN	RAY GIDEON
STARRY EYED - S	MONTE MERRICK
STARS - S	ROB THOMPSON
STARS AND BARS	WILLIAM BOYD
STARS FELL ON ALABAMA - S	THOMAS RICKMAN
STARS MY DESTINATION, THE - S	LORENZO SEMPLE
STARSHIP INVASIONS	ED HUNT
STARSTRUCK	STEPHEN J. MACLEAN
START OVER, THE - S	EBBE ROE SMITH
START THE REVOLUTION WITHOUT ME	FRED FREEMAN
START THE REVOLUTION WITHOUT ME	LAWRENCE J. COHEN
STARTING OVER	JAMES L. BROOKS
STARWRECK - S	CHRISTOPHER CLUESS
STARWRECK - S	STUART G. KREISMAN
STATE & MAIN - S	DAVID MAMET
STATE OF GRACE	DENNIS MCINTYRE†
STATE OF MIND - S	STEVEN SODERBERGH
STATEN ISLAND FERRY (P)	JAMES KENNEDY
STATES OF SHOCK (P)	SAM SHEPARD
STATIC	KEITH GORDON
STATIC	MARK ROMANEK
STATION CHIEF - S	MARC NORMAN
STATION SIX-SAHARA	BRIAN H. CLEMENS
STATION SIX-SAHARA	BRYAN FORBES
STATIONMASTER'S WIFE, THE	RAINER WERNER FASSBINDER†
STAVISKY	JORGE SEMPRUN
STAY HUNGRY	BOB RAFELSON
STAY HUNGRY	CHARLES GAINES
STAY TUNED - S	JIM JENNEWEIN
STAY TUNED - S	TOM S. PARKER
STAYING ALIVE	NORMAN WEXLER
STAYING ALIVE	SYLVESTER STALLONE
STAYING ON TOP - S	STEPHEN NEIGHER
STAYING TOGETHER	MONTE MERRICK
STEAGLE, THE	PAUL SYLBERT
STEAL THE NIGHT - S	MICHAEL ALAN EDDY
STEAL THE SKY (CTF)	DOROTHY TRISTAN
STEAL THE SKY (CTF)	CHRISTOPHER WOOD
STEALING HEAVEN	CHRIS BRYANT
STEALING HOME	STEVEN W. KAMPMANN
STEALING HOME	WILL ALDIS
STEALING THUNDER	PAUL F. EDWARDS
STEALING THUNDER - S	REED STEINER
STEAM HEAT - S	DEBORAH BARON
STEAMING	PATRICIA LOSEY
STEEL	LEIGH CHAPMAN
STEEL	PETER S. DAVIS
STEEL	ROB EWING
STEEL	WILLIAM N. PANZER
STEEL & LACE	DAVE EDISON
STEEL & LACE	JOSEPH DOUGHERTY
STEEL ANGEL - S	RICHARD PRICE
STEEL ARENA	MARK L. LESTER
STEEL DAWN	DOUG LEFLER
STEEL MAGNOLIAS	ROBERT HARLING
STEEL ROSE - S	JOHN SACRET YOUNG
STEEL TRAP, THE	ANDREW STONE
STEELE JUSTICE	ROBERT BORIS
STEELYARD BLUES	DAVID S. WARD

379

St-Su

Title	Writer
STEEPLECHASE - S	JAMES BRENDAN PATTERSON
STELLA	ROBERT GETCHELL
STEP RIGHT UP - S	JOHN MCNAUGHTON
STEPFATHER, THE	BRIAN GARFIELD
STEPFATHER, THE	CAROLINE LEFCOURT
STEPFATHER, THE	DONALD E. WESTLAKE
STEPFATHER II	JOHN P. AUERBACH
STEPFATHER III - S	MARC RAY
STEPFORD WIVES, THE	WILLIAM GOLDMAN
STEPHEN D - S	HUGH LEONARD
STEPHEN KING'S CAT'S EYE	STEPHEN KING
STEPMOTHER - S	PETER HUNE
STEPPENWOLF - S	JOHN SARGENT
STEPPING - S	GERALD AYRES
STEPPING OUT - S	DAVID A. SILVERMAN
STEREO	DAVID CRONENBERG
STERILE CUCKOO, THE	ALVIN SARGENT
STEVE DUNLEVY STORY, THE - S	LINDA YELLEN
STEVIE	HUGH WHITEMORE
STEVIE WANTS TO PLAY THE BLUES (P)	EDUARDO MACHADO
STEWARDESS SCHOOL	KEN BLANCATO
STICK	ELMORE LEONARD
STICK	JOSEPH C. STINSON
STICK UP, THE	JEFFREY BLOOM
STICKS AND BONES (P)	DAVID RABE
STICKY FINGERS	CATLIN ADAMS
STICKY FINGERS	MELANIE MAYRON
STIFFS - S	CHRIS COLUMBUS
STIFFS - S	GEORGE HAGEN
STILL CRAZY - S	BILL KERBY
STILL CRAZY - S	JIM HART
STILL FRIENDS - S	DEBORAH BARON
STILL LIFE (P)	EMILY MANN
STILL OF THE NIGHT	DAVID NEWMAN
STILL OF THE NIGHT	ROBERT BENTON
STILL SMOKIN'	CHEECH MARIN
STILL SMOKIN'	TOMMY CHONG
STILLWELL - S	CALDER WILLINGHAM
STILLWELL - S	GEORGE MACDONALD FRASER
STING, THE	DAVID S. WARD
STING II, THE	DAVID S. WARD
STINGER, THE - S	RICHARD HEFT
STIR	BOB JEWSON
STIR CRAZY	BRUCE JAY FRIEDMAN
STIR IT UP - S	SEAN MCCARVER
STIRRUPS - S	GAIL FISHER
STIRRUPS - S	MARC CHESLER
STITCH IN TIME, A	JACK DAVIES
STITCH IN TIME, A - S	FRANK DARABONT
STITCHES	MICHAEL PASEORNEK
STITCHES	MICHAEL CHOQUETTE
STOCK CARS FOR CHRIST - S	ROBIN SWICORD
STOLEN FLOWER - S	GEORGE GALLO
STOLEN FLOWER - S	HILARY HENKIN
STOLEN HEAVEN	ANDREW STONE
STOLEN KISSES	FRANCOIS TRUFFAUT†
STOLEN MOMENTS - S	JULIAN BARRY
STOLEN THUNDER - S	ALLAN WEISBECKER
STOMPING GROUND - S	DENIS HAMILL
STOMPING GROUND - S	JOHN HAMILL
STONE - S	JAY PRESSON ALLEN
STONE BOY, THE	GINA BERRIAULT
STONE COLD	WALTER DONIGER
STONE COLD DEAD	GEORGE MENDELUK
STONE WINGS - S	BLAIR FERGUSON
STONEY ISLAND	ANDREW DAVIS
STONEY ISLAND	TAMAR SIMON HOFFS
STONYBROOK - S	ALAN M. SHAPIRO
STOOGEMANIA	CHUCK WORKMAN
STOOGEMANIA	JIM GEOGHAN
STOP AT NOTHING (CTF)	STEPHEN JOHNSON
STOP ME BEFORE I KILL	VAL GUEST
STOP OR MY MOM WILL SHOOT	BLAKE SNYDER
STOP THE WORLD - I WANT TO GET OFF	LESLIE BRICUSSE
STOP THE WORLD - I WANT TO GET OFF	ANTHONY NEWLEY
STORK, THE - S	DAVID ODELL
STORM AND SORROW (CTF)	LEIGH CHAPMAN
STORM CENTER	DANIEL TARADASH
STORM FEAR	HORTON FOOTE
STORM WARNING	RICHARD BROOKS
STORM WARNING - S	WES CLARRIDGE
STORMY MONDAY	MIKE FIGGIS
STORMY SUMMER	CHARLOTTE BRANDSTROM
STORMY WEATHER - S	RICHARD MURPHY
STORY OF A THREE-DAY PASS, THE	MELVIN VAN PEEBLES
STORY OF ADELE H., THE	JEAN GRUAULT
STORY OF ADELE H., THE	SUZANNE SCHIFFMAN
STORY OF MANKIND, THE	CHARLES BENNETT
STORY OF MANKIND, THE	IRWIN ALLEN
STORY OF WOMEN	CLAUDE CHABROL
STORY OF WOMEN	COLO TAVERNIER O'HAGAN
STORYVILLE - S	MARK FROST
STRAIGHT MAN, THE - S	ROGER L. SIMON
STRAIGHT OUT OF BROOKLYN	MATTY RICH
STRAIGHT TALK - S	CRAIG BOLOTIN
STRAIGHT TALK - S	PATRICIA RESNICK
STRAIGHT THROUGH THE HEART	DORIS DORRIE
STRAIGHT TIME	EDWARD BUNKER
STRAIGHT TIME	JEFFREY BOAM
STRAIGHT TIME	ALVIN SARGENT
STRAIGHT TO HELL	ALEX COX
STRAITJACKET	ROBERT BLOCH
STRANDED	ALAN CASTLE
STRANDING, THE - S	FRASER CLARKE HESTON
STRANGE AFFAIR, THE	STANLEY MANN
STRANGE BEHAVIOR	MICHAEL LAUGHLIN
STRANGE BEHAVIOR	WILLIAM CONDON
STRANGE BREW	DAVE THOMAS
STRANGE BREW	RICK MORANIS
STRANGE BREW	STEVE DEJARNATT
STRANGE HEARTS - S	CAROL WATSON
STRANGE INVADERS	MICHAEL LAUGHLIN
STRANGE INVADERS	WILLIAM CONDON
STRANGE ONE, THE - S	CALDER WILLINGHAM
STRANGER CAME HOME, THE	MICHAEL CARRERAS
STRANGER IN A STRANGE LAND - S	LEE REYNOLDS
STRANGER IN A STRANGE LAND - S	LEWIS JOHN CARLINO
STRANGER IN LEADVILLE, A - S	ETHAN WILEY
STRANGER IS WATCHING, A	EARL MAC RAUCH
STRANGER IS WATCHING, A	VICTOR MILLER
STRANGER THAN PARADISE	JIM JARMUSCH
STRANGER, THE	DAN GURSKIS
STRANGERS IN LEADVILLE - S	FRANK DARABONT
STRANGERS IN THE NIGHT - S	PAUL ATTANSIO
STRANGERS KISS	BLAINE NOVAK
STRANGERS KISS	MATTHEW CHAPMAN
STRANGERS WHEN WE MEET	EVAN HUNTER
STRANGLEHOLD - S	HARLAN ELLISON
STRANGLEHOLD - S	MARK ROSNER
STRANGLERS OF BOMBAY, THE	DAVID Z. GOODMAN
STRAPLESS	DAVID HARE
STRAT - S	ED NEUMEIER
STRAT - S	MICHAEL MINER
STRAW DOGS	DAVID Z. GOODMAN
STRAWBERRY - S	BETH HENLEY
STRAWBERRY BLONDE, THE	JULIUS J. EPSTEIN
STRAWBERRY BLONDE, THE	PHILIP G. EPSTEIN†
STRAWBERRY FIELDS - S	HENRY C. PARKE
STRAWBERRY STATEMENT, THE	ISRAEL HOROVITZ
STRAY DOG	AKIRA KUROSAWA
STRAY DOG - S	JULE SELBO
STRAY DOG - S	PAUL MORRISSEY
STREAMERS	DAVID RABE
STREET	KEVIN ELDERS
STREET DANDY - S	THOMAS HEDLEY JR.
STREET GIRLS	BARRY LEVINSON
STREET HEARTS - S	LESLIE RAY
STREET HEAT - S	ZALMAN KING
STREET HERO	JAN SARDI
STREET HUNTER	JOHN A. GALLAGHER
STREET HUNTER	STEVE JAMES
STREET JUSTICE	JAMES J. DOCHERTY
STREET LEGAL - S	THOMAS LEE WRIGHT
STREET OF NO RETURN	SAMUEL FULLER
STREET PEOPLE	ERNEST TIDYMAN†
STREET PEOPLE	RANDAL KLEISER
STREET SMART	DAVID FREEMAN
STREET SMARTS - S	MICHAEL JENNING
STREET TRASH	ROY FRUMKES
STREET WARS	JAMAA FANAKA
STREET WHERE YOU LIVE, THE - S	JASON BRETT
STREET WIRED - S	DANIEL YOST
STREET WITH NO NAME, THE	HARRY KLEINER
STREETFIGHT (AF)	RALPH BAKSHI
STREETFIGHTER - S	VINCENT GUTIERREZ
STREETHUNTER	JOHN A. GALLAGHER
STREETRACERS - S	KEM NUNN
STREETS	ANDY RUBEN
STREETS	KATT SHEA RUBEN
STREETS OF FIRE	LARRY GROSS
STREETS OF FIRE	WALTER HILL
STREETS OF GOLD	DEZSO MAGYAR
STREETS OF GOLD	HEYWOOD GOULD
STREETS OF GOLD	RICHARD PRICE
STREETS OF GOLD	TOM COLE
STREETWALKIN'	DIANE GONCIARZ
STREETWALKIN'	JOAN FREEMAN
STREETWALKIN'	ROBERT ALDEN
STREETWISE - S	DAVID CHISOLM
STREETWISE - S	DAVID FALLON
STRETCH, THE - S	ALLEN HOLLEB
STRICTLY DISHONOURABLE	NORMAN PANAMA
STRIKE IT RICH	JAMES SCOTT
STRIKE THREE CALLED - S	MICHAEL KANE
STRIKEBOUND	RICHARD LOWENSTEIN
STRIKER - S	GARNER SIMMONS
STRINGS - S	JULIAN BARRY
STRIPES	DAN GOLDBERG
STRIPES	HAROLD RAMIS
STRIPES	LEN BLUM
STRIPPED TO KILL	ANDY RUBEN
STRIPPED TO KILL	KATT SHEA RUBEN
STRIPPED TO KILL 2	KATT SHEA RUBEN
STROKE OF GENIUS - S - S	CLIFTON CAMPBELL
STROKER ACE	HAL NEEDHAM
STROKER ACE	HUGH WILSON
STROKES - S	DAVID SHABER
STRONG MEDICINE	RICHARD FOREMAN
STRUCK BY LIGHTNING	TREVOR A. FARRANT
STRYKER	HOWARD R. COHEN
STRYKER	LEONARD HERMES
STUCK IN THE MIDDLE - S	RANDY SCHLOSSMAN
STUCK ON YOU!	LLOYD KAUFMAN
STUCK ON YOU!	WARREN D. LEIGHT
STUD, THE	JACKIE COLLINS
STUDENT BODIES	MICKEY ROSE
STUDENT TEACHERS, THE	DANNY OPATOSHU
STUDS LONIGAN	PHILIP YORDAN
STUFF, THE	LARRY COHEN
STUNT MAN, THE	LAWRENCE B. MARCUS
STUNT MAN, THE	RICHARD RUSH
SUBJECT WAS ROSES, THE	FRANK D. GILROY
SUBLET - S	R. TIMOTHY KRING
SUBMARINE X-1	DONALD SANFORD
SUBSTANCE OF FIRE (P)	JON ROBIN BAITZ
SUBURBIA	PENELOPE SPHEERIS
SUBURBIA (P)	ERIC BOGOSIAN
SUBWAY	LUC BESSON
SUBWAY RIDERS	AMOS POE
SUCCESS	LARRY COHEN
SUCCESS	WILLIAM RICHERT
SUCCESS - S	JAMES KENNEDY
SUCCESS - S	LARRY GROSS
SUCCESS - S	MARY ROBISON
SUCCESS IS THE BEST REVENGE	JERZY SKOLIMOWSKI
SUCCESS STORY - S	ANDREW BERGMAN
SUCH GOOD FRIENDS	ELAINE MAY
SUCKERS - S	MICHAEL THOMAS
SUDDEN DEATH	SIG SHORE
SUDDEN IMPACT	CHARLES B. PIERCE
SUDDEN IMPACT	EARL E. SMITH†
SUDDEN IMPACT	JOSEPH C. STINSON
SUDDENLY	RICHARD SALE
SUDDENLY LAST SUMMER	GORE VIDAL
SUDIE AND SIMPSON (CTF)	KEN KOSER
SUDIE AND SIMPSON (CTF)	SARA FLANIGAN CARTER
SUGAR & SPIKE - S	ED KAPLAN
SUGAR (P)	PETER STONE
SUGAR CANE ALLEY	EUZHAN PALCY
SUGARBABY	PERCY ADLON
SUGARLAND EXPRESS, THE	HAL BARWOOD
SUGARLAND EXPRESS, THE	MATTHEW ROBBINS
SUGARLAND EXPRESS, THE	STEVEN SPIELBERG
SUGARPUSS - S	WILLIAM RICHERT
SUICIDE IN B-FLAT (P)	SAM SHEPARD
SUITOR, THE	JEAN-CLAUDE CARRIERE
SULLIVAN'S PAVILLION	FRED G. SULLIVAN
SULLIVAN'S STATION - S	WALTER NEWMAN
SUM OF US, THE (P)	DAVID STEVENS
SUMMER	ERIC ROHMER
SUMMER CAMP NIGHTMARE	BERT L. DRAGIN
SUMMER CAMP NIGHTMARE	PENELOPE SPHEERIS
SUMMER GARDEN (P)	TERRY CURTIS FOX
SUMMER HEAT	MICHIE GLEASON
SUMMER INTERLUDE	COLO TAVERNIER O'HAGAN
SUMMER INTERLUDE	DANIEL VIGNE
SUMMER JOB - S	JEFFREY C. SHERMAN
SUMMER LOVERS	RANDAL KLEISER
SUMMER MADNESS	DAVID LEAN†

Title	Writer
SUMMER NIGHT WITH GREEK PROFILE	LINA WERTMULLER
SUMMER OF '42	HERMAN RAUCHER
SUMMER OF THE FALCON - S	CLAIRE LABINE
SUMMER RENTAL	JEREMY STEVENS
SUMMER RENTAL	MARK A. REISMAN
SUMMER RUN	LEON CAPETANOS
SUMMER SCHOOL	DAVID DASHEV
SUMMER SCHOOL	JEFF FRANKLIN
SUMMER SCHOOL	STUART BIRNBAUM
SUMMER STORY, A	PENELOPE MORTIMER
SUMMER WISHES, WINTER DREAMS	STEWART STERN
SUMMERFIELD	CLIFF GREEN
SUMMERHOUSE - S	ED KAPLAN
SUMMERTIME	DAVID LEAN†
SUMMERTIME - S	PATRICK READ JOHNSON
SUMMERTREE	ED HUME
SUMMIT KILL - S	PAT PROFT
SUN, THE - S	JONATHAN HEAP
SUN, THE - S	PHILIP MORTON
SUN ALSO RISES, THE	PETER VIERTEL
SUN BEARING DOWN - S	LARRY KETRON
SUNBELT - S	CLAYTON S. FROHMAN
SUNBURN	JAMES BOOTH
SUNDAY BEER - S	RICHARD BURRIDGE
SUNDAY IN AUGUST	FRANCO BRUSATI
SUNDAY IN THE COUNTRY, A	BERTRAND TAVERNIER
SUNDAY IN THE COUNTRY, A	COLO TAVERNIER O'HAGAN
SUNDAY LOVERS	FRANCIS VEBER
SUNDAY LOVERS	GENE WILDER
SUNDAY LOVERS	LESLIE BRICUSSE
SUNDAY RUNNERS IN THE RAIN (P)	ISRAEL HOROVITZ
SUNDOG - S	TERRELL TANNEN
SUNDOWN: THE VAMPIRE IN RETREAT	ANTHONY HICKOX
SUNDOWN: THE VAMPIRE IN RETREAT	JOHN BURGESS
SUNLIGHT AND SHADOWS - S	A. MARTIN ZWEIBACH
SUNNY WITH RAIN	KEN FINKLEMAN
SUNNYSIDE	TIMOTHY GALFAS
SUNSET	BLAKE EDWARDS
SUNSET	ROD AMATEAU
SUNSET BOULEVARD	BILLY WILDER
SUNSET UNLIMITED - S	BLAINE NOVAK
SUNSHINE (P)	WILLIAM MASTROSIMONE
SUNSHINE BOYS, THE	NEIL SIMON
SUNSHINE FLYER - S	DENNIS O'FLAHERTY
SUNSTROKE - S	TERRY CURTIS FOX
SUPER FUZZ	SERGIO CORBUCCI
SUPER MARIO BROS: THE MOVIE - S	BARRY MORROW
SUPER, THE - S	NORA EPHRON
SUPER, THE - S	SAM SIMON
SUPER, THE - S	STU SILVER
SUPERCOPS, THE	LORENZO SEMPLE
SUPERGIRL	DAVID ODELL
SUPERGRASS	PETER RICHENS
SUPERGRASS, THE	PETER RICHARDSON
SUPERMAN	DAVID NEWMAN
SUPERMAN	LESLIE NEWMAN
SUPERMAN	MARIO PUZO
SUPERMAN	ROBERT BENTON
SUPERMAN II	DAVID NEWMAN
SUPERMAN II	LESLIE NEWMAN
SUPERMAN II	MARIO PUZO
SUPERMAN III	DAVID NEWMAN
SUPERMAN III	LESLIE NEWMAN
SUPERMAN IV	CHRISTOPHER REEVE
SUPERMAN IV	LARRY KONNER
SUPERMAN IV	MARK ROSENTHAL
SUPERNATURALS, THE	JOEL SOISSON
SUPERNATURALS, THE	MICHAEL S. MURPHEY
SUPERSTAR (FD)	CHUCK WORKMAN
SUPERSTAR: THE KAREN CARPENTER STORY (SHORT)	TODD HAYNES
SUPERSTITION - S	STEPHEN H. FOREMAN
SUPERTANKER - S	SCOTT MORGAN
SUPERVIXENS	RUSS MEYER
SUPPOSE THEY GAVE A WAR AND NOBODY CAME?	DON McGUIRE
SURE THING, THE	JONATHAN ROBERTS
SURE THING, THE	STEVEN L. BLOOM
SURF II	R.M. BADAT
SURF NAZIS MUST DIE	JON AYRE
SURFIN' USA - S	JOE ANSOLABEHERE
SURFIN' USA - S	STEPHEN VIKSTEN
SURPRISE OF THE DEEP - S	STANFORD SHERMAN
SURRENDER	JERRY BELSON
SURRENDER DOROTHY - S	SCOTT FROST
SURRENDER THE PINK - S	CARRIE FISHER
SURROGATE, THE - S	FAY KANIN
SURVIVAL GAME	HERB FREED
SURVIVAL GAME	P.W. SWANN
SURVIVAL GAME	SUSANNAH DE NIMES
SURVIVAL QUEST	DON COSCARELLI
SURVIVAL RUN	LARRY SPIEGEL
SURVIVAL RUN	FREDERIC SHORE
SURVIVAL RUN	G.M. CAHILL
SURVIVALIST, THE	ROBERT DILLON
SURVIVALIST, THE - S	NICHOLAS KAZAN
SURVIVALISTS, THE - S	JONATHAN REYNOLDS
SURVIVING DAUGHTER (P)	RON NYSWANER
SURVIVOR, THE	DAVID AMBROSE
SURVIVOR, THE (P)	SUSAN NANUS
SURVIVORS, THE	MICHAEL LEESON
SUSPECT	ERIC ROTH
SUSPECT BEHAVIOR - S	DAVID SIMKINS
SUSPENSE	PHILIP YORDAN
SUSPICIOUS MINDS - S	DAVID HAY
SUSPIRIA	DARIO ARGENTO
SUZI AND THE MECHANIC - S	EVERETT LEWIS
SVENGALI - S	BRAD BUCKNER
SVENGALI - S	EUGENIE ROSS-LEMING
SWANN IN LOVE	PETER BROOK
SWAMP THING	WES CRAVEN
SWAMPOUT - S	DAVID ODELL
SWANN IN LOVE	JEAN-CLAUDE CARRIERE
SWARM, THE	STIRLING SILLIPHANT
SWASHBUCKLER	JEFFREY BLOOM
SWEENEY 2	TROY KENNEDY MARTIN
SWEET BERLIN - S	ROBERT BORIS
SWEET BIRD OF YOUTH	RICHARD BROOKS
SWEET CHARITY	PETER STONE
SWEET CHARITY (P)	NEIL SIMON
SWEET DIRTY TONY	CHUCK WORKMAN
SWEET DREAMS	ROBERT GETCHELL
SWEET HEARTS DANCE	ERNEST THOMPSON
SWEET HOURS	CARLOS SAURA
SWEET KILL	CURTIS LEE HANSON
SWEET LIBBY - S	JAMES BRIDGES
SWEET LIBERTY	ALAN ALDA
SWEET LIES - S	ROB DUNN
SWEET LORRAINE	GEORGE MALKO
SWEET LORRAINE	MICHAEL ZETTLER
SWEET LORRAINE	SHELLY ALTMAN
SWEET LORRAINE	STEVE GOMER
SWEET MOVIE	DUSAN MAKAVEJEV
SWEET NOVEMBER	HERMAN RAUCHER
SWEET PEA - S	ROB THOMPSON
SWEET POISON (CTF)	WALTER KLENHARD
SWEET REVENGE	STEVEN M. KRAUZER
SWEET REVENGE	TIM McCOY
SWEET REVENGE (CTF)	JANET BROWNELL
SWEET RIDE, THE	TOM MANKIEWICZ
SWEET SMELL OF SUCCESS	ERNEST LEHMANN
SWEET SOUNDS	RUTH PRAWER JHABVALA
SWEET SUE (P)	A.R. GURNEY
SWEET SUZYI	RUSS MEYER
SWEET SWEETBACK'S BAADASSSSSS SONG	MELVIN VAN PEEBLES
SWEET TALKER	BRYAN BROWN
SWEET TALKER	TONY MORPHETT
SWEET WILLIAM	BERYL BAINBRIDGE
SWEETER THAN HONEY - S	STANFORD SHERMAN
SWEETHEART - S	R.M. BADAT
SWEETHEARTS - S	L.M. KIT CARSON
SWEETIE	GERARD LEE
SWEETIE	JANE CAMPION
SWEETWATER - S	TONY YERKOVICH
SWEETZER - S	SCOTT SPENCER
SWEPT AWAY	LINA WERTMULLER
SWIFT AND NATURAL - S	BASHAR SHBIB
SWIFTY (P)	JAMES KENNEDY
SWIM VISIT (P)	WESLEY MOORE
SWIMMER, THE	ELEANOR PERRY†
SWIMMING POOL, THE - S	RICHARD HEFT
SWIMMING TO CAMBODIA	SPALDING GRAY
SWING KIDS - S	JONATHAN FELDMAN
SWING LOW, SWEET HARRIET - S	HARLAN ELLISON
SWING SHIFT	BO GOLDMAN
SWING SHIFT	NANCY DOWD
SWING SHIFT	RON NYSWANER
SWINGER - S	JULIAN BARRY
SWINGER, THE	LAWRENCE ROMAN
SWINGIN' MAIDEN, THE	LESLIE BRICUSSE
SWINGIN' SUMMER, A	LEIGH CHAPMAN
SWINGS - S	STEVEN KLOVES
SWITCH	BLAKE EDWARDS
SWITCHING - S	BO GOLDMAN
SWITCHING CHANNELS	JONATHAN REYNOLDS
SWORD AND THE SORCERESS, THE	ALBERT PYUN
SWORD AND THE SORCERESS, THE	JOHN STUCKMEYER
SWORD AND THE SORCERESS, THE	THOMAS KARNOWSKI
SWORD OF GIDEON (CTF)	CHRIS BRYANT
SWORD OF HEAVEN	JAMES BRUNER
SWORD OF LANCELOT	CORNEL WILDE†
SWORD OF THE VALIANT	HOWARD C. PEN
SWORD OF THE VALIANT	STEPHEN WEEKS
SWORD OF THE VALIANT	PHILIP M. BREEN
SWORDKILL	TIM CURNEN
SWORDMAN OF SIENA, THE	MICHAEL KANIN
SWORDMAN OF SIENA, THE	FAY KANIN
SWORDS OF HEAVEN	BRITT LOMOND
SWORDS OF HEAVEN	JOSEPH RANDAZZO
SWORDS OF HEAVEN	WILLIAM P. O'HAGAN
SYLVESTER	CAROL SOBIESKI†
SYLVIA (1985)	MICHAEL FIRTH
SYLVIA	SYDNEY BOEHM†
SYLVIE - S	LYNN SIEFERT
SYNCOPATION	PHILIP YORDAN
SYNANON	S. LEE POGOSTIN
SYNGENOR	BRENT V. FRIEDMAN
SYNGENOR	MICHAEL CARMODY
SYSTEM, THE	JO EISINGER

T

Title	Writer
T.R. BASKIN	PETER HYAMS
TABLE DANCING - S	JOHN CARLEN
TABLE DANCING - S	RITA MAE BROWN
TABLE FOR FIVE	DAVID SELTZER
TAFFIN	DAVID AMBROSE
TAG	NICK CASTLE
TAGGET (CTF)	JANIS DIAMOND
TAGGET (CTF)	PETER S. FISCHER
TAGGET (CTF)	RICHARD T. HEFFRON
TAI PAN	JOHN BRILEY
TAI-PAN	STANLEY MANN
TAILS, I DIE - S	JOHN HERZFELD
TAKE A GIANT STEP	JULIUS J. EPSTEIN
TAKE CARE OF MY LITTLE GIRL	JULIUS J. EPSTEIN
TAKE CARE OF MY LITTLE GIRL	PHILIP G. EPSTEIN†
TAKE DOWN	KEITH MERRILL
TAKE IT BACK - S	BART BAKER
TAKE ME OUT TO THE BALLGAME	HARRY TUGEND†
TAKE THAT - S	JULIAN BARRY
TAKE THE HIGH GROUND	MILLARD KAUFMAN
TAKE THE MONEY AND RUN	WOODY ALLEN
TAKE THE MONEY AND RUN	MICKEY ROSE
TAKE THIS JOB AND SHOVE IT	BARRY SCHNEIDER
TAKE THIS JOB AND SHOVE IT	JEFFREY BERNINI
TAKE, THE	DEAN RIESNER
TAKEN IN MARRIAGE (P)	THOMAS BABE
TAKING CARE OF BUSINESS	JEFFREY ABRAMS
TAKING CARE OF BUSINESS	JILL MAZURSKY
TAKING CHANCES - S	HARRIS ORKIN
TAKING CHARGE	DYANNE ASSIMOW
TAKING LUCY - S	TERREL SELTZER
TAKING OF BEVERLY HILLS, THE	DAVID BURKE
TAKING OF BEVERLY HILLS, THE	DAVID FULLER
TAKING OF BEVERLY HILLS, THE	RICK NATKIN
TAKING OF BEVERLY HILLS, THE	SIDNEY J. FURIE
TAKING OF PELHAM 1-2-3, THE	PETER STONE
TAKING OFF	JEAN-CLAUDE CARRIERE
TAKING OFF	JOHN GUARE
TAKING OFF	MILOS FORMAN
TAKING STEPS (P)	ALAN AYCKBOURN
TALE OF SPRINGTIME, A	ERIC ROHMER
TALENT FOR THE GAME	DAVID HIMMELSTEIN
TALENT FOR THE GAME	LARRY FERGUSON
TALENT FOR THE GAME	TOM DONNELLY
TALES FROM THE CRYPT	MILTON SUBOTSKY
TALES FROM THE DARKSIDE: THE MOVIE	GEORGE A. ROMERO
TALES FROM THE DARKSIDE: THE MOVIE	MICHAEL McDOWELL

Ta-Th

FILM WRITERS GUIDE

INDEX OF FILM TITLES

Title	Writer
TALES FROM THE DARK SIDE: THE MOVIE II - S	GAHAN WILSON
TALES FROM THE DARKSIDE: THE MOVIE II - S	MICHAEL MCDOWELL
TALES FROM THE VIENNA WOODS	CHRISTOPHER HAMPTON
TALES OF HOFFMAN, THE	EMERIC PRESSBURGER†
TALES OF HOFFMAN, THE	MICHAEL POWELL†
TALES OF TERROR	RICHARD MATHESON
TALES OF THE NEW DEPRESSION - S	MICHAEL A. KAPLAN
TALES OF THE UNKNOWN	GARY ELLIS
TALES OF THE UNKNOWN	GREG BEEMAN
TALES OF THE UNKNOWN	JEFF COPELAND
TALES OF THE UNKNOWN	MICHAEL MATLOCK
TALES OF THE UNKNOWN	ROGER NYGARD
TALISMAN, THE - S	ARLENE SARNER
TALISMAN, THE - S	JERRY LEICHTLING
TALISMAN, THE - S	RICHARD LAGRAVENESE
TALK RADIO	ERIC BOGOSIAN
TALK RADIO	OLIVER STONE
TALKIN' DIRTY AFTER DARK	TOPPER CAREW
TALKING DIRTY - S	LYNNE GILER
TALKING PICTURES (P)	HORTON FOOTE
TALKING TO THE MOOSE - S	STEVEN SLAVKIN
TALL BLOND MAN WITH ONE BLACK SHOE, THE	FRANCIS VEBER
TALL DOG - S	ANDREW BERGMAN
TALL GUY, THE	RICHARD CURTIS
TALL STORY	JULIUS J. EPSTEIN
TALL STRANGER, THE	CHRIS KNOPF
TALL T, THE	BURT KENNEDY
TAMARIND SEED, THE	BLAKE EDWARDS
TAMER OF HORSES (P)	WILLIAM MASTROSIMONE
TAMING OF THE SHREW, THE	FRANCO ZEFFIRELLI
TAMMY AND THE BACHELOR	OSCAR BRODNEY
TAMMY AND THE DOCTOR	OSCAR BRODNEY
TAMMY TELL ME TRUE	OSCAR BRODNEY
TAMPOPO	JUZO ITAMI
TANGERINE - S	JOHN BEAIRD
TANGO & CASH	RANDY FELDMAN
TANGOS: THE EXILE OF GARDEL	FERNANDO E. SOLANAS
TANK	DAN GORDON
TANK MALLING	JAMES MARCUS
TANK MALLING	MICK SOUTHWORTH
TANNER '88 (CMS)	GARRY TRUDEAU
TAP	NICK CASTLE
TAPEHEADS	BILL FISHMAN
TAPEHEADS	PETER MCCARTHY
TAPEHEADS	JIM HERZFELD
TAPIOCA MISANTHROPA, THE (P)	WALTER HALSEY DAVIS
TAPPING THE SOURCE - S	EARL MAC RAUCH
TAPPING THE SOURCE - S	KEM NUNN
TAPPING THE SOURCE - S	RON KOSLOW
TAPS	DARRYL PONICSAN
TAPS	ROBERT MARK KAMEN
TARAS BULBA	WALDO SALT†
TARGET	DON PETERSON
TARGET	HOWARD BERK
TARGET	LEONARD B. STERN
TARGET - S	RON BASS
TARGETS	PETER BOGDANOVICH
TARGETS	POLLY PLATT
TARZAN AND THE VALLEY OF GOLD	CLAIR HUFFAKER†
TARZAN, THE APE MAN	GARY GODDARD
TARZAN, THE APE MAN	THOMAS L. ROWE
TARZANA (SHORT)	STEVE DEJARNATT
TASTE OF EXCITEMENT, A	DON SHARP
TASTE OF FEAR	JIMMY SANGSTER
TASTE OF HONEY, A	SHELAGH DELANEY
TASTE OF HONEY, A	TONY RICHARDSON
TASTE OF SIN, A	ULLI LOMMEL
TATIANA - S	ANDREI KONCHALOVSKY
TATIANA - S	FLOYD BYARS
TATIE DANIELLE	FLORENCE QUENTIN
TATTOO	JOYCE BUNUEL
TATTOO	ROBERT BROOKS
TATTOOED HITMAN, THE	JACK SHOLDER
TAX MAN - S	ERIC ESTRIN
TAX MAN - S	MICHAEL BERLIN
TAXI DRIVER	PAUL SCHRADER
TAXI TO GLORY	DAVID PEOPLES
TAXI!	JOHN BRIGHT†
TAXING WOMAN, A	JUZO ITAMI
TAXING WOMAN'S RETURN, A	JUZO ITAMI
TCHIN-TCHIN	RONALD HARWOOD
TEA AND SYMPATHY	ROBERT ANDERSON
TEA IN THE HAREM	MEHDI CHAREF
TEACH 109 (SHORT)	RICHARD C. KLETTER
TEACH ME TONIGHT - S	JAMES PASTERNAK
TEACHER'S PET	FAY KANIN
TEACHER'S PET	MICHAEL KANIN
TEACHERS	BILL MCKINNEY, JR.
TEARJERKER - S	KENNY A. SOLMS
TEARS OF THE SUN - S	RON BASS
TECHNICOLOR TIME MACHINE, THE - S	CHRIS MILLER
TECHNICOLOR TIME MACHINE, THE - S	MICHAEL D. SUTTON
TEEN GENIE - S	GEORGE SAUNDERS
TEEN GENIE - S	JOHN B. HEDBERG
TEEN TOUR - S	JEFFREY C. SHERMAN
TEEN WITCH	ROBIN MENKEN
TEEN WITCH	VERNON ZIMMERMAN
TEEN WOLF	JOSEPH LOEB III
TEEN WOLF	LEONARD B. STERN
TEEN WOLF	MATTHEW WEISMAN
TEEN WOLF	R. TIMOTHY KRING
TEENAGE GHOST STORY - S	ROBERT DELAURENTIS
TEENAGE KILLER ZOMBIES - S	ROBERT WUHL
TEENAGE MUTANT NINJA TURTLES	BOBBY HERBECK
TEENAGE MUTANT NINJA TURTLES	TODD W. LANGEN
TEENAGE MUTANT NINJA TURTLES 2	TODD W. LANGEN
TEENAGE WEDDING (P)	JOHN STEPPLING
TEETH'N' SMILES - S	GEOFFREY BAERE
TELEFON	PETER HYAMS
TELEFON	STIRLING SILLIPHANT
TELEGRAPH HILL - S	WESLEY MOORE
TELEGRAPH ROAD - S	DOUG RICHARDSON
TELEKINETIC MAN - S	DAN O'BANNON
TELEKINETIC MAN - S	DON JAKOBY
TELEMACHUS (P)	LEWIS JOHN CARLINO
TELEPATHY - S	STEPHEN VOLK
TELEPHONE JACK - S	JOHN KAYE
TELEPHONE, THE	HARRY NILSSON
TELEPHONE, THE	TERRY SOUTHERN
TELL ME A RIDDLE	JOYCE ELIASON
TELL ME A RIDDLE	ALEV LYTLE
TELL ME THAT YOU LOVE ME, JUNIE MOON	MARJORIE KELLOGG
TELL ME TRUE - S	LARRY ATLAS
TELL THEM WILLIE BOY IS HERE	ABRAHAM POLONSKY
TELL-TALE HEART, THE	BRIAN H. CLEMENS
TELLING TALES - S	CINDY MYERS
TELLING TIME - S	REBECCA KALIN
TELLTALE HEART, THE - S	ART WALLACE
TEMP, THE - S	KEVIN FALLS
TEMPEST	LEON CAPETANOS
TEMPEST	PAUL MAZURKSY
TEMPEST, THE	DEREK JARMAN
TEMPORARY INCONVENIENCE - S	DAVID CASCI
TEMPTING FATE - S	A.J. CAROTHERS
TEMPTING FATE - S	RAYMOND HARTUNG
TEN FROM YOUR SHOW OF SHOWS	MEL BROOKS
TEN GENTLEMEN FROM WEST POINT	RICHARD MAIBAUM†
TEN LITTLE INDIANS	GERRY O'HARA
TEN LITTLE INDIANS	HARRY ALAN TOWERS
TEN LITTLE INDIANS	JACKSON HUNSIKER
TEN LITTLE INDIANS	PETER YELDMAN
TEN MILLION DOLLAR GETAWAY, THE (CTF)	CHRISTOPHER CANAAN
TEN NORTH FREDERICK	PHILIP DUNNE
TEN RILLINGTON PLACE	CLIVE EXTON
TEN TENTHS - S	GUSTAVE REININGER
TEN WANTED MEN	HARRIET FRANK JR.
TEN WANTED MEN	IRVING RAVETCH
TENANT, THE	GERARD BRACH
TENANT, THE	ROMAN POLANSKI
TENDER, THE - S	ROY CARLSON
TENDER HEART, THE - S	MICHAEL SERAFIN
TENDER IS THE NIGHT (CMS)	DENNIS POTTER
TENDER MERCIES	HORTON FOOTE
TENDER TRAP, THE	JULIUS J. EPSTEIN
TENDER, THE	ROBERT STITZEL
TENDERFOOT - S	MONTE MERRICK
TENEBRAE	DARIO ARGENTO
TENLEY'S MEN - S	KEVIN FALLS
TENNESSEE NIGHTS - S	LAIRD KOENIG
TENNIS - S	JULIAN BARRY
TENTACLES	STEVEN W. CARABATSOS
TENTH KINGDOM, THE - S	SIMON MOORE
TENTH VICTIM, THE	TONINO GUERRA
TENUE DE SOIREE	BERTRAND BLIER
TEQUILA SUNRISE	ROBERT TOWNE
TERATOMA - S	W.D. RICHTER
TERESA	STEWART STERN
TERMINAL BLISS	JORDAN ALAN
TERMINAL CHOICE	NEAL BELL
TERMINAL CHOICE	PETER LAWRENCE
TERMINAL MAN, THE	MIKE HODGES
TERMINAL STATION - S	MICHAEL J. AUERBACH
TERMINAL VELOCITY - S	D.T. TWOHY
TERMINATOR, THE	GALE ANNE HURD
TERMINATOR, THE	JAMES CAMERON
TERMINATOR 2	JAMES CAMERON
TERMINATOR 2	WILLIAM WISHER
TERMINI STATION	COLLEEN MURPHY
TERMINUS (FD)	JOHN SCHLESINGER
TERMS OF ENDEARMENT	JAMES L. BROOKS
TERRA NOVA (P)	TED TALLY
TERRIFIC...TERRIFIC! (P)	STEVE SHAGAN
TERROR	DAVID MCGILLIVRAY
TERROR IN THE AISLES (FD)	MARJORIE DOPPELT
TERROR IN THE WAX MUSEUM	JAMESON BREWER
TERROR OF MANHATTAN - S	MICHAEL J. MURRAY
TERROR OF THE TONGS, THE	JIMMY SANGSTER
TERROR ON DUNCAN ISLAND - S	W.D. RICHTER
TERROR RANCH - S	DANIEL SULLIVAN
TERROR SHIP - S	W.D. RICHTER
TERROR TRAIN	T.S. DRAKE
TERROR WITHIN, THE	THOMAS M. CLEAVER
TERROR WITHIN II, THE	ANDREW STEVENS
TERRORISTS, THE	PAUL WHEELER
TERRORVISION	TED NICOLAOU
TERRY & THE PIRATES - S	JULES FEIFFER
TERRY FOX STORY, THE (CTF)	ED HUME
TESLA - S	MICHAEL ALMEREYDA
TESLA - S	J. RANDAL JOHNSON
TESS	GERARD BRACH
TESS	ROMAN POLANSKI
TEST OF LOVE, A	CHRIS BORTHWICK
TEST OF LOVE, A	JOHN PATERSON
TESTAMENT	JOHN SACRET YOUNG
TESTIMONY	DAVID RUDKIN
TESTIMONY	TONY PALMER
TETHER DISORDER (P)	CLIFTON CAMPBELL
TETSU JIBA	AKIRA KUROSAWA
TEX	CHARLIE HAAS
TEX	TIM HUNTER
TEXANS - S	HUGH WILSON
TEXAS CHAINSAW MASSACRE, THE	KIM HENKEL
TEXAS CHAINSAW MASSACRE, THE	TOBE HOOPER
TEXAS CHAINSAW MASSACRE PART 2, THE	L.M. KIT CARSON
TEXAS JACK - S	ALEX HENDRIE
TEXAS LEAD AND GOLD - S	JIM GORMAN
TEXAS LEAD AND GOLD - S	MICHAEL BECKNER
TEXAS LIGHTNING	GARY GRAVER
TEXAS RANGERS - S	TODD DURHAM
TEXASVILLE	PETER BOGDANOVICH
THAI PIRATES - S	TIMOTHY B. MCCANLIES
THAI PIRATES (CTF) - S	DENNIS L. CLARK
THANK GOD IT'S FRIDAY	ARMYAN BERNSTEIN
THANK GOD IT'S FRIDAY	ROBERT KLANE
THANK GOD THERE'S A ROOF - S	MONICA JOHNSON
THANK YOUR LUCKY STARS	NORMAN PANAMA
THANKS DAD - S	HAL DRESNER
THAT CERTAIN FEELING	NORMAN PANAMA
THAT CHAMPIONSHIP SEASON	JASON MILLER
THAT KIND OF WOMAN	WALTER BERNSTEIN
THAT LUCKY TOUCH	JOHN BRILEY
THAT MAN FROM RIO	JEAN-PAUL RAPPENEAU
THAT MAN FROM RIO	PHILLIPE DE BROCA
THAT NIGHT - S	CRAIG BOLOTIN
THAT OBSCURE OBJECT OF DESIRE	JEAN-CLAUDE CARRIERE
THAT SINKING FEELING	BILL FORSYTH
THAT SUMMER	JANEY PREGER
THAT SUMMER OF WHITE ROSES	RAJKO GRLIC
THAT SUMMER OF WHITE ROSES	SIMON MACCORKINDALE
THAT TOUCH OF MINK	STANLEY SHAPIRO†
THAT WAS THEN, THIS IS NOW	EMILIO ESTEVEZ

Title	Writer
THAT'LL BE THE DAY	RAY CONNOLLY
THAT'S ADEQUATE	HARRY HURWITZ
THAT'S ALL FOLKS - S	BRIAN LEVANT
THAT'S LIFE!	BLAKE EDWARDS
THAT'S LIFE!	MILTON WEXLER
THAT'S LIFE, 1986 - S	PETER KRIKES
THAT'S LIFE, 1986 - S	STEVE MEERSON
THE BIG BROKERS - S	JOEL OLIANSKY
THE BIG LOVE (P)	JAY PRESSON ALLEN
THE DREAMER EXAMINES HIS PILLOW (P)	JOHN PATRICK SHANLEY
THELMA AND LOUISE	CALLIE KHOURI
THEO - S	ANDY LEWIS
THERE GOES MY BABY	FLOYD MUTRUX
THERE GOES THE BRIDE	TERRY MARCEL
THERE IS NO THIRTEEN	WILLIAM SACHS
THERE MUST BE A PONY (P)	JAMES KIRKWOOD†
THERE SHOULD HAVE BEEN CASTLES? - S	HERMAN RAUCHER
THERE WAS A CROOKED MAN	DAVID NEWMAN
THERE WAS A CROOKED MAN	ROBERT BENTON
THERE'S A RUSSIAN IN MY FRIDGE - S	CRISTINE BEATO
THERE'S MAGIC IN MUSIC	ANDREW STONE
THERE'S SOMETHING ABOUT MARY - S	EDWARD DECTER
THERE'S SOMETHING ABOUT MARY - S	JOHN J. STRAUSS
THESE ARE THE DAMNED	EVAN JONES
THESE MEN (P)	MAYO SIMON
THEY ALL LAUGHED	PETER BOGDONAVICH
THEY ARE US - S	MAX PROSS
THEY ARE US - S	TOM GAMMILL
THEY CALL ME BRUCE?	DAVID RANDOLF
THEY CALL ME BRUCE?	ELLIOTT HONG
THEY CALL ME BRUCE?	JOHNNY YUNE
THEY CALL ME BRUCE?	TIM CLAWSON
THEY CALL ME MISTER TIBBS!	ALAN R. TRUSTMAN
THEY CAME FROM WITHIN	DAVID CRONENBERG
THEY CAME TO ROB LAS VEGAS	JO EISINGER
THEY DARE NOT LOVE	CHARLES BENNETT
THEY DON'T DANCE MUCH - S	MARI KORNHAUSER
THEY LIVE	JOHN CARPENTER
THEY MIGHT BE GIANTS	JAMES GOLDMAN
THEY SHALL NOT PASS - S	STEVE SHAGAN
THEY SHOOT HORSES, DON'T THEY?	ROBERT E. THOMPSON
THEY SLEEP BY NIGHT - S	BRUCE WAGNER
THEY STILL CALL ME BRUCE	JOHNNY YUNE
THEY WENT THAT-A-WAY & THAT-A-WAY	TIM CONWAY
THEY WENT WEST - S	STEPHEN VIKSTEN
THEY'RE PLAYING WITH FIRE	HIKMET AVEDIS
THEY'RE PLAYING WITH FIRE	MARLENE SCHMIDT
THEY'VE LANDED - S	DAVID LOUCKA
THICKER THAN WATER - S	DARRYL WIMBERLY
THIEF	MICHAEL MANN
THIEF OF HEARTS	DOUGLAS DAY STEWART
THIEF OF TIME - S	GINNY CERRELLA
THIEF WHO CAME TO DINNER, THE	WALTER HILL
THIEVES	HERB GARDNER
THIEVES LIKE US	CALDER WILLINGHAM
THIEVES LIKE US	JOAN TEWKESBURY
THIEVES LIKE US	ROBERT ALTMAN
THIN ICE - S	JOHN HILL
THIN ICE - S	STEVEN DE SOUZA
THIN ICE - S	JACK BEHR
THIN LINE, THE	MICHAEL GRAIS
THIN LINE, THE	MARK VICTOR
THIN MAN'S LAST CASE, THE - S	GEN LEROY
THIN WALLS - S	RON HUGO
THING, THE	BILL LANCASTER
THINGS ARE TOUGH ALL OVER	CHEECH MARIN
THINGS ARE TOUGH ALL OVER	TOMMY CHONG
THINGS CHANGE	DAVID MAMET
THINGS CHANGE	SHEL SILVERSTEIN
THINGS INVISIBLE TO SEE - S	JAIME B. KLEIN
THINGS OF LIFE, THE	CLAUDE SAUTET
THINGS THAT GO BUMP IN THE NIGHT - S	ANTON DIETHER
THINK BIG	JIM WYNORSKI
THINK BIG	DAVID TAUSIK
THINK BIG	EDWARD KOVACH
THINK BIG	JON TURTLETAUB
THINK BIG	R.J. ROBERTSON
THINK PIECE, A (P)	JULES FEIFFER
THINNER - S	MICHAEL M. MCDOWELL
THIRD AND OAK: THE POOL HALL (CTF)	MARSHA NORMAN
THIRD DEGREE BURN (CTF)	DUNCAN GIBBINS
THIRD DEGREE BURN (CTF)	YALE UDOFF
THIRD TIME LUCKY - S	STANLEY MANN
THIRST	JOHN PINKNEY
THIRTEEN - S	DENNIS L. CLARK
THIRTEEN CLOCKS, THE - S	A.J. CAROTHERS
THIRTEENTH DUKE, THE - S	RICHARD MANNING
THIRTEENTH DUKE, THE - S	WILLIAM CONDON
THIRTEENTH LETTER, THE	HOWARD KOCH
THIRTEENTH STEP - S	JOHN JACOBSEN
THIRTY IS A DANGEROUS AGE, CYNTHIA	DUDLEY MOORE
THIRTY SIX EXPOSURES - S	GARY WALKOW
THIRTY-NINE STEPS, THE	CHARLES BENNETT
THIS GUN FOR HIRE (CTF)	NEVIN SCHREINER
THIS HAPPY BREED	DAVID LEAN†
THIS HAPPY FEELING	BLAKE EDWARDS
THIS IS ELVIS (FD)	ANDREW SOLT
THIS IS ELVIS (FD)	MALCOLM LEO
THIS IS MY AFFAIR	ABRAHAM POLONSKY
THIS IS SPINAL TAP	CHRISTOPHER GUEST
THIS IS SPINAL TAP	HARRY SHEARER
THIS IS SPINAL TAP	MICHAEL MCKEAN
THIS IS SPINAL TAP	ROB REINER
THIS IS YOUR LIFE - S	NORA EPHRON
THIS IS YOUR LIFE - S	DELIA EPHRON
THIS PROPERTY IS CONDEMNED	FRANCIS FORD COPPOLA
THIS SPY'S IN LOVE WITH YOU - S	CLYDE DERRICK
THIS TIME FOREVER	BILL LAMOND
THIS YEAR'S MODEL (SHORT)	JANICE SHAPIRO
THOMAS CROWN AFFAIR, THE	ALAN R. TRUSTMAN
THORNY HAWKINS - S	ANDREW DEUTSCH
THOSE BEAUMONT GIRLS - S	ANN DONAHUE
THOSE DARING YOUNG MEN IN THEIR JAUNTY JALOPIES	JACK DAVIES
THOSE DARING YOUNG MEN IN THEIR JAUNTY JALOPIES	KEN ANNAKIN
THOSE GLORY, GLORY DAYS	JULIE WELCH
THOSE LIPS, THOSE EYES	DAVID SHABER
THOSE MAGNIFICENT MEN IN THEIR FLYING MACHINES	JACK DAVIES
THOSE MAGNIFICENT MEN IN THEIR FLYING MACHINES	KEN ANNAKIN
THOSE OF US WITHOUT KEYS - S	JOHN HILL
THOSE WONDERFUL MOVIE CRANKS	JIRI MENZEL
THOUSAND CLOWNS, A	HERB GARDNER
THOUSAND PIECES OF GOLD	ANNE MAKEPEACE
THRASHIN'	ALAN SACKS
THRASHIN'	PAUL BROWN
THREE	JAMES SALTER
THREE AFTER THIRTY - S	PATRICIA RESNICK
THREE AMIGOS	LORNE MICHAELS
THREE AMIGOS	RANDY NEWMAN
THREE AMIGOS	STEVE MARTIN
THREE BAD MEN IN A HIDDEN FORTRESS	AKIRA KUROSAWA
THREE BRAVE MEN	PHILIP DUNNE
THREE BROTHERS	FRANCESCO ROSI
THREE C S, THE - S	ANN BIDERMAN
THREE DAYS IN HELL - S	PETER MCBRIDE
THREE DAYS OF THE CONDOR	DAVID RAYFIEL
THREE DAYS OF THE CONDOR	LORENZO SEMPLE
THREE DAYS, FOUR NIGHTS - S	DIANE ENGLISH
THREE FEET TO GERMANY - S	HERMAN RAUCHER
THREE FOR THE ROAD	MIGUEL TEJADA-FLORES
THREE FOR THE ROAD	RICHARD MARTINI
THREE FOR THE ROAD	TIM METCALFE
THREE FOR THE SHOW	LEONARD B. STERN
THREE FUGITIVES	FRANCIS VEBER
THREE GUYS NAMED MIKE	SIDNEY SHELDON
THREE HATS FOR LISA	LESLIE BRICUSSE
THREE HOTELS (P)	JON ROBIN BAITZ
THREE KINDS OF HEAT	LESLIE C. STEVENS
THREE MEN AND A BABY	JAMES ORR
THREE MEN AND A BABY	JIM CRUICKSHANK
THREE MEN AND A LITTLE LADY	CHARLIE PETERS
THREE MEN AND A LITTLE LADY	JOSAN MCGIBBON
THREE MEN AND A LITTLE LADY	SARA PARRIOTT
THREE MUSKETEERS, THE	GEORGE MACDONALD FRASER
THREE O'CLOCK HIGH	RICHARD CHRISTIAN MATHESON
THREE O'CLOCK HIGH	TOM SZOLLOSI
THREE OF HEARTS - S	ADAM GREENMAN
THREE ON A COUCH	MARVIN WORTH
THREE ON A MATCH	JOHN BRIGHT†
THREE POSTCARDS (P)	CRAIG LUCAS
THREE RING CIRCUS	DON MCGUIRE
THREE RIVERS - S	ROWDY HERRINGTON
THREE SECRETARIES - S	JOHN HUGHES
THREE STRANGERS	HOWARD KOCH
THREE STRIPES IN THE SUN	RICHARD T. MURPHY
THREE TO GO	PETER WEIR
THREE WORLDS OF GULLIVER, THE	ARTHUR ROSS
THRESHOLD	JAMES SALTER
THRILL OF IT ALL, THE	CARL REINER
THRILL, THE (P)	JOHN STEPPLING
THROB - S	LARRY GROSS
THRONE OF BLOOD	AKIRA KUROSAWA
THROUGH A GLASS DARKLY	INGMAR BERGMAN
THROW MOMMA FROM THE TRAIN	STU SILVER
THROWIN' BASS - S	MICHAEL MAYSON
THUNDER - S	ROBERT CASWELL
THUNDER ALLEY	J.S. CARDONE
THUNDER AND LIGHTNING	WILLIAM HJORTSBERG
THUNDER BAY	JOHN MICHAEL HAYES
THUNDER IN THE SUN	STEWART STERN
THUNDER ON THE HILL	OSCAR SAUL
THUNDER RUN	CAROL HEYER
THUNDER RUN	CHARLES DAVIS
THUNDERBALL	JOHN HOPKINS
THUNDERBALL	RICHARD MAIBAUM†
THUNDERBIRD SIX	GERRY ANDERSON
THUNDERBOAT - S	DENNIS HACKIN
THUNDERBOAT - S	STUART BIRNBAUM
THUNDERBOLT AND LIGHTFOOT	MICHAEL CIMINO
THUNDERHEART - S	JOHN FUSCO
THURSDAY'S CHILD - S	DENNIS PALUMBO
THX 1138	GEORGE LUCAS
THX 1138	WALTER MURCH
TICKET OUTTA HERE, THE	JEFFERSON DAVIS
TICKET TO HEAVEN	ANNE CAMERON
TICKET TO HEAVEN	R.L. THOMAS
TICKET TO RIDE - S	DAVID TAYLOR
TICKETS	ALAN MANDEL
TICKETS - S	CHARLES SHYER
TICKING MAN, THE - S	BRIAN HELGELAND
TICKING MAN, THE - S	MANNY COTO
TIDES, THE - S	AMOS POE
TIDY ENDINGS (CTF)	HARVEY FIERSTEIN
TIE ME UP! TIE ME DOWN!	PEDRO ALMODOVAR
TIES THAT BIND - S	JOANNA MCCLELLAND-GLASS
TIGER MAKES OUT, THE	MURRAY SCHISGAL
TIGER RAG - S	MICHAEL THOMAS
TIGER WARSAW	ROY LONDON
TIGER'S TALE, A	PETER VINCENT DOUGLAS
TIGERTOWN (CTF)	ALAN M. SHAPIRO
TIGHT QUARTERS - S	JEFF LANTOS
TIGHT QUARTERS - S	JEFF LEVIN
TIGHT QUARTERS - S	LEANN LANTOS
TIGHTROPE	RICHARD TUGGLE
TIGHTROPE MAN, THE - S	BARRY KEEFFE
TIGRESS, THE - S	KARIN HOWARD
TIL DEATH DO US PART - S	GREG ANTONACCI
TIL DEATH DO US PART - S	RENEE ORIN
TIL MARRIAGE DO US PART - S	ALI MATHESON
TIL MARRIAGE DO US PART - S	JON COOKSEY
TIL THERE WAS YOU - S	MICHAEL THOMAS
TILDEN (P)	WALTER HALSEY DAVIS
TILT	DONALD CAMMELL
TIM	MICHAEL PATE
TIMBUCTOO (P)	TOM KEMPINSKI
TIME & AGAIN - S	NICHOLAS KAZAN
TIME AFTER TIME	NICHOLAS MEYER
TIME BANDITS	MICHAEL PALIN
TIME BANDITS	TERRY GILLIAM
TIME BETWEEN, THE - S	STEPHEN METCALFE
TIME BOMB	DAVID PEOPLES
TIME CAPSULE - S	JOHN A. GALLAGHER
TIME FLIES - S	STEPHEN METCALFE
TIME FOR WEDDING CAKE - S	LOUIS LARUSSO II
TIME LOST AND TIME REMEMBERED	DESMOND DAVIS
TIME OF DESTINY, A	ANNA THOMAS
TIME OF DESTINY, A	GREGORY NAVA
TIME OF THE CUCKOO, THE (P)	ARTHUR LAURENTS
TIME OUT OF JOINT - S	MICHAEL DUNCAN
TIME OUT OF JOINT - S	SAM HAMM
TIME SCAVENGERS	NEAL SHUSTERMAN
TIME STEPS - S	BO GOLDMAN

Ti-Tr

FILM WRITERS GUIDE

INDEX OF FILM TITLES

Title	Writer
TIME TO REMEMBER, A	THOMAS TRAVERS
TIME WALKER	KAREN LEVITT
TIME WALKER	TOM FRIEDMAN
TIMERIDER	MICHAEL NESMITH
TIMERIDER	WILLIAM DEAR
TIMERS - S	IAN SEEBERG
TIMES SQUARE	VALERIE BENNETT
TIMES SQUARE	JACOB BRACKMAN
TIMES SQUARE	ALLAN MOYLE
TIMES SQUARE	LEANNE UNGER
TIMOTHY GEDGE - S	MICHAEL AUSTIN
TIN DRUM, THE	JEAN-CLAUDE CARRIERE
TIN DRUM, THE	VOLKER SCHLONDORFF
TIN LIZZIE TROOP, THE - S	MILES HOOD SWARTHOUT
TIN MAN - S	TOM DONNELLY
TIN MEN	BARRY LEVINSON
TINGLER - S	RON HUGO
TINKER'S DAMN, A - S	DARRYL WIMBERLY
TINTIN - S	MELISSA MATHISON
TIRADE (P)	RICHARD MAIBAUM†
TITAN - S	GARNER SIMMONS
TO BE OR NOT TO BE	RONNY GRAHAM
TO BE OR NOT TO BE	THOMAS MEEHAN
TO DIE A STRANGER - S	JOHN BRILEY
TO FIND A MAN	ARNOLD SCHULMAN
TO KILL A MOCKINGBIRD	HORTON FOOTE
TO KILL A PRIEST	AGNIESZKA HOLLAND
TO KILL A PRIEST	JEAN-YVES PITOUN
TO LIVE AND DIE IN L.A.	GERALD PETIEVICH
TO LIVE AND DIE IN L.A.	WILLIAM FRIEDKIN
TO SIR, WITH LOVE	JAMES CLAVELL
TO SLEEP WITH ANGER	CHARLES BURNETT
TO THE DEVIL A DAUGHTER	CHRISTOPHER WICKING
TO THE END OF THE SILVER MOUNTAINS	AKIRA KUROSAWA
TO THE MANOR BORN - S	ELIZABETH BRADLEY
TO THE MANOR BORN - S	STEPHEN MCPHERSON
TO THE VICTOR	RICHARD BROOKS
TOAST OF THE TOWN (P)	JEROME LAWRENCE
TOAST OF THE TOWN (P)	ROBERT E. LEE
TOBY MCTEAGUE	DJORDJE MILICEVIC
TOBY MCTEAGUE	JAMIE BROWN
TOBY MCTEAGUE	JEFFREY P. MAGUIRE
TODD KILLINGS, THE	JOEL OLIANSKY
TODDLERS - S	ANDREW BRECKMAN
TOKYO BAY - S	THOMAS MCGUANE
TOKYO DIAMOND - S	MONTE MERRICK
TOKYO POP	FRAN RUBEL KUZUI
TOKYO POP	LYNN GROSSMAN
TOKYO WOES - S	BRUCE JAY FRIEDMAN
TOKYO-GA (FD)	WIM WENDERS
TOM CAT - S	PETER FILARDI
TOM DOOLEY PROJECT, THE - S	PAUL THEROUX
TOM HORN	THOMAS MCGUANE
TOM HORN	BUD SHRAKE
TOM JONES	JOHN OSBORNE
TOM MIX & PANCHO VILLA	DERIC WASHBURN
TOM MIX AND PANCHO VILLA - S	THOMAS POPE
TOM WEST - S	ROBERT J. COMFORT
TOM, DICK AND HARRY - S	DAVID CASCI
TOM, NICK AND MARY - S	STANFORD SHERMAN
TOMB OF LIGEIA	ROBERT TOWNE
TOMB, THE	KENNETH J. HALL
TOMBOY	BEN ZELIG
TOMMY	KEN RUSSELL
TOMMY SWIFT - S	JEREMY IACONE
TOMORROW	HORTON FOOTE
TOMORROW NEVER COMES	DAVID PURSALL
TOMORROW THE WORLD	RING LARDNER JR.
TOMORROW THE WORLD (P)	ARNAUD D'USSEAU†
TONIGHT AT 8:30 (P)	JONATHAN LYNN
TONIGHT FOR SURE	FRANCIS FORD COPPOLA
TONIGHT'S THE NIGHT	JACK DAVIES
TOO BEAUTIFUL FOR YOU	BERTRAND BLIER
TOO CONFUSED, THE ANGEL (P)	LORING MANDEL
TOO DEEP FOR TEARS - S	MARTIN COPELAND
TOO FAR TO WALK - S	WILLIAM GOODHART
TOO GOOD TO BE TRUE - S	ALEC LORIMORE
TOO GOOD TO BE TRUE - S	TERRY WINKLESS
TOO LATE BLUES	JOHN CASSAVETES†
TOO LATE BLUES	RICHARD CARR
TOO LATE FOR HEROES - S	DOUGLAS DAY STEWART
TOO LATE FOR TEARS	ROY HUGGINS
TOO LATE THE HERO	LUKAS HELLER†
TOO MUCH	ERIC ROCHANT
TOO MUCH SUN	AL SCHWARTZ
TOO MUCH SUN	LAURA ERNST
TOO MUCH SUN	ROBERT DOWNEY
TOO OUTRAGEOUS!	DICK BENNER†
TOO SCARED TO SCREAM	GLENN LEOPOLD
TOO SCARED TO SCREAM	NEAL BARBERA
TOO SMART FOR LOVE - S	AMY SPIES
TOOTH OF CRIME (P)	SAM SHEPARD
TOOTS IN SOLITUDE - S	DOUG WHEELER
TOOTSIE	LARRY GELBART
TOOTSIE	DON MCGUIRE
TOOTSIE	MURRAY SCHISGAL
TOP, THE - S	LOUIS VENOSTA
TOP GUN	JACK EPPS JR.
TOP GUN	JIM CASH
TOP SECRET!	DAVID ZUCKER
TOP SECRET!	JERRY ZUCKER
TOP SECRET!	JIM ABRAHAMS
TOP SECRET!	MARTYN BURKE
TOP SECRET (1952)	JACK DAVIES
TOP STORY - S	ALLYN WARNER
TORCH SONG	JOHN MICHAEL HAYES
TORCH SONG TRILOGY	HARVEY FIERSTEIN
TORCHLIGHT	ELIZA MOORMAN
TORCHLIGHT	PAMELA SUE MARTIN
TORCHLIGHT - S	THOMAS LEE WRIGHT
TORMENT	JOHN HOPKINS
TORMENT	SAMSON ASLANIAN
TORN - S	DAVID H. FRANZONI
TORN APART	MARC KRISTAL
TORN CURTAIN	BRIAN MOORE
TORPEDO RUN	RICHARD SALE
TORPEDO RUN	WILLIAM WISTER HAINES†
TORPEDOS - S	JOHN MCCORMICK
TORPEDOS - S	ROSS LA MANNA
TORRENTS OF SPRING	JERZY SKOLIMOWSKI
TORRID ZONE, THE - S	MARI KORNHAUSER
TORTURE GARDEN	ROBERT BLOCH
TOTAL ABANDON - S	LARRY ATLAS
TOTAL ECLIPSE OF THE HEART - S	DAVID PIRIE
TOTAL RECALL	RONALD SHUSETT
TOTAL RECALL	DAN O'BANNON
TOTAL RECALL	GARY GOLDMAN
TOTAL RECALL	JON POVILL
TOUCH - S	HAMPTON FANCHER
TOUCH AND GO	ALAN ORMSBY
TOUCH AND GO	ROBERT L. SAND
TOUCH AND GO	HARRY COLOMBY
TOUCH AND GO (1980)	PETER YELDMAN
TOUCH LUCK - S	PETER LENKOV
TOUCH OF A STRANGER	BRAD GILBERT
TOUCH OF A STRANGER	JOSLYN BARNES
TOUCH OF CLASS, A	JACK ROSE
TOUCH OF LARCENY, A	GUY HAMILTON
TOUCH OF THE COWBOY - S	GEORGE E. SIMPSON
TOUCH, THE	INGMAR BERGMAN
TOUCH, THE - S	STEVE MARTIN
TOUCHED	LYLE D. KESSLER
TOUCHED BY LOVE	HESPER ANDERSON
TOUGH COOKIES - S	CARL G. SAUTTER
TOUGH CUSTOMERS - S	DAVID FREEMAN
TOUGH CUSTOMERS - S	JULIAN BARRY
TOUGH ENOUGH	JOHN LEONE
TOUGH GUYS	JAMES ORR
TOUGH GUYS	JIM CRUICKSHANK
TOUGH GUYS DON'T DANCE	NORMAN MAILER
TOUGH TANGO - S	THOMAS HEDLEY JR.
TOUR '85 - S	BENNETT TRAMER
TOUR, THE - S	BOB DOLMAN
TOUR, THE - S	WILLIAM GOODHART
TOURIST TRAP, THE	DAVID SCHMOELLER
TOURIST, THE - S	CLAIRE NOTO
TOURIST, THE - S	PATRICIA L. KNOP
TOURISTS, THE - S	JEFF BERMAN
TOURISTS, THE - S	JERRY RAPP
TOUTE UNE VIE	CLAUDE LELOUCH
TOWER, THE - S	BILL KERBY
TOWERING INFERNO, THE	STIRLING SILLIPHANT
TOWN ON TRIAL	KEN HUGHES
TOWN THAT DREADED SUNDOWN, THE	EARL E. SMITH†
TOWNIES - S	JOHN FUSCO
TOXIC AVENGER, THE	JOE RITTER
TOXIC AVENGER, PART II, THE	GAY PARTINGTON TERRY
TOXIC AVENGER, PART III, THE	GAY PARTINGTON TERRY
TOXIC AVENGER, PART III, THE	LLOYD KAUFMAN
TOY SOLDIERS (1991)	DAN PETRIE JR.
TOY SOLDIERS (1991)	DAVID KOEPP
TOY SOLDIERS (1984)	DAVID FISHER
TOY SOLDIERS (1984)	WALTER FOX
TOY, THE	CAROL SOBIESKI†
TOYS - S	BARRY LEVINSON
TOYS - S	VALERIE CURTIN
TRACE, THE - S	DANILO BACH
TRACER - S	FRANK GALATI
TRACERS (P)	SHELDON B. LETTICH
TRACES - S	MARK FROST
TRACK 29	DENNIS POTTER
TRACKDOWN	PAUL F. EDWARDS
TRACKDOWN - S	JOHN A. GALLAGHER
TRACKDOWN - S	ROBERT GINTY
TRACKER EAST - S	THOMAS LEE WRIGHT
TRAINING EXERCISE - S	THOMAS LEE WRIGHT
TRACKS	HENRY JAGLOM
TRACKS END - S	ERIC BERCOVICI
TRADEOFF - S	RON BASS
TRADER HORN	WILLIAM NORTON SR.
TRADING HEARTS	FRANK DEFORD
TRADING PLACES	HERSCHEL WEINGROD
TRADING PLACES	TIMOTHY HARRIS
TRAFFIC SCHOOL - S	BRIAN REHAK
TRAFFIC SCHOOL - S	DANA OLSEN
TRAGEDY OF A RIDICULOUS MAN	BERNARDO BERTOLUCCI
TRAGEDY OF FLIGHT 103, THE (CTF)	MICHAEL EATON
TRAIL OF THE FOX - S	JOHN ROMANO
TRAIL OF THE PINK PANTHER	BLAKE EDWARDS
TRAIL OF THE PINK PANTHER	FRANK WALDMAN†
TRAIL OF THE PINK PANTHER	GEOFFREY EDWARDS
TRAILBLAZERS - S	DENNIS L. CLARK
TRAIN RIDE TO HOLLYWOOD	DAN GORDON
TRAIN ROBBERS, THE	BURT KENNEDY
TRAIN, THE	WALTER BERNSTEIN
TRANCERS	DANNY BILSON
TRANCERS	PAUL DEMEO
TRANCERS II - S	JACKSON BARR
TRANSFORMERS: THE MOVIE, THE (AF)	RON FRIEDMAN
TRANSYLVANIA 6-5000	RUDY DELUCA
TRANSYLVANIA MUSICAL - S	ROBERT KLANE
TRANSYLVANIA TWIST	R.J. ROBERTSON
TRANSYLVANIA-PENNSYLVANIA - S	NEIL LANDAU
TRANSYLVANIA-PENNSYLVANIA - S	TARA ISON
TRANSYLVANIA-PENNSYLVANIA - S	RICHARD OUTTEN
TRAP, THE	NORMAN PANAMA
TRAP DOOR - S	BILL KERBY
TRAP DOOR - S	CHARLIE HAAS
TRAP DOOR - S	TIM HUNTER
TRAPPED	JOHN BEAIRD
TRAPPED (CTF)	FRED WALTON
TRAPPED (CTF)	STEPHEN J. FEKE
TRASH PATROL - S	RAYMOND HARTUNG
TRAVELING LIGHT - S	JEAN VALLELY
TRAVELING MAN (CTF)	DAVID TAYLOR
TRAVELING PLAYERS, THE	THEO ANGELOPOULOS
TRAVELLING LIGHT - S	JAN ELIASBERG
TRAVELLING NORTH	DAVID WILLIAMSON
TRAVELS WITH MY AUNT	HUGH WHEELER†
TRAVELS WITH MY AUNT	JAY PRESSON ALLEN
TRAVESTIES (P)	TOM STOPPARD
TRAXX	GARY DEVORE
TREACHEROUS - S	DAVID AMBROSE
TREASURE - S	BRIAN DEPALMA
TREASURE - S	DOUGLAS STEFEN BORGHI
TREASURE HUNT - S	DAVID AMBROSE
TREASURE HUNT - S	JOHN MCTIERNAN
TREASURE HUNT - S	TAB MURPHY
TREASURE ISLAND (1971)	WOLF MANKOWITZ
TREASURE ISLAND (CTF)	FRASER CLARKE HESTON
TREASURE ISLAND - S	DAVID FREEMAN
TREASURE OF GUNSIGHT BUTTE - S	DAVID A. CHAPPE
TREASURE OF MATECUMBE, THE	DON TAIT
TREASURE OF THE FOUR CROWNS	JERRY LAZARUS
TREASURE OF THE FOUR CROWNS	JAMES BRYCE
TREASURE OF THE FOUR CROWNS	LLOYD BATTISTA
TREASURE OF THE YANKEE ZEPHYR	EVERETT DEROCHE
TREE, THE (P)	RICHARD MAIBAUM†
TREMORS	BRENT MADDOCK
TREMORS	S.S. WILSON
TRENCHCOAT	JEFFREY PRICE
TRENCHCOAT	PETER SEAMAN
TREVOR (P)	JOHN BOWEN
TREVOR - S	BARRY MORROW

Title	Writer
TREVOR - S	ROBERT KAUFMAN
TRIAL BY COMBAT	JULIAN BOND
TRIAL BY JURY - S	JORDAN KATZ
TRIAL OF THE PINK PANTHER	TOM WALDMAN†
TRIALS & TRIBULATION - S	DANILO BACH
TRIALS AND TRIBULATIONS OF CHINAMEN - S	NICK W. THIEL
TRIALS OF OSCAR WILD, THE	KEN HUGHES
TRIANGLE - S	NAOMI FONER
TRIANGLE FACTORY, THE - S	DAVID RAYFIEL
TRIBES - S	JETTE RINCK
TRIBUTE	BERNARD SLADE
TRICK BABY	LARRY YUST
TRICK OR TREAT	GARY GRAVER
TRICK OR TREAT	RHET TOPHAM
TRICK OR TREAT	JOEL SOISSON
TRICK OR TREAT	MICHAEL S. MURPHEY
TRICK OR TREAT - S	RAY CONNOLLY
TRICKS - S	STEVE SHAGAN
TRIMMING THE FAMILY TREE	DAVID MIRKIN
TRIMMING THE FAMILY TREE - S	JOHN WARREN
TRINITY - S	MICHAEL CRISTOFER
TRIP BACK DOWN, THE - S	JOHN BISHOP
TRIP TO BOUNTIFUL, THE	HORTON FOOTE
TRIPLE ECHO	ROBIN CHAPMAN
TRIPWIRE	JAMES LEMMO
TRIPWIRE	B.J. GOLDMAN
TRISTAN - S	GERARD BRACH
TRIUMPH OF LINCOLN CLUN, THE - S	DAVE LEWIS
TRIUMPH OF LINCOLN CLUN, THE - S	ANDY LEWIS
TRIUMPH OF THE SPIRIT	ANDRZEJ KRAKOWSKI
TRIUMPH OF THE SPIRIT	LAURENCE HEATH
TRIUMPH OF THE SPIRIT	SHIMON ARAMA
TRIUMPH OF THE SPIRIT	ZION HAEN
TRIUMPHS OF A MAN CALLED HORSE	JACK DEWITT
TRIUMPHS OF A MAN CALLED HORSE	KENNETH G. BLACKWELL
TROIKA - S	ALEC TEAGUE
TROIS PLACES POUR LE 26	JACQUES DEMY
TROJAN WOMEN, THE	MICHAEL CACOYANNIS
TROLL	ED NAHA
TROLL IN CENTRAL PARK, A (AF) - S	STU KRIEGER
TROLLENBERG TERROR, THE	JIMMY SANGSTER
TROLLOPS - S	JONATHAN BENAIR
TRON	STEVEN LISBERGER
TROOP BEVERLY HILLS	MARGARET GRIECO OBERMAN
TROOP BEVERLY HILLS	PAMELA R. NORRIS
TROOP BEVERLY HILLS	AVA OSTERN-FRIES
TROP BELLE POUR TOI	BERTRAND BLIER
TROPICAL WHOLESALE - S	THOMAS MCGUANE
TROPICANA - S	RON SHELTON
TROPICS, THE - S	STEPHEN J. MACLEAN
TROPPO - S	TROY KENNEDY MARTIN
TROUBLE ALONG THE WAY	JACK ROSE
TROUBLE ALONG THE WAY	MEL SHAVELSON
TROUBLE IN BIG D - S	JIM HART
TROUBLE IN MIND	ALAN RUDOLPH
TROUBLE IN TARZANA - S	LINDA A. SEGALL
TROUBLE MAN	JOHN D.F. BLACK
TROUBLE WITH ANGELS, THE	BLANCHE HANALIS
TROUBLE WITH DICK, THE	GARY WALKOW
TROUBLE WITH GIRLS, THE - S	WILL JACOBS
TROUBLE WITH HARRY, THE	JOHN MICHAEL HAYES
TROUBLE WITH LARRY, THE - S	RONNI KERN
TROUBLE WITH SPIES, THE	BURT KENNEDY
TROUBLEMAKER, THE	BUCK HENRY
TROUBLEMAKER, THE (P)	FRANCIS VEBER
TROUBLESHOOTER - S	ALICE ARLEN
TROUT, THE	JOSEPH LOSEY†
TROUT, THE	MONIQUE LANGE
TRU (P)	JAY PRESSON ALLEN
TRUCK TURNER	LEIGH CHAPMAN
TRUE AS A TURTLE	JACK DAVIES
TRUE BELIEVER	WESLEY STRICK
TRUE BLOOD	FRANK KERR
TRUE COLORS	KEVIN WADE
TRUE CONFESSIONS	JOAN DIDION
TRUE CONFESSIONS	JOHN GREGORY DUNNE
TRUE CRIME MAGAZINE - S	ALLYN WARNER
TRUE HEARTS - S	ALLEN COULTER
TRUE LOVE	NANCY SAVOCA
TRUE LOVE	RICHARD GUAY
TRUE LOVE - S	JULIE HICKSON
TRUE ROMANCE - S	MARK FROST
TRUE SPORT - S	PATRICK DUNCAN
TRUE STORIES	BETH HENLEY
TRUE STORIES	DAVID BYRNE
TRUE STORIES	STEPHEN TOBOLOWSKY
TRUE STORY OF JESSE JAMES, THE	WALTER NEWMAN
TRUE TO LIFE	NEIL LANDAU
TRUE TO LIFE - S	TARA ISON
TRUE WEST (P)	SAM SHEPARD
TRUEST SPORT - S	MARK VICTOR
TRUEST SPORT - S	MICHAEL GRAIS
TRUEST SPORT, THE - S	DARRYL PONICSAN
TRULY, MADLY, DEEPLY	ANTHONY MINGHELLA
TRUST	HAL HARTLEY
TRUST - S	MIKE MAHERN
TRUST ME	BOBBY HOUSTON
TRUST ME	GARY RIGDON
TRUST ME ON THIS - S	TOM SZOLLOSI
TRUTH, THE - S	DAVID LOUCKA
TRUTH ABOUT SPRING, THE	JAMES LEE BARRETT†
TRUTH ABOUT SWEDES, THE - S	JEFF BUHAI
TRUTH ABOUT SWEDES, THE - S	STEVEN R. ZACHARIAS
TSUBASA NO GAIKA	AKIRA KUROSAWA
TUBESTEAK	ADAM DUBOV
TUBESTEAK - S	JANICE SHAPIRO
TUCK EVERLASTING	FREDERICK KING KELELR
TUCKER: THE MAN AND HIS DREAM	ARNOLD SCHULMAN
TUFF TURF	JETTE RINCK
TUFF TURF	GREG COLLINS O'NEILL
TUFF TURF	MURRAY MICHAELS
TUG OF WAR - S	ROBERT CARNEY
TULIPS	HENRY OLEK
TULKU - S	PAUL F. EDWARDS
TULSA (P)	SHEM BITTERMAN
TUMBLEDOWN (CTF)	CHARLES WOOD
TUMBLIN' DICE - S	NICHOLAS ST. JOHN
TUNA HELL - S	DAVID CHASE
TUNE IN TOMORROW	WILLIAM BOYD
TUNNEL BOYS - S	BLAIR FERGUSON
TUNNEL IN THE SKY - S	TIM CURNEN
TUNNEL VISION	NEAL ISRAEL
TUNNELS OF CU CHI - S	JIM CRUMLEY
TUNNELS OF LOVE - S	JULIE HICKSON
TUPAC AMARU - S	MICHAEL THOMAS
TURK 182	DENIS HAMILL
TURK 182	JAMES GREGORY KINGSTON
TURK 182	JOHN HAMILL
TURN LEFT OR DIE - S	MARK VICTOR
TURN LEFT OR DIE - S	MICHAEL GRAIS
TURN OF THE SCREW, THE	RUSTY LEMORANDE
TURNAROUND, THE (P)	MARK MEDOFF
TURNER & HOOCH	DANIEL PETRIE, JR.
TURNER & HOOCH	DENNIS SHRYACK
TURNER & HOOCH	JACK EPPS JR.
TURNER & HOOCH	JIM CASH
TURNER & HOOCH	MICHAEL BLODGETT
TURNING POINT, THE	ARTHUR LAURENTS
TURTLE BEACH - S	DAVID WILLIAMSON
TURTLE BEACH - S	ANNE TURNER
TURTLE DIARY	HAROLD PINTER
TUSKE GI ARMEN - S	MARCEL MONTECINO
TUTTO A POSTE E NIENTE IN ORDINE	LINA WERTMULLER
TUTTO E. FINITO - S	HERMAN RAUCHER
TUXEDO PARK - S	DAVID SMITH
TUXEDO TERRACE - S	MICHAEL PREMINGER
TUXEDO TERRACE - S	RICK PODELL
TWELVE ANGRY MAN	REGINALD ROSE
TWELVE CHAIRS, THE	MEL BROOKS
TWENTY MILLION MILES TO EARTH	CHRIS KNOPF
TWENTY-FIFTH HOUR, THE	WOLF MANKOWITZ
TWENTY-ONE	DON BOYD
TWENTY-ONE	ZOE HELLER
TWENTY-ONE THE HARD WAY - S	RICHARD CHAPMAN
TWICE AROUND THE DAFFODILS	NORMAN HUDIS
TWICE AROUND THE PARK (P)	MURRAY SCHISGAL
TWICE DEAD	BERT L. DRAGIN
TWICE DEAD	ROBERT MCDONNELL
TWICE IN A LIFETIME	COLIN WELLAND
TWICE UPON A TIME (AF)	BILL COUTURIE
TWICE UPON A TIME (AF)	JOHN KORTY
TWICE UPON A TIME (AF)	CHARLES SWENSEN
TWICE UPON A TIME (AF)	SUELLA KENNEDY
TWILIGHT - S	CAMILLE THOMASSON
TWILIGHT TIME - S	JOHN SINGLETON
TWILIGHT ZONE - THE MOVIE	GEORGE CLAYTON JOHNSON
TWILIGHT ZONE - THE MOVIE	JOHN LANDIS
TWILIGHT ZONE - THE MOVIE	JOSH ROGAN
TWILIGHT ZONE - THE MOVIE	RICHARD MATHESON
TWILIGHT'S LAST GLEAMING	RONALD M. COHEN
TWIN SISTERS - S	DAVID PRESTON
TWINKLE - S	JULIA CAMERON
TWINKLE, TWINKLE, KILLER KANE	WILLIAM PETER BLATTY
TWINKY	NORMAN THADDEUS VANE
TWINS	HERSCHEL WEINGROD
TWINS	TIMOTHY HARRIS
TWINS	WILLIAM J. DAVIES
TWINS	WILLIAM OSBORNE
TWISSLEMAN - S	E. MAX FRYE
TWIST AND SHOUT	BILLE AUGUST
TWIST OF FATE	LAIRD KOENIG
TWISTEDI - S	ALAN ORMSBY
TWISTED JUSTICE	DAVID HEAVENER
TWISTED NERVE	ROY BOULTING
TWISTER	MICHAEL ALMEREYDA
TWO + TWO - S	LARRY GELBART
TWO ARE GUILTY - S	ALISON CROSS
TWO BIT ROMANCE - S	JUNE ROBERTS
TWO BIT ROMANCE - S	RANDI MAYEM SINGER
TWO BITS - S	LARRY DAVID
TWO BITS - S	JOSEPH STEFANO
TWO COPS - S	GREGORY FLEEMAN
TWO COPS - S	ROBERT MEGGINSON
TWO FACES OF DR. JEKYLL, THE	WOLF MANKOWITZ
TWO FOR THE ROAD	FREDERIC RAPHAEL
TWO GUYS FROM ITALY - S	GEOFF GRODE
TWO GUYS FROM SPACE - S	ELLIOT M. STERN
TWO GUYS IN TUXEDOS - S	MICHAEL VARHOL
TWO IDIOTS IN HOLLYWOOD	STEPHEN TOBOLOWSKY
TWO JAKES, THE	ROBERT TOWNE
TWO JOHNNIES - S	DON CIRILLO
TWO LANE BLACKTOP	RUDOLPH G. WURLITZER
TWO LEFT FEET	JOHN HOPKINS
TWO LITTLE RICH GIRLS - S	DIANE WILK
TWO LITTLE RICH GIRLS - S	KEN FINKLEMAN
TWO LIVES - S	ALVIN SARGENT
TWO LUCKY PEOPLE - S	VALERIE CURTIN
TWO MOON JUNCTION	ZALMAN KING
TWO MOON JUNCTION	MACGREGOR DOUGLAS
TWO OF A KIND	JOHN HERZFELD
TWO OF THE MISSING - S	LEE REYNOLDS
TWO ON THE AISLE - S	MICHAEL SERAFIN
TWO SOLITUDES	LIONEL CHETWYND
TWO VIRGINS - S	LINDY LAUB
TWO WAYS TO GO - S	HERMAN RAUCHER
TWO-MINUTE WARNING	ED HUME
TWO-PENNY SPARROW - S	THOMAS RICKMAN
TYPHOON LAGOON - S	GARY K. WOLF

U

Title	Writer
U.H.F.	AL YANKOVIC
U.H.F.	JAY LEVEY
U.S. MARSHALL - S	DAVID HIMMELSTEIN
UFO - S	BRAD BUCKNER
UFO - S	EUGENIE ROSS-LEMING
UFORIA	JOHN BINDER
UGLY AMERICAN, THE	STEWART STERN
UGLY DUCKLING, THE	SID COLIN†
UGLY DUCKLING - S	NICK W. THIEL
ULTIMATE SOLUTION OF GRACE QUIGLEY, THE	A. MARTIN ZWEIBACH
ULTIMATE GAME, THE - S	GARY THOMPSON
ULTIMATE WARRIOR, THE	ROBERT CLOUSE
ULTIMATUM - S	LAURENCE DWORET
ULTIMATUM - S	ROBERT ROY POOL
ULZANA'S RAID	ALAN SHARP
UMA	AKIRA KUROSAWA
UMBERTO D.	CESARE ZAVATTINI†
UMBRELLAS OF CHERBOURG, THE	JACQUES DEMY†
UN -MAN - S	WILLIAM TEPPER
UN CHAMPE EN VILLE	JACQUES DEMY†
UN PAPILLON SUR L'EPAULE	JEAN-CLAUDE CARRIERE
UN PAPILLON SUR L'EPAULE	TONINO GUERRA
UN SEMAINE DE VACANCES	BERTRAND TAVERNIER
UNASSIGNED TERRITORY - S	KEM NUNN
UNBEARABLE LIGHTNESS OF BEING, THE	JEAN-CLAUDE CARRIERE
UNBEARABLE LIGHTNESS OF BEING, THE	PHILIP KAUFMAN

Un-Vi

FILM WRITERS GUIDE

INDEX OF FILM TITLES

Title	Writer
UNBELIEVABLE TRUTH, THE	HAL HARTLEY
UNBELIEVABLES, THE - S	ED SOLOMON
UNBORN, THE	HENRY DOMONIC
UNCHAINED	HALL BARTLETT
UNCLE, THE	DESMOND DAVIS
UNCLE BUCK	JOHN HUGHES
UNCLE JOE SHANNON	BURT YOUNG
UNCLE WILLIE - S	MICK GARRIS
UNCOMMON VALOR	JOE GAYTON
UNCOMMON WOMEN AND OTHERS (P)	WENDY WASSERSTEIN
UNCONQUERED	CHARLES BENNETT
UNDEFEATED, THE	JAMES LEE BARRETT†
UNDER COVER	JOHN STOCKWELL
UNDER COVER	SCOTT G. FIELDS
UNDER COVER OF DAYLIGHT - S	DONALD L. STEWART
UNDER FIRE	CLAYTON S. FROHMAN
UNDER FIRE	RON SHELTON
UNDER MILK WOOD	ANDREW SINCLAIR
UNDER MY THUMB - S	FRANCIS VEBER
UNDER ONE ROOF - S	STEVE DUNCAN
UNDER PRESSURE - S	STANFORD SHERMAN
UNDER SURVEILLANCE - S	JIM FISHER
UNDER SURVEILLANCE - S	JIM STAAHL
UNDER THE BOARDWALK	ROBERT KING
UNDER THE CHERRY MOON	BECKY JOHNSTON
UNDER THE GUN	ALMER JOHN DAVIS
UNDER THE GUN	JAMES DEVNEY
UNDER THE GUN	JAMES SBARDELLATI
UNDER THE GUN - S	JEFFREY ABRAMS
UNDER THE GUN - S	JILL MAZURSKY
UNDER THE GUN - S	RICHARD WHITLEY
UNDER THE RAINBOW	FRED BAUER
UNDER THE RAINBOW	HARRY HURWITZ
UNDER THE RAINBOW	MARTIN SMITH
UNDER THE RAINBOW	PAT BRADLEY
UNDER THE RAINBOW	PAT MCCORMICK
UNDER THE ROCK PILE - S	FRANK DEESE
UNDER THE SIGN OF CANCER - S	ALEXANDER TANA
UNDER THE SUN OF SATAN	MAURICE PIALAT
UNDER THE VOLCANO	GUY GALLO
UNDER THE WIRE - S	J.S. CARDONE
UNDER THE YUM YUM TREE	DAVID SWIFT
UNDER THE YUM YUM TREE	LARRY ROMAN
UNDER WRAPS - S	ALAN BERGER
UNDER WRAPS - S	KATHY GORI
UNDER WRAPS - S	APRIL DAMMANN
UNDERCOVER MAN, THE	MALVIN WALD
UNDERCOVER MAN, THE	SYDNEY BOEHM†
UNDERCOVERS HERO	ROY BOULTING
UNDERCURRENTS - S	THOMAS LEE WRIGHT
UNDERWATER	WALTER NEWMAN
UNDERWORLD	CLIVE BARKER
UNDERWORLD (1960)	SAMUEL FULLER
UNDERGROUND	ANDY LEWIS
UNDERGROUND	LUKAS HELLER†
UNDERGROUND - S	CORT CASADY
UNDERGROUND - S	DAVID WILTSE
UNDERGROUND - S	FRANK KERR
UNDERGROUND - S	ROBERT ROY POOL
UNDERGROUND ACES	ANDREW PETER MARIN
UNDERGROUND ACES	JIM CARABATSOS
UNDERGROUND ACES	LENORE WRIGHT
UNDERSHORTS: THE MOVIE	BRYAN MICHAEL STOLLER
UNDERSTUDY - S	NICHOLAS MEYER
UNDERTOW - S	ERIC RED
UNDERTOW - S	KATHRYN BIGELOW
UNE SEMAIN DE VACANCES	COLO TAVERNIER O'HAGAN
UNEMPLOYED - S	NICHOLAS ST. JOHN
UNEMPLOYMENT BLUES - S	FRED LEBOW
UNFAITHFULLY YOURS	BARRY LEVINSON
UNFAITHFULLY YOURS	ROBERT KLANE
UNFAITHFULLY YOURS	VALERIE CURTIN
UNFINISHED BUSINESS - S	DENIS O'NEIL
UNFINISHED BUSINESS - S	HENRY C. PARKE
UNFINISHED BUSINESS - S	LEAH APPET
UNFINISHED BUSINESS - S	RENEE ORIN
UNFINISHED BUSINESS - S	DON MCLENNAN
UNFORGETTABLE - S	ADAM DUBOV
UNFORGETTABLE - S	JANICE SHAPIRO
UNGODLY, THE - S	OLIVER STONE
UNGUARDED MOMENT, THE	LAWRENCE B. MARCUS
UNHEALTHY TO BE PLEASANT (P)	JAMES KIRKWOOD†
UNHEARD MELODIES - S	BILL STEWART
UNHOLY, THE	FERNANDO FONSECA
UNHOLY, THE	PHILIP YORDAN
UNIDENTIFIED FLYING ODDBALL	DON TAIT
UNFINISHED BUSINESS - S	CAROL MONPERE
UNINVITED, THE - S	JONATHAN TYDOR
UNION CITY	MARK REICHERT
UNION STORY - S	THOMAS RICKMAN
UNITED STATES - S	LARRY GELBART
UNIVERSAL SOLDIER - S	LESLIE BOHEM
UNIVERSAL SOLDIER - S	RICHARD ROTHSTEIN
UNKNOWN SOLDIER, THE - S	ED NAHA
UNLAWFUL ENTRY - S	LEWIS A. COLICK
UNMARRIED WOMAN, AN	PAUL MAZURKSY
UNNAMEABLE, THE	JEAN-PAUL OULLETTE
UNNATURAL ACTS - S	GINNY CERRELLA
UNNATURAL HISTORY - S	ROBIN SHEPHARD
UNNATURAL HISTORY - S	STEVE MORRIS
UNRAVELLED - S	LINDSAY MARACOTTA
UNRAVELLED - S	THOMAS BAUM
UNREMARKABLE LIFE, AN	MARCIA DINEEN
UNSANE	DARIO ARGENTO
UNSEEN HAND, THE (P)	SAM SHEPARD
UNSEEN, THE	KIM HENKEL
UNSEEN, THE	NANCY RIFKIN
UNSEEN, THE	PETER FOLEG
UNSEEN, THE	MICHAEL L. GRACE
UNSUITABLE JOB FOR A WOMAN, AN	ELIZABETH MCKAY
UNTIL SEPTEMBER	JANICE LEE GRAHAM
UNTIL THE END OF THE WORLD	PETER CAREY
UNTIL THE END OF THE WORLD	WIM WENDERS
UNTITLED A-GO-GO - S	RICHARD WHITLEY
UNTOUCHABLES, THE	DAVID MAMET
UNTYING THE KNOT - S	REX MCGEE
UNWANTED ATTENTIONS - S	JIM CARABATSOS
UP FOR GRABS - S	NEAL ISRAEL
UP FOR GRABS - S	PAT PROFT
UP FROM THE BEACH	STANLEY MANN
UP FROM THE DEPTHS	ALFRED SWEENEY
UP IN ARMS	ROBERT PIROSH†
UP IN SMOKE	CHEECH MARIN
UP IN SMOKE	TOMMY CHONG
UP IN THE CELLAR	THEODORE J. FLICKER
UP IN THE WORLD	JACK DAVIES
UP ON THE ROOF (P)	SIMON MOORE
UP THE ACADEMY	JAY TARSES
UP THE ACADEMY	TOM PATCHETT
UP THE CREEK	JEFFREY C. SHERMAN
UP THE CREEK	JIM KOUF
UP THE CREEK	DOUGLAS GROSSMAN
UP THE CREEK (1958)	VAL GUEST
UP THE GARDEN PATH - S	GEORGE E. SIMPSON
UP THE GARDEN PATH - S	NEAL R. BURGER
UP THE SANDBOX	PAUL ZINDEL
UPI	RUSS MEYER
UPHILL ALL THE WAY	FRANK Q. DOBBS
UPSIDE DOWN - S	MICHAEL MINER
UPSTATE MURDERS, THE	DAVID PAULSEN
UPTIGHT	JULES DASSIN
UPTOWN SATURDAY NIGHT	RICHARD WESLEY
UPWARD BOUND - S	DAVID H. SMILOW
UPWORLD - S	JOHN WATSON
URANIUM CONSPIRACY, THE	DAVID PAULSEN
URBAN COWBOY	AARON LATHAM
URBAN COWBOY	JAMES BRIDGES
URBAN LEGENDS - S	ETHAN WILEY
URBAN LEGENDS - S	RANDY JOHNSON
URBAN LEGENDS - S	GREGORY C. WIDEN
URIAH - S	BRYAN GORDON
URIAH - S	LAWRENCE J. BLOCK
US - S	ERIC ROTH
US AND THEM - S	GREG DAVIS
US AND THEM - S	LARRY GARCIA
USED CARS	BOB GALE
USED CARS	ROBERT ZEMECKIS
USED PEOPLE - S	TODD GRAFF
USS TEAKETTLE	RICHARD T. MURPHY
UTILITIES	DAVID GREENWALT
UTILITIES	JIM KOUF
UTILITIES - S	PAUL PRICE
UTILITIES - S	STEVE NATHAN
UTU	GEOFF MURPHY
UTZ - S	HUGH WHITEMORE

V

Title	Writer
V.I. WARSHAWSKI	DAVID AARON COHEN
V.I. WARSHAWSKI	EDWARD TAYLOR
V.I. WARSHAWSKI	NICK THIEL
VACANCY IN PARADISE (P)	JAMES KIRKWOOD†
VACATION	JOHN HUGHES
VAGABOND	AGNES VARDA
VAGRANT, THE - S	RICHARD JEFFERIES
VALACHI PAPERS, THE	STEPHEN GELLER
VALDEZ HORSES - S	STEWART STERN
VALDEZ IS COMING	DAVID RAYFIEL
VALDEZ IS COMING	ROLAND KIBBEE†
VALENTINE - S	LEAH APPET
VALENTINO	JOHN BYRUM
VALENTINO	KEN RUSSELL
VALENTINO PLACE - S	THOMAS HEDLEY JR.
VALENTINO RETURNS	LEONARD GARDNER
VALET GIRLS	CLARK CARLTON
VALET PARKING - S	ELLIOT M. STERN
VALHALLA'S WAKE - S	KEVIN JARRE
VALLEY BOYS - S	DENNIS CLARK
VALLEY GIRL	ANDREW LANE
VALLEY GIRL	WAYNE CRAWFORD
VALLEY GIRL II - S	JOSEPH LOEB III
VALLEY OBSCURED BY CLOUDS, THE	BARBET SCHROEDER
VALLEY OF GWANGI, THE	WILLIAM BAST
VALLEY OF THE KINGS	ROBERT PIROSH†
VALMONT	JEAN-CLAUDE CARRIERE
VAMP	RICHARD WENK
VAMPING	MICHAEL P. HEALY
VAMPING	FREDERICK KING KELLER
VAMPIRA	JEREMY LLOYD
VAMPIRE BLUES - S	L.M. KIT CARSON
VAMPIRE LUST	DJORDJE MILICEVIC
VAMPIRE LUST	JEFFREY P. MAGUIRE
VAMPIRE'S KISS	JOSEPH MINION
VAMPIRES IN KODACHROME (P)	DICK BEEBE
VAN GOGH	MAURICE PIALAT
VAN GOGH'S LAST PORTRAIT - S	JEFF LEWIS
VAN NUYS BLVD.	WILLIAM SACHS
VANITIES - S	MICHAEL CRISTOFER
VAPOR OF GLORY (P)	CHARLES EDWARD POGUE
VARIETY LIGHTS	FEDERICO FELLINI
VASECTOMY, A DELICATE MATTER	ROBERT BURGE
VASECTOMY, A DELICATE MATTER	ROBERT HILLIARD
VAULT OF HORROR	MILTON SUBOTSKY
VEIL, THE - S	JOHN BRILEY
VENGEANCE OF FU MANCHU, THE	HARRY ALAN TOWERS
VENGEANCE VALLEY	IRVING RAVETCH
VENOM	ROBERT CARRINGTON
VENUS DESCENDING - S	MARK FROST
VENUS IN BLUE JEANS - S	ROBIN SCHIFF
VENUS PETER	CHRISTOPHER RUSH
VENUS PETER	IAN SELLAR
VERDICT, THE	DAVID MAMET
VERNA, THE USC GIRL - S	DAVID SHABER
VERONICO CRUZ	MIGUEL PEREIRA
VERONIKA VOSS	RAINER WERNER FASSBINDER†
VERY GOOD GIRLS - S	NAOMI FONER
VERY IMPORTANT PERSON	JACK DAVIES
VERY OLD MONEY - S	JOSEPH DOUGHERTY
VERY SPECIAL FAVOR, A	NATHAN MONASTER†
VERY SPECIAL FAVOR, A	STANLEY SHAPIRO†
VETERAN'S DAY (P)	DONALD FREED
VIBES	BABALOO MANDEL
VIBES	LOWELL GANZ
VIBES	DEBORAH BLUM
VICE ACADEMY	RICK SLOANE
VICE SQUAD	ROBERT VINCENT O'NEIL
VICE SQUAD	KENNETH PETERS
VICE SQUAD	SANDY HOWARD
VICE SQUAD (1953)	LAWRENCE ROMAN
VICE VERSA	DICK CLEMENT
VICE VERSA	IAN LAFRENAIS
VICE VERSA (1948)	PETER USTINOV
VICIOUS LIPS	ALBERT PYUN
VICTOR, THE - S	DAVID M. CHASKIN
VICTOR, THE - S	RICHARD C. KLETTER
VICTOR/VICTORIA	BLAKE EDWARDS
VICTORS, THE	CARL FOREMAN†
VICTORY	EVAN JONES
VICTORY	JEFF MAGUIRE
VICTORY	DJORDJE MILICEVIC
VICTORY	YABO YABLONSKY
VICTORY - S	MARK PEPLOE
VIDA - S	BILL LANCASTER
VIDEO KILLED THE RADIO STAR - S	LESLIE BOHEM

Title	Writer
VIDEODROME	DAVID CRONENBERG
VIETNAM NURSES - S	APRIL SMITH
VIETNAM, TEXAS	C. COURTNEY JOYNER
VIETNAM, TEXAS	TOM BADAL
VIEW FROM POMPEY'S HEAD, THE	PHILIP DUNNE
VIEW FROM THE BRIDGE, A (P)	ARTHUR MILLER
VIEW FROM THE SQUARE, A - S	JOHN HOPKINS
VIEW FROM THE TOP, A - S	MATT COOPER
VIEW TO A KILL, A	MICHAEL G. WILSON
VIEW TO A KILL, A	RICHARD MAIBAUM†
VIEWING, THE (P)	LYLE D. KESSLER
VIGIL	VINCENT WARD
VIGILANTE FORCE	GEORGE ARMITAGE
VIGIN AND THE GYPSY, THE	ALAN PLATER
VIKING (P)	STEPHEN METCALFE
VIKING QUEEN, THE	CLARKE REYNOLDS
VIKING, THE - S	JOHN MILLIUS
VIKINGS, THE	CALDER WILLINGHAM
VILLA RIDES	ROBERT TOWNE
VILLAGE OF DAUGHTERS	DAVID PURSALL
VILLAGE OF THE DAMNED	STIRLING SILLIPHANT
VILLAGE OF THE DAMNED	DAVID J. HIMMELSTEIN
VILLAIN	DICK CLEMENT
VILLAIN	IAN LAFRENAIS
VILLAIN, THE	ROBERT G. KANE
VINCE AND AL GO TO WAR - S	ROBERT J. COMFORT
VINCENT (SHORT)	TIM BURTON
VINCENT AND THEO	JULIAN MITCHELL
VINCENT THE DUTCHMAN	MAI ZETTERLING
VINDICATOR	DAVID PEOPLES
VIOLENT DEATH, A MUSICAL (SHORT)	CHRIS RUPPENTHAL
VIOLENT ENEMY, THE	EDMUND WARD
VIOLENT MEN, THE	HARRY KLEINER
VIOLENT ZONE	DAVID PRITCHARD
VIOLENT ZONE	JOHN BUSHELMAN
VIOLETS ARE BLUE	NAOMI FONER
VIRGIN - S	DIANA HAMMOND
VIRGIN - S	NICHOLAS KAZAN
VIRGIN SOLDIERS	JOHN HOPKINS
VIRGIN, THE- S	NEAL JIMENEZ
VIRGINIA REEL - S	JANUS CERCONE
VIRTUE - S	ELISA BELL
VISION QUEST	DARRYL PONICSAN
VISIONS OF SUGAR-PLUMS (SHORT)	TODD DURHAM
VISIT TO A CHIEF'S SON	ALBERT RUBEN
VISIT TO A SMALL PLANET (P)	GORE VIDAL
VISIT, THE	BEN BARZMAN†
VISITING HOURS	BRIAN TAGGERT
VISITOR, THE	ROBERT MUNDY
VISITOR, THE	MICHAEL J. PARADISE
VISITOR, THE - S	DAVID NEWMAN
VISITOR, THE - S	LIZ COMICI
VISITOR, THE - S	LOU COMICI
VISITORS, THE	ELIA KAZAN
VITAL SIGNS	JEB STUART
VITAL SIGNS	LARRY KETRON
VIVA MARIAI	JEAN-CLAUDE CARRIERE
VIVA MARIAI	LOUIS MALLE
VIVEMENT DIMANCHE	SUZANNE SCHIFFMAN
VODONE - S	ALEC LORIMORE
VODONE - S	TERRY WINKLESS
VOICE IN THE MIRROR, THE	LAWRENCE B. MARCUS
VOICE OF A STRANGER - S	CHRISTOPHER WOODEN
VOICE OF A STRANGER - S	JACKSON BARR
VOICE OF THE HEART (CTF)	RITA LAKIN
VOICE OF THE MOON, THE	FEDERICO FELLINI
VOICES (1979)	JOHN HERZFELD
VOICES (1973)	GEORGE KIRGO
VOICES (1973)	ROBERT ENDERS
VOLUNTEERS	DAVID ISAACS
VOLUNTEERS	KEN LEVINE
VOLUNTEERS	KEITH CRITCHLOW
VON RYAN'S EXPRESS	WENDELL MAYES
VOODOO - S	DAVID ODELL
VOODOO - S	GINNY CERRELLA
VOODOO - S	PETRU POPESCU
VOODOO DAWN	EVAN DUNSKY
VOODOO DAWN	JEFFREY DELMAN
VOODOO DAWN	JOHN A. RUSSO
VOODOO DAWN	THOMAS RENDON
VOODOO QUEEN - S	CYNTHIA CIDRE
VORTEX	BETH B
VORTEX	SCOTT B
VOSA - S	LOUIS GARFINKLE
VOSA - S	QUINN REDEKER
VOYAGE OF THE DAMNED	DAVID BUTLER
VOYAGE OF THE DAMNED	STEVE SHAGAN
VOYAGE TO THE BOTTOM OF THE SEA	CHARLES BENNETT
VOYAGE TO THE BOTTOM OF THE SEA	IRWIN ALLEN
VOYAGER	RUDY WURLITZER
VOYAGER	VOLKER SCHLONDORFF
VULGARIANS - S	JEFF BUHAI
VULGARIANS - S	STEVE ZACHARIAS
VULGARIANS, THE - S	DANA OLSEN
VULGARIANS, THE - S	ROBERT COLLECTOR
VULGARIANS, THE - S	TED MANN

W

Title	Writer
W	GERALD DI PEGO
W	RONALD SHUSETT
W.C. FIELDS AND ME	BOB MERRILL
W.W. AND THE DIXIE DANCEKINGS	THOMAS RICKMAN
WACKIEST SHIP IN THE ARMY, THE	RICHARD T. MURPHY
WACKO	DANA OLSEN
WACKO	DAVID GREENWALT
WACKO	JIM KOUF
WAGES OF FEAR	WALON GREEN
WAGES OF SIN - S	PIERS ASHWORTH
WAGES OF THIN, THE(P)	TREVOR GRIFFITHS
WAIT UNTIL DARK	ROBERT CARRINGTON
WAIT UNTIL SPRING, BANDINI	DOMINIQUE DERUDDERE
WAITING FOR THE LIGHT	CHRIS MONGER
WAITING FOR THE MOON	MARK MAGILL
WAITRESSI	CHARLES KAUFMAN
WAITRESSI	MICHAEL STONE
WAKE IN FRIGHT	EVAN JONES
WAKE OF JAMIE FOSTER (P)	BETH HENLEY
WAKE UP AND LIVE	HARRY TUGEND†
WAKEFIELD TRILOGY, THE (P)	ISRAEL HOROVITZ
WALK IN THE SPRING RAIN, A	STIRLING SILLIPHANT
WALK LIKE A DRAGON	JAMES CLAVELL
WALK LIKE A MAN	ROBERT KLANE
WALK PROUD	EVAN HUNTER
WALK WITH ANGELS - S	GUSTAVE REININGER
WALKER	RUDOLPH G. WURLITZER
WALKING MY BABY BAK HOME	DON MCGUIRE
WALKING MY BABY BACK HOME	OSCAR BRODNEY
WALKING ON GLASS - S	FRANK NORWOOD
WALKING TALL	MORT BRISKIN
WALKING THE EDGE	CURT ALLEN
WALKING TO WALDHEIM (P)	MAYO SIMON
WALL STREET	STANLEY WEISER
WALL STREET	OLIVER STONE
WALLRAFF - S	BOBBY ROTH
WALLS - S	BILL STEWART
WALLS - S	KURT LUEDTKE
WALLY'S CAFE (P)	RON CLARK
WALTER AND JUNE	DAVID COOK
WALTZ ACROSS TEXAS	BILL SVANOE
WALTZ IN MARATHON - S	REX MCGEE
WALTZ OF THE TOREADORS, THE	WOLF MANKOWITZ
WANDA NEVADA	DENNIS HACKIN
WANDERER, THE - S	DAVID SEAY
WANDERERS, THE	PHILIP KAUFMAN
WANDERERS, THE	ROSE L. KAUFMAN
WANDERLUST - S	ANDY TENNANT
WANDERLUST - S	ROBERT LENSKI
WANTED - S	DUSTY KAY
WANTED - S	LYNN GROSSMAN
WANTED - S	MICHAEL TOLKIN
WANTED DEAD OR ALIVE	BRIAN TAGGERT
WANTED DEAD OR ALIVE	GARY A. SHERMAN
WANTED DEAD OR ALIVE	MICHAEL PATRICK GOODMAN
WANTED DEAD OR ALIVE II - S	TOM DESIMONE
WANTING OF LEVINE, THE - S	PETER STONE
WAR AND LOVE	ABBY MANN
WAR BABIES - S	FRANK KERR
WAR BABIES - S	JONATHAN KAUFER
WAR BETWEEN MEN AND WOMEN, THE	MEL SHAVELSON
WAR BOYS - S	IRA BEHR
WAR DANCE - S	ERIC HUGHES
WAR GODS OF THE DEEP	CHARLES BENNETT
WAR GODS OF THE DEEP	LOUIS M. HEYWARD
WAR HORSE, THE - S	BILL KERBY
WAR HUNT	STANFORD WHITMORE
WAR IS OVER, THE	JORGE SEMPRUN
WAR LORD, THE	MILLARD KAUFMAN
WAR LOVER, THE	HOWARD KOCH
WAR OF CHRISTMAS, THE	RAY DEFELITTA
WAR OF THE ROSES, THE	MICHAEL LEESON
WAR PARTY	SPENCER EASTMAN†
WAR REQUIEM	DEREK JARMAN
WAR WAGON, THE	CLAIR HUFFAKER†
WARBIRDS	ULLI LOMMEL
WARD B	VINCENT MONGOL
WARFMAN MASTER OF A MILLION SHAPES (P)	MICHAEL WELLER
WARGAMES	LAWRENCE LASKER
WARGAMES	WALTER F. PARKES
WARHEAD	RENE BALCER
WARLOCK	D.T. TWOHY
WARLOCK HOLMES - S	BRIAN STRASMANN
WARLORD - S	CHARLES ROBERT CARNER
WARLORDS - S	ANDREW DETTMAN
WARLORDS - S	DANIEL TRULY
WARLORDS OF ATLANTIS	BRIAN HAYLES
WARLORDS OF THE 21ST CENTURY	HARLEY COKLISS
WARLORDS OF THE 21ST CENTURY	IRVING AUSTIN
WARLORDS OF THE 21ST CENTURY	JOHN BEECH
WARM DECEMBER, A	LARRY ROMAN
WARM NIGHTS ON A SLOW MOVING TRAIN	BOB ELLIS
WARM SUMMER RAIN	JOE GAYTON
WARNING SHOT	MANN RUBIN
WARNING SIGN	HAL BARWOOD
WARNING SIGN	MATTHEW ROBBINS
WARP - S	MARK VICTOR
WARP - S	MICHAEL GRAIS
WARPED ARROWS - S	CHRIS COLUMBUS
WARRIOR - S	DALE HEARD
WARRIOR - S	JOHN RAFFO
WARRIOR - S	ROB THOMPSON
WARRIOR AND THE SORCERESS, THE	WILLIAM STOUT
WARRIOR AND THE SORCERESS, THE	JOHN BRODERICK
WARRIOR BLUE - S	JIM HART
WARRIOR OF THE RAINBOW - S	WILLIAM GOODHART
WARRIOR QUEEN	HARRY ALAN TOWERS
WARRIOR QUEEN	RICK MARX
WARRIORS - S	GARY GOLDMAN
WARRIORS OF THE RAINBOW - S	JOHN BRILEY
WARRIORS, THE	DAVID SHABER
WARRIORS, THE	WALTER HILL
WASH, THE	PHILIP KAN GOTANDA
WASHINGTON GIRLS - S	TOM MANKIEWICZ
WASHINGTON PAGES - S	ALEC LORIMORE
WASHINGTON PAGES - S	TERRY WINKLESS
WASSAJA - S	HESPER ANDERSON
WASTED - S	WALON GREEN
WASTELAND - S	LEE DRYSDALE
WATCH THE SKY - S	JOHN BEAIRD
WATCHER IN THE WOODS, THE	BRIAN H. CLEMENS
WATCHER IN THE WOODS, THE	HARRY SPALDING
WATCHER IN THE WOODS, THE	ROSEMARY ANNE SISSON
WATCHERS	BILL FREED
WATCHERS	DAMIAN LEE
WATCHERS II	HENRY DOMONIC
WATCHING THE DETECTIVE - S	RICK KING
WATCHMEN - S	SAM HAMM
WATER	BILL PERSKY
WATER	DICK CLEMENT
WATER	IAN LAFRENAIS
WATER BABIES, THE	MICHAEL ROBSON
WATER DANCE, THE	NEAL JIMENEZ
WATER DANCER - S	JEREMY LARNER
WATER ENGINE, THE (P)	DAVID MAMET
WATERING PLACE, THE - S	LYLE D. KESSLER
WATERLOO	H.A.L. CRAIG
WATERMELON MAN	HERMAN RAUCHER
WATERSHIP DOWN (AF)	MARTIN ROSEN
WATERWORLD - S	PETER RADER
WATUSI	JAMES CLAVELL
WAVELENGTH	MIKE GRAY
WAVES - S	HENRY OLEK
WAXWORK	ANTHONY HICKOX

Title	Writer
WAXWORK II	ANTHONY HICKOX
WAY AHEAD, THE	PETER USTINOV
WAY OF A GAUCHO	PHILIP DUNNE
WAY OUT WEST - S	KEVIN QUINN
WAY OUT, THE - S	MAURICE E. HURLEY
WAY TO THE GOLD, THE	WENDELL MAYES
WAY WE ARE, THE - S	LEAH APPET
WAY WE WERE, THE	ARTHUR LAURENTS
WAYNE'S WORLD - S	MIKE MYERS
WAYS AND MEANS - S	JANUS CERCONE
WAYSIDE MOTOR INN, THE (P)	A.R. GURNEY
WAYWARD ANGEL - S	LYLE D. KESSLER
WAYWARD STORK, THE (P)	HARRY TUGEND†
WE HAVE MANY NAMES	MAI ZETTERLING
WE THE PEOPLE...200 (P)	LIONEL CHETWYND
WE THINK THE WORLD OF YOU	HUGH STODDART
WE THREE - S	FREDERIC RAPHAEL
WE WERE STRANGERS	PETER VIERTEL
WE'RE IN THE MONEY - S	CHRIS RUPPENTHAL
WE'RE NO ANGELS	DAVID MAMET
WEATHER WAR - S	STIRLING SILLIPHANT
WEATHERCHILD - S	TOM CAMP
WEATHERMAN - S	STEVE TESICH
WEATHERMEN, THE - S	BEN STILLER
WEB OF DECEIT (P)	SANDOR STERN
WEDDING, THE - S	SOLLACE MITCHELL
WEDDING BAND - S	TED ALLAN
WEDDING IN WHITE	WILLIAM C. FRUET
WEDDING PARTY, THE	BRIAN DEPALMA
WEDDING WAS BEAUTIFUL, PEOPLE WERE CRYING, THE - S	ANDRZEJ KRAKOWSKI
WEDDING, A	ALLAN F. NICHOLLS
WEDDING, A	PATRICIA RESNICK
WEDDING, A	ROBERT ALTMAN
WEDLOCK - S	JOE IDE
WEEDS	DOROTHY TRISTAN
WEEDS	JOHN HANCOCK
WEEGEE - S	GARY DRUCKER
WEEGIE - S	MARDIK MARTIN
WEEK'S VACATION, A	BERTRAND TAVERNIER
WEEK'S VACATION, A	COLO TAVERNIER O'HAGAN
WEEKEND AT BERNIE'S	ROBERT KLANE
WEEKEND OF SHADOWS	PETER YELDMAN
WEEKEND PASS	LAWRENCE BASSOFF
WEEKEND WARRIORS	BRUCE BELLAND
WEEKEND WARRIORS	ROY M. ROGOSIN
WEEKEND WARRIORS - S	DAVID LOUCKA
WEEKEND WARRIORS - S	DENISE DE CLUE
WEEKEND WARRIORS - S	MARK KRAM
WEEKEND WITH KATE	HENRY TEFAY
WEEKEND WITH KATE	KEE YOUNG
WEEKENDS - S	ROBERT KAUFMAN
WEIRD SCIENCE	JOHN HUGHES
WELCOME HOME	MAGGIE KLEINMAN
WELCOME HOME - S	VINCENT GUTIERREZ
WELCOME HOME - S	THOMAS M. CLEAVER
WELCOME HOME, ROXY CARMICHAEL	KAREN LEIGH HOPKINS
WELCOME HOME SOLDIERS	GUERDON TRUEBLOOD
WELCOME HOME, WELL DONE - S	DAVID RAYFIEL
WELCOME TO 18	JUDITH SHERMAN WOLIN
WELCOME TO ANDROMEDA (P)	RON WHYTE†
WELCOME TO BLOOD CITY	STEPHEN SCHNECK
WELCOME TO BUZZSAW - S	DANIEL GOLDIN
WELCOME TO BUZZSAW - S	JOSHUA P. GOLDIN
WELCOME TO HARD TIMES	BURT KENNEDY
WELCOME TO L.A.	ALAN RUDOLPH
WELCOME TO ZIMM'S - S	JERRY WINNICK
WELDER, THE (SHORT)	NORTHROP DAVIS
WELL, THE - S	DAVID M. CHASKIN
WENDELL WILCOX AND THE MONSTER MAKERS - S	CHARLES KAUFMAN
WENDELL WILCOX AND THE MONSTER MAKERS - S	LARRY B. WILLIAMS
WEST POINT STORY, THE	IRVING WALLACE†
WEST SIDE STORY	ERNEST LEHMAN
WEST SIDE WALTZ (P)	ERNEST THOMPSON
WEST WITH THE NIGHT - S	JOHN BRILEY
WESTLANDER - S	JEFFREY KINDLEY
WESTWORLD	MICHAEL CRICHTON
WET RAINBOW	DJORDJE MILICEVIC
WETHERBY	DAVID HARE
WHALES OF AUGUST, THE	DAVID BERRY
WHALESONG - S	ROGER S. HOLZBERG
WHAT A WAY TO GO	ADOLPH GREEN
WHAT A WAY TO GO	BETTY COMDEN
WHAT ABOUT BOB?	ALVIN SARGENT
WHAT ABOUT BOB?	TOM SCHULMAN
WHAT ABOUT BOB?	LAURA ZISKIN
WHAT ABOUT LOVE - S	ERIC SCHAEFFER
WHAT CHANGED CHARLEY FARTHING	DAVID PURSALL
WHAT DID YOU DO IN THE WAR, DADDY?	BLAKE EDWARDS
WHAT DID YOU DO IN THE WAR, DADDY?	WILLIAM PETER BLATTY
WHAT DO I TELL THE BOYS AT THE STATION?	WILLIAM REILLY
WHAT DREAMS MAY COME - S	RICHARD MATHESON
WHAT EVER HAPPENED TO LOVE AT FIRST SIGHT - S	ERIC SCHAEFFER
WHAT EVERY WOMAN WANTS - S	JUDITH FEIN
WHAT HAPPENED TO HARRY - S	SARAH C. PALEY
WHAT HAVE I DONE TO DESERVE THIS?	PEDRO ALMODOVAR
WHAT I DID LAST SUMMER (P)	A.R. GURNEY
WHAT I DID THAT SUMMER - S	FRANK D. GILROY
WHAT I DID WITH THE PRESIDENT'S DAUGHTER - S	ROSIE SHUSTER
WHAT MAKES SAMMY RUN? - S	BUDD SCHULBERG
WHAT NICK SAW - S	JONATHAN HEAP
WHAT NICK SAW - S	PHILIP MORTON
WHAT'S NEW PUSSYCAT?	WOODY ALLEN
WHAT'S SO BAD ABOUT FEELING GOOD?	ROBERT PIROSH†
WHAT'S UP DOC?	BUCK HENRY
WHAT'S UP DOC?	DAVID NEWMAN
WHAT'S UP DOC?	ROBERT BENTON
WHAT?	GERARD BRACH
WHAT?	ROMAN POLANSKI
WHATEVER HAPPENED TO BABY JANE?	LUKAS HELLER†
WHEELS - S	DAVID SHABER
WHEELS OF TERROR (CTF)	ALAN B. MCELROY
WHEN A MAN LOVES A WOMAN - S	STEPHEN FISCHER
WHEN A STRANGER CALLS	FRED WALTON
WHEN A STRANGER CALLS	STEPHEN FEKE
WHEN A STRANGER CALLS BACK - S	FRED WALTON
WHEN DINOSAURS RULED THE EARTH	VAL GUEST
WHEN EIGHT BELLS TOLL	ALISTAIR MACLEAN
WHEN FATHER WAS AWAY ON BUSINESS	ABDULAH SIDRAN
WHEN HARRY MET SALLY	NORA EPHRON
WHEN I GROW UP	MICHAEL KANIN
WHEN IT'S OVER (P)	EDUARDO MACHADO
WHEN NATURE CALLS	CHARLES KAUFMAN
WHEN STRANGERS MARRY	PHILIP YORDAN
WHEN THE WHALES CAME	MICHAEL MORPUGO
WHEN THE WIFE'S AWAY - S	MITCHEL KATLIN
WHEN THE WIFE'S AWAY - S	NAT BERNSTEIN
WHEN TIME RAN OUT	CARL FOREMAN†
WHEN TIME RAN OUT	STIRLING SILLIPHANT
WHEN WE WERE VERY YOUNG (P)	THOMAS BABE
WHEN WILLIE COMES MARCHING HOME	RICHARD SALE
WHEN WORLDS COLLIDE - S	MICHAEL BURTON
WHEN YOU COMIN' BACK RED RYDER?	MARK MEDOFF
WHERE ANGELS GO, TROUBLE FOLLOWS	BLANCHE HANALIS
WHERE ARE THE CHILDREN	JACK SHOLDER
WHERE DANGER LIVES	CHARLES BENNETT
WHERE DOES IT HURT?	ROD AMATEAU
WHERE EAGLES DARE	ALISTAIR MACLEAN
WHERE HAS TOMMY FLOWERS GONE? (P)	TERRENCE MCNALLY
WHERE LOVE HAS GONE	JOHN MICHAEL HAYES
WHERE THE BOYS ARE	STU KRIEGER
WHERE THE BOYS ARE	JEFF BURKHART
WHERE THE BUFFALO ROAM	JOHN KAYE
WHERE THE DAY TAKES YOU - S	KURT VOSS
WHERE THE GIRLS WERE - S	ANNE BEATTS
WHERE THE GREEN ANTS DREAM	WERNER HERZOG
WHERE THE HEART IS	JOHN BOORMAN
WHERE THE HEART IS	TELSCHE BOORMAN
WHERE THE HOT WIND BLOWS	JULES DASSIN
WHERE THE RAIN IS BORN - S	ALLYN WARNER
WHERE THE RED FERN GROWS	DOUGLAS DAY STEWART
WHERE THE RIVER RUNS BLACK	NEAL JIMENEZ
WHERE THE RIVER RUNS BLACK	PETER SILVERMAN
WHERE THE SPIES ARE	WOLF MANKOWITZ
WHERE THE SPIES ARE	VAL GUEST
WHERE THE SUN NEVER SETS - S	LORENZO SEMPLE
WHERE THERE'S A WILL - S	DENIS HAMILL
WHERE THERE'S A WILL - S	JOHN HAMILL
WHERE THERE'S LIFE	MEL SHAVELSON
WHERE'S POPPA?	ROBERT KLANE
WHERE'S THE BODY? (P)	JOHN H. KOSTMAYER
WHEREABOUTS - S	JACK EPPS JR.
WHEREABOUTS - S	JIM CASH
WHEREABOUTS - S	JONATHAN REYNOLDS
WHICH WAY HOME (CTF)	MICHAEL LAURENCE
WHICH WAY IS UP?	CARL GOTTLIEB
WHICH WAY TO THE FRONT?	DEE CARUSO
WHICH WAY TO THE FRONT?	GERALD GARDNER
WHIFFS	MALCOLM MARMORSTEIN
WHIMPER OF WHIPPED DOGS, THE - S	HARLAN ELLISON
WHIPLASH	HARRIET FRANK JR.
WHIPLASH - S	JEREMY BERTRAND FINCH
WHIRLIGIG - S	WILLIAM D. WITTLIFF
WHISKEY MAN - S	A.J. CAROTHERS
WHISPER TO A SCREAM, A	ROBERT BERGMAN
WHISPERERS, THE	BRYAN FORBES
WHISPERS	ANITA DOOHAN
WHISPERS	DON CARMODY
WHISPERS - S	CHRIS BRYANT
WHISPERS IN BEDLAM - S	DARRYL PONICSAN
WHISTLE BLOWER, THE	JULIAN BOND
WHISTLE STOP	PHILIP YORDAN
WHISTLIN' DIXIE - S	DAVID SELTZER
WHISTLING DIXIE - S	JACK KAPLAN
WHITE SAVAGE	RICHARD BROOKS
WHITE ANGEL - S	CLIFFORD GREEN
WHITE ANGEL - S	ELLEN GREEN
WHITE BUFFALO, THE	RICHARD SALE
WHITE CAMELEON (P)	CHRISTOPHER HAMPTON
WHITE CHRISTMAS	NORMAN PANAMA
WHITE COVER - S	THOM EBERHARD
WHITE CROW, THE: EICHMANN IN JERUSALEM (P)	DONALD FREED
WHITE DAWN, THE	THOMAS RICKMAN
WHITE DOG	CURTIS LEE HANSON
WHITE DOG	SAMUEL FULLER
WHITE FANG	DAVID FALLON
WHITE FANG	JEANNE ROSENBERG
WHITE FANG	NICK THIEL
WHITE GIRL, THE	TONY BROWN
WHITE GOLD - S	FIONA LEWIS
WHITE HEAT - S	DON MCLENNAN
WHITE HOT	ROBBY BENSON
WHITE HOTEL - S	DENNIS POTTER
WHITE HOUSE, THE - S	MICHELE WOLFF
WHITE HUNTER, BLACK HEART	BURT KENNEDY
WHITE HUNTER, BLACK HEART	JAMES BRIDGES
WHITE HUNTER, BLACK HEART	PETER VIERTEL
WHITE HUNTERS - S	MAGGIE KLEINMAN
WHITE LIES - S	HENRY C. PARKE
WHITE LIGHTNING	WILLIAM NORTON SR.
WHITE LINE FEVER	JONATHAN KAPLAN
WHITE LINE FEVER	KEN FRIEDMAN
WHITE LIONS, THE	COREY BLECHMAN
WHITE MAJIC - S	STEPHEN J. CURWICH
WHITE MAN'S BURDEN - S	NATALIE COOPER
WHITE MAN'S BURDEN - S	RICHARD LAWTON
WHITE MEN CAN'T JUMP - S	RON SHELTON
WHITE MISCHIEF	JONATHAN GEMS
WHITE MISCHIEF	MICHAEL RADFORD
WHITE NIGHTS	ERIC HUGHES
WHITE NIGHTS	JAMES GOLDMAN
WHITE OF THE EYE	DONALD CAMMELL
WHITE OF THE EYE	CHINA CAMMELL
WHITE ON WHITE - S	LEON CAPETANOS
WHITE PALACE	ALVIN SARGENT
WHITE PALACE	TED TALLY
WHITE ROCK (FD)	TONY MAYLAM
WHITE ROOM	PATRICIA ROZEMA
WHITE ROSE - S	LEM DOBBS
WHITE SANDS - S	DANIEL PYNE
WHITE SHEIK, THE	FEDERICO FELLINI
WHITE SHERPA, THE - S	STEVEN HAYES
WHITE TRASH - S	ED NEUMEIER
WHITE TRASH - S	MICHAEL MINER
WHITE WATER SUMMER	ERNEST KINOY
WHITE WATER SUMMER	MANYA STARR
WHITE WEDDING - S	SAM HAMM
WHITE ZONE, THE - S	C. COURTNEY JOYNER
WHITER SHADE OF PALE - S	D. SHONE KIRKPATRICK
WHITEWATER - S	DARRYL WIMBERLY
WHO DARES WINS	REGINALD ROSE

Title	Writer
WHO DONE IT, DARLING? (P)	CHARLES EDWARD POGUE
WHO FRAMED ROGER RABBIT	JEFFREY PRICE
WHO FRAMED ROGER RABBIT	PETER SEAMAN
WHO HAS SEEN THE WIND?	PATRICIA WATSON
WHO IS HARRY KELLERMAN AND WHY IS HE SAYING ALL THESE TERRIBLE THINGS ABOUT ME?	HERB GARDNER
WHO IS KILLING THE GREAT CHEFS OF EUROPE?	PETER STONE
WHO SHOT SAMUEL RAY? - S	REX PICKETT
WHO SLEW AUNTIE ROO?	JIMMY SANGSTER
WHO SLEW AUNTIE ROO?	ROBERT BLEES
WHO YOU KNOW - S	HENRY BEAN
WHO'LL STOP THE RAIN	JUDITH RASCOE
WHO'S AFRAID OF VIRGINIA WOLF?	ERNEST LEHMAN
WHO'S BEEN SLEEPING IN MY BED?	JACK ROSE
WHO'S GOT THE ACTION?	JACK ROSE
WHO'S HARRY CRUMB?	PETER MARTIN WORTMANN
WHO'S HARRY CRUMB?	ROBERT CONTE
WHO'S MINDING THE STORE?	HARRY TUGEND†
WHO'S THAT GIRL	ANDREW SMITH
WHO'S THAT GIRL	KEN FINKLEMAN
WHO'S WHO - S	AMY SPIES
WHO'S WRITING THIS? (P)	PHILIP MORTON
WHODUNNIT (P)	ANTHONY SHAFFER
WHOLLY MOSES	GUY THOMAS
WHOOPEE BOYS, THE	DAVID OBST
WHOOPEE BOYS, THE	JEFF BUHAI
WHOOPEE BOYS, THE	STEVEN R. ZACHARIAS
WHOPPER - S	ED RUGOFF
WHOPPER - S	MICHAEL GOTTLIEB
WHORE	DEBORAH DALTON
WHORES GOLD	DAVID PEOPLES
WHOSE LIFE IS IT ANYWAY?	BRIAN CLARK
WHOSE LIFE IS IT ANYWAY?	REGINALD ROSE
WHOSE WOODS THESE ARE - S	RICHARD CHRISTIAN MATHESON
WHOSE WOODS THESE ARE - S	TOM SZOLLOSI
WHY BOTHER TO KNOCK	FREDERIC RAPHAEL
WHY DID I EVER LEAVE HORSES? - S	JOHN BRILEY
WHY ME?	DONALD E. WESTLAKE
WHY ME?	LEONARD MAAS JR.
WHY SHOOT THE TEACHER?	JAMES DEFELICE
WHY TO REFUSE (P)	EDUARDO MACHADO
WHY WOULD I LIE?	PETER STONE
WICKED AS THEY COME	KEN HUGHES
WICKED LADY, THE	MICHAEL WINNER
WICKED STEPMOTHER	LARRY COHEN
WICKER MAN, THE	ANTHONY SHAFFER
WIDE SARGASSO SEA - S	SHELAGH DELANEY
WIDE SARGASSO SEA - S	JOHN DUIGAN
WIDOW (CTF) - S	JOEL GROSS
WIDOW CLAIRE, THE - S	HORTON FOOTE
WIDOW'S BLIND DATE, THE (P)	ISRAEL HOROVITZ
WIDOWS - S	DAN GOLDBERG
WIDOWS - S	LEN BLUM
WIDOWS - S	RICHARD LAGRAVENESE
WIFE MISTRESS - S	NEAL MARSHALL
WILBY CONSPIRACY, THE	HAROLD NEBENZAL
WILBY CONSPIRACY, THE	ROD AMATEAU
WILD	NORMAN MAILER
WILD AND THE WILLING, THE	MORDECAI RICHLER
WILD ANGELS, THE	CHARLES B. GRIFFITH
WILD ANGELS, THE	PETER BOGDONAVICH
WILD AT HEART	DAVID LYNCH
WILD BIG RED, THE	PAUL F. EDWARDS
WILD BILL BEETHOVEN - S	TODD DURHAM
WILD BILLY - S	MICHAEL AUSTIN
WILD BLUE	RICHARD SMITH
WILD BLUE YONDER - S	BILL LAMOND
WILD BLUE YONDER - S	JO LAMOND
WILD BOYS - S	HARLEY PEYTON
WILD BUNCH, THE	WALON GREEN
WILD CHILD, THE	JEAN GRUAULT
WILD DUCK, THE	HENRI SAFRAN
WILD GEESE II	REGINALD ROSE
WILD GEESE, THE	REGINALD ROSE
WILD HEART, THE	EMERIC PRESSBURGER†
WILD HEART, THE	MICHAEL POWELL†
WILD HEARTS CAN'T BE BROKEN	MATT WILLIAMS
WILD HEARTS CAN'T BE BROKEN	OLEY SASSONE
WILD HORSE	KEVIN WILSON
WILD HORSE HANK	JAMES LEE BARRETT†
WILD IS THE WIND	ARNOLD SCHULMAN
WILD LIFE, THE	CAMERON CROWE
WILD ORCHID	PATRICIA L. KNOP
WILD ORCHID	ZALMAN KING
WILD ORCHID II	ZALMAN KING
WILD PAIR, THE	JOHN CROWTHER
WILD PAIR, THE	JOSEPH GUNN
WILD RIDE - S	ADAM DUBOV
WILD RIDE - S	JANICE SHAPIRO
WILD ROVERS	BLAKE EDWARDS
WILD SANCTUARY - S	EARL MAC RAUCH
WILD SANCTUARY, A - S	ROGER L. SIMON
WILD SIDE, THE	PENELOPE SPHEERIS
WILD STRAWBERRIES	INGMAR BERGMAN
WILD THING	JOHN SAYLES
WILD THING	LARRY STAMPER
WILD WEST SHOW - S	WES CLARRIDGE
WILD WOMEN DON'T HAVE NO BLUES - S	CARL G. SAUTTER
WILDCARD - S	DIANA HAMMOND
WILDCATS	EZRA SACKS
WILDER NAPALM - S	VINCE GILLIGAN
WILDERNESS - S	JOSEPH C. STINSON
WILDERNESS - S	OLIVER STONE
WILDEST DREAMS	CHUCK VINCENT
WILDEST DREAMS	CRAIG HORRALL
WILDFIRE	MATTHEW BRIGHT
WILDFIRE	ZALMAN KING
WILDFIRE (CTF) - S	SARA FLANIGAN CARTER
WILDROSE	EUGENE CORR
WILDROSE	JOHN HANSON
WILDROSE	SANDRA SCHULBERG
WILL ROGERS FOLLIES, THE (P)	PETER H. STONE
WILL SUCCESS SPOIL ROCK HUNTER (P)	GEORGE AXELROD
WILL TO KILL - S	HARVEY WARREN
WILL TO KILL - S	JOY WARREN
WILLIE - S	ERIC ROTH
WILLIE AND PHIL	PAUL MAZURKSY
WILLIE THE HAT'S KID - S	JEREMY IACONE
WILLOW	BOB DOLMAN
WILLOW	GEORGE LUCAS
WILLY MILLY	CARLA REUBENS
WILLY MILLY	WALTER CARBONE
WILLY WONKA AND THE CHOCOLATE FACTORY	ROALD DAHL†
WIMPS FROM SPACE - S	TODD DURHAM
WIND - S	RUDY WURLITZER
WIND ACROSS THE EVERGLADES	BUDD SCHULBERG
WIND AND THE LION, THE	JOHN MILIUS
WIND IN THE WILLOWS - S	GREG DAVIS
WIND IN THE WILLOWS - S	LARRY GARCIA
WINDOWS	BARRY SIEGEL
WINDRIDER	BONNIE HARRIS
WINDRIDER	EVERETT DEROCHE
WINDS OF AUTUMN, THE	CHARLES B. PIERCE
WINDWALKER	RAY GOLDRUP
WINDWARD PASSAGE - S	RON BASS
WINDY CITY	ARMYAN BERNSTEIN
WINGED FEET (P)	BILL CORBETT
WINGING IT - S	W.D. RICHTER
WINGO - S	RICHARD PRICE
WINGS - S	EZRA LITWAK
WINGS - S	MARJORIE SCHWARTZ
WINGS OF DESIRE	PETER HANDKE
WINGS OF DESIRE	WIM WENDERS
WINGS OF EAGLES, THE	WILLIAM WISTER HAINES†
WINGS OF FAME	HERMAN KOCH
WINGS OF FAME	OTAKAR VOTOCEK
WINNER, THE - S	RON NYSWANER
WINNERS CIRCLE, THE (P)	JAMES KENNEDY
WINNERS TAKE ALL	CHRISTOPHER KNIGHT
WINNERS TAKE ALL	EDWARD S. TURNER JR.
WINNERS TAKE ALL	TOM TATUM
WINNIE - S	EMILY MANN
WINNING STREAK - S	JOSEPH C. STINSON
WINNING TICKET, THE	ROBERT PIROSH†
WINNING UGLY	DANIEL PYNE
WINSLOW'S MUSE - S	JIM STRAIN
WINSTON (SHORT)	STEVEN SODERBERGH
WINSTON COME HOME, YOUR DOG DIED TUESDAY - S	BILL MCKINNEY, JR.
WINTER - S	JIM HART
WINTER - S	THOMAS HEDLEY JR.
WINTER CARNIVAL	BUDD SCHULBERG
WINTER CHILDREN - S	JEREMY IACONE
WINTER FLIGHT	ALAN JANES
WINTER KILLS	WILLIAM RICHERT
WINTER LIGHT	INGMAR BERGMAN
WINTER OF OUR DREAMS	JOHN DUIGAN
WINTER PEOPLE	CAROL SOBIESKI†
WINTER SONG - S	DENNE BART PETITCLERC
WINTER'S TALE - S	MELISSA MATHISON
WINTER'S TALE (P)	ANDY WOLK
WINTERHAWK	CHARLES B. PIERCE
WIRED	EARL MAC RAUCH
WISDOM	EMILIO ESTEVEZ
WISE BLOOD	BENEDICT FITZGERALD
WISE BLOOD	MICHAEL FITZGERALD
WISE GUYS	GEORGE GALLO
WISH YOU WERE HERE	DAVID LELAND
WISHBONES - S	MATTHEW MCDUFFIE
WISHFUL THINKING - S	LEE REYNOLDS
WISHFUL THINKING - S	JERRY JACOBIUS
WISHFUL THINKING - S	NICK GORE
WIT'S END - S	JAMES CRESSON
WITCH DOCTOR - S	MARC D. SOTKIN
WITCH STORY (P)	JAMES KIRKWOOD†
WITCH, THE - S	ERIC LUKE
WITCHBOARD	KEVIN S. TENNEY
WITCHCRAFT	HARRY SPALDING
WITCHCRAFT - S	CELIA GITTLESON
WITCHCRAFT - S	CHRIS MILLER
WITCHCRAFT - S	MICHAEL D. SUTTON
WITCHCRAFT - S	TONY GITTLESON
WITCHERY	DANIELE STROPPA
WITCHES - S	SCOTT SPIEGEL
WITCHES OF EASTWICK, THE	MICHAEL CRISTOFER
WITCHES,THE	ALLAN G. SCOTT
WITCHES, THE (1966)	NIGEL KNEALE
WITH A VENGEANCE - S	GERALD DI PEGO
WITH DEADLY INTENT - S	MIGUEL TEJADA-FLORES
WITH OPEN ARMS - S	ROD MCCALL
WITHNAIL AND I	BRUCE ROBINSON
WITHOUT A CLUE	GARY MURPHY
WITHOUT A CLUE	LARRY STRAWTHER
WITHOUT A TRACE	BETH GUTCHEON
WITHOUT MERCY - S	CHRISTIAN STOIANOVICH
WITHOUT MERCY - S	PHOEBE DORIN
WITHOUT WARNING	LYN FREEMAN
WITHOUT WARNING	STEVE MATHIS
WITHOUT WARNING	DANIEL GRODNIK
WITHOUT WARNING: THE JAMES BRADY STORY (CTF)	ROBERT BOLT
WITHOUT YOU I'M NOTHING	SANDRA BERNHARD
WITHOUT YOU I'M NOTHING	JOHN BOSKOVICH
WITNESS	EARL WALLACE
WITNESS	PAMELA WALLACE
WITNESS	WILLIAM KELLEY
WITNESS FOR THE PROSECUTION	BILLY WILDER
WITNESS TO MURDER, A - S	GARNER SIMMONS
WITNESS TO WAR - S	JACK BEHR
WITNESS TO WAR - S	SANDY KROOPF
WITNESSES - S	HAL BARWOOD
WITNESSES - S	MATTHEW ROBBINS
WIVES - S	DORIS BAIZLEY
WIVES AND LOVERS	EDWARD ANHALT
WIZ, THE	JOEL SCHUMACHER
WIZARD FROM FLATBUSH, THE - S	HARV ZIMMEL
WIZARD FROM FLATBUSH, THE - S	JOEL SALTZMAN
WIZARD OF LONELINESS, THE	NANCY LARSON
WIZARD OF SANTA MONICA, THE - S	IAN ABRAMS
WIZARD, THE	DAVID CHISOLM
WIZARDS (AF)	RALPH BAKSHI
WIZARDS OF THE LOST KINGDOM	TOM EDWARDS
WOLF AND ROSE - S	RON KOSLOW
WOLF AT THE DOOR, THE	CHRISTOPHER HAMPTON
WOLF LARSEN	JACK DEWITT
WOLF MAN, THE	CURT SIODMAK
WOLFEN	DAVID EYRE
WOLFEN	MICHAEL WADLEIGH
WOLFPACK	WILLIAM P. MILLING
WOLVERINES (P)	TOM PATCHETT
WOMAN ALONE, A	AGNIESZKA HOLLAND
WOMAN ALONE, A (1936)	CHARLES BENNETT
WOMAN AT DEAD OAKS (P)	JAMES KIRKWOOD†
WOMAN IN HIDING	OSCAR SAUL
WOMAN IN JEOPARDY - S	ANABEL DAVIS-GOFF
WOMAN IN MIND (P)	ALAN AYCKBOURN
WOMAN IN THE DARK - S	KARIN HOWARD
WOMAN IN THE ROOM, THE - S	FRANK DARABONT
WOMAN IN THE WILDERNESS - S	STEPHEN H. FOREMAN
WOMAN INSIDE, THE	JOSEPH VAN WINKLE

Wo-Ze

FILM WRITERS GUIDE

WOMAN NEXT DOOR - S .... THOMAS POPE
WOMAN OF INDEPENDENT
  MEANS, A - S .... LAWRENCE D. COHEN
WOMAN OF STRAW .... STANLEY MANN
WOMAN OF THE RING - S .... VINCENT GUTIERREZ
WOMAN OF THE YEAR .... MICHEAL KANIN
WOMAN OF THE YEAR .... RING LARDNER JR.
WOMAN OF THE YEAR (P) .... PETER STONE
WOMAN ON HER OWN .... AGNIESZKA HOLLAND
WOMAN UNDER THE
  INFLUENCE, A .... JOHN CASSAVETES†
WOMAN WANTED - S ..... JOANNA MCCLELLAND-GLASS
WOMAN WARRIOR (CTF) - S .... RANCE HOWARD
WOMAN'S GUIDE TO
  ADULTERY, A - S .... RAMA LAURIE STAGNER
WOMAN'S PLACE, A - S .... JANET KOVALCIK
WOMAN'S PLACE, A - S .... JOHN ROMANO
WOMAN'S WORLD .... RICHARD SALE
WOMAN, THE - S .... ANN BIDERMAN
WOMBLING FREE .... LIONEL JEFFRIES
WOMEN BEHIND BARS - S ..... MICHAEL MCDOWELL
WOMEN IN LOVE .... LARRY KRAMER
WOMEN IN RED, THE .... GENE WILDER
WOMEN NEXT
  DOOR, THE .... FRANCOIS TRUFFAUT†
WOMEN NEXT DOOR, THE .... JEAN AUREL
WOMEN NEXT DOOR, THE ... SUZANNE SCHIFFMAN
WOMEN OF BEVERLY
  HILLS - S .... LINDSAY HARRISON
WOMEN OF
  MANHATTAN (P) .... JOHN PATRICK SHANLEY
WOMEN ON THE VERGE OF A NERVOUS
  BREAKDOWN .... PEDRO ALMODOVAR
WOMEN ON THE VERGE OF A NERVOUS
  BREAKDOWN (REMAKE) - S .... TOD CARROLL
WOMEN WHO RODE
  AWAY, THE - S .... HESPER ANDERSON
WOMEN'S CLUB,
  THE .... SANDRA WEINTRAUB ROLAND
WOMEN'S WORK - S .... JOAN TAYLOR
WOMEN, MONEY &
  RESTAURANTS - S .... LLOYD FONVIELLE
WOMEN, THE - S .... ANNE BEATTS
WON TON TON, THE DOG WHO SAVED
  HOLLYWOOD .... ARNOLD SCHULMAN
WONDER BOY - S .... ERIC ROTH
WONDER WHEELS - S .... TERRY BRENNAN
WONDERFUL WORLD OF THE BROTHERS
  GRIMM, THE .... WILLIAM ROBERTS
WONDERLAND .... FRANK CLARKE
WONDERLAND - S .... ALEX WINTER
WONDERLAND .... TOM STERN
WOO WOO KID, THE .... PHIL ALDEN ROBINSON
WOODS, THE (P) .... DAVID MAMET
WOODSIDE PROPHETS .... ABBE WOOL
WORDS AND MUSIC - S .... W.D. RICHTER
WORD OF HONOR - S .... THOMAS POPE
WORDS (SHORT) .... CHUCK WORKMAN
WORK OF ART, A - S ...... PETER VINCENT DOUGLAS
WORKING CLASS HERO - S .... RAY CONNOLLY
WORKING GIRL .... KEVIN WADE
WORKING GIRLS .... LIZZIE BORDEN
WORKING TRASH - S .... DENNIS PALUMBO
WORKS , THE - S .... JULIA CAMERON
WORKS, THE - S .... DENNIS PALUMBO
WORLD ACCORDING TO
  GARP, THE .... STEVE TESICH
WORLD APART, A .... SHAWN SLOVO
WORLD GONE WILD .... JORGE ZAMACONA
WORLD IS FULL OF MARRIED
  MEN, THE .... JACKIE COLLINS
WORLD ON FIRE - S .... ANDREW CHAPMAN
WORLD'S GREATEST
  ATHLETE, THE .... DEE CARUSO
WORLD'S GREATEST
  ATHLETE, THE .... GERALD GARDNER
WORLD'S GREATEST HUMAN FLY - S ...... JOHN HILL
WORLD'S GREATEST LOVER, THE .... GENE WILDER
WORLD'S OLDEST LIVING
  BRIDESMAID, THE - S .... JANET KOVALCIK
WORLD, THE - S .... PAUL D. ZIMMERMAN
WORLDBEATER - S .... THOMAS RICKMAN
WORST MOVIE EVER
  MADE, THE - S .... ALAN JAY GLUECKMAN
WORST PERSON IN N.Y. - S ..... SUZANNE O'MALLEY
WORTH WINNING .... JOSAN MCGIBBON
WORTH WINNING .... SARA PARRIOTT
WORTH WINNING - S .... BRYAN GORDON
WOULD YOU DO IT FOR
  A PENNY? - S .... HARLAN ELLISON
WOUNDED KNEE - S .... DJORDJE MILICEVIC
WOUNDED KNEE (CTF) - S .... DENNIS L. CLARK
WR - MYSTERIES OF THE
  ORGANISM .... DUSAN MAKAVEJEV
WRAITH, THE .... MIKE MARVIN
WRIGHT BROS., THE - S .... MARK MALONE
WRINKLE IN TIME, A - S ...... CHRISTOPHER DEVORE
WRINKLE IN TIME, A - S .... ERIC BERGREN
WRINKLE IN TIME, A - S .... SUSANSHILLIDAY
WRITER'S BLOCK (CTF) .... ELISA BELL
WRITING ON THE
  WALL (P) .... BARRY MICHAEL COOPER
WRONG BOX, THE .... LARRY GELBART
WRONG DOOR, THE - S .... SCOTT PARKER
WRONG GUYS, THE .... DANNY BILSON
WRONG GUYS, THE .... PAUL DE MEO
WRONG IS RIGHT .... RICHARD BROOKS
WRONG MAN, THE - S .... ROY CARLSON
WRONG MOVE, THE .... PETER HANDKE
WRONG PLANET .... LEE ROSE
WRONG PLANET - S .... PATRICIA RESNICK
WRONG TURN AT
  LUNGFISH (P) .... GARRY MARSHALL
WUSA .... ROBERT STONE
WUTHERING HEIGHTS (1970) .... PATRICK TILLEY

X

X - THE MAN WITH THE
  X-RAY EYES .... ROBERT DILLON
X THE UNKNOWN .... JIMMY SANGSTER
XANADU .... MARC RUBEL
XANADU .... RICHARD CHRISTIAN DANUS
XTRO .... ROBERT SMITH

Y

YAKOMAN AND TETSU .... AKIRA KUROSAWA
YAKUZA, THE .... LEONARD SCHRADER
YAKUZA, THE .... PAUL SCHRADER
YAKUZA, THE .... ROBERT TOWNE
YAMASHITA'S GOLD .... DERIC WASHBURN
YANKEE WHITE - S .... ROY CARLSON
YANKS .... COLIN WELLAND
YANKS .... WALTER BERNSTEIN
YARD WARS - S .... EDWARD DECTER
YARD WARS - S .... JOHN J. STRAUSS
YARMAKOV TRANSFER, THE- S ...... CHRIS BRYANT
YEAR AND A DAY, A - S .... MICHAEL LEESON
YEAR MY VOICE BROKE, THE .... JOHN DUIGAN
YEAR OF LIVING DANGEROUSLY, THE .... C.J. KOCH
YEAR OF LIVING
  DANGEROUSLY, THE .... DAVID WILLIAMSON
YEAR OF LIVING
  DANGEROUSLY, THE .... PETER WEIR
YEAR OF THE
  COMET, THE - S .... WILLIAM GOLDMAN
YEAR OF THE DRAGON .... MICHAEL CIMINO
YEAR OF THE DRAGON .... OLIVER STONE
YEAR OF THE GUN - S .... DAVID AMBROSE
YEAR OF THE TIGER .... WES CLARRIDGE
YELLOW JERSEY - S .... COLIN WELLAND
YELLOW RAFT IN BLUE
  WATER, A - S .... GLORIA KATZ
YELLOW RAFT IN BLUE
  WATER, A - S .... WILLARD HUYCK
YELLOW SUBMARINE (AF) .... ERICH SEGAL
YELLOWBEARD .... BERNARD MCKENNA
YELLOWBEARD .... GRAHAM CHAPMAN†
YELLOWBEARD .... PETER COOK
YELLOWHAIR AND THE FORTRESS
  OF GOLD .... JOHN KERSHAW
YELLOWHAIR AND THE FORTRESS
  OF GOLD .... MATT CIMBER
YELLOWSTONE KELLY .... BURT KENNEDY
YENTL .... BARBRA STREISAND
YENTL .... JACK ROSENTHAL
YERMAKOV TRANSFER,
  THE - S .... ALLAN G. SCOTT
YES, GIORGIO .... NORMAN STEINBERG
YES SIR, THAT'S MY BABY .... OSCAR BRODNEY
YESTERDAY'S HERO .... JACKIE COLLINS
YO' JULIETTE - S .... RANDY WEINER
YO' JULIETTE - S .... ROB HANNING
YO OLIVER - S .... FRANK PUGLIESE
YOJIMBO .... AKIRA KUROSAWA
YONADAB (P) .... PETER SHAFFER
YOR, THE HUNTER FROM
  THE FUTURE .... ANTHONY M. DAWSON
YOR, THE HUNTER FROM
  THE FUTURE .... ROBERT BAILEY
YOSHIKO - S .... MURDO LAIRD
YOU BETTER WATCH OUT .... LEWIS JACKSON
YOU CAN'T HAVE
  EVERYTHING .... A. MARTIN ZWEIBACH
YOU CAN'T HURRY LOVE .... RICHARD MARTINI
YOU DON'T DIE OF LOVE - S ..... THOMAS THONSON
YOU FOR ME .... WILLIAM ROBERTS
YOU FOR ME - S .... BO GOLDMAN
YOU LIGHT UP MY LIFE .... JOSEPH BROOKS
YOU ONLY LIVE TWICE .... ROALD DAHL†
YOU SHOULD SEE THE CONKLIN'S
  LIVING ROOM - S .... ROBERT NEWCOMBE
YOU TALKIN' TO ME? .... CHARLES WINKLER
YOU'RE A BIG
  BOY NOW .... FRANCIS FORD COPPOLA
YOU'RE IN THE NAVY NOW .... RICHARD T. MURPHY
YOU'RE NEVER TOO YOUNG ...... SIDNEY SHELDON
YOUNG AND WILLING .... MORDECAI RICHLER
YOUNG AT HEART .... JULIUS J. EPSTEIN
YOUNG BILLY YOUNG .... BURT KENNEDY
YOUNG BUCKS - S .... ANDY BOROWITZ
YOUNG CATHERINE (CTF) .... CHRIS BRYANT
YOUNG COMMANDOS .... BOAZ DAVIDSON
YOUNG DOCTORS IN LOVE .... MICHAEL ELIAS
YOUNG DOCTORS IN LOVE .... RICHARD EUSTIS
YOUNG EINSTEIN .... DAVID ROACH
YOUNG EINSTEIN .... YAHOO SERIOUS
YOUNG EVE - S .... CHARLES ROBERT CARNER
YOUNG FRANKENSTEIN .... GENE WILDER
YOUNG FRANKENSTEIN .... MEL BROOKS
YOUNG GIRLS OF
  ROCHEFORT, THE .... JACQUES DEMY†
YOUNG GUNS .... JOHN FUSCO
YOUNG GUNS II .... JOHN FUSCO
YOUNG LILLY - S .... NATALIE COOPER
YOUNG LIONS, THE .... EDWARD ANHALT
YOUNG LOVERS - S .... BENNETT YELLIN
YOUNG LOVERS - S .... PETER FARRELLY
YOUNG LUST .... ROBIN MENKEN
YOUNG LUST .... BRUCE WAGNER
YOUNG MAFIA .... THOMAS LEE WRIGHT
YOUNG MAN WITH A HORN .... CARL FOREMAN†
YOUNG MEN WITH UNLIMITED
  CAPITAL - S .... JOHN BYRUM
YOUNG SAVAGES, THE .... EDWARD ANHALT
YOUNG SHERLOCK HOLMES .... CHRIS COLUMBUS
YOUNG TEDDY ROOSEVELT - S .... THOMAS POPE
YOUNG WARRIORS .... LAWRENCE D. FOLDES
YOUNG WARRIORS .... RUSSELL W. COLGIN
YOUNG WARRIORS, THE .... RICHARD MATHESON
YOUNG WINSTON .... CARL FOREMAN†
YOUNGBLOOD .... PETER MARKLE
YOUNGBLOOD .... JOHN WHITMAN
YOUNGBLOOD .... PAUL CARTER HARRISON
YOUR BASIC LOUSY
  MARRIAGE - S .... BRUCE JAY FRIEDMAN
YOUR WISH IS MY COMMAND - S .... DANA OLSEN
YOUR WISH IS MY
  COMMAND - S .... ROBERT COLLECTOR
YOURS, MINE AND OURS .... MEL SHAVELSON
YOUTH, SPRING, LOVE (P) .... JAMES KIRKWOOD†

Z

Z .... COSTA-GAVRAS
Z .... JORGE SEMPRUN
Z .... BEN BARZMAN†
ZABRISKIE POINT .... CLARE PEPLOE
ZABRISKIE POINT .... MICHELANGELO ANTONIONI
ZABRISKIE POINT .... SAM SHEPARD
ZABRISKIE POINT .... TONINO GUERRA
ZADARI COW FROM HELL .... MERLE KESSLER
ZANDALEE .... MARI KORNHAUSER
ZANDE - S .... ANDY LEWIS
ZANDY'S BRIDE .... MARC NORMAN
ZAPPEDI .... BRUCE RUBIN
ZAPPEDI .... ROBERT J. ROSENTHAL
ZARAK .... RICHARD MAIBAUM††
ZARDOZ .... JOHN BOORMAN
ZAZIE .... LOUIS MALLE
ZEBRAHEAD, THE GREY
  BOY - S .... ANTHONY DRAZAN
ZEBVLON - S .... RUDOLPH G. WURLITZER
ZED AND TWO NOUGHTS, A ... PETER GREENAWAY
ZELIG .... WOODY ALLEN

Ze-Zu

Title	Writer
ZELLY & ME	TINA RATHBORNE
ZERO CLUB, THE - S	AARON LATHAM
ZERO HOUR!	HALL BARTLETT
ZERO POSITIVE (P)	HARRY KONDOLEON
ZERO VISIBILITY - S	NICHOLAS BOGNER
ZIGZAG MAN, THE - S	ALEXANDER TANA
ZIG-ZAG MAN, THE - S	THOMAS RICKMAN
ZIPPYVISION - S	DIANE NOOMIN
ZODIAC - S	CHIP PROSER
ZODIAC - S	KENNETH H. FRIEDMAN
ZODIAC - S	SNOO WILSON
ZONE TROOPERS	DANNY BILSON
ZONE TROOPERS	PAUL DE MEO
ZONE TWO - S	RICHARD HEFT
ZOO GANG, THE	DAVID DASHEV
ZOO GANG, THE	JOHN WATSON
ZOO GANG, THE	PEN DENSHAM
ZOO GANG, THE	STUART BIRNBAUM
ZOO PLANE - S	GARRY TRUDEAU
ZOOMAN AND THE SIGN (P)	CHARLES H. FULLER
ZOOT SUIT	LUIS VALDEZ
ZORBA THE GREK	MICHAEL CACOYANNIS
ZORRO - S	NANCY LARSON
ZORRO, THE GAY BLADE	BOB RANDALL
ZORRO, THE GAY BLADE	DON MORIARTY
ZORRO, THE GAY BLADE	GREG ALT
ZORRO, THE GAY BLADE	HAL DRESNER
ZPG	FRANK DE FELITTA
ZULU	CY ENDFIELD
ZULU DAWN	ANTHONY STOREY
ZULU DAWN	CY ENDFIELD

★★★★

IF HE'S IN THE BACK OF A POLICE CAR TODAY, WHERE WILL HE BE TOMORROW?

He's not a bad kid, really. But one night, while spraying graffiti on a brick wall, this 12 year-old had his first brush with the law.

Where do you go before things get out of hand?

He got help at a local Youth Center. They got help from the United Way. All because the United Way got help from you.

Your single contribution helps provide therapy for a child with a learning disability, rehabilitation for a cocaine abuser, and a program that sends a volunteer to do the shopping for a 79 year-old woman.

Or, in this case, a place where a kid can toss a basketball around after school. A place where a basically good kid can stay that way.

United Way

It brings out the best in all of us.™

UNITED WAY OF AMERICA CAMPAIGN
NEWSPAPER AD NO. UW-89-1490—2 COL.

FILM WRITERS
ACADEMY AWARDS AND NOMINATIONS
1960-1990

★★ = winner in category

1960

Original Screenplay

THE ANGRY
  SILENCE .... Richard Gregson, Michael Craig, Bryan Forbes
THE APARTMENT .... Billy Wilder, I.A.L. Diamond ★★
THE FACTS OF LIFE .... Norman Panama, Melvin Frank
HIROSHIMA, MON AMOUR .... Marguerite Duras
NEVER ON SUNDAY .... Jules Dassin

Adaptation

ELMER GANTRY .... Richard Brooks ★★
INHERIT THE
  WIND .... Nathan E. Douglas, Harold Jacob Smith
SONS AND LOVERS .... Gavin Lambert, T.E.B. Clarke
THE SUNDOWNERS .... Isobel Lennart
TUNES OF GLORY .... James Kennaway

1961

Original Screenplay

BALLAD OF A SOLDIER .... Valentin Yoshov, Grigori Chukhrai
GENERAL DELLA
  ROVERE .... Sergio Amidei, Diego Fabbri, Indro Montanelli
LA DOLCI
  VITA .... Federico Fellini, Tullio Pinelli,
                                         Ennio Flaiano, Brunello Rondi
LOVER COME BACK .... Stanley Shapiro, Paul Henning
SPLENDOR IN THE GRASS .... William Inge ★★

Adaptation

BREAKFAST AT TIFFANY'S .... George Axelrod
THE GUNS OF NAVARONE .... Carl Foreman
THE HUSTLER .... Sidney Carroll, Robert Rossen
JUDGMENT AT NUREMBERG .... Abby Mann ★★
WEST SIDE STORY .... Ernest Lehman

1962

Original Screenplay

DIVORCE—ITALIAN
  STYLE .... Ennio de Concini, Alfredo Giannetti,
                                                         Pietro Germi ★★
FREUD .... Charles Kaufman, Wolfgang Reinhardt
LAST YEAR AT MARIENBAD .... Alain Robbe-Grillet
THAT TOUCH OF MINK .... Stanley Shapiro, Nate Monaster
THROUGH A GLASS DARKLY .... Ingmar Bergman

Adaptation

DAVID AND LISA .... Eleanor Perry
LAWRENCE OF ARABIA .... Robert Bolt
LOLITA .... Vladimir Nabokov
THE MIRACLE WORKER .... William Gibson
TO KILL A MOCKINGBIRD .... Horton Foote ★★

1963

Original Screenplay

AMERICA, AMERICA .... Elia Kazan
FEDERICO FELLINI'S
  8 1/2 .... Federico Fellini, Ennio Flaiano, Tullio Pinelli,
                                                         Brunello Rondi
THE FOUR DAYS OF
  NAPLES .... Pasquael Festa Campanile, Massino
                          Franciosa, Nanni Loy, Vasco Pratolini, Carlo Bernari
HOW THE WEST WAS WON .... James R. Webb ★★
LOVE WITH THE PROPER STRANGER ..... Arnold Schulman

Adaptation

CAPTAIN NEWMAN,
  M.D. .... Richard L. Breen, Phoebe and Henry Ephron
HUD .... Irving Ravetch, Harriet Frank Jr.
LILIES OF THE FIELD .... James Poe
SUNDAYS AND
  CYBELE .... Serge Bourguigon, Antoine Tudal
TOM JONES .... John Osborne ★★

1964

Original Screenplay

FATHER
  GOOSE .... S.H. Barnett, Peter Stone, Frank Tarloff ★★
A HARD DAY'S NIGHT .... Alun Owen
ONE POTATO, TWO
  POTATO .... Orville H. Hampton, Raphael Hayes
THAT MAN FROM
  RIO .... Jean-Paul Rappeneau, Ariane Mnouchkine,
                                        Daniel Boulanger, Philippe de Broca

Adaptation

BECKET .... Edward Anhalt ★★
DR. STRANGELOVE OR: HOW I LEARNED TO STOP
  WORRYING AND LOVE THE BOMB .... Stanley Kubrick,
                                           Peter George, Terry Southern
MARY POPPINS .... Bill Walsh, Don DaGradi
MY FAIR LADY .... Alan Jay Lerner
ZORBA THE GREEK .... Michael Cacoyannis

1965

Original Screenplay

CASANOVA '70 .... Age Scarpelli, Mario Monicelli,
                           Tonino Guerra, Giorgio Salvioni, Susi Cecchi D'Amico
DARLING .... Frederic Raphael ★★
THOSE MAGNIFICENT MEN IN THEIR
  FLYING MACHINES .... Jack Davies, Ken Annakin
THE TRAIN .... Franklin Coen, Frank Davis
THE UMBRELLAS OF CHERBOURG .... Jacques Demy

1965 (continued)

Adaptation

- CAT BALLOU .... Walter Newman, Frank R. Pierson
- THE COLLECTOR .... Stanley Mann, John Kohn
- DOCTOR ZHIVAGO .... Robert Bolt ★★
- SHIP OF FOOLS .... Abby Mann
- A THOUSAND CLOWNS .... Herb Gardner

1966

Original Screenplay

- BLOW-UP .... Michelangelo Antonioni, Tonino Guerra, Edward Bond
- THE FORTUNE COOKIE .... Billy Wilder, I.A.L. Diamond
- KHARTOUM .... Robert Ardrey
- A MAN AND A WOMAN .... Claude Lelouch, Pierre Uytterhoeven ★★
- THE NAKED PREY .... Clint Johnston, Don Peters

Adaptation

- ALFIE .... Bill Naughton
- A MAN FOR ALL SEASONS .... Robert Bolt ★★
- THE PROFESSIONALS .... Richard Brooks
- THE RUSSIANS ARE COMING THE RUSSIANS ARE COMING .... William Rose
- WHO'S AFRAID OF VIRGINIA WOOLF? .... Ernest Lehman

1967

Original Screenplay

- BONNIE AND CLYDE .... David Newman, Robert Benton
- DIVORCE AMERICAN STYLE .... Norman Lear
- GUESS WHO'S COMING TO DINNER? ..... William Rose ★★
- LA GUERRE EST FINIE .... Jorge Semprun
- TWO FOR THE ROAD .... Frederic Raphael

Adaptation

- COOL HAND LUKE .... Donn Pearce, Frank R. Pierson
- THE GRADUATE .... Calder Willingham, Buck Henry
- IN COLD BLOOD .... Richard Brooks
- IN THE HEAT OF THE NIGHT .... Stirling Silliphant ★★
- ULYSSES .... Joseph Strick, Fred Haines

1968

Original Screenplay

- THE BATTLE OF ALGIERS ...... Franco Solinas, Gillo Pontecorvo
- FACES .... John Cassavetes
- HOT MILLIONS .... Ira Wallach, Peter Ustinov
- THE PRODUCERS .... Mel Brooks ★★
- 2001: A SPACE ODYSSEY ...... Stanley Kubrick, Arthur C. Clarke

Adaptation

- THE LION IN WINTER .... James Goldman ★★
- THE ODD COUPLE .... Neil Simon
- OLIVER! .... Vernon Harris
- RACHEL, RACHEL .... Stewart Stern
- ROSEMARY'S BABY .... Roman Polanski

1969

Original Screenplay

- BOB & CAROL & TED & ALICE ...... Paul Mazursky, Larry Tucker
- BUTCH CASSIDY AND THE SUNDANCE KID .... William Goldman ★★
- THE DAMNED ... Nicola Badalucco, Enrico Medioli, Luchino Visconti
- EASY RIDER .... Peter Fonda, Dennis Hopper, Terry Southern
- THE WILD BUNCH ...... Walon Green, Roy N. Sickner, Sam Peckinpah

Adaptation

- ANNE OF THE THOUSAND DAYS .... John Hale, Bridget Boland, Richard Sokolove
- GOODBYE COLUMBUS .... Arnold Schulman
- MIDNIGHT COWBOY .... Waldo Salt ★★
- THEY SHOOT HORSES, DON'T THEY? .... James Poe, Robert E. Thompson
- Z .... Jorge Semprun, Costa-Gavras

1970

Original Screenplay

- FIVE EASY PIECES .... Bob Rafelson, Adrien Joyce
- JOE .... Norman Wexler
- LOVE STORY .... Erich Segal
- MY NIGHT AT MAUD'S .... Eric Rohmer
- PATTON .... Francis Ford Coppola, Edmund H. North ★★

Adaptation

- AIRPORT .... George Seaton
- I NEVER SANG FOR MY FATHER .... Robert Anderson
- LOVERS AND OTHER STRANGERS .... Renee Taylor, Joseph Bologna, David Zelag Goodman
- M*A*S*H .... Ring Lardner, Jr. ★★
- WOMEN IN LOVE .... Larry Kramer

1971

Original Screenplay

- THE HOSPITAL .... Paddy Chayefsky ★★
- INVESTIGATION OF A CITIZEN ABOVE SUSPICION .... Elio Petri, Ugo Pirro
- KLUTE .... Andy and Dave Lewis
- SUMMER OF '42 .... Herman Raucher
- SUNDAY, BLOODY SUNDAY .... Penelope Gilliatt

Adaptation

- A CLOCKWORK ORANGE .... Stanley Kubrick
- THE CONFORMIST .... Bernardo Bertolucci
- THE FRENCH CONNECTION .... Ernest Tidyman ★★
- THE GARDEN OF THE FINZI-CONTINIS .... Ugo Pirro, Vittorio Bonicelli
- THE LAST PICTURE SHOW .... Larry McMurtry, Peter Bogdanovich

1972

Original Screenplay

THE CANDIDATE .... Jeremy Larner ★★
THE DISCREET CHARM OF THE
    BOURGEOISE .... Luis Bunuel, Jean-Claude Carriere
LADY SINGS THE
    BLUES .... Terence McCloy, Chris Clark, Suzanne de Passe
MURMUR OF THE HEART .... Louis Malle
YOUNG WINSTON .... Carl Foreman

Adaptation

CABARET .... Jay Presson Allen
THE EMIGRANTS .... Jan Troell, Bengt Forslund
THE GODFATHER ..... Mario Puzo, Francis Ford Coppola ★★
PETE'N'TILLIE .... Julis J. Epstein
SOUNDER .... Lonne Elder III

1973

Original Screenplay

AMERICAN
    GRAFFITI .... George Lucas, Gloria Katz, Willard Huyck
CRIES AND WHISPERS .... Ingmar Bergman
SAVE THE TIGER .... Steve Shagan
THE STING .... David S. Ward ★★
A TOUCH OF CLASS .... Melvin Frank, Jack Rose

Adaptation

THE EXORCIST .... William Peter Blatty ★★
THE LAST DETAIL .... Robert Towne
THE PAPER CHASE .... James Bridges
PAPER MOON .... Alvin Sargent
SERPICO .... Waldo Salt, Norman Wexler

1974

Original Screenplay

ALICE DOESN'T LIVE HERE ANYMORE ...... Robert Getchell
CHINATOWN .... Robert Towne ★★
THE CONVERSATION .... Francis Ford Coppola
DAY FOR NIGHT .... Francois Truffaut, Jean-Louis Richard,
                                                   Suzanne Schiffman
HARRY AND TONTO .... Paul Mazursky, Josh Greenfeld

Adaptation

THE APPRENTICESHIP OF
    DUDDY KRAVITZ .... Mordecai Richler, Lionel Chetwynd
THE GODFATHER
    PART II .... Francis Ford Coppola, Mario Puzo ★★
LENNY .... Julian Barry
MURDER ON THE ORIENT EXPRESS .... Paul Dehn
YOUNG FRANKENSTIEN .... Gene Wilder, Mel Brooks

1975

Original Screenplay

AMARCORD .... Federico Fellini, Tonino Guerra
AND NOW MY LOVE .... Claude Lelouch, Pierre Uytterhoeven
DOG DAY AFTERNOON .... Frank R. Pierson ★★
LIES MY FATHER TOLD ME .... Ted Allan
SHAMPOO .... Robert Towne, Warren Beatty

1975 (continued)

Adaptation

BARRY LYNDON .... Stanley Kubrick
THE MAN WHO WOULD BE KING ... John Huston, Gladys Hill
ONE FLEW OVER THE CUCKOO'S
    NEST .... Lawrence Hauben, Bo Goldman ★★
SCENT OF A WOMAN .... Rugero Maccari, Dino Risi
THE SUNSHINE BOYS .... Neil Simon

1976

Original Screenplay

COUSIN,
    COUSINE .... Jean-Charles Tachella, Daniele Thompson
THE FRONT .... Walter Bernstein
NETWORK .... Paddy Chayefsky ★★
ROCKY .... Sylvester Stallone
SEVEN BEAUTIES .... Lina Wertmuller

Adaptation

ALL THE PRESIDENT'S MEN .... William Goldman ★★
BOUND FOR GLORY .... Robert Getchell
FELLINI'S CASANOVA ... Federico Fellini, Bernardino Zapponi
THE SEVEN-PER-CENT SOLUTION .... Nicholas Meyer
VOYAGE OF THE DAMNED .... Steve Shagan, David Butler

1977

Original Screenplay

ANNIE HALL .... Woody Allen, Marshall Brickman ★★
THE GOODBYE GIRL .... Neil Simon
THE LATE SHOW .... Robert Benton
STAR WARS.. George Lucas
THE TURNING POINT .... Arthur Laurents

Adaptation

EQUUS .... Peter Shaffer
I NEVER PROMISED YOU A ROSE
    GARDEN .... Gavin Lambert, Lewis John Carlino
JULIA .... Alvin Sargent ★★
OH, GOD! .... Larry Gelbart
THAT OBSCURE OBJECT OF
    DESIRE .... Luis Bunuel, Jean-Claude Carriere

1978

Original Screenplay

AUTUMN SONATA .... Ingmar Bergman
COMING
    HOME .... Nancy Dowd, Waldo Salt, Robert C. Jones ★★
THE DEER HUNTER .... Michael Cimino, Deric Washburn,
                                                Louis Garfinkle, Quinn K. Redeker
INTERIORS .... Woody Allen
AN UNMARRIED WOMAN .... Paul Mazursky

Adaptation

BLOODBROTHERS .... Walter Newman
CALIFORNIA SUITE .... Neil Simon
HEAVEN CAN WAIT .... Elaine May, Warren Beatty
MIDNIGHT EXPRESS .... Oliver Stone ★★
SAME TIME, NEXT YEAR .... Bernard Slade

FILM WRITERS GUIDE

ACADEMY AWARDS & NOMINATIONS

1979

Original Screenplay

ALL THAT JAZZ .... Robert Alan Arthur, Bob Fosse
....AND JUSTICE FOR ALL ...... Valerie Curtin, Barry Levinson
BREAKING AWAY .... Steve Tesich ★★
THE CHINA
   SYNDROME .... Mike Gray, T.S. Cook, James Bridges
MANHATTAN .... Woody Allen, Marshall Brickman

Adaptation

APOCALYPSE NOW .... John Milius, Francis Coppola
KRAMER VS. KRAMER .... Robert Benton ★★
LA CAGE AUX
   FOLLES .... Francis Veber, Edouard Molinaro,
                                              Marcello Danon, Jean Poiret
A LITTLE ROMANCE .... Allan Burns
NORMA RAE .... Irving Ravetch, Harriet Frank Jr.

1980

Original Screenplay

BRUBAKER .... W.D. Richter, Arthur Ross
FAME .... Christopher Gore
MELVIN AND HOWARD .... Bo Goldman ★★
MON ONCLE D'AMERIQUE .... Jean Gruault
PRIVATE
   BENJAMIN ..... Nancy Meyers, Charles Shyer, Harvey Miller

Adaptation

BREAKER
   MORANT ..... Jonathan Hardy, David Stevens, Bruce Beresford
COAL MINER'S DAUGHTER .... Tom Rickman
THE ELEPHANT
   MAN .... Christopher Devore, Eric Bergren, David Lynch
ORDINARY PEOPLE .... Alvin Sargent ★★
THE STUNT MAN .... Lawrence B. Marcus, Richard Rush

1981

Original Screenplay

ABSENCE OF MALICE .... Kurt Luedtke
ARTHUR .... Steve Gordon
ATLANTIC CITY .... John Guare
CHARIOTS OF FIRE .... Colin Welland ★★
REDS .... Warren Beatty, Trevor Griffiths

Adaptation

THE FRENCH LEIUTENANT'S WOMAN .... Harold Pinter
ON GOLDEN POND .... Ernest Thompson ★★
PENNIES FROM HEAVEN .... Dennis Potter
PRINCE OF THE CITY .... Jay Presson Allen, Sidney Lumet
RAGTIME .... Michael Weller

1982

Original Screenplay

DINER .... Barry Levinson
E.T.-THE EXTRATERRESTRIAL .... Melissa Mathison
GANDHI .... John Briley ★★
AN OFFICER AND A GENTLEMAN ...... Douglas Day Stewart
TOOTSIE .... Don McGuire, Larry Gelbart, Murray Schisgal

1982 (continued)

Adaptation

DAS BOOT .... Wolfgang Petersen
MISSING .... Donald Stewart, Costa-Gavras ★★
SOPHIE'S CHOICE .... Alan J. Pakula
THE VERDICT .... David Mamet
VICTOR/VICTORIA .... Blake Edwards

1983

Original Screenplay

THE BIG CHILL .... Lawrence Kasdan, Barbara Benedek
FANNY & ALEXANDER .... Ingmar Bergman
SILKWOOD .... Nora Ephron, Alice Arlen
TENDER MERCIES .... Horton Foote ★★
WARGAMES .... Lawrence Lasker, Walter F. Parkes

Adaptation

BETRAYAL .... Harold Pinter
THE DRESSER .... Ronald Harwood
EDUCATING RITA .... Willy Russell
REUBEN, REUBEN .... Julius J. Epstein
TERMS OF ENDEARMENT .... James L. Brooks ★★

1984

Original Screenplay

BEVERLY HILLS COP .... Daniel Petrie Jr., Danilo Bach
BROADWAY DANNY ROSE .... Woody Allen
EL NORTE .... Gregory Nava, Anna Thomas
PLACES IN THE HEART .... Robert Benton ★★
SPLASH .... Lowell Ganz, Babaloo Mandel,
                                    Bruce Jay Friedman, Brian Grazer

Adaptation

AMADEUS .... Peter Shaffer ★★
GREYSTOKE: THE LEGEND OF TARZAN,
   LORD OF THE APES .... P.H. Vazak, Michael Austin
THE KILLING FIELDS .... Bruce Robinson
A PASSAGE TO INDIA .... David Lean
A SOLDIER'S STORY .... Charles Fuller

1985

Original Screenplay

BACK TO THE FUTURE .... Robert Zemeckis, Bob Gale
BRAZIL .... Terry Gilliam, Tom Stoppard, Charles McKeown
THE OFFICIAL STORY .... Luis Puenzo, Aida Bortnik
THE PURPLE ROSE OF CAIRO .... Woody Allen
WITNESS ... Earl W. Wallace, William Kelley, Pamela Wallace ★★

Adaptation

THE COLOR PURPLE .... Menno Meyjes
KISS OF THE SPIDER WOMAN .... Leonard Schrader
OUT OF AFRICA .... Kurt Luedtke ★★
PRIZZI'S HONOR .... Richard Condon, Janet Roach
THE TRIP TO BOUNTIFUL .... Horton Foote

1986

Original Screenplay

"CROCODILE"
  DUNDEE .... Paul Hogan, Ken Shadie, John Cornell
HANNAH AND HER SISTERS .... Woody Allen ★★
MY BEAUTIFUL LAUNDRETTE .... Hanif Kureishi
PLATOON .... Oliver Stone
SALVADOR .... Oliver Stone, Richard Boyle

Adaptation

CHILDREN OF A
  LESSER GOD .... Hesper Anderson, Mark Medoff
THE COLOR OF MONEY .... Richard Price
CRIMES OF THE HEART .... Beth Henley
A ROOM WITH A VIEW .... Ruth Prawer Jhabvala ★★
STAND BY ME .... Raynold Gideon, Bruce A. Evans

1987

Original Screenplay

AU REVOIR, LES ENFANTS .... Louis Malle
BROADCAST NEWS .... James L. Brooks
HOPE AND GLORY .... John Boorman
MOONSTRUCK .... John Patrick Shanley ★★
RADIO DAYS .... Woody Allen

Adaptation

THE DEAD .... Tony Huston
FATAL ATTRACTION .... James Dearden
FULL METAL
  JACKET ..... Stanley Kubrick, Michael Herr, Gustav Hasford
THE LAST EMPEROR ...... Bernardo Bertolucci, Mark Peploe ★★
MY LIFE AS A DOG .... Lasse Hallstrom, Reidar Jonsson,
                                        Brasse Brannstrom, Per Berglund

1988

Original Screenplay

BIG .... Gary Ross, Anne Speilberg
BULL DURHAM .... Ron Shelton
A FISH CALLED
  WANDA .... John Cleese, Charles Crichton
RAIN MAN .... Ronald Bass, Barry Morrow ★★
RUNNING ON EMPTY .... Naomi Foner

Adaptation

THE ACCIDENTAL
  TOURIST .... Frank Galati, Lawrence Kasdan
DANGEROUS LIAISONS .... Christopher Hampton ★★
GORILLAS IN THE MIST ..... Anna Hamilton Phelan, Tab Murphy
LITTLE DORRIT .... Christine Edzard
THE UNBEARABLE LIGHTNESS
  OF BEING .... Jean-Claude Carriere, Philip Kaufman

1989

Original Screenplay

CRIMES AND MISDEMEANORS .... Woody Allen
DO THE RIGHT THING .... Spike Lee
DEAD POETS SOCIETY .... Tom Schulman ★★
SEX, LIES AND VIDEOTAPE .... Steven Soderbergh
WHEN HARRY MET SALLY... .... Nora Ephron

Adaptation

BORN ON THE FOURTH
  OF JULY .... Oliver Stone, Ron Kovic
DRIVING MISS DAISY .... Alfred Uhry ★★
ENEMIES, A
  LOVE STORY .... Roger L. Simon, Paul Mazursky
FIELD OF DREAMS .... Phil Alden Robinson
MY LEFT FOOT .... Jim Sheridan, Shane Connaughton

1990

Original Screenplay

ALICE .... Woody Allen
AVALON .... Barry Levinson
GHOST .... Bruce Joel Rubin ★★
GREEN CARD .... Peter Weir
METROPOLITAN .... Whit Stillman

Adaptation

AWAKENINGS .... Steven Zaillian
DANCES WITH WOLVES .... Michael Blake ★★
GOODFELLAS .... Nicholas Pileggi, Martin Scorcese
THE GRIFTERS .... Donald E. Westlake
REVERSAL OF FORTUNE .... Nicholas Kazan

★★★★

This is one of the most powerful weapons in the fight for human rights.

It can help more innocent people get out of prison and free from torture than all the guns in the world. It's a guarantee to human rights everywhere on the globe. Everyday.

Amnesty International uses this weapon very effectively. Since 1961, A.I. has helped more than 25,000 women, men and children win their freedom from prison and torture. With simple, yet effective letters. Write today. It may be the most powerful letter you've ever written.

Write a letter, save a life.

Yes, I want to become a member of Amnesty International and make a difference.
Enclosed is my tax-deductible contribution for: ☐$25 ☐$35 ☐$50 ☐$75 ☐$100 ☐ Other $ _____
Minimum annual contribution is $25. $15 for students, senior citizens and limited income.

Name _____
Address _____
City _____ State _____ Zip Code _____
LE89

Amnesty International USA
322 Eighth Avenue, New York, New York 10001

AGENTS & MANAGERS

A

ABRAMS ARTISTS & ASSOCIATES
9200 Sunset Blvd.
Suite 625
Los Angeles, CA 90069
213/859-0625

420 Madison Ave.
Suite 1400
New York, NY 10017
212/935-8980

Harry Abrams

BRETT ADAMS, LTD.
448 West 44th Street
New York, NY 10036
212/765-5630

ADDIS-WECHSLER & ASSOCIATES
(In Association with the Robert Littman Co.)
955 S. Carrillo Drive
3rd Floor
Los Angeles, CA 90211
213/954-9000

Keith Addis
Nick Wechsler

THE ADLER AGENCY
12725 Ventura Blvd., Suite D
Studio City, CA 91604
818/769-5003

Jerry Adler

THE AGENCY
10351 Santa Monica Blvd.
Suite 211
Los Angeles, CA 90025
213/551-3000

AGENCY FOR CREATIVE TALENT
10351 Santa Monica Blvd.
Suite 211
Los Angeles, CA 90025
213/277-4909

AGENCY FOR THE PERFORMING ARTS, INC. (APA)
9000 Sunset Blvd.
Suite 1200
Los Angeles, CA 90069
213/273-0744

888 Seventh Avenue
New York, NY 10106
212/582-1500

IRVIN ARTHUR ASSOCIATES, LTD.
9363 Wilshire Blvd.
Suite 212
Beverly Hills, CA 90210
213/278-5934
FAX 213/276-7493

ARTISTS AGENCY, INC.
(In Association with Favored Artists)
230 West 55th Street
Suite 29D
New York, NY 10019
212/245-6960

THE ARTISTS AGENCY
10000 Santa Monica Blvd.
Suite 305
Los Angeles, CA 90067
213/277-7779

ARTIST'S CREATIVE MANAGEMENT
12001 Ventura Place
3rd Floor
Studio City, CA 91604
818/769-0469

THE ARTISTS GROUP, LTD.
1930 Century Park West
Suite 403
Los Angeles, CA 90067
213/552-1100

ASSOCIATED TALENT INTERNATIONAL
9744 Wilshire Blvd.
Suite 312
Beverly Hills, CA 90212
213/271-4662

B

BARRETT, BENSON, McCARTT & WESTON
9320 Wilshire Blvd.
Suite 300
Beverly Hills, CA 90212
213/247-5500
FAX 213/247-5599

Christopher Barrett
Jeff Benson
Bettye McCartt
Richard A. Weston

BENNETT AGENCY
150 S. Barrington Ave.
Suite 1
Los Angeles, CA 90049
213/471-2251

Carole Bennett

J. MICHAEL BLOOM, LTD.
233 Park Avenue South
10th Floor
New York, NY 10003
212/529-6500

9200 Sunset Blvd.
Suite 710
Los Angeles, CA 90069
213/275-6800

GEORGES BORCHARDT LITERARY AGENCY
136 East 57th Street
New York, NY 10022
212/753-5785

BORINSTEIN ORECK BOGART AGENCY
8271 Melrose Ave.
Suite 110
Los Angeles, CA 90046
213/658-7500

Mark Borinstein
Mary Oreck
Bari Bogart

THE BRANDT COMPANY
12700 Ventura Blvd.
Suite 340
Studio City, CA 91604
818/506-7747

Geoff Brandt

BRESLER-KELLY-KIPPERMAN
15760 Ventura Blvd.
Suite 1730
Encino, CA 91436
818/905-1155

111 West 57th St.
Suite 1409
New York, NY 10019
212/265-1980

Sandy Bresler
John S. Kelly
Perri Kipperman (NY)

THE BRILLSTEIN COMPANY
9200 Sunset Blvd.
Suite 428
Los Angeles, CA 90069
213/275-6135

Bernie Brillstein

BRODER-KURLAND-WEBB-UFFNER AGENCY
8439 Sunset Blvd.
Suite 402
Los Angeles, CA 90069
213/656-9262
FAX 213/650-9713

Bob Broder
Norman Kurland
Elliot Webb
Beth Uffner

CURTIS BROWN, LTD.
606 North Larchmont
Suite 309
Los Angeles, CA 90004
213/461-0148

Ten Astor Place
New York, NY 10003
212/473-5400

NED BROWN AGENCY
10551 Wilshire Blvd.
West Los Angeles, CA 90024
213/456-8068

THE BRUSTEIN CO.
10850 Wilshire Blvd.
Suite 350
Los Angeles, CA 90024
213/470-8342

Richard Brustein

C

CAMDEN-ITG
(Camden Artists incorporating International Talent Group)
822 S. Robertson Blvd.
Suite 200
Los Angeles, CA 90035
213/289-2700
FAX 213/289-2718

729 Seventh Ave.
16th Floor
New York, NY 10019
212/221-7878

WILLIAM CARROLL AGENCY
120 South Victory Blvd.
Burbank, CA 91502
818/845-3791

CASAROTTO COMPANY LTD.
2nd Floor, National House
60-66 Wardour Street
London W1V 3HP, England
01/287-4450
FAX 01/287-9128

Jenne Casarotto

THE CHASIN AGENCY
190 North Cañon Drive
Suite 201
Beverly Hills, CA 90210
213/278-7505

Tom Chasin

CHATTO & LINNIT
Prince of Wales Theatre
Coventry Street
London W1, England

CINEMA TALENT INTERNATIONAL
8033 Sunset Blvd.
Suite 808
West Hollywood, CA 90046
213/656-1937

CIRCLE TALENT ASSOCIATES
433 N. Camden Dr.
Suite 400
Beverly Hills, CA 90210
213/285-1585
FAX 213/285-1580

CONTEMPORARY ARTISTS, LTD.
132 S. Lasky Drive
Beverly Hills, CA 90212
213/278-8250

THE COOPER AGENCY
10100 Santa Monica Blvd.
Suite 310
Los Angeles, CA 90067
213/277-8422
FAX 213/277-8433

Frank Cooper
Jeff Cooper

THE COPPAGE COMPANY
11501 Chandler Blvd.
North Hollywood, CA 91601
818/980-1106

Judy Coppage

CREATIVE ARTISTS AGENCY (CAA)
9830 Wilshire Blvd.
Beverly Hills, CA 90212
213/288-4545
FAX 213/288-4800

PETER CROUCH & ASSOCIATES
59 Frith Street
London W1, England
011/441/734-2167

D

JUDY DAISH AGENCY
122 Wigmore Street
London W1H 9FE, England
011/441/486-5405

DYTMAN & ASSOCIATES
433 N. Camden Dr.
Suite 600
Beverly Hills, CA 90210
213/288-1827
FAX 213/288-1801

Jack Dytman

E

ROBERT EISENBACH AGENCY
967 Hammond
Suite 1
Los Angeles, CA 90069
213/962-5809

EPSTEIN-WYCKOFF
280 S. Beverly Drive
Suite 400
Beverly Hills, CA 90212
213/278-7222

Gary Epstein
Craig Wyckoff

F

FAVORED ARTISTS AGENCY
8150 Beverly Blvd.
Suite 201
Los Angeles, CA 90048
213/653-3191

MAGGIE FIELD AGENCY
12725 Ventura Blvd.
Suite D
Studio City, CA 91604
818/980-2001

FILM ARTISTS ASSOCIATES
7080 Hollywood Blvd.
Suite 704
Hollywood, CA 90028
213/463-1010

KURT FRINGS AGENCY, INC.
139 S. Beverly Dr.
Suite 328
Beverly Hills, CA 90210
213/227-1103

G

THE GAGE GROUP INC.
9255 Sunset Blvd.
Suite 515
Los Angeles, CA 90069
213/859-8777
FAX 213/859-8166

315 W. 57th St.
Suite 4H
New York, NY 10019
212/541-5250
FAX 212/956-7466

Martin Gage

HELEN GARRETT AGENCY
P.O. Box 889
Hollywood, CA 90028
213/871-8707

THE GERSH AGENCY
232 N. Cañon Drive
Beverly Hills, CA 90210
213/274-6611

130 West 42nd St.
Suite 2400
New York, NY 10036
212/997-1818

Bob Gersh
Dave Gersh
Phil Gersh

HARRY GOLD & ASSOCIATES
12725 Ventura Blvd.
Suite E
Studio City, CA 91604
818/769-5003

THE GOLDSTEIN COMPANY
864 S. Robertson Blvd.
Suite 304
Los Angeles, CA 90035
213/659-9511

Gary W. Goldstein

GORES/FIELDS AGENCY
10100 Santa Monica Blvd.
Suite 700
Los Angeles, CA 90067
213/277-4400

Sam Gores
Jack Fields

THE GORFAINE/SCHWARTZ AGENCY, INC.
3301 Barham Blvd.
Suite 201
Los Angeles, CA 90068
213/969-1011
FAX 213/969-1022

Michael Gorfaine
Samuel Schwartz

GRAY/GOODMAN, INC.
205 South Beverly Drive
Suite 210
Beverly Hills, CA 90212
213/276-7070

Stephen Gray
Mark Goodman

ARTHUR B. GREENE
101 Park Avenue
43rd Floor
New York, NY 10178
212/661-8200

HAROLD R. GREENE, INC.
8455 Beverly Blvd.
Suite 309
Los Angeles, CA 90048
213/852-4959

LARRY GROSSMAN & ASSOCIATES
211 S. Beverly Drive
Suite 206
Beverly Hills, CA 90212
213/550-8127

THE GURIAN AGENCY
10249 Century Woods Drive
Los Angeles, CA 90067
213/550-0400

Naomi Gurian

H

REECE HALSEY AGENCY
8733 Sunset Blvd.
Suite 101
Los Angeles, CA 90069
213/652-2409

THE MITCHELL J. HAMILBURG AGENCY
292 S. La Cienega Blvd.
Suite 312
Los Angeles, CA 90211
213/657-1501

HARRIS & GOLDBERG TALENT AND LITERARY AGENCY, INC.
1999 Avenue of the Stars
Suite 2850
Los Angeles, CA 90067
213/553-5200
FAX 213/557-2211

Scott Harris
Howard Goldberg

RICK HASHAGEN & ASSOCIATES
157 West 57th Street
New York, NY 10019
212/315-3130

HATTON & BAKER
18 Jermyn Street
London W1, England
011/441/439-2971

HEACOCK LITERARY AGENCY
1523 Sixth Street
Suite 14
Los Angeles, CA 90401
213/393-6227

HENDERSON/HOGAN AGENCY, INC.
247 S. Beverly Drive
Suite 102
Beverly Hills, CA 90212
213/274-7815

405 W. 44th Street
New York, NY 10036
212/765-5190

Margaret Henderson
Jerry Hogan (NY)

HERMAN & LEWIS TALENT AGENCY
9601 Wilshire Blvd.
Suite 333
Los Angeles, CA 90210
213/550-8913

Richard Herman
Michael Lewis

I

MICHAEL IMISON PLAYWRIGHTS
011/441/354-3274 (London)
212/874-2671 (New York)

INTERNATIONAL CREATIVE MANAGEMENT (ICM)
8899 Beverly Blvd.
Los Angeles, CA 90048
213/550-4000
FAX 213/550-4108

40 West 57th Street
New York, NY 10019
212/556-5600

in Italy, known as
TNA (The New Agency)
Viale Paroli, 41
Rome, Italy 00197
011/396-87.87.98

388-396 Oxford Street
London, W1 England W1N 9HE
01/629-8080

INTERTALENT AGENCY, INC.
131 South Rodeo Dr.
Suite 300
Beverly Hills, CA 90212
213/858-6200
FAX 213/858-6222

J

JANKLOW & ASSOCIATES
1900 Avenue of the Stars
Suite 770
Los Angeles, CA 90067
213/785-9550

Janklow & Nesbit
598 Madison Avenue
New York, NY 10022
212/421-1700

Morton Janklow
Lynn Nesbit

MELINDA JASON COMPANY
c/o Walt Disney Studios
500 S. Buena Vista, Tower
28th Floor
Burbank, CA 91521
818/560-5000

K

THE KAPLAN-STAHLER AGENCY
8383 Wilshire Blvd.
Suite 923
Beverly Hills, CA 90211
213/653-4483

Mitch Kaplan
Elliot Stahler

PATRICIA KARLAN AGENCY
4425 Riverside Drive
Suite 102
Bubank, CA 91505
818/846-8666

WILLIAM KERWIN AGENCY
1605 N. Cahuenga Blvd.
Suite 202
Los Angeles, CA 90028
213/469-5155

PAUL KOHNER, INC.
9169 Sunset Blvd.
Los Angeles, CA 90069
213/550-1060
FAX 276-1083

KOPALOFF COMPANY
1930 Century Park West
Suite 403
Los Angeles, CA 90067
213/203-8430

Don Kopaloff

LUCY KROLL AGENCY
390 West End Avenue
New York, NY 10024
212/877-0627

L

LAKE & DOUROUX INC.
445 S. Beverly Drive
Suite 310
Beverly Hills, CA 90212
213/557-0700

Candace Lake
Michael Douroux

THE LANTZ OFFICE
(In Association with The Roberts Company)
888 Seventh Avenue
25th Floor
New York, NY 10106
212/586-0200

IRVING PAUL LAZAR AGENCY
120 El Camino Drive
Suite 108
Beverly Hills, CA 90212
213/275-6153

One East 66th Street
New York, NY 10021
212/355-1177

THE LIBERTY AGENCY
10845 Lindbrook Dr.
Suite 200
Los Angeles, CA 90024
213/824-7937

Glennis Liberty

THE ROBERT LITTMAN COMPANY
(In Association with Addis-Wechsler & Associates)
409 N. Camden Dr.
Beverly Hills, CA 90210
213/278-1572

LONDON MANAGEMENT
235/241 Regent Street
London W1 2J7, England
011/441/493-1610

STERLING LORD LITERISTIC
One Madison Avenue
New York, NY 10010
212/696-2800

M

SHERI MANN AGENCY
8228 W. Sunset Blvd.
Suite 303
Los Angeles, CA 90046
213/655-6266

STEPHANIE MANN AGENCY
8323 Blackburn Avenue
Suite 5
Los Angeles, CA 90048
213/653-7130

HAROLD MATSON COMPANY, INC.
276 Fifth Avenue
New York, NY 10001
212/679-4490

MEDIA ARTISTS GROUP
6255 Sunset Blvd.
Suite 627
Hollywood, CA 90028
213/463-5610

HELEN MERRILL
435 West 23rd Street
Suite 1-A
New York, NY 10011
212/691-5326

MLR REPRESENTATION
200 Fulham Road
London SW10, England

THE MONTEIRO ROSE AGENCY
17514 Ventura Blvd.
Suite 205
Encino, CA 91316
818/501-1177
FAX 818/501-1194

Candy Monteiro
Fredda Rose

WILLIAM MORRIS AGENCY
151 S. El Camino Drive
Beverly Hills, CA 90212
213/274-7451
FAX 213/859-4462

1350 Avenue of the Americas
New York, NY 10019
212/586-5100

2325 Crestmoore Road
Nashville, TN 37215
615/385-0310

31-32 Soho Square
London W12 5DG, England
01/434-2191

Via Giosue Carducci, 10
00187 Rome, Italy
48-6961

Lamonstrasse 9
Munich 80, West Germany
011/47/608-1234

THE MORTON AGENCY
11011 1/2 Strathmore Dr.
Los Angeles, CA 90024
213/824-4089

N

CNA & ASSOCIATES
1801 Avenue of the Stars
Suite 1250
Los Angeles, CA 90067
213/556-4343
FAX 213/556-4633

19 West 44th St.
Suite 812
New York, NY 10036
212/840-7330
FAX 212/840-7527

Christopher Nassif

O

THE DANIEL OSTROFF AGENCY
9200 Sunset Blvd.
Suite 402
Los Angeles, CA 90069
213/278-2020

P

PARAMUSE ARTISTS ASSOCIATION
1414 Avenue of the Americas
New York, NY 10019
212/758-5055

THE PARKS AGENCY
138 East 16th St.
Suite 5B
New York, NY 10003
212/254-9067

Richard Parks

THE PARNESS AGENCY
9220 Sunset Blvd.
Suite 204
Los Angeles, CA 90069
213/273-2233

Leslie Parness

THE PARTOS COMPANY
3630 Barham Blvd.
Suite 2108
Los Angeles, CA 90068
213/876-5500

Walter Partos

BARRY PERELMAN AGENCY
9200 Sunset Blvd.
Suite 531
Los Angeles, CA 90069
213/274-5999

PETERS, FRASER & DUNLOP
The Chambers, Chelsea Harbour
Lots Road
London, SW10 OXF, England
71/376-7676

PHOENIX LITERARY AGENCY
315 South F Street
Livingston, Montana 59047
406/222-2848

PLESHETTE & GREEN AGENCY
2700 North Beachwood Drive
Los Angeles, CA 90068
213/465-0428

Lynn Pleshette
Richard Green

BARRY POLLACK
9255 Sunset Blvd.
Suite 404
Los Angeles, CA 90069
213/550-4525

PREFERRED ARTISTS
16233 Ventura Blvd.
Suite 1421
Encino, CA 91436
818/990-0305

JIM PREMINGER AGENCY
1650 Westwood Blvd.
Suite 201
Los Angeles, CA 90024
213/475-9491

R

DOUGLAS RAE MANAGEMENT
28 Charing Cross Road
London, WC2 England
011/441/836-3903

MARGARET RAMSAY LTD.
London, England
071/240/240-0691

THE RICHLAND/WUNSCH/ HOHMAN AGENCY
9220 Sunset Blvd.
Suite 311
Los Angeles, CA 90069
213/278-1955
FAX 213/278-1156

Daniel A. Richland
Joseph Richland
Robert J. Wunsch
Robert Hohman

THE ROBERTS COMPANY
(In Association with The Lantz Office)
10345 W. Olympic Blvd.
Penthouse
Los Angeles, CA 90064
213/552-7800
FAX 213/552-9324

Nancy Roberts

FLORA ROBERTS, INC.
157 West 57th Street
New York, NY 10019
212/355-4165

ROBINSON, WEINTRAUB, GROSS & ASSOCIATES, INC.
(In Association with The Marion Rosenberg Office)
8428 Melrose Place
Suite C
Los Angeles, CA 90069
213/653-5802
FAX 213/653-9268

Stu Robinson
Bernie Weintraub
Ken Gross

ROGERS & ASSOCIATES
3855 Lankershim Blvd.
North Hollywood, CA 91604
818/509-1010

Stephanie Rogers

THE MARION ROSENBERG OFFICE
(In Association with Robinson, Weintraub, Gross & Associates)
8428 Melrose Place
Suite C
Los Angeles, CA 90069
213/653-7383

ROSENSTONE/WENDER
Three East 48th Street
New York, NY 10017
212/832-8330

Howard Rosenstone
Phyllis Wender

S

SANFORD, SKOURAS, GROSS & ASSOCIATES
1015 Gayley Avenue
3rd Floor
Los Angeles, CA 90024
213/208-2100
FAX 213/208-6704

Geoffrey Sanford
Spyros Skouras
Brad Gross

THE SARNOFF COMPANY, INC.
12001 Ventura Place
Suite 300
Studio City, CA 91604
818/761-4495

Jim Sarnoff

JACK SCAGNETTI AGENCY
5330 Lankershim Blvd.
Suite 210
North Hollywood, CA 91601
818/762-3871

THE IRV SCHECHTER COMPANY
9300 Wilshire Blvd.
Suite 410
Beverly Hills, CA 90212
213/278-8070
FAX 213/278-6058

SUSAN SCHULMAN LITERARY AGENCY, INC.
454 West 44th Street
New York, NY 10036
212/713-1633
FAX 212/581-8830

KATHLEEN SCHULTZ
11846 Ventura Blvd.
Suite 100
Studio City, CA 91604
818/760-3100

SELECT ARTISTS
337 West 43rd St.,
Suite 1B
New York, NY 10036
212/586-4300

DAVID SHAPIRA & ASSOCIATES
15301 Ventura Blvd.
Suite 345
Sherman Oaks, CA 91403
818/906-0322
FAX 818/783-2562

THE SHAPIRO/LICHTMAN AGENCY
8827 Beverly Blvd.
Los Angeles, CA 90048
213/859-8877
FAX 213/859-7153

Martin Shapiro
Bob Shapiro
Mark Lichtman

KEN SHERMAN & ASSOCIATES
9507 Santa Monica Blvd.
Suite 211
Beverly Hills, CA 90210
213/273-8840

SHORR, STILLE & ASSOCIATES
800 S. Robertson Blvd.
Suite 6
Los Angeles, CA 90035
213/659-6160

Fred Shorr
Lucy Stille

LINDA SIEFERT & ASSOCIATES
8A Brunswick Gardens
London W8 4AJ, England
011/441/229-5163

JEROME SIEGEL ASSOCIATES
7551 Sunset Blvd.
Suite 203
Los Angeles, CA 90046
213/850-1275

SUSAN SMITH & ASSOCIATES
121 N. San Vicente Blvd.
Beverly Hills, CA 90211
213/852-4777
FAX 213/658-7170

192 Lexington Ave.
New York, NY 10016
212/545-0500
FAX 212/545-7143

SMITH/GOSNELL/NICHOLSON & ASSOCIATES
P.O. Box 1166
1294 Calle de Sevilla
Pacific Palisades, CA 90272
213/459-0307

Creighton Smith
Ray Gosnell
Skip Nicholson

SOLOMON WEINGARTEN & ASSOCIATES
10530 Santa Monica Blvd.
Los Angeles, CA 90025
213/474-8703

S.T.E. REPRESENTATION, LTD.
9301 Wilshire Blvd.
Suite 312
Beverly Hills, CA 90210
213/550-3982

888 Seventh Avenue
Suite 21-F
New York, NY 10106
212/246-1030

Clifford Stevens (NY)
David Eidenberg

STONE MANNERS AGENCY
9113 Sunset Blvd.
Los Angeles, CA 90069
213/275-9599

Tim Stone
Scott Manners

THE STRICK AGENCY
9220 Sunset Blvd.
Suite 204
Los Angeles, CA 90069
213/273-0919

Shirley Strick

SUTTER/WALLS ASSOCIATES
8322 Beverly Blvd.
Suite 200
Los Angeles, CA 90048
213/658-8200

Curry Walls

H. N. SWANSON, INC.
8523 Sunset Blvd.
Los Angeles, CA 90069
213/652-5385
FAX 213/652-3690

THE TANTLEFF OFFICE
375 Greenwich St.
Suite 700
New York, NY 10013
212/941-3939

Jack Tantleff

THAL LITERARY MANAGEMENT
8721 Sunset Blvd.
Penthouse #8
Los Angeles, CA 90069
213/659-4946
FAX 213/659-4619

Jeffrey Thal

TRIAD ARTISTS, INC.
10100 Santa Monica Blvd.
16th Floor
Los Angeles, CA 90067
213/556-2727
FAX 213/551-0501

888 Seventh Avenue
Suite 1602
New York, NY 10109
212/489-8100

THE TURTLE AGENCY
12456 Ventura Blvd.
Suite 1
Studio City, CA 91604
818/506-6898

Cindy Turtle

TWENTIETH CENTURY ARTISTS
3800 Barham Blvd.
Suite 303
Los Angeles, CA 90068
213/850-5516

UNITED TALENT AGENCY
9560 Wilshire Blvd.
Beverly Hills, CA 90212
213/273-6700
FAX 213/247-1111

V

VANGUARD ASSOCIATES
2730 Wilshire Blvd.
Suite 500
Santa Monica, CA 90403
213/829-5000

W

WARDEN & WHITE ASSOCIATES
8444 Wilshire Blvd.
4th Floor
Beverly Hills, CA 90211
213/852-1028
FAX 213/852-1028

David Warden
Steve N. White

SANDRA WATT & ASSOCIATES
8033 Sunset Blvd.
Suite 4053
Los Angeles, CA 90046
213/653-2339

WILE ENTERPRISES, INC.
2730 Wilshire Blvd.
Suite 500
Santa Monica, CA 90403
213/828-9768

Shelly Wile

WRIGHT CONCEPT TALENT AGENCY
1015 N. Cahuenga Blvd.
Hollywood, CA 90038
213/461-3844
FAX 213/461-2958

Marcie Wright

WRITERS & ARTISTS AGENCY
11726 San Vicente Blvd.
Suite 300
Los Angeles, CA 90049
213/820-2240
FAX 213/207-3781

70 West 36th St.
Suite 501
New York, NY 10018
212/947-8765

★ ★ ★ ★

GUILDS

WRITERS GUILD OF AMERICA-WEST, INC.
8955 Beverly Blvd.
Los Angeles, CA 90048
213/550-1000

WRITERS GUILD OF AMERICA-EAST, INC.
555 West 57th St.
New York, NY 10019
212/245-6180

WRITERS GUILD OF GREAT BRITAIN
430 Edgeware Road
London W21 EH, England
011/4471/723-8074

DIRECTORS GUILD OF AMERICA
7920 Sunset Blvd.
Los Angeles, CA 90046
213/289-2000

SCREEN ACTORS GUILD
7065 Hollywood Blvd.
Hollywood, CA 90028
213/851-4301

BE THE FIRST ON YOUR BLOCK!

Stop worrying whether you have the most up-to-date Lone Eagle directories.

Get on our standing order list and receive your copy of all Lone Eagle guides, *hot off the press* <u>automatically</u> and, at a five percent discount.

Send (or fax) us a note on your letterhead and we'll take care of the rest.

Just look at what you'll be getting:

- ★ MICHAEL SINGER'S FILM DIRECTORS: A COMPLETE GUIDE
- ★ FILM WRITERS GUIDE
- ★ FILM PRODUCERS, STUDIOS, AGENTS AND CASTING DIRECTORS GUIDE
- ★ SPECIAL EFFECTS AND STUNTS GUIDE
- ★ CINEMATOGRAPHERS, PRODUCTION DESIGNERS, COSTUME DESIGNERS AND EDITORS GUIDE
- ★ FILM COMPOSERS GUIDE
- ★ TELEVISION WRITERS GUIDE
- ★ TELEVISION DIRECTORS GUIDE
- ★ FILM ACTORS GUIDE

LONE EAGLE PUBLISHING CO.

2337 Roscomare Road, Suite 9
Los Angeles, CA 90077
213/471-8066 or
1/800-FILMBKS • FAX 213/471-4969

ISN'T IT TIME YOU HAD YOUR OWN COPIES?

CALLING ALL CREDITS!

The **Fourth Edition of FILM WRITERS GUIDE** is now in preparation. It will be published in the fall of 1992. We update our records continuously. If you are a film writer and you qualify to be listed (please read the Introduction for qualifications), then send us your listing information **ASAP**.
Photocopy the form on the next page.

Our editorial deadline is June 1, 1992.

(Please do not wait until then.)

Send all film writers listing information to:

> **FILM WRITERS GUIDE**
> **Fourth Edition**
> **2230 North Gower Street**
> **Los Angeles, CA 90068**
> **213/471-8066 or 1/800-FILMBKS**

If you are a television writer, a director (*film or television*), film composer, film actor, cinematographer, production designer, costume designer, editor, agent, producer or studio executive, casting director, special effects or stunts coordinator and want to find out about getting listed in our other directories, call **213/471-8066** or **1/800-FILMBKS** or write to:

LONE EAGLE PUBLISHING CO.
2337 Roscomare Road, Suite 9
Los Angeles, CA 90077
213/471-8066 • 213/471-4969 (FAX) • 1/800-FILMBKS

★ ★ ★

The FOURTH EDITION of FILM WRITERS GUIDE
is now in preparation.

WGA Member? Yes ☐ No ☐

DON'T BE LEFT OUT!!! Guarantee your *FREE* listing (for qualified flm writers) by filling out and returning this form to us *IMMEDIATELY*. *(Photocopy as many times as necessary).*

WRITER'S INFORMATION

Name
Company
Address
City/State/Zip
Area Code/Phone
Birth Date & Place
Home ☐   Business ☐

PLEASE PRINT OR TYPE

REPRESENTATIVE'S INFORMATION

Agent ☐   Personal Manager ☐   Attorney ☐
Business Manager ☐   Other ☐   AFM ☐

(List as many representatives as you would like. Continue listing on reverse, if necessary.)

Name
Company
Address
City/State/Zip
Area Code/Telephone
Other Guild Affiliations

PLEASE PRINT OR TYPE

CREDITS

List your credits as follows: Please note alternate titles in parentheses. Pease note Academy nominations/awards for your work. If you need more space, please continue on reverse side.

FEATURES: GHOST ★★ Paramount, 1990, w/Peter Barsochini
PRETTY WOMAN *3000* Buena Vista, 1990
TELEFEATURES: THIRD DEGREE BURN (CTF) HBO Pictures, 1989, w/Yale Udoff, directed

---

MAIL or FAX form *IMMEDIATELY* to
FILM WRITERS GUIDE
Fourth Edition
2230 North Gower Street
Los Angeles, CA 90068
213/471-8066 or 213/471-4969 (FAX)

Questions ???
Problems ???
Call 213/471-8066

We couldn't have said it better ourselves...

If you ever get muddled on director's credits (who hasn't?), there's one book truly worthy of being called a "must," namely "Film Directors: A Complete Guide." It's an elephantine volume...compiled and edited by Michael Singer, and now out in its sixth annual edition, and best one so far. Like the earlier Singer deliveries, this one is a lulu, chock-full of screen credits of every working director from Paul Aaron to Edward Zwick, listed both by the director's name and by film title. Want to know who directed "Dynamite Chicken"? Want to know Oliver Stone's first film? It's all there, including, for the first time, a separate section with the full credits of 180 deceased directors, allowing one also a quick reference to the full body of screen work by everyone from the late Ernst Lubitsch (including his numerous German-made features) to Charles Laughton (who directed only one film, the excellent 1955 "The Night of the Hunter")... By Singer's own admission, "It's primarily aimed for industrites, including actors who might want to check out a director's credits before a reading or a meeting. But I think it also offers a lot of fun for anyone who's just crazy about the movies." Indeed it does. Singer's even included a full listing of all the screen credits of Alan Smithee (that's the pseudonym designed by the DGA for members who want to remove their real names from the credits of a film). And among other oddities there's the director, one of the best, who guided a 1973 Fox film under the pseudonym of "Bill Sampson"; that, of course, was the name of the fictional director in the Oscar-winning "all About Eve." Singer's book includes his real identity.

More on "Film Directors": A valuable thing about Michael singer's book is the fact it doesn't encompass just selected credits but each director's full portfolio, warts and all. This year's volume includes at leat 300 new additions as well as one major corrected omission from past volumes: Richard Thorpe, director of some 177 films in his heyday, and still very much alive. (Says Singer, who's also a publicist at Fox, "I'm embarrassed but I'd thought he was dead. But I talked to him on the phone and he's 92 now and sounds just as feisty as you'd expect the director of movies like 'Ivanhoe' and 'Jailhouse Rock' would be. He told me he didn't want to be interviewed anymore. He said, 'I'm too old to go over all that old stuff. I'll just let the work speak for itself.'") ...Singer's book, done with major help from Joan-Carrol Baron, also speaks for itself, and deserves a spot on anyone's bookshelf. As an invaluable reference, it's at the head of the class.

Robert Osborne
The Hollywood Reporter

Michael Singer's FILM DIRECTORS: A COMPLETE GUIDE
Eighth Annual International Edition—$59.95

TO ORDER YOUR COPIES:
Send $59.95 plus $6.00 postage/handling for first copy and $2.50 for each additional copy.
Inquire for foreign shipping rates.
California residents must add $4.95 tax per book.

Use the handy post-paid order form in the front of the book, or send order and payment to:
LONE EAGLE PUBLISHING COMPANY
2337 Roscomare Road, Suite 9
Los Angeles, CA 90077
213/471-8066 •1/800-FILMBKS 213/471-4969 (fax)

NOTES

INDEX OF ADVERTISERS

A special thanks to our advertisers whose support makes it possible to bring you the **third edition of FILM WRITERS GUIDE.**

AIDS Project Los Angeles	322
Amnesty International USA	398
Arizona Film Commission	Cover 3
Bruder Releasing, Inc.	5
Chicago Film Office	17
Screenplay Systems	Cover 4
Starlight Foundation	vi
United Way	392

★ ★ ★

ABOUT THE EDITOR

SUSAN AVALLONE was a magazine editor for four years before entering the entertainment industry. She is currently a development executive.

A native of New York, Susan has resided in Los Angeles for three years with her husband Carr D'Angelo.